HANDBOOK OF ANTHROPOLOGY IN BUSINESS

HANDBOOK OF Anthropology in Business

RITA DENNY

PATRICIA SUNDERLAND

EDITORS

Left Coast Press Inc.

Walnut Creek
California

Left Coast Press, Inc.
1630 North Main Street, #400
Walnut Creek, ca 94596
www.LCoastPress.com

ISBN 978-1-61132-171-5 hardback
ISBN 978-1-61132-768-7 consumer eBook

Library of Congress Cataloging-in-Publication Data

Handbook of anthropology in business / edited by Rita M. Denny, Patricia L. Sunderland.
pages cm
Includes bibliographical references and index.
ISBN 978-1-61132-171-5 (hardback) –
ISBN 978-1-61132-768-7 (consumer eBook)
1. Business anthropology.
I. Denny, Rita Mary Taylor, 1956- II. Sunderland, P. L. (Patricia L.)
GN450.8.H36 2014
302.3›5—dc23

2014005444

Printed in the United States of America
∞ ™ The paper used in this publication meets the minimum requirements of American National Standard of Information Sciences—Permanence of Paper for Printed Library Materials, ANSI/NISO Z39.48—1992.

This book is dedicated to:

Karen Kruse Eskew,
Whose perspective in life is unfailing
and
Jennifer Collier Jennings,
Without whom this book would not exist

CONTENTS

ACKNOWLEDGMENTS

This volume is the result of tremendous effort invested by people situated in multiple fields of work, geographies, and career trajectories. Like anthropological analysis itself, the process in creating this volume was immersive, inductive, and iterative. We flung the net widely. As editors, and anthropologists, we saw no other way to embark on the task of illuminating a nascent, and perhaps disruptive, set of practices if we were to capture the spirit, breadth, and depth of work conducted at the intersection of anthropology and business. Our goal was to curate what emerged in a way that makes otherwise closed, fragmented silos more visible and, as a result, more permeable in the future. Our commitment to this process depended on the heart, wisdom, thoughtfulness, and diligence of many people. It could not have been done otherwise.

To the authors of these chapters: thank you for multiple iterations of your chapters, your work as reviewers, and for persevering when the task sometimes seemed endless. Since multiple eyes reviewed these chapters multiple times, the review process was not an easy one. In the editorial attempt to make divergent trajectories visible and understandable across the landscape, we consciously assigned authors to review chapters that shared a common interest but not necessarily a shared background. Thank you for taking part in this process and for bearing with us.

Beyond the authors, thank you to those who filled in needed expertise and vantage points in reviewing manuscripts: ken anderson, Katja Battarbee, Allen Batteau, Russell Belk, Jeanette Blomberg, Kevin Bohrer, Elizabeth Briody, Francoise Brun-Cottan, Susan Byrne, Jennifer Chase, Lily Chumley, Tomoko Hamada Connolly, David Crockett, Michael Donovan, Luther Elliott, Heather Ford, Fred Gleach, Julia Gluesing, Michael Griffiths, David Howes, Erica Herman, Gavin Johnston, Brigitte Jordan, Jelena Karanovic, Ed Liebow, Gerald Lombardi, Tracey Lovejoy, Nushina Mir, Alexandra Mack, George Marcus, Robert Moïse, Pedro Oliveira, Stephen Pace, Krzysztof Polak, Christophe Robert, Rick Robinson, Benjamin Rossi, Vilma Santiago-Irizarry, Stas Shectman, Donald Stull, Susan Terrio, Arvind Venkataramani, Melanie Wallendorf, Michelle Weinberger, and Bob Yovovich. Some people reviewed multiple manuscripts, often in the face of tight deadlines, and they did so as though they had all the time in the world: Marietta Baba, Melissa Cefkin, Franck Cochoy, Bernard Cova, Jay Hasbrouck, Ed Liebow, Maryann McCabe, Brian Moeran, Dawn Nafus, Stephen Pace, Rick Robinson, Vilma Santiago-Irizarry, Charley Scull, and John F. Sherry, Jr. Thanks also go to Steve Barnett, Katja Battarbee, Allen Batteau, Tonya Bradford, Heather Ford, Michael Griffiths, Elliot Hedman, Suzanne Gibbs Howard, Panthea Lee, Sam Ladner, Sidney Levy, Rick Robinson, Jane Fulton Suri, Brad

Trainor, and Yang Xiaomin for their voices, effort, and contributions to this endeavor.

The catalyst in creating this *Handbook* was a request from Mitch Allen and Jennifer Collier Jennings at Left Coast Press. We are indebted to their wisdom and foresight, their patience in allowing a shared vision to emerge, and their faith in us as editors. Jennifer, our Left Coast editor, was a muse, guide, and source of perspective (and humor) throughout the process. Hers is a voice of great clarity. Without it, and without the tremendous amount of effort and time she dedicated to helping us make the process work, the volume literally would not exist.

Thank you to our advisory board: Melissa Cefkin, Bernard Cova, Dominque Desjeux, Patricia Ensworth, Natalie Hanson, Dawn Nafus, and John F. Sherry, Jr. You were instrumental in getting the *Handbook* off the ground and helping us in the effort to make divergent trajectories visible. Melissa Cefkin was an indefatigable being in responding to our queries, both large and small, throughout the last two years.

We had muses: people whose chapters, reviews, emails, insightful minds, and wonderful spirits simply kept us going. Moments for needing a muse were many—and really all of the authors and reviewers could be listed—but we especially note Melissa Cefkin, Franck Cochoy, Dominique Desjeux, and Dawn Nafus. Thank you for keeping us going. There were also colleagues, friends, and family who offered encouragement, gems of practical advice, or assistance at *just* the right moment: Charlotte Bradford, Sue Byrne, Alessandro Caliandro, Christopher Denny, Donald Denny, Karen Eskew, Belain Eyob, Mekonnen Ketsela, Rita McElwee, Joan E. O'Brien, Shailesh Patel, Irene Patner, Sarah Schacht, Steve Schacht, Donald Stull, Elizabeth Sunderland, Susan Terrio, William Mazzarella, and Christine Yarbrough.

With 65 authors, 43 chapters, and 6 introductions, keeping track of everything and everyone was no small feat and was only possible given the incredible organizational abilities of Jennifer Collier Jennings, the Left Coast staff, and our copy editor, Michelle Treviño. Michelle seems to channel the *Chicago Manual of Style* even in sleep; she assured coherence of thoughts, figures, hyperlinks, and conventions of references, spelling, and punctuation. Oversights, omissions, mistakes, and errors of judgment are our own.

Last, but not least, this volume reflects Patti's tenacious commitment to the wide view of possibility and Rita's tenacious commitment to making what *is* the best it can be. It exists with great heart and huge effort.

Rita Denny & Patricia Sunderland
February 2014

INTRODUCTION

PATRICIA SUNDERLAND & RITA DENNY

Anthropology in business is a matrix of multiple endeavors that on the one hand has existed for a very long time and on the other is just coming into view. Actors in this terrain include anthropologists, their sociological kin, designers, and ethnographers of other disciplinary origins who have found themselves working with or for business or who take business as an object for study. Historically there are traceable lines of activity—in fields of technology and design, organizational and workplace studies, advertising and market research—but also myriad, deviating instantiations: social entrepreneurship; journalism; management consulting; service design; product, brand, workplace, and policy innovation; commercial semiotics; and cultural dubbing, to name a few. There are calls to install chief culture officers in the C-suite. Some argue that such activities should not even exist; others argue for their ascendance. Although futures are unpredictable, at present there is great momentum in these trajectories of activity.

Our choice of "Anthropology in Business" rather than "Business Anthropology" as the title of this handbook was purposeful. To call it the latter seemed too great a presupposition of an existing field with established parameters and boundaries. Rather than presupposing a field, our goal with this volume was to gather together and present prominent examples of activities occurring at the intersection of anthropology and business. Some of these activities are, in fact, creative of the contemporary emergence of a field as well as the academic discipline of "Business Anthropology"—and undoubtedly the creation of a volume is also a gesture that aids in the production of a discipline—but our goal was to retain the flavor of this emergent moment, to give a taste of the lines of development as well as multiple instantiations. This goal is reflected in the five sections that organize this volume: Dynamics of Tension, Forces of Change (Section I); Boundaries Breached and Blurred (Section II); Plying the Trade (Section III); The Energy of Memes (Section IV); and Muses for Engagement (Section V).

Handbook of Anthropology in Business, edited by Rita Denny and Patricia Sunderland, 13–31.

If one accepts that change happens at the boundaries of endeavors, and that innovation often occurs at the intersection of domains, there are currently frame-breaking collisions occurring at the intersections of anthropology and business, and the boundaries of both business and anthropology are expanding. The activities are considerable. In October 2013, LinkedIn, an important social media resource in business realms, had almost a thousand members in the "Business Anthropology" group. The "Consumer Anthropology–Anthropology Applied to Business" group had more than 3,000 members; a search for "organizational anthropology" returned results for more than 25,000 people and an English-Dutch group "Anthropology in Organizations" with almost 700 members.[1] Numerous other related groups abound, such as Career Anthropologist, Ethnography Forum, Ethnographers, and Ethnography; in fact, there are more than 200 groups that include either anthropology or ethnography as key *raison d'être.* Leaning toward scholarly and academic activities, there are also LinkedIn groups for the American Anthropological Association's National Association for the Practice of Anthropology (NAPA), The Ethnographic Praxis in Industry Conference (EPIC), and for *The Journal of Business Anthropology* (JBA).

The launch of two business anthropology journals, *International Journal of Business Anthropology* in 2010 and *Journal of Business Anthropology* in 2012 have been two highly significant events of the making of the field. The I*nternational Journal of Business Anthropology,* edited by Guang (Robert) Tian, Daming Zhou, and Alfons van Marrewijk, is sponsored by The College of Sociology and Anthropology of Sun Yat-Sen University in China and The Faculty of Social Science of Vrije Universiteit in the Netherlands. The *Journal of Business Anthropology* was launched under the editorial direction of anthropologists Brian Moeran at the Copenhagen Business School and Christina Garsten in the Department of Social Anthropology at Stockholm University. As disciplinary makers and markers, the geographic, locational details of these journals are telling.

Anthropology in business is a global endeavor, taking place within the disciplinary boundaries of anthropology and social science as well as business schools and in business. We have tried to reflect the range and diversity of these developments in the inclusions to the volume. Thus, we have included chapters that focus on anthropological incursions in business schools in the United States (Arnould and Thompson) and China (Tian) as well as the development of business-oriented curriculum within anthropology and interdisciplinary programs in France (Desjeux), Sweden (O'Dell and Willim), and the United States (Squires et al.; DiCarlo et al.). Roberts' chapter, focused on the British experience since 1950, is also grounded in issues of academic training.

Reflecting the global aspect of anthropology in business in this volume proved simultaneously both extremely easy and an enormous, virtually insurmountable challenge. The aspects that made a global view easy perhaps have to do with the fact that both anthropology and business traditionally have seen the world as their purview. Thus, four of the chapters in Plying the Trade, a section focused on the kinds of work done at the intersection of anthropology and business, include endeavors that entailed fieldwork in multiple countries (Cova; Erickson; Hasbrouck and Scull; Hunt and Barton). Other chapters in that and other sections detail endeavors in Australia (Agafonoff et al.), China (Wang), the Czech Republic (Ailová et al.), Finland (Tamminen et al.), France (Alami; Cochoy), Italy (Pant), Japan (McCreery and Yamaki), Norway (Hepsø), Russia (Shatokhina), and the United Kingdom (Kimbell). At the same time, even if to our chagrin, there is little question that this volume has also reproduced a North American bias. It is a bias to which Roberts points in his chapter, a bias born of operating with the United States as starting point, inherently giving priority to US developments and lending them the status of explicit as well as implicit comparative frame (see and compare Oliveira 2013). While we tried to overcome this limitation with invitations to authors from other countries, we would note that language is its own source of bias. The task of writing in English was clearly not a seamless one for many of the authors and in turn not an easy one for us as editors. Undoubtedly an American bias was reinserted as we edited the language of chapters; making them more understandable inherently meant putting them in our terms, as much as we may have tried to do otherwise.

Moreover, as much as we saw our task as neither creating nor reinforcing silos, as the *Handbook* took form, we realized that the inclusions echoed established traditions and formations of theory in American academic anthropology. Theory in American anthropology has garnered its frames from its own thinkers, but in doing so has always relied heavily on traditions emanating from Britain and France, with a bit of an open ear for what was occurring in Scandinavia. So it is here for most of the authors as well as the volume as a whole. We note this and point to the need for future works to include Latin American, southern European, African, Middle Eastern, and southeast Asian voices, along with additional voices from China and Japan, Australia, New Zealand, and Germany. The traditions are varied and the intersections important for both anthropology and business.

Even accepting the circumscribed space of anthropology in business addressed in this volume, the current flourishing and the range and variety of endeavors taking place still makes both this volume and this introduction a necessarily partial one. We can only hope that these 43 chapters, along with these words of introduction, serve as a means to inform and orient readers to some of the swirls, flows, and knots at the intersection of anthropology and business at this point in time.

PLURAL POLYSEMIA

> . . . an old city: a labyrinth of little streets and squares, of old and new houses, and of houses with additions from various periods; and this surrounded by a multitude of modern sections with straight regular streets and uniform houses.
>
> —Ludwig Wittgenstein[2]

In setting up her discussion of the intersection of anthropology and medicine, Diasio (1999:17) drew on Wittgenstein's description of an old city, a comparative metaphor he had used to depict language. Geertz (1983:73) also drew on Wittgenstein's metaphor in "Common Sense as a Cultural System" to set up his analysis of the kinds of places anthropologists tended to look for insight as well as the topics they tended to pursue. Diasio, noting that anthropology was encircled by contiguous fields, used it for the field of medical anthropology. We believe that Wittgenstein's city metaphor can equally serve to depict the situation of anthropology in business. Notably, we take both anthropology and business as labyrinths of the old and new, and the mixture as a matter of intertwined mazes. There is not one kind of anthropology, just as there is not one kind of business, and like language at the root of the metaphor, both are polysemic: there are multiple meanings associated with and attributable to both.

One can witness the polysemia in action in the vocabulary surrounding endeavors. Is it corporate anthropology, commercial anthropology, or business anthropology? As Moeran points out in his chapter, this "terminological confusion" also extends to "the varieties of anthropological subdisciplines currently associated with business: industrial, corporate, organizational, enterprise, and economic anthropologies, as well as the anthropologies of work and management." And even if one settles on the gloss of business anthropology, as Moeran also notes, the term "business" does not always translate well in non-European languages. Thus scholars in countries such as China and Japan "are obliged to come up with neologisms of one sort or another for their interpretations of 'business anthropology,' which they then supplement with age-old words like 'administration,' 'commerce,' 'management,' 'work,' and so on." (See, for example, McCreery and Yamaki's chapter "The Anthropology of Business and Administration in Japan.")

The terminological heterogeneity reflects the ascendency of varied theoretical and practical incursions of anthropology with business at different points in time, the different houses built, along with their additions and new neighbors. In the 1930s, "industrial anthropology" was the term (A. Jordan 2010, 2013), a designation that resonated with the industrial focus of business at that time. The ascendency of the corporation and framing of anthropological work in corporate terms is one of the more recent developments (Cefkin 2009a; A. Jordan 2013; Urban and Koh 2013). One can also add some of the subfields of anthropological endeavor in business to this ascendency, many used (at least sometimes) as the first word of an anthropology compound noun: "advertising anthropology" (Malefyt and Moeran 2003; Malefyt and Morais 2012), "design anthropology" (Clarke 2010; Gunn and Donovan 2012a), "consumer research" (Sunderland and Denny 2007), "workplace studies" (Szymanski and Whalen 2011), and, again, "organizational anthropology" (Caulkins and Jordan 2013; van Marrewijk 2010). Walking about and through the city, exploring and leaving traces across domains, one finds—beyond the contributors to this volume—consultants such as Grant McCracken[3] (1988, 2005, 2009, 2012a, 2012b) and Douglas Holt (2003, Holt and Cameron 2010); the academically located Daniel Miller (1997, 1998, 2008, 2010, 2012; Horst and Miller 2012) and George Marcus (Marcus 1999, 2012a, 2012b; Marcus and Fischer 1986,; Holmes and Marcus 2005); Gillian Tett (2009, 2010, 2012), who has managed an extremely successful journalism career at *The Financial Times* and retains her anthropological ties and voice;[4] the many anthropologists who work or have worked in technology companies, including Genevieve Bell (Dourish and Bell 2011), Jeanette Blomberg (2005, 2009; Blomberg et al. 1993, 2003), Brigitte Jordan (lifescapes.org, 2011, 2013), Julien Orr (1996), and Lucy Suchman (2011, 2013); and relative newcomers such as Pedro Oliveira, whose recent book (Oliveira 2013) is in many ways a travelog tracing some of the paths of earlier city dwellers while eruditely adding his own Portuguese–clinical psychologist–British–social anthropologist viewpoint, which, in fact, could change some of the lenses through which the rest of us see the terrain.

In this volume, we have tried to retain some sense of the bustling heterogeneity of this city by not organizing the volume in terms of usual silos indicated on the contemporary landscape, such as design, organizational, consumer research, consumer culture theory, corporate consulting, or academia versus practice. Several important contemporary edited volumes and review articles, focused exclusively on particular subfields, provide excellent vantage points from which to gain insight into these area activities: Caulkins and Jordan (2013) for organizational anthropology; Gunn et al. (2013) for design anthropology; Joy and Li (2012) for consumer culture theory; Szymanski and Whalen's (2011) collection of ethnographic work practice studies; and Maurer (2006) along with Maurer and Mainwaring (2012) for the anthropology of money and finance. In this volume, note also Cefkin's review and overview of work practice studies and Arnould and Thompson's chapter on consumer culture theoretics.

Our goal is to give a broader view of the anthropology-business domain and its vibrant as well as problematic intersections. Although some of the authors

(Roberts; Høyem; Kitner) point explicitly or implicitly to the structural and emotional vestiges of the "off-limits" status of business for anthropologists during the 1960s and 1970s, this home is not one on which we dwell. In essence, this resides on a path that has become a well-worn cul-de-sac, one that tends to obstruct vision in terms of what is really happening in the city as well as its possibilities. Rather, with this volume we highlight the heterogeneous and polysemic nature of business as well as the actual activities of actors within business domains. This heterogeneity is illustrated in the varied type of business contexts in which anthropology currently has a voice. Among those included in this volume are: health care (Alami); finance (Ensworth); family-owned enterprises (Pant); technology (Cefkin; Nafus; Kitner; Hanson; Cotton); energy (Hepsø); foundations (Hasbrouck and Scull; Kimbell); design (Erickson; Neese; Darrah and Dornadic); branding and marketing from an academic, business school perspective (Diamond et al.); and advertising, branding, and marketing from a practicing and consumer research perspective (Malefyt; McCabe; Morais; Tamminen et al.) and their combination (Agafonoff et al.; Cova; Shatokhina). The polysemia is also manifest in the varied realities experienced in domains; for instance, on the question of sustainability, compare the chapter by Kitner with that of Hasbrouck and Scull. The spirit we hope this volume conveys is that business is not a monolith, neither inherently good nor inherently bad, just as anthropology is neither monolithic, nor inherently good or bad. Business, like anthropology, is made up of actors with strategic goals and interests, enmeshed in material and practical realties, built up in the past and the present. And business and anthropology are intertwined, in the corners of the academy as well as commerce.

VIBRANT, PROBLEMATIC INTERSECTIONS

Perhaps not surprising, the vibrant intersections, the ones of considerable activity and engagement of anthropology in business, are simultaneously those authors have called out as not only of considerable movement, but also as sites of problems and tension. In the present moment, the resurgence of the ontological and epistemological power of quantitative frameworks, often in the form and gloss of "Big Data," is a force to be reckoned with (see Maxwell 2013; Slobin and Cherkasky 2010).

In the first section of this volume, amid a larger discussion of the decoupling of ethnography from anthropology within business domains, Baba notes the competitive pressure of Big Data analytics, ultimately arguing that it may also be an arena of opportunity for anthropologists: on the one hand for supplying the missing contextualization of quantitative patterns; on the other, through the ethnographic study of Big Data industries. Approaching the issue from a sociological stance, Patel also suggests that anthropologists need to be prepared to fuse quantitative and qualitative approaches to remain innovative. Moreover, he argues persuasively that the seeming oppositions of quantitative and qualitative methodologies are a false divide, based on a "misreading of our scholarly heritage." To move forward, Patel maintains, we must in essence dismantle some of the renovations we have done on our epistemological foundations, and look back to see what new, relevant forms can be built for contemporary data-driven environments. These are urgently voiced calls, answered, at least in part, by the stellar example Nafus provides in Section II. Acknowledging the performative role of numbers as well as their status as a more powerful form of knowledge, she tells the story of a different kind of quantitative index she and colleagues at Intel developed to address questions of emerging markets for technology adoption. Notably, the changed index also shifted development discussions away from otherwise recurrent rehearsals of the implicit problematic assumptions of West-centric development discourse. Note also comments on these issues in chapters by Kozinets, Arnould and Thompson, and Hunt and Barton.

Embedded in these discussions of quantitative ascendency are issues and concerns regarding the anthropological voice. A prevailing wish voiced by contributors to the second issue of *Journal of Business Anthropology*'s Opinion forum (JBA 2012) was that the anthropological voice be an effective counterbalance to prevailing psychological, economic, and marketing discourses in the world of commerce, industry, and business. Yet, success in this regard is contingent on how others view anthropologists and anthropology and, importantly, is fueled by anthropologists' positionality in the workplaces inhabited. It is one of the knottier city intersections, made more complicated by the diagonal boulevards of the trade press's (and anthropologists') imaginaries of anthropology and corporations, and traffic lights that are on the blink.

Anthropology in the corporate imaginary, and in material practice, Suchman (2013) argues, is brought into view through a lens of new frontiers for corporate action. Wilner, in her analysis of representations of anthropology in the trade press in this volume, would agree. Drawing on articles spanning several decades, Wilner notes that the journalistic frame renders anthropological contributions to the corporate landscape in embarrassing terms, trivializing the meaning of human experience and the endeavor. The new-frontier positioning of anthropology draws on problematic public imaginaries: anthropologists study (exotic) others, and corporations are nonreflexive pragmatists driving for competitive edge. Anthropologists in business, in these prevailing discourses, are inserted into existing research and design processes (discovery) while optimizing them (accessing new frontiers). The danger in this positioning of anthropology, and anthropologists, is twofold. First, in action, anthropologists risk being subsumed by the dominant community of practice that perpetuates existing ways of doing and thinking in the marketplace and, subsequently, in public imaginaries. Second, the ethnographic method becomes/remains disengaged from anthropology. Instead, its use in business contexts (whether in marketing, design, product innovation, or work practices) is appropriated—a "mining of method" (Maurer and Mainwearing 2012) from the discipline's perspective—or becomes a commoditized service in the market, as Baba documents in her chapter. This elision of anthropology, Baba argues, must be taken seriously by those working in business.

For anthropologists working in business realms, having their voice heard, having their theories make a difference, and making a contribution—as anthropologists and to the matters at hand—are keenly felt. In fact, as we have argued elsewhere, these are often emotionally experienced as moral imperatives (Denny 2013; Sunderland 2013). In the chapters by Ailová et al. writing from the Czech Republic, Erickson citing a project with Boeing, and Høyem caught in the suburbs of fast-food outlets, the frustration and struggle to effectively implement an anthropologically inflected voice is evident. Kozinets, describing the uptake of netnography by corporations, rues the elision of the cultural voice in the corporate embrace of the method. The blog post by sociologist Sam Ladner with the provocative heading, "Does Corporate Ethnography Suck?" that Teitler uses as the opening example in her chapter on the blogosphere captures the tonal angst.

Positioned in arenas in which communication does not take place using the register of anthropology, but rather of the specific business domain in which they work, anthropologists—if they want to be heard at all—must use the language of that domain. Quite often, to retain their sense of personal and professional identity, they must also find a way to translate and transliterate their concepts, an excellent example of which is provided in Cefkin's chapter. It is not easy, though, as Cohn's (1987) classic article detailing her experience studying defense intellectuals poignantly illustrated; the language used tends to create its own encompassing, often inescapable frame. As Suchman (2011) has noted, reflecting on her experiences at Xerox PARC, being "in the frame" of design processes limits the ability to problematize the process when doing the work.

But, as the authors in this volume demonstrate, to be an anthropologist in work one must of necessity be an anthropologist of the work, whether it be activities, teams, development, branding, design, or innovation. One's lot is to never stop ruminating. Erickson, reporting on a project conducted for Boeing for redesigning airline travel, keeps thinking and circling back to the problem long after the project has ended. Malefyt's examination of theories of the senses held by anthropologists compared with those of advertisers led to recasting his clients' focus onto product experience. McCabe turns her work on pet food brand positioning into a rumination on a shifting US ontology of humans in relation to the animal world. As Rabinow et al. (2008) note, reflecting on the needs of contemporary anthropological fieldwork, the anthropological position is both timely—by being immersed in the present—but also untimely, by virtue of analytic position. Silletoe (2007) noted "detachment" as a hallmark of anthropological contribution while at the same time ceding the need for mastering the practices and discourses of one's field of practice. Tett (2010) maintains it is the anthropologists' "filter" that is distinguishing, allowing a distinctive vantage point on the ways power structures and discourses are replicated, granting an acute ear for the unsaid and great ability to fit things together systemically. Anthropologists in business are hybrid as a matter of course (Blomberg 2005). A random walk through the chapters in this volume will demonstrate the duality of roles, the immersed and the reflective.

The label of anthropologist can be extremely helpful as Darrah and Dornadic, Ensworth, and Morais describe in their chapters: it can confer competitive advantage in obtaining work, or confer desired distinctiveness of voice on a workplace team or in a business practice; it is both a selling point and a point of deeply seated pride. It is a both/and. At the same time, anthropologists-as-others risk perpetuating a public (trade press) imaginary that stereotypes the discipline as exotic and that simultaneously obscures the anthropological difference that, for example, recontextualizes the problem to be solved and/or reexamines the epistemology of knowing. In managing the material realities of their work, contributors to this volume sometimes illustrate a productive tension they bring to bear: Kitner thinks of her task as being a "burr in the saddle"; Nafus reconfigures assumptions high-tech product mangers make about developing markets in a register intelligible to her internal clients; Hepsø describes the need to adhere to workplace practices while incrementally changing them in practice. Using Viveiros de Castro's (2004) notion of controlled equivocations as his muse, Oliveira (2012) suggests that anthropologists, enmeshed in networks of client constituencies, are brokers of epistemologically incompatible views. For Oliveira, partial resolution of equivocations is achieved through a process of co-creation designed so that constituencies become materially enmeshed in another's ontological view.

Language and discursive practices are at the heart of the problem of positionality and voice. It is not just a matter of bilingualism and the necessity for anthropologists in business to become bilingual; rather, the difficulty rests with the performativity of language (Callon 1998; Holmes 2009; Silverstein 2006). Discursive practices are located within institutional structures where status, power, or identity is actively negotiated though language events at the same time that the terms of talk are the means by which "what is going on" is established (Denny 2013). For the bilingual anthropologist, discursive choices, opportunities for code-switching, even fostering a new client register, are an ongoing process (and vibrant problematic intersection) precisely because ethnographic ways of knowing and analysis so often constitute a different frame. This is illustrated in the beginning of Cefkin's chapter as she recounts a moment of giving tips to a computer scientist on how to conduct an ethnographic investigation. Hasbrouck and Scull, reflecting on the role of language in their multidisciplinary, multicountry project on sustainable fishing practices, recount the analysis process the reassembled interdisciplinary team engaged in at the completion of the fieldwork:

> [W]hile interdisciplinary teams are an excellent way to expand thinking and challenge assumptions, they require a significant amount of time dedicated to negotiating the meaning of terms, as well as understanding when and where each person should variously assert or abandon their disciplinary biases. Yes, egos can get in the way! But the negotiation, as processed through analyzing the data collected, is often very productive, and sometimes revelatory.

Tied within practices of the work, entailing powers of hierarchy, language, and discursive practices are not always easy to manage. But when successfully managed, as Hasbrouck and Scull demonstrate, the possibilities of hybridities are powerful.

To counterbalance prevailing economics or corporate discourses, one must embrace productive tensions in voice and positionality, which, in turn, entails grappling with issues of language, translation, and cross-disciplinary communication and negotiation, all of which become means for changing the ways anthropology is imagined by others and practiced at the intersection with business. As Wilner and Morais both note in their chapters, there is a need for a louder voice. For Morais this means becoming part of strategic decision-making; for Wilner this means becoming an author of what is circulated and consumed in public spaces. Actions at all these levels are necessary for, as Baba notes in her chapter, the decoupling of anthropology and ethnography in corporate spaces is systemically grounded, not only by historical trajectories of the discipline but by market dynamics as well. The rise of techno-ethnography (see also Malefyt 2009), with its elision of analysis and assumed transparency of meaning, is its own formidable trajectory, the pedestrian tunnel, perhaps, of this knotty intersection.

AVENUES OF INTEREST

As many of the chapters demonstrate, commitment and attention to issues of method—in what manner, with what approaches, with whom and in what ways research is conducted and communicated—are large arenas of concern (note also Lury and Wakeford's 2012 volume on methods). Ladner's blog post asking whether corporate ethnography sucked was provocative precisely because of these underlying concerns. Who would want their research domain to be seen—or actually be—substandard?

In fact, there remains a deep engagement and commitment to fieldwork and the ethnographic process. The reality of this commitment is vividly illustrated by Moynié, an ethnographic filmmaker, whose chapter details his own phenomenological experiences in building rapport and conducting fieldwork with his camera. Høyem's evocative contribution, conveying painful aspects of being in the field in a fast-food restaurant, is in many ways a "Tale of the Field" (Marcus 2009; van Maanen 2011). In keeping with the anthropological genre of personal accounts, a few literary liberties are perhaps taken, but in doing so the process of ethnographic research and realities of being in the field, as well as a commitment to anthropological traditions—in research process and narrative form—are simultaneously illustrated. Wang's chapter, "Live Fieldnoting," can also be read as a plea for excellence in the field, with matters of rapport, ethics, interlocutors, analytic influences, and audience all interrelated. Her chapter brings to the fore some of the contemporary realities and possibilities of fieldwork in faraway places, where the faraway of friends and colleagues in New York or California are moments away from Wuhan and Shanghai via Instagram.

As a discipline, there has rightfully been a lot of agita and soul searching among anthropologists concerning not only ways to be relevant with the contemporary, but also how to have methods relevant amid social realities of interconnected technologies and communicative channels, new forms of social life in space, time, and kind (e.g., Faubion and Marcus 2009; Rabinow 2008; Rabinow et al. 2008; note also chapters in this volume by Caliandro and Kozinets on ethnography in digital spaces). Contemporary fieldwork often involves other experts and interdisciplinary teams, often simultaneously as subject, object, interlocutor, and synthesizer of research (Holmes and Marcus 2005; Rabinow and Stavrianakis 2013) and methodological innovations that have occurred at intersections of anthropology in business—for instance, at the intersection of anthropology and design—have been called out as examples of possibilities and paradigms (see Gatt and Ingold 2013; Murphy and Marcus 2013).

The chapter by Hasbrouck and Scull serves as an example that encompasses and illustrates many of these methodological issues. Their uniquely written account of an international, multisited, interdisciplinary investigation in search of sustainable models for the fishing industry led them to trace the journey of fish from the source through processing, distribution, and consumption, or as they poetically put it, "from hook to plate." In their account, one can witness the workings and wonders of being in the field, presented as offset texts that also include genre narratives such as arrival scenes, surprises, and confusion followed by insight. In conducting this research, however, they used what they called "an adapted form of anthropological research" carried out by interdisciplinary teams that conducted research simultaneously in different locations both geographically and on the "hook to plate" journey. These methods included facility tours, informal interviews, photojournaling, and shadowing; these and similar methods are often used in consumer, design, and other business research as the other chapters in the Plying the Trade section, as well as those by Ensworth, Morais, and Malefyt show. There are useful and replicable models being bred "in the impatient world of corporate anthropology," as Hasbrouck and Scull so aptly characterize the terrain.

Matters of pedagogy, inextricably linked with issues of anthropological theory, methods, and ethnographic practice, are also a major avenue of interest in the *Handbook*. A concern with adequate academic training has been a catalyst, or at least a cornerstone, in much of the recent writing that Marcus, Rabinow, and colleagues have undertaken on the need to rethink ethnographic practice. Chapters from innovators of curricula in anthropology-business as well as interdisciplinary design, are spread throughout the volume's five sections. The chapter by Desjeux, describing the professional doctoral program he has developed in France, includes discussion of the analytic models with which he tries to equip students, with particular explication of the itinerary method he has developed. The method, with roots in Desjeux's work on agricultural itineraries in Madagascar and the Congo, as well as experience with Michel Crozier's strategic analysis for organizations, has proved an extremely useful modality for studies of consumption. This method, passed on to students in France, has also been picked by Erickson, a consumer researcher based in the United States, as he notes in his chapter on airline interior redesign for Boeing.

The avenues of training are internationally intersected and interdisciplinary. The international influence and exchange is perhaps most evident in Tian's chapter on the history of business anthropology and training in China, and the interdisciplinary aspect most evident in DiCarlo et al.'s discussion of the integration of anthropology into the core curriculum of the undergraduate College of Design, Engineering, and Commerce at Philadelphia University, yet all of the chapters on training evidence these factors.

HANDBOOK & CITY STRUCTURE

There are many other avenues, shared streets, lanes, *petites rues,* and *bâtiments* one could call out. For example, one could note the permeation of theoretical frameworks emanating from Bruno Latour, Michel Callon, and actor-network theory in the work and analyses of several of the authors (Cochoy; Kimbell; Nafus; O'Dell and Willim). One could put the *Handbook* back together in terms of traditional disciplinary or practice domains; for example, consumer culture theory (Arnould and Thompson; Diamond et al; Kozinets), design and design thinking (Kimbell; Erickson; Hasbrouck and Scull; Neese), consumer and marketing research (Ailová et al; Agafonoff et al.; Cova; McCabe; Malefyt; Tamminen et al.), and organizational anthropology (Cefkin; Ensworth; Hanson; Hepsø; McCreery and Yamaki; Pant). Or, one could focus on hybridity, and note the enthusiasm for combinations as well as the creativity that ensues in the usage of insight, styles, and building materials from other domains (Baba; Cochoy; DiCarlo et al.; Nafus; Neese; Hunt and Barton) as well as note the ways that interdisciplinary combinations become new styles, new objects, domains in their own right (see Diasio 1999).

In our own structuring of sections we have organized chapters that highlight large social and historical dynamics in the first section: Dynamics of Tension, Forces of Change. We move to a closer-in view of the kinds of disciplinary, theoretical, and methodological boundaries that have been and are being breached and blurred in the mixing of anthropology and business in the second section: Boundaries Breached and Blurred. The third section, Plying the Trade, consists of chapters grounded by case studies which illustrate in greater detail the kinds of work being done, and the methodological and analytic frameworks applied. The Energy of Memes, the fourth section, brings the focus back to culturally salient ideas and practices that have been taken up and circulated at the intersections of anthropology and business. The final section, Muses for Engagement, is about the sources of inspiration and motivation that keep people able and willing to work at the intersection of anthropology and business. These muses include academic developments and theorizing as well as popular culture and professional as well as personal predilections. In the introductions to each of these sections, we highlight more of the opportunities and challenges we see occurring at the intersections of anthropology and business. But our purpose for now is simply to invite readers to discover the city, to be *flaneurs*, to investigate aspects of the city they do not yet know. And while we are acutely aware that our city metaphor has by now become dangerously tiring—and it is high time for us to switch to the compositional metaphor used by O'Dell and Willim in the *Handbook*'s final chapter—we have stayed with the metropolitan muse for a reason.

A significant difference of this *Handbook* from other collections is the diversity of authors, some located inside, some outside of the academy; some of those outside of the academy working inside corporations, others not; some are academically trained as anthropologists, some as sociologists, others as designers, and others as marketers. Some reside betwixt and between, holding academic positions and also acting as business consultants, or working in business full-time while also university-affiliated. Some are established scholars with considerable reputations; others have arrived on the scene relatively recently.

To us, this diversity is both a reflection of the anthropology in business domain and a contribution that the anthropology-business intersection and this *Handbook* offer the field. The domain of anthropology in business has been one where scholarship has gone outside the bounds of anthropology departments, as in the case of consumer culture theory emanating from marketing departments. Scholarship outside the walls of academia has also been particularly active. The Ethnographic Practice in Industry Conference (EPIC) and its published proceedings since 2005 as well as the books published in an academic vein, often by academic presses, by those working full-time in or for businesses are cases in point. (e.g., Cefkin 2009a; B. Jordan 2013; Malefyt and Morais 2012; Squires and Byrne 2002; and this volume). It is also a domain where there has been a distinct and dynamic interchange among organizations and individuals operating from within and outside the academy. Again, EPIC is a case in point in that the American Anthropological Association publishes its proceedings (see also Cefkin 2012). The development of academic programs geared to preparing students for careers in anthropology-business domains beyond academia are also cases in point.

These developments are understandable in the context of contemporary training of more graduate students than the academic marketplace could possibility accommodate, a dynamic that many of the authors of the chapters focused on academic training point out. These developments in outside-of-academia scholarship also fit within the current technologically aided and abetted social milieu of "openness" and exchange of ideas (see chapters by Wang and Teitler). For example, for those working in the anthropology in business domain, especially those working at the nexus of anthropology and design, the Anthrodesign listserv begun by Natalie Hanson in 2002 has become a very active source of exchange of ideas and references. It is now a community, not just a listserv.[5] Open access journals, Google Scholar and Google Books, self-publishing via Amazon, and TED talks could also all be brought forth as examples. And while there were other historical eras when these mediated possibilities did not exist and scholarship took place beyond the institutional confines of universities (e.g., Benjamin Whorf), these media are helpful to non–university-affiliated scholars in the current moment.

There is also clear movement from the academic side. The Society for Applied Anthropology's increasing, or more aptly stated, returning openness (A. Jordan 2010) to business topics; Wasson's (2006) advocacy for the role of scholar-practitioners (see also Squires et al.'s chapter); the American Anthropological Association's relationship and support of EPIC; and the French Association of Anthropologists noting that business domains were possibilities for anthropologists (see chapter by Desjeux) are all significant. In March 2013, Alladi Venkatesh, a professor of marketing and board member of the Center for Ethnography at the University of California at Irvine, co-organized with George Marcus the Anthropology of Consumption and Markets Conference. This conference, which included speakers and attendees from academia and practice, lived up to the stated goal for the Center for Ethnography : ". . . sustained and diverse theoretical and methodological conversations across disciplines, academic and applied, both to probe the state of ethnographic practice and to influence the current changes in how ethnography is conducted, reported, received, and taught" (Center for Ethnography 2013). While the "corridor talk" as well as some of the official comments of the conference indicated that the event was unique in bringing together faculty from business schools as well as anthropology (and other) departments, the spirit and hope of the conference was that the "unique" status should not remain. Melanie Wallendorf, sociologist and participant in the Consumer Behavior Odyssey (Belk 1991), an exemplary research project that Arnould and Thompson call out in their chapter as the "most spectacular gesture" of the early wave of cultural approaches taking place in marketing departments, mentioned in her podium comments that she looked forward to the day when campus paths between university business school and social science buildings were literally well-worn from all the students who walk back and forth.

In Urban and Koh's (2013) review article of ethnographic research in corporations, they make a distinction of anthropological research "in" corporations and "for" corporations.[6] These prepositional distinctions, plus "with," "of," "on," and "against," are also used by Moeran in his contribution to this volume, as they were in his provocative coda (Moeran 2012) to the foundational set of opinion essays regarding business anthropology included in the second issue of the *Journal of Business Anthropology.* The conclusion these authors draw regarding all of these linkages between anthropology and business, as well as from the implicitly prepositional "business anthropology," is, in fact, that it is their linking and grouping that counts. Their point and *the* point, as Cefkin (2009b) has also so aptly framed it, is that when we *engage* with them all, we benefit. The benefit is in theory and practice: the rejuvenation of theory, practice, and anthropology, inside and outside of academic and commercial walls. As Roberts' chapter reminds us in the opening section, developments inside and outside of academic departments *are* intertwined. And so, while we are aware that there is likely to be a tendency to read this book in terms of predefined interests and to start, as well as perhaps conclude, with the known names of colleagues, competitors, and friends, we invite you to engage with something or someone new. In fact, there is perhaps no better place to start than with the final section: Muses for Engagement.

REFERENCES

Belk, Russell, ed. 1991. *Highways and Buyways: Naturalistic Research from the Consumer Behavior Odyssey.* Provo, UT: Association for Consumer Research.

Blomberg, Jeannette. 2005. "The Coming of Age of Hybrids: Notes on Ethnographic Praxis." EPIC 2005:67–74.

_____. 2009. "Insider Trading: Engaging and Valuing Corporate Ethnography." In *Ethnography and the Corporate Encounter: Reflections on Research in and of Corporations,* edited by M. Cefkin, 213–26. New York: Berghahn.

Blomberg, Jeanette, Mark Burrell, and Greg Guest. 2003. "An Ethnographic Approach to Design." In *Human-Computer Interaction Handbook: Fundamental, Evolving Technologies and Emerging Applications,* edited by A. Sears and J. Jacko, 965–84. Philadelphia, PA: Lawrence Erlbaum Associates.

Blomberg, Jeanette, Jean Giacomi, Andrea Mosher, and Pat Swenton-Wall. 1993. "Ethnographic Field Methods and Their Relation to Design." In *Participatory Design: Principles and Practices,* edited by D. Schuler and A. Namioka, 123–55. Hillsdale, NJ: Lawrence Erlbaum Associates.

Callon, Michel, ed. 1998. *Laws of the Market.* Oxford, UK: Blackwell.

Caulkins, D. Douglas, and Ann Jordan, eds. 2013. *A Companion to Organizational Anthropology.* Malden, MA: Wiley-Blackwell.

Cefkin, Melissa, ed. 2009a. *Ethnography and the Corporate Encounter: Reflections on Research in and of Corporations.* New York: Berghahn.

_____. 2009b. "Introduction: Business, Anthropology, and the Growth of Corporate Ethnography." In *Ethnography and the Corporate Encounter: Reflections on Research in and of Corporations,* edited by M. Cefkin, 1–37. New York: Berghahn.

_____. 2012. "Close Encounters: Anthropologists in the Corporate Arena." *Journal of Business Anthropology* 1(1):91–117.

Center for Ethnography. 2013. "Welcome." http://www.ethnography.uci.edu/ (accessed October 28, 2013).

Clarke, Alison J., ed. 2010. *Design Anthropology: Object Culture in the 21st Century.* New York: Springer Vienna.

Cohn, Carol. 1987. "Sex and Death in the Rational World of Defense Intellectuals." *Signs* 12(4):687–718.

Denny, Rita. 2013. "The Cry of Practicality." In *Advancing Ethnography in Corporate Environments,* edited by B. Jordan, 136–50. Walnut Creek, CA: Left Coast Press.

Diasio, Nicoletta. 1999. *La Science impure: Anthropologie et médecine en France, Grande-Bretagne, Italie, Pays-Bas* [*Impure Science: Anthropology and Medicine in France, Great Britain, Italy, and the Netherlands*]. Paris: Presses Universitaires de France.

Dourish, Paul, and Genevieve Bell. 2011. *Divining a Digital Future: Mess and Mythology in Ubiquitous Computing.* Cambridge, MA: MIT Press.

Faubion, James, and George E. Marcus, eds. 2009. *Fieldwork Is Not What It Used To Be: Learning Anthropology's Method in a Time of Transition.* Ithaca, NY: Cornell University Press.

Gatt, Caroline, and Tim Ingold. 2013. "From Description to Correspondence: Anthropology in Real Time." In *Design Anthropology: Theory and Practice,* edited by W. Gunn, T. Otto, and R. C. Smith, 139–58. London: Bloomsbury.

Geertz, Clifford. 1983. *Local Knowledge: Further Essays in Interpretive Anthropology.* New York: Basic Books.

Gunn, Wendy, Ton Otto, and Rachael Charlotte Smith, eds. 2013. *Design Anthropology: Theory and Practice.* London: Bloomsbury.

Gunn, Wendy, and Jared Donovan, eds. 2012a. *Design and Anthropology.* Burlington, UK: Ashgate.

_____. 2012b. "Design Anthropology: An Introduction." In *Design and Anthropology,* edited by W. Gunn and J. Donovan, 1–16. Burlington, UK: Ashgate.

Holmes, Douglas. 2009. "Economy of Words." *Cultural Anthropology* 24(3):381–419.

Holmes, Douglas, and George E. Marcus. 2005. "Cultures of Expertise and the Management of Globalization: Toward the Re-Functioning of Ethnography." In *Global Assemblages: Technology, Politics, and Ethics as Anthropological Problems,* edited by A. Ong and S. Collier, 145–73. Oxford, UK: Blackwell.

Holt, Douglas. 2003. *How Brands Become Icons: The Principles of Cultural Branding.* Boston: Harvard Business School Press.

Holt, Douglas, and Douglas Cameron. 2010. *Cultural Strategy: Using Innovative Ideologies To Build Breakthrough Brands.* Oxford, UK: Oxford University Press.

Horst, Heather, and Daniel Miller, eds. 2012. *Digital Anthropology.* Oxford, UK: Berg.

Jordan, Ann T. 2010. "The Importance of Business Anthropology: Its Unique Contribution." *International Journal of Business Anthropology* 1(1):15–25.

_____. 2013. *Business Anthropology.* 2nd edition. Long Grove, IL: Waveland Press.

Jordan, Brigitte. 2011. "Transferring Ethnographic Competence: Personal Reflections on the Past and Future of Work Practice Analysis." In *Making Work Visible: Ethnographically Grounded Case Studies of Work Practice,* edited by M. H. Szymanski and Jack Whalen, 344–58. Cambridge, UK: Cambridge University Press.

_____, ed. 2013. *Advancing Ethnography in Corporate Environments: Challenges and Emerging Opportunities.* Walnut Creek, CA: Left Coast Press.

Joy, Annamma, and Eric P. Li. 2012. "Studying Consumption Behavior through Multiple Lenses: An Overview of Consumer Culture Theory." *Journal of Business Anthropology* 1(1):141–73.

Lury, Celia, and Nina Wakeford, eds. 2012. *Inventive Methods: The Happening of the Social.* London: Routledge.

Malefyt, Timothy de Waal. 2009. "Understanding the Rise of Consumer Ethnography: Branding Technomethodologies in the New Economy." *American Anthropologist* 111(2):201–10.

Malefyt, Timothy de Waal, and Brian Moeran, eds. 2003. *Advertising Cultures.* New York: Berg.

Malefyt, Timothy de Waal, and Robert J. Morais. 2012. *Advertising and Anthropology: Ethnographic Practice and Cultural Perspectives.* London: Berg.

Marcus, George E., ed. 1999. *Corporate Futures: The Corporation as a Culturally Sensitive Form.* Chicago, IL: University of Chicago Press.

_____. 2009. "Introduction: Notes toward an Ethnographic Memoir of Supervising Graduate Research through Anthropology's Decades of Transformation." In *Fieldwork Is Not What It Used To Be: Learning Anthropology's Method in a Time of Transition,* edited by J. Faubion and G. Marcus, 1–34. Ithaca, NY: Cornell University Press.

_____, ed. 2012a. "Opinion: What Business Anthropology Is, What It Might Become . . . and What, Perhaps, It Should Not Be." *Journal of Business Anthropology* 1(2):265–72.

_____. 2012b. "The Viral Intimacies of Ethnographic Encounters: Prolegomenon to a Thought Experiment in the Play of Metaphors." *Cultural Anthropology* 27(1):168–74.

Marcus, George E., and Michael Fischer. 1986. *Anthropology as Cultural Critique: An Experimental Moment in the Human Sciences.* Chicago, IL: University of Chicago Press.

Maurer, Bill. 2006. "The Anthropology of Money." *Annual Review of Anthropology* 35(1): 15–36.

Maurer, Bill, and Scott Mainwaring. 2012. "Anthropology with Business: Plural Programs and Future Financial Worlds." *Journal of Business Anthropology* 1(2):177–96.

Maxwell, Chad R. 2013. "Accelerated Pattern Recognition, Ethnography, and the Era of Big Data." In *Advancing Ethnography in Corporate Environments,* edited by B. Jordan, 175–92. Walnut Creek, CA: Left Coast Press.

McCracken, Grant. 1988. *Culture and Consumption: New Approaches to the Symbolic Character of Consumer Goods and Activities.* Bloomington: Indiana University Press.

_____. 2005. *Culture and Consumption II: Markets, Meaning, and Brand Management.* Bloomington: Indiana University Press.

McCracken, Grant. 2009. *Chief Culture Officer: How To Create a Living, Breathing Corporation.* New York: Basic Books.

_____. 2012a. *Culturematic: How Reality TV, John Cheever, a Pie Lab, Julia Child, Fantasy Football, Burning Man, the Ford Fiesta Movement, Rube Goldberg, NFL Films, Wordle, Two and a Half Men, a 10,000-Year Symphony, and ROFLCon Memes Will Help You Create and Execute Breakthrough Ideas.* Boston: Harvard Business Review Press.

_____. 2012b. "Culture To Advance Innovation: Grant McCracken at TEDxHarlem." August 3. http://www.youtube.com/watch?v=5V-8SbhFAEo (accessed October 29, 2013).

Miller, Daniel. 1997. *Capitalism: An Ethnographic Approach.* London: Berg.

_____. 1998. *A Theory of Shopping.* Cambridge, UK: Polity Press.

_____. 2008. *The Comfort of Things.* Cambridge, UK: Polity Press.

_____. 2010. *Stuff.* Cambridge, UK: Polity Press.

_____. 2012. *Consumption and Its Consequences.* Cambridge, UK: Polity Press.

Moeran, Brian. 2012. "Coda to Opinions: What Business Anthropology Is, What It Might Become . . . and What, Perhaps, It Should Not Be." *Journal of Business Anthropology* 1(2):290–97.

Murphy, Keith M., and George E. Marcus. 2013. "Ethnography and Design, Ethnography in Design . . . Ethnography by Design." In *Design Anthropology: Theory and Practice,* edited by W. Gunn, T. Otto, and R. C. Smith, 251–68. London: Bloomsbury.

Oliveira, Pedro. 2012. "Ethnography and Co-Creation in a Portuguese Consultancy." *Journal of Business Anthropology* 1(2):197–217.

_____. 2013. *People-Centered Innovation: Becoming a Practitioner in Innovation Research.* Columbus, OH: Biblio.

Orr, Julian E. 1996. *Talking About Machines: An Ethnography of a Modern Job.* Ithaca, NY: ILR Press.

Rabinow, Paul. 2008. *Marking Time: On the Anthropology of the Contemporary.* Princeton, NJ: Princeton University Press.

Rabinow, Paul, George E. Marcus, James Faubion, and Tobias Rees. 2008. *Designs for an Anthropology of the Contemporary.* Durham, NC: Duke University Press.

Rabinow, Paul, and Anthony Stavrianakis. 2013. *Demands of the Day: On the Logic of Anthropological Inquiry.* Chicago, IL: University of Chicago Press.

Sillitoe, Paul. 2007. "Anthropologists Only Need Apply: Challenges of Applied Anthropology." *Journal of the Royal Anthropological Institute* 13:147–65.

Silverstein, Michael. 2006. "Old Wine, New Ethnographic Lexicography." *Annual Review of Anthropology* 25:481–96.

Slobin, Adrian, and Todd Cherkasky. 2010. "Ethnography in the Age of Analytics." *EPIC* 2010:188–98.

Squires, Susan, and Bryan Byrne, eds. 2002. *Creating Breakthrough Ideas: The Collaboration of Anthropologists and Designers in the Product Development Industry.* Westport, CT: Bergin & Garvey.

Suchman, Lucy. 2011. "Anthropological Relocations and the Limits of Design." *Annual Review of Anthropology* 40:1–8.

_____. 2013. "Consuming Anthropology." In *Interdisciplinarity: Reconfigurations of the Social and Natural Sciences,* edited by Andrew Barry and Georgina Born, 141–60. London: Routledge.

Sunderland, Patricia. 2013. "The Cry for More Theory." In *Advancing Ethnography in Corporate Environments,* edited by B. Jordan, 122–35. Walnut Creek, CA: Left Coast Press.

Sunderland, Patricia L., and Rita M. Denny. 2007. *Doing Anthropology in Consumer Research.* Walnut Creek, CA: Left Coast Press.

Szymanski, Margaret H., and Jack Whalen, eds. 2011. *Making Work Visible: Ethnographically Grounded Case Studies of Work Practice.* New York: Cambridge University Press.

Tett, Gillian. 2009. *Fool's Gold: The Inside Story of J. P. Morgan and How Wall Street Greed Corrupted Its Bold Dream and Created a Financial Catastrophe.* New York: Free Press.

Tett, Gillian. 2010. "Silence and Silos: The Problems of Fractured Thought in Finance." Paper presented at the 109th Annual Meeting of the American Anthropological Association, November 19, New Orleans, LA. vimeo.com/17854712 (accessed October 29, 2013).

______. 2012. Anthropology in the World conference keynote lecture. Royal Anthropological Institute's Discover Anthropology Programme. http://www.youtube.com/watch?v=QJKLqWiIh8k (accessed October 29, 2013).

Urban, Greg, and Kyung-Nan Koh. 2013. "Ethnographic Research on Modern Business Corporations." *Annual Review of Anthropology* 42:139–58.

van Maanen, John. 2011. *Tales of the Field: On Writing Ethnography.* Second edition. Chicago, IL: University of Chicago Press.

van Marrewijk, Alfons. 2010. "European Developments in Business Anthropology." *International Journal of Business Anthropology* 1(1):26–44.

Viveiros de Castro, Eduardo. 2004. "Perspectival Anthropology and the Method of Controlled Equivocation." *Tipití: Journal of the Society for the Anthropology of Lowland South America* 2(1):3–20.

Wasson, Christina. 2006. "Making History at the Frontier." *NAPA Bulletin* 26:1–19.

NOTES

1 See van Marrewijk (2010) for an overview of organizational anthropology in the Nether-lands, often neglected in US discussions of anthropology in business.

2 This quotation, in French in Diasio's text, uses Geertz's translation, with the replacement of labyrinth for maze. We would also like to acknowledge the inspiration that Diasio's analysis provided for our approach in this introduction.

3 See McCracken's 2012 TEDX Harlem presentation regarding Culturematics (McCracken 2012b; http://www.youtube.com/watch?v=5V-8SbhFAEo). This talk is a vivid demonstration of McCracken's tremendous ability to see and make connections across cultural domains as well as his boundless energy, including for walking.

4 See, as an example, Gillian Tett's keynote lecture for the 2012 Anthropology in the World Conference in London, part of the Royal Anthropological Institute's Discover Anthropology Programme (Tett 2012; http://www.youtube.com/watch?v=QJKLqWiIh8k).

5 See the Anthrodesign website at http://anthrodesign.com.

6 Notably, these kinds of "in," "of," "with," and "for" discussions also surface in discussions of anthropology and design; see Gunn and Donovan (2012b).

Section I

DYNAMICS OF TENSION, FORCES OF CHANGE

INTRODUCTION

PATRICIA SUNDERLAND & RITA DENNY

The six chapters of this introductory section engage matters of anthropology and ethnography in business at a bit of a distance. To employ a metaphor often used in business domains, the point of entry is at the widest end of the funnel. These chapters render the gaze as an encompassing one: looking over, around, and at trends, and interrogating practices. From this vantage point, one of the crucial dynamics that comes into focus is the interdependence and intertwining of theory and practice within and outside the walls of academic institutions and disciplines. As Arnould and Thompson point out in their chapter, "certain approaches, problematics, or theoretical positions emerge from historically specific institutional arrangements and opportunities." Chapters in this section are an invitation to consider dynamics surrounding the theories and methods of anthropological work and to interrogate assumptions surrounding the history, practice, and purpose of anthropological endeavors.

A crucial aim of Roberts' chapter, a sketch of the development of business anthropology in the United Kingdom since the late 1940s, is to elucidate ways developments in anthropology's application in business are integrally related to developments in the academy. He notes that early on, Oxford, Cambridge, and the London School of Economics—the elite universities in which anthropology was established in the United Kingdom—produced too few graduates to have any significant number of anthropologists at work in positions beyond the academy. Whatever leanings there were—or not—toward the value of anthropological engagement with business, the opportunity for significant impact was minimal, at least numerically. The arithmetic favored replacement of academic teaching positions within these founding universities and supplied the faculty to fill positions as the discipline expanded to other universities. An anthropology practice in business arose only after the discipline expanded and produced a significant number of graduates. Importantly, he notes that now institutions are in turn responding to labor markets and opportunities in terms of programmatic

Handbook of Anthropology in Business, edited by Rita Denny and Patricia Sunderland, 35–41.

developments, for instance by offering degrees in digital anthropology at University College London and design anthropology at University of Aberdeen.

Baba's historical chapter revolves around the coupling and decoupling of ethnography and anthropology. Because this coupling is located at the heart of the establishment of anthropology as an academic discipline, Baba worries that a contemporary decoupling may have significant identity consequences for anthropology. She locates roots of the current decoupling in the commodification of ethnography as a business service that can be carried out by others, combined with the hybridization of anthropology with other fields (such as design). Baba also argues that the decoupling is rooted in the anthropological embrace of Foucaultian analysis. Noting that Foucault became one of the most-cited and influential theorists in American academic anthropology, Baba links this disciplinary development with postmodernism, the "crisis of representation," and Marcus and Fisher's (1986) influential call for the reframing of anthropology's mission to one of cultural critique. Baba points to Foucault's concepts of power/knowledge, his interest in topics related to science and technology, and the intertwined interest and influence of the interrogation of domains of technology, science, and power within contemporary anthropology. She sees a root of the contemporary decoupling of ethnography from anthropology in Foucaultian "problematizations" and analytic commitment to the value of second-order understanding and explication. In fact, drawing on Foucault, Rabinow (2003) has maintained that acknowledging the intellectual difference between engaging in ethnography and anthropology is necessary for an anthropology of the contemporary. Rabinow and Stavrianakis (2013) have also argued that the decoupling of participant observation and anthropology was necessary to analyze and comprehend less-than-successful collaborative fieldwork experiences with synthetic biology and nanotechnology experts.

As Roberts, Baba, and other authors in this section are keen to clarify, one cannot draw simplistic, non-overlapping circles for academic anthropology and "professional anthropology," the compound term that Desjeux uses rather than the more usual—though significantly less precise—formulation of "practicing anthropology" often used in the United States. For Desjeux the point is that the analytic requirements are the same. As he maintains for "fieldwork carried out and financed at the request of clients, whether the anthropologist is an entrepreneur, a research manager, or an academic," the request may not be anthropological, but the answer is. Notably, embedded in Desjeux's formulation is also the recognition that anthropology can be and is "applied" by anthropologists who are affiliated with universities as well as those who are not. In essence, the boundaries are porous both practically and theoretically, a reality also instantiated in Roberts' chapter by his discussion of academic research on the career trajectories of PhD anthropologists, research on which he relies as part of his narrative and data, and in which he was also involved as "informant."

Moeran addresses the intertwining of theory and practice as he simultaneously disentangles and defines parameters and a programmatic statement for business anthropology. Providing details of his own fieldwork in Japan, which he conducted as an academic anthropologist, Moeran maintains that these experiences, which included selling his own crafted pots in a department store and helping to write advertising taglines, have reinforced his view that "for fieldwork to be really 'successful,' the fieldworker has to do (or have done) what his or her informants are doing." Adding that this "is something that, ideally, every anthropologist of business should aim for when in the field," Moeran notes that this process of doing-what-informants-do is in fact often experienced by anthropologists who work in and with business for extended periods of time.

The very real truism that theory resides in methods and methods reside in theories, explicitly noted by Moeran, is a dynamic that quite obviously animates the analyses of all of the authors of chapters in this section. It is a central component in Baba's detailing of the coupling and decoupling of anthropology and ethnography as well as Desjeux's explication of the actual analytic similarity and symmetry of anthropological analyses catalyzed by client requests or academic theoretical puzzles. This reality is also visible in Arnould and Thompson's tracing of consumer culture theory within the business school context in terms of three discernable epistemic moments: humanistic/romantic, social constructivist, and global-network. As they note, for example, the humanistic/romantic moment arose as a countermove to the disciplinary view of consumers as "rational, information-driven, utility-maximizing decision-makers" and attempted to replace positivist standards of objectivity and methods with those that revealed the consumer meanings of consumption via researchers' more "empathetically, emotionally, and experientially attuned" endeavors. In the current global-network epistemic moment, attention and efforts have shifted to digital methodologies and a larger scale and scope in addition to local phenomena and cultural forms. Here, as they point out, "consumers, consumption, and consumer culture" are construed as "polyvocal and polysemic phenomena that are diffuse across heterodoxic and glocalized spaces." Given this epistemic moment, careful readers may ponder whether our depiction in the opening introduction of the terrain of anthropology and business in the terms of a plural, polysemic metropolis could possibly be entirely coincidental.

The chapter by Patel also encourages us to go back and rethink our assumptions regarding divisions between quantitative and qualitative methods in the wake of "Big Data," a phenomenon that Arnould and Thompson note has been a challenge for culturally oriented researchers in business schools, even as the shift to the examination with and through global digital methodologies has occurred (see Caliandro in Section IV and Kozinets in Section V). Patel's review and recontexualization of the positions of Comte, Durkheim, Simmel, and Geertz are helpful grounding, and his analysis is extremely stimulating food for thought. His conclusions also mesh with those of Baba, in her contention that as anthropologists we need to engage with both technology and Big Data and to not be afraid. In the end, and underneath it all, they both contend that as anthropological researchers, we have nothing to fear except fear itself.

Patel's point is that we need to move beyond the epistemologically at-odds bifurcation of quantitative and qualitative frameworks as well as the stance of using quantitative frameworks to validate qualitative findings and qualitative frameworks to validate the quantitative findings. Simultaneously holding these frameworks as at-odds as well as covalidators is at once oxymoronic but also true in practice. Desjeux's explication of the scales of observation method, one of the four primary frameworks he emphasizes in the professional anthropology doctoral program at the Sorbonne, offers a way out of this impasse. For Desjeux, it is a question of magnification and relevance: "[W]hat is visible on one scale can become invisible or change shape at another level of observation . . . and the interest of the scales is to shift focus to bring out contextual effects that vary from one scale to another."

More than a century's worth of ink has been spilled on the quantitative-qualitative epistemological divide in the social sciences. If Patel, Desjeux, and Baba are looking for ways to move beyond this divide in the anthropology in business domain, what they and all of the authors in this section are asking anthropologists to do is to interrogate the dynamics surrounding the theories and methods by which they carry out their work and to interrogate the assumptions they have about those theories and methods. Patel's point that "many practicing ethnographers continue to believe the spoken word of subjects embodies the only form of defensible truth, at once superior to any form of empirical measurement" does hold more than a faint ring of truth. Embraces of materiality, the value of behavioral observation, and attention to assemblages may be part of the milieu, but once one moves to the scale of larger, global assemblages and to Big Data, we do need to face the terrain head on and with eyes—even if not arms—open.

One of the reasons to face these matters, which authors of chapters in this section explicitly note, is survival. The stakes implicated are the survival of anthropology as discipline, the survival of professional anthropology, the survival of the anthropological subfield, the survival of the anthropological voice. While it can be easy to categorize survival calls as mildly alarmist and to then just "get on with things," what survival calls remind us is that there are stakes in the game, that just "getting on with things" can lead us down paths we might not want to go, including the road to extinction. Survival calls are also a reminder of the larger-than-disciplinary dynamics that affect our work.

For instance, the concluding section of Arnould and Thompson's chapter tracing and reviewing cultural approaches within the business school context is aptly titled "Whither the Cultural Turn in Consumer Research." They point out significant challenges, among them an absence of corporate funding for chairs and programs in culturally oriented research in US business schools (such funding is often a significant departmental resource in US business schools). The lack of attention to the cultural turn in business schools by the "parent disciplines of anthropology and sociology" is also called out as a factor. The latter is by no means a unique phenomenon, as Rabinow (2003:5) eloquently spelled out in his discussion of the routine mutual neglect between "interpretive communities." In Rabinow's terms, the debates (and the fights) within communities tend to be internal ones, and those external to the system do not much care. But there are stakes and there are consequences, and the lack of attention by the fields of anthropology and sociology to the work of colleagues in business schools is meaningful because outside-the-field attention and support can make a difference, as Arnould and Thompson's point about funding makes clear (see also Fischer 2003:166–9). Thus, we might all also ponder what it means that, as Roberts alerts us in his chapter, an anthropologist received the award as "UK Designer of the Year" for innovative work on public services under the auspices of the Design Council.

Roberts' chapter also makes it clear that as important as the increased numbers of available anthropologists were to the growth of anthropologists working outside the academy in the United Kingdom, funding sources also made a difference. Notably, he points out that in the 1990s, evaluations for funding for anthropological research through research councils included assessments regarding the "likelihood to positively affect the UK economy." At the same time, other funding sources arose from entities "specifically focused on policy or business settings"; both of these funding initiatives helped support the development of anthropological research in business-related settings, including his. In the end for Roberts, the situation that has fostered the contemporary proliferation of anthropologists in business is multiplicative: increased demand, increased publicity, and increased academic training.

We must note, however, that we highlight this funding focus with some trepidation. Undoubtedly buttressed by the history of anthropology's humanistic legacy, pointed to in the chapter by Arnould and Thompson as well as that by Baba, combined with the legacy of Marxian analysis (see chapter by McCreery and Yamaki in Section II), there is a resonant danger in locating matters of money in any sort of causative role. Money too easily turns into the ultimate ruler and dictatorial arbiter, analytically encased in a negatively inflected box of capitalism—at the current moment the box of global corporate capitalism—and stops there. Despite nuanced ethnographic works that examine global assemblages and financial worlds (Fisher and Downey 2006; Ho 2009; Ong and Collier 2005; Tsing 2005), and despite anthropologists' own interests in increased salaries, organizations, institutional support, and funding—which Baba's chapter reminds us has been both a concern and an integral part of the development of anthropology as a discipline—assumptions about corporations often remain in a sealed box of negativity. As Moeran notes in his chapter, the subtext is "that money is the root of all evil: a subtext that perhaps inflects current interest in the excellent anthropological work being carried out in the field of finance." Concerns regarding corporate action and the subtext of money have fueled excellent analyses of contemporary human and ecological crises (Dumit 2012; Farmer 2010; Fortun 2001; Sunder Rajan 2012), and many anthropologists have embraced an activist stance. What we must nonetheless guard against is a halt in thinking, a halt in nuance, and the quick assumption that corporate activity is evil and anthropologists are now needed—not just to salvage cultures or to let the subaltern speak—but to save the world. Such a scope is to be applauded (How can one be against saving the planet? And anthropology would be well positioned if it could save the world). But in the embrace of this scope, we cannot be simultaneously myopic and grand. It will behoove us not to traffic in unexamined boxes of whatever sort; they get us nowhere. At the least, they get us nowhere as anthropologists. In business circles, "culture" has often been appropriated too easily and simply and reified as a causative and unexamined variable (see Mazzarella 2003; Orta 2013; Sunderland and Denny 2007). We need not make the same conceptual mistake in terms of "corporations." As Latour (2013:384) reminds in reference to critiques of capitalism: "But isn't this a new exaggeration? Doesn't it attribute too much power to this monster? More seriously still, isn't it a way of agreeing to conspire with Capitalism by taking it too hastily as a cancer with terrifying destructive power?"

In 2013, Heather Paxson's award-winning book *The Life of Cheese: Crafting Food and Value in America* was published. Paxson moves easily back and forth between national data and finely detailed ethnographic data in this explication of artisanal cheesemakers—and sellers—in the United States. Should studies like this one, focused on a product but conducted by an anthropologist with an academic position, or the efforts of activist scholars such as Fortun (2012), be seen as necessarily different—as in of a different breed—than those of anthropologists working in applied circles? The answer to draw from the arguments in Desjeux's and Moeran's chapters is that fundamentally they should not. Both Desjeux and Moeran conclude that topically and analytically the similarities tend to outweigh the differences. The challenge is to view the work done from many positionalities seamlessly, rather than as across a great divide. As part of his effort to unite and define business anthropology, Moeran evoked trade as one common thread: "Riggers, weavers, dealers, planters, farmers, bankers, and camel drivers are all involved in business of some sort or other. They all *trade.*" We do all trade, and it is time to trade stories.

REFERENCES

Dumit, Joseph. 2012. *Drugs for Life: How Pharmaceutical Companies Define Our Health.* Durham, NC: Duke University Press.

Farmer, Paul. 2010. *Partner to the Poor: A Paul Farmer Reader.* Edited by Haun Saussy. Berkeley: University of California Press.

Fischer, Michael M. J. 2003. *Emergent Forms of Life and the Anthropological Voice.* Durham, NC: Duke University Press.

Fisher, Melissa S., and Greg Downey, eds. 2006. *Frontiers of Capital: Ethnographic Reflections on the New Economy.* Durham, NC: Duke University Press.

Fortun, Kim. 2001. *Advocacy after Bhopal: Environmentalism, Disaster, New Global Orders.* Chicago, IL: University of Chicago Press.

———. 2012. "Ethnography in Late Industrialism." *Cultural Anthropology* 27(3):446–64.

Ho, Karen. 2009. *Liquidated: An Ethnography of Wall Street.* Durham, NC: Duke University Press.

Latour, Bruno. 2013. *An Inquiry into Modes of Existence: An Anthropology of the Moderns.* Translated by Catherine Porter. Cambridge, MA: Harvard University Press.

Marcus, George E., and Michael M. J. Fischer. 1986. *Anthropology as Cultural Critique: An Experimental Moment in the Human Sciences.* Chicago, IL: University of Chicago Press.

Mazzarella, William. 2003. "Critical Publicity/Public Criticism: Reflections on Fieldwork in the Bombay Ad World." In *Advertising Cultures,* edited by Timothy D. Malefyt and Brian Moeran, 55–74. New York: Berg Publishers.

Ong, Aihwa, and Stephen J. Collier, eds. 2005. *Global Assemblages: Technology, Politics, and Ethics as Anthropological Problems.* Malden, MA: Blackwell Publishing.

Orta, Andrew. 2013. "Managing the Margins: MBA Training, International Business, and the 'Value Chain of Culture.'" *American Ethnologist* 40(4):689–703.

Paxson, Heather. 2013. *The Life of Cheese: Crafting Food and Value in America.* Berkeley: University of California Press.

Rabinow, Paul. 2003. *Anthropos Today: Reflections on Modern Equipment.* Princeton, NJ: Princeton University Press.

Rabinow, Paul, and Anthony Stavrianakis. 2013. *Demands of the Day: On the Logic of Anthropological Inquiry.* Chicago, IL: University of Chicago Press.

Sunderland, Patricia L., and Rita M. Denny. 2007. *Doing Anthropology in Consumer Research.* Walnut Creek, CA: Left Coast Press.

Sunder Rajan, Kaushik, ed. 2012. *Lively Capital: Biotechnologies, Ethics, and Governance in Global Markets.* Durham, NC: Duke University Press.

Tsing, Anna Lowenhaupt. 2005. *Friction: An Ethnography of Global Connection.* Princeton, NJ: Princeton University Press.

1

De-Anthropologizing Ethnography: A Historical Perspective on the Commodification of Ethnography as a Business Service

MARIETTA L. BABA

INTRODUCTION

The relationship between anthropology and ethnography has evolved significantly in the past two centuries, and it has influenced our understanding of both fields (Marcus and Fischer 1986; Pels and Salemink 1999; Stocking 1995). At various points in the past (e.g., the mid- to late nineteenth century), the diverse practices we now associate with ethnography were separate and more or less distinct from what was then called anthropology, while at other times (e.g., the mid-twentieth century) anthropology and ethnography were closely intertwined and identified with one another. Methodology is constructed within a social, political, and historical context (Pels and Salemink 1999:34), so what we think of as ethnography in the contemporary context continues to evolve, just as anthropology has changed in its relationship to the sciences and humanities (see Faubion 2001; Kuper 2011). The association between these two fields is in a state of flux, and nowhere is this more apparent than in the domain of anthropological business practice (e.g., Cefkin 2009; Malefyt 2009; Malefyt and Morais 2012; Sunderland and Denny 2007). Here, anthropology and ethnography are under constant pressure to justify and rationalize themselves, not necessarily as one integral entity, but as multiple and potentially quite different approaches to representing and/or understanding human and social phenomena.

A major premise of this chapter is that intellectual developments within the discipline of anthropology and cognate fields have converged to open the space between anthropology and ethnography, and as a result ethnography has become less dependent upon anthropology for its identity and practices. At the same time, anthropology has evolved toward a highly heterogeneous state with diverse and some might even say fragmented perspectives on its mission (Kuper 2011). These developments have taken place within a capitalist context in which

Handbook of Anthropology in Business, edited by Rita Denny and Patricia Sunderland, 43–68.

much of the value added in developed economies is associated with service(s).[1] Within this context, ethnography has emerged as a service that is provided not only by business anthropologists but also by social science, humanities, or even technical professionals in consultancies and market research firms that claim to bring consumer knowledge to design, development, or production (Malefyt 2009). Through the process of commodification (defined later in this chapter), ethnographic services can be denuded of craft knowledge or skill base and rendered less expensive or more pliable (Braverman 1974). This need not be (consciously) motivated by "scientific management" (i.e., Taylorism [Taylor 1911]) but may stem from other contemporary trends, such as the "industrialization of services" described by Karmarkar (2004), in which business services become more standardized and automated through the use of information and communication technologies (ICT). Alternatively, business services that represent information to a client may be influenced by the wave of "Big Data" that is challenging firms to access, organize, and interpret the ever-increasing volume of digital information available as a result of networking and information technology (see Maxwell 2012). The twentieth-century concepts of anthropology and ethnography (e.g., expertise in the exotic, interpretation of the other, attention to detail and difference [Marcus and Fischer 1986; Suchman 2013]) may not have caught up with these tendencies.

In this chapter, I elaborate on some of the mediating forces that have widened the distance between anthropology and ethnography, while propelling the latter into the slipstream of commoditized services. One of the main influences on this shift has been the relationship between anthropology and technology stemming from the discipline's increasingly humanistic orientation. This has affected the anthropological gaze upon technology, both as subject and as object, just as businesses have become increasingly interested in streams of digital data from sources that did not exist even a few years ago (see PCAST 2013). This confluence of forces has altered the juxtaposition of anthropology, technology, and businesses in a manner that has serious implications for business anthropology.

ANTHROPOLOGY & ETHNOGRAPHY: THE STANDARD MODEL

For centuries, a variety of professions conducted ethnography-like practices long before anthropology was established as a discipline. These included not only explorers' journals and travelogues but also aspects of classical ethnography, including long stays in the field, participant observation, in-depth discussions with local people, and translation across linguistic boundaries (e.g., see Pels and Salemink 1999:34–7). It was only with the rise of anthropology as an academic discipline that such practices became known as ethnography, and were closely affiliated with the nascent academic discipline, including points at which the boundaries between ethnography and anthropology were blurred (Stocking 1995:16).

Long before anthropology became institutionalized as an academic discipline in the 1920s and 1930s, "armchair philosophers" read and analyzed the works of writers, travelers, explorers, missionaries, and colonial administrators who engaged in ethnographic or "proto-ethnographic" observations and thinking (Pels and Salemink 1999:7) without doing any fieldwork themselves. Alternatively, colonial administrators took government-sponsored courses on anthropology and became semi-professional anthropologists, undertaking a self-styled form of ethnography.

By the early twentieth century, a quasi-professional ethnography emerged. For example, British government officials in Africa, such as those in Nigeria and on the Gold Coast, could be seconded to anthropological work, gathering demographic census data and other ethnological information (Stocking 1995:369–86). On the Gold Coast, for example, Robert Sutherland Rattray established an Anthropological Department of Ashanti as part of his colonial administration, through which he undertook detailed studies and produced a series of published works that remain of value to students of the Ashanti (e.g., Rattray 1923, 1956, 1959).

Yet it was academics such as Frazer who aimed to provide a more rigorous and objective analytic framework for raw material collected in the field by practicing professionals and who developed more grounded theories about the evolution of humanity and the development of its institutions, even though the practitioners (e.g., missionaries) provided valuable ethnographic evidence and insights for the grand schemes of anthropologists such as Tylor (Stocking 1995:17–46). This reflected the state of anthropology up through the early decades of the twentieth century.

In none of these earlier guises was ethnography a full-fledged profession standing on its own merits. One did not pursue a career as an "ethnographer." Rather, proto-ethnography was the idiosyncratic practice of individuals following other career paths, each of whose ethnographic labors were identified and made manifest by anthropologists. Nevertheless, "amateur" or co-vocational ethnography could be practiced without anthropological sanction.

Toward the turn of the twentieth century, scholars started to shape the discipline of anthropology and ethnographic fieldwork into a more unified endeavor that combined empiricism and theorization. This era saw the rise of positivist social science, and anthropologists were expected to develop theory regarding the nature of humanity and the development of society (Bulmer and Bulmer 1981). There was a political charge to the emergence of the social sciences, as the question of colonial power was looming on the transatlantic horizon, as well as the stirrings of sociobiology and eugenics (Kohler 1978; Ross 1991). These issues became important in the relationship of anthropology and ethnography in both Europe and the United States in the coming decades.

In the mid-twentieth century two British social anthropologists developed a theory of practice for ethnography and a theoretical framework for socio-cultural anthropology that in turn influenced American anthropology. Bronislaw Malinowski established a framework for integrating ethnographic fieldwork and anthropological analysis of field data that was superior to the separation of these activities (Stocking 1995). Radcliffe-Brown's structural-functionalism, based upon Durkheimian functionalism, was crucial in establishing an anthropological (or comparative sociological) theory developed upon the basis of ethnographic field data collected by the same anthropologist(s) who constructed the theory (see Harris 1968:515–16). These were substantial intellectual breakthroughs that legitimized social anthropology and led to an increase in academic chairs at universities in Great Britain (Mills 2002:186).

Though proponents tried to "sell" this combined anthropological-ethnographic science, potential consumers often were scarce. Colonial administrators did their own ethnography, and some were alienated by poor producer-consumer relationships: for example, early anthropologists promised policy-relevant research but then studied whatever they chose (Kuper 1983). Even serious "applied anthropologists" such as Malinowski found it difficult to fulfill overly optimistic expectations for policy-oriented research (Stocking 1995). Anthropology's first "brand" identity was not ideal for its intended sponsors (i.e., colonial government) in a number of respects, and this probably affected relationships with other external constituents such as commercial concerns over the long term (see for example Mills 2006). The sponsors that eventually supported the anthropology-ethnography combination were not colonialists but American philanthropists (forerunners of later state sponsors) with their own agenda pertaining to the establishment of empirical social science and long-range hopes for social welfare and perhaps "control" (Fisher 1993:12).

After anthropology became established as an academic discipline in the early decades of the twentieth century, ethnography emerged as a distinct career. Under anthropology, ethnography is both a literary genre (writing that portrays cultural practices and beliefs) and a qualitative fieldwork practice (observation of and participation in people's lives, recording and describing social and cultural processes, interpretation of the point of view of the people being observed, and the production of accounts of their cultural beliefs and practices [Marcus and Fischer 1986:18–25]). Holistic representation in ethnography is an effort to contextualize cultural elements and make systematic connections among them, a goal early ethnographers had not envisioned prior to the twentieth century.

It is important to note that these two meanings of ethnography—a product and a process—are closely related in anthropology, not just because one produces the other but also because the product of the process was used to train students in the practice of ethnography. Rather than break ethnography down into component parts and teach students how to perform them, many academic departments taught ethnography by having professors lead seminars in which students read and discussed ethnographic works, including works in which the anthropologist confronts the issues of producing ethnography (see Marcus and Fischer 1986:21).

The process of producing ethnography is perhaps the central rite of passage in sociocultural anthropology; to become a full-fledged professional anthropologist in the subfield of sociocultural anthropology, one must conduct ethnography and produce it (Macdonald 2001). This suggests that the practice of ethnography within the discipline of anthropology remains a form of "craft knowledge," generally held tacitly by the practitioner. The informal rule of "one anthropologist, one field site" has discouraged repeat studies that might invalidate previous research and expose actual practices. The exception here "proves the rule," so to speak, in that in perhaps the most famous case in which one anthropologist challenged the validity of another's fieldwork (the Mead-Freeman controversy), the consensus has been that the challenger is the one who is suspect on both personal and professional grounds (Freeman 1983; Marcus and Fischer 1986:3).

Anthropological ethnography cannot be considered a true craft profession, since training is not conveyed through "apprenticeship." Rather, students are immersed in the product and then thrown into the process, to sink or swim. Anthropology departments may rationalize and teach the components of ethnographic practice (e.g., qualitative fieldwork methods; textual analysis methods) as "skills" required for a degree. There has been no discipline-wide effort to certify or accredit practitioners. This is a point of vulnerability: any other field could appropriate the ethnographic method, since anthropology has not formalized, validated, or certified its approach. This may be related, at least in part, to the crisis of representation.

THE RISE OF CRITICISM & THE DISTANCING OF ANTHROPOLOGY & ETHNOGRAPHY

A number of developments led to a gradual decoupling of anthropology and ethnography. Many of these resulted from challenges to the authority of anthropology as a "science of man" and were linked to the epistemological uncertainty arising from critical movements associated with postmodernism. Over time, anthropology and ethnography became more distinctive and not necessarily coupled endeavors. It was through this process that the practices of ethnography were incorporated or hybridized into those of other disciplines and professions, which initiated the emergence of ethnography as a business service.

The integral relationship of anthropology and ethnography was sustained through the middle of the twentieth century, as American anthropology moved beyond structural-functionalism and split theoretically into orientations that attribute causal primacy in cultural patterning either to tangible material forces and interests (materialist) or to the forces of the human mind (mentalist). The materialist school was influenced by Marxian theory, while the mentalist school, which became more influential over time, was shaped by the work of cognitive and interpretive anthropologists such as Clifford Geertz and David Schneider (Ortner 1984).

Geertz's view that cultures could be "read" by the observer, just as texts are read, marked a difference between materialist behavioral science approaches and cultural interpretive accounts in anthropology. Of course, the observed also interpret, and this idea inspired interest in how interpretations are constructed by anthropologists, who really are working from interpretations by informants (Clifford 1988; Marcus and Fischer 1986). This led to wider-ranging critical reflections upon the practices of ethnography, which was considered a social science methodology: but was it?

The split between the materialist, behavioral science, and interpretive approaches to culture was not resolved in anthropology, in part because the discipline was overtaken by postmodernism, a movement that reflects a set of critical and rhetorical practices that destabilized epistemological certainty across the human sciences and related professions (Aylesworth 2012). The postmodern critique that began in the 1960s called into question some of the most fundamental conceptual foundations of anthropology. This criticism is important because it has relevance for anthropology's orientation toward professional fields such as computation, design, and other industry practices.

In *Anthropology and the Colonial Encounter* (1973), Talal Asad and his coauthors pointed out that anthropological ethnography did not acknowledge the circumstances that shaped the phenomenon that anthropologists studied, and that the subjects formed under colonialism could not be separated from that context. Anthropologists were criticized for distancing themselves from the relationships between their own native societies and those of their subjects and by "essentializing" selected traits, not only of the observed but also of the observer.

In the practice of ethnography, anthropologists classically established a dyadic relationship with a subject of research, who is a coproducer of knowledge but who receives little or no benefit (or recognition) from the process. Thinkers such as James Clifford (1988) questioned whether anthropologists can presume an authoritative stance with respect to the Other, when ethnographic relationships presume rapport and trust that may not exist, and embed an implicit relationship with readers whose interests and conceptions are encoded in texts but never raised to the level of consciousness. Through such criticism, anthropological ethnographies faced a "crisis of representation," illustrated by Derek Freeman's (1983) assertion that Margaret Mead's representation of Samoan society and its childrearing practices in *Coming of Age in Samoa* ([1929] 1949) was romanticized and naive, since Mead, as a young white woman, did not have access to all of the key actors in Samoan society.

This critique also raised doubts about anthropology's construct of "culture," forged in the context of colonialism and its successor regimes. Ascribing essentialized, set traits or integrated, coherent features to the "essence" or nature of a subject that cannot or do not change is suspect (Faubion 2001). It also seems unlikely that we can know that such traits exist or existed when the anthropologists engaged in "salvaging" a culture also are allied with the institutions that aim to "develop" it (see Stocking 1995). Many anthropologists represent "cultures" as if they are pristine isolates even when they are enmeshed in relationships with external economic and political forces, and some have had reasons to overlook such complications (e.g., see Miller 1995). Anthropology never resolved the problem of how to preserve cultures while engaging in the process of changing them, and the idea of culture now is less a scientific construct than a literary or vernacular one that has been widely adopted but is poorly understood.

George Marcus and Michael Fischer (1986) have argued that anthropology lost its *raison d'être* as decades of twentieth-century criticism took their toll upon its founding vision. The idea of "salvaging" vanishing cultures could not animate a discipline in a world where most societies were connected to global networks. The public appetite for learning about exotic peoples waned, and people began to question the importance of cultural differences.

Marcus and Fischer (1986) thought anthropology might have another mission in which ethnography could play a vital role. They reminded anthropologists that criticism of their own society was a major justification for social research in fields across the social sciences, and that anthropology could engage in such critique if the discipline compiled accounts that recognized and distinguished homogenizing factors compared with substantive distinctions in the contemporary world. Examining what is the same and what is different across human societies, within the context of globalization, would require anthropologists to become students of the contemporary and to become cross-cultural rather than studying only one society: both major challenges. They suggested two forms of cultural critique, neither of which had been fully accomplished by anthropologists in their view: (1) defamiliarization by epistemological critique (finding things that are exotic and using them to illuminate a unity among people and inspire reflection upon our own practices) and (2) defamiliarization by cross-cultural juxtaposition (ethnographic study in one society, compared with ethnographic study in the home society, developed to show the opportunities for recombination).

Marcus and Fischer's (1986) seminal work attempts to distinguish between the components of epistemology and methodology that are ethnographic and those that are anthropological. Ethnography focuses upon detail in situ, while anthropology respects context and recognizes ambiguities and multiple possibilities inherent in any situation (which are necessary for theorization). They not only emphasize that the prerequisites for criticism come from anthropology (they are not inherent within ethnography), but also recognize the overall strengths and limitations of the two distinct endeavors.

Marcus and Fischer (1986) noted that the social consensus on anthropology's role had broken down, and they proposed a new mandate that redirected anthropology toward cultural criticism. The question was whether anthropologists would agree with their proposal, and whether society would buy in to it, since a disciplinary mandate requires broader social legitimization if it is to stand (Kuklick 1991).

Just prior to the publication of Marcus and Fischer's book, American anthropologists were introduced to the work of the French historian and philosopher Michel Foucault. One of Foucault's key interlocutors is Paul Rabinow, an anthropologist at the University of California at Berkeley whose work focuses on contemporary knowledge-production practices and relations of power in institutional venues. Rabinow's study of Foucault was part of an investigation of anthropology as an interpretive science. In subsequent research, Rabinow developed an anthropology of the contemporary in which he elaborated upon the ramifications of Foucault's concepts, especially power/knowledge for the discipline.

Despite the fact that he is not an anthropologist, Foucault has become one of the most cited intellectuals in the literature of contemporary American anthropology. One of the reasons that Foucault may have been so widely accepted in the United States is that his writings and lectures appeared on the American scene in parallel with the crisis of representation, offering a means for thinking through the crisis of representing others who are less powerful by engaging analytic frameworks of power/knowledge. Foucault steers anthropology away from colonial subjects and toward the contemporary, while providing an original epistemology for critique that is relevant to cross-cultural contexts, resonating well with Marcus and Fisher's influential call to cultural criticism.

Foucault's influence on anthropology's relationship to ethnography stems from a particular methodological approach to critical study, his interest in subjects related to science and technology, and the increasing importance of these subjects in the evolution of contemporary ethnography, especially in the United

States. His way of thinking "problematizes" a situation space, which means that he uses an "ensemble of discursive and non-discursive practices that makes something enter into the play of true or false and constitute it as an object of thought (whether in the form of moral reflection, scientific knowledge, political knowledge)" (Foucault 1994:670; compare with Collier et al. 2004). His method suggests an intellectual framework that has been highly conducive to the practice of contemporary anthropology in America. "Problematizations" are framed as intellectual challenges when "something prior must have happened to introduce uncertainty, a loss of familiarity; that loss, that uncertainty is the result of difficulties in our previous way of understanding, acting, relating" (Foucault 1994:598). Most remarkably, he suggested that such situations may be studied from the perspective of the second-order observer; that is, it is not necessary to be present in the moment to do a Foucaultian analysis, a possibility that further opens the distance between anthropology and ethnography. Anthropologists need not be ethnographers to conduct Foucaultian analysis and criticism. The goal is to see a situation not only as a given but equally as a question: to see how there are multiple constraints and multiple responses (see Collier et al. 2004). From this perspective, Foucault's analytic mode connects with Marcus and Fischer's recommendations for cultural critique (e.g., alternative possibilities), but may lose some of the face validity of classical ethnographic fieldwork.

IMPLICATIONS OF THE CRITICAL TURN FOR THE COMMODIFICATION OF ETHNOGRAPHY

Not all of the influences of the critical turn in anthropology are fully understood at this point, and some of them are still in motion. Nevertheless, it is possible to discern the outlines of some of them upon the relationship between anthropology and ethnography and the position of ethnography in business. Ethnography has been increasingly hybridized with the methods of other disciplines, and ethnography has continued to evolve into a commodity service in the business domain.

The Hybridization of Anthropology & Ethnography

Starting in the 1970s, anthropologists began to explore venues and modes of discovery outside of former colonies and traditional cultural field sites (Faubion 2001; Macdonald 2001). This shift reflected not only resistance to Western anthropologists' presence in former colonies and anthropologists' increasing discomfort with their position in these locales, but also a crisis of representation in anthropological ethnography and a gradual decline in the scientific status of the culture construct. Experimentation within anthropology led to a situation in which a range of ethnographic fieldwork practices were repatriated to the United States and other first-world locations where political resistance was less acute and other disciplines were exploring ethnography as a means to address their own methodological crises. Laura Nader at Berkeley made her famous challenge to "study up" (Nader 1969), meaning to shift our locus of analysis from relatively less powerful to relatively more powerful subjects, and this gave legitimacy to those who wanted to pursue research in venues other than typically remote and exotic locations. The hold that anthropology had over ethnography was loosened as anthropologists radiated over many different field sites and came into contact with other disciplines and professions eager to learn about ethnography. Gradually, a process of hybridization unfolded, as anthropologists and members of other fields worked their knowledge(s) and practices together (Suchman 2013). Many new "institutional anthropologies" (e.g., medical, legal, educational, and so forth; see Bennett [1996]) emerged, each with its own hybridized constructs, methods, and approaches.

Among these is a new interdisciplinary field that some have called "design ethnography" or "ethnographically informed design," which reflects a hybridization of anthropology, ethnography, participatory design, industrial engineering, and several other cognate fields in which practitioners are interested in making a difference in the development of new products, services, and systems (Squires and Byrne 2002). The relationship between anthropology, ethnography, and the design industry can be used as an illustration of the way in which hybridization loosens the hold of anthropology upon ethnography and moves ethnography toward the business domain. From an anthropological perspective, the hybridized design field can be traced to the critical wave in anthropology and its influence on graduate students in the 1970s and 1980s to conduct research outside the academy.

One such student was Lucy Suchman, who decided to conduct her doctoral research at Xerox PARC. Suchman conducted an ethnomethodological[2] study of computer supported work—video studies of engineers working with a copying machine compared with engineering instructions for use of that machine—that led to the discovery that natural human interaction and communication practices were unlike those envisioned by the designers of equipment. This led Xerox to make changes in the way it designed its equipment, and gave Suchman credibility to organize the research group that established the Work Practice and Technology area at Xerox PARC in 1989 and advanced ethnographically informed design of prototype technology in research and development.

Suchman's group at Xerox PARC was involved for a decade in interdisciplinary research and development oriented toward understanding the workplace of the future and the kinds of work environments and designs that might emerge with it. Funding for the Workplace Project came from Steelcase and

Xerox, which were brought together by the design firm Jay Doblin and Associates of Chicago. Suchman hired a talented group of individuals to work on the project, and Doblin Group research director Rick Robinson created a methodology combining ethnography and design, which became the basis for Robinson's start-up firm E-Lab. From the research laboratory environment of the Workplace Project, E-Lab spun off a sophisticated methodology for multidisciplinary "design ethnography": how to conduct ethnographic studies of consumers in the field for clients to use as input for design and development projects. E-Lab integrated ethnographic practices into all of its client projects, which were conducted by multidisciplinary teams. However, Robinson acknowledged that business clients did not appreciate the value of anthropology or ethnography, and worked to demonstrate ways in which his approach could be *added in* as a complementary feature to what the client was already doing (Reese 2002:41). In other words, the design ethnography was not a standalone value-added service but at most a "chunk" of the product development process.

Wasson, a project manager at E-Lab in 1996 and 1997, provides a detailed description of the firm's methodology (Wasson 2002). E-Lab made extensive use of technology in its approach, including videotaping, software for analysis and mark-up of video clips, team-based analysis sessions, verbal and graphical frameworks for client presentations, and other means to enable anthropologists, other social scientists, designers, and other technologists to participate in all phases of the creative process. In working out the methodology, it was necessary for anthropologists to explain and demonstrate the elements of ethnography so that other members of the team could participate and learn. Even so, Wasson (2002:87) suggests that ethnography became a "pale shadow" of itself in this new incarnation:

> In its most emaciated form, the term [ethnography] is simply used to refer to a designer with a video camera. Even in somewhat richer versions, the term has become closely identified with the act of observing naturally occurring consumer behaviors. The need to analyze those behaviors and situate them in their cultural context is poorly understood, even though these activities are essential parts of developing a model of user experience that leads to targeted and far-reaching design solutions.

E-Lab established a template that was imitated and improved by other design and market research firms. Anthropology was not an essential element of the equation, since it was not considered necessary that ethnographers be anthropologists. Hybridizing ethnography and design required that the componential elements of ethnography be made explicit and tangible, so that they could be learned (copied) by others and fit within the multidisciplinary frame. Once made explicit, the elements could be rationalized or enhanced through various means (e.g., conducted by other employees with different skill levels, replaced or improved by technology, left out altogether if not budgeted). Thus, at its inception, design ethnography established a model for what was to become the commoditization of ethnography as a service to other firms, which even at this early stage was alarming to anthropologists. Anthropology was experiencing its "crisis of representation" and so was not in a strong position to argue against such developments.

Commodification of Services: The Rise of Techno-Ethnography

Business services to other businesses (or "producer services") comprise a large and growing sector of the economy in developed nations (Bryson et al. 2004:75). Such services may represent virtually any aspect of a firm's operations, from human resources to marketing and advertising to manufacturing, all contingent upon how the firm defines its core operations. The reasons for this expansion of business-to-business services are complex, and include anticipated reductions in transaction costs, improvements in flexibility, risk reduction, and concentration on core skills. E-Lab's innovative business-to-business service provided a means by which clients could investigate contemporary or future consumer experience worlds.

Services often are portrayed as fundamentally different from manufacturing and agriculture, with the distinction centering upon intangibility (Bryson et al. 2004:24). In many ways, however, manufacturing and other forms of tangible production are intertwined with services, and one could not happen without the other. Services support tangible production in various ways, and the deeper one delves into the fine details of tangible production processes, the more "services" one discovers (e.g., planning, maintenance, delivery, collection, accounting). Such complexity means that it can be difficult to distinguish between manufacturing and service.

The increasing division of labor in capitalist economies that Adam Smith described more than two hundred years ago is now occurring in service economies as a process of increasing specialization (Karmarkar 2004; Levitt 1976). Business services are experiencing a wave of change that in some ways resembles that which overtook manufacturing: services are gradually becoming "industrialized"[3] through the processes of standardization, automation, and resulting commodification (i.e., a tendency toward outsourcing [Davenport 2005; Karmarkar 2004]). This is being driven by developments in ICT that make it possible to automate services, with sophisticated hardware and software taking over roles that previously were performed by people. Technology enables supply chains to be shortened, creating an "information assembly line" in which data in digitized form can be standardized: "built to order, assembled from components, picked, packed, stored, and shipped, all using processes resembling manufacturing" (Karmarkar 2004:2). The most important aspects of business services now are labor and intellectual property, which cannot be automated. How this process affects anthropology and ethnography depends upon the extent to which our practices have or may be standardized or automated.

Another feature of services "industrialization" is self-service. This process usually means that occupations or professions that provided such services previously lose status and control (or shrink and disappear), and competition in the market intensifies (Karmarkar 2004:6). Such changes are increasingly affecting more complex services such as market research and other information-intensive fields. The increasing availability of standards for various processes is expected to make standardization and automation of services more widespread in the future (Davenport 2005).

The standardization and automation of ethnographic research services has been reported previously in the anthropological literature, following the distancing of ethnography and anthropology and the operationalization of ethnographic components and their substitution with people and processes other than those developed within anthropology. In a recent paper, Malefyt (2009) observed the rise of consumer research firms that brand themselves through the offering of technology-enhanced ethnography as a service. These companies offer a specific form of "technomethodology" (Malefyt 2009), with the anthropological analysis missing or invisible (Sunderland and Denny 2007). Malefyt notes that it is no longer difficult to find anthropologists who offer consumer research services, so technology enhancement may do more to distinguish brands than the anthropological component. Firms use cell phone calls, digital photo-reporting, blogging, and other technologies to support "ethnography," which may be conducted by just about anyone who can wield the equipment, including the consumers themselves.

Ironically, Malefyt's observation is almost the reverse of Suchman's assessment that anthropology in the late twentieth century became a brand that companies wanted to publicize as a means to signal that they were exploring the exotic and therefore were innovative and on the cutting edge (Suchman 2013). This brand image for anthropology (exoticism and interpretation of the Other) follows the development of academic anthropology in mid–twentieth-century America, when most academics preferred to conduct research in exotic locales (Shankman 2000).

Now, a kind of reversal may be in progress, at least in certain business domains such as marketing. Boutique consulting firms that specialize in technology-enhanced ethnographic services are shedding or at least squeezing anthropologists—cutting out the middle man, so to speak—and using various forms of ICT to connect their clients directly to the consumer. According to Malefyt (2009), a high degree of agency is assigned to consumers, and technology is the means to access them.

Vendors may rename ethnography in terms of their own proprietary technology (e.g., "cellnography," "photo-ethnography," "blography")[4] while claiming that consumers engage in self-service fieldwork "without the aid of an outside observer," yielding insights that are not possible with traditional ethnography. Techno-ethnography replaces longer-term anthropological approaches to fieldwork and the authenticity of "being there" with the rapid mode of "fast" technology, engaging modern self-aware consumers without anthropological theory, questions, or interpretations. A transparency of meaning is taken as self-evident (Malefyt 2009). This is a radical departure from the work of anthropologists representing others through the analysis of one's own experience in the world of these others.

Again, the irony is deep, given anthropology's "crisis of representation" and all of the intellectual angst that has gone into the effort to counter distortions created by the postcolonial observer. Is the anthropologist just a "middle man" who slows down the process and can be eliminated with the click of a mouse? Have we come full circle to the age of exploration when just about anyone could write a narrative about the "natives," including the natives themselves? After all, the anthropologists are doing this too (e.g., native ethnography), so could it be so wrong?

Vendors don't necessarily worry as much about the play of truth and falsity as about whether their brand of ethnography sells. But business anthropologists should worry about whether the anthropological brand is becoming obsolete, and all anthropologists should take more seriously the elision of anthropology from ethnographically branded consumer research firms. Malefyt (2009) suggests that technology-enhanced, ethnography-branded consumer research firms are reifying a version of social relations based on an ideology of technology, progress, and innovation. That particular ideology could be derived from or related to the implicit truth claims underpinning science-based modes of representation (e.g., technology) and their cultural dominance over the more humanistic narratives presented by anthropology, which has drifted away from science in recent decades.

A parallel explanation or hypothesis is that anthropology is not being "consumed" in the marketplace (Suchman 2013): what is being incorporated into business practice is not the anthropology but the bits of ethnography that can be operationalized and commoditized, and anthropologists are being deskilled out of the process where cost-effective. This follows Braverman's theory of monopoly capital, in which many knowledge-based work skills eventually are broken down into component parts and taken over by lesser-skilled roles and technology. New ICT enables techno-ethnography–branded firms to shorten their supply chains from consumer to client, whereas self-service consumers are not paid for their labor. We know that business clients do not always understand or value anthropological knowledge (Malefyt and Morais 2012; Sunderland and Denny 2007; Wasson 2002). This explanation has the advantages of a Marxian inflection, while it also "problematizes" the aestheticization of ethnography in the discipline of anthropology for those interested in history and criticism.

The deskilling of ethnographers engaged in business services was observed by Lombardi (2009:46), who described his clients' desire for the immediacy of direct experience at a "pre-analytic level" as a substitute for costly data interpretation.[5] He linked this tendency to Lyotard's body of theory when he noted that clients appear to be increasingly disinterested in ethnographic metanarratives regarding consumers (Lyotard 1984:xxv, 37; compare with Lombardi 2009:46).

Lombardi (2009:43–44) criticized the development of a software tool for coding visual image data that allowed part of a complex qualitative data analysis project to be outsourced to India, where the work could be accomplished at much less cost. He objected to this practice on several grounds, noting that outsourcing created a multitier work force, rendered levels of accuracy unpredictable, and created a congealed set of database entries that were resistant to further evolution and revision. Indeed, this process would be a questionable practice in anthropology; data torn from context means the value of interpretation declines, even if the "business proposition" appears reasonable on the surface. In this paper, Lombardi never mentions the discipline of "anthropology," leading to the inference (from this and other evidence presented here) that the decoupling of anthropology and ethnography within the context of late–twentieth-century capitalism has hastened the process of commodification.

The de-anthropologization of ethnography in consumer research is not an unexpected turn, given the developments in both anthropology and in technology. Sociocultural anthropology has not fully embraced the pragmatic aspects of technology, which is one of the means by which business services are commoditized (e.g., see Hakken's [1999:65] discussion on the marginalization of the technical in anthropology). Without command of technology, anthropologists have less influence in the development of trends such as techno-ethnography. Although there are important exceptions (e.g., the National Science Foundation [NSF] Summer Field School for Anthropological Methods and the University of Florida's online methodology courses)[6], the tendency within academic anthropology is to view technology as a "problematized site" to be examined and explored from a critical angle, rather than as a means to enhance ethnography. Meanwhile, more of society is being infused by technology, and it is becoming a medium of social discourse and action, leaving anthropologists at risk of falling out of step with the culture. Anthropology departments are not necessarily equipped to teach students to use digital technology; students may need to go elsewhere to acquire these skills. Yet, in the job market, if one does not want to become an academic, the capacity to manipulate social media is vital, and anthropologists who are not cognizant and facile with these tools will not be on the cutting edge.

Technological developments in other fields continue to automate higher functions of data analysis, further challenging the need for skilled researchers in remote areas. For example, probabilistic topic models are a "suite of algorithms whose aim is to discover the hidden thematic structure in large archives of documents" (Blei 2011:1). This computational modeling technique permits an unsupervised approach to textual analysis where no *a priori* information exists about the nature of the text. The technology accepts a collection of documents as input and produces output representations as topics that underlie the texts. As an illustration, Mark et al. (2012) used topic modeling and pronoun analysis to study Iraqi blog contents as an indicator of the health or state of an affected population in a war zone from 2003 to 2011. They found that people exhibited a collective identity when blogging about the war, as exhibited by higher use of the first-person plural pronoun ("we") when writing about the war compared with blogging about other topics. They also showed that blogging about daily life decreased as war-related violence increased, as correlated with validated body counts from independent sources (Mark et al. 2012:37). This is only one example of the ways in which technology is gradually making inroads into the practice of qualitative research.

Anthropology was created not only to give people calling themselves anthropologists a more systemically connected, empirically grounded, and theoretically sophisticated approach to describing and explaining what was going on "out there" compared with just any other gatherer of datum or storyteller, but also for larger political reasons. In Great Britain, the government needed a justification for remaining in and "developing" the colonies, and a "scientific" anthropology helped provide it (Mills 2002). Similarly, "applied anthropology" exploded in the United States and was institutionalized only after Americans began moving into Britain's former colonial areas (see Baba and Hill 2006). Globalization and neoliberalism tend to reduce the need for our discipline because these political economies work toward greater homogenization, although this is a very long project (and may never be realized). However, it is necessary to keep in mind the possibility that the larger reasons for retaining anthropology may be on the wane.

ANTHROPOLOGICAL "BRAND IDENTITY" & THE CHALLENGES AHEAD

So far we have explored three eras in the relationship between anthropology and ethnography, each of which suggests a different potential "brand identity" for anthropological ethnography. Brand identity in this context suggests a mark of difference or distinction that anthropological ethnography carries compared with other approaches to quests for knowledge about the human world (e.g., demography, psychology, economics, and so forth). This difference may be sustained when aspects of anthropological ethnography are combined with components from other disciplines and professions (i.e., hybridization). However, there is also the possibility that the anthropological features may be elided and only the ethnographic elements sustained, such that a new brand is created (e.g., techno-ethnography with no anthropology).

In the first era, anthropology and ethnography were coupled as a distinctive enterprise in which the same individuals engaged in both endeavors together. This was a new premise, joining theory and practice in a brilliant move that created a new discipline. Ethnography became a kind of "theory of practice" for anthropology: a way to obtain knowledge through practice. But these endeavors are not one and the same, and they have different historical origins, so it is not a simple matter to keep them conjoined. The early proponents of the anthropological-ethnographic union tried to create a distinctive "brand" identity that would be useful to potential sponsors (i.e., colonial administration) because the practitioners needed to have financial support, but the initial phase of this campaign has been deemed largely unsuccessful (Kuper 1983; Stocking 1995).

In the second era, anthropological ethnography found private-public sponsorship for its union and was given a legitimate place within the academy to pursue a "science of humanity" (Marcus and Fischer 1986; Mills 2002). This "golden age" was rather short-lived, spanning from the 1920s to the 1960s or so (Faubion 2001:45). The "brand" was a science of the exotic and esoteric (but serving hegemonic interests [Baba and Hill 2006]), which laid the basis for businesses' initial interest in anthropologists as sources of fresh, innovative, and counterintuitive information (Suchman 2013).

Since then, anthropology and ethnography have drifted apart once again, each finding other partners, at times even repudiating the former relationship. In this third era, the "brand" of ethnography has taken on a life of its own and in some ways is scarcely recognizable. As Wasson (2002) noted, the "brand" could be any design employee E-Lab sanctioned wielding a video camera. It is not clear that anthropology has a "brand" at this point; the members of the discipline probably would disagree on the nature of such a thing, which exacerbates the problems identified earlier concerning the distinctive value of anthropology.

None of these depictions are the "truth" or the "way things are": they are all partial views from different angles, and there are doubtless others that could be brought forth. Anthropologists are still engaging in powerful ethnographic fieldwork that brings to life substantial narratives of other worlds. I recommend Caitlin Zaloom's *Out of the Pits* (2006) or Karen Ho's *Liquidated* (2009) for different visions of the financial past and present in America through the lens of modern ethnography. There is a contemporary conjunction of anthropology and ethnography that brings us new understanding of business realities in a way that is different from any other discipline. This is important and significant, but it is not especially "branded" in the marketplace. Does this matter? Is there any possibility of learning from our own practice to strategically reposition anthropological ethnography in business at the higher end of the services market, where the specialized talents of knowledge workers are factored into price in acknowledgement of superior results?

Some observers, such as Robert Morais (2012), suggest that the conflation of anthropology with ethnography, and its delivery as such by anthropologists, established conditions for the situation described here as commodification. He recommends that anthropologists become more strategic (see also Morais in this volume) in delivery to sponsors and clients; that is, crafting "blueprints" or conceptual frameworks for the embedding of research results that would incorporate creative and novel ways of thinking about the world designed to attract new constituents and sponsors. Strategic thinking may be distinguished from the purely analytical because it places research within a larger (macro) problem-oriented frame of reference that unites disciplinary knowledge with knowledge(s) from other sources (e.g., other disciplines, institutions, or competitive analyses) and seeks the achievement of societal goals or other specific aims. Institutional anthropologists in fields such as medical anthropology or educational anthropology are acquainted with strategic approaches because their sponsors (e.g., National Institutes of Health) may explicitly seek such solutions. Morais notes that anthropologists, who are uniquely positioned to learn from other disciplines and to learn about clients' businesses, have the means to become highly creative strategic consultants who will produce valuable insights. This may be a way to move toward the higher end of the services market and reverse the process of commodification.

Some cultural critics would like to turn anthropology into a moral and political enterprise, although it is not clear whether this mandate will garner the broad social legitimization that leads to the permanent university positions needed to ground the discipline. Regardless, there is little question that anthropology in America has taken a decided turn toward the humanities, and this has been clear in its theoretical orientation since the 1980s. A humanistic orientation for anthropology has significant implications for the future because of new data collection, analysis, and interpretation challenges facing the social sciences, which are evident in the direction of federal funding agencies.

The NSF recently published "Rebuilding the Mosaic," a document summarizing the results of a two-year study of the social, behavioral, and economic science communities, projecting where these fields are going in the next decade.[7] The information was drawn from a crowdsourcing initiative in which 252 authors from around the world wrote white papers on the future of their fields (primarily social science). The NSF analyzed the documents via a text mining or topic extraction technology at the Institute for Quantitative Social Science at Harvard.

The summary reveals that the social science community predicts its future research will be interdisciplinary, data intensive, and collaborative. For example, papers about environmental and climate change point to the importance of integrating data and synthesizing results across archaeology and anthropology, sociology, politics, technology, ecology, and other natural sciences, including astronomy.

Ideas about collaboration, data, technology, and infrastructure are closely intertwined. Accessing and working with data and collections, especially heterogeneous data, data at scale, or data that are sensitive pose significant issues. The challenges of working with very large quantities of data were addressed in many of the papers. Some addressed the need for centers to support computation resources, training, and access to analytic and modeling tools, diverse data and expertise that could be assembled to test different models in a culture where interdisciplinary, collaborative research is nurtured. Others discussed the equivalent of clinical trials for possible interventions, or the value of mounting large proof-of-concept projects that exceed the funding typically available for small-scale research projects. Still others considered the relatively large-scale simulations of the results of proposed interventions and an evaluation of the utility of the models being proposed.

All of these approaches would require that NSF change the way in which it conceptualizes and funds the social, behavioral, and economic sciences, and the way in which these sciences are organized. This is not the kind of change that happens quickly, given that the federal government and academia are involved, although both are facing the need for major changes, and quickly. Both the NSF and the National Institutes of Health displayed willingness to move in new directions that "will advance the core scientific and technological means of managing, analyzing, visualizing, and extracting useful information from large and diverse data sets. This will accelerate scientific discovery and lead to new fields of inquiry that would otherwise not be possible" (from the NSF's Grant Proposal Guide).[8]

Such public sector proposals complement discussions going on in the commercial world about large data sets or "Big Data," defined as data sets whose size is beyond the ability of typical database software tools to capture, store, manage and analyze" (Manyika et al. 2011). Organizations are capturing an increasing volume and detail of digital information through multimedia and social media, and the "internet of things" that are expected to fuel innovation and economic growth. The major domains for the growth of Big Data are health care, retail, manufacturing, personal location data, and the public sector in Europe. A number of features distinguish digital technology-driven data collection (Maxwell 2012). Often these data are passive or automated in their mode of collection, meaning that the individual whose behavior is being recorded could be unaware of that fact, leading to privacy issues. The data also are more granular (i.e., fine-grained) than would be possible through traditional social science methods (e.g., video surveillance with digital enhancement), yielding highly detailed evidence that may be mined and cross-referenced to other data. Another distinguishing feature is hybridity; data sets combine information from diverse sources that previously would have been distinguished as either quantitative or qualitative, but now are combined into a unified system (e.g., an electronic health record containing insurance codes, medical history, and laboratory test results).

Traditional statistical methods are not well suited to the nature and scale of Big Data, a situation that has provided an opportunity for commercial producers of software to create specialized tools (analytics) that support the aggregation, analysis, and interpretation of digitized data sets. These tools work more quickly and are able to analyze more data at a lower cost than ethnography, and are increasingly more "mechanized, commoditized, assumed and culturally embedded"; yet at the same time, their underlying algorithms often are proprietary "black boxes" based upon non–open source rules and norms that cannot be validated (Maxwell 2012:183). One consequence of overreliance upon nontransparent analytic models is an increased risk of system vulnerability and the potential for collapse, as witnessed in the 2008 financial crisis. Another risk relates to the privacy and security of individuals whose identities may be revealed within the data array.

New strategic roles for anthropologists and ethnographers emerge as opportunities from the competitive pressures of Big Data and its analytics. Two distinct realms of opportunity may be noted: (1) contextualization and probing of patterns reported from analysis of Big Data; and (2) deeper understanding of the organizations and institutions of Big Data industries.

First, there should be checks and balances upon on patterns reported by data analytics, as well as means to further examine the underlying realities. Social scientists, including anthropologists with ethnographic skills, can put their legacy knowledge and mission to work with other fields to probe and validate the patterns and ask even more fundamental questions about the nature of the data that are being collected. For example, very large data sets available through electronic medical or health records can be analyzed to identify patterns and trends related to disease occurrence. Kaelber et al. (2012) showed that data from nearly one million patients could be pooled and searched through a Health Insurance Portability and Accountability Act of 1996 (HIPAA)–compliant, patient-blinded web application that standardized and normalized the data using common ontologies.[9] In this study, patient race and ethnicity were correlated with the incidence of venous thromboembolic events (VTEs). According to the study authors, Hispanic individuals had the lowest VTE rate, both for women and men, compared with white individuals, and this trend persisted among the studied body mass index (BMI) and height categories. The study also found that African-American individuals had the highest VTE rate (women and men) compared with white individuals. White individuals had generally two to three times the odds of VTE compared with Hispanic individuals, whereas African-American individuals had three to four times the odds of VTE compared with similarly sized whites (Kaelber et. al. 2012:3). Remarkably, the study does not provide reasons for these differences or factors that may underlie them, even though the stated intent of the study is to demonstrate the potential value of data mining electronic health records using analytic tools. These findings raise questions regarding the context in which race and ethnicity information is collected and interpreted, and the more general issue of health disparities. We may ask: to what extent is the information encoded in electronic health records valid and accurate for the patient population represented? Although race and ethnicity are mandatory demographic fields in electronic health records (EHRs) implemented under the American Recovery and Reinvestment and Health Information Technology for Economic and Clinical Health (HITECH) Acts (see Ulmer et al. 2009), the accuracy of physicians' records on patient race and ethnicity is not clear, nor do we know whose perspective is represented in the recording of this information. We may ask also to what extent the racial and ethnic differences reported in the study reflect health disparities such as access to health care for different segments of the population. These are sensitive sociotechnical matters that require investigation by persons with the skills to interpret across linguistic and cultural domains. These questions represent contextual information missing from the data mining exercise; without this information, the findings cannot be interpreted with confidence. These are questions that anthropologists, working with colleagues in health care and technology fields, could address with their interpretive and critical skills, and in doing so make a significant contribution to the evolution of Big Data, as well as illustrate through a strategic approach joining organizational/business and medical anthropology.

A second opportunity for anthropological ethnographers is the emergence of a new industry and contemporary field site (Maxwell 2012). Each application domain for Big Data (e.g., retail, health care, public sector) is defined by a distinctive set of institutional actors such as software vendors, consulting firms, large corporations, public agencies, and so forth, whose interactions define the nature and evolution of an institutional field.[10] There is a need for more fundamental understanding of the organizations and institutions that comprise these fields, including the cultural rules and norms of their engineers, code developers, systems creators, and other professionals, not only to "demystify" the analytic tools they produce (Maxwell 2012:186), but also to better comprehend the interactions of these professions and their technological products with other social actors (e.g., consumers) and their larger social contexts. Anthropologists also can partner with analytics practitioners in adding value to their explanations; data mining pattern-recognition does not preclude the incorporation of sociocultural knowledge, to the extent that these fields are not alienated from one another. If anthropology becomes and remains a humanistic enterprise with the tendency of its practitioners to stand back and ask critical questions regarding technological phenomena rather than getting into the field site and grappling with the first-order data "on the ground"—including an understanding of technology on its own terms—then the next culture to be salvaged may be our own.

CONCLUSION

We should consider the possibility that business clients may be willing to forego anthropological analysis and link directly to the consumer for understanding because we (anthropologists) have not yet done all that we could to enhance and explain our discipline-based and interdisciplinary expertise as means to analyze and interpret the world. It could be a matter of our disciplinary trajectory over a long period of time and an unanticipated consequence of that pathway. But history may be interpreted in many ways. As we have learned about our past, we have changed our practices so that our field is strengthened. Still, there has not emerged an integration of this knowledge to bring anthropology to new understanding(s) of itself. The fragmentation of the field makes us vulnerable.

While we might not want to fully revive any of anthropology's past brand images, it may be prudent to reassert the value of anthropological ethnography as an enterprise dedicated to understanding the complexity of the world we are living in now and to explain how the distinctive advantages of this union brings insight in *this* new world, whether it is continuing to explore new worlds that are emerging every day, or through finding ways to recognize patterns in massive quantities of data, or asking questions about the nature of such data and what it means to whom and why. There should be a place for business anthropology here in its role as a field that is interested in human difference and similarity while remaining grounded in the epistemological and methodological fundamentals that have made anthropology distinctive throughout time, including the moral and ethical questions that anthropology has always addressed. The "most humanistic of the sciences and most scientific of the humanities" could become a critical nexus for the interdisciplinary world of the future.

REFERENCES

Asad, Talal, ed. 1973. *Anthropology and the Colonial Encounter.* London: Ithaca Press.

Aylesworth, Gary. 2012. "Postmodernism." In *The Stanford Encyclopedia of Philosophy (Fall 2012 Edition),* edited by Edward N. Zalta. http://plato.stanford.edu/archives/fall 2012/entries/post modernism (accessed December 19, 2013).

Baba, Marietta L. and Carole E. Hill. 2006. "What's in the Name Applied Anthropology? An Encounter with Global Practice." In *The Globalization of Anthropology,* edited by C. E. Hill and M. L. Baba, NAPA Bulletin 25:176–207. Washington DC: American Anthropological Association.

Bennett, John. 1996. "Applied and Action Anthropology." *Current Anthropology* 36(Supplement): S23–S53.

Blei, David. 2011. Introduction to Probabilistic Topic Models. http://www.cs.princeton.edu/~blei/topicmodeling.html (accessed March 7, 2012).

Braverman, Harry. 1974. *Labor and Monopoly Capital.* New York: Monthly Review Press.

Bryson, John R., Peter W. Daniels, and Barney Warf. 2004. *Service Worlds: People, Organizations and Technology.* London: Routledge.

Bulmer, Martin, and Joan Bulmer. 1981. "Philanthropy and Social Science in the 1920s: Beardsley Ruml and the Laura Spelman Rockefeller Memorial, 1922–29." *Minerva* 19:347–407.

Cefkin, Melissa, ed. 2009. *Ethnography and the Corporate Encounter: Reflections on Research in and of Corporations.* Volume 5: Studies in Applied Anthropology. New York: Bergham Books.

Chesbrough, Henry, and James Spohrer. 2006. "A Research Manifesto for Services Science." *Communications of the ACM* 49(7):35–40.

Clifford, James. 1988. *The Predicament of Culture: Twentieth-century Ethnography, Literature and Art.* Cambridge, MA: Harvard University Press.

Collier, Stephen J., Andrew Lakoff, and Paul Rabinow. 2004. "Biosecurity: Towards an Anthropology of the Contemporary." *Anthropology Today*. 26:78–107.

Davenport, Thomas H. 2005. "The Coming Commiditization of Processes." *Harvard Business Review* 83(6):100–108.

Faubion, James D. 2001. "Currents of Cultural Fieldwork." In *Handbook of Ethnography,* edited by P. Atkinson, A. Coffey, S. Delamont, J. Lofland, and L. Lofland, 39–52. London: Sage Publications.

Fisher, Donald. 1993. *Fundamental Development of the Social Sciences: Rockefeller Philanthropy and the United States Social Science Research Council.* Ann Arbor, MI: The University of Michigan Press.

Freeman, Derek. 1983. *Margaret Mead and Samoa: The Making and Unmaking of an Anthropological Myth.* Cambridge, MA: Harvard University Press.

Foucault, Michel. 1994. *Dits et Ecrits: 1954–1988.* 4 volumes. Paris: Editions Gallimard.

Hakken, David. 1999. *Cyborgs@Cyberspace: An Ethnographer Looks to the Future.* New York: Routledge.

Harris, Marvin. 1968. *The Rise of Anthropological Theory: A History of Theories of Culture.* New York: Thomas Y. Crowell Company.

Ho, Karen. 2009. *Liquidated: An Ethnography of Wall Street.* Durham, NC: Duke University Press.

Kaelber, David C., Wendy Foster, Jason Gilder, Thomas E. Love, and Anil K. Jain. 2012. "Patient Characteristics Associated with Venous Thromboembolic Events: A Cohort Study Using Pooled Electronic Health Record Data." *Journal of the American Medical Informatics Association.* Published online July 3, 2012. DOI: 10.1136/amiajnl-2011-000782. http://jamia.bmj.com/content/19/6/965.full.pdf+html.

Karmarkar, Uday. 2004. "Will You Survive the Services Revolution?" *Harvard Business Review* 82(6):100–107.

Kohler, Robert. 1978. "A Policy for the Advancement of Science: The Rockefeller Foundation 1924–9." *Minerva* 16:480–515.

Kuklick, Henrika. 1991. *The Savage Within: The Social History of British Anthropology,* 1885–1945. Cambridge, UK: Cambridge University Press.

Kuper, Adam. 1983. *Anthropology and Anthropologists: The Modern British School.* London: Routledge and Kegan Paul.

_____. 2011. "Anthropologists Unite!" *Nature* 470:166–68.

Levitt, Theodore. 1976. "The Industrialization of Service." *Harvard Business Review* September-October:63–74.

Lombardi, Gerald. 2009. "The De-Skilling of Ethnographic Labor: Signs of an Emerging Predicament." EPIC 2009, 41–49

Lyotard, Jean Francois. 1984. *The Postmodern Condition: A Report on Knowledge.* Minneapolis: The University of Minnesota Press.

Macdonald, Sharon. 2001. "British Social Anthropology." In *Handbook of Ethnography,* edited by P. Atkinson, A. Coffey, S. Delamont, J. Lofland, and L. Lofland, 60–72. London: Sage Publications.

Malefyt, Timothy. 2009. "Understanding the Rise of Consumer Ethnography: Branding Technomethodologies in the New Economy." *American Anthropologist* 111(2):201–10.

Malefyt, Timothy, and Robert J. Morais. 2012. *Advertising and Anthropology.* London: Berg.

Manyika, James, Michael Chui, Brad Brown, Jacques Bughin, Richard Dobbs, Charles Boxburgh, and Angela Hung Byers. 2011. *Big Data: The Next Frontier for Innovation, Competition, and Productivity.* McKinsey Global Institute. http://www/mckinsey.com/insight/business_technol ogy / big_data_the_next_frontier_for_innovation (accessed December 19, 2013).

Marcus, George E., and Michael M. J. Fischer. 1986. *Anthropology as Cultural Critique: An Experimental Moment in the Human Sciences.* Chicago, IL: University of Chicago Press.

Mark, Gloria, M. Bagdouri, L. Palen, J. Martin, B. Al-Ani, and Kenneth Anderson. 2012. "Blogs as a Collective War Diary." In *Proceedings of the CSCW* 2012, 37–46.

Maxwell, Chad R. 2012. "Accelerated Pattern Recognition, Ethnography, and the Era of Big Data." In *Advancing Ethnography in Corporate Environments: Challenges and Emerging Opportunities,* edited by B. Jordan, 175–92. Walnut Creek, CA: Left Coast Press.

Mead, Margaret. (1929) 1949. *Coming of Age in Samoa.* New York: Mentor Books.

Miller, Daniel. 1995. *Acknowledging Consumption: A Review of New Studies.* London: Routledge.

Mills, David. 2002. "British Anthropology at the End of Empire: The Rise and Fall of the Colonial Social Science Research Council, 1944–1962." *Revue d'Histoire des Sciences Humaines* 6:161–88.

Mills, David. 2006. "Dinner at Claridge's? Anthropology and the 'Captains of Industry,' 1947–1955." In *Applications of Anthropology: Professional Anthropology in the Twenty-first Century*, edited by S. Pink, 55–70. Oxford: Berghahn Books.

Morais, Robert J. 2012. "Anthropology and Ethnography." *Journal of Business Anthropology* 1(2): 273–77.

Nader, Laura. 1969. "Up the Anthropologist—Perspectives Gained from Studying Up." In *Reinventing Anthropology*, edited by D. Hyme, 284–311. New York: Random House.

Ortner, Sherry B. 1984. "Theory in Anthropology Since the Sixties." *Comparative Studies in Society and History*. 26(1):126–66.

PCAST (President's Council of Advisors on Science and Technology). 2013. "Report to the President and Congress. Designing a Digital Future: Federally Funded Research and Development in Networking and Information Technology." January 2013 http://www.whitehouse.gov/sites/default/files/microsites/ostp/pcast-nitrd2013.pdf (accessed December 19, 2013).

Pels, Peter, and Oscar Salemink. 1999. "Introduction: Locating the Colonial Subjects of Anthropology." In *Colonial Subjects: Essays on the Practical History of Anthropology*, edited by P. Pels and O. Salemink, 1–52. Ann Arbor, MI: University of Michigan Press.

Reese, William. 2002. "Behavioral Scientists Enter Design: Seven Critical Histories." In *Creating Breakthrough Ideas: The Collaboration of Anthropologists and Designers in the Product Development Industry*, edited by S. Squires and B. Byrne, 17–43. Westport, CT: Bergin & Garvey.

Rattray, R. S. 1923. *Ashanti*. Oxford, UK: The Clarendon Press.

______. 1956. *Ashanti Law and Constitution*. London: Oxford University Press.

______. 1959. *Religion and Art in Ashanti*. London: Oxford University Press.

Rhea, Darrel, and Lisa Leckie. 2006. "Digital Ethnography, Sparkling Brilliant Innovation." *Innovation* Summer:19–21. http://www.idsa.org/sites/default/files/2526-Rhea.pdf (accessed December 29, 2008).

Ross, Dorothy. 1991. *The Origins of American Social Science*. Cambridge, UK: Cambridge University Press.

Scott, W. Richard. 2008. *Organizations and Institutions: Ideas and Interests*. 3rd edition. Los Angeles, CA: Sage Publishers.

Shankman, Paul. 2000. "The 'Exotic' and the 'Domestic': Regions and Representations in Cultural Anthropology." *Human Organization* 59(3):289–99.

Stocking, George W. Jr. 1995. *After Tylor: British Social Anthropology* 1888–1951. Madison, WI: University of Wisconsin Press.

Squires, Susan and Bryan Byrne, eds. 2002. *Creating Breakthrough Ideas: The Collaboration of Anthropologists and Designers in the Product Development Industry*. Westport, CT: Bergin and Garvey.

Suchman, Lucy. 2013. "Consuming Anthropology." In *Interdisciplinarity: Reconfigurations of the Social and Natural Sciences*, edited by A. Barry and G. Born, 141–60. Routledge.

Sunderland, Patricia, and Rita M. Denny. 2007. *Doing Anthropology in Consumer Research*. Walnut Creek, CA: Left Coast Press.

Taylor, Frederick Winslow. 1911. *The Principles of Scientific Management*. New York: Harper.

Ulmer, Cherly, Bernadette McFadden, and David R. Nerenz (eds.). 2009. *Race, Ethnicity, and Language Data: Standardization for Health Care Quality Improvement*. Institute of Medicine. Washington, D.C.: The National Academies Press.

Wasson, Christina. 2002. "Collaborative Work: Integrating the Roles of Designers and Ethnographers." In *Creating Breakthrough Ideas: The Collaboration of Anthropologists and Designers in the Product Development Industry*, edited by S. Squires and B. Byrne, 71–90. Westport, CT: Bergin & Garvey.

Zaloom, Caitlan. 2006. *Out of the Pits: Traders and the Technology from Chicago to London*. Chicago, IL: The University of Chicago Press.

NOTES

The author would like to acknowledge the valuable insights gained from suggestions and critiques on earlier versions of the paper provided by Jeanette Blomberg, Melissa Cefkin, Elizabeth Drexler, and Emily Altimare, as well as two anonymous reviewers. Any shortcomings of the paper are strictly my responsibility.

Earlier versions of this paper were presented at the Computer-Supported Cooperative Work (CSCW) Conference, an Interest Group of the Association of Computing Machinery, in Seattle, WA, February 11–15, 2012, and at the First International Conference on Business Anthropology in Guangzhou, China, May 17–20, 2012.

1 Service(s) in this context means a "negotiated exchange between a provider and an adopter (supplier and customer) for the provision of (predominantly) intangible assets" (Chesbrough and Spohrer 2006:37).

2 Ethnomethodology is a sociological method that represents human action and interaction by describing phenomena from the perspective of the participant(s), making visible the participants' methods for establishing the coherence of the phenomena.

3 Industry is defined as production on a large scale.

4 The following examples were selected from Malefyt (2009), but all are still current as of this writing based on a web search. *Research International, USA* calls its brand of ethnography—a self-service fieldwork that consumers conduct using cellphones—"cellnography." "Photo-ethnography" is a trademark that claims that consumers conduct their own ethnography in which the consumer monitors, organizes, and assesses his or her own thoughts and assumptions. Technology instantly transfers "facts" through self-aware individuals without interference from a researcher. Cheskin claims that their version "innovates" upon the standard of ethnography because "ethnography is no longer a leading-edge research method" (Rhea and Leckie 2006:20–1; compare Malefyt 2009:205). Digital technology applies new technology to the process of ethnographic observation. Now What Research combines face-to-face interviews with consumer blogs in a branded technique called "blography," and Red Dot Square emboldens consumers through virtual animated 3-D shopping.

5 Lombardi (2009:46) also described "disintermediating technologies that create a simulacrum of identity with the consumer's point of view." Corroborating Malefyt (2009), he reported on a French market research firm that used a video camera hidden in the nosepiece of a wearer's glasses to allow one to experience the visual reality of the wearer "remotely and in real time" (Lombardi 2009:46).

6 See the NSF field school's website at http://qualquant.org/methodsmall/ethnographic-field-school/; see UF's website at http://catalog.distance.ufl.edu/course.aspx?s=21449.

7 The results may be viewed at http://www.nsf.gov/sbe/sbe_2020_.

8 See the NSF's Grant Proposal Guide at http://www.nsf.gov/funding/pgm_summ.jsp? pims_id504767.

9 An ontology is a formal representation of knowledge; in this case, for clinical information that exists in an electronic health record.

10 An institutional field may be described as a diverse set of social actors operating within a specific domain or arena, in which all actors seek to advance their interests and impose their conception of "the rules of the game" upon the others (Scott 2008:183).

2

Theorizing Business & Anthropology

BRIAN MOERAN

WORDS & MEANINGS

It isn't all that easy to say what "business anthropology" is. Is it a kind of anthropology whose proponents study "business" organizations and forms of one sort or another in a more or less objective manner? Or are these anthropologists themselves somehow involved in the businesses concerned, as formally identified anthropologists, or consultants, or marketers, or something like that? In which case, is business anthropology something that anthropologists do *for* (and sometimes *with*), as well as *in*, business? If so, can or should it be distinguished from the kind of research conducted *on* business relations by academic anthropologists?

The answers given to each of these questions necessarily influence the way in which one talks about how best to theorize this emergent field of anthropology. I think it fair to say that it is currently populated by two kinds of anthropologists: those employed full-time in universities, business schools, and other institutions of higher learning; and those who make their living practicing anthropology in all kinds of different business situations. There are cross-overs, of course: business anthropologists head back into academia, while academic anthropologists occasionally take the plunge into the world outside their ivory towers. As a result, there should be a fruitful cross-fertilization of ideas, experiences, methods, and analyses (and this *Handbook* is just such a welcome endeavor).

This distinction in employment may reflect and reinforce an already existent one in intellectual leanings. There is a perception that those employed in academia (whom I shall call "anthropologists of business") are somehow different from those making a living out of their anthropological training ("anthropologists in business"). The former are seen to strive for an "objective" understanding of a business organization and to make use of age-old anthropological theories

Handbook of Anthropology in Business, edited by Rita Denny and Patricia Sunderland, 69–82.

based on studies of gift-giving, magic, totemism, social dramas, and so on. The latter work in and for a business organization and may be more concerned with immediately practical results that have a positive effect on their employer's financial baseline.

Such a perception is, of course, misplaced, in that anthropologists in business also make use of age-old theories in their analyses and they can hardly not be "objective" in their findings. At the same time, it hints at and so sustains earlier prejudices regarding the notions of "applied" and "business" in anthropology. Business anthropology can easily be dismissed by "purists" (including those veering towards the anthropology of business) as yet another, faintly disreputable, example of applied anthropology (Evans-Pritchard 1946), whereas the anthropology of business may, perhaps, be allowed to takes its place among the many more-or-less acceptable subdisciplines (for example, aesthetic, cognitive, design, development, educational, feminist, humanistic, legal, media, medical, political, psychological, sensory, symbolic, and urban anthropologies) that constitute the discipline as a whole.

Why this prejudice against business anthropology (or even the anthropology of business)? First, anthropologists who work in, for, with, and even on various forms of business organizations are tainted by a perceived "commercialism." The implication here is that either they are paid by the business organization concerned, or that their research will be used to further that organization's business aims and profits (usually, it is further implied, at the expense of some underprivileged group or other). In this respect, the world of anthropology resembles that of cultural production in general, where we find a distinction clearly made between "creative" and "humdrum" personnel (Caves 2000), with the former praised for their lofty "artistic" ideals and the latter damned for being concerned with management and financial administration. "Pure" anthropologists, then, are to film directors and editors, for instance, as "applied" anthropologists are to producers and publishers. The subtext here is that money is the root of all evil: a subtext that perhaps inflects current interest in the excellent anthropological work being carried out in the field of finance (e.g., Fisher 2012; Ho 2009; Maurer 2005; Riles 2011; Zaloom 2006).

Second, until comparatively recently, most anthropologists carried out their fieldwork in nonindustrialized societies typically characterized as "tribal" and assumed to have no knowledge of, or much interest in, the modern industrial, highly urbanized societies from which the anthropologists came. Rather like William Morris and others involved in the formation of Britain's Arts and Crafts Movement in the latter half of the nineteenth century, these earlier anthropologists developed in their writings an implicit critique of both industrialism and, to a lesser extent, urbanization: writings that exhibited a fond romanticism for, and exoticization of, "the rest" against "the West."

Although anthropology has moved to embrace the study of complex societies and no longer concentrates exclusively on nonwestern or "primitive" societies (Hannerz 1986), many of the discipline's proponents seem to hold fast to a romantic idea that "small-scale" is good, while "complex" is somehow bad. Better pigs and ancestors than mills in Manchester; better the circulation of *kula* objects than of advertising agency accounts. It is precisely because most business anthropology, as it has taken place hitherto, is conducted in highly (post-) industrialized societies like those found in the United States, Europe, and Japan, that it receives the Evans-Pritchard treatment of faint, but damning, distaste.

There is a third, slightly different, issue arising from the semantic density of the English word "business," which can mean anything from "occupation" or "trade" to the place or organizational form in which it takes place, by way of earnestness, harsh treatment, and even defecation (according to Webster's *Encyclopedia Unabridged Dictionary of the English Language*). This semantic density can cause confusion both historically and across cultures. On the one hand, six or seven centuries ago, our ancestors thought of "business" as "industry" (in the meaning of "diligence") and only through this interpretation arrived at "occupation." This terminological confusion extends to the varieties of anthropological subdisciplines currently associated with business: industrial, corporate, organizational, enterprise, and economic anthropologies, as well as the anthropologies of work and management. On the other hand, while European languages may have equivalent words that cover at least some of the same meanings as "business" does in English, Chinese and Japanese, among others, do not. As a result, scholars in these countries are obliged to come up with neologisms of one sort or another for their interpretations of "business anthropology," which they then supplement with age-old words like "administration," "commerce," "management," "work," and so on.

So, how best might we say what business anthropology is, in a manner that is comprehensible both to ourselves as native English speakers and to those who live and work in other languages? While it might be argued that there is nothing to connect the social relations found, for example, on a Norwegian oil rig, or in a Peruvian craft market; in a tea plantation in the Himalayan foothills, or in irrigated rice paddy fields along the Yangtze River basin; among hedge fund managers in a multinational bank, or drivers of a camel train in the Saudi Arabian desert, I would propose that, in spite of initial appearances to the contrary, there is, indeed, a common thread. Riggers, weavers, dealers, planters, farmers, bankers, and camel drivers are all involved in business of some sort or other. They all *trade*. And in trade they engage in practices that form many of the building blocks of anthropological theory: material culture and technology; gifts, commodities, and money; labor and other forms of social exchange; (fictive) kinship, patronage, quasi-groups, and networks; rituals, symbolism, and power; the development and maintenance of taste; and so on. It is through trade and through analyses of trade that the different anthropologies (corporate, organizational, economic, industrial, and so on), and other anthropological traditions (like those found in Japan and China) become united into a single "business" anthropology. And precisely because business anthropology is an anthropology of trading relations, it also reaches out to other disciplines such as business history, cultural studies, management and organization studies, some parts of sociology, and even cultural economics.

So far, so good. But it seems to me that a major problem in the theoretical and practical development of business anthropology is that most anthropologists who have studied, for example, family businesses in northern Italy (Yanagisako 2002), the Shanghai stock market (Hertz 1998), or a corrugated board manufacturer in Japan (Clark 1979), do not immediately see themselves as "business" anthropologists per se, but as *anthropologists* pure and simple. They apply anthropological theories to contemporary social and cultural phenomena that happen to be found in business environments. In this sense, perhaps, they are anthropologists of business.

Still, it begs the question: what is it that a business anthropology, or anthropology of business, can contribute to anthropology in general? What can it achieve that anthropology on its own cannot? To answer this question, I am going to resort to personal experience, since it is this that has led to my being classified as a "business anthropologist" in recent years, and to my being asked to write this chapter. Although such personal experience may not be shared by many of my colleagues in the field, it can, in Lévi-Strauss's famous phrasing, be "good to think" (*bonne à penser*). And thinking, right now, is what business anthropology needs, if it is to make any mark at all on the intellectual landscape of both businessmen and anthropologists.

A COMMUNITY OF FOLK ART POTTERS

Way back from 1977 to 1979, I conducted fieldwork for my PhD in Sarayama (Onta), a 14-household pottery community in southern Japan. The topic of my research was the Japanese folk art (or *mingei*) movement and how potters coped, or did not cope, with aesthetic ideals initially promulgated by philosophers and elite artist-craftsmen (including the English potter Bernard Leach) based hundreds of miles away in Tokyo, before being blown up—mainly by the media—into a full-scale consumer "boom" for people living in Tokyo and other urban conglomerations in Japan. And yet, here was I, living on the first floor of a *sake* shop in a remote mountain community, populated by generation after generation of farmer-potters whose view of their pottery making and the "outside" world (which began 200 yards down the road) was somewhat different from that which I had been led to believe by all the learned articles and books on folk art aesthetics that I had been reading some months previously back in London.

In spite of all the finely written words about beauty, nature, harmony, and being "at one with" one's materials, I quickly learned that money (a topic never mentioned in aesthetic treatises) was extremely important to the potters of Sarayama. After all, they were caught up in the midst of a consumer boom. So, the challenge was how to find out about it. Although this was difficult, it proved possible: thanks to sly persistence, plenty of luck, and an extended period of fieldwork that resulted in potters forgetting why I was there in the first place! After two years in Sarayama I *did* obtain a lot of financial details for households. I knew—through gossip, access to one household's detailed records over time, and (slightly deviously explained) measurement of potters' climbing kiln chambers—more or less exactly the yield of each firing. This I was able to set against expenses for materials (such as they were) and hired labor (such as it was outside the household), and use to show the economic effects of the folk art boom on pottery households. And because I also spent some time in the local city, and elsewhere, tracing the various degrees of mark-up in retail over wholesale prices, I also began to learn a little about Japanese craft retailing practices and to get a more nuanced impression of the nature of "consumer demand."

As a result, my thesis ended up looking not just at the practice of folk art aesthetic ideals, but at issues of pottery production and the market as they affected both aesthetic ideals and the community of potters in Sarayama. But could this be labeled a form of business anthropology? I realized, of course, that pottery households in Sarayama—like traditional Japanese households throughout the country—were first and foremost economic organizations, and that family and kinship came second. But my disciplinary leaning was towards a melding of "economic" and "aesthetic" anthropology that, to my mind, was absolutely necessary to, but generally lacking in, the "anthropology of art" (although I was reluctant to give the craft that I had studied the status of "art"). If anything, then, I thought of my work as representing an uncomfortable mixture of economic anthropology and the anthropology of art.

And yet, because it dealt with trading relations, the thesis—and the book that followed (Moeran 1997)—was indeed, I now realize and accept, an incursion into the field of business anthropology. There are many, many other such monographs of which the same might be said, from Malinowski's *Argonauts of the Western Pacific* (1922) to Bestor's *Tsukiji* (2004), by way of Powdermaker's analysis of the Hollywood film industry (1950), Watson's study of emigration and the lineage system in the New Territories of Hong Kong (1975), and Lien's ethnography of a Norwegian food company (1997).

CERAMIC ART & DEPARTMENT STORES

My second period of fieldwork in Japan was as a postdoctoral student and extended my interest in pottery into the ceramic art world. The research question underlying this fieldwork was simple enough: how did a potter manage to elevate himself to such an extent that his work came to be considered "art" rather than mere "craft"? And how, as a result, did he attain the honor of designation by the Japanese Cultural Agency as the holder of an "important intangible cultural property"? The answer was a little more complex. Potters who wished their work to be seen as "ceramic art" used to exhibit it in department stores, which regularly held one-man, group, and competitive exhibitions of one sort or another on a weekly (or, if very important, fortnightly or three-weekly) basis. Potters would start by holding shows in local department stores, and gradually move further afield as success encouraged them and opportunity arose. Their choices were motivated by an informal ranking system of stores, based on both sales generated and their cultural capital (including tradition and regional location).

I therefore found myself visiting numerous shows in department stores around Kyushu, where I lived, as well as further afield in Osaka and Tokyo. These visits, however, together with interviews with store representatives, yielded basic information only, which came to be repeated almost word for word by one informant after another: department stores put on cultural activities like art and ceramics exhibitions to give "culture" back to their loyal customers who had spent their money elsewhere in the store over the years. In other words, exhibitions were a straight swap of economic for cultural capital.

This was fine insofar as it went, but, after listening to the third recounting of exactly the same reasoning, my fieldworker's hackles were raised and I grew (as it proved, rightly) suspicious. But, until I was able somehow to break down this wall of the "public face" of a department store, I realized that I was going to get nowhere. That I was in fact able to move backstage was pure chance. By hooking up with an active, but slightly disillusioned, gallery owner, I found myself visiting both potters and department stores with a different hat on my head. I was no longer a "scholar," but an "assistant": partly invisible behind my informant, the front man in all negotiations that took place before my very eyes (and in my ever-present notebook).

What I learned from this research—which included my holding my own pottery exhibition in a Kyushu department store—was how different people in an art world emphasized different values regarding what made an art object (or, in my case, pot) "good," "bad," or merely "indifferent." Both potters and retailers recognized three sets of value that made up the "price" or overall "worth" of a pot: aesthetic, commodity, and social. While potters tended to stress aesthetics over price (commodity value), they did not ignore the latter; after all, they had a living to make. But their considerations of what made a pot good or indifferent were not necessarily the same as those of dealers and department store representatives, nor indeed of critics (who virtually ignored the fact that a pot was a commodity other than as a potential *objet d'art*). What united, and separated, them all were social values: the estimation of quality based on *who* you knew in the world of art pottery. The idea that Potter A's work could be considered "good" because he or she had been apprenticed to Potter B might hold good among those who liked the latter's work. But it came to be a criticism among those who preferred Potters C, D, or E, each of whom had their own coteries of aficionados.

Needless to say, perhaps, steering a course between these different networks of relations was a difficult and tiring task. Although located in a particular business world, what I encountered was not that different from kinship relations or political networks in other fieldwork contexts. So, was this investigation of would-be "artist potters" an example of business anthropology, or just anthropology in general? Was I then just studying markets and forms of exchange (including bribery), like many economic anthropologists (e.g. Plattner 1996), while also adhering to my interest in art and aesthetics?

AN ADVERTISING AGENCY

If anything counts towards my being a business anthropologist, I suppose it is my fieldwork in a medium-sized Tokyo advertising agency, then called Asatsū, conducted throughout 1990, just as Japan's economic "bubble" burst (Moeran 1996). Although this research provided a wonderful mixture of mental and bodily understanding of what it meant to be employed in advertising (more of which a little later), it was also disturbingly preplanned. Before I arrived in January 1990, the manager of the CEO's office sent me a timetable for my research: the first two weeks of January would be spent in his office; the following week in magazine buying; the next in newspaper buying; then television and radio, before spending a month in marketing, and the following months in accounts, creative, merchandizing, special promotions, the international division, personnel, finance, and information technology (IT), before returning to the CEO's office to round things up.

I can still vividly recall my very first day in Sarayama, when I was having lunch in the noodle shop, wondering what on earth I was going to do, now that I had finally arrived in "the field." How should I start my study? As I looked at a hand-drawn map of the names and locations of the 14 houses in Sarayama on the wall above me, I decided that maybe the best way to start would be to find out who lived in each household. That way, I could at least get to know who was who, how old they were, where they were born, where the wives had come from, and so on and so forth. So, that afternoon, I started asking people about their families, which turned out to be a stroke of luck because, in spite of their fame throughout the land, Sarayama's potters had *never* been asked about their families. It was always pots, pots, pots. In this I unwittingly endeared myself to everyone in the community (and it was probably this that saved me from being thrown out of the community when I started calculating a kiln's economic yield a few weeks later!).

But now, more than a decade later, I was being *told* what to study and when. This was both a great relief, and an initial source of worry. What if the agency was trying to steer my research in particular directions, in which I might not necessarily wish to go? After all, I wasn't dealing with a bunch of "country bumpkins" (as one critic once referred to the potters of Sarayama in my presence). Now I was seriously "studying up." Power relations were inverted, and who knew where I, as an anthropologist, would end up?

In fact, the carefully concocted schedule was designed to allow anyone in the agency to know where I might formally be found, should the necessity arise. By being officially located in one department or another, a manager or other employee would know how to trace me, even though I might be somewhere else at that particular time. So, in mid-April, for example, the accounts divisional manager's secretary would be able to tell an enquirer that I was in fact attending the trainees' induction classes that week, or helping with the Mercedes Benz presentation in the international division the next. In short, the timetable was an exercise in information for others, rather than in control over the fieldworker.

Two other aspects of fieldwork were exceptional and thus worth mentioning. First, every time I moved from one section, department, or division to another, agency personnel would give me more or less formal lectures about their work before letting me experience it for myself in practice. On my first day in the magazine buying department, for example, I was given a two-hour lecture covering the overall field of magazine advertising and the agency's activities therein. This was followed in the afternoon by two one-hour lectures by two different media buyers about particular aspects of their work. The next morning, the departmental manager suddenly turned to me and said:

> Right, professor! Now we're going off to the biggest publisher in Japan, Kodansha, to negotiate the purchase of ad pages over the next year in all its magazines. You may sit quietly in the meeting and take notes, but you say nothing. OK? We'll fill you in on what's gone on when we come back to the office later on in the day.

And so I sat in on two hours of negotiations, of the kind already described to me in some detail secondhand by those who had lectured me the day before, but including a lot of tacit knowledge that I was unable to grasp then and there.

When it was over, I was asked if I had any questions, and Kodansha's advertising manager answered them quite frankly, before inviting us to lunch, where conversation (aided by a bottle of beer each) voiced some of that tacit knowledge and soon encompassed all kinds of topics I would never have dreamed of asking about! This, surely, was *business* anthropology!

Second, my informants in Asatsū allowed me to get involved in their projects in such a way that I was not simply asking them questions and observing what was going on, but was actively participating in working out how best to solve a marketing problem or come up with a campaign tagline. This was not the first time that I had engaged in observant participation—my pottery exhibition in a Kyushu department store had been just that—but it provided me with the kind of illumination that, by the end of my fieldwork, made me feel more like an "ad man" than an academic!

The fact that I was able to make a contribution to the agency's collective thinking about how best to present two of its campaigns to potential clients has over the years reinforced my view that, for fieldwork to be really "successful," the fieldworker has to do (or have done) what his or her informants are doing: exhibited pots in a department store, worked as a hedge fund manager, been a boxer, ballet dancer, school teacher, or whatever. It is this physical experience that allows the fieldworker to understand things somewhere down in his or her solar plexus, rather than just in the head (Wacquant 1995). And I think that it is something that, ideally, every anthropologist of business should aim for when in the field. It is certainly something that applied business anthropologists often experience in their everyday work over long periods of time.

BODY & MIND

So, where do these fieldwork accounts take us? First, my call for a shift from participant observer to observant participant in fieldwork has theoretical, as well as methodological, implications. By holding my own pottery exhibition in a department store and by working on an ad agency account team for a potential client, I experienced *physically* what otherwise was an *intellectual* endeavour. Until I was prevailed upon to exhibit my own pots, I had listened to potters, dealers, department store representatives, and newspaper journalists criticizing one another and the pots on show in the various exhibitions then popular in urban Japan. I had even joined in with my own bits of gossip gleaned during interviews with informants and observations at exhibitions far afield, and learned to be as cynical as those populating the art world of contemporary Japanese ceramics. But once I had to make pots for my own one-man show, things changed drastically. I became extremely self-conscious and unsure of myself and my work, which I saw as amateurish and very far from the kind of perfection that I sought in my imagination. When somebody actually paid me a compliment, I felt a glow of pleasure that offset the disappointment of watching others displaying no interest at all as they walked quickly past the works on display. When my first pot was sold—a quarter of an hour after the show opened—I nearly embraced the middle-aged woman who had fallen for a plate on which I had drawn a picture of Snoopy in a bath, with the words *Happy Bathday* written round its rim! I quickly learned the meaning of "thank you" as people whom I had never seen before and would never see again decided to pay for a set of dishes or a vase or a *sake* cup, each of which, I felt, cost far more than it should have, and which contained a little bit of "me" that they were taking home.

I also, of course, experienced firsthand the negotiations that took place among different stakeholders in my exhibition, and even made my own contributions to them: for example, by bringing in an organization (the British Council) to which my main sponsors had no access. These experiences impressed upon me the fact that being a potter or "ceramic artist" required more than technical skills in throwing, glazing, and firing pots. Social skills were also crucial to public recognition and acceptance of one's work. I, too, had to learn to spin a tale around my pots and so provide a hook upon which people could hang their expectations. Such realizations, stemming from my physical engagement with pottery, later were reflected in my intellectual analysis of the ceramic art world, allowing me to be multifaceted and more nuanced in my explanations than I might otherwise have been (Moeran 2014:60–81).

The same can be said of my engagement with advertising, which, as anyone who has read anything written by scholars in the field of cultural studies knows, is an easy target for criticism. The fact that I was myself able to come up with taglines and slogans for clients and participate directly in campaign proposals taught me an awful lot about the kinds of stress that advertising executives go through every day for months, years, decades at a time. It also taught me that, in spite of all appearances to the contrary, advertising campaigns came into being through teamwork and that those involved in different business spheres—creative, marketing, media buying, accounts—somehow had to resolve their inevitable differences if they were to make an idea work. Finally, it taught me about how difficult it actually is for people employed in a business like advertising (or, for that matter, fashion magazine or book publishing) to disengage themselves, to reflect upon what they are doing or being asked to do, and to make moral and ethical decisions that could radically change that business. It made me realize just how privileged academics are, and how luxurious is their way of working that allows them to be disengaged, objective, reflexive, and critical.

THEORIZING BUSINESS & ANTHROPOLOGY

All of which brings me back, perhaps a little circuitously, to the topic of this entry in this book: how to theorize the anthropological study of business. Clearly, our theories are in our methods, and vice versa. Business anthropologists—that is, anthropologists who work in or for a business organization—are often obliged to carry out research and analysis according to the expectations of a particular client. A manufacturer may frame a problem in terms of the unionized workers it employs; a city education council in terms of its high-school students. But what if fieldwork reveals that the cause of the "problem" is the manufacturer's middle managers and not its workers, or the teachers and not the students of a high school? Will the client be open-minded enough to accept such a finding, or not?

There are a number of issues like this (including access, client confidentiality, and publication rights) that anthropologists in and of business face, but it strikes me that, first and foremost, business anthropology, by whatever name, needs to develop a programmatic statement of what it should be about. By so doing, it will enable those interested in the subject to focus on issues that become common to them all. Such commonality is essential if this emergent subdiscipline of anthropology is to be anything other than a passing fad, temporarily attracting scholars and practitioners who otherwise feel out of place. One has only to look at another recently emerged "discipline," fashion studies, to understand what I mean. The last thing we want as anthropologists interested in business is an endless stream of descriptive, only partially critical, navel-gazing studies.

So, what might a program for business anthropology look like?

For a start, it must *engage* with the discipline as a whole at both practical and theoretical levels. By this I am referring to two things. First, it should fight to revitalize current anthropology programs taught in universities and other institutions of higher learning. In an era when most anthropology students can only get jobs in business organizations of one sort or another, shouldn't "academic" anthropologists be preparing their students specifically for such job opportunities, rather than giving them endless doses of ethnographic and theoretical discussions that are in large part irrelevant to their future careers? Isn't it time academic anthropology made concessions to the modern world in which their universities are almost entirely located, and made use of contextualized business case studies, methodologies, and theories that together would provide a practical and pertinent foundation for future anthropological research? As business anthropologists we must *engage with colleagues in our discipline* far more, perhaps, than we already do.

Second, in anthropology, as in many other disciplines, there is far too much citation for citation's sake of other people's work. We need to go beyond making passive use of anthropological or sociological theories by *recontextualizing* them. How far can we usefully apply theories of animism and contagious magic in "primitive" societies to branding in contemporary marketing, for example, or frame analysis of business settings? Other theoretical topics developed in nonbusiness contexts that immediately come to mind include in no particular order: family businesses; gender; law; entrepreneurship; markets, money, and exchange; material culture; power relations; economic, social, and cultural capital; limited stock companies; networks; bureaucracies; frame analysis; meetings; ritual, symbolism, and religion; CCT (consumer culture theory; see Arnould and Thompson in this volume); and globalization. We have, therefore, a lot of anthropological theories out there that may be put to the test in contemporary business contexts. As business anthropologists, we need to *engage with theories* (more on this in a minute or so).

This invites a second programmatic statement that is so obvious it shouldn't need saying. We must be *comparative.* Those anthropologists working in, on, for, or against businesses must compare their findings with those of their colleagues working both in other branches of business *and* in other societies. Are analogies to be drawn between north Italian silk manufacturing family firms, on the one hand, and family restaurant owners in Chinatown in London, on the other? If so, what are they? And how do they compare with the ideals and practices of Japanese corporate "familism"? What are the mechanisms sustaining a preference for family forms as a means of making a living from different kinds of business activities over generations and across cultures? An essential aspect of engagement, then, is adoption of a broad perspective.

Third, we should be discussing *methodology* far more than we do. As anthropologists, we have been brought up to learn about and practice—occasionally even to worship—the defining feature of our discipline: participant observation–style fieldwork. In recent years, some of our colleagues have argued over its former practices and suggested acceptable new ways of going about our craft: multisited fieldwork, for example, or para-ethnography. With the digital revolution, anthropologists have turned to other ways of recording ethnographic material than by traditional means of pencil and notebook. Some use video and audio equipment; others resort to various interactive fora made available by the internet. Business anthropologists are in the forefront of these trends. They often take for granted their everyday practices that would surprise their academic colleagues (like the fact that consultants of one sort or another may have to share their video material with their clients at the end of each day, for example). It strikes me that they could, and should, be leading the way in this particular field of anthropological interest.

As I suggested here, we might think about focusing our theoretical endeavors to "configure" our field of study. The question then becomes: what directions should such theoretical endeavors take?

We all have our different theories about theories, but what I personally would like to see over—say—the next ten years is anthropologists in and of business, engaging with:

1. Social relations and structures of power in, between, and dependent upon business organizations of all kinds, but particularly firms;
2. Explicit comparison between these social forms (companies, industries, conglomerates, and so on) and the various cultures (work, management, professional, regional, national, and so forth) that, in one way or another, impinge upon and form them, and by which they themselves are developed and sustained;
3. The materials, technologies, and things (goods, commodities, equipment, tools) with which business people of all kinds engage, in which they are entangled, and which afford their organizational forms (see Suchman 1987); and
4. Ethnography and fieldwork methods (see also Baba and Patel in this volume).

If we could do all that, and do it well, and in the course of doing it, provide detailed ethnographic studies of business situations of all kinds, perhaps then our colleagues in anthropology might reluctantly agree that the anthropologies in, of, for, and with business are "good to think." And that, without the customary cynical smirk, Lévi-Strauss can be a brand of jeans as well as a long-lived anthropologist.

REFERENCES

Bestor, Theodore. 2004. *Tsukiji: The Fish Market at the Center of the World.* Berkeley & Los Angeles: University of California Press.

Caves, Richard. 2000. *Creative Industries: Contracts between Art and Commerce.* Cambridge, MA: Harvard University Press.

Clark, R. 1979. *The Japanese Company.* New Haven: Yale University Press.

Evans-Pritchard, E. E. 1946. "Applied Anthropology." *Africa* 16:92–8.

Fisher, Melissa S. 2012. *Wall Street Women.* Durham, NC: Duke University Press.

Hannerz, Ulf. 1986. "Theory in Anthropology: Small Is Beautiful? The Problem of Complex Cultures." *Comparative Studies in Society and History* 28(2):362–7.

Hertz, Ellen. 1998. *The Trading Crowd: An Ethnography of the Shanghai Stock Market.* Cambridge, United Kingdom: Cambridge University Press.

Ho, Karen. 2009. *Liquidated: An Ethnography of Wall Street.* Durham, NC: Duke University Press.

Lien, Marianne. 1997. *Marketing and Modernity.* Oxford, United Kingdom: Berg.

Malinowski, Bronislaw. 1922. *Argonauts of the Western Pacific.* London: Routledge & Kegan Paul.

Maurer, Bill. 2005. *Mutual Life, Limited: Islamic Banking, Alternative Currencies, Lateral Reason.* Princeton, NJ: Princeton University Press.

Moeran, Brian. 1996. *A Japanese Advertising Agency: An Anthropology of Media and Markets.* London: Curzon/Honolulu: University of Hawai'i Press.

_____. 1997. *Folk Art Potters of Japan.* London: Curzon/Honolulu: University of Hawai'i Press.

_____. 2014. *The Business of Creativity.* Walnut Creek, CA: Left Coast Press.

Plattner, Stuart. 1996. *High Art Down Home: An Economic Ethnography of a Local Art Market.* Chicago, IL: University of Chicago Press.

Powdermaker, Hortense. 1950. *Hollywood, the Dream Factory: An Anthropologist Looks at the Movie-makers.* Boston: Little, Brown.

Riles, Annelise. 2011. *Collateral Knowledge: Legal Reasoning in the Global Financial Markets.* Chicago, IL: University of Chicago Press.

Suchman, Lucy. 1987. *Plans and Situated Actions: The Problem of Human-Machine Communication.* Cambridge, United Kingdom: Cambridge University Press.

Wacquant, Loïs. 1995. "The Pugilistic Point of View: How Boxers Think and Feel about Their Trade." *Theory and Society* 24(4):489–535.

Watson, James. 1975. *Emigration and the Chinese Lineage: The Mans in Hong Kong and London.* Berkeley & Los Angeles: University of California Press.

Yanagisako, Sylvia. 2002. *Producing Culture and Capital: Family Firms in Italy.* Princeton, NJ: Princeton University Press.

Zaloom, Caitlin. 2006. *Out of the Pits: Traders and Technology from Chicago to London.* Chicago, IL: University of Chicago Press.

Suggested Further Readings

Cefkin, Melissa, ed. 2010. *Ethnography and the Corporate Encounter: Reflections on Research in and of Corporations.* Oxford, United Kingdom: Berghahn.

Jordan, Ann T. 2013. *Business Anthropology.* Prospect Heights, IL: Waveland Press.

Jordan, Brigitte., ed. 2013. *Advancing Ethnography in Corporate Environments: Challenges and Emerging Opportunities.* Walnut Creek, CA: Left Coast Press.

Journal of Business Anthropology. 2012. Open Access. Available at rauli.cbs.dk/jba.

Malefyt, Timothy. de Waal, and Robert. J. Morais. 2012. *Advertising and Anthropology: Ethnographic Practice and Cultural Perspectives.* Oxford, United Kingdom: Berg.

Marcus, George., ed. 1998. *Corporate Futures: The Diffusion of the Culturally Sensitive Corporate Form.* Chicago, IL: University of Chicago Press.

Moeran, Brian. 2005. *The Business of Ethnography: Strategic Exchanges, People and Organizations.* Oxford, United Kingdom: Berg.

Schwartzman, Helen. 1989. *The Meeting: Gatherings in Organizations and Communities.* New York: Plenum.

Sunderland, Patricia. L., and Denny, Rita M. 2007. *Doing Anthropology in Consumer Research.* Walnut Creek, CA: Left Coast Press.

3

Decentering the Origin Story of Anthropology & Business: The British Experience Since 1950

SIMON ROBERTS

A quick survey of the journalistic work that has reported on anthropology in business could lead you to believe that use of anthropology in business is a recent phenomenon. That survey might also create the impression that it is primarily an American phenomenon. The origin myths of corporate anthropology tend to locate the genesis of the practice in the United States: enter tales of Xerox PARC and the campuses of other American technology corporations such as Intel and Microsoft. This tendency towards geographical bias in the story of anthropology's application can therefore also be seen as an institutional one. And yet, perhaps unsurprisingly, the story is a little more complex and a lot more interesting than business and mainstream journalism would initially contend. This essay seeks to fill in some of the gaps in the story of anthropology's engagement with business with a particular focus on British anthropology and its development in the second half of the twentieth century.

TRANSATLANTIC INTERACTION

The long history of business anthropology, which can be traced to the early 1920s, is not a solely American affair: there was interaction between British academic institutions and anthropologists during the period when anthropology in business was starting to develop. However, the bias in the story towards American activity and individuals is somewhat legitimate in that it was in the United States, at least for the most part, where the early experimentation and interaction between industrialists and anthropologists occurred.

A definitive story of anthropology in business does not exist, but a number of accounts tell the story of engagement that involves individuals from Britain

Handbook of Anthropology in Business, edited by Rita Denny and Patricia Sunderland, 83–99.

and the United States. For example, three essays by Baba (2006, 2009, 2012) provide a rich picture of the interwoven efforts of philanthropists, pioneering social scientists (not just anthropologists), and industrialists that are both international and interdisciplinary in nature. For example, Baba's 2012 introductory essay to the first edition of the *Journal of Business Anthropology* emphasizes Radcliffe-Brown and Malinowski's contribution to the early application of anthropology in industrial contexts in America. More pertinent to the argument in this essay, Baba's essays demonstrate the importance of the financial assistance provided by the Laura Spelman Rockefeller Memorial to Malinowski and the London School of Economics (Baba 2012:27).

This New York–based foundation simultaneously supported the earliest forms of business anthropology in the United States and sustained what, at the time, was one of the only UK academic departments teaching anthropology. The picture that emerges from Baba's accounts, and from that of Mills (2002), is one of exchange: British or British-trained anthropologists were active in the United States and participated in some of the earliest efforts to define the practical ways in which anthropology could be applied to business and industrial welfare problems. For example, the contributions of Radcliffe-Brown were central to the development of the Human Relations School, a group founded in Chicago that focused on direct observation of organizations and behavioral interactions (see Baba 2012:42). On the other hand, philanthropic support flowed back across the Atlantic to support the academic and colonial research endeavors of key British departments.

However, when it comes to the very earliest practical explorations of how anthropology could engage in business the action is, without doubt, in the United States, the earliest examples being the "Hawthorne Project" at Western Electric (led by Elton Mayo and W. Lloyd Warner) and the Yankee City research project, led by Warner (see Baba 2012:38–40). A series of detailed accounts of such work has been published elsewhere (see Baba 2009, 2012); however, it is worth noting Baba's conclusion that "without the conceptual contributions of British social anthropology" this work would not have been possible (Baba 2012:42).

Even more relevant here is that the literature records no such sustained efforts or success in Britain between 1920 and 1930, when this pioneering work was taking place in the United States. As Mills' (2006) account suggests, the earliest efforts to foster engagement between industry and anthropology did not occur until the late 1940s, when, as in the United States, the focus was on industrial and social welfare of workers. In the United Kingdom, the overtures came from industrialists to anthropologists, not the other way around. Baba attributes this in part to a greater focus on pragmatism in the United States. It certainly seems as if British anthropologists were happy to be involved in the

United States, and British institutions happy to receive financial support from the philanthropic funds of industrialists such as Rockefeller, but the unease with actually applying anthropology in industrial contexts in the United Kingdom held back British anthropology longer.

The early start that anthropology in business got in the United States and the existence of corporate environments that more obviously nurtured sustained anthropological involvement in business over the course of the twentieth century has resulted in a tendency for accounts such as Cefkin's volume *Ethnography and the Corporate Encounter* (2009) or Sunderland and Denny's *Doing Anthropology in Consumer Research* (2007) to be tilted, geographically and institutionally, to the United States. But, I would suggest, there is another absence in these stories. While they both provide very rich and complementary accounts of how an academic discipline was incorporated into a variety of business contexts, neither of these volumes explicitly relates that story to the discipline of anthropology itself during the same period, in the United States or elsewhere.

This chapter will neither belabor the point about a bias in previous accounts toward the United States, nor deny that there exist some good, if partial, accounts of the endeavors of anthropologists in business within Europe (Pink 2006). Instead, I have two more specific aims. The first is to sketch some features of the story of the development of business anthropology in the United Kingdom from the late 1940s to the present day. I use the word "sketch" advisedly because there are gaps in the story (which are opportunities for deeper research). The second is to demonstrate that the story of anthropology's application in business (or elsewhere for that matter) should not be divorced from an understanding of the development of the discipline itself. I attempt to link these two through telling the intertwining story of anthropology's development inside and outside British academic departments.

I argue that for much of the twentieth century, at least until its expansion in the 1980s, British anthropology was a relatively niche discipline that did not create many anthropologists. Since very few anthropologists were "produced" overall, even fewer anthropologists existed to craft careers as anthropologists outside academe. Further, the elite universities of Oxford, Cambridge, and the London School of Economics (LSE) dominated the discipline. These departments were led by conservative figures who largely resisted the idea that anthropology should engage with nonacademic fields of practice. In that sense, the central concern of these departments was the establishment and reproduction of the discipline. The fact that the discipline was small and dominated by a small number of (conservative) departments held back the development of a cadre of self-consciously applied anthropologists and any recognizable brand of applied anthropology, be it in business or any other setting.

However, two environmental factors—one threatening, and the other nourishing—created the conditions in the 1980s and 1990s, respectively, for anthropology's expansion outside of British academic departments. By the 1980s the discipline had strengthened—both in terms of the numbers of students it was producing and the diversity of the departments in existence—such that the conditions for its flourishing outside of academe were in place.

The result is that in the second decade of the twenty-first century it is possible to argue that, happily, the prospects for doing things "beyond the department" with an anthropology degree in the United Kingdom look as good as they ever have. There are strong departments in many universities and a growing awareness of the career paths that are available to graduate anthropologists, evidenced by an increasing appetite to engage with and learn from those practicing anthropology in business, and to develop courses (such as design anthropology and digital ethnography) that are consciously angled towards new applied directions that have emerged in the last decade or so.

My interest in writing this story is not to provide some strictly chronological account of the relationship in the form of a "who, why, and when" history but to develop an account that accentuates the different trajectories of anthropology and anthropologists in this period and explores the attitude of different academic bodies and individuals to these developments. The account leans on my own journey from anthropology student in the 1990s to my current status as a consulting business anthropologist. My story is not unique or outstanding, but it is underpinned by two important propositions: namely, it fits into a wider narrative about British anthropology and career possibilities for those with an anthropology degree in Britain, and it is representative of a shift towards engagement with industry by the discipline.

FROM DINNERS AT CLARIDGE'S TO AN EVENING AT PIZZA EXPRESS

In 2003 three British anthropologists, Jonathan Spencer, Anne Jepson, and David Mills, explored career possibilities for postgraduates by setting out to establish the career journeys of a 10-year cohort of PhD anthropologists from UK universities between 1992 and 2002. That Spencer had taught me as an undergraduate, and subsequently supervised my PhD research, further encouraged my interest in his research when I received the survey his team had produced.

The stimulus for Spencer, Jepson, and Mills' work was a clear sense that postgraduate career paths were changing. Their objective was to inform the development of teaching to better prepare students for their likely occupational future. If, as they suspected, more anthropology PhDs were being produced than ever before, and the number of jobs in anthropology departments was shrinking, what might the future hold for those embarking on postgraduate research? By charting the career journeys of a 10-year cohort of PhD students from UK universities, they intended to produce a high-fidelity picture of the opportunities or challenges presented to these students and British anthropology departments.

Their research quickly identified that a unified record of the 765 anthropology postgraduates between 1992 and 2002 did not exist, and would have to be created, and that finding those operating outside of academe would require a certain amount of sleuthing, use of personal networks, and "targeted Googling." What they found out from the 309 of those 765 that they were able to contact was consistent with Gerald Mars' characterization in an *Anthropology Today* editorial (2004) of anthropology as an "exploding discipline" whose members had dispersed throughout the workplace galaxy. However, many were self-consciously labeling themselves as anthropologists even if their job, in their own or others' estimations, did not resemble something anthropological in nature. The anthropological identity was, it seems, enduring, whatever the career path that had been chosen.

The snapshot that Spencer, Jepson, and Mills were able to create was in some ways consistent with their initial expectation: the anthropology departments at Cambridge, Oxford, and LSE were most successful in producing anthropologists who went on to establish academic careers in anthropology departments. In that sense, the historical dominance of a few key departments that produce academic anthropologists continues. Elsewhere, anthropologists were found in other departments ranging from sociology, religious studies, development, and nursing studies. Overall, Spencer and Mills concluded that between 60 and 65 percent of the cohort were in academic employment somewhere in the world (Spencer et al. n.d.).

Of those in the United Kingdom working outside of academe, they found 21 percent working in national or local government and another 17 percent working within UK and international nongovernmental organizations and in the charity sector, both as managers or social researchers. Finally, they identified that 13 percent of the cohort worked in commercial organizations, such as research and consultancy firms.

I completed my PhD in anthropology in 2000. I had been in touch with Jonathan Spencer not long before he started work on the survey project, and I recall feeling somewhat sheepish about admitting that I was working in the private sector. My own hesitancy about '"breaking cover" betrayed my own squeamishness about "selling out" (or being accused of having done so). Of course Spencer's response was more gracious than I might have been expecting, and he

Figure 3.1. Employment of anthropology PhDs completed in the UK between 1992 and 2002 now working outside academia (Spencer et al. n.d.).

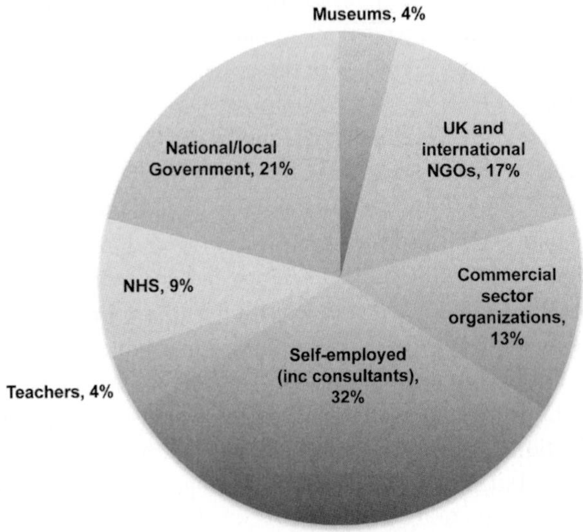

was more than a little intrigued by what I was up to. As his research was to discover, my own career choice was not one pursued by many postgraduates in the 10-year cohort.

My own sense that I had transgressed an unwritten but well-understood boundary demarcating the "pure" environs of an academic career and the impurity of the private sector has a long tradition in British anthropology, and elsewhere. As David Mills (2006) has argued, there is (or at least had always been) a "serial ambivalence" about the virtue and utility of anthropology being applied outside of academe (Mills 2006:56). As he outlines in his entertaining account of British anthropology's prandial relationship with "Captains of Industry" in the late 1940s and 1950s, neither party could quite decide on the value of that relationship. As his essay makes clear, anthropologists like Edmund Leach and Meyer Fortes were unclear about the morality of applying anthropology to the workplace to help solve some of the issues faced by industrialists in postwar Britain. Further, and more troubling in their mind, they questioned the suitability of the subject's methodologies to examine these questions. Leach was particularly cautious about the scale of the claims made on behalf of anthropologists, noting in a letter to Israel Sieff, a British industrialist who was leading the efforts to establish a relationship between anthropologists and British industrialists: "The fact is that the anthropologist really does not know whether or not his subject has any important practical applications, but when anyone holds out a financial carrot he tends to invent them" (Mills 2006:60).

And yet, on the other side of the fence, the "Captains of Industry" with whom they had a series of meetings, from companies such as Unilever, ICI, and Marks & Spencer, found the arcane language and predilection for conceptual thinking of these "anthropological mandarins" hard to penetrate. On reading a memo from Meyer Fortes, one industrialist admitted to another that having read the document several times over, he still did not understand it: "I think there is a difficulty of communication. It would seem there is considerable difference between the nomenclature in general use in anthropological circles and in the business world" (Mills 2006:63). Equally, they found these anthropologists' unwillingness to truly consider how their discipline might be of use to industry mildly off-putting. As a result of this hesitancy, the proto-relationship between the Royal Anthropological Institute (RAI) and industry (as personified by the leaders of these large businesses) never blossomed despite the best efforts of its two main boosters, Israel Sieff (son of one of the founders of Marks & Spencer, a large British retail chain) and Robert Hyde, one of the founders of the Industrial Welfare Society.[1]

During that early dalliance between industry and anthropology, industry had used dinners at Claridge's, an iconic and expensive hotel in London's Mayfair district, to create commensal bonds between themselves, academics and members of the RAI. More than 50 years later, Spencer and Mills bought dinner for anthropologists working outside academe, this time in the Mayfair branch of Pizza Express. The evening was designed to allow them to share the early findings of their cohort research and learn more about the careers of those, like myself, who they subsequently described as those "successfully selling their anthropological skills in more commercial settings—for example with short-term ethnographic projects for independent research institutes, often in areas like IT and communications technology" (Spencer et al. n.d.). And while it is likely that the dinners at Claridge's would have been of higher quality than our pizzas, dough balls, and salads, those present welcomed the opportunity to share their experiences. Spencer and Mills concluded that the evening had been satisfactory and that they received "particularly rich material" from the guests, concluding that "mutually beneficial links could be usefully established between academic and non-academic anthropologists" (Spencer et al. n.d.). Gillian Tett, a journalist at *The Financial Times* in London, a member of the 1992–2003 cohort and one of the more widely known anthropologists attending the dinner, later wrote an article about anthropology careers beyond academe for the paper (Tett 2005).

THE DEVELOPMENT OF A DISCIPLINE & ITS INTERACTIONS

The history of UK anthropology's engagement with the world outside the department is clearly more than the sum of the interaction between individuals on each side of the fence. It is also about the history and development of anthropology as a *discipline* in the United Kingdom. During the years of anthropology and industry's early courtship, as recounted here, anthropology in the United Kingdom had a very different complexion compared with today, both in terms of its size and structure. That is important to consider when thinking about the development of its relationships with the business world.

In the early period, the 1940s and 1950s, when the discipline was small and governed by a relatively homogenous (white, middle class, male) establishment with quite antipathetic views about the appropriateness and suitability of anthropology's engagement with industry, it is unsurprising that neither the resources nor will existed to find meaningful forms of engagement.

At the time that Meyers Fortes and Edmund Leach were thinking through what a relationship with industry could or should look like, they were figureheads of an extremely small discipline extending, in the United Kingdom, to only three departments (at Cambridge, Oxford, and LSE) and numbering only 30 academics (Spencer 2000:3). The Association of Social Anthropologists (ASA) had been established in 1946 as an association for professional anthropologists (i.e., those in academia) in distinction to the RAI, which was more of a society for colonial administrators and gentlemen scholars. The ASA was an outfit that would represent, it was hoped, an emergent cadre of academic anthropologists. The material point is that anthropology was a small discipline feeling its way through some of the issues created by its own development. Any history of the interaction between business and anthropology, or its absence, in the United Kingdom in the mid-twentieth century needs to recognize the simple fact that, notwithstanding the unwillingness of the few anthropologists that there were to engage with business, the total number of anthropologists available for any such interaction was in any case very small.

By 1963, there were 50 anthropologists working in British universities, but they were predominantly still in the same few institutions. However, British higher education expanded in the 1960s, and new universities and polytechnics, informally and derogatorily known as the "red brick" institutions, emerged (Spencer 2000:4). With that expansion came the establishment of new anthropology departments, sometimes alongside sociology departments; while the growth of anthropology in this period looks solid, when compared with that of sociology it was less impressive, with sociology finding more of a market within the bureaucracies of postwar Britain. One reason, Spencer suggests, is demographic: there were simply not enough anthropologists to drive the expansion (Spencer 2000:4).

By 1973 there were about 90 anthropologists in post, rising to nearly 120 by 1983 (with departments at St. Andrews and Goldsmiths in London added to the roster of institutions teaching the subject). And, by 1993, there were 160 anthropologists in British universities. During that period there had been a rise in the number of undergraduate and postgraduate students. Between 1970 and 1994, 964 anthropology PhDs were awarded, 460 of them from the triumvirate of Oxford (187), Cambridge (137), and LSE (136).

Aside from the dominance of these three institutions, which managed, between 1970 and 1994, to produce 50 percent of all PhDs awarded in anthropology, the records also show that a great increase in PhD production occurred in the 1980s and has continued thereafter, running at roughly 40 a year since the mid-1980s (Spencer 2000:8).

So at one level the picture is of a steady growth in the raw number of PhDs being produced. These students were a necessary but still insufficient requirement for anthropology to engage with the world, since a steady supply of postgraduate surplus to those required to actually reproduce the discipline itself is a sine qua non of their engagement. To adopt the language of demographers, from the 1960s on anthropology as a discipline had achieved replacement fertility: it was growing, and with growth could come an expansion in terms of application. But numbers alone do not account for the increasing engagement and application. The next section discusses the other factors in play.

NECESSITY AS THE MOTHER OF INVENTION

Looking at the landscape of British anthropology departments in more detail helps us see why certain types of novel engagement outside of these departments took hold. During the 1980s, departments which had been founded in the 1970s (such as those at Kent and Sussex) had fallen on hard times during the lean early Thatcherite years, and under the leadership of Ralph Grillo and others they pioneered vocational courses (Spencer 2000:14). These courses prepared students for working in the field of social development. The goal at this stage in the discipline's history in Britain, if not for Oxford, Cambridge, and LSE, then at least for other departments, was merely survival in an era of harsh higher education cuts that were focused on the social sciences. As Spencer reports, the tone of the ASA Decennial in Cambridge in 1983 was one of crisis, but Edmund Leach was still keen to assert that the role of the ASA was to keep anthropologists out of colonial hands; if the only employment route for a British PhD anthropologist was social development, then the discipline best "shut itself down" (Spencer, personal communication, November 2012; see also Spencer 2000:14).

This innovation from a new breed of departments and academics, despite the resistance of some within British anthropology, can be seen with the benefit of hindsight to have revitalized the discipline. This innovation led to the development of new avenues for the application of British anthropology. Although these were largely in social development, a mold had been broken. In the past, a comparatively small number of students from a small number of institutions worked on research funded by government or its agencies, or were groomed as academics of the future. By the mid- to late 1980s this picture had evolved: there were more anthropologists, more courses that strayed from the classic mold, and clearer career options for anthropologists outside of research and teaching in anthropology departments. They might work in other departments, in social development, or in other applied settings. However, the residual ideas of impurity connected to such routes, espoused most vehemently by Leach, still continued to colonize the anthropological mind.

I started as an undergraduate at Edinburgh University in 1991. This department was a beneficiary of the development described here, able to offer its students courses taught by academics with strong regional expertise (especially in south Asian and African anthropology) and, by virtue of a strong relationship with the ODA (Overseas Development Agency), later known as DiFD (the Department for International Development), experience in applied work. The department provided evaluation of development projects on a contract basis. Looking back, the Edinburgh anthropology department seems to have displayed a healthy "mixed economy" approach to anthropological engagement. This was a department at ease with the idea of hiring anthropologists to work in a dedicated fashion on development-related contracts.

Outside of work in the field of social development and the traditional routes of university employment, the 1990s were a time when funding opportunities through research councils (for anthropology the Social Science Research Council, later the Economic and Social Research Council [ESRC]) were evaluated, in part, according to their likelihood to positively affect the UK economy. But outside of those channels a welter of new funding opportunities arose, and European money and British government funding avenues increased markedly. It seems reasonable to assert that the combination of these funding trends—one to do with applicability, the other with increased funding opportunities from entities specifically focused on policy or business settings—further drove anthropology to become ever more applied in social policy and business settings.

In my PhD funding application to the ESRC I had asserted the likely benefits to the UK economy and media industry of an anthropological study of the satellite television revolution unfolding in India at the time. I did so because in 1993, the Conservative government had, as Anthony Cohen, my head of department at the time, noted, "explicitly adopted 'wealth creation' as the test of acceptable scientific research and scholarship, a standard which was quickly and supinely adopted by the Economic and Social Research Council" (Cohen 1994:196).

I am not sure that any *direct* benefits as hoped for by the ESRC have subsequently accrued from this study, although the fact that in my estimation my PhD did establish the foundation for a career in business may retrospectively satisfy the Research Council auditors. Perhaps the fact that this area of research was funded at all suggests prescience on the part of the funding authorities that such a PhD topic might actually be a good foundation for a career consulting for technology and media companies after all? However, what was regarded by many at the time as a travesty—the introduction of criteria in funding decisions that favored research that could demonstrate some potential application—appears after the fact to be a policy that has pushed anthropology as a discipline, and individual funding applicants, to consider how their work might be useful beyond its strictly and legitimately academic concerns. There may be anecdotal (or more formal) evidence demonstrating that anthropological research applications exhibiting no aspiration toward wealth creation or application are *not* funded. That is difficult to judge without a large evaluative survey. However, I suspect that a mix of research topics continue to be funded, and that just as harsh environment of the 1980s produced conditions that led to innovation which has turned out to be positive for the discipline, the same may be true of this turn in policy because it forced a conversation about what might legitimately be considered applicable research.

THE BIRTH OF PUBLIC-PRIVATE ANTHROPOLOGY

The harsh economic environment of the 1980s created a sense of necessity that led to innovation in the form of courses tailored towards a growing job market opening in development. Ralph Grillo and others had exploited an elective affinity between anthropology and development to great and enduring effect. Jobs in social development became the "obvious" choice for anthropologists seeking work outside of academe. However, the United Kingdom of the 1990s offered a different, more nourishing economic environment that coincided with the strengthening discipline and the growing number of postgraduates. One area where opportunities arose was in government.

The 1990s was the decade when "evidence-based" policymaking became the vogue and, relative to the 1970s and early 1980s, and certainly to the current period of austerity, there was financial abundance in the public sector. A growing number of research roles in government departments and agencies opened up opportunities for anthropologists. By the early 2000s there were anthropologists in the heart of Whitehall, in departments such as the Ministry of

Defence, the Foreign and Commonwealth Office, and the Civil Contingencies Secretariat at Cabinet Office. Anthropologists also found employment in the Defence Science and Technology Laboratory (founded 2001), and in research roles at the Department of Transport. This was in addition to anthropologists working within the "home" of the discipline in government, the Department for International Development.

Social research budgets boomed with an influx of European funding into the so-called "quangos" (quasi-nongovernmental organizations) and other national bodies such as the Design Council and NESTA (the National Endowment for Science Technology and the Arts, founded in 1998), both of which started to advocate the use of research-led innovation in product and service design. NESTA's Public Services Innovation Lab connected a research-focused approach with a growing commitment to investigating how public services could meet major social challenges such as aging and chronic disease. Elsewhere, a unit called RED was set up in 2004 by the Design Council to "tackle social and economic issues through design-led innovation"[2] and led by Hilary Cottam, an Oxford-educated anthropologist who was awarded "UK Designer of the Year" in 2005 for her work on innovative approaches to public service reform. Cottam has continued to work on public service innovation through her consulting firm called Participle, where she is engaged in reconceptualizing the welfare state and "designing and developing large-scale projects that demonstrate the next generation of public services."[3]

Numerous other links between anthropology and public policy and public service design emerged in this period of reform-focused government. Policy entrepreneurs such as Geoff Mulgan, founder of the think tank Demos and later director of the Prime Minister's Strategy Unit, began to take a strong interest in what anthropology and ethnographic approaches could add to public policy development. The Young Foundation (founded by Michael Young, author of the classic urban sociology text *Family and Kinship in East London*), an organization that Mulgan led between 2004 and 2011, developed a strong ethnographic research capability; its research team is currently led by Will Norman, an LSE anthropology postgraduate.

The context for the emergence of this field of employment possibilities is the tendency, still strong despite more straitened economic times, to think about public policy, social issues, and public services through a customer-centric, "user-led," or "user-centered" lens. Arguably, this approach was given a formal blessing in October 2001 by then–Prime Minister Tony Blair, who declared that "the key to reform [of public service] is redesigning the services around the user—the patient, the pupil, the passenger, the victim of crime" (Public Administration Select Committee 2004:3–4).

In the same period, numerous private companies emerged to offer research-led strategy and design services to both private and public sectors and increasingly made a point of the fact that they had anthropologists on staff. Two examples of such companies are Live|work, a service design company founded in 2002, which refers to its "unique multi-disciplinary team of designers, technologists, social anthropologists, marketers, management consultants, operations professionals and entrepreneurs". ESRO, a research company founded in 2004 by another LSE postgraduate, Robin Pharoah, "to bring an ethnographic approach to social and commercial research challenges" (http://www.esro.co.uk/), has developed a strong reputation in the social and market research market, a reputation cemented by winning several Market Research Society awards for their work on public sector research.

These are but two examples of what is now an increasingly crowded market where a formal training in anthropology is not always seen as a prerequisite to claiming expertise in anthropological or ethnographic approaches. Britain has a very large market research and marketing services sector, with the market research sector estimated to be worth more than £3 billion (Market Research Society 2013), and one trade directory of research companies lists a total of 53 organizations claiming an ability to provide ethnography as a research approach or "service" (Association of Qualitative Research 2013). It is interesting to reflect then on the popularity of the methods, their probable commoditization (see Suchman 2007), and the "market potential" (but also competition) for those with degrees that they regard as providing credibility to their claims to be bona fide ethnographers.

Having myself set up Ideas Bazaar in 2002 in an attempt to bridge commercial and academic research, I was fortunate enough to find myself with a role within a think tank, which had been central, in the guise of one of its founders Robert Hyde, in the early discussions between industry and anthropology that I describe in this chapter. The Industrial Society, later to become known as The Work Foundation, had established a technology think tank, iSociety. I become a part of the team, and was given the somewhat tongue-in-cheek title of "ethnographer in residence." At iSociety we ran studies exploring the rise of networked technologies in British life, with projects on mobile phones, broadband internet, and technology in the workplace. The high premium attached to the communication of these findings (a clear benefit for the two principal funders of iSociety, Microsoft, and the professional services firm PwC), gave work using an anthropological approach significant airtime that it might not otherwise have received. This publicity did my fledgling ethnographic research consultancy no harm either, and we secured other work that allowed us to continue to document, albeit in a proprietary context, the everyday use of technology in a period of rapid growth in the mobile phone, mobile internet, and broadband markets. We also went on to receive a large number of commissions from the BBC, an organization I had listed as a potential beneficiary of my PhD work on television in India, although that work for the British public service broadcaster more often took me to Birmingham than Banaras, India, my PhD fieldsite.

DEVELOPMENTS, NOT GRAND DESIGNS

One key feature in the story of corporate anthropology's development in the United States is the predominance of the research and development labs of technology corporations as the key site of employment opportunities, with the obvious and iconic example being Xerox PARC's Palo Alto labs. But while there are some anthropologists employed by large technology companies in the United Kingdom, for example at Microsoft in Cambridge, the UK operations of American technology corporations have not, on the whole, created research and innovation labs that have employed anthropologists or other social scientists in significant numbers or for sustained periods of time. Hewlett Packard began a multidisciplinary lab in Bristol in the mid-1990s, employing anthropologists and sociologists such as Abi Sellen, Richard Harper, and Kenton O'Hara (all now at Microsoft Research in Cambridge), but this interdisciplinarity waned in the early 2000s as the "peripheral" disciplines (i.e., anthropology) lost out in favor of a focus on engineering. Sellen, Harper, O'Hara, and others had previously worked at EuroPARC in Cambridge (founded in 1987 as European branch of the successful Xerox PARC research center). Although EuroPARC is no longer in existence, it was noteworthy for its specific focus on interdisciplinarity, and on the integration of social science into a technology research context.

With echoes of Spencer and Mills' cohort research work with which I began this essay, Crucible, a research network at the University of Cambridge dedicated to promoting research collaboration between technologists and researchers in the Arts, Humanities and Social Sciences (AH&SS), has sought to investigate the influence of some of the alumni of EuroPARC through a series of interviews.[4] The results of this work are not currently available, but it seems reasonable to posit that the influence of these individuals, given their profile within corporate research and academic contexts, and through their establishment of research and innovation consultancies, has been important. For example, one alumna of EuroPARC, Rachel Jones, went on to establish a successful research and innovation consultancy, Instrata, in 2001 after working at the consulting firm Sapient in the preceding years.

However, given the obvious absence of a strong tradition of industrial research and development lab employment for anthropologists in the United Kingdom, it would be unwise to privilege this relatively short-lived lab in any account. Rather, my aim has been to chart the role of pioneers and believers, of innovation and invention, and to consider the socioeconomic forces and institutional developments that have combined to create a discernible career path for anthropologists outside of academe in the United Kingdom in the last 60 years.

The story is not one of grand designs—of a set of policies or strategies being laid out and then explicitly pursued—but instead of slow evolution. I hope to have shown how the development of anthropology in its disciplinary settings in the United Kingdom is a vital component of the story. I hope also to have shown that when this history is combined with a consideration of the wider forces at play beyond academe, it gives a better sense of what has developed, and why.

The efforts of early believers in the United Kingdom, such as Sieff and Hyde, who were working some 20 years after the early US pioneers, were designed to foster engagement between industry and anthropology. Although ultimately unsuccessful in their stated aims in the short term, they did succeed in forcing a debate about the appropriate basis for engagement. Innovators like Ralph Grillo within academe were adept at seeing the demand for anthropology in the field of social development and responded by creating appropriate courses. The result was new opportunities and the development of a "convention" within the discipline that this field of employment was one well suited to the skills of trained anthropologists. In a context of a growing discipline—both in terms of the number of departments and graduates and postgraduates being trained—Grillo's approach was quickly replicated, and other development focused courses emerged.

The same pattern of institutions responding to changing labor markets and opportunities is repeating itself today. With the emergence of a demand for anthropologists within the sort of public and private research settings that I have described, courses have been developed to meet those demands. Notable among these are the Digital Anthropology Masters at University College, London, and the Design Anthropology Masters at Aberdeen. However, within more conventional degree programs, attempts are being made to ensure that students are aware of new forms of disciplinary practice. For example, at the University of Manchester, a course module is "Introduction to Business Anthropology: Consumers, Companies and Culture."[5] In these departments and elsewhere, postgraduates as well as undergraduates are exposed to alternative career trajectories. For example, an annual "retreat" for anthropology PhD students in Scottish universities makes a point of using those who have fashioned careers for themselves beyond academic departments—be it in technology companies, the Civil Service, or as independent consultants—to inform current students about the career opportunities beyond academe.

The net result of all of this activity is the emergence of a multiplier effect. The growing awareness of the demand for anthropologists in a variety of workplace settings, the increased publicity of their work in business, and the laying down of discernible patterns to employment has been matched by obvious and committed engagement within academic departments. The understanding that anthropology can lead to work in development is now being repeated in other areas of application, such as design, research, and innovation in and beyond technology companies.

Changes in the labor market and shifts in public and private sector priorities will coalesce with an increasing willingness on the part of many anthropology departments to interact with, and learn from, those pursing new types of careers with anthropology degrees. Therefore, we can expect the conventional careers for anthropology graduates to continue to be reinvented in ways that are difficult to anticipate today. The original visions of Sieff and Hyde—that industrialists and anthropologists could work together—did come to pass. However, that relationship took longer to gel than they had anticipated, developed by an indirect route, and took different forms from those they had envisaged.

REFERENCES

Association of Qualitative Research. 2013. http://www.aqr.org.uk (accessed 12 March 2013).

Baba, M. 2006. "Anthropology and Business." In *Encyclopedia of Anthropology*, edited by H. Birx, 83–117. Thousand Oaks, CA: Sage Publications.

_____. 2009. "Disciplinary-Professional Relations in an Era of Anthropological Engagement." *Human Organization* 68(4):380–91.

_____. 2012. "Anthropology and Business: Influence and Interests." *Journal of Business Anthropology* 1:20–71.

Cefkin, M., ed. 2009. *Ethnography and the Corporate Encounter: Reflections on Research in and of Corporations*. Oxford, United Kingdom: Berghahn.

Cohen, A. 1994. *Self Consciousness: An Alternative Anthropology of Identity*. London: Routledge.

Market Research Society. 2013. "UK Research Market Worth over £3bn, Says First Comprehensive Sector Review." http://www.mrs.org.uk/article/item/556 (accessed 10 March 2013).

Mars, G. 2004. "Refocusing with Applied Anthropology." *Anthropology Today* 20(1):1–2.

Mills, D. 2002. "British Anthropology at the End of Empire: The Rise and Fall of the Colonial Social Science Research Council, 1944–1962." *Revue d'Histoire des Sciences Humaines* 6:161–88.

_____. 2006. "Dinner at Claridge's? Anthropology and the Captains of Industry 1947–1955." In *Applications of Anthropology: Professional Anthropology in the Twenty-first Century*, edited by S. Pink, 55–70. Oxford, United Kingdom: Berghahn.

Pink, S., ed. 2006. *Applications of Anthropology: Professional Anthropology in the Twenty-first Century*. Oxford, United Kingdom: Berghahn.

Public Administration Select Committee. 2004. *Choice, Voice and Public Services: House of Commons. Public Administration Select Committee Written Evidence*. London: The Stationery Office Limited.

Spencer, J. 2000. "British Social Anthropology: A Retrospective." *Annual Review of Anthropology* 29:1–24.

Spencer, J, A. Jepson, and D. Mills. n.d. "Where Do All the Anthropologists Go? Research Training and 'Careers' in Social Anthropology." http://www2.lse.ac.uk/anthropology/events/Conferences/Anth-in-London-2009/careers_in_social_anthro-pology.pdf (accessed January 5, 2013).

Suchman, L. 2007. "Anthropology as 'Brand': Reflections on Corporate Anthropology." Paper presented at the Colloquium on Interdisciplinarity and Society, Oxford University, Oxford, United Kingdom, February 24.

Sunderland, P., and R. Denny. 2007. *Doing Anthropology in Consumer Research.* Walnut Creek, CA: Left Coast Press.

Tett, G. 2005. "Office Culture." *The Financial Times* May 20. http://www.ft.com/cms/s/0/cd6cfbd4-c75c-11d9-9765-00000e2511c8.html#axzz2H32WqEfU (accessed 10 March 2013).

NOTES

I want to thank Jonathan Spencer for an illuminating conversation about the history of British anthropology that inspired my treatment of this essay. More generally, I also thank him for his support as a teacher, PhD supervisor, and in subsequent years. I wish to thank Adam Drazin and my father Bill Roberts for close readings of the essay and to the two anonymous reviewers; all their suggestions and comments helped improve it. Any remaining errors and omissions remain, of course, my own.

1 The Industrial Welfare Society, which changed its name to The Industrial Society in 1965 (and to The Work Foundation in 2002), was established originally by Hyde to ensure the good physical working conditions of men and boys working in munitions factories, but over time widened its remit to the fostering of good human relations in industry in general.

2 See the RED website at http://www.designcouncil.info/RED/.

3 See the Participle website at http://www.participle.net/.

4 Alumni of EuroPARC include William Newman, Bill Gaver, Richard Harper, Abigail Sellen, Quentin Stafford-Fraser, Rachel Hewson, Satinder Gill, Kenton O'Hara, Rachel Jones, Mark Stringer, and Carey Young.

5 The course description can be found at http://www.socialsciences.maschester.ac.uk/ubdergraduate/courses/modules/module.html?code=SOAN10361.

4

Professional Anthropology & Training in France

DOMINIQUE DESJEUX

INTRODUCTION

This chapter describes the history of professional anthropology in France and the content of a professional doctoral program to show how the professional anthropology of consumption can—with an empirical, inductive approach—produce practical epistemological innovation. When I speak of professional anthropology, I refer to fieldwork carried out and financed at the request of clients, whether the anthropologist is an entrepreneur, a research manager, or an academic. This could be called Research on Demand (ROD), on the model of Video on Demand. This phrase does not imply an opposition between theoretical anthropology and applied anthropology: the analytic requirements of studies are the same whether carried out in an academic context or an industrial one. It refers to the origins of the research topic and the choice of the field to be studied. Professional anthropologists do not devise their own topics. They do not begin by formulating questions theorized in seminars; they begin from practical problems that must be solved. Paradoxically, however, professional anthropology actually fosters new types of theorizing.[1]

Researchers may carry out several studies each year, which forces them to constantly reposition themselves mentally, to reexamine their explanatory models, and to shift their viewpoints as they respond to specific requests to provide anthropological analysis. Starting off with practical problems, they must find new methods of observation and new angles of interpretation to understand human behavior. They constantly explore unknown territories: the worlds emerging from developments in new technologies, new diseases, new efficient consumption, new cultures, new entrepreneurs, new poor, new markets, new environmental risks, and new military tensions.[2] Anthropologists then can relate these phenomena to structures that are more or less stable. Through their train-

---

Handbook of Anthropology in Business, edited by Rita Denny and Patricia Sunderland, 100–115.

ing in comparative intercultural methods, they have learned to distinguish between and harmonize what is particular and what is universal, what is permanence, and what is change: the structural model of Claude Lévi-Strauss and the dynamism of Georges Balandier.

THE RISE OF PROFESSIONAL ANTHROPOLOGY & ACADEMIC OPPORTUNITIES

Between 1945 and 1990, French anthropologists had little involvement in professional anthropology, even though applied anthropology did exist to a certain extent. They worked largely in Africa at first, studying above all rural and urban indigenous communities in former French colonies. This was the heyday of the anthropology of kinship, with Lévi-Strauss as the main reference, and the anthropology of dynamic change, with Balandier as father figure. After African independence, many French anthropologists continued to work on agricultural development projects, studying changes in peasant communities, problems of disease and witchcraft, and the new African business class. Others returned to France and studied the poor on the outskirts of cities, migrants, the transformation of rural society, and rural magical-religious phenomena. Publicly funded classic research was thus largely limited to the poor, immigrants, the sick, disappearing farmers, and some "exotic" societies. Post-industrial society was largely ignored and, despite the profound transformations of the *trente glorieuses,* the "30 glorious" years of prosperity between 1945 and 1975 (which saw the arrival of mass consumption, distribution, and marketing), anthropological research generally ignored consumption.

In the late 1980s, due to rising unemployment and anthropologists' difficulty in finding university and publicly funded positions, the journal of the French Association of Anthropologists (*Bulletin de l'Association Française des Anthropologues*) began questioning the "purposes of anthropological research" (1987). The journal followed up with other articles in this vein, citing marketing and management as possible applications of anthropology in an issue on contract ethnology (1989; No. 35), and presenting in "Training in Anthropology" (1990; No. 42) the only professionally oriented anthropology program, the Sorbonne Magistère of Social Sciences Applied to Intercultural Relations. Jean-François Baré confirms in *Les Applications de l'anthropologie* (1995) that in the early 1990s, professional anthropology in France was still in its infancy. Rural societies and Africa remained dominant themes for a major research group, the Euro-African Association for the Anthropology of Social Change and Development headed by Jean-Pierre Olivier de Sardan. There were only two or three ethnological studies of companies and professions, and one course on intercultural management.[3]

In France psychology was the first academic discipline in the social sciences to really engage in professional intervention, with the creation of the Association for Psycho-sociological Research and Intervention by Guy Palmade in 1958. Sociology followed shortly afterward, with Michel Crozier at the Centre National de la Recherche Scientifique (CNRS) recruiting researchers and conducting contracted research for private companies and government agencies from 1960 on. Renaud Sainsaulieu, within Crozier's network in the human resources sector, founded the Association of Sociology Professionals in Business in 1998, affiliating most of the researchers who worked with private companies. Researchers such as Norbert Alter, professor of sociology of innovation at the University of Paris IX-Dauphine, in turn trained professionals who worked outside the university. Many of these researchers have become consultants, some working only in the public sector, others with private companies.

In the early 1990s, there were still only three small, private contract firms that used anthropology: Argonautes and SHS Consulting in Paris and IRIS in Toulouse. However, change was occurring. The 1990s marked the advent of ethnomarketing, which became one of the major activities of professional anthropology, and it was also a time of renewal for marketing, with two important authors, Olivier Badot and Bernard Cova. Their book *Néo-marketing* (1992 [2009]) emphasized the importance of social ties among consumers and between consumers and businesses. This marked the beginning of the cross-fertilization of anthropology with management sciences that led to the founding of the Consumption and Society network in 2001, with Marc Filser, Oliver Badot, Joël Bree, Eric Rémy, Isabelle Garabuau Moussaoui, and Jean-François Lemoine. It should be noted, however, that mixing does not occur in the core of academic anthropology but rather on its margins, and in business schools and universities.

Another trend emerged at the same time with Franck Cochoy in Toulouse, researchers working under Michel Callon at the École des Mines de Paris, and the actor-network theory of Bruno Latour, who developed the field of sociology of the market. In *Une Sociologie du Packaging* (2002), Cochoy shows with intelligence and humor that marketing's "control" of the consumer refutes the liberal theory of the market. If the laws of the market functioned on their own, there would be no need for advertising or packaging to "enhance" consumer choice.

The 2000s marked the full-fledged development of professional anthropology (and thus ROD) mainly in three fields: consumption and innovation as a single process,[4] from mass consumption to new communication technologies; intercultural applications for organizations in France and abroad; and immigration. Professional training was developed through interdisciplinary and international networks[5] combining anthropology, microsociology, economics, management science, and methods of group facilitation and change management.

The main characteristic of ROD is that it starts from a request—a problem to solve—rather than solely from an academic's theoretical question. Although the request is not anthropological, the answer is, or at least is produced by anthropological methods. Learning how to carry out professional anthropology thus means first learning how to understand a specific problem involving consumption, innovation, education, social inclusion, or decision-making and then translating it into an ad hoc method of anthropological inquiry, with a different angle than a psychologist, engineer, marketer, lawyer, or economist would have. Anthropology is effective not because it is a better science but because it allows actors, customers, activists, journalists, and everyone who uses it to shift the way in which they inquire about their problem when a situation seems blocked.

In practice, professional anthropology often tends toward hybridization, crossing public and private professional worlds, scientific and practical results, research and development and marketing, doctors and patients, or businesses and consumers. It is this "in-between" work that determines the training of professional anthropologists, as can be shown with the example of the doctoral program established at the Sorbonne (Université Paris Descartes Sorbonne Paris Cité).

DOCTORAL TRAINING IN PROFESSIONAL ANTHROPOLOGY: INDUCTIVE INQUIRY & A VARIETY OF METHODS

In the past 10 years, some French universities have lost up to 40 percent of their social science students, academic positions have become scarce, and funding has decreased, yet the number of doctorates has not diminished much. How is it possible to find work for everyone? Sophie Alami and I established the Professional Doctoral Program in Social Sciences in 2007 to train professional anthropologists, helping them to acquire both the methodological frameworks of anthropology and sociology and the problem-solving skills that their clients require. Their studies are designed to prepare them to become research managers, although some do go on to teach in higher education.

Course content covering both anthropology and sociology is only part of this process. The objective is to train students to manage studies on their own, from start to finish, in an often-unknown domain. This involves a complex alchemy of reasoning methods, tools, information collection techniques, and professional know-how, all of which is reinforced with a large amount of practical fieldwork in diverse and often unexpected fields. By conducting ROD studies in areas such as uses of the car, energy savings in the household, practices involved in having breakfast, online gaming, genealogy, the homeless, makeup and body care, waste disposal, and medication, they learn to manage the interface between an organization's research needs and a socioanthropological response.

This three-year program at the Sorbonne includes one week per month of courses, consisting of monitoring students' fieldwork, theoretical contributions, discussion of readings, and seminars with professional experts. Each student must find an employer, a nongovernmental organization (NGO), a government agency, or a private company that wishes to recruit a young doctoral student to perform research for them with a Convention Industrielle de Formation par la Recherche (CIFRE)–supported thesis (public funding that cofinances the student's salary), a thesis scholarship, a research tax credit (national-level tax assistance), or a fixed-term study contract as an employee, an independent freelancer, or part of a sponsoring company. Their contracts allow them to work and conduct research at the same time, in France or abroad.

Students receive a University Diploma (DU) for each year completed. Awarding a diploma every year reduces the chances that students will embark on a thesis project and not complete it, nevertheless giving certification for work completed to those who do leave the program. It also provides the sponsoring organization with concrete results every year. Students carry out a three-week field study within their company for each of three years to acquire exposure to a variety of fields and scales of observation. In the first year, students carry out microsocial-scale qualitative surveys of 20 to 30 stakeholders, who may be consumers, professionals, or applicants for social assistance, and obtain a DU1 degree in consumer-study management in France and abroad. In the second year, their anthropological research relates to systems of action on a mesosocial scale, and the coursework features organizational sociology, anthropology, intercultural project management, and group facilitation. The DU2 degree is awarded in team management. The third year is more flexible. It includes a collective quantitative survey on a macrosocial scale with geopolitical implications, and students obtain the DU3 professional doctoral degree in social sciences. This is coupled with the classic doctorate thesis which, defended at the Sorbonne, is drawn from their three research projects and their theoretical formulations, much like the HDR degree, which confers authority to supervise research.

Anthropology teaches students to conduct research in an inductive mode, without a priori assumptions, but nevertheless with methodological tools that structure their exploration in areas often with no points of reference. I would argue that anthropologists in the field are like sixteenth-century navigators embarking on a new coast without knowing where they were. Early navigators only had a sextant to gauge their position relative to the sun, a compass to indicate directions, and a sounding line to avoid the shallows. They plotted the coastline and then drew a map, gradually putting everything into perspective.

Anthropologists' instruments are the methods that allow them to map the contours of social phenomena and the paths that lead through the maze of decision-making; we focus on four of these. The first is the scales of observation method, which focuses on the effects of how reality is sectioned; what is visible on one scale can become invisible or change shape at another level of observation. This method also shows that social causation may vary according to the scale, and an independent variable that seems explanatory on one given scale might become a dependent variable on another. The second approach is the itinerary method, which fits neatly into the anthropological tradition. A framework helps reconstruct the series of practices involved in the acquisition and use of goods and services, not as individual, one-time practices but as part of a collective decision-making process that can be analyzed in terms of three major forces that shape all reality: material, social, and symbolic. The third is that of the life course or life cycle, a starting point for constructing social and cultural identities through the accumulation of many micro-rites of passage. The fourth is that of action systems. This approach can be used to analyze the family, for example, as a system of actors who undergo constraints, areas of uncertainty, and power relations. This approach to constrained action is akin to Crozier's interactionist, utilitarian, strategic tradition in sociology. For illustration, I describe in more detail the first two methods, the scales of observation and itinerary method, with brief allusions to the life course and action system approaches embedded in these descriptions (see Clochard and Desjeux 2013; Desjeux 2004, 2006, 2009, 2011; Dias Campos 2010; and Yang 2006).

THE SCALES OF OBSERVATION METHOD

In epistemological terms, the scales of observation method shows that causality and the explanation of phenomena vary from one scale to another, depending on whether they emphasize the correlation effect, the effect of situation, or the effect of meaning (described in Desjeux [2004]). These three systems of causality show that social reality can be explained by several different systems. Thus, no scale is in the absolute more relevant than another; the interest of the scales is to shift focus to bring out contextual effects that vary from one scale to another. Moreover, when changing scales of observation, a phenomenon that was visible on, say, the macrosocial level, becomes invisible under microsocial observation. A phenomenon that on the macrosocial scale is an explanatory independent variable might become a dependent variable in a microsocial analysis. Beneath the scales of observation method, there is an epistemology that both shows the diversity of scientific explanations and also emphasizes the importance of constraints in explaining human behavior on mesosocial and microsocial scales.

For example, consumption can be analyzed geopolitically—that is, on a broad *macrosocial* scale—largely conditioned today by the growth of a global middle class, particularly significant in China. The global upper middle class has, in the 10 years between 2000 and 2009, increased from 200 million to 560 million people with greater disposable income than ever before. As a consequence there is a growing demand for raw materials, energy, and protein-based food, leading to a sharp increase in commodity prices in international trading. In Western countries, these increases have weighed most heavily on the purchasing power of the poorest social classes, for whom food expenditure is proportionately higher in their budget. Because of their reduced purchasing power, they tend to consume less now than they did before 2000.

This example shows that consumption is not limited to an individual making decisions in the aisles of a supermarket; it can also be analyzed on a macroscopic scale. The macrosocial scale makes it possible to analyze the major cleavages that structure society, such as social strata and social classes, age and generation, sex and gender, and ethnic, political, or religious cultures. This macrosocial sectioning of reality can reveal causal effects of social class, such as a correlation between belonging to an impoverished social class and dietary behaviors that lead to obesity.

However, if the focus of the observation is changed, analyzing consumption on a *mesosocial* scale brings out quite different results. Here the researcher focuses on the internal functioning of nations, political systems, or administrations in interaction with industrial operators and services, consumer pressure groups, the media, and scientists. On this scale, it is possible to observe power relations and cooperation among different actors, negotiating the rules that may organize a market in favor of a particular group. The American debate between Republicans and Democrats on the issues of taxes, budget deficits, and social welfare can be analyzed on this scale: the solutions chosen will directly affect the ability of different social strata to consume. Similarly, in China, the establishment of a new social security system will undoubtedly have an influence on the development of Chinese domestic consumption. Without social protection and retirement pensions, the Chinese have generally put about 25 percent of their income in savings. Here causality is no longer a correlation; it is a factual situation that reveals to what extent the actors have to mobilize the economic, political, or administrative situation in their favor. The *mesosocial* scale is the most suitable one for analyzing the public policies that organize the field of consumption and the ability to consume.

The *microsocial* level of observation reveals interactions within a household. It helps identify the actors, their constraints, and their practices: everything that organizes their behavior and decisions. On this scale, for example, it is easy to observe the French family squabbles among mothers and children between

7:00 and 8:30 a.m. over getting up, washing, having breakfast, and going to school. On this scale, it can be seen that consumers have a certain leeway to decide whether to make a purchase or adopt an innovation. They are neither entirely free nor entirely driven by their desires. They maneuver to fit within the constraints of society.

Finally, observation at the *microindividual* scale allows researchers to determine the meaning that individuals give to their purchases and their consumption, identifying the trade-offs that an individual might be dealing with in choosing among an array of products. This is the scale of observation and interpretation most often used in marketing. It helps researchers understand the tacit motivations that may lead to a purchase. At this scale, causality may come from a correlation effect, shown in the context of experimental research in the psychology of purchase, but more often it stems from the meaning that individuals give to their more or less conscious actions and motivations, which organize their choice. At this scale, meaning is often an after-the-fact justification for decisions made within constraints allowing actors to resolve the cognitive dissonance that may arise from the gap between intent and constraints.

Household consumption can thus be profitably studied on a microsocial level of observation, and certain other methodological frameworks work well at this level. Here the life cycle method may be used, for example, to show how the meaning and the use of cosmetics vary at the different life stages of childhood, adolescence, youth, adulthood, middle age, and old age. This framework provides the information needed to show how certain consumer goods are markers of different stages of the life cycle or how others mark the transition between two stages of the life cycle. At each at step of the life cycle, consumers acquire the goods that go into constructing their identity, whether by means of conformity or transgression.

THE ITINERARY METHOD

The itinerary method (see Alami et al. 2009) is based on my work reconstructing agricultural itineraries for rice cultivation in the highlands of Madagascar and for cassava and vegetable production in the Congo basin between 1971 and 1979. It incorporates a type of strategic analysis for organizations developed in France by sociologist Michel Crozier, in his book *The Bureaucratic Phenomenon* (1963), which I applied to the analysis of families, both nuclear and extended.

It is an inductive method based on description by the actors in a situation, collected through interviews and observations on the site of the practice. Consumption in urban societies is analyzed by observing end consumers in their homes as well as in the places where they make their purchases. The anthropologist may conduct interviews in the kitchen to talk about culinary practices, in the bathroom to talk about body care, or in the living room to discuss the household's practices involving television, computer, video games or the phone, studying the discussions that may develop within the family and determining whether a particular commodity is acquired or not. The home, used itself as a stimulus for data collection, is analyzed as a place for using goods and services and also as a space for social interaction.

The itinerary starts with a "triggering event" and continues through acquisition, use, and disposal. The "trigger" may be a special event such as a birthday, an anniversary, or a regular occurrence or moment; Saturday morning, for example, is often the moment for shopping in France. In China, grandparents who care for their (only) grandchild often shop in the morning, whereas professional young urban couples do their shopping in the late afternoon. Or it may be a spontaneous or conditioned desire of one or more family members, such as a Chinese young woman's decision to buy makeup: the desire of a young adolescent coming of age or a requirement for a new job. Depending on the explicit or implied norms that organize each culture, different purchases may thus be socially permitted, prescribed, or prohibited.

The trigger, however, is not an absolute starting point. It is set in the context of interactions that actors may have in their lives or with their relations. Other family members may oppose a young woman's decision for makeup: parents consider their daughter too young or a stepmother worries that her daughter-in-law may actually be seeing another man. Purchasing decisions are thus the result of a series of microdecisions and microinteractions. In the end, either the outcome of the interaction is positive or the plan to make a purchase is thwarted. In the case of a new product or innovation, the result will be either that it is tried . . . or that it will fail to convince.

The second step of the itinerary follows the consumer to the place of acquisition. The term *acquisition* generally indicates monetary purchases, but it also includes receiving items as gifts, free samples, exchanges, and the like, without the use of a monetary equivalent. Theft is another mode of acquisition, representing 2 to 3 percent of the turnover of supermarkets in France; this illegal practice appears to have increased since the 2008 crisis and a diminution of purchasing power. The trajectory is identified, in particular the means by which an individual travels to acquire a good or service. This mobility may involve a car, a bicycle, travel by foot, public transportation, and also the internet; today the internet and e-commerce are important steps in the itinerary of consumption, used to buy new products but also to compare prices, to find secondhand goods, and to make payment. The focus of data collection in the itinerary method is on actors, practices, and material objects; meaning and values are determined afterwards. This makes it easier to see how a new system of objects can alter practices of acquisition. Changes in the supply chain, which organizes mobility, can lead to changes in consumer behavior, and logistical transformations—the notion of proximity changes with a car—also alter representations.

The third step is the selection among the array of products in a store aisle or on a computer screen. At this stage we try to reconstruct the criteria involved in consumer choice, in particular what constitutes and signals quality in a product. For example, when working on beauty and body care products in China, women look for reliable, effective merchandise. A foreign brand may signal these qualities, although counterfeiting introduces uncertainty as to whether the foreign brand is authentic or not. Examining the place of purchase, accompanying the interviewee to a department store or a supermarket, helps researchers identify the concrete criteria for a consumer's choices, such as signs of authenticity and security, which may be very closely linked to the history and culture of a country.

The fourth stage of the itinerary is the researcher's observation of how the purchases are dealt with back in the home. As for body care products in China, some items are stored in the bathroom, but other, more intimate ones may be placed in the bedroom; to a certain extent, the bathroom is not considered as private as the bedroom is in France or the United States. Talking with interviewees about objects in front of a kitchen cupboard or a bedroom closet is a rewarding technique of gathering information about the importance of the objects to them. Having them describe how objects were purchased or who gave them to them, or how complicated it is to throw things away to move, for example, is an effective way to create a link with the interviewees and to enable them to express their rationality, their emotions, and the problems in their daily lives that are not resolved. Furthermore, eliciting interviewees' comments on visible, palpable, specific objects and their uses and related practices significantly increases the reliability of what they relate. Rather than seeking frequencies, opinions, or values, the anthropologist has informants describe and tell "stories" about these objects, including practices, tensions, and emotional moments that are related to them. In addition, eliciting explanations of how the objects are stored in a closet or elsewhere is a very effective way to understand how each culture classifies pure versus impure, noble versus shameful, practicality versus aesthetics, ordinary versus luxurious, and so on.

The next stage of the itinerary may be preparing a product for use, such as assembling and preparing ingredients for cooking. Chinese cuisine is a good example of the relationship between culinary practices and systems of objects. Because Chinese food is eaten with chopsticks and knives are not commonly used at the table, components are all prepared with a cleaver and a chopping block and rapidly cooked in a wok on a gas stove. Dishes are served on plates and rice served in bowls, both easily manipulated with chopsticks, which are mastered in early childhood. Chopping block, knives, gas, woks, bowls, and chopsticks form a system of objects that does not include ovens, baking pans, and many appliances used in other cultures. The system of objects can also be used to examine the social interactions involved in food preparation and eating and to get a sense of the significance of these practices and the imagination that is associated with them.

Here action systems are also in play: the use of a product or service is embedded in a system formed of material, social, and symbolic elements. A corollary of this fact is that if you change one element of the system, it alters or upsets the entire system. The system can be viewed both as a constraint and also as a potential for innovation, for the adoption of a new product or service, which helps explain consumer behavior. Consumers are more likely to adopt a new product if it fits into their system of actions, objects, and symbols than if the innovation increases the mental load for potential adopters, if it causes too great a conflict with their group's social norms, or if it threatens the identity of male or female actors Other considerations, of course, also come into play: if the new item does not fit in the budget, if the home is too small, if the consumer is short on time, or if the product is too complicated to learn how to use, as is the case for some of the new technologies, the chances that it will be adopted are also greatly reduced.

The following stage of the itinerary is the actual use of the product, be it for food, do-it-yourself chores, body care, managing medicines, watching TV, or communicating on a computer or cell phone. This step is extremely informative in terms of buying behavior, and most crucial in determining whether the item will be purchased again. This stage is very much influenced by the effects of age and generation—the distinction between them is not always easy to make in a qualitative survey on a microsocial scale—which seems to be the case for Chinese women's use of cosmetics and body care. The youngest members of the urban middle class are the most avid users of cosmetics and body care products, "officially" beginning around age 18: makeup is forbidden in schools. Nevertheless, in terms of social norms, makeup is a practice allowed today. The traditional concept of "face" (*mianzi*; 面子) is at play—makeup and body care are used on the parts most exposed to the gaze of others, the face as well as the hands, neck, and feet—but makeup has been reinterpreted in a new set of social appearances. Makeup has become more sophisticated, and a more natural, "naked" look (*luo zhuang*; 裸妆) has come into style (read: become a norm). This practice is thus one of many analyzers of often-invisible changes within Chinese society, and its positive and negative norms have been reconstructed thanks to the interviews concerning product use that we conducted in bathrooms in China.

The final stage of the itinerary method is disposal. The article may be left to "cool off" in a closet, an attic, or a cellar; it may be given away or resold; it may be recycled; it may be thrown away. The question of recycling is extremely strategic today because of the need to conserve raw materials and to engage in a more economical consumption.

The itinerary method shows that a consumer decision can be analyzed and described as a social process over time (and space), not just as a single arbitration conducted in one moment in front of a store display. In operational terms, this means that the decision-making process may be hindered and stopped at any stage if it encounters too strong a material, social, or symbolic constraint. These constraints account for the limited power of persuasion and advertising. It is important also to understand the system of concrete objects that contribute to the use of a particular product. The difficulty of selling bath salts and cake mixes to the middle class in a China where bathtubs and ovens are imported luxuries and therefore limited to a small number of wealthy people becomes readily apparent thanks to the onsite observation afforded by this method.

NAVIGATING THE CONSTRAINTS

Professional anthropological training thus requires students to reexamine the rules of classical epistemology, which were often established in the framework of a "pure" science without situational constraints.[6] Inductive empirical epistemology enables students to learn how to distinguish the effects of scale; to take the ambiguity of phenomena into account; and to distinguish between practices and the meaning that stakeholders ascribe to their actions, in their positive and negative dimensions. To understand values, imagination, and culture, researchers must identify the material, social, and symbolic constraints that lie between meaning and practices. They then generalize on the basis of the *diversity* of practices and social mechanisms, not their frequency, as in quantitative approaches. Qualitative approaches are regularly alleged to be insufficiently scientific, accused of dealing with too small a sample. However, the scales-of-observation method can show that experimental and quantitative approaches are not the only models for science. It relativizes scientific criteria that were designed as absolutes for all scales and situations, contrasting in vitro experimental sciences that examine single causes and in vivo social sciences that confront situations with multiple causes. The method allows us to maintain rigor but also to show diversity and a limited legitimacy for each system of explanation.

Professional anthropology does not involve seeking the purity, often phantasmagorical, of an ideal science. Instead, it seeks to apply what is fundamental to anthropology: analyzing differences without associating value judgments that would deem one method, profession, or approach inherently superior to another. Of course this is easier said than done. Nevertheless, professional anthropologists do not try to enchant reality; their main function is to show clients that if they want to succeed in expanding their market or carrying out their development project, they must take into account the unresolved problems that actors face in their daily lives. Values and meaning, even though very important to individuals, only partially explain consumer behavior: individual intent is only part of the explanation of social interplay within a family. The final outcome exceeds individual calculations, which are conditioned by the situation of collective social interplay. The originality of the method is to focus on the external forces that influence individual intentions and motivations. Thus, unlike with marketing, consumer behavior is not observed as individual behavior but as collective behavior, with interactions between partners, between parents and children, and with in-laws, friends, and colleagues. Not only are the actor's decisions subject to these constraints, they also involve ambivalence and oppositions between the ordinary and enchantment, imagination and practices, constraints and values. Thus, if a business wants to succeed in placing an innovation, a new product, or a new service, it must take into account constraints, areas of uncertainty, power relations, and cooperation or alliances that determine the decisions of different members of the family. These are best analyzed as they impact a new product's production, distribution, use, and consumption, as well as how it is recirculated or disposed of.

Anthropologists must learn to deal with constraints, like any actors: academics, business executives, journalists, or activists. Academic anthropologists face the pressure to publish, the standards of tenure committees, and the relations between networks and intellectual movements, whereas professional anthropologists deal more with the constraints of the market. In addition, the anthropologist-entrepreneur also faces the stress of economic survival, payroll, and charges and taxes at the end of the month. When students enter the profession, they will have to manage a heavy workload, negotiating contracts, respecting budget constraints, conducting several studies simultaneously, doing several interviews a day, finding the time to keep up on reading, working between several disciplines, translating the results of the research, coping with the stress related to keeping a contract, doing accounts, and finalizing reports. Report-writing is indeed a skill to be learned. Professional anthropologists must communicate the results of their study, remaining as close to the truth as possible while respecting the constraints of the client. Thus, first-year students learn not only to write reports, articles, and summaries but also to produce PowerPoint presentations and films. The pioneers of anthropological observation, such as Gregory Bateson and Margaret Mead in Bali and Jean Rouch in Africa, used visual techniques to document and to enrich their work. Visual techniques have been greatly enriched since their time, and these methods enable researchers to capture intimate moments that would otherwise be invisible. Thus, in addition to conducting at least 20 90-minute interviews on practices, each first-year student learns how to make a 10-minute film.[7]

The work-study alternation of our program allows students to learn about the constraints specific to ROD, in particular regarding time management. The procedures and the quality of research expected in both basic and applied research are more or less the same, but the timelines are much shorter in professional anthropology. By carrying out studies in a limited time—several months or even several weeks—they learn to comply with deadlines so as to avoid forfeiting payment or losing a customer. Time for theorizing and reflection are reduced, and they must be able to shift viewpoints rapidly to maximize the analysis of the data they produce.

Anthropological results, like all information, represent a risk, and they must fit into the interplay of interests among all the stakeholders, including those of the professional anthropologist. The report must deal with the fact that results may conflict with the objectives of the company's marketing and communications department, whose concern is positive brand image. A study may show negative aspects of the phenomenon studied as well as positive ones, such as research on online gambling or lotteries that encounters the idea of play but also the risk of addiction. In any case, the research results are reinterpreted within the action system that commissioned the study, and stakeholders use the information to legitimize decisions, to counter another participant, to support an innovation or bury it, and so on. Anthropologists often do not see the actual results of their action because their reports are generally absorbed by the effects of network, sets of stakeholders, and relations of power and cooperation that exist in any public or private organization. A provisional confidentiality clause in a contract often minimizes the risk of resistance, allowing the researcher to present the results of a study relatively freely. The information in the report may not be available to everyone at the end of a study, but this is very often simply a short-term compromise: two to four years after the results are submitted, the client may allow studies to be published as articles or posted online, which ultimately is not much longer than the time it takes to have an article published in a scientific journal.

From the colonial era through today, anthropologists have been faced with uses of the knowledge that they produced that were intended or unintended, positive or negative. Beyond any ethical or political controversy, what makes the substance and strength of anthropology is a diversity of modes of reasoning, seeking both permanent structures and dynamic innovations. The particular skill of applying this very real, very inductive practice to the discovery of societies in all their diversity is the most important thing that we can transmit in teaching students and training anthropologists.

REFERENCES

Alami, Sophie, Dominique Desjeux, and Isabelle Garabuau-Moussaoui. 2009. *Les Méthodes Qualitatives.* Paris: Presses Universitaires de France.

Bulletin de l'Association Française des Anthropologues. Paris: Association Française des Anthropologues (AFA). No. 26/27, 1987; No. 35, 1989 ; No. 42, 1990 (renamed *Journal des Anthropologues*).

Badot, Olivier, and Bernard Cova. 1992 [2009]. *Néo-marketing*, 2nd edition. Paris: Éditions EMS.

Baré, Jean-François. 1995. *Les applications de l'anthropologie* [Applications of Anthropology]. Paris: Kartala.

Clochard, Fabrice, and Dominique Desjeux, eds. 2013. *Le consommateur malin face à la crise* (2 tomes) [*The Smart Consumer Dealing with the Crisis* (2 volumes)]. Paris: L'Harmattan.

Cochoy, Franck. 2002. *Une sociologie du packaging* [*A Sociology of Packaging*]. Paris: Presses Universitaires de France.

Crozier, Michel. 1963. *The Bureaucratic Phenomenon.* Chicago, IL: University of Chicago Press.

Desjeux, Dominique. 2004. *Les sciences sociales* [*The Social Sciences*]. Paris: Presses Universitaires de France.

______. 2006, *La consommation* [*Consumption*]. Paris: Presses Universitaires de France.

______. 2009. "2009 un supermarché à Guangzhou (Chine) entre tradition et modernité, du vrac au paquet." www.youtube.com/watch?v=ELoGPfohd3E.

______. 2011. "Anthropology of Process of Innovation." In *Innovation and Entrepreneurship from the Idea to Organization*, edited by Alain Bloch and Sophie Morin Delerm, 121–32. Portland, OR: Eska Publishing.

Dias Campos, Roberta. 2010. "La consommation de la beauté comme analyseur de la construction sociale du corps féminin: Une étude comparée France et Brésil." [Consumption of Beauty [products] as analyzer of the social construction of the female body: A comparative study, France and Brazil]. Thesis, Department of Consumer Anthropology, UFRJ/University Paris Descartes, Rio de Janeiro and Paris.

Diaso, Nicoletta. 1999. *La Science Impure: Anthropologie et Médecine en France, Grande-Bretagne, Italie, Pays-Bas* [*Impure Science: Anthropology and Medicine in France, Great Britain, Italy, the Netherlands*]. Paris: Presses Universitaires de France.

Douglas, Mary. 1966. *Purity and Danger: An Analysis of Concepts of Pollution and Taboo.* London: Routledge and Kegan Paul.

Mariampolski, Hy. 2006. *Ethnography for Marketers: A Guide to Consumer Immersion.* Thousand Oaks, CA: Sage.

Sunderland, Patricia, and Rita Denny. 2007. *Doing Anthropology in Consumer Research.* Walnut Creek, CA: Left Coast Press.

Yang, Xiao Min. 2006. *La fonction sociale des restaurants en Chine.* Paris: L'Harmattan.

NOTES

1 The tension between academic anthropology and professional anthropology in France is longstanding and, in a sense, normal. For some, it is linked to the fear of pollution, to echo the work of British anthropologist Mary Douglas (1966), that the contact with colonial administration, customers, entrepreneurs, politics, or media power would seem to imply; for others, it may involve a fear of purity that is considered deadly. Notions of purity are embedded in the issue of whether anthropology should work only on questions posed by the academic environment or if it can take up questions that come from external demands. This is why the term *professional anthropology* is used here in the sense of field studies carried out and financed at the request of customers, whether the anthropologist is an entrepreneur, a research manager, or an academic.

2 For example, a quantitative field study on how smart consumers were dealing with the crisis of 2008 (Clochard and Desjeux 2013).

3 My own professional career began as a sociologist of organizations in Michel Crozier's laboratory between 1969 and 1971, before leaving for Africa, where I trained agricultural engineers in Madagascar and then the Congo. Thereafter, I taught social sciences for eight years at the School of Agriculture in Angers. This was followed, in 1988, by university teaching at the Sorbonne (Université Paris Descartes Sorbonne Paris Cité), as full Professor in the Magistère of Social Sciences Applied to Intercultural Relations. In 1990 I created a small anthropology business, Argonautes, with Sophie Taponier. In 2007, along with Sophie Alami, I started the professional doctoral program described in this chapter.

4 See Desjeux (2011); for the United States, see Sunderland and Denny (2007) and Mariampolski (2006).

5 These included Patricia Sunderland, Rita Denny, Ken Erickson, and Hy Mariampolski in the United States; Zheng Lihua and Yang Xiaomin in China; and Roberta Dias Campos in Brazil.

6 In 1999, Presses Universitaires de France published Nicoletta Diasio's *La Science Impure* (*Impure Science*) on the relationship between anthropology and medicine in France, Italy, Great Britain, and the Netherlands in the past 150 years. The book points out that at its inception, European anthropology had ties with colonization and with physical and medical anthropology. Anthropology was thus born in a context of ambiguity, which explains the conflicts that characterize it today, especially the controversy concerning the question of the purity of scientific practices in anthropology. It is a moral, epistemological, and ontological question central to the conflict between professional and academic anthropology.

7 At present, new social anthropology companies in France such as Méthos, Monde Moderne, ETE-ICOS, and Cinqsixproduction use ethnographic films as a basis for their work.

5

Living in Business Schools, Writing Consumer Culture

ERIC J. ARNOULD & CRAIG J. THOMPSON

In this historical reflection, in which we combine realist and confessional modes of representation (van Maanen 2011), we argue that writing consumer culture in the business school context is best conceived as historically situated discursive practice (Foucault 1970, 1972) emergent from prevailing conditions of knowledge creation. We consider the question of how writing consumer culture while living the B-school context has evolved with attendant points of disjuncture, slippage, and friction in the establishment of consumer culture theoretics (CCT; Arnould and Thompson 2005, 2007), an emergent discipline now organized through an organization the Consumer Culture Theory Consortium and an annual conference in its ninth year in 2014 (CCT Consortium 2013).

From this standpoint, certain approaches, problematics, or theoretical positions emerge from historically specific institutional arrangements and opportunities. As these institutional arrangements change, new salient theoretical questions, new status games, standards of legitimacy, and competitions for resources arise in the academic "field" (Bourdieu 1990), providing an impetus to reconfigure discursive practices. In this case, the field is the global network of academic marketing departments and related journals in which writing culture became possible at a historical moment (Sherry 1991), but which also evolves in response to institutional contingencies in the B-school that challenge the legitimacy of this practice.

Against this backdrop, three discernible epistemic moments mark the CCT experience of writing culture in the B-school, each characterized by distinctive discursive practices: (1) humanistic/romantic (roughly speaking 1979 to early 1990s); (2) social constructivist (approximately early 1990s to 2000); and (3) global-network (2000 to the present; see Latour 2005). Each discursive system

---

Handbook of Anthropology in Business, edited by Rita Denny and Patricia Sunderland, 116–134.

encodes a dominant view of consumers and their relationships to consumer culture and privileges certain kinds of research questions and issues (i.e., expressed through ontological axioms).[1] These discursive systems also manifest underlying strategies for attaining legitimacy and credibility within the governing institutional field and prevailing epistemic moment (expressed through epistemological and axiological maxims).

Our general point is that evolving discursive systems evoke an array of rhetorical gestures that signal fluency in operative rules, motifs, and core assumptions tacitly expressing background knowledge that can "go without saying" (Barthes 1972 [1957]). When shifting institutional/political contingencies precipitate a new discursive system, previously established rhetorical conventions are not necessarily displaced. Instead, they can linger on as routines that can anachronistically impede emerging systems of analysis and obstruct particular research projects. Our reflection does not address the full spectrum of specific paradigmatic orientations that influence CCT scholars writing culture in the B-school. To transform a limitation into a benefit, we use our deconstructive analysis of cultural consumption studies and multisited research experiences, drawing from the first author's confessional tales from the field.

THE HUMANISTIC/ROMANTIC MOVE (1979–1990)

A first discursive system took shape in an epistemic moment when the disciplinary identity of cultural approaches to consumption were primarily defined through oppositional contrasts to research steeped in positivistic, realist, and managerial normative expectations engendered during the Cold War (Belk 1987; Holbrook and Hirschman 1982; Sherry 1990). This discursive system drew from the vernacular of humanistic social psychology (Rogers 1961), but its most spectacular gesture, the Consumer Behavior Odyssey (Belk 1991), invoked both anthropological and sociological classics and the expeditionary trope of early twentieth century ethnographic practice thanks to the participation of anthropologist John F. Sherry and sociologist Melanie Wallendorf. It brokered the cultural legacy of romanticism and its veneration of the particular over the abstract; the artistic over the technical; the emotional and expressive over the rational and utilitarian; and the organic over the mechanical (Brown et al. 1998; Campbell 1987).

Accordingly, humanistic/romantic CCT discourses called into question the prevailing disciplinary view of consumers as rational, information-driven, utility-maximizing decision-makers. Holbrook and Hirschman's treatises on experiential (1982) and hedonic consumption (Holbrook and Hirschman 1982)—and the Consumer Behavior Odyssey (Belk 1991; Belk et al. 1988, 1989)—played pivotal roles in establishing these romantic motifs in consumer research and importantly become canonical epistemological templates for subsequent research in this discursive tradition. Eschewing positivistic standards of objectivity, detached observation, and measurement, the humanist/romantic move invited consumer researchers to become empathetically, emotionally, and experientially attuned to the lives of consumers to reveal the deep meaning of consumption. Participant observation in naturalistic settings and other ethnomethodological techniques were heralded as means to capture the subjective/emotive/aesthetic/experiential aspect of consumption that were systematically elided by lab-based experimental studies of consumer choice processes. Evident here is a depth ontology; truths lie within and below the surface of things.

Researchers rebelled against the technocratic/instrumental axiology-defining consumers as targets of profit-seeking managerial action (Belk 1987; Holbrook 1987) and substituted the goal of studying consumption for its intrinsic merit in comprehending everyday life in consumer culture (Thompson et al. 1989). On a different axiological level, however, little signs of revolt against the norms of the B-school as an institution or academic publishing as a metric are evident in this period. Indeed, proponents of the cultural turn ardently pursued publications in top-tier marketing journals as a source of institutional credibility. And indeed, B-school recruitment into marketing departments of a number of anthropologists—Janeen Costa, Annamma Joy, and John Sherry, for example—thanks in part to a favorable supply-demand situation in the early 1980s, seemed to support this model of institutional legitimation.

Back on the epistemological front, humanistic/romantic discourses exhibited a concession to the positivistic view of legitimate science during this epistemic moment (see Belk 1990). Proponents tactically embraced Lincoln and Guba's (1985) version of ethnographic research—naturalistic inquiry—and its epistemological analogs to reliability (dependability), validity (trustworthiness), generalizability (transferability), and intersubjective certifiability (member checks and triangulation; Wallendorf and Belk 1989). In this rhetorical move, legitimacy hinges on the claim that human experience is inherently subjective. Thus, discovery-oriented, inductive methodologies that offer moments of shared experiential/emotional understanding (i.e., *verstehen*)—via interpersonal empathy, contextual immersion, introspective reflection, and so on—are empirically truer to these realities (in the sense of imposing fewer distorting biases) than "sciencey" quantitative, hypothetico-deductive methods (Thompson et al. 1989).

In retrospect, participants drastically under appreciated the roots of the critical rejection of these early discursive moves in mainstream marketing and consumer research (Calder and Tybout 1987; Cohen 1989; Hunt 1990, 1993). As Tadajewski (2006) cogently argues, modern marketing is deeply implicated in the modernist project generally and especially the postwar American, global hegemon; while epithets typical of the Cold War years were not generally hurled at the practitioners of the humanist/romantic brand of consumer research, stand-ins such as "relativist" were indeed flung about.

The first author's initial forays into this world took advantage of the optimistic opening afforded by the epistemological, ontological, and axiological questioning that cut across the fields of marketing and consumer research, while participating in the predominant discursive gestures contributors to the cultural turn in consumer research initiated. He entered the arena through field work on marketing systems in Niger: a serendipitous research relationship with a marketing professor, James McCullough, who invited him to meet people active in the humanist/romantic cultural turn, led him to Melanie Wallendorf, then a new assistant professor. Unlike some European scholars for whom the cultural turn was precipitated later by postmodernism (Cova and Maclaren 2012), for Arnould as an anthropologist, culture was the frame through which he, like John F. Sherry and fellow Arizona alumnus Richard Wilk, approached consumer behavior.

Arnould's first publication in the field appears as an advocacy piece from the anthropological disciplinary leverage point offered in support of colleagues working from within the marketing discipline, calling into question managerial axiology, positivist epistemology, and the choice-making ontology of consumption referred to here (Arnould 1983). The paper commented on three foundational pieces of research that have since blossomed in the interpretive traditions of consumption studies, one focusing on consumption ritual, the second on consumer experience and identity, and the third on consumer acculturation and materiality, a kind of proto-archaeology of consumption.

Arnould and Wilk (1984) was a more full-throated intervention to foreground the then-limited ethnological understanding of consumption. This study basically offered an interpretation of the selectivity of the diffusion of elements of western consumer culture into nonwestern contexts inspired by Mary Douglas. It was in fact the kind of classic "Black Swan" contribution with which economic anthropologists have confronted economics since the work of Boas, Malinowski, and Mauss, and continuing through the contemporary contributions of M.A.U.S.S. (Anti-Utilitarian Movement in the Social Sciences) and, in the development context, FSR (Farming Systems Research).

For Arnould, the apotheosis of this first moment in writing culture in the B-school came with two articles in *Journal of Consumer Research* (*JCR*). In Wallendorf and Arnould (1988), the authors sought to turn the tables on positivist inquiry by using a multimethod, cross-cultural approach including Arnould's data from Niger—the first *JCR* article to draw on African materials—to critique ethnocentric accounts of materialism while showing how ethnographic insight could enrich conventional methods. In Arnould (1989), he used all of the tropes of realist ethnography (van Maanen 2011) as rhetorical warrant for claims made about Nigerien consumers. The work was unabashedly ethnographic, and it used the exotic context in a double move; first, it bolstered the enterprise of culturally oriented consumer research by extending its applicability to the African context, and thereby sought to establish the author's legitimacy in writing about it. At the same time, it insisted upon Maussian ethnology: the comparative method of using ethnographic cases to develop, amend, and extend social theory. To do so it chose a foil: conventional diffusion of innovations theory. The paper foresaw CCT's later concern with globalization, but via world systems theory rather than the Appadurian tropes that came after, to argue that multiple consumption globalities operated in Niger.

THE SOCIAL CONSTRUCTIVIST MOVE (1990–2001)

As the humanistic/romantic discursive system gained visibility and legitimacy in consumer research, some researchers began to criticize its concessions to positivistic epistemological orthodoxy, and its ontological reproduction of subjectivist versus objectivist dualisms (Firat and Venkatesh 1993; Hirschman 1993; Murray and Ozanne 1991; Thompson 2002). In a related turn, consumer culture researchers, less constrained by demands for epistemological justifications, began to draw more inspiration from the narrative turn (Clifford and Marcus 1986), such as Geertzian-styled ethnographies (Arnould and Price 1993; Celsi et al. 1993; Peñaloza 1994; Schouten and McAlexander 1995), hermeneutics (Arnold and Fischer 1994; Thompson et al. 1994), and reader response theory (Mick and Buhl 1992; Scott 1994), all of which placed interpretation, reflexivity, and narrativity at the center of the research enterprise. These parallel developments coalesced into a new discursive system: social constructivist CCT, which portrayed consumers as culturally constituted actors whose experiences and identity projects were expressions not of essentialized selves, but rather webs of sociocultural meanings (Holt and Thompson 2004; Stern et al. 1998).

Through these social constructive discursive practices, CCT researchers began to formulate consumers as creative, embodied agents who produced their identity by drawing from cultural resources, including commercially produced ones. Rather than expressing their romantic inner essence through consumption, this discursive system portrayed consumers as *bricoleurs*. Formulating consumers as creative producers of identity is evident in Haytko and Baker (2004), as presaged in Schouten's (1991) paper on symbolic self-completion, and in Gainer and Fischer's (1991) study of home shopping and ultimately in the idea of multiple consuming selves (Bahl and Milne 2010; Goulding et al. 2002).

From an epistemological standpoint, the reflexive turn pushed back against the positivistic prescriptions of the humanistic/romantic system (Murray et al.

1994:563) and the promotion of more explicitly socially constructed accounts of knowledge production (see also Hudson and Ozanne 1988). Stephen Brown, in a series of playfully astute articles and books (Brown 1996; Brown et al. 1998; Brown and Turley 1997), significantly expanded the discursive limits of CCT while infusing the emerging social constructive tradition with a highly refined deconstructionist sensibility. Along with Stephen Brown, Morris Holbrook, Douglas Brownlie, and Maurice Patterson, among others, advocated and demonstrated the use of alternative research narrative forms that disrupted the omniscient, objectivist, scientistic conventions that dominated academic consumer research and that continued to frame consumer culture studies (e.g., Schau et al. 2001). Though less flamboyant in narrative style, other practitioners of CCT's social constructivist discourses brought to the disciplinary foreground and further developed a theoretical vernacular for addressing the socio-historic forces which shape and discipline consumer behavior (Hirschman 1993; Holt 1997; Thompson and Hirschman 1995).

Another ontological aspect of the social constructivist turn was a more extensive engagement with sociology of knowledge issues that called attention to the power structures that shape research narratives and their portrayal of the research subject. Gender bias became prominent among these topics (Bristor and Fisher 1993; Hirschman 1993). Building on early work (Wallendorf and Reilly 1983), social constructivist CCT also began to develop theoretical accounts that highlighted cultural (and subcultural) differences and particularities (Applbaum and Jordt 1996; Kates 2002; McCarty 1989; Oswald 1999; Peñaloza 1994), initiating a research stream on ethnicity (Özçağlar-Toulouse and Béji-Bécheur 2012) that has become more vivid as researchers appreciate the liquidity of the world (Bardhi et al. 2012).

Finally, as suggested here, the social constructivist turn marked a more critical axiological engagement with, rather than a rebellious rejection of, marketing. In other words, researchers recognized that consumer projects were not merely contingently related to commercial contexts and resources, but deeply imbricated in them. Peñaloza and Gilly's (1999) work on retailers' socializing role was pivotal, as was John Schouten, Jum McAlexander, and Susan Fournier's ethnographic consulting for Harley-Davidson, Jeep, and other brands.

Arnould's work found a formative and reactive place in this moment in consumer culture studies. Still seeking legitimacy for ethnography, he found it useful to leverage ethnographic work in discursive fields more congenial to mainstream axiologies. A project on adoption of the market orientation in public education (Kennedy et al. 2003) is an example. Similar were a string of studies focused on the emergent co-constructive outcomes of experiential service encounters in extreme environments and the dramaturgical framing of such encounters. This multimethod research showed how certain socio-historical resources such as ideas about wilderness or friendship could be drawn upon to produce valued identity outcomes (Arnould and Price 1993; Arnould et al. 1998; Price and Arnould 1999). What may have made these studies palatable was embedding them in another discourse that was building legitimacy in the marketing canon at the same time: services research. Perhaps the most constructivist account was that which argued that consumer authenticity could be decomposed into performative modalities: one a self-authoring project, which was called an authenticating act; and the other a socially integrating gesture, known as an authoritative performance (Arnould and Price 2000). Some of this work found a favorable resonance within more mainstream quarters; some took directions that strayed too far from the realist ontology that continues in US B-school marketing departments. A coauthored paper confronted issues of epistemology and ontology, drew upon critical narrative and feminist discourses, and argued for nonrepresentational and nonconvergent modes of interpretation (Thompson et al. 1998).

From the first author's confessional perspective, an institutional high-water mark of this moment was the heretical consumer research workshop organized in 1996 by Professors Alladi Venkatesh and Fuat Firat at the now-shuttered Arizona State University–East campus. It marked a first high-water mark in terms of the number of culturally and critically oriented scholars actively working in better US B-schools, and acceding to leadership positions in certain professional organizations. Also, from the first author's perspective it marked a high point in his belief in the possibility of a sea change in B-school culture. Since then, a rhizomatic rather than revolutionary process has ensued. While Arizona, Wisconsin, and York remain institutionally committed to the cultural turn, colleagues have also disbursed to non–B-schools such as the Medill School of Journalism at Northwestern University, to non–PhD-granting institutions such as Notre Dame, and to a host of other business schools. Moreover, research and teaching inspired by the cultural turn now flourishes in Scandinavia, Turkey, the United Kingdom, France, and Italy; tender offshoots have even appeared in Germany and the Netherlands. A push is on to extend the movement to South America. Institutionally, CCT has diffused, but like market capitalism generally, B-school culture has assimilated much that was once radical.

THE GLOBAL-NETWORK MOVE (2001–PRESENT)

Since the turn of the millennium, a third discursive system among adherents to the cultural turn has taken shape. Global-network discourses amplify certain implications that had been latent to the social constructivist system. In the global-network system, consumers and global consumer culture are cast in a vernacular of flows, scapes, nodes in networks, practices, interconnectivity and interactivity, decentered or diffused agency, coproduction, structures of common difference, hybridity, syncreticism, and creolization (Appadurai 1990; Hannerz 1996; Wilk 1995). While this theoretical vernacular previously gained currency in sociological and anthropological studies of globalization, the ubiquity of the internet and other digital technologies in mainstream managerial thought, as in everyday life, create potent incentives to more widely adopt and apply these network tropes in culturally oriented B-school writing.

Institutionally, the embrace of global-network discourses also enhances the disciplinary status of CCT as a haven of innovation and cutting-edge ideas. Many researchers have recognized that the digital world creates new spaces of self-creation and community (Kozinets 1997, 1998, 1999; Schau and Gilly 2003; Schau et al. 2009). The ontological opening has spurred epistemological innovation, with the high-profile addition of netnography to tools researchers use (Kozinets 2002a), no doubt with massively multiplayer online role-playing games (MMORPGs) and crowd-sourcing following on. However, cultural approaches have had to contend vigorously with scholars associated with top B-schools for whom the internet primarily comprises a large dataset, so-called Big Data, from which to compute causal models related to standard business outcomes (Dholakia and Vianello 2011; Hoffman and Fodor 2010).

Global-network discursive practices formulate consumers as agents embedded in market systems, and market systems as emerging through intersections of global and local cultural forms, often through digital media. The ontology has also broadened to de-privilege persons relative to things, increasingly recognizing the agentic qualities of the latter (Zwick and Dholakia 2006). Furthermore, this discursive system has opened toward experimentation with alternative modes of representation (film, poetry, dance) and toward explorations of post-natural and post-human ontologies, the latter of which radically decenters the concept of consumer agency that predominated in both humanistic/romantic and social constructivist discourse (Campbell 2013; Giesler and Venkatesh 2005). Of course, actor-network theory and post-humanism pose a significant, potential threat to cultural epistemologies and ontologies; the former as it treats culture as epiphenomenal, the latter as it decenters humans from the center of social inquiry.

Institutionally, the attenuation of some epistemological controversies around the epistemological and ontological claims of the first and second waves reflects a certain degree of institutional legitimacy and competition for other disciplinary resources, such as impact factor ratings of articles and demonstrations of relevance in B-school environments. An annual CCT conference was initiated in 2006, and the Consumer Culture Theory Consortium was formalized in 2011. There has also been a florescence of interest in the cultural turn in business, as seen in the success of the Ethnographic Praxis in Industry Conference and the related vogue for design thinking. Among B-schools globally, a series of international doctoral seminars proliferate rhizomatically at Bilkent University, Ankara, Turkey; Southern Denmark University; and more recently, Royal Holloway, United Kingdom, and Université Lille 2, France. Benchmarking papers appear in European journals (Özçağlar-Toulouse and Cova 2010). But this institutional legitimacy sparks a critical backlash from the left that deplores a new "orthodoxy" in consumer culture theoretics (Bradshaw and Dholakia 2012).

Global-network CCT presents a different set of axiological aims from its predecessors by directly engaging research questions and issues conventionally addressed in the marketing management literature, such as branding (Beverland 2009; Holt 2004; Thompson et al. 2006), global marketing (Cayla and Eckhardt 2008; Cayla and Elson 2012; Giesler 2012; Peñaloza et al. 2011), and word-of-mouth (Kozinets et al. 2010). Simultaneously, global-network discourses provide a warrant to pursue other forms of relevance related to the enhancement of consumer welfare and critical analyses of the societal conditions that produce asymmetrical distributions of cultural resources (Crockett and Wallendorf 2004; Elliott and Cova 2008; Adkins and Ozanne 2005; Lee et al. 1999; Ozanne and Saatcioglu 2008). This includes critical efforts aiming to destabilize hegemonic, and often neoliberal, northern discourses with perspectives drawn from the global south (Bonsu and Polsa 2011; DeBerry-Spence 2010; Scott et al. 2012). Naturally, the turn towards "relevance" also exposes cultural work to additional critique from the left (Cova et al. 2011).

In terms of ontology, global-network discursive practices construe consumers, consumption, and consumer culture as polyvocal and polysemic phenomena that are diffused across heterodoxic and glocalized spaces. Global-network discourses represent consumers as actors whose actions emerge in contingent relation to collective influences and connections to social networks, whether in the form of family (Epp and Price 2008), brand community (Muniz and O'Guinn 2001), global-local interpellations (Kjeldgaard and Askegaard 2006), or temporary tribe-like formations (Canniford and Shankar 2013; Shankar et al. 2007). These portrayals of consumption are exemplified by multilayered ethnographies of themed retailers on the one hand (Kozinets et al. 2004; Diamond et al. 2009) and ephemeral culture-generating manifestations (Goulding and Saren 2009; Kozinets 2002b) on the other.

Researchers using global-network perspectives have begun to address how consumption and marketing practices unfold across post-national and postcolonial networks (Kimura and Belk 2005; Strizhakova et al. 2008; Varman and Belk 2009; Viswanathan et al. 2005). Research in Turkish contexts has raised the most powerful systematic critique so far of Euro-American perspectives on consumption insisting on the sociocultural and dialogic particularities of Turkish consumption (Karababa and Ger 2011; Sandikci and Ger 2010; Üstüner and Holt 2007), but there are hopeful signs from Africa as well (Bonsu 2009; DeBerry-Spence 2010).

The first author has sought to navigate all of these turns, but would argue that institutionally, the turn has moved in unanticipated directions because of institutional forces in play that threaten the cultural turn. Thus, he has participated in the effort to expand the frontiers of the cultural turn into managerial marketing spaces, especially in services and retailing. In services, he and others have tried to forge an intellectual alliance with service dominant logic research (Arnould 2008; Arnould et al. 2006; Peñaloza and Venkatesh 2006). However, for institutional reasons having to do with credentialing, the latter current has evolved in more resolutely managerial (services science) and foundationalist directions.

At this point, it appears that social constructivist social science has gone in related directions, that of practice theory and that of actor-network theory (Latour 2005). While the latter has made a limited appearance in the work of consumer researchers inspired by the cultural turn (Epp and Price 2010), the former is experiencing a vogue. Inspired by Warde (2005), we and others apply practice theoretical arguments to the production and consumption of value within the consumption collectivities that have moved to the center of much cultural work (Arsel and Bean 2013; Askegaard and Eckhardt 2011; Schau et al. 2009; Woermann 2012).

WHITHER THE CULTURAL TURN IN CONSUMER RESEARCH

These final reflections emerge from efforts to navigate the discursive space of the cultural turn in consumption studies. From the first author's confessional perspective, several institutional conditions pose significant challenges to ongoing fruition of the cultural turn in US B-schools. First, marketing's enduring infatuation with the modernist project of discovering universalizing and foundationalist explanations—now manifested through the reductionistic rhetorics of neuro-marketing (see Schneider and Woolgar 2012) and evolutionary psychology, as well as the quantification of Big Data analytics—continues to cast cultural modes of analysis as propaedeutic knowledge. Second is the absence of corporate funding for chairs and programs in CCT-oriented research despite its ubiquity in the corporate world. Third are the knowledge/power dynamics in the parent disciplines of anthropology and sociology, for which the cultural turn in consumer research in the B-school goes largely unremarked (Graeber [2011] is telling; see also Moeran, this volume).

On the other hand, if we look at CCT as a field of rhizomatic resistance to status quo knowledge/power structures (Deleuze and Guattari 1987), we see a growing host of colleagues invested in the cultural turn throughout the world, identify fellow travelers in many corners of the global academy, and register a significant presence in the blogosphere and in popular business publishing. Moreover, we clearly have in hand a set of epistemological alternatives to foundationalist science: phenomenological inquiry, constructivist ethnography, feminist and postcolonial standpoint interpretivism, practice, and actor-network approaches. And we have elaborated alternatives to much of the ontological apparatus of modernist consumer research as shown in Table 5.1. The knowledge game is changing so rapidly we may optimistically presume a future based on the realist tale we've also told here. Thus, CCT is even now becoming an institutionalized track at the annual American Marketing Association conferences.

Whereas the primary challenge to writing culture in North American B-schools has been marginalization, a looming threat is appropriation without attribution of consumer culture constructs by the "mainstream." Path-breaking cultural work on identity, brand community, status consumption, consumer co-creation, and the hedonic, emotive, and social properties of consumption experience, once excoriated for exoticism and irrelevance, is now appropriated in this way (e.g., Berger and Ward 2010; Chernev et al. 2011; Dholakia and Vianello 2011; Han et al. 2010).

Fortunately, the critical perspective among practitioners of the cultural turn promises maneuvers to flank mainstream recuperation. Moving beyond a white Euro-American vision represents a major opening for research reflected in efforts to grasp the dynamics of nonwhite (Ainscough and Motley 2000; Crockett and Wallendorf 2004), and non-Western consumer behavior (Creighton 1991; Dong and Tian 2009; Karababa and Ger 2011; Sandikci and Ger 2010; Üstüner and Holt 2007). In other terms, more work both on the shape of global flows of resources (Appadurai 1990), an approach that combines interests in marketplace cultures, ideology, and on the socio-historic patterning of consumption (Wilk 1995), evades appropriation. This postcolonial shift (Thompson et al. 2013) offers opportunities to open up conventional consumer identity research beyond the *bricoleur* self. Jafari and Goulding's (2008) "torn self" and Üstüner and Holt's (2007) "shattered identity project" concepts, and Luedicke's (2011) work on contested acculturation, begin this critique.

The postmodern legacy (Cova and Maclaren 2012) presages a dedicated effort to develop more critical approaches to consumer culture that question the ontological status of consumers, consumer goods, sites, and borders (Bardhi et al. 2012; Campbell 2013; Zwick and Dholakia 2006). In this vein, global-network discursive practices produce a critical reflection on consumption. This provides an opening to engage in two critical inquiries. First, we can question the scolding rhetoric of modernist critiques of "materialism" and "overconsumption" to consider how to extend the benefits of market culture to base of the pyramid consumers (Geiger-Oneto and Arnould 2011; Kjellberg 2008; Miller 2012;

Table 5.1. Contrasting elements of marketing and consumer culture theoretic ontologies.

	Concepts from Marketing (Economics and Cognitive Psychology)	CCT-derived Concepts (Anthropology, Sociology, and Design)
1	Subjects, consumers	Actors, *bricoleurs*, partners, prosumers, avatars, makers
2	Needs, wants, motivations	Intentions, projects, desires
3	Knowledge, memory	Competences, commitments
4	Involvement	Teleo-affective engagement
5	Personality	Identity
6	Segments	Networks, tribes, communities
7	Inside the consumer's head	Consumption fields, lifeworlds
8	Purchase decisions	Acquisition, consumption, and disposition strategies and tactics
9	Utility, benefits	Value and meaning creation
10	Ownership	Access, participation, experience, guardianship
11	Goods	Objects, images, narratives
12	Possessions	Experiences, appropriations

Visnathawan et al. 2005) while overcoming market imperialism (Dolan 2005, 2008; Varman and Belk 2009) and moving to more sustainable consumer culture (Cherrier et al. 2012; Markkula and Moisander 2012; Peattie and Collins 2009). Furthermore, combining practice theory with a global-network perspective can shed light on the ecological consequences of mundane consumption practices. Consider studies that situate the consumption of air, water, and energy within frameworks of global nodes, scapes, flows, and practices, and as sites for political controversy (Hargreaves 2011; Press and Arnould 2009; Strengers 2011; Wilhite and Nakagami 1996; Wilk 2006; Wilk and Wilhite 1995).

To conclude, we have adopted realist narrative conventions to identify three distinctive modes of discursive practices that have shaped the intellectual trajectory of the cultural turn manifest in CCT in consumption studies in B-school marketing departments: the humanistic/romantic, the social constructivist, and the global-network. And we leavened this with a confessional tale of the first author's mixed experience of this cultural turn. We hope to inspire scholars to consider where we have come and reflect on how to contest power/knowledge moves that incent the repetition of well-rehearsed topics and discursive strategies, and equally that produce mainstream appropriation. Now more than ever, we also invite authors and reviewers to declare, coordinate, and respect the distinct and not necessarily convergent ontological, epistemological, or axiological choices made by contributors to the cultural turn in consumption studies, recognizing the healthy heterodoxy and heteroglossia that produces innovation and resists recuperation.

REFERENCES

Adkins, Natalie Ross, and Julie L. Ozanne. 2005. "The Low Literate Consumer." *Journal of Consumer Research.* 32(June):93–105.

Ainscough, Thomas L., and Carol M. Motley 2000. "Will You Help Me Please? The Effects of Race, Gender and Manner of Dress on Retail Service." *Marketing Letters* 11(May):129–36.

Appadurai, Arjun. 1990. "Disjuncture and Difference in the Global Cultural Economy." *Theory, Culture and Society* 7:295–310.

Applbaum, Kalman, and Ingrid Jordt. 1996. "Notes toward an Application of McCracken's 'Cultural Categories' for Cross-Cultural Consumer Research." *Journal of Consumer Research* 23(December):204–18.

Arnold, Stephen J., and Eileen Fischer. 1994. "Hermeneutics and Consumer Research." *Journal of Consumer Research.* 21(June):55–70.

Arnould, Eric J. 1983. "Glimmers and Fancies: Culture and Consumer Behavior." In *Advances in Consumer Research* 10:702–4.

_____. 1989. "Toward a Broadened Theory of Preference Formation and the Diffusion of Innovations: Cases from Zinder Province, Niger Republic." *Journal of Consumer Research* 16(September):239–67.

_____. 2008. "Service-dominant Logic and Resource Theory." Special Issue on Service Dominant Logic. *Journal of the Academy of Marketing Science* 36(1):21–4.

Arnould, Eric J., and Linda L. Price. 1993. "'River magic': Hedonic Consumption and the Extended Service Encounter." *Journal of Consumer Research* 20(June):24–45.

_____. 2000. "Authenticating Acts and Authoritative Performances: Questing for Self and Community." In *The Why of Consumption: Contemporary Perspectives on Consumers' Motives, Goals, and Desires,* edited by S. Ratneshwar, D. G. Mick, and C. Huffman, 140–63. New York and London: Routledge.

Arnould, Eric J., Linda L. Price, and Avinash Malshe. 2006. "Toward a Cultural Resource-based Theory of the Customer." In *The New Dominant Logic in Marketing,* edited by R. F. Lusch and S. L. Vargo, 91–104. Armonk. NY: M. E. Sharpe.

Arnould, Eric J., Linda L Price, and Patrick Tierney. 1998. "Communicative Staging of the Wilderness Servicescape." *Service Industries Journal* 18(July):90–115.

Arnould, Eric J., and Craig J. Thompson. 2005. "Consumer Culture Theory (CCT): Twenty Years of Research." *Journal of Consumer Research* 31(March):868–83.

_____. 2007. "Consumer Culture Theory (and We Really Mean Theoretics): Dilemmas and Opportunities Posed by an Academic Branding Strategy." In *Consumer Culture Theory: Research in Consumer Behavior,* Vol. 11, edited by R. W. Belk and J. F. Sherry, Jr., 3–22. Oxford, UK: Elsevier.

Arnould, Eric J., and Richard R. Wilk. 1984. "Why Do the Natives Wear Adidas?" In *Advances in Consumer Research,* 11:748–53.

Arsel, Zeynep, and Jonathan Bean. 2013. "Taste Regimes and Market-mediated Practice." *Journal of Consumer Research* 39(5):899–917.

Askegaard, Søren, and Giana M. Eckhardt. 2011. "Glocal Yoga: Re-appropriation in the Indian Consumptionscape." *Marketing Theory* 12(1):45–60.

Bahl, Shalini, and George Milne. 2010. "Talking to Ourselves: A Dialogical Exploration of Consumption Experiences." *Journal of Consumer Research* 37(June):176–95.

Bardhi, Fleura, Giana Eckhardt, and Eric Arnould. 2012. "Liquid Relationship to Possessions." *Journal of Consumer Research* 39(October):510–29.

Barthes, Roland. 1972 [1957]. *Mythologies.* New York: Hill and Wang.

Belk, Russell W. 1987. "A Modest Proposal for Creating Verisimilitude in Consumer Information Processing Models and Some Suggestions for Establishing a Discipline to Study Consumer Behavior." In *Philosophical and Radical Thought in Marketing,* edited by R. Bagozzi, N. Dholakia, and A. F. Firat, 361–72. Lexington. MA: Lexington Press.

______. 1990. "Participant Observation: A Methodology for Human Studies/Interpretive Interactionism." *Journal of Marketing Research* (JMR) 27(August):368–70.

______, ed. 1991. *Highways and Buyways: Naturalistic Research from the Consumer Behavior Odyssey.* Provo, UT: Association for Consumer Research.

Belk, Russell W., John F. Sherry Jr., and Melanie Wallendorf. 1988. "A Naturalistic Inquiry into Buyer and Seller Behavior at a Swap Meet." *Journal of Consumer Research* 14(March):449–70.

Belk, Russell W., Melanie Wallendorf, and John F. Sherry Jr. 1989. "The Sacred and the Profane in Consumer Behavior: Theodicy on the Odyssey." *Journal of Consumer Research* 16(June):1–38.

Berger, Jonah, and Morgan Ward. 2010. "Subtle Signals of Inconspicuous Consumption." *Journal of Consumer Research* 37(December):555–69.

Beverland, Michael. 2009. *Building Brand Authenticity.* Basingstoke, UK: Palgrave Macmillan.

Bonsu, Samuel K. 2009. "Colonial Images in Global Times: Consumer Interpretations of Africa and Africans in Advertising." *Consumption, Markets & Culture* 12(March):1–25.

Bonsu, Samuel K., and Pia Polsa. 2011. "Governmentality at the Base-of-the-Pyramid." *Journal of Macromarketing* 31(September):236–44.

Bourdieu, Pierre. 1990. *The Logic of Practice.* Stanford, CA: Stanford University Press.

Bradshaw, Alan, and Nikhilesh Dholakia. 2012. "Outsider's Insights: (Mis)understanding A. Fuat Fırat on Consumption, Markets and Culture." *Consumption, Markets & Culture* 15(1):117–31.

Bristor, Julia M., and Eileen Fischer. 1993. "Feminist Thought: Implications for Consumer Research." *Journal of Consumer Research* 19(March):518–36.

Brown, Stephen. 1996. "Consumption Behaviour in the Sex 'n Shopping Novels of Judith Krantz: A Post-structuralist Perspective." *Advances in Consumer Research* 23:43–8.

Brown, Stephen, Ann Marie Doherty, and Bill Clark, eds. 1998. *Romancing the Market.* London and New York: Routledge.

Brown, Stephen, and Darach Turley, eds. 1997. *Consumer Research: Postcards from the Edge.* Oxon and NewYork: Routledge.

Calder, Bobby J., and Alice M. Tybout. 1987. "What Consumer Research Is." *Journal of Consumer Research* 14(June):136–40.

Campbell, Colin. 1987. *The Romantic Ethic and the Spirit of Modern Consumerism.* Cambridge, MA: Blackwell.

Campbell, Norah. 2013. "The Posthuman Consumer." In *The Routledge Companion to Digital Consumption,* edited by R. W. Belk and R. Llamas, 39–50. London and New York: Routledge.

Canniford, Robin, and Avi Shankar. 2013. "Purifying Practices: How Consumers Assemble Romantic Experiences of Nature." *Journal of Consumer Research* 39(March): 1051–69.

Cayla, Julien, and Giana M. Eckhardt. 2008. "Asian Brands and the Shaping of a Transnational Imagined Community." *Journal of Consumer Research* 35(August):216–30.

Cayla, Julien, and Mark Elson. 2012. "Indian Consumer *kaun hai?* The Class-based Grammar of Indian Advertising." *Journal of Macromarketing* 32(December):295–308.

Celsi, Richard L., Randall L. Rose, and Thomas W. Leigh. 1993. "An Exploration of High-Risk Leisure Consumption through Skydiving." *Journal of Consumer Research* 20(June):1–23.

Chernev, Alexander, Ryan Hamilton, and David Gal. 2011. "Competing for Consumer Identity: Limits to Self-expression and the Perils of Lifestyle Branding." *Journal of Marketing* 75(May):66–82.

Cherrier, Hélène, Mathilde Szuba, and Nil Özçağlar-Toulouse. 2012. "Barriers to Downward Carbon Emission: Exploring Sustainable Consumption in the Face of the Glass Floor." *Journal of Marketing Management* 28(March):397–419.

Clifford, James, and George W. Marcus, eds. 1986. *Writing Culture: The Poetics and Politics of Culture.* Los Angeles and Berkeley: University of California Press.

Cohen, Joel B. 1989. "An Over-extended Self?" *Journal of Consumer Research* 16(June): 125–8.

CCT Consortium. 2013. Consumer Culture Theory. http://consumerculturetheory.org/.

Cova, Bernard, Daniele Dalli, and Detlev Zwick. 2011. "Critical Perspectives on Consumers' Role as 'Producers': Broadening the Debate on Value Co-creation in Marketing Processes." *Marketing Theory* 11(September):231–41.

Cova, Bernard, and Pauline Maclaran. 2012. "Rethinking Consumer Culture after Postmodernism: In Search of a New 'Turn'?" Paper presented at the 2012 Consumer Culture Theory Conference, 16–19 August, Oxford, United Kingdom.

Creighton, Millie R. 1991. "Maintaining Cultural Boundaries in Retailing: How Japanese Department Stores Domesticate 'Things Foreign'" *Modern Asian Studies* 25(October): 675–709.

Crockett, David, and Melanie Wallendorf. 2004. "The Role of Normative Political Ideology in Consumer Behavior." *Journal of Consumer Research* 31(December):511–28.

DeBerry-Spence, Benét. 2010. "Making Theory and Practice in Subsistence Markets: An Analytic Autoethnography of MASAZI in Accra, Ghana." *Journal of Business Research* 63(June):608–16.

Delueze, Gilles, and Felix Guattari. 1987. *A Thousand Plateaus.* Translated by Brian Massumi. Minneapolis. MN: University of Minnesota Press.

Dholakia, Utpal M., and Silvia Vianello. 2011. "Effective Brand Community Management: Lessons from Customer Enthusiasts." *IUP Journal of Brand Management* 8(March): 7–21.

Diamond, Nina, John F. Sherry Jr., Albert M. Muñiz Jr., Mary Ann McGrath, Robert V. Kozinets, and Stefania Borghini. 2009. "American Girl and the Brand Gestalt: Closing the Loop on Sociocultural Branding Research." *Journal of Marketing* 73(May):118–34.

Dolan, Catherine S. 2005. "Fields of Obligation." *Journal of Consumer Culture* 5(November):365–89.

_____. 2008. "In the Mists of Development: Fairtrade in Kenyan Tea Fields." *Globalizations* 5(June): 305–18.

Dong, Lily, and Kelly Tian. 2009. "The Use of Western Brands in Asserting Chinese National Identity." *Journal of Consumer Research* 36(October):504–23.

Elliott, Richard, and Bernard Cova. 2008. "Interpretive Consumer Research as Cultural Critique." *Consumption, Markets & Culture* 11(June)71–2.

Epp, Amber M., and Linda L. Price. 2008. "Family Identity: A Framework of Identity Interplay in Consumption Practices." *Journal of Consumer Research* 35(June):50–70.

Epp, Amber M., and Linda L. Price. 2010. "The Storied Life of Singularised Objects: Forces of Agency and Network Transformation." *Journal of Consumer Research* 36(February):820–37.

Firat, A. Fuat, and Alladi Venkatesh. 1993. "Postmodernity: The Age of Marketing." *International Journal of Research in Marketing* 10(September):227–49.

Foucault, Michel. 1970. *The Order of Things.* New York: Pantheon.

_____. 1972. *The Archaeology of Knowledge.* London and New York: Routledge.

Gainer, Brenda, and Eileen Fischer. 1991. "To Buy or Not To Buy? That Is Not the Question: Female Ritual in Home Shopping Parties." *Advances in Consumer Research* 18:597–602.

Geiger-Oneto, Stephanie, and Eric J. Arnould. 2011. "Alternative Trade Organization and Subjective Quality of Life: The Case of Latin American Coffee Producers." *Journal of Macromarketing* 31(September):276–90.

Giesler, Markus. 2012. "How Doppelgänger Brand Images Influence the Market Creation Process: Longitudinal Insights from the Rise of Botox Cosmetic." *Journal of Marketing* 76(6):55–68.

Giesler, Markus, and Alladi Venkatesh. 2005. "Reframing the Embodied Consumer as Cyborg: A Posthumanist Epistemology of Consumption." *Advances in Consumer Research* 32:661–9.

Goulding, Christina, and Michael Saren. 2009. "Performing Identity: An Analysis of Gender Expressions at the Whitby Goth Festival." *Consumption, Markets & Culture* 12(March):27–46.

Goulding, Christina, Avi Shankar, and Richard Elliott. 2002. "Working Weeks, Rave Weekends: Identity Fragmentation and the Emergence of New Communities." *Consumption, Markets & Culture* 5(December):261–84.

Graeber, David. 2011. "Consumption." Current *Anthropology* 52(August):489–511.

Han, Young Jee, Joseph C. Nunes, and Xavier Drèze. 2010. "Signaling Status with Luxury Goods." *Journal of Marketing* 74(July):15–30.

Hannerz, Ulf. 1996. *Transnational Connections: Culture, People, Places.* London: Routledge.

Hargreaves, Tom. 2011. "Practice-Ing Behavior Change: Applying Social Practice Theory to Pro-Environmental Behaviour Change." *Journal of Consumer Culture* 11(1):79–99.

Haytko, Diana L., and Julie Baker. 2004. "It's All at the Mall: Exploring Adolescent Girls' Experiences." *Journal of Retailing* 80(Spring):67–84.

Hirschman, Elizabeth C. 1993. "Ideology in Consumer Research, 1980 and 1990: A Marxist and Feminist Critique." *Journal of Consumer Research* 19(March):537–55.

Hoffman, Donna L., and Marek Fodor. 2010. "Can You Measure the ROI of Your Social Media Marketing?" *MIT Sloan Management Review* 52(Fall):41–9.

Holbrook, Morris B. 1987. "O, Consumer, How You've Changed: Some Radical Reflections on the Roots of Consumption." In *Philosophical and Radical Thought in Marketing,* edited by Firat Firat, Nikhlesh Dholakia, and Richard Bagozzi, 156–77. Lexington, MA: D. C. Heath.

Holbrook, Morris B., and Elizabeth C. Hirschman. 1982. "The Experiential Aspects of Consumption: Consumer Fantasies, Feelings, and Fun." *Journal of Consumer Research* 9(September):132–40.

Holt, Douglas B. 1997. "Poststructuralist Lifestyle Analysis: Conceptualizing the Social Patterning of Consumption." *Journal of Consumer Research* 23(March):326–50.

———. 2004. *How Brands Become Icons: The Principles of Cultural Branding.* Cambridge, MA: Harvard Business School Press.

Holt, Douglas B., and Craig J Thompson. 2004. "Man-of-Action Heroes: The Pursuit of Heroic Masculinity in Everyday Consumption." *Journal of Consumer Research* 31 (September):425–40.

Hudson, Laurel Anderson, and Julie L. Ozanne. 1988. "Alternative Ways of Seeking Knowledge in Consumer Research." *Journal of Consumer Research* 14(March):508–21.

Hunt, Shelby D. 1990. "Truth in Marketing Theory and Research." *Journal of Marketing* 54(July):1–15.

———. 1993. "Objectivity in Marketing Theory and Research." *Journal of Marketing* 57(April):76–92.

Jafari, Aliakbar, and Christina Goulding. 2008. "'We Are Not Terrorists!' UK-based Iranians' Consumption Practices and the 'Torn Self.'" *Consumption, Markets & Culture* 11(June):73–91.

Karababa, Eminegül, and Güliz Ger. 2011. "Early Modern Ottoman Coffeehouse Culture and the Formation of the Consumer Subject." *Journal of Consumer Research* 37(February):737–60.

Kates, Steven M. 2002. "The Protean Quality of Subcultural Consumption: An Ethnographic Account of Gay Consumers." *Journal of Consumer Research* 29(December):383–99.

Kennedy, Karen Norman, Jerry R. Goolsby, and Eric J. Arnould. 2003. "Implementing a Customer Orientation: Extension of Theory and Application." *Journal of Marketing* 67(October):67–82.

Kimura, Junko, and Russell W. Belk. 2005. "Christmas in Japan: Globalization versus Localization." *Consumption, Markets & Culture* 8(September):325–38.

Kjeldgaard, Dannie, and Søren Askegaard. 2006. "The Glocalization of Youth Culture: The Global Youth Segment as Structures of Common Difference." *Journal of Consumer Research* 33(September):231–47.

Kjellberg, Hans. 2008. "Market Practices and Over-Consumption." *Consumption, Markets & Culture* 11(June):151–67.

Kozinets, Robert V. 1997. "'I Want To Believe': A Netnography of the X-Philes' Subculture of Consumption." *Advances in Consumer Research* 24:470–5.

———. 1998. "On Netnography: Initial Reflections on Consumer Research Investigations of Cyberculture." *Advances in Consumer Research* 25:366–71.

Kozinets, Robert V. 1999. "E-Tribalized Marketing? The Strategic Implications of Virtual Communities of Consumption." *European Management Journal* 17(June):252–65.

_____. 2002a. "The Field Behind the Screen: Using Netnography for Marketing Research in Online Communities." *Journal of Marketing Research* 39(February):61–72.

_____. 2002b. "Can Consumers Escape the Market? Emancipatory Illuminations from Burning Man." *Journal of Consumer Research* 29(June):20–38.

Kozinets, Robert V., John F. Sherry Jr., Diana S. Storm, Adam Duhachek, Krittinee Nuttavuthisit, and Benet Deberry-Spence. 2004. "Ludic Agency and Retail Spectacle." *Journal of Consumer Research* 31(December):658–72.

Kozinets, Robert V., Kristine de Valck, Andrea C. Wojnicki, and Sarah J. S. Wilner. 2010. "Networked Narratives: Understanding Word-Of-Mouth Marketing in Online Communities." *Journal of Marketing* 74(March):71–89.

Latour, Bruno. 2005. *Reassembling the Social: An Introduction to Actor-Network-Theory.* New York: Oxford University Press.

Lee, Renée Gravois, Julie L. Ozanne, and Ronald Paul Hill. 1999. "Improving Service Encounters Through Resource Sensitivity: The Case of Health Care Delivery in an Appalachian Community." *Journal of Public Policy & Marketing,*18:230–48.

Lincoln, Yvonna S., and Egon G. Guba. 1985. *Naturalistic Inquiry.* Newbury Park, CA: Sage.

Luedicke, Marius K. 2011. "Consumer Acculturation Theory: (Crossing) Conceptual Boundaries." *Consumption, Markets & Culture* 14(September):223–44.

Markkula, Annu, and Johanna Moisander. 2012. "Discursive Confusion over Sustainable Consumption: A Discursive Perspective on the Perplexity of Marketplace Knowledge." *Journal of Consumer Policy* 35(March):105–25.

McCarty, John A. 1989. "Current Theory and Research on Cross-Cultural Factors in Consumer Behavior." *Advances in Consumer Research* 16:127–9.

Mick, David Glen, and Claus Buhl. 1992. "A Meaning-Based Model of Advertising Experiences." *Journal of Consumer Research* 19(December):317–38.

Miller, Daniel. 2012. *Consumption and Its Consequences.* London: Polity Press.

Muniz Albert M. Jr., and Thomas C. O'Guinn. 2001. "Brand Community." *Journal of Consumer Research* 27(March):412–32.

Murray, Jeff B., and Julie L. Ozanne. 1991. "The Critical Imagination: Emancipatory Interests in Consumer Research." *Journal of Consumer Research* 18(September):129–44.

Murray, Jeff B., Julie L. Ozanne, and Jon M. Shapiro. 1994. "Revitalizing the Critical Imagination: Unleashing the Crouched Tiger." *Journal of Consumer Research* 21(December):559–65.

Oswald, Laura R. 1999. "Culture Swapping: Consumption and the Ethnogenesis of Middle-Class Haitian Immigrants." *Journal of Consumer Research* 25(March):303–18.

Ozanne, Julie L., and Bige Saatcioglu. 2008. "Participatory Action Research." *Journal of Consumer Research* 35(October):423–39.

Özçağlar-Toulouse, Nil, and Bernard Cova. 2010. "Une Histoire de la CCT Française: Parcours et Concepts Clés." *Recherche et Applications en Marketing* 25(2):69–91.

Özçağlar -Toulouse, Nil, and Amina Béji-Bécheur 2012. *L'Ethnicité, Fabrique Marketing?* Paris: Editions EMS.

Peattie, Ken, and Andrea Collins. 2009. "Guest Editorial: Perspectives on Sustainable Consumption." *International Journal of Consumer Studies* 33(March):107–12.

Peñaloza, Lisa. 1994. "Atravesando Fronteras/Border Crossings: A Critical Ethnographic Exploration of the Consumer Acculturation of Mexican Immigrants." *Journal of Consumer Research* 21(June):32–54.

Peñaloza, Lisa, and Mary C. Gilly. 1999. "Marketer Acculturation: The Changer and the Changed." *Journal of Marketing* 63(July):84–104.

Peñaloza, Lisa, and Alladi Venkatesh. 2006. "Further Evolving the New Dominant Logic of Marketing: From Services to the Social Construction of Markets." *Marketing Theory* 6(September): 299–316.

Peñaloza, Lisa, Nil Toulouse, and Luca Massimiliano Visconti, eds. 2011. *Marketing Management: A Cultural Perspective.* London and New York: Routledge.

Press, Melea, and Eric J. Arnould. 2009. "Constraints on Sustainable Energy Consumption: Market System and Public Policy Challenges and Opportunities." *Journal of Public Policy & Marketing* 28(Spring):102–13.

Price, Linda L., and Eric J. Arnould. 1999. "Commercial Friendships: Service Provider-Client Relationships In Social Context." *Journal of Marketing* 63(October):38–56.

Rogers, Carl. 1961. *On Becoming a Person: A Therapist's View of Psychotherapy.* New York: Houghton Mifflin.

Sandikci, Özlem, and Güliz Ger. 2010. "Veiling in Style: How Does a Stigmatized Practice Become Fashionable?" *Journal of Consumer Research* 37(June):15–36.

Schau, Hope J., Stephen Brown, and Anthony Patterson. 2001. "Suburban Soundtracks." In *Imagining Marketing: Art, Aesthetics and the Avant-Garde,* edited by Stephen Brown and Anthony Patterson, 225–32. London and New York: Routledge..

Schau, Hope J., and Mary C. Gilly. 2003. "We Are What We Post? Self-Presentation in Personal Web Space." *Journal of Consumer Research* 30(December):385–404.

Schau, Hope J., Mary C. Gilly, and Mary Wolfinbarger. 2009. "Consumer Identity Renaissance: The Resurgence of Identity-Inspired Consumption in Retirement." *Journal of Consumer Research* 36(August):255–76.

Schau, Hope J., Al Muniz Jr., and Eric J. Arnould. 2009. "How Brand Community Practices Create Value." *Journal of Marketing* 73(September):30–51.

Schneider, Tanja, and Steve Woolgar. 2012. "Technologies of Ironic Revelation: Enacting Consumers in Neuromarkets." *Consumption, Market & Culture* 15(June):169–89.

Schouten, John W. 1991. "Selves in Transition: Symbolic Consumption in Personal Rites of Passage and Identity Reconstruction." *Journal of Consumer Research* 17(March): 412–25.

Schouten, John W., and James H. McAlexander. 1995. "Subcultures of Consumption: An Ethnography of the New Bikers." *Journal of Consumer Research* 22(June):43–61.

Scott, Linda M. 1994. "Images in Advertising: The Need for a Theory of Visual Rhetoric." *Journal of Consumer Research* 21(September):252–73.

Scott, Linda M., Catherine Dolan, Mary Johnstone-Louis, Kimberly Sugden, and Mary Alice Wu. 2012. "Enterprise and Inequality: A Study of Avon in South Africa." *Entrepreneurship: Theory & Practice* 36(May):543–68.

Shankar, Avi, Bernard Cova, and Robert Kozinets, eds. 2007. *Consumer Tribes.* Oxford, UK: Butterworth-Heinemann.

Sherry, John F., Jr. 1991. "Postmodern Alternatives: The Interpretive Turn in Consumer Research." In *Handbook of Consumer Behavior;* edited by Thomas Robertson and Harold Kassarjian, 548–91. Englewood Cliffs, NJ: Prentice Hall..

Stern, Barbara B., Craig J. Thompson, and Eric J. Arnould. 1998. "Narrative Analysis of a Marketing Relationship: The Consumer's Perspective." *Psychology & Marketing* 15(May):195–214.

Strengers, Yolande. 2011. "Negotiating Everyday Life: The Role of Energy and Water Consumption Feedback." *Journal of Consumer Culture* 11(3):319–38.

Strizhakova, Yuliya, Robin A. Coulter, and Linda L. Price. 2008. "Branded Products as a Passport to Global Citizenship: Perspectives from Developed and Developing Countries." *Journal of International Marketing* 16(4):57–85.

Tadajewski, Mark. 2006. "The Ordering of Marketing Theory: The Influence of McCarthyism and the Cold War." *Marketing Theory* 6(June):163–99.

Thompson, Craig J. 2002. "A Re-Inquiry on Re-Inquiries: A Postmodern Proposal for a Critical Reflexive Approach." *Journal of Consumer Research* 29(June):142–5.

Thompson, Craig J., and Elizabeth C Hirschman. 1995. "Understanding the Socialized Body: A Poststructuralist Analysis of Consumers' Self-Conceptions, Body Images, and Self-Care Practices." *Journal of Consumer Research* 22(September):139–53.

Thompson, Craig J., William B. Locander, and Howard R. Pollio. 1989. "Putting Consumer Experience Back into Consumer Research: The Philosophy and Method of Existential-Phenomenology." *Journal of Consumer Research* 16(September):133–47.

Thompson, Craig J., Howard R. Pollio, and William B. Locander. 1994. "The Spoken and the Unspoken: A Hermeneutic Approach to Understanding the Cultural Viewpoints that Underlie Consumers' Expressed Meanings." *Journal of Consumer Research* 21(December):432–52.

Thompson, Craig J., Aric Rindfleisch, and Zeynep Arsel. 2006. "Emotional Branding and the Strategic Value of the Doppelgänger Brand Image." *Journal of Marketing* 70(January):50–64.

Thompson, Craig J., Barbara B. Stern, and Eric J. Arnould. 1998. "Writing the Differences: Postmodern Pluralism, Retextualization, and the Construction of Reflexive Ethnographic Narratives in Consumer Research." *Consumption, Markets & Culture* 2(September):105–60.

Thompson, Craig J., Eric Arnould, and Markus Giesler. 2013. "Discursivity, Difference, and Disruption: Genealogical Reflections on the CCT Heteroglossia." *Marketing Theory* 13(June):149–74.

Üstüner, Tuba, and Douglas B. Holt. 2007. "Dominated Consumer Acculturation: The Social Construction of Poor Migrant Women's Consumer Identity Projects in a Turkish Squatter Community." *Journal of Consumer Research* 34(June):41–56.

van Maanen, John. 2011. *Tales of the Field: On Writing Ethnography.* Second edition. Chicago, IL: University of Chicago.

Varman, Rohit, and Russell W. Belk. 2009. "Nationalism and Ideology in an Anticonsumption Movement." *Journal of Consumer Research* 36(December):686–700.

Viswanathan, Madhubalan, José Antonio Rosa, and James Edwin Harris. 2005. "Decision Making and Coping of Functionally Illiterate Consumers and Some Implications for Marketing Management." *Journal of Marketing* 69(January):15–31.

Wallendorf, Melanie, and Eric J. Arnould. 1988. "'My favorite things': A Cross-Cultural Inquiry into Object Attachment, Possessiveness, and Social Linkage." *Journal of Consumer Research* 14(March):531–47.

Wallendorf, Melanie, and Russell W. Belk. 1989. "Assessing Trustworthiness in Naturalistic Consumer Research." In *Interpretive Consumer Research,* edited by Elizabeth C. Hirschman, 69–84. Provo, UT: Association for Consumer Research.

Wallendorf, Melanie, and Michael D. Reilly. 1983. "Ethnic Migration, Assimilation and Consumption." *Journal of Consumer Research* 10(December):292–302.

Warde, Alan. 2005. "Consumption and Theories of Practice." *Journal of Consumer Culture* 5(July): 131–53.

Wilhite, Harold, and Hidetoshi Nakagami. 1996. "A Cross-Cultural Analysis of Household Energy Use Behavior in Japan and Norway." *Energy Policy* 24(September): 795–804.

Wilk, Richard R. 1995. "Learning To Be Local in Belize: Global Systems of Common Difference." In *Worlds Apart,* edited by D. Miller, 110–33. London: Routledge.

_____. 2006. "Bottled Water." *Journal of Consumer Culture* 6(November):303–25.

Wilk, Richard R., and Harold Wilhite. 1985. "Why Don't People Weatherize Their Homes? An Ethnographic Solution." *Energy* 10(5):621–9.

Woermann, Niklas. 2012. "On the Slope Is on the Screen: Prosumption, Social Media Practices, and Scopic Systems in the Freeskiing Subculture." *American Behavioral Scientist* 56(April):618–40.

Zwick, Detlev, and Nikhilesh Dholakia. 2006. "The Epistemic Consumption Object and Postsocial Consumption: Expanding Consumer-Object Theory in Consumer Research." *Consumption, Markets & Culture* 9(March):17–43.

NOTE

1 Our tripartite organizing framework is based on a related article coauthored with Markus Giesler (see Thompson et al. 2013).

6

Methodological Rebellion: Overcoming the Quantitative-Qualitative Divide

NEAL H. PATEL

This chapter is about methodological rebellion. I argue that the prevailing opposition between qualitative and quantitative methods is flawed, is a misreading of our scholarly heritage, and stands in the way of our evolution as researchers. It must be overcome to facilitate innovation in our research practice.

Before Karl Marx became famous for his critique of the political economy, he described his intellectual mission as a "*ruthless criticism of everything existing*" (1843; Marx and Engels 1978). "Ruthless" in the sense that Marx was unafraid of where his results would take him and "just as little afraid" of conflict with the powers that be (Marx 1843). By "everything existing," he meant discarding all the prevalent thinking of his day and starting over from basic presumptions (Marx 1843). He proceeded by reconstructing the historical terms leading to the dominant paradigms of his era. Along the way, Marx discovered flaws in the old way of thinking upon which he could lay the foundation of a new direction.

Borrowing Marx's framework, I will demonstrate that a deep, "ruthless" engagement with the scholarly tradition will challenge and transform our assumptions about the divisions between quantitative and qualitative methods.

WINTER IS COMING

Professional ethnographic researchers tend to distinguish their approach to consumers by explaining how "conventional" market research disregards the complex patterns, hidden meanings, and latent needs implicit in everyday life that subjects cannot easily articulate (Slater and Narver 1998). In this way, the ethnographic, customer-centric turn in business renders the syndicated techniques of

Handbook of Anthropology in Business, edited by Rita Denny and Patricia Sunderland, 135–156.

market research at odds with innovation in products and services (Hamel and Prahalad 1994). Yet Slobin and Cherkasky (2010) point out that risk-averse businesses increasingly turn to quantitative web analytics and business intelligence for new customer insights. In place of the ethnographer, web-application logs capture the real-time behavior of millions of customers, while fine-tuned algorithms promise a "perfectly calibrated" set of products and services (Slobin and Cherkasky 2010). Although Slobin and Cherkasky (2010) demonstrate that, in practice, this approach leads to "data hoarding" more than experiential understanding, quantitative and computational techniques are rapidly catching up with technology. "Data is the sword of the 21st century," remarked Jonathan Rosenberg, former Google, Inc. Senior Vice President of Product Management "and those who wield it well, the Samurai" (Rosenberg 2009).

Whereas a thoughtful integration of quantitative methods with qualitative research practice appears to follow, this is a troubling evolutionary proposition to many in a research community founded on the *deficiencies* of outdated quant methods, not to mention the value proposition of qualitative research:

> This community of researchers has qualitative methods at the heart of our core competencies and a sudden shift to quantitative research, especially when some clients view it as a way to jump strait [*sic*] to validating their hypothesis, hunch or concepts without examining the context for its relevance, through qualitative research is not a good sign. . . . For those clients who want to achieve a breakthrough in delivering value to their audience, quantitative is only a way of shirking responsibility from finding new directions and a way of playing safe (Dandavante 2009).

Indeed, the enmity towards quantitative research shared by many professional ethnographers parallels a longstanding debate within marketing research, the very discipline ethnographers have sought to distance themselves from. Since the 1980s, marketing researchers have grappled deeply with the question of whether their craft is truly scientific, a debate over the validity of "science" itself. Based on his analysis of Kuhn's *Structure of Scientific Revolutions* (1962), Paul Anderson (1983, 1986) argued that marketing shouldn't aspire to "canonical" conceptions of scientific research, because the philosophy of science provides no clear consensus "as to the nature or very existence of a unique scientific method" (Anderson 1983:25). Instead, Anderson rejects the notion that scientific claims are valid because they can be disproven, observing that all claims justifiable on this basis can be widely divergent, even incompatible (Anderson 1986:167). Shelby Hunt (1990), on the other hand, found Anderson's analysis overlooked Kuhn abandonment of relativism as nihilistic. "The frequent arguments that strive to use the absolute or relative incommensurability of scientific theories as a reason for thinking that they are inaccessible to purely scientific (rational) comparisons are simply fallacious" (Hunt 1990:3). Indeed, Hunt continues, the truth of a scientific proposition "is not to claim that it is certain; rather, it is to claim that the world is as the proposition says it is" (Hunt 1990:12). Moreover, Hunt's interrogation of Anderson's argument fails to find a viable relativistic alternative to scientific realism. "Many marketing researchers, either explicitly or implicitly," Hunt argues, "already are guided by scientific realism. Understandably so: scientific realism is coherent and intelligible" (1990:13).

Yet ethnographers, with the winter of Big Data looming on the horizon, have yet to see a way out of our own methodological stalemate. In our era, ethnography is an established practice within market research, replete with its own conventions, syndicated techniques, and researchers who have become implicitly suspicious of numbers. "Quant" and "qual" only encounter each other in terms of "either/or," "better-than," "one validating the other," or as "ceremonial" gestures to appease numbers-obsessed clients (Boehm 2009). Statistical "snake-handling" is somehow more preferable than meaningful dialogue between qualitative and quantitative analysis. Meanwhile, the gathering forces of evolution—driven by Big Data, the internet's increasing share of social life, and the floundering economy—offer research practitioners a single choice: *adapt,* or prepare for marginalization. For anthropology to have a future in business, it must be allowed to innovate: in the current context, this means reevaluating our collective suspicion of quantitative research.

Therefore, starting with a "ruthless" interrogation of the philosophical roots of quantitative and qualitative methods, then reconstructing some of the history embodied in the present-day divide, I will explain how the mutual exclusivity of qualitative and quantitative methods is not intrinsic, but socially constructed. Finally, I will introduce a basic framework for how research can move forward, along with some brief examples.

THE ORIGIN OF THE SPECIES

Discourse among professional ethnographers tends to deploy the term "positivism" interchangeably with quantitative methods. Indeed, the quantitative empirical turn in American sociology, which gave birth to professional market research, traces its origins to the positivist tradition. However, closer inspection of the philosophical tradition suggests that positivism is far from the reckless belief in the self-evident veracity of numbers that it is currently portrayed to be.

Comte

"Positivism" originates in the Positive philosophy of French philosopher August Comte (Levine 1995). Comte divides all knowledge into three basic categories:

"the theological, or fictitious; the metaphysical, or abstract; and the scientific, or positive" (Comte 1975:71). By "positive," Comte simply meant things we can be "positive" about: he authoritatively debars to human reason any speculation about origin, meaning, or other sublime mysteries best left to the domain of the theological, or metaphysical. "Our real business," Comte declares, "is to analyze accurately the circumstances of phenomena, and to connect them by the natural relations of succession and resemblance" (Comte 1975:75).

Consider gravity: "We say that the general phenomena of the universe are *explained* by it, because it connects under one head the whole immense variety of astronomical facts," but, Comte argues, "as to *what* weight and attraction *are*, we have *nothing* to do with that. . . . [T]heologians and metaphysicians may imagine and refine about such questions, but positive philosophy rejects them all" (Comte 1975:75; emphasis added). Thus, "facts" insofar as they are "positive" facts, must be universally observable and expressed through sufficiently general means, such as measurement.

Comte's concern with a measurable universe traces back to his historical context. Born in 1798, four years after the Reign of Terror (1793–1794) in the chaos of post-Restoration France, Comte lived in an era that utterly confused fact with ideology. His wariness of "truth" in the hands of power is apparent in his writing. He found metaphysical and theological abstraction, along with their sway over the human imagination, to be powerful, perhaps useful, but nonetheless *dangerous* forms of knowledge, which "offered the powerful charm of unlimited empire over the external world" (Comte 1975:74).

Alternatively, Comte saw certainty—anything one can be "positive" about—as the basis for a more democratic consensus. Under conditions of anarchy, Comte argued, consensus serves as a means to society forward constructively toward a common good. He depicted human development in terms of a historical progression from theological, to metaphysical, to positivist thinking (Comte 1975).

But such consensus is only possible because positive facts can be *disputed* "without once inquiring into [*their*] nature" (Comte 1975:75). Comte does not claim that a fact is infallible because it is measurable. On the contrary, "there is no science," Comte concedes, "that, having attained the positive stage, does not bear marks of having passed through the others" (Comte 1975:72). "Measuring" is making an assumption. Positive facts are a form of *convention* that can be shared, contested, and constructively debated: that's why they're valuable.

Thus, the true origins of "positivism" belie the contemporary stigma levied at—and in some cases, incorrectly promulgated by—statisticians: that mere numbers are self-evident. In Comte's view, positive truth is always a form of convention required to describe the observable features of something otherwise imponderable.

Durkheim

Comte connected with later generations of social scientists through the work of Emile Durkheim—who directly influenced early anthropology and sociology—and Georg Simmel, whose critical reception of positivism inspired the methodological development of the Chicago School of sociology.

Durkheim believed that positive social science would evolve into the pursuit of "social facts"—sociological laws explaining social life "in the nature of society itself"—the way, say, Newton's Laws or the Laws of Thermodynamics explain the physical universe (Durkheim 1982:7). Discovering social facts would render sociologists capable of "maintaining" the proper functioning of society in its normal equilibrium, or "re-establish[ing] it if disturbed," and, if necessary, "rediscover[ing] the conditions of normality if they happen to change" (Durkheim 1982:104). However, distinguishing the "normal" state from the abnormal required a science of facts, "determined by some sort of mental calculus," upon which "no limit can be laid" in the search for optimal social laws (Durkheim 1982:104).

In other words, Durkheim dreamed of sociology as "natural science," aimed at maintaining the integrity of social order. He thereby made consensus-as-social-good—the way Comte meant it—his explicit scientific aim. He even cites Comte as the first scholar to tap into the altruistic, rather than economic, dimensions of the division of labor in society, which Durkheim would later identify as an engine of social solidarity (Durkheim 1984:23,306).

Indeed, Durkheim eventually extends Comte's idea into full-scale functionalism. Durkheim's concern with social solidarity is founded on his vision of a society in which individuals are primarily a loose bundle of biological drives, feelings, and intentions, barely distinguishable from animals (Durkheim [1897] 1951:213). Society, on the other hand, offers individuals the means to acquire "higher-order" elements of culture, or even religion and politics, through social exchange and collective identification (Durkheim [1897] 1951:213). Solidarity, in the form of laws, professional codes, and cultural norms, guides human beings through life and provides us with a sense of belonging (Durkheim 1984:284).

Whereas an integrated society works towards a collective purpose, a disintegrated society is a jumble of individuals, who exist without purpose. "Because society is the end on which our better selves depend," Durkheim argued, we cannot escape society "without a simultaneous realization that our activity is purposeless" (Durkheim [1897] 1951:213). Thus, in the absence of solidarity, *anomie*, depression, and disillusionment don't emanate from the individual, but are the individual's expression of "*society*'s state of integration" (Durkheim [1897] 1951:213).

Understanding Durkheim's journey from positivism to functionalism is instructive because Durkheim had significant influence over early anthropologists. For instance, A. R. Radcliffe-Brown (Radcliffe-Brown and Evans-Pritchard 1952) studied "primitive" societies to develop universal generalizations about social structure. "Societies differ from one another in their structure and constitution and therefore in the customary rules of behavior," Radcliffe-Brown conceded, but institutions like religion, for example, invariably function to maintain social order (Radcliffe-Brown and Evans-Pritchard 1952:160). The particulars may vary according to the specifics of a given society, but function remains the same (Radcliffe-Brown and Evans-Pritchard 1952:161). Indeed, Radcliffe-Brown's language invokes Durkheim's quantitative positivism:

> It is this theory that I propose for your consideration. Applied, not to single society such as ancient China, but to all human societies, it points to the correlation and co-variation of different characteristics or elements of social systems (Radcliffe-Brown and Evans-Pritchard 1952:160).

Durkheim was so influential that even early social anthropologists—the other side of the proverbial house—who disagreed with Radcliffe-Brown's structural functionalism formulated their understanding of qualitative methods in positivist terms. For example, Bronislaw Malinowski ([1922] 1978)—who coined the very phrase "ethnography"—identified the "concrete, statistical documentation" of the organization of the "tribe" as a "goal of ethnographic field-work," alongside the "anatomy" of its culture, the "imponderabilia of actual life," and minute, detailed observations, "made possible by close contact with native life" (Malinowski [1922] 1978:24).

For that matter—whether or not Malinowski disagreed with Radcliffe-Brown's notion of the collective, rather than individual, structuration of society—he certainly seemed to embrace the notion of ethnography as a form of objective science aimed at producing general law. "Ethnographic work is creative in the same sense as the construction of general principles in the natural science," Malinowski argued, "where objective laws of very wide application lie hidden till brought forth by the investigating human mind (Malinowski [1922] 1978:397). "Perhaps man's mentality will be revealed to us," Malinowski speculated, leading researchers "along some lines which we have never followed before" (Malinowski [1922] 1978:25). Moreover, "as the principles of natural science are empirical," Malinowski argued, "so are the final generalizations of ethnographic sociology because, although expressly stated for the first time by the investigator, they are nonetheless objective realities of human thinking, feeling and behavior" (Malinowski [1922] 1978:397).

Once again, we find little in early formulation of anthropological methods that prohibits ethnographers from engaging in the allegedly positivist enterprise of empirical measurement and analysis (and much to suggest they *should*). Despite this, many practicing ethnographers continue to believe the spoken word of subjects embodies the only form of defensible truth, at once superior to any form of empirical measurement. However, like Durkheim and Malinowski, even Radcliffe-Brown and Evans-Pritchard (1952) oriented themselves around a positivist framework, understood in terms of the simple necessity of empirical fact as the basis for universal scientific consensus.

Perhaps those same ethnographers might recoil in Lovecraftian[1] horror to learn that somewhere, in the primordial epistemological goo of philosophical prehistory, they may be descended from positivists.

Simmel

Simmel, unlike Durkheim, was more directly influential on the early sociologists. A victim of anti-Semitism in his native Germany, Simmel went unappreciated by German academic departments despite public support from the likes of Max Weber and Edmund Husserl. Yet Simmel had a profound impact on early American sociology, with six publications in the American *Journal of Sociology* by 1906. Titanic figures in the Chicago School like Robert Park, Ernest Burgess, Everett Hughes, and Louis Wirth learned at the feet of Simmel (Bulmer 1984).

In further contrast to Durkheim, Simmel was more or less preoccupied with the limits of scientific empiricism, but *advocated* for the role of abstract, theoretical, and metaphysical knowledge (Simmel 1971). Although positive knowledge can neither answer nor discard certain ontological questions—such as the absolute origin of things—to Simmel, these questions remained relevant to scientific inquiry. "If the history of the sciences really does reveal that the philosophical mode of cognition is the primitive mode," Simmel observed, "then this provisional procedure is nevertheless *indispensable* when confronted with certain questions . . . namely those questions . . . that we have so far been unable either to answer or dismiss" (Simmel 1978:53).[2] According to Simmel, "even the empirical in its perfected state might no more replace philosophy as an interpretation...than would the perfection of mechanical reproduction of phenomena make the visual arts superfluous" (Simmel 1978:53).

In other words, to Simmel's mind, abstract inquiry is useful because it provides insight into the meaning of phenomena that cannot be captured through empirical measurement: it is as useful as *even the most perfect* statistical analysis. This led Simmel to advocate an interpretive framework for understanding social phenomena (Simmel 1978:54).

Thus, the early Chicago School sociologists were more pragmatists than positivists, and favored observational fieldwork and interpretive methods. Robert Park and Ernest Burgess ([1925] 1984), W. I. Thomas and Florian Znaniecki

(1918–1920), and scores of other sociologists sought empirical validation in examination of the real, lived social world (Bulmer 1984). After the arrival of William F. Ogburn, scholars like Burgess became more interested in ideas and techniques embodied in statistics (Bulmer 1981:315). Simmel's influence on sociological theory and methods foreshadows an interdisciplinary period of collaboration across the qualitative-quantitative line, which will be disrupted due to a series of historical developments.

Geertz

Nearly everyone who identifies as a practicing ethnographer, in either academic or professional circles, encounters Geertz. His work is usually where the conversation on ethnography begins. In evolutionary parlance, Geertz is a pivotal, keystone organism, like the *archaeopteryx*, that reoriented the evolutionary trajectory of his species.

The best route to understanding Geertz's perspective, for our purposes, is through his rejection of Lévi-Strauss's ([1949] 1969) structural anthropology. Lévi-Strauss, like Radcliffe-Brown, drew inspiration from Durkheim as well as Ferdinand de Saussure (himself an admirer of Durkheim) (Lévi-Strauss [1949] 1969, [1979] 1995). Lévi-Strauss believed that human characteristics are ultimately the same everywhere, because the both "primitive" and "civilized" societies are based on universal structures, transcending individual experience. Using de Saussure's ([1965] 1986) formal semiotics and their binary conception of meaning, Lévi-Strauss sought universal structures in things like myth and ritual (Lévi-Strauss [1979] 1995). Like Radcliffe-Brown, Lévi-Strauss ([1949] 1969) came to see the formal identification of irreducible social structures as the heart of anthropology.

This point of view frustrated Geertz (1973a, 1973c) for two reasons: first, anthropology had been telling more or less the same story since the days of Durkheim; second, structural anthropology had evolved into a kind of "fastidious Mandarinism," obsessed with *sui generis* structures at the expense of understanding individual, "lived" experience (Geertz 2000:75). So, in place of Durkheim, Geertz drew insights from Edmund Husserl (1999), transmitted through the work of Alfred Schütz ([1962] 1982) and Ludwig Wittgenstein ([1953] 2009).

Husserl (1999) argued that experience envelops and explains reality, placing him squarely at odds with Lévi-Strauss (Geertz 1973c:356). He contended that every individual apprehends meaning from the perspective of their own reality (Husserl 1999:33–4). Communication between one reality and another thereby requires a confluence of shared signs and gestures, but the process is always indeterminate.

Writing about Husserl's student, Schütz ([1962] 1982), Geertz observed that "common sense" is really the individual's informal grasp of socially constructed reality. "The world of everyday life" is itself "a cultural product, for it is framed in terms of the symbolic conceptions of 'stubborn fact' handed down from generation to generation. . . . Like Mt. Everest, it is just there" (Geertz 1973a:111). Yet the terms in which individuals apprehend "common sense"—though pivotally important to Geertz—are invisible to the structuralist perspective.

Wittgenstein (2009), moreover, conceived of language as an interdependent, socially constructed web of reference reinforced through usage, in stark contrast to Saussure's formal conception of signs and signifiers. As a cultural product, language is less an act of comprehension than it is acquired through games circumscribed by the rules of grammar, conferring meaning upon words in terms of their association with everyday life (Wittgenstein 2009).

For Geertz, Wittgenstein's "attack" upon Saussure's formal conception of signs and signifiers "brought thought out of its grotto in the head into the public square where one could look at it" (Geertz 2000:xii). He regarded Wittgenstein's work as almost "custom designed" to enable his brand of ethnography (Geertz 2000:xii). Geertz thereby formulated the object of anthropological inquiry as a "historically transmitted pattern of meanings embodied in symbols, a system of inherited conceptions expressed in symbolic forms by means of which men communicate, perpetuate, and develop their knowledge about and attitudes toward life" (Geertz 1973a:89). In other words, culture is not *sui generis,* but inseparably bound to context, place, and even the life of the subject itself.

Consider the position of ethnography: Geertz suggested our data are the "means by which people communicate, perpetuate, and develop . . . knowledge about and attitudes toward life" (1973a:89). We translate and interpret, but, if we believe Wittgenstein, as Geertz certainly did, the subjective structures that facilitate translation are "slippery" enough to ensure *something* is going to get lost (Geertz 2000:xii).

Geertz believed in the interpretive and narrative virtuosity of the observer, but he didn't claim it somehow transcends the phenomenological problem of meaning. The "thickest" description, as Geertz put it, still "strains to read over the shoulder" of the subject (Geertz 1973b:452). Interpretive data is, therefore, subject to the same conditionality as quantitative data. Data is always *convention,* an act of abstraction: in this case, from the metaphysical rather than the positive. "All ethnography is part philosophy," Geertz wrote, "and a good deal of the rest is confession" (Geertz 1973c:346).

Thus, a closer reading of Geertz undercuts the idea that modern ethnographic methods make a superior claim to "truth" than quantitative methods. Geertz identifies the contribution of "thick description" as sensitivity to a "symbolic" reality not easily captured or understood in the formal qualitative empiricism favored by his forebears.

Taking the conclusions of the previous sections together, it becomes clear that—in their original formulations—neither quantitative nor qualitative social science makes any claim to either "superiority" or "objectivity." Qualitative research concerns itself with understanding and decoding *subjective*, phenomenological (symbolic, mental, gestural) content because it regards these as the structure of social order. Quantitative research conscientiously limits itself to what is objectively (tangibly, materially) measurable, because it cannot confidently treat "subjective" content. The difference is in the type of method demanded by the unit of analysis, more than it is a commitment to one epistemological system over another. The next section reconstructs the historical events that shaped the contemporary schism between qualitative and quantitative methods.

SELECTION & ADAPTATION

The Character Education Movement & Quantitative Sociology

Sociologists published a variety of influential urban ethnographies after World War I, such as *The City* (Park and Burgess [1925] 1984) and *The Polish Peasant in Europe and America* (Thomas and Znaniecki 1918–1920), a highly anticipated, $50,000 research project that sold in excess of 1,500 copies in its first press (Bulmer 1984). William F. Ogburn's arrival at Chicago led sociologists to experiment with quantitative statistical techniques and survey research (Bulmer 1981). During this period, W. I. Thomas ([1933] 1951) and others began making contributions to the field of "Culture and Personality."

Founded on the research design of Lawrence Frank (1948), the study of culture and personality linked the behavioral sequences of early childhood with the psychological dynamics inherent in culturally sanctioned norms and behavior (Sapir [1938] 1956). Thomas worked alongside Frank's students such as Edward Sapir (1934), Ruth Benedict (1934), John Dollard (1936), Margaret Mead (1946, 1951b, 1952), and others (Bateson [1942] 1956, [1942] 1972). These scholars took anthropological and psychological data, such as informant autobiographies, life histories, and artistic products, and combined them with statistical analysis of Rorschach or Thematic Apperception Tests to analyze human culture into a system relating early childhood to psychosocial dynamics (Henry 1947). In other words, the prevalent method of feeding or toilet training children in a given society would be related to the way adults interact or respond to ideas and events.

This interdisciplinary episode created some of the first qualitative marketing research techniques. Sidney Levy (2003) characterized this as a "second" Chicago School that contributed new concepts such as cognitive dissonance, diffusion, and social influence, coupled with qualitative market research techniques such as oral histories and group interviews, later known as "focus groups" (Levy 2003:101).

On the East coast, Paul Lazarsfeld conducted the first scientific survey of radio listeners in 1930 and 1931, just two years after he first came to the United States. Five years later, Lazarsfeld joined the sociology faculty at Columbia, where he founded a school of quantitative social research. In 1948, Lazarsfeld produced a landmark study on the effect of the mass media on social control, shifting cultural trends, and complex social organization (Lazarsfeld and Merton [1948] 1957).

Throughout this period, competition over scant financial resources pushed social scientists of the era to shore up their standing in the academic universe, which meant going to great lengths to present themselves as a rational, morally neutral "objective science" (Camic 1986). Concurrently, the American "Character Education Movement" funded a watershed of "moral character studies" with civic, religious, and government support. The goal was to instill loyalty, patriotism, and obedience—"good character"—in young people. They even funded "academic" research, which implicated the type of social science research favored by the Culture and Personality School in an evaluative discourse on virtue (Camic 1986). Moreover, by the late 1940s, McCarthyist hostility towards Freudian psychological methods raised unhealthy suspicions about mixed-method qualitative research (Mead 1954). The political climate, coupled with the dangerous association between social psychology and popular pseudoscience, forced sociologists to choose between an aggressively rational, value-neutral scientific framework for research and political, even financial, disaster.

This tension crept into academic circles, where it sparked contention between "the advocates of measurement and those committed to the prewar (World War II) emphasis upon qualitative methods and field research methodologies, with the latter resisting the incoming proponents of quantitative methods," not least of which between Lazarsfeld and his colleague Merton (Levy 2003:104). Levy cited a comment by David Riesman, who recalled grad students routinely translated "acidulous comments by faculty members into actual prescriptions of what would pass muster," leading to a generation of students who "feared to write a dissertation without tables in it" (Levy 2003:105). It was within the interest of social scientists to embrace hard-nosed quantitative methods to earn recognition as "*scientific*" discipline relative to others. The qualitative marketing research techniques developed in the Culture and

Personality School became displaced to for-profit consulting organizations like Social Research, Inc. (Levy 2003).

Thus, emerging from a period of interdisciplinary collaboration across methodological lines, American sociology faced a direct threat to its survival. It adapted, but at the cost of deep divisions between quantitative and qualitative social scientists that persist to this day. In fact, more than 50 years later, Levy's recounted this note from a graduate student enrolled in his qualitative research workshop at Chicago:

> Why do we have to constantly justify the use of certain techniques . . . why are we ashamed to be purely qualitative, just as we are not ashamed to be purely quantitative? . . . I am constantly grappling with this . . . and would like to find a way of dealing with this issue, so that we can have other ways of collecting, analyzing, and presenting data (Levy 2003:105).

The National Character Movement & Ethnographic Practice

Meanwhile, a parallel set of historical circumstances led anthropologists to cast aside quantitative methods in favor of strict adherence to qualitative methods. It began with the buildup to World War II, when the US military sought to better understand how enemies, allies, and the public would respond to military operations and psychological warfare and recruited the Culture and Personality School into the war effort (Mead 1951a).

Ruth Benedict, Margaret Mead, and their colleagues soon went to work for the Office of Strategic Services (OSS) and the Office of War Information on "national character studies" (Mead and Metraux 1953; Office of Strategic Services Assessment Staff 1948). "National Character" was an applied science, analogous to our own industry-driven ethnographic practice (Gorer 1953). They would gather data on a given country, draw conclusions about patterns of early childhood experience, and let psychoanalytic theories of character fill in the rest (Bateson [1942] 1972; Gorer 1953). National Character borrowed the Culture and Personality School techniques, but aimed for "ideal types" that could inform predictions about the behavior of national groups, rather than reconstruct specific processes of social adaptation.[3]

Researchers had no access to their subjects, just fragments such as art, literature, and radio broadcasts (Mead and Metraux 1953). Simply working out what childhood experiences would generally be in a given culture was itself an obstacle to researchers. Nevertheless, this work was incredibly influential. Benedict's (1946) and Gorer's ([1943] 1956) work on Japanese national character served as the foundation for wartime intelligence efforts, as did Gorer's (1953; Gorer and Rickman 1950) work on Russia. Bateson and Mead (1941) engineered the morale-building campaign which imagined the Allied troops with their "backs against the wall," having determined that the American public would approve more aggressive troop commitments in response to cognitively dissonant military asymmetry (Bateson [1942] 1972; Gorer 1953; Mead 1948, 1951c).

Nevertheless, National Character came crashing down after World War II. The memory of Nazism made the academy very uneasy with its blatant, essentialist determinism (Mead 1952, 1954). Some interpreted the emphasis on childhood as a racist attempt to "blame" nations for innate, unalterable traits (Dallin 1949; Wolfe 1951). Furthermore, McCarthyists were eager to portray everyday Russians as psychologically identical to everyday Americans, so they attacked Mead and Gorer, specifically their mixed psychometric and psychoanalytic methods, discrediting them as "racist diaperologists" (Dallin 1949). Even the qualitative researchers at Social Research Inc. could not escape the confused ideological wrath of McCarthyism and social critics who found the notion of studying consumers offensive and characterized their work as "work of the devil or as a Freudian aberration" (Levy 2003:104).

The next generation of anthropologists sought to distance themselves from National Character, just as a young Clifford Geertz began his career. Geertz nodded to anthropology as a "science" in his early work (Geertz 1957), but rejected it about 15 years later in favor of "thick description," participant observation, and the "lived" experience of the subject as both the means and the object of ethnographic study (Geertz 1973a, 1973b). Even in private industry, the interdisciplinary research borne out of Culture and Personality and National Character schools by Social Research Inc. continued on as qualitative research (Levy 2003).

JUPITER & BEYOND THE INFINITE

The principal aim of this chapter has to been to demonstrate that the modern opposition between qualitative and quantitative research has less to do with actual methodology and more to do with the selective forces of history. Thus, the evolutionary origins of the qualitative-quantitative divide are now laid bare for consideration. A "ruthless" interrogation of the epistemological origins of both qualitative and quantitative social science—*in the words of their very architects,* no less—does not reveal strong philosophical grounding for the widespread contention between qualitative and quantitative methods. There were, on the other hand, a series of historical events that drove qualitative and quantitative social science apart, culminating in the current divide, which insists on an "either/or" or "one-validating-the-other" perspective as an epistemological necessity.

But, if we discard the current paradigm in favor of the perspective that methods are determined by the unit of analysis, more than a commitment to one epistemological system over another, we open ourselves to new trajectories for advancing the collection, analysis, and presentation of data. This section discusses three principles of empirical research intended to advance research practice.

First, both qualitative and quantitative methods determine what is *generally* true about a population by analyzing a "sample." For statisticians, these are a series of observations, *objects* of cultural, social, or environmental production that can be positively accounted for (i.e., measured). Researchers want to understand and predict what is true "on average," subject to a series of enumerated, measurable conditions. Polling predictions are only true, for example, *within a specified standard error.* These specified "errors" let us compare, refine, and discuss generalizations about society.

Ethnographers seek *subjective* structures: the implicit assumptions shared between individuals in a population that allow them to correctly interpret and respond to social gestures, symbols which are never articulated but mutually understood. These "imponderabilia" are the object of qualitative research because they are normatively transmitted, telling researchers something about how society *teaches,* or even *expects,* a given population to think.

Second, both methods are limited by the "scale" of the sample. Conventional statistical analyses require a sample size of $x \geq 35$ to assume that the sampling distribution of probability approximates a normal curve (Allison 1999). The larger the number of observations, the lower the standard error on predicted values of x. Thus, quantitative methods tend to require a larger scale of observations to make reliable inferences. This also limits quantitative inferences to that which can be measured, and what is true "on average," as opposed to in the individual case.

The typical ethnographic study, on the other hand, requires in-depth conversations with subjects, participant observation, and the preparation of field notes and observations. This mode of research benefits from intensive observation of a small number of subjects, who cultivate trust with researchers, thereby permitting access to the inner reaches of their mental life. This does not scale well, and expanding the number of subjects involved reduces the available memory and attention of the individual researcher, resulting in poor data based on cursory, and therefore superficial, interactions with subjects.

Third, the intersection of these two principles encourages the formation of *hybrid "statistico-ethnographic"* methods, driving methodological innovation in two ways. First, a *hybrid* method might be anything that expands the scale of qualitative inference to the level of an entire population, or enables quantitative models to produce valid, precise generalizations about a mere handful of individuals. These can be loosely summarized in Figure 6.1.

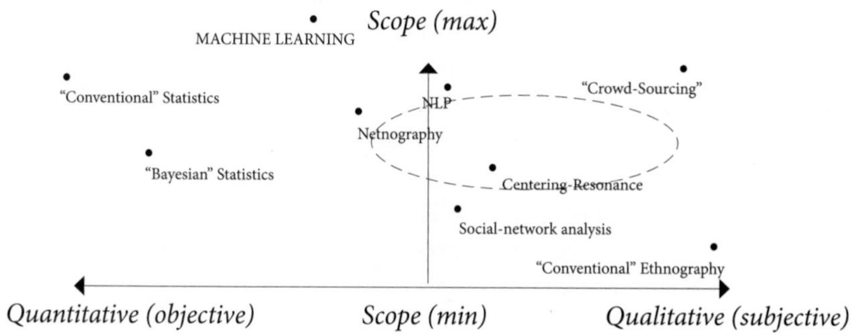

Note: The labels "Objective and "Subjective" describe units of analysis: *objective* refers to material constructs that can be measured; *subjective* refers to mental, gestural, or symbolic constructs that must be interpreted.

Figure 6.1. Hybrid qual-quant methods.

Second, individuals express their subjectivity by producing objective cultural forms, to the extent that these forms can be measured, they can be quantified. Meanwhile, the unexplained remnants of predictive models, the "outliers" and "residual" cases, point ethnographic researchers to individuals whose deviation from what is *generally* true about a cultural population may be instructive.

This formal elaboration is useful for two reasons. First, it is a *heuristic* of discovery that encourages further exploration in the field of hybrid research methods along these various axes (Abbott and Alexander 2004). Anything social scientists can do to make "Conventional Statistics" move to the lower right—such that quantitative models generalize at finer levels of observation, or help to quantify what would normally be subjective elements of mental life—is a breakthrough. Similarly, anything that moves "Conventional Ethnography" toward the upper left, thereby increasing the scale of rich qualitative observation, should be considered innovation.

Second, formal elaboration allows us to distinguish between legitimate hybrid methods—those that remain true to the underlying epistemological assumptions of qualitative and quantitative research—and those that *do not.* For instance, more than a few firms understand "hybrid methods" as ethnographic research served up to clients alongside survey analysis. This is often done for cosmetic rather than empirical reasons: it is an attempt to "dress up" ethnographic research as rigorous and comprehensive by associating it with survey results.

Unfortunately, this commonly results in serious violations of empirical logic. For instance, when two survey results lead to contradictory conclusions, they are either eliminated or, more commonly, linguistically strung together in a single narrative interpretation of the results. Collected text data are "cherry-picked" and pruned to corroborate the explanation. The problem, of course, is that survey respondents don't answer questions as a *group;* they treat each survey item individually. But text data offers a veneer of spoken truth, creating the illusion that the context of the response does not change from question to question.

Conversely, results of ethnographic studies are often presented in terms of survey results: 5 percent of subjects believed "x," while 15 percent believed "y." In a study limited to 15 or 20 people, presenting results in this way not only belies the object of ethnographic study—which is not objective measurement, but *subjective* investigation—but leads to absurd conclusions. It is a strange argument, indeed, that suggests 20 percent of a 20-person sample, or *four people,* have *anything at all* to say that is statistically representative of an entire population! Yet this sort of tendency is very common, even in presentations from researchers at the highest echelons of Fortune 500 companies.

"Statistico-Ethnography"?

We conclude with brief examples of how social scientists are advancing research methods along the trajectory defined in this chapter. The term "statistico-ethnography" is offered both as provocation and to describe methods that abjure the quantitative-qualitative divide in favor of deploying appropriate methodological means to gain the most insight from each unit of analysis.

One of the earliest instances of this is "netnography." Whereas previous ethnographic studies have devoted attention to behavior within and among virtual information networks (Knorr-Cetina and Bruegger 2002), netnography is a branch of ethnography that uses the internet to extend the scope of the usual 30-person ethnographic field study to virtual societies made up of millions of individual users.

Although "netnography" refers to a specific group of scholars concerned with the symbolic, cultural, social, and commercial structures that emerge on the internet (Jones 1995; Kozinets 1998; Rheingold 1993), the practice of mining web traffic for consumer analytics has become so common that mere attention to online data no longer distinguishes netnography. However, early netnography painted a rich picture, not only of the internal dynamics governing listservs, newsgroups, websites, chat forums, and massively multiplayer online role-playing games (MMORPGs),[4] but of the implicitly shared rules, symbols, and gestures that govern them, coupled with statistical analysis of recurrent behaviors and trends (Rheingold 1993).

Indeed, the rapid diffusion of data-mining as a means of apprehending consumer trends created a glut of new data, creating unique opportunities for social scientists developing new, computational methods of analysis. Machine learning refers to a range of methods for processing streams of data into discrete signals that may further trigger a desired behavior. For example, while a social network insight captures comments, preferences, and tastes, a machine-learning algorithm determines how these fit together into subjects, whether they are positive or negative, and how to predict individual preferences on the basis what has been learned.

Applied to social science, researchers can expand the scale of their qualitative insights from pages of field notes to the infinite utterances of online communities (Stone et al. 1996). In addition to being able to classify and categorize text data at a scale impossible to achieve with human researchers, machine learning overcomes the inherent cognitive limitations of the human brain. Computers process an entire body of text or "corpus" instantaneously. Human beings, on the other hand, must read each page individually, then recall it, and place it in context, inviting the inevitable consequences of memory, fatigue, and cognitive load. Subject matter on one page may "prime" reception of the next; disposition toward a given idea may cause it to "jump out" to the researcher. This is undesirable if researchers are at all concerned with ruling out their own bias in their interpretation of qualitative results.

Indeed, Yahoo! researcher Bo Pang (Pang et al. 2002) determined that human subjects were about 60 percent accurate when classifying the sentiment of movie reviews, while an algorithm achieved 70 percent using the corpus' most statistically prominent words. There are many variations of machine learning, including supervised or unsupervised text clustering (Seo and Sycara 2004), or centering resonance analysis, or CRA (Corman et al. 2002). CRA ranks influential word pairings, using the influence of one word to predict the influence of another. Researchers use these prevalent semantic structures to reconstruct themes, revealing implicit symbolic relationships. This sort of linguistic analysis transcends the logistical limits of verbal transcription and enables detailed interpretation of linguistic exchanges that occur freely at massive scale.

But there are limits to machine learning. Datasets must be substantial, numbering in the tens to hundreds of thousands of observations (Pang and Lee 2008). The baseline accuracy of sentiment analysis can also vary substantially depending on the type of data, as much as 15 percent across the dataset (Pang and Lee 2008).

There are also methods that attach precise, quantitative metrics to the dynamics of small-scale social order. Social network analysis (Wasserman and Faust 1994) lets researchers analyze and quantify social structure as an outcome of the limitless informal interdependencies we might uncover through qualitative fieldwork, or test hypotheses about where subjects fit into social order

(Hanneman and Riddle 2005). Measurement and prediction of institutional phenomena—status, mimetic tendencies, even the contagion of ideas—are possible through the medium of social network analysis (Centola and Macy 2007). Computational demands have historically limited social network analysis to small-scale datasets, though the introduction of larger datasets through online social networking and advances in cloud-computing technology are making large-scale social network analysis possible (Mislove et al. 2007).

Finally, not all statistical models imagine probability in the same way. Consider a multivariate regression model. Its inferences are based on the assumption that our observed data, if we collected it over and over again *ad infinitum*, would behave in a somewhat predictable way, and base our inferences on that. To be sure, we can quantify the extent to which all of this is true, which allows us to refine our regression models and make comparisons (Allison 1999).

But this mediation between the actual data and our inferences chafes ethnographers who favor a "deep" engagement with the observed data, leading to criticism. However, Bayesian statistics do not require these sorts of assumptions.[5] Bayes' theorem dictates that, since we are uncertain about the true value of some parameter—some data point we would like to draw inferences from—we will consider it random, and any statement about that data point is *subjective* until we gather more data, and revise our beliefs. This means "the inference is based on the actual occurring data, not all possible data sets that might have occurred but didn't!" (Bolstad 2007:7). Thus in the framework offered here, Bayesian statistics are a noteworthy "advance" because they transcend the larger scale required by "frequentist" statistical methods.[6] I could, for example, make a series of Bayesian predictions about the preferences and choices of a small, previously interviewed subject population to test some of the hypotheses developed from my interpretation of field data (Gill 2002).

Epilogue

The illustrations here are simplified examples of qual and quant working together. In closing, I put the question to you, the reader: what does the future look like? I think the answer only begins with this chapter: I don't know where it ends. So I close where I began, with the words of Karl Marx:

> It will transpire that the world has long been dreaming of something that it can acquire if only it becomes conscious of it. It will transpire that it is not a matter of drawing a great dividing line between past and future, but of carrying out the thoughts of the past. And finally, it will transpire that mankind begins no *new work*, but consciously accomplishes its old work (Marx 1972).

REFERENCES

Abbott, Andrew, and Jeffrey Alexander. 2004. *Methods of Discovery: Heuristics for the Social Sciences.* New York: W. W. Norton & Company.

Allison, Paul D. 1999. *Multiple Regression: A Primer.* Thousand Oaks, CA: Pine Forge Press.

Anderson, Paul F. 1983. "Marketing, Scientific Progress, and Scientific Method." *Journal of Marketing* 47:18–31.

_____. 1986. "On Method in Consumer Research: A Critical Relativist Perspective." *Journal of Consumer Research* 13:155–73.

Bateson, Gregory. (1942) 1972. "Morale and National Character." In *Steps to an Ecology of Mind,* edited by Gregory Bateson, 88–106. New York: Ballantine Books.

_____. (1942) 1956. "Some Systematic Approaches to the Study of Culture and Personality." In *Personal Character and Cultural Milieu,* edited by Douglas Haring, 131–8. Syracuse, NY: Syracuse University Press.

Benedict, Ruth. 1934. *Patterns of Culture.* Boston: Houghton Mifflin Co.

_____. 1946. *The Chrysanthemum and the Sword: Patterns of Japanese Culture.* Boston: Houghton Mifflin Co.

Boehm, Matthew. 2009. Post to Anthrodesign mailing list, February 18, 2009. http://groups.yahoo.com/neo/groups/anthrodesign/conversations/messages/7179 (accessed January 2, 2014).

Bulmer, Martin. 1981. "Quantification and Chicago Social Science in the 1920s: A Neglected Tradition." *Journal of the History of the Behavioral Sciences* 17:312–31.

_____. 1984. *The Chicago School of Sociology.* Chicago, IL: The University of Chicago Press.

Camic, Charles. 1986. "The Matter of Habit." *American Journal of Sociology* 91:1039–87.

Centola, Damon, and Michael Macy. 2007. "Complex Contagions and the Weakness of Long Ties." *American Journal of Sociology* 113:702–34.

Comte, August. 1975. *August Comte and Positivism.* Edited by Gertrud Lenzer. New York: Harper & Row.

Corman, Steven R., Timothy Kuhn, Robert D. McPhee, and Kevin J. Dooley. 2002. "Studying Complex Discursive Systems: Centering Resonance Analysis of Organizational Communication." *Human Communication Research* 28:157–206.

Dallin, David J. 1949. "Exterminate the Russians?" *New Leader.* October 29:2.

Dandavante, Uday. 2009. Post to Anthrodesign mailing list, February 18, 2009. http://groups.yahoo.com/neo/groups/anthrodesign/conversations/messages/7178 (accessed January 2, 2014).

De Saussure, Ferdinand. (1965) 1986. *Course in General Linguisitics.* Lima, Peru: Open Court Publishing.

Dollard, John. 1936. *Criteria for the Life History.* New Haven, CT: Yale University Press.

Durkheim, Emile. (1897) 1951. *Suicide.* Translated by John A. Spaulding and George Simpson. New York: Free Press.

_____. 1982. *Rules of the Sociological Method.* Edited by Steven Lukes. New York: Free Press.

_____. 1984. *The Division of Labor in Society.* Translated by Lewis A. Coser. New York: Free Press.

Frank, Lawrence. 1948. *Society as Patient.* New Brunswick, NJ: Rutgers University Press.

Geertz, Clifford. 1957. "Ritual and Social Change: A Javanese Example." *American Anthropologist* 59:32–54.

_____. 1973a. "Religion as a Cultural System." In *The Interpretation of Cultures,* edited by Clifford Geertz, 87–125. New York: Basic Books.

_____. 1973b. "Deep Play: Notes on the Balinese Cockfight." In *The Interpretation of Cultures,* edited by Clifford Geertz, 412–54. New York: Basic Books.

_____. 1973c. "The Cerebral Savage: On the Work of Claude Lévi-Strauss." In T*he Interpretation of Cultures,* edited by Clifford Geertz, 345–61. New York: Basic Books.

Geertz, Clifford. 2000. *Available Light: Anthropological Reflections.* Princeton, NJ: Princeton University Press.

Gill, Jeff. 2002. *Bayesian Methods: A Social and Behavioral Sciences Approach.* Boca Raton, FL: Chapman& Hall/CRC Press LLC.

Gorer, Geoffrey. (1943) 1956. Comment on Japanese Personal Character. In *Personal Character and Cultural Milieu,* edited by Douglas Haring, 405–23. Syracuse, NY: Syracuse University Press.

_____. 1953. National Character: Theory and Practice. In *The Study of Culture at a Distance,* edited by Margaret Mead and Rhoda Metraux, 57–84. Chicago, IL: University of Chicago Press.

_____. (1953) 1956. Japanese National Character. In *Personal Character and Cultural Milieu,* edited by Douglas Haring, 424–37. Syracuse, NY: Syracuse University Press.

Gorer, Geoffrey, and John Rickman. 1950. *The People of Great Russia.* New York: Chanticleer Press.

Hamel, G., and C. K. Prahalad. 1994. *Competing for the Future.* Boston: Harvard Business School Press.

Hanneman, Robert, and Mark Riddle. 2005. "Introduction to Social Network Methods." http://faculty.ucr.edu/~hanneman/nettext/.

Henry, William E. 1947. "The Thematic Apperception Technique in the Study of Culture Personality Relations." *Genetic Psychology Monographs* 35:3–135. http://www.ccs.neu.edu/home/amislove/publications/SocialNetworks-IMC.pdf.

Hunt, Shelby D. 1990. "Truth in Marketing Theory and Research." *Journal of Marketing* 54:1–15.

Husserl, Edmund. 1999. *The Essential Husserl: Basic Writings in Transcendental Phenomenology.* Edited by Donn Welton. Bloomington, IN: Indiana University Press.

Jones, Stephen G. 1995. "Understanding Community in the Information Age." In *Cybersociety: Computer-mediated Communication and Community,* edited by Stephen G. Jones, 10–35. Thousand Oaks, CA: Sage.

Kardiner, Abram. 1945. *The Psychological Frontiers of Society.* New York: Columbia University Press.

_____. (1945) 1956. "The Concept of Basic Personality Structure as an Operational Tool in the Social Sciences." In *Personal Character and Cultural Milieu,* edited by Douglas Haring, 469–82. Syracuse, NY: Syracuse University Press. Originally published in *The Science of Man in the World Crisis,* edited by Ralph Linton. New York: Columbia University Press.

Knorr-Cetina, Karin D., and Urs Bruegger. 2002. "Global Microstructures: The Virtual Societies of Financial Markets." *American Journal of Sociology* 107(4):905–50.

Kozinets, Robert V. 1998. "On Netnography: Initial Reflections on Consumer Research Investigations of Cyberculture." *Advances in Consumer Research* 25:366–71.

Kuhn, Thomas S. 1962. *The Structure of Scientific Revolutions.* Chicago, IL: University of Chicago Press.

Lazarsfeld, Paul F., and Robert K. Merton. (1948) 1957. "Mass Communication, Popular Taste, and Organized Social Action." In *The Communication of Ideas,* edited by Lyman Bryson, 95–118. New York: Harper.

Levine, Donald N. 1995. *Visions of the Sociological Tradition.* Chicago, IL: University of Chicago Press.

Lévi-Strauss, Claude. (1949) 1969. *Elementary Structures of Kinship.* Boston: Beacon Press.

_____. (1979) 1995. *Myth and Meaning: Cracking the Code of Culture.* New York: Schocken Books.

Levy, Sidney. 2003. "Roots of Marketing and Consumer Research at the University of Chicago." *Consumption, Markets and Culture* 6: 99–110.

Lovecraft, Howard P. (1920) 1999. "Facts Concerning the Late Arthur Jermyn and His Family." In *The Call of Cthulhu and Other Weird Stories,* edited by S. T. Joshi, 14-23. New York: Penguin Books.

Malinowski, Bronislaw. (1922) 1978. *Argonauts of The Western Pacific.* Oxon, UK: Routledge.

Marx, Karl. "Letter to Ruge." In *The Marx-Engels Reader,* translated by Ronald Rogowski and edited by Robert Tucker, 7–10. New York: Norton.

Marx, Karl, and Friederich Engels. 1978. *The Marx-Engels Reader.* Edited by Robert C. Tucker. New York. W. W. Norton.

McGrayne, Sharon Bertsch. 2011. *The Theory That Would Not Die: How Bayes' Rule Cracked the Enigma Code, Hunted Down Russian Submarines, and Emerged Triumphant from Two Centuries of Controversy.* New Haven, CT: Yale University Press.

Mead, Margaret. 1946. "Personality: Cultural Approach To." In *Encyclopedia of Psychology,* edited by Philip Lawrence Harrimon, 477–87. New York: Philosophical Library.

_____. 1948. "A Case History in Cross-National Communications." In *The Communication of Ideas,* edited by Lyman Bryson, 209–29. New York: Harper.

_____. 1951a. "The Study of National Character." In *The Policy Sciences: Recent Developments in Scope and Method,* edited by Daniel Lerner, 70–85. Stanford, CA: Stanford University Press.

_____. 1951b. "The Anthropologist and the Historian: Their Common Problems." *American Quarterly* Spring:3-13.

_____. 1951c. "What Makes Soviet Character?" *Natural History* LX:296+.

_____. 1952. "Social Anthropology and Its Relations to Psychiatry." In *Dynamic Psychiatry,* edited by Franz Alexander, 401–47. Chicago, IL: University of Chicago Press.

_____. 1953. "National Character." In *Anthropology Today: An Encyclopedic Inventory,* edited by A. L. Kroeber, 642–67. Chicago, IL: University of Chicago Press.

_____. 1954. "The Swaddling Hypothesis: Its Reception." *American Anthropologist* 56:338–47.

Mead, Margaret, and Rhoda Metraux, eds. 1953. *The Study of Culture at a Distance.* Chicago, IL: University of Chicago Press.

Mislove, Alan, Massimiliano Marcon, Krishna P. Gummadi, Peter Druschel, and Bobby Bhattacharjee. 2007. "Measurement and Analysis of Online Social Networks." *Proceedings of the 5th ACM/USENIX Conference on Internet Measurement,* 29–42.

Office of Strategic Services Assessment Staff. 1948. *The Assessment of Men: Selection of Personnel for the Office of Strategic Services.* New York: Rinehart.

Pang, Bo, and Lillian Lee. 2008. "Opinion Mining and Sentiment Analysis." *Foundations and Trends in Information Retrieval* 2:1–135.

Pang, Bo, Lillian Lee, and Shivakumar Vaithyanathan. 2002. "Thumbs up? Sentiment Classification Using Machine Learning Techniques." *Proceedings of the Conference on Empirical Methods in Natural Language Processing (EMNLP)* 1:79–86.

Park, Robert W., and Ernest Burgess. (1925) 1984. *The City: Suggestions for Investigation of Human Behavior in the Urban Environment.* Chicago, IL: The University of Chicago Press.

Radicliffe-Brown, A. R., and E. E. Evans-Pritchard. 1952. *Structure and Function in Primitive Society: Essays and Addresses.* New York: Free Press.

Rheingold, Howard. 1993. *The Virtual Community: Homesteading on the Electronic Frontier.* Reading, PA: Addison-Wesley.

Rosenberg, Jonathan. 2009. "From the Height of this Place." Post to Google Blog, February 16. http://googleblog.blogspot.com/2009/02/from-height-of-this-place.html.

Sapir, Edward. 1934. "Emergence of the Concept of Personality in the Study of Culture." *Journal of Social Psychology* 5:408–15.

_____. (1938) 1956. "Why Cultural Anthropology Needs the Psychiatrist." In *Personal Character and Cultural Milieu,* edited by Douglas Harding, 719–27. Syracuse, NY: Syracuse University Press.

Schütz , Alfred. (1962) 1982. *The Problem of Social Reality.* The Hague: Martinus Nijhoff Publishers.

Seo, Young-Woo, and Katia Sycara. 2004. "Text Clustering for Topic Detection." *Robotics Institute.* CMU-RI-TR-04-03. Pittsburgh, PA: Carnegie Mellon University.

Simmel, Georg. 1971. *On Individuality and Social Forms.* Edited by Donald N. Levine. Chicago, IL: University of Chicago Press.

_____. 1978. *The Philosophy of Money.* Translated by Tom Bottomore and David Frisby. London: Routledge & Kegan Paul.

Slater, Stanley F., and John C. Narver. 1998. "Customer-Led and Market-Oriented: Let's Not Confuse the Two." *Strategic Management Journal* 19:1001–6.

Slobin, Adrian, and Todd Cherkasky. 2010. "Ethnography in the Age of Analytics." *Ethnographic Praxis in Industry Conference Proceedings,* 188–98. Oxford, UK: Blackwell Publishing Ltd.

Stone, Philip J., and others. 1996. *General Inquirer: A Computer Approach to Content Analysis.* Boston: MIT Press.

Thomas, William Isaac. (1933) 1951. "Outline of a Program for the Study of Personality and Culture." In *Social Behavior and Personality: Contributions of W. I. Thomas to Theory and Social Research,* edited by Edmund Volkhart, 289–317. New York: Social Science Research Council.

Thomas, William Issac, and Florian Znaniecki. 1918–1920. *The Polish Peasant in Europe and America: Monograph of an Immigrant Group Vols. 1–4.* Boston: Gorham Press.

Wasserman, Stanley, and Katherine Faust. 1994. *Social Network Analysis: Methods and Applications.* New York: Cambridge University Press.

Wittgenstein, Ludwig. (1953) 2009. *Philosophical Investigations.* Translated by G. E. M. Anscombe, P. M. S. Hacker, and Joachim Schulte, edited by P. M. S. Hacker and Joachim Schulte. Malden, MA: Blackwell.

Wolfe, Robert. 1951. "The Swaddled Soul of the Great Russians." *New Leader.* January 29, pp. 15–18.

NOTES

This paper solely expresses the opinions and ideas of the author and does not in any way represent, or opine on, the views or opinions of, Google, Inc., Motorola Mobility, Inc. ("MMI") or Google/MMI personnel.

1 See H. P. Lovecraft, *Facts Concerning the Late Arthur Jeryman and His Family* ([1920] 1999).

2 When Simmel says, "this provisional procedure" in this quote, he means "philosophical or metaphysical abstraction." When he says "primitive," he means, "primary."

3 Kardiner (1945a, [1945b] 1956) came close to a causal explanation of character adaptation, but he was subsumed by Mead (1951b, 1953) and others (Gorer [1953] 1956), who wanted to emphasize the National Character School's attention to cultural particularity and flexibility of analysis.

4 "Massively-Multiplayer Online Role Playing Games" (MMORPGs), what Kozinet referred to as MUDs, or "Multi-User Dimensions" or "Dungeons" in his early work. MMORPGs are the more widespread, modern instantiation of MUDs.

5 For a witty introduction to Bayesian Theory, see McGrayne and Bertsch's (2011) recent book.

6 Bayesian statistics have been around for a very long time; they're just not as popular as "frequentist" techniques like multiple regression analysis or factor analysis, which are common in the market research toolkit.

Section II

BOUNDARIES BREACHED & BLURRED

INTRODUCTION

PATRICIA SUNDERLAND & RITA DENNY

The eight chapters in this section illuminate ways disciplinary and methodological boundaries are being breached and blurred at the intersection of anthropology and business. The lens authors use is focused slightly tighter than the large, broad view provided in Section I: Dynamics of Tension, Forces of Change, but still a bit broader than the case study focus provided in Section III: Plying the Trade. Among the anthropological interventions in business domains included here are four that fall more into the "organizational" side of things: Pant's discussion of management consulting among family-owned firms in Italy, Ensworth's chapter on informational technology at the global "Megabling Bank," Nafus' reflections on the social life of numbers at Intel, and Cefkin's overview and explication of work practice studies. Design is central in Kimbell's discussion of a public service initiative as it is in DiCarlo et al.'s chapter focused on a new curriculum at Philadelphia University. Alami's chapter provides an overview of anthropological approaches in the domain of health care in France; McCreery and Yamaki's describes the work of the anthropology of administration group at the National Museum of Ethnography in Osaka, Japan. These chapters bring to light some of the tensions and opportunities that arise in the doing of anthropology in business terrains as well as speak to anthropology's purpose and position today and what these might be in the future.

One of the most striking disciplinary boundaries that is breached and blurred in the course of anthropological incursions in business involves the purpose of anthropological research. As the chapters in this section make clear, anthropological interventions in business are just that: interventions. Anthropological research within business domains is often commissioned so that a status quo can be changed; a crucial *raison d'être* of the research is to make a difference. As Cefkin notes in her discussion of business' embrace of work practice studies, "Work practice studies intersect neatly with the paradigm of 'problem-solving,' a paradigm driving many efforts in business generally, including much that goes on in the name of innovation and development." Or,

---

Handbook of Anthropology in Business, edited by Rita Denny and Patricia Sunderland, 159–166.

as Ensworth characterized the work of her information technology consulting project once it was flowing, "accumulating insights and developing solutions." The consulting projects described in the chapters by Pant, Kimbell, and Alami also have effecting a change in current practices at their core.

The fact that research is carried out to effect change may seem like an obvious point given the "practicing," "applied," or "professional" status of the anthropology-in-business terrain, yet this intervention is a boundary breach that strikes at the heart of identity issues for the discipline of anthropology as well as individual anthropologists. To be a researcher—to conduct research—is central in what it means to be an anthropologist. As a discipline, core identity resides in the explication and elucidation of physical, material, and sociocultural phenomena, not in intervention. Moreover, in the United States from at least the 1970s until quite recently, with the exception of protection and advocacy for the less powerful, a stance toward active nonintervention reigned. To be an anthropologist has meant to do research for the sake of illumination. Without question, the process and analytic frameworks of research act upon and enact worlds, a point to which we will return, but the centrality of research in anthropological identity is a point worth pondering. It is helpful to read the chapters in this section with this core disciplinary and personal identity framework in mind and to consider ways the centrality of the research role fuels what are deemed to be contributions of the discipline.

The chapter by DiCarlo et al. is a case in point of viewing the benefits of anthropology in terms of research perspectives. Written in the form of a three-party conversation, the authors focus on the ways that anthropology has been incorporated into the core curriculum of the College of Design, Engineering, and Commerce at Philadelphia University. To incorporate the anthropological perspective, an ethnographic method course was created as one of the four fundamental core courses. As they point out, while not always taught by anthropologists, the course was developed in consultation with anthropologists, and method texts written by anthropologists are used. Moreover, in the discussion of why the anthropological perspective was deemed essential to incorporate into the common core curriculum, research experiences are consistently invoked as the means by which anthropological insight is built. The authors discuss the ways students learn and become critical observers by exploring examples in their own lives, as well as discuss how students learn inductive thinking and analysis techniques, pattern recognition, and to look at contexts as systems through the interpretation of ethnographic data. Fostering the ability to work in teams is also a goal of the curriculum, and collaborative ethnographic fieldwork "becomes the true team-building experience." Learning how to communicate interpretations, ideas, and conclusions in compelling ways from the ethnographic methods course is seen to help prepare students communicate ideas in general and thus to "negotiate any workplace landscape in the future." The point is that not only is research at the heart of what an anthropological perspective means, but that anthropological insight is located in the doing of ethnographic research.

In line with the centrality of research to anthropological identity, anthropologists in business realms are often called upon as experts in ethnographic methods and to act as trainers for others in ethnographic approaches. These expert abilities are also often a topic for discussion. When the Megabling Bank managing director queried Ensworth about how anthropology would factor into her work as consultant, she writes that her answer began, "for 20 years I had been applying ethnographic research concepts and methods to help build software and manage information systems." She also notes that an initial challenge of the research process conducted collaboratively with bank employees "was to train the task force in ethnographic concepts and methods." Cefkin opens her chapter with a vignette about giving tips to a computer scientist who was planning her first ethnographic investigation, and includes discussion of Blomberg et al.'s (1993) early and generative publication "Ethnographic Field Methods and Their Relation to Design," as well as other writings that are used to explain ethnographic methods and anthropological understanding to others in the corporation.

In the realm of business, the borders between the fields of anthropology and design are increasingly interwoven. This is seen not only in the curriculum that DiCarlo et al. describe, but in the foundation-sponsored effort to find new solutions for the provision of elder care in the United Kingdom, which Kimbell details in her chapter. Kimbell's design ethnography approach is one that thoughtfully and skillfully incorporates analytical perspectives, not only from design but also anthropology and sociology (see also Neese's discussion in Section IV). As Kimbell's chapter attests, design as a field is increasingly moving beyond the design of products to the design of services and realms of policy and, for some scholars, a form of social inquiry and a way of producing knowledge (Ehn et al. 2013; Kilbourn 2013; Otto and Smith 2013). There is also disciplinary interest in design as a process model for contemporary anthropological fieldwork (Faubion and Marcus 2009; Gatt and Ingold, 2013; Murphy and Marcus 2013; Rabinow et al. 2008).

The interweaving interests of anthropology and design create conundrums. If anthropology and the anthropological have been, at heart, about elucidating social worlds, design is about intervening in and introducing things into the world (Gunn and Donovan 2012; Otto and Smith 2013). As Murphy and Marcus (2013:259) have noted, design is embedded in a context of creating things that sell, whereas success in anthropological ethnography is emmeshed in standards and judgments for conducting ethical research. These differences can create tensions for anthropologists working in business realms. The discursive power of "design" is also resonant in business, where a priority is placed on problem-solving, action, and change; and resonant in the academy with respect to consumer-oriented practices (see Urban and Koh 2013). The "creativity" of design is a potent beacon in anthropology and business alike. Yet the central position of research in anthropological identity—to elucidate rather than to create—means that anthropological contributions risk being subsumed by the design process. Anthropology might be "used" only at the beginning of the process, with the insights at risk of being discarded when "the real" matters of designing products or solutions are under way (see Darrah and Dornadic in Section v; also see Murphy and Marcus 2013). The noninterventionist "researcher" stance may also propel anthropologists to be reticent and less than forceful in pushing forward their point of view.[1] As more activist orientations, including the embrace of design, develop in the discipline and in commercial arenas, the researcher-foremost anthropological identity may be significantly revised. Nonetheless, the implications of research identity at the heart of anthropology may need to be closely monitored if the anthropological aspects of a conjoined enterprise with design are to fully thrive.

The chapters in this section also illuminate how analytic categories are interrupted or breached by anthropologists working in business arenas. The process and analytic frameworks of research act upon and enact worlds. Many of the authors point out that one of the key contributions of anthropology in business worlds is moving beyond the individual-actor focus of other forms of research and explanation. For instance, Pant notes in terms of management consulting that anthropological approaches that consider not only the actors, but also the socioecological context, "produce a more coherent picture and a holistic management strategy." In Alami's review of anthropological inroads in the French healthcare industry, she calls out the opportunity that socio-anthropology affords for overcoming "the 'trap' of patient-centric approaches, which only consider the patient perspectives." She points to the importance of taking into account not only all of the actors involved, but also relevant representations, as well as the social context and power dynamics thereof. As she concludes: "Socio-anthropological studies in the health field make it possible to highlight material, social, and symbolic factors that direct, organize, and constrain individual behavior in health and illness while encompassing the action system in which medical action takes place." In a similar vein, Kimbell argues that an important value of the design ethnography approach in the arena of policy is not that it allows for a more human-centered perspective, as it is often argued, but rather that design ethnography's methods "reveal how public and collective issues exist as *assemblages of people, organizations, and things*." Her point is that design ethnography approaches are not "human-centered" but rather are a means to understand complex political, financial, social, and technological sociomaterial assemblages "at human scale." As she points out, the potential lies not only in helping find solutions to public issues, but also in reframing and reconstituting the issues themselves.

Nafus' chapter is a compelling demonstration of reframing and reconstituting issues. As does Kimbell, Nafus interrupts prevailing discourses that frame the problem to be solved. Drawing on insights regarding the reality of research performativity from both Callon (the performativity of market analyses) and Geertz (models *of* becoming models *for*), Nafus provides a contextual account of a new technology index she and colleagues developed at Intel. The new index not only helped Intel select promising markets for new technologies, but also simultaneously interrupted problematic intrusions of traditional framing in terms of development and "emerging" markets and their "readiness," a discursive framework that had been previously difficult to circumvent despite realizations of its problematic assumptions and predictive inaccuracies. Akin to Kimbell's chapter, what the chapter by Nafus also explicitly demonstrates is the way that anthropological analytic frameworks become combined, merged, and interwoven with other analytic frameworks in the doing of the work. In Nafus' work, the analytic engagement involves the quantitative world of numbers, a crucial context at Intel, as it is in industry and business more generally. Noting that numbers have social lives, with abilities to sustain as well as subvert practices, Nafus found a way to sustain numbers while subverting West-centric development discourse. As she perspicaciously put it: "We qualitative researchers may not like numbers as our preferred tools of the trade, but we do need to acknowledge them as things in the world, with their own social lives. In a world full of numbers, our encounter with the quantitative cannot be limited to raising epistemological objections to its assumptions."

The need to work with—not only around—other analytic frameworks is more implicit in the chapters by Ensworth, Pant, and Cefkin, but is clearly in play in these chapters too. For Pant, the quotidian assumptions and practices of management consulting are the point of entry. For Ensworth, it is project management. As Ensworth noted regarding her engagement, in the classification scheme of the bank's managing director who hired her, "I was a project manager specializing in business analysis, requirements engineering, and quality assurance for information systems at large global organizations." For Cefkin, work practice studies intercede in mechanistic perspectives that permeate business organization and operations while meshing with paradigms of "actionable findings" and "problem solving." Moreover, as these chapters and the chapters by Nafus and Kimbell also illustrate, the work and the research invariably involves not only engaging with these perspectives but also participation of others trained and immersed in these frameworks as part of the team, often as co-ethnographers. In that sense, anthropology in business entails an embrace of the paraethnographic in which the ontological and epistemological viewpoints of expert others are not simply inscribed as data, but incorporated analytically (Cefkin 2009; Holmes and Marcus 2006; Marcus 2012). One could also argue that by engaging in business milieus, anthropologists are embracing the role of anthropologists as diplomats, a metaphoric role that Latour (2013) has postulated is both apt and desirable for the field.

What is at stake here is whether anthropological engagements in business can play a positive role: positive for the field of anthropology and positive in terms of the issues many anthropologists hold dear. While Baba's warning (Section 1) that a decoupling of anthropology and ethnography in business risks dissolution of the anthropological voice remains quite real, chapters in this section also illustrate the potential promise of an anthropological voice when boundaries are breached and blurred. For Cefkin, an important aspect of work practice studies is that in addition to "actionable results," the studies produce rich, complex, uncertain stories. As she maintains, "work practice studies inevitably derive understandings that exceed the parameters of the study as initially framed." A crucial point of this is that the social and cultural insights derived in work practice studies' commitment to understanding the doing of work are a means to see not only "enduring business and market forms, but emerging ones as well." In essence, work practice studies not only hold the potential to contribute to business concerns, but also the explication of sociocultural dynamics central to anthropology as a discipline. As Cefkin argues, given the consequential, pervasive agency that businesses have in people's lives, this matters.

If the answer to the question of having a positive impact is an explicit affirmative in terms of the sociocultural research that anthropologists hold dear, the answer the authors provide in their chapters is also both explicitly and implicitly affirmative in terms of the humanistic and activist orientations discussed in Section 1. The chapter by Pant is a demonstration of these orientations in action. In his role as management consultant helping Italian family-run businesses remain viable amid daunting national and global economic challenges, he focuses on the value of "place-based branding," an emphasis supported by a hypothesis that "the source of competitiveness in the next economy, after the saturation and decline of the current industrial model, is going to be this 'quality of context' [which Pant defines as "quality of services and infrastructures, environmental health, safety, social tranquility, cultural vivacity, recreational facilities, and civic bonds"], not merely the quality of products." As he notes: "From a more critical postindustrial perspective, the 'old economy' may be identified with 'rubble' (pollution, waste, manmade debris, and industrial wastelands).... [I]t has no future unless it smartens itself up and prepares itself to respond to the fundamental ecological limits, social imperatives, and existential angst that challenge us today." The viability of these ideas in action is being tested in the *Terre di Cuore* campaign, a sustainability and place-branding project in which both businesses and business organizations are involved. As Pant maintains in his conclusion, should these local initiatives become multilocal, there is hope for both humanism and a way out of ecological crises.

If Pant's conclusion is one of humanism and hope, and Nafus' example shows that analytically and morally troubling discursive practices can be subverted, McCreery and Yamaki's chapter on the anthropology of business and administration in Japan in many ways serves as the classic anthropological reminder that ontological worlds are not shared. Their discussion is centered on the work of the anthropology of administration group at the National Museum of Ethnology, work which they point out involves an anthropology *of* business. McCreery and Yamaki's chapter reminds that critiques of business are embedded in traditions of analytic thought, traditions that are also socially and culturally embedded. As they note, in Japan, "the academic aversion to business, grounded both in aristocratic attitudes that see trade as demeaning and theories of class struggle in which the owners and workers are enemies, seem less pronounced that it is elsewhere." The examples they include regarding the ways religion and business are explicitly intertwined in Japanese business practice are also compelling, perhaps especially so for those unfamiliar with Japan. These include on-site shrines with "departments that see to the worship of the gods enshrined in them" as well as rituals from new employee purification to company funerals. The fact that in this scholarship anthropological fieldwork was informed by management theory as a starting point may not surprise, but that the analysis and insights of F. W. Taylor, seen as "the father of scientific management," and E. B. Tylor, "the father of modern anthropology," are deemed traceable to Quaker upbringing may give pause.

These realities, like the realities that unfold and the characters that come to life in other chapters in this section, are a reminder that both business and anthropological analyses are populated by people. They also remind that theories, like people, embody socioculturally, materially mediated thoughts, feelings, and agendas.

REFERENCES

Blomberg, Jeanette, Jean Giacomi, Andrea Mosher, and Pat Swenton-Wall. 1993. "Ethnographic Field Methods and Their Relation to Design." In *Participatory Design: Principles and Practices*, edited by D. Schuler and A. Namioka, 123–55. Hillsdale, NJ: Lawrence Erlbaum Associates.

Cefkin, Melissa, 2009. "Introduction: Business, Anthropology, and the Growth of Corporate Ethnography." In *Ethnography and the Corporate Encounter: Reflections on Research in and of Corporations*, edited by M. Cefkin, 1–37. New York: Berghahn.

Ehn, Pelle, Keith Murphy, Carl DiSalvo, Joan Greenbaum, and Maria Hellström Reimer. 2013. "(New) Public Goods: Design, Aesthetics and Politics." Presented at the Stephan Weiss Lecture Series, Parsons The New School for Design, October 3, New York, New York. http://justpublics365.commons.gc.cuny.edu/2013/10/02/new-public-goods-thursday-oct-3-new-school-930-1230/ (accessed January 7, 2014).

Faubion, James, and George E. Marcus, eds. 2009. *Fieldwork Is Not What It Used To Be.* Ithaca, NY: Cornell University.

Gatt, Caroline, and Tim Ingold. 2013. "From Description to Correspondence: Anthropology in Real Time." In *Design Anthropology: Theory and Practice*, edited by Wendy Gunn, Ton Otto, and Rachel Charlotte Smith, 139–58. New York: Bloomsbury.

Gunn, Wendy, and Jared Donovan. 2012. "Design Anthropology: An Introduction." In *Design and Anthropology*, edited by W. Gunn and J. Donovan, 1–16. Burlington, UK: Ashgate.

Holmes, Douglas R., and George E. Marcus. 2006. "Fast Capitalism: Para-Ethnography and the Rise of the Symbolic Analyst." In *Frontiers of Capital: Ethnographic Reflections on the New Economy*, edited by M. S. Fisher and Greg Downey, 33–57. Durham, NC: Duke University Press.

Kilbourn, Kyle. 2013. "Tools and Movements of Engagement: Design Anthropology's Style of Knowing." In *Design Anthropology: Theory and Practice*, edited by Wendy Gunn, Ton Otto, and Rachel Charlotte Smith, 68–82. New York: Bloomsbury.

Latour, Bruno. 2013. *An Inquiry into Modes of Existence: An Anthropology of the Moderns.* Translated by Catherine Porter. Cambridge, MA: Harvard University Press.

Marcus, George E. 2012. "Opinion: What Business Anthropology Is, What It Might Become . . . and What, Perhaps, It Should Not Be." *Journal of Business Anthropology* 1(2):265–72.

Murphy, Keith M., and George E. Marcus. 2013. "Ethnography and Design, Ethnography in Design . . . Ethnography by Design." In *Design Anthropology: Theory and Practice*, edited by Wendy Gunn, Ton Otto, and Rachel Charlotte Smith, 251–68. London: Bloomsbury.

Otto, Ton, and Rachel Charlotte Smith. 2013. "Design Anthropology: A Distinct Style of Knowing." In *Design Anthropology: Theory and Practice*, edited by Wendy Gunn, Ton Otto, and Rachel Charlotte Smith, 1–29. New York: Bloomsbury.

Rabinow, Paul, and George Marcus with James Faubion and Tobias Rees. 2008. *Designs for an Anthropology of the Contemporary*. Durham, NC: Duke University.

Urban, Greg, and Kyung-Nan Koh. 2013. "Ethnographic Research on Modern Business Corporations." *Annual Review of Anthropology* 42:139–58.

NOTES

1 We thank Christian Madsbjerg of ReD Associates for the insights he shared on these dynamics during a conversation in his office in the spring of 2013.

7

Making Markets Emerge: Enumeration, "Development," & Technology Markets

DAWN NAFUS

INTRODUCTION

Market relationships, both as people live them and as anthropologists talk about them, soon encounter quantitative measurement in one form or another. As an anthropologist in industry, I am occasionally asked for my point of view on the numbers produced by marketing firms or industry analysts. On other occasions, my point of view is treated as secondary to numbers, as if numbers, rather than ethnographic description, were self-evidently the more legitimate form of knowledge. Anthropologists in industry often encounter these numbers in Cefkin's (2012) sense of an encounter. Following Asad (1973), Cefkin treats encounters as unexpected events, at times a clash, that require us to wrestle with how we might be both complicit in, and resistant to, more powerful forms of knowledge.

Other kinds of scholarship have had their encounters with numbers too. Within business schools, consumer culture theory succeeded in developing new perspectives on markets beyond the firm-centric views that dominate business schools (see Arnould and Thompson, this volume). Developing this perspective required getting beyond numbers as the only possible form of knowledge production. This took place in a context where business schools had been shaped by Cold War–era politics in that enumerating knowledge about markets was a politically convenient way of narrowing the frame of enquiry and avoiding the politically problematic questions that the other social sciences raised about capitalism (Tadajewski 2006).

Economic sociology inspired by Michel Callon (1998) could be added to this list of disciplines encountering the quantitative. It has entirely reframed the role of quantitative measures in markets, focusing on numbers as self-fulfilling performances. If we believe, as many of us did before the Great Recession, that

Handbook of Anthropology in Business, edited by Rita Denny and Patricia Sunderland, 167–185.

universal, mathematical laws of the markets apply everywhere, then that belief sets those "laws" into practice regardless of whether they are "true." The "market value" of a derivative may have had more to do with abstractions upon abstractions of economic modeling, which few people actually understand, and which eventually brought the whole thing tumbling down, but it also became "true," at least for a time, if enough people act as if they are convinced by it. In a context where credit default swaps and algorithmic trading no longer merely model the market, but actively perform in it, the consequences of the numbers we produce in the world are serious. We qualitative researchers may not like numbers as our preferred tools of the trade, but we do need to acknowledge them as things in the world, with their own social lives. In a world full of numbers, our encounter with the quantitative cannot be limited to raising epistemological objections to its assumptions.

My own encounter with the quantitative has centered on questions of economic development, and whether development does or does not indicate promising technology markets. At minimum, development organizes markets through measurements that divide the world into either emerging markets or mature ones. This organization is simple, but its making involves a highly complex set of social practices. Here I reflect ethnographically on how discourses of economic development are operationalized and practiced through numbers. It is not enough to simply critique the assumptions on which those numbers are based. I also wish to suggest a role for numbers in changing things. This requires us to consider not just the assumptions these numbers make, but also their social lives: how they are circulated within and between institutions, and the kinds of relationships they sustain or subvert.

Like most anthropologies of development (de Soto 2003; Escobar 1994; Ferguson 1994), I do not take development to be an *a priori* economic fact that some countries are considered more developed than others. Instead, I view it as a historically and socially situated discourse that organizes hierarchical relationships. If we look at development in this way, it is not hard to see how quantitative measurements of economic development, and the subsequent measures of market opportunities, are shaped not just by the brute "facts" of wealth, but also beliefs about what constitutes progress, and what social groupings can be said to have it (cities, countries, etc.). As the measures get more complex, and embedded in daily economic life, the relations among wealth, neoliberal public policies, and technology adoption get more deeply intertwined. From a firm's point of view, beliefs about what development is prefigures whether a market exists at all. Even before goods are made and marketed, firms routinely make decisions about which people are "ready" to be consumers at all. Conversely, places said to lack development are deemed "not ready" and thus not even a market. In this sense, seeing like a corporation in some ways is similar to seeing like a state (Scott 1998): with a certain gaze, people and places that cannot be counted literally do not count as a market. By looking at how quantitative measurements and notions of economic development figure in these decisions of who is and is not in a market, and the social and institutional constraints that people working in companies face when making decisions about markets, we can better understand what it is like to see like a company.

Applied anthropologists are often called upon to narrow the distance between consumer and producer. Economic anthropology, sociology, and consumer culture theory have in various ways focused on how consumers and producers actively co-create the meaning of both objects and brands. Firms and their customers are always acting in some relationship to one another, often rely-ing on shared cultural meanings. By asking questions about where markets are and where markets are not, we can also see how the distance between consumers and producers has its own social organization. It is not there simply because the two kinds of actors are distinct; it has its own configuration. The networks that otherwise tie producers and consumers together are also cut in certain ways (Strathern 1996), so that not each and every connection between consumer and producer can be made.

In this case, the connections between producers and would-be consumers are cut by assumptions about which consumers are "ready" for which technologies. The story will come as no surprise to anthropologists working in development. What might come as more of a surprise is the idea that parts of that network might be reassembled in different form. Simakova and Neyland (2008) show how information and communication technology (ICT) marketing works by creating and mobilizing constituencies around the creation of tellable stories about the value of new technologies. Securing a tellable story in the mess of constantly shifting actors and perpetually new products is difficult at best in the ICT industry. Indeed, it is a preoccupation among anthropologists in this industry (see also Cefkin 2010). Yet there are some tellable stories, like those about development, that do not shift so easily or quickly. In fact, critics of development (de Soto 2003; Escobar 1994; Ferguson 1994) point to a suspicious lack of uncertainty, where states of development become a too easily rendered just-so story about the triumph of Western industrialization as the only possible desirable end state for all countries. Development discourse is persistent, even though there are many indications that it has overstayed its welcome. As I describe in this chapter, the marketers and new product developers I work with are not unaware of problems with "development." At minimum, they know that something is amiss when they land in an emerging market city like Shanghai to find there is little there that has yet to "emerge." They are keenly aware that people with low incomes in the global South do not appreciate producers talking down to them (Kuriyan et al. 2012). There are robust debates about whether "emerging" is even the right word for the profound changes in the geography of revenue generation. And yet, development remains a center of gravity, difficult to shake.

There is something odd going on with development. It is both as securely dominant as ever, and yet simultaneously loudly contested. It endures as a framing device, problematically immune to the endemic change that otherwise characterizes the technology industry. The role of measurement can give us a clue as to why its dominance has outlasted its convincingness.

My encounter with these issues came to a head in a project that created an alternative way of measuring technology adoption. I used this project to inform my firm's prioritization of emerging markets, its strategies to engage those markets, and the design of technologies for first-time computer buyers. My reflections are grounded in this experience. First, I take a step back to look at the broader context of academic scholarship and practitioner reports that produce and sustain the West-centric assumptions that currently underlie marketing and new product development practices. Next, I show why the conflation of technology "readiness" with economic development is so difficult to overcome, and how the use of quantitative measurement firmly entrenches them. I do this through the now unfashionable, but nevertheless serviceable, insight from Geertz (1973) that models *of* some phenomena quickly become models *for* those phenomena. A Geertzian view works particularly well in this case because indices are literally a mathematical "model of" that can easily be traced to prescriptions of various kinds. The chapter then turns to the consequences of this conflation. While there are empirically grounded associations between wealth and technology adoption, there are also significant constraints and economic costs associated with the assumption that they are one and the same thing. I then discuss the alternative we developed, the Technology Distribution Index (TDI), to overcome these business constraints while also making alternative social imaginations more possible. The measurement retains some of the dominant epistemic frameworks of a multinational firm, but it does not resort to West-centric assumptions about the development status of a country. I conclude by discussing the ways that this encounter with the quantitative loosens the connection between development as a discourse versus a daily practice.

THE BUSINESS CONTEXTS THAT MAKE MARKETS EMERGE

Intel employs anthropologists within its research and development (R&D) organization to provide insight into why and how products are likely to be used. Though the use of anthropology to conduct user-driven innovation is now fairly commonplace in product development processes, multinational corporations continue to privilege standardized quantitative measurements (Flynn et al. 2009). Anthropologists and designers might arrive at a compelling design, but whether product managers believe the design is likely to win in the marketplace is in part a function of quantitative measurements. Clashes as well as corroborations can occur between the quantitative knowledge that suggests there is a scalable market and the qualitative knowledge that informed the product development in the first place.

These two issues of geography and the privileging of numbers come to a head when multinational corporations seek to develop products for emerging markets. Specifically, classifications such as "mature" and "emerging" markets, based on national income levels, are simple rules of thumb that focus product developers' ideas of whom they are developing for, and simultaneously market strategists' plans for which customers matter more, and how. These categorizations have descriptive merit: the market messages, design, and distribution channels that would make a computer compelling in Bangladesh are not the same ones that would be compelling in the United States. Digital divide research confirms a strong association between technology diffusion and income (Caselli and Coleman, 2001; Dedrick et al. 2003; Kiiski and Pohjola 2002). While the relation between wealth and technology clearly exists, the causality that underlies it has proved elusive to economists and policy scholars (de Ridder, 2007; Kolko 2010; Taylor and Zhang 2007).

The social shaping of technology and science and technology studies (STS) literature (Bijker and Law 1994; MacKenzie and Wajcman 1999; Oudshoorn and Pinch 2005) suggests good reasons for this elusiveness. The associations between wealth and technologies are the result of the mutual coevolution between designers and users. ICTs are, by and large, made for the wealthy and middle classes by middle class and wealthy people. PCs were designed for offices, not agricultural communities. They were designed for individual use and were assumed to have an individual owner, even though much of the world does not use them that way (Pal et al. 2006). This is a historical process that made technologies by and for wealthy people, but it is still only a history, not an inevitable trajectory for all time.

While the social shaping of technology scholarship makes its way into large firms primarily through applied anthropologists, mainstream management and economics scholarship also makes its way in via consultants and participation in policymaking processes. Even this scholarship has also found the technology/wealth conflation more difficult to maintain, if for totally different reasons. They find that when they expand their ideas about what technology is, and seek to account for the breadth of information services that are available, the correlation between adoption and wealth breaks down (de Laiglesia 2008; Mahajan and Banga 2006; Paltridge 2008). They find not just surprising rates of mobile phone adoption in poorer countries, but more innovation related to mobile phones (services, power supply, payment models, mobile banking, etc.) than in wealthier countries. It is in these currents of mixed academic knowledge and practice where we find careful economists aware that causality problems vex the wealth/adoption relationship, and marketers and product developers intrigued by the innovation happening in poorer areas.

Despite the increasing tellability of stories that question the conflation of technology with developedness, the wealth/technology association persists. Following the longstanding view of culture formation that culture takes shape when a model *of* some phenomenon becomes a prescriptive model *for* it (Geertz 1973), we might start by asking what makes this conflation so powerful when so few find it satisfying. The language and concepts available to think about new markets are linked to the long-troubled history of development. Ferguson (1994) shows that by claiming that non-Western parts of the world are in need of development, Western policymakers positioned themselves to treat countries that do not meet Western standards of wealth as if they were somehow childlike. They created a cultural logic that made it seem as if following the path of earlier industrialized countries were as natural and inevitable as the physical maturation of a person. In turn, the only possible debates to be had were what kinds of technology or education would best bring about development, not whether the West really was the best model for what other countries should aspire to, or whether endless wealth was really the best end state. In this way, development is not a neutral description of change but a teleological one in which the West has set the terms of betterment.

This history sets the unavoidable background to distinctions between mature and emerging markets. At this company and well beyond it, the BRICs (Brazil, Russia, India, and China) were countries that were said to be emerging because they exhibited high rates of economic growth, and not because they had particular needs for certain kinds of technologies. Higher levels of disposable income do make purchasing products easier. But these high economic growth rates serve as indicators only, and what they indicated carried cultural meaning for the people I worked with that went far beyond this basic business logic: a sense that upper-middle class Westerners could understand BRIC consumers even if product developers knew that people in those places were not entirely the same as them. What made citizens of BRIC countries emerge to people for whom they were previously invisible was the new wealth that made commonality imaginable. What was now in common was the consumption of mass-manufactured commodities itself. This made it possible to believe that "they" were now at some level "just like us." This new commonality made people in the emerging markets now part of the stories people in the firm were prepared to tell each other about technology.

This dynamic is easiest to see concretely when the sense of commonality breaks down and things go awry. I attended a planning session to decide R&D directions for a new generation of location-aware technologies. Under consideration were new ways of making use of the data generated by these technologies. A social scientist had suggested that there were lead users of a specific kind of global positioning system (GPS) technology among an ethnic group in Cameroon. The group used the technology to mark trees of cultural significance to them, enabling loggers to harvest around those trees and gain sustainability certifications so that they can sell in European markets (Lewis 2012). The researcher was pointing out that the location-aware technologies could make new conversations possible between social groups. This turned out to be an unthinkable idea when substantiated by the Cameroon example. The claim that this was a leading use of technology was met with laughter, after which it was suggested, with some degree of empathy for the proposer, that the example did not help to show the underlying power of the proposal. Another person added that the example used to substantiate that there was a lead use should be something that "scales." GPS tagging for sustainable logging did not "scale." Yet another person asked for an example that was more "relatable."

These were people who were otherwise supportive of the underlying concept, and shared with the researcher the belief that there was value in sharing location data between different kinds of social groups. Indeed, the negative response was intended to help this researcher ensure that it made its way further along the product development process. Despite the Cameroon case being a well-documented, working example of using location data for this purpose, it proved unhelpful in enabling the team to imagine future products. Instead, the researcher was asked to re-present the otherwise compelling argument, but this time to do so using "relatable" examples that "scale." In the end, he used a completely fictional scenario placed in the United States to substantiate his case for the concept, and the team considered it more convincing than the real one.

I would propose that there is a relationship between unrelatability, scale, and development that went unsaid in this discussion. It is difficult to believe that scale was the real problem in any absolute sense, because there were less empirical grounds to believe the new, fictional proposal was scalable, and his was a group that was otherwise committed to empirically grounding one's arguments. Furthermore, the Cameroonian technology was already embedded in a large resource extraction industry. No one around the table knew enough about logging to say whether it could become a larger part of that trade or similar industries. The crossborder trade of which the Camaroonians were a part was discussed as if it did not exist or had nothing to do with "scale." The interaction dissuaded the researcher from investigating numerically whether this technology use was scalable throughout that industry or industries with similar issues. For these reasons, scale could be interpreted not as a literal demand for higher profitability, but a more vague social operation. Scale appeared to me to work as a cultural hinge that connects "lead users" to some larger market *that in turn included people sitting in the room.* It appeared there had to be some imaginable relation between those sitting in the room and the technology users under discussion for those users to be seen as lead users: the harbinger of something much larger to come. That the proposed example "didn't scale" betrayed the limits of imagination that people encounter when social difference cannot be elided. Nobody in the room was ever going to geotag information about whether the trees around them contained edible insects for foraging. It was hard to imagine those who did as leaders of a new market. The trope of emergence, with its connotations of visibility, cannot be coincidental in these circumstances.

The most likely marker of what made someone relatable in this context was whether he or she could be thought of as "developed" or put in the position of needing development. As the product was intended for "mainstream" markets, and not to "enable development," the example did not fit the frameworks in play. In fact, I have witnessed other discussions about Intel's role in developing technologies "for development" that resembled more closely this sort of technical direction. On the other hand, if what we are talking about is mainstream markets, these are thought of in terms of their similarities, not differences. Possible differences among those who had development, whether between American consumers or between American product developers and China's middle class, were easily elided and went unquestioned. For example, research to evaluate the merit of this or that device often takes place across (say) the United States, Germany, and China precisely to ensure that any differences between them can be glossed. Rejection of the technology in one country could be a fluke, but rejection in a large country, or more than one, breaks the notion that there is a market for the thing at all. Such research strategies suggest an assumption that profitable markets are a mass, not an assembly of multitudes, and that emerging markets are those newly included in those masses whose similarities can be stretched and glossed, but not broken. Here, new wealth gave product developers just enough room to act *as if* BRIC consumers were similar enough to be targeted as a worldwide group with a "global" orientation, regardless of how slippery such appearances are (Mazzarella 2003; Ong 2006). That same "as if" quality did not extend to others. In this example we can also see how notions of markets as abstractions, rather than actually existing exchanges between people, become important. In the context of producing new technologies, speaking about markets in "as if" terms is par for the course, if not central. If a product is so new that it has never been transacted, the existence of a market for it is at best virtual. New markets are models in its purest sense.

The underlying issue is much wider than the discussions that take place within one particular firm. For example, normative language is rampant in the recent attention to so-called "reverse" innovation, where products are developed in the third world and diffuse to the first. The reverse innovation literature questions the necessity of high levels of wealth for innovation (Hang et al. 2010; Immelt et al. 2009). Indeed, there is a good deal of enthusiasm for reverse innovation within the ICT industry. However, the term points to the wider beliefs about wealth that underlie it. That there is a "reversal" assumes that innovation otherwise belongs to the first world, and diffuses outward. It does not question what those roles are or how they came into being. How much "reverse" innovation there has to be before people stop treating it as a reversal from the norm has yet to be seen. Similarly, through the controversial trope of the "bottom of the pyramid" (Prahalad 2004), reaching less wealthy customers has become important to technology firms. Yet this too presumes a well-trodden norm where the producers and profit-takers remain firms from wealthy countries.

Such loose language, so frequently wielded as to be unremarkable, is not simply uncareful speech, but reflects a widespread cultural model that has taken a historical association and rendered it predictive. What is remarkable about the model is the ability to maintain alternatives as anomalies rather than challenges. It does not deny alternatives, but renders them perpetual surprises when the association between wealth and technology turns out not to be an *a priori* necessity, as when Indian car manufacturers sell in the United States or when Ugandans buy mobile phones before they do refrigerators, or when mobile phone-based banking takes off in Kenya before anywhere else. These are not untellable stories. They hang together (Mol 2002) in some way, but in the face of the practical need to get a product to market, they are encountered as bracketed-off exceptions to the seemingly more practical (practicable?) rule of thumb that mass markets with wealth are the ones worth considering.

QUANTITATIVE MODELS OF & FOR

Not only are alternatives to the development/technology conflation treated as surprising anomalies, there are also ways that the conflation is embedded in day-to-day market activities. One way is with quantitative technology adoption indices. These indices embed the cultural model of what a developed country should look like into a quantitative model. They tidily conflate Geertz's "models of" with "models for," and set them into operation. They are produced equally by public sector organizations seeking to develop countries with the aid of technology and the private sector looking for places to adopt them. So conflated are "models of" and "models for" that the public sector, private sector, and academic measurements are hardly distinguishable from one another despite serving supposedly different goals (for a survey, see Vaezi and Bimar 2009). One example is the Economist Intelligence Unit (EIU)'s E-Readiness Index. The EIU defines E-Readiness as:

> a measure of the quality of a country's ICT infrastructure *and* the ability of its consumers, businesses and governments to use ICT to their benefit. When a country uses ICT to conduct more of its activities, the economy can become more transparent and efficient. Our ranking allows governments to gauge the success of their technology initiatives against those of other countries. (EIU 2009:3; my emphasis).

Following the cultural model, the quantitative model treats technology as *both* a driver of development and an outcome. The EIU measures the ability to use and benefit from ICTs through a weighted constellation of factors, which includes macroeconomic environment, literacy rates, ease of registering businesses, trade legislation and competition law, level of e-commerce use, ICT spending per capita, entrepreneurship rates, and broadband penetration. By EIU's own admission (2009), the weightings were not derived from any scholarship that might pinpoint the strength of how these factors affect a highly nebulous concept like "readiness" (see also Maugis et al. 2005), but were simply asserted as a reasonable approximation. This gives us the unsurprising result that high-scoring countries are ready to benefit from that which they already have. The E-Readiness report goes on to note the remarkable gains made by emerging markets while retaining the Organization for Economic Cooperation and Development (OECD) countries as top scorers. This is not remarkable at all, of course, but set by the terms of measurement.

Bundled indices such as E-Readiness affect market selection processes for many firms. While the EIU does not make any claims about causality, and cannot be judged in these terms, it does convert cultural assumption into a quantitative index, and in doing so both sustains and operationalizes a worldview. They sustain it in the sense that the outcome challenges no one: countries that increasingly bear some resemblance to OECD countries rise in rankings. They operationalize it in the sense that when firms make decisions about which emerging markets constitute priorities, those that fail to emerge onto EIU's list, regardless of their affinity for this or that technology, cannot be seen. Precisely because indices circulate outside the firm, they create a broader, stable referent that people can use when proposing a new product or market. To violate the consensus, such as suggesting a country off the culturally validated list, is a lot to ask of a product manager when so much else about new technology markets is uncertain. This is so regardless of his or her personal attitudes toward development.

THE COST OF MATURE/EMERGING DISTINCTIONS

While there is clearly a highly complex relationship between economic conditions and technology, when it becomes a starting point from which other arguments flow, it incurs significant economic costs beyond the usual anthropological criticisms. The first cost is that the distinction can distort the scale of opportunities. The mature/emerging distinction takes the country as the unit of analysis, although it may not always be a useful proxy for how a market might scale. Data are designed so that countries can be said to have *a priori* characteristics, such as gross domestic product (GDP) growth, foreign direct investment (FDI), broadband availability, etc. They can be convincingly analyzed as a unit regardless of whether they act as such. In politically fragmented and socially heterogeneous places like India, they do not. Indeed, the Cameroonians mentioned earlier were quite obviously only a subset of all the people in Cameroon, which may have contributed to the sense that their practices were not scalable. The paucity of regional or city-level statistics, as well as geographically disbursed ethnic groups, creates strained ways of conceptualizing technology adoption, such that some countries are seemingly stuck in a perpetual state of "emergingness" even when they are at the same time considered hotbeds of technical innovation.

While the inadequacies of data are not something we were able to change, what we can change is the cost paid in terms of the product opportunities missed simply because countries were not perceived to be ready for them. For example, the rapid growth of the African phone market appears surprising to the product developers I worked with because much of the continent appears to lack the infrastructure and economic forms that have supported the growth of earlier technologies in industrialized nations. Once this adoption became undeniable, the cultural model kept it as an anomaly. I heard repeated comments that of course mobile phones have taken off in emerging markets, as building the network is so much less expensive. Yet the commonplace understanding within both the private sector and among development agencies is that Africa is not investable because of its political instability and the supposed lack of demand for anything more than basic needs (Konkel and Heeks 2009). The levels of political stability in Africa have not significantly changed in time to be "ready" for mobile phones (Heeks 2009), and yet "unaffordable" handsets are widely purchased. By aggregating factors believed to be conducive to technology adoption in a more general way, indices make it hard to see the technology adoption that is in fact possible. It is through numerical indices of readiness that the case of mobile phones in Africa appears more of an anomaly than it actually is.

These are both high costs to pay. At Intel, the constraints set by these measurements became pressing. Its business had been diversifying to include more kinds of computer hardware, and as part of that diversification it launched a computer designed specifically for classrooms in emerging markets. These were not technologies targeted to the new wealthy within emerging markets, but were designed for those with more serious economic constraints. With a social mission to help build local economies, and goal of keeping costs low, tracking rising disposable income levels would provide little in the way of guidance. The countries that had the traditional neoliberal package as embodied in E-Readiness measures would not necessarily make ideal sites for pilot programs and early sales. What constituted an emerging market for this product, then, could no longer be elided as part of a preconceived mass market. As this was an entirely new class of product, and no money had changed hands, how to measure this market was a nontrivial problem.

THE TECHNOLOGY DISTRIBUTION INDEX

I worked with colleagues ken anderson and Phil Howard, the latter a University of Washington political scientist, to develop a measurement that got beyond the mature/emerging dyad. We set out to identify a set of countries that had relatively high technology adoption rates but did not necessarily rank highly in terms of development indicators. The result was the Technology Distribution Index (TDI). Further details of the measure are found in Howard et al. (2009). I offer a brief summary here. The TDI is a calibrated measure that allows us to relate a country's share of the global stock of a particular technology to its share of global GDP dollars. This measure, which can be applied to any technology, allows us to say whether the country has higher, lower, or a middling amount of technologies for its level of economic capacity. This helps identify countries where political and social factors have brought ICTs more rapidly than might have otherwise been expected as a function of economic development alone.

This index is created through a ratio of two ratios. First, we calculated a ratio of a country's economic output to the output of all countries in a given year. Then we calculated a ratio of a country's technology consumption to the technology consumption of all countries in a given year. The ratio of these two ratios reveals whether the proportion of ICTs is in some balance with economic productivity. A natural log is taken to balance the scale as a distance from zero so that, unlike technology adoption per dollar of GDP, the TDI does not suffer from ceiling or floor effects (Figure 7.1).

The reader will have guessed by now that the translation of the empirical problem into mathematical form was entirely Phil Howard's work. Nevertheless, through close collaboration with him (and generous patience on his part),

Figure 7.1. Technology distribution index value calculation.

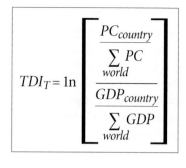

$$TDI_T = \ln\left[\frac{\dfrac{PC_{country}}{\sum_{world} PC}}{\dfrac{GDP_{country}}{\sum_{world} GDP}}\right]$$

I too have been able to use the method to calculate scores for various technologies. The experience was roughly analogous to conducting field research in a new place: it changes a person, but not in ways that force her to hand back her anthropology degree. Regardless of one's affinity for math, we can see the difference measurement makes by visualizing the data as a global map. Figure 7.2 shows the penetration of various technologies. It shows a clear pattern of concentrated adoption in the OECD countries, though more weakly

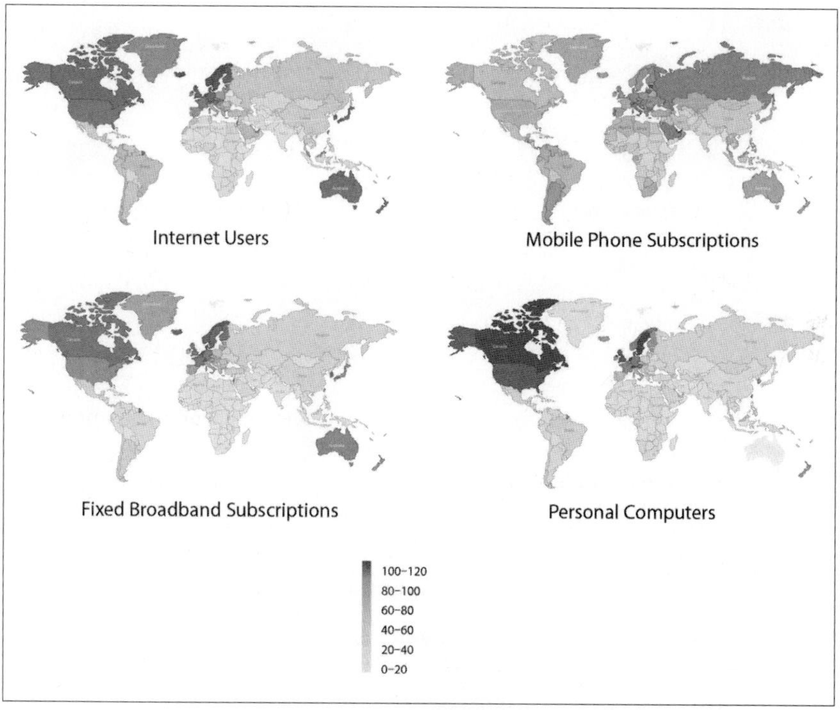

Figure 7.2. Technology ownership/use per 100inhabitants, various technologies.

Number of technologies specified per 100 inhabitants. In the case of internet users, the population of active internet users was used, regardless of whether the user owned a PC or method of access. Source: ITU (2008). Visualization created on IBM Many Eyes. For interactive, full-color map, see http://www-958.ibm.com/software/analytics/many eyes/visualizations/technology-per-100-inhabitants.

for mobile phones. The TDI creates a more complicated picture (Figure 7.3). It is only possible to pick out individual country scores through the color image (which can be found at the IBM Many Eyes website[1]. However, even in grayscale, it is still possible to see that the overall pattern is broken up, and emerging market powerhouses like India and China are largely in the middle of the pack. The sensitivity of technology adoption to cost is clear in the color online version. Fixed broadband is expensive, and its subscribers are concentrated in wealthy countries, but the world's internet users are more evenly scattered, suggesting shared use is important in making the internet accessible. The exceptional mobile phone adoption in Russia still translates into a high score in the TDI, but not as much. This suggests that some of the growth in mobile phone ownership is explained by rising incomes, while some is explained by other

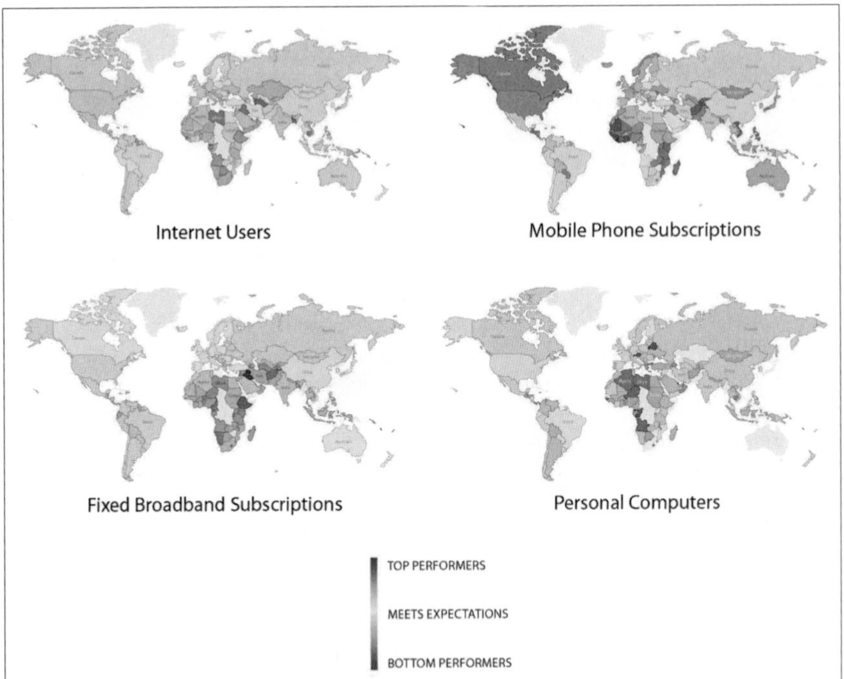

Figure 7.3. TDI scores, various technologies .

"Meets expectations" scores are scores near zero. The extremes on both ends represent divergence from zero. Source: Author's calculations based on 2008 World Bank and ITU data. Visualization created on IBM Many Eyes. For interactive map, see http://www-958.ibm.com/software/analytics/manyeyes/visualizations/technology-distribution-index-vari.

factors such as consumer affinity, social structures that enable adoption, etc. Kenya scores three times as much as Russia in mobile phone adoption under the TDI. This means that in Kenya adoption is much more strongly explained by factors other than rising economic wealth compared to Russia.

The data may serve multiple purposes. A firm looking for a single market to pilot a new product and establish its credibility as a concept might wish to pick a country with historically high scores across multiple product categories to minimize the risk of unanticipated barriers to adoption. The TDI does not assume to know what constitutes a barrier, but if multiple technologies are succeeding despite low incomes, we can surmise for practical purposes there are few. A firm can also use it to identify places where it has had relative success with its technologies, but where that success was hidden in other measurements. A strategy for scaling products globally can be arrived at through more careful observation of adoption patterns as measured in this way. Because the scores are not aggregated overall, marketers can draw conclusions about the adoption of technologies not yet on the market based on similarities and differences with previous technologies without resorting to notions of developedness. For example, a country with a surprisingly high rate of internet users but a low rate of broadband subscribers might mean there is demand for a new connectivity solution, not a naiveté about what the internet is and does. Indeed, at Intel the TDI has been used in all of these ways for various emerging markets projects.

CONCLUSION: MAKING A DIFFERENT MARKET EMERGE

There are threads that make the TDI traceable back to development discourse. It did, after all, incorporate GDP figures, but created a different relationship to those figures so that they do not control the ultimate assessment. The network that connected GDP to technology adoption was cut differently, although the actors remained the same. At least in this iteration, the TDI also did not challenge the notion of countries as sites of adoption. We remained constrained by the available data, which were from secondary sources that did take countries to be an appropriate unit of analysis. The firm, for that matter, was organized as if countries were the sites of adoption, and in this way this empirical liability became an organizational asset. Nevertheless, in the ways outlined in this chapter, we made new markets emerge.

The ease with which Intel adopted the TDI, compared with the difficulty of explaining why ethnic minority groups in Cameroon are a perfectly reasonable place to start a new product development discussion, is telling. In practice, development was a notion relatively easy to dispose of provided other dominant frameworks were maintained, such as scalability as connections and similarities between identified countries. In sharing it with my colleagues around the company, I had relatively little convincing or cajoling work to do. The main communication work was to explain the merits of a relative measure, rather than an absolute measure, and to help people get a more embodied feel for them. The numbers that the method produces are abstract distances from zero. They are not felt in the way that claims of so many billions of dollars are felt, though when I worked with them I did develop an intimacy with them. "-2.7" came to mean something to me over time. Still, explaining this did not encounter difficulties, and the measurement was used in many parts of the company. The relatively easy adoption of the TDI cannot be explained by the mere economic incentive to make use of it. Maintaining the fiction that markets emerge solely as a function of rising incomes was quite costly, yet maintained nevertheless.

Returning to the notion of the tellable story, I would argue that a tellable story must be augmented by other resources that set them into practice: resources that do not always look like stories. If we would like to see a tellable story in the TDI, we are likely to find much that falls short of a narrative. The TDI does not say what factors make for high levels of technology adoption, only that there is a measurable remainder after the effects of income are taken into account. It gives only a limited sense that there is something interesting going on in a particular country for which we do not have a model and might not need one. In this, it points to what it cannot explain, and also cannot be explained in traditional models.

Indeed, as a numerical device, the TDI could in fact say many things. The issue, however, was not necessarily what was sayable, but how numbers set the "model of" into motion, cohering markets together as if they were more than abstractions. The TDI did create a kind of representational frame, but it was a frame that in this context could also perform a market (Callon 1998). In this sense the significance of the TDI has less to do with its representational claims, and more to do with its performance of a market that relieves actors of the need to tell a certain kind of story, or rely on dubious stories. The TDI opened up the possibility to shift the focus to day-to-day practice without directly challenging the supposed consensus other measurements represent. In market selection discussions that involved the TDI, states of development were usually not discussed. These conversations instead focused on the technologies that *had* been adopted, and what that configuration said about the presence or absence of enabling factors without naming what those were. Just as critiques of development had been known, but set aside, when it came to the practice of market assessments, here it was development that was set aside.

The consensus that development was necessary for technology adoption had already begun to unravel: the TDI would not have been a good way to start that undoing. But by paying attention to which parts of the network had started to unravel, and which had been hanging on too long, the shift in register to the numerical did reconfigure connections between producers and consumers. This suggests a more complex role for numbers. They are not just embodiments of dominant discourse, or epistemological trump cards. Instead, numbers can be designed to point to alternatives, and open up the context in which other kinds of stories might take greater hold. Here, we did this by designing a number that performed its partialities as well as its claims. It does not attempt to explain everything away, but shows what remains when the dominant frame is taken away.

In a context where development was both peculiarly persistent, yet increasingly questioned, treating numbers as active participants in the making of markets alleviated the need for rules of thumb that have overstayed their welcome. The politics of doing so will not be to everyone's taste. The TDI is unsatisfying as a form of critique. The TDI remains silent on matters many academic anthropologists would prefer to tackle as an extended deconstruction of ways that global markets reproduce a neocolonial impulse. The politics of the TDI are partial, as all situated knowledge is. Here, it is situated between these critiques and the actions of firms. This situatedness makes it possible to partially rearrange the connections between people and calculations. This sort of work requires an ethnographic sensitivity to not just the anthropologically objectionable assumptions that traditional measures make, but also to numbers as entangled, fraught social entities that work in particular ways. Perhaps an engaged anthropology requires not just a theory of development, but a theory of numbers as well.

REFERENCES

Asad, Talal, ed. 1973. *Anthropology and the Colonial Encounter*. Ithaca, NY: Cornell University Press.

Bijker, Wiebe, and John Law. 1994. *Shaping Technology/Building Society: Studies in Sociotechnical Change*. Cambridge, MA: MIT Press.

Callon, Michel. 1998. *Laws of the Markets*. Oxford, UK: Wiley-Blackwell.

Caselli, Francesco, and Wilber Coleman. 2001. "Cross-Country Technology Diffusion: The Case of Computers." *American Economic Review* 91(2):328–35.

Cefkin, Melissa, ed. 2010. *Ethnography and the Corporate Encounter*. New York: Berghan Books.

______. 2012. "Close Encounters: Anthropologists in the Corporate Arena." *Journal of Business Anthropology* 1(1):91–117.

de Laiglesia, Juan. 2008. "Innovation, Investment and Access to Telecommunications in Latin America." Paper presented at the Joint OECD-World Bank Conference on "Innovation and Sustainable Growth in A Globalised World," November 28, 2008, Paris.

de Ridder, John 2007. "Catching Up in Broadband: What Will It Take?" Paper presented at the Technology Policy Research Conference (TPRC), August 15, 2007, Arlington, VA. http://papers.ssrn.com/sol3/papers.cfm?abstract_id=2118202.

de Soto, Hernando. 2003. *The Mystery of Capital: Why Capitalism Triumphs in the West and Fails Everywhere Else*. New York: Basic Books.

Dedrick, Jason, Vijay Gurbaxani, and Kenneth Kramer. 2003. "Information Technology and Economic Performance: A Critical Review of Empirical Evidence." *ACM Computing Surveys* 35(1):1-28.

Economist Intelligence Unit (EIU) 2009. "E-Readiness Rankings 2009: The Usage Imperative." http://graphics.eiu.com/pdf/E-readiness%20rankings.pdf (accessed January 18, 2011).

Escobar, Arturo. 1994. *Encountering Development*. Princeton, NJ: Princeton University Press.

Ferguson, James 1994. *The Anti-Politics Machine: "Development," Depoliticization and Bureaucratic Power in Lesotho*. Minneapolis: University of Minnesota Press.

Flynn, Donna, Tracey Lovejoy, David Siegel, and Susan Drey. 2009. "Name That Segment!: Questioning the Unquestioned Authority of Numbers." *Ethnographic Praxis in Industry Conference Proceedings* (1):81–91.

Geertz, Clifford. 1973. *The Interpretation of Cultures*. New York: Basic Books.

Hang, Chang-Cheih, Jin Chen, and Annapoornima Subramian. 2010. "Developing Disruptive Products for Emerging Economies: Lessons from Asian Cases." *Research Technology Management* 53(4):21–6.

Howard, P., K. Anderson, L. Busch, and D. Nafus. 2009. "Sizing Up Information Societies: Towards a Better Metric for the Cultures of ICT Adoption." *The Information Society* 25:208–19.

Heeks, Richard. 2009. "Emerging Markets, IT and the World's 'Bottom Billion'." *Communications of the ACM* 52(4):22–4.

Immelt, Jeffery, Vijay Govindarajan, and Chris Trimble. 2009. "How GE Is Disrupting Itself." *Harvard Business Review* October:3–11.

Kiiski, S., and M. Pohjola. 2002. "Cross-Country Diffusion of the Internet." *Information Economics and Policy* 14(2):297–310.

Kolko, Jed. 2010. "Does Broadband Boost Local Economic Development?" Public Policy Institute of California, January. www.ppic.org/content/pubs/report/R_110JKR.pdf (accessed January 12, 2011).

Konkel, Agnieszka, and Richard Heeks. 2009. "Challenging Conventional Views on Mobile-Telecommunications Investment: Evidence from Conflict Zones." *Development in Practice* 19(3):414–20.

Kuriyan, Renee, Dawn Nafus, and Scott Mainwaring. 2012. "Consumption, Technology, and Development: The 'Poor' as 'Consumer'." *Information Technologies & International Development* 8(1):1–12.

Lewis, Jerome. 2012. "Technological Leap-Frogging in the Congo Basin. Pygmies and Geographic Positioning Systems in Central Africa: What Has Happened and Where Is It Going?" *African Study Monographs* 43(Supplementary Issue):15–44

MacKenzie Donald, and Judith Wajcman, eds. 1999. *The Social Shaping of Technology*. London: Open University.

Mahajan, Vijay, and Kamini Banga. 2006. *The 86% Solution: How To Succeed in the Biggest Market Opportunity of the Next 50 Years*. Upper Saddle River, NJ: Wharton School Publishing.

Maugis, Vincent, Nazli Coucri, Stuart Madnick, Michael Siegel, Sharon Gillet, Farnaz Haghseta, Hongwei Zhu, and Mike Best. 2005. "Global E-Readiness—For What? Readiness for e-Banking." *Information Technology for Development* 11(4):313–42.

Mazzarella William. 2003. *Shoveling Smoke: Advertising and Globalization in Contemporary India*. Durham, NC: Duke University Press.

Mol, Annamarie. 2002. *The Body Multiple: Ontology in Medical Practice*. Durham, NC: Duke University Press.

Ong, Aiwa. 2006. *Neoliberalism as Exception: Mutations in Citizenship and Sovereignty*. Durham, NC: Duke University Press.

Oudshoorn, Nelly, and Trevor Pinch. 2005. *How Users Matter: The Co-Construction of Users and Technology*. Cambridge, MA: MIT Press.

Pal, Joyojeet, Udai Pawar, Eric Brewer, and Kentaro Toyama. 2006. "The Case for Multi-User Design for Computer Aided Learning in Developing Regions." *ACM Proceedings of the 15th International Conference on the World Wide Web*, 781–9.

Paltridge, Sam. 2008. "Liberalisation and User Driven Innovation in Africa." Paper presented at the Joint OECD-World Bank Conference on "Innovation and Sustainable Growth in A Globalised World," November, 28, 2008, Paris.

Prahalad, C. K. 2004. *The Bottom of the Pyramid: Eradicating Poverty through Profits*. Philadelphia, PA: Wharton School Publishing.

Scott, J. 1998. *Seeing Like a State: How Certain Schemes To Improve the Human Condition Have Failed*. New Haven, CT: Yale University Press.

Simakova, Elena, and Daniel Neyland. 2008. "Marketing Mobile Futures: Assembling Constituencies and Creating Compelling Stories for an Emerging Technology." *Marketing Theory* 8(1):91–116.

Strathern, Marilyn. 1996. "Cutting the Network." *Journal of the Royal Anthropological Institute* 2(3):517–35.

Tadajewski, Mark. 2006. "The Ordering of Marketing Theory: The Influence of McCarthyism and the Cold War." *Marketing Theory* 6(2):163–99.

Taylor, R., and B. Zhang. 2007. "Measuring the Impact: Theories of Information and Development." Paper presented at the Telecommunications Policy Research Conference (TPRC), September 26, 2007, Washington, DC. http://s3.amazonaws.com/academia.edu.documents/29720127/TPRC_08_Taylor_and_Zhang_Final.pdf?AWSAccessKeyId=AKIAJ56TQJRTWSMTNPEA&Expires=1387503077&Signature=20Q4LL6eYQ3Og9PQOmttMLHPjmI%3D&response-content-disposition=inline.

Vaezi, Seyed Kamal, and H. Sattary I. Bimar. 2009. "Comparison of E-Readiness Assessment Models." *Scientific Research and Essay* 4(5):501–12.

NOTES

The author would like to thank ken anderson, Phil Howard, Sarah Wilner, Suzanne Thomas, Jeanette Bloomberg, Melissa Cefkin, and the editors of this volume for their inspiration, encouragement, and editorial eye. All errors of fact and misuses of theory are my own.

1 The IBM Many Eyes website can be found at http://www-958.ibm.com/software/analytics/manyeyes/visualizations/technology-distribution-index-vari.

8

Design Ethnography, Public Policy, & Public Services: Rendering Collective Issues Doable & at Human Scale

LUCY KIMBELL

This chapter discusses the take-up of design ethnography in public policy contexts in the developed world. It shows how a design-ethnographic approach reconfigures how collective issues, and responses to them—in the form of new services or ventures—are constituted. Although the focus in this chapter is aging, there are increasing numbers of examples of this approach being used to craft new ways of responding to challenges such as families in crisis, inequality, chronic disease, and worklessness, far removed from the contexts in which anthropological research has been used to help design new computer systems for workplaces.

Literature on recent examples of design ethnography include the creation of the cross-ministerial innovation unit MindLab in Denmark (Bason 2010; MindLab 2012); "experience-based design" in the United Kingdom's National Health Service (Bate and Robert 2008); a federal social innovation team called TACSI (The Australian Centre for Social Innovation) in Australia (TACSI 2012); design-led approaches to regional policy issues involving design students, designers, and researchers (Art Center College of Design 2012; DESIS Network 2012); the articulation of a new agenda combining design and ethnography in the context of security and disarmament (Miller et al. 2010); and several experiments prompting teams of designers, technologists, and policymakers to address social issues using ethnographic research as a starting point (Design Council 2012; Nesta 2012) in the United Kingdom. Although organized in different ways, these projects share a commitment to bringing a people-centered perspective to complex policy issues by combining methods based on ethnography and creative design research. Further, they exemplify how design-ethnographic approaches are shifting "into the wild"—into the domains

---

Handbook of Anthropology in Business, edited by Rita Denny and Patricia Sunderland, 186–201.

of social entrepreneurship, service provision, and public policy—so they are no longer the preserve of people with design or social science training.

Many of these examples emphasize design ethnography as a process that pushes policy to become more human-centered rather than technocratic (OPM 2004; Parker and Heapy 2006). Indeed, this focus is commonly asserted as the value of ethnography. However, I argue that this formulation misses the way design ethnography's methods reveal how public and collective issues exist as *assemblages of people, organizations, and things*. Far from being human-*centered*, the interviews, videos, photographs, storyboards, and service concepts practitioners create and deploy rest on the entanglement of people with many other human and nonhuman actors. Such artifacts are not just stories of how users of services interact with digital and material stuff, but rather offer up analyses of how an issue is constituted. Further, they have the potential to reconstitute what an issue is, reframing or intervening directly into public issues, not just helping find solutions to them.

In this chapter I show how design ethnography can help create new understandings of what makes up an issue and how one might engage with it. I emphasize the productive collision of ethnographic and design practices; in the service of organizations and communities engaging with complex collective issues in which numerous organizational actors are involved, problems are sometimes described as "wicked" (Rittel and Webber 1973), and facts and values are hard to untangle.

DESIGN ETHNOGRAPHY IN THE CONTEXT OF AGING

To explore further the possibilities of design ethnography in the context of collective issues, I describe a contemporary challenge for which I was involved briefly as a design consultant: the care of older people, and how this care can be organized and resourced. The project I describe combined ethnography and design approaches in an effort to find new organizational solutions to providing care for older people in the United Kingdom.

Aging is not a single issue. The institutional actors involved in constituting the collective issue of aging include policymakers; professionals concerned with the health and well-being of older people and their families and carers; other academics and professionals such as economists and pensions practitioners; civil servants and managers working in local, regional, and central government; activists and members of voluntary and community groups; businesses such as providers of services or homes for older people; older people and their families, friends, and neighbors; and other institutions such as the media and online worlds. Discussions about aging are shaped by sociocultural practices around caring, health and well-being, end of life, and by the ways familial and community responsibilities are enacted. Some of the questions that are currently discussed in the United Kingdom include: Who should look after older people? What is the role of the state or local government in their care? How can it be organized and resourced? What are the costs? What is a good quality of life for an older person? How do physical and mental changes such as dementia affect older people and carers, families, and the communities they live within? Where will the resources to create better quality of life and well-being for older people and their carers come from? Are older people a deficit or drain on society, or are they active contributors? As economic uncertainty and changes in the political landscape lead to politicians cutting budgets for social care and public health provision, how can service managers access or combine resources in new ways to provide care for older people? Several organizations have explored bringing together approaches from ethnography and design to create new models of care for older people. Examples are UK consultancy Participle's social enterprise called Circles, which involves older people as active participants in a local network for teaching, learning, and sharing (Participle 2012).

The approach I describe is primarily instantiated within my professional practice as a design consultant and educator. This practice involves a blurring and broaching of boundaries that combines concepts and methods from several fields, including a close attention to the situated practices in and around a (potential) service or venture, and an awareness of the challenges of using analyses of existing states of affairs when designing for change. From Participatory Design (Binder et al. 2011; Ehn 1988), I inherit a practical orientation toward involving nonspecialists in doing design work through making artifacts that prompt and make available the social interactions that constitute a service. From workplace studies and Science and Technology Studies (Barad 2007; Latour 2005; Suchman 2002), my approach borrows an analysis of the world of care and caring as made up of the performative interactions of heterogeneous actors, including, for example, older people and their carers and family members and support staff, but also newsletters, straight-backed chairs, websites, tea bags, and procedures for giving injections. From speculative design (DiSalvo 2012) and design anthropology (Halse 2008), this practice recognizes the agency of designed things in creating opportunities to inspire, provoke, or set up future sets of relations between actors. Sometimes called "social design"—an uneasy term suggesting that there are kinds of design that are *not* social—the approach I describe in this chapter is a rich site for exploring how ethnography and design can reconstitute collective issues and social problems.[1] This approach, which I call "design ethnography," aims to engage productively with the following challenges:

- Working within extremely short timescales, allowing perhaps only a few days for fieldwork, interviews, and workshops.

- The risk of ethnography being reduced to data gathering, losing its analytical purpose.
- Making ethnographic research useful within a change process.
- Ethnographic methods being used by people who are not trained in ethnography or the social sciences, and who do not share anthropology's and sociology's commitments to relating fieldwork to bodies of literature.
- Design being reduced to a toolkit of methods, detached from a culture of designerly practice when no longer practiced by designers but by managers and policymakers.

GENERATING KNOWLEDGE & REVEALING CAPACITIES

My colleagues and I undertook a project for a UK provider of housing and support services for older and vulnerable people. The organization wanted to design a new befriending service involving unpaid volunteers visiting older people in their homes, or accompanying them on short trips outside their homes. Although the organization used volunteers for other activities, at that stage they did not make extensive use of volunteers for befriending. As lead consultant, I constructed a project that combined ethnographic and design approaches to help the organization in their design of this new service. At the stage we engaged with them, their small team was running a pilot with three older people and a few volunteer befrienders. In total we spent about 22 days on the project over four months.

To start our work, a researcher spent several days doing semistructured ethnographic interviews with older people, professionals involved in their care and support, and volunteers engaging with older people. The selection of people to interview was agreed upon jointly among the manager in charge of the service, my researcher colleague, and I, and was significantly shaped by how easy it was to get in touch with them, and who was available for interview within our timeframe. The choice of interview questions was influenced by the storyworld template, which aims to analyze a person's lifeworld, including their relationships with other people and things (see Figure 8.1), and is a version of the persona method frequently used in product and interaction design. Having completed the interviews, the researcher then wrote up anonymized interview notes to give to the client. In addition, she created eight single-page personas of older people and four volunteers, which combined aspects of these interviews, which a colleague with a clinical background and I both reviewed. One of these is shown in Figure 8.2. Among social scientists working in consumer research there is often discomfort with the persona method as reducing research subjects to mere caricatures. However, given our limited resources on this project and the client's request for help with user research, we felt it was appropriate to

Figure 8.1. Storyworld template used to create personas or guide interviews. Courtesy of Lucy Kimbell and Joe Julier.

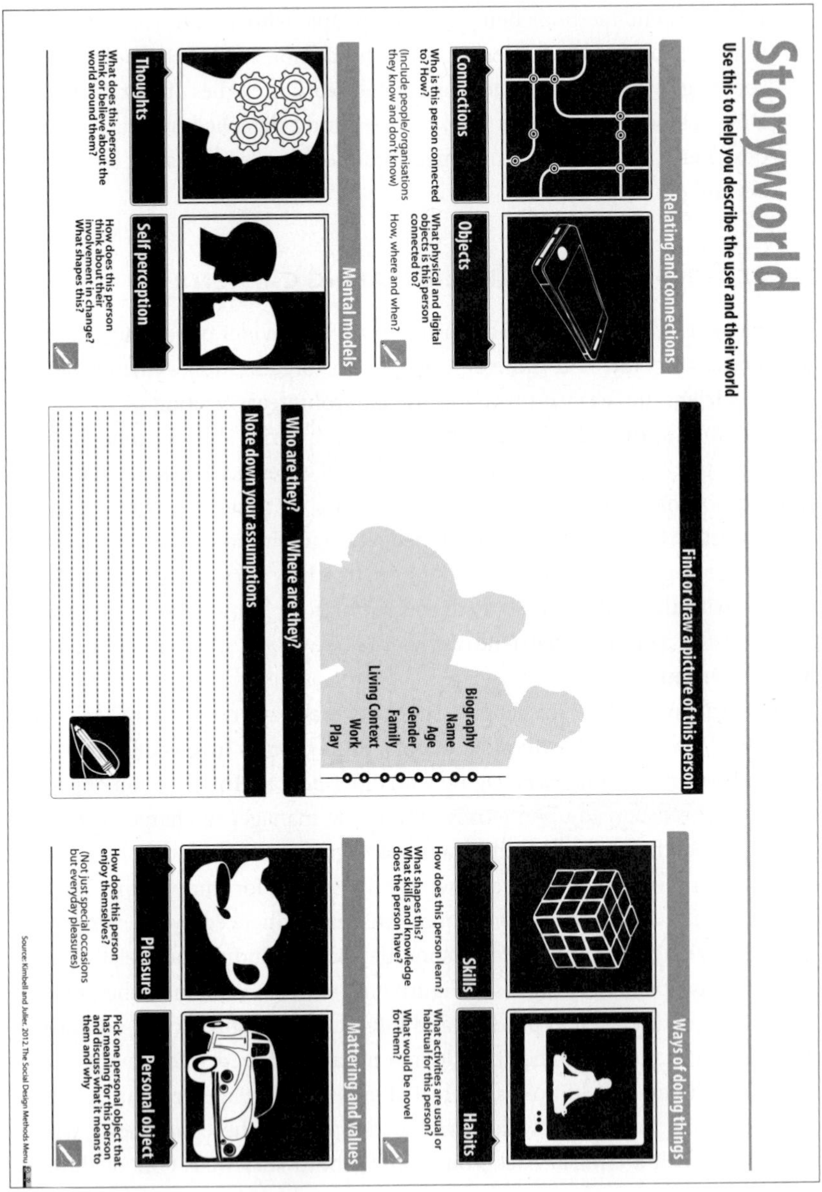

Figure 8.2. Persona of older man George, derived from interviews, and annotated in the workshop. Reproduced with permission.

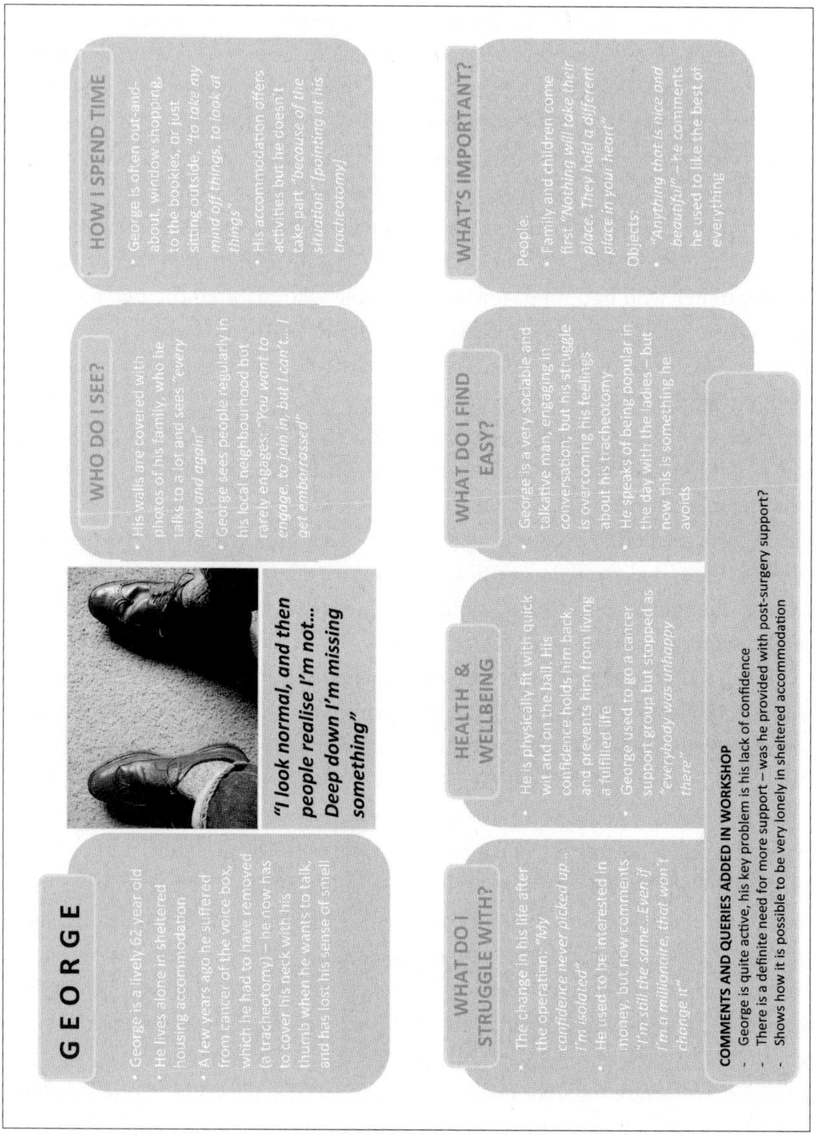

create personas to use with them as part of a method assemblage to reconstitute the issue we were working on (see Wilkie 2010).

With my colleagues I then organized and facilitated a workshop with six staff members and two service users. Our aims were to share, develop, and validate the eight personas we had created, elicit themes emerging across all of them, and help the organization's staff clarify which themes they wanted to focus on.

During the workshop, we asked participants to "get to know" the set of personas by reading them, discussing them in pairs, and writing notes onto the printouts, which we later added to the digital versions as shown in Figure 8.2. As the group read and discussed each of the personas, we asked participants to assess if they recognized the person being described, and invited them to query the researcher who had interviewed the people who inspired the personas. We also invited participants to add extra information to the personas, drawing on their knowledge of older people and the health and care systems. For example, when reviewing the persona named George, who lives in sheltered housing, participants began to query the support and services around George. George had undergone a tracheotomy and had lost confidence when interacting with other people. One participant said, "There is a definite need for more support: was he provided with postsurgery support?" This illustrates how the personas were not viewed as fixed descriptions of a state of affairs, but opened up conversations among participants about older people's particular needs and resources, and how these could be reconfigured.

We then asked them to work in pairs to create additional personas on blank templates, to include examples of older people they thought were missing or people they thought might be potential users of the service they were designing. Working in pairs, the staff members created four new personas based on people known to them: one person who was unable to leave their bed, another with dementia, one who was himself a carer of a son with learning difficulties, and a fourth who was an older person with learning difficulties. The participants then shared these new personas with one another, again adding layers of detail to one another's descriptions and querying or challenging aspects. In their discussions the staff made numerous references to people they worked with, drawing on their detailed knowledge of older people's lived realities from their work as support staff and service managers. The two service users also contributed to the activities. The group together created a revised set of 12 personas of older people, which brought into view the lived experiences of some of the people the organization wanted to support through the befriending service. The nuances and details in these discussions brought the hybrid users to life as distinct people, situated within particular contexts with specific needs and resources.

Our next activity was to discuss themes emerging from this collection of personas. Examples suggested by participants included making distinctions between older people who pay for services versus those who do not; those who are active versus those who are less active; older people who live in the community versus those who live in supported housing; those who are isolated versus those who are not isolated; those who benefit from one-on-one interactions versus those who function better in groups; and those who have carers versus those who live alone and have few visitors. However, as facilitators, we identified and proposed two other themes we had heard in the conversation, which, in discussion, participants agreed were a useful way to distinguish between older people. These were people with lots of meaningful connections versus those with fewer connections, and those who are in a stable situation versus those whose situation was worsening.

We then drew up on the wall a matrix with these two themes as axes, as shown in Figure 8.3. We asked participants to place each of the personas in the quadrants. For example, participants described the persona George shown in Figure 8.2 as midway down the y-axis because he was in a stable situation, but quite far to the right on the x-axis, as he had few meaningful connections. This activity led to productive discussions about the lives of the different personas and in some cases the older people they were based on. On reviewing all the personas placed on the matrix, participants identified that the target group they wanted to address with their service was people "going downhill" who were slipping into a less sustainable situation, and who had few meaningful connections (the top-right quadrant of Figure 8.3).

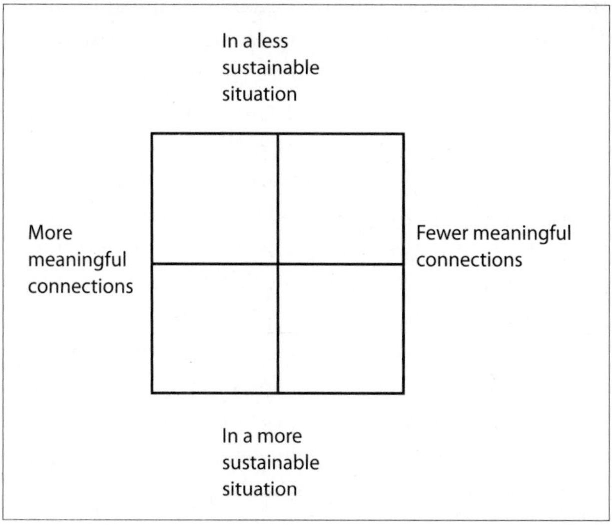

Figure 8.3. Matrix developed in workshop to analyze older people targeted by the befriending service.

By developing and populating this matrix, the participants now had a shared conceptual apparatus for distinguishing between the older people their service might support. Instead of asking "How do we get people to pay for a befriending service?" as at the beginning of the project, the staff had shifted towards identifying groups who they thought the service could benefit and could articulate a reason why the older person, or family members or carers, might now see value in a befriending service.

In summary, this workshop provided the organization with a way to engage productively with design ethnography. Although we also delivered interview notes to our client, we decided that our focus should be finding a way to enable staff to access their *own* detailed knowledge of the older people they worked with, and to help them access the few days of research we had done for them. The workshop was thus a performative encounter between different kinds of knowledge: the staff members' embodied knowledge about older people, families, and the health and social care systems; ethnographic rendering of the interviewees' worlds captured in the interviews and personas which made this knowledge less familiar and more analytical; and the participants' lack of knowledge about how to use this to design a befriending service. It was not a situation where we acted as researchers, handing over our analysis from my colleague's interviews, but rather an event that staged a mutual elaboration between activities based in ethnography (observation and understanding of the world) and design (acting on the world) (Halse 2008). Reviewing and annotating the eight personas we had created and then producing additional ones allowed the staff to engage with the activities of researching and designing. In short, this workshop approach made design ethnography doable for these staff members. Our persona-creating process and workshop design brought into view their working practices and knowledge, resulting in a collective activity that made available the complex, situated lives of the people the organization wanted to reach, and posed questions about the volunteers who could support them.

This design-ethnography approach had another function. As personas were reviewed, annotated, and created in the workshop, some of the participants made present resources that were not previously evident or available. In the organization's documents and in our emails, phone calls, and meetings with them, staff members had used language consistent with the existing care paradigm: the older people had "needs," whereas the volunteers had "resources," so the task of the befriending service was to engage the latter to address the former. However, the design-ethnographic approach enacted in the workshop prompted staff and service users to highlight something different: the older people's *capacities*. They both saw the older people as having something to offer the (presumably younger) people coming into their homes. The older people were not just people with needs who needed care. Rather, they were active participants in the encounter in their homes, and this insight should be built into the design of the befriending service. Similarly, when we went through a similar exercise in a later workshop reviewing, annotating, and creating volunteer personas, this activity shifted the group from seeing the befrienders as volunteers with something to offer to seeing them as having requirements themselves and the service as having outcomes for them.

The result was to move the project team from understanding older people as individuals needing support and care to people situated within their own social networks and localities, who were also a resource supporting the befriending service. In our subsequent work to support their design of the befriending service, we were able to cast the befriending service as an encounter of mutual value between an older person and a volunteer, rather than a service primarily to support older people.

SERVICES AS CONFIGURING SOCIOMATERIAL RESOURCES

I turn now to another workshop some weeks later, which further advanced the project. This brought an operational focus to thinking through what resources were required to deliver and support interactions between older people and others in their living environment, with the befrienders, and with the organization itself. To help the managers and staff work out what the service needed to offer and how this should be resourced, we organized a workshop that used a version of the service blueprint method. This method draws on research in services marketing (Bitner et al. 2008) that sees a service as a configuration of people and artifacts over time and distinguishes between "frontstage" and "backstage" operations. The template shown in Figure 8.4 combines this with an ethnographically informed understanding of situated interactions between humans and digital and material artifacts over time. The project team had already designed a first version of many of these interactions, such as preparing interview protocols for volunteers, but at this stage, the discrete events and artifacts they were planning had not been brought together.

We organized a collaborative visual activity in two stages. First, on large sheets of paper we stuck to the wall, we drew out a grid based on the blueprint template, adapted to the vocabulary used by the organization's staff. If the x-axis represents time, then the various phases from left (present) to right (future) allowed participants a way to describe important events in the interactions between people and artifacts in the service they were designing. In this workshop, participants decided to distinguish these phases: inquiring (finding out about the service), assessment (signing up or joining it), induction (training and matching older people and befrienders), first visit or meeting, second and subsequent visits, feedback, and ending.

Figure 8.4. Service blueprint template. Courtesy of Kimbell and Julier.

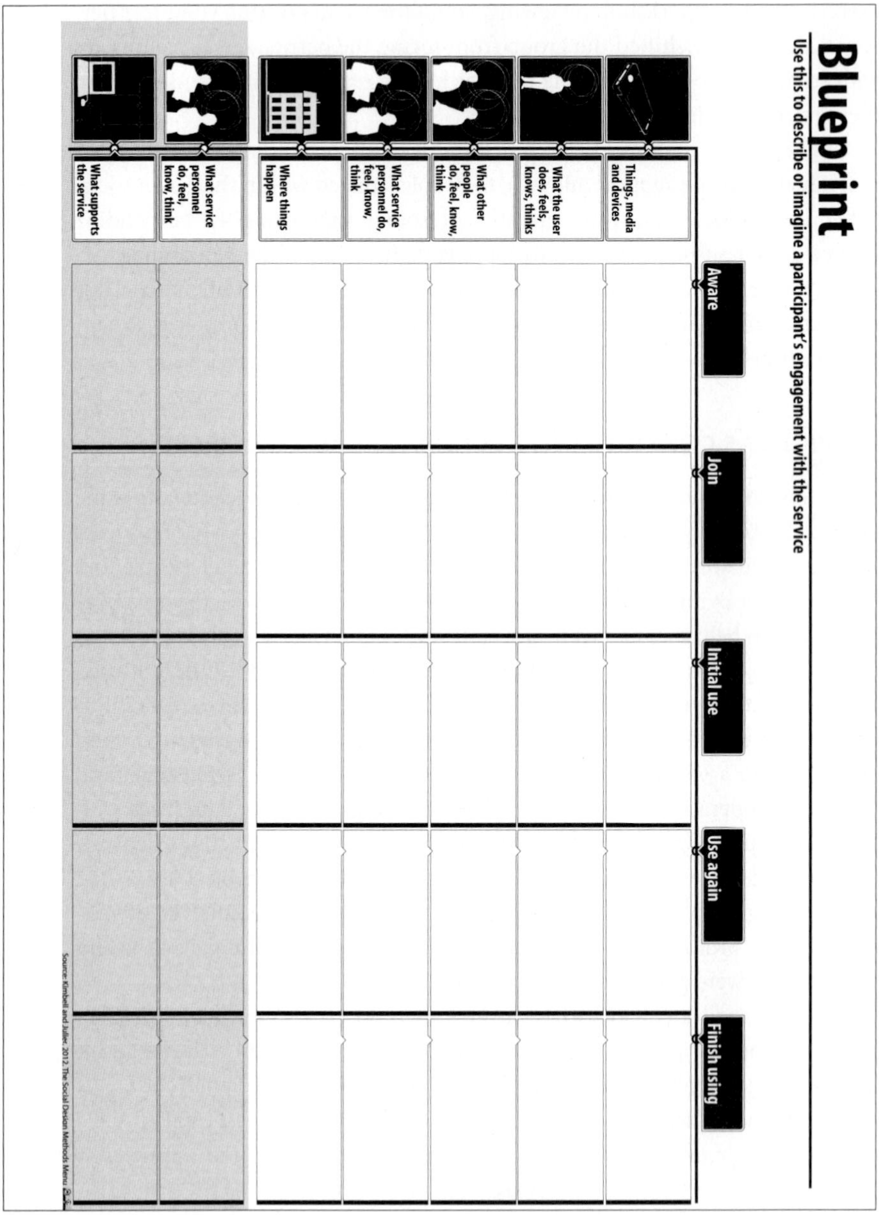

We then asked participants to tell a story based on this framework, describing in detail the imaginary encounter of one of the older people personas and one of the befriender personas, matched by the staff member whose actual job this would be, while we captured aspects by writing and drawing on the framework on the wall. As they went about this, participants referred again and again to the personas (who they were familiar with from previous workshops), describing what might happen in the imagined interactions between them and with staff members and organizational artifacts such as forms, letters, and websites. After the whole narrative had been completed, we then asked participants to reflect on how the description of the service they had created would be different if we had used other personas. This led to a discussion that resulted in the team concluding that the service interactions they described worked for most of the personas but highlighted some of the meanings the interactions had for older people, volunteer befrienders, and members of staff. This, then, was now a nearly stable description of the service they wanted to offer.

The second stage of this workshop involved a closer focus on the backstage operations of the service: the resources available (or not) internally within the organization required to constitute the interactions they hoped for between these older people and these befrienders. For this activity, we asked participants to describe the teams and organizational functions they thought were required to support the service, using vocabulary they were familiar with based on a structure we proposed that distinguished between operations, human resources, marketing and communications, finance and accounting, information technology (IT), and research. Again, we captured this on large sheets of paper on the wall, and we later wrote this up in digital form for later use (Figure 8.5). This activity led to extensive discussions between managers and staff members about how their team and the new service interacted with the rest of their organization, and to what extent its aims were being realistically resourced.

Throughout this workshop, the collective temporal ordering enacted by doing the blueprinting allowed the participants to put into relation different human and organizational resources. The activities moved them from thinking about what might happen between *this* older person, and *this* befriender (based on the personas) during a home visit toward considering how resources within and beyond their own organization were implicated in the service in which this interaction was a key activity. The shared visual activity of the blueprinting method brought into view the multiple actors involved in the service over time, as well as important artifacts such as application forms and databases and interactions between people via phone calls and face-to-face encounters. The befriending service was now in view as an unfolding configuration of all these elements, both digital and material artifacts and the events and practices in which they were given meaning. What this method helped the project team do

Figure 8.5. Service operations blueprint for the befriending service. Reproduced with permission.

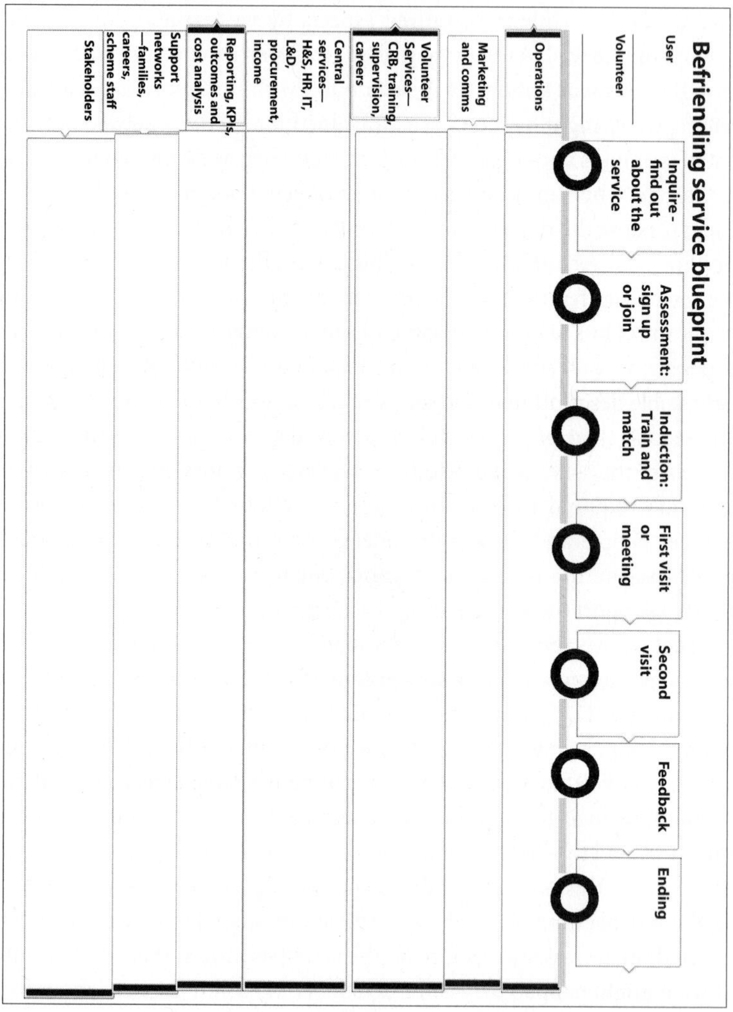

was rethink the entity they were designing as something in which digital and material artifacts as well as the practices played important roles and in which the interrelationships between them were contingent and open to query.

DOABLE & AT HUMAN SCALE

What I have tried to do is show how in the context of one contemporary topic—aging—an approach that combines ethnography and design can be used to change the way the issue is made up in practice. In my description of a project in which I was involved, I have illustrated how methods that combine aspects of design and ethnography can serve to reconstitute the issue and render it accessible for the professionals involved, even when resources are limited. I showed how the creation, development, and use of personas in a workshop with staff members allowed them to shift away from seeing their work as designing a befriending service for older people with needs to a reconfiguration of the caring issue: it was not just something "done to" older people, but rather an interaction of two active participants in the process. Here, the older people were recast as having capacities and resources, and similarly, the volunteers had requirements and the service had impacts on them. In addition, the workshop helped the staff better describe the older people they wanted to target and why the befriending service would be of value to them. I also described how the use of blueprinting created a temporal ordering of heterogeneous actors including human and institutional resources, resulting in the team having a new, shared view of what the service was that they were designing.

These methods can be used by professionals not trained in (or even familiar with) design or ethnography. I showed how these were deployed in only a few hours in workshops to make the policy or collective issue of aging a different issue. In doing so, I tried to show how this approach:

- Revealed capacities and resources that were previously not evident;
- Constituted the issue of aging in a different way, as a sociomaterial assemblage of people, organizations, and things such as phones, databases, and buildings, but also as skills and knowledge unfolding in practice; and
- Supported recombining these capacities and resources in new ways.

Rather than being primarily concerned with coming up with new solutions to the challenge of caring for old people, I argue that design ethnography can constitute the aging issue differently. Design ethnography can render aging a different kind of problem, one that is social and material, and made up of diverse actors with capacities and resources.

Many of the practitioners and policymakers using ethnographic approaches and design methods claim they are of value because they are human-*centered* in contrast to technology-, policy-, or organization-centered approaches. I would argue that such approaches are not human-centered but rather work *at human scale*. The methods of design ethnography are centrally concerned with mobilizing people as a resource, for example when configuring new solutions in providing a service, particularly attending to old people, their carers and families, and frontline staff or volunteers involved in care. People are central to design ethnography, but they are always situated in particular worlds and in relation to other people and things and ways of living, working, and caring. Some of the methods of design ethnography that make available this relational view of people include creating personas and service blueprints. The point here, however, is not that they are human-centered but rather they provide a way to understand sociomaterial assemblages involving complex political, financial, social, and technological systems at human scale. Further, the approach and methods of design ethnography serve to make the design of a new venture or service doable when time and funds are limited. This approach is a powerful resource for engaging professionals and others involved in complex collective issues.

This account exemplifies the increasingly blurred boundaries between design and ethnography and their new locations in public policy contexts, not just workplaces or technology firms. Like other chapters in this volume, it shows how even given limited resources, the analytical orientation of ethnography is productive for asking different questions and provoking new thinking. Not simply bringing back data from the field, the central activity in this case was using an ethnographic approach to help design new services underpinned by a practice orientation. The blurring between research, design, and entrepreneurship in this chapter shows how design ethnography can be enacted as a collective practice, open to nonspecialists whose knowledge and expertise can be mobilized in participatory workshops. Further, it helps illuminate why such an approach cannot be reduced simply to toolkits for social design. By describing the active co-constitution of a collective enquiry, this chapter showed how a design-ethnographic approach recombines the analysis of fieldwork with the creativity of the studio as practice unfolds. This continues the emerging trajectory of anthropology away from the academy into different kinds of organizations, and into projects and ventures in which public policy grapples with collective issues. This casts design ethnography as a co-constituent in policy and practice.

REFERENCES

Art Center College of Design. 2012. "Designmatters." www.artcenter.edu/accd/programs/designmatters.jsp (accessed September 16, 2012).

Barad, Karen. 2007. *Meeting the Universe Halfway: Quantum Physics and the Entanglement of Matter and Meaning*. Durham, NC: Duke University Press.

Bason, Christian. 2010. *Leading Public Sector Innovation: Co-Creating for a Better Society*. Bristol, UK: Policy Press.

Bate, Paul, and Glenn Robert. 2007. *Bringing User Experience to Healthcare Improvement: The Concepts, Methods and Practices of Experience-Based Design*. Abingdon, UK: Radcliffe Publishing.

Binder, Thomas, Giorgio de Michelis, Pelle Ehn, Giulio Jacucci, Per Linde, and Ina Wagner. 2011. *Design Things*. Cambridge, MA: MIT Press.

Bitner, Mary Jo, Amy Ostrom, and Felicia Morgan. 2008. "Service Blueprinting: A Practical Technique for Service Innovation." *California Management Review* 50(3):66–94.

Blyth, Simon, and Lucy Kimbell. 2011. *Design Thinking and the Big Society*. London: Actant and Taylor Haig.

Design Council. 2012. "Design Challenges." www.designcouncil.org.uk/our-work/challenges/ (accessed September 16, 2012).

DESIS Network. 2012. "Design for Social Innovation and Sustainability." www.desis-network.org/ (accessed September 16, 2012).

DiSalvo, Carl. 2012. *Adversarial Design*. Cambridge, MA: MIT Press.

Ehn, Pelle. 1988. *Work-Oriented Design of Computer Artifacts*. Hillsdale, NJ: Lawrence Erlbaum Associates.

Halse, Joachim. 2008. "Design Anthropology: Borderland Experiments with Participation, Performance and Situated Intervention." Doctoral thesis, The IT University of Copenhagen, Denmark.

Kimbell, Lucy, and Joe Julier. 2012. *Social Design Methods Menu*. London: Fieldstudio Ltd.

Latour, Bruno. 2005. *Reassembling the Social: An Introduction to Actor-Network-Theory*. Oxford, UK: Oxford University Press.

Miller, Derek, Lisa Rudnick, Lucy Kimbell, and Gerry Philipsen. 2010. "Strategic Design and Public Policy: The Glen Cove Conference on Strategic Design and Public Policy." unidir.org/pdf/activites/pdf3-act535.pdf (accessed September 16, 2012).

MindLab. 2011. "About MindLab." www.mind-lab.dk/assets/116/ml_folder_eng.pdf (accessed July 15, 2011).

Nesta. 2012. "Public Services Lab." www.nesta.org.uk/areas_of_work/public_services_lab (accessed September 15, 2012).

Office for Public Management (OPM). 2004. "Every Child Matters: Change for Children. The Management, Organisational and Governance Implications." Briefing Paper, December 2004. www.commissioningsupport.org.uk/idocc09c.pdf?docid=5ce752d3-14ec-45da-837a-626ab8b452e2&version=-1 (accessed July 15, 2011).

Parker, Sophia, and Joe Heapy. 2006. *The Journey to the Interface: How Public Service Design Can Connect Users to Reform*. London: Demos.

Participle. 2012. "The Circle Movement." www.participle.net/projects/view/5/101/ (accessed December 15, 2012).

Rittel, Horst, and Martin Webber. 1973. "Dilemmas in a General Theory of Planning." *Policy Sciences* 4:155–69.

Suchman, Lucy. 2002. "Practice-Based Design of Information Systems: Notes from the Hyperdeveloped World." *The Information Society* 18(2):139–44.

The Australian Centre for Social Innovation (TACSI). 2012. "How Can We Enable Great Living in Late Adulthood?" www.tacsi.org.au/our-projects/caring/ (accessed September 16, 2012).

Thorpe, Adam, and Lorraine Gamman. 2011. "Design and Society: Why Socially Responsive Design Is Good Enough. *CoDesign: International Journal of Cocreation in Design and the Arts* 7(3-4):217–30.

Wilkie, Alex. 2010. "User Assemblages in Design: An Ethnographic Study." Doctoral thesis, Goldsmiths, University of London.

NOTES

The case described was a project undertaken by The Young Foundation in 2012.

1 For a fuller discussion, please see Bason (2010), Blyth and Kimbell (2011), Kimbell and Julier (2012), and Thorpe and Gamman (2011).

9

The Anthropologist as IT Troubleshooter on Wall Street

PATRICIA ENSWORTH

INTRODUCTION

Among large global organizations, the keywords in the human resources job database seldom include "anthropologist." In the domain of information technology (IT) systems, the notion that anthropology might provide useful concepts or methods to address real-life business issues often provokes a skeptical first response. Yet in the past 25 years, throughout my career as a manager and consultant, the theories, perspectives, and skills instilled by my education in anthropology have helped solve critical problems time and again. The four-field body of knowledge has provided a framework for investigating an organization's culture, language, physical characteristics, and historical artifacts. The research principles and methods of ethnography have shaped my approach to learning about people's beliefs, values, and behaviors in their occupational environment. The metaphor of a work process community as a cultural group with unique social structures, myths, customary practices, and so on has influenced my data-gathering techniques, analytical assumptions, and recommendations for fixing broken systems.

Here is a tale of one such adventure.

CASE STUDY: MEGABLING BANK

Recruitment

Detective stories often begin when the private investigator receives an appeal for help from someone in trouble. So it is with management consultants. On a spring morning in 2005, the call came from the mother of one of my child's elementary school classmates who worked as a senior project manager in the

Handbook of Anthropology in Business, edited by Rita Denny and Patricia Sunderland, 202–222.

IT department of Megabling Bank.[1] I did not know her well personally. Because we both worked in IT we had met for lunch a few times and traded professional war stories along with observations about school life.

"We need a consultant to help us get some projects back on track," she said. "Can you come in and meet with my managing director?"

Like any anthropologist preparing for fieldwork, I researched the Megabling "tribe" and practiced their native language. Megabling was one of the world's top five investment banks. The division that employed the managing director (MD) created investment products and traded securities both for the bank's own account and on behalf of its customers. Among the types of securities were derivatives based upon equities, bonds, mortgages, credit card debt, interest rates, currencies, and commodities. The IT environment included Windows, Unix, mainframe, and telecommunications platforms. The firm's operations spanned major offices in New York, London, Frankfurt, Zurich, Hong Kong, and Tokyo, with smaller offices in Rio de Janeiro, Glasgow, Paris, Budapest, Dubai, Shanghai, and Sydney. At the most senior levels of management the leaders of the company were European, although more than half of the investment capital came from China and oil-producing Middle Eastern countries.

As we met in his spacious private office overlooking midtown Manhattan, interrupted frequently by incoming calls and messages on his BlackBerry, the MD explained the situation. He was in trouble because he had bent some rules and now faced unpleasant consequences.

To implement their Y2K defense strategy, in the late 1990s Megabling had outsourced most of the testing and some of the maintenance development work for its proprietary software applications and IT systems to a leading vendor in India. Over a period of five years Megabling's corporate sourcing and risk management groups had worked closely with the Indian supplier to ensure compliance with industry standards for data security and privacy, disaster recovery, project management, documentation, and other key elements of a mature, reliable offshore outsourcing engagement. This Indian company had been designated as the only approved supplier with whom Megabling's IT managers were allowed to do business.

The Indian engineers were well educated, skilled, and hard-working. Their employer ensured that they received ongoing training in new technologies and global business practices. However, they were accustomed to a structured work environment and hierarchical chain of command. They had been educated to follow instructions, but not to propose ideas. In the domain of finance, they were familiar with traditional investment products: the sort of stocks, bonds, and options that even the most sophisticated, risk-taking investor traded until powerful computers and internet connectivity arrived on Wall Street in the mid-1990s.

The MD told me that when Megabling's new types of derivatives were being created soon after Y2K, the Indian testers and developers had performed poorly. They seemed unable to cope with the complex algorithms underlying the structures of these unconventional securities, and they also had difficulty keeping up with the fast pace at which innovative products were being designed, sold, and traded.

Hoping to solidify Megabling's leadership position in this dynamic market, the MD had taken matters into his own hands. Bypassing the firm's procurement and risk management departments, and signing several small contracts for which he did not need budget approval from a higher authority, the MD initiated a stealth pilot project. He established outsourcing engagements with two suppliers not on the approved vendor list, one in Toronto and the other in Kiev. Both firms were boutiques staffed by testers and developers more experienced in collaborative design, mathematical creativity, and agile project management methodologies than their counterparts in India.

It had been a good idea at first: so good, in fact, that within two years the number of applications and systems tested in Kiev had doubled and the number in Toronto had quadrupled. Mindful of their turbulent recent history in the post-Soviet era, the Kiev supplier had taken the initiative to comply with procurement and risk management department requirements, but the Toronto supplier felt no such urgency. As a result, critical work on many of Megabling's most profitable and cutting-edge products was now in the hands of an unauthorized vendor (Figure 9.1).

There was more bad news. In Toronto, the volume of work had grown beyond the supplier's ability to handle it. Delivery schedules were slipping and error rates increasing. The office had run out of space and equipment but could not afford to expand unless the supplier raised their rates. Turnover among the staff had increased, and the new hires seemed less competent. In the New York Megabling office, tensions were running high between the onsite employees of the rival outsourcing vendors. The previous week a fight had broken out: a male Canadian tester had insulted a female Indian tester with X-rated profanity, and she had thrown hot coffee in his face. Since legally this constituted a workplace assault, the female tester had been immediately fired and deported. Debates about the fairness of the punishment had divided the office, and morale was terrible. Worst of all, the risk management auditors had discovered some serious operational and security failures during an inspection of the Toronto facility. Unless these violations were corrected within 60 days, the contracts with the Toronto supplier would be broken and the engagement terminated at once. The Megabling products they worked on would be abruptly withdrawn from the markets. The MD would certainly lose his job and would probably be pilloried in the financial media.

Figure 9.1. Megablinginformation technology outsourcing logistics.

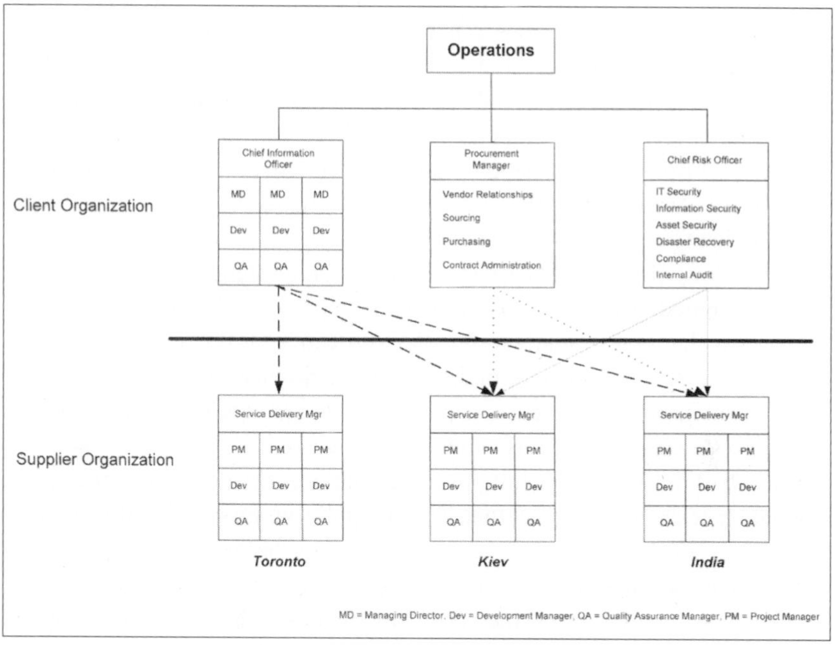

The MD had seen this crisis coming for a while, and he had tried a number of tactics to address the situation, but there had been no improvement. Now he had reached the point where he realized he needed help from outside: an expert consultant.

When it comes to hiring consultants, senior executives have three choices. They can engage the services of a big enterprise partner such as IBM, Deloitte and Touche, Accenture, or Infosys. They can go to a boutique firm with between a dozen and a hundred employees and/or associates who specialize in an esoteric business domain and/or technical skill. Or they can recruit a soloist, who then brings in other professionals as needed.

Each approach has advantages and disadvantages. The big enterprise partners offer vast resources. Their brand name opens doors and confers a sense of security among the client's personnel. But they tend to accept the lines of authority depicted in the client's organization chart at face value, and they avoid challenging the status quo. Establishing the engagement is bureaucratic, time-consuming, and requires a great deal of involvement from the client's procurement department and the vendor's service delivery staffs. Most important, it draws senior management attention to the seriousness of the problem.

Relationships with consultants from boutique firms are easier and quicker to initiate, and these experts often provide access to more state-of-the-art tools and techniques. However, they can be very expensive. Certain experts can be difficult to schedule because they service many clients simultaneously. The solutions they propose can be inflexible because they are structured according to the firm's signature methodology or custom software. Some boutique firms are also notorious for information leaks: the client's senior management might not become alarmed about the problem, but there could be gossip on the street and the client's competitors might find out.

The soloist might at first appear to be the riskiest solution. He or she might quit, get injured, fall ill, or turn out to be incompetent. Balancing these disadvantages is the soloist's ability to serve as a detective, mediator, and therapist. One can more easily operate under senior management's radar and cross-departmental silo boundaries to map actual power structures and networks of influence. Tactics of grassroots community organizing can be more effectively employed so that stakeholders support the solutions they create and the implementation takes into account their specific political, financial, and technical realities. A soloist's independence and objectivity become important assets when the engagement in question is an innovation or a turnaround project. Under those circumstances, the consultant acts as a change agent, bringing together diverse stakeholders who do not normally interact with each other and enabling them to make a difference.

It was not necessary for me to make much of a sales pitch to the MD, because I had been referred by a trusted colleague and he already had a good idea of who I was and what I had done. He was a mathematician and computer scientist in charge of more than 300 IT workers around the world. According to his classification schema, I was a project manager specializing in business analysis, requirements engineering, and quality assurance for information systems at large global organizations.

When he asked me how anthropology factored into the equation, I explained that for 20 years I had been applying ethnographic research concepts and methods to help build software and manage information systems. As an analyst at a retail brokerage, I had started out focusing on usability issues for international applications. For 10 years as a manager at a credit rating agency I had led a multicultural group responsible for process reengineering. After publishing a technical reference book of advice for new project managers, I had become an independent consultant and had started my own company. Only half-joking, I told him that from my experience working as a consultant and a business owner I had realized that project leadership involved elements of shamanism: the project team needs to believe in one's magical powers to conjure creative spirits, heal organizational disease, and give the tribe courage to deal with an uncertain future. He laughed, but he got it.

For the MD, I believe the key selling point was that my anthropology "secret sauce" had somehow earned me a reputation for being good at getting difficult people to communicate and collaborate better. For me, the application of anthropology in a Wall Street firm was more a matter of variations on a proven and widely known recipe. Over the years through my participation in committees and initiatives of the Society for Applied Anthropology, the National Association of Practicing Anthropologists, and the American Anthropological Association's Committee on Practicing, Applied, and Public Interest Anthropology, I had discovered many similarities between my work with information systems in global organizations and my colleagues' work in tourism, cultural/natural resource management, and public health. At conferences we debated the same questions of ethics and objectivity, and we compared notes on our respective symptoms of "going native." One advantage of my professional domain was that I rarely needed to use sunblock, insect repellent, or hand sanitizer on the job.

While his BlackBerry flashed and buzzed, we discussed the evolution of information technology in finance from standalone punch card mainframe computers to interconnected high-speed planetary digital networks. We traded war stories about preparations for Y2K and recovery from the 9/11 attacks. At the end I was hired and provided with an ID badge, a system login, and a budget. To form a task force I was given matrixed supervisory authority over seven test managers and development managers with projects in the Toronto pipeline.

Research Process

The first challenge we faced was to train the task force in ethnographic concepts and methods. These were busy people; they needed to know just enough to be motivated and effective.

During my previous consulting engagements I had learned to omit lengthy discourses on anthropological fieldwork. Unless specifically asked, I would not disclose that my historical role model was Bronislaw Malinowski, or that I felt his study of the trading practices and nautical technology among the Trobriand Islanders provided a useful template for cultural analysis of capitalist high-tech organizations (Malinowski 1961). Likewise, I seldom found that business colleagues related well to Arjun Appadurai's concept of a translocal ethnoscape as a multisited community united by common cultural customs, values, and activities (Appadurai 1988). The idea elaborated by Rita Denny that linguistic practices define the terms of engagement (Denny 2012) might provide me with a good conceptual framework for my research strategy, but like people seeking to build a new house, my clients wanted to see the design rather than hear about underlying architectural principles.

If some of the client team members were old enough to remember how users operated computers before the introduction of the graphical user interface, the mouse, or the laser printer, I might mention the Xerox Palo Alto Research Center (or PARC, where all three were invented). I could tell them about PARC's ethnographic research for projects in its Work Practice and Technology laboratory (Szymanski and Whalen 2011). Younger members were usually impressed by recent anecdotes of ethnography at companies such as IBM, Intel, Google, Yahoo, Microsoft, and Facebook (Cefkin 2010).

Generally it is most effective to present the skillset of ethnography to IT professionals as an adaptation and enhancement of techniques they already use. For example, project managers are already familiar with "stakeholder identification" (Ensworth 2001; Kerzner 2009; Project Management Institute 2008). Business analysts and software developers practice "requirements elicitation" (International Institute of Business Analysis 2009; Wiegers 2003). Quality assurance specialists study workers' motivation and communication when they attempt to improve operational procedures (Juran 1992; Walton and Deming 1988).

During my presentation to the Megabling task force I stated that an essential concept of the ethnographic approach is its focus upon the lived experience of the people affected by the organizational problem that management wants to solve. In the domain of information technology, the problem often arises if a system developed in the past no longer accurately models the relationships, rules, and transactions of the present. When a system is first built, business analysts and requirements engineers interview users and stakeholders to create the design. They document their research in the form of use cases, flowcharts, and system architecture diagrams. These techniques may work well enough for version 1.0 because the cyberspace model matches the user community's lived experience. But over time, the model and the reality increasingly diverge. Later, when those business analysts and requirements engineers go back to the users and stakeholders and try to gather data about why Version 6.3 is generating so many errors and causing so many headaches, two factors frequently prevent them from making a good diagnosis. First, their tools (the use case, the flowchart, the system diagram) are ill-suited to capturing the panoply of weird adaptive behaviors that evolve in isolated locations. Second, many members of the user community are ashamed or afraid to admit their actual behaviors. They know how the process was designed and what they are supposed to do; in effect, the system has acquired the moral authority of law (Lessig 2006).

Therefore, another important concept of the ethnographic approach I stressed is that obtaining valid information about a person's actions demands more data sources than the individual's self-reported account. Even if the subject is not deliberately lying, he or she may misinterpret the question, accidentally leave things out, or omit messy details in an attempt to provide a coherent narrative and/or please the interviewer. From the ethnographer's perspective, this situation does not indicate a rule violation or moral failing: it's just the way things are in the field (Bernard 2011).

Fortunately, these concepts have some theoretical parallels and precedents in the IT world. Coders who have studied the psychology of computer programming may understand the dynamic relationship between system models and human behavior (Weinberg 1998). Battle-scarred managers with years of experience mediating between uncooperative groups of stakeholders may have acquired a more humanistic view of the "peopleware" that keeps the enterprise in business (DeMarco and Lister 1999). User interface designers and usability testers may already be lobbying for more focus on the variety of lived realities (Schumacher 2009) and against the software's tendency to enforce binary thinking (Lanier 2010).

The Megabling task force listened without comment. Unlike in academia, I find there is rarely an intellectual appetite for debates about concepts in a business environment. What matters is getting things done: the action plan.

The first step in our action plan would be to establish a steering committee. The committee would include our core task force and be augmented by representatives from the operational functions necessary for the success of an offshore outsourcing engagement. We would select three systems for which the Toronto supplier provided development or testing services. The systems would comprise different technical architectures, business functions, and user communities. Members of the core task force would study each system's work processes from end to end. From our data analysis, we would discover common issues. We would also identify subject matter experts, influential users, and other stakeholders who cared about fixing the problems. These people would be invited to form a working group. The working group would prioritize the issues and propose solutions. The steering committee would review and approve the solutions, and if necessary procure additional resources and funding. Both the steering committee and the working group would meet biweekly and make presentations on their milestones, deliverables, and progress toward their solutions. A collaboration website would be created on the firm's intranet for posting announcements and storing documents. When special expertise was needed, I would engage the services of other consultants with whom I regularly collaborated to design surveys, organize and analyze data, and create training. Once the problems with the Toronto supplier had been resolved, the steering committee would disband, the working group would transition to a permanent self-governing Community of Practice, and I would depart.

Initially the task force responded that this action plan seemed quite similar to other organizational development initiatives they had participated in both at Megabling and elsewhere. The differences began to emerge when I described the ethnographic methods we would use.

For our research exploring a system's end-to-end work processes we would select a sample of users to study. Typically, with what we might call "conventional" methods, senior management would select the research subjects. We would accept senior management's list, but we would also create our own list based upon the snowball sampling technique. To show the structure of the user community we would use organization charts as well as social network diagrams.

Conventional methods included researchers interviewing their "subjects"[2] for a half-hour by phone and reviewing artifacts the subjects sent via e-mail. Researchers also would secretly examine the data logs produced by the subjects' usage of the IT systems. Instead, we would personally visit the people at their work locations. Depending upon their role, these one-to-one encounters would last from a half-day to two days. We would conduct both open-ended interviews and structured surveys. We would observe the subjects doing their work and handling their artifacts. We would ask a subject to teach the researcher his or her job and allow the researcher to perform it as a participant-observer under supervision. We would shadow the subjects to meetings, meals, and social gatherings such as team member baby showers and fantasy baseball drafts. We would make audio and video recordings. We would show the subjects their data logs and solicit their comments. Rather than acting like inspectors, we would strive for an attitude of relaxed guests just hanging out and taking a friendly interest in their world.

In addition, the conventional approach to classification of data seemed too narrow for our ethnographic methods. Usually researchers began their data gathering with checklists of definitions and categories prescribed by the functionality of the system. We would encourage the subjects to tell stories, and from those narratives we would derive "native" taxonomies. Whereas conventional organizational development techniques might rank subjects' occupational roles based upon a hierarchy of influence into groups such as "expert," "partner," or "pair of hands," we would also explore our subjects' social roles within their user community: warlord, den mother, sidekick, peacekeeper, hostess, guidance counselor, etc. Our reports presenting our findings would show photographs of actual users and provide quotations in the subjects' own words.

Our action plan estimated four months for data gathering and analysis, a long time by Megabling IT standards. We also requested a relatively large budget for international travel and research tools such as video equipment, transcription services, and statistical software. The MD approved a schedule of two months, most of the travel, and none of the tools.

Our data collection started with the instigators of the trouble: the procurement and risk management departments. We moved on to the accounting, legal, and training departments. Other important sources included the managers of each hardware platform; the owners of all the relevant internal workflow, office productivity, software engineering and change management tools; and the administrators of enterprise databases. We spent days with the developers of the applications and systems who were interfacing with resources in Toronto, and even more time with their end users in several countries. At the Toronto supplier we shadowed the service delivery manager, and we apprenticed as testers in the various groups supporting the applications and systems. We worked alongside the Toronto business and operations managers to understand their interactions with a large and valued client such as Megabling. We traveled to India to compare that supplier's structured and hierarchical methodologies with the more agile and democratic Canadian style.

Some members of the task force proved adept at the ethnographic methods and enjoyed the work; others did not. The enthusiasts became the lead researchers who developed relationships with the subjects, while the less sociable, more skeptical members preferred to help organize and analyze the data. All of the information was stored on spreadsheets. Filters, macros, and pivot tables set the boundaries of our quantitative number-crunching abilities. Content analysis of interviews and observations was performed by the researcher who interacted with the subject and then conveyed in the form of summary notes.

At first we had difficulty gaining access to our subjects, but after we discovered and resolved a management issue our work became much easier (see the Findings section for details). Fortunately when the two months ran out we were given a one-month extension in recognition of the obstacles we had initially faced. We completed about two-thirds of the data gathering and analysis we hoped for. Nevertheless, the steering committee felt that we had generated enough insights for the working group to begin implementing solutions to the issues we documented.

Senior management acknowledged that among the most important benefits of our ethnographic research was an improvement in awareness and communication between different factions of the user community for each system. Time and again we found ourselves in the position of describing to members of Group A what members of Group B thought, felt, and did, and the members of Group A would look at each other and say, "Huh. Really? That's odd. Well no wonder then. . . ." We would arrange for representatives from each group to contact each other and compare their practices, and out of the ongoing dialog would emerge suggestions for better process alignment and resource allocation.

While the solutions were being planned and implemented, my role as an ethnographer mostly consisted of ensuring that the working group and the steering committee continued to focus upon all the stakeholders affected by the changes under way. I deliberately amplified the voices of those users of the system who ordinarily would be ignored because of their low status, poor communication skills, or lack of access to decisionmakers. Such users are often the ones who develop the most creative workarounds and unique local practices, which can either serve as an inspiration to others or derail the entire system. Anthropologists might interpret this agenda as advocating industrial democracy; among business executives it is known as risk management. I also lobbied for ongoing ethnographic research to determine the impact of the solutions on the people whose work practices and relationships were altered.

Finally, when the project transitioned to an operational process, several of our ethnographic research methods were endorsed by the Megabling's central project management office as effective techniques for system design and risk mitigation.

The Findings

Management Issues

As mentioned earlier, in contrast to a sample selection process based upon organizational charts, the exploratory snowball method helps map social networks and delineate boundaries of ideology, territory, and allegiance. This proved invaluable early in our data collection when we encountered difficulties scheduling meetings with many people whom we had identified as essential interviewees. Of course, access problems are normal in ethnographic research. But our subjects' resistance seemed unusually anxious.

We kept on snowballing, asking questions about patterns of communication, past troubles, disagreements over strategy. Eventually we dug deep enough to find the root cause: a bully with a hidden agenda.

Every outsourcing engagement at Megabling was supervised by a vendor relationship manager (VRM). The role of the VRM was to ensure that the supplier met its Key Performance Indicators (KPIs) set forth in the contract's Master Services Agreement (MSA).

The VRM for the Toronto and Kiev suppliers also managed the Indian supplier. In fact, he had set up the Indian outsourcing engagement five years earlier. He had become friends with his colleagues in India and enjoyed visiting them twice a year. Any increase in work given to the Toronto or Kiev suppliers translated into a lost opportunity for the Indian supplier.

In person, one-on-one, the VRM had been charming and helpful to me and the other task force members. But whenever his name came up during our interviews, people seemed to get tense and change the subject. Then, as part of my research I attended a meeting between the VRM and the Toronto supplier's service delivery manager. The purpose of the meeting was to discover why the supplier's KPIs had been below the levels mandated in the MSA for four consecutive months.

The Toronto service delivery manager was a quiet, analytical, chess-playing engineer. He brought along several spreadsheets documenting resource constraints and workflow bottlenecks, and proceeded to describe how his testers' and developers' activities had been prioritized.

The VRM was from a tough neighborhood in Baltimore. He had worked as a debt collector, a public middle school teacher, and an auditor before he obtained his position with Megabling in the procurement department.

"Listen!" the VRM suddenly shouted, ripping the papers out of the service delivery manager's hands and tossing them in the direction of a nearby trash can. "Just cut the crap! I'm sick of your excuses. If these numbers aren't better next month I'm personally going to tear you a new asshole!"

The service delivery manager blinked a few times and nodded. Meeting adjourned.

Afterward I asked the VRM about his negotiating tactics.

"These vendors are all thieves," he informed me. "Remember that, and don't believe anything they say."

I asked about the tone of his communication. He smirked.

"Hey, it works with the Indian guys. If you don't put them in their place they won't take you seriously."

At our next steering committee meeting we considered the potential impact of the VRM's behavior upon our goal of improving trust and communication among members of the supplier-client work process community. It was agreed that his attitudes and behavior created a risk. After our MD conferred with procurement, the bully was "promoted" to *Strategic* VRM, and his role redefined as limited to advisory. A more diplomatic test manager from our task force was appointed as the day-to-day *Operational* VRM for the Toronto outsourcing engagement.

The effect was immediate. We had sent a clear signal to stakeholders at both Megabling and the Toronto supplier that our steering committee could make change happen. People were suddenly much more willing to talk to us and let us hang out with them. The pace of our data collection accelerated. Soon we were accumulating insights and developing solutions.

Business Analysis

The most urgent problem with the outsourcing engagement was a blockage in the payment of the supplier's invoices. Due to a lack of alignment between the categories of the Toronto supplier's invoices and the data fields in the Megabling accounting system, more than half of the invoices submitted were processed incorrectly, leading to time-consuming investigations among the accounting clerks on both sides. Megabling owed the Toronto supplier more than $2 million: an amount that could finance the architectural renovations and infrastructure enhancements necessary to correct the violations without any rate increase. The Toronto supplier customized its invoice format, the payment backlog gradually cleared, and remediation work began.

Risk management's checklist of operational and security safeguards had been developed for the Indian supplier. It assumed an environment of unreliable electricity, multiple religions and languages among the staff, inefficient transportation, and political instability. The senior management of the Toronto supplier felt that many of the items on the checklist were unnecessary in Canada and resisted Megabling's pressure to comply. Risk management eventually agreed and created more appropriate and affordable evaluation criteria.

For every application and system outsourced to the Toronto supplier, the Megabling test or development manager was required to create a task order. This addendum to the MSA established the outsourced work's deliverables, deadlines, quality standards, and roles and responsibilities. All task orders were written using a standard template provided by the legal department. Like the risk management checklist, the task order template had been developed for use with the Indian supplier. It assumed a degree of stability, predictability, and repeatability in the outsourced work that simply did not exist because the investment products being designed, sold, and traded were brand-new and continuously changing. As a result, the Megabling managers often ignored the task orders: they left sections blank, drafted vague specifications, or cloned versions from old and mismatched projects. In effect, there were no rules of engagement: or the rules could be revised at the whim of the client manager. The Toronto supplier did not like this state of affairs, but they did not feel empowered to protest. To improve the process, the legal department introduced an alternative task order template more suitable for agile methodologies. In addition, the training department recorded a mandatory video briefing for client managers about the importance of correct task orders and the recommended practices for writing them. Procurement also implemented a periodic audit of task orders on file with review comments for the authors.

Whenever a new hire at the Toronto supplier joined a Megabling project, the Megabling IT administrators of all the hardware platforms, workflow tools, human resources systems, time-tracking systems, and relevant applications and databases needed to add the person to their list of users and configure appropriate levels of permissions for access. Each individual access request required a separate e-mail or intranet form, and most were sent to different IT administrators. Many requests could not be granted until they had been sent several levels up the management hierarchy for review and approval. In addition, all permissions expired periodically and needed to be renewed, but the person holding the permission was not always notified before, during, or after the expiration, leaving him or her to cope with a sudden mysterious loss of connectivity. Delays were common, resulting in idle, unproductive time for the Toronto supplier resources and frantic scrambles when deadlines loomed or failures occurred. It appeared that the Toronto supplier was being unfairly blamed for a problem actually caused by dysfunctional Megabling processes.

This sort of inefficient cyberbureaucracy had become the bane of all IT system users' existence in many organizations, and everyone just put up with it the way they endured commuter traffic. However, the contractual issues of the vendor-client relationship and the dependence of critical revenue-generating investment products on high levels of response time, operational throughput, and quality standards motivated Megabling senior management to pay attention and order immediate remedial action. In this case no new checklists, templates, or procedures were necessary: it was simply a matter of telling everyone at Megabling to use the same forms and processes as they already did for onboarding new hires at the Indian supplier. The MSA was amended to give the Toronto service delivery manager responsibility for ensuring that new hire permissions were granted within a certain time, and an escalation path to follow at Megabling if he encountered delays. At the Toronto supplier each team created a permissions template for their application or system, and they began tracking the issue and expiration dates. Within a few months the unproductive time due to lack of access significantly declined.

Requirements Engineering

At the beginning of the outsourcing engagement, the Toronto supplier employed only six testers and three developers assigned to two Megabling applications. The Megabling development managers invested time and effort in explaining the bank's business, describing the IT environment, and demonstrating the software. The Toronto resources got to know the Megabling developers and end users in New York and London; they communicated daily by e-mail, instant messages, teleconferences, and phone calls. The tone of communication was informal, with lots of banter and commentary on nonwork topics. Under these circumstances, when a requirement submitted by Megabling seemed ambiguous—for example in the interpretation of a business rule, user type, or design layout—the Toronto tester or developer was often able to make an educated guess about the intent and get it right. Otherwise, a quick message or phone call to a Megabling developer or end user would usually resolve the issue.

As the engagement grew, this informal teamwork gave way to a more impersonal, document-based mode of interaction. The metaphorical bandwidth of communication between Megabling and the Toronto supplier narrowed, and exchanges become less frequent. New hires in Toronto began their work without ever having met or spoken to anyone from Megabling except for a telephone job interview with the development manager. They understood Megabling was some kind of bank, but many thought it was a consumer retail business with checking and savings accounts. Their software demos were conducted hurriedly by the senior members of the Toronto teams. At Megabling, development managers no longer remembered the names of the Toronto people working for them, much less their individual areas of technical expertise or their favorite sports.

This alienation would probably not have mattered as much if the applications and systems under development had been associated with services commonly used by the general public. Yet the investment products were both esoteric and constantly evolving as the capabilities of computer technology expanded. Rather than simply writing code to implement design specifications they had been given, developers were co-creators of the new cybermarkets. Misunderstandings among the developers, testers, and end users hindered the research and development (R&D) process, undermined quality, and delayed product releases.

To reconnect the vendor and client groups on the development teams, first the Megabling training department adapted the welcome packet and orientation video they used for the company's new hires so that the materials were suitable for outsourcing engagements. The Toronto supplier added content describing the bank's business—information that was unnecessary for Megabling recruits because they would have learned it in the process of applying for jobs—and made the training a mandatory step in the new hire onboarding procedures.

Meanwhile, we took photographs of the Megabling development teams and their partner teams in Toronto, both individual and group pictures. Every application or system had its own collaborative workspace on the Megabling intranet, and the photos were posted on a new "People" page along with brief "Notes" sections beside the individuals containing personal data they provided ("Father of 3 kids under age 5." "Just bought a camper." "My aviary has 14 parakeets, 8 canaries, and a cockatiel." "I hate the Yankees."). In each team, one member at Megabling and one in Toronto were appointed to update the group photos and notes at least monthly. In effect, we were creating the equivalent of a neighborhood directory and newsletter. At first the development managers considered this effort to be a waste of precious time. Nevertheless, members of all the application and system groups appreciated it and reported that they found it easier to get the information they needed to do their work. After a few months most of the development managers grudgingly accepted the procedure and incorporated the effort into their resource plans.

A more critical gap was the disconnect between the Toronto supplier's staff and the end users of the applications and systems they supported. In the most extreme cases, testers in Toronto were being asked to verify functionality for which they had no context: the "right" answer could depend upon a number of factors, but they were unable to judge which ones mattered. Although they could consult the developers, the developers seldom had enough knowledge of the boundary conditions to enable the testers to create negative tests or stress tests.

We arranged for the lead Toronto tester from each application and system to travel to his or her primary end-user Megabling site and spend a week among their end-user community. Each was instructed to learn the application or system from multiple perspectives based upon various end-user roles, including upstream and downstream interfaces and data feeds. Another assignment was to create a simplified version of user experience personas: record audio interviews with representatives of each end-user role, videotape or photograph them in their work environments, and write descriptions of their backgrounds, job functions, attitudes toward IT, likes and dislikes for the application or system, usage challenges, etc. Besides raising eyebrows over the travel expenses billed to Megabling, this initiative annoyed some of the end-user managers because they felt it was disruptive to their operations. Some of the end users were suspicious about why they were being singled out and investigated. Nevertheless, after our MD called in favors from his executive counterparts in the end-user communities, most of the groups cooperated. One unexpected benefit was that it raised the end users' consciousness about the expertise and dedication of the human beings behind their applications and systems. The testers returned to Toronto with a much better understanding of their test requirements and passed along the knowledge to their colleagues. They reported more cordial relationships with end-user representatives whom they could now contact to answer questions quickly, accurately, and thoroughly.

A less-visible undertaking that reduced the amount of time the Toronto supplier staff devoted to administrative tasks was the negotiation of modifications to Megabling IT operations' standard requirements document template and configuration management system. To understand the impact of these recommendations in non-IT terms, imagine that you are writing a shopping list for your partner to take to the grocery store. On the shopping list you want to include milk, butter, eggs, coffee, and a few other things you aren't sure about yet until you check a recipe. Under the old procedures, you would fill out a separate one-page form for each item describing the nutritional content; package weight, size, and color; latest acceptable expiration date; desired geographical origin; etc. You would make a copy of the first version, index it, and lock it in a safe deposit box. While you consulted the recipe, changed your mind a few times about the ingredients, and added and subtracted items, you would copy and store each updated version until you were ready to hand the list to your helpful shopper. Under the new procedures, you would include only as much information as the shopper needed to find what you wanted, and the only version of the list you would copy and save would be the final one. Although common sense might suggest the latter approach, in a financial company the former is often dictated by government regulations, internal audits, security protocols, and knowledge management programs. Persuading the bank compliance officers that agile IT methodologies with less documentation would not entail greater risk freed the Toronto supplier resources to focus on more productive work.

Quality Assurance

Many development managers at Megabling dismissed the concerns of quality assurance practitioners on the theory that the occupation attracts whiners, pessimists, and malcontents who are never satisfied. This attitude was unwise: if testers and quality control technicians are unable to perform their jobs effectively, in the end the entire organizations suffers along with their customers. The task force researchers felt that the testers working at the Toronto supplier had plenty of valid complaints.

Due to budgetary constraints, their equipment was inadequate. The end users of their applications and systems had two display screens on their desks; the testers had only one, which made it impossible for them to verify certain user interface behavior. The Megabling standard test management tool did not run properly on their outdated computer configuration. The slow speed of their Toronto network and the manner in which they remotely accessed Megabling's virtual private network (VPN) through the bank's firewall made response time frustratingly sluggish. The lack of a dedicated, isolated server for a testing environment allowed developers to modify code and data at will and prevented the testers from monitoring the impact of changes against a baseline. All of these issues were real and significant, and all of them could easily have been resolved by spending money. However, the Toronto supplier claimed it could not afford to do so without raising rates. Procurement countered that unless the Toronto supplier made the investment, Megabling would terminate their contracts. This standoff lasted for several months. Ultimately Megabling helped the president of the Toronto supplier craft a presentation for its board of directors showing how infrastructure upgrades could enable larger outsourcing engagements and attract new clients. The board authorized a line of credit from their bank to finance the expenditures, and the equipment was upgraded.

Money alone could not overcome the testers' other major obstacle. When users reported errors, acrimonious finger-pointing ensued. For many applications and systems, it was unclear who should be responsible for verifying each different element of the deliverables. Unit tests, system tests, integration tests, localization tests, performance tests, stress tests, failover tests, penetration tests, usability tests, acceptance tests: there was plenty of blame to go around. It was easier for Megabling developers and end users to vilify the outsourced supplier than to admit any negligence on their own part. To rebuild trust and cooperation, we created RACIN charts showing who was **R**esponsible, **A**ccountable, **C**onsulted, **I**nformed, and **N**ot Involved in the various testing phases. The RACIN charts did not lower the number of defects, but they did increase the defect detection percentage levels and improve the collaboration to identify root causes.

The Outcome

My engagement with Megabling lasted a year and a half. It was by no means smooth sailing all the way. Any turnaround project causes change, and change produces stress. Change results in winners and losers. Change forces people to develop new habits and temporarily demands more work. Many stakeholders deliberately created delays, invented obstacles, or plotted sabotage. Veteran project managers expect this behavior. Yet most stakeholders realized that the working group's solutions to the problems would eventually be implemented because they were necessary for the business, and because they represented the lesser of two evils. The greater evil was the high probability that managers who failed to cooperate would find themselves under intense scrutiny from Internal Audit.

At the conclusion of the assignment, the success criteria had been met. The Toronto supplier had implemented the risk management auditors' operational and security specifications, and the procurement department had added the company to Megabling's list of approved vendors. The agile methodology for new product development had become an accepted practice throughout the IT department, with the Toronto supplier as the preferred outsourcing partner for that type of work. Delivery schedules and error rates were occasionally troublesome but no longer a constant, pervasive worry. The volume of Megabling IT work performed in Toronto was steadily growing.

The cost of the consulting services provided by myself and by the specialists I had brought in for particular tasks was less than a third of the value of the

Toronto supplier's revenue from additional Megabling business. For Megabling, my value was measured in terms of a reduction in the Toronto supplier's operational and security risk: for any business, risk is costly because the capital that must be set aside to cover potential losses cannot be put to more productive use.

The MD was pleased and relieved. His reputation was safe, his rivals no longer had grounds for criticizing his pilot project, and the more ambitious development managers admired him for his bold vision. Now he could turn his attention to more interesting matters, such as the increasingly strange results the software testers were reporting from systems that handled mortgage-backed securities.

It would be tempting to end the story there, with all the loose ends tied up, but of course real life is not so neat.

Soon afterward, the MD quit, hired away by a bigger bank that had been impressed by his pragmatic, out-of-the-box thinking. He was replaced by an MD who believed that Canadian resources were overpaid in the global market for IT skills and that the same work could be accomplished adequately in other countries with lower wages. Procurement agreed, and they began devising a long-range strategy to relocate outsourced headcount based solely on labor arbitrage.

The Toronto supplier's success in improving its operations to meet Megabling's standards, and the resulting expansion of its business, made it an attractive acquisition. The company was sold within six months. The new owners demanded revisions to the MSA and a large rate increase.

The new MD brought back the old VRM ("they're all thieves") to negotiate with the new owners of the Toronto supplier. This could have undermined the ongoing productive vendor-client working relationships, but in the short term it had surprisingly little impact because by then the Megabling IT Outsourcing Community of Practice had become a strong, cohesive grassroots council whose wide-ranging expertise and collective authority commanded more respect than the VRM's bluster.

Longer-term plans to expand the application of ethnographic concepts and methods for IT governance were abruptly shelved following the collapse of the financial markets, when cost-cutting became the entire industry's top priority.

CONCLUSION

The scenario of a nonconformist manager who launches a groundbreaking pilot technology project that succeeds beyond all expectations but endangers regular operations is a challenge faced by many industries. Organizational leaders everywhere struggle to maintain a balance between freedom and control, especially for their most creative, visionary talent. Information technology regulates that balance through the rules encoded in workflow software. Data systems must be constantly adjusted as circumstances change, or else they cease to accurately model reality and they break down.

Anthropologists are good at understanding and explaining the lived experience of diverse stakeholders within a work process community. As IT troubleshooters, we can shine a metaphorical flashlight into a corner where nobody else has looked and discover missing puzzle pieces. This revelation often happens when "technical" problems mask "people" problems. It happens in organizations where a climate of fear prevents people from answering questions honestly because the truth will get them fired. It happens on multicultural, virtual, and/or geographically distributed teams where local groups evolve unique adaptive work practices. Finally, sometimes it happens when operations have become dysfunctional, regulators are pawing at the door, senior management has tried everything they know to try in vain, and an anthropologist assumes the role of shaman.

REFERENCES

Appadurai, Arjun. 1988. *The Social Life of Things*. Cambridge, UK: Cambridge University Press.

Bernard, Russell. 2011. *Research Methods in Anthropology, Fifth Edition*. Lanham, MD: AltaMira Press.

Cefkin, Melissa, ed. 2010. *Ethnography and the Corporate Encounter: Reflections on Research in and of Corporations*. New York: Berghahn Books.

DeMarco, Tom, and Tim Lister. 1999. *Peopleware: Productive Projects and Teams*. New York: Dorset House.

Denny, Rita. 2012. "The Cry of Practicality." In *Advancing Ethnography in Corporate Environments*, edited by Brigitte Jordan, 136–50. Walnut Creek, CA: Left Coast Press.

Ensworth, Patricia. 2001. *The Accidental Project Manager: Surviving the Transition from Techie to Manager*. New York: John Wiley and Sons.

International Institute of Business Analysis. 2009. *Guide to the Business Analysis Body of Knowledge (BABOK Guide), Version 2*. Toronto, Canada: International Institute of Business Analysis.

Juran, Joseph. 1992. *Juran on Quality By Design: The New Steps for Planning Quality Into Goods and Services*. New York: Free Press.

Kerzner, Harold. 2009. *Project Management: A Systems Approach to Planning, Scheduling and Controlling, 10th Edition*. Hoboken, NJ: John Wiley and Sons.

Lanier, Jaron. 2010. *You Are Not a Gadget*. New York: Alfred A. Knopf.

Lessig, Lawrence. 2006. *Code Version 2.0*. New York: Basic Books.

Malinowski, Bronislaw. 1961. *Argonauts of the Western Pacific*. New York: E. P. Dutton.

Project Management Institute. 2008. *Guide to the Project Management Body of Knowledge (PMBOK Guide), Fourth Edition*. Newtown Square, PA: Project Management Institute.

Schumacher, Robert. 2009. *Handbook of Global User Research*. Burlington, MA: Morgan Kaufman.

Szymanski, Margaret H., and Jack Whalen, eds. 2011. *Making Work Visible: Ethnographically Grounded Case Studies of Work Practice*. Cambridge, UK: Cambridge University Press.

Walton, Mary, and W. Edwards Deming. 1988. *The Deming Management Method*. New York: Perigee Books.

Weinberg, Gerald. 1998. *The Psychology of Computer Programming*. New York: Dorset House.
Wiegers, Karl. 2003. *Software Requirements, Second Edition*. Redmond, WA: Microsoft Press.

NOTES

1 To comply with nondisclosure and intellectual property rules, the organization described is a fictionalized composite portrait of several real businesses that share similar characteristics.

2 "Subjects" was the terminology we used deliberately to evoke laboratory experiments. In the domain of finance, ethnography is often regarded as suspiciously touchy-feely and unscientific. Our credibility among stakeholders in an environment ruled by quantitative analysis was enhanced by the association with behavioral sciences.

10

Management Consulting in Times of Austerity: Sustainability & the Business-Place-Community Nexus in Italy

DIPAK R. PANT

ANTHROPOLOGY, MANAGEMENT CONSULTING, & FAMILY BUSINESS

This chapter demonstrates how anthropology is ideally suited to reconfigure the terms and tasks of management consulting. To make the case, I explore broad issues regarding the nature of family firms and their role in the industrial economy based on my experience with Italian family-run businesses and coaching a new generation of Italian family entrepreneurs on how to compete effectively in times of turmoil and austerity. More specifically, I show how an anthropologist's perspective and emphasis on the "quality of context" can help us think about family businesses as place-based brands in a global world and help address intergenerational succession issues while, at the same time, enhancing competitiveness in a globalized marketplace.

Business communities all over the world are heterogeneous mosaics, diverse not just in size and sector but also culturally. Their organizational cultures are derived from three predominant value streams: the business founder's (or the current leader's) personal values, vision, and behavior; the sociocultural milieu of the locality; and the organizational dynamism stimulated by actions and reactions of workers and stakeholders as adaptive response to their company's identity, memory, and leadership.

In the case of businesses established, owned, and led by a family's members, organizational culture is shaped by the shared identities and memories that provide a connectedness to time-tested core values and standards of behavior that may lead to stability and success (Denison et al. 2004). More than 20 years ago Europe-wide comparative surveys showed that family businesses tended to

Handbook of Anthropology in Business, edited by Rita Denny and Patricia Sunderland, 223–233.

be led and managed by generalists who needed consensus from family members' close circuits and community, rather than by specialists (experts) from professional management. Therefore, family businesses were said to be more introspective and cautious in entrepreneurial actions and quite stable factors in a society, rather than progressive or dynamic social elements (Donckels and Fröhlich 1991). In an era of economic austerity and uncertainty, however, family businesses are looking for new ideas. This chapter, then, presents my work across two boundaries: anthropology and management consulting, and family business and management consulting.

THE ITALIAN BUSINESS COMMUNITY & THE CLIMATE OF UNCERTAINTY

More than 90 percent of Italy's approximately 6 million businesses are owned and operated by families, forming a successful and relatively stable core of the Italian business community. A full 93 percent of firms have 50 or fewer employees (ISTAT 2012; Movimprese 2012; Paolazzi and Traù 2012), and around 40 percent of the largest Italian firms are owned by families whose members are directly involved in management. Around 50 percent of Italian family firms, particularly the small ones, cease to operate as an independent business in the second generation, in the lifetime of the immediate heirs and successors of the founders; only 15 percent of family firms continue to operate beyond the third generation. More than half of family firms are actively headed by a senior family member around 60 years of age. Every year, tens of thousands of family businesses undergo the intergenerational passage and transition in management (Cicogna and Devecchi 2007).

Italian family firms are facing daunting challenges posed by a widespread crisis of consumer confidence, a severe credit crunch (related to the volatility of the global financial market and the indebtedness of local banks), a heavy tax burden, and deepening recession in the Italian economy.[1] For the foreseeable future, it seems impossible for the Italian government to introduce fiscal incentives and cheap credit to help the ailing industrial sectors or reduce the very heavy tax burden and fiscal pressure on Italian companies because of the country's enormous sovereign debt.

Italy's global business competitiveness is poor compared to most European Union countries because of low labor productivity, high value-added tax (IVA), high tariffs paid for utilities and facilities, complicated industrial relations (frequent strikes and protests), aging infrastructures, and pervasive inefficiency and delay in regulatory institutions; it is currently ranked 42nd in global competitiveness (World Economic Forum 2012). The capacity of Italian entrepreneurs to make long-term decisions is made more difficult by the persistent climate of political instability at the national level and, to some extent, also by the recent crisis of confidence in the common European currency.[2]

While Italian industry is well known for products of the highest quality in the sectors of food and drink, clothing and apparel, design and decor, furniture and construction, and machine tools and components, Italian businesses, particularly in the manufacturing sectors where family-owned and family-run businesses are concentrated, have suffered an inexorable decline in the past two decades. Industrial production has moved to cheaper labor markets (Paolazzi and Traù 2012), reducing many parts of the country to industrial wasteland. Another massive problem is chronic alienation of manpower from the socio-economic mainstream due to widespread underemployment and massive unemployment: Italy's high numbers of young people aged 15 to 29 who are not in education, employment, or training ranks among the worst of the 27 countries in the European union (ISTAT 2012). The social legitimacy of business has fallen to levels unseen in recent history (Porter and Kramer 2011).

In this difficult, unnervingly confused period, Italian entrepreneurs are looking to management consultants for clarity and foresight. At the same time, however, professional management consultants, both academic and corporate, have been largely discredited because they failed to foresee or subsequently handle the recent economic crisis. The declining reputation of professional management consultants in Italy may also be related to the widespread contempt and anger shown by ordinary people in Italy and other industrialized countries against politicians, technocrats, bureaucrats, and other members of the power establishment where professional management consultants are seen to belong.

Looking for a radically different perspective, the heads of a few Italian businesses have turned to me, an anthropologist (and accidental economist[3]), for advice. As a result of this request, I began to provide advisory support to Italian business organizations, at first using a logico-experimental procedure of observation and experience led by ethnographic research. As the works progressed, I introduced more intense, continuous dialog with company owners and top operators; because I worked with family businesses, these people were mostly family and close kinship networks. This research has produced insights of the world of Italian business and has encouraged me to launch new experiments in corporate strategy focused on "sustainability": business profitability, employee wellness, environmental care, and social legitimacy.

Given that anthropology is actor (human)-centered and context (socioecological complex)-focused, its approach to business strategy is more inclusive, comprehensive, and balanced than any single social or economic or management discipline. Anthropology views business from a dual perspective: first, as a human being's state of engagement and livelihood ("busy-ness") in an empirical survey of the microcosm (human actors); and second, as a component of the human ecosystem in an overview of the macrocosm (habitat-community complex). Anthropology is also quintessentially interdisciplinary; it is capable of bridging the distances that separate societal, economic, and biophysical data and information, and may integrate and explain diverse types of data and information to produce a more coherent picture and a holistic management strategy. Thus, the anthropological difference rests with holism and a long-range view, in contrast to the compartmentalized (specialized) vision and short-termism of conventional economics and management studies.

INDUSTRIAL DECLINE, CHALLENGES, & THE "SUSTAINABILITY" IMPERATIVE

A salient feature of Italian industrial districts (*distretti industriali*) is the central roles of families, kinship, and friendship in defining the local business cluster. That is why Italian businesses are crucial stakeholders, not only in their local economy but also in the local cultural identity and prestige of their place-system (Pant 2005). They are under constant social scrutiny and bear great social responsibility because of their family roots, kinship and friendship networks, territoriality, and place-based identity.

The industrial decline of Italy that began in the 1990s has been aggravated by the waves of recession in rich Western markets that usually import high-quality, comparatively expensive Italian products. Manufactured on small scales by family-run companies that emphasize tradition and quality, these products are unable to compete on price with the products of large-scale economies of transnational corporations whose managers are global corporate professionals and whose operational units are located in the world's low-tax/cost zones. The business-friendliness of public institutions seems to be a burning issue for the Italian business world. Italian entrepreneurs, privately and publicly, complain about the level of interference, overlapping standards, complex regulations,[4] and administrative inefficiency of Italy's public institutions. Accredited international observers tend to substantiate their claims. According to the Global Competitiveness Index, Italy's competitiveness score for public institutions was a relatively poor 92nd, while, as mentioned here, Italy's overall competitiveness ranking was 42nd (World Economic Forum 2012).

Key challenges for the Italian business community are their comparative disadvantages vis-à-vis larger transnational corporations and emerging markets; interregional imbalances in entrepreneurial dynamism and the need to develop a robust and balanced domestic market; generation gap, intergenerational passage, and management transitions and the need for a better intergenerational dialog; knowledge and value-sharing processes; and better cooperation with public institutions. These challenges are common to all organizations in Italy, so the search for a strategy starts with repositioning the specific organizational and operational needs of family-owned/run enterprises in the context of the common challenges being faced by the Italian business community as a whole, with maximum awareness of changing circumstances and shifting paradigms at European economy and globalized markets.

Place-Systems in the Context of Globalization

Globalization is also multilocalization, which demands more attention to local contexts and networking, and overcoming problems of intra/interlocal linkages. Globalization is something more than internationalization, more than the inflow and outflow of products and services across national borders. In business, it is the optimal allocation of resources and skills through worldwide networking, or multilocalization, which means running businesses deeply rooted in multiple/different geocultural contexts, combining the resources and skills of diverse professional and social origins. Multilocalization demands more attention to local issues and to complementarity and networking, first at the local level, within and around a place-system; then with the outer world. Globalization demands local competitiveness.

I believe that the speed and complexities of globalization in an average person's life and surroundings is provoking a desperate search for an organic sense of belonging. Along with the advance of globalization, "local-ness" is regaining new importance (and sometimes also new political distortions). Global movement of people, resources, and information across national and cultural boundaries has undermined the concept and practice of national sovereignty; at the same time, radicalization of identities is on the rise everywhere, even in the largely homogenized and secular Western societies, including Italy.

Despite their capillary territorial presence and (legitimate) coercive force, the strength of national governments is being undermined by transnational corporations (multinationals) and multilocal (regional, global) linkages in almost every sector. Intergovernmental institutions (multilateral bodies like the United Nations, World Bank, International Monetary Fund, World Trade Organization, etc.) have not proved as effective in leadership, regulation, and enforcement as the situation would demand; they are even weaker than the individual governments of the member-states that constitute these global institutions. More narrowly defined contexts of self-governance (like cities and regions) are gaining importance because there is a fierce competition for attention and investment among place-systems (territories). Place-systems will have to reorganize and market themselves to retain existing resources and to attract new ones in terms of business ventures and a skilled workforce. Place-brand[5] is important more than ever. As I have written elsewhere (Pant 2005), "place-branding" means a set of public-private cooperative actions: requalifying the habitat and community through comprehensive infrastructural, environmental, and social investments to design a "place-system" with a distinct quality of context.

In Italy, the brand-image of a place-system (territory) already exists. Many Italian products, particularly in the food and drink sector, enjoy strong place-brand advantage. In the food and drink sector, advantages of these have been consolidated by the legal protection of their trademarks associated with the identification of the place of production and the typical procedures of that place (traditional local craftsmanship); for example, *indicazione geografica tipica* (IGT), *denominaziome di origine controllata* (DOC), *denominaziome di origine controllata e garantita* (DOCG), and *denominazione di origine protetta* (DOP). There is also a movement in some quarters to extend similar legal protection to manufacturing products through total transparency in the entire supply chain and the traceability of ingredients, production process, and workforce. Such place-system advantage is important because it is becoming a crucial element for business in today's hypercompetitive global market. Business ventures are associated with their venues; they will need to become known also for their "quality of context" (quality of services and infrastructures, environmental health, safety, social tranquility, cultural vivacity, recreational facilities, and civic bonds). The source of competitiveness in the next economy, after the saturation and decline of the current industrial model, is going to be this "quality of context," not merely the quality of products. To achieve this, effective and accountable governance and efficient micromanagement of place-systems is required. Therefore, private businesses and civic organizations are well positioned to adopt a new, more constructive (and assertive) posture vis-à-vis public institutions at the local level.

Growing Prominence of Human & Social Preoccupations

The inclusion of human and social preoccupations in strategic management is likely to give social legitimacy to businesses, particularly in Italy, the cradle of humanism and the Renaissance. Yet, moral legitimacy and social consensus for business cannot be taken for granted: these need to be routinely articulated through the civic and human purposefulness of business. A business's moral and social legitimacy is articulated and affirmed through the way it does business and by other collateral (extra-business) actions in its place-system that are directly noticeable to its fellow citizens. Social legitimacy and consensus enable businesses to improve their relations with public institutions (at least on a local level).

In Italy, as in most advanced industrialized countries, the "old economy" is usually identified with hardware, while the "new economy" is identified with software. From a more critical postindustrial perspective, the "old economy" may be identified with "rubble" (pollution, waste, manmade debris, and industrial wastelands) and the "new economy" with "bubbles" (volatile finance, sudden booms, and crashes). Is there anything safer and saner in sight, beyond the rubble and the bubbles? The "old economy" is quantitatively growth-oriented, urban and industrial, and finance-dominated; it has no future unless it smartens itself up and prepares itself to respond to the fundamental ecological limits, social imperatives, and existential angst that challenge us today. The "new economy" (high-tech, dot-coms, telecoms, software, the internet, information and communications technology–aided global financial transactions, etc.) is not actually "new" but merely the most recent, vibrant, and volatile appendix of the "old" economy. It will survive as long as the most consistent parts of the "old economy" keep on dispensing goods, incomes, infrastructures, and, thus, demand for services. The genuinely new economic horizons are represented by a clever combination of the old and new economies that transcends both of them and ignites an entrepreneurial race in the direction of "wellness" and "sustainability." The future of Italian businesses lies in the relentless pursuit of excellence and in striving for absolute quality: quality not only of their products and services but, above all, of the "context" where they are located, where the destiny of a business is interwoven with that of its owners, managers, workers, stakeholders, and their families and communities.

A STRATEGY & METHOD

There are limited opportunities for reducing the cost of doing business in Italy, so competing in mass markets is impossible without further dislocating manufacturing to low-cost production zones or lowering product quality to an extent that would destroy brand value. But it is feasible to target specific niche markets in different parts of the world, as has been done successfully by some famous Italian companies, usually in fashion, food, and drinks. The viable marketing strategy is multitarget "narrowcasting" rather than mass-target "broadcasting." A possible strategy to offset the "comparative" disadvantage of Italian business on the global market may lie in a redefinition of "competitive" advantage: competence, workforce productivity, excellence and distinction, and enhancing the value of the product brand, corporate brand, and place-brand. The relentless pursuit of "competitive" (not "comparative") advantages implies continuous improvements in quality of products, procedures, and place in the business system as a whole. The key variable for the success or failure of such a strategy is human capital: augmenting competence, efficiency, loyalty, and cooperation becomes a top priority for its management. Italian business leaders may start with the requalification of both exterior (physical aspects of workplace habitat) and interior (skills, knowledge, and relationships) assets.

Workplace habitat requalification—for example, improving the eco-efficiency of material structures and processes and raising the aesthetic appeal of the workplace buildings, courtyard, surroundings, and landscaping—is a potent strategic tool of internal corporate branding since it encourages a sense of belonging, identity, and wellness among workers and stakeholders alike. In my experience, initiating and sustaining the process of workplace habitat requalification is a peaceful and powerful strategy in the liquefaction of inertia, resistance, unbusinesslike attitudes or even some hostility from the employees of a business organization.

Once workplace habitat requalification begins to move forward, it becomes easier to initiate the requalification process of interior assets: workforce quality and loyalty, skills, knowledge, competence, and coordination. The external (workplace habitat) requalification process generates an anticipation of change among all. Then, collaborative foresight exercises consisting of interactive discussions with the company-owning family's members, managers, workers, and stakeholders about the future of the business are possible. Such exercises seem to be helpful in improving internal communication, in sharing experience and vision, and in synergizing personal agenda and workers' ambitions with the vision and mission of an organization. A collaborative foresight exercise in a corporate setting is a step-by-step imagination process that is not aimed at predicting the future but raises awareness about possibilities, direction, and purpose: fore*sight*, not fore*cast*.

Collaborative foresight exercises help business owners (family members) and executives (some also from outside the family) to realize quickly the importance of a long-range planning perspective. It also makes business owners and top executives acutely aware of their organization's inner and intangible resources such as identity, memory, distinction, prestige, corporate community cohesion, and relationships. The most interesting, and unexpected, outcome of collaborative foresight exercises have been in finding a unique correlation between a "sustainability" orientation and time range: the longer the time range of foresight, the more sustainability-oriented thinking was expressed by owners and executives. As owners and executives stretch their imagination ahead into future, they become aware of the inseparability of the four dimensions of business sustainability: long-term economic-financial viability (profitability); environmental and landscape quality; social cohesion and civic tranquility; and ethical-existential legitimacy in the eyes of family members, workers, stakeholders, institutions, and community.

This idea of enlarging, encompassing, and inclusive progression in entrepreneurial action, from family-owned firm to community-owned place-system, while developing businesses as profitably as possible, is based on corporate strategy that integrates *value-adding* with *value-sharing*. My experiences lead me to a hypothesis that sustainability becomes achievable if the business organizations are made aware of the critical nexus between their organization's success, survival, and continuity with the value of their place-system and its attractiveness (livability-visitability-investability; in Italian, *vivibilità-visitabilità-investibilità*). The family firms with strong territorial identity and community ties—such as those in Italy—may be more sensitive to this "business-place-community" nexus and, eventually, may prove themselves to be successful actors in improving the social and environmental quality of their place-system.

Terre di Cuore

This hypothesis is being tested in a few localities of Italy through a social (inter-firm) campaign (opinion-mobilizing) project called *Terre di Cuore*,[6] launched with the help of a few Italian entrepreneurs whose family-run firms operate in manufacturing, construction, commerce, and service sectors. Between 2010 and 2012, a number of public conferences and joint workshops (with the participation of businesses, nongovernmental organizations, and local administrative authorities) were organized in several towns in Italy[7] under the (informal) banner of the campaign *Terre di Cuore*, with logistic and financial support from business organizations. In 2013, even more events were organized, thanks to the enthusiasm of some entrepreneurs. The *Terre di Cuore* campaign is a multilocal sustainability and place-branding project. It is a social project of cultural and economic revitalization through combined volunteer/charity efforts by local stakeholders to requalify their common economic, environmental, and civic assets and to project local sustainability and its habitants' wellness to give them a competitive edge in everything: business, profession, and lifestyle as well as in perception, image, and place-brand.

The aim of the *Terre di Cuore* project is to create "zones of wellness and sustainability" in the place-systems where businesses are rooted. Business organizations initially move on their own, without involving public institutions, in several ways:

- by mapping local "values" in terms of specialties and particular skills (*genius loci*) and environmental and cultural resources (*la mappa dei valori*); by mapping local "vulnerability" and critical situations in habitat, business, and social security (*la mappa dei dis-valori*);
- by elaborating an alternative image of local future (collaborative foresight to agree on a best, plausible scenario of reference) by taking stock of the "values" and "vulnerabilities"; and
- by drawing (and locally managing) a viable (pragmatic) road map that lead/tends to the best plausible alternative image of local future (scenario of reference).

It is a movement to encourage multilocal place-brand strategy. In this way, local business leaders of multiple localities become the promoters of their place-brand. Place-brand promotion by entrepreneurs enables the business community to have a better dialog and positive cooperation with public institutions. It also helps them to foster moral legitimacy and social consensus for the business. Workforce productivity and loyalty are likely to benefit from the place-branding process.

Once promoted, the place-brand protects and promotes all those who contribute to its development. *Terre di Cuore* is a multilocal place-branding campaign through the collective action of local business organizations; it is based on shared values and measurable (and enforceable) social and environmental quality standards. It may help to foster trade, attract investments, and develop tourism. Even without much development in trade and tourism, it certainly mobilizes local resources (and public opinion) towards sustainability and wellness, and enhances collective well-being and social cohesion through the quality of local human capital and landscape. The *Terre di Cuore* campaign may prove to be a win/win strategy.

STRATEGIC APPLICATIONS OF ANTHROPOLOGY IN BUSINESS & ETHICS

Anthropology can produce business strategies that capitalize on human capital and place-based local knowledge (*genius loci*) and, at the same time, point toward profitability (business continuity) and sustainability (quality of context) through constant focus on the value of the place-brand. An ethical balance can be achieved in the business applications of anthropology by aligning the drive for sustainability (quality of context, place-brand) with the legitimate drive for profitability (business vitality and continuity). Ultimately, the alignment of profitability with sustainability helps to favor the supreme interests of community and habitat, at least at the local level. If the local becomes multilocal, then it is possible to foresee a new wave of planetary humanism and a global renaissance led by the entrepreneurs and workers together.

REFERENCES

Cicogna, A., and C. Devecchi. 2007. "L'impresa familiare italiana: una specie da proteggere." in *Challenge 2000* (*La rivista di Management per l'Azienda Evolutiva*, Data Consult Group Srl) 23:36–43.

Daniel Denison, D., C. Lief, and J. L. Ward. 2004. "Culture in Family-Owned Enterprises: Recognizing and Leveraging Unique Strengths" *Family Business Review* 17(1):61–70.

Donckels, R., and E. L. Fröhlich. 1991. "Are Family Businesses Really Different? European Experiences from STRATOS." *Family Business Review* 4(2):149–60.

ISTAT (2012). Rapporto Annuale 2012—La Situazione del Paese. Rome: Istituto Nazionale di Statistica.

Movimprese (2012). "Infocamere: la Società Informatica delle Camere di Commercio Italiane" (online resource center for the Italian Chambers of Commerce). http://www.infocamere.it/movimprese.

Pant, D. R. 2000. *The Armenian Scenarios: Strategic Foresight of Business, Security and Culture in the Republic of Armenia*. Varese, Italy: LIUC/Crespi.

______. 2005. "A Place Brand Strategy for the Republic of Armenia: 'Quality of Context' and 'Sustainability' as Competitive Advantage." *Journal of Place Branding* 1(3):273–82.

Paolazzi, L., and F. Trau', eds. 2012. *Scenari Industriali* (No. 3, June 2012). Rome: Centro Studi Confindustria (Confederation of Italian Industries).

Porter, M. E., and M. R. Kramer 2011. "Creating Shared Value." *Harvard Business Review* (January–February). http://hbr.org/2011/01/the-big-idea-creating-shared-value (accessed January 9, 2014).

World Economic Forum. 2012. *The Global Competitiveness Report 2012–2013*. Geneva: World Economic Forum.

NOTES

1 In its annual rate of economic growth, Italy ranks last among the 27 member states of European Union (EU), some way below both Euro (common Euro currency)–area countries average and the average of all EU (including non–Euro currency) countries.

2 In the 66 years between 1945 and 2012, Italy had 25 prime ministers who presided over 62 governments.

3 Since 1995, I have been teaching courses related to economic policy, planning, and strategic management in Italian universities as well as in a few higher education and research institutions in other countries of Europe, Asia, and in the Americas as a visiting professor. My direct involvement as a practitioner in economic planning and management dates back to the period between 1987 and 1990 when I used to provide field survey and advisory services to rural development agencies and business organizations in Nepal while teaching at Tribhuvan University's Central Department of Sociology & Anthropology, Kathmandu (Nepal). Since then, practical works in the fields of economics and management have remained a constant parallel practice alongside my main academic duties, and the practical assignments have taken me to various places (Armenia, Brazil, Cambodia, Mongolia, Peru, Sierra Leone, and Venezuela) for significant periods of time.

4 Not only Italian national institutions but also the EU institutions are facing similar complaints from European business communities as the economic recession and credit crisis persist in the Euro currency zone.

5 My discovery of "place-brand" was an unintended consequence of a field survey in northern Armenia (southern Caucasus) in October 1999; the first time I used the term "place-brand" and suggested it as an economic strategy for Armenia's government in a published report (Pant 2000:107–8). In October 1999, I was in a survey mission of Armenia's archaeological sites in the Shirak region to explore proper ways of integrating the restoration of historical monuments with broader local (rural) development strategy; the mission was commissioned by an Italian nongovernmental organization (Centro Studi e Documentazione sulla Cultura Armena, Venice) in collaboration with Armenia's National Board for the Restoration of Historical Monuments (Ministry of Culture). In that case, as the requalification of the "place system" proceeded, a global marketing strategy to replace the common international perception of Armenia as a remote and trouble-prone ex-Soviet land by highlighting Armenia's distinction in heritage, landscape, and lifestyle was also needed.

6 *Terre di cuore* literally means "lands of the heart"; proper translation would be "places/lands that are in your heart" or "the land where your heart dances."

7 Bari (Apulia), Brindisi (Apulia), Campobasso (Molise: http://www.youtube.com/watch?v= n35s CBOFXLE); Manfredonia (Foggia, Apulia), Motta di Livenza (Treviso, Veneto), Palmanova (Udine, Friuli-Venezia-Giulia: http://www.youtube.com/watch?v=IuVaQMBASpg); Perignano/Lari (Pisa, Tuscany: http://www.youtube.com/watch?v=EK9Lk89oaoA); Prato (Tuscany: http://www.youtube.com/watch?v=sgqOiVgxeek); Salerno (Campania), Serravalle Sesia (Vercelli, Piedmont), Siena (Tuscany), and Terni (Umbria).

11

Opportunity & Challenge in the Health Care Industry: Anthropological Inroads in France

SOPHIE ALAMI

INTRODUCTION

Despite inroads of ethnographic methods in French consumer research, until recently socio-anthropology has generally remained quite marginal in private–business research practices in the health sector. This chapter outlines the current dynamics framing opportunities and challenges in the healthcare field in France and illustrates the contributions that socio-anthropology can make in this sector.

This chapter not only illustrates what it takes to cross into the health care sector and inhabit it successfully, but also reveals the entanglements within. Social, economic, and regulatory changes in the health care field have created an environment receptive to a "rediscovery" of the value of socio-anthropological research. In France, it is a moment of collaboration for the pharmaceutical industry, medical research, health care practitioners, and social anthropologists. The realm of anthropologists' incursions extends from public agencies to patients' associations and from pharmaceutical marketing to clinical practice. In this chapter, I provide a brief overview of the dynamics of this market shift followed by examples drawn from health sector research I have carried out in the last decade. At the end of the chapter I discuss some of the challenges of interdisciplinary dialog, highlighting methodological and epistemological issues. I call out in particular the opportunity social anthropology and the itinerary method afford for breaching the "trap" of patient-centered approaches, which only consider the patient perspective.

Handbook of Anthropology in Business, edited by Rita Denny and Patricia Sunderland, 234–246.

THE RISE IN DEMAND FOR SOCIO-ANTHROPOLOGY IN THE HEALTH SECTOR

Anthropology has been interested in health, illness, and traditional therapeutic behaviors since the nineteenth century, but medical anthropology did not become a clearly defined academic specialty in France until the second half of the twentieth century (Diasio 1999). Similarly, the sociology of health emerged in France in the 1970s and really began developing in the 1980s (Carricaburu and Ménoret 2004). Among French private research firms, however, interest in this area is quite new.[1] In recent years, attracted to a sector with substantial economic weight and potential growth, major private national marketing research institutes have developed specific firms or departments[2] dedicated to health care research.[3]

This chapter highlights some of the economic, regulatory, and societal changes underlying this market shift. Health care companies are facing new regulatory requirements and confronting more rigorous government health care cost-control policies. At the same time, their business models have had to adjust to a decrease in the number of new drugs launched and an increase of generics: in France, out of 348 classes, the number of classes with generics increased from 64 in 2002 to 90 in 2008. As a consequence, new sources of value have been identified and the focus has shifted to prevention, early detection, individual services, and therapeutic education (Industries de Santé 2010).

In the 2010 French Health Industries report, economic stakeholders emphasized, in addition to issues of health governance and economic performance, a "societal" challenge: to control health care costs, this report states that France must consider the issues of quality and equal access to health care; improve prevention, compliance, and health education; optimize the overall care of patients; and involve patients and public opinion (Industries de Santé 2010).

At the same time, changes in medicine (specialization, fragmentation, and complexification) and new issues related to the development of chronic diseases[4] have meant that treatment options other than drugs must henceforth be considered. The increase in patients who suffer from chronic diseases in Western countries has led to the emergence of the concept of "therapeutic education," designed to help people deal with their illnesses over time. In 1998, the Regional Office for Europe of the World Health Organization (WHO) published recommendations promoting the education of both health care providers and patients (WHO-Europe 1998). In 2004, WHO launched a Patient Safety program. This program was meant to lead "a global drive to build on patient safety education, its principles and approaches that lead to a future health care workforce educated to practice patient-centered care anywhere in the world" (WHO 2011b). A program component titled "Patients for Patient Safety" emphasizes "the central role patients and consumers can play in efforts to improve the quality and safety of health care around the world," and officially asserts patients as "partners" of health care professionals whose voices have to be heard and learned from (WHO 2011a). The centrality of the perspective of "patients and families, consumers and citizens" is clearly affirmed; it is considered a necessary condition for "safety improvements" and "systemic quality" (WHO 2011c).

These new requirements have been adopted at the national level. In June 2007, the French Haute Autorité de Santé (HAS) edited recommendations promoting Therapeutic Patient Education and identified the improvement of patients' quality of life as part of health care professionals' concern, along with biological and clinical goals (HAS 2007). Similarly, the US Food and Drug Administration (FDA) guidelines have also emphasized the relevance of patients' perspectives to medical product development (FDA 2006, 2009). These guidelines broaden the traditional perspective of medicine and of the pharmaceutical industry by shifting from a focus on product (drugs) to the notion of "treatment benefit." They stress the need to question patients directly to enrich the drug evaluation process with indicators of what "really matters" for patients, showing patients' perspectives on treatment benefits and risks (such as side effects and inconvenience).

These environmental changes are all conducive to socio-anthropological approaches. Just as marketing has become "customer-centric," in health care, it has also become important to hear the patient's voice beyond the mere detection of symptoms. Health care professionals and medical institutions are attempting to figure out how to deal with this new approach, to be more "patient-centric," with the politically correct empowerment of the patient showing the limits of a medical decision-making process that fails to consider patients' views and has difficulty involving patients in health care design.

These elements, combined with the rise of patient organizations, have led the health sector to "rediscover" the relevance of socio-anthropological approaches and have opened new areas of collaboration among the pharmaceutical industry, medical researchers, and socio-anthropologists.

SOCIO-ANTHROPOLOGY APPLICATION: DOMAINS FOR CONTRIBUTIONS

These new "environmental constraints" have favored interdisciplinary collaborations and new types of research opportunities. At first, research opportunities were mainly linked to public funding, dealing for instance with AIDS or projects in the Third World; when the private sector was involved, it was mainly in the management of drug marketing issues. In 1995, for instance, I was appointed by the Moroccan Ministry of Public Health to work on the prevention of sexually transmitted diseases and AIDS in urban areas and to design a study to analyze women's vulnerability in this matter. Later on, in early 2000, I was introduced to issues in the pharmaceutical industry and commissioned to analyze doctors' practices of diagnosis and drug prescriptions for specific diseases. I was called upon to study health issues ranging from public health issues to more commercial ones, with a greater diversity of questions asked. Since then, the change in the health sector environment has contributed to the rise of new opportunities that have led to new research objectives and new partnerships.

Socio-anthropological studies indeed have the potential for improving the health care process, training of health care professionals, patient education, development of medical tools, marketing and communication (both marketing and scientific), and a combination of these outcomes. Contributions of some specific interdisciplinary collaborations that do not fall within the usual scope of products and brands are shown in Table 11.1, illustrating targets as diverse as

Public Agencies	Health Industry (Marketing and Clinical Departments)	Health Professionals	Patients' Associations
Evaluate, control, improve, and optimize healthcare quality and cost Design and execute actions for public health Formalize recommendations and share best practices Fight against inequalities in healthcare access	Identify and exploit potential prescriptions Segment targeted populations Promote product sales Consolidate the image of company and its products Gain customer loyalty Develop new products and services Create and successfully use a network of medical experts Develop training for health professionals	Develop, test, and evaluate instruments for common healthcare procedures Evaluate and improve patient care Develop therapeutic education for patients	Communication Lobbying Actions for patient support Foster research

Table 11.1. Possible outcomes of socio-anthropological qualitative studies in the field of health.

health care training, patient education, and research tools that can help health professionals manage and develop treatment.

In recent years, I have seen that socio-anthropological studies also have a place in certain clinical research by fostering reflection on innovation in medical instruments. Qualitative research provides a "database" that can enrich and inform the viewpoints of health care professionals and industrials. A study on knee arthritis, for instance, was the context for that type of work. A pharmaceutical firm sponsored a socio-anthropological study jointly designed with physicians. The expected outcome was the development of tools (Benhamou et al. 2013a; Benhamou et al. 2013b) to evaluate patients' expectations, fears, and beliefs towards arthritis, which would be designed for use in doctors' routines to improve patient–physician relationships, patient information, and therapeutic adjustment. The first part of the research project was a qualitative study based on in-depth interviews and life histories (Alami et al 2011b). The study analyzed and compared representations and practices concerning arthritis and its management among patients, doctors, and professionals delivering alternative medicine. The results of the study were used to identify, through a Delphi[5] procedure, items that could help physicians record patients' expectations, fears, and beliefs related to their condition. For the first round of the Delphi procedure and the generation of items, the experts were asked to read the results of the qualitative study and extract items that they found most relevant. The Delphi procedures ended with the generation of questionnaires that were tested by means of a national multicenter cross-sectional survey of patients in a primary care setting. In this project, socio-anthropology was first used in an innovative research design to develop a medical instrument.

Socio-anthropological studies also have been useful in designing training programs. For instance, a qualitative study on pain induced by physical therapy programs (Alami et al. 2011a) provided the opportunity to foster medical training and patient information and education. Chronic painful conditions are increasing among the aging in developed countries. People facing painful conditions are frequently referred to physical therapy programs, but those programs may provoke pain and lead to less compliance; the impact of the neglected pain may include the denial of symptoms and the discontinuation of therapy. The qualitative project that I worked on was based on semistructured interviews with both patients and care providers. It examined individual behaviors, personal feelings and interpretations, social interactions, and material background throughout the patients' journey. Among other results, the study underlined that doctors lack knowledge and recognition of the specific pain induced by exercise or mobilization (PIEM) executed during physical therapy programs and patients' ambivalent views of this specific pain—seen both positively as a necessary part of the healing process or as a protective signal indicating a pain threshold, and negatively as an indicator of the care providers' lack of competency—and that patients had difficulty expressing it. The study identified barriers to PIEM recognition and needs for medical information, and continued with a second step of collaborative work with physicians aimed at determining what information was useful to improve therapist and practitioner practices through a Delphi procedure involving both patients and medical experts.

Socio-anthropological studies can also help identify ways of improving patient care when no therapeutic progress is expected in the short term. This was the case with two projects on rare diseases, systemic sclerosis and pulmonary arterial hypertension, that I was invited to work on. In the case of incurable disease, one of the current challenges is to optimize care for patients and improve their "quality of life" (Sitbon et al. 2012). Confronting the different views of patients, relatives, and practitioners can provide a comprehensive picture of the illness and enrich medical knowledge by adding stakeholders' concerns, goals, and expectations. It also makes it possible to understand the scientific uncertainties, the controversies, and the diversity of professional practice that patients may face in fields where medical knowledge is limited and unsure. Socio-anthropological analysis can thus have an impact on medical decision-making when it indicates divergences between health care professionals' practices or questions the way the therapeutic contract between physicians and their patients should be built, and should evolve. Socio-anthropology helps broaden the picture by determining what benefits patients seek beyond healing and eliminating symptoms and also by identifying how they define their "quality of life" and what is important to them.

Those projects shed light on the question of how to improve medical practice as well as that of the "co-construction" of therapeutic decisions and the role of the ill in this process. Beyond the analysis of the patient perspective, they focus on how disciplinary and professional issues are also involved in the organization of care through questions such as managing patient flow and gaining scientific authority (Castel 2002).

Socio-anthropological approaches have also allowed me to focus on the environment in which individual representations of health, illness, and healing practices of the body are developed. These representations are crucial to how individuals relate to their bodies and their health, and they help explain why patients do or do not adhere to the therapies offered. Analyzing the information-gathering practices of those facing health issues—particularly on news websites, discussion forums (Gaglio 2010; Scull 2009), and traditional media—fosters understanding of images and collective representations that feed individual representations and the ambivalences and controversies that they face; it also highlights the nature of interactions that develop between health care professionals and the people who consult them. Analyzing the information circulating in the media and identifying the semantic registers developed, the metaphors used, and the types of argumentation can provide a more precise identification of cultural determinants that condition individual practices.

Finally, socio-anthropological studies can make relevant contributions to decision-making in health issues. Health and illness deserve to be thought of in more than strict biological terms; disease is also a social construct, and biological data "make sense" through a system of beliefs, social relationships, and specific environmental contexts. Furthermore, intervention in health may not be effective if no thought is given to the "end users."

CHALLENGES WITH INTERDISCIPLINARY DIALOG

The projects that I focused on presented an interdisciplinary dialog that appeared to be useful dynamics but also a form of stress. I would like to illustrate this by focusing on two methodological points, both of them leading to epistemological issues.

Conducting socio-anthropological research requires, by definition, collecting personal data. This concept is legally defined in France, and the administration of surveys and studies is controlled by different public entities.[6] Therefore, the first step of any health study, including socio-anthropological ones, is legal. Aside from the length of this compliance process (two or three months at least), the main issue at this step is to reconcile the interests of all the stakeholders without getting caught up in their constraints or weakening the study's methodology. The public committees in charge of the process are mainly composed of physicians and scientists, who may be quite unfamiliar with qualitative research and socio-anthropological research in general even though they are mandated to evaluate research objectives and methodologies, and the relevance of collecting personal data. Socio-anthropologists working in the health sector must thus deal with, more than those in fields used to qualitative approaches, the eternal questions of sample justification (social representativeness and triangulation rather than statistical representativeness), the reliability of the approach (induction versus hypothetical-deductive research), the formalization of qualitative data collection tools (closed-ended questions and strict data collection protocol versus open-ended questions and a more "co-constructed" approach, which allows flexibility of the topics covered from one interviewee to another), generalization (statistical generalization versus analytical), etc. Although these questions are legitimate and they require reasoned answers in epistemological terms, the "challenge" often seems to lie in the complexity of interdisciplinary dialog that is implied and in the discussion that underlies the assessment of the quality of a socio-anthropological approach.[7] The challenge then is to preserve an open methodological design, consistent with an inductive approach that guarantees wealth of study results and is honest about its limitations.

The second point I would like to underline may be designated as the patient-centric trap. Adopting a patient-centered approach does not mean considering the perspective of patients alone. Sources of information must be triangulated, because the social realities studied are constructed in the interaction between patients and their social environment. This means that the patients' views must be put into perspective with, depending on the topics under study, the point of view of their family, their nonprofessional caregivers, their doctors, and the health professionals with whom they are in contact.

Triangulating data collection techniques also helps to avoid overinterpretation or misinterpretation of data. For example, when studying actual patient practices, the use of techniques other than interviews, such as direct observation, photography, and even journals as a medium to facilitate memory, allows for both greater reliability of the data collected and also for better interpretation. Thus, when asked about the impact of illness on daily activities, an interviewee may, for example, have a sincere but inaccurate assessment of his or her functional abilities (see Cefkin, this volume, on the "Say-Do Distinction," and Ensworth pointing out the limits of self-reported account). How each person faces illness—phases of denial or depression, for example—may affect the evaluation and lead the researcher to under- or overestimate the activities performed, involuntarily and unconsciously. Persons in the interviewee's environment might be key informants in identifying the reality of the impact of the disease on an individual. Similarly, the circle of family and friends can be a relevant indicator of therapeutic paths taken by individuals—whether medical or alternative—and provide perspective on patients' requests for information or expectations.

Here, triangulation goes beyond mere methodological triangulation and takes on a more theoretical aspect. The challenge is to develop an approach that attempts to articulate the dynamics and the structure, social interplay, and determinants that characterize the social phenomena under study. These two dimensions are not, however, observable simultaneously, as Dominique Desjeux rightly pointed out (Desjeux 2004). By structure, I mean especially the cultural and symbolic dimensions analyzed through social representations expressed by the interviewees. By dynamics, I mean ways in which individual practices are constructed through the interplay of interaction and of power relationships, subject to situation effects: dynamics involve a short time frame, negotiations, and arbitrations, whereas representations are more long term.

Improving the treatment of a medical condition requires considering both the meaning that individuals attribute to the situation in which they find themselves (Augé and Herzlich 1984; see also Ensworth, this volume, who refers to "native taxonomies") and the action system (Crozier and Friedberg 1977) in which they operate. The representation of the disease, its cause, the therapeutic solutions available, drugs in general, and in particular the medicine proposed are all social representations that sustain health-related behaviors. In the context of discussions on improving patient care, these representations may be in harmony or in conflict with biomedical and therapeutic prescription, possibly disrupting, from the point of view of biomedical institutions, a care procedure. Similarly, lifestyle, daily activities, and physical environment affect how a medical prescription is "received." The physical adaptations implemented by those dealing with the illness sometimes also offer a number of interesting ways of improving the lives of patients. Thus, the issue of adherence is a major issue for health care professionals, highlighting the need to identify the dovetailing or the tension that may exist between practices and social representations in certain situations marked by the illness. Analyzing both the practices and the representations involved is part of the process of objectifying social reality.

Calling for the analysis of both representations and practices also implies analyzing interactions, because individual interpretations concerning health and illness are also conditioned by the partners (spouse, children, employer, nurse, intern, or professor of medicine, etc.) and the balance of power involved. The sick person is in effect part of a system of action (in the Croziérian meaning of the term) that illness helps to devise. Analyzing the system highlights what matters to them or what they want and also the constraints that they face, the resources they can deploy, and the manner in which they react to the situations they face. Even if meaning usually appears first in individuals' statements, a socio-anthropologist does well to show how meaning is embedded in power games, physical constraints, and institutions (Desjeux 2004) to grasp the specific rationality behind each individual behavior.

I have found the itinerary method (Desjeux and Garabuau-Moussaoui 2000; also Desjeux, this volume) helpful to reach these goals on a micro-social level of observation. The issue is particularly "remembering, without eliminating its existence, that consumer choices (in this case health care) are not limited to arbitration; they are part of strategic social, emotional, and symbolic interplay" (Desjeux et al. 1998). This is all the more important in that individuals' views and practices change all along their complex therapeutic path. Not only do their attitudes change in the psychological sense, but also their social position, the persons with whom they interact, and the information they have access to: all of these may change as their journey leads them from the onset of the illness, its diagnosis, then its management or its chronic nature. The challenge then is to understand both the structure of these courses, the individual logical constructs at work in different situations and their rationality, and the sense that sick persons make of these factors throughout therapeutic itineraries that are sometimes quite complex.

Following a therapeutic itinerary also means taking into account all the actors involved. The data collected from ill persons constitute a mere layman's view on sickness and health, but the words of health professionals should not necessarily be considered incontrovertible. They provide, as do the views of "laymen," a social construction to be deconstructed, as in the work begun by Latour and Woolgar (1979), an ethnography of the neuroendocrinology laboratory of Professor Guillemin in San Diego. Analysis of the process of medical decision-making, of doctors' actions and hesitations, can be critical to improving patient care. The anthropologist is in a good position to examine the practices of biomedicine. Doctors are not only conditioned by scientific considerations, which are also subject to change, and their decision-making routines are not homogeneous.

Adopting a patient-centric approach thus means much more than interviewing patients on their beliefs, fears, or expectations—issues of frequent interest for health care professionals—and directing communications to them. The whole social system must be examined, and caregiver perspectives and the dynamics of power relations in health care contexts must also be discussed. Therapeutic Patient Education advocates thus should go beyond a simplistic view of therapeutic education that postulates that patients are the ones to be changed and that delivering information to patients changes individual behavior mechanically. A more contingent and systemic approach is needed, in which information is viewed as a part of a larger decision process, informed by culture, and is reinterpreted through people's objectives, practices, and interests.

CONCLUSION

Socio-anthropological studies in the health field make it possible to highlight material, social, and symbolic factors that direct, organize, and constrain individual behavior in health and illness while encompassing the action system in which a medical action takes place. They generally are part of an interdisciplinary framework of collaboration and research that demands attention to the legal requirements related to the protection of persons, regulations governing the relationship between health professionals and the health industry, and the medical and/or industrial objectives of the study sponsor. The challenge is to reconcile those requirements with the epistemological ones that are specific to socio-anthropological research.

REFERENCES

Alami, Sophie, Dominique Desjeux, Marie-Martine Lefèvre-Coleau, Anne-Sophie Boisard, Eric Boccard, François Rannou, and Serge Poiraudeau. 2011a. "Management of Pain Induced by Exercise and Mobilization during Physical Therapy Programs: Views of Patients and Care Providers." *BMC Musculoskeletal Disorders* 12:172. doi:10.1186/1471-2474-12-172.

Alami, Sophie, Isabelle Boutron, Dominique Desjeux , Monique Hirschhorn, Gwendoline Meric, François Rannou, and Serge Poiraudeau. 2011b. "Patients' and Practitioners' Views of Knee Osteoarthritis and Its Management: A Qualitative Interview Study." *PLoS One* 6(5). doi:10.1371/journal.pone.0019634.

Augé, Marc, and Claudine Herzlich. 1984. *Le Sens du Mal: Anthropologie, Histoire, Sociologie de la Maladie*. Paris: Éditions des Archives Contemporaines, Collection Ordres Sociaux.

Barbour, Rosaline S. 2001. "Checklists for Improving Rigour in Qualitative Research: A Case of the Tail Wagging the Dog?" *British Medical Journal* 322:1115.

Benhamou, Mathilde, Isabelle Boutron, Marie Dalichampt, Gabriel Baron, Sophie Alami, François Rannou, Philippe Ravaud, and Serge Poiraudeau. 2013a. "Elaboration and Validation of a Questionnaire Assessing Patient Expectations about Management of Knee Osteoarthritis by Their Physicians: The Knee Osteoarthritis Expectations Questionnaire." *Annals of the Rheumatic Diseases* 72(4):552–9.

Benhamou, Mathilde, Gabriel Baron, Marie Dalichampt, Isabelle Boutron, Sophie Alami, François Rannou, et al. 2013b. "Development and Validation of a Questionnaire Assessing Fears and Beliefs of Patients with Knee Osteoarthritis: The Knee Osteoarthritis Fears and Beliefs Questionnaire (KOFBeQ)." *PLOS One* 8(1):e53886. doi:10.1371/journal.pone0053886.

Carricaburu, Danièle, and Marie Ménoret. 2004. *Sociologie de la Santé, Institutions, Professions et Maladies*. Paris: Armand Colin, Collection U.

Castel, Patrick. 2002. "Normaliser les Pratiques, Organiser les Médecins. La Qualité comme Stratégie de Changement. Le Cas des Centres de Lutte Contre le Cancer." PhD dissertation, Institut d'Etudes Politiques, Centre de Sociologie des Organisations, Paris, France.

Claudot, Frédérique, François Alla, Jeanne Fresson, Thierry Calvez, Henry Coudane, and Catherine Bonaïti-Pellié. 2009. "Ethics and Observational Studies in Medical Research: Various Rules in a Common Framework." *International Journal of Epidemiology*. 38(4):1104–8.

Crozier, Michel, and Erhard Friedberg. 1977. *L'Acteur et le Système*. Paris: Seuil, Collection Points.

Desjeux, Dominique. 1998. "Les Échelles d'Observation de la Consommation." http://www.argonautes.fr/sections.php?op=printpage&artid=85 (accessed December 16, 2013).

_____. 2004. Les Sciences Sociales. Vendôme: Presses Universitaires de France, Collection Que sais-je: No. 3635.

Desjeux, Dominique, and Isabelle Garabuau-Moussaoui, eds. 2000. *Objet Banal, Objet Social: Les Objets Quotidiens comme Révélateurs des Relations Sociales*. Paris: L'Harmattan, Collection Dossiers Sciences Humaines et Sociales.

Diasio, Nicoletta. 1999. *La Science Impure*. Paris: Presses Universitaires de France.

Gaglio, Gérald. 2010. "Consommation d'Informations sur Internet et Modulation de la Relation aux Médecins. Le Cas d'Aidantes de Malades Atteints d'une Pathologie Lourde." *Sociologies Pratiques* 1(20):63–74.

Haute Autorité de Santé (HAS). 2007. "Recommandations. Éducation Thérapeutique du Patient. Définition, Finalités et Organisation." www.has-sante.fr/portail/upload/docs/application/pdf/etp_-_definition_finalites_-_recommandations_juin_2007.pdf (accessed September 10, 2012).

Industries de Santé. 2010. États Généraux de l'Industrie. "Rapport du Groupe de Travail Industries de Santé." www.industrie.gouv.fr/archive/sites-web/etats-generaux-industrie/fileadmin/documents/Nationnal/documents/Industrie_de_sante/EGI_-_industrie_de_sante.pdf (accessed September 13, 2012).

Latour, Bruno, and Steve Woolgar. 1979. *Laboratory Life: The Social Construction of Scientific Facts*. Los Angeles: Sage Publications. Translated into French in 1988 (*La Vie de laboratoire. La production des faits scientifiques*). Paris: La Découverte.

Scull, Charley. 2009. "Market Research, Webnography, and Chronic Disease." Paper presented at the American Anthropological Association Annual Meeting, December 2–6, Philadelphia, PA. http://www.practicagroup.com/pdfs/Market_Research_Webnography_and_Chronic_Disease.pdf (accessed September 24, 2012).

Sitbon, Olivier, Sophie Alami, Luc Mouthon, Vincent Cottin, Dominique Desjeux, Esther Quessette, and Serge Poiraudeau. 2012. "Patients', Relatives', and Practitioners' Views on Pulmonary Arterial Hypertension." Poster presented at the 22nd European Respiratory Society Annual Congress, Vienna, Austria, September 1–5, 2012.

U.S. Department of Health and Human Services Food and Drug Administration (FDA). 2006. "Guidance for Industry: Patient Reported Outcome Measures: Use in Clinical Medical Product Development to Support Labeling Claims: Draft Guidance. *Health and Quality of Life Outcomes* 4:79.

_____. 2009. "Patient-Reported Outcome Measures: Use in Medical Product Development To Support Labeling Claims." *Clinical/Medical* 74(35):65132–33.

World Health Organization (WHO). 2005. "Preventing Chronic Diseases: A Vital Investment." http://www.who.int/chp/chronic_disease_report/full_report.pdf. (accessed January 13, 2013).

_____. 2011a. "Patients Have a Voice Too!" http://www.who.int/patientsafety/patients_for_patient/en/ (accessed September 14, 2012).

_____. 2011b. "Patient Safety Curriculum Guide: Multi-Professional Edition." http://www.who.int/patientsafety/education/curriculum/PSP_DG_Forewords_2011.pdf(accessed September 14, 2012).

_____. 2011c. "Patients for Patient Safety—Statement of Case." http://www.who.int/patientsafety/patients_for_patient/statement/en/index.html (accessed December 16, 2013).

WHO-Europe. 1998. "Therapeutic Patient Education—Continuing Education Programmes for Healthcare Providers in the Field of Chronic Disease." http://www.euro.who.int/__data/assets/pdf_file/0007/145294/E63674.pdf (accessed September 12, 2012).

NOTES

1 I am not dealing here with contract research organizations (CROs), which focus on clinical research and medical-marketing studies.

2 This is the case for the Institut Français d'Opinion Publique (IFOP), which gave birth to Global Healthcare in 2009, since renamed IFOP Healthcare. IFOP was founded in 1938 by a professor of social psychology and has been a pioneer in the opinion poll and market research sector in France. Others companies followed, such as TNS Sofres (Kantar group), and midsized firms Harris Interactive in 2009 and Opinion Way in 2010.

3 They joined the few pioneering specialized institutes such as Intercontinental Marketing Services Health (IMS Health), a leading market research company founded in 1954 specializing in the health care sector.

4 See WHO's report *Preventing Chronic Disease: A Vital Investment* (2005). The report shows that the impact of chronic diseases is growing in many countries. Chronic disease was responsible for 60 percent of all deaths in the world in 2005, half of which were people younger than 70 years.

5 The Delphi technique was developed by the RAND Corporation (supported by the US Air Force under Project Rand) in the 1950 and 1960s. It is a systematic method for eliciting expert opinion on specific topics either for forecasting purposes, decision-making processes, evaluation generation, or to explore a problem area or uncharted domain. It relies on successive rounds of questioning of experts, each expert interviewed separately. The Delphi method thus aims to highlight convergences of opinion and to identify consensus.

6 The Commission Nationale de l'Informatique et des Libertés (CNIL) is the French public authority in charge of applying the data privacy law. Studies in the health sector may also require evaluation by the Comité Consultatif pour le Traitement de l'Information en Matière de Recherche dans le Domaine de la Santé (CCTIRS, the advisory committee on information processing in material research in the field of health). Its role is to instruct the CNIL by evaluating the research methodology, the necessity of using personal data, and the relevance of personal data according to the research objectives. Transposing the Helsinki Declaration into national regulations, these two national authorities deliver scientific opinion and legal authorization. Another authority, the Comité de Protection des Personnes (CPP; People Protection Committee) delivers an ethical evaluation. For a detailed presentation of the French system, see Claudot et al. (2009).

7 For an illustration of the debate, see Rosaline S. Barbour (2001) and the responses to this article published in the *British Medical Journal* (http://www.bmj.com/content/322/7294/1115?tab=responses).

12

Anthropology in a Design, Engineering, & Commerce Curriculum

LISA DICARLO, HEATHER MCGOWAN, & SARAH ROTTENBERG

INTRODUCTION

Philadelphia University, previously Philadelphia College of Textiles and Science, was founded in 1884 in response to industry need for better textiles knowledge. Over 125 years the college grew to a university that includes programs in design, engineering, business, health science, and the liberal arts. In 2007, Steve Spinelli Jr., PhD, president of Philadelphia University, led a strategic planning effort. He recognized that students today are graduating into a world that is "VUCA": volatile, uncertain, complex, and ambiguous.[1] VUCA is a term from military vocabulary that is increasingly used in strategic leadership in a wide range of organizations to tackle wicked problems such as access to clean water, sustainable energy, and health care, where multidisciplinary solutions are required. Spinelli subscribes to the belief that innovation rarely occurs as a result of the advancement of a single discipline, but rather that innovation occurs in the overlaps and "white spaces" between disciplines. As a result, it was determined that while disciplines and majors still needed to exist, the boundaries needed to be removed. The key mandate from the university's strategic plan, focused on students achieving an innovation mindset, called for reorganizing half of the university into a new College of Design, Engineering, and Commerce (DEC). Spinelli searched for an advisor who could connect the thinking across the disciplines and bring a broader external network to advise the faculty. In 2008, Spinelli hired Heather McGowan, who held academic degrees in both design and business and had extensive professional experience in design strategy, product development, and business model innovation, to work with faculty.

After reviewing the learning outcomes (see interactive flash map[2]) from the academic programs in design, engineering, and business, we (the strategic planning team at Philadelphia University) found that most programs introduce

Handbook of Anthropology in Business, edited by Rita Denny and Patricia Sunderland, 247–265.

collaboration too late, with too few skills to facilitate collaboration (Figure 12.1). We discovered that the single-discipline focus, which may be ideal for entry-level jobs, created barriers to higher levels of career growth where the emphasis on discipline expertise lessens and the ability to coordinate, manage, and then strategize across functions becomes essential (Figure 12.2). We then looked at the spectrum of innovation from the formulation end of opportunity creation or problem finding to the delivery and optimization end of value delivery. We recognize the spectrum of innovation as defined by Clay Christensen from sustaining or incremental innovation generally centered around product or service improvements to radical, revolutionary, or disruptive innovation, which refers to innovation that requires a greater change either internally in the organization or external in the market (Christensen et al. 2008). Disruptive innovation can create new markets. We propose that incremental or sustaining innovation includes the development and optimization of products and services with a focus on solving known problems and that radical, revolutionary, or disruptive innovation requires white space discovery and formulation of new methods and processes, and entirely new value propositions. We found that both the disciplines of engineering and business emphasize development and optimization where design stretches further into discovery and formulation (Figure 12.3). We also found that the VUCA world requires greater exploration in the opportunity creation end of the spectrum. To best prepare students to collaborate in this environment, we needed to create courses and experiences that offered greater exposure to discovery and formulation in a manner that is connected and relevant to business and engineering's discipline strengths in development and optimization (Figure 12.4).

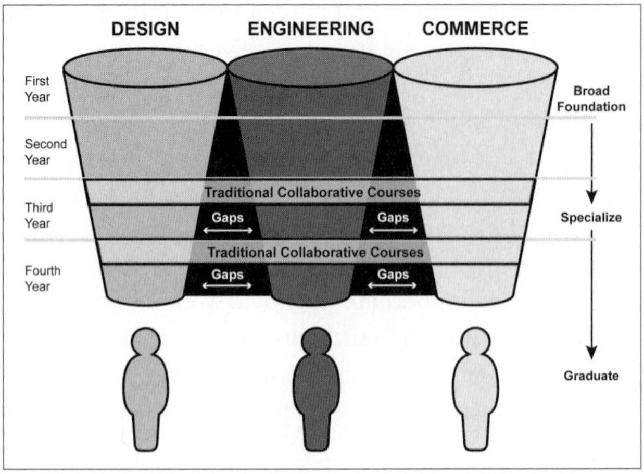

Figure 12.1. The gap effect of belated collaboration.

Figure 12.2. Career limits of the single-discipline mindset.

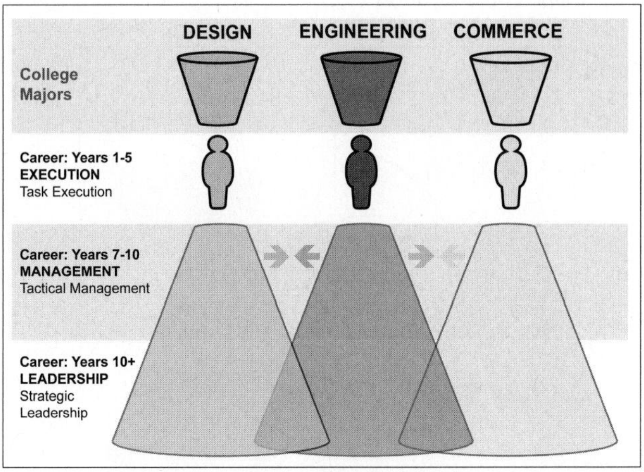

With this in mind we identified a fundamental set of common connective skills and developed the first beta courses into what we called a core framework. This represents a common core curriculum for all students in the 14 undergraduate majors that make up DEC. The courses are designed to spiral through phases of discovery and formulation with tangible opportunities to integrate their growing discipline knowledge, culminating in an integrative senior thesis capstone. There are four courses in the core curriculum:

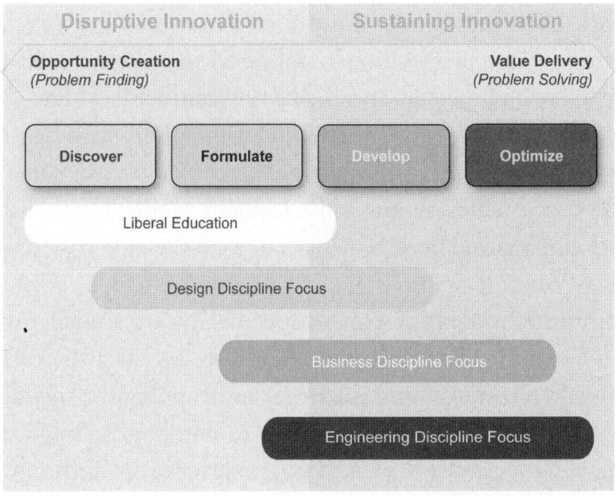

Figure 12.3. Spectrum of innovation and discipline foci.

Figure 12.4. Integration of DEC core curriculum, liberal education, and discipline concentration.

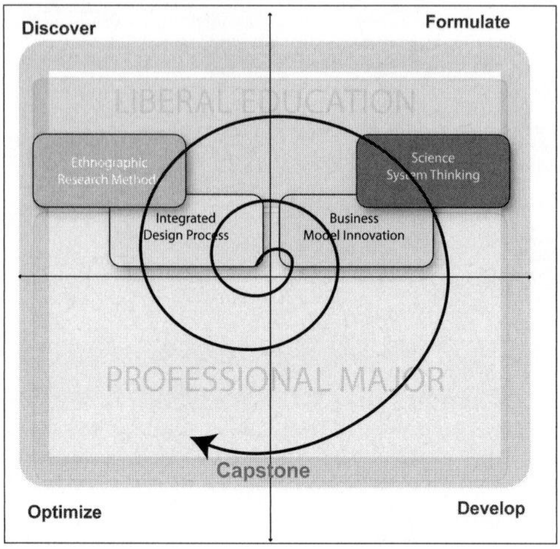

- **Process: Integrative Design Processes (IDP)** introduces students to dealing with ambiguity and propositional thinking through finding problems, prototyping, and iterating solutions while working in diverse teams of students.
- **Methods: Ethnographic Research Methods** continues the emphasis on inquiry, teamwork, and dealing with ambiguity from IDP, exclusively focuing on people and behavior with unique insights into behavior and belief, the cultural construction of everything, and the concept of sameness and difference. Above all, the course emphasizes developing empathy.
- **Frameworks: Business Model Innovation** introduces students to the concept of how a value proposition is delivered to customers through infrastructure to create financial, social, and environmental value.
- **Systems:** Students then choose between **Sustainability** and **Eco-innovation** as options to explore their discipline expertise or industry in a more systemic way using nature as the most resilient model. Causality and complexity are emphasized here.

In building the ethnography course specifically, we sought to bring in a diverse team of experts: both corporate anthropologists with experience in real-world industry challenges and academic anthropologists, specifically those experts well versed in teaching anthropology to nonmajors and in diverse settings. Heather sought advisors with deep experience in anthropology from both academic research and applied corporate perspectives. She engaged Lisa

DiCarlo, who teaches applied anthropology, and Sarah Rottenberg, who brings a perspective on using the tools of anthropology for design research and has more than 15 years of experience as an innovation/design consultant. We offer our experience in creating this core curriculum as a conversation.

ANTHROPOLOGY IS A CORE SKILL FOR MANAGING AMBIGUITY

HEATHER: We had three primary goals in building the core curriculum: (1) to simultaneously prepare students for the jobs that exist today and the ones that will emerge tomorrow; (2) to prepare students to adapt to forces of change in their professions; and (3) to prepare students to work effectively in teams. Why did we decide that anthropological skills are essential in this common core to help us achieve those goals?

LISA: What I have gathered from teaching anthropology to business majors who go on to a variety of careers is that the anthropological perspective offers some unique insights, and these insights are important regardless of someone's major or the industry she works in. People tend to describe behavior in terms of ideals and live it in terms of how they negotiate their conditions. Anthropology examines that intersection of behavior and belief and offers a way to understand why the two differ. When students start to explore examples of this in their own lives, it raises their awareness about how important it is to examine contexts and to question what they hear. In essence, they become more critical observers. Exploring the extent to which our lives are culturally constructed gives students a couple of useful ways of looking at the world. First, they develop empathy for other cultural worlds and may start to examine cultural differences in a more useful way. Second, they begin to look at their own contexts as systems that have developed and persisted through the efforts and beliefs of the people who came before them. If it's that basic, they realize, then surely those systems can be tweaked. In other words, they become aware of how negotiable constructs really are. In the book Where Good Ideas Come From, Steven Johnson (2010) describes innovative societies as ones in which people have access to different ideas and can question existing systems (among other things). The implications of cultural construction are irresistible to ponder. Understanding that concept leads to raised awareness about how we differ and how we are similar in terms of lived lives. There are universal experiences and needs, and then there are context-dependent negotiations and solutions. Whoever gets this will be more empathic with respect to cultural difference.

Maybe the students *won't* become anthropologists . . . what if instead they become politicians, ad reps, bankers, religious leaders, teachers of any discipline, law enforcement, or simply community members with an anthropological perspective? It's not just about how these methods will serve them in their careers. It's also about how these methods will serve them in life. I'm okay with that.

SARAH: I'm not just okay with that; I'm thrilled by it! And I think bringing in anthropological approaches teaches students even more than empathy. It teaches them inductive thinking and pattern recognition, both of which are necessary to recognize that you're in an ambiguous situation, to make sense of why things are changing, and to begin to identify how you can respond to that change. Students become open to looking for the unexpected through observation and immersion in new cultural contexts. But just finding new perspectives is not enough. Anthropology also teaches students to interpret their ethnographic data, to make sense of what they see. We teach inductive analysis techniques that work from individual bits of data up towards theories and hypotheses, which enable students to truly generate new ideas about how the world works rather than just confirm or refute their suspicions. They learn to recognize patterns, look for links between seemingly unrelated bits of data, and to probe behind what they are seeing and ask the question why is it happening.

A good example of how this works can be found in the work that Jump Associates did with General Electric Company's plastics division many years ago. We were helping GE expand into a new market and started by spending time with potential customers in that market, employees and owners of small businesses for whom GE wanted to develop products. Through the course of our research, we heard several stories about play and experimentation. One person was experimenting with a new ingredient that he discovered growing on the side of the road while driving to work one day. Another had a mini-processing plant in his garage. A third was experimenting with the fuzz on tennis balls. Rather than ignoring these stories or poking fun at these quirky behaviors, GE paid attention to them and pondered the implications for their own business. In doing so, the team realized that to win business with companies in this particular industry, GE needed to tap into the culture of experimentation, and work differently with them than they did with other customers. GE needed to engage them creatively in the early stages of the product development process and partner with them to co-create new products. This new partnership made entering into the new market both less expensive and faster, as GE could tap into their partners' resources and existing manufacturing capabilities instead of building their own. It also meant that the co-developed products were easy to sell, because they had been made alongside their customers. Noticing the pattern and correctly interpreting these stories resulted in GE succeeding in the new business earlier and with less investment than they had initially projected. Empathy and pattern recognition seem like soft skills, but they can have incredibly hard benefits.

PRACTICING ANTHROPOLOGY TEACHES TEAMWORK

HEATHER: From my experience in both product design and entrepreneurship, I found people often rushed into problem-solving: designing prototypes and business plans before they really understood the problem. That is one of the fundamental reasons I wanted to push for more problem finding and framing in the DEC core, which anthropology does very well. In addition to this emphasis, we are also introducing students to working effectively in teams. People tend to think of the lone anthropologist in a mud hut in a third-world country. That hardly conjures up notions of building teamwork. How does ethnography come into play in developing team players? Does adding anthropology into the core actually work against our goals of getting students to learn to collaborate?

SARAH: Not at all. Anthropologists in academic and corporate settings frequently work as part of a research team, and fieldwork can be a big part of creating a successful team. At the beginning of each client project, we try to erase the line between the client team and the consulting team to create a single, unified working group with shared expectations and goals. It's difficult. Everyone comes from different perspectives. Organizational cultures create different ideas of what a team is and how a great team should function. Even when we use the same words to talk about consumers, ideas, and innovation, we doubtless have different specifics in mind (see Neese as well as Hasbrouck and Scull, this volume). A project kick-off meeting, designed to get everyone on the same page, is in reality most likely an exercise in finding out how many different pages everyone is on. When the project actually gets under way, the first activity is typically going out into the field to collect data and learn about people and their lives. Fieldwork becomes the true team-building experience. It's like a road trip: it puts both client and consultants out into the unknown, in an unfamiliar city, with unfamiliar people, touring unfamiliar homes, stores, and offices. Unexpected things happen, and people are forced to deal with the unexpected together. Along the way team members get to know each other much better than they ever would around a conference room table, or even a dinner table. Collaboration happens because it must: when you're in a participant's home, someone asks the questions, someone else holds the camera, someone else takes notes. Everyone is engaged because everyone has a job to do, and you can't exactly check your smartphone in the middle of an interview. Gathering great data about people and their lives also helps. The data provide everyone with a new, shared set of information to work with, and everyone begins to work with the same information instead of just focusing on what each individual knew before the project started. Without fail, by the next big meeting, folks who have been in the field doing research together have begun to form a collective sense of team identity. This collaborative approach to fieldwork, which intentionally helps build relationships between team members, is what our students are learning.

LISA: The most effective way I've found to get students to see the importance of working in teams is to lead them through exercises that demonstrate the conspicuous gaps in knowledge that result from one person's attempt to assess a situation or come up with a solution. Simple observation exercises requiring students to go in teams to a common location and write down everything that happens (not everything they see, but everything that happens) in a 10-minute period are very effective. They complete the exercise without speaking to one another before, during, or afterwards. When they return to class and report their findings, they realize that they are capable of being in the same place and noticing what happens in very different ways. So when they collect information to understand or solve problems, they want to work with other people, and they often choose team members who see things very differently. The person concentrating on dialogs wants to work with the person who notices traffic flows, or the one who focuses on people interacting with their gadgets. It also gets them to think in terms of "an" answer as opposed to "the" answer. "An" answer can accommodate another answer. "The" answer has a harder time with that.

How many ethnographic studies would have been written differently if the fieldwork had been a collaborative effort?

INSERTING ANTHROPOLOGY INTO THE CURRICULUM THROUGH INTEGRATIVE EXPERIENCES

HEATHER: Collaboration and shared gained insights are great goals and outcomes, but how do you institutionalize this beyond a single course experience and really affect the program?

LISA: I would also say that it depends on how anthropology is *added* to the curriculum. If it is tacked on as a separate course, or as an elective, it reinforces the belief that anthropology is optional, or something that belongs in a mud hut by itself. The DEC research methods course, Learning from Fieldwork, was designed to be user-friendly on a couple of levels. It is clear that the methods taught in the course come from anthropology. Many of the texts are ethnographic methods texts written by anthropologists (e.g., Bernard 2011; Kutsche 1997; Wolcott 2008), the jargon of anthropology is present throughout the syllabus, the course was co-created with anthropologists as consultants, and anthropologists are among those who teach the course. The course is also taught by faculty from different disciplinary backgrounds, and will no doubt be taught differently from their perspective. To give the course some uniformity of methods taught, faculty interested in teaching the course attend workshops to learn specifically how these research methods fit into anthropological research. The larger message here is that faculty from many disciplines can teach such a course because they also conduct fieldwork and use ethnographic research methods. Students come to understand that while ethnographic methods are most commonly associated with the discipline of anthropology, they are applicable to other areas of study. In my opinion, this is a true integration of both the anthropological perspective as well as ethnographic methods into the DEC curriculum. If it is truly integrated as it is in the DEC curriculum, students will experience it as part of a core set of skills or perspectives that they need to master to be effective at whatever they do next. I've seen courses in other programs in which students form teams with one engineering major, one business major, and one anthropologist. This is a good start, and it presents a format where three disciplines are equally important to problem-solving, fact-finding, design, etc. Knowing how to work with anthropologists, engineers, or entrepreneurs represents one level of skills integration. Knowing how to think and see like an anthropologist, and an engineer, and an entrepreneur, is a deeper level of integration.

HEATHER: Part of our intent in the DEC core was to go beyond the decades-old collaborative course form of simply coordinating functions: design it (design), build it (engineering), and sell it (business). The type of collaboration Sarah mentions in the field is exactly what inspired us to create this core, common set of experiences and tools, and anthropology comes in as an excellent Swiss army knife of sorts. Given this collaborative field experience, what are some of the key exercises or experiences you present to orient students to this way of thinking?

SARAH: One of the first things you have to do is get students out of their classrooms, off the computer, and out into the world together. You can't build empathy with another person without stepping into their world. One of my favorite in-class exercises is borrowed from the Stanford University Needfinding course taught by Dev Patnaik called Moccasins.[3] It requires teams of students to spend several hours across multiple days with someone whose life is completely different from theirs and to come back and tell the class this person's story from their point of view, as if they're standing in their shoes. Before they begin, each person writes down their expectations of what they'll see. At the end, they have to tell a new story. I've had students spend time with campus police, Chipotle managers, drycleaners, surgeons, and people living in assisted living facilities, with great results. Without fail, the teams find that the more time they spend with another person, in the other person's environment, the more they are truly able to understand who that person is, why they act as they do, and what matters to him/her.

LISA: I use a similar exercise in the field course I teach in Turkey, which is also open to students who have just finished their first year, as well as upper-level students. I divide a class of 15 into five groups, pair each group with someone who lives in Istanbul, and send the groups out with the assignment to see the city. The Istanbul residents have been prompted to take their groups to very different places within the city. At the end of the day we regroup, and the students begin to describe the "Istanbul" they saw. Of course, there are lots of contested opinions that get passed around in that discussion: lots of "That's not how I saw it" or "Where did you see that?" The point here, much like your Moccasins exercise, is to learn to ask about the experiences of others, to question one's own experience and the significance of it, and to have more awareness about how knowledge is created. This pushes students to be able to identify and to think critically about culturally constructed meanings and categories. How can we read what we see before us? What does "dirty" mean? What is success? What constitutes a good marriage? What does it mean to be healthy? How are these concepts defined, and why or how do they change across or within cultural contexts? If students can situate meanings and practices within a broader, longer spectrum of human behavior, they are beginning to think like anthropologists.

HEATHER: What other aspects of a classic anthropological point of view inform what you teach in the Ethnographic Research Methods course?

LISA: The anthropological perspective teaches us that meanings are culturally constructed and context dependent. Letting the field site "speak to us" and shape our research is a cornerstone of an anthropological approach. Similarly, project conditions should determine the research approach when conducting research to inform an entrepreneurial venture or new design.

SARAH: Depending on what other training you've had, it can be hard to accept that there isn't one single way to conduct good research, that what's good in one project is not the same as what's good in another project, given different contexts and goals.

I struggled with this issue in my first job as a design researcher, at Doblin Group in Chicago. I had just graduated with a master's degree in social science from the University of Chicago and had learned about scientific method, rigorous data collection, and validity of research. My colleagues told me what our research questions were and asked my opinion on how we should go about answering the questions. The plan I initially devised took three times as long and cost twice as much as we could afford. The research plan was whittled down considerably. The path we took worried me. I didn't believe that it was "real research." But in the end, we generated insights for our clients, and developed a point of view about what they should do. Since then, I have a more nuanced understanding about the difference between research that's conducted to be predictive and comprehensive and research that's conducted to be stimulating, provocative, and inspirational. In reality, the appropriate question to ask isn't "Is this a valid research process or not?" but "What is the purpose of the project?" and "What kinds of research can achieve that goal?" Different projects require different kinds of research depending on how people plan to use that research. Only once you can articulate the goal of your research can you can design a project that accomplishes your goals. Then, you choose different methods of data collection and analysis, using appropriate numbers of participants based on whether you're trying to inspire new ideas, to develop a statistically valid understanding of consumer behaviors, or to evaluate the potential success of existing ideas.

This seems like common sense, but in practice, it is tricky to implement. People often plan new projects based on what has worked well in the past. We get into the habit of doing something a certain way, and it takes time and effort to question that approach with each new project.

THE CHALLENGES OF TEACHING ETHNOGRAPHY ACROSS DISCIPLINES

HEATHER: Taking this line of thinking a bit further, what are the other challenges that you've encountered doing this work professionally, and how does it inform your approach to teaching ethnographic methods for design, entrepreneurship, engineering, or product/service development?

SARAH: Perhaps the most challenging part of using ethnographic methods in this way is ensuring that your insights are actionable, not just valid and illuminating. The research process has to provide data that are useful. And it's difficult to tell how actionable a research finding is without actually using it.

So when I teach these methods at the University of Pennsylvania, I try to get my students to close the loop as quickly and as often as possible. As soon as they start conducting analysis, I ask them to start generating ideas and implications based on their research. And if there's no clear "so what" from what they're finding, if they can't generate new ideas for the design of a product, an experience, or a business, I send them back to work. Unfortunately, this is not always the way that design research is implemented in business today.[4] Too often, data are collected, analysis is completed, and then the ideation begins.

Sometimes a company will enlist one team or company to do the data collection and analysis and another to do the ideation, strategy, or product development work. That approach leads to weaker research and weaker ideas. I teach students to consciously mix ideation into the research process. Closing the loop in the process, going from seeing something out there in the world, to drawing conclusions about what you see, to deriving implications for your project helps student learn what is well-executed research versus poorly executed research.

The DEC curriculum is set up to help students learn how to get to the "so what." The first class they take, the Integrated Design Process, introduces students to the entire process, exposes them to how ethnographic methods fit into the process, and requires them to apply their learning to a real project. This immediately helps them understand why and how it's valuable. Then, they have a chance to get better at implementing those methodologies through more practice in the Ethnographic Research Methods course.

HEATHER: Great point about mixing ideation into the research process and seeking focused results that are actionable. One of the objections I received early on from faculty is that students are not emotionally ready, let alone cognitively prepared, to tap into this level of empathy. Do you find this to be true and, if so, how do you address this?

LISA: I think undergrads are ready for this as soon as they arrive, when they are first-year students. When I was at Babson, there was a foundation course for first-year students in History and Society called Crises in Citizenship and Community, and I taught that course for several years. We used Appiah's *Cosmopolitanism* (2006) to try to get students to think beyond their own perspectives. Again, it's easy to read about the concept of caring for people you don't know and have never seen, or to even understand how they are similar or different. It is more of a challenge to get students to question their unexamined assumptions about how much of their experience is a shared experience among the people they see every day. To that end, I would start that course with an exercise in defining community. The students had to write what they knew to be a truthful statement about Babson culture on the whiteboard. We would then go through the statements one by one to see how many of the statements rang true for all of the students. For example, one student would write that Babson is a friendly place. Another student would write Babson students don't seem to have any fun . . . or that Babson has a partying culture. In a class of 30, there were usually two or three general statements that the class would identify as a common experience. That simple exercise usually resulted in students asking, "Who is we?" throughout the rest of the course when someone would make a general statement about how "we" feel or what "we" believe. So even in the very first weeks of the first semester of the first year, it is possible to get them to examine their assumptions about shared experiences, shared identity, shared beliefs.

They get it at that age. I think their ability to grasp the concept depends more upon our ability to design effective learning experiences for them. (Both of these exercises are part of the DEC curriculum now.)

SARAH: I agree, Lisa. I think the sooner we help students get outside of their comfort zones, and the sooner we start helping them see how their experience is unique and not universal, the better. And starting early means that students have less to unlearn. It does stretch them developmentally and cognitively, but it stretches them in the right direction; the more students exercise these muscles, the better they'll be at it. The ability to develop empathy with others is one of those lifelong skills that will serve students in a number of ways once they start developing it, and I think it will help make them more competitive in the job market and serve them in their careers as well as in the classroom.

HEATHER: That is encouraging. If teaching empathy isn't a problem, what concepts are problematic? Have you identified concepts that are particularly difficult for students to grasp at this stage? How do you teach them?

LISA: Anthropology is all about how knowledge and behavior of all types, or what we "know" to be true and right, is culturally constructed and context dependent. And fieldwork is a process that starts as broadly as "What's going on?" and gets more defined along the way. We can never predict how long it will take or exactly where it will lead. So with students who are used to learning just to test well, I make experiencing the ambiguity, the failure, and the revisions part of the grade. It sounds very mechanical, but it works. For every research plan that my students write, they are expected to revise it at least twice in the semester. They get more credit for keeping track of more revisions. They get bonus points for sharing their crappy first drafts of their research plan and explaining the parts that turned out to be unfeasible or unrealistic. They are marked down if they don't report any revisions. I assume that they will fail or misfire during fieldwork, as we all occasionally do. They are required to report those experiences and they are marked down if they don't 'fess up. Finally, they are required to describe ways in which they dealt with ambiguity (I called it "not knowing"). In other words, they're not evaluated on getting THE ANSWER regarding a particular topic of inquiry. They're evaluated in terms of how they go through the process of fieldwork, and how they contribute to other students' learning by sharing their experiences with the class. In a sense, they're no different from us, from faculty members. If we were rewarded in some way for reporting the false starts, the misfires, for showing the crappy first drafts, we would do the same.

SARAH: It is hard for students to grasp the idea that there is no one right answer. It's also hard for them to develop the flexibility to revise, adapt, and iterate their work as they're doing it. Teaching ethnography can act as a Trojan horse for teaching flexibility and adaptability, too. To do ethnographic research well, students need to learn to give up control of their interviews to their research participants. In the course of an interview, they need to be prepared to throw out their research protocols and follow the direction that the conversation takes, picking up cues from the participants' language and environment to direct their questions. In the course of a project, they often realize that their incoming hypothesis is absolutely incorrect. Sometimes, that means they just need to shift the line of questioning. Sometimes, they need to recalibrate their entire research plan, including both who they are talking to and what they observe. This kind of flexibility and acknowledging that you don't have the answer is not easy, for students or for professionals. We've literally had clients break down in tears during fieldwork because they've just realized that they don't know their business or their customers as well as they thought they did. But hopefully, by giving students the chance early in their careers to experience not knowing as an empowering experience, they'll be open to putting themselves in situations where they need to feel their way towards the answer in the future.

FACULTY DEVELOPMENT: INTEGRATING LIBERAL & PROFESSIONAL EDUCATION

HEATHER: Absolutely! Teaching students to move outside of their comfort zones is critical, but what about faculty? We developed a liberal and professional co-teaching model. We have one faculty member somewhat grounded in the discipline and the other from outside the discipline. This absolutely pushed them outside of their comfort zone. However, we found that the faculty experience teaching the pilot courses was the single biggest conversion moment in getting them enthusiastic about further experimentation. We simulated experiences throughout building DEC in workshops and charrettes and workgroups, etc. Have you had different or similar experiences engaging faculty at your institutions or enterprises?

SARAH: I noticed the same thing you did, Heather, with the DEC faculty. When I worked with the first faculty team that was going to teach the IDP core course the summer before the course was taught, I observed a little fear and apprehension. This kind of work is scary! Amazingly, when I met up with the same faculty members five months later, the level of confidence had shot up. Not because everything had gone exactly according to plan, because it hadn't, but because each person had become more accustomed to teaching new materials, bringing the diverse disciplines of design, engineering, and commerce into conversation with each other, and taking students on a journey that was almost as new to them as it was to the students.

I don't think we should underestimate how hard this transition is for faculty, and how deeply it challenges ingrained notions of what a professor is, what constitutes expertise, and what it means to be part of the discourse of a discipline. (The fact that we call a field of study a discipline says it all!) In the United States, people who have been successful in academia have been successful because they have specialized. They know things about their fields that no one else knows, and they have claimed a territory for expertise. But asking people from different disciplines to integrate their work with each other and teach multidisciplinary content pushes us outside that territory. It forces us to discuss, reflect upon, and teach things that we're not experts in. This pushes everybody outside of their comfort zone. We feel like it is only our right to speak about that which we know cold, topics where we can quote the literature. But if we're asking it of our students, we need to model it ourselves.

The only way we can get there is through starting the dialog and setting up opportunities for faculty to experience the power of collaboration and integration. The IDP course is one of those opportunities.

LISA: Good point, Sarah. We do know things about our field that no one else knows but we fall short somehow on knowing how to explain all of the ways in which our field, whatever that is, contributes to the larger cross-disciplinary exploration of particular topics. In academia we are trained to be "back of the store" scholars. We produce knowledge for and within our respective disciplines. We have inward discussions about the merits of our perspectives, often to the discredit (can I say that?) of other disciplinary perspectives. We don't generally teach our students about being the "front of the store" scholar, one who connects with other disciplines, shares the merits of one's disciplinary perspective with colleagues from different traditions, and communicates easily across those boundaries.

It will be easier to get faculty on board for specific collaborative initiatives if there is more openness on campus to collaborating in general. There are always examples of faculty members who collaborate on an informal basis. Aside from my position in the sociology department and in the interdisciplinary Business, Entrepreneurship and Organizations program, I find other opportunities to work across departments that aren't part of my formal duties. This semester, I'm a guest lecturer in a Rhode Island School of Design course on product development taught by an industrial design professor. Another colleague from engineering is also participating. We haven't made any formal announcement about this experiment, but we are experimenting nonetheless. I think this happens a lot. Finding these examples and sharing them with the rest of the faculty might lead to the discovery of even more instances of informal collaboration. In the absence of an administrative mandate, I think it starts like that.

EXPECTATIONS & PARTING THOUGHTS

HEATHER: What do we hope will be the fruit of all of this labor? Aspirationally, when we look at graduates now and 10 years from now, how do you expect these professionals to operate in their professions?

SARAH: I hope that graduates excel at both generating new ideas and getting people in their world excited about those ideas, so that they are able to make a difference in their professional worlds. When students learn ethnographic research methods in the DEC courses, they also learn how to communicate their interpretations, ideas, and conclusions in compelling ways through stories about the people and places that they study. Knowing which stories best embody your point of view and which are most likely to persuade other people of your point of view is a skill that will help students negotiate any workplace landscape in the future. In my time at Jump Associates, we worked closely with a team within General Mills called the iSquad. The team of internal consultants was responsible for facilitating brand teams through the innovation process and helping them come up with new products, new marketing campaigns, and new packaging ideas. Because they were a part of the organization, they had a great sense of what kinds of stories would resonate with their internal audience. In their work, they spent an equal amount of time communicating the results from their research as they did gathering and analyzing research. During the time that we worked together, they had a hand in the majority of big, profitable innovations within the company and were responsible for the big shifts in how the company related to their consumers because they were able to tell persuasive stories that galvanized internal teams into action. I would love to see DEC graduates be able to have that kind of impact.

LISA: Isn't there an iterative relationship between professionals and the workplace? We change the workplace and it changes us? It is hard to say what the workplace will be like. As for DEC graduates as future professionals, I hope they will take their lateral-thinking, hybrid perspectives with them and become collaboration catalyzers. If they have learned in college to see across disciplinary divides and to build an eclectic portfolio of problem-solving approaches, they will want to be able to continue working that way once they move into their professions.

HEATHER: We've talked a lot about what we've been trying to accomplish, why we're undertaking these initiatives, and how we're approaching it. I'd like to take also take a moment to look ahead into the future. When we succeed, what will success look like? What is the long-term impact you would like to see more broadly?

SARAH: I would like to see more and more of this kind of initiative taking place at a variety of scales, across a broad range of academic institutions. American universities currently face an innovator's dilemma not so different from the one faced by the disk drive industry that Clayton Christensen (1997) wrote about. For universities, the potential disruptors are multiple: technological, economic, and social forces are all driving towards change. The very skills and abilities that we're trying to teach DEC students—how to interpret and adapt to change and prepare for an uncertain future—are the skills that faculty and staff throughout academia will also need to learn. Not every school will address their innovators dilemma in the same way—some will reorganize their programs, some will embrace online learning, some will engage in international expansion—but every school will have to do something. At the University of Pennsylvania, where I teach, teams are currently experimenting with all of these different kinds of initiatives, as well as several more. My hope is that in teaching these skills to our students we learn them ourselves, and end up leading change rather than becoming its victims. What Philadelphia University is doing with DEC is a bold experiment; we need to see more of them!

LISA: I like that. From my view, faculty will follow the lead of administration and what they incentivize. When we are at our most inspired stage, after the dissertation, we all learn that success will come from aiming for tenure and nothing else. In a sense, we are also striving to pass the test, and the test is the tenure review process. Believe me, if innovation experiments were a requirement for tenure, faculty would be innovative: or the ones who are already innovative would be more public about it. We are trained to master our disciplines, not to innovate on them. As a cultural anthropologist who jumped over to the entrepreneurship division (aka THE DARK SIDE) earlier in my career, I was considered a lost or unfocused colleague and not an example of how valuable the liberal arts perspective really is in the study of entrepreneurship. A colleague of mine from graduate school is now working at Intel. She regularly offers to go back to our department to talk with students about what it's like to work as an anthropologist outside of academia. I don't know that they have ever taken her up on that offer. I would like to see an attack on two fronts: demand from the outside for more innovative approaches, which is already happening to a certain extent; and university administrators who reward academics early on for thinking outside the compartment. Of course, graduate programs would also have to encourage students to look at their disciplines as constructs that can survive visiting the intersections with other disciplines. Now that would be interesting. Heather, you have been asking all the questions here, but what do you think? What long-term impact would you like to see?

HEATHER: I suspect, and have thus far experienced, that students are ready for this and even hungry for it. They want the applied, the relevant, and the real world even if it is messy. My hopes are similar to yours in that this experiment will force changes in one small institution in Philadelphia that may catalyze changes at other institutions. Philadelphia University is not the only to try this: Rotman School of Management at the University of Ontario, Stanford, Franklin W. Olin College of Engineering, University of Pennsylvania, Babson College, Brown University, Rhode Island School of Design, Carnegie Mellon University, and many other institutions have been working at this at the course and program levels for decades. Universities will need to rethink many processes and structures such as organizing faculty and students around functional disciplines and related identities, rewarding lifetime employment based upon singular, isolated expertise, and process rigidities that discourage experimentation at many places. For the students, my hope is that they push this farther than what we started and that the first and second graduating classes from DEC, along with graduates from the University of Pennsylvania and Brown, stay engaged in their institutions as active alumni who influence the next iterations. One of the biggest next hurdles is how to really leverage teaching something like anthropological tools and skills across an entire field such as marketing or engineering. In creating DEC we purposefully created an integrated core so the design thinking, anthropology, business models, etc. are taught in an applied, integrated way, but that is only 10 percent of the student's course load. Traditionally, education is delivered in a somewhat transactional way through the consumption of independent, often disconnected courses, frequently with a large division between liberal and professional education. Philadelphia University has its sights set on tearing down those walls. It was a privilege to be part of the first phase of the experiment, and I look forward to watching their evolution and, I hope, the impact across other institutions. Thank you both for helping with this; your contributions were absolutely invaluable!

SARAH: Heather, thanks for including us in this conversation. I think I can speak for Lisa when I say it has been a privilege for both of us to be part of the experiment as well.

REFERENCES

Appiah, Kwame A. 2006. *Cosmopolitanism: Ethics in a World of Strangers*. New York: W. W. Norton.

Bernard, H. Russell. 2011. *Research Methods in Anthropology: Qualitative and Quantitative Approaches*. 5th edition. Lanham, MD: AltaMira Press.

Christensen, Clayton M. 1997. *The Innovator's Dilemma: When New Technologies Cause Great Firms to Fail*. Boston: Harvard Business School Press.

Christensen, Clayton M., Michael Horn, and Curtis Johnson. 2008. *Disrupting Class: How Disruptive Innovation Will Change the Way the World Learns*. New York: McGraw Hill.

Johnson, Steven. 2010. *Where Good Ideas Come From: A Natural History of Innovation*. New York: Riverhead Books.

Kutsche, Paul. 1997. *Field Ethnography: A Manual for Doing Cultural Anthropology*. New York: Prentice Hall.

Wolcott, Harry. 2008. *Ethnography: A Way of Seeing*. Lanham, MD: AltaMira Press.

NOTES

The team would like to acknowledge the faculty and leadership from Philadelphia University, without whom many of the discussed experiences would never have occurred, notably President Steve Spinelli, Provost Randy Swearer, Vice Provost Gwynne Keathley, Executive Dean Ronald Kander, Dean Susan Lehrman, Dean Michael Leonard, Associate Dean Phillip Russel, and the entire DEC faculty development team, most notably from the research methods course: Rick Shain, Marcella Deh, and Sharon Kornelly.

1 VUCA is a military term that migrated into business leadership management in the early 2000s. It was adopted as a central mindset in planning the new College of Design, Engineering, and Commerce.

2 See http://www.philau.edu/strategicinitiatives/flash/DEC.Integrated.Model.swf.

3 A human-centered, empathy-oriented approach to design engineering was first introduced to Stanford University in 1958 with the introduction of the design program into the mechanical engineering department. This was a novel way of thinking through how to best approach design and engineering problems. Ultimately, the perspective and methodology was formalized though the introduction of a course called Needfinding, which is currently taught by Dev Patnaik, who is also the CEO of Jump Associates. The thinking also underlies the approach of the Hasso Platter Institute of Design at Stanford University, which was established by IDEO founder David Kelly.

4 The practice of design research in business today is a topic that is thoroughly discussed and hotly debated regularly in anthrodesign, an online community that discusses the intersection of anthropology and design. To see some of these discussions, see Anthrodesign.com.

13

The Anthropology of Business & Administration in Japan

JOHN L. MCCREERY & KEIKO YAMAKI

> The distinctive features at the heart of Umesao's scholarship were three: persistence, boundary-crossing, and discovery.
>
> —Masatake Matsubara (2011:3)

In Japan, the anthropological study of business has a long and distinguished history. Chie Nakane's *Japanese Society* (1967) makes the social structure of large Japanese corporations the centerpiece of a classic study of Japanese society as a whole. Subsequent studies include white collar workers (Rohlen 1979), industrial familism (Noguchi 1990), Japanese factories (Dore 1973; Roberts 1994), the wedding industry (Goldstein-Gidoni 1998), department stores (Matsunaga 2002), an advertising agency (Moeran 1996), and American firms doing business in Japan (Hamada 1991). And even this is only a partial list of anthropological research conducted in business settings in Japan and published in English. This chapter, however, investigates a body of work, published in Japanese and largely unfamiliar to scholars outside Japan, which is notable for its success in crossing boundaries: disciplinary divides, national frontiers, and the schism between academy and business. The work in question is that of the Anthropology of Administration Group (*Keieijinruigaku*) at the National Museum of Ethnology (*Minpaku*) in Osaka, and is extraordinary in three respects:

1. Breadth and longevity: Rooted in an academic partnership between an anthropologist from a national museum and a professor of business administration, the group has, from the start, combined anthropological and management perspectives. It has also included specialists in sociology, folklore, and Japanese history. The group's founders and core members worked together for more than two decades.

Handbook of Anthropology in Business, edited by Rita Denny and Patricia Sunderland, 266–283.

2. Global perspective: The founders met as participants in a research project on comparative civilizations, with global and world historical dimensions. In the group's research, participant observation and the anthropologist's passion for local detail is informed by big-picture concerns.
3. Religion: A topic largely, if not completely, avoided in Western anthropological and other research on how businesses are managed has from the start taken center stage in the group's research.

Part 1 begins with the history of the group's formation as told by several of its core members. Part 2 examines the ideas and approaches found in those publications, to explore how they have changed over time and were affected by the historical context in which they appeared. Part 3 then turns to the question how this research, which is unabashedly academic in character, relates to anthropology in business, applied business anthropology. It also considers the importance of the Japanese experience to that in the United States and Europe.

PART 1: THE ORIGINS OF *KEIEIJINRUIGAKU*

Hirochika Nakamaki is the charismatic academic entrepreneur who is one of the group's two founders. He has taken responsibility for securing grants to support its research and arranging its publications (Nakamaki and Hioki 1997, 1999, 2003, 2007, 2009, 2012). In interviews conducted with Nakamaki in 2012, he described himself as a disciple of National Museum of Ethnology founder Tadao Umesao. An article in the museum's newsletter summarizes Umesao's work:

> The distinctive features at the heart of Umesao's scholarship were three: persistence, boundary-crossing, and discovery. Umesao pursued topics ranging from comparative civilization and comparative religion to women's studies, information industries, technologies for intellectual production, and cultural development—for periods that sometimes spanned decades. His persistence was incredible. At the same time, he never confined himself to a single academic specialty but was constantly crossing boundaries between existing disciplines (Matsubara 2011:3).

Nakamaki says that he met Koichiro Hioki, his collaborator for more than 20 years, through The Japan Society for the Comparative Study of Civilizations (*Hikakubunmei gakkai*). When they met, Hioki was teaching at Kyushu University and engaged as a consultant by the president of Hasegawa Corporation, a manufacturer of *butsudan,* Buddhist home altars. The president wanted to build an altar museum to collect and exhibit religious altars from all over the world. Hioki did not know much about museums, but he knew someone who did: Nakamaki.

That project never came to fruition. The collapse of the economic bubble of the late 1980s left many Japanese corporations with their finances in perilous shape. At Hasegawa, other senior executives banded together to put a stop to the president's extravagance. But when Hioki moved to Kyoto University, their opportunities to meet increased. Nakamaki says that it may have been over a beer that the possibility of their organizing a joint research project came up.

At this point Nakamaki had recently published *Once There Were* Daimyo, *Now There Are Companies* (Nakamaki 1992); Hioki may already have been working on *The Company As Cultural Apparatus* (*Bunmei no sōchi toshite no Kigyo*; 1994). Nakamaki explained that Hioki had been working with sociologists on a joint research project but was unhappy with their reliance on survey research. He thought that anthropological methods, participant observation, and in-depth interviews would allow him to probe more deeply into company cultures.

Much of what happened next is chronicled by Izumi Mitsui, professor of management at the Nihon University Business School (Mitsui 1997).

An Insider's Story

> It is rush hour. The herds of salarymen are rushing up the stairs looking terribly busy. The trains are packed with salesmen with cell phones pressed to their ears. There are smiles on the faces of the fathers having a drink after work with their friends. The office lady's back is twitching as she shops at the convenience store after working overtime. Mother and children are gathered round the table, missing the husband and father who has been posted by himself to a job far away. A group of elderly retirees who used to work together are throwing a party. All are examples of modern *jōmin* (ordinary people) who live in the shadows of companies (Mitsui 1997:63).

This is the way Mitsui, a born storyteller, begins her account of the group's formation. She observes that most previous studies of companies have been conducted from the perspectives of economics or management, more rarely sociology. All see the company as a "rational," "functional," and "efficient" mechanism. During the postwar years of rapid economic growth, this view of companies seemed plausible. The vision it embodied boosted productivity. People were willing to see themselves as gears in the corporate machine and to perceive the self-discipline demanded by the workplace as a sign of adulthood.

Then, things changed. Economic collapse destroyed the myth of endless growth. The "company men" on whose backs the image of the company as a "rational mechanism" was built were suddenly behaving like refugees under attack. The mass media became filled with reports of corporate scandals and maltreatment of employees. The blind admiration of the Japanese management, whose "mysteries" seemed inexplicable in terms of European and American management theory, was gone. As Mitsui put it, we needed new stories to understand what was going on.

Companies are, in fact, both rational and functional in many respects. They gather information, forecast the future, set targets, refine their processes, and appoint managers to make necessary adjustments, trying to do everything as efficiently as possible. When, however, we turn our attention to the people who make up companies, we discover behavior that seems irrational.

Executives whose decisions affect their companies' futures turn to fortune-tellers or pray to gods or Buddhas. Japan's largest companies often have shrines on their premises and departments that see to the worship of the gods enshrined in them. New employees undergo "purification," are introduced to the sacred ground on which the company was founded, and rise each morning to collectively sing the company song and recite the company creed. Some may be saboteurs and refuse to follow the rules, but others are corporate saints whose achievements or sacrifices earn them company funerals or a place in the company cemetery. From a purely rational perspective, these findings are unexpected.

Mitsui's account turns to the first stirrings of what would become the "Anthropology of Administration." Specialists in anthropology, management, religion sociology, history, and education debated the meaning of "company" and "salaried worker." These early discussions included a strong vein of humor. The origins of salaried worker habits were traced to Edo-period samurai, caricatured as malingerers, lazy, incompetent, or afraid of their wives. Then the discussion turned serious. Mental illness among salaried workers was an issue of growing concern. Members of the group felt they were on the edge of something new, and it was exciting.

The group's first grant was for "Comprehensive Research on Company Cultures." It anticipated extended fieldwork and participant observation, but the barriers to getting researchers into Japanese companies proved too high. The theme was switched to "Anthropological Research on Company Cultures and Company Museums."

Nakamaki explained that the difficulty of gaining access to companies was not the only barrier. The group's participants were all full-time academics and, while there were grants for field trips overseas, there was neither funding nor freedom from teaching and other responsibilities for those doing research in Japan. It was Hioki who suggested that the theme be changed to corporate museums, which were accessible and public displays of company culture.

According to Yoshiyuki Takeuchi, Mitsui's husband and a professor of applied statistics and econometrics, Mitsui dragged him along when she joined the group. He was the designated driver for the museum project and was, he says, appalled that the anthropologists had not collected financial data on companies before going to see their museums. In the written synopsis he prepared for our 2012 interview, Takeuchi observes that the group began with broadly defined goals similar to those of classic anthropological research: ethnographic research on companies and salaried workers (Takeuchi 2012). It would approach companies as groups with distinctive cultures and use participant observation to explore in detail the lives and habits of company employees. At the end of the day, however, the research focused on topics related to religion and ritual. Other topics that might have been explored include ethnicity, mid-career hires, local hiring overseas, part-time workers, retirees, and the impact of mergers and acquisitions.

PART 2: THE OUTPUT

The group's founders, Hirochika Nakamaki (National Museum of Ethnology) and Koichiro Hiroki (Kyoto University), have edited six volumes: *Toward an Anthropology of Administration* (1997), *The Anthropology of Administration: Company Funerals* (1999), *The Anthropology of Administration: Company Museums* (2003), *The Globalization of Company Culture* (2007), *Religion in the Company* (2009), and *The Anthropology of Administration: Company Mythology* (2012). Core group members Noriya Sumihara, Izumi Mitsui, and Yusuke Watanabe edited the volume *Corporate Ideals: Anthropology of Administration Research on Succession and Dissemination* (2008), the first major collection of papers not edited by Nakamaki and Hioki. What follows is taken largely from the editors' introductions to these works.

Why Companies and Salaried Workers?

Toward an Anthropology of Administration (Nakamaki and Hioki 1997) opens with a powerful case for making companies and salaried workers core topics in the anthropology of Japan. In 1990, there were more than 2 million companies in Japan, including the smallest as well as the largest firms. Given Japan's population of around 120 million, roughly 1 in 60 Japanese was a company president. In a labor force of 66 million, company presidents accounted for 1 in 33 workers.

In 1960, salaried employees accounted for 50 percent of Japanese workers. By 1990, that figure had risen to more than 80 percent. The population share of farmers living in rural villages—once considered the Japanese prototype—had declined precipitously. Anyone who wished to understand Japan from an anthropological perspective would have to include the company, along with households and localities, as institutions of central importance in Japanese society. *Shaen*, the ties that bound workers to their companies, would have to be considered along with *ketsuen,* literally "blood ties" (i.e., kinship), and *chien,* local ties.

Why, then, were these topics neglected by both ethnology/social and cultural anthropology (*minzokugaku*) and folklore studies (*minzokugaku*—the same pronunciation but a different Chinese character for *zoku*)? Ethnology was seen as the study of hunters, gatherers, or pastoralists living on the margins of nation states. These were not to be found in Japan, and Japan's rapidly growing economy had made it possible for young anthropologists to do fieldwork outside Japan. Folklorists continued to study rural traditions in Japan but turned increasingly to their adaptation or reinvention in the cities to which migrants from the countryside flocked in search of employment. Companies and salaried workers were off the radar for both. That left the gap that *Keieijinruigaku* would fill.

Focused on Cultural Differences

The group would also address something missing in management theory: cultural differences. Anthropologists do not assume that capitalism will work the same way in all societies. Differences between Japanese and American forms of capitalism had, for example, become a major stumbling block in trade negotiations related to the automobile industry.

Cross-cultural issues are not confined to nation-states. Even in Japan, corporate cultures differ depending on industry and locality (finance versus manufacturing, Tokyo versus Osaka). Cultural differences also divide management-track from ordinary employees and employees of different generations. To understand these issues demanded close study of the values and habits of temporary and part-time workers, freelancers, and suppliers, as well as full-time employees.

How To Think about Companies

A central issue was how to think about companies. Were they, to borrow the conceptual framework created by German sociologist Ferdinand Tönnies, *gemeinschaft* (community) or *gesellschaft* (corporation)?[1] From the perspective of management theory, organizations are *gesellschaften* whose members are driven by instrumental rationality to maximize efficiency in pursuit of profit. But why, then, are Mt. Koya in Wakayama Prefecture and Mt. Hiei on the outskirts of Kyoto, once occupied by the graves of *daimyo,* the lords of Tokugawa Japan, also the sites of corporate monuments to those who have died in the service of their companies or played important roles in their founding and growth? Why did the construction of such monuments become popular in the mid-1950s as Japan's postwar economy took off? Why were companies involved in ancestor worship? A variety of research all pointed in the same direction: companies were presenting themselves as *gemeinschaften*, intimate communities, often portrayed as families, bound together by emotional ties that transcend purely economic relations.

It would be naive, however, to understand Japanese corporations exclusively in *gemeinschaftlich* terms. Business reality was laid bare when workers who had taken for granted lifetime employment, age-based promotion, and annual raises found themselves restructured following the collapse of the economic bubble of the late 1980s.

How To Write about Companies

If how to think about companies was one key issue, another was how to write about them. Writing for a Japanese audience, it was necessary to distinguish company ethnography from company history. In Japan, the typical company history is a chronological account of the founding that celebrates the founders and others who have contributed to the company's growth. Like the monuments on sacred mountains and the rituals performed before them, the company history is a corporate assertion of company identity, showcasing vision and values.

In contrast, a company ethnography would describe a company synchronically and introduce a comparative perspective that highlighted differences from other companies. It would challenge conventional management theory trapped by reliance on Anglo-American models. In previous work, Hioki had written:

> Business administration has developed by importing theories and models from economics and the behavioral sciences (sociology and psychology), which have themselves followed the model of natural science. We have been like a marathon runner who is always looking at the backs of faster runners. Now, suddenly, no one seems to be in front. It would be a mistake, however, to think that people are interested in our research—the interest is in management itself! (Hioki 1994:1–2)

A company ethnography would not be confined to behavior on company premises. It would also include advertising and sales promotion, volunteer and philanthropic activities (still relatively new concepts in Japan in the early 1990s), social interaction within and across industries, even sport (many Japanese major league baseball and other teams are associated with companies instead of cities).

Salaried Workers as *Jōmin*

Were Japan's salaried workers members of a privileged elite or simply people with decent jobs? Becoming a salaried, white-collar worker and climbing the management track in a government agency or major corporation had become an ideal to which many aspired. Contemporary images of salaried workers could be traced to Edo-period samurai, whose livelihoods depended on government stipends. In early Meiji, however, former samurai accounted for no more than 6 percent of Japan's population. As of 1990, salaried workers accounted for more than 80 percent of Japan's workforce. No longer an elite, salaried workers had become Japan's new *jōmin* (ordinary people).

While interviewing Nakamaki, I suggested that calling salaried workers the new *jōmin* was both descriptive and politically astute. Use of this old-fashioned word connected the Anthropology of Administration to the work of Yanagita Kunio, the father of folklore studies in Japan. *Jōmin* was the term used by Yanagita to describe the rural villagers whose traditions he studied.

This usage served two purposes. First, it implied that the group's members would study companies as Yanagita had studied rural villages, as communities with distinct local traditions, collecting detailed information on the customs and habits of their employees. Second, it legitimized the group's research at Minpaku, a national museum where folkloric research still had a strong presence. I also observed how labeling salaried workers as *jōmin* positioned *Keiei-jinruigaku* as salvage anthropology: research directed at recording traditions that might soon disappear. Nakamaki agreed with all three points.

Corporate Ancestor Worship

Again, the group's original intention had been to focus on company ethnography, using participant observation to explore company cultures. When that proved impossible, the focus shifted first to company museums. For various reasons, however, publication of that research was delayed. The next book published was *Anthropology of Administration: Company Funerals* (Nakamaki 1999).

The other volumes in this series all begin with extended essays on the theory that informs the research. In contrast, this volume begins with photographs, scenes from company funerals that vividly illustrate the ethnographic observations mentioned in the preface:

> The cherry blossoms fall as if fleeing from the cold rain. The solemn executives arrive in their black limousines and enter the funeral hall in Aoyama. The employees assigned to welcome them are wearing plastic raincoats, rushing out to open the doors of each car and hold umbrellas over the heads of the VIPs as they make their way into the hall. The very special VIPs are split off and guided to a special waiting room. The others are led directly into the hall and guided to seats behind the first row reserved for their superiors.
>
> The service begins at 1:00 p.m. By 2:00 p.m., more than a hundred latecomers are lined up, waiting in the cold in the temporary tent outside the hall. Most are silent, listening intently to the sounds from inside the hall

> heard over the public address system. Inside the hall, the head of the funeral committee and the representative of the friends of the deceased are making the necessary formal remarks. When the head of the funeral committee has finished his speech, as the offering of the sacred branches begins, those who will participate in this final offering hand their name cards to the receptionists before they line up and are given the flower they will place on the table in front of the deceased's photograph. As those who have completed their offerings leave the hall, they are handed small packets of salt, to ward off misfortune . . . (Nakamaki 1999:1).

This particular funeral was unusual, a Shinto instead of a Buddhist service (in Japan, most funerals are Buddhist), but the overall pattern of events would be the same at both and at increasingly popular nondenominational alternatives. Nakamaki suggests that the way in which this pattern transcends differences in religious belief or affiliation with particular religions represents something fundamental in Japanese culture. It asserts the enduring presence and significance of the group mourning the loss of an important figure: in this case, the company. This classic anthropological proposition becomes this volume's central theme.

Museums as Corporate Temples

We return now to museums. Like the religious beliefs associated with company funerals, corporate museums take many forms. Some celebrate company history or the founders' great achievements. Others explain how the company's products are manufactured or display the products themselves. Companies that build museums range from small *sake* breweries to giant automakers, banks, and nuclear power plants as well as manufacturers. The terminology used to describe them is equally diverse. Common alternatives include "museum," "hall," "house," "gallery," and "center." Besides museums proper, there are also libraries; archives; memorial halls; culture, science, and technology halls; and the displays and visitor centers connected with company tours.

Instead of a definition, the authors turn to a simile. When they ask themselves what company museums most closely resemble, the answer is temples. Like temples, museums are consecrated spaces and dedicated expressions of collective identity. New employees' initiations include visits to company museums to help them better appreciate company history and values.

These generalizations are, however, only a first step. The diversity of company museums is yet more evidence that companies cannot be understood completely if conceived only as efficient mechanisms or economic actors making calculated choices.

The Impact of Globalization

Awareness of culture change has been a core element for Anthropology of Administration since the beginning. In the first three volumes, however, the focus was on the contrast between the assumed rationality of Anglo-American management theory models and an anthropological approach that treated companies as communities with distinct cultures. As a new millennium began, however, change became a prominent theme. From a backward-looking salvage anthropology, the group's attention turned to a now-and-future–oriented exploration of how change was affecting Japanese companies and Japanese society as a whole. The inevitable topic was globalization. The volume *Globalization of Company Culture* (Nakamaki and Sedgwick 2003) addressed its implications for Japan.

A New Commercial Code

On May 1, 2006, Japan introduced a new Commercial Code, the first major revision since 1899. The objective was to unify the law affecting companies and equip Japanese companies to adapt to globalization. Major features included lowering barriers to company formation and mergers and acquisitions. The new law also strengthened demands for corporate compliance and corporate social responsibility by making external directors, disclosure, and risk management obligatory. Companies were plunged into a whirlpool of legal, regulatory, and ethical restructuring.

Behind the wording of the new law lay a radical change in values and worldview. Companies long accustomed to the old legal framework had to reinvent themselves. Top management was given broader discretion in decision-making. At the same time, rules governing personal responsibility and corporate governance became more rigorous, disrupting established practices. Anthropology of Administration research on the globalization of corporate culture did not focus, however, on how companies, *qua* organizations, conformed to the new law. The group's members wanted to know how the new law affected company cultures, particularly in ways not spelled out in laws or contracts.

Market Individualism

First, it was necessary to understand the new business model that globalization implied. A key concept was "market individualism," which according to Ronald Dore has three distinctive features:

1. Emphasis on self-reliance instead of protecting labor
2. Market-driven compensation
3. Acceptance of growing inequality.

These principles are antithetical to those embodied in the Japanese-style management that developed starting in the mid-1950s, with its one-for-all and all-for-one sense of collective responsibility, seniority-based pay, and a Gini coefficient low enough that Japanese salaried workers, both blue and white collar, identified themselves as middle class.

Challenging Convergence Theory

Another aspect of globalization is the prominence of "convergence theory," the idea that as forms of human organization become increasingly rational they will naturally come to resemble each other. Max Weber, whose thinking gave rise to this model, distinguished between value and instrumental rationality; however, living in a world where European-style bureaucracy appeared to be the peak of organizational evolution, he had focused on the latter instead of the former. The result was, Nakamaki observes, a view of companies and, indeed, whole societies that resembles Tolstoy's description of families: "Happy families are all alike; every unhappy family is unhappy in its own way." Cultural difference would thus be read as a symptom of unhappiness, of lagging behind in pursuit of progress. Progress meant greater happiness but also the disappearance of cultural differences.

Suppose, however, that value rationality and instrumental rationality vary independently. If so, different types of management could embrace different values while continuing to implement them as efficiently as possible. The Japanese-style management model had once been seen in this light and thus was important evidence against convergence theory.

Research that challenged convergence theory identified several culturally distinct management styles. The three most notable were the Anglo-American, German-Scandinavian, and Japanese models developed during the 1960s. All three addressed the problem of worker alienation, but in strikingly different ways. Along with lifetime employment, seniority-based pay, and company unions, Japanese management used company ancestor worship, company museums, and other forms of company ceremonial to build an emotional bond to the company. The German-Scandinavian approach was to build solidarity among different types of workers and involve their unions in management. Instead of company or worker solidarity, the Anglo-American model focused on the individual worker, making "quality of working life" the key to recruiting and retaining skilled workers. It thus anticipated the rise of market individualism.

Cultural Perspectives on Standardization

Convergence theory implies that globalization will lead to cultural homogenization in products and behavior as well as management styles. Homogenization, however, requires standardization, and here again the evidence is mixed. In ways well known to savvy users of personal computers, smartphones, and other digital devices, the world of electronics is a world of global and not-so-global standards. Some are imposed by national or international regulatory bodies. Others are de facto standards, created when a new innovation takes the market by storm.

National electric power grids are another familiar example. Some deliver 100-volt current; others, 200 volts. Electrical outlets and plugs vary from country to country. Looking deeper into history, we discover silk and tea, where standardization of thread weight and quality made possible long-distance trade in silk, but standards for tea varied by region. Japanese preferred green tea, while Chinese preferred half-fermented oolong, and South Asians and Europeans fully fermented black teas.

The Impact of Colonialism

Proponents of Weberian and, more recently, Anglo-American management models present them as supremely modern and rational, pointing for evidence to their spread around the world. They neglect, however, the role of colonialism in promoting their spread. In colonies and formerly colonized new nations, the latest management models from the West were often adopted (or simply imposed) as a total package. In Japan this was not the case. When Japan's industrialization began following the Meiji restoration, Western management ideas were modified by managers who had no direct experience of how they were implemented in the West. Instead, they were adapted to fit familiar Japanese models of large-scale social organization: the quasi-feudal domains into which Tokugawa Japan was divided. Here is where Japanese-style management found its local roots.

Returning to Religion

The preface to *The Globalization of Company Culture* begins with a description of Japan's new Commercial Code, designed to prepare Japanese companies for competition in global markets. The preface to *Religion in the Company* begins with a challenge to globalization: "Global prosperity was in retreat in 2008, a year of financial crisis marked by the subprime loan issue and the bankruptcy of Lehman Brothers" (Nakamaki 2009:1).

Manufacturing industries were hit especially hard, leading to downward adjustments in production and hiring plans and "once-in-a-century" difficulties in procuring new capital. While bankruptcy and recession are recognized elements of capitalism, the carelessness with which companies so easily fired temporary and foreign workers called into question its ethical grounds. The layoffs may have been legal under the contracts signed with temp staff suppliers; the lack of consideration for workers' basic human rights was nakedly exposed. Moral and ethnical issues led directly back to religion; to meanings, values, and worldviews; to questions about companies' *raisons d'être* and to wondering what significance ethics and religion have for companies.

The authors observe once again that while economics treats capital and labor as quantifiable variables, anthropologists prefer to focus on concrete details of workplaces and worker lives. Consider, for example, the company cafeteria. What is management trying to accomplish by providing this facility? What does it mean to workers to eat lunch there every day? What are we to make of an entrepreneur who rejects the "buy low and sell high" wisdom of the market to follow the teachings of the founder of the new Japanese religion Tenrikyo to "buy high and sell low"? Examples like these have profound meaning for our understanding of economic behavior.

In the introduction, the authors observe that companies and religions seem so fundamentally different that to speak of them together may seem like a meaningless exercise. While companies appeared in modern times as a way to organize labor, religions emerged in ancient times as spiritual bodies. While companies pursue profit, religions offer peace of mind. The goals and social organization in these two domains seem utterly different. This conventional view is, however, superficial. Companies and religion are connected in all sorts of ways. Besides the company shrines and contributions to local festivals, funerals, initiations, and temples (museums) mentioned in previous volumes, there are also deeper connections. While business practices and techniques for achieving salvation may differ, both have a spiritual and intellectual side.

There have been many studies that examine the overlap between religion and economic behavior, the most famous being, of course, *The Protestant Ethic and the Spirit of Capitalism* by Max Weber. In a different tradition, Marx characterizes religion as the opiate of the people, a tool by which the bourgeoisie control the workers. The research reported in this book begins, however, from a different starting point, that of anthropological fieldwork informed by management theory. Its intellectual ancestors are F. W. Taylor, the father of scientific management, and E. B. Tylor, the father of modern anthropology with its core idea that culture is a complex whole comprising everything acquired by human beings as members of society.

Both Taylor and Tylor, these Japanese scholars observe, were raised as Quakers. Quakers (more formally the Society of Friends) are a Protestant sect founded in seventeenth-century Britain by George Fox. For Quakers, religious authority is found in the "inner light" of each believer's conscience. Worship takes the form of the "meeting," at which every believer is free to speak his or her mind.

Taylor, who is often portrayed as a key architect of the modern assembly line with its deskilling of workers and their transformation into cogs in the machine, was, it turns out, a more complex and sympathetic character than this caricature allows. As a Quaker who believed in the sanctity of work, he was deeply disturbed when, working on the line at his father-in-law's factory, he found his fellow workers restricting output to prevent the owner from lowering the piecework rate that determined their wages. His intention, however, was not to reduce wages. On the contrary, his aim was to remove every barrier to more efficient production, increasing productivity and allowing the owner to pay higher wages while also reaping a higher profit.

Besides his definition of culture, Tylor's contributions to *Keieijinruigaku* include his treatment of animism, conceived as a universal ground of religious belief and feeling, and his effort to describe its relation to modern, rational thought. This approach, these Japanese researchers assert, is also rooted in Quaker beliefs, in this case the belief that the inner light of the conscience offers access to an invisible spiritual world accessible to all human beings. Also important for these researchers is Tylor's interest in survivals, elements of culture that persist as societies evolve. Animism and survivals point to what are, from a rational-choice perspective, irrational aspects of company culture.

Tylor's evolutionary theories may seem at odds with the project of approaching companies as groups with distinct cultures whose differences have to be understood in their own, specifically local, terms. From a broader comparative perspective, however, especially one in which change over time is included, his thinking suggests similarities in knowledge, symbol, and belief found worldwide that cannot be ignored.

Myths, Ideals, & Management Crises

The last two volumes considered here develop previous ideas in complementary directions. *The Anthropology of Administration: Company Mythology* (Nakamaki and Hioki 2012) returns to the stories that companies tell about their founders and the legendary exploits of those who have saved the company in times of crisis. This book has done well in Japan, perhaps because the themes on which it focuses are popular with Japanese executives struggling to rebuild or maintain corporate morale in the face of recession and restructuring.

Management Ideals: Inheritance and Dissemination—Research in the Anthropology of Administration (Sumihara et al. 2008) has a more sociological focus. It is motivated by news reports of corporate scandals that have damaged even once-impeccable reputations to examine the processes by which corporate ideals, proudly announced in corporate philosophies and corporate brand definitions, are reinterpreted, transformed, or ignored, as business environments change and founders and their early disciples are replaced by new generations of managers. As indicated in the subtitle, "Inheritance and Dissemination," management transitions and issues related to reformulating corporate identities in an era of mergers and acquisitions are themes of particular interest.

PART 3: IMPLICATIONS FOR BUSINESS ANTHROPOLOGY

Is It Business Anthropology?

The Anthropology of Administration is a Japanese project, conceived and implemented by Japanese scholars strongly focused on the implications of globalization for Japan and Japanese companies. How does this body of work compare with what has come to be called "business anthropology" outside of Japan?

Outside Japan, business anthropology claims a long history but occupies a peripheral position in academia. In the inaugural issue of the *Journal of Business Anthropology,* Allen Batteau and Carlolyn Psenka explain why the status of business anthropology as "anthropology" remains contested ground, at least in the United States. In terms of academic hierarchy, pure anthropology sits at the top, with applied anthropology a stepchild corrupted by practical concerns, and business anthropology the even more corrupted stepchild of applied anthropology, polluted by enabling corporations to achieve their profit-making goals (Batteau and Psenka 2012).

In Japan, however, the academic aversion to business, grounded both in aristocratic attitudes that see trade as demeaning and theories of class struggle in which the owners and workers are enemies, seems less pronounced than it is elsewhere. We have to remember that in Japan shareholders, workers, and companies prospered together during the rapid growth that began in the mid-1950s and continued, only briefly interrupted by the oil shocks of the 1970s, until the collapse of the economic bubble in 1991. The Japanese critique of globalization and market individualism is grounded in a worldview in which business is seen as playing a positive role in society. The focus of the critique is what business has become as companies encouraged by national policy have imitated Anglo-

American models in an effort to compete more effectively in a globalized economy. It is not directed at business per se.

Keieijinruigaku is not antibusiness, in the characteristic style of academically dominant "pure" anthropology; but neither is it uncritical in the way it thinks about business. It is an anthropology *of* business; it is not (or at least not yet) an anthropology *in* business, dedicated to helping business achieve its profit-making goals. Its big-picture, global perspective is strikingly different from that of recent work that focuses on anthropologists who work as employees or consultants to corporations (Cefkin 2010; Guang Tian et al. 2011; Jordan 2013; Sunderland and Denny 2007).

Driven from the start by consciousness of changes in Japanese company behavior, aware of the difficulties of exporting Japanese-style management to other countries, and increasingly focused on the growing impact of globalization on Japanese company cultures and the relation of Japanese companies to Japanese society, *Keieijinruigaku* embodies a third way, addressing large social and global issues through close attention to ethnographic detail. Its thick descriptions challenge simplistic models of companies and their workers conceived as wholly rational actors obsessed with increasing efficiency. Its persistent concern with religion and ethics raise important questions of meaning in a manner that accepts the contributions of social science but also insists that scientific analysis be tempered by reality-based humanism.

On a Practical Note

In conclusion, we return to where we began and the first of the ways in which the *Keieijinruigaku* group represents an extraordinary achievement: its longevity and the breadth of the academic disciplines from which its members have been recruited. Group founder Hirochika Nakami says that he has always taken responsibility for recruiting new members to the group, finding funding to support its research, and ensuring that the results of its research were published. Izumi Mitsui remarks that Nakamaki has been an entrepreneur par excellence, someone who took it upon himself to organize the people, resources, and output that make up a successful enterprise.

Nakamaki says that part of his strategy has been to be sure that the group's publications are always books. Its members' contributions would thus appear together. They did not publish in academic journals, where their research results would become only scattered individual achievements.

From the start, this group has been about sharing. Its members met to share diverse perspectives and create something new. Their teamwork has been exceptional, a model that deserves emulation.

The scope of the group's research has, however, been limited by lack of access to the inner workings of Japanese corporations, the result of corporate cultures strongly suspicious of outsiders and academic policies that made research on corporations not the kind of anthropology that receives the leaves and funding required for long-term ethnography. The English-language anthropology of business mentioned in the introduction to this chapter suggests that foreign anthropologists have had an edge here. Besides the funding and leave required for sustained ethnographic research, they may also have been seen as less dangerous. They may have been, as complete outsiders, regarded as more easily controlled outsiders than Japanese natives, who might have other local loyalties. Whatever the case, the *Keieijinruigaku* group's research does not include the intimate detail concerning work practices and business processes found in other chapters in this volume (e.g., those by Cefkin and Ensworth). At the end of the day, what business anthropologists from other parts of the world may find most useful in this body of research is its combination of global perspective and attention to global changes affecting the business world worldwide, a perspective often missing in studies tightly focused on specific situations and problems.

REFERENCES

In English

Batteau, Allen W., and Carolyn E. Psenka. 2012. "Horizons of Business Anthropology in a World of Flexible Accumulation." *Journal of Business Anthropology* 1(1):72–90.

Cefkin, Melissa, ed. 2010. *Ethnography and the Corporate Encounter: Reflections on Research in and of Corporations*. New York, Oxford: Berghahn Books.

Dore, Ronald. 1973. *British Factory—Japanese Factory: The Origins of National Diversity in Industrial Relations, With a New Afterword*. Berkeley: University of California Press.

Goldstein-Gidoni, Ofra. 1998. *Packaged Japaneseness: Weddings, Business and Brides*. Honolulu: University of Hawaii Press.

Guang Tian, Robert, Daming Zhou, and Alfons van Marrewijk. 2011. *Advanced Readings in Business Anthropology*. Atlanta: North American Business Press.

Hamada, Tomoko. 1991. *American Enterprise in Japan*. New York: SUNY Press.

Jordan, Brigitte, ed. 2013. *Advancing Ethnography in Corporate Environments*. Walnut Creek: Left Coast Press.

Matsubara, Masatake. 2011. "Tadao Umesao's Ecological View of History." *Minpaku Anthropology Newsletter*. Osaka: National Museum of Ethnology Osaka.

Matsunaga, Louella. 2002. *The Changing Face of Japanese Retail: Working in a Chain Store*. London: Taylor & Francis.

Moeran, Brian. 1996. *A Japanese Advertising Agency: An Anthropology of Media and Markets*. Honolulu: University of Hawaii Press.

Nakane, Chie. *Japanese Society*. 1970. Berkeley: University of California Press.

Noguchi, Paul. 1990. *Delayed Departures, Overdue Arrivals: Industrial Familialism and the Japanese National Railways*. Honolulu: University of Hawaii Press.

Roberts, Glenda. 1994. *Staying on the Line: Blue-Collar Women in Contemporary Japan*. Honolulu: University of Hawaii Press.

Rohlen, Thomas. 1979. *For Harmony and Strength: Japanese White-Collar Organization in Anthropological Perspective.* Berkeley: University of California Press.

Sunderland, Patricia L., and Rita M. Denny. 2007. *Doing Anthropology in Consumer Research.* Walnut Creek: Left Coast Press.

In Japanese

Hioki Koichiro. 1994. *Bunmei no sōchi toshite no Kigyo* (*The Company as Cultural Apparatus*). Tokyo: Yuhikaku.

Mitsui Izumi. 1997. "Keieijinruigaku' Monogatari: Nijūisseki he no Furonteia" ("The Anthropology of Administration: To the 21st Century Frontier"). *Minpaku Tsushin* 77:63–8.

Nakamaki Hirochika. 1992. *Mukashi daimyo, ima kaisha: Kigyo to Shukyo* (*Once It Was* Daimyo, *Now It Is Company: Business and Religion*). Kyoto: Tankosha.

———, ed. 1999. *Shasō no Keieijinruigaku* (*Anthropology of Administration: Company Funerals*). Osaka: Toho Shuppan.

Nakamaki Hirochika, and Koichi Hioki, eds. 1997. *Keieijinruigaku Kotohajime* (*Toward an Anthropology of Administration*). Osaka: Toho Shuppan.

———. 2003. *Kigyo Hakubutsukan no Keieijinruigaku* (*The Anthropology of Administration: Company Museums*). Osaka: Toho Shuppan.

———. 2007. *Kaishabunka no gurūburuka* (*Globalization of Company Culture*). Osaka: Toho Shuppan.

———. 2009. *Kaisha no naka no shūkyō: Keieijinruigaku no shiten* (*Religion in Companies: An Anthropology of Administration Perspective*). Osaka: Toho Shuppan.

———. 2012. *Kaisha shinwa no Keieijinruigaku* (*The Anthropology of Administration: Company Mythology*). Osaka: Toho Shuppan.

Nakamaki Hirochika, and Mitchell Sedgwick, eds. 2003. *Nihon no soshiki: Shaen bunka to infoumaru katsudo* (*The Anthropology of Japanese Organizations: Corporate-bond Culture and Informal Behavior*). Osaka: Toho Shuppan.

Sumihara Noriya, Mitsui Izumi, and Watanabe Yusuke, eds. 2008. *Keieirinen: Keishō to denpa no keieijinruigaku kenkyu* (*Management Ideals: Inheritance and Dissemination—Research in the Anthropology of Administration*). Kyoto: PHP Interface.

Takeuchi Yoshiyuki. 2012. "Nakamaki, Hioki 'Keijinruigaku' wa nani wo yatte kita no ka?" ("Nakamaki, Hikoki and the Anthropology of Administration, What Have They Achieved?") Unpublished document.

NOTE

1 *Gemeinschaft* and *gesellschaft* are sometimes translated as "association" and "society," but these translations miss the force of the Japanese understanding of them, in which *gemeinschaft* refers to a community whose members identify with the group and have strong emotional attachments to it, while *gesellschaft* refers to a group whose members are linked only by instrumental ties, making it easy to leave one and join another.

14

Work Practice Studies as Anthropology

MELISSA CEFKIN

During a brief trip to Sao Paulo in 2012 I spoke with a Brazilian computer scientist whose main area of specialization was medical informatics. Tatiane (not her real name) was exploring how to provide social services for differently abled people in the city, keeping in mind the opportunities afforded by mobile, networked, and sensor-enabled technologies. Her effort intersected with trends in local governments to offer solutions to ease traffic congestion and monitor air quality and its everyday effects on citizens, for example, through the use of distributed sensor technology together with social media data. One aspect of her project concerned technical infrastructures for supporting vocational training for those with disabilities.

Tatiane was planning to "do some ethnography" and she, never having engaged in research of this type, wanted some tips. We talked about the problem at hand. We talked about what she hoped to gain from the ethnographic investigation. She described briefly how she and her team members were conceptualizing the population of relevance. We discussed the relative value of interviews compared with observations, how she might record the data, and how long she might take to do the study.

We touched on a range of topics. I interjected frequently with tips, cautions, and ideas for how the investigation might best take advantage of the things ethnography is especially geared to produce. I encouraged Tatiane to focus on open-ended questions in her interviews, on questions that would allow participants to describe their experiences rather than a survey-like list (though I suggested she might want to also supplement with a survey). I mentioned that it was important to think about the broader life context of participants, beyond the instructional setting of the classroom. (This was a big surprise for her.) I

Handbook of Anthropology in Business, edited by Rita Denny and Patricia Sunderland, 284–298.

advocated a view that vocational learning would have something to do with how participants saw themselves in the world, their identities, and influences. Her ears perked up when I suggested that understanding people's "networks"—assistive networks including role models, influencers, co-learners, and so on—might help to identify existing informal resources that could possibly be leveraged. (The notion of a "network" tends to lend comfort in such contexts given its potential to be rendered algorithmically.) In short, I urged her to recognize that what matters is not only what she observed people doing in the moment but who they understood themselves to be, who they were becoming, and the social and cultural world views that shape their perception and which they in turn reproduce.

Tatiane seemed to readily grasp the value of gaining this kind of understanding for designing and developing technical solutions. But then came "the question," posed less as a designer and more as a scientist: "How do I ensure objectivity?" I reminded her that the ethnographic approach aims to understand what things mean to participants and not, in the first instance, what they mean to investigators; that is, that the aim is to look "at" the situation, rather than "for" evidence for or against the researchers' *a priori* assumptions. I described many of the things that can be done to ensure the robustness of the data and the validity of the study, pointing to sampling and coverage strategies, leveraging data capture tools (i.e., video) to test and better assess emerging patterns, and maintaining a self-reflective stance so as to exercise a perspective of "suspended judgment." But, I asserted, at the end of the day this is an interpretive science, not a positivist one. Tatiane's eyes got big as she looked around the research lab and commented, "But my colleagues here are all scientists and they expect objectivity."

Indeed they do. Her colleagues are like my colleagues, members of a corporate scientific research lab. Corporate research labs have been among the core sites of applied anthropological studies of work since the 1980s. Eleanor Wynn and then Lucy Suchman, Brigitte Jordan, Jeanette Blomberg, Julian Orr, and others brought anthropology into the lab at Xerox Palo Alto Research Center (PARC) in the late 1970s. Other corporate research labs beyond Xerox, including Microsoft, Intel, Pitney Bowes, IBM, and others, have also employed anthropologists.

A key form of applied anthropological work performed in such business settings falls under the rubric of work practice studies. What kind of anthropology is this? Work practice analyses, together with the concomitant change efforts they participate in (hereafter I use the term "work practice studies" to refer to the full set of data gathering, analysis, recommendations, designing, prototyping, and testing of changes that commonly constitute the whole of a project that starts with work practice analysis), are a particular construct of social research within a broader scene of ethnographic and anthropological studies in business. Work practice studies focus on "work as doing" rather than focusing particularly on the fact of "work as activities explicitly prescribed in the relationship of employment" (Orr 1996:149). Work practice studies highlight the actions and practices of doing work, including the many social, material, and cultural factors and dynamics (including but not exclusive to the employment relationship) that produce and are reproduced in the doing of work. As such, work practice studies occur at a critical juncture in business activity, the site where potentially powerful socioeconomic forms emerge and are reproduced.

My aim in this chapter is twofold. First, I explore the ways in which work practice studies, by engaging such sites of socioeconomic production, perform a kind (albeit a particular kind) of social and cultural work in and for business. Work practice studies have proven to be an attractive form of social research in enterprise contexts. I explore some likely reasons for its popularity, perhaps first among those, for the ways in which they offer "actionable" findings. Work practice studies act to engage anthropological perspectives directly within sites of business through the advocacy and embodiment of principles adapted from anthropological theory and ethnographic practice. Second, while advocating for the value of intervening in such (admittedly contested) sites of social production, I offer this appraisal with the aim of pressing for even more from work practices studies. Work practice studies hold the potential of not only examining the strengths and weaknesses of existing business forms but also identifying the emergence of new ones. I believe that they are especially well poised to offer significant insight on the dynamics and actions that give rise to these forms, and to move from addressing today's problems to revealing the very dynamics shaping socioeconomic developments more broadly.

Here I explore the anthropological foundations of work practice studies. Following an introductory description of some notable examples of work practices studies, I discuss some of the perspectives shaping work practice studies. From there I turn to an exploration of the salience of work practice studies for business and consider the ways work practice studies are suited to advising business actions. I end by posing some thoughts about the potential of work practice studies to further inform social and cultural understandings of practice, work, and business more broadly.

THE ANTHROPOLOGICAL BASES OF WORK PRACTICE STUDIES

Introduction to Work Practice Studies

There is a small but thriving body of literature on work practices, one that specialists themselves turn to in particular. Articles from a work practices perspective are spread across a range of journals, many focused at the intersection of human-computer interaction; there is not yet a journal dedicated particularly to work practice studies. One monograph and two edited volumes are worth calling out as notable signposts for this work in the last two decades for their specificity of focus on applied work practice studies.

Most notable among the few anthropological monographs dedicated to a study of work practices is Julian Orr's *Talking about Machines* (1996). Orr focuses on how work gets done in the world of Xerox field service technicians, the people who travel from client site to client site to repair and maintain office equipment. Drawing especially from Lucy Suchman's treatment of situated action, Orr puts the actual performance of the work at the center of his exploration. Orr's core argument is that the ability of service technicians to perform is deeply situated in the *particular* social and technical configurations of their work. He hones in on the ways service tech reps construct an understanding of the problems at hand, highlighting the role of "war stories." War stories are the stories tech reps tell each other about prior cases of repair and tricky fixes, of working with the idiosyncratic characteristics of particular machines (and customers and coworkers), and of the ingenuity tech reps use to overcome them (or apocryphal cases in which they didn't). Orr's argument is especially illuminating in light of the ways knowledge is more typically abstracted and codified in organizational settings; rendered, for example, into standard form workflow diagrams or guidelines.

Two edited volumes have consolidated dedicated treatments of work practice. *Workplace Studies: Recovering Work Practice and Informing System Design* (2000) by Luff, Hindmarsh, and Heath includes both case studies and methodological and conceptual arguments for work practice studies and how they are performed, with particular attention to technology and design as encountered in the workplace. The kinds of cases they are interested in are those that offer "detailed naturalistic" (Luff et al. 2000:xiv) ways of understanding technologies in action. Examples include such things as document production in law firms and the functioning of control rooms of transportation systems. They argue that such studies not only provide empirical depth to previously assumed understandings of technologies in action (especially by designers and decision-makers for business), but in so doing enables a rethinking (they use Garfinkel's ethnomethodological notion of "respecifying" [1991]) of sociotechnical forms. Through this lens, concepts often taken for granted in everyday business practice, such as the notions of "user," "communication," and "routine work," are reexamined.

The second collection of work practice studies is the 2011 *Making Work Visible: Ethnographically Grounded Case Studies of Work Practice*, edited by Szymanski and Whalen. This volume presents examples of the work practice–centered analysis that has been performed throughout the Xerox research community, often in the Xerox business, in the last 30 years. The goal of this volume is to show "how the research has been carried out and its constructive impact on the ways people work and the technologies that support that work" (Szymanski and Whalen 2011:1). They position work practice analysis itself as follows: "As work practice analysts, our job is to make unbiased observations despite business goals or technology design requirements. If we do our job well, our insights are obvious in retrospect, but by making those insights visible, they become a resource, and we are able to build on them" (Szymanski and Whalen 2011:1). The volume includes sections on work practice studies in historical context, methods, and competency transfer. It also includes sections clustered around notable areas of focus reoccurring in various studies: work with documents, interactions with customers, and learning and knowledge sharing.

Work practice studies look beyond the often taken for granted constructs of business practice to focus on how people's ability to perform work emerges through interactions and meaning-making practices created and re-created in sites of business production. The value of thinking and observing at the level of practice is not obvious (as my conversation with Tatiane reminds us). Some basic anthropological precepts sit at the core of these contributions.

Principles & Perspectives

In 1993, Blomberg, Giacomi, Mosher, and Wall published the article "Ethnographic Field Methods and Their Relation to Design." They presented the idea that ethnography offers designers "an alternative methodology" in which to "gain a clearer view of the users for whom they design technologies" (Blomberg et al. 1993:124). They position this assertion vis-à-vis a desire in the 1980s to shift the focus of system designers "away from the view that technology supported individual tasks and toward the view that human activities were in large part carried out in cooperation with others" (Blomberg et al. 1993:124). Concern with cooperation has often translated directly to a focus on the collaborative (if distributed and asynchronous) dimensions of group work. Blomberg et al.'s perspective rests on the recognition that interactions with technical and business artifacts hold social and cultural meanings. It intimates broader views of the sociality of practice, how people's actions and motivations are always already formed in interaction with social constructs of meaning and participation, even when performed solely.

Blomberg et al. advance four "guiding principles of ethnography" for design: (1) natural settings, (2) holism, (3) descriptiveness, and (4) the native's point of view. The first, natural settings, is described in terms of a "commitment to study the activities of people in their everyday settings" (Blomberg et al. 1993:125). This leads to the second principle, holism, the view that behaviors can only be understood in light of the "everyday context" in which they occur. The "descriptive" principle focuses on the effort to maintain fidelity to what is observed to have happened rather than idealized or normative ideas of what should happen, and in particular as an approach suggests that it "leads ethnographers to assume a nonjudgmental stance with respect to the behaviors they study" (Blomberg et al. 1993:126). The "native's (or "member's") point of view" illustrates the perspective that what is of interest is "how people organize their behavior and make sense of the world around them" (Blomberg et al. 1993:127). Thinking back to Tatiane, it was clear she had absorbed the view that ethnography focuses on "natural settings"; it is questionable the extent to which she had recognized the remaining principles prior to (and perhaps even after) our chat.

Having established these four principles, Blomberg et al. elaborate methodological approaches for doing ethnography, covering observation, and interviewing; forms of data capture (notetaking, video and audio recording, and analysis); discussions of the significance of locations of research; and more. They conclude with a valuable and still relevant discussion of what it means to be engaged in ethnographic work as a process of intervention and change. They reassert the need for attention to ethical issues, extending concern of what counts in these settings to consideration of who is involved in both the construction and use of the data, and to issues of access and reciprocity. They also affirm a point of view that the ethnographic stance leads towards an advocacy of the users while acknowledging the potential ethical dilemma posed by the fact that the analyst may at the same time represent purveyors of the technology.

In 2003, Blomberg published with Burrell and Guest a chapter for *The Human-Computer Interaction Handbook* titled "An Ethnographic Approach to Design" (this piece was reedited by Blomberg and Burrell for a second edition in 2012). Here, the four principles are repeated, with the implications and uses of these principles elaborated with a broader range of ethnographic techniques for data gathering, analyzing, and communicating ethnographic findings. They also add mini–case studies of "ethnography in action." The chapter leans towards technologies-in-use, particularly as encountered in and developed by business settings, though the subject remains broadly the "user."

It is worth noting that these articles are framed through the lens of ethnography and do not explicitly draw their arguments back to broader claims about the discipline of anthropology. (See Baba, this volume, for a sensitive account of the dynamic and changing relationship between ethnography and anthropology, particularly that taking shape in business settings.) At the same time, consistent with work practice studies more generally and likely in recognition of the potential livelihood of ethnography in business settings, they stop short of insisting on "participant observation," a core principle of anthropological ethnography since Malinowski. The formal and legally binding actions and roles of work practitioners mean that the opportunities to actually participate are limited.

Vinkhuyzen (2011) discusses a case where they were able to do just that, but more often practitioners instead pursue adjacent activities, such as enrolling in the training courses offered to employees (a route Orr took) or listening in on calls fielded by call center reps (but not responding to those calls).

Moreover, these articles are not about work or work practice per se. They do not, for instance, focus attention on accounting for the organizational constructs commonly addressed in work practice studies, such as incentive and reward systems or management practices. Orr, for instance, in his analysis of field service technicians, elaborates on the way that organizational constructs such as "the team" or the "territory" shape the work and experience of service tech reps. They have addressed this articulation toward design, and in fact the kind of design shaped by the technical settings in which many practitioners operate, including of tools, systems, and processes.

Blomberg et al.'s framing of principles articulates, nonetheless, a common thread underlying work practice studies for design more generally. Their formulation of core principles productively point towards the value and desire to render social and cultural understandings within technical and business settings. As articulated, their principles aim to guide the doing of the work, pointing to techniques and tips useful in performing ethnographically informed studies in work settings.

Together with Blomberg and other colleagues (notably Susan Stucky, also previously of the Institute for Research on Learning), I participated in the development of a yet further rearticulation of core principles as an argument for the salience of anthropological understanding in business strategy and design efforts. Drawing essentially from the same set of four notions articulated by Blomberg et al., here we foregrounded the principles in epistemic terms, as forms of knowledge required to appreciate and deepen social and cultural insight, more than as guidelines for conducting ethnography.

We also called out four principles: (1) the say-do distinction, (2) situated actor perspective, (3) "emic" point of view, and (4) a system framework. The principles are described in detail in the excerpt that follows, preserving the articulation we used with our business counterparts at the time, members of a corporate training and learning group at IBM participating in an initiative aimed at enhancing the learning embedded in people's everyday work experience. We designed a methodology for use by learning specialists and managers for recognizing work practices as the site of work-embedded learning and to leverage the learning opportunities afforded by close attention to work practice. This extract from our internal documentation formed part of that methodology.

This effort exemplifies a form of anthropological intervention at work. Just as my conversation with Tatiane illustrates one way we might engage business counterparts in reconciling anthropologically informed perspectives, this articulation represents another. It demonstrates a specific example of how we have communicated our perspective and used them to inform business actions. Extracted from their contexts of use, anthropologists may find these treatments of complex and still-debated concepts overly simplified. At the same time, many anthropologists working in business, who are exhorted to speak in plain terms and discouraged from using referential statements and technical language, are likely to find this particular rendering of perspectives especially academic.

Say-Do Distinction

Research in anthropology and sociology shows that how people talk about what they do and what they actually do can differ significantly. The reasons for this are three-fold—limitations of human memory, the desire to present a particular self image, and the limited accessibility humans have to the taken for granted, everyday ways of doing things (tacit understanding). Research on child rearing practices by Whiting and Whiting (1970) and more recent studies by Tope and colleagues (2005) have clearly reconfirmed this perspective.

Th[is] methodology employs techniques that provide ways to triangulate between what people say and what they do (e.g. real time observations and in context interviews). This enables the development of learning solutions that fit people's ways of working and that increase both the adoption and effectiveness of the learning solutions.

"Emic" Point of View

The notions of "emic" and "etic" originated in analysis of language and pointed to distinctions between phonemic and phonetic analysis (Pike, 1967). In Pike's work the phon*etic* analysis is the description of the sounds or phonemes that made up a language. Phon*emic* analysis identifies only those sounds that carry meaning within the language (e.g., sounds that distinguish one word from another).

When applied to social systems, the emic view is the insider view and represents the *meaningful* distinctions made by people inside the practice (e.g., how sales people distinguish among their clients). The emic units of analysis can only be identified *in context* since that is where meaning is constructed. Th[is] methodology provides ways of gaining views on to the work from inside the practice and from the perspective of the work practitioners themselves. The effectiveness of th[is] methodology builds on the emic perspective to point to opportunities for work-based learning solutions that make sense to workers because they are informed by an understanding of their experiences.

Situated Actor Perspective

Research shows that the capabilities of individuals are inextricably tied to how individuals are situated in relation to other people, their environment, and the material artifacts available and/or in use, including information technologies. These ideas have been articulated most clearly in sociology (ethnomethodology), anthropology, and cognitive psychology (Garfinkel, 1964; Suchman, 1987; Hutchins, 1995) and have been further explored by scholars in the learning sciences (Engstrom, 2001; Lave and Wenger, 1991).

The implication of this perspective is that individual capabilities and performance must be understood in relation to the work system composed of people, places, and things. Individual capabilities both find expression and are developed in the context of participation in social life. Th[is] methodology provides the means to understand how individual capabilities are constituted in practice.

Systemic Framework

Th[is] methodology takes a systemic view, focusing on relationships and interactions between people and between people and things. The systemic framework recognizes that changes in one part of the system can affect other parts. Recent advances in system theory have extended this notion to apply to dynamic (not mechanistic) systems such as organizations. In anthropology, the notion of *holism* has directed attention to the social whole—the context—that surrounds any particular occurrence. Social Network Analysis also draws on notions of the value created in the interconnections between people. Th[is] methodology supports the identification of how the parts of a whole (the work system) are interconnected and it positions particular tasks or people in relation to a system of action (Blomberg et al., 2006) (IBM 2006).

The significance of these principles as a way of intervening in normative business thinking should not be underestimated. The principles work to counter the individualistic bias dominant in business. The cultural model of individual-as-hero persists broadly throughout the business landscape. A focus on advancing and ensuring individual skill and knowledge dominates. Orr's (1996) attention to war stories and the occasions in which they are told and retold strongly makes that point that even where any given individual performs a particular act of repair, the social, technical and procedural knowledge they demonstrate comes through the collective body of knowledge created and re-created through storytelling.

Another instance of how the principles disrupt normative business thinking comes by realizing that things do not operate neatly in functionalist terms. They counter pervasive mechanistic perspectives shaping the models that underlie many aspects of business organization and operations, from the design of business processes to organizational structures. Whereas there may already be recognition (and dismay) that people do not always behave as proscribed by business designs, there tends to be less recognition of how this can also be true of other business elements. Organizational units, strategic plans, policies, and even technical artifacts such as copiers and computer systems do not always behave as proscribed either, despite their engineered basis. A telling example can be seen in Mack and Kaplan's case study of a policy change regarding mail delivery in a large organization (2009). The decision was made to cut internal standard mail delivery (personal mail, journals, catalogs, advertisements) to one day a week. The declared aim was to decrease environmental impact and increase efficiency. The results, however, for reasons beyond what are often cavalierly attributed to peoples' resistance to change, were anything but straightforward. Indeed, resistance because people felt they had no say in the change and the poor communication around the policy change did have ramifications for employee engagement. But challenges resulting from the failure to recognize how the changes would affect people's work also became evident. For example, what counted as standard mail to those in the unit sorting mail did not necessarily match that of the recipient. Items that mail sorters identified as advertisements were among the documents the marketing department used to analyze their competitors and determine advertising plans. Similar disconnects were experienced by others in other divisions. The change, in other words, far from manageable as a simple change of process, had a negative impact on the work of the people across the organization.

This specification of principles, like any other, invites critical assessment of what could be more or less emphasized, and what is left out. These principles do not, for example, present a view of social change. We might hesitate, similarly, at the absoluteness with which the principles are claimed. The notion of "emic" categories, for example, provides work practice analysts a powerful frame for making sense of variations in practice, allowing them to recast actions that may be seen by others as inefficient or even irrational and show them to be meaningful and logical for those close to the practice. At the same time, anthropologists know that notions of "emic" and "etic" are not absolute, and advancing this distinction risks overdetermining notions of inside and outside.

Nonetheless, by applying these perspectives to our work and engaging others in considering them, work practice analysts reflect upon workings of the business world that might otherwise go unexamined. Through these principles, we help prompt reflexive consideration within the organization itself as to why things are the way they are. When enacted through the actions of anthropologists in business contexts, such principles can productively disrupt and expand business thinking, particularly where normative models for understanding business and the markets fail and alternatives and more nuanced means of understanding are sought. Like Nafus' Technology Distribution Index (this volume) and Kimbell's active working through assemblages of people, organization, and things embodied in storyworlds and workshops (this volume), these principles play a performative role in engaging and reframing business forms.

REFLECTIONS ON THE RELEVANCE OF WORK PRACTICE STUDIES FOR BUSINESS

Work practice studies sit within a broader field of anthropological studies of work, organization, and business enterprise. This broader field includes works that focus on sites of market production and ethnographies of producers such as Brondo and Baba's study of General Motors assembly plants (2010). Many studies are construed, in particular, via their relationship to consumers or users of their products such as work in the area of marketing and advertising (see, for instance, Malefyt and Morais [2012] and Sunderland and Denny [2007]). In such studies, descriptions of work practice may appear but are not foregrounded as the focus of analysis.

Work practice studies give rise to particular opportunities for innovation, development, design, and deployment, engaging others in the organization with a stake in those dynamics along the way. Thus, business locations where insight on workplace practitioners' actual practices can give rise to novel innovations, including such research divisions as the one that employed Tatiane, form one of the core sites for the performance of work practice studies. Another common site is in product and service development groups, which are interested in enhancing the likelihood of the take-up and usefulness of tools, systems, and programs. It is easy to imagine, for example, that once the products and systems Tatiane and her team envisioned for supporting vocational training for differently abled people are developed, understanding where they fit into the landscape of state and local social service organizations would follow, and in particular the way in which the systems will be deployed and supported by workers in those organizations. (The example of work presented by Kimbell in this volume suggests just such a chain of investigation and intervention.)

Yet another common site for performing work practice studies are the locations where new practices are expected to actually emerge and be performed: sites of business operations. Vinkhuyzen (2011) offers detailed descriptions of the work of customer interaction in document reproduction stores, the practices of reprographics employees in order taking and fulfillment. He details a number of rich social research themes, such as sorting out the "grammar of customer requests" (2011:214) and the nature of "money talk" (2011:218), and he indicates how the work identified significant opportunities for improving interactions at the counter, where the employee meets the customer.

Given the direct applicability of work practice studies, it is common for other technical researchers and engineers to collaborate in the studies. Further collaborators might include line, production, or operations managers, those responsible for and accountable to the implementation of systems and programs in their divisions. These are functions and roles that are at the center of business performance.

Why are work practice studies considered attractive in such core business functions? Work practice studies intersect neatly with the paradigm of "problem-solving," a paradigm driving many efforts in businesses generally, including much that goes on in the name of innovation and development. This is not to say that work practice studies are singularly geared to such problem-solving. Rather, however constructed and however broad the findings and implications, they also almost certainly render at least some relatively concrete results (see Ensworth, this volume), potentially with measurable impact. Vinkhuyzen and his colleagues (2011), for example, were able to offer up specific recommendations for everything from order form design to enhanced learning programs. In such cases the translation from research to design, as advanced by Blomberg et al. (1993, 2003), is readily evident.

Moreover, work practice studies can be designed to work effectively within the contours of broader business rhythms and processes. The boundaries of a problem, subjects of study, and general directions of desired results can be relatively circumscribed in advance. For example, any given study may revolve around those who intersect with a particular tool or data set, or be designed to track the unfolding of a particular transformation for a particular period of time. This facilitates working across groups, divisions, functions, and roles, for the structure and form of the work is at least somewhat recognizable and attendant to the constraints of the context. This is not to say working within these contours is always easy or unfettered. Any number of constraints can be imposed. For instance, as I have explored elsewhere (Cefkin 2012), issues of time and temporality—most evidently the periods or lengths of time spent in the data gathering and analysis phases—must constantly be negotiated and may on occasion be compromised.

In addition, and most important, results from work practice studies point toward (at least some) implications within the control of business partners with whom the work is being conducted. Whether it is strategists advancing new directions, designers building new concepts, or developers actually creating products, services, systems, and tools, work practice studies produce "actionable" results.

At the same time, when done well, findings and results from work practice studies also tell a much richer, and often complex and uncertain, story. Indeed, work practice studies inevitably derive understandings that exceed the parameters of the study as initially framed. These may call attention to failures and challenges far beyond the immediate control of the business at hand, even calling into question formations upon which the very basis of the enterprise is founded. Whereas for the anthropologist this may be exactly the point at which we feel we are succeeding in bringing about broader understandings of the dynamics at play, in terms of informing business action, these can be discomforting moments. These tellings are not understood to be "actionable" for the purposes of the business at hand, either because they fall outside the purview of the involved parties or because they do not tell a story serviceable within the business construct. It is no wonder Tatiane had not planned to step outside the classroom in her "ethnographic" examinations of people with disabilities. Wasn't her job to design technology platforms for learning, and not to address challenges of living with disabilities more broadly? It is such moments that I have in mind as I turn, in conclusion, to thoughts about the potential of work practice studies to more actively inform understandings of broader social and cultural processes.

THE FUTURES OF WORK PRACTICE STUDIES

The articulation and embedding of foundational principles based in anthropological ways of knowing and the concomitant methods used to realize these ways of knowing can be celebrated as contributions of anthropological understanding on work and organizations. Work practice studies have focused attention on the social life of the materials and constructs—documents, customers, learning, coordination, and so on—of everyday business actions, constructs of social significance that might have otherwise escaped consideration.

Work practice studies open windows to ways that experiences of work tie to concepts central to social and cultural theories and knowledge. Take the notion of identity, for example. Orr suggests that "a focus on the work itself" offers insight missing from other studies of work to help answer questions such as "What role do the events of a day's work play in the process of defining identity?" (Orr 1996:152). Orr identifies competence in the work as the thing that creates technician identity and speaks to the embrace of the notion of technician "defined as someone who fixes the world and makes it right" (1996:160). Tech rep identity, it is suggested, has to do with more than just a job performed or a role held; it embodies a way of being in the world.

Another example touching on broader social and cultural interests considers cultural modes of sensorial experience. Drawing from numerous studies of the work practices of sales representatives, I have begun to explore instances of market formation and to consider what shapes sellers' experiences in this process. The participation of sales representatives in ritualized weekly activities related to building and maintaining sales forecasts, I previously suggested (Cefkin 2007), constitutes a pervasive cultural pattern for their participation in the market. Repeated week after week in enterprises large and small, sales pipeline management serves to experientially reinforce the requirement of sales reps to drive market activity through meeting their sales obligations. This happens, I argue, not only through repeated review and tweaking of spreadsheets and databases (the kinds of practices that feed forms of economic modeling referenced by Nafus in this volume), but also more implicitly through forms of encouragement performed through the patterns and rhythms of call-and-response used in the meetings managers run to manage the sales pipeline.

The understandings rendered through such observations do not "need" resolution. They do not actively demand business decisions. They remain dynamic, even indeterminate. They appear less immediately useful to the problem at hand. And yet, given the critical sites in which work practice studies occur, the moments and locations out of which business constructs emerge and are reproduced, such insights hold great potential. Such examinations concern interests at the heart of anthropology and social sciences and humanities more generally. Most significantly, they point to emerging social forces and dynamics. Given that the work considered here is being done in the context of applied anthropological and ethnographic work, do such contributions matter?

I believe they do. Work practice studies occur at key sites of social and cultural production. Businesses, through the resources they employ and consume and the concepts and objects they produce, act as pervasive and powerful agents of people's lives. Businesses are among the most consequential institutions in today's world. Committed to an understanding of the doing of work, work practice studies have the potential to reveal how these forms develop. They also provide a route to recognizing not just enduring business and market forms, but emerging ones as well. They can help identify the strengths of existing business structures and discourses by understanding how they are created and re-created in a day-to-day practice and identify the dynamics and actions giving rise to changes. Through these examinations, they can observe whose interests are enabled and what is omitted along the way. Investigating enduring and emerging business in its making demands a particular kind of awareness. The commitment to reflexive practice brought to work practice studies via anthropology promises an important if subtle way to enact and enable new awarenesses as a part of business practice. Work practice studies have the potential to go beyond encapsulated "just so" stories, to go beyond a telling of how things work in particular places, to examining the very dynamics extending and shaping socioeconomic developments more broadly.

REFERENCES

Blomberg, Jeanette, Mark Burrell, and Greg Guest. 2003. "An Ethnographic Approach to Design." In *Human-Computer Interaction Handbook: Fundamental, Evolving Technologies and Emerging Applications*, edited by A. Sears and J. Jacko, 965–84. Philadelphia, PA: Lawrence Erlbaum Associates.

Blomberg, Jeanette, Jean Giacomi, Andrea Mosher, and Pat Swenton-Wall. 1993. "Ethnographic Field Methods and Their Relation to Design." In *Participatory Design: Principles and Practices*, edited by D. Schuler and A. Namioka, 123–55. Hillsdale, NJ: Lawrence Erlbaum Associates.

Brondo, Keri, and Marietta Baba. 2010. "Last In, First Out: A Case Study of Lean Manufacturing in North America's Automobile Industry." *Human Organization*. 69(3):263–74.

Cefkin, Melissa. 2007. "Numbers May Speak Louder than Words, but Is Anybody Listening? Rhythms of Sales Pipeline Management." *Proceedings of the Ethnographic Praxis in Industry Conference*, 187–99. American Anthropological Association.

_____. 2012. "The Limits to Speed in Ethnography." In *Advancing Anthropology in Corporate Environments: Challenges and Emerging Opportunities*, edited by B. Jordan, 108–22. Walnut Creek, CA: Left Coast Press.

Garfinkel, Harold. 1991. "Respecification: Evidence for Locally Produced, Naturally Accountable Phenomena of Order, Logic, Reason, Meaning, Method, etc. in and as of the Essential Haecceity of Immortal Ordinary Society, (I): An Announcement of Studies." In *Ethnomethodology and the Human Sciences*, edited by Graham Button, 10–19. Cambridge, UK: Cambridge University Press.

IBM. 2006. "A Practice-Based Learning Methodology." IBM unpublished report.

Luff, Paul, Jon Hindmarsh, and Christian Heath, eds. 2000. *Workplace Studies: Recovering Work Practice and Informing System Design*. Cambridge, UK: Cambridge University Press.

Mack, Alexander, and Joshua Kaplan. 2009. "Policy Change Inside the Enterprise: The Role of Anthropology." *Ethnographic Praxis in Industry Conference Proceedings*, 59–71, American Anthropological Association.

Malefyt, Timothy de Waal, and Robert Morais. 2012. *Advertising and Anthropology: Ethnographic Practice and Cultural Perspectives*. London, New York: Berg Publishers.

Orr, Julian E. 1996. *Talking About Machines: An Ethnography of a Modern Job*. Ithaca, NY: ILR Press.

Sunderland, Patricia, and Rita Denny. 2007. *Doing Anthropology in Consumer Research*. Walnut Creek, CA: Left Coast Press.

Szymanski, Margaret H., and Jack Whalen, eds. 2011. *Making Work Visible: Ethnographically Grounded Case Studies of Work Practice*. Cambridge, UK: Cambridge University Press.

Vinkhuyzen, Erik. 2011. "Interactions at a Reprographics Store." In *Making Work Visible: Ethnographically Grounded Case Studies of Work Practice*, edited by M. Szymanksi and J. Whalen, 205–24. Cambridge, UK: Cambridge University Press.

NOTE

I would like to thank Jeanette Blomberg, Francoise Brun-Cottan, Dawn Nafus, Susan Stucky, and the editors for their helpful comments on drafts of this chapter.

Section III

PLYING THE TRADE

INTRODUCTION

RITA DENNY & PATRICIA SUNDERLAND

Many of the volume's chapters could have fallen into this "Plying the Trade" section. As in the volume as a whole, our purpose in this section is to illuminate the nature of the work at the intersection of anthropology and business. Our goal is not to present a set of tools or a pedagogical how-to on methods; instead, the chapters in this section are grounded by details of case studies to illustrate the kinds of work done; the range of methods, interests, and applications; and the resulting impact. It is a collection of work that is indicative, not exhaustive. It speaks to breadth of scope mirrored in the larger world: working as consultants/suppliers and as employees within "client organizations." The focus is myriad: rum, pets, technology of various forms, airplanes, global fishing, oil rigs, telecom, and beer, which captures the breadth of industries we have observed anthropologists are working within: hi-tech, electronics, telecom, consumer goods, automotive, hard goods (e.g., Whirlpool), retail, food and beverage, insurance, pharmaceutical, financial services, advertising and communication, journalism, design firms, brand or business consultancies, and consumer research. The 11 chapters in this section are partial glimpses, particular instantiations at the intersection of anthropology and business. The stories told, the methods embraced, the locations of practice, and the frames for thinking reflect varied trajectories: some convergent, some divergent. These stories and countless others—now and in the future—were not (and will not be) created in a vacuum, so it is worth calling out some of the historical context for the three main trajectories—design, marketing, and semiotics—underpinning many of the chapters in this section.

The design trajectory in the United States is usually located in the work at Xerox PARC in the late 1970s and early 1980s, conducted by Eleanor Wynn, Lucy Suchman, Jeanette Blomberg, Brigitte Jordan, Julian Orr, and their collaborators (Cefkin 2009; A. Jordan 2013; Otto and Smith 2013; Reese 2002). Interests in human computer interfaces, workplace practices, and human factors

Handbook of Anthropology in Business, edited by Rita Denny and Patricia Sunderland, 301–308.

sparked what is now commonly called "design ethnography" and, more recently, "design anthropology." The ethnographic approach at Xerox PARC migrated into industrial design firms in the late 1980s (with, for example, The Work Project for Steelcase that combined Suchman's efforts at Xerox PARC and Rick Robinson's at Doblin Group in Chicago. Integration of ethnographic practices in the design process via companies like E-Lab, IDEO, and SonicRim in the 1990s had a significant impact on design firm process (Reese 2002; Wasson 2000, 2002). There were intertwined trajectories with Europe at about the same time in the form of participatory design. Contextualized by different social and political concerns than in the United States, user- or human-centered approaches to design constituted the common ground (see Otto and Smith 2013).

While an early trajectory of anthropology in marketing in the United States dates to the 1950s at the University of Chicago with the interdisciplinary effort of Social Research, Inc. (Levy 2003), a significant reintroduction took place in New York in the late 1970s and early 1980s when University of Chicago–trained Steve Barnett focused his attention on Madison Avenue advertising firms and consumer product manufacturers (Sunderland and Denny 2007; see also Wilner in Section IV). Numerous US anthropologists now working in the consumer research arena worked with Barnett, including Maryann McCabe, whose chapter in this section theorizes the meaning of pets and a shift in natural cosmology in the United States, an analysis that fueled her recommendations for repositioning a pet food brand. At about the same time that Barnett and other anthropologists began conducting cultural analysis in New York, anthropologists Grant McCracken and John F. Sherry, Jr., took up their positions at the Royal Ontario Museum and the Kellogg School of Business at Northwestern University, respectively, in the mid-1980s. McCracken's indomitable spirit in illuminating all things cultural since then is well established (2013; www.cultureby.com). Similarly, John Sherry's contributions to marketing and brand theory, including consumer culture theory, remain unchecked (Sunderland and Denny 2007; also see Arnould and Thompson in Section I and Diamond et al. in Section IV).

Also in the early 1980s, Virginia Valentine in Britain, drawing on Lévi-Strauss and Roland Barthes, founded what is now the UK trajectory of applied semiotics. With her firm, Semiotic Solutions, she introduced a distinctly cultural perspective to European market research (Valentine and Gordon 2000). The current state of commercial semiotics as it is practiced in the United Kingdom is the topic of Hunt and Barton's chapter. While semiotic applications in marketing also developed in France (Floch [1990] 2001; Mick et al. 2004), and more recently in the United States (Oswald 2012), Valentine had a significant impact on the institutionalization of commercial semiotics in the United Kingdom and Europe.

What is important to note is that design, marketing, and semiotics trajectories are increasingly convergent, as design firms have become brand architects and brand and research firms have taken on product and service innovation. This is illustrated in the chapter by Ailová et al., who institute a combination of anthropology and design thinking in developing their consumer research practices in the Czech Republic. As semioticians, Hunt and Barton draw the distinction between cultural insight and consumer insight, the latter historically the domain of marketing research in Britain. That the cultural turn in branding practices in the United Kingdom was significantly influenced through the impetus of semiotic analysis is suggested by the actions of Britain's Market Research Society in the creation of the Virginia Valentine Award in 2011 for cultural insights. (See also Neese's chapter in Section IV, describing the integration of cultural analysis into the design process.) The blurring borders between consumer culture theory, consumer research, and design are displayed in both Agafonoff et al.'s as well as Cova's case studies as the authors take the opportunity of work with Diagio and HP, respectively, to theorize brands. Hepsø's modeling of work practices in the oil industry no doubt reflects historic crosscurrents between research conducted at Xerox PARC and the Institute for Research on Learning (B. Jordan 2011; Suchman 2011). The blurring borders between industry or for-profit models and interests usually in the domain of nonprofit organizations—addressing or solving social or public needs or problems—is also resonant, referenced in Kitner's chapter in her work at Intel and documented in detail in Hasbrouck and Scull's chapter, whose project falls squarely within the realm of social entrepreneurship.

Emergent trajectories are grounded by constellations of relationships. Training programs reflect particular histories of their faculty, as seen in the chapter by Squires et al. University of North Texas faculty are cross-teaching and cross-fertilizing ideas with other programs, globally. Amid activities in multiple countries, with multiple traditions as context, what is still striking is the extent to which the authors in this section, in this volume, and no doubt in the world more generally, have forged their own paths. Looking forward, there are more convergent possibilities made possible globally by virtue of institutionalized formats in the form of new journals or conferences such as EPIC (Ethnographic Praxis in Industry) and vibrant online interaction in the form of blogs, listservs, or discussion groups, all of which transcend geography.

If this section is more populated by the stories of consultant/suppliers than employees (Hepsø and Kitner chapters to the contrary), as a whole it speaks to centrality of the client relationship, which exists whether one's client is internal or external. These chapters illustrate what the commitment to the social and cultural looks like when the goal is to encourage clients to reconceive sometimes deeply embedded understandings of their product, brand, or service.

Hunt and Barton want to be agitators in the corporate boardroom. Agafonoff and his coauthors, on a project for Bundaberg rum, capture methodological dilemmas: "Diageo took some convincing about the approach: the client was anxious about the a small sample size, iterative approach, focus on social and cultural investigation using immersive participant-observation techniques, and the absence of a concrete schedule for fieldwork and analysis." Cova documents Hewlett Packard's (HP) reluctance to break tradition in how it thought about and thus talked about the iconic HP 12c calculator. It was not easy for the 12c team to cede control to consumer ideas and practices. Kitner's chapter includes a poignant tale of her work in fisheries management. Her failure to successfully mediate prevailing views of fishery solutions became an ethical abyss when she was asked to temper her assessment. Her tale reminds us that there are no monoliths, only particularities, in actual practice. As these chapters amply illustrate, it is not the fish, calculator, laptop computer, pets, rugby league fans, airline spaces, beer, or oil field that is the object of study but rather the social, cultural, and contextual systems—within which these phenomena gain meaning and materiality—that sustain the authors' gazes.

These chapters also document openness toward methods and the proclivity to improvise in the service of ethnographic fieldwork, analysis, and reporting. There is a fondness for inductive analysis and situationally grounded activities that are leavened by a good dose of uncertainty. As Hepsø notes, collaborative work is inherently emergent. In the study for Boeing, Erickson's quest for permission to conduct fieldwork while in flight is its own tale; his call to Chile's future president, then CEO of LAN Airlines, in the attempt to gain permission for inflight filming captures the nerve and nervousness often required to execute ideas. In Agafonoff's fieldwork, a study of rugby league fans in the bourbon belt of Australia, contingency—in terms of who, what, where, and when—was designed into the process. There is also openness to new methods or sources of data that can illuminate one's task. Hunt and Barton, for example, view algorithm-produced digital texts for application of semiotic analysis as one of potential insight and opportunity.

Not surprisingly, a comparative lens is a ubiquitous heuristic in these chapters whether the source is multiple geographies or comparative social groups. Comparison is also evident another way—in analytic perspective—what Hasbrouck and Scull describe as the multiple focal lengths' perspective the anthropologists on the team provided, or what Agafonoff and his coauthors refer to as the individual, social, and cultural levels of inquiry (akin to Desjeux's micro-, meso-, and macrosocial scales in the first section of this volume).

Experiential materiality in the analysis process and/or in conveying analysis is also highlighted in these chapters. As a pedagogical practice, Squires and her colleagues describe making analytic work tangible by rendering it visible through collaborative efforts of students in the classroom, incorporating artifacts produced outside of the classroom. The tangibles produced—arrowed thoughts on paper, video, photos, diagrams—then become fodder for targeted exploration and ongoing analysis by student teams. In Cotton's case study on product development for mobile computing, the process included building distinct environments as the basis for client team immersion so that Microsoft designers would tangibly experience what consumers with laptops are doing and thinking. The built environments included excerpted video and photos. Erickson, in his multicountry project for Boeing, created a team blog for people in the field and clients in Seattle; midstream, it came to include one of the research participants as well. In addition, one of the primary deliverables to Boeing was a group of edited videos of disabled traveler experiences (examples included in his chapter). Ailová and her colleagues instituted pre-fieldwork training sessions for clients; improvisation ruled the day in Hunt and Barton's in situ exploration with clients in a study for Tiger Beer; Hasbrouck and Scull, akin to the kind of design anthropology models which Murphy and Marcus (2013) have maintained can serve as innovation possibilities for contemporary ethnography, intentionally paired team members with different backgrounds to experience links in the global fishing chain together.

While the impact of design on ethnographic practices is surely visible in many of these chapters—as well as the impact of videographic traditions in consumer research (Belk and Kozinets 2005; Pink 2001, 2006; Sunderland and Denny 2002, 2007)—a question to ask is whether the material creations that emerge through process can capture the public imagination in ways parallel to archaeology's beloved artifacts. As Duranti (2013) observes, anthropology as a discipline has always been seen as delivering material objects that connect us with others. If archaeology has had a heyday historically in capturing the public imagination because of the palpable connection that comes from materiality of their stories, what are the materialities anthropologists in business can offer?

A great delight in reading this collection of stories is the myriad forms of success in endeavors. In some stories there are tangible, expected outcomes: new tariff plans for mobile phones, a redesigned service strategy for a telecom's enterprise customers, a communication strategy for a brand of pet food, a product optimization model for oil rig operations, a strategic plan for Bundy rum to become a regional brand in Australia, a framework for solution sets to achieve sustainable global fishing, a positioning for Tiger beer in Asia, product concepts for innovation in mobile computing.

Yet it is equally worth considering what wasn't produced. Frustration in achieving impact is not surprising because, even given what an anthropological or cultural lens can offer, any deliverable confronts existing ways of doing and circulates within practices and power relationships that reflect organizational issues (Cefkin 2009; Denny 2013; Flynn 2009; B. Jordan 2013; Sunderland 2013; Sunderland and Denny 2011). But more important, the nature of impact glimpsed through frustration can be illuminating (see also Moeran 2012). What is it that sticks?

As Cotton ruefully notes, their mobile computing project changed how the Microsoft client team thought about their design task (via a more nuanced understanding of users), but the project, in which the explicit goal was innovation, had little impact on new product designs. Similarly, Erickson reports no appreciable impact on airplane design. What he does note, though, is the impact on Boeing's frame for thinking about onboard practices. Ultimately, Erickson observes, design efforts would have to take on the central assumption of time as the optimal calibrator of air travel practices, as well as make the (passenger and employee) work of air travel visible. This is no small feat. We would observe that change is often incremental, in this section seen in Hepsø's chapter, where bringing about change to the machine metaphor that guides the modeling of work practices in the extraction industry is more tortoise than hare.

Notably, the centrality of the social and cultural comes to the fore in what sticks. Despite their initial misgivings about approach, the Diageo brand team thought differently about rum by the end: the team now considered the social fabric of Bundy rum, which led to a reframing of the marketing strategy. Boeing pondered the implications of liminality in designing air travel. Mars contemplated the cultural metaphors framing relationships with pets. Hasbrouck and Scull, based on the success of their project, speak of the opportunity for anthropologists to engage:

> As complex global system issues continue to demand not one but many solutions, it is clear to us the important role that anthropologists can play not just in helping to make sense of the data, but also by helping the various disciplinary perspectives needed to fully understand the complexity of these systems communicate with one another. Furthermore, global issues, though constituted by a range of culturally varied iterations, are by definition issues that have virtually universal implications: implications that include the anthropologists who study them.

It is a multiplicity of roles: being the agent in making complex social systems visible at multiple levels; articulating problems that, if solved, would make a difference in achieving client ends; and, finally, being able to facilitate problem-solving. Researcher, consultant, strategist, facilitator: the anthropologists, semioticians, and social scientists in these chapters are often "facilitating-provokers" (Kilbourn 2013). These chapters are enactments of the desire to change how clients—internal or external—think, whether in the context of a particular project or as a more general stance, by being, to use Kitner's formulation in the opening chapter of this section, "a burr in the saddle."

REFERENCES

Belk, Russell, and Robert Kozinets. 2005. "Videography in Marketing and Consumer Research." *Qualitative Market Research: An International Journal* 8:128–41.

Cefkin, Melissa. 2009. "Introduction." In *Ethnography and the Corporate Encounter: Reflections on Research in and of the Corporation*, edited by M. Cefkin, 1–37. New York: Berghahn.

Denny, Rita. 2013. "The Cry of Practicality." In *Advancing Ethnography in Corporate Environments*, edited by B. Jordan, 136–50. Walnut Creek, CA: Left Coast Press.

Duranti, Alessandro. 2013. "On the Future of Anthropology: Fundraising, the Job Market and the Corporate Turn." *Anthropological Theory* 13(3):201–21.

Floch, Jean Marie. (1990) 2001. *Semiotics, Marketing and Communication: Beneath the Signs, the Strategies*. Translated by Robin Orr Bodkin. New York: Palgrave.

Flynn, Donna. 2009. "'My Customers Are Different!' Identity, Difference and the Political Economy of Design." In *Ethnography and the Corporate Encounter: Reflections on Research in and of the Corporation*, edited by M. Cefkin, 41–57. New York: Berghahn.

Levy, Sidney J. 2003. "Roots of Marketing and Consumer Research at the University of Chicago." *Consumption, Markets and Culture* 6(2):99–110.

Jordan, Ann T. 2013. *Business Anthropology*. 2nd edition. Long Grove, IL: Waveland Press.

Jordan, Brigitte. 2011. "Transferring Ethnographic Competence: Personal Reflections on the Past and Future of Work Practice Analysis. In *Making Work Visible*, edited by Margaret H. Szymanski and Jack Whalen, 344–58. New York: Cambridge University Press.

______, ed. 2013. *Advancing Ethnography in Corporate Environments: Challenges and Emerging Opportunities*. Walnut Creek, CA: Left Coast Press.

Kilbourn, Kyle. 2013. "Tools and Movements of Engagement: Design Anthropology's Style of Knowing." In *Design Anthropology: Theory and Practice*, edited by Wendy Gunn, Ton Otto, and Rachel Charlotte Smith, 68–82. New York: Bloomsbury.

McCracken, Grant. 2013. "How To Be a Self-Supporting Anthropologist." In *A Handbook of Practicing Anthropology*, edited by Riall Nolan, 104–13. West Sussex, UK: Wiley-Blackwell.

Mick, David Glen, James E. Burroughs, Patrick Hetzel, and Mary Yoko Brannen. 2004. "Pursuing the Meaning of Meaning in the Commercial World: An International Review of Marketing and Consumer Research Founded on Semiotics." *Semiotica* 152(1):1–74.

Moeran, Brian. 2012. "Coda to Opinions: What Business Anthropology Is, What It Might Become . . . and What, Perhaps, It Should Not Be." *Journal of Business Anthropology* 1(2):290–7.

Murphy, Keith, and George E. Marcus. 2013. "Ethnography and Design, Ethnography in Design . . . Ethnography by Design." In *Design Anthropology: Theory and Practice*, edited by W. Gunn, T. Otto, and R. C. Smith, 251–68. London: Bloomsbury.

Oswald, Laura R. 2012. *Marketing Semiotics*. Oxford, UK: Oxford University Press.

Otto, Ton, and Rachel Charlotte Smith. 2013. "Design Anthropology: A Distinct Style Of Knowing." In *Design Anthropology: Theory and Practice*, edited by Wendy Gunn, Ton Otto, and Rachel Charlotte Smith, 1–29. New York: Bloomsbury.

Pink, Sarah, ed. 2001. *Doing Visual Ethnography: Images, Media and Representation in Research*. Thousand Oaks, CA: Sage.

______. 2006. *The Future of Visual Anthropology*. London: Routledge.

Reese, William. 2002. "Behavioral Scientists Enter Design: Seven Critical Histories." In *Creating Breakthrough Ideas*, edited by S. Squires and B. Byrne, 17–44. Westport, CT: Bergin & Garvey.

Suchman, Lucy. 2011. "Work Practice and Technology." In *Making Work Visible*, edited by Margaret H. Szymanski and Jack Whalen, 21–33. New York: Cambridge University Press.

Sunderland, Patricia. 2013. "The Cry for More Theory." In *Advancing Ethnography in Corporate Environments*, edited by B. Jordan, 122–35. Walnut Creek, CA: Left Coast Press.

Sunderland, Patricia, and Rita Denny. 2002. "Performers and Partners: Consumer Video Documentaries in Ethnographic Research. In *Qualitative Ascending: Harnessing Its True Value*, 285–303. Amsterdam: ESOMAR.

_____. 2007. *Doing Anthropology in Consumer Research.* Walnut Creek, CA: Left Coast Press.

_____. 2011. "Consumer Segmentation in Practice: An Ethnographic Account of Slippage." In *Inside Marketing*, edited by Detlev Zwick and Julien Cayla, 137–61. Oxford, UK: Oxford University Press.

Valentine, Virginia, and Wendy Gordon. 2000. "The 21st Century Consumer: A New Model for Thinking." *International Journal of Market Research* 42(2):185–206.

Wasson, Christina. 2000. "Ethnography in the Field of Design." *Human Organization* 59(4):377–88.

_____. 2002. "Collaborative Work: Integrating the Roles of Ethnographers and Designers." In *Creating Breakthrough Ideas*, edited by S. Squires and B. Byrne, 71–90. Westport, CT: Bergin & Garvey.

15

The Good Anthropologist: Questioning Ethics in the Workplace

KATHI R. KITNER

The night was warm and dusty as we waited for the research team to gather at a popular restaurant perched atop a seven-story tower in downtown Ahmedabad. I had joined my Australian and Indian academic colleagues on a project in northwestern India to look at the role of mobile phones and related communication technologies in economic development. Some of the researchers I had known just a few days; we were still learning about each other, both personally and professionally. Standing a bit apart from the others, Tripta and I smoked our cigarettes quietly in the shadows of the ungainly concrete building. Suddenly she took a deep drag, shifted her weight, jutted her hip, and asked, "How do you continue as an anthropologist and work at a place like Intel?"

Her dark eyes stared at me intently and with fiery challenge in them. I sighed and dragged deeply on my own cigarette. I knew what she really meant. Don't they suck your soul out from within you? Don't you hate having to sell out people's lives for a corporate profit? What is it like to be working from the belly of a capitalistic beast? How can you work under such *unethical* conditions? Haven't you *sold out*?

I have heard some version of this question before, not only in my current position as a senior research scientist and anthropologist at Intel Labs, but in almost all my previous jobs as an applied anthropologist,[1] from cultural resource management (CRM)[2] archaeology to fisheries management, as well as at academic conferences including that of the American Anthropological Association. That the question has resurfaced continually over the years points to its lasting currency and the difficulty of finding a definitive answer. There are anthropologists who have dedicated significant parts of their careers to understanding the conundrum of ethics and anthropology; I am not one of them. But

Handbook of Anthropology in Business, edited by Rita Denny and Patricia Sunderland, 309–320.

I have thought deeply about this question over many years, so rather than present a formal review of the extensive literature on ethics in the discipline (AAA 2013; Treitler and Ramagosa 2009; Whiteford and Trotter 2008), this chapter shines a light on the experience of facing ethical challenges in daily practice in business anthropology.

What constitutes the daily practice of anthropology in general is shifting: whereas in decades past most anthropologists (or sociologists, or historians, linguists, etc.) with graduate degrees assumed they would end up in some variant of an academic position, more recent PhDs are looking for jobs in sectors other than university-level research and teaching. Many end up in corporate settings (although current numbers on this trend are lacking; see Bureau of Labor Statistics 2012) due to the lack of growth in academic positions in the United States. But labor statistics aside, there on that dusty evening in northwest India, the question came laden—burdened, perhaps—with the additional hand baggage of antiglobalization, North versus South, Occidentalism and Orientalism, right versus left, postcolonialism, and more. The meaning seemed clear: in the battle of Good versus Evil, which side are you on? The contrasts between anthropology as a discipline born of colonialism yet attuned to less powerful people and the global corporatism that ate those same disempowered people for breakfast was stark. Tripta wanted to know how I lived with myself in such a seemingly duplicitous way. Even worse, she implied, maybe I was not an anthropologist at all.

Of course, my answer was hesitant at first as I tried to tease out the complicated mix of points that should comprise all good anthropological answers. Instead of claiming purity and vigilance while living in the labyrinth of corporate practices, I told her a story, which I will retell here, with some twists, showing how I—an "everyday anthropologist"—have acted in the face of different ethical conflicts. I believe ethics—whether in academic, medical, legal, political, or even engineering fields—is not a clear topic with neatly drawn rules. It does not matter whether you are at the top of your career, a student, or working in a for-profit business or a nonprofit nongovernmental organization (NGO): the dilemmas swirling around the concept of "doing the right thing" are still difficult, usually contentious, and often intellectually and emotionally painful. Even the Society for Applied Anthropology and the American Anthropological Association have seen fit to develop only "guidelines" for ethical behavior, with no enforcement capability or means to punish those errant in their ethical ways. In such gray areas, it can be more helpful to discuss examples rather than formalized abstractions.

In this chapter I look back at one particular ethical dilemma I faced while working in the fisheries industry, and although the path I chose was not without compromise, I believe that considering the circumstances, it was the best one for me to travel. If anthropologists know little else, they know that one's life is not a series of well-chiseled, clearly demarcated events, but rather is more a jerky meandering through a holistic web of human interactions. From a detailed examination of this dilemma, I will turn to my current role as an anthropologist at Intel Corporation, and examine how my work here compares with my position in fisheries, and why. I ask readers to keep in mind the conundrums we all face every day as anthropologists employed in myriad locations, from the college classroom to a NGO-funded health program in an impoverished community to a large corporation like Intel or Proctor and Gamble. We know every single place we occupy or action we take poses potential pitfalls in the practice of ethical behavior; therefore, how can we hope to not only confront these complex, even convoluted challenges every day in our practice, and in turn make the outcomes better, more ethical, and more humane? Furthermore, how do we know when we have lost the fight, and the only answer to the conflict is to leave it and walk far away?

SNAPPER-GROUPER UNDER SIEGE

The laws of US federal fishery management dictate that should the stocks of a certain species or complex of fish fall below a scientifically determined level (and how that level is determined is itself a contentious issue, characterized by full faith in the supremacy of numeracy and statistical modeling), then federal fishery managers and their public and civil counterparts must co-construct a "plan" to rebuild the depleted stocks of fish.[3] This process is not simple or straightforward, and the answers to questions such as who "owns" the fish or has the right to exploit publically held resources are unclear and hotly contested. The entire process becomes politicized and fraught with tension and angst because of all the varying interests with a stake in the fishery. In particular, those who fish and those who earn a living from fishing—for both commercial and recreational purposes—stand to lose not only income, but also their future rights to fish should more restrictive regulations be implemented. Under federal law, fishery plans must conform to a set of regulatory "standards."[4] For social scientists, the most important one is National Standard 8: "Conservation and management measures shall, consistent with the conservation requirements of this chapter (including the prevention of overfishing and rebuilding of overfished stocks), take into account the importance of fishery resources to fishing communities" (NOAA 2013).[5]

In the 1990s, US fisheries in general (both the fish and those who catch the fish) were under a great deal of stress from a variety of factors. The fishing communities where I worked (in the southeastern United States) were being squeezed in many ways: entire demographic shifts bringing wealthier, mostly northern, residents to "quaint" seaside towns; an increase in the number of those participating in the recreational side of fishing, bringing a different ethos to fishing in general; the early signs of global warming effects on the oceans and their fish stocks; the importation of inexpensive seafood from either aquaculture farms or less-regulated foreign fisheries; the rising cost of fuel; and the increasingly stringent cuts in allowable catches by fishery managers made in hope of rebuilding the declining fish stocks.

Within this turbulent context, fishery scientists (a varied lot of specialized fishery biologists and statisticians) determined that the snapper-grouper complex of fish (containing more than 70 distinct species) was being overfished: so many fish were being caught that their ability to maintain a healthy level of reproduction was being threatened. The scientific finding of "overfished" triggers a process of creating mandatory regulatory interventions aimed at rebuilding the stocks to a predetermined level. The biological side of this equation alone is a highly complex and sometimes contentious process. However, human behaviors and associated artifacts lie within cultural systems, and no matter how much the biologists tried to argue that it was only a problem of the fish, it was always a problem of fish intertwined in cultural systems.

The differences between the cultural systems of the various stakeholders became clear as the process of creating new fishery management plans began to unfold. Federal law demands that each group's needs and desires must be accounted for in a rebuilding plan for threatened fish stocks; typically their worldviews clash because of their closely held and deeply nuanced cultural differences.

First, there are the federal managers, or policymakers, who are employed by the US government or their proxies: they are both the judge and the executioner, as they will have final say in the creation of the plan and will implement the new regulations. Second are the fishermen, made up of two general groups: commercial fishermen, who in this case were small businesses (and not the larger factory-type boats common in the Alaskan fisheries, for example) and the recreational fishermen, who ranged from wealthy sport fishermen to the working class family out on a "party boat" for a vacation treat. Around these two groups exists the entire ecosystem of related economic activities and players: boat dealers, bait and tackle shops, fish houses, seafood shops, tourists, restaurants, hotels, and more. The third group is composed of environmental interests, ranging from large, well-run institutions such as the Environmental Defense Fund to smaller groups that reflect perhaps a town or local conservation gathering. Last, there is the "general public," the rather amorphous grouping of US citizens who, by virtue of their citizenship, hold a stake in the fate of public resources.

As an anthropologist, I was tasked with determining the social impacts of the proposed regulations on each grouping of stakeholders and reporting back to the policymakers the outcomes of my analysis. This was no easy task, and it was often carried out in concert with other academic anthropologists well versed in fishery issues and with economists also employed by the federal and state governments. After conducting field research with all the different stakeholders, data analysis, and consultations with other colleagues, I determined that the regulations proposed in this case to restrict fishery catches might be beneficial to the public and to fishery stocks. However, particularly in the context of all the other aforementioned changes occurring (demographic, economic, climate), the regulations would be seriously detrimental to the continued survival of the Southeast's fishing communities.

My assessment was problematic for the policymakers, who believed that rebuilding the fish stocks would benefit the communities by enabling larger catches in the future. The problem, however, was that this predicted increase in bounty would not come about for another human generation or two, long after most of the aging fishermen had died and their fish houses had been turned into restaurants selling "locally caught" but really Chilean cultured salmon. Nor were the policymakers taking into account any of the other events that were impinging on the small fishing businesses and their communities.[6] The fishery scientists, meanwhile, claimed that the "human side" of the picture was out of their legal purview and that they were charged only with rebuilding fisheries, not communities. My argument that a fishery is a cultural construct and does not exist unless humanly defined and as part of an ecosystem that also contains humans fell squarely on deaf ears.

I may have been able to live with all of that professionally and continued to work in this field. I loved the work and the people, and I believed the questions about common property resource allocation and climate change that were being addressed were critical to the future well-being of all. But when I received the official review of my social impact assessment,[7] I was asked by federal fishery biologists to temper my anthropological assessment and make it more "positive." It was also suggested that my assessment was most likely wrong, as there was no way to prove the coming negative impacts I had predicted for many of the fishing communities.[8] This feedback was not the same assessment I had received by other social scientists in the field, but rather from key biologists and policymakers. Concerned that they may be facing another lawsuit, fishery managers wanted to present a united front for their regulations, and I was not playing by the unspoken rules.

It was then that I realized that my position—my job—was no longer *ethically* possible for me. I could not just stand up and lie to the public about what I, to the best of my professional understanding, believed to be true. I could not put a happier gloss on what I saw was an unfair steamrolling of a group of people who had historically been less empowered than those who governed their livelihoods. I strongly believed that there was a breach of social justice occurring and I wanted no part of it. I was being asked to cooperate in what I felt to be unethical behavior that would lead to harming a community, changing their way of life—in many cases destroying it—and I could not justify my continued complicity and employment. Sadly, after much self-examination, I came to the realization that if I stayed, I would lose my self-respect as an anthropologist and as a human being. I began to search for another job.

EVERYDAY ANTHROPOLOGY IN THE SILICON FOREST

From fisheries I moved into an entirely new area of anthropology that I had never even imagined existed: the world of "high tech" and user experience, interaction design, and technology for development. However, before I accepted this position, I had questions of my own for my new, potential colleagues that boiled down to: "Do you feel 'wrong' working at a large, for-profit multinational corporation?" Yes, I had asked essentially the same question that Tripta and so many others would pose to me years later. After all, when I was in graduate school and for years afterward, the big multinational corporations were the enemy of "the people," and this worldview remains strong among many anthropologists today when they fail to see the corporation as an institution similar to many others: governments, nonprofits, universities. Let us then peer a bit more purposefully into what my anthropological life looks like in a corporate environment and the common challenges I face in terms of living an ethical life now that I am in what some might call the "belly of the beast."

In comparison with my work in fisheries, my job within a research lab at a technology corporation is quite different, and yet still similar in many ways. In general, my days consist of moving back and forth between the roles of anthropologist as technology researcher and anthropologist as educator. As a researcher, I have worked on various projects, from using communication technologies for community development projects in places like Chicago, Peñalolen, and Chapleau, to studying the impact of broadband rollout in Brazil. Other topical areas have been the examination of unequal, gendered access to the internet in different countries (Intel 2012), the creation of the consumer in the global economy (Kitner et al. 2011), and most recently, the role of the smartphone in different development and consumer scenarios (e.g., Tacchi et al. 2012). As an applied anthropologist, I am also a type of educator: I use research results to influence or guide product design and affect how technology is used and placed in the larger world. While the foci are different, the basic practices are very similar to my previous job: research used to influence future outcomes, whether in products or in policy.

An important difference from my fisheries work is that I no longer work in isolation from other anthropologists or social scientists. It is still true, however, that as a social scientist, I labor in the minority, now among engineers, before amid biologists. Previously, when I had riddles to solve about fishermen, I could call on only a few people, and other than an economist who was colocated with me, my social science colleagues were far away. That was not so bad, but the sense of isolation that had built up was perhaps too much. The power of sharing a cup of coffee and one's thoughts or worries about work with a coworker of a similar mindset is absolutely invaluable, particularly if one doubts one's research or work process. Real examples of questions we discuss at work include what methods are best to understand women's phone behavior in Mumbai, how do governments work in concert with small businesses to create the image of the consumer, or how can research within a corporation avoid a colonial stance vis-à-vis the new knowledge economies now rising globally. Because of the interdisciplinary team structure of my workplace, and because of the relative wealth of anthropologists working alongside me (five, not counting those in other business groups within the corporation), I find not only intellectual sounding boards, but real grounding and critique of my work and point of view.

I have not yet had the same dull and throbbing pain I experienced many years ago, that dark sense of crossing my ethical boundaries. I believe that one critical aspect of my daily work is that I do not believe I am complicit in actions that compromise the well-being of people that I study or work alongside directly. I know where my work output goes and how it will be used, as much as any other anthropologist can know how their work will be used. The research results I produce go to product design groups, where increasingly our findings directly inform the product or services being developed, and I publish in the same journals as my academic and other counterparts. Unlike many academics, I do not compete for funding for research; my funding is generally part of the year's operating budget and is not solicited from entities that might pose for me an ethical conflict with my anthropological values. However, I do realize that the money that funds my work comes from sales of technology, and that the products sold may be used in ways that are problematic for an anthropologist, or any other well-meaning person; but to deconstruct the possibilities *ad infinitum* would be paralyzing. This is a dilemma all anthropologists—in fact, one that all people in research—face every day. For example, there are those who sometimes ask me why I work to foist unnecessary stuff on people who can often barely afford it. The unspoken text is that I somehow spend my days hatching plots to expose people's cultural secrets so that the marketing masters in their advertising agencies can exploit those weak spots. However, I know that understanding consumption, from the conspicuous kinds to the sustainable kinds, is important and critically needed in the broken world we inhabit today. But ethically—and it is an ethical question—I must ask how it is that we as anthropologists have the right or mandate to decide what others should be allowed to yearn for or consume? This question itself is heavy with tension in our discipline, hungover as we often are with our historical legacy of being the handmaiden to wars, colonial oppression, and neoliberal regime imposition. James Ferguson (2006) offers a bit of clarification and way-clearing when he cautions us to not confuse the question of "cultural difference with the question of material inequality" (2006:20), and calls for a better appreciation of social inequality that may masquerade as "global culture." I cannot say then that selling a smartphone to a street trader in Johannesburg will be in itself good or bad ethically. But making the opportunity available so that the trader can decide for himself is the right thing, and not a nefarious act on my or others' parts.

The lack of perfect control over one's work is a gray area; we must reflect on it and personally acknowledge that we must draw our own limits. While my work here at Intel does not resemble in the least, for example, the Human Terrain System (Forte 2011) work that caused such anguish for many anthropologists, it is important to explore and understand what potential harm one's research may cause in both the long and short term.

TO BE THE BURR UNDER THE SADDLE

A company like Intel, much like a large state university, employs thousands of people engaged in various endeavors in different but linked departments: engineering, manufacturing, business and market analysis, and social research. Each group performs according to their specific disciplinary mandates, yet works in some degree of articulation with other groups in this joint endeavor to create an institution, a corporation, or a university. Researchers at Intel create and propose their own research agendas, which are then vetted for approval and funding by senior management. Here at Intel, yes, there are some researchers who work with US Department of Defense researchers, or with the US Department of Energy National Laboratories network, or in conjunction with the US Agency for International Development (e.g., USAID 2012) and other similar agencies. However, their involvement with these government programs is quite similar to academics who are involved in like research and applications. Furthermore, much research that is ongoing is conducted in close collaboration with university-based colleagues, and addresses issues surrounding poverty, economic development, climate change, sustainable cities, and gender discrimination—the list is long—and often in collaboration with academic counterparts.

As we consider the ethical dimensions of this arena, there is a central yet often unspoken question: are we to be ethics police over all our colleagues, anywhere and everywhere we work? Are we responsible—and culpable—for the ethical behavior of everyone in our organization? Does our identity as anthropologists give us more moral responsibility to address ethical questions than that of our colleagues in other disciplines? Csikszentmihályi has argued, "Engineering education and professional identity doesn't so much inculcate ethics as systematically separate technical work from ethical thought and action. Ultimately, a professional engineer must subsume their own moral, political, and intellectual agency, channeling instead the interests of their clients" (Csikszentmihályi 2012). I agree that this does happen to some extent, and yet it is an oversimplification to think of all who work in a corporation as robots responding to the same siren song of "the client." The question, again, is at what level our ethical responsibility lies: here the blurry areas again creep in like fog. Whether we are employed in the academy, or in a corporation like Intel, how much of what we do demands our neverending vigilance to make light shine on potential wrongdoing? Here I see two types of challenges. One is where the ethical breach is actually occurring and can be concretely confronted; for example, if our university has its endowment invested in a company that manufactures weapons, or our employer markets agricultural chemicals harmful to the environment. But the other challenge is trickier: what if, as mentioned, there is just the *potential* to create an ethical mess; for example, the selling of unneeded products to an unsuspecting consumer? Can we tease apart the probable or improbable outcomes with any degree of certainty? Are we even intellectually—or emotionally—capable of juggling all these ethical balls at once and for longs stretches of time, sometimes decades of time?

We—all of us—seem to live in a space of what some have called "bounded ethicality," the idea that people by nature desire to be good, but when confronted with the boundaries of their own life context (created by cultures and subcultures) may lose their moral compass and not see clearly the ethical breaches right under their noses. The idea is based on Simon's (1982) concept of "bounded rationality," which he developed to help explain why people did not always (rarely, I would argue) act as rational beings with regard to economic decision-making because of cultural milieu in which they find themselves daily. The idea of our actions being bound or guided by our life circumstances is not new, but when applied to the field of ethics, as Bazerman and Tenbrunsel (2012) have, the resultant concept of bounded ethicality helps to show how our situational and psychological contexts impact how we behave. We would like to think that anthropologists, trained to be all at once participant, observer, and analyzer, may have a better chance to stand above any fray of boundedness and see right from wrong. Being able to see the problems is but one part of the challenge, however. If we are honest with ourselves, we see that sometimes being ethical also demands courage, conviction, and a willingness to lose much both professionally and personally. Such qualities and actions are sometimes in short supply regardless of who we want to be or where we work. How much does fear of reprisal, social isolation, or economic loss play into whether or not we act ethically to expose wrongs? How many of us can afford suddenly to lose our paychecks for standing up for what we believe? I know we all think we would, but the reality is often more complicated.

My approach to ethical behavior within my own organization is to be the anthropological burr under the saddle. What do I mean by that? I mean that the anthropologist should be the one to constantly nudge in the right direction, to prick a bit more if the process is running the wrong way, and to offer guidance when necessary or requested. In other words, I try to work as effectively as possible to influence the processes and products within the organization. This can be practiced in the smallest ways and still have a good effect. For example, let us say that there is a project where women in smaller Bangladeshi villages will be interviewed about their use and knowledge of computer and phone technologies. How do we guarantee the confidentiality of a young Bangladeshi woman who, when the interview occurs, is watched by her brother, father, or other male community member and may face punishment later for not answering a question in the "right" way? Different field methods and interview techniques can be discovered, debated, and remedied before they become an issue. How can researchers protect her? Is the research even worth carrying out if there is any cause to think it might harm a participant? To ask these questions, and ask them until a good answer is received, is to be the burr under the saddle of "business as usual." Only when there are dilemmas of such a nature that I am sure there is no resolution and that continuing will breach my ethical standard do I consider walking away. Understanding where this breaking point exists in one's professional identity is, I believe, critical to being a good anthropologist.

So, what are the questions and challenges we face as anthropologists at work in the corporate world, and how should we face them? For the most part, I am surrounded by people (not just anthropologists) driven by a desire to explore the ways that different technological things can enhance the human condition, not deteriorate it. Could the best ethical role of the anthropologist in a corporation be that of a burr under the saddle? Is this the moral and ethical path to travel as we attend to our work? I think that the answer lies uniquely within each of us, and must be learned through experience and knowing oneself.

"Know oneself." "Do no harm." These are the two phrases that come to mind first when I think of the ethical dimensions of working as an anthropologist. Since my days as an undergraduate, through my first anthropological employment as a "shovelbum" traveling from one archaeological dig to the next, I always somehow felt guided by the idea that anthropologists were, by their training, driven to be good and to defend the practice of "goodness" in their work. Perhaps some of this strong conviction comes from my first mentor, Olaf Prufer, who drove home the notion that the inviolability of human rights should be respected by the anthropologists. The notion that anthropologists have a great and serious responsibility to the people with whom we work continues to be a guiding principle of my career.

Know yourself, your limits, and your biases, and state these publicly and up front: only then can you develop an honest approach to ethical behavior. Knowing yourself, you can draw your own lines. Be bold enough to redraw or erase completely the poorly drawn lines so that in so doing, we strive as anthropologists and human beings to be good.

REFERENCES

American Anthropological Association. 2013. "Committee on Ethics, Resources." http://www.aaanet.org/cmtes/ethics/Ethics-Resources.cfm (accessed September 4, 2013).

Bazerman, Max H., and Ann E. Tenbrunsel. 2011. *Blind Spots: Why We Fail to Do What's Right and What to Do about It.* Princeton, NJ: Princeton University Press.

Bureau of Labor Statistics. 2012. "Anthropologists and Archeologists." *U.S. Department of Labor Occupational Outlook Handbook, 2012–13 Edition.* http://www.bls.gov/ooh/life-physical-and-social-science/anthropologists-and-archeologists.htm (accessed January 23, 2013).

Csikszentmihályi, Chris. 2012. "Engineering Collectives: Technology from the Coop." *Limn* 2: Crowds and Clouds. http://limn.it/engineering-collectives-technology-from-the-coop/ (accessed December 10, 2013).

Ferguson, James. 2006. *Global Shadows: Africa in the Neoliberal World Order.* Durham, NC: Duke University Press.

Forte, Maximilian C. 2011. "The Human Terrain System and Anthropology: A Review of Ongoing Public Debates." *American Anthropologist* 113(1):149–53.

Ingles, Palma, ed. 2007. Special Issue: Anthropology and Fisheries Management in the United States: Methodology for Research. *NAPA Bulletin* 28(1).

Intel Corporation. 2012. "Women and the Web: Bridging the Internet Gap and Creating New Global Opportunities in Low and Middle-Income Countries." http://www.intel.com/content/www/us/en/technology-in-education/women-in-the-web.html.

Kitner, Kathi R., Renee Kuriyan, and Scott Mainwaring. 2011. "Cracking Representations of Emerging Markets: It's Not Just About Affordability." Paper presented at the 7th Ethnographic Praxis in Industry Conference, Boulder, CO, September 18–21, 2011.

NOAA Fisheries. 2007. Magnuson-Stevens Fishery Conservation and Management Act. May 2007, Second Printing, U.S. Department of Commerce.

______. 2013. "National Standard Guidelines, Office of Sustainable Fisheries." http://www.nmfs.noaa.gov/sfa/laws_policies/national_standards/documents/national_standard_8_cfr.pdf, Code of Federal Regulations, 2010 (accessed December 10, 2013).

Simon, Herbert. 1982. *Models of Bounded Rationality: Empirically Grounded Economic Reason.* Cambridge, MA: MIT Press.

Society for Applied Anthropology (SfAA). 2012. "Statement of Strategic Values and Goals." http://www.sfaa.net/sfaagoal.html (accessed January 28, 2013).

Tacchi, Jo, Kathi R. Kitner, and Kate Crawford. 2012. "Meaningful Mobility: Gender, Development and Mobile Phones." In *Feminist Media Studies*, edited by Larissa Hjorth and Sun Lim, 12(4):528–37.

Treitler, Inga, and Frank Ramagosa. 2009. "Ethnographer Diasporas and Emergent Communities of Practice: The Place for 21st Century Ethics in Business Ethnography Today." *Proceedings of the 5th Ethnographic Praxis in Industry Conference* 2009:50–8.

USAID. 2012. "USAID Launches New Network to Engage Students and Universities in Solving International Development Challenges Seven Top U.S. and Foreign Universities Join Forces with USAID to Create Development Labs and Discover Development Solutions." November 9. http://www.usaid.gov/news-information/press-releases/usaid-launches-new-network-engage-students-and-universities.

Whiteford, Linda M., and Robert T. Trotter. 2008. *Ethics for Anthropological Research and Practice.* Long Grove, IL: Waveland Press.

NOTES

1 Some anthropologists do not like the distinction made by using the term "applied anthropologist," claiming that all anthropology is practiced *and* applied. However, I use it in the sense of the Society for Applied Anthropology's description of the Society's *Strategic Values and Directions* that states that applied anthropology is problem-solving focused "building partnerships in research and problem solving; acknowledging the perspectives of all people involved; focusing on challenges and opportunities presented by biological variability, cultural diversity, ethnicity, gender, poverty and class; and addressing imbalances in resources, rights, and power," (SfAA 2012).

2 CRM can be seen through a lens of various disciplines such as history or architectural preservation; I am using the term here to refer to "applied archaeology," or the archaeology often done outside academia and with the intent of recovering or preserving as much of the past as possible in the face of, for example, large construction projects, transportation system enhancements, or military base expansions.

3 The case described here refers to US fishery regulations at the national level. Although similar, distinct processes for management of fisheries exist at the state and international levels.

4 "The National Standards are statutory principles that must be followed in any fishery management plan (FMP). The guidelines summarize interpretations by the Secretary of Commerce that have been, and will be, applied under these principles. The guidelines are intended as aids to decision-making; FMPs formulated according to the guidelines will have a better chance for expeditious review, approval, and implementation by the Secretary of Commerce . . ." (NOAA Fisheries 2013).

5 This standard was updated in 2007 along with the reauthorization of the Magnuson-Stevens Fishery Conservation and Management Act (NOAA Fisheries 2007). In the amended version, the rule requires the use of the best available economic and social science data, a requirement that did not exist when I was employed. This rule was also important in that it gave anthropologists an entrée into the world of federal fishery management; when I started my work there, I was one of the first to be employed in such a setting. For a good overview of anthropologists in federal fishery management, see Ingles (2007).

6 The other events deemed to have had an impact—positive and negative—were shifting demographics along the southeastern US coast with an influx of more wealthy, often retired northerners whose movement was causing a building boom and a related real estate sell-off; changes in the property tax structure that made it difficult to continue owning waterfront property; the globalization of the seafood industry and the advent and boom of inexpensive imports of fish and shrimp; sharp increases in the cost of fuel; and the change in worldview that the public held regarding fishing from a romantic view of fishermen to one of ruthless plunderers.

7 All assessments—biological and otherwise—were always peer-reviewed and then taken to public hearings in the hopes of (1) getting the right answers and (2) allowing input from all parties.

8 There was also no way to prove the predicted positive impacts on the fishery stocks, but I did not say that at the time. As noted earlier, the biological assessments, based on complex mathematical modeling, seemed to seem more real to many people than "simple qualitative" and ethnographic data.

16

The Sustaining Impact of Anthropology in Business: The "Shelf Life" of Data

MARTHA COTTON

INTRODUCTION

The promise and value of anthropology and business ultimately depends on the ability of our work to have a sustaining impact. As a veteran consultant who plays in the intersection of anthropology and business, I have a longstanding interest in tracing the "shelf life" and impact—or lack thereof—of the outcomes of our work. What happens after the anthropologist consultants leave? How are the results socialized, adopted, and integrated within the organization they are meant to serve? Or *are* they? What remains from the original intent of the work, and what evolves? What proves transformational or memorable? What has sustained value and a long shelf life, and what dies from meaninglessness or neglect?

The successful and effective consultant whose work has a long shelf life has to accomplish many things: the consultant must be able to communicate what is learned through the data and take the important step of building clients' convictions for what might be done about it. She must nurture a client to be both willing to take up the mantle of what is meaningful about the work, as well as enthusiastically socialize colleagues within her own internal working groups and organization to also find it meaningful. This chapter supports the growth of successful, effective consultants by looking at ways of developing a strong collaboration with clients and detailing different ways of helping the consumers of our work be as immersed and engaged in the data as we, the anthropologist consultants, are.

To bring tangibility to these themes, I focus on a specific ethnographic study I conducted as part of a consulting engagement in 2008. In 2012, I asked several members of our original client team to reflect on not only what happened during our engagements, but also after we (the consultants) delivered our results

Handbook of Anthropology in Business, edited by Rita Denny and Patricia Sunderland, 321–335.

and left them to take the actions we recommended. I will articulate what "sticks" and why so readers can better understand key components of work that has longstanding value and impact.

WHAT MAKES WORK STICK?

If you were a kid in the United States in the 1970s, you will be familiar with "Schoolhouse Rock!" a series of musical cartoon vignettes that appeared on Saturday morning between the Flintstones and the Jetsons. It was an educational series intended to teach the young of America about things ranging from grammar to history to the United States Constitution. But one particular vignette, "I'm Just a Bill,"[1] which explores how a bill becomes a law, has particular resonance to the topic of this chapter. In the cartoon, poor Bill, an anthropomorphized scroll of paper with a tuft of unruly hair, languishes on the steps of Capitol Hill, waiting to be noticed so that he might one day become a law. A dominant message is that in our democracy, although designed with the best possible intentions, it is very, very hard to get things done. And the young minds singing along learn that a lot of cute little Bills waiting on the steps of the Capitol never, for a whole host of reasons, become laws. They meet the saddest possible end. They die, unnoticed and forgotten.

I raise this as a metaphor that is particularly meaningful for the ethnographer/consultant. We trade in insights (sometimes called an "actionable insight"), findings, frameworks, and observations. We develop them from our research with the best possible intentions. We dress them up and present them to our clients, hopefully in their most flattering outfit, expecting that the inherent goodness of the work will ensure its uptake. We trust that our metaphorical "Bill on Capitol Hill" will get taken inside the building and have the desired impact. Much of our work of course does get taken in; a good consultant will see to it. But let's not kid ourselves: once the ethnographer consultant wraps up her project and leaves, even the most successful work may, for many reasons, never get picked up off the steps and brought inside. What actually happens? Why are some parts of the work brought inside and others not? How can we better prepare them for adoption? And I mean actually, not theoretically.

A good consultant knows all about the best ways to give action to insight, to frame human experience in a meaningful way, to articulate the "so what" of it all to ensure impact. But I mean how the insight actually gets picked up and championed within a client's organization: carried through the extensive stage-gated, supply-chained, brand-positioned, market-researched, Six Sigma-ed, lean-manufactured, politically charged minefield that is organizational product or service development (you thought democracy was hard for little Bill; try making a new kind of toothpaste!).

To deconstruct the trajectory of stickiness, allow me to introduce a project code named Nomad, conducted in the fall of 2008, when gravitytank (the innovation consultants) collaborated with Microsoft Hardware (the client). We'll see what stuck and what didn't. We'll see what is left, four years later, to be proud of. And we'll see what was left to languish on the steps, unnoticed and forgotten.

PROJECT OVERVIEW

Our client, one of the world's largest software companies, also had a small hardware business. They made mostly mice and keyboards. They noticed that the sale of laptops was far outpacing the sale of desktops. Remember, this is prehistoric 2008: netbooks were new and tablets were nonexistent. The rise of the laptop was generally not good news for computer accessories: there's not a lot of room for an external keyboard in your backpack. Cognizant of this growing trend (and most likely knowing more than I did about what technologies were in development that would continue to alter the picture), Microsoft Hardware wanted to better understand the mobile laptop user: the person doing this thing called "mobile computing." But it got more interesting. They had identified an interesting and growing type of mobile computing, and asked us not to look at the classic "road warrior" type you'd immediately think of (the management consultant, the pharmaceuticals sales rep), but to look at people who primarily used laptops within and around their home, for work as well as personal productivity, and who were mobile in more mundane ways: on the couch, in the living room, in bed, at the coffee shop, and at the library.

Objectives & Methodology

The objectives of the project were twofold:

- Develop a point of view and conviction around mobile laptop users and their accessory needs.
- Create actionable, tangible value propositions for concept ideation and development.

So we did some self-documentation methods. We had people write online diaries about their mobile computing experiences, and document their inventories of what they used and when. We asked them to tell us what mobility meant to them. We then did ethnographic interviews in their homes and in other relevant locations. For instance, if one of our participants routinely worked at a coffee shop, we went there with him and watched him work, paying special attention to how he prepared for the trip, what he took, how he set up once there, and how he worked there.

Post-Fieldwork Workshop

Once back from the field, we prepared for a two-day workshop at gravitytank's dedicated workshop space with attendance from about 15 Microsoft Hardware team members representing functional areas ranging from product planning, product strategy, marketing, design, and user research. The workshop was designed to be immersive, interactive, and generative, and was considered a key step in developing the stated objective of an aligned "point of view and conviction" that all team members could share. But it was also a moment where key findings from the research would start to be brought to life via concept brainstorming.

Linda, who was our main point of contact on the Nomad project, has said, "One of my most significant accomplishments at Microsoft was getting 15 people to fly to Chicago for that workshop. It was a moment in time." The accomplishment was "significant" in that her team had never been through a two-day intensive workshop of this sort before, and it was a "moment in time" because she was able to do it during a specific time when there was enthusiasm for investing significantly in this kind of alignment activity. Another stakeholder, Andy, indicated that several years after the workshop happened, attendees still talked about the impact the experience had on them.

Workshop attendees ranged from industrial designers, to marketing managers, to ergonomists, to product platform managers. The objectives for the two days were to immerse Microsoft Hardware in the learnings from fieldwork, present frameworks that reveal opportunity areas, and generate hypotheses about ways to capitalize on opportunities. But as another, less explicit objective, Linda felt very strongly that her team be introduced to not only actionable insights, but newer ways of thinking about their business. I suspect that not everyone on the team was fully aware of the urgency of the problem at hand. It is very easy to get tunnel vision about the relative importance of the thing you spend your days working on when it consumes your life but not necessarily the user's life. Linda wanted her team to think differently about their user, and this workshop's not-too-secret objective was to reintroduce that user to the team in a meaningful way. In building conviction for her team we would not only help everyone feel strongly about WHO they were designing for, but WHY they needed to think differently and commit to perhaps painful change in their organization.

We communicated our findings in a variety of ways. We did a short presentation of key themes from the research, but quickly got people up on their feet so we could tangibly introduce their user, and the environment in which their user used their products. As depicted in the images that follow, we built five discrete environments where we saw mobile computing happen and where we saw interesting, sometimes surprising behaviors (Figures 16.1–16.5). Now it may sound obvious that mobile computing happens in a Starbucks or on an airplane (indeed, much of this chapter was written using a laptop on a tiny airplane tray table!), but we forced our clients to become hyperaware of the space itself by standing in a replicated environment. We asked them to think about the contextual implications of each space, and what that space affords for the use (or lack thereof) of their products. We divided the group into smaller

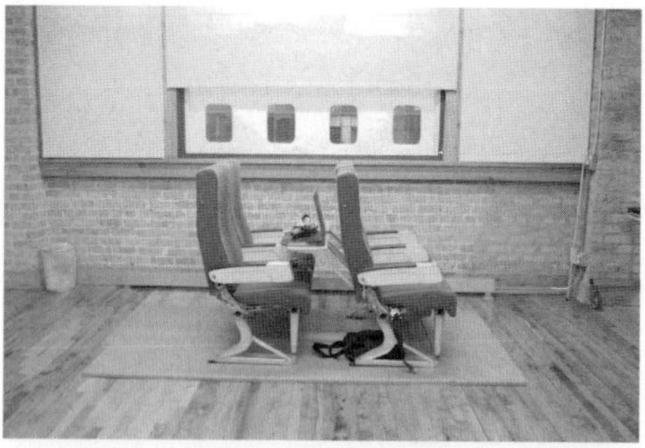

Figure 16.1. The airline seat is probably the most obvious space for awkward computing. But we asked our client to rethink an experience they themselves have frequently. We had them think about productivity, comfort, battery life, and the context as it relates to computer accessories.

Figure 16.2. Your local coffeehouse. Yes, a great place to sit and work, but also a place for home office denizens who just want to see another face every once in a while.

Figure 16.3. The kitchen setup showed laptops as cookbooks, homework helpers, printers on kitchen counters, and improvised "offices" in the most unlikely (and potentially lethal for consumer electronics) of places.

Figure 16.4. This living room setup gave an early glimpse into what tablet technology ultimately brought to the fore: your laptop is your companion for all things relating to media consumption.

Figure 16.5. The traditional "home office," the most expected place for in-home computing. Yet the permanent computer setup in the home is a dying breed.

teams and had them rotate around each environment "station," where they watched video of real people in these environments, read content on posters about the benefits and shortcomings of each environment, and (importantly) were encouraged to discuss what they were learning.

After exploring these environments, we broke for lunch and then jumped into an opportunity presentation, quickly followed by a variety of brainstorming activities that basically led the agenda for the rest of the workshop. Our brainstorming focused on creating storyboards where we redesigned a person's experience, solving for real-world pain points, and ideating solutions to meet their needs at key points. By the workshop conclusion, we had four to five key scenarios, supported by many, many concepts. All were developed in a collaborative fashion: gravitytank working with Microsoft.

The final phase of the project was the shortest: we analyzed the workshop outcomes, iterated on the brainstormed concepts, and developed four product platforms. These platforms were "families" of product concepts united by a single consumer value story, with illustrations of specific product concepts to bring those platforms to life.

THAT'S THE PROJECT OVERVIEW: HERE'S WHAT ACTUALLY HAS HAPPENED

By all accounts, the project went well. It was successfully executed and well received (indeed, about 18 months later, gravitytank worked with the same team at Microsoft to expand on some of the work). Alignment was created across the organizations team, and minds were changed. The client team members were great collaborators, and gravitytank was very proud of the quality of work delivered. Although product platforms were well received, they didn't actually result in any new product introductions to the market.

As preparation for this chapter, I interviewed several members of the original team who participated on the Microsoft side, many of whom have since left that company and gone on to other things. In my analysis of their comments about the highs and lows of the project, I have organized my diagnoses of what "stuck" into four themes:

1. Building unity through immersion
2. Creating empathy through tangibility
3. Framing and naming
4. Behaviors versus technology trends

Interestingly, these themes tend to cluster more around the less-tangible outcomes of the work (building conviction) than the tactical product strategy ones (product concepts). You will notice also that nowhere is there going to be mention of a "report" or a tangible "deliverable." In short, four years later, what seems to have stuck are things that affected the way they think and talk about their consumers, not outcomes that addressed the more explicitly stated project goals of creating new products. That is a humbling realization for an innovation firm.

Building Unity through Immersion

Justyn, one of our research participants for this project, was at the time of the study a creative writing graduate student. On a lovely fall day, he prefers to work in the park near his school (Figure 16.6). He scours the park to find power, and grabs free wifi from the café across the street. He carries in his briefcase a collapsible stenographer desk, which just fits his laptop. Regardless of the extra heft, he is very pleased with this creative solution, which allows him to get work done, but also enjoy the outdoors. "I feel like I'm cheating," he says with a smile on his face.

Figure 16.6. Justyn in the park.

There was much to learn from Justyn and our other research participants. But we wanted to make sure the lesson wasn't that people will (as Justyn did) carry their office on their backs to support their mobile computing needs. What was more meaningful about Justyn's behavior was that his tenacious passion for working outside in his own little spot of the park had him seeking homegrown solutions. The "working" solution was far from perfect, but the environment delivered.

We realized that immersion was key for our client to get beyond the surface insight that the ethnography revealed. We decided to push immersion as far as we could in the collaborative workshop.

The workshop worked. Why? Immersion. We went short on presentations and long on creating experiences. We wanted to help our client understand that people adapt extremely well to the sometimes odd environments where they find themselves using a laptop, as is evidenced by Justyn. We took cues from our research participants, like Justyn, who so clearly embraced his mobile computing as an environmental experience.

As mentioned in the previous section, we took the approach of introducing our research findings via a physical immersion in a re-created environment. What was sticky about this approach was making the research findings super-tangible by immersing them in these environments. It was also efficient in terms of time; we spent about an hour getting the groups rotated through each station. At the end of that hour, workshop attendees had quite tangibly walked in their end users' shoes. It built unity because in sharing the experience, they all lived it together. We did follow that hour with a short presentation where we simplified the story into a consumer framework (more on that later), but this presentation built on the shared understanding attendees already had gleaned for themselves. I believe that through this immersive exercise, we transferred ownership of the research findings, and unity was the natural outcome.

Lessons learned about unity through immersion

- Think about delivering experience rather than "findings." We know that the best way to learn is through experience. There is a massive amount of unhealthy behavior in the client/consultant relationship when the latter begins to present to the former. Lights go out, PowerPoints go on, smartphones come out, the consultant is half-listened to, and the client is scanning ahead for "ah has." Find ways to help them experience what is surprising or insightful.
- Strive for efficiency. Too quickly can your immersive objective delve towards overindulgence. Never assume that your client cares as much about every nook and cranny as you do. Crystalize the story you want to communicate and drive the point home.
- Beware the true but useless. Most researchers I work with are well intentioned in their passion for the peculiarities and mundanities of human behavior. Be mercenary about immersing your client in what is both "true" but also actually helpful to their goals.

Creating Empathy through Tangibility

At the time of our study, Renee was a busy mom of two school-aged girls, working part-time out of her home doing sales for sporting magazines. She also had a large organizational role with her kids' afterschool sports programs. She traveled once a month or so for work, but for the most part, worked out of her kitchen (Figure 16.7). Renee used to have a home office on the main floor of her house but, in a remodel a year before our study, she gave up that room to make a separate dining room off the family room. She had a theoretical commitment to re-create her home office in the basement.

Figure 16.7. Renee working in her kitchen.

Figure 16.8. Renee's kitchen setup.

But as a "temporary" office, she worked out of her kitchen. You can see in Figure 16.8 her laptop, mouse, printer, folders, and phone all set up on the kitchen counter. Hardly ideal, but this is how it worked for her: she had a direct line of view into the family room and dining room where her daughters would do homework after school or watch TV. She could very handily multitask: attend to email and then empty the dishwasher; start working on dinner while working on a spreadsheet. But it was far from perfect: One of the side effects of this setup was that Renee had developed a nasty callous on her right wrist where it would bump against the kitchen counter granite as she used her mouse. Also, when she had company over, she had to dismantle the setup, only to set it up again after they left. Regardless of how well it did or didn't work, this "temporary" setup had been in place for close to a year, and we got the feeling that that basement home office would remain theoretical.

Imagine being an ergonomist who designs computer mice and keyboards with the users' comfort in mind. If you were told this story about Renee you might respond with a mixture of bewilderment and annoyance. Why would anyone willingly work in such a nonideal arrangement? You might dismiss her story, saying "she's crazy," and not take the time to empathize with why someone would chose to live with these tradeoffs.

We knew we needed to build a good dose of empathy creation into our deliverables to think about solving the right problem for Renee. Was Renee's problem that she was trying to set up a home office in a place where a home office doesn't belong? Or was her problem that her home office was in exactly the place it should be, but the products she had to put there were not compatible with that space? The empathetic response to that question would be to think about the latter. There is a very good reason she is set up in the kitchen: it is the command center for her home, and she is the captain in charge.

Enter the value of the workshop again. We used the stations as described in the previous section not only to immerse our client in the user experience, but hopefully to develop a healthy empathy for that user and a clear perspective on the role of their product offerings in their lives. A loss of perspective is a dangerous thing in product strategy.

Scott, who at the time was the product unit manager for the organization, mentioned to me that this project was a great catalyst for change, and that "the greatest thing was to hear an engineer say 'that's not a good experience.'" I believe the workshop was in essence the first step in practicing empathy. We needed those on the Microsoft team not as prone to being empathetic to understand that seeing weird behavior doesn't mean the person is weird and the behavior should be discounted. It means that the person is actually wholly human and is making accommodations with the stuff in her life to make her life work better.

I don't believe the workshop delivered empathy wholesale, but I do believe that the tangible environments we had people step into in the immersion stations helped the team start to think empathetically. They could begin to understand that a person who had a home computing setup that physically hurt her was neither weird nor masochistic, but just a busy multitasking mom who wants to work in the center of her family life.

Lessons learned about creating empathy through tangibility

- There are certainly those who are more empathetic by nature, and those who need to practice it. So think less of empathy being "taught" but more "practiced."
- Use the notion of tangibility as an aid to practicing empathy. Ask yourself how you can make an experience real enough to be empathized with.

Framing & Naming

Each immersion station (detailed in the previous section) was given a name. The names of these environments became key touchstones for the remainder of the project. We called them "configurations." A configuration is a place, the stuff you put it in, and the way the two (place and stuff) work together in that given environment. We identified six configurations:

- **Nesting:** A permanent setup in the home, dedicated to laptop usage and "office" supplies. Tends to look most like a traditional home office.
- **Command Centering:** A semipermanent setup in the home where the user is positioned strategically to engage in home life and computing tasks simultaneously. Happens in places like the kitchen or family room.
- **Camping:** A purposeful (mobile computing) excursion to a temporary place. Tends to happen in places like coffee shops, quick-service restaurants, libraries, and parks.

- **Touching Down:** Improvised use of the laptop during "captive" times or places. Happens on airplanes, in buses, or in cars waiting to pick kids up from school.
- **Cross-Pollinating:** Using the laptop in a secondary role to support another activity that is the main focus, like to display a cookbook for cooking or sheet music for guitar playing.
- **Standing By:** A passive form of laptop use where the machine plays a companion role; it's up and running nearby, and used only intermittently.

The very act of giving language to these experiences allowed our client to continue to tell each other the story of what real people are doing in the real world. This language apparently continues to be used to this day. Linda, when reflecting on the relative importance of the act of naming, said that having named these environments, ". . . without having to overthink it, the design team went off and designed. They were sometimes using the language incorrectly, but I don't care. It was a mechanism to evangelize the work to other teams."

Giving the Microsoft team a language they could speak to each other proved invaluable for not only their ongoing design challenges but also for them to fundamentally keep their user in focus. This language was then organized into a framework (Figure 16.9).

The framework, as Linda says, "gave us words to describe what people were doing and why." The original version of the framework had multiple layers and complexities, but almost immediately the language took on prominence, the

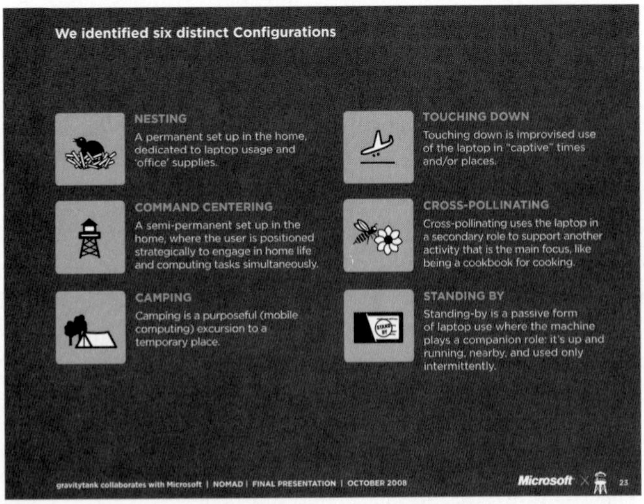

Figure 16.9. Configurations framework.

extra layers fell away, and the naming of those six configurations remains the key touchstone of the framework.

In the workshop, the framework was introduced to the team in an immersive fashion. First, they literally walked into each component of the framework (via the immersion stations described earlier in this chapter); they then were introduced to how these concepts organized themselves into a framing device.

The framework was flexible and reusable. Linda indicated that she presented the work several times after our official engagement ended, and the clarity of the framework ensured that "everyone walks out of the presentation and uses the language."

Lessons learned about framing and naming

- Be ethnographic with your client. Discover what kind of language will have the most impact for them and their organization. Make it highly accessible to the topic at hand, but also to the nuances of their business.
- Beware of too many clever things, or "Russian Doll-ing," as we frequently say at gravitytank. A framework inside a framework inside a framework is a map for getting lost inside clever ideas.
- Pitch and iterate. Frameworks will get simpler in the telling of them. Tell the story of the framework to someone less familiar with the project. Their feedback will help you see what is clear and unclear, what is core to the telling, and what is extraneous. Be prepared to sacrifice some beloved parts for the greater good of a working framework.
- Remember Linda's comment about evangelizing. To you, framing and naming might be the hard-won result of endless analysis and creativity, debates with your teammates, and your desire to capture each important nuance of a human experience. To your client, framing and naming are efficient communication tools intended to be touchstones to a bigger idea, and intended to help people make better decisions.

Behaviors versus Technology Trends

If you think of the trajectory of mobile computing since 2008, and what has changed in the space of "mobile computing," it seems intimidating to try to keep up. The introduction of tablets, the growth of smartphones and social networks, and the proliferation of wifi have monumentally and positively affected peoples' ability to access information and produce content in a variety of contexts.

So, yes, technology has exploded. And people have altered their expectations for what technology can and should do for them. They get more and they demand more. You might rightly ask, given all these changes, how work done at the end of the previous decade might still have relevance. Why indeed is some of this stuff still sticky?

I would hypothesize that the reason some of the language from Project Nomad has stuck is it describes more fundamental human drivers that technology merely enables. Has Renee's desire to be in the center of things in her home changed with the introduction of the tablet? Has Justyn's delight in working in the park on a beautiful fall day been affected by the growth of smartphones? Of course the answer is not at all; if anything, their nascent needs are much better supported by these devices. Certainly the ethnography consultant's bias is that the world is better for mobility not necessarily because of the devices, but because of the things people were doing anyway.

Lessons learned about behaviors versus technology trends

- When it comes to understanding user behavior, be neither afraid nor blinded by the relative speed of innovation. Ask yourself what fundamental human behaviors the technology is addressing. Chances are the core of those needs existed a hundred years ago.
- When it comes to stickiness in the context of shifting and innovative technologies, remember Renee and Justyn: try to deconstruct what uses the device affords (the ability to work in your kitchen because of the size of your laptop) from the things people want to get done anyway (the ability to multitask). Affordances and human drivers will have a symbiotic relationship for sure, but it is a good way to ensure that what you ultimately learn has stickiness, because in this example it's the need for multitasking that is the most interesting and the most sticky observation.

CONCLUSION: WHAT ABOUT PRODUCTS?

As I mentioned in the beginning of this chapter, it is difficult to draw a hard line between the outcomes of this project and actual products that made it to market. I learned from Steve, who was the product unit manager for the group at the time, that while there was a concept informed by Project Nomad put on the roadmap for a while, a shift in focus for the business made it die on the vine. But Steve did say that the work drove his team to decide who they were and were not, so we seemed to have made an impact on decisions of what concepts *not* to pursue, rather than what to try to bring to market.

So, to think back to poor little Bill sitting on Capitol Hill, it is clear that in many ways, much of the intent of the work was left on the steps. If I were to catalog the sum total of what actually stuck, the list is mortifyingly short:

- The memory of an immersive, empathetic workshop experience
- About a dozen words
- A clarifying framework

So, four years later, if you were to judge the success of this project based on ethnographic research–informed product ideas that have ultimately generated revenue for our client, it would appear to be a failure. Our metaphorical Bill is still sitting on the steps of Capitol Hill, or more than likely was swept up and unceremoniously thrown away.

However, if you were to judge based on the less-tangible impacts of helping our client think differently, and perhaps behave differently as they went about their jobs, adopting fundamentally new language to describe a core component of their end users' experience, if you think about the lasting effect of these relatively small but essential components of the work, it could be called a success. Our little Bill made it inside and was sanctified in the hallowed halls of the organization. He does not look like the same Bill we placed on the steps four years ago, but ultimately he was never ours (the consultants') to adorn.

NOTE

1 See the video at http://www.youtube.com/watch?v=tyeJ5503Elo.

17

Notes from the Periphery: Ethnography & Business in the Czech Republic

KATEŘINA AILOVÁ, JAROSLAV CÍR, & KATEŘINA SV. GILLÁROVÁ

During the Czech Velvet Revolution in 1989, it was commonly repeated that the country was 20 years behind the West because of the Iron Curtain, which effectively separated the central and eastern European countries from western Europe. After 24 years of "catching up with the West" (in the postsocialist parlance), the country is now economically on a par with fellow European Community countries, integrated through consumer markets, business relationships, and media.[1] From the business point of view, local markets are as saturated and commoditized as in the rest of Europe, and the slowing growth curves are causing companies to ask not "what shall we do to grow," but rather "what should we do not to decline so fast." Some Czech companies started using ethnography in their efforts to innovate and to respond better to the local market and its customers.

The position of the Czech Republic remains peripheral in the production of anthropological knowledge as well as the practice of ethnography applied in business. Nonetheless, ethnography has woken businesses up to "getting real" about customers, and has shown that products and services that respond to customer needs do matter. This customer focus directly challenges business's at-times lethargic attitude in addressing customer complaints, which is partially a legacy of socialist times. In contrast to the action-oriented American "let's change the world" attitude, there is the Czech phrase "*To je jedno . . .*" ("It's all the same, no matter"), which was an oft-repeated phrase during the Czech socialist past. For those not familiar with the socialist-time mentality, the "*to je jedno*" attitude is well articulated in this old joke, a key to how deeply the socialist regime affected behavior:

Handbook of Anthropology in Business, edited by Rita Denny and Patricia Sunderland, 336–345.

> Lenin, Stalin, and Brezhnev are taking a trip by train. Suddenly, the train stops in the middle of nowhere. The three leaders start debating what to do to get moving. "Lets explain to the engine-driver that it is in the interest of the proletariat to immediately fix the problem!" says Lenin. "Let's shoot the son of a bitch!" shouts Stalin. "No," says Brezhnev, "let's just hop up and down on our seats and pretend that the train is still running."

Ethnography in the Czech Republic has helped corporate clients (e.g., marketing, product, brand managers) understand customer insights in real and authentic contexts, and to reveal links between causes and consequences. It also helped to provoke empathy, which in turn has made corporate decision-makers care, and change the world for the better: at least for the customers. Making people care is part of stepping out from the shadows of the Czech totalitarian past. Ethnography helped Czech companies realize that they may be vainly "hopping up and down" in their seats instead of accepting the challenge to address customers' real concerns.

This chapter describes the challenges of introducing and practicing ethnography in a business environment much different from those of the world's leading industrialized countries. It explores the extent to which ethnography is becoming a generally known and accepted practice in consumer research and corporate life in the Czech Republic. We look at successful projects that used the ethnographic approach, and how they have changed the thinking about consumers in corporations. We also try to untangle some of the reasons ethnography remains a niche approach to solving business challenges in the Czech Republic, despite successful efforts in pioneering and publicizing it.

ETHNOGRAPHY IN CZECH BUSINESS PRACTICES

Adopting ethnographic methods to the Czech business practice was by no means a smooth transfer of knowledge. Lack of professional ethnographic research experience and resources slowed the development of a local professional community. At the same time, the trendy demand for ethnography led to shorthand approaches labeled as ethnography, yet without adequate data collection and analysis standards.

Early use of participant observation in Czech business emerged with the opening of multinational corporations' branch offices in the 1990s. Fast-moving consumer goods (FMCG) companies with expatriate managers encouraged their local colleagues to visit consumers' homes. Later promoters of ethnography were usually brand managers who had had the opportunity to participate in global consumer ethnographies carried out by Procter & Gamble, Unilever,

Philip Morris, or Kraft in Western Europe or North America. While managers tried to replicate research techniques suited to those markets in the Czech branch offices, they were often ill equipped to professionally analyze Czech consumer realities.

The word "ethnography" eventually became popular. Yet, much was lost in translation. The label of ethnography was sometimes used for customer video intercepts by advertising agencies. At other times, consumer diaries were combined with standard focus groups and then called ethnography. In the late 1990s, the first practitioners of ethnography were nonanthropologists. They were interested in ethnography as a technique. Some had access to ethnography manuals through multinational corporate hubs; others studied literature on the topic. Today, there is a small group of professional anthropologists applying the ethnographic approach in business; slowly, a small community of practice (Wenger 1998) is shaping up.

Despite the compromises and limitations existing in the Czech context, there have been a number of successful projects. In the following examples, we convey the effects of an ethnographic approach on the local business practices.

Challenging Preconceptions

Ethnography changes how clients—corporate decision-makers—think about their customers. Sometimes, ethnography helps to crack the shell of clients' professional blindness, giving them feelings of revelation ("I was blind, but now I see"). But in other cases, the marketers' preconceptions about how consumers use products are firmly entrenched (Flynn 2009). In ethnography, we see customers do unexpected or "strange" things. When a client labels some behavior strange,[2] it can be a red flag, signaling a clash between consumer reality and the corporate imagination of it. In those moments, some clients welcome and value the discovery of a new perspective, a new understanding. But some clients do not. Their first reaction in encountering the consumer reality may be to challenge researchers about the quality of recruitment, or even to doubt the value of ethnographic approach overall (see also Flynn 2009).

When ethnography conflicts with corporate preconceptions, there is an opportunity to disrupt the stereotypes about customers held in the corporate imagination. For example, a mobile provider was planning to launch a new generation of mobile services tariff plans for the Czech market. The marketing team had designed numerous concepts for the new plans based on price modeling, consumer segmentation data, and other mostly quantitative data, such as usage behavior analyses. Multiple rounds of focus groups were conducted, with the consistent result that none of the concepts resonated with consumers. Therefore, the marketing team turned to the research team, which recommended starting with customer ethnography. In the weeks that followed, the team shadowed customers during their decision-making process, accompanied customers while they shopped the competition, conducted in-depth interviewing, read customer diaries, and was engaged in co-creation workshops. Together these methods created a deep immersion for the marketing team in the customers' way of thinking and making decisions.

Some of the findings that particularly challenged the preconceptions of the marketing team were, for example, that customers frequently did not know, nor did they care much, about the details of their own current calling plans. Customers wanted quality coverage for calling and they wanted to use mobile services as cheaply as possible. They wanted to pay only for the services they would use—not pay for a plan that bundles services they would not use—and they wanted to pay about the same amount every month, without having to monitor their usage too closely. They certainly wanted to avoid the shock of unexpectedly high bills. When deciding what provider to choose, customers were by far not as economically rational as the marketing team expected. Ethnographic observations showed that customers frequently abandoned rational calculations, instead choosing the mobile provider where they had a better shopping experience: friendlier sales representatives who helped the customer understand what the services were about in human rather than technical terms, and who made the customer believe that the price was among the lowest on the market.

Overall, the marketing team had built their prior concepts on the idea that customers make rational decisions, that minute differences in price matter to them, and that they have a good knowledge of the patterns of their own usage. Participation in the ethnographic exploration helped the team see that the new plans would be relevant only if they are simple to understand, flexible enough to adjust to individual needs, and charge a flat monthly fee. The plans should also "speak" to customers in a human and friendly way in advertising, promotional materials, and during the sales process. The ethnographic experiences of the marketing team led to a radical change in the product offering. The new tariff plans were successful. The learning from this project also proved that starting concept development with ethnography can make the time-to-market significantly faster than concept development solely based on quantitative indices.

Client Immersion

Once clients have experienced immersion in the consumer world, it is seductive for them to get attached to details that confirmed their opinions, thus endangering a meaningful synthesis. The solution that has worked for us is to bring clients into the field with us. In our experience, clients have always benefited from ethnographic work when they were well motivated and trained to observe, ask questions, notice details, see patterns, and synthesize meanings. There are further benefits to engaging clients deeply in research projects. For one, more eyes see more. And for another, the more different the eyes, the more varied the observations. Ethnographers and clients have different experiences and backgrounds. When synthesizing insights with the participation of clients who went through fieldwork, we were able to draw on a wider pool of knowledge than we otherwise would. Yes, this process of collaborative analysis with clients needs to be well managed, but we believe in the process.

We have seen repeatedly that clients who were actively engaged in fieldwork and insights generation eventually made more customer-focused decisions. Another crucial benefit of engagement is the opportunity for ongoing involvement with the implementation of solutions. Usually, once the ethnography results are passed on to the client side, the agency that supplied the ethnographic research does not play any further role in how insights are implemented (see Morais, this volume). It is more rare that insights directly influence solutions, unless there is a close collaboration between researcher and marketing team, or conversely, unless the marketing team is already involved in the data collection phase. In our varying practices we have found that ethnography can be effectively mined if clients are well trained to collect data, get involved in participant observation, experience self-reflective exercises, or participate in interviewing.

Adequate training and motivation of clients who come with ethnographers to the field can help overcome many barriers. What has worked for us is bringing clients to the field frequently, engaging them in interviewing and data gathering (while not giving them the sole responsibility for it), allowing them generally plentiful face time to get to know the customer as a person, and also—and this is crucial—engaging the client in postfield insight-generation.

Involvement of both executives and ethnographers throughout the duration of the project from fieldwork and collaborative analysis to solution design helps to maintain the original insights without their pieces being carved out to a formless stereotype, and without losing the original focus and contexts of findings. Managers use stories from the field to aid their memory more frequently than citing quantitative data (though these are certainly part of the final decision-making). Because ethnography illustrates insights visually and with emotional contexts it brings out a more reflexive thinking about "what is really going on" from the consumers' point of view.

Contexts, Details, & Decisions

Ethnography privileges details in the doing and in reporting (e.g., to see the "rich detail," the "detailed insights"), details that illustrate how people think.

Details constitute the Geertzian "rich texts" (Geertz 1973). Rich detail disappears in corporate thinking quite fast. It is not unusual that once the ethnographic data detail a lively customer portrait, the clients respond with a demand list asking for anything from shopping behavior drivers to emotional benefits ranking. It goes something like this: "All of this is quite nice, but how should we work with it? Customer stories are not exactly useful for us. We don't see the point. We need a summary picture. We need high-level comparisons. Tell us what we should do."

Details are usually undervalued (in Czech the idiom "*utopit se v detailech*": "to drown in details"), because they are not considered "representative"; details distract and are seen as exceptional. The quest for representativeness on which corporate decision-making overly relies is interestingly counterproductive. We try to make clear that understanding details leads to understanding root causes, and therefore helps not only to inspire but also to solve real issues. Managers nevertheless hesitate to work with details and their contexts. Complexity, rich detail, and contextuality of ethnographic insights lack the clear-cut numbers, comparative graphs, and representativeness to a population, which managers often require. On a certain level, the charm of graphs and numbers is that they give an illusion of clarity and correctness (as in the common English idiom that "numbers speak for themselves"). We have often faced the requirement of quantitative proofs, which ethnography can rarely deliver.

The preference for the quantitative partially stems from Czech education (Santiago 2012): elementary schools to universities mostly require students to memorize at the expense of critical thinking or synthesis of ideas (Straková 2009). Prevalent essentializing of the quantitative paradigm, together with lack of training in critical reflection, makes it harder for managers to see value in ethnography. Yet, there have been cases when ethnography substantially contributed to solving perplexing problems.

The Gordian Knot

A project for a large telecom provider, aptly named the Gordian Knot, combined customer and corporate ethnography. The objective was ambitious: to transform enterprise customers' experience along the entire customer lifecycle, with the aim to increase sales and to reach better overall satisfaction by making customer-focused changes in the internal delivery processes. The core project team consisted of ethnographers and the E-level executives (i.e., division directors) across relevant departments. The ethnographic approach, together with design thinking, was integral to the solutions, even if it was occasionally challenged by the research department and Six Sigma team (who had previously worked on the problems without being able to fully resolve them).[3] The core team participated in numerous sales visits to enterprise customers, outage and complaints resolution visits, regular customer care visits, and finally in a deep-dive workshop with enterprise customers. They worked through a pile of customer complaints, mapping pain points that customers experienced. These engagements showed how creatively customers could compensate for the company service inefficiencies. The work continued: the team subsequently went through a number of workshops where customer experiences were mapped along the phases of customer lifecycle from the perspectives of sales, operations, and care teams. The insights and learning were continuously synthesized into problem areas, which were filled with more detailed insights as the project went along. Once the definition of problem areas was specified, we ran creative workshops that collected the involved teams' ideas for particular problem solutions. And to properly triangulate the data, we also interviewed sales, operations, and care employees on details of particular problematic processes. We videotaped their work, especially with the customer relationship management (CRM) system, the systems enabling provisioning of end-user technology solutions, and the billing system. From this massive data (imagine a room covered with large-scale mind maps and hundreds of Post-its organized in clusters), which were systematically collected and placed into a common overarching framework of a customer lifecycle, the team was able to reveal a network of related causes for each of 16 problem areas. From the analysis, the numerous team discussions and particularly the ethnographic immersions, the team defined a list of 64 solutions that included both fix-the-basics projects and innovative future-focused solutions.

This complex transformation program eventually mended inefficiencies that both customers and employees were experiencing, and resulted in clearly targeted changes that positively affected customer experience. Ethnographic experience and the richness of detail allowed the cross-functional team to build solutions stemming not from top-down executive decisions, but from the real-life details up. The solutions were then clear and systematically solving problems from their root causes, and in cross-functionally agreed and feasible ways. The action plan resulting from this project proved that executives changed their general attitudes and involvement in designing solutions because of the rich understanding and human empathy, and the fact that they knew precisely how positively their solutions would affect customers' experiences. They started caring more about the impact of their work on customers, and stepped out of the "*to je jedno*" ("it does not matter") attitude.

Bringing the Experiences Together

There are a number of benefits in combining ethnography with cross-functional collaboration, such as the common experience of drawing insights from customer perspectives, developing strategic directions based on insights, and co-creating the ideas for products, marketing, and communication. Collaboration contributes to creating the consensus among core team members. The results are faster decision-making, substantiated by shared understanding, and unifying the diversity in cross-functional team into a common focus on implementing solutions, aptly likened by Moeran (2011:27) to Victor Turner's (1964) concept of ritual communitas.

The second benefit of client involvement in ethnography is in the strength of decisions and the buy-in of decision-makers who participated in the project from the early customer immersion on. Because of contextual understanding, the engaged decision-makers (such as the executive board of the company) were better able to foresee the effects of proposed solutions. They also were less likely to allow for compromises, such as when the budget was limited for a full-scope implementation.[4] If top managers were involved in projects from the consumer immersion phase, they understood the customer needs and their contexts. If they also participated in the design phase, they had a sense of ownership of the solution. This was invaluable support in delivering customer-focused solutions and innovation to the market.

ON THE PERIPHERY

Despite a number of successful ethnographic projects with Czech companies, we still ask ourselves why there are not more. We see two ends of a continuum that are in tension. At one end there is the evangelizing work that researchers, research agencies, and other advocates of ethnography do within companies, pushing ethnography as a backdrop to quantitatively based decision-making. This includes implementing ethnography's benefits, creatively building ideas on insights gained from ethnography, and encouraging clients to work with qualitative understanding of consumers. On the opposite end of the continuum, ethnography has proved to be a useful selling tool for a number of companies and research agencies. Paradoxically, in such situations, ethnography in the Czech Republic has faced the risk of ossifying into a standardized "black box" process, which is then used as a run-of-the mill technique.

There are three broad reasons that may explain the particular forms in which ethnography has been adopted into the Czech business environment. The first reason is that in the last 20 years, the Czech Republic has been more of a sales market for multinational corporations rather than a center of product or technology development with a global impact. This is visible in the sales focus of local subsidiaries, translation-focused services of local advertising agencies (Czech-dubbed versions of foreign advertising), and in the limited budgets and development opportunities for local subsidiaries of global corporations. The distant echo of the center-periphery phenomenon resonates here (Said 1979; Zarycki 2007). The periphery position combines lost-in-translation issues with the lack of knowledge and resources for a wide awareness of how ethnography can contribute to business.

The second reason is the lack of professional and academic discourse on the topic. University and business schools make no mention of ethnography in the courses on consumer research methods, and managers graduate with little or no social science training. Therefore, practitioners are few. A review of the academic literature on the topic of ethnography in business in the Czech realm yields no results. There has been only one short introduction to the topic, published in a business trade journal (Ailova 2004) by a professional anthropologist.[5] Not even at the 2010 conference "Consumer Culture: Between Aesthetics, Social Distinction and Ecological Activism" (Consumer Culture 2010) was there any mention of ethnography as a method for researching consumer behavior.

There is also a third phenomenon that contributes to ethnography's particular and often limited forms in the Czech business context. We can call it "local *bricolage*," which essentially refers to making the best out of limited resources.[6] In adopting business ethnography into the Czech context, a missing know-how and experience has led to adaptations and compromises. In the worst cases, ethnography is only appropriated by its name.

One of the key achievements of Czech business ethnography is its ability to erase the border between the manufacturers and their agencies on one hand and the consumers on the other. By erasing the border, ethnography forces companies "to get real," to see the consumer as a fully rounded human being, to acknowledge their needs and problems, and to try to solve them. Too frequently do we see in the Czech businesses such vain "hopping up and down" as in the Stalin-Brezhnev joke, without meaningful decisions being made. Czechs could afford to "hop up and down" when the postsocialist economy was booming and consumers were eager to buy. Today the boom is over, as the economic crisis hit our part of Europe, and it is clear that Czech companies need to look increasingly for ways to deliver better product and services. Ethnography is among the productive tools that proved to be able to help them along the way.

REFERENCES

Ailova, Katerina. 2004. "Etnografické metody ve výzkumu spotřebitelů" ["Ethnographic Methods in Consumer Research"]. *Trend Marketing* 1(12):34–5.

Consumer Culture. 2010. "Between Aesthetics, Social Distinction and Ecological Activism" conference, October 7–9, 2010, Art Centre of Palacký University, Olomouc, Czech Republic. oltk.upol.cz/consumerculture/.

Eurostat. 2012. "GDP Per Capita in the Member States Ranged from 45% to 274% of the EU27 Average in 2011." Eurostat News Release 97/2012, 20 June 2012. epp.eurostat.ec.europa.eu/cache/ITY_PUBLIC/2-20062012-AP/EN/2-20062012-AP-EN.PDF.

Flynn, Donna K. 2009. "'My Customers are Different!' Identity, Difference, and the Political Economy of Design." In: *Ethnography and the Corporate Encounter: Reflections on Research in and of Corporations,* edited by Melissa Cefkin, 41–57. New York: Berghahn Books.

Geertz, Clifford. 1973. "Thick Description: Toward an Interpretive Theory of Culture." In *The Interpretation of Cultures*, 3–30. New York: Basic Books.

Myant, Martin R. 2003. *The Rise and Fall of Czech Capitalism: Economic Development in the Czech Republic since 1989*. Cheltenham, UK: Edward Elgar Publishing Ltd.

Moeran, Brian. 2011. "Perspectives in Business Anthropology: Cultural Production, Creativity and Constraints." *International Journal of Business Anthropology* 2(1):16–30.

Said, Edward. 1979. *Orientalism*. New York: Vintage.

Santiago, Paulo, Alison Gilmore, Deborah Nusche, and Pamela Sammons. 2012. *OECD Reviews of Evaluation and Assessment in Education: Czech Republic 2012*. Paris: OECD Publishing. dx.doi.org/10.1787/9789264116788-en.

Straková, Jana. 2009. "Vzdělávací politika a mezinárodní výzkumy výsledků vzdělávání v ČR" ["Educational Policy and the Results of International Studies of Czech Education"]. *Orbis Scholae* 3(3):103–18.

Turner, Victor. 1964. "Betwixt and Between: The Liminal Period in Rites de Passage." In *Proceedings of the American Ethnological Society, Symposium on New Approaches to the Study of Religion*, 4–20. Seattle: University of Washington Press.

Wenger, Etienne. 1998. *Communities of Practice: Learning, Meaning, and Identity*. Cambridge, UK: Cambridge University Press.

Zarycki, Tomasz. 2007. "An Interdisciplinary Model of Centre-Periphery Relations: A Theoretical Proposition." *Regional and Local Studies* (Special Issue), 110–30.

NOTES

We would like to thank Tomáš Rudolf (Insiqua), Jiri Michal (Kraft Foods), Tomas Hrivnak (Idealisti), Boris Stepanovic (Philip Morris), Radka Dvorakova (Confess Research), and David Masilka (TNS AISA) for contributing to this chapter. For insightful comments and help with the text, we would like to also thank Inga Treitler (Anthropology Imagination) and Rudolf Cihak (IdeaSense).

1 In 1990, per capita GDP in Czechoslovakia was 52 percent of EU average when compared by purchasing power parity (Myant 2003:10). In 2011, this measure was at 80 percent (Eurostat 2012).

2 We have seen client reactions range from giggling to derogatory remarks, as far as outright refusal of insights based on such observation (see also Flynn 2009).

3 The particular failure of previous Six Sigma work on the topic was due to the fact that they relied only on internal managers' perspective, while completely ignoring customer point of view and experience. They also failed to look at details within the internal processes and their contexts to deeper understand the consequences of daily practices, for example in the sales or operations teams.

4 We were witness to internal negotiations within a company for particular features of a customer-facing solution and adequate budget to implement it. The impact of power, politics, and the personal interests of executives are often stronger than the best customer-focused designs. It would be interesting to compare differences in boardroom negotiations cross-culturally. Here, we cannot testify to how Czech culture locally influences these negotiations, since we have no comparative data.

5 The Slovak version of this article (Ailova 2004) even stirred an online debate on the pitiful fate of anthropologists if their future is in reducing their skills to consumer research (http://kyberia.sk/id/3620507).

6 A great example of such *bricolage* is the invention of hydrogel contact lenses by the prominent Czech chemist Otto Wichterle. For a lack of better equipment, he constructed the first prototype of his lenses on a homemade apparatus made from a children's building kit called Merkur, a bicycle dynamo, and a bell transformer.

18

Training the Next Generation: Business Anthropology at the University of North Texas

SUSAN SQUIRES, CHRISTINA WASSON, & ANN JORDAN

INTRODUCTION

As business anthropology has developed into a recognized field, important questions about how universities might effectively prepare future generations of practitioners have been raised by those currently working in business. How to maintain high standards of work "in our professional traditions" arises at every Ethnographic Praxis in Industry Conference (Lombardi 2009:42; Squires and Mack 2012; Tian 2011; Wasson and Metcalf 2006). The first generation of anthropologists employed full-time in industry faced a steep on-the-job learning curve, as they gained business-specific expertise in the cultural logics and practices of the business world while improvising ways to demonstrate the value of their anthropology training (Benson 2001; Bodo 2001; Briody and Pester 2012; Flynn and Lovejoy 2008; Ikeya et al. 2007; Sachs 2006; Squires 2006). Patricia Sachs, a pioneer in the field, had this to say about her learning process:

> As an anthropologist [in business], I have bushwhacked my career. There was no clear trail to follow, and many of the brambles that pricked my skin along the way were unfortunately provided by members of my very own discipline. While bushwhacking clearly suits my style, it is time that alternative career paths become better options for anthropology graduates (2006:161–2).

No longer do new practitioners have to face a steep on-the-job learning curve in the business world. Now that business anthropology has become more widely established, a number of universities have developed targeted graduate programs that specifically prepare students to enter the field. Depending on the university, such programs may be housed in colleges of design (University of Dundee, Swinburne University of Technology), interdisciplinary institutes

Handbook of Anthropology in Business, edited by Rita Denny and Patricia Sunderland, 346–361.

(University of Southern Denmark), or anthropology departments (Wayne State University, University of North Texas).

While many students who apply to these programs seek training on how to operate effectively in corporate settings, there is also a second group of students with a different set of needs. These students already have well-established professional careers in the business world. They do not need to learn about the cultural logics and practices of business per se. What they seek from a graduate program in business anthropology is training in anthropology. However, they are still looking for a program that can show them how to connect anthropological theories and methods with applications in fields such as design, marketing, and management. The needs of both groups—students at the start of their careers, who may have more anthropology background, and students further along in their careers, who bring the wisdom of work experience—converge and interact productively in the class setting.

This chapter offers a case study of how the next generation of business anthropologists is being trained at one institution, the University of North Texas (UNT). Our goal is to identify lessons learned and practices that may be useful to other emerging programs. We also want to stimulate discussion with the community of practicing business anthropologists on how to best train the next generation of practitioners. We begin by placing the business anthropology program in context by discussing the history of the anthropology department at UNT and the development of our master's program in both its on-campus and online versions. Next, we describe the department's pedagogical commitment to strong training in theory coupled with strong training in practice. Then, we turn to the particular areas of expertise we offer: our established foci in design anthropology and organizational anthropology, and the current growth areas of marketing and strategy. In conclusion, we will offer insights from our 13 years of experience with a master's program in applied anthropology, which we hope provide value to other programs.

THE UNIVERSITY OF NORTH TEXAS & APPLIED ANTHROPOLOGY

UNT is situated in the Dallas–Fort Worth metroplex, home to diverse ethnic communities, important business and corporate headquarters, non-governmental organizations (NGOs) and other agencies that provide students a wide range of opportunities to practice engaged anthropology. Located in Denton, it is the fourth-largest university in the state, has 36,000 students, 12 colleges, a budget of $750 million, and brings in $1.3 billion to the regional economy annually. As a state university, it is responsible to the state legislators and, as a consequence, must justify its cost to the legislature and to the people of Texas. This is accomplished in part by large enrollments and the dollars university employees, students, and former students bring into the economy (Henry et al. in press).

The anthropology department is in a school of applied social and behavioral science, which gives the faculty engaged in applied anthropology legitimacy in the university. The department offers a master's degree in applied anthropology with five specialty areas: business, technology, and design anthropology; migration and border studies; medical anthropology; anthropology of education; and environmental and ecological anthropology. All students take the same core courses and are free to take courses in other specialty areas. For example, non–business anthropology students take organizational anthropology because they will be working with and for complex organizations. In addition, faculty members sit on committees for students in other specialty areas. The requirements for the applied thesis are the same across the specialty areas. Faculty participation in other specialty areas benefits the students and allows the department to maximize the use of its resources. The anthropology department at UNT prides itself in providing students with a strong theoretical foundation in combination with extensive experience working on client projects to prepare them for the world of practice.

Among the five areas of specialization, business anthropology has thrived for four reasons. First, it dates to the beginning of the master's program in 2000, which allowed business anthropology faculty to help shape the overall program. Second, since it is located in an anthropology department, rather than a business or design school, the training is embedded in anthropological theory and case studies. Third, it is located in a department entirely focused on applied anthropology; there is no tension over the merits of traditional versus applied work. The department members can focus all their energy on building the applied program. Fourth, it is located in a college entirely focused on applied social science. This is an advantage when making tenure decisions because there is no argument at the college level over the merits of applied work.

UNT hired its first business anthropologist in 1990 (Jordan); a second was hired in 2001 (Wasson), and a third in 2010 (Squires). In 2000, the department initiated its master's program in applied anthropology, which included business anthropology as one of five specialty areas. This was the first graduate program in applied anthropology and first graduate concentration in business anthropology in the state of Texas. Today, the department has a faculty of 12 applied cultural and linguistic anthropologists, a four-field undergraduate program, and an on-campus and online applied anthropology master's program.

Master's students in the program are required to take a set of five core courses: Thought and Praxis I and II, Ethnographic and Qualitative Methods, Quantitative Methods, and Preparation for Practice and the Applied Thesis. Business anthropology students are also required to take Organizational Anthropology and Design Anthropology. Students take three additional courses, two of which must be outside of the department: in business, in design, or in a third field relevant to their interests.

As it launched the graduate program, the department also developed online classes for its undergraduates. The success of those undergraduate courses and the university's desire to develop online education convinced the department to develop an online master's program in applied anthropology. Online opportunities allowed individuals tied geographically to regions where there were no appropriate local education facilities to take anthropology courses. The department wanted the online program to serve the needs of students around the world who could not move to Texas, including many who were already seasoned professionals and wanted to take their work in a new direction.

The faculty began meeting regularly to plan such a program in 2003, with Christina Wasson as lead, and launched the program in 2006 (Re Cruz et al. 2007; Wasson 2007). The online program tends to attract students who have established careers in the business world, but it also includes students at the start of their careers. Its biggest advantage is the high quality of the students; this is likely to be a result of the paucity of online options for such individuals as well as their enthusiasm at finding a program that enables them to pursue a deeply held interest within the constraints of their geographic location and work and family commitments.

INTEGRATION OF THEORY & PRACTICE

Our faculty is committed to giving master's students strong training in theory coupled with strong training in practice. We subscribe to a "theory of practice" that regards "theory and practice as interdependent elements in a spiral of new knowledge" within the discipline of anthropology (Baba 2000:36). To become effective practitioners, we believe that our students need a rich and diverse toolbox of theories, grounded in the historical evolution of anthropological approaches. We also recognize the contributions practice can make to new theory development. "Applied work has . . . helped to shape theory in anthropology, by opening new fields of research and contributing to the revision of theories, especially in the areas of intercultural relations, social change, development, and organizational culture" (Rylko-Bauer et al. 2006:185). We seek to inculcate an awareness of this reciprocal relationship between theory and practice in our students and encourage them to develop an integrated identity as "scholar-practitioners" (Wasson 2006; Wasson et al. 2012). Our hope is that they will both develop sophisticated, theoretically informed work approaches as practitioners and contribute to future theory development by continuing to publish and present at conferences.

This view of the interdependence of theory and practice shapes the design of our master's program. In their first year, students take a sequence of two courses, Anthropological Thought and Praxis I and II, that examines the history of approaches to theory and practice in anthropology. The first course mainly provides an overview of the last hundred years of anthropological theory, while integrating theory with practice. At the start of the course, students are given a case study: the surprisingly high mortality rate of Chicago's 1995 heat wave (Klinenberg 2002). Then, for each theoretical approach they study, students discuss how that approach might have analyzed the mortality rate of the heat wave, and what kinds of solutions the approach would have generated. Over the course of the semester, students come to see how different theoretical frameworks lead to widely varying ways of addressing social problems. The second course mainly exposes students to the history of anthropological practice, but highlights interdependencies between theory and practice: developments in practice are linked to the theoretical context of their time, and threads between the two courses are woven back and forth.

Our master's program is also designed to give students as much experience as possible with client projects. We regard client projects as the best opportunity for students to discover, firsthand, what it is like to use theories and methods they have learned in the pursuit of client goals (see Aiken in press). These projects also provide opportunity to discover how they can contribute to theory development. In their first year, master's students are required to take Qualitative Methods. The course is organized around a semester-long client project, and students learn about the relationship between client goals, research questions, and research design. The two electives in business anthropology also include semester-long client projects. The capstone experience for master's students is a two-semester applied thesis project conducted for a client. It results in two kinds of outputs: applied findings for the client, and a theoretically framed ethnography submitted to the university as a thesis.

DEPARTMENTAL AREAS OF FOCUS WITHIN BUSINESS ANTHROPOLOGY

The business anthropologists at UNT have diverse expertise. Ann Jordan specializes in organizational anthropology and has studied health care systems, organizational culture and change, mergers, self-managed work teams, and global organizational networks. Christina Wasson's work is motivated by a passion for three "C"s: communication, collaboration, and community building. She investigates how technology can bring together people who are geographically separated and applies her findings to the design of technologies and organizational change processes. Susan Squires specializes in the technology sector and is a recognized expert on customer insights research (Baba 2012). She has helped develop easy-to-use tele-health communications devices for older adults, mapped workflow of computational scientists, and inspired the design of telecommunication and medical support products. Given the expertise of the business anthropology faculty at UNT, we focus on two primary areas: (1) organizations and (2) design and technology. We also have several new growth areas, which will be addressed in the following section.

Organizations

Ann Jordan teaches Organizational Anthropology, which includes readings on theory, case studies, methods, and ethics. It demonstrates how anthropologists have put theory into practice in organizational settings. The readings on anthropological methods focus on applying methods in organizational settings and the class session on ethics focuses on the particular ethical issues that organizational work entails. Studying the anthropological literature comprises half the class; the other half is a class project for an organizational client. While the literature provides valuable understandings and examples and gives students the material to use in their later working lives, it is the class project that teaches them how to do organizational anthropology and gives them the confidence to realize they can do such work on their own. Prior to the start of class, the instructor finds a client who has a project with relevant research questions about organizational issues. Projects always begin with a class session in which the client describes the organization and the issues the students will examine. Following the initial session, Jordan guides the class in brainstorming about the research questions, appropriate methods to use, and ultimately an interview schedule. Students then conduct four field contacts with the client organization, which are typically participant observation, interviews, or focus groups. While gathering this field data, the class continually reassesses the direction of the project by discussing the results of these contacts and determining what types of contacts should follow and with which groups of employees. Students then transcribe their audiotaped notes and interview texts. The class develops a coding list, and all interviews are coded using Atlas.ti. The class is then divided into groups to analyze the coded content. This leads to further class discussion of the analysis and ultimately the development of findings and recommendations in a PowerPoint presentation to the client in the final class of the semester.

For the on-campus class, the client is always a local nonprofit that can benefit from free consulting. Client projects have included a study of student and staff perceptions of education, services, and facilities for a community college; a project focused on creating a stronger volunteer program for a local family resource center; and research defining the organizational culture and providing steps for organizational change for a nonprofit organization providing services to low-income and homeless citizens.

For the online class, determining a client is an added challenge because the students are located all over the world; thus, the organization to be studied must have units globally or in some way be able to be studied in locations worldwide. These classes have worked on the impact that restructuring the headquarters of the American Red Cross had on regional operations; consumer perceptions of General Motors vehicles while GM was negotiating with the US government over bankruptcy and an infusion of funds; and the franchise as an organizational form and the motivations for individuals to start franchise businesses during an economic downturn.

While students may not work as organizational anthropologists in the future, they will certainly be working with and for organizations. For students who become managers in organizations, the course provides an anthropological perspective on organizations that one former student described as "managing paradigms."

The on-campus and online courses cover the same content. The readings are identical and the projects require the same assignments from students. Obviously, there is a difference in the delivery system. With regard to the readings, on-campus students meet weekly in a seminar to discuss the readings. The online students contribute several times a week to a discussion board to discuss the readings and write critiques of the readings for the instructor. The online requirements are an attempt to generate the same interactive engagement with the readings that the on-campus class has during its seminar sessions. To learn from the project, the students need to collectively discuss and strategize at regular intervals. The on-campus class does this during its weekly seminars. The online class participates in 10 synchronous meetings during the semester to achieve the same objective. We use software that allows all voices to be heard while we view the same whiteboard computer screen. The greatest difficulty with the synchronous meetings is finding a time when all can participate. The online students are typically professionals with day jobs and frequently have other commitments in the evenings. Some of them are in other countries. We always manage to find a time, but students in other countries usually have to get up in the middle of the night to participate. The online class requires more time from the student than the on-campus class.

On-campus students tend to be younger and more likely to have just finished undergraduate school compared with the older, established professionals typically found in the online program. Mixing the two groups in class is an advantage. The less-experienced students learn from the older ones, while the older ones frequently have less anthropological training and learn about anthropology from the younger ones.

Applied Theses with an Organizational Focus

Students have conducted a variety of organization-focused studies for their applied thesis projects. Jose Mendez Andino evaluated the executive assistant job position at a Fortune 500 company. He assessed the hiring, promotion, training, and career ladder of executive assistants. Given the critical role of the executive assistants to the overall productivity of its executive offices, the company believed it was important to continue to identify, grow, and develop a strong pipeline of executive assistants in anticipation of future business needs. Lauri Lillie carried out an impact assessment and evaluation of the home ownership program for Dallas Area Habitat for Humanity, which included an analysis of the priorities of key stakeholders in the organization. Brianne Moore studied the challenges midsize organizations perceive in "going green." This included organizational members' definitions of a green organization, their perceptions of the incentives and barriers to increasing their organization's ecologically sustainable practices, and their views on environmental legislation relevant to their organization. Mohammedali Zolfagharian studied franchise organizations to determine how franchisors and franchisees viewed the successes and failures of their partnerships.

Graduates are working as organizational anthropologists in a variety of settings. For example, Kelly Moran graduated in 2007 with the goal "to make products a better fit for their users." Now a manager of applied anthropology with VHA, she describes herself as "the company's ethnographic expert":

> I serve on a multidisciplinary team of mostly remote coworkers who travel to high-performing hospitals around the country to determine what these organizations are doing right. We use an evaluative research approach to discover implicit enablers to success. I explain to research participants that what we mean by this is that they have implemented work processes and techniques that have become to them as second nature as breathing. They aren't the things they think about when they describe their job, but they are absolutely essential. By teasing out and documenting these gems, we help other hospitals in our network improve their own clinical and supply chain processes. It is immensely interesting and rewarding work, and I think not far from my original goal. Rather than making a product better by studying its user, I am optimizing an indispensable service by studying its provider.

Design & Technology

Wasson and Squires were both early practitioners in the field of design anthropology (Squires and Byrne 2002; Wasson 2000). Wasson teaches the on-campus Design Anthropology course; Squires teaches the online version.

Christina Wasson developed the on-campus Design Anthropology course at UNT in 2002. She seeks to have each class consist of about half anthropology students and half design students. One of her pedagogical goals is to have design and anthropology students learn from each other, and learn how to collaborate with each other. In addition to advanced undergraduates and master's students in anthropology and design, Wasson accepts a few doctoral students from fields such as marketing and information science.

Like Jordan's Organizational Anthropology course, Wasson's Design Anthropology course interweaves two equal goals: critical reflection on the literature in design anthropology and hands-on experience with a client (Wasson and Metcalf 2013). Field methods vary, depending on the research topic; they typically include some combination of in-depth interviews, participant observation, shadowing, intercept interviews, and photo diaries. Most fieldwork is video-recorded. Students collect data in cross-disciplinary pairs. Field notes, video clips, and other data are placed on a password-protected website so students can access each other's data. Much of the analysis is conducted during class time by all the students working together as a group. Wasson serves as guide and facilitator. Each team presents findings from its fieldwork. Students describe their fieldwork experience, illustrating key moments and insights with video clips. Examples and emergent insights from class discussions are noted by Wasson in a Word document visible to the whole class via an LCD projector. As the Word document becomes longer, students start to group ideas. Information is organized into the categories of instances, patterns, and design ideas. Over time, chapter topics for the final report emerge and are divided up among students. Students then conduct further analysis on their own to ensure a thorough review of all data for each topic.

Examples of client projects from the on-campus Design Anthropology course include research on travelers' use of concessions at the Dallas/Fort Worth International Airport; a study of how 18- to 24-year-olds use and understand their mobile devices for Microsoft; and an investigation of how the design of a mobile phone could communicate that it was ecologically friendly for Motorola.

In 2011, Squires developed an online version of the Design Anthropology course. The course design was influenced by her experience teaching Design Anthropology on campus in 2010, where she drew on Wasson's approach. While retaining many of the readings in the face-to-face course and the client project, she reorganized the flow and added course content based on previous experience conducting design ethnography workshops for business and design professionals, and from interviews she and Alexandra Mack conducted with senior practitioners about the skills and knowledge needed for practitioners in industry today (Mack and Squires 2011). These senior practitioners pointed out that "no one can just be a field worker" anymore; for new practitioners, success in the job requires "leadership, management, consulting, innovation, and marketing" (Mack and Squires 2011:22). The new content included a theoretical frame for understanding material culture that could be used to innovate, leadership and collaborative principles for team-building, management and consulting opportunities within teams, and interacting with customers. Squires developed innovative ways to expose students to these areas. In adapting the course to an online format, Squires drew on the experience of other departmental faculty who had developed online courses (Davenport and Henry 2007:12–15; Nuñez-Janes and Re Cruz 2007:20–3).

For the client project, she invited Alexandra Mack, an anthropologist working for Pitney Bowes, to be the industry partner. In line with the need to prepare students for current jobs, the course is based on the four objectives identified earlier as departmental goals in training master's students, and explicitly reflects what senior practitioners consider necessary skills and knowledge. The online course has been taught once, and is still evolving. It is scheduled to be taught regularly in the future. For the first class, the client project looked at the communication needs of small businesses for Pitney Bowes.

The faculty in the anthropology department has a commitment to active learning and student engagement. Squires reflects this commitment in the online Design Anthropology course, which is based on constructivist pedagogy, one of several approaches that incorporates hands-on experience. In her adaptation of this pedagogical approach for the course, the student carries out a task or activity and reflects on its outcome. The concrete experiences are then analyzed and translated into the general principles or explanatory models under which the task or activities fall (Kolb and Fry 1975). Finally, the student applies anthropological theory for deeper insights and hypothesis testing. Working in teams, the students engage in the entire process from the first meeting with the client (Mack) through writing a proposal, conducting the research, analyzing the data, and creating a final deliverable of findings and recommendations to presenting the final report to the client during the final week of the course.

To build the students' theoretical knowledge, each phase of the course project is accompanied by theoretical readings relevant to the current project phase. The course has 10 learning modules woven into the 16-week course project. Topics include the anthropological perspective, the concept of culture, comparisons of theoretical models used by different disciplines, theories on team-building and practical manuals on developing a field guide, and various methods for coding data and finding themes. By the end of the course, students are expected to pull this knowledge together to develop explanatory models to explain findings supported by research literature. While each learning module includes a theoretical overview of the weekly topic, we realize one course cannot give all the theory students need. However, what is provided has two benefits: the theory provides a foundation on which students will build, and it allows them to work with the theory as it connects to practice and vice versa (Squires and Mack 2012).

Applied Theses with a Design & Technology Focus

Students have conducted numerous applied thesis projects related to design and technology. For example, Matthew Baline, who was employed at Cisco, investigated user needs for the design of a mobile version of Cisco's online support services (the "help desk"). His study targeted Cisco "partners" who install Cisco products. He uncovered previously unknown problems with support services and surprising constraints in the daily work experience of those who install Cisco products. Diana Harrelson conducted a study for Red Hat on what motivates members of an open-source community, the Fedora Project, to join and to remain active contributors. Her recommendations included reducing the technical challenges to joining the community, improving communication methods, and showing participants how their work made a difference. Jennifer Cardew Kersey helped Intrepid Consultants, a market research company, develop a suite of virtual ethnography methods. She developed and tested these virtual research methods over the course of three client projects, and then developed a training program for employees. Her thesis exhaustively reviewed previous research on virtual ethnographic methods and reflected on the challenges of translating between academic and applied approaches.

After graduation, our design anthropology students begin the work of building a career. Megan Bannon, a 2007 graduate, was hired by her applied thesis client, the marketing agency RAPP: "I was hired on originally as a strategist, but given the visibility of my thesis project within the agency, I was soon asked to head up the creation of an anthropology-based research department. Working directly with the global Chief Strategy Officer, we built a global group that conducted primary, secondary, and social media research." Later, she joined SapientNitro's Experience Research team and now lives in London: "I'm at an interesting juncture in my career now, straddling research and strategy, and trying to blur the lines between the two. My ultimate goal is to become a Chief Culture Officer, as Grant McCracken outlines in his book *Chief Culture Officer*, but that's quite a few years off at this point."

CURRENT GROWTH AREAS

In addition to the established foci of organizational anthropology and design anthropology, business anthropology at UNT is starting to expand into two additional areas, based on student interest and interviews with senior business anthropologists (Mack and Squires 2011). We describe them briefly to highlight the emergent nature of our program.

Marketing

Anthropology is a popular minor for marketing doctoral students at UNT. Marketing products and services are coming under increasing pressure from rapid technical and sociocultural changes, and business executives now ask marketing professionals for deeper insights into the lives of consumers so they can "reframe" product placement and messaging. Squires brings consulting experience in market research to our program (Squires and Wall 2002). Given the strong interest in this topic by both marketing and applied anthropology students, we continue to explore how best to provide anthropological theory and methods to support students who want to build skills and knowledge about customer research that will support appropriate product placement and advertising messaging based on customer needs and preferences.

Strategy

Senior business anthropologists are taking on leadership roles in their organizations. In these new roles, they find themselves informing strategy and organizational change (Flynn and Lovejoy 2008; Mack and Squires 2011; see also Morais, this volume). For instance, DePaula and his Intel colleagues described themselves as "decision-makers in the corporate business environment" who are being asked "to contribute as product and business strategists" (DePaula et al. 2009:3). While the next generation of business anthropologists may not immediately find jobs that contribute to corporate strategy, some will eventually find themselves in such roles, and we are exploring ways to prepare our students not only for that first job, but for subsequent roles as they are promoted. This topic is relevant to all specialty areas in the UNT anthropology master's program, although the specifics of leadership may vary in different sectors. The required course, Preparation for Practice and the Applied Thesis, includes lessons about future management and leadership challenges. It draws on Riall Nolan's *Anthropology in Practice* to explore these issues (2003).

CONCLUSIONS

In reflecting on the last 13 years of the UNT master's program in applied anthropology, we have identified a somewhat heterogeneous collection of insights that might be valuable to other programs. Some of them are lessons learned, some of them are best practices, some are fundamental philosophical perspectives. Most also apply more generally to any applied anthropology master's program.

The Value of an All-Applied Department & College

The program at UNT has several advantages that other programs may not have: (1) having business anthropologists involved in the development of the applied program allowed us to create a favorable atmosphere for our work; (2) being in an anthropology department allowed us to develop a program that made extensive use of anthropological theory; and (3) being located in an applied department and an applied school prevented the tensions that often arise between applied and traditional social scientists and allowed us to focus our energy on applied work. We feel these three advantages have been valuable in allowing us to develop a strong program.

The Need for a Pre-Practicum Course

At first, the new master's program in applied anthropology included a two-semester practicum sequence as students' capstone experience but no pre-practicum course. Based on her experience with the National Association for the Practice of Anthropology (a unit of the American Anthropological Association) Mentor Program and her research on best practices in applied anthropology programs concerning internships and practicums, Wasson recommended adding a pre-practicum course to the requirements for the master's degree. Most programs had a pre-practicum course. Moreover, there seemed to be a need for such a course at UNT; students expressed concern about not feeling adequately prepared to find a practicum site and not knowing how to successfully conduct a practicum project. The suggestion was accepted, and Wasson was asked to develop the course. It has been taught every year since 2003, and is valued by students.

The Political Consequences of Labeling the Capstone Project

From its beginnings in 2000, the UNT master's program in applied anthropology included a two-semester practicum sequence as the students' capstone experience. The practicum was a research project for a client. Students were required to deliver two kinds of outputs. First, they prepared deliverables for the client, which might take the form of a written report, a verbal presentation, a video, a website, a training module, or some combination of these. Second, they prepared a scholarly report for the anthropology department.

In 2011, the department decided to rename the "practicum" to an "applied thesis." The name change did not represent any substantive change in the requirements for students. The new name was selected to raise the status of the degree in the eyes of the university administration. For many in the administration, the term "practicum" connoted a project lacking in theoretical sophistication. Furthermore, some funding sources for graduate students were only available to students working on a "thesis." The decision to rename the capstone project was therefore based on a recognition of university politics and a wish to enable our students to access as much funding as possible.

Our Fundamental Philosophy: The Merging of Theory & Practice

For us, theory and practice are interdependent knowledge sets within the discipline of anthropology and fundamental to any applied anthropology program. To become effective practitioners, we believe our students need a solid knowledge base in anthropological theory in combination with extensive experience working on client projects to prepare them for the world of practice; this shared understanding of practice has shaped our master's program. All master's students are required to take Anthropological Thought and Praxis I and II. Further, many of our required courses include a client project that provides our students with a firsthand opportunity to apply the theories and methods that they have learned in the pursuit of client goals. By the time they graduate, our goal is to prepare our students to be sophisticated, theoretically informed practitioners.

REFERENCES

Aiken, Jo. In press. "Close Encounters of the Client Kind." *Practicing Anthropology* 36(2). Special issue, "Practicing Anthropology in the Private Sector."

Baba, Marietta. 2000. "Theories of Practice in Anthropology: A Critical Appraisal." *NAPA Bulletin* 18:17–44.

______. 2012. "Anthropology and Business: Influence and Interests." *Journal of Business Anthropology* 1(1):20–71.

Benson, J. 2001. "Challenging a Paradigm in Two Directions: Anthropologists in Business and the Business of Practicing Anthropology." In *Careers in Anthropology: Profiles of Practitioner Anthropologists*, edited by P. L. W. Sabloff. *NAPA Bulletin* 20(1):23–7.

Bodo, D. 2001. "Communicating Anthropology." In *Careers in Anthropology: Profiles of Practitioner Anthropologists*, edited by P. L. W. Sabloff. *NAPA Bulletin* 20(1):28–30.

Briody, Elizabeth, and Tracy Meerwarth Pester. 2012. "Corporate Work: Countering the Stereotypes." Paper presented at the American Anthropological Association Annual Meeting, San Francisco, CA, November 14–18, 2012.

Davenport, Beverly, and Doug Henry. 2007. "Building a Sense of Community in an Online Class." *Practicing Anthropology* 29(1):12–15.

DePaula, R., S. Thomas, and X. Lang. 2009. "Taking the Driver's Seat: Sustaining Critical Enquiry while Becoming a Legitimate Corporate Decision Maker." Proceedings of the 2009 Ethnographic Praxis in Industry Conference. *EPIC 2009*:2–16.

Flynn, D., and T. Lovejoy. 2008. "Tracing the Arc of Ethnographic Impact: Success and (In)visibility of Our Work and Identities." Proceedings of the 2008 Ethnographic Praxis in Industry Conference. *EPIC 2008*:238–50.

Henry, Lisa, Ann Jordan, Mariela Nuñez-Janes, and Alicia Re Cruz. In press. "Synonyms for Engagement: Forging an Engaged Anthropology in North Texas." In *Annals of Anthropological Practice*, edited by Linda Bennett and Linda Whiteford.

Ikeya, N., E. Vinkhuyzen, J. Whalen, and Y. Yamauchi. 2007. "Teaching Organizational Ethnography." Proceedings of the 2007 Ethnographic Praxis in Industry Conference. *EPIC 2007*:270–82.

Klinenberg, Eric. 2002. *Heat Wave: A Social Autopsy of Disaster in Chicago (Illinois)*. Chicago, IL: University of Chicago Press.

Kolb. D. A., and R. Fry. 1975. "Toward an Applied Theory of Experiential Learning." In *Theories of Group Process*, edited by C. Cooper, 33–58. London: John Wiley.

Lombardi, G. 2009. "The Deskilling of Ethnographic Labor: Signs of an Emerging Predicament." Proceedings of the 2009 Ethnographic Praxis in Industry Conference. *EPIC 2011*:41–9.

Mack, A., and S. Squires. 2011. "Evolving Ethnographic Practitioners and Their Impact on Ethnographic Praxis." Proceedings of the 2011 Ethnographic Praxis in Industry Conference. *EPIC 2011*:18–28.

Nolan, Riall W. 2003. *Anthropology in Practice: Building a Career Outside the Academy*. Boulder, CO: Lynne Rienner Publishers.

Nuñez-Janes, Mariela, and Alicia Re Cruz. 2007. "The Pedagogy of Teaching Online Graduate Courses in the Program of Applied Anthropology." *Practicing Anthropology* 29(1):20–3.

Re Cruz, Alicia, Christina Wasson, and Tyson Gibbs. 2007. "The Whys and Hows of an Online Applied Anthropology Program: The University of North Texas Case." *Practicing Anthropology* 29(1):1–6.

Rylko-Bauer, Barbara, Merrill Singer, and John Van Willgen. 2006. "Reclaiming Applied Anthropology: Its Past, Present, and Future." *American Anthropologist* 108(1):178–90.

Sachs, Patricia. 2006. "Bushwhacking a Career." *NAPA Bulletin* 26:152–62.

Squires, Susan. 2006. "Solving Puzzles." *NAPA Bulletin* 26:191–208.

Squires, Susan, and Bryan Byrne, eds. 2002. *Creating Breakthrough Ideas: The Collaboration of Anthropologists and Designers in the Product Development Industry*. Westport, CT: Bergin and Garvey.

Squires, Susan, and Alexandra Mack. 2012. "Renewing Our Practice: Preparing the Next Generation of Practitioners." Proceedings of the 2012 Ethnographic Praxis in Industry Conference. *EPIC 2012*:296–310.

Squires, Susan, and George Wall. 2002. "From Discovery to Launch: Unpacking the Fuzzy Front End." Paper presented at the Annual International Conference of the Product Development Management Association, Orlando, FL, October 1–3.

Tian, Robert G. 2012. "We Need Business Anthropology Education: Editorial Commentary." *International Journal of Business Anthropology* 3(1):11–14.

Wasson, Christina. 2000. "Ethnography in the Field of Design." *Human Organization* 59(4):377–88.

_____. 2006. "Making History at the Frontier." *NAPA Bulletin* 26:1–19.

_____. 2007. "Designing the First Online Master's Program in Applied Anthropology." *Practicing Anthropology* 29(1):7–11.

Wasson, Christina, Mary Odell Butler, and Jacqueline Copeland-Carson, eds. 2012. *Applying Anthropology in the Global Village*. Walnut Creek, CA: Left Coast Press.

Wasson, Christina, and Crysta Metcalf. 2006. "Modeling a Corporate-Academic Collaboration: Motorola and UNT." Workshop, Ethnographic Praxis in Industry Conference, Portland, OR, September 24–26, 2006.

______. 2013. "Teaching Design Anthropology through University-Industry Partnerships." In *Design Anthropology: Between Theory and Practice*, edited by Wendy Gunn, Ton Otto, and Rachel Charlotte Smith, 216–31. London: Berg.

NOTES

We would like to thank the following: the University of North Texas, the College of Public Affairs and Community Service, and the Department of Anthropology for supporting the business anthropology program; our former students, Jennifer Kersey, Kelly Moran, and Megan Bannon, for contributing their stories to this chapter; and Rita Denny and Patricia Sunderland for flexibility and assistance in writing this chapter.

19

Configuring Family, Kinship, & Natural Cosmology: Branding Pet Food

MARYANN MCCABE

INTRODUCTION

An article about Take Your Dog to Work Day recently published in a local newspaper caught my eye (Manning 2012). It reminded me of Take Our Daughters to Work, the program founded by Gloria Steinem and the *Ms.* Foundation for Women in 1993. The program on taking dogs to work was started in 1999 by Pet Sitters International. Participation in these two annual celebrations, taking children to work in April and dogs in June, has grown since each program began. The goals of these events clearly differ, but I was struck instead by their similarities: and I was startled by the pet event, despite being both a mother and pet owner. What does inclusion of dogs and children in the same kind of program encode about cultural views of pets in our everyday lives?

These popular events reflect ways that people negotiate the home-work boundary through personal possessions (Tian and Belk 2005). Displaying photos of pets in corporate offices, for example, introduces an aspect of the home-self into the work environment (Tian and Belk 2005:304). But why do pets have power to represent the home-self? The number of pet-owning households has grown steadily in the United States; today, more than half of all households owns pets. What is the cultural meaning of pets in our society?

Pet food manufacturers care about this question because of interactivity between producers and consumers in the branding process (McCabe and Malefyt 2010). Anthropologists also care about this question, and the discipline has a long tradition of work on the interaction between human and nonhuman animals. This chapter explores the deployment of anthropological concepts in consumer research through a case study of a research project for Mars Inc. The company was seeking to understand cultural assumptions underlying pet-keeping practices to reposition its brand of dog and cat food. Mars wanted to

Handbook of Anthropology in Business, edited by Rita Denny and Patricia Sunderland, 362–378.

identify an emotion-based positioning that would capture and express the relationship between humans and their pets. The case study highlights the value of anthropological analysis in the business environment of consumers and competitors.

My research colleague and I discovered that pet-keeping practices raise core anthropological issues of family, kinship, and natural cosmology. Anthropology has long addressed relations between human and non-human animals because of animism, totemic practices with species of animals, and cross-cultural pet-keeping practices with individual animals (Gray and Young 2011). Much of the anthropological literature focuses on the liminality of nonhuman animals based on animal-human, nature-culture, and wild-tame dichotomies in the work of Lévi-Strauss ([1962] 1966), Douglas (1966), and Tambiah (1969).

My analysis of how families are constituted with dogs and cats is fueled by the new processual view of kinship (Bamford and Leach 2009b:14). In line with more recent scholarship eschewing predetermined oppositions (Bamford and Leach 2009a; Carsten 2000, 2004; Franklin and McKinnon 2001a), I seek the meaning of pets in indigenous terms through pet-keeping practices and metaphors in folk discourse. Key metaphors of pet ownership are "blood," "home," and "complete family." I explore these metaphorical expressions for their meaning in the historical and social context of pet-keeping in the United States, and then see where the pet metaphors break down (Belk 1996) and lead to contradictions in folk discourse and the play of tropes (Fernandez 1991). Analysis of these metaphors opens a window on consumption creating culture (Arnould and Thompson 2005; Wallendorf and Arnould 1991).

In this chapter, I first look at processes whereby pets are incorporated into the family through a kinship trope and how people use pets to create family in everyday life. Then I explore what rescue reveals about human relationships with pets because most cats and dogs are now obtained through rescue from animal shelters and given a home. Finally, I discuss how pet-keeping practices are changing perceptions of the human-animal boundary and reconfiguring beliefs about natural cosmology. Nature, like kinship, is whatever we imagine it to be, and the category of nature has become problematized as a shifting classificatory process (Franklin et al. 2000). The meaning of pet ownership emerging from this analysis provided symbolic material for crafting a new positioning.

METHODOLOGY

I have conducted marketing research for three pet food companies. This project for Mars and its advertising agency, TBWA\Chiat\Day, was done at a time when the brand was a fairly new player in a crowded marketplace (2008). Mars had initially positioned the brand as a good-tasting, healthy meal, but the company and its agency wanted to differentiate it by developing a unique positioning in the pet food industry.

Mars chose Philadelphia and Nashville as research sites because they were strong and representative markets for the brand. I asked anthropologist Mark Rogers to do the fieldwork with me; each of us worked in one city. We conducted 12 in-home interviews of three-and-a-half hours that included a home tour, observation of the families' interactions with their pets, and a shop-along when we accompanied respondents on visits to stores where they usually buy pet food. During these store visits, respondents provided "stream of consciousness" narration of their thoughts and feelings as they perused pet food aisles and made purchase selections. We also conducted six small group interviews with six participants each; these were done in local market research facilities and each lasted two hours.

Prior to the individual and group interviews, all respondents completed two homework assignments: they created a collage of what having dogs and cats means to them, and took photos to show their pets' personalities, behavior patterns, favorite activities, and interactions with family members. All of our respondents were women, 25 to 54 years old with children under 18 living in the household. A national recruiting firm recruited a group representing a demographic mix (in terms of employment, household income, marital status, education, and ethnicity) as well as a variety of brand choices across the pet food price spectrum.

The in-home interviews were oriented to learning about the women's daily lives, values, and worldviews; histories of pet ownership; current experiences with pets at home; and pet care, including food. The purpose of the small group interviews was to explore and hone positioning ideas identified during the in-home interviews. Members of the company and advertising team joined us for interviews in the field, and our exchange was productive and conducive to identifying key elements for new positioning of pets as social connectors.

PETS & PET FOOD

Pet ownership has become widespread in the United States and Europe since the second half of the nineteenth century (Irvine 2004). The most recent survey of the leading trade association, the American Pet Products Association, indicates that in the United States it rose from 56 percent of households in 1988 to 62 percent in 2012. Cats and dogs are by far the largest categories of pets owned: there are 86.4 million cats and 78.2 million dogs living in US households (APPA 2012). Pet-keeping has expanded to a point of overpopulation. Approximately 6 million dogs and cats are euthanized in animal shelters in the United States each year (Serpell 1996).

Not surprisingly, sales in the pet industry also continue to rise. Pet owners spent $53 billion on food and accoutrements for their pets in 2011, up from $17 billion in 1994 (APPA 2012). This high rate of spending, coupled with increasing pet ownership, indicates that something remarkable is happening with pet relationships in our society. Zoologist James Serpell (1996) encourages us to consider the anomaly of our loving treatment of pets compared with the brutal treatment animals receive in agribusiness. The anthropological lens of this case study brings to light how pets are incorporated into family life and the human world while connecting us to the animal and natural world.

Of the total amount that consumers spent on their pets in 2011, the largest category is pet food, which accounts for 39 percent of total spending, or $20 billion (APPA 2012). Commercial pet food first appeared in the United States in the early twentieth century (Grier 2007) and today is generally considered safe and scientifically formulated (Nestle and Nesheim 2010) despite recalls from manufacturers (Nestle 2008). Nutritionists have argued that studies provide limited evidence for the benefit of commercial diets, though they provide no evidence for harm (Nestle and Nesheim 2010:272). There is oversight of the pet food industry, but it is complex and there are both gaps and overlaps in the regulatory authority of the US Food and Drug Administration, feed control officials in each state, and the American Association of Feed Control Officials (AAFCO), a nonprofit, voluntary organization that sets standards for ingredients in pet food (Nestle and Nesheim 2010:90).

Pet food brands have formed a rather homogenous positioning field based on healthy food—promoting concepts such as wholesome, natural, nutritious, or scientifically formulated—because there is impetus to earn the coveted "complete and balanced" label from AAFCO (Nestle and Nesheim 2010:31). Although this positioning speaks to people's desire to give their pets good food, it represents very limited brand differentiation in the marketplace. In this context, Mars, the largest pet food manufacturer worldwide, sought to develop new positioning through insight gained from ethnography. Previous experience working with anthropologists led the company and its ad agency to believe that ethnography would provide valuable insight into cultural practices relating to pet-keeping in homes.

PETS AS SOCIAL CONNECTORS

We discovered that mothers use pets to create family in everyday life. Pets provide focus for interaction among human family members. They are a catalyst, something to talk about, a cause for interacting. "Not a day goes by in our house," commented one mother, "without discussion of our pets, like how cute they are or the silly things they do." Pets shape shared experiences when, for example, parents and children take their dog to the dog park or dress up their cat for Halloween. Women participating in our research emphasized their continual need to find ways to get family members to talk, share thoughts and feelings, and do things as a family. Pets become adjuncts in the process of creating and strengthening bonds in the family. This reflects a notion of relatedness in defining kinship as a "process rather than a state of being" (Bamford and Leach 2009b:10).

For our respondents, pets are subjects, not objects or things, possessions, or commodities. Through anthropomorphism, pet owners recognize their dogs and cats as minded and sentient beings. They attribute human-like characteristics such as thoughts, feelings, intentions, and personalities to their pets. Our respondents said that when you look into your pet's eyes, you know intelligence and emotion are there. They told stories about pets being smart and feeling happy, sad, angry, and jealous. To grant subjectivity through anthropomorphism, says geographer Rebekah Fox, is "a human means of acknowledging the animal's role in an active reciprocal relationship" (2006:531). This is a step beyond thinking of animals acting solely on instinct. Anthropomorphism is one way pets become members of the family.

We learned from our respondents how pets are drawn into the reciprocity of family life. Based on our observations, spontaneous interactions with pets engender playful behavior and conversations among children, parents, and grandparents in the home. We observed more purposeful interactions involving pets and children where, for instance, a mother praises a pet for "licking its plate clean" and gives voice to the pet to encourage the child to eat the food on his or her plate. Pets are resources for communication (Tannen 2007). As linguist Deborah Tannen explains, when a mother speaks out loud for a dog, she frames the dog as participant in family interaction. Speaking through, for, and to dogs can buffer criticism, deliver praise, teach values, resolve conflict, and create a family identity that includes the dog as a family member.

The identity of a pet-owning family is contoured through the sensory and emotional experience of interacting with the animal over its lifetime. This experience with a dog or cat produces memories for the family in much the same way as Sutton (2001) discusses food and memory. A pet provides shared embodied intimacy with mnemonic power. When human family members hear, see, touch, and smell their dogs and cats while playing with them and tending to their needs, they become closer and develop memories. Keeping pets is a generative process for families insofar as interactions create family bonds in the present and memories for the future.

According to our research participants, pets are necessary to "complete the family." Pets make the family whole because they are part of the perceived natural order. With their distinct species' intelligence and sentience, pets demonstrate "nature" and the world around us. One mother, for instance, recalled the time the family cat came to the front door with a still-wiggling rodent in its mouth. It was a moment for teaching her children about the knowledge, skills, and lifeways of animals. They bring something unique and nonhuman to our lives. Mothers raise their children with pets so that the children develop empathy, compassion, and responsibility caring for the animal and gain life experience through the animal's growth and eventual death. A home with lots of warm and fun interactions between human and nonhuman species is considered complete.

Blood, Family, & Kinship

We found that people who have pets speak of them in kinship terms. Our respondents claim their cats and dogs are "like blood" and members of the family. Using the metaphor of blood in reference to pets reprises David Schneider's seminal idea that kinship in the United States rests on the concept of blood as a substance that relates people to one another (Schneider 1968). Schneider realized that kinship is not a natural system based on the biogenetic substance of blood but a symbolic system where the concept of blood is used to create relationality. Blood is a cultural means by which pet owners incorporate animals as members of the family. It creates a form of interspecies relatedness between humans and animals that are pets in the family. As an analytic term, blood has unbounded properties, can move between domains including those of human and animal, and does not connote an immutable essence but something subject to change depending on context (Carsten 2011). Cross-culturally, blood is only one of the substances configuring kinship. Others include semen, milk, bone, flesh, soul, and genes. Relatedness comes into practice through the symbolic action of these substances. Yet in the case of pets, the idea of shared blood exists in tandem with awareness of species difference. This is what makes relationships with pets so powerful. We simultaneously inhabit different symbolic spaces, where pets are like us and not like us, creating dynamic force that connects family and family with nature.

Pet-keeping practices demonstrate how kinship is constructed through performance. Recognizing subjectivity in dogs and cats and conferring family membership on them configures kinship with animals on the basis of constructivism, the dominant theory of kinship in anthropology. Sahlins claims that all means of constituting kinship, whether through procreation or performance, are essentially the same (Sahlins 2011a:14), and therefore defines kinship as "mutuality of being" or people intrinsic to each other's existence (Sahlins 2011a:2). This definition moves away from predetermined notions of kinship as consanguinity and affinity that are Western cultural categories. According to practices of pet owners in the United States, pets are active subjects in constituting families through the everyday interactions of life in the household. As Viveiros de Castro relates, kin ties are created or produced "by purposeful acts of feeding, caring, sharing, loving and remembering" (2009:257).

Although kinship with pets is performative and constituted metaphorically through blood, home, and complete family, these metaphoric relationships break down in pet-keeping practices in two ways. First, when a family surrenders a dog or cat to a shelter for any reason, the constructed kinship bond with the animal comes to an end. Kinship through blood or another symbolic substance is fluid and can be done and undone because it is brought into being in practice (Franklin and McKinnon 2001b:13). The metaphors incorporating pets into families also break down in relation to power. While pets are considered members of the family in a reciprocal relationship with humans, the humans retain control over the animal's life and death (Fox 2006). Power represents an unbalance of "mutual being" (Sahlins 2011b).

Antidote to Technology

For mothers participating in our study, pets resolve imbalances between technology and sociality that occur in everyday family life. Technology, sometimes a centrifugal force separating individual family members when they spend time connected to phones, tablets, computers, and other technological devices, constrains the sense of family togetherness. The busy lives that people lead with family members each pursuing different interests and activities adds to the atomization of the family. When this happens, our respondents say pets are "free therapy." They act as a centripetal force stimulating interaction and restoring balance between private and public time and space in the household. Pets become a respite from isolating experiences with technological devices by encouraging family interaction. In this sense, pets are interlocutors in the performance of kinship.

Pets let people negotiate family relationships in the technological culture of the United States. Psychologist Sherry Turkle (2011) suggests that technology is the architect of our intimacies because we are lonely but fearful. We would rather text than talk, she argues, to avoid the messy, frustrating and complex world of people and, as a result, machines substitute for connecting with each other face-to-face. Fear of public exposure is a common theme in the domestication of new media technologies as people worry about maintaining privacy while making connections (Horst 2012; Miller 2012). Of course, virtual pets can become members of the family and stir interaction among family members, but the virtualness of pets and pet games like Tamagotchi means loss of embodied animals and opportunity to learn directly from them about their world and ours (Davies 2000).

RESCUE, HOME, & MORALITY

The animal welfare and the animal rights movements in the United States have strongly influenced attitudes and behavior toward animals and pets in this country. Their activities have created a voice often heard in the media. Although the two movements are different in origin and mission, they form key parts of the broader cultural and historical context shaping pet-keeping practices in the family and treatment of animals in society. Adopting animals from shelters has become a popular way of adding pets to the family. This section examines what rescuing animals means to people and discusses contested public discourse on the morality of pet ownership. The analysis leads to an important part of positioning strategy for pets as social connectors not only within the family but also between the family and nature.

Animal Welfare

Known through its humane societies, the animal welfare movement has roots in the late nineteenth century and concern over cruelty to animals at a time when pet ownership was beginning its long and continuing rise in the United States. This movement is oriented to reforming treatment of animals and to educating the public (Sperling 1988). In response to the problem of pet overpopulation, the animal welfare movement has successfully promoted acquisition of pets through adoption from shelters operated by local humane societies. The American Humane Association website,[1] for example, says that the best place to find a dog or a puppy is your local animal shelter or breed rescue group, and encourages people to give a dog a second chance at finding a home. Buying a pet from a pet store is discouraged because pet stores typically buy animals from puppy mills, the high-volume, low-standard facilities where dogs are often kept in gruesome conditions as they churn out litter after litter of merchandise for the nation's pet stores (Schaffer 2009).

We learned from our research participants who obtained dogs or cats from shelters that a compelling metaphor is the "cage"; that is, rescuing animals from a confined space where they are kept in the shelter. They described the emotional experience of walking through shelters, being attracted to certain animals, and wanting to free them from life in a cage. On display in a shelter, animals are a collection of objects of desire (Stewart 1993). As a collection, they are reordered not as existing naturally in the shelter but temporarily there, available for adoption and ready for rehoming. Stewart writes that a collection is "a form involving the reframing of objects within a world of attention and manipulation of context" (1993:151). Bringing animals home frees them not only from the cage but also from being objects on view. Adoption makes them subjects in the family.

To rescue is a heroic act for our research participants. They feel pulled toward saving animals from confinement and display as well as the euthanasia that results from overcrowding in shelters. A "no-kill" policy has become popular among shelter advocates, but only a small percentage of shelters pursue this policy. It requires organization and maintenance of a foster care system in the community that provides care until animals are ready for adoption. Rescue enhances the sense of self by making people feel they are doing something positive in the world.

Giving a dog or cat a home underlies motivation for rescue. "Home" has several referents in this context. According to our respondents, giving a pet a home means providing a safe and secure place to sleep, making food available morning and evening, meeting the animal's medical needs, giving affection, and making the animal part of your family. As one woman said, "Rescuing animals means preventing them from being euthanized and giving them a good life in which they are secure, active, nurtured physically and emotionally, and loved." Rescue is a galvanizing and polarizing issue. "It's like religion and politics. We don't discuss it," said another woman angry with her sister for getting a puppy through a breeder instead of rescue. The power of the rescue idea resides in the cultural values of freedom (no cage) and home (being part of a family) and is so potent that giving a home to a pet is important even to homeless people (Kidd and Kidd 1994).

Animal Rights

If the animal welfare movement counsels reform, the animal rights movement urges revolution (Sperling 1988). The animal rights movement has raised questions about the morality of pet ownership because animal rights advocates recast the boundary between humans and animals in a more limited way than previously posited in public discourse. This grassroots movement, which organized in the late 1970s to protest treatment of animals in laboratories for biomedical and behavioral research, has been critical of technological society and domination of the body and nature by science and medicine (Sperling 1988). State laws in the post–World War II era helped to foster use of animals for lab research by allowing universities access to abandoned animals and seizure from pounds.

Although the animal rights movement is not unitary, including advocates, activists, and rescuers from diverse ideological perspectives (Greenebaum 2009), adherents generally subscribe to ideas proposed by philosopher Peter Singer in *Animal Liberation* (1975), considered the movement's bible. Singer based his thinking on Jeremy Bentham's utilitarian notions put forward in 1781 in *The Principles of Morals and Legislation* that animals can suffer regardless of their inability to think or speak. Singer advanced the concept of "speciesism," calling for equal consideration of human and animal rights and suggesting that humanity's treatment of animals constitutes illegitimate and immoral oppression because use of animals in lab research makes them victims of patriarchal and capitalist forces (Sperling 1988). When animal rights proponents claim that a significantly great gap does not exist between humans and animals, a moral red flag is raised over pet ownership. In discourse, the issue becomes a philosophical one of whether animals have intrinsic worth. As anthropologist Elizabeth Lawrence (1995) poses the question, are the differences between humans and animals morally relevant and therefore let us exclude animal interests when they conflict with our own? According to the animal rights movement, the answer is no: humans and animals are moral equals. This point is contested among scholars. Sociologist Leslie Irvine (2004) argues that moral equality would mean the end of pets. She writes, "For if animals have the right not to be treated as things, then we cannot justify breeding them simply to serve as our companions. If we recognize the intrinsic value of animals' lives, then it is immoral to keep them for our pleasure, regardless of whether we call them companions or pets" (2004:14). In contrast, anthropologist Susan Sperling (1988) openly questions the central assertion of the animal rights movement that animals and humans share equal moral status and supports regulation to ensure humane treatment of lab animals. Geographer Rebekah Fox takes a centrist position that recognizes similarities and differences between humans and animals and proposes an ethics of care that is rejected in animal rights ideology (2006:534).

This contested discourse on moral parity reflects the fact that we are grappling with the relationship between humans and animals in our society. Scientific representations are changing as a result of new research on human-animal boundaries, and this affects popular as well as academic thinking (Fox 2006). Pet-keeping practices reveal shifts in the perceived cosmological relationship of humans and animals.

SHIFTS IN NATURAL COSMOLOGY

When our research participants described the process of choosing animals to adopt, they spoke about going to a shelter and "falling in love" with a specific animal. This metaphor was elaborated in the romantic experience of "love at first sight," "immediate attraction," and "instant connection." Captured in the metaphorical expression are two different notions of emotional relationship with pets. One notion is based on anthropomorphism. As a respondent said, "The kitten had an adorable face and I just fell in love with her." An adorable face anthropomorphizes the animal. The other notion implies a sense of relating to animals having consciousness and agency. A respondent, commenting on a dog selected for adoption, said, "I could tell he was just looking for a loving home." This involves reciprocity between human and animal or a relationship where there is "co-construction of emotional experience" (Cheetham and McEachern 2012:5).

Thus, among pet owners, tension exists in the perceived relationship of humans to animals. Because anthropomorphism is rooted in domination and human attempt to elevate the human species from the rest of the animal kingdom (Bettany and Belk 2011), the tension likely reflects ideological movement from the Judeo-Christian tradition of domination where the earth and everything in it is created to serve man, and other animals are considered inferior to man (Serpell 1996), toward a posthumanist reconceptualization positing an interdependence of society and nature and asserting that humans are an animal species no more or less important than any other (Charles and Davies 2008).

As a socially constructed practice, pet-keeping is historically contingent and depends on how the boundary between human and animal is defined (Irvine 2004; Thomas 1983). In the United States, imaginaries about the boundary have shifted over time. Sperling writes, " Natural cosmology is not static, and important aspects of the relationship between humanity and the natural world have been contested and redefined in modern industrial society" (1988:131). Cultural perceptions about natural cosmology have altered with the move from rural agricultural life to urban industrial life amid widespread anxieties about the incursions of technologies into nature, including the ecological crisis, endangered species, genetic engineering, and industrialized agriculture (Sperling 1988).

Scientific Representations

The perceived boundary between animals and humans now stands at its narrowest point in scientific representation and the cultural history of the United States. There are several reasons for the current thin construction of the boundary marker. First is anthropomorphism of pets. For pet owners, anthropomorphizing is a step in becoming a member of the family as quasi-human (Belk 1996), although this is contested by posthumanist discourse that equates anthropomorphism with human domination of other species. Second is the ideology of the animal rights movement, which accords intrinsic value to animals and grants moral equality to animal and human species. Taken to its extreme, posthumanist thought defines pet ownership as immoral control of one species over another. Third is scientific research on animal capabilities that has profoundly affected how the boundary between humans and animals is imagined

(Hurn 2012; Lawrence 1995). Animal behavior studies, especially in primatology, have revealed cognitive and communicative skills of nonhuman primates not previously realized. Results of these studies on sentience and use of language and tools, which make animals seem more like humans, have been brought to public attention through television, print, and online media. Scientific representations have influenced popular attitudes toward animals and blurred the boundary between animals and humans that had been defined so widely in Christian theology and Cartesian dualism (Sperling 1988).

The thinness of the line constructed between humans and animals is nowhere more apparent than in recent scholarship ascribing agency to animals (McFarland and Hediger 2009). Granting nonhuman agency moves beyond anthropomorphism to regarding animals as active subjects with self-awareness or consciousness, allowing them to affect people with whom they are interacting. From this perspective, anthropologist Samantha Hurn says animals may have "capacity to impact on the relationships between the humans involved, leading some researchers to refer to these multi-species interactions as 'intersubjective'" (Hurn 2012:125). For example, ethnographic studies on chimps and the people who care for them (Taylor 2007) and horses and the people who ride and groom them (Cassidy 2002) suggest some form of intersubjective relationship exists between humans and animals. Intersubjectivity assumes that human and animal actors recognize mindedness and intentionality in each other and empathize with each other (Hurn 2012). This line of thinking extends to recognizing animal personhood. Yet it is a "flexible personhood," argues anthropologist Dafna Shir-Vertesh (2012), based on pet-keeping practices in Israel that are similar to those in the United States and Europe. When a pet is surrendered to a shelter, the animal's connection to the family and the animal's personhood are both altered. As Shir-Vertesh writes, ". . . . the termination of the familial relationship with the animals is related to the termination, at least to a certain extent, of their personhood" (2012:427).

Broadening the Human-centric World

For our research participants, pets create links to nature. A respondent mused, "I grew up with dogs and value what they bring to the family: responsibility, companionship, love, and a lot of fun. I also believe that having a dog or a cat helps you to be considerate and compassionate toward the nonhuman world: animals, plants, trees, waters, et cetera." Pets expand a human-centric world. Belonging to a different species, they bring the natural world, however imagined, to the family. This experience of nature is something to enjoy and celebrate because it enriches family life.

Anthropologist Tim Ingold (1994a) speaks about the historically placed boundary between humans and animals in terms of people's attitudes toward animals. He argues that trust characterized the attitude toward animals in hunter-gatherer societies and then domination once domestication occurred. Pet-keeping practices in the United States reveal a newly emergent attitude. A sense of partnership connects pet owners to animals and the natural world in a single field of relationships. Dogs and cats as pets are partners participating in the work of creating family and inhabiting a shared interspecies planet. When pet owners say that having a pet completes the family, they mean becoming more aware of nature by living with a unique and nonhuman but sentient species. This draws humans and pets into the same sociocosmic frame of reference.

CONCLUSION

For a new positioning strategy, Mars embraced the idea of pets as social connectors based on our ethnographic research. This idea provided a way of making emotional connections with pet owners. Going beyond the concept of health typical of pet food brands in the marketplace, it yielded a point of differentiation for the Mars brand. The company's advertising agency developed a brand narrative drawing links between nutritious food, healthy pets, connecting people, and closer family. Mars was able to draw on the understanding of pets as catalysts for family interaction, antidotes to isolating technology, and links to the natural world. In this case study, we see that anthropological analysis helps to shape business strategy.

We proposed to the company and its advertising agency that brand strategy orient outreach to mothers and the role they play in creating family life. The idea of pets as social connectors would lend itself to images of families interacting with their pets, a point of differentiation for Mars because other brands were using images of individuals with their pets. Our ethnographic research indicated that this approach to strategy and communications would resonate with women, who tend to be the primary pet food shoppers. It would express the affect of giving the pet healthy and tasty food not only to maintain the animal's health but also show appreciation to the pet for bringing the family closer together.

An ad campaign for a Mars pet food brand produced after our research results were delivered seems to have implemented the new positioning. The campaign featured a dog and a cat, anthropomorphized characters, living in a home with a family. From a semiotic glance at a set of print advertisements, it is apparent that the pets are part of family life. A child plays with them, and they join the family for a ride in the car together. The cat and dog, both sentient and smart beings, know they must pose for photos in costumes designed by their owners. The dog and cat display feelings like fear at thunder and lightening. They cuddle but then swear secrecy about their human-like behavior, giving evidence of species difference, and also show typical animal behavior such as hissing to ward off predators. These print ads use humor to portray the fun of family life among humans with animals from the natural world. Visualized in the print ads is the positioning idea of pets as a point of connection within the family and with nature.

Scientific representations of the relation between humans and animals have assumed a human-animal boundary portrayed in terms of either differences in degree or differences in kind (Ingold 1994b). Recent studies on human-animal intersubjectivity push the degree of difference to a thin point. However, perception of a boundary between humans and animals is not a cultural universal, as the ethnography of Amazonia illustrates (Allen 2002; de la Cadena 2011). In the Andean case, humans, ancestors, gods, animals, and features of the natural world are integrated in the indigenous definition of community.

Although natural cosmology in the United States is conceived less holistically, pet-keeping practices reflect a change in the way humans perceive themselves in relation to animals and the natural world. Humans are now imagined to coexist more in partnership with nonhuman animals than in domination of the natural world. These cross-cultural differences in natural cosmology between Amazonia and the United States are based on distinct ontological assumptions (Fausto 2007; Viveiros de Castro 2009). In the US case, as we have seen, the assumptions have been predicated on a human-animal divide in the western tradition that is now contested by a posthumanist discourse in which humans are considered an animal species no more or less important than any other (Charles and Davies 2008).

Pet-keeping practices indicate how consumption creates culture. The continuing rise in number of pet-owning households in the United States and increasing purchase of pet food and the many other provisions that people buy for their pets constructs the family in a new way. Human relationships with pets configure kinship as a symbolic and performative process where blood renders animals family members necessary to complete the domestic unit. Adopting dogs and cats through rescue and bringing them into the home makes them subjects in the family. Mothers and pets become partners in fostering interaction within the family. This grants agency to animals, since they are perceived to have ability to connect us to each other and to the natural world. Pets also become actors in the wider social context. They counter isolating tendencies of technology in home environments and help to create warm and fun family experiences and memories.

REFERENCES

Allen, Catherine J. 2002. *The Hold Life Has: Coca and Cultural Identity in an Andean Community*, 2nd edition. Washington, DC: Smithsonian Books.

American Pet Products Association (APPA). 2012. 2011–12 APPA National Pet Owners Survey. www.americanpetproducts.org/press_industry trends.acp (accessed August 21, 2012).

Arnould, Eric J., and Craig J. Thompson. 2005. "Consumer Culture Theory (CCT): Twenty Years of Research." *Journal of Consumer Research* 31:868–82.

Bamford, Sandra, and James Leach, eds. 2009a. *Kinship and Beyond: The Genealogical Mode Reconsidered.* New York: Berghahn.

_____. 2009b. "Introduction: Pedigrees of Knowledge: Anthropology and the Genealogical Method." In *Kinship and Beyond: The Genealogical Mode Reconsidered,* edited by S. Bamford and J. Leach, 1–23. New York: Berghahn.

Belk, Russell W. 1996. "Metaphoric Relationships with Pets." *Society and Animals* 4(2):121–45.

Bettany, Shona, and Russell W. Belk. 2011. "Disney Discourses of Self and Other: Animality, Primitivity, Modernity, and Postmodernity." *Consumption, Markets & Culture* 14:163–76.

Carsten, Janet. 2000. *Cultures of Relatedness: New Approaches to the Study of Kinship.*

Cambridge, UK: Cambridge University Press.

_____. 2004. *After Kinship.* Cambridge, UK: Cambridge University Press.

_____. 2011. "Substance and Relationality: Blood in Contexts." *Annual Review of Anthropology* 40:19–35.

Cassidy, R. 2002. *The Sport of Kings: Kinship, Class and Thoroughbred Breeding in Newmarket.* Cambridge, UK: Cambridge University Press.

Charles, Nickie, and Charlotte Aull Davies. 2008. "My Family and Other Animals: Pets as Kin." *Sociological Research Online* 13(5)4. doi:10.5153/sro.1798.

Cheetham, Fiona, and Morven G. McEachern. 2012. "Extending Holt's Consuming Typology To Encompass Subject-Subject Relations in Consumption: Lessons from Pet Ownership." *Consumption, Markets & Culture* doi:10.1080/10253866.2011.652826.

Davies, Gail. 2000. "Virtual Animals in Electronic Zoos: The Changing Geographies of Animal Capture and Display." In *Animal Spaces, Beastly Spaces: New Geographies of Human-Animal Relations,* edited by C. Philo and C. Wilbert, 243–66. London: Routledge.

de la Cadena, Marisol. 2011. "Alternative archives: Understanding indigenous politics the Andean way." Presented at Henry Lewis Morgan Lectures, University of Rochester, New York, October 19, 2011.

Douglas, Mary. 1966. *Purity and Danger: An Analysis of Concepts of Pollution and Taboo.* London: Routledge.

Fausto, Carlos. 2007. "Feasting on People." *Current Anthropology* 44: 497–514, 521–4.

Fernandez, James W. 1991. *Beyond Metaphor: The Theory of Tropes in Anthropology.* Stanford, CA: Stanford University Press.

Fox, Rebekah. 2006. "Animal Behaviours, Post-Human Lives: Everyday Negotiations of the Animal-Human Divide in Pet-Keeping." *Social and Cultural Geography* 7:525–37.

Franklin, Sarah, and Susan McKinnon, eds. 2001a. *Relative Values: Reconfiguring Kinship Studies.* Durham, NC: Duke University Press.

_____. 2001b. "Introduction." In *Relative Values: Reconfiguring Kinship Studies,* edited by S. Franklin and S. McKinnon, 1–25. Durham, NC: Duke University Press.

Franklin, Sarah, Celia Lury, and Jackie Stacey. 2000. *Global Nature, Global Culture.* London: Sage.

Gray, Peter B. and Sharon M. Young. 2011. "Human-Pet Dynamics in Cross-Cultural Perspective." *Anthrozoos* 24:17–30.

Greenebaum, Jessica. 2009. "'I'm not an activist!': Animal Rights vs. Animal Welfare in the Purebred Dog Rescue Movement." *Society and Animals* 17(4):289–304.

Grier, Katherine C. 2007. *Pets in America: A History.* New York: Mariner Books.

Horst, Heather A. 2012. "New Media Technologies in Everyday Life." In *Digital Anthropology*, edited by H. Horst and D. Miller, 61–79. London: Bloomsbury.

Hurn, Samantha. 2012. *Humans and Other Animals: Cross-cultural Perspectives on Human-Animal Interactions.* London: Pluto Press.

Ingold, Tim. 1994a. "From Trust to Domination: An Alternative History of Human-Animal Relation." In *Animals and Human Society: Changing Perspectives*, edited by A. Manning and J. Serpell, 1–22. London: Routledge.

_____. 1994b. "Humanity and Animality." In *Companion Encyclopedia of Anthropology: Humanity, Culture and Social Life*, edited by Tim Ingold, 14–32. London: Routledge.

Irvine, Leslie. 2004. "Pampered or Enslaved? The Moral Dilemmas of Pets." *The International Journal of Sociology and Social Policy* 13:5–17.

Kidd, Aline H., and Robert M. Kidd. 1994. "Benefits and Liabilities of Pets for the Homeless." *Psychological Reports* 74:715–22.

Lawrence, Elizabeth Atwood. 1995. "Cultural Perceptions of Differences between people and Animals: A Key to Understanding Human-Animal Relationships." *The Journal of American Culture* 18:75–82.

Lévi-Strauss, Claude. (1962) 1966. *The Savage Mind.* Chicago, IL: University of Chicago Press.

Manning, Sue. 2012. "Take Your Dog to Work Day: Dogs at Work (and Play)." *Democrat and Chronicle*, June 19, C1–C2.

McCabe, Maryann, and Timothy de Waal Malefyt. 2010. "Brands, Interactivity and Contested Fields: Exploring Production and Consumption in Cadillac and Infinity Automobile Advertising Campaigns." *Human Organization* 69:252–62.

McFarland, Sarah, and Ryan Hediger, ed. 2009. *Animals and Agency: An Interdisciplinary Exploration.* Boston: Brill Academic Publishers.

Miller, Daniel. 2012. "Social Networking Sites." In *Digital Anthropology*, edited by H. Horst and D. Miller, 146–61. London: Bloomsbury.

Nestle, Marion. 2008. *Pet Food Politics: The Chihuahua in the Coal Mine.* Berkeley: University of California Press.

Nestle, Marion, and Malden C. Nesheim. 2010. *Feed Your Pet Right: The Authoritative Guide to Feeding Your Dog and Cat.* New York: Free Press.

Sahlins, Marshall. 2011a. "What Kinship Is (Part One)." *Journal of the Royal Anthropological Institute* (N.S.) 17:2–19.

_____. 2011b. "What Kinship Is (Part Two). *Journal of the Royal Anthropological Institute* (N.S.) 17:227–42.

Schaffer, Michael. 2009. *One Nation under Dog: Adventures in the New World of Prozac-Popping Puppies, Dog-Park Politics, and Organic Pet Food.* New York: Henry Holt and Company.

Schneider, David M. 1968. *American Kinship: A Cultural Account.* Englewood Cliffs, NJ: Prentice-Hall.

Serpell, James A. 1996. *In the Company of Animals: A Study of Human-Animal Relations*, 2nd edition. Cambridge, UK: Cambridge University Press.

Shir-Vertesh, Dafna. 2012. "'Flexible Personhood': Loving Animals as Family Members in Israel." *American Anthropologist* 114:420–32.

Singer, Peter. 1975. *Animal Liberation.* New York: Avon.

Sperling, Susan. 1988. *Animal Liberators: Research and Morality.* Berkeley: University of California Press.

Stewart, Susan. 1993. *On Longing: Narratives of the Miniature, the Gigantic, the Souvenir, the Collection.* Durham, NC: Duke University Press.

Sutton, David E. 2001. *Remembrance of Repasts: An Anthropology of Food and Memory.* Oxford, UK: Berg.

Tambiah, Stanley J. 1969. "Animals Are Good To Think and Good To Prohibit." *Ethnology* 8:423–59.

Tannen, Deborah. 2007. "Talking the Dog: Framing Pets as Interactional Resources in Family Discourse. In *Family Talk: Discourse and Identity in Four American Families,* edited by D. Tannen, S. Kendall, and C. Gordon, 49–69. Oxford, UK: Oxford University Press.

Taylor, Nicola. 2007. "Never an It: Intersubjectivity and the Creation of Personhood in an Animal Shelter." *Qualitative Sociology Review* 3:59–73.

Thomas, Keith. 1983. *Man and the Natural World: A History of the Modern Sensibility.* New York: Pantheon.

Tian, Kelly, and Russell W. Belk. 2005. "Extended Self and Possessions in the Workplace *Journal of Consumer Research* 32:297–310.

Turkle, Sherry. 2011. *Alone Together: Why We Expect More from Technology and Less from Each Other.* New York: Basic Books.

Viveiros de Castro, Eduardo. 2009. "The Gift and the Given: Three Nano-Essays on Kinship and magic." I*n Kinship and Beyond: The Genealogical Model Reconsidered,* edited by S. Bamford and J. Leach, 237–68. New York: Berghahn.

Wallendorf, Melanie, and Eric J. Arnould. 1991. "'We gather together': Consumption Rituals of Thanksgiving Day." *Journal of Consumer Research* 18(June):13–31.

NOTES

The author wishes to thank Mark Rogers for collaboration on fieldwork and insightful analysis of data in this project.

1 See the American Humane Society website at http://www.americanhumane.org/.

20

Ethnography Guiding Brand Strategy: Rum & Real Blokes

NICK AGAFONOFF, JULIEN CAYLA, & BELINDA HEATH

INTRODUCTION

There is a rich literature on corporate ethnography focusing on new product design and development (Flynn et al. 2009; Salvador et al. 1999), but we still know relatively little about the role ethnography can play in guiding brand strategies. In a tale of rum, rugby, and urban tribes, this chapter describes how ethnography facilitated strategic change for an established brand by attending to the intricate system of differences between various fan groups of Australian rugby. Our work further illustrates how ethnography can help organizations deal with the complexity and ambiguity of markets (Cayla and Arnould 2013).

Indeed, the company that owns the Australian Bundaberg Rum, or "Bundy," could not understand its relative lack of success at a regional level, specifically its lack of success among fans of rugby league teams associated with mid-sized towns and suburbs in New South Wales. Extensive observations and interviews provided localized and nuanced interpretations of Australian male identity narratives, eventually helping redesign Bundy's branding strategy.

In considering the social fabric from which brand meanings emerge, we especially draw from recent work on the significance of urban tribes (Cova et al. 2007). Urban tribes are a feature of late modern sociality representing social groupings not bound by geography or kinship, but instead by the sharing of a particular sensibility, common leisure pursuits, and passions (Maffesoli 1996). In Australia, sports fandom is particularly important for the articulation of male tribal identities. Hence, sport helps maintain "mateship"—a historic Anglo-Australian form of masculinism (Evans 1992; Tacey 1997)—and operates as a cultural resource for the articulation of group identities aligned with specific sports and teams. Indeed, the groups of Australian fans we studied revealed an array of rituals, vocabularies, and other symbolic practices, including

Handbook of Anthropology in Business, edited by Rita Denny and Patricia Sunderland, 379–395.

brand loyalties, demarcating insiders from outsiders, which facilitate rivalries between groups. Brands ignore this degree of nuance at their peril.

This chapter begins by situating the ethnographic project within its particular cultural and strategic context. Then we outline key stages of the study and describe our findings, highlighting the complexity of Australian masculinities, social identities, and tribal memberships we uncovered. Finally, we draw from this case study to analyze more generally the benefits and challenges of projects that problematize the regional specifics of consumer culture. Overall, this original case study illuminates the role of corporate ethnographic research in deciphering the cultural meanings of iconic brands as produced by diverse groups of consumers.

STRATEGIC CONTEXT

Diageo, the commissioning client for this research, is a large British multinational company with a portfolio of leading alcohol brands such as Guinness beer, Smirnoff vodka, and Bundaberg Rum. Bundaberg is an icon in Australian consumer culture, an important nexus through which brand-loyal Australian males construct their identity as laid-back, friendly mates.

Bundaberg's mascot, the "Bundy bear," personifies these qualities. Introduced in 1961, the polar bear mascot originally connoted how the drink could ward off a winter chill, an attempt to expand the brand's geographical reach by enticing drinkers from the colder southern Australian states. The bear's constructed persona also evoked positive qualities of "mateship," a discourse from Australia's colonial history and the frontier survival mentality in which "a man will do anything to protect or support a mate" (Tacey 1997:135). By deploying this socio-semiotic strategy, the Bundaberg brand successfully positioned itself as a national symbol representing a distinctively Australian form of masculinity (see the Bundaberg website).[1] Despite its national status, Bundaberg, a brown rum, hails from its namesake town in the state of Queensland. Cultural loyalties have translated into uneven brand penetration across different Australian states: consumption in Queensland remains high at 53 percent of sales compared with New South Wales at 18 percent and 28 percent for the rest of the country (Diageo, personal communication, 2012).

Brown rum also has a long history of consumption in the bush dating back to early settlement and the Rum Rebellion of 1808 (Hughes and Ramson 1990). This legacy, in conjunction with rum as the traditional drink of sugar cane farmers, established Bundaberg as the authentic brown spirit for the hard-drinking "man of the land" in Queensland and rural areas of Australia. The brown spirits market includes a complicated mix of local, regional, and national identities and loyalties. In 2000, Bundaberg Rum became the key sponsor of the

Wallabies—the national rugby union team—in an attempt to meld the brand's signification with national pride. Yet in Australia, rugby union is a product of the exclusive private school system and thus is associated with economically privileged classes. Rugby league, in contrast, is the sport of working-class values, hard physicality, and regionalized identities.

A significant market weakness for Bundy was in an area that Diageo managers appropriately labeled "the bourbon belt." This region incorporates more traditional working class suburbs in the state of New South Wales, predominantly in Sydney's west and southwest, in addition to industrial areas of Wollongong and Newcastle. Essentially, the bourbon belt was rugby league territory.

This situation posed a key question for Bundaberg and Diageo: how could the brand appeal to the traditional working class suburbs of New South Wales, and what factors were currently inhibiting consumption in these markets? Brands such as Jack Daniels and Jim Beam were the highest-selling brown spirit labels in the belt. Even lowly bourbon, such as Woodstock—commonly known as "car park" bourbon—outstripped consumption of Bundaberg Rum.

Historically, these markets are also strong consumers of rugby league (Williams 2009), so Diageo committed large amounts of money to make Bundaberg Rum the main sponsor of the National Rugby League competition (NRL). The strategy was straightforward: win over rugby league fans in traditional working class suburbs of New South Wales through a sponsorship deal. As it turned out, penetration of this elusive market would not be so simple. Thus, Diageo approached research and branding consultancy Galileo Kaleidoscope with these key questions: what continued to inhibit its uptake in bourbon belt markets, despite big marketing dollars and the NRL sponsorship? Rugby league is a sport for "tough" men and brown rum is traditionally a tough man's drink in Australia, but bourbon belt men were not buying Bundy. What would happen if NRL sponsorship continued?

In many ways, this was a dream marketing challenge for the research team: Brett Donahay, account director at Galileo Kaleidoscope, and Agafonoff, a freelance market ethnographer, are both die-hard rugby league fans with extensive knowledge of rugby codes and their cultural significance. This familiarity enabled them to propose two factors that potentially influenced consumer reception of Bundaberg's NRL sponsorship: First, New South Welshmen and Queenslanders are traditional sporting rivals, so Bundaberg's Queensland heritage could alienate fans in New South Wales. Second, Diageo's high-profile sponsorship of the Wallabies potentially played into a rivalry of class and culture that alienated other fans. The national rugby union represents the nobility; the fans of rugby league represent the "Aussie battler," who maintains parochial loyalty for a local or childhood club.

The researchers told Diageo that more knowledge about local cultural identification was imperative before a sponsorship roll-out. What did it mean to belong to a rugby league consumption tribe located in the bourbon belt? Although not specifically referencing sociological theorists such as Maffesoli (1996) at the outset of the commercial proposal, Donahay and Agafonoff wanted to stress socially cohesive values, lifestyles, and attitudinal dispositions among NRL consumer groups. For example, who represented "outsiders" versus "insiders" and why? What tensions surrounded male local identities? How might these tensions be relieved or leveraged for the benefit of sponsorship? In summary, Diageo and the researchers needed to understand what Bundy represented as a cultural symbol.

At the core of the proposal was sociocultural thinking: getting beyond a focus on the individual to comprehend the relationship between individuals and groups, groups and society, society and identity, and identity in relation to consumption. To this end, the research team proposed conducting ethnographic research into the lives of rugby league followers and bourbon drinkers in traditional working-class suburbs. Donahay and Agafonoff nominated two sample regions: Penrith, in Sydney's outer-west, and Wollongong, a coastal industrial center 80 kilometers south of Sydney. Each region acts as a major social, cultural, and economic hub in the wider bourbon belt area.

DOING THE RESEARCH

The design of the ethnographic project targeted the overlapping domains of individual, social, and cultural inquiry. For example, at an individual level, how did young male NRL fans from Wollongong develop salient forms of personal identity from their geographic region and as followers of rugby league? More broadly, the researchers queried the relationship between consumers' physical worlds (Where do I live?), and how they extracted various forms of meaning from this platform (What do I live for? What do I view as integral to my identity? What does a typical day in my life/week look and feel like? What are my key challenges? What sorts of things do I aspire to/work towards/dream about?).

At a social level, the research team sought to comprehend what it meant to consume rugby league in respect to local group discourses. For example, to follow the NRL with your mates, what do you have to do to maintain social inclusion? What does this sociocultural landscape look and feel like? Who is in competition for what and why? How do groups of NRL consumers express and resolve tensions? What are the symbols of success and failure, status and power? What are the symbolic theatres through which affiliated groups of young men create and consecrate their folklore? What can these places tell us about shared values, beliefs, and aspirations? How does rugby league define shared rituals, practices, and identity?

In terms of the cultural dimensions of brand identity, the researchers also explored the relationship between individual and social identities, discourses of masculinity, and their reification as various consumption practices. What brown spirit brands did local NRL consumers esteem, and how were these perceptions manifested through group behavior? What roles did different brands play in defining shared loyalties and origins? How did "insiders" consume various brown spirit brands within the context of communal rituals and rites of passage?

The research team tailored their objectives to extract three, interrelated levels of understanding:

1. **Individual:** how does what I consume interact with my identity and why?
2. **Social:** what influences the research participants' immediate social circles and their decision-making around consumption?
3. **Macro-cultural:** what embedded narratives and discourses structure consumption patterns?

The researchers identified appropriate individuals and groups to participate in the ethnography, established rapport, and immersed themselves in participants' worlds to explore the process of belonging. Agafonoff's role as a video ethnographer ensured that the team provided ethnographically rich, salient footage and allowed both researchers to triangulate perspectives for more robust findings. Cultivating a deeper immersion process, the research team collaborated with participants to unlock collective cultural codes while creating space to consolidate insights and implications from outsider/theoretical vantage points. Furthermore, presentation of the study's key findings and observations through video allowed the client, Diageo, to connect with lived experiences in "the field."

The researchers initially recruited only two individuals, and to ensure successful "snowballing," Donahay and Agafonoff conducted a workshop with a large group of potential respondents selected by a professional agency according to key market specifications provided by the client. They identified potential collaborators and "tribal gatekeepers" as well as contexts for further exploration such as significant places and salient themes or issues such as the role of women in local identity politics. Next, a four-stage research program enabled progression from a contextual understanding of the individual, to contextual understanding of groups, to a contextual understanding of the role of consumption in defining these layers of consumer identification.

While the ethnography included a set program for engagement with the proposed sample group, the researchers stressed to the client that it was crucial for the inquiry to develop through contextual observation. Generally speaking, the holistic nature of ethnographic research means that cultural knowledge would accrue and evolve through the course of immersion in participants' social worlds, moving from the stances of outsiders to insiders, observers to participants. An iterative approach allowed the research team to return to cultural content that may have been unclear at an earlier stage of research. Hence, the researchers generated a basic framework for inquiry, trusting that specific questions would arise from the immersion.

Primary Considerations: Documenting/Analyzing Findings "Iteratively"

While engaged in fieldwork, Agafonoff and Donahay examined local rituals, practices, performances, and language pertaining to young men and rugby league consumption tribes. The researchers sought to understand places of significance and rites of passage embedded in participants' narratives, gaining a deeper perspective of their consumption culture. Participants also recorded video diaries to share and discuss with the research team, documenting distinctions between "insiders" and "outsiders" in relation to objects, brands, rituals, and practices. Both streams of video content additionally captured participants' regard for inalienable objects and practices, in contrast to those considered stigmatized or profane. Through these discussions, demonstrations, and visual tours, participants revealed important status hierarchies, individual/social tensions, aspirational frameworks, and how these values are expressed as a cultural form.

Secondary Considerations: Ramifications for Brand/Marketing Strategy

During the fieldwork period, Agafonoff and Donahay iteratively referenced emergent findings with five key queries, specifically devised by the research team to address strategic implications for the Bundaberg Rum brand.

1. How should Bundaberg/Diageo position Bundy in relation to particular regions?
2. What events should be sponsored and when?
3. What sort of promotional material/tactics are best suited for a regional marketing strategy?
4. What language should marketers use in these messages?
5. How should Bundaberg/Diageo best characterize competitor brands?

These analytical processes consisted of informal and formal discussion to generate thematic findings. However, as the researchers' video documented much of the field context, Donahay and Agafonoff remained mindful to investigate participants' vantage points before imposing theoretical perspectives onto data.

It was important for the research team to emphasize to the client that timing and outputs were contingent. They estimated that fieldwork and analysis could take between three and five months to allow for a more organic development of the project: for relationships to form, to build trust, and for researchers to gain a comprehensive understanding of the sociocultural landscape in each immersive stage. In the end, from planning to final presentation, the project took 3.5 months. This duration permitted the team to identify social and cultural phenomena that required deeper exploration that was evident only after engagement in the field.

Diageo took some convincing about the approach: the client was anxious about the a small sample size, iterative approach, focus on social and cultural investigation using immersive participant-observation techniques, and the absence of a concrete schedule for fieldwork and analysis. Departure from a focus on the individual to a sociocultural domain and from psychographic/demographic factors toward cultural geographic/ritualistic characteristics also appeared unusual. Why did Diageo sign off on the research design? In addition to personal trust, it was clear that the failure of conventional market research practices to explain Bundy's lack of success in the bourbon belt helped sell the ethnographic approach.

FINDINGS

Regional Cultural Gatekeepers

Chris, 22 years old, was a third-generation Wollongong resident and a keen surfer with a steady girlfriend. He was finishing his undergraduate degree while working in administration for a local engineering firm. After graduation, Chris wanted to go backpacking overseas. A passionate rugby league supporter, he attempted to attend every St. George/Illawarra Dragons home game. But the game itself was just the beginning: to celebrate a win, he would take a 1.5-hour train journey into the heart of Sydney for a night of drinking and partying with his mates. Chris and his mates typically met at local pubs and clubs to watch other league games on television matches.

Ryan, 24 years old, was a local Penrith high school teacher who still lived at home with his parents. He supported the Penrith Panthers as his local team, but simultaneously barracked for the Balmain Tigers of inner-western Sydney due to family loyalties across several generations. His grandfather and great grandfather had lived and worked in the Balmain area as blue-collar dockworkers and even played rugby league for lower divisions in the Balmain club. Without fail Ryan, his mates, and his family watched every Panthers and Balmain match. Like Chris, they attended home games unless the opponent was too weak to make the game competitive. They went to Penrith Leagues club to watch other big matches on cable television, especially on Friday and Saturday nights. The club houses several nightclubs, bars, eating, and a gambling area, so the venue provided a total environment for them. In another dimension of rugby league consumption, Ryan frequently made bets on games.

Chris and Ryan shared an interest in the Wallabies as the national rugby union side. The attraction in watching a Wallabies match was that the team represented "them" as Australians, a nation performing on the world stage. However, neither one of them ever considered watching a local rugby union match. Rugby league was the game that represented them at a local level, encapsulating their origins and their whole sense of community as boys who grew up in Wollongong and Penrith. To quote Ryan: "I don't mind watching the Wallabies because I like sport, but I could never follow rugby union. . . . [I]t doesn't have the same heart or guts that league has. . . . [L]eague is for real blokes." Rugby league, their local team, going to games and betting on the games, is all part of expressing Chris and Ryan's local identity and loyalties, as well as defining what they are not. To quote Chris: "What am I not? I'm not a north shore, private school, rugby union boy . . . a wanker."

Ryan explained that another reason for the social divide was that people from the eastern suburbs of Sydney thought people from the Penrith region were "bogans," a ubiquitous slur meaning uneducated, devoid of fashion sense, and lazy (see Nichols 2011). Chris expressed similar views about Wollongong, especially in relation to the lower-income Dapto area near the industrial works ("they give the rest of the 'Gong a bad name"). Both men however, wanted to express pride in their local environment:

> We don't have Bondi, but we have the Nepean . . . a big beautiful river with some of the best bass fishing of its kind in Australia. We don't want people from the East to know about how good we have it, so they can just keep thinking that we are a bunch of bogans. We will take revenge on the footy field. —Ryan

> We have some of the best surf beaches in the world, but we keep them our secret. We know that we have some rough types in our community, but so

does everyone. What bothers me the most is that the rest of us get lumped in with these lower socioeconomic groups. Just because I am from the 'Gong it doesn't mean I wander around in old tracky-dacks and have no standards. —Chris

Both Chris and Ryan took time to show the research team around their local neighborhoods, where they explored the people, places, and groups that they were proud of, that brought shame, or that had particular meaning. They searched for cultural theatres rich with folklore. Significant places of meaning included the beach, the Nepean River, nature reserves, public parks, schools, sports ovals, pubs, clubs, take-away shops, skate parks, and public car parks. Every one of these places conjured strong memories of local people, events, childhood experiences, and rites of passage. Examples included the first time they caught a wave on the infamous riptide and became local legends; their first fist fight with a group of invaders from Campbelltown who were socializing with local girls in the car park; an endless summer of drinking and smoking marijuana on the banks of the river; the place they lost their virginity.

The Playful Plunderers of the 'Gong

The researchers stumbled upon a particularly interesting—and infamous—cultural theatre in Chris's region: The Barn. It was a cheap rental house occupied by three young bachelors who threw continuous open-house parties, many of which became legendary events. Because the house sat on a property opposite one of the best surfing beaches in Wollongong—some of the best real estate in the area—the landlord was planning to demolish it and the occupants could do whatever they wanted to the house without the threat of eviction. Graffiti completely covered the house. The renters told story after story about it, how it originated and what it represented to them. The décor at the Barn commemorated specific events, people, and experiences: one marker pen piece documented a threesome involving a pot of honey; a photo plaque showed the number of Jack Daniels and Cokes—in excess of 1,000—consumed at a party; photographs showed scantily clad women in a tub that Barn residents filled with milk; and Dragons team paraphernalia included flags, jerseys, and a picture of a resident standing with local legend Mark Gasnier.

The Barn held an elevated social status in Wollongong because it was where "things happened." It hosted, celebrated, and consecrated discourses of mateship and masculinity, becoming the ultimate expression of bourbon belt aspiration in this area. To be accepted meant being "one of the boys" and not pretending to be better than anyone else. They pitted themselves against other towns, such as Newcastle, where they had tested the physical and ideological supremacy of their social group.

A cultural-identity tension, however, became evident among the Wollongong tribe. On one hand, they existed as kings of the neighborhood and custodians of the beach. They reveled in machismo, talking about *their* local women as if they were cattle, assets to protect from marauding hoards from the southeast. These acts of local "protection" manifested in physical violence, such as car-park brawls or intimidation of visiting surfers. Yet on the other hand, they strived for a life far removed from the Barn's parochialism. The men shared an ability to laugh at themselves and each other, consuming media in a cosmopolitan fashion. Many harbored plans to travel overseas and most were pursuing a tertiary qualification. Others planned to move out of the area in the future. Yet, their loyalties to the 'Gong were collectively anchored by stories and experiences shared in relation to local places, events, and other groups.

As the researchers continued to immerse themselves in the fabric of the Wollongong scene, they were able to construct a clearer picture of the tribal distinctions that the research participants were making. The research team speculated that Bundy needed to appeal to Wollongong's "Northies," a social group who represented the most powerful and iconic tribe in the region, typified by life at the Barn. However, Donahay and Agafonoff also speculated that if Bundy became an aspirational brand, it could alienate young working class men from Wollongong's south and social groups from surrounding suburbs. This realization prompted the researchers to focus on the role of rugby league in the Wollongong area and on expression of local tensions in this cultural forum.

The researchers discovered that rugby league acted to smooth social identity conflicts, bringing unity and channelling regional pride toward the local team. Social-class differences temporarily evaporated as everyone celebrated their "local boys": brutal, hard men, but also committed professionals seeking to improve their game and compete on an equal footing with Sydney's eastern suburbs. In other words, league still encapsulated working class values, yet simultaneously addressed middle class aspirations for personal development to the extent whereby a 'Gong player became good as or better than an urban Sydney player. League hence enabled young men to voice their local entitlements, parochialism, and traditional constructs of masculinity in contrast to other men and women, while attending to desires for self-improvement, celebrity, and cosmopolitanism.

The implications for the Bundy brand in Wollongong became clearer: Bundy needed to foster an authentic symbolic relationship with the local NRL team. Yet subsequent research in Penrith destabilized this neat conclusion, as participants honored their regional identities in a very different pattern.

The Local Pride of Penrith Boys

Hanging out with Ryan and his mates in Penrith at Panthers Nightclub (the local NRL club-complex), it soon became apparent to the research team that it was less acceptable to aspire to alternative places and lifestyles in this context. Ryan and his social group instead valorized their greater western regional identity in opposition to perceived inner-city lifestyles. Despite being closer to Sydney, it was actually more difficult for Ryan and his Penrith tribe to reach the urban center. The train station closed early in the evening, resulting in a dangerous late-night trip. In addition, Penrith is a basin for the greater western Sydney area, so Ryan and his mates viewed themselves as part of a cultural-geographic center rather than a satellite. Their social pilgrimages also took them across a much wider region than evidenced by the tribes from the 'Gong.

The Penrith men shared local pride, overtly defensive of all things Penrith. They shared folkloric stories, emphasizing the importance of relationships and noble character traits over performance or sophistication. Being a man meant loyalty and respect, trust and responsibility. It did not translate into having fun with your mates and participating in practical jokes. It did mean bringing pride to your community by being a "top bloke" and a true local.

A walk through Ryan's house revealed an honorific, clean, and tidy environment. He displayed pictures of grandfathers and great-grandfathers who had fought in both wars. His treasured artefacts demonstrated respect for local cultural symbols, such as a large photograph of the Nepean River and a beautifully framed rugby league jersey worn by a past premiership captain for the Penrith NRL team. Ryan's home exuded a relaxed and comfortable feeling in relation to his local Penrith identity, consistent with how other young men in his community also spoke about the area.

The great challenge for the Penrith region was not about placating local tensions between divergent groups and tribes, but finding a coherent expression across geographic space. Once again, rugby league and local team support played an important cultural-identity role. For example, groups of men and young families undertook an hour's train journey from Katoomba in the Blue Mountains down to a local Penrith Panthers match, or drove to Windsor or Blacktown. These townships are dotted across the greater western region of Sydney. While the Wollongong tribe considered inner-city Sydney teams to be their main rivals, the Penrith tribes viewed other regional-based teams, such as the Newcastle Knights, Canberra Raiders, and St. George-Illawarra, as cultural opponents.

LOCATING COMMON GROUND AMONG REGIONAL TRIBES

Although significant differences existed between Wollongong and Penrith tribes, they both consumed a lot more bourbon than rum. A deeper exploration into each set of consumption preferences revealed a surprise. For both, Bundy represented a class-status problem due to its sponsorship of the Wallabies rugby union, and a concentrated source of state-based loathing by all. But otherwise, the brand was a blank narrative, especially in Penrith. Bundy rum was quite simply an outsider, lacking local familiarity. Jack Daniels and Jim Beam were closer brand "insiders." Both brands had accompanied regional young men through important "rites of passage" and previously supported local clubs and events. These bourbon brands thus remained integral to a sense of manhood and mateship.

How could Bundy become one of them? Chris used the example of a new person moving to the community. Acceptance would come slowly. You could not be showy. You needed to get to know the locals, not the other way around. Jack Daniels and Jim Beam understood them, and that is what Bundy must do. It could not just sweep in and sponsor the NRL as an outsider. Bundy needed to support the community, local teams and clubs, surf competitions and fishing events. The Wallabies sponsorship had failed to spark aspirational connotations; Bundy therefore needed to leverage *local* aspiration, as understood within regional tribal discourses. The brand ultimately needed to become a "local," not a national icon.

This analysis had several strategy implications. In the presentation to Diageo, we included the following key cultural insights about the brand:

1. Regional tribes did not reject Bundy. Rather, it was misinterpreted and didn't enter their worlds.
2. It was hard for the bourbon belt to identify a clear role for the brand. Bundy remained an outsider.
3. In no way did the brand behave as a local. Bundy was not as masculine as Wollongong/Penrith locals needed it to be because the brand was distant from local initiation rituals/events. Bundy also failed to connote aspiration as it was understood in a regional context.
4. Bundy should strive for local acceptance and ultimately become a "local hero."

The research team concluded that Bundy should represent a more potent form of masculinity. It needed to crack the symbolic sphere of special moments and rite-of-passage events, and meaningfully align itself with local matches (beyond being merely available at the game). At that time, big nights, big games, and classic moments all pivoted on bourbon brands. Cultural custodians, such as popular local players, were also not recommending the brand. Ultimately, Bundy needed to do what the locals do, which was to support the regional NRL teams and not the game as a whole; for example, by creating hype for local matches via radio and print, associating the brand with local symbolism and language, connecting the Bundy bear to local heroes, and featuring local imagery on communications or even issuing special edition cartons.

Diageo found inspiration in the findings and was careful to integrate its insights into subsequent marketing strategy. The Bundaberg Rum brand could not feasibly support direct affiliation with every local NRL club, nor sacrifice a potentially broader market to court regional perspectives. Bundy hence needed to pitch widely, while addressing regional tensions across the bourbon belt. Diageo responded in two key ways: first, the semiotic codes of working class hardness and personal aspiration were reconciled with the introduction of Bundaberg Red, advertised as a smoother, multifiltered product with a refined, subtle flavor. This brand extension became widely known via the Bundaberg Red Cup, a supporter of competition matches between local NRL divisions. Hence, Bundy appealed to regional loyalties and cross-class values, yet avoided semiotic clashes between various regional teams and associated social groups. Second, later promotions also downplayed ironic humor (too connotative of urban, middle class "union" cultures) and increased an on-ground presence during regional team matches. In these ways Diageo steadily enhanced Bundy's authenticity as a regional brand, becoming firmly entrenched within what was formerly the bourbon belt of New South Wales.

THEORETICAL & MANAGERIAL IMPLICATIONS

Cultural Branding

Although there has been a considerable amount of research into the cultural dimension of brands (Cayla and Arnould 2008; Diamond et al. 2009; Holt 2004; Manning and Uplisashvili 2007), academic scholarship on branding remains dominated by economic (Erdem and Valenzuela 2006) and psychological approaches (Keller 2008). These approaches treat brands either as information signals or as bundles of cognitive associations. Forging a similar critique, Sherry writes, "traditionally, marketers have framed branding as a cognitive or structural enterprise in models of strategic management, slighting the lived experience consumers have of brands, neglecting the cultural complexity that animates brands in so many distinctive ways" (Sherry 2005:40).

Holt's work (2004) in this area is especially compelling, demonstrating that vibrant and sustainable branding strategies can emerge from brands when they are harnessed to alleviate societal anxieties. In their work on cultural strategy, Holt and Cameron (2010) describe the historical development of several brands to illustrate the complex, socioculturally inflected semiotic bricolage that lies behind the success of iconic brands. For example, they show how Philip Morris, after several marketing debacles, was eventually able to weave together different signs into a narrative about a distinctively outdoorsy, rugged, and individualistic American masculinity. This narrative found special resonance in the context of the 1950s when American men were anxious that they were becoming "organization men," working in large bureaucracies.

A limitation of Holt's work on iconic brands is that while drawing from archival material, we know little about the way consumers relate to iconic brands. More specifically, while we know about the deep loyalties brands like Apple and Harley have developed among a core group of consumers (Muniz and Schau 2005), such work says little about the relationship that other, less-involved and less-passionate consumers entertain with national iconic brands like Bundy.

The ethnographic case we presented here, about Bundaberg's forays into the Bourbon belt, extends Holt and Cameron's work in showing that at times brands also need to attend to regional affiliations, and articulate brand strategies that resonate at a more localized level. Holt's work makes a strong case about the necessity for brands to attend to contradictions occurring at the societal level in the American context. Harley-Davidson, Levi's, or Marlboro are powerful examples of how brands resolve national anxieties and contradictions by offering powerful narratives about what it means to be an American man. Yet in the Australian context, we also show that brand managers have to deal with complex social arrangements involving regional rivalries (Queensland versus New South Wales), social class dynamics expressed through sports fandom (rugby league versus rugby union), and center/periphery distinctions (Penrith versus Sydney).

Other cases have already highlighted the challenges of negotiating community affiliations. The efforts of Salomon are especially noteworthy here in trying to move away from its associations with skiing to be embraced by the snowboarding community (Cova 2005). Like the Bundy case, Salomon trod lightly in its approach to the snowboarding community by creating a separate unit dedicated to snowboarding products, avoided big ad campaigns, and focused on "being there," close to the snowboarders. Hewlett-Packard's handling of the 12c calculator (Cova, this volume) also demonstrates that marketing managers must be very careful in the way they deal with brands that help articulate professional identities (in the case of the 12c, membership in the community of financial wizards). Similarly, Bundy approached the rugby league tribe with care and subtlety, eventually choosing to sponsor local teams rather than the NRL team, and investing at a local level. Bundaberg's approach mirrors other branding efforts in progressively infiltrating particular spaces (Bradshaw et al. 2006).

Cultural branding, as illustrated in the Harley-Davidson (Schouten and McAlexander 1995), Hewlett-Packard (Cova, this volume), Salomon (Cova 2005), or the Bundy case, recognizes the social dimensions of identity projects (e.g., what it means to be a snowboarder, a member of the financial community, or a rugby league fan). These branding strategies also acknowledge the complexity of social dynamics that demarcate insiders from outsiders. Here we share others' interpellations that the management of identity (e.g., brand identity, organizational identity) should be a corporate priority (Bouchikhi and Kimberly 2008; Hatch and Schultz 2008). We emphasize the relevance of ethnographic approaches in understanding and deciphering social identity dynamics, and how such dynamics assist the design of marketing strategies. However, although social identity dynamics have long been recognized as central to the politics and dynamics of consumption (Bourdieu [1979] 1984), ethnographic projects realized in the corporate world still rarely explicitly engage with this body of work to consider the more social dimension of branding work.

Ethnography & Branding Strategy

Ethnography's ability to "zoom out" is particularly important for marketing managers to consider, for the world of brands is intensely symbolic and social. For example, we know that very loyal customers can develop quasireligious, parasocial relationships with their favorite brands (Fournier 1998). The Bundy project similarly demonstrated that brands can also became profane, in the way that the brand became an object of contempt for the playful plunderers of the Wollongong Barn we studied.

Importantly, while this project started with a branding question (should Bundy sponsor the NRL?), the project helped articulate original insights about the social fabric of Bundy's landscape. The research team was allowed to largely ignore the micro-lens of psychologizing branding questions (e.g., how strong is the relationship between Bundy and its customers) to analyze the complexity of social group memberships.

Here we are reminded of Dominique Desjeux's insights about ethnographic projects operating at a meso-level of analysis, as ethnographers try to analyze the structuring of macrodynamics (gender; social class) on small group interactions (households; peer groups; tribes). Ethnographic approaches have much to contribute to the world of branding strategy, especially when branding research is allowed to zoom out of consumers' minds, and reframe client briefs in more social terms.

Along with other anthropologists (see Alami et al. 2009), we recognize that an ethnographic approach can be at odds with the dominant discourses and practices of marketing departments, which tend to focus on consumer psychology and consumer attitudes towards brands, while ignoring the materiality and practice-based foundations of our lives. For corporate ethnographers, reconciling marketers' focus on consumer psychology with an ethnographic sensibility privileging objects, practices, and the social fabric of consumer culture can prove relatively difficult. In our experience, corporate clients have often been more comfortable with projects involving visiting several households, and examining their consumption experiences in different domains. In this kind of work, corporate ethnographers have often had to struggle to move beyond the psychologizing focus of motivations and attitudes to try to surface culturally inflected ways of being and behaving (Sunderland and Denny 2003). While ethnography emerged to capture and understand the complexity of social worlds, in the corporate world ethnography has often been reduced to a more individualizing frame at the expense of a wider social lens on communities, peer groups, tribes, and other social groupings.

Our chapter has shown how an ethnographic approach can become an important strategic tool for helping organizations decipher the complexity of the marketplace, whether that complexity lies in the different shades of social identity projects, the intricacies of material culture, or the rituals and practices structuring mateship. Such concerns intimately relate to commercial questions about the situational relevance of a brand, market penetration, brand rejuvenation, and other important business concerns. In these different areas, ethnography is an important approach to guide strategic action.

REFERENCES

Alami, Sophie, Dominique Desjeux, and Isabelle Garabuau-Moussaoui. 2009. *Les Méthodes Qualitatives*. Paris: Presses Universitaires de France.

Bouchikhi, H., and J. R. Kimberly. 2008. *The Soul of the Corporation: How To Manage the Identity of Your Company*. Upper Saddle River, N.J.: Wharton School Publishing.

Bourdieu, Pierre (1979) 1984. *Distinction: A Social Critique of the Judgement of Taste*. Translated by R. Nice. London: Routledge.

Bradshaw, Alan, Pierre McDonagh, and David Marshall. 2006. "No Space—New Blood and the Production of Brand Culture Colonies." *Journal of Marketing Management* 22(5–6):579–99.

Cayla, Julien, and Eric Arnould. 2008. "A Cultural Approach to Branding in the Global Marketplace." *Journal of International Marketing* 16(4):86–112.

_____. 2013. "Ethnographic Stories for Market Learning." *Journal of Marketing* 77(4):1–16.

Cova, Bernard. 2005. "Thinking of Marketing in Meridian Terms." *Marketing Theory* 5(2):205–14.

Cova, Bernard, Robert Kozinets, and Avi Shankar. 2007. *Consumer Tribes*. Oxford, UK: Butterworth-Heinemann.

Diamond, N., J. F. Sherry, Jr., A. M. Muniz, Jr., M. A. McGrath, R. V. Kozinets, and S. Borghini. 2009. "American Girl and the Brand Gestalt: Closing the Loop on Socio-Cultural Branding Research." *Journal of Marketing* 73:118–34.

Erdem, T., J. Swait, and A. Valenzuela. 2006. "Brands as Signals: A Cross-Country Validation Study." *Journal of Marketing* 70(1):34–49.

Evans, Raymond. 1992. "A Gun in the Oven: Masculinism and Gendered Violence." In *Gender Relations in Australia: Domination and Negotiation*, edited by Raymond Evans and Kay Saunders, 182–203. Sydney, Australia: Harcourt, Brace, Jovanovich Group.

Flynn, Donna K., Tracey Lovejoy, David Siegel, and Susan Dray. 2009. "'Name that Segment!' Questioning the Unquestioned Authority of Numbers." *Ethnographic Praxis in Industry Conference Proceedings* (1):81–91.

Fournier, Susan. 1998. "Consumers and their Brands: Developing Relationship Theory in Consumer Research." *Journal of Consumer Research* 24:343–73.

Hatch, Mary Jo, and Majken Schultz. 2008. *Taking Brand Initiative: How Companies Can Align Strategy, Culture, and Identity through Corporate Branding*. San Francisco: Wiley/Jossey-Bass.

Holt, Doug B. 2004. *How Brands Become Icons: The Principles of Cultural Branding*. Boston: Harvard Business School Press.

Holt, Doug B., and Douglas Cameron. 2010. *Cultural Strategy: Using Innovative Ideologies to Build Breakthrough Brands*. Oxford, UK: Oxford University Press.

Hughes, Joan, and Bill Ramson. 1990. "A Dinkum Dialogue with the Demon Drink." *English Today* 6:66–9.

Keller, Kevin L. 2008. *Strategic Brand Management: Building, Measuring, and Managing Brand Equity*. Upper Saddle River, NJ: Pearson/Prentice Hall.

Maffesoli, Michel. 1996. *The Time of the Tribes: The Decline of Individualism in Mass Society*. London: Sage.

Manning, Paul, and Ann Uplisashvili. 2007. "'Our Beer': Ethnographic Brands in Post-socialist Georgia." *American Anthropologist* 109(4):626–41.

Muniz, Albert M., Jr. and Hope Jensen Schau. 2005. "Religiosity in the Abandoned Apple Newton Brand Community." *Journal of Consumer Research* 31(4):737–47.

Nichols, David. 2011. "The Bogan Delusion: Myths, Mischief and Misconceptions." Affirm Press NRL New South Wales. www.nrlnsw.com.au (accessed December 22, 2012).

Salvador, T., G. Bell, and K. Anderson. 1999. "Design Ethnography." *Design Management Journal* (Former Series), 10:35–41.

Schouten, J. W., and J .H. McAlexander. 1995. "Subcultures of Consumption: An Ethnography of the New Bikers." *Journal of Consumer Research* 22:43–61.

Sherry, John F. 2005. "Brand Meaning." In *Kellogg on Branding*, edited by T. Calkins and A. Tybout, 40–69. New York: John Wiley.

Sunderland P. L., and R. Denny. 2003. "Psychology versus Anthropology: Where Is Culture in Marketplace Ethnography?" In *Advertising Cultures*, edited by T. D. Malefyt, and B. Moeran, 187–202. London: Berg.

Tacey, David. 1997. *Remaking Men: Jung, Spirituality and Social Change*. London: Taylor & Francis.

Williams, Terry. 2009. "The Lost Tribes of League: The Fate of Axed and Merged Clubs and Their Fans." 11th Annual Tom Brock Lecture for The Australian Society of Sports History, September 23. www.tombrock.com.au (accessed July 31. 2013).

NOTE

1 www.bundabergrum.com.au (accessed December 17, 2012).

21

The Life of a Cult Object Before, During, & After an Ethnographic Study: The HP 12c Financial Calculator

BERNARD COVA

Matthew Rothman bought an HP 12c financial calculator for his first job out of college in 1989. Years later, he still has the same calculator. And he still uses it constantly, just like thousands of other 12c enthusiasts. "Whenever I switch jobs, I just peel the old business card that is on the back and tape my newest one on," says Mr. Rothman, head of quantitative equity strategies at Barclays Capital in New York (Peterson 2011).

INTRODUCTION

Around 30 years after the launch of the 12c calculator by Hewlett-Packard (HP), it's still commonplace for financial analysts filing into a conference room to set down their calculators next to their papers and cellphones. Indeed, the 12c, which costs around $70 (versus about $10 for a standard calculator), remains HP's best-selling calculator of all time. Sales of the device, which debuted in 1981, continued to grow even after HP introduced more advanced products as well as a 12c iPhone application, which replicates all of the calculator's functions. The slim and rectangular 12c, which comes in black and white, is just over 5 inches wide by 3 inches high. It runs on an unconventional operating system called "Reverse Polish Notation" (RPN)[1], which eschews parentheses and equal signs in an effort to increase calculation efficiency (Figure 21.1).

In other words, the HP 12c is a cult object with an unusually long commercial life. Like the cult movie *Casablanca* (Eco 1986) and the cult scooter Vespa (Eco and Calabrese 1996), we define a cult object as an object that creates a world completely structured in a manner such that the fans can cite episodes and protagonists of the life of the object as if they were aspects of the life of the

Handbook of Anthropology in Business, edited by Rita Denny and Patricia Sunderland, 396–411.

Figure 21.1. The original HP 12c, launched in 1981.

fan her/himself. This chapter describes a multicountry ethnographic study as an episode in the life of this cult object, tracing its history before, during, and up to 10 years after the study. It illustrates the various interests at stake, the outcomes of the ethnographic project, and its lasting impacts.

However fantastic the 12c has been for HP, this kind of cult object raises strategy and marketing management questions for the company. Collective powers are projected onto cult objects (Schiermer 2011), and its societal dynamics are such that it often transcends (or runs counter to) the intentions of its creator (Cova and Svanfeldt 1993). "Like a sorcerer's apprentice, he has created something that escapes him" (Maffesoli 1992:124). The end effect is that the product becomes an icon, its functional dimension disappearing behind its aesthetic meaning. Thus, firms seeking to regain control want studies that can help them understand the phenomenon. Quantitative research can't achieve this goal (Belk 2006), which is why companies have come to rely, sometimes grudgingly, on qualitative and even ethnographic studies.

THE PROBLEM IN 2001, ACCORDING TO HP

In 2001, HP was a multinational company that had embedded its competitive advantage for more than 30 years in its ability to repeatedly take a technological leap forward. Recognized as one of the world's most innovative companies in its sector, the company established a number of global standards, including the 12c calculator, launched in 1979, which has been adopted by financial specialists as an indispensable professional accessory. However, at the beginning of the new millennium, the calculator's performance was very limited compared with the new models that had come out in the previous 20 years, notably HP products such as the 17b or 20c, which were supposed to replace the 12c but failed to do so. All efforts to withdraw the 12c from the market encountered strong resistance from customers. Similarly, any effort to alter it on an aesthetic or technical level was boycotted; HP had to return to square one every time, much as Coca-Cola had to do after its misfortunes launching New Coke.[2] HP was even forced to lower the new software version's speed and performance to accommodate characteristics of the previous 12c version. In the end, the 12c became the global top seller in its category.

HP Financial Services' marketing and new products department, based at the time in Grenoble (France), compared the advantages and disadvantages of maintaining the 12c in its product range (Table 21.1). HP's marketing and new products department—much like any entity that considers technological innovation a core value for its brand—struggled to deal with this extraordinary success. In-house brainstorming sessions carried out in conjunction with financial specialists identified certain key factors. The 12c:

- enabled a rapid visualization and summary of customers' financial calculation;
- fit into a coat pocket and was therefore easy to carry;
- used specific RPN, which was hard to learn but performed well; and
- was recommended by business school professors from North America to Europe and South America and used in their lessons.

HP was aware that 12c customers tended to repurchase the product whenever their current calculator came to the end of its working life; even owning several was not uncommon. In part because of the behavior of these loyal customers, HP's marketing and new products department agreed to abandon its customary market study approaches. Members of the department asked whether, in today's world, numbers and demographics could communicate

Advantages	**Disadvantages**
The HP 12c, one of a kind	But . . .
· Launched in September 1981; 20 years old!	· Calculator looks old
· Expensive for its market segment	· Technology is obsolete, too costly to maintain under today's standards
· World's bestselling financial calculator	· Competitors getting better every day
· Price-inelastic; any change harms sales	· Need to be proactive in defending market share and leadership
· Quantitative market research shows no alterations should be made to the product	· HP wants to be considered an evolving, dynamic brand
· Consumers love it, consider it beautiful	

Table 21.1. The 12c's advantages and disadvantages to HP in 2000.

how consumers behave toward a product. They shared the view that the only way to leverage the 12c's history was by exploring the product's market "life" by understanding consumers' experience with the 12c. HP's marketing and new products department contacted me, and I advised them to consult Argonautes, France's premier ethno-marketing company, founded by the anthropologist Dominique Desjeux.

For the department, this nontraditional approach was risky and raised several challenges. The research sample was accused of being insignificant. Senior management was doubtful about the value of the research, in part because observing one person costs 10 times more than quantitative research and twice as much as observing focus groups. Moreover, in-house procurement procedures required a minimum of three competitive bids to get on HP's list of approved providers, but a limited number of qualitative research agencies able to develop this kind of approach existed, adding procurement irregularities to the list of difficulties managers were already facing.

After several meetings with Argonautes that allowed managers to better understand the potential contribution of an ethnographic approach, HP's marketing and new products department—having no other choice!—decided to hire Argonautes to understand what meaning the 12c had for its enthusiastic users. This involved visiting financial specialists in their workplaces, spending days with them, and monitoring everything they did with the 12c: how they would use it at the beginning of the day, how the devices would be transferred from one worker to another, whether people took it with them on a trip, and so on. This first stage of work was supplemented by onsite interviews discussing the product. Observations were structured around four dimensions: consumers' shared experience with the 12c; how the 12c was used; the 12c's application in social interaction; and consumers' mental representations of the 12c.

HP's marketing and new products department expected the ethnographic research to enhance their understanding of the 12c by creating awareness of how customers live with the 12c as well as providing further insight into general trends in calculator use above and beyond this product. The research focus specifically revealed risks surrounding certain "untouchable" aspects of the 12c that consumers did not wish to see changed in future product innovations and gave strategic direction for the next-generation 12c, including a possible top-grade version. In return, the project created a precedent in the way that HP marketed its products and itself.

RESEARCH BY ARGONAUTES

HP decided to conduct the ethnographic study in four countries: the 12c's largest market (United States); the second largest market (Brazil); a big market for

HP calculators in general (Norway); and a reference country (France). Seven to nine interviews (including related observations) were conducted in interviewees' offices or homes in each of these countries. Interviews were not restricted to finance specialists alone and included people between the ages of 27 and 55. Interviews and observations were carried out by various trained ethnographers speaking the local language. The length of the interviews and related observations varied, depending on the contents and consumers' level of cooperation, from one hour to half a day, and explored the following specific questions:

- What was the 12c's itinerary from purchase to use: where was it stored, exactly who used it, who had bought it (as a gift, for example), was the family involved, etc.?
- What practices were involved in the 12c's use (website forums, collector and user clubs); what objects were associated with it (suitcase, suit, shirt, car, etc.); what spaces were associated with it (living room, office, street, etc.); what uses were prescribed, permitted, or prohibited?
- What were the symbolic representations of the 12c?

In this chapter I provide a brief overview of the findings related to the life of the 12c and practices surrounding its use followed by details on the meanings users invested in the 12c.

Itinerary & Practices Involving the 12c

Most users who purchased a 12c for themselves already had knowledge, familiarity, and experience with the calculator. To want a 12c, potential customers had to know and like it already, meaning they had been in a position where they had to use it. This is because the 12c was not conducive to "immediate" or spontaneous use; as one respondent noted, people rarely had a spontaneous need for the 12c. Rather, in many financial companies it was regular practice to provide new employees with a 12c, so that introducing it and requiring that it be used was creating a social norm. Initiation was crucial under such circumstances: there was neither immediate accessibility nor instant satisfaction, but the reward and gratification of hard effort.

> Once you get a feel for the RPN, it gets under your skin!

> It takes a little getting used to, but it's like driving on the right or left side of the road. It depends on which way you start; if you change, it takes a bit of a learning curve.

For the uninitiated, RPN is an incomprehensible mystery that, for most, can only be mastered after a long initiation period; anyone who got past this initial hurdle, however, found it a powerful and elegant tool that was ultimately easy to use. It seemed entirely logical, in part because of the way it avoided extra symbols and parentheses, reducing the number of keystrokes required for complex expressions. Once consumers got used to RPN, it was hard for them to change to another calculation system. The positive image of the 12c and the personal attachment users formed may have been proportionate to people's investment in the learning process, specifically the final gratification of manipulating the device at will.

The 12c was never the only tool that users wielded for their calculation needs. The 12c appears to complement applications like Excel, which have the advantage of offering more precise calculations. The 12c did not disappear with computerization, but it did assume another role because it was appreciated for its other qualities: simplicity of use, rapidity, accessibility, and mobility. Users tended to position the 12c between ordinary calculators and other technical calculators that they described as overly sophisticated.

> One of my colleagues has got a 17B and a 19B. I've tried both, but I wouldn't change my 12c for them. My HP is simple, nice, and it's got all the functions I need. It doesn't need to be more advanced.

The 12c gradually acquired the status of a lifecycle object, particularly observed when users acquired one at the beginning of their careers and kept it as they rose through the ranks (Figure 21.2). While new uses were different from the original one, the 12c was still being used for professional purposes and was being integrated into people's private sphere among their other objects of affection, following them through various phases of their life.

Figure 21.2. "My 15-year-old HP 12c." Photo courtesy of Hale Stewart.

Figure 21.3. "My HP 12c." Photo courtesy of Gillis Heller.

> It's not ugly, it's not looking good either. I like the design. It hasn't changed over the years.

The 12c was clearly a major conversational tool that facilitated and galvanized exchanges. It had become the object that people would systematically take with them to meetings or negotiations.

> You don't go to meetings without your HP. Lots of times in a meeting, the CEO will ask you a question, and he expects an answer immediately: not tomorrow, not when you go back to your computer and think about it. Without the 12c, I don't know how long you would have lasted in the company.

> For a broker to appear professional, he needs all the proper tools to make his appointments run smoothly. The 12c is the right tool!

The 12c was also a "hot item": owners worried that it might be stolen or that borrowers would not return it, and as a result tended to engrave or carve their name or nickname on it, "like a jewel" (Figure 21.3). Many people we interviewed would loan their 12c for a short time, but never for an entire day; many ritualistically made sure it was on their desk before they left at the end of every day.

Representations of the 12c: A Plurality of Meanings

Dominique Desjeux and I offered a number of parallel interpretations for this ethnographic study. These were discussed with HP's marketing and new products department managers to emphasize the fact that with ethnographic studies, "[m]arketing executives and managers need to reject the idea that there is 'one truth to be discovered' and accept the basic assumption that all empirical phenomena are open to multiple interpretations" (Moisander and Valtonen 2012:257). Far from being a simple universal tool with a very specific meaning, by 2001 the 12c had become a polyglot product given very different meanings across the world, and diverse interpretive frameworks (authenticity, generation, sustainability, tribalism, and so on) were needed to comprehend these meanings.

In Brazil (São Paulo), it was a cult object with strong connection value. Here, the 12c had become a stable reference in an otherwise constantly changing environment, something that people would bring out as part of a professional rite of passage so they could feel they belonged to the (largely imaginary) community of Wall Street financiers. Learning to use the 12c required sacrifice. Keeping it maintained required enthusiasm. In the United States (New York), the 12c had a high use value, explained in part by the way that professionals and consultants prescribed it as a market standard ("the right tool"; "the real thing") thanks to its clever operating system, the ease with which it could be used to make customer presentations, its useful size, and aesthetically pleasing traditional golden borders.

In Norway (Oslo), the 12c was considered a user-friendly (and even rustic) object that companies would purchase on behalf of their employees. It was much praised for a timeless design reflecting stability and solidity, making this a natural working tool. It also symbolized a break from the concept of infinite progress or hyper-choice because, despite being relatively limited, it satisfied most everyone's needs, as opposed to other new products deemed overly complicated. The operating system was also conducive to users adapting and reappropriating the device. Last, people liked the "click" sound that the 12c made when turned off. In France (Paris), the 12c was perceived as a mixture of the three aforementioned countries: it was viewed as a simple but useful device with a strong connection value that was combined with a relatively French appreciation for the status gained by owning this kind of product.

Despite the many different meanings attributed to the 12c, users worldwide agreed that it should be left alone. Its tangible and intangible "untouchables," to be retained for any new version, included its key click, golden plate, handy format, easy access to key functions, RPN, and programming capabilities. Above and beyond these untouchables, the idea of HP Financial Services' marketing and new products department—even before starting its ethnographic research—was to capitalize on the 12c's success by launching a top-grade version that could almost be classified as a luxury product. Toward this end, it took on board the following strategic points evoked during the research project:

- Don't position the new product offer as something "new"
- Respect the 12c's identity as a product characterized by its stability, authenticity, legitimacy, and the feeling of power it gives owners

- Develop the 12c's dual positioning as a situational product (customer meetings) in the United States and as a bridge to an imaginary financial community in the rest of the world.

STRATEGIES DEVELOPED BY HP (POST-2001)

Limited Series

Based on the study findings, HP's marketing and new products department imagined several strategic operations to take advantage of the 12c's surprising success. Options ranged from the modest (not changing anything) to the ambitious (creating an autonomous 12c business unit):

- No change/milk the cash cow
- Special 12c/limited edition including design changes, packaging changes (box, case, etc.), and communication changes
- 12c with a distribution partner/co-marketing
- 12c as a brand range in finance/umbrella brand
- 12c co-branded with a name from outside the world of finance
- 12c as a specific business unit/autonomous approach including specific range of products, partners, and markets.

Some of these options seemed too difficult to develop within HP's corporate culture. For example, the option of having a 12c brand name for a range exceeding this one calculator (possibly having other calculators, accessories, and textbooks) required a major commitment by HP's top management to move the corporate culture away from technologically driven growth. Instead, HP thought of launching a limited series bearing the code name "12cx." There would only be one or two possibilities for changing the original settings, with the product positioning now highlighting stability, authenticity, and reassurance in a fast-moving world. One advantage would be that the same distribution channels could be followed.

To ensure that the target audience of cult consumers would accept this higher-end version of the 12c, the idea developed by HP's marketing and new products department managers was not to present this as an HP initiative but as something driven by legitimate users (academics, business writers, advisors to international institutions, so-called financial wizards) who wanted to change the 12c. In this way, HP would appear to be responding to a kind of grassroots initiative driven by charismatic cult users, and the company could be construed as nothing more than the party adopting and generalizing their initiative. To this end, it had to invent a story that looked consistent with reality even if it was not "real." This interpretation took some elements of the 12c's history and wove them into a plausible scenario. The idea was to create a story lacking any real names or places, one where consumers could project their own imagination (thereby maintaining some degree of mystery) reflecting their own trajectories. The story was to be told in a way that enabled a modicum of identification and "translation" in each culture (Brazil, France, United States, etc.). Local groups would ascribe their own detailed meaning to it. Nonetheless, this thinking about the limited series did not translate into HP's actually launching anything in 2002, but demonstrated instead the path that would have to be taken when designing the 12c Platinum, whose launch was programmed for 2003.

Launching the 12c Platinum in 2003

The launching of the 12c Platinum in 2003 can be analyzed within the wider framework of retromarketing (Brown 2001) that was very fashionable at the time among automakers. The new model was for all intents and purposes a clone of the neverending 12c. Against all expectations, however, it did not replace its predecessor, which HP continued to manufacture. In part, the 12c Platinum owed its existence to the original version's difficulties in finding processors. Above all, it allowed HP to perpetuate a successful model without upsetting traditionally minded users. The only real differences were that the HP 12c Platinum's first model was a dark blue box with a gray background, followed by a black model in a chrome framework (Figure 21.4). The new processor was also much faster (up to 10 times) than its predecessor. There was a major difference in the ways that data could be entered in the HP 12c and HP 12c Platinum: the HP 12c only had one mode (RPN), whereas the HP 12c Platinum had two: RPN and the more traditional algebraic mode. Like all the latest HP models, manufacturing was subcontracted to the Chinese company Kinpo.

Figure 21.4. The 12c Platinum, launched in 2003.

The 12c Platinum caused panic among 12c fans, who temporarily feared that it would displace the old model. This led to a run on stocks of the original version—renamed the 12c Gold—even as HP advertising about the new model helped to launch Platinum sales. As a result, total 12c sales boomed in 2003 and in 2004. Moreover, fans of the cult object would often become double consumers. As one financial specialist reviewed on Amazon: "Many people wonder: Should I get the HP 12c Platinum or the old standby, the HP 12c Gold. Personally, I'd recommend getting both. Like most things, each model has advantages and disadvantages, but both are still among the finest feats in engineering in terms of a calculator."[3]

The 12c's 25th Anniversary in 2006

The Platinum's successful launch seems to have bolstered the 12c's status as a cult object to the extent that HP abandoned its functional traditions and decided in 2006 to celebrate the 12c's 25th anniversary. HP introduced a special edition of the HP 12c Platinum, commemorating the 25th anniversary of its "iconic consumer electronics product that has remained virtually unchanged since its debut" (from the HP website at the time). A further celebration of this milestone was the "Tales of the Amazing HP 12c Calculator Contest," a nationwide competition in the United States asking entrants to submit their most creative and incredible real-life HP 12c calculator success stories.

Reproducing ideas highlighted during the ethnographic study, HP began looking for real stories that could elucidate people's perception of the 12c: "If you've got a good story to tell using the HP 12c as a student, instructor, or professional, enter the contest to win an HP 37-inch LCD flat-panel TV or other prizes." The contest ran from February 10 to May 1, 2006, and was open to US residents who owned or had owned the HP 12c calculator. The winning essay was "The Boon of B-School," written by Srinivasa Rajan, East Brunswick, NJ. On the HP website at that time, the following paragraph was posted:

> At Columbia Business School in 1999, we were required to have and taught to use a 12c. When we started the hardest course of all—Business Finance—we were taught to use MS Excel for large valuation projects. For the final exam, we had laptops and were given Excel files with the annual financial statements of a complex fictional company to create a sale price valuation. Unfortunately, as soon as the test started, my laptop died! There was no spare computer available, so the attending TA gave me a printed copy of the financial statements and blank exam booklet. I took the test with only my 12c and a pencil. 24 hours later, grades were published, and thanks to my 12c I had earned an A! Despite the "advantage" of using laptops and Excel, only seven

others matched my A-grade! After hearing my story, the professor made 12c's mandatory for students!

The 12c's 30th Anniversary in 2011

HP did the same thing in 2011 for the 30th anniversary of its cult object, bringing out a special and limited edition launched at an evening gala in New York. A classic 12c financial calculator was marketed for this occasion as a special 30th anniversary limited-edition release. Each HP 12c 30th Anniversary Edition calculator came stamped with a unique production number. Displayed in an elegant gift box, it became the perfect gift for any business professional, student, or collector (Figure 21.5). For the occasion, HP opened a mini-website where people could order these "collectors' items." On August 30, 2011, HP held a 30th anniversary celebration for the 12c calculator at Harry's Cafe & Steak in New York, a favorite haunt of traders who attended to celebrate or commiserate over the state of the market.

Figure 21.5. The 12c Limited Edition 30th Anniversary version.

CULT OBJECTS & THEIR ETHNOGRAPHIES

The story of the life of the HP 12c before, during, and after the Argonautes' ethnographic research shows how the marketing, design, and product planning of a cult object (Belk and Tumbat 2005) could benefit from ethnographic insights and how marketing and new product development have to be "moderate" or "humble" not to turn consumers away from evolution/new versions of cult objects. The HP 12c is not an isolated case. Other products benefit from the same cultish fame and the same plurality of meanings ascribed to them.

As I have written elsewhere (Cova and Cova 2002), some cult objects have lived through a period of deterioration followed by resurrection, surrounded by what can be called "satanic myth" in the deterioration phase and myth in the rebirth, such as the Lomo LC-A camera launched in Russia during the 1980s by the Lomo corporation, which from 1914 onwards had been a leading maker of optical instruments. In the early 1990s, the camera was considered cheap and not very good: pictures came out with dark edges and were blurred, distorted, abstract. Yet some Austrian students who discovered a Lomo LC-A in a shop in Prague somehow found all this quite exciting, leading to the birth of what became known as Lomography. What started as a small community of friends became an astounding analog movement featuring several million fans devoted to the cultish Lomo camera.

A second category of cult objects have disappeared from the market and then reappeared in the form of retro products and brands (Hemetsberger et al. 2011). This is the case of retro cars such as the Mini and the New Beetle, for example, and specifically the Fiat 500 (Pattuglia 2011). Between 1957 and 1975, Fiat sold as many as 3.8 million Fiat 500 cars. Then, the Fiat 500 continued its life outside of the market. However, on July 4, 2007, exactly 50 years after the launch of the first 500, the Fiat Group launched the third millennium edition. The new Fiat 500 was designed to conjure up the past, but definitely without being a copy or an unimaginative revival. "The new Fiat belongs to everybody" was the claim that wrapped up the commercial and the campaign, emphasizing the capability of everyone to ascribe his or her own meaning to the car, based on individual history. In addition, cult objects had been ironically summed up in the advertising campaign featuring the Fiat 500 together with other magic little items, such as the Bic cigarette lighter and the Rubik's cube (Pattuglia 2011).

Finally, certain cult objects forming a third category have already totally disappeared from the market and gained cult status after that. This is the case of the East German Trabant automobile (Berdahl 2000). The Trabant was designed as the communist answer to the Volkswagen Beetle, but it was built on the cheap and altered little before production halted in 1991. This vehicle, known affectionately as the Trabi or perhaps less affectionately as the "*Rennpappe*" ("racing cardboard") due to its flimsy bodywork, was often the butt of jokes regarding its quality. The anthropologist Berdahl (1999, 2000) talked of a "special word" used by former East German citizens to describe their relationships to the vehicle: "*hasslieben*," or a mixture of loving and hating. Soon after reunification, a nostalgic fixation on the Trabi, as part of a broader wave of nostalgia for certain aspects of the GDR (*ostalgia*), emerged (Berdahl 2000). The Trabi then moved from the jokebooks of 1989 to a new status as the "cult automobile" of the late 1990s. An internet search returned a list of 130 fan clubs for the Trabant around Germany and others throughout Europe and in the United States.

For each of the three categories of cult objects, ethnographic research allows one to delve deeply into their multiplicity of meanings, both personal and social (Leigh et al. 2006). It details what practices are involved in their use, what objects are associated with them, and what spaces are associated with them. It shows how people gain a sense of authenticity in the consumption context via the cult object and its ownership; what are tangible and intangible "untouchables," to be retained for any new version of this object. However, the use of ethnographic methods in commercial settings for understanding the life of such cult objects is not disseminated via writing because the insights gained are applied to a company process of marketing. This chapter proposes a unique view on this phenomenon through the life of a cult object before, during, and after an ethnographic research.

CONCLUSION

In conclusion, it is worth noting that HP carried out this ethnographic study on the 12c because it did not see how any of the other methods that it used customarily could offer an alternative. Managers in HP's marketing and new products department greeted the study findings with great interest, having worked together with us to develop a host of potential strategies for the 12c, ranging from limited series production to an independent business unit. Senior managers from HP's Calculators division only implemented a few of their marketing specialists' recommendations, however, reflecting both a lack of confidence in the findings of a purely qualitative study (the company generally relies on quantitative data) and a misunderstanding of the cultural role that objects and brands play in society today (Kornberger 2010). In reality, the 12c Platinum's launch should be construed as a compromise between the novel ideas being conveyed in the ethnographic study and the much more traditional strategic approach that top management decided to follow. Senior managers' resistance to the proposal that the new 12c be launched as something driven by its legitimate users meant that all throughout 2002, no really new thinking took place in this area. It was only in 2003 that plans were relaunched for a new 12c, culminating in the 12c Platinum, which only adopted some of the ideas contained in the initial proposal. Having said that, HP Calculator's top management also ended up—more or less unintentionally—giving birth to a cult object strategy that would ultimately mobilize its fan communities to celebrate the 12c's 25th (and later 30th) anniversary. In this sense, the ethnographic study undertaken in 2001 paved the way for HP to adopt a new vision of the 12c, even if the company's senior managers never converted fully to ethnographic or cultural approaches to branding and marketing.

REFERENCES

Belk, Russell W., ed. 2006. *Handbook of Qualitative Research Methods in Marketing*, Cheltenham/ Northampton, UK: Edwar Elgar.

Belk, Russell W., and Gülnur Tumbat. 2005. "The Cult of Macintosh." *Consumption, Markets & Culture* 8(3):205–17.

Berdahl, Daphne. 1999. "'(N)Ostalgie' for the Present: Memory, Longing, and East German Things." *Ethnos* 64(2):192–211.

_____. 2000. "'Go, Trabi, Go!': Reflections on a Car and Its Symbolization over Time." *Anthropology and Humanism* 25(2):131–41.

Brown, Stephen. 2001. *Marketing: The Retro Revolution*. London: Sage.

Cova, Bernard, and Véronique Cova. 2002. "Tribal Marketing: The Tribalisation of Society and its Impact on the Conduct of Marketing." *European Journal of Marketing* 36(5/6):595–620.

Cova, Bernard, and Christian Svanfeldt. 1993. "Societal Innovations and the Postmodern Aestheticization of Everyday Life." *International Journal of Research in Marketing* 10(3):297–310.

Eco, Umberto. 1986. "*Casablanca*: Cult Movies and Intertextual Collage." In *Travels in Hyper Reality*, edited by Umberto Eco, 197–211. New York: Harcourt, Brace Jovanovich.

Eco, Umberto, and Omar Calabrese, eds. 1996. *The Cult of Vespa*. Milan: Lupetti.

Hemetsberger, Andrea, Christine Kittinger-Rosanelli, and Barbara Mueller. 2011. "'Grandma's Fridge is Cool'—The Meaning of Retro Brands for Young Consumers." In *Advances in Consumer Research*, edited by Darren W. Dahl, Gita V. Johar, and Stijn M. J. van Osselaer, 38:242–8. Duluth, MN: Association for Consumer Research.

Kornberger, Martin. 2010. *Brand Society. How Brands Transform Management and Lifestyle*. Cambridge, UK: Cambridge University Press.

Leigh, Thomas W., Cara Peters, and Jeremy Shelton. 2006. "The Consumer Quest for Authenticity: The Multiplicity of Meanings within the MG Subculture of Consumption." *Journal of the Academy of Marketing Science* 34(4):481–93.

Maffesoli, Michel. 1992. *La transfiguration du politique* [*The Political Transfiguration*]. Paris: Grasset.

Moisander, Johanna, and Anu Valtonen. 2012. "Interpretive Marketing Research." In *Marketing Management: A Cultural Perspective*, edited by Lisa Peñaloza, Nil Toulouse, and Luca M. Visconti, 246–60. Oxon, UK: Routledge.

Pattuglia, Simonetta. 2011. "Integrated Marketing Communication and Brand Management: The Case Study of Fiat 500." DSI Essays Series, Dipartimento di Studi sull' Impresa, University of Rome "Tor Vergata," Vol. 18. http://ideas.repec.org/a/tov/dsiess/v18y2011.html.

Peterson, Kristina. 2011. "Wall Street's Cult Calculator Turns 30." *The Wall Street Journal* May 4. http://online.wsj.com/news/articles/SB10001424052748703841904576257440326458056.

Schiermer, Bjørn. 2011. "Quasi-objects, Cult Objects and Fashion Objects on Two Kinds of Fetishism on Display in Modern Culture." *Theory, Culture & Society* 28(1):81–102.

NOTES

1 Reverse Polish Notation is a way of expressing arithmetic expressions that avoids the use of brackets to define priorities for evaluation of operators. In ordinary notation, one might write (3 + 5) * (7 – 2); the brackets tell us that we have to add 3 to 5, then subtract 2 from 7, and multiply the two results together. In RPN, the numbers and operators are listed one after another, and an operator always acts on the most recent numbers in the list. The numbers can be thought of as forming a stack, like a pile of plates. The most recent number goes on the top of the stack. An operator takes the appropriate number of arguments from the top of the stack and replaces them by the result of the operation.In this notation, the above expression would be 3 5 + 7 2 – *

2 On April 23, 1985, Coca-Cola, in an attempt to stay ahead of its rival Pepsi-Cola, decided to scrap the original Coca-Cola and introduced New Coke in its place. A few days later, the production of original Coke was stopped. This joint decision has since been referred to as "the biggest marketing blunder of all time." Sales of New Coke were low and public outrage was high at the fact that the original was no longer available. It soon became clear that Coca-Cola had little choice but to bring back its original brand and formula. The simple fact is that all the time and money and skill poured into consumer research on the new Coca-Cola could not measure or reveal the deep and abiding emotional attachment to original Coca-Cola felt by so many people (See Roberto Goizueta, CEO in 1985, speak about this piece of Coke's history, at http://www.youtube.com/watch?v=BmQs8g9ytRA).

3 See the review at http://www.amazon.com/HP-113394-12C-Platinum-Calculator/product-reviews /B00009WNV9.

22

Able to Fly: Temporality, Visibility, & the Disabled Airline Passenger

KENNETH C. ERICKSON

A TRAVEL SCRAPBOOK

Japan is a graying country. Japan Airlines (JAL), serving this nation with the highest proportion of employed senior citizens in the developed world (Kingston 2012), wanted to know what the commercial airplane manufacturer Boeing was doing to make the travel experience easier, safer, and more accessible for older people. JAL was an important customer: their questions could not be ignored and in fact coincided with a stream of work on this issue that Boeing's designers were already undertaking. Boeing had engaged a team of anthropologists, myself among them, to help understand airline travel and the range of conditions known as "disability" in four very different parts of the world.[1]

This chapter recounts the contribution of those anthropologists: I explore how the research was done and point out important turns along the research path to convey what enterprise anthropology is like by showing, as Geertz suggested, "what the practitioners of it do" (Geertz 1973:5). I also tell stories of how we captured some opportunities but missed others. All ethnographers know the frustration of missed opportunity, insight that fails to reach the client, or not knowing how the research was put to use. These are all standard challenges faced by anthropologists for hire. It often seems that by the time our ethnographic teams have discovered what questions really matter, the final report is due and (if we are lucky) we're off to the next tactical project in some other part of the world. Did our research continue to influence cabin design? We aren't sure. We discovered interesting patterns and put some venerable anthropological theory to work explaining and expanding them, but very few really substantive changes to the process of airplane travel appeared in any clear way in our report, and the few possible tactical changes in airplane and service design that emerged from the work have not yet been manifest.

Handbook of Anthropology in Business, edited by Rita Denny and Patricia Sunderland, 412–428.

Why was this? Is this just the nature of anthropological work for hire in business, the inevitable condition of applied anthropological travels? By the time our team finished the work time had run out: the report was complete and we were rushing on to the next thing. I might say that we had no time to address emerging questions that surfaced in our work or to follow through on the implementation of our ideas. It would be easy to say that, and it would be partly true. But this chapter shows that the value of anthropological thinking goes beyond the narrow question, "What did Boeing do with this work?" In this case, it brings out the larger themes of visibility and temporality that were inspired by the Boeing analysis and that would condition significant change in airline travel for all of us, whether we are disabled or not.

At first, reviewing and writing about the Boeing work seemed an exercise in re-presenting the facts in temporal order, from project beginning to project end, like an airplane journey is supposed to be. But by adding in scraps of experience drawn from many additional flights, this travel scrapbook may call out the wider differences among accommodating, user-friendly public spaces and the industrially rationalized spaces (and cultural assumptions) that discourage an awareness of human suffering: symptoms of aging, illness, and disability that all humans will one day share and experience.

RESERVATIONS

Our team's journey began as all commercial airline travel begins: with a contract, a ticket, a bill of lading. In this case, our research shop Pacific Ethnography was contracted to move a project from its beginning to a final report. Boeing has a team for designing everything in the passenger area behind the cockpit: the Payloads Concept Center. They became our client, our co-researchers, and colleagues in fieldwork done in Chile, China, India, and the United States.

Boeing's designers at the Payloads Concept Center wanted an international and cross-cultural view: the easy choices were China and India, centers of growth in the airline industry, and the United States, the world's largest national market for commercial airplanes. We argued for the inclusion of a Latin American carrier, which might offer interesting contrasts. I had taught a short course in ethnography in Chile for a few years, I like the place, and have good friends there; knowing some ethnographic researchers in Chile would help us get the work done. We gathered a research team of anthropologists: me in Los Angeles, longtime colleagues Jo Yung in Hong Kong and filmmaker/ethnographer Bruno Moynié in Toronto, Canada; former research intern and student Benjamin Ross in Fujian, China; Sergio Poblete in Santiago, Chile; and frequent collaborator and ethnographer Ramanathan Haridoss in Pondicherry, India. Hai Nguyen, a designer with a background in design ethnography, also joined us. We were supported by Boeing's project team of three engineers, including Vicki Curtis, our project director at Boeing, who were detailed to the project at least part of the time. We enlisted the help of another anthropologist, Martin Høyem, to build a team ethnographic blogging tool and to help oversee our insights from his office in Pasadena, California. We worked up a research plan, and in the process we began to learn, with our Boeing colleagues in Everett, Washington, just how humans—especially humans whose bodies present special limitations—experience airline travel.

Planning a research itinerary, like planning travel, means deciding where to go and how to get there. How will we get the work done? With whom should we talk, and how might we document the experience of disabled people during an airplane trip? We had a sense that the airplane is not just a means of moving bodies from point A to point B: it is also a workplace (and a highly gendered one, as Hochschild's 1983 essay shows). Could our work encompass that point of view? And what, really, did the Boeing team want to do with this work? What did they already know, and what would be most helpful to them? To frame some answers, we needed to check in with our research sponsors.

CHECK-IN

The Boeing Payloads Concept Center is housed in a nondescript office park a short distance from Boeing's enormous manufacturing and office facilities. In Boeing's cavernous hangers, airplanes-to-be move down assembly lines at a couple of inches every hour. The 747 and 767 lines and the new 787 Dreamliner line are all just up the hill behind the Concept Center. But the design shop where our colleagues were working was not as intimidating as the assembly floors.

Hai Nguyen and I made an initial visit, and were surprised by the informality of the designers and engineers. Project design teams were free to dream up and model new ideas in their own rooms. Vicki, for example, had recently spent some time at the Palm Springs airport, collecting trash bags from airplane galleys and weighing and sorting what she found.[2]

The initial description of our task focused on the experiences of older travelers. But the Boeing designers had a broader view based on their understanding of universal design, the notion that when designers target so-called special needs, the results can benefit anyone, whether they have "special" needs or not (Goldsmith 2012). Disability advocates are often asked: Why design for just a few? How many of our end users really have these problems? Boeing people outside the design team were likely to ask the same questions. Universal design is one answer.

The iconic example of universal design can be seen on most street corners in any city in the United States: curb cuts. These cuts, or ramps graded down from the surface of the sidewalk, may have first been developed in Kalamazoo, Michigan, where a young man named Jack Fischer, recently returned from World War II and experiencing some mobility issues, convinced the city to try out some ramps for his fellow veterans who were in wheelchairs. They did, and the curb cuts benefited all pedestrians. That's universal design: designed for special needs but offering benefits for everyone (see Neese, this volume, for a designer's perspective).

Boeing's designers had been exploring aging and design for quite a while. Vicki had developed a workshop using a "third age" suit, a weighted suit that simulated the symptoms of aging. Engineers and designers wore the suits on flights to gain a firsthand understanding of the older passenger's experience (Spicer 2006). So people at Boeing had some initial ideas for our team. One senior engineer wondered aloud if it wouldn't make sense to meet the growing Asian airlines' needs for profitability by designing airplane cabins without seats. After all, he said, people there are accustomed to crowded trains and subways! Some of us raised our eyebrows at that one, but it raised an interesting point: just how are people's expectations about air travel shaped by the travel experience, generally, within their local context? Our efforts to understand local context began there, with local fieldworkers sorting out the ways in which disability was represented and acted upon in daily life in all four settings.

PREBOARDING

Doing research in applied cultural anthropology is, at base, about understanding human life up close, in lived contexts, drawing on the expansive toolkit of ethnographic research to frame up useful solutions to human problems. It means creating some kind of useful knowledge. This kind of work should recognize that for the ethnographer, anything could be a datum. That means it is unwise to front-load the work with too many predesigned questions. One has to be open to learning what questions matter to the people who are doing what they do in the contexts that are discovered to exist in and around the problem one is interested in.

Framing things in this way should mean considering just what is meant by useful knowledge. What is use? Who is doing the using? Eventually, anthropologists teasing out the usefulness of their work will find that reason "exhausts itself searching for the last end" (Augé 1998:76). New and unpredictable uses, some of them not terribly helpful for the human condition, are always possible outcomes of anthropological work. Spending time with the folks who commissioned the work helped us understand how they thought the work might be useful. There were other players, too: the research participants who held additional desires about how the work might be a lever for some kind of change.

So, everything from figuring out where to go, finding out how to get permission to be there, learning how to use the structured, password-protected team blog, and figuring out who we would finally be talking to and hanging out with were all grist for the ethnographic research mill.

Like any ethnographic project, the work began with a research plan: ours included expert interviews with people who knew about disability or air travel; interviews with recent travelers who had physical problems; a look at the literature on disability and universal design; and participant observation as disabled people flew on commercial airplanes. This last element demanded an answer to the researcher's first research design question: *Where can we go to see this process, this product, or this service actually being used, or shared, or discussed, in someone's real life?* Then, research plans must figure out sampling among those places. What are the meaningful physical and temporal contexts and people in and around that place that we should not miss? How can this be done within the constraints of a staffing and travel budget and a client's timeline?

Naturally, airplanes and airports had to be part of the answer. We knew we wanted to fly along and participate in air travel with disabled people. But what were the wider contexts to consider? When, for example, does travel really start?

Boeing viewed the travel process as something that began long before landing gear leaves tarmac and is retracted into the belly of the plane. This fit with our understanding of an itinerary, a notion borrowed from Dominique Desjeux, which we often use in so-called "consumer research" (see Desjeux, this volume). An itinerary approach looks for the culturally significant moments during which humans are interacting with objects (or services) that are bought or sold. One could begin a study of air travel's itinerary with the decision to go somewhere, or one might begin before that, as people engage in conversation about air travel with others or engage with public messages about air travel. So air travel certainly includes travel from home to the airport and possibly quite a bit before that, all of which sets the stage for the next trip. How might we capture all—or most—of those steps along the itinerary?

I confess, we did not. In a way, we became so wrapped up in (often, fascinated by) the process of obtaining permission to videotape, that we did not allow ourselves the chance to be present for nonmanufactured, naturally occurring pretravel planning. We learned about it in interviews, certainly. But we missed our flight on this one. It would have taken a long time, a year or more (as most of our travelers flew only a few times a year, if at all) to be present for naturally occurring preflight experiences. We made the reservations in accord with the permissions we finally gained, and we relied on interviews and in-flight conversations to gain a beginning understanding of the wider temporal frame of air travel.

But we certainly had included some time to learn about what Boeing had been doing. We listened to Vicki tell us about her experience finding a third age suit from Ford Motor Company, borrowing it, and putting it on some engineers at Boeing. We learned that her team had compiled lists of physical symptoms and sorted out those that seemed actionable and significant as a way to extend the field of inquiry beyond the specific request that JAL had made to study elderly passengers. These included upper- and lower-limb mobility issues, obesity and issues related to physical size and body shape, visual and aural difficulties, and difficulties with touch or sensation. (Emotional or mental health problems were on the list, but these were left aside for this project.) We discussed with the Boeing team how we could make the project collaborative, how we could lean on them for connections to airlines to get in-flight videography permission, and how we might share results and insights as they emerged on the team's blog. Then we settled on ways to extend the research beyond the in-flight experience to include expert interviews and interviews with recent travelers.

After meeting with the Boeing team we crafted our three-part plan. First, expert interviews in each national setting with disability advocates and air travel experts—flight attendants, flight attendant trainers, or other relevant airline personnel—would help us understand what disability meant in each national setting, and how daily life practices and ideas about disability and public policy shape local meanings about physical symptoms, human mobility, and other forms of physical limitation. We had at least a basic understanding of the many anthropological approaches to disability: that it is a dimension of human difference that can, in some cases, be hidden; that it crosscuts other categories of difference like race and gender and sexuality in ways that ineluctably affect every human at some point; and that responses to disability—from accommodation to hiding the disabled or worse—are culturally, institutionally, and historically mediated (see Rapp and Ginsberg 2012 for a recent discussion).

After our discussions with disability experts, we aimed to interview recent travelers who had experienced a symptom of some kind or were limited in their mobility, vision, hearing, or touch. Perhaps they had been wearing a cast, or had a relative with whom they were traveling who had limited hearing, sight, or mobility. We decided to snowball out from our expert interviews, and also planned to spend time in airport waiting areas, talking informally with people who might be using a cane or a wheelchair, or who could tell us something about the experience of traveling with some sort of physical difference. We hoped the recent traveler and expert interviews would connect us with possible fly-along participants.

PREFLIGHT

For a while, we discussed the possibility of identifying differently abled passengers who were planning a trip, and then flying along with them. This proved much too ungainly for our purposes. While we could find some frequent travelers with special needs in California, their schedules did not match up with our research timeline or with our airline permissions: Boeing had a deadline in mind, and we were bound to keep it. So we elected to find people with a range of backgrounds and physical issues and offer them a free overnight trip, a cash thank-you gift, and food and lodging for a stay away from home. As it turned out, the people who participated were not joining up for the compensation. They joined in because they wanted to help us understand the needs of people like them.

In our expert interviews with disability advocates we learned that progress in public accommodation was an ongoing struggle, everywhere. Anyone outside of the so-called mainstream was usually given short shrift in service design, if considered at all. In the nineteenth and through much of the twentieth centuries in the United States, people with disabilities were often hidden away. Despite the visibility—and well-known heroic advocacy—of Deng Xiaoping's wheelchair-bound son, Deng Pufeng, disabled people in China inhabit an especially challenging (and often invisible) social space (Kohrman 2005). Special accommodations are designed into the rapidly renovating public spaces of Tier I and Tier II Chinese cities, while appropriate education and rehabilitation services are just beginning to take shape. The differently abled travelers who helped us knew that their fellow passengers and many airline staff regarded them as "problems." They were excited about the prospect of helping Boeing—and airline companies—do better.

Because of this, finding people to join us for a flight turned out to be easy. We kept a fairly open sample frame so that we could capture people with upper- and lower-body issues, people who were usually in wheelchairs, people with visual issues, people dealing with obesity, and people with aural issues. We chose the United States as an initial location: we only sought one fly-along person there. In Los Angeles, we found Andy Arias, an actor with mild cerebral palsy, by combing an internet social networking site. Our colleague in Chile, Sergio Poblete, reached out to the Chilean disability advocacy association, a group that had just then pushed through legislation to require accessibility for disabled people in Chilean public facilities. Through them he found Santiago residents Luís Méndez, a blind poet and call-center worker, and Leonora Parrau, a student with partial hearing in just one ear. Andy, Luís, and Leonora had all flown before. In India, visits to a South Indian residential rehabilitation center for young people brought Ramanathan in touch with a mathematics graduate student, Mr. Vasudevan, who used a wheelchair to compensate for his malformed legs. He was a first-time flier. Then, we were lucky to secure the participation of Mr. Shivaguru, the father of our Indian anthropologist's neighbor and friend. Mr. Shivaguru was obese and usually traveled by train or car because of the discomfort involved in air travel. Deng Pufeng's China Disabled Person's Federation put us in touch with Ms. Zhong in Guangzhou, a small shopkeeper whose lower body had been paralyzed by polio, and Huang Janhai, now a watch repair man who had lost both arms in a childhood electrical accident. It turned out that Janhai had already been the photogenic subject of a Chinese documentary and was something of a hero in the Chinese disability community.

Each of these participants brought a different set of experiences and expectations to flying. Andy had flown often; Luís had flown to Spain, once, for a conference; Leonora was an infrequent flier. Mr. Shivaguru hated flying. Mr. Huang was quite familiar with telling his story to video cameras in his hometown of Beijing but like his colleague from Guangzhou, he had never flown before. Both were looking forward to their first long-distance out-of-town excursion.

While all this recruiting happened, we began our interviews. Our team spoke with regional and national leaders in disability advocacy. We interviewed flight attendants, supervisors, and in-flight directors. We spoke with designers in India and China, prosthetic specialists, and government disability services coordinators. I began a friendship with Carmen Applegren, a communications specialist with the Braille Institute who would soon be flying up to northern California to train with her first seeing-eye dog. As we got the lay of the land we noted findings on our blog. We planned our first fly-along with Andy Arias, from Los Angeles to Oakland and back.

We knew that in the post-9/11 environment, bringing lots of bulky electronic equipment on board and aiming cameras at flight attendants and our disabled colleagues might be a tricky business. So we sought permission. We tried to break through the airline bureaucratic barriers, something of an ethnographic study in itself.

We started with Alaska Airlines in the United States since Boeing had a company contact for us from a prior design project. Alaska needed a written project description. We faxed one over. And we waited. We followed up, and while we waited some more, we reached out to Southwest Airlines. We found their service support staff interested, willing, and able to quickly provide us with permission to do the work. They would alert a flight crew once we knew which Los Angeles to Oakland flight we wanted to take for a quick hop up and back, and they would allow us to film Andy's experience.

Chile was a bit more difficult. LAN Airlines directed us to their in-flight service department, but although they understood and appreciated our request, approval could only come from the office of the corporate CEO, who was at that time the man who would later become the President of the Republic of Chile. At one point, I telephoned his office, and the CEO (it could have been the future president's operations chief, my notes are muddy as I was so nervous about the high-level call) graciously took my call, said he understood the notion of anthropologists working on design issues, and referred me back to another official in the airline. They, in turn, asked for further documentation. As Sergio waited for a reply, we directed our attention to a smaller organization: Sky, the other Chilean airline. Their smaller size may have made it easier for us to break through the red tape, and we were granted permission to do our work on their flights.

Similarly, Rama's efforts to secure formal permission from Jet Airways for flights from Chennai to Delhi met with endless barriers. Rama's solution was to board the plane with Bruno and negotiate his permissions with the crew on the spot. This worked, though in one instance it resulted in a request that we not use an in-flight interview fragment from a flight crew member, a request which Rama's team quickly granted by providing the crew member with the recorded footage and an apology to the supervisor who had voiced some concern about our informal discussions with the crew member.

China presented other challenges. We knew that a top-down approach to one of China's carriers might cause more problems than it solved, but anthropologist Jo Yung had a friend who worked as a flight crew member for China Southern, China's largest airline. China Southern is among the largest passenger carriers in the world. Jo's friend was part of a flight crew that always flew the same route: Urumchi in the west of China, to Beijing, to Guangzhou, then back again the next day. Our plans called for Yunlang in Guangzhou to fly to Beijing, and Mr. Jinhai in Beijing to fly to Guangzhou. With just one crew, two problems were solved. Jo's friend arranged for the crew to meet Bruno, Jo, and our participants at the door of their flights, and with Bruno taking care to film discreetly in the waiting areas at Baiyuan Airport in Guangzhou and Beijing Capital Airport in Beijing, the China crew had no problems capturing the experience in video. Video from Chile and China are available online.[3]

IN FLIGHT

With all the expert interviews and most of the recent flier interviews completed, we began the fly-along process. Bruno, at the time, used a standard-definition mini-DV camera with wireless Sennheiser microphone sending and receiving units. Since the goal was to produce four standalone videos, each one telling the story of the respondent's travel experience, his single-camera rig meant that respondents sometimes had to back up and restart an entrance to a plane, so that Bruno could shoot from different angles. There is, of course, a balance to be struck between the demands of creating a meaningful narrative and not directing the experienced reality so much that important details become hidden or reshaped. This raises a common question: how would the presence of the researchers change things?

We answered that question just as other anthropologists do: we triangulated our observations against what we had learned in multiple interviews. And team members and respondents compared notes about what they had just experienced. While some extra attention was clearly given to our respondents by the flight attendants, the difficult moments in their interactions were still very much visible.

In some cases, respondents were able to comment immediately about the things that had happened during the flight, as Bruno interviewed them between the safety rituals, distribution of food and drink, and visits to the lavatory. Leonora spoke about the impossibility of hearing the safety announcements and about the challenge of convincing people that her invisible aural limitation was, indeed, a real problem. Luís talked after takeoff about his past overseas trip, during which he felt that had there been an emergency he would not have known how to help himself since all the instructions had been given visually. Mr. Shivaguru was unable to enjoy a meal or a drink because he could not manage the drop-down seat-back tray. Ms. Yunlan spoke not only of the difficulty of getting to the lavatory but the difficulty she had locating and using the awkwardly positioned flush button once she was finished in the restroom and ready to be carried back to her seat. Mr. Jianhai simply managed to show off how he was fully able to manage the airplane interior, with just a few modifications to his space. For example, he used the armrest tray table belonging to the vacant seat next to him rather than his own as his bare feet transformed into skillful hands.

Plenty of patterns came to light. One was the difficulty that disabled passengers had with service people on the ground. This offered a considerable contrast to the efforts made by in-flight crew members, who made a point of suggesting, when the physical limitation was obvious, how the passenger might best stow a backpack, fasten a belt, use the call button, or adjust a meal tray. The disabled passengers took active roles, gently guiding the flight crew so that they understood what they were capable of, demonstrating what they already knew about how the cabin would limit their ability, and asking for help when they needed it.

On the ground, people rarely seemed to know what to do. This was especially true with regard to mobility issues. Ms. Lihuan was pushed right into the plane in a bulky airport wheelchair. The ground attendant stumbled through the textbook difficulties that Boeing had told us about: an unmanageable 90-degree turn on entering the plane, a wheelchair too wide to pass through the first-class aisle, no special chair to help Ms. Lihuan to her seat, and even glaringly annoying questions, asking her if she could manage her luggage while lifting her up and carrying her to her bulkhead seat.

Andy and Vasudevan were quite capable of mobility in the aisle without their chairs, but had to negotiate with both ground and flight crews to see that their chairs would be properly stowed in the belly of the plane. Andy made a point of not taking the aisle seat in the front row that was offered to him. That's the seat that makes things easier for flight crew members. Andy wanted a window seat, a few rows back, a demonstration of his independence and his discomfort with being singled out.

Luís was directed to his seat first with hand signals (despite his white cane and obvious lack of vision), then by tentative touches by a flight attendant who seemed to be learning, willingly and at that very moment, how best to guide Luis. After a wrong turn into the galley, Luis reached for the crew member's shoulder and she directed him to his seat.

In two cases, preflight safety instructions were given by flight attendants who were standing behind the bulkhead, so that people in the window seats of the first row, behind the bulkhead, could not see the demonstrations, a common violation of international protocol. The Sky Airlines crew, though, were careful to provide tactile support for Luís, allowing him try out the demonstration oxygen mask while they instructed him in its use. Leonora was ignored—her auditory limitation was invisible—and she and Mr. Shivaguru received no special attention at all. Among all the passengers with whom we flew, Mr. Shivaguru had by far the most discomfiting experience. He knew it would be this way. As an obese man, he much preferred to travel by train, where he could move around and enjoy a meal in comfort.

The team used the blog regularly; in the process, Vicki at Boeing prompted us to rethink our notion of collaboration. All of the "official" research team members were among the presently able-bodied. Vicki was wondering, for example, why didn't we invite Andy Arias to blog? Wouldn't he have some questions to ask of the other bloggers? Couldn't Andy make some blog posts of his own? Good questions. We invited Andy to blog along with us, and he engaged Vicki in a round of questions and answers about his experience and the experience of the other passengers that challenged the boundaries between researchers and passengers (see Wang, this volume).

LANDING

Coming back to the United States with hours of footage, Bruno started to build short videos about each experience. The team began the analytic task of making sense of the range of experiences in which we had been a part. Marc Augé's work on hypermodern spaces had prompted us to understand the airport—and the airplane—as a kind of homogenized non-place, one in which the physical space and the highly regulated human activities within it would presumably constrain the range of human experiences, perceptions, and meanings that we might find expressed, experienced, or contested by our participants (Augé 1995). We expected the forms of sociability, including problem-solving, to be limited by the airplane's enclosed space. And during flight, we found that highly regular, sometimes plainly ritual practice (rites of passage, of course, as in van Gennep's 1909 work) shaped the ways in which our respondents experienced flight. But the in-flight experience was, in many ways, better than the experience of our participants in other daily-life contexts. On board, there were opportunities to reshape space and negotiate interpersonal exchanges with people who were trying to help. And while the interior of an airplane can be disabling, it is in many ways no less disabling than ordinary public facilities in most places in the world. And both the disabled and those of us who were, at the time, temporarily able-bodied, experienced similar constraints to ordinary overall mobility, range of motion, ordinary hearing, and even ordinary taste and smell (think of the limited range of things to eat and drink). While flying, all of us—able-bodied or not—were fully capable passengers, although confined to and strapped into our conveyance.

ARRIVAL

As we came to the end of our flights, final ritual announcements and practices were offered up: marking imminent departure from the liminal space of strapped-in seating, noisy engines, limited visibility (only cockpit crew can see where the plane is going), and ritualized (or absent) meals. Bodies were rearranged and rebelted, and personal space was reconfigured; uniformed crew inspected and disciplined passenger noncompliance; and the flight-deck specialist made her or his ritual chant to familiarize passengers with local weather, arrival time, and last-minute safety directives. Ritual specialists bid passengers goodbye from the plane. Exiting the arrival area, everyone passed once more through a security checkpoint, but this one required only that travelers pass in one direction and, like Lot's wife, not turn back. There was no going back. It was official: differently abled or not, we had arrived.

After our own project landing, a few months after turning in our report, we asked our team leader at Boeing, Vicki, for guidance about what Jo Yung and I might share in a planned public presentation at a Hong Kong airline interiors conference. We had anticipated that we would be enjoined from discussing the tactical design issues we had found but we didn't expect that we'd be asked to hold back much from our final report when we presented our results publicly. Aside from an interruption by the director of the Payloads Concept Center during our final presentation, who asked us to replay and discuss the video of Andy's problems with the never-redesigned seatbelt, much of what we brought to light during our videography and interviews was simply real-world documentation of what engineers and designers had already noticed on their own. But it was not the tactical information that Vicki asked us to withhold from our Hong Kong presentation. Instead, it was the idea of the liminality of air travel, the ritual process model—drawing on Turner (1999)— that we had used to frame up some of our discussion of passenger experience that she asked us not to include. Ritual process theory, laid out in preanalysis by Martin Høyem on the project blog, was what Boeing wanted us not to talk about, at least for a while.

Why was this the case? Perhaps the ritual process model was the only part of the work that Boeing had not yet integrated into their design thinking. The ritual process model highlighted the liminality of the air travel experience, its apartness from ordinary life, and its division into the phases of separation, transition, and reintegration (boarding and takeoff, flight, and landing). It foregrounded the ritual marking of the boundaries between these periods with safety messages, periods of confinement, and special food (or the lack thereof), all administered by ritual specialists. How this helped Boeing rethink the travel experience is not quite clear. Nevertheless, it is fair to say that our work painted faces and emotions on the engineering and design canvases that had already sketched out the basic problems and possible passenger workarounds against which designers could create improved flight experiences. The anthropological theory about ritual process, though, offered a perspective about liminality, with the special rules, opportunities for inversion, and ritual response to real or imagined danger, that helped explain some of the things people did—or said they did—while flying in commercial airplanes. If nothing else, a close attention to the extraordinary nature of travel in general might have opened a path to greater attention to time and visibility—for all travelers—but more will be said about that at the end of this chapter. For our report to Boeing, we noted how the liminal space of the airplane produces behaviors and expectations that are of the ordinary—everyone has limited mobility, everyone has limited hearing, and everyone endures new disciplines on eating, drinking, smoking, or using the bathroom. It was not the case that Ndembu ritual participants and airplane passengers have a lot in common; rather, it was the combination of ritual action, danger, and remarkably global ritualized instructions that seemed to offer Boeing a different perspective on disabled flight.

FREQUENT FLIER MILES

After all these flights, what had been gained? Certainly the fieldworkers gained a new appreciation of the experiences of differently abled passengers and the people who see to their safe arrivals. Vicki Curtis at Boeing offered this assessment:

> I read in an IATA [International Air Transport Association] report a really shocking statement: "The most powerful substitute to aircraft travel is not an alternative mode of transport, but the decision not to travel." If we don't fix it, they won't go. If they don't go, we all lose money. I am still preaching that we need to change things: and I think people at Boeing are getting the picture. They are working on designs (preliminarily) that unbeknown to them accommodate disabilities. They don't realize it, but their designs are better. I don't think we focus on aging or disabilities; it is just better design. We are starting to get it. (Curtis, personal communication, 2012).

"Getting it" will involve more than tweaking the inflight experience for differently abled people. Getting it may entail rethinking the meaning and process of air travel for everyone. That's a tall order. And it is one that JAL has already taken to heart in their rethinking of air travel.

Japan Airlines—a company known to develop Japan's leaders from among Japan's political elite (Tett 2003)—sought and found new leadership as it successfully clawed its way out of a sea of red ink. The company's interim CEO in charge of the JAL turnaround was Kazuo Inamori, an entrepreneur who founded Kyocera and a Zen priest in the Rinzai tradition. He was certainly concerned with the bottom line. But he has said in several interviews that the foundation for changing the JAL fortunes was a thorough rethinking of corporate goals, of what the company's purpose was. The new JAL view did not stress time or money. It focused on happiness. "It wasn't for shareholders, and it wasn't for executives. It was for all the employees working at the company. We put that at the very beginning of our philosophy statement. 'This is your company, and its goal is to make all of you happy'" (Maxwell 2012). As of this writing, JAL has become the most profitable airline in the world. This was the result of better organizational design.

To design a better experience, time has to move from its powerful position at the core of what air travel is about. Likewise, making the work of air travel visible—that of passengers and employees alike—must become a focus for design efforts; our work was part of that. This is not a new idea for designers, for they realize that the invisibility of work is a problem for ethnographers and designers to solve rather than a production goal to be achieved (Suchman 1995). Invisibility in service work extends worker alienation from the tools of production even farther, pushing workers away not only from their tools but from the products of their work, the service they provide, the people they care for. That seems a good recipe for rotten service and unhappy people. This has been the longstanding and generally failed strategy followed by most systems of rationalized production (Braverman 1998). The same is true for services. Designers informed by ethnographic approaches, and, evidently, the CEO responsible for the JAL turnaround, stress the importance of social, interpersonal connections—the exchanges of information, of requests for assistance or assessments of customer well being or happiness—in addition to the more easily measured but less intimate aspects, like on-time performance, time spent getting into and out of a seat, or the nearly invisible automaticity of ticketing, flight, baggage handling, and flight arrival. Time and rationalized, deskilled processes are the stock in trade of ordinary thinking about the design, operation, and maintenance of airplanes. These are the instrumentalities of ordinary management, not the extraordinary acts of communicative ritual that are required for the intimate human exchanges that take place prior to embarking on the cultural (and physical) dangers of travel.

The specialists engaged in comforting and caring for people engaged in what has always been the scary business of travel are ritual specialists. Thus, travel has its own saints: the apocryphal Saint Christopher in the so-called West and Jizo Bodhisattva in Japan. Each, like flight attendants, have their own ready-made ritual and conceptual equipment (Bays 2002). Travel's ritual specialists help people deal with the imagined fears and real dangers of travel—the small dangers of missing a flight or losing ones clothing, or the bigger danger of being stuck on the tarmac for hours or involved in an emergency evacuation. Airlines rarely account directly for intimate, emotional components that inhere in these ritual details. Airlines mostly measure time, not well being. And in so doing, they increase the anxiety of passengers who are constantly confronted with the manipulation of time: the extension of flight times to account for delays, or airline willingness to book people for 45-minute connections when only a sprinter could make it across three arrival halls to the next flight. And airlines rarely indicate how long it may take to recover one's luggage (or your own wheelchair if you have one). Instead, passengers wait for bags to emerge from behind the wall, where invisible hands manage the stuff that is expelled, somehow, from the belly of the plane.

Airlines, like so many enterprises, have made work invisible and make rationalized time the only temporal reality. Collaborative design and design research make work visible, and can treat time differently.

Boeing, like JAL, is indeed starting to "get it." Boeing knows how important it is to see where you are, where you are going, and what things look like outside the airplane window. They've reconfigured the interior of the new Dreamliner so that windows are actually at what is, for most passengers, roughly eye-level. The carbon-fiber fuselage allows greater structural strength and affords bigger windows, while light-sensitive glass obviates the need for those window shades that used to be difficult for passengers to manage (though Mr. Huang had no trouble using his feet to control his shade). And although we think of Boeing as making only the airplane, they also make jet-bridges and some of the display technology that shows seat availability for passengers waiting at the gate. This is evidence that Boeing already knows that air travel does not begin when passengers enter the plane; it is not inconceivable that they may broaden their view of travel further and include the entire process of baggage handling, making it, too, more transparent.

At the end of the day, passengers are willing to endure a certain level of hardship in travel. Without it, proud travelers would have fewer travel stories to tell and there would be no problems for designers or anthropologists to work on. But there should be some physical and emotional comfort for travelers. There should be support for ritual specialists—Jizo, Saint Christopher, or flight attendants—who make air travel manageable. Without such ritual attention the globalized, airline-enabled shrinking world expands again. The short flight that compressed time and erased difference and distance expands mightily and uncomfortably into its own rationalized disability through an inability to make visible and provide for human difference. The proudly endured hardship of travel becomes suffering—or a decision not to travel at all—to the degree that airlines hide their own work. And air travel disables itself further when it becomes suffused only with time, or, as a Zen master might say, concerned only with being *on time* instead of *being-in-time* (Dogen [1240] 1985). Time in properly ritualized travel need not be something that is "dealt with," something waited impatiently upon, or begrudged on either end of a trip. When comfort happens, when one is at home in one's seat, time stops and the present moment is there to be appreciated, as in Andy's a view from his window, or Luis's calm sense of well-traveled, visually impaired (but fully capable) security. And the work of flight attendants on the ground and in the air, *seeing to* the needs of passengers, can be made visible and appreciated, so they, in turn, may see and appreciate those whose bodies—and luggage—they care for. That's where universal design fosters a good kind of globalization: through it we recognize our common, traveling humanity, and the difference between the temporarily able-bodied and others dissolves, for a time, into thin air.

REFERENCES

Augé, Marc. 1995. *Non-Places: Introduction To An Anthropology of Supermodernity*. New York: Verso.

_____. 1998. *A Sense for the Other: The Timeliness and Relevance of Anthropology*. Stanford, CA: Stanford University Press.

Bays, Jan Chozen. 2002. *Jizo Bodhisattva: Modern Healing and Traditional Buddhist Practice*. Boston: Tuttle.

Braverman, Harry. 1998. *Labor and Monopoly Capital: The Degradation of Work in the Twentieth Century*. New York: Monthly Review Press.

Brown, S. E. 1999. "The Curb Ramps of Kalamazoo: Discovering Our Unrecorded History." *Disability Studies Quarterly* 19(3):203–5. www.independentliving.org/docs3/brown99a.html (accessed October 10, 2012).

Dogen, Eihei. (1240) 1985. "Uji: The Time Being." In *Moon in a Dewdrop: The Writings of Zen Master Dogen*, edited by Kazuaki Tanahashi, 76–9. New York: North Point.

Geertz, Clifford. 1973. *The Interpretation of Cultures: Selected Essays.* New York: Basic.

Goldsmith, Selwyn. 2012. *Universal Design*. Oxford, UK: Architectural Press.

Hochschild, Arlie Russell. 1983. *The Managed Heart: The Commercialization of Human Feeling.* Berkeley: University of California Press.

Kingston, Jeff. 2012. *Contemporary Japan: History, Politics, and Social Change since the 1980s.* New York: John Wiley & Sons.

Korhman, Matthew. 2005. *Bodies of Difference: Experiences of Disability and Institutional Advocacy in the Making of Modern China.* Berkeley: University of California Press.

Maxwell, Kenneth. 2012. "'Mikoshi Management': How Kazuo Inamori Lifted Japan Airlines." Japan Realtime Blog. *Wall Street Journal Online.* blogs.wsj.com/japanrealtime/2012/07/30/mikoshi-management-how-kazuo-inamori-lifted-japan-airlines/ (accessed September 1, 2013).

Rapp, Rayna, and Faye Ginsburg. 2012. "Anthropology and the Study of Disability Worlds." In *Medical Anthropology at the Intersections: Histories, Activisms, and Futures*, edited by Marcia C. Inhorn and Emily A. Wentzell, 163–83. Durham, NC: Duke University Press.

Spicer, Kathleen. 2006. "Engineers, Designers Walk in the Shoes of Older Passengers to Understand Needs of Future Air Travelers." *Boeing Frontiers* 4(8). www.boeing.com/news/frontiers/archive/2005/december/i_ca1.html (accessed October 1, 2012).

Suchman, Lucy. 1995. "Making Work Visible." *Communications of the ACM* 38(9):56–64.

Tett, Gillian. 2003. *Saving the Sun: How Wall Street Mavericks Shook Up Japan's Financial World and Made Billions.* New York: HarperCollins.

Turner, Victor. 1969. *The Ritual Process: Structure and Anti-structure.* New York: Aldine.

van Gennep, Arnold. (1909) 1981. *Les Rites de Passage* [*The Rites of Passage*]. Paris: Picard.

NOTES

While the author is responsible for errors of omission and commission here, the work was a team effort in multisited ethnography. In addition to the support from Vicki Curtis and her team at The Boeing Company's Payloads Concept Center, thanks are due to Carmen Applegren, Andy Arias, Ramanathan Haridoss, Martin Høyem, Huang Jianhai, Luís Mendez, Bruno Moynié, Hai Nguyen, Ben Ross, Leonora Parrau, Sergio Poblete, Sivaguru, Vasuydevan, Jo Yung, Zhong Yunlan, and crew members and administrators from Southwest Airlines, Sky Airlines, Air India, Jet Airways, and China Southern Airlines.

1 Although the term "disability" carries with it a negative connotation (and the thankfully less often used Spanish "*menos valido*" sounds even worse), the English term is used frequently by advocates for the rights of people who are differently abled. Our respondents in English used the words "disabled" and "disability" to talk about their own bodies as they experience what we came to understand as disabling environments. Here, the terms "differently abled" and "disabled" are intended to have the same value and are used interchangeably.

2 Her work on trash had also focused on the airplane as a workplace, and although we might have enjoyed spending more time with the questions surrounding the airplane cabin as a workplace, we were directed to focus our efforts on passenger experience, and leave aside the experiences of the cabin crew, except as they directly touched upon passenger experience.

3 Mr. Huang, China: http://www.youtube.com/watch?v=ywDKiMrV_WQ; Mr. Mendez, Chile: https://vimeo.com/4421999.

23

Mediating Business Process Models with an Anthropological Voice: "Double-Level Language" in the Norwegian Oil Industry

VIDAR HEPSØ

INTRODUCTION

Collaborative work can be fluid and chaotic. Creating representations of work activities for people in and across domains to implement change in work processes is never easy. I have been involved in studying work as an anthropologist and researcher for more than 20 years, primarily doing evaluation and development of collaborative computer systems in an oil company. This experience has taught me that anthropology can provide support for sense-making activities in a multidimensional interactional space where the understanding of and representation of work are key issues. For heuristic reasons I argue that this interactional space has two broad modes of communication. I have borrowed the term "double-level language" from the design of collaborative information systems (Robinson 1991; Robinson and Bannon 1991) to describe these two modalities of communication. I explore the communication and representation of a specific type of artifact used in double-level language communication—flow charts—to illuminate the role of the anthropologist in this interactional space. My key claim as an anthropologist supporting change and development work in industry is that using double-level language is a crucial feature of our practice when we help workers, managers, and clients make sense of their world, represent their world, and take action based on the insights they have developed.

The first mode in this double-level interaction space is *formal and rule-based;* it views work as a prescription of temporal task sequences. It uses rather stringent representations, and action is constrained by formation and transformation rules. The second mode is *informal and cultural;* it deals with the development of interpretations, sense-making, and articulation of work. This mode entails natural, emergent, and fairly unrestricted communication.

Handbook of Anthropology in Business, edited by Rita Denny and Patricia Sunderland, 429–446.

Both modalities are necessary. Double-level language enables participants to point at aspects of the situation that they are discussing. Developing shared understanding and addressing ambiguity happen through shifting between the cultural and formal aspects of language (Robinson 1991:41–3). Cooperative work and communication are both discursive (setting rules and conventions, achieving agreements) and indexical (grounded in the objects of work). People need to discuss their work using their own situated language. Still, formal representations are essential because they provide a common reference point for a group (Robinson 1991:43). People engaged in change efforts need to create and abide to formalism using rules to agree upon and change practice. They must share a minimum understanding of formalism that describes communication, coordination, roles, and dependencies. Finally, they must also be able to describe an external world where things can be pointed out and in which behavior is rule-governed and predictable. Stability and predictability facilitates and grounds dialog and negotiation.

An interesting setting for addressing the implications of double-level language is the domain of business process management (BPM). BPM is used to study, identify, change, and monitor work activities in organizations. Business process modeling is a formal technique and method to identify and modify existing work activities and align them with an envisioned organizational state. A business process is a structured, measured set of activities designed to produce a specified output for a particular customer or market. It defines activities to be undertaken by which roles and what information requirements these roles and activities need for their execution. Such a model is often depicted through a flow chart (see Figures 23.2 and 23.4), which represents the first mode in double-level language.

Over the years BPM has become pervasive in many types of businesses, from manufacturing and extractive industries to health care and government. The theory and method of BPM is instrumental and reductionist in the sense that it objectifies human action and meaning to entities and relations among entities. It uses a strict mechanical and machine-like metaphor. Patricia Sachs (1995:36–9) describes this approach as an organizational view of work that is represented by sets of defined tasks and operations such as those described in methods and procedures.

The BPM view of work differs from what Sachs calls an "activity-oriented approach," which is comparable to the second mode in double-level language. The range of activities, communication practices, relationships, and coordination it takes to accomplish business functions (or work activities) are complex and repeatedly mediated by workers and managers alike. Sachs argues that an activity-based view analyzes everyday work practices to demonstrate the ways employees actually make the business function effectively. It means taking a look at whole activities as distinct from only particular tasks and sequences, thereby focusing on how working people communicate, think through problems, forge alliances, and learn as a way of getting work done (Sachs 1995:39).

Anthropologists have a long tradition in criticizing the first-mode approaches to studying work (Hepsø 1997; Suchman 1994, 1995, 2007). However, there are also good examples of modeling[1] frameworks that incorporate anthropological perspectives and an activity-based understanding of work. The business agent-based holistic modeling system (BRAHMS) was originally developed by Maarten Sierhuis and others (Clancey et al. 1998; Sachs 1995; Sierhuis 1996) to analyze or design human organizations and work processes. It had the capability to incorporate rich ethnographic and unstructured data through a rule-based activity programming language. The formal language of BRAHMS is based on a theory of work practice and situated cognition.

In this chapter, I show how such "thin description" (Geertz 1973) modeling activities (first mode) can be a catalyst for thicker descriptions of work practice (second mode). As a practitioner in industry, I try to use double-level language by developing thick descriptions of work, though this must be done within a framework of formalism. It is the dialectic between the first and second modes that is of particular interest to me, since this perspective is used to inform the development of collaboration practices within the oil company where I work.[2] This approach is useful for anthropologists working in industry with the design and representation of work, as well as for process consultants, software engineering/modeling experts, and others who are interested in a more open discussion around modeling and representation of human practice.

I present three vignettes that show how anthropological knowledge can contribute in developing work. Each vignette represents a unique instantiation of double-level language processes. The first vignette is related to envisioning the operations of a new oil and gas organization where I helped to develop new business models or work activities in the planning of future operations. Anthropological knowledge developed elsewhere in the organization was used to scrutinize the outcomes of the modeling process. The second vignette describes how ethnography and ethnographic data were used to develop new collaborative business processes for production optimization in another part of the organization. These activities were visualized as new business process models with my help. The third and final vignette shows how these new business process models, once objectified through the models and charts, were translated into a new setting in another part of the organization. A process was undertaken in which a richer, active content was created around the formal charts. For each case I give some background and describe the project goals, the challenge, my role, the outcome, and why I am presenting this story. All these elements are summarized in Table 23.1.

Table 23.1. Double-level language processes.

	Vignette 1: The social construction of a new oil and gas organization	Vignette 2: Developing a new model of production optimization	Vignette 3: Translating a model of production optimization to a new setting
Background	A group of operational people has been assigned the job to plan future work activities of a new oil and gas installation.	A group of production engineers have been co-located in a collaborative environment to experiment with their current way of working during a three-month period.	An existing group of production/reservoir engineers is trying to make sense of the formalized work process descriptions and translate it to their own work setting.
Project Goals	Formally envisioning operations of a new oil and gas organization.	Evaluating and describing work practices in an emerging area of real-time production optimization.	Implementing the new business model of production optimization in a different oil field.
The Challenge	How not to become too instrumental in describing new work activities.	Maintain focus on the situated setting to describe the emerging new practice but still be able to convey the essence of the new work practices to the rest of the organization using a more formal approach.	Applying formal descriptions developed elsewhere to a new setting. The challenge was to be compliant to company policy and at the same time be responsive to local work practices and needs.
My Role	Project manager and facilitator helping to develop new business models and work activities for future operations.	Ethnographer and facilitator helping a group of production engineers articulate their work practice.	Ethnographer and facilitator helping production and reservoir engineers adjust a new model to fit their own needs.

Table 23.1. continued

	Vignette 1: The social construction of a new oil and gas organization	Vignette 2: Developing a new model of production optimization	Vignette 3: Translating a model of production optimization to a new setting
Outcome	Flow charts and descriptions of how future work should be conducted.	Report describing new second-mode practice and flow charts describing a new company standard for production optimization.	Report describing emerging second-mode practices based on first-mode (company) requirements and expectations.
Why Am I Telling This Story?	The corporate need for formalism when a large group of people plans the future.	The critical importance of a situated understanding of emerging work practices, while at the same time adhering to a corporate need for simplification.	The potential fallacy of first-mode representations as models when applied across space and time.

VIGNETTE 1: THE SOCIAL CONSTRUCTION OF A NEW OIL & GAS ORGANIZATION

Statoil, Norway's state-owned oil company, was developing a new oil producing organization: the oil production ship Norne (Figure 23.1). This installation started production in 1997. It was Statoil's first floating production ship and very different from the permanent concrete and steel megaliths that the company managed on the Norwegian continental shelf. Compared with those giant structures, Norne required a lean organization to make money. All the same oil-producing functions had to be accomplished, but these efforts had to be executed differently. Thus, Norne challenged the company's existing work practices and demanded the development of new ways of working, not only on the boat itself, but also in cooperative onshore-offshore functions inside Statoil and in vendor relationships with companies outside Statoil.

A group of people with diverse operational backgrounds from various parts of the company was tasked with planning work activities on and with Norne. I participated in the project as a team member together with several colleagues who were engineers. My role was project manager for documenting the creation

Figure 23.1. The Norne production ship, 2010. Photo by Kenneth Engelsvold, Statoil.

of the business processes and facilitating the development process. The difficulty in this case was not to become too instrumental (first-mode biased) in describing new work activities. The group was expected to produce flow charts and textual descriptions of how future work activities should be conducted. But whereas my engineer colleagues helped Norne articulate the specific first-mode operational activities, my role, as I will soon come back to, was to help Norne address the second-mode issues, and I was challenged to balance this strong need for formalism in planning the start-up of a new oil installation with an ethnographic and activity-oriented approach.

Business process modeling was used as a method to define the future Norne operational practice and the major business processes (Gjersvik and Hepsø 1998; Hepsø 1997). My research included face-to-face meetings and workshops where Norne employees described new work practices. I also spent two to three days every week over a seven-month period doing observations in the office area where the Norne personnel worked, did participant observation in meetings and workshops; and conducted 20 interviews with the key operational people from Norne who participated in developing the work activities. My field notes reveal the challenging duality of double-level language that I faced in this project.

The maintenance team consisted of offshore first-line and middle managers, process technicians, mechanics, and telecom/data technicians. Except for a woman in her mid-20s they were all men in their 30s and 40s. A group of around 10 team members were assembled during the start-up meeting that took place in Norne's meeting room. A skilled engineer colleague facilitated these sessions because of his thorough understanding of the maintenance work process. He had put a large sheet of brown paper on the meeting room table on which the group started to capture the sub-activities of maintenance and the outcomes of the maintenance activities using Post-it notes.

The facilitator asked: "Who is maintenance's customer?" The group discussed who their major internal company customers were. One process technician argued that operations was their customer: "Maintenance delivers things to operations so operations will be able to run the vessel under the best possible conditions." The group offered a number of definitions of maintenance activities: plan and carry out work orders, get spare parts, and replace malfunctioning equipment. A senior Norne technician elaborated: "Operations are dependent on maintenance in terms of its ability to keep the installation up and running. Maintenance must deliver availability of the technical systems for operational activities to take place. Availability means a proper technical condition of the installation."

Using the process modeling method the group came up with a number of activities that enhanced their understanding of the new operational model. On the brown paper participants created a flow chart listing major activities, their temporal sequence, and some interdependencies between them. This chart, reproduced in Figure 23.2, depicts the basic routines of plant maintenance in a sequential manner. The roles are defined at left in the chart, separated by lines. The boxes represent the activities undertaken by the roles, and the circles are products or outcomes of the activities. In a number of follow-up meetings, the work activities were articulated and broken down through more detailed flow charts. If a vital new element in maintenance had been defined, the group discussed it and some of the team members were given the task to write down the details. In subsequent interviews, workshop participants told me that this first-mode development of work processes clarified both internal and external demands in the group. The process modeling enabled collaboration across the group and was instrumental for working towards a common objective: the Norne operational model.

What could I do as anthropologist? How could a "culture expert" help develop the necessary second-mode qualities that a high-risk organization like Norne needed? I helped to describe the goals of the new organization, the qualities of the espoused routines: quality assurance, maintenance, and routines for experience transfer. These are mainly first-mode activities. However, the sharing of responsibilities between work teams, the ability to take important decisions under pressure in crisis situations, the management in daily operations, and the development of a safety culture was something that Norne had to take seriously if they were to succeed. I could point to this during discussions with

Norne personnel, but they had to walk the line of uniting their flow charts with a future operational practice themselves. My problem was that since the Norne organization was in the midst of preparations for operations (and not in operations yet), it was very difficult to do a traditional workplace study of operational practice. So, in meetings with the Norne employees, I discussed their world as they wanted it to be in the future.

For example, in a meeting with the Norne employees responsible for developing the maintenance process, one of the team members reviewed the latest changes in the operational model. After a short brainstorming session, he added comments to the model as the different members spoke up. Then I spoke up to shift the group's attention:

> Go back to the platform maintenance overview chart [Figure 23.2]. Take a look at the "create work order" sub-activity [utarb.arb.anmodn.]. I know from past fieldwork I have conducted that the "bureaucracy" with work orders takes considerable time. You have said that Norne will try to reduce the number of work orders by 75 percent. How do you plan to do this when you are in operation, since both you and I know that it is easy to fall back on old practice?

The Norne technician answered:

> You have seen our criteria to differentiate between work orders; they are fairly clear [he navigates in the flow chart and clicks on the circular box "Kriterer for forenklet gjennomføring"]. However, I do agree that we have to do something more than just define these criteria, these things will not happen by themselves.

I asked: "How do you plan to do this?" He answered:

> Good question! We have already taken measures to present this way of thinking during our presentation to newly recruited Norne people. Another idea is to live by and learn from using these principles during our commissioning phase before we get the first oil. I think this is the only way we can make Norne staff understand what this really is about. I want you [addressing his other colleagues in the meeting] to help me plan how we can take steps to live by these principles before we come into operations.

By addressing a small instrumental feature in the first-mode flow chart that had inherent weaknesses, I was able to challenge them on a second-mode level, making them work more with the noninstrumental issues that had to be developed alongside the first mode. Such weaknesses could often be presented as concrete challenges, as I did in another example, an instrumental-cultural dis-

Figure 23.2. The offshore plant maintenance process.

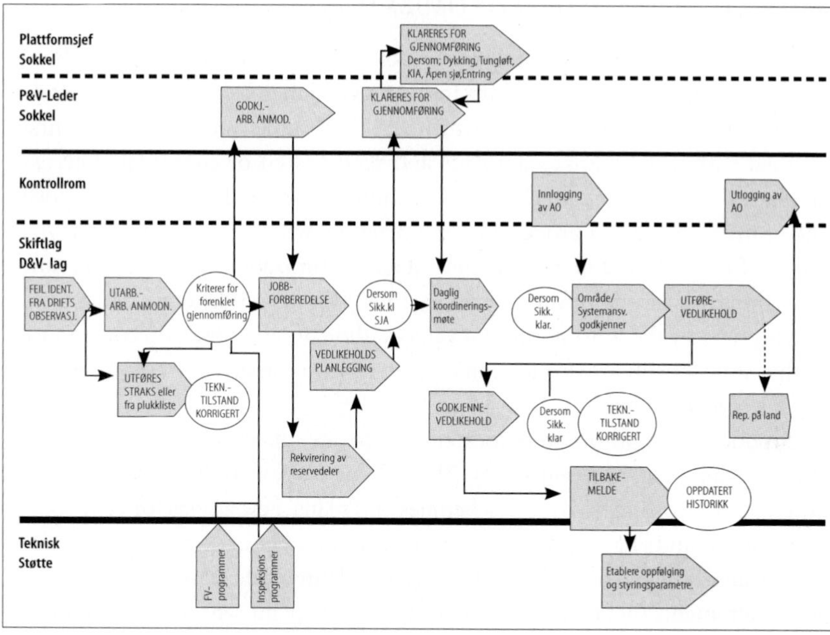

course on "safety in maintenance." A new safety practice had to be developed for Norne. To initiate a discourse to make "zero accident" philosophy the future practice I had to go back to my previous ethnographic work, study reports on accidents or "close calls" at both Statoil and other high-risk industries, and take this information back to discuss with the modeling teams. Detailed information in accident reports provided second-mode input that could be used during discussions and workshops with Norne personnel and help answer the question of how Norne should develop a safety culture through the organization of work. Juxtaposing their planned operational concept with concrete examples from past accidents triggered second-mode communication that went beyond the instrumental first mode.

In sum, I was faced with a situation in which a pretty stringent formalism was needed to help various groups develop and structure a future operational model. The first-mode flow charts were dense but lacked details; describing work in its nitty-gritty detail was not an option. Still, by introducing second-mode communication on the cultural level, where their natural language was used to discuss their experience and practice, I helped the team escape the worst instrumentalism and make sense of the formal representations.

VIGNETTE 2: DEVELOPING A NEW MODEL OF PRODUCTION OPTIMIZATION

An oil and gas company's workforce works both onshore and offshore. Those that are offshore work 12-hour shifts for 14 days and then have 4 weeks off, while those onshore work ordinary working hours. Most tasks and activities are first planned within disciplinary domains and then shared or coordinated across domains. Onshore personnel provide administrative and technical support; one of their domains is production optimization, which can be defined as the process for short- and long-term control and optimization of oil and gas flow from the reservoir via offshore facilities to export from offshore installations. This is probably the most important value-adding process for all oil companies. Within this domain are production engineers, who can give input to reservoir engineers or vice versa.

Production engineers were located in separate offices, and there was very little collaboration between peers. Their focus was on individual wells and production according to overall schedules and plans. Few arenas for collaboration existed, and sharing of information within and across communities was complicated. They also had limited access to real-time data: continuous streams of measurements that come from well and process plant sensors and comprise parameters that can be adjusted to tune the performance of the wells and production facilities. The production engineers responsible for this oil field saw the need for change themselves. They were a group of young people that took interest in sitting and working together. They argued that sitting together was a more social and fun way of working where they could learn and get help from their colleagues.

A three-month pilot project was designed to test new collaborative work practices among production engineers, a new collaborative office environment, and several new information systems. During the pilot the production engineers moved to a collaboration room with PCs, whiteboards, Smartboards, large visual displays, and telephone-videoconferencing facilities (Figure 23.3). They also had increased access to real-time production data. During the pilot the space became the day-to-day work environment for the production engineers and was soon domesticated as their space. Here they could discuss their ideas and conduct analytic work among peers much easier than before. The work also boosted the confidence of production engineers because it gave them more attention and new opportunities to show their capabilities.

The main activities of the production engineers were to monitor well performance and flow line performance, diagnose wells with deviating behavior, and monitor water breakthrough in the wells. Their work was very knowledge intensive. Several morning and ad hoc coordination meetings were held with

Figure 23.3. Illustration from a collaborative environment, the workplace of production engineers. Photo by Gorm Kallestad, Statoil.

various groups onshore and offshore. During these meetings the status of the wells was on the agenda, and some short- and long-term action points were taken back to the community for more detailed analysis or immediate troubleshooting. The production engineers had close to 50 wells to follow; 30 of these wells were producers, and the rest were injectors. The injectors were used to inject water back into the reservoir to keep up the reservoir pressure. Each well in this dispersed network was located at strategic points in the reservoir. Contrary to the belief that an oil reservoir is a homogeneous "tank of oil," the reservoir is complex, with faults splitting it into segments with diverging vertical and horizontal flow conditions. A production engineer explained:

> We develop an increased understanding of how wells interact through the production history. The key is to see the wells together since the optimization of one well might lead to loss of overall production given the right circumstances. When doing this evaluation and analysis work we juggle between parameters: temperature, pressure, water production, production rates, gas, and availability of equipment in the offshore process plant.

As a company ethnographer I was asked to follow the work of production engineers as they increasingly used real-time data and video collaboration to work across boundaries (Hepsø 2006, 2009). My job and objective was to describe the emerging collaboration practices in production optimization that developed across professional domains and geographical locations during the pilot. My challenge as ethnographer and facilitator was to understand the emerging new practice and its context in an ethnographically rich way while also developing ways to document and communicate the practices in formal terms. Over the course of the pilot project I observed the engineers' collaboration environment, activities, and work with real-time data. Real-time data here are continuous streams of measurements that come from well and process plant sensors. Together these measurements comprise parameters that can be adjusted to tune the performance of the wells and production facilities. I also conducted interviews with people directly or indirectly involved in the pilot. In the end, I helped the production engineers write an experience report that documented their new practices. After the evaluation I also helped a larger team of production engineers describe the new practice in flow charts. These flow charts eventually became the new corporate standard (Figure 23.4).

A second-mode approach is vital to grasp the emerging practice of knowledge professionals, even when the final objective is to document new standards in first-mode terms. Much of their highly skilled work involves double-checking and back and forth communication among professionals, and it is hard to grasp the essence of the work using a temporal sequence or flow of activities. The key second-mode issues here were to help the production engineers improve this double-checking data/information capability through improved communication among the peers. Such activities were not visible in the formal representations. Reflecting on the representation in the flow chart, one production engineer acknowledged:

> The flow chart represents the main structure of our DPO [detailed production optimization] work, but it does not go into details around how we assess weaknesses in the data sets and discuss these shortcomings between us. This is a far more complex communication process.

Ethnographic observation revealed how the engineers used real-time data and how they analyzed and aggregated data using numerous production engineering software tools to develop a situated understanding of the reservoir (Almklov and Hepsø 2011; Hepsø 2006, 2009; Monteiro et al. 2012; Østerlie et al. 2012). Important activities to understand in this work involved the validation of information and data, comparing and contrasting and double-checking the information. The communication among peers around ongoing work was frequent and intensive. These conversations and discussions took up much of the day and were integrated in the more sequential but knowledge-intensive work they did. To see this required a second-mode understanding, a perspective difficult to envision with a first-mode sequential understanding of work.

Figure 23.4. The DPO work practice objectified as a process model.

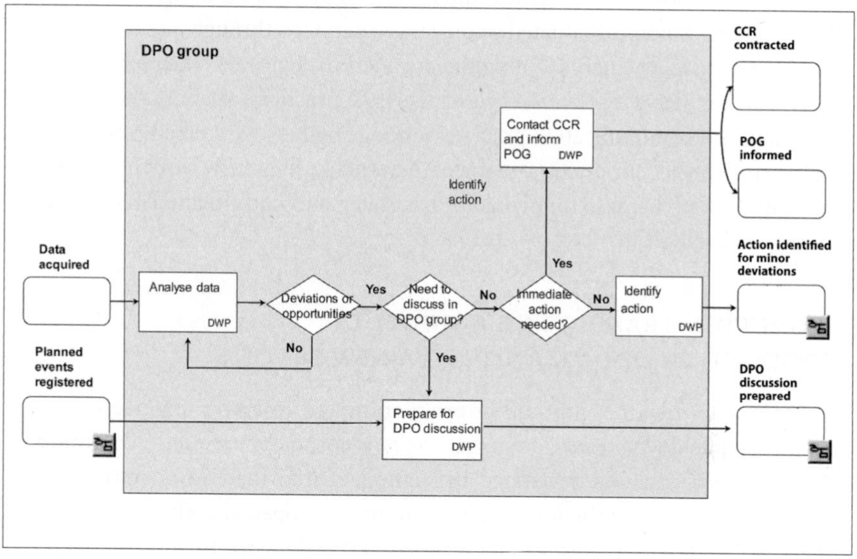

The three-month pilot was repeated in other oil fields in the same geographical area. The work practices were later defined as detailed production optimization (DPO). Since pilots could document a substantial increase in production, the DPO concept was sanctioned as a new practice for all of the company's oil fields in Norway. The basic principles behind the DPO concept were to be documented as process model charts, since the company had started using process models to describe work and procedures throughout its business. Ethnographic input from past pilot evaluations was vital for the group of domain advisors and production engineers that finally received the mandate to create the business processes of DPO in Statoil. Since I had a role in following up several of these pilots, I became a member of this team. The situated practice had to be simplified: a number of roles were described, new collaboration principles were defined, and new office environment features associated with collaboration spaces and information and communications technology (ICT) requirements (common information spaces) were set up in this process of generalizing the DPO concept. The flow chart (Figure 23.4) has the same sequential flow; the round rectangle represents a product or a new start condition. The rectangles are activities, and the final box represents decisions that must be taken. The communicative and knowledge-intensive work between the various production engineers is too complex to represent, so the DPO group is defined as an overall category.

The double-level language approach in this vignette starts with the second mode; it is ethnographic in nature and has the opposite goal compared with the first vignette. Emerging situated practices are depicted through a second-mode perspective as they emerge among the production engineers. The second mode is critical for grasping the essence of the new practices, such as the double-checking and communication practices among engineers described earlier. Still, in the end I helped production engineers externalize these new work practices as first-mode flow charts so they could be translated and implemented in a broader corporate setting.

VIGNETTE 3: TRANSLATING A MODEL OF PRODUCTION OPTIMIZATION TO A NEW SETTING

This vignette describes a group of production and reservoir engineers in yet another oil field who tried to translate the new corporate production optimization standard that was developed in Vignette 2 into their work setting. The challenge was to take the formal descriptions developed elsewhere and adjust them, both complying with company policy and at the same time taking advantage of situated practices in an environment that is older and has a more complex and tightly integrated technical infrastructure.

I participated in a team of colleagues with backgrounds in informatics and computer science. We observed the oil field during several phases of their development process, over a period of one and a half years. The first objective was to develop a report describing emerging second-mode situated practices and come up with suggestions for how the company's DPO first-mode requirements and expectations could be translated into a stepwise plan later to be implemented. The second task was to execute the plan and document the emergence of new second-mode practices (Hepsø et al. 2009). This example is important because it shows the potential fallacy of first-mode representations and why they always have to be adjusted to situated practices when they move across space and time.

The ethnographic study in this organization was done concurrently with the deployment of the DPO first-mode model. This work concluded (not surprisingly) that the situation in this organization was very different from that in Vignette 2 and that it was impossible to develop a blueprint of the DPO process model in this new setting. While the DPO originated at newer oil fields, this oil field was a "tail producer": the peak production phase was over, and it was just a question of time before the field would have to close down. When income decreases, so does investment (in information systems or rig hardware), and the fields has to live with existing infrastructure. The three old platforms at this field were heavily integrated with each other and the infrastructure was very complex, which brought tough challenges to coordination and dependencies. In addition, the field had a more complex oil reservoir, so the production engineers were more dependent on collaboration with reservoir engineers. The real-time data infrastructure was old. Most staff was located in a traditional office environment; open spaces and collaboration rooms were scarce. The production engineers were separated in different locations in the building, and there were strong cliques divided either by age/experience or by which wells and production systems they supported. Among the production engineers were several key people with long experience and dominating worldviews. They took great pride in their present way of working, were resistant to changing their established work practice, and were not comfortable with using sophisticated collaboration systems. The DPO concept was unfamiliar, and it threatened the power and existing status of the senior personnel.

Still, among the younger crew, several production engineers welcomed the idea that the oil field needed a way of working that moved more in the direction of the DPO concept. They saw the need to be better informed and coordinated across the three aging platforms and office environments. Putting production engineers in the same collaboration room would increase the notion of a shared situational awareness. A small part of the organization tested out the concept first and co-located themselves in a collaboration room. This group created an environment in which they learned faster when sitting together, improved

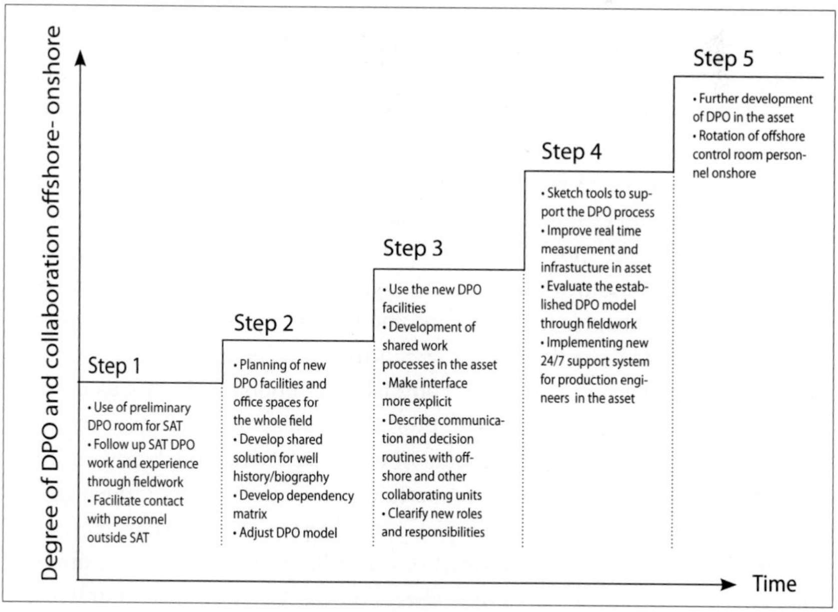

Figure 23.5. A "staircase" for developing situated practices.

their shared situational awareness and experience transfer, and reported similar experiences as those presented in Vignette 2.

To facilitate the translation of DPO in this oil field, our team arranged several workshops with the production engineers and set up a study trip to other DPO locations elsewhere in Norway. A stepwise improvement process was developed (Figure 23.5). This "staircase" described how management of this oil field could move closer to the corporate standard by setting up new, targeted activities. Workshops helped to flesh out how the DPO should be translated. One example was that a detailed plan for an ideal DPO group work week was set up. This new plan was based on ethnographic input that captured the existing work week of production engineers, and also incorporated the engineers' own improvements to their schedules. Ethnographic input and interviews provided input both in step 1 and step 4 of the staircase (see Figure 23.5). Much of this knowledge was used when the oil field implemented a new organizational model for the production engineers with new roles and responsibilities. We followed the work practices of this group until the spring of 2008, when it moved into a new office environment specially designed for their needs. Production engineers had become co-located in collaborative environments and the DPO work process had found its situated practice, though tensions between the younger and older staff continued.

CONCLUSION

Business processing modeling brings to mind what Clifford Geertz (1973) called "*models of*." The problem is, as Geertz pointed out, *models of* often become *models for*. If *models of* are insufficiently informed by larger ideas and concepts—what second-level mode insights provide—then realizing these "blueprints" in practice (*models for*) will inevitably be ineffective. In a larger conceptual sense, business processing models are metaphorical. Moreover, in this or in other cases, whatever root metaphor of a model is chosen—for instance, that of a machine—it becomes difficult to change in the next incarnation. The key argument in this chapter is that to become something more than an instrumental activity (and not be trapped within the machine analogy), there must be a combined focus on formalism and dialog: a "double-level language." My three vignettes are different configurations that display the dualism in the first and second modes of communication. There is an interactional space in this dualism that can improve the illumination of work in process modeling. In this interactional space, the anthropologist can have an important role, and the three cases represent typical situations we will meet. We have to retain the situated understanding of work. It is always the discourse on the cultural level that gives power and meaning to the formal representations. Still, as an anthropologist working in industry, I have to go from my "thick descriptions" of work practices to "thin descriptions" that can be communicated and taken to new locations. This means that I cannot escape the first mode of work no matter how much I try. If we want to "catch" work practice, we have to externalize it in one way or another, thereby risking making it simplified and stereotyped.

REFERENCES

Almklov, Petter, and Vidar Hepsø. 2011. "Between and Beyond Data: How Analogue Field Experience Informs the Interpretation of Remote Data Sources in Petroleum Reservoir Geology." *Science, Technology and Human Values* 41(4):539–62.

Clancey, William J., Patricia Sachs, Maarten Sierhuis, and Ron van Hoof. 1998. "BRAHMS: Simulating Practice for Work Systems Design." *International Journal of Human-Computer Studies* 49:831–65.

Geertz, Clifford. 1973. *The Interpretation of Culture*. New York: Basic Books

Giere, Ronald N. 2004. "How Models Are Used To Represent Reality." *Philosophy of Science* 71:742–52.

Gjersvik, Reidar, and Vidar Hepsø. 1998. "Using Models of Work Practice as Reflective and Communicative Devices: Two Cases from the Norwegian Offshore Industry." Paper presented at the Participatory Design Conference, November 12–14, Seattle, WA.

Hepsø, Vidar. 1997. "The Social Construction and Visualization of a Norwegian Offshore Installation." *Proceedings of the Fifth European Conference on Computer Supported Cooperative Work*. Amsterdam: Kluwer Academic Publishers. http://www.ecscw.org/1997/08.pdf (accessed June 2, 2012).

_____. 2006. "When Are We Going To Address Organizational Robustness and Collaboration as Something Else than a Residual Factor?" Society of Petroleum Engineers Paper No. 1000712. Presented at the SPE Conference on Intelligent Energy, April 11-13, Amsterdam, the Netherlands.

_____. 2009. "'Common' Information Spaces in Knowledge Intensive Work: Representation and Negotiation of Meaning in Computer Supported Collaboration Rooms." In *Handbook of Research on Knowledge-Intensive Organizations*, edited by Dariusz Jemielniak, Leon Kozminski, and Jerzy Kociatkiewicz, 279–94. Hershey PA: Idea Group Publishing.

_____. 2012. "Doing Corporate Ethnography as an Insider." In *Advancing Ethnography in Corporate Environments*, edited by Brigitte Jordan, 151–62. Walnut Creek, CA: Left Coast Press.

Hepsø, Vidar, Glenn Munkvold, Knut R. Rolland, and Hans Hysing Olsen. 2009. "Ny praksis produksjonsoptimalisering muliggjort av integrert operasjon. Spredningen av detaljert produksjonsoptimalisering (DPO)" ["New Practice Production Optimization Enabled by Integrated Operations"). In *Forskning som endringsverktøy i organisasjoner* [*Research as Change Method in Organizations*], edited by Irene Lorentzen Hepsø and Trond Kongsvik, 55-73 Trondheim: Tapir.

Monteiro, Eric, Gasparas Jarulaitis, and Vidar Hepsø. 2012. "The Family Resemblance of Technologically Mediated Work Practices." *Information and Organization Journal* 22(3):169–87.

Østerlie, Thomas, Petter G. Almklov, and Vidar Hepsø. 2012. "Dual Materiality and Knowing in Oil and Gas Production." *Information & Organization* 22(2):85–105.

Robinson, Mike. 1991. "Double Level Language and Co-operative Working." *AI & Society* 5:34–60.

Robinson, Mike, and Liam Bannon. 1991. "Questioning Representations." *Proceedings of the Second European Conference on Computer Supported Cooperative Work*. Amsterdam: Kluwer Academic Publishers.

Sachs, Patricia. 1995. "Transforming Work: Collaboration, Learning and Design." *Communications of the ACM* 38(9):36–44.

Sierhuis, Marten. 1996. "Selective Ethnographic Analysis Qualitative Modeling for Work Place Ethnography." Nynex Science and Technology. http://216.122.146.242/documentation/papers/aaa.pdf (accessed 2.June 2012).

Suchman, Lucy A. 1994. "Do Categories Have Politics?" *Computer Supported Cooperative Work Journal* 2(3):177–90.

______. 1995. "Making Work Visible." *Communications of the ACM* 38(9):56–64.

______. 2007. *Human-Machine Reconfigurations: Plans and Situated Actions.* Cambridge, UK: Cambridge University Press.

NOTES

1 A model seeks to describe the relationships between a specified set of phenomena and tries to represent them in a simplified form. It is a heuristic device, more or less arbitrary to the empirical reality it is supposed to represent. Its only test of validity is the degree it helps to improve our understanding of a phenomenon we approach. The perspective of modeling described here is rooted in a practice perspective associated with an embodied and noncognitive anthropology. Models are primarily tools that we use and relate to through practice (see Almklov and Hepsø 2011; Giere 2004; Østerlie et al. 2012). They do not exist just in the heads of people, but are also embodied in the world of artifacts that we use and create through our practice.

2 For more than 20 years I have worked in a large oil company as a researcher and consequently as an insider in this organization. Insider research is not a topic that I address in this essay; see Hepsø (2012) for more details on this approach. For the last five years I have also been an adjunct professor at a management school and a university in Norway, a position that enables me to spend some time pursuing my academic writing and interests.

24

Decoding Culture: Cultural Insight & Semiotics in Britain

CATO HUNT & SAM BARTON

> The world is pallid, ill organized, and hard to read. We distribute meanings to make them more meaningful (McCracken 2012:120).

Brands and consumers are suspended in what Clifford Geertz famously called "webs of significance" (Geertz 1973:5), and a canny marketer needs to understand how cultural meanings and ideas come into being and are communicated. Without this understanding, marketers cannot meaningfully weave their brands into the fabric of consumers' lives. As McCracken puts it, "Culture supplies us with knowledge we don't know we know, that operates invisibly to shape our understanding of the world" (2009:47).

This chapter explores commercial semiotics and the role it plays in helping brands reflect and capitalize on the cultural context in which they exist. We give a brief history of the evolution of the industry with a focus on Britain, an overview of key approaches, and then shed some light on the ways in which the industry could evolve in the future.

The applied semiotic discipline has had a varied and complex history, having grown up in different geographies and with different theoretical lineages. There have been two key paradigms at play, that of Ferdinand de Saussure ([1916] 1974) and Charles Sanders Peirce (1867), who coined the terms "semiology" and "semiotics," respectively. Saussure was a linguist; his structural approach to analyzing textual materials has heavily influenced thinking in continental Europe.[1] Peirce's approach was based in philosophy, logic, and interpreting evidence. His ideas around the interpretation of meaning as an active process between signs in culture and the way they are understood by people continues to resonate through much contemporary semiotic thinking.[2]

Handbook of Anthropology in Business, edited by Rita Denny and Patricia Sunderland, 447–462.

However, commercial semiotics in Britain has forged its own, more eclectic path. It began in the early 1980s, in a literary theory class taught by Malcolm Evans at North London Polytechnic (now London Metropolitan). One of his students, Virginia Valentine, an advertising copywriter turned qualitative researcher, began to think about the implications of applying semiotics to business and branding questions. She was particularly inspired by Claude Lévi-Strauss and his use of myth in resolving cultural contradiction, Vladimir Propp's use of structure and narrative, and the cultural meanings and codes of Roland Barthes (Evans 2010). After some persuading from Valentine, Evans joined her at the agency she founded with her husband Monty Alexander in 1989, Semiotic Solutions.

At this stage, Evans was already incorporating ideas from a broader scope of theory than solely semiotics. His introduction of Raymond Williams' ([1980] 2005) model of culture that identifies residual, dominant, and emergent patterns was central to the development of the field, as it established the capability to make well-founded predictions about the future trajectories of culture (Evans and Shivakumar 2010). Williams also draws a valuable distinction between the study of the "object" and the study of the "practice" ([1980] 2005:48). He spoke about looking at sets of objects collectively to identify the driving forces beneath, rather than exclusively assessing the meaning of individual objects of study. There is a strong argument that the field has more in common with the British cultural studies of Raymond Williams and Stuart Hall, or the work of Marshall McLuhan, than pure semiotics as established by Saussure and Peirce. The approach is marked out by the pragmatic application of different approaches in addition to—and often blended with—semiotics, such as cultural studies, anthropology, or psychology. This is perhaps the reason that the term "cultural insight" rather than purely semiotics in the United Kingdom has gained some precedence in recent years.[3] The emerging discipline in Britain continues to expand its methodological toolbox, absorbing influences from a broad range of academic theory and practice. Indeed, many commercial practitioners in Britain have diverse academic backgrounds. At Added Value, for instance, academic backgrounds span art history, English, modern languages, psychology, sociology, linguistics, anthropology, and cultural studies. This brings a constant flow of new ways of thinking and approaching clients' challenges. Alex Gordon talks about the need to embrace the "postmodern inter-textual fabric of our world" (2004:14); this is perhaps a defining point of view for the British school of semiotics. He goes on to urge the industry "to take imaginative hypothetical leaps between different disciplines, drawing them together in a web of connection, which strengthens the brand at the centre" (Gordon 2004:23). Since its inception, commercial semiotics in Britain has emerged as a hybrid methodology that, like a magpie (see Dexter 2007), draws on multiple theoretical strands.

But how does this actually play out in the commercial context? We begin with a review of some of the key approaches in the commercial semiotician's toolbox, followed by some case studies on their practical application for brands.

ANALYZING A CULTURAL "TEXT"

Semiotics is an analysis of cultural meaning produced through signs. Applied to marketing, the semiotic (or "decoding") process involves making sense of a brand's expression as a communication text: from product design, packaging, and advertising through to retail design, websites, and experiential events. We break the text down into its constituent parts (color, imagery, shape and form, materials, typeface, language, audio, and so on) to uncover an implicit cluster of meanings. It is through this assemblage of texts and signs that a brand conveys its point of view on the world.

We would suggest that we don't just see things: we interpret signs, whose meanings draw from history, myth, and ideology. As Holt and Cameron explain, "All mass-cultural expressions—whether a film or a retail store design or packaging graphics—rely on elements for which the meaning has been well established historically in the culture" (2010:175). Think of an apple; now think what an apple can communicate or signify. It signifies a fruit that grows on trees, tastes sweet, and is often green. If we dig a little deeper and think about what the picture of the apple suggests as a cultural symbol, then things begin to get interesting. On one level we could say that an apple signifies freshness, health, nature. Take yet another step towards uncovering the meaning of the apple, and we encounter Johnny Appleseed, the Big Apple, "an apple a day keeps the doctor away," the Apple technology company, Eve's temptation, and Halloween apple bobbing, to mention just a few.

Now let's look at this in action. The ad campaign for the DKNY fragrance Be Delicious is a wonderful example of how a brand can play with signs to create a complex and compelling story. In the print ad,[4] we see a beautiful young woman staring at us, lips parted. She's just taken her first bite of an apple, juice (or water?) drips down her finger, and her knitted cardigan has fallen off her shoulders to reveal the straps of her lingerie. She's surrounded by a golden halo of sunshine (borrowing from religious iconography of the Virgin Mary), and the New York skyline is reflected in the sleek apple-shaped bottles placed in front of her, suggesting breasts. The brand is cleverly playing with a culturally resonant tension between sexuality and innocence.[5]

The real power of commercial semiotics comes when interpreting patterns that emerge through a larger corpus of cultural texts. We look for how similar ideas are communicated and expressed across texts, theming and clustering as we go. This is valuable when applied to the central idea or concept that a brand is founded upon, for example, masculinity, softness, indulgence, empowerment, Italianness. So, if we wanted to locate the DKNY ad within a broader context of "femininity," we would not only look at other brand communication in fragrance, but would also look outside the category to personal care, fashion, jewelry, and cosmetics. We can then add another layer and look at how femininity is expressed in broader culture by reading books, news stories, magazines, and blogs; watching TV shows and films; visiting stores and trade shows; and immersing ourselves in cultural events and experiences. (In the past our immersions have included learning how to dance to "feel Latinness" by a former Miss World contestant in Miami, fishing with a rural community in Thailand to understand "freshness," and staying in fancy hotels to understand the "luxury experience.") By looking outside the category, we are able to identify the broader patterns around the concept we are exploring; these patterns are formed around clusters of signs and meanings, which we call "codes." The value of drawing codes from adjacent categories is their ability to clarify and enrich current expressions, as well as to introduce innovative and emergent expressions not currently in the core category. Once we have identified codes, we are able to locate the brand and its competitors within this wider context, which creates new ways for us to think about the client issue.

CULTURAL MAPPING

Getting to codes is only part of the process. To identify potential opportunities for the brand moving forward, the codes are typically "mapped" in terms of key tensions and binary oppositions. Mapping codes in this way locates a brand's strategy within a broader landscape of meaning, whether at the category level (e.g., fragrance) or the identity level (e.g., femininity).

Such "code maps" are developed on a project-by-project basis, according to the client issue. Another way of mapping cultural meaning is Virginia Valentine's "myth quadrant"[6] based on the structuralist thinking of Claude Lévi-Strauss. "The purpose of a myth," Lévi-Strauss stated, "is to provide a logical model capable of overcoming a contradiction" (1963:229). Valentine asserted that the "power of the brand myth seems to stand in direct proportion to the dynamism of the contradiction it resolves: i.e., the stronger the oppositions, the stronger the myth—and, consequently, the stronger the brand positioning" (2001:9).

We've drawn up a myth quadrant for skin care (Figure 24.1). The quadrant is defined by two cultural "norms"—"traditional nature" (e.g., plants, herbs, homemade preparations, folklore, old wives' tales) and "modern science" (e.g., laboratories, doctors, scientific formulas)—and two contradictions—"modern nature" (e.g., a departure from "green nature" to geology such as crystals and

Figure 24.1. A myth quadrant for skin care.

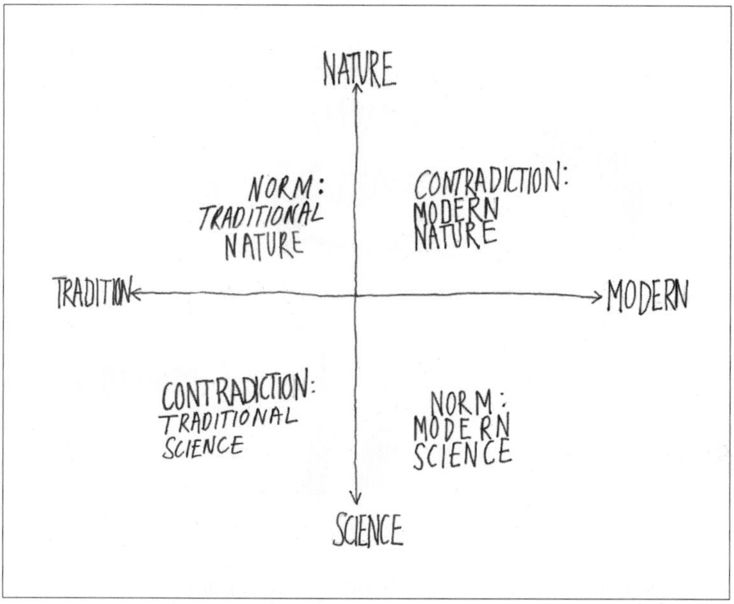

volcanic ash to natural forces like magnetism) and "traditional science" (e.g., ancient rituals revisited and "proven" with modern science). The latter two have provided fertile ground for many skin care brands to explore: for example, Jurlique and Korres play in "modern nature," and Aesop, Kiehl's, and Pukka in "traditional science."

Cultural meaning is constantly changing, or as McCracken asserts, "culture is hyperactive" (2009:52). It is messy, chaotic, and mercurial in nature. And as meaning shifts, so do the ways in which ideas are expressed. The casting of James Bond, for example, brilliantly adapts and responds to prevailing ideals of masculinity to stay relevant (Figure 24.2). One of the core methods used to understand this flow of change is drawn from Raymond Williams ([1980] 2005), who asserted that at any given time there are residual, dominant, and emergent cultural forms.

Residual codes are dated; those which have been around for some time and are out of touch with the culture around it. Dominant codes are "everywhere" and reflect the dominant mood of present-day society. You might say they are so normative, they appear middle of the road.

By contrast, emergent codes are what surf at the cusp of the wave. They are evidence of a new infiltration of thinking and approach. We identify these by looking for things that disrupt the pattern, what McCracken calls the "weak

Figure 24.2. The changing face of masculinity. Illustration by Sam Barton, 2012.

signals" (2009) that herald future change, or the "oddities" that he goes on to define as "Culturematics" (McCracken 2012). Ten years ago, when Rachel Lawes presented her paper "Demystifying Semiotics," she described how the color gold is no longer a reliable cue for luxury. Referencing biscuits specifically, she explained that the real luxury brands were more likely to be wrapped in "corrugated cardboard in subdued, natural colours" (Lawes 2002:2). Looking at this a decade later, we have had our fill of brown paper packaging. In the last few years of economic uncertainty, it seems we are all ready for some bling again, evidenced by a carnival of color and pattern. And a bit of gold. Here we have a sign that reemerges with the cultural meaning it once had. Thus goes the ebb and flow of meaning.

Tapping into emergent codes is important for brands looking to pave their way to future success. Very often, the search for these emergent codes goes beyond a brand's own category. If, for example, we wanted to understand how to embed luxury as a central element of a brand's positioning, we would look at a range of luxury categories such as fashion, liquor, motor vehicles, jewelry, hotels, and objects d'art for inspiration on what the most current expression of luxury might look like. But we wouldn't stop here. We would venture to the fringes and niches of society to find the things that aren't easily visible in the mainstream.

Yet by emergent we don't necessarily mean "trendy." To quote Charles Leech, semioticians specialize in "the art of thinking profoundly about banal things" (2012:7). Good semioticians will get excited by exploring the evolution of household cleaning products or the humble loaf of bread. We scope a wide range of cultural texts. We need to find the DIY biotech labs, retiree-only universities, dissolvable packaging, the community cooperative projects that are changing the way we do business. When we're looking for the "emergent" we often don't know what we are looking for (although we'll have a few hunches). This is often the antithesis of our technical analysis as it's almost impossible to have a clearly defined corpus of texts to analyze. We have to use our instinct to spot the patterns, make connections between disparate cultural signifiers, and, finally, identify the movement of changing codes.

TURNING IT INTO STRATEGY

Semiotics and other cultural insight methods are increasingly being used as strategic tools for clients, offering a new perspective on how to view brands. Semiotics enables clients to see the world differently, and, as a consequence, allows clients to build stronger, more meaningful brands. It provides a different kind of map, one through which they can locate themselves within the world around them. We like to think of it as a brand satellite navigation system. Which roads are already clogged by the competition? Which are quiet and pose an opportunity? Which routes are unchartered or still being built, revealing emerging future potential? When done well, it vividly brings to life the cultural landscape a brand lives in, and can help map out potential future opportunities.

When used in brand positioning, semiotics can be used to explore an idea central to the brand, such as empowerment, joy, indulgence, or naturalness. For instance, a recent project for Asia Pacific Breweries saw us delve into the idea of "Asian Energy" for Tiger beer, one of their flagship brands. For several years, Tiger had communicated the idea of "winning," but this was becoming less relevant as cultural attitudes in Asia shifted away from overt self-congratulation. The brand team had decided that moving forward, it wanted to own the idea of "Asian Energy," having identified it as a fertile positioning area. However, the Tiger team were unsure of exactly what "Asian Energy" could mean and, most important, how Tiger beer was going to communicate this in a relevant way to consumers across a variety of Asian markets. Since "Asia" is made up of an immensely diverse array of cultures, we explored widely, from looking at the architecture and design scene in Singapore, to pop-up retail collectives in Jakarta, to underground club promotion in Hong Kong. Tiger knew that it needed a take on "Asian Energy" as seen from the perspective of Asia, so we also interviewed cultural experts in each geography to ensure our findings were grounded locally. We developed nine unique potential expressions of "Asian Energy," vividly brought to life. One of our codes, "Dynamic Diversity," explored the idea that Asian cities are hotbeds of multiculturalism, the crossroads of cultures that collide and combine to create incredible contrasts: ancient iconography with street art, traditional puppetry with rap music, modern skyscrapers cradling small, centuries-old restaurants. Rather than being disjointed, the Asian megacity displays harmony through its rich tapestry of contrasts. The energy this creates is one of excitement and discovery, where inspiration is drawn from this rich diversity. Another code—"Alive at Night"—brought to life the idea that a new day starts when the sun goes down, that Asian Energy is brightest and most exuberant at night. The cities pulse here with the hum of neon more than any other place on earth. The "Asian Megacity" was highlighted as the key source of Asian Energy, an idea which was developed into new creative concepts to be tested with consumers. The final campaign launched across Asia in the spring of 2013 (Figure 24.3).

As we are living in an experience economy, we have pushed the boundaries in terms of conducting semiotic analysis in the real world, through our creation of culturally immersive experiences. In 2011, Philips presented us with the challenge of providing them with a deep understanding of the global trends of hair care to inform their 10-year innovation pipeline, to carry the brand from being a background player to a leader in the category. Understanding global hair care is no mean feat given the incredible global variation in styles, hair type, fashion influences, care routines, and rituals. We realized that we needed a different kind of cultural insight methodology, one that didn't rely too heavily on mediated sources such as advertising, which would play back what the category was already doing. We created an approach that drew on ethnographic methods and cultural insight, alongside consumer workshops, trends, and expert panel sessions with industry style movers and shakers, typifying an increasingly hybrid approach.

Figure 24.3. The Asian megacity brought to life in this campaign for Tiger beer. Courtesy of APB Breweries.

The Added Value and Philips teams worked together during our week-long "cultural immersions" across five markets, propelling everybody into the real-world spaces shaping the meanings of the category. We brought Philips face-to-face with the source material, helping them navigate the intricate cultural contexts framing their challenge: the in-home hair rituals in Mumbai, the style-crazed teens in Shanghai, the future of coloring as seen in a hidden salon in East London.

By guiding Philips through the exploration of leading-edge sites of cultural creation, we were able to capture spontaneous and emergent expressions and give them the unique opportunity to become a participant observer. The immersion provided the client with a more intuitive understanding of the semiotic process, while allowing them to collaborate in the research giving a depth of client buy-in that traditional approaches rarely offer. Our clients "lived" the research with us: we were scrutinized by a trichologist, had our hair "laminated," and one of the team even returned from Paris with pink hair. Philips emerged with a rich and inspiring array of potential global and local innovation areas, which we built into an interactive desktop tool, mapping out their innovation pipeline. The process ensured the ideas were fully supported internally; indeed, they are already being implemented. It was a totally new way of doing cultural insight for us and the client, and has consequently completely changed the way they do future-focused innovation.

These projects have shown clients how culture can inform big strategic questions: Where to invest? Where to innovate? What to change? And how to do it?

LOOKING TO THE FUTURE

Although still modest in number, specialist agencies and semiotic and cultural insight departments in larger consultancies (like Added Value) are flourishing. We think we are finally at a tipping point; a moment in time where "culture" is becoming the new "consumer." The last three years have seen marketing books such as McCracken's *Chief Culture Officer* (2009) and *Culturematic* (2012), Holt and Cameron's *Cultural Strategy* (2010), the inaugural Semiofest[7] conference in the summer of 2012, and, at Added Value, we've seen cultural insight propelled to the top of the CEO's global priorities. This shift, we think, is due to two key factors. First, brand owners are waking up to the fact that traditional consumer insight is not enough to win in the new marketing economy: weaving multiple insight strands together to make sense of the problem is becoming the smart way to do research. Second, practitioners have worked hard to leave behind the reputation of semiotics as being overly intellectualized and "black box"

(Valentine 2007) to something more accessible and useful for clients. But herein lies one of the biggest tensions in the industry; the desire to stay true to theoretical frameworks and processes versus the need to provide pragmatic and useful solutions to our clients. Malcolm Evans has said that in academia we can talk of "interesting things for hours on end; in the commercial world we need to talk about things that are useful for clients" (Malcolm Evans quoted in MacFarquhar 1994:60). Increasing demand for cultural and semiotic insight has come from this refocus, as practitioners become more comfortable with the balancing act. As Alex Gordon explains, "It's the less disciplined, the less rigid, which brings a level of richness and provides a deeper level of insight that's more powerful, relevant, and useful" (2012).

As cultural insight develops at a rapid pace, we can start hypothesizing about how it will shape shift in the future. What will it draw on and be influenced by? How will our roles change? It's not hard to imagine how "managing meaning" will become a more focused exercise across many walks of life. Semioticians will increasingly be working at advertising and design agencies, in architecture practices, and in the public sector. Indeed, before we know it there will be semiotic spin doctors working for celebrities and heads of state.

For the industry to evolve, there will undoubtedly be an increasing blurring of boundaries between semiotics and other fields of study such as psychology, neuroscience, the applied humanities, computer science, statistics, anthropology, and behavioral economics. For example, developments in brain science will likely have an affect on how we view, understand, and research cultural meaning. We know that "culture wires the brain" (Park and Huang 2010), that the social and the mind are inseverable. The interplay between how meanings exist in the world and how individuals perceive and experience them is a marketer's dream, even if it's one we may never fully understand. Another area that will be fruitful for semioticians is the work being advanced in psychoanalysis and psychological anthropology, which looks at the interaction of mental and cultural processes. Gananath Obeyesekere describes "the work of culture" as "the process whereby symbolic forms existing on the cultural level get created and recreated through the minds of people" (1990:xix). Given the role of brands in identity formation, there is a real opportunity here to understand the relationships between human motivations, how they operate throughout conscious and unconscious thought, and the impact this has on cultural meaning.

The net will be cast far and wide as truly groundbreaking insight approaches are sought, with both academics and commercial semioticians needing to collaborate to make this happen. The following section explores some of the future directions we think will shape the industry in the next decade.

Socio-Semiotics

Although not a new field, the full, practical application of socio-semiotic approaches have yet to be realized. By linking semiotics to core methods of social anthropology, we are able to widen desk-based investigations to the exploration of sociocultural spaces, to examine the production of meaning at the level of social interaction between brands and consumers. The opportunity to conduct an extensive co-reading alongside consumers permits rich and multilayered interpretations of the facets of their daily life, and of their relationship and usage of brands. Understanding the whole person and not just some of their prominent needs helps us to understand people's deeper repertoire of experience, not only their associations and familiarity with brands. In the research community, the integrated co-reading of consumer and semiotic insight is happening more and more. Ethnography, and increasingly netnography (see Kozinets and Caliandro, this volume), is an obvious bedfellow. It works particularly effectively when we need to understand the dynamics within particular environments: understanding meal preparation and the role of the kitchen for example, or the experience of the retail space and the signs and meanings that play in these spheres.

The Digital & "Big Data" Revolution

The Big Data revolution is upon us. People follow, record, map, post, blog, share, create, tweet. It has opened the floodgates to unprecedented amounts of cultural data that we can access, analyze, and make useful. It is not new in market research (your loyalty cards and shopping habits have been put to good use by retailers for many years), but we are now seeing the development of breakthrough software resources and techniques that will enable semioticians to analyze digital "multimodal" texts: photos, images, music, video content, interactive websites, and so on.[8] By creating tagging protocols, we can create algorithms to link and cluster data based on meaning. In a similar vein, Chris Arning (2011) talks about the potential for crowdsourced semiotics, referencing Tim Berners-Lee et al.'s (2001) vision for a Semantic Web that understands and connects the "meanings" of data. The notion of a global, searchable, open-source database of semiotically tagged cultural texts would be an exciting development for the industry. The hope is that this could revolutionize the way we work by helping us to get to meaning clusters and codes more quickly. This would give more time for "deep thinking" since gathering the right corpus of material can be very labor intensive, especially when working in different geographies. It's possible to track cultural shifts on a massive scale, as seen with the emergence of "culturomics," a new discipline developed by a team from Harvard and Google

Books, which focuses on the quantification of cultural trends. In 2010, Google Books Ngram Viewer was launched, the world's first culturomic browser. It contains more than 500 billion words from digitized books across seven languages published between 1500 and 2008. From the data emerge fascinating tales of our cultural evolution, from linguistic and grammatical changes over time, to the quest for fame, to stories of censorship and suppression. By using the Google Ngram Viewer we are able to type in our own words and phrases, enabling students and researches to chart the cultural developments of interest to them. (Beware, it's addictive.) The project has begun with books but it's clear the vision is grand, to include "newspapers, manuscripts, maps, artwork and a myriad of [*sic*] other human creations" (Michel et al. 2010:181).

The idea of being able to quantify meaning across different cultures and languages has huge implications for how marketers monitor their brand. We'll see a shift in techniques that enable brands to track and manage their meaning and cultural relevance over time. This is pattern recognition on a huge scale.

Experiential Semiotics

A sign can be interpreted through different sensory modalities: not just visual, but auditory, kinesthetic, tactile, olfactory, gustatory. Our experiences, perceptions, and memory can be shaped by the different modes through which we experience something. Gunther Kress cites an experiment in which schoolchildren are asked to describe a visit to the British Museum via a story or drawing. Those who write the story describe salient events in the order they happened, whereas the drawings focus on "the simultaneous presence of entities, shown in spatial relations within a framed space," demonstrating that each "conforms to the semiotic logic of its mode" (Kress 2010:75).

In the next decade, brands are going to engage the senses in ways we haven't seen before: taste, touch, aural, and olfactory cues; 3D and HD; augmented and virtual reality. In their paper "Sonic Semiotics" (Arning and Gordon 2006), Alex Gordon and Chris Arning point to the lack of attention given to the "aural consumer landscape" in the brand experience. They emphasize the powerful role music can play in the branding process, lamenting the fact that it is so often a last-minute addition in the editing suite. The work of Giorgio Grignaffini (1998) on the semiotics of taste enables us to think about it as more than a psychological manifestation. He discusses three "nuances" or ways in which we experience taste: perceptual sense, aesthetic judgement, and the social dimension which relates to preferences being linked to certain groups such as social class. Building on this, Jean-Jacques Boutaud (1999) talks about a broader field he calls "synesthesic semiology," which seeks to understand interactions between the senses. Chiva describes the powerful effect of "synesthesia" as "more than the mere sum of the sensory inputs" (1996). No sense works in isolation, and thus it will help us "establish the procedures surrounding the drawing up of a product's 'sensory map'"(Boutaud 1999). Semiotics could play a critical role in helping understand and craft the multisensory world of the brand and translating how our senses convey emotional experience to consumers (see also Malefyt, this volume).

CREATIVE INNOVATION

Within the context of marketing innovation, the key role for commercial semioticians is to be a provocateur or "agitator" (Gordon 2012). We are comfortable working with extremes, oppositions, and otherness. We will be the people in the room suggesting that a product's "darkness" should be dramatized by using "light." This sense of energy and change is echoed by McCracken's vision of the Chief Culture Officer as being "an internal entrepreneur, and innovation agent inside the corporation" (2009:107).

We envision a future that sees semioticians working more closely with the "creative" arms of marketing and branding from the start of the creation process. Working alongside product and packaging designers, copywriters, retail designers, digital designers, 3D printing experts, social network developers, and experience curators, the role would be to provide inspiration on the most culturally resonant ways to breathe life into a brand.

Semiotic and cultural analysis are increasingly being used at the core of innovation, and indeed this is exactly what Douglas Holt and Douglas Cameron argue for in their book *Cultural Strategy.* They demonstrate through a series of case studies that "innovating in cultural expression—what we call cultural innovation—is a powerful tool for building new business and reviving failing ones" (Holt 2010:183).[9] Strong cultural expression, they say, is at the heart of iconic brands. Absolutely, if a semiotic approach enables us to break down the signs and signifiers of meaning, then we are also perfectly placed to take the creative leaps in the reconstruction, distortion, and creation of new ones. We think the role of cultural analysts and semioticians will increasingly move from being the "deconstructors" of meaning to the "constructors": the people loading up the creative springboard into the development of new categories, new products, new brands, and new, vibrant, culturally relevant brand expressions.

CONCLUSION

Commercial semiotics in Britain has been on an exciting journey. As it moves into the mainstream of market research, we expect to see more eclectic and richly layered approaches to understanding cultural meaning, which is becoming more broadly known as cultural insight.

As this happens, the role of the commercial semiotician will increasingly become that of a cultural guide and provocateur, at the heart of creating the strategic blueprint for brands and categories by influencing and disrupting cultural meaning, making creative leaps, and helping brands create a vision of their future self.

REFERENCES

Arning, Chris. 2011. "Semiotics in the Age of Digital." Paper presented at the Insight Show, London, June 30. Reproduced on SlideShare. www.slideshare.net/Semiotico/insight-show-slides-final-june-2011-text (accessed August 29th 2012).

Arning, Chris, and Alex Gordon. 2006. *Sonic Semiotics: The Role of Music in Marketing Communications.* Paper presented at the ESOMAR Congress, London, United Kingdom, September 17–20.

Arning, Chris. 2012. Interview with Cato Hunt, August 22.

Barthes, Roland. (1957) 1972. *Mythologies.* Translated by Annette Lavers. London: Paladin.

Berners-Lee, T., James Hendler, and Ora Lassila. 2001. "The Semantic Web." *Scientific American* 284(5):34–43.

Boutaud, Jean-Jacques. 1999. "Sensory Analysis: Towards the Semiotics of Taste." *Advances in Consumer Research,* edited by Eric J. Arnould and Linda M. Scott, 337–40. Provo, UT: Association for Consumer Research. http://www.acrwebsite.org/search/view-conference-proceedings.aspx?Id=8273.

Chandler, Daniel. 2007. *Semiotics: The Basics.* London: Routledge.

Chiva M. 1996. "Le Mangeur et le Mangé: La Complexité d'une Relation Fondamentale, Identités des Mangeurs, Images des Aliments." ["The Eater and the Eaten: The Subtle Complexity"]. In *Identités des Mangeurs, Images des Aliments,* edited by I. Giachetti, 11–30. Paris: Polytechnica.

Cobley, Paul. 2001. *The Routledge Companion to Semiotics and Linguistics.* London: Routledge.

Danesi, Marcel. 2004. *Messages, Signs, and Meanings: A Basic Textbook in Meanings and Communication.* Toronto: Canadian Scholars' Press.

de Saussure, Ferdinand. (1916) 1974. *Course in General Linguistics.* Translated by Wade Baskin. London: Fontana/Collins.

Dexter, Andy. 2007. "The Charm of Magpies: How New Disciplines Emerge in Market Research." Paper presented at the Market Research Society Golden Jubilee Conference, Brighton, United Kingdom, March 21–23.

Evans, Malcolm. 2010. "Virginia Valentine." *Semionaut* (blog), December 7. http://www.semionaut.net/virginia-valentine/ (accessed August 20, 2012).

Evans, Malcolm, and Hamsini Shivakumar. 2010. "Insight, Cultural Diversity, Revolutionary Change: Joined Up Semiotic Thinking for Developing Markets." Paper presented at the ESOMAR Congress, Athens, Greece, September 12–15.

Floch, Jean-Marie. (1990) 2001. *Semiotics, Marketing and Communication: Beneath the Signs, the Strategies.* Translated by Robin Orr Bodkin. New York: Palgrave.

Geertz, Clifford. 1973. "Thick Description: Towards an Interpretive Theory of Culture." In *The Interpretation of Cultures,* 3–32. New York: Basic Books.

Gordon, Alex. 2004. "Signs and Wonders: The Transformative Power of International Semiotics." Paper presented at the ESOMAR Worldwide Qualitative Research Conference, Cannes, Monaco, November 28–30.

_____. 2012. Interview with Cato Hunt, September 12th.

Greimas, Algirdas Julien. 1983. *Structural Semantics: An Attempt at a Method.* Translated by Daniele McDowell, Donald Schleifer, and Alan Velie. Lincoln: University of Nebraska Press.

_____. 1990. *The Social Sciences. A Semiotic View.* Translated by Frank Collins and Paul Perron. Minneapolis: University of Minnesota Press.

Grignaffini G. 1998. "Pour une sémiotique du goût: de l'esthésie au jugement, sémiotique gourmande. Du goût entre esthésie et sociabilité." *Nouveaux Actes Sémiotiques* 55–6:29–39, cited in Boutaud, Jean-Jaques, 1999.

Holt, D., and D. Cameron. 2010. *Cultural Strategy Using Innovation Ideologies To Build Breakthrough Brands.* Oxford, UK: Oxford University Press.

Kress, G. 2010. *Multimodality: A Social Semiotic Approach to Contemporary Communication.* London: Routledge.

Lawes, Rachel. 2002. "De-mystifying Semiotics: Some Key Questions Answered." *The International Journal of Market Research* 44(3):251–65.

Leech, Charles. 2012. *Introduction to Market Research Semiotics.* Unpublished paper. ABM Research. Used with permission from author.

Lévi-Strauss, Claude. 1963. "The Structural Study of Myth." In *Structural Anthropology, Vol. 1.* Translated by Clair Jacobson and Brooke Grundfest Shoepf, 206–31. New York: Basic.

MacFarquhar, Larissa. 1994. "A Semiotician Goes to Market." *Lingua Franca* September/October, 59–79.

McCracken, G. 2009. *Chief Culture Officer: How to Create a Living, Breathing Corporation.* New York: Basic.

_____. 2012. *Culturematic: How Reality TV, John Cheever, a Pie Lab, Julia Child, Fantasy Football, Burning Man, the Ford Fiesta Movement, Rube Goldberg, NFL Films, Wordle, Two and a Half Men, a 10,000-Year Symphony and ROFLCon Memes will Help You Create and Execute Breakthrough Ideas.* Boston: Harvard Business Review Press.

Michel, Jean-Baptiste, Yuan K. Shen, Aviva P. Aiden, Adrian Veres, Mathew K. Gray, the Google Books Team, et al. 2011. "Quantitative Analysis of Culture Using Millions of Digitized Books." *Science* 331:176–82.

Mick, David Glen, James E. Burroughs, Patrick Hetzel, and Mary Yoko Brannen. 2004. "Pursuing the Meaning of Meaning in the Commercial World: An International Review of Marketing and Consumer Research Founded on Semiotics." *Semiotica* 152(1/4):1–74.

Obeyesekere, Gananth. 1990. *The Work of Culture: Symbolic Transformation in Psychoanalysis and Anthropology.* Chicago, IL: University of Chicago Press.

Park, Denise C., and Chih-Mao Huang. 2010. "Culture Wires the Brain: A Cognitive Neuroscience Perspective." *Perspectives on Psychological Science* 5:391–400.

Peirce, Charles Sanders. 1867. "On a New List of Categories." In *Proceedings of the American Academy of Arts and Science* 7:287–98.

Valentine, Virginia. 2001. "The 'Notness' Principle." Paper presented at the Market Research Society Training Seminar, London, February.

_____. 2007. "Semiotics, What Now, My Love?" Paper presented at the Market Research Society Golden Jubilee Conference, Brighton, United Kingdom, March 21–23.

Williams, Raymond. (1980) 2005. *Culture and Materialism: Selected Essays.* London: Verso.

NOTES

Thanks to Inka Crosswaite for her contribution to shaping early drafts of this chapter, and to Marcus Alfonsetti, Hazel Barkworth, Izzy Pugh, Ian LaPoint, Alec Donald, Scotty Hawkes, Malcolm Evans, Alex Gordon, Chris Arning, Charles Leech, Rachel Lawes, Paul Cobley, Janis Wilson, Mark Foster, Nina De Grave, and Ray Poletti.

1 de Saussure influenced theorists such as Roland Barthes (e.g., 1972) and Algirdas Julien Greimas (e.g., 1983, 1990), who laid the groundwork for much contemporary semiotic thinking by using it to reveal hidden cultural meaning in everyday life. They subsequently influenced another generation of semiotians such as Marcel Danesi (e.g., 2004) and Jean Marie Floch (e.g., [1999] 2001), who applied semiotics directly to marketing.

2 For a comprehensive overview of semiotics and its application to marketing, see Mick et al. (2004).

3 The Market Research Society's Virginia Valentine Award, created in 2011, is for "Cultural Insights"; Sign Salad, the agency founded by semiotician Alex Gordon, calls itself "a semiotics and cultural insight agency"; and Added Value, a strategic marketing consultancy, has called its offer Cultural Insight since 2005.

4 http://www.dknyfragrances.co.uk/bedelicious/pdfs/Be1.pdf.

5 Independently, other semioticians have homed in on this as a case study, such as Susana Aktories Gonzalez in ESOMAR semiotics training workshops.

6 Another example would be Greimas' semiotic square (1983), in which a greater number of oppositions are able to be held in tension with one another. For more, see Chandler (2007) and Cobley (2001).

7 Semiofest was organized by Chris Arning, Lucia Neva, Hamsini Shivakumar, and Kishore Budha, and was borne out of a desire "to create a forum for knowledge sharing within the industry" (Arning 2012).

8 See the work of the Multimodal Analysis Lab based at the University of Singapore (http://multimodal-analysis-lab.org).

9 In their approach to "cultural innovation," Holt and Cameron do not call out semiotics as a specific tool or methodology, but they do use associated techniques such as discourse analysis. Their approach is informed by an array of sociocultural theories from history, politics, media studies, cultural sociology, cultural anthropology, and geography (Holt and Cameron 2010). They describe their "cultural strategy model" as a "detailed blueprint guiding the development of a cultural innovation" (Holt and Cameron 2010:14).

25

Hook to Plate Social Entrepreneurship: An Ethnographic Approach to Driving Sustainable Change in the Global Fishing Industry

JAY HASBROUCK & CHARLEY SCULL

INTRODUCTION: OUR CHALLENGE

This chapter explores how an adapted form of anthropological research can serve as a platform for the collaborative, dispersed, and interdisciplinary approach needed to stimulate innovation within social entrepreneurship. It does so through the lens of a project that focused on developing sustainable economic models for the fishing industry. We begin with the project design brief and an overview of social entrepreneurship and sustainability. We then contrast the scope and scale of traditional ethnographic research (one or a few researchers examining a particular culture or social phenomenon through extended field stays) with large-scale projects focusing on entire industries (multiple research teams examining different industry sectors), and link the benefits of the latter to the cross-pollination of perspectives critical for successful social entrepreneurship. This includes a consideration of the challenges of managing and coordinating the diverse perspectives and disciplinary biases of these research teams. In the end, we argue that the tenets of anthropology can drive solutions inspired not by institutional priorities, but by the naturally occurring behaviors, priorities, and motivations in the everyday lives of those for whom solutions are intended to work. We conclude by considering how anthropology is uniquely situated to identify principles of change by offering culturally focused methods for understanding complex problems, and guiding solution sets built on those understandings that are as diverse as the lives of those who inspired them.

Handbook of Anthropology in Business, edited by Rita Denny and Patricia Sunderland, 463–485.

The Hook

Where does the fish we buy come from? I was off to China to find out. When I (Charley) stepped off the plane in Haikou, China, on the tropical southern island of Hainan, it was almost midnight local time, but it was more than 24 hours since I had left New York City. I was there to meet a fish buyer, whose company sells to a major American grocery wholesaler, and a research colleague with a background in journalism and a wealth of experience in social entrepreneurship. The buyer was coming from Vancouver and the journalist from San Francisco; so, in part for logistical ease and in part because we had never met one another in person, we planned our flights to arrive at around the same time. As luck would have it, I was the first to arrive. Speaking neither Cantonese nor Mandarin, I was pleased to find a sign with my name written on it, and delighted to find it being held by a woman who turned out to be our translator. The time flew by while I peppered her with a million annoying anthropological questions, about food, migration, identity, labor, and fishing most of all, until my field partners eventually arrived.

The next morning we were bumping along a dirt road in a Jeep on our way to visit a giant open-air tilapia aquaculture operation. Although there is no current sustainability rating for aquaculture, tilapia has become a "fish farm" favorite because of its adaptability, its middling position in the fish food chain as a herbivorous but high-protein fish,[1] and its universal generic white fish quality. From an aquaculture standpoint, the main advantages of tilapia are the combination of the prolific breeding, the speed with which they reach maturity, hardy resistance to disease, and ability to live in fresh or salt water. Originally from North Africa and the Levant, tilapia are now the third most farmed fish in the world, after salmon and carp. The tilapia industry came to Hainan just over 10 years ago as part of the vision of a farsighted Chinese entrepreneur. The tropical climate was ideal for them, and they're now a major industry on the island and an important source of tilapia for the North American market.

Figure 25.1. Fish dinner bell, Hainan, China. Photo courtesy of Charley Scull.

We jumped out of the Jeep and watched as a fish bell was rung and then food dumped into the water. Who knew fish came when you rang the dinner bell? (Figure 25.1). Our guide then threw out a net to catch some of the greediest fish to show to our buyer. Later that day these same tilapia would become our lunch. From the farm we went to a giant processing plant, where we donned sterile suits and rubber boots to watch an army of color-coded jumpsuit–clad workers bleed, gut, and fillet the fish by hand. The final product is then seal-packed and frozen solid in less than an hour before being stacked in cold storage rooms until the full order is assembled for shipping (Figures 25.2 and 25.3).

Our buyer opened several random boxes to do some quality control checks, weighing and visually inspecting sample packets, before being whisked off to a long and elaborate lunch: sand worm soup, anyone? Business cards were exchanged and strategic meetings were held. In the meetings, our buyer showed his high-quality packaging and spoke passionately about his vision for the company and the role that the quality of the product played in that vision, and the supplier continuously brought the conversation back to price point. Of course, all of this happened through a translator, who I suspect may have been more savvy about the fish trade than she was about translating.

And so this pattern, of visiting farms, touring processing plants, and sitting through long formal lunches that were deemed so important in the courtship of our high-powered buyer by the Chinese processors, but which the buyer secretly found to be the height of tedium (as a teetotaling vegetarian), continued over the next few days as we criss-crossed the island in a blur of business cards.

Figure 25.2 (top). Dressed for the occasion, Hainan, China. Photo courtesy of Charley Scull.

Figure 25.3 (bottom). Fish processing plant, Hainan, China. Photo courtesy of Charley Scull.

Confusing and interesting as this all was, and made more confusing still by difficulties of language and inadequate sleep, the question of how it might all relate to the challenges of sustainability in the global fishing industry remained. However, as the anthropologist and lead researcher on the Hainan field team, I was still just in the research phase of aggregating vast quantities of information, from the minutiae of the fish lunch bell to the global network of trade partners, with all of it run through the filter of local culture and custom; prior experience had taught me not to panic and to just embrace this early ambiguity. At this stage I just wanted to take it all in as I had no idea yet which observations or insights might prove most useful when my research team gathered with the other field team for the collaborative storytelling and synthesis sessions.

The Plate

What does a sustainable fish look like when it hits the plate? Surprisingly familiar. For one restaurateur in Portland, Oregon, it looks like a very nice sushi restaurant. When I (Jay) first walked in to Kristofor Lofgren's Bamboo Sushi,[2] I was struck first by how much thought and care had gone into the interior, and how subtle he and his staff are with placing educational materials at various places around the restaurant. Small wallet-sized lists of sustainable species are at each table, and certifications that the restaurant has earned for adhering to sustainable purchasing practices are displayed near the entrance next to food reviews. Other than that, Kristofor relies primarily on a well-informed staff to convey messages about sustainable fishing to guests, but usually only when they ask. More often the staff emphasizes new menu choices and high quality, although their background in sustainability is surprisingly deep. During my visit, I had the opportunity to join Kristofor while he interviewed a potential new server. The conversation focused almost entirely on the job candidate's passions, personal growth, and interest in sustainability. Kristofor and his staff's holistic approach illustrates the ways in which ecological sustainability, business interests, and the larger social good can mesh seamlessly. Check out more from an interview with Kristofor Lofgren,[3] CEO of Bamboo Sushi.[4]

A GLOBAL CRISIS: OUR RESEARCH PLAN

Like any project involving global change, the design brief for this project was a bit overwhelming at first: identify areas of opportunity for viable models and practices for sustainable fishing. Just deciding where to begin tackling a problem like this was a challenge. Before our research began, Ashoka, a social entrepreneurship foundation, conducted a preliminary review of the topic that provided good background information for understanding the context in which our research would begin. They broke the problem into three objectives:

1. Survey the entrepreneurial efforts addressing unsustainable fishing and distill from those a set of frameworks for understanding why these solutions succeed;
2. Recommend potential funding strategies in existing solutions, given the context of those entrepreneurial frameworks; and
3. Identify areas of opportunity where the David and Lucile Packard Foundation could help invent and incubate a new solution.

Ashoka's work also included a round of information gathering and key industry stakeholder identification. A report of their findings, *Changing the Future of Wild Fish: An Entrepreneurial Approach to Sustainable Solutions*,[5] includes an apt description of the industry setting:

> The threat of overfishing and extinction of marine life is as complex a problem as one could imagine in our modern, hyper-connected world. It is a story whose span touches fishing villages in Sri Lanka, corporate executives at Walmart, and diners at both four-star restaurants and McDonald's. At every link in this chain, as roles change, the incentives and motivations shift for the human beings involved. At many junctures, the links are not really links at all, but diffuse cascades of related, dependent events that seem impossible to trace to a single moment with the potential for change.

In this initial report, Ashoka also identified frameworks for understanding how three key segments of the industry (consumers, buyers, and fisheries) relate to the fish supply chain, and used these frameworks to identify an initial set of opportunities and challenges for increasing sustainable practices. Among other things, these included broadening the consumer target, increasing focus on fish processing, encouraging more hybrid and cross–industry segment thinking, and aligning sustainability strategies with new business opportunities. While useful in framing context and identifying the most promising areas of the industry to enact change, it was clear that acting on these opportunities and challenges was going to require more. In particular, catalyzing change that would resonate with industry stakeholders was going to require gaining a deep understanding of their relationship to the industry, including historical, cultural, and economic interactions.

To give readers a sense of the cultural implications of this challenge, 95 percent of fisheries jobs are in the world's poorest countries. Many fishermen are faced with conflicting motivations as they struggle to reconcile profit, conservation, and survival. The industry has also been dominated by solo entrepreneurs who typically come from a long line of fishermen extending back multiple generations. Many own and operate their own boats. More recent entries include large-scale, vertically integrated, multinational fishing companies, which handle all aspects of the trade, from catching to processing to distributing. These companies compete directly with smaller-scale solo fishermen.

After considering the magnitude and complexity of the challenges the industry and its stakeholders face, the project focus shifted to include a deeper look at the problem across all of its diverse vectors. With the next phase of funding from the Packard Foundation, Cheryl Dahle (the project's primary lead) enlisted Central, an innovation consultancy founded by Damien Newman, to drive the social entrepreneurship directive further by applying design thinking[6] to the challenge. This approach involves framing a problem as a design challenge, from initial human-centered research to insight generation, ideation, and rapid prototyping (Cross 2011; Kelly 2001, 2005). Of course, applying design thinking to a challenge as global in scope and scale as the fishing industry was a daunting task. Damien likened the process to the "design squiggle,"[7] in which a project's uncertain beginnings, often messy and tangled, gradually gain clarity through a process of pattern finding, theme building, framework development, and insight generation. All of this needed to be built on in-depth ethnographic research. Cue the anthropologists.

We knew that understanding the daily lives, challenges, and interactions of those "on the water" was going to be complex, and that any effort to change any stakeholder's behavior would necessarily be as varied as the trade itself. Add to this the equally complex social realms of consumers and buyers, and the need for a systemic approach to the challenge of catalyzing sustainable fishing became obvious to us. Thus, an ethnographic understanding of each segment of the supply chain—paired with a design-thinking approach to synthesizing ethnographic insights and developing new ideas tailored to them—was the methodological and analytic core we embraced to meet the project's goal to drive sustainable change in the global fishing industry.

The following ethnographic methods were used to elicit data during the course of this study:

- **Facility tours:** Informal, guided visits hosted and led by research participants.
- **Informal interviews:** Unscripted dialog with participants guided by a predetermined set of discussion topics.
- **Photojournaling:** Participant-created series of photos or short video clips that reflect their response to a series of prompts designed by the researcher. Often "assigned" to the participant at the end of a visit and returned to the researcher at a later date.
- **Shadowing:** Researchers follow and observe research participants throughout a typical day or set of activities (often conducted in a mode similar to that of an "apprentice").

Strategically planned ethnographic methods were essential for developing a deeply rooted understanding of the pulls, pushes, and other forces at play within and between complex systems. The mix of methods chosen provided a grounded understanding of the multiple, competing problems at play, and helped identify where the leverage points and real opportunities for change could be found.

Three key data sources fed into our research strategy for this project: the diverse and sometimes competing range of stakeholder identities, their practices, and their interactions within and between fishing industry systems. Our sample included industry stakeholders such as fish processors, cold storage companies, fish buyers and wholesalers, nongovernmental organizations (NGOs), fish farmers, restaurateurs, and industry innovators of varied stripes.[8]

SOCIAL ENTREPRENEURSHIP & SUSTAINABILITY: OUR WORKING LEXICON

The research planning described in this chapter all took place within the context of two interrelated fields: social entrepreneurship and sustainability. With respect to the first, most social entrepreneurs are pragmatic visionaries who prioritize social change. As Ashoka, the NGO that conducted the initial information-gathering for this project, points out: where traditional entrepreneurs are known for innovating within a particular industry, "[s]ocial entrepreneurs act as the *change agents for society*, seizing opportunities others miss and improving systems, inventing new approaches and creating solutions to change societies for the better" (Ashoka website;[9] emphasis added).

As an organization, Ashoka's mission is not only to identify social entrepreneurs but also to find ways to support them, which they do most prominently through their Global Fellows program. Influential and inspirational social entrepreneur/innovators from the past that continue to inspire that organization include figures as diverse as Susan B. Anthony, Maria Montessori, Florence Nightingale, Vinoba Bhave, and John Muir. As is the case with all of these historical figures, identifying a pressing social need was only part of the solution; it quickly becomes clear that the most successful social entrepreneurs recognize that the success of their enterprise is, in fact, as important as the social problems they address. In the end, the best ideas are ones that are relatively easy to implement, generate widespread support, and are geared to generate system-wide impact.

While the principles of sustainability (MacPherson 2004; McDonough 1992) necessarily form the core of any solutions that attempt to address a challenge as large as sustainable fishing, actual working solutions are only possible with full participation from, and realistic incentives for, key industry players. Just as Walmart's sustainability initiatives,[10] have driven their suppliers to reevaluate and reinvent their source, production, and shipping processes in ways that both increase profit and facilitate change, truly sustainable fishing practices had to integrate industry needs as part of any solution. This approach to sustainability is often framed as the holistic integration,[11] of environmental, economic, political, and social, in which the needs of each are met (and their interdependencies recognized) without compromising the ability of future generations to meet them as well (see McDonough and Braungart 2002; Satterthwaite 1999; United Nations 1987).

For a topic like sustainable fishing, the moral and conservation arguments put forth by a wide range of NGOs, though often valid, frequently concentrate on specific issues, often ecological. And while NGOs certainly drive real change, those in the industry frequently view them as antagonistic. Our tactical decision to leverage the pragmatically minded social entrepreneur model for this project was an attempt to discover opportunities to make inroads within the fishing industry and to find ways to influence key stakeholders' behavior there, rather than attempt to change their entire worldview.

This approach shifts traditional advocacy-based research away from privileging conservation alone, and toward a broader integration of needs throughout a complex global system (be they environmental, economic, political, or social). We argue that this latter approach is aligned well with the tenets of anthropology because it seeks inspiration for solutions not from institutional priorities but from the naturally occurring behaviors, priorities, and motivations in the everyday lives of those for whom solutions are designed. This type of research seeks to broaden the definition of advocacy beyond a certain group or species, and to provide solutions that work in the daily lives of many different system players and their various motivations. In short, research at the intersection of social entrepreneurship and sustainability is inherently needs driven, participatory, systems-aware, and empathetic.

As for the ways in which sustainability set the context for our work on this project, the term itself has exploded into public consciousness within the discourse surrounding conservation, environmentalism, and resource management. In regards to fisheries, an industry with its own fair share of confusing jargon, sustainability is used to refer both to the quantity of fish taken from a given fishery (measured culling that allows fish stock to replenish itself) and the manner in which the fish are caught, a practice that accounts for the health of the entire aquatic ecosystem and not just the specific fish for which the quota applies. Unfortunately, definitions of what practices and what quantities qualify as "sustainable" often vary among governmental policies, biologists, and independent "eco-labels."

The imprecision surrounding the definition of "sustainability" has been passed on to consumers, who are largely confused about what it is that "sustainability" means when it comes to fish. "Sustainability," as a food label term, stands out in its ambiguity even among other ethical food choice labels, whose names are varyingly self-explanatory, such as "free-range," "shade-grown," "cruelty free," and "fair trade." Perhaps "organic" is the closest example of a food label similar to "sustainability" in that "organic" experienced initial confusion surrounding its meaning—some of which lingers—but it has, over time, gained acceptance as at least representing a generally positive association (see Ashoka Innovators for the Public 2008:19). In the realm of fish-purchasing decisions, "sustainability," though also seen as a generally positive trait, has yet to reach the level of familiarity that "organic" has and is further confused in the eyes of consumers over other uncertain ethical decisions, such as whether "farm" or "wild" caught fish is better for the body, the environment, and so on.

Despite this ambiguity, or perhaps made possible because of its ambiguity, "sustainability" was certainly ubiquitous in the branding and messaging of industry vendors when we walked the floor of the massive European Seafood Exposition in Brussels. Industry players had received the message that the public is increasingly concerned about the diminishing seafood supply, at least on some level, and the language of responsible resource management, if not the practice of it, was everywhere to be seen (Figures 25.4 and 25.5).

Digging deeper into the etymology of sustainability reveals older definitions that are less directly implicated in the politics of conservation.[12] To some big-market vendors who have become unexpected allies in the sustainable fishing movement, it means *consistency* of the supply. To an industry insider from an Alaskan community development co-op fishery, with whom we spoke at the massive European Seafood Exposition in Brussels, sustainability means *continuity,* not just of fish stocks, but of the communities, traditions, and cultures who

Figure 25.4. European Seafood Exposition, 2009, Brussels, Belgium. Photo courtesy of Charley Scull.

Figure 25.5. Selling sustainability, Brussels, Belgium. Photo courtesy of Charley Scull.

interact with and subsist off of the fishery (see Kitner, this volume). As he put it, while surrounded by the ubiquitous "sustainable" signage at the exposition:

> When you look around at the show, how many booths say sustainability on them? Half of them, at some point, right? And I can honestly say I think that—I think we think about sustainability a little bit different, and I think, frankly, in a deeper way than most of them do, because to me, sustainability is not only affecting fishing resources. Our company turns 100 years old next year, right. So we need fish to stay in business. If we kill them all we go out of business. That's not in our best interest. But sustainability's not only an eco-

logical and biomass issue and health of the sea, it's an issue of these coastal communities and these rural areas where people have had this lifestyle for hundreds or thousands of years that's still going to be viable or not. And so what it really has meant for us is really thinking about sustainability in a way that integrates not only the biomass, the raw material that comes out of the ocean, but it integrates that into the human interaction with it.

UNDERSTANDING A GLOBAL SUPPLY CHAIN: OUR MAP

As always, the research challenge that emerged for us lay in how best to execute our research plan, given the time and resources available. Because the scale of our study needed to encompass an entire supply chain—a tall order for anthropology in the academy and one that is virtually unheard of in the impatient world of corporate anthropology—we needed to craft a map of that supply chain, however subjectively, as an entry point for our work.

In basic terms the various steps of the fishing supply chain, irrespective of scale, are:

1. Source the fish: either through catching wild fish or through aquaculture
2. Process the fish: this can involve freezing, filleting, and storing the fish
3. Distribute the fish: through stores, restaurants, sharing
4. Consume the fish: who is the end consumer?

In tracing the journey of the fish, from its watery habitat to the consumers' digestive tract or "from hook to plate," as we have called it, these essential steps are consistent, whether in relation to a single fish or an entire industry. This schema is, of course, vastly simplified here, but one can easily imagine how factors such as geography and scale quickly make it more complex.

Take the example of a common scenario for a fish caught off the coast of Alaska. The fish is minimally processed on site (i.e., fish are bled and *gutted*, removing the head and inner organs) and then frozen before being transported across the Pacific Ocean to China. Once in China, the fish are thawed and hand-filleted—a process that allows for significantly less waste than automated filleting—before being refrozen, packed back into ships, and transported back across the Pacific.[13] They then travel through the Panama Canal and up the Atlantic coast to Baltimore, at the end of the long narrow Chesapeake Bay, where they are placed in cold storage facilities. From Baltimore, the fish are now ideally positioned for quick and easy distribution along the major railways and roadways of the country. Although shipping is still a relatively good value from a carbon footprint standpoint, that still seems like a lot of food miles for your Alaskan pollock.[14]

Our model of the supply chain was an abstraction of very basic steps, and we were well aware of the numerous ways in which specific examples might quickly change the look and emphasis of this simplified schema. For example, other layers that could be added to this model include distinguishing primary from secondary processing, adding in other players like fish buyers and brokers, shipping and land transport industries, the variety of retail vendors, and even the range of consumer markets. Other additions might include international and local regulations of resource management, labor rights, and food safety as well as tariffs and customs, environmental lobbyists, industry and legal standards concerning weights, measures, and packaging, marketing boards, and so on and so forth. Suffice it to say the model could become very crowded, very quickly. For the purposes of our paper and for the purposes of our study, it became important to develop this relatively simple, though admittedly subjective model, to give our diverse research team some common language and to give ourselves some ideas about the ideal entry points of the system.

FIELDWORK APPROACH: OUR ACTIONS

With an eye toward both understanding the global supply chain and identifying key areas of opportunity where levers for change might be most effective, Phase One of this project identified fish processing as an underexposed "opportunity area." Although processors have some reach in both directions along the chain, they possess no control over the way the fish are caught nor over the way they are sold and marketed to consumers. What's more, processors are vulnerable to the fluctuations of supply and the whimsy of buyers, as well as the pricing instability that comes with both. Furthermore, because of their "middle of the chain" role, they have often been excluded from engaging in conversations about sustainability. We speculated that they were actually in an important position in terms of linking supply to demand. And since processing was deeply implicated in the global scale of the industry, positive changes introduced in that space could have potentially far-reaching impact on the system as a whole.

However, because of their limited reach and their general exclusion from sustainability conversations, we recognized that getting processors to share their thoughts on sustainability and the state of the industry seemed likely to give us a somewhat narrow view of the system. In light of that, we chose fieldwork entry points that were more broadly representative of stakeholders throughout the supply chain. To do this we looked at big global-network players, smaller closed-network players, and also dynamic examples of innovators and outliers, knowing from previous research how often key insights are generated from learning about the way industry innovators think and act.

In the end, our fieldwork included multiple sites across four countries. Among the players on the periphery, we visited an aboveground tank salmon farmer who was part of a local farming network in British Columbia, Canada, as well as education-oriented sustainable seafood restaurants in Portland, Oregon, and Sausalito, California. Other small, closed-systems research included observations with Great Lakes fishermen, who were selling their local catch directly to high-end Chicago-area restaurants, as well as high-volume fish brokers working the phone lines to unload fresh-caught local fish. Finally, our work also included much larger global systems: shadowing a Canadian-based buyer for a major American wholesaler; touring processing plants and aquaculture farms in Hainan, China; walking the floor at a major global industry trade show in Brussels, Belgium; and visiting a cold storage facility in Baltimore.

Looking Forward: Tank-based Fish Farming

We (Jay and Colleen, our research partner on this trip) began our visit with Swift Aquaculture at the end, so to speak: the day they were cleaning waste from the fish tanks. Bruce Swift, his son, cat, and dog all led us down a gravel road to what looked like a barn. Bruce answered a call on his cell phone, and then asked us to step out of the way as a huge tanker truck backed up and sidled next to the barn. When it was eventually in position, Bruce's neighbor Ralph (son-in-law of the dairy farmer who employs Bruce's son) leaned out of the driver seat of the truck and swung a huge pipe into a tank on the side of the barn. With the flip of a switch and a puff of diesel, the engine began drawing gallons of fish waste into the truck's tank. The smell instantly pushed us back on our heels. When he finished, Ralph pulled the pipe up and drove the truck over to a nearby crop of beans, where he sprayed the waste as fertilizer. This is all part of Bruce's larger vision for sustainable tank-based fish farming, and it's intimately tied to farming his land, a tight-knit community of like-minded farmers, and a passion for salmon.

Having "cleaned house," our next task was to accompany Bruce through a series of feedings and other maintenance of his operation. We began with a look at his broodstock tanks, which are outside and covered with netting to prevent birds from feeding on the young fish. Stopping to feed them a fishmeal custom-designed by Bruce's wife, Mary Lou, we then headed inside the barn to check on the three giant, constantly recirculating tanks. Each holds a different age cohort, and all are swimming vigorously "upstream" as Bruce checks water quality, temperature, and other readings. Another round of feeding and we headed back outside to survey the full range of crops Bruce integrates into the "ecosystem" he designed. In addition to the beans and garlic he fertilizes with fish waste, Bruce also grows several cash crops using recirculated, nutrient-rich water from the fish tanks. These include wasabi, watercress, and nasturtium, as well as a small group of crayfish he's begun raising. A huge pump keeps the water flowing from the fish tanks to the filter drum, into the hydroponic crops, and back to the fish tanks.

Over the course of our three-day visit with Bruce, we also helped harvest, clean, weigh, and deliver watercress to a local dairy and cheese shop (part of a network of local farmers and food producers), visited on-site farm-based restaurants, and learned (or rather watched) how to fillet a salmon and prepare wasabi. Walking away from this field experience left us keenly aware of how skillfully balanced and fully integrated Bruce's efforts are: both in terms of his own aquaculture "ecosystem" on his five-acre farm, and his relationship with the local community of like-minded farmers and food suppliers. Here's a closer look at our visit with Swift Aquaculture.[15]

Unexpected Insights: Cold Storage

In exploring the global seafood supply chain, we wanted to leave no link unexamined, but even so, a visit to a cold storage facility in Baltimore was a step we almost passed over. In the end it got a single day of observation, as I (Charley) took an early morning train to Baltimore and was back in New York in time for dinner that same night. The time proved well spent, however, and practices observed there later provided vital fuel for fresh thinking during analysis.

Far from viewing themselves as an incidental link on the journey of goods from production to consumption, the storage workers I visited spoke with pride about the noble history of their trade, tracing its roots back to the early Phoenicians in the dawn of Western history. Despite this important legacy, a source of pride often similarly invoked in conversations with fishermen, incidentally, they also saw themselves as a segment in the chain with little potential to influence people on either side of themselves (producers and wholesalers), leaving them vulnerable within the supply chain. In this respect, they shared a great deal with fish processors as necessary but often overlooked middlemen. Often thought of only when something goes wrong, their reputation for reliability remains one of their most valued commodities. Other key vulnerabilities are tied to fluctuations in the economy and in the energy market. Their ability to keep their warehouses full and energy efficient, particularly in the case of cold storage, as well as their ability to keep their reputations clean, represent their few and limited controls over profitability.

Although this particular facility was somewhat of an industry thought leader,[16] the principles of energy conservation and good reputation as the keys to good business are critical across the cold storage industry. This facility had implemented a number of key changes to address these vulnerabilities. From an energy efficiency standpoint, they had built a new facility closer to the seaport, in recognition that the time between containers being unloaded off of ships and transported to the storage facilities was one of the most problematic moments in the integrity and efficiency of the cold storage chain. By situating themselves closer to the ships, they reduced this time period significantly. They also implemented a range of other innovations, from simple modifications like installing motion-sensitive lights and better-sealed loading docks, and painting their roofs white, to inventive new ideas like using their giant warehouse roofs and prime unobstructed locations to install solar panels on their roofs (offsetting their energy costs by 20 percent and increasing cost stability against a volatile market of energy costs).[17] Reputation was a more difficult task, but they made an important change to the way they communicated with their clients by instituting a transparent and interactive inventory system that shifts the onus of ordering from themselves to their clients. This client-operated system helped them demonstrate their openness and broke down siloed systems of knowledge in the process. In effect, they were minimizing the chances for miscommunication and blame by openly giving more information access to their customers while also improving and protecting their reputation.

Like the social entrepreneurship mindset that was driving our greater project, we saw, in the cold storage example, an instance in which best practices for the "bottom line" can also be best practices for the environment. The lessons about rethinking the system by reimagining warehouses as mobile, or warehouses as energy opportunity spaces, or the benefits of creating openness in a system that has always been closed and cryptic, are the type of mindset shifts that we used to rethink core assumptions of the fishing industry, where many traditions are perceived as unassailable and where secrecy and deception have long played important roles.

INTERDISCIPLINARY TEAMWORK: OUR STRUGGLES

Reaching a collective understanding in projects of this scope and scale is often a matter of finding a common language. And while interdisciplinary teams are an excellent way to expand thinking and challenge assumptions, they require a significant amount of time dedicated to negotiating the meaning of terms, as well as understanding when and where each person should variously assert or abandon their disciplinary biases. Yes, egos can get in the way! But the negotiation, as processed through analyzing the data collected, is often very productive, and sometimes revelatory.

In addition to the two anthropologists (Jay and Charley), other members of the field teams came from a mix of disciplinary backgrounds, including designers, scientists, sociologists, and journalists. In interdisciplinary pairs, we spread out across the globe to collect ethnographic data on the key practices, interactions, and identity characteristics of industry stakeholders. When we returned, we were faced with the challenge of sharing, analyzing, and developing insights from data that were gathered using the same methods, but had been interpreted through very different disciplinary lenses.

This is when the team's range of expertise paid off. The accumulated experience from team members in each of these disciplines allowed the team to set observations in context and situate team member insights within broader cultural phenomena and industry frames of reference. They also provided "macro" lenses that helped us understand the dynamics and interactions in and between the various components of the fishing industry, as well as tie together recommended solution streams at the end of our analysis.

We found that the key to integrating our disparate worldviews began with finding a common language to share our field experiences and pull relevant data into a collective pool. This took more than two weeks, during which the team developed a process for categorizing and prioritizing different forms of data (scientific, policy, emotional, procedural, etc.). Dialog and patience were our best allies at this stage, as we eventually developed a platform for sharing data effectively.

Narrowing the challenge a bit, the biases of the discipline of anthropology can sometimes run counter to the design-thinking process. First, as most anthropologists know, the discipline is steeped in the lore of the lone anthropologist who ventures out into the exotic and unknown to bring back their "discoveries" (there's a reason the average PhD in cultural anthropology takes 8 to 10 years). However, unlike a process that takes one person 10 years to complete, projects driven by design thinking and social entrepreneurship don't have the luxury of that much time. Instead, they're much more likely to deploy a team of 10 over the course of a year (often less). This puts the impetus on anthropologists to not only work more collaboratively, but also to tease out the anthropological significance of data contributed by those not trained in its practice or in anthropological interpretation, all while leaving room for different forms of making sense of that data. It can be a difficult balance to strike, but we saw that many of the interpretive and listening skills that anthropology values so highly can be applied directly to facilitating team collaboration and hosting data analysis sessions.

SHAPING THE FUTURE: OUR INSIGHTS

Borrowing from human-centered design protocols, we used boards to post quotes, observations, images, and artifacts from each field visit to begin our analysis. We then collectively reviewed all boards to find patterns between them. Of course, with such wide-ranging field experiences, finding patterns within our huge data set of observations and interviews was both time consuming and taxing. After a great deal of storytelling, scribing, reviewing transcripts, diagramming, and clustering, our patterns eventually coalesced. We identified basic commonalities, important differences, and telling links that spanned across our observations. Barriers to sustainability became our inevitable focus, and we found many, from consumers, to buyers, to fisheries. Among them were consumers' lack of reliable information, buyers' sourcing difficulties and skepticism about the definition of "sustainable," and fisheries' powerful incentives to fish unsustainably in an industry that is increasingly hostile toward their interests. But this was only the beginning. We then used these patterns as the basic material from which we derived larger themes that could help us define the current set of cultural conditions within the industry, as well as how they interrelate. For this, we concentrated heavily on sketching frameworks that visually depicted these relationships in form of charts and diagrams (see Ashoka Innovators for the Public [2008] for some examples) and then developing statements that represented the dynamics of these frameworks. Among the most important themes we discovered were:

- **Demand bullies supply**: Middlemen in fish distribution are currently incentivized to do primarily one thing: provide a reliable source of fish for ever-demanding customers. Yet they're in a position to provide valuable supply-end information on species and conditions that could be leveraged.
- **Daily catch mentality rules**: Manually entered data and other tasks scoped entirely within the time frame of one day leave little time or energy to consider long-term goals or threats.
- **Story and platform are a critical pairing for change**: Although many people in the industry have a good story to tell about fishing sustainably, they

tend to lack the platform for relaying their message within a system focused on price, daily catch, and reliable supply.

- **Innovators are stranded:** Innovators within the industry currently lack a common means of connecting with one another across industry segments. This means that sustainable solutions can't grow to scale effectively.

From these themes, and a set of typologies that emerged from them, we developed a series of design principles that were used to shape the rough "rules" and range for potential solution sets. These are slightly more abstract in nature than themes to allow for a wide variety of ideas that can collectively address the challenges identified. Here, from the Future of Fish (FoF) executive summary (Future of Fish 2010) are the four that stood out most:

- "Counselors" connect ideas with people and organizations that can help expand their thinking around the possible ways they might be a more powerful advocate for change. Give them a clear path to incorporate new ideas.
- "Catalysts" connect support, knowledge, and structure to grow their ideas for a more significant impact. Give them a path to embed their ideas into the mainstream.
- "Conduits" need motivation (i.e., story) to help them see how to use their platform differently. They have tremendous reach and power. It's just a matter of inventing (or revealing) an incentive for them to change focus. Give them a sense of how innovative ideas can be grounded and practical.
- "Compilers" are perfectly happy to function and excel within a given set of boundaries. But those boundaries need to be shifted. They need a new story that connects their self-interest to the bigger picture. Give them a better script.

With these "rules" in hand, a range of solution sets were then developed, each aimed at providing incentives for sustainable fishing practices across industry sectors, and adapted to the varying roles and motivations of key players. In the end, the project outcomes went beyond catch limits and fishing regulations, and into areas of the industry like processing, storage, retail messaging, new farming methods, and other approaches. For example, two outcomes included establishing a global network for species tracing to empower fishermen to command better prices for sustainably caught species, and developing new loan models for land-based aquaculture to encourage this practice and reduce dependence on wild species. Critical to most outcomes were programs designed specifically to enable entrepreneurship and local empowerment as part of the solution.

But standalone solutions are only part of the picture. Without a systematic and integrated approach to addressing globally declining fish stocks, these ideas can't grow to scale effectively. The final, and arguably most important, outcome of this project was to kickstart an innovation hub for the industry that can serve as an integrative holding body connecting people across different sectors of the industry to incubate new ideas, disseminate critical information, and accelerate systemic change. That hub is now known as the Future of Fish (FoF),[18] a platform for engaging the entire supply chain, including fishermen, processers, distributors, and consumers.

FoF is a nonprofit organization led by Cheryl Dahle that serves as an "accelerator for entrepreneurs launching market-based initiatives that drive sustainability, efficiency, and traceability in the seafood supply chain." As their mission explains: "We focus specifically on industry pioneers whose planned initiatives are directly aligned with our mission and whose ideas are considered too nascent to secure traditional financing without the additional strategic and operational support we provide" (from the FoF website). They do this by facilitating partnerships and forming cooperative cohorts among stakeholders at all levels of the fish supply chain, and helping them develop and grow their ideas for sustainable fishing practices. A key benefit cohorts receive is support from stakeholders in different parts of the supply chain, as well as customized business services from FoF that lower barriers to getting started and encourage collaboration. As they put it on their website: "We collaborate with our entrepreneurs and partners to produce scalable and investable businesses or partnerships that generate significant financial and environmental returns."

Today, FoF has more than 20 participating entrepreneurs. Some of their projects have included facilitating partnerships between fish distributors and IT companies to develop improved species tracking; forging partnerships between food service companies and chefs to increase awareness (and sales) of high-quality flash-frozen fish; and programs that encourage fishing companies to pay fishers by the hour (rather than by number of fish caught) to encourage more careful handling, and therefore a better quality, of fish. Of course, these partnerships are just the beginning of change that is expected to set new standards and encourage sustainable practices in the industry.

ANTHROPOLOGY, DESIGN, & GLOBAL SYSTEMS: OUR CALL TO ACTION

Traditional anthropological training fosters a critical, empathetic, and relativistic mindset that is in part the result of the embedded observational approach of ethnography. At the heart of what makes anthropology useful to improving our understanding of humans is its multiple focal lengths approach: its ability to tack back and forth between the micro and the macro and between the physical and the conceptual without ever losing sight of the contextual systems that influence and constrain human beliefs and behaviors. Beyond the types of data *created* by anthropologists, it further distinguishes itself from other forms of observational research through the ways that anthropologists think, frame, write, and talk about their findings (see Sunderland and Denny 2007). However, there is little in the conventional training of anthropologists that teaches them how to attach purposeful action to their observations and analysis.[19]

By contrast, design is inherently geared towards thinking about new solutions, new products, improved functionality, and ways to make systems operate more efficiently, fluidly, or elegantly, but can at times exist in a conceptual space that is detached from a deep and critical understanding of real-world behaviors. Combining these two disciplines, and drawing on the complementary strengths of each of them, has become a familiar approach in the research industry; it was at the heart of how our team hoped to understand key opportunity areas on this project.[20]

The value of ethnography in the analysis of complex global systems (like sustainable fishing) is realized best when the innovation process is reconceptualized. Rather than framing it solely as a method for fulfilling "unmet needs," research for systemic change requires a deep understanding of organizational, cultural, network, and behavioral subsystems to inform and drive creative solutions that align with each. To do this, we need to understand the diverse range of motivations and barriers that individuals within these systems, as well as the relations of power, and systemic barriers or enablers that make these systems persist as they currently do. Only then can we design solutions for "disrupting" them productively.

The role of ethnographic research in this process becomes one of "knowledge arbitrage" and engagement. First, it fills gaps in knowledge by laying open these complex systems to greater scrutiny and enabling the identification of the key problems that might be solved to create social innovation and business opportunities. Then, through narrative and a deep understanding of the lives of people operating within these systems, ethnographic insights can energize a broad community of problem-solvers and enlist their knowledge to address those key problems.

In contrast to most market research, the synthesis of ethnographic data in projects addressing complex systems doesn't necessarily narrow in focus to drive toward one best solution. Instead, we found that while our synthesis sessions did bring increased clarity to the project, the complexity of the industry and diverse range of motivations, barriers, moments of change, social networks, and choice logics of its players drove toward a series of parallel solution "streams" that varied in scope, scale, and by potential players.

While the resolution of the challenges that continue to affect the global fishing industry remains a work in progress, the multiplicity of opportunity areas that anthropology helped to identify are encouraging. As complex global system issues continue to demand not one but many solutions, it is clear to us the important role that anthropologists can play not just in helping to make sense of the data, but also by helping the various disciplinary perspectives needed to fully understand the complexity of these systems communicate with one another. Furthermore, global issues, though constituted by a range of culturally varied iterations, are by definition issues that have virtually universal implications: implications that include the anthropologists who study them. For this reason, we see projects like this one as an example of a global-scale challenge that anthropology and anthropologists have both a unique ability and perhaps even a moral responsibility to help address.

REFERENCES

Ashoka Innovators for the Public. 2008. *Changing the Future of Wild Fish: An Entrepreneurial Approach to Sustainable Solutions.* Prepared by the Discovery Group, an Ashoka Initiative. Commissioned by the David and Lucile Packard Foundation. http://www.futureoffish.org/assets/pdfs/FutureFishReportPH_ONE.pdf.

Brown, Tim. 2009. *Change By Design: How Design Thinking Transforms Organizations and Inspires Innovation.* New York: HarperCollins.

Cross, Nigel. 2011. *Design Thinking: Understanding How Designers Think and Work.* Oxford, UK, and New York: Berg.

Future of Fish. 2010. "Future of Fish: The Executive Summary." 2010. www.futureoffish.org/assets/pdfs/FOF_EXECUTIVESUMMARY_2010.pdf.

Grescoe, Taras. 2008. *Bottomfeeder: How to Eat Ethically in a World of Vanishing Seafood.* New York: Bloomsbury.

Gunn, Wendy, and Jared Donovan, eds. 2012. *Design and Anthropology: Anthropological Studies of Creativity and Perception.* Burlington, VT: Ashgate.

Gunn, Wendy, Ton Otto, and Rachel Charlotte Smith. 2013. *Design Anthropology: Theory and Practice.* New York: Bloomsbury.

Kelly, Tom. 2001. *The Art of Innovation.* New York: Doubleday.

______. 2005. *The Ten Faces of Innovation: IDEO's Strategies for Beating the Devil's Advocate & Driving Creativity Throughout Your Organization.* New York: Doubleday.

Lang, Tim, David Barling, and Martin Caraher. 2009. *Food Policy: Integrating Health, Environment, and Society.* Oxford, UK: Oxford University Press.

Lockwood, Thomas. 2009. *Design Thinking: Integrating Innovation, Customer Experience, and Brand Value.* New York: Allworth Press.

MacPherson, Mandana. 2004. "Sustainability for Designers." Report from The Natural Step–US, San Francisco, CA.

McDonough, William. 1992. *The Hannover Principles: Design for Sustainability.* William McDonough Architects, Charlottesville, VA.

McDonough, William, and Michael Braungart. 2002. *Cradle to Cradle: Remaking the Way We Make Things*. New York: Northpoint Press.

Pilloton, Emily. 2009. *Design Revolution: 100 Products that Empower People*. New York: Metropolis Books.

Pincetl, Stephanie. 2002. *Practice and Theory of Urban Sustainability in the Developed and Developing Nations*. Los Angeles: USC Center for Sustainable Cities.

Satterthwaite, David, ed. 1999. *The Earthscan Reader in Sustainable Cities*. London: Earthscan Publications.

Sunderland, Patricia, and Rita Denny. 2007. *Doing Anthropology in Consumer Research*. Walnut Creek, CA: Left Coast Press.

United Nations. 1987. "Our Common Future, Report of the World Commission on Environment and Development, World Commission on Environment and Development, 1987." Published as Annex to General Assembly document A/42/427, Development and International Cooperation: Environment, August 2.

NOTES

A special thanks to Cheryl Dahle of the Future of Fish and Damien Newman of Central for their leadership and to the David and Lucile Packard Foundation for supporting this research. We would also like to thank all our interdisciplinary research partners on this project and the many participants who gave of their time, thoughts, and experiences so generously and unreservedly.

1 Compare with *Bottomfeeder* (2008) by Taras Grescoe for more discussion on sustainability as it relates to consumption choices based on the place of a fish species within the food chain.

2 More on Kristofor Logfren at futureoffish.org/cohort/category/entrepreneurs/kristofor-lofgren#kristofor-lofgren.

3 See vimeo.com/6799361.

4 See http://www.youtube.com/watch?v=QIOwVtyxYBI&feature=youtu.be.

5 See http://www.futureoffish.org/assets/pdfs/FutureFishReportPH_ONE.pdf.

6 For more discussion on the relationship between design and anthropology, look at Gunn et al. (2012, 2013); for a more in-depth exploration of design thinking, see Brown (2009) and Lockwood (2009).

7 See more about the Design Squiggle at vimeo.com/5787721.

8 The original research plan for this work also included analogous field observations from other industries and practices, through which we intended to find inspiration and discover new ways for approaching the challenge of sustainable fishing. These included ethnographic research with the following: resource managers of dwindling or limited supplies such as directors of organ transplant programs or beekeepers; energizers such as political campaign organizers or event planners; change agents such as personal trainers or crisis management consultants; and observations within parallel industries such as sustainable sugar cane and nut cultivation. Unfortunately, time and budget prevented us from conducting this portion of research for this project.

9 See http://www.ashoka.org/.

10 See corporate.walmart.com/global-responsibility/environment-sustainability.

11 See citiesprogramme.com/aboutus/our-approach/circles-of-sustainability. Wikipedia also provides a useful synthesis at wikipedia.org/wiki/Sustainability.

12 The difficulty of defining sustainability is made more complex in cases where differences in political, economic, and social systems contrast starkly. Any global challenge faces these questions, as well as how to navigate those differences within postcolonial contexts. For sustainability, the issue is particularly prevalent in matters related to development, where historically poorer nations are still building infrastructure. For more, see Pincetl (2002).

13 The reasons behind why processing is done in China are myriad, but include overfishing of areas that may have historically had processing capabilities but no longer maintain enough locally caught stock to keep them running. As a result, it is often the case that neither the skill level nor the capacity for processing are available closer to where the fish are caught or at least not at what is considered an "affordable" rate, in terms of economies of scale.

14 Much has been written about "food miles" as an effective metric for revealing the hidden ecological, social, and economic consequences of the consumption of nonlocal food (compare with Lang et al. 2009), but for a conversation about how fish, in particular, are implicated in the global transportation industry, see the "Fast Fish, Slow Fish" chapter of *Bottomfeeder* (Grescoe 2008). Wikipedia also provides a useful synthesis of some of the controversy surrounding "food miles" as a concept: wikipedia.org/wiki/Food_miles.

15 See vimeo.com/6041764.

16 In fact, it was awarded the 2012 "top green provider" award by a leading trade magazine.

17 Go to the storage company website (mtccold.com/) to learn more about this solar panel project, including this short video (mtccold.com/2011/04/29/mtc-goes-solar/) that shows the installation of the panels.

18 See http://www.futureoffish.org/.

19 Many anthropologists may feel like identifying solutions is an important and natural next step to their research and analysis, and indeed many of them become strong advocates for social change within their constituent fieldwork communities. While others are independently good at thinking about pragmatic solutions, typically there is nothing in the training of anthropologists that fosters the development of these skills.

20 While the anthropologist may still be more often associated with academia than industry in the minds of the general public, designers are similarly more often thought of as creators of new objects than as agents for social change. However, principles of good design, or "design thinking" as it has been labeled (compare with Brown 2009), favor a holistic approach in which the same design ideals apply equally to designing a better mobile phone, a better way to transport water in the developing world (compare with Pilloton 2009), or finding opportunities to improve better practices across a global supply chain.

Section IV

THE ENERGY OF MEMES

INTRODUCTION

RITA DENNY & PATRICIA SUNDERLAND

Our goal in bringing together these particular chapters is to bring into focus and address the impact of memes in the framing of work and activities of practices. We want to consider how particular memes have been taken up and circulated in the intersections of anthropology (or anthropologists) and business. While memes as originally conceived by Dawkins (1976) are units of cultural transmission—the cultural counterpart to genes—as we conceive them, memes are culturally salient ideas or practices and best thought of as signs: discursive vehicles of accrued meaning with overlapping orbits of circulation. Memes in this volume include tribe, culture, anthropology, Big Data, VUCA (volatility, uncertainty, complexity, and ambiguity), and design; in this section, memes include anthropology, user, empathy, agile, strategy, nationalism, business anthropology, branding, live, open, and digital.

Memes gain substance and legitimacy by virtue of their popularized existence. Often underpinned by metaphors of progress or virus, they are afforded an implicit inevitability. Rather than accept their inevitability, we wish to call out their semiotic foundations. Memetic transfer is not coterminous with meaning transfer. Words are polysemic in that signification accrues in particular instantiations by particular interlocutors in particular organizational contexts (see Hankins 2013). Language is performative (Gal 2012; Hanks 1996, 2005; Schieffelin et al. 1998; Silverstein 2004, 2006). While each chapter in this section stands simultaneously on its own as topical analysis, case study, essay, or review of current practices at the intersection of anthropology and business, we want to call out the significance of discursive forms in framing actions.

Memes are significant sources of momentum and action serving to organize corporate or institutional action and practices: journalistic stories (Wilner); business school curricula (Tian); design process (Neese); software development protocols (Hanson); advertising creative strategy (Morais, Tamminen et al.); marketing discourses (Shatokhina). Ideas about brands (Diamond et al.)

Handbook of Anthropology in Business, edited by Rita Denny and Patricia Sunderland, 489–496.

have organized efforts of scholars and practitioners since at least the 1950s. As discursive signs, memes also frame and are framed by larger sociocultural discourses: memes of "live," "open," or "digital" simultaneously constrain and open up possibilities for ethnographic practices (Wang, Caliandro).

In this section we get glimpses of memes in the making. For example, in the development of business anthropology in China, business anthropology can be seen as a particular instantiation of a Western idea taken up by Chinese anthropology departments and business schools as a way to optimize business management education (Tian). How this discursive sign is played out, or negotiated, in practice has an impact on what "business anthropology" comes to mean beyond these particular institutions. We also get glimpses of the generative processes that keep signs in play. In China, incorporating business anthropology is supported by a desire to make China globally competitive. In the chapters by Shatokhina and Tamminen et al., nationalism-as-meme emerges through, and is organized by, brand communications; advertising, rather than academic department curricula, is the locus for discursive activity. Shatokhina argues that post-Soviet Russian identity is being negotiated through a lens of consumption, "contemporary ideologies . . . appear as sets of images, stereotypes, narratives introduced and articulated through the design of products and ad campaigns," that then revises history in the process.

By virtue of their different orbits of circulation in and by which meaning is accrued, memes are sometimes irreconcilable, as, for example, in the meme of tribe. The origin of "tribe" in academic marketing scholarship is often attributed to Maffesoli's (1996) *Time of the Tribes* (*Le Temps des Tribus*), in which he argues for the importance and existence of social affinity groups (tribes) in postmodern life. *Consumer Tribes*, edited by Cova, Kozinets, and Shankar (2007), draws on Maffesoli's theorizing (as does Agafonoff et al. in Section III). Canniford and Shankar's chapter in the same volume discusses the appropriation of tribal-as-in-primitive tropes by media and marketing discourses about surfing (Canniford and Shankar 2007). But one might also ask the extent to which this academic volume's title, *Consumer Tribes*, might perform similarly. Anthropologists, especially in the United States, might cringe at what seems a not sufficiently considered (or ill-considered) use of "tribe." Meanwhile, a startup in Texas, taking on the mantle of "anthropology" (as meme), can name itself Tribus and coopt early homo sapiens iconography (http://www. wearetribu .com/what-we-can-learn-from-anthropology/) to market themselves, and in the trade press, including the *Harvard Business Review* (anderson 2009), tribe is a signal of the anthropological approach. Tribe is made irreconcilable by virtue of different intellectual histories in which partially shared denotations are insufficient for shared understanding.

The semiotic orbits of memes also result in unlikely juxtapositions. VUCA, as in "a VUCA world," was originally a military term then adopted by business management leadership in the 1990s. Philadelphia University President Stephen Spinelli, himself a former entrepreneur, revamped undergraduate education to deal with this new world by integrating an anthropology-inspired curriculum in its newly formed College of Design, Engineering and Commerce (DiCarlo et al. in Section II). Business anthropology in China can result in alignment of anthropology departments and business schools in ways that are, perhaps, unfathomable in other places. What the terms, or memes, of anthropology, business anthropology, and tribe signify is only partially shared; histories are elided; new usages in new contexts propel orbits of new meaning which, depending on the audience, are incommensurate.

Wilner's chapter tracing the construct of "anthropology" in the trade press and Neese's chapter tracing the construct of "the user" in design practice show us why memes are important to deconstruct. "Word choices highlight assumptions," as Neese says. Like other discursive signs, "anthropology" and "the user" obscure as much as show, erase as much as highlight (Gal 2005). Wilner argues that anchoring "anthropology" in the popular and trade press to iconic figures in anthropology, such as Margaret Mead or primatologist Dian Fossey, is not particularly helpful to the discipline because the discursive constructions are inevitably partial. In the case of "the user," naturalization of the person as the central consideration of the design process risks ignoring (not seeing) the social world and assemblages in which objects and people are enmeshed. Neese suggests that designers should shift from the reification of person to sociocultural understandings of objects as a source for design inspiration and "consideration" (also see Kimbell in Section II).

Reliance on "person" is also implicit in the emphasis placed on empathy as a distinguishing aspect of ethnographic process and mode for understanding in design discourse. (See also the chapters by DiCarlo et al. in Section II and Cotton in Section III.) As Neese notes, "empathic thinking is methodically learned." Prevalent in design process and discourse, the empathy meme becomes problematic when "being in your shoes" falls short in denaturalizing what is experienced, leaving us with a notion that empathy for "users" is the necessary and sufficient consideration for understanding what is going on. A decided emphasis on the personal rather than the social is an ongoing challenge in making the social and cultural, and the materiality of assemblages, visible.

Thus, memes are most productively thought of not as fads or random ideas with fans, or units of cultural evolution, but as discursive signs whose meanings are in flux and contingent and made substantial through indexicalized usages of interlocutors (wherever they sit), situated in particular historical, social, and political contexts. What it means to be Finnish, for example, has changed significantly in the last 20 years, as the country has shifted reference points from the Soviet Union to a global, commercial world (Tamminen et al.). In Russia, there is a re-indexicalization of "ours" in post-Soviet society constituted partially through discourses of consumption (Shatokhina). We might wish that "anthropology" has undergone similar indexical change in the popular and trade press, but it has not, Wilner argues in her chapter. Anthropology-as-meme remains an exoticized discipline in journalistic discourse, a constant, new discovery that can provide deep insight in an uncertain world (in which an uncertain world in need of help is itself a well-worn trope of the last 30 years).

NEGOTIATING, PROPELLING, & CONTESTING MEMES

As a whole, the chapters in this section illustrate larger economic, social, and political arenas within which the practices of the anthropology-business intersection are situated. The chapters illustrate prevailing cultural or market discourses that anthropologists contend with, or find inspiration from, in forging their own routes. The meme of anthropology in trade journalism frames how anthropologists' work is understood by business, as Wilner shows in her parsing of popular and trade press treatment of anthropology as a discipline. "Weaving in and out of caricature" and describing what anthropology in business is by describing what it isn't, all in a tone of entertainment, might reflect journalists' own needs to craft a compelling read, but doing so, Wilner argues, does damage. Each instantiation undermines the work and potential contribution (whether practical or reflexive) to innovation, design, creative strategy, and, importantly, the discipline of anthropology. These journalistic instantiations, as discursive activity, frame expectations of colleagues, employers, C-suite executives, and potential coworkers in counterproductive ways.

Memes also frame work processes: design process often glorifies "the user" (Neese); Agile software development glorifies nimbleness of action (Hanson). The Agile process that Hanson describes in her chapter is iterative, incremental, and collaborative. Like design more generally, it too situates the user centrally but ties the concept of product optimization to market flux and contingency. "Agile," as in quick to respond, fleet of foot, with athletic grace and movement, becomes the metaphor for being sensitive to the demands of business stakeholders, design engineers, product managers, and, presumably, users. Strategy, in Morais' chapter, is a meme that organizes actions of advertising development: Morais describes the activities that strategy codification organizes, arguing that anthropologists gain authority to the extent that they behave and engage in these activities. Both Hanson and Morais speak to the importance of understanding not only the processes organizing work, but in mastering the business issues. Anthropologists have to fit in and find ways to contribute, these authors argue, to gain a needed position of influence. There is opportunity to make one's craft and point of view visible, but it must be done through integration into existing work paradigms, a tension to be sure (Cefkin 2010; Denny 2013; Sunderland 2013). Hanson reminds us that this can take time. Both chapters, in their details of process, specify the requirements (so to speak) of activities, the processes themselves seemingly subject to "design" thinking.

The chapter by Diamond et al. on the American Girl brand lays the foundation for the concept of brand fortitude, a newly theorized brand property. Their focus in this chapter is how brands retain vitality; how, in this case, American Girl dolls retain their branded-by-marketer meanings along with their singularized-by-household meanings. The decade of work by these researchers on this brand (see Borghini et al. 2009; Diamond et al. 2009; Sherry et al. 2008) builds on decades of work by marketing scholars on the topic (or meme) of brand. The brand meme is persistent; the notion of brand as symbolically constructed goes back to Levy (1959) and since then has been animated by marketing scholars and managers alike. (See Manning 2010 and Agafonoff et al.'s chapter in Section III.)

The chapters by Tamminen et al. and Shatokhina reflect the intersection of two memes, branding and nationalism, from two different vantage points. For Tamminen et al., nationalism is an inspirational muse and resource for strategizing Finnish brands. Recognizing nationalism as a discourse, the authors suggest that nationalism remains a potent discursive sign in the context of sociopolitical change and globalized markets. Shatokhina, in her chapter, examines ongoing national identity-making, or remaking, through current branding discourses and practices in Russia and former USSR countries. Through a set of semiotic snapshots she explores how the borders of national identity are being negotiated. Packaging, for example, might draw on the golden age of a Soviet past through naming (e.g., 48 Kopek) or design cues that are reminiscent of Soviet goods. In parsing A/Olenka chocolate wrappers, Shatokhina illuminates how packages become canvases for establishing and contesting "us" versus "them," not only in Russia, but in Ukraine and Belarus. In both chapters we see how nationalism is reflected and renegotiated through consumption and market activities.

If memes sometimes constrain anthropological endeavors in business, they can also clearly inspire action, as the chapters by Morais, Hanson, Tamminen et al., and Tian attest. In the chapters by Wang and Caliandro, memes of open and digital are also muses and sources of inspiration. In these cases, though, these discursive signs circulate in larger sociocultural orbits that then frame or provide trajectories for ethnographic practices and, in so doing, simultaneously constrain and open up possibilities for anthropological analysis and thinking.

Wang's chapter on live fieldnoting brings two particularly salient cultural ideas into focus (and into interrelationship): live and open. Wang advocates use of social media tools for posting field observations, actions, or moments; her chapter is studded with examples from her own fieldwork. The difficulty of "live" in connection with fieldwork is that "live" as a discursive sign entails a sense of immediacy and a value of authenticity by virtue of its apparently unscripted (not contrived), current (now), unmediated state. Its discursive value is perhaps derived from a society-wide embrace of the constantly and iteratively new, itself grounded in metaphors of technological process and progress. In relationship to fieldwork, the problematic of "live" is, as Malefyt (2009) notes, that technomethodologies popularly embraced by purveyors of ethnography in business elide the notion of analysis, conflating real-time data with "what is going on" analytically. (Baba in Section 1 eloquently describes the risks inherent in commodification of ethnography as a business service.) "Live" carries with it a notion of unmediated, though in practice, of course, it is not so. In practice, as Wang notes, what is posted involves selection, writing involves consideration, and posts have viewers; social media has followers. Interlocutors cannot help but be co-present in the formulation of "live" data. Data are produced, not gathered, something that the meme of "live" obscures.

Co-occurring with "live" in Wang's chapter is the meme of "open." In her argument for live fieldnoting, Wang intentionally draws on the open source movement as a model in advocating a more collaborative, inclusive fieldwork practice. One of Wang's motivations in doing so is to make the ethnographic contribution more robust and more visible: live fieldnotes are illustrations of sometimes collaborative thinking and analysis that make ethnography-as-analytic-framework visible, even when glimpsed via Instagram. Wang's collaborative inclination is a theme echoed in many of the volume's chapters. A collaborative process towards understanding is being institutionalized, whether the collaborative group is internal or external clients; multifunctional teams composed of executives, designers, developers, researchers, agency creatives, and brand managers (or whomever); fellow colleagues; or followers of all kinds via social media.

If digital is implicit in Wang's chapter, it is explicit in Caliandro's review of ethnographic approaches in digital spaces. If, as a discursive sign, "digital" is enveloped by notions of modernity and at this point is a "catchall for novelty" (Miller and Horst 2012:5), Caliandro's chapter reminds us that virtual is no less real (and no more mediated) than offline life; that discourses in digital spaces are social and cultural texts offering new forms of data; and that it is an additional resource for theorizing brands, consumption, and consumers. Online is life, as Horst and Miller's (2012) edited volume demonstrates; sites for transformation, a means for reflexive understanding of the culturally normative, a nexus of media engagement. And as Miller and Horst argue, there is a need to make the networks afforded by digital technologies, including networked information that is Big Data, visible: "If we ignore these new forms of knowledge and inquiry, we succumb to yet another version of the digital divide" (2012:17).

Caliandro's review of key approaches to work in the digital domain demonstrates that it is not the method (or "fieldsite") that constrains, but the questions we ask of data. It is the analytic questions (and embedded assumptions) that matter; data wherever derived are fodder for analysis. The meme need not define the action. Wang, Caliandro, Neese, Diamond et al., Tamminen et al., and Shatokhina all point to the value in searching for meanings or the process of meaning-making, the importance of materialities and material practices, and the need for decoding ideologies, whether the goal is branding, innovation, or design.

These chapters amply illustrate the power of discursive signs to organize, constrain, inspire, or propel actors at the intersections of anthropology and business, with subsequent implications for fieldwork practices, branding activities, advertising strategies, design of objects, services, software, and academic programs. Given divergent orbits in the circulation of discursive signs, deconstructing, subjecting to scrutiny, and contesting would seem a must. Wilner notes that anthropologists in business must author and circulate other forms of representation since "relegating representation is fraught with peril." Wang would concur in the need for better representation of ethnographic analysis. Actively countering extant understandings is sometimes needed, as is querying assumptions of process; we need to make our own indexical contributions to the meanings of things.

REFERENCES

anderson, ken. 2009. "Ethnographic Research: A Key to Strategy." *Harvard Business Review* (March): 24.

Borghini, Stefania, Nina Diamond, Robert V. Kozinets, Mary Ann McGrath, Albert M. Muniz, Jr., and John F. Sherry, Jr. 2009. "Why Are Themed Brandstores So Powerful? Retail Brand Ideology at American Girl Place." *Journal of Retailing* 85(3):363–75.

Canniford, Robin, and Avi Shankar. 2007. "Marketing the Savage: Appropriating Tribal Tropes." In *Consumer Tribes*, edited by B. Cova, R. Kozinets, and A. Shankar, 35–47. Oxford, UK: Butterworth-Heinemann.

Cefkin, Melissa. 2010. "Practice at the Crossroads: When Practice Meets Theory, a Rumination." *EPIC* 2010:46–58.

Cova, Bernard, Robert V. Kozinets, and Avi Shankar, eds. 2007. *Consumer Tribes*. Oxford, UK: Butterworth-Heinemann.

Dawkins, Richard. 1976. *The Selfish Gene*. New York: Oxford University Press.

Denny, Rita. 2013. "The Cry of Practicality." In *Advancing Ethnography in Corporate Environments*, edited by B. Jordan, 136–50. Walnut Creek, CA: Left Coast Press.

Diamond, Nina, John Sherry, Jr., Albert Muniz, Jr., Mary Ann McGrath, Robert Kozinets, and Stefania Borghini. 2009. "American Girl and the Brand Gestalt: Closing the Loop on Socio-Cultural Branding Research." *Journal of Marketing* 73(3):118–34.

Gal, Susan. 2005. "Language Ideologies Compared." *Journal of Linguistic Anthropology* 15(1):23–37.

_____. 2013. "Sociolinguistic Regimes and the Management of 'Diversity.'" In *Language in Late Capitalism: Pride and Profit*, edited by Alexandre Duchêne and Monica Heller, 22–42. London, UK: Routledge.

Hankins, Joseph. 2013. "Semiotics of Organizations." In *A Companion to Organizational Anthropology*, edited by D. Caulkins and A. Jordan, 204–18. Malden, MA: Wiley-Blackwell Publishing.

Hanks, William F. 1996. *Language and Communicative Practice*. Boulder, CO: Westview Press.

_____. 2005. "Pierre Bourdieu and the Practices of Language." *Annual Review of Anthropology* 34:67–83.

Horst, Heather A., and Daniel Miller, eds. 2012. *Digital Anthropology*. London, UK: Berg.

Levy, Sidney J. 1959. "Symbols for Sale." *Harvard Business Review* (July–August):117–12.

Maffesoli, Michel. 1996. *The Time of the Tribes*. Translated by Don Smith. London, UK: Sage.

Malefyt, Timothy de Waal. 2009. "Understanding the Rise of Consumer Ethnography: Branding Technomethodologies in the New Economy." *American Anthropologist* 111(2):201–10.

Manning, Paul. 2010. "The Semiotics of Brand." *Annual Review of Anthropology* 39:33–49.

Miller, Daniel, and Heather A. Horst. 2012. "The Digital and the Human: A Prospectus for Digital Anthropology." In *Digital Anthropology*, edited by H. Horst and D. Miller, 3–38. London, UK: Berg.

Schieffelin, Bambi B., Kathryn Ann Woolard, and Paul V. Kroskrity, eds. 1998. *Language Ideologies: Practice and Theory*. New York: Cambridge University Press.

Sherry, John, Jr., Stefania Borghini, Albert Muniz, Jr., Mary Ann McGrath, Nina Diamond, and Robert Kozinets. 2008. "Allomother as Image and Essence: Animating the American Girl Brand." In *Explorations in Consumer Culture Theory*, edited by J. F. Sherry, Jr. and E. Fischer, 137–49. London, UK: Routledge.

Silverstein, Michael. 2004. "'Cultural' Concepts and the Language-Culture Nexus." *Current Anthropology* 45(5):621–52.

_____. 2006. "Old Wine, New Ethnographic Lexicography." *Annual Review of Anthropology* 25:481–96.

Sunderland, Patricia. 2013. "The Cry for More Theory." In Advanc*ing Ethnography in Corporate Environments*, edited by B. Jordan, 122–35. Walnut Creek, CA: Left Coast.

26

A Crisis of Representation? Anthropology in the Popular Business Media

SARAH J. S. WILNER

> The famous anthropological absorption with the (to us) exotic . . . is essentially a device for displacing the dulling sense of familiarity with which the mysteriousness of our own ability to relate perceptively to one another is concealed from us (Geertz 1973:14).

Anthropology, in its central engagement with the other, is said to "make the strange familiar and the familiar strange." In this chapter, I argue that anthropology itself is presented as an exotic form of activity in popular American business media accounts. Ethnographic practices in particular are made both strange and familiar in narratives that find them at turns palliative and peculiar, and their authors baffled or bemused. Offering evidence of the exoticization of anthropology, I sketch what critical historian James Clifford called a "specification of discourses": "Who speaks? Who writes? When and where? With or to whom? Under what institutional and historical constraints?" (Clifford 1986:13). And, because these discursive concerns have strange symmetry with journalism's "Five Ws" (who? what? where? when? and why?)—the structuring device employed to ensure that a report's account is complete—I use those questions as an organizing aid for the discussion. Finally, I highlight some of the reasons anthropology's representation in the business press is problematic, for reviewing a broad collection of articles reveals journalists engaged in an ironic turnabout: reporting on the activities of business anthropologists creates the quasi-ethnographic task of appraising an unfamiliar group's behaviors, practices, and values and then attempting to convey them in a compelling written account. This is significant, for while the poetics of contemporary trade journalism are distinct from that of ethnography, journalism's products not only have equal power to construct reality through representation, arguably they

Handbook of Anthropology in Business, edited by Rita Denny and Patricia Sunderland, 497–520.

have much more influence (particularly if the size of the audience who consumes these accounts is considered a relevant metric).

To gather material for this exercise, I searched online media databases using relevant keywords and phrases, narrowing the search by specifying newspapers and magazines as article sources to better capture a sense of the popular discourse surrounding applied business anthropology.[1] Titles included: *Money; Fortune; Forbes; Bloomberg; BusinessWeek; The Economist; Fast Company; Wall Street Journal; New York Times; The Atlantic; USA Today; Advertising Age; Harvard Business Review; Technology Review* (MIT); and *Design Management Journal*. Early volumes of *Journal of Marketing* (from its first printing in 1936 to 1965) were also surveyed because during this period the *Journal* was written largely by and for practitioners. Initial searches resulted in hundreds of articles that referred, at least in passing, to applied anthropology in the corporate sector. These were then read for relevant content, and this additional assessment reduced the set to 88 articles containing enough content to afford and warrant further analysis, with most appearing in print since 1986; the most recent article appeared February 20, 2013. I examined the articles by informally open-coding them, looking for emergent patterns and themes. It is on the basis of many of those themes that I make the assertions in this chapter.

ESTABLISHING RAPPORT

To understand the narrative arc of cultural anthropology in the popular and trade press, it is useful to trace the representation of anthropology in the business media over time.[2] I present an overview of business anthropology's representation in the popular media from the 1950s to the present (see Table 26.1). Note that the table's contents are not definitive; in every category there are exceptions.

Although the first corporate anthropological research is said to have been conducted in the 1930s (see Jordan 2010), and trade magazines such as *Advertising Age* reported on company-sponsored research in the 1940s (Jordan 2010; Levy 2006), the first articles in the subset examined here appeared in the 1950s. The first, by Allan R. Wilson, appeared in the *Harvard Business Review* in 1952. Wilson's article may have inadvertently provided a template for future writing about qualitative research, as most of the examples in the set follow this format. Early in the article, Wilson offers an illustrative account of the successful application of qualitative methods, a revelatory instance of deep insight that would have been overlooked using other methods of research. Next, he further supports his claim of the benefit of the technique (here, interviewing users) by enumerating the deficiencies of "traditional" methods, a rhetorical device still very much in use in contemporary accounts. Finally, the need to overcome these deficiencies with the methods outlined is given additional urgency by framing the status quo as disrupted by the (apparently enduringly) growing complexity of market conditions and consumer behavior: "The kind of situation in which qualitative market research is particularly effective—a situation in which the market tides are muddy and changing—demands that the new method be used with skill and understanding," asserts Wilson. "The use of [such] methods . . . offers an improved means for solving the new and complex problems of business managements caught in the tide rips [*sic*] of a changing economic environment" (Wilson 1952:76,86).

Compare Wilson's assertions to an excerpt of an article that appeared in *BusinessWeek* a half-century later:

> For Best Western International Inc., [ethnography] . . . convinced the hotel chain that it didn't need to boost its standard 10% senior citizen discount. The tapes showed that seniors who talked the hotel clerk into a better deal didn't need the lower price to afford the room; they were after the thrill of the deal. . . . [E]thnographic research is quickly becoming a standard agency offering [and] . . . it's not hard to see why. As products mature and differences in quality diminish, marketers are anxious to hook into subtle emotional dimensions that might give them an edge. This up-close approach can also help marketers figure out how different ethnic and demographic groups react to their products, especially important in a fragmenting marketplace. . . . [E]thnographic insights can even help with humdrum products. By videotaping consumers in the shower . . . Moen Inc. uncovered safety risks. . . . Uncovering such design flaws by simply asking questions is almost impossible (Khermouch 2001:94).

The elements are all there: the new insight, the critique of a "traditional" technique, and the reference to an uncertain and potentially dangerous world made safer and more accessible through this novel technique that renders meaning.

Part and parcel of the growth and accompanying tumult of a postwar economy and consumer culture in the 1950s, social scientists began applying their theories and research methods to corporate market research activities. For example, an early article that might have been published before its audience was ready for it, "Anthropology's Contributions to Marketing" (Winick 1961), was written by the former director of marketing research for J. Walter Thompson. Despite the claim that "A good case could be made for the thesis that marketing researchers do more anthropological research on modern cultures than do anthropologists" (Winick 1961:60), it is difficult to know how many practicing marketing researchers reading the article might have known enough about the field to recognize how their work could be characterized as anthropological.

However, at that time a small group of academics did begin to merge practice and theory by establishing their own consulting firms. A prime example is Social Research Inc. (SRI), believed to be the first management consulting firm to include business anthropologists and applied anthropological techniques (Jordan 2010). Founded by faculty from the University of Chicago, they applied their expertise—and graduate students—to understanding changing markets and consumer behavior. One of those students, Sidney Levy, went on to become not only a principal at SRI, but also a professor of marketing at Northwestern University and the University of Arizona. While Levy (and colleagues) exhorted practitioners to consider qualitative methods (Gardner and Levy 1955), symbols (Levy 1959), and holistic systems of consumption (Boyd and Levy 1963) in the pages of the *Harvard Business Review*, his work explicitly referencing anthropological theory and method was primarily published in books and journal articles rather than news reports (see Levy and Rook [1999] for a sampling of these articles).[3]

In the 1960s, the internationalization of the marketplace provoked new concerns about existing modes of consumer research, and so globalization and cross-cultural consumer behavior became a common refrain motivating the commission of cultural anthropological research. A somewhat surprising example of internationalism comes from Ernest Dichter (1963), who mused in the *Harvard Business Review*: "For top management in companies with foresight to capitalize on international opportunities . . . an understanding of cultural anthropology will be an important tool of competitive marketing" (Dichter 1962:113). The example is unexpected in part because Dichter, a psychologist, consumer behavior scholar, and marketing consultant known as "the father of motivational research" was promoting a profession to which he did not belong.[4] His statements, delivered in the authoritative register of his era, convey an idiosyncratic blend of personal travel experience, psychological prognosis, and ethnocentrism. Nevertheless, his assertion that "cultural anthropology will become an important tool of competitive marketing" is both prescient and early evidence of the growing interest in commercial applications for anthropology.

In the 1960s and 1970s, ethical concerns about the role of anthropologists employed by the government, combined with rising popularity of other research methods such as focus groups and the use of business anthropology, declined. However, the 1980s saw a resurgence of interest in anthropology and ethnography, a shift Jordan playfully summarizes: "In the 1980s, management sciences discovered culture" (2010:11). Such swings of the methodological pendulum are, however, not new. Among other reasons, Holt (2002) has argued that historically the relationship between marketers and consumer culture is dialectic, insofar as marketers' strategic salvos are met with consumer resistance, culminating in a new system of relationships until the cycle begins anew. This tendency, coupled with social shifts and technological disruptions, invariably brings market research techniques in and out of favor as marketers seek new means of apprehending consumers.[5] And so, as innovation in work processes as well as computing technology accelerated, it further provoked companies to hire anthropologists to inform new product development (Wasson 2000) as well as account for and anticipate shifting organizational structures and consumer behaviors. Accounts of these anthropologists and their practices started filling newspaper columns: Steve Barnett's consulting work for Union Carbide, Procter & Gamble, and Kimberly-Clark (Lewin 1986); the pathmaking activities of Lucy Suchman's team at Xerox's Palo Alto Research Center (PARC) (Deutsch 1991); and the research practices of advertising agency Young & Rubicam (Alsop 1986), among others, were brought to the attention of readers of the *New York Times* and *Wall Street Journal*. The media's interest in the "novelty" of anthropology and ethnography has continued, unabated, ever since.

MEDIA'S AMBIVALENT RELATIONSHIP WITH ANTHROPOLOGY

Reflecting upon the ongoing attention of popular media to anthropological and ethnographic practice, Sunderland and Denny (2007) speculate whether it speaks to the normalization of the presence of anthropologists and ethnographers in the business world or, drawing on Sidney Levy's insights, signals their work as inexorably anomalous. The answer is probably both, if one considers that journalists' job is also to make the strange familiar (i.e., explain the subject of their article) and the familiar strange (luring readers with titillating topics to increase engagement and sell copies). However, when the necessary narrative parsimony of popular print media is added to the equation, the unfortunate result is often perfunctory characterization that can sometimes trivialize the nuanced and demanding craft of cultural insight.

THE FIVE Ws

The vast majority of articles examined conformed to the basic structuring mechanism for journalistic exposition: the Who, What, When, Where, and Why of corporate anthropology. However, for those working as or with business anthropologists in the past 30 years, this perennial introduction can be perplexing, requiring quotation-marked qualification.[6] Equally off-putting, the business news reporters in this sample frequently played in gray areas of journalistic conventions for accuracy in representation (see the Society of Professional Journalists 1996) with a sensationalist tone more common in entertainment reporting,

Table 26.1. Conceptualizations of anthropology in the media.

	Early (1950s–1980s)	Mid-range (1990s)	Recent (2000–2012)
Who is the primary author of the account?	• Academic-practitioners writing in hybrid trade/scholarly journals	• Staff writers • Selected voices are added: directors of market research at agencies and practicing anthropologists	• Staff writers • Anthropology practitioners and design ethnographers begin to author their own accounts • Corporate managers hiring ethnographers
Who is an anthropologist or ethnographer in business?	• Anthropologists who apply their tools and training to business problems (social scientists)	• Market researchers, especially ad agency staff • People who interview and/or uses observational methods (including video) • Designers/R&D specialists • PhDs, especially as "staff anthropologists" rather than consultants	• Designers • PhDs in anthropology, psychology, sociology • People who interview and/or uses observational methods (including video) • Hybrids (academics who consult for companies)
What is anthropology or ethnography in business?	• Academic anthropology used on business problems • Work being done by ad agencies and consulting firms is "observational research"	• Any observation of consumers in "natural habitats" • "A sure-fire way to impress clients"	• "An observation technique" • "Immersion in a consumer's world" • Resistance begins: "A fad"; "verbal hype"; "branding jargon"; "voyeurism"
Where is it being done?	• Fieldwork is often not described; anthropologists with expertise in a specific (sub)culture apply it to problems they are given by the firm	• Inside major corporations • In private (homes) • In public (airports, stores "shoppers' habitats")	• "Wherever the product is important" • In private (homes) • Servicescapes

Table 26.1. Continued

When do you need to use it?	• If managers are stuck: they can't discern why the product is not more popular • Product development • When you need to know how to talk to specific consumers or use symbols (e.g., for advertising)	• If managers are stuck and they need new ideas • If managers are stuck and they want to improve internal processes • To help develop advertising campaign language	• When you're developing, not validating a product or concept (focus groups are for validating) • To help develop an advertising campaign • If managers are stuck: consumers aren't behaving as anticipated
Why is it employed?	• Managers are stuck and can't figure out the solution to a problem • What people say and what they do is different	• To understand customers and/or employees • Designing products • Need to understand new culture to expand internationally • "Unique insights" • What people say and what they do is different	• To gain new consumer insight, especially over competitors • To insure innovation is relevant • To target subcultures • Because people don't know what they want • What people say and what they do is different
Illustrative Source	Winick (1961)	Kane (1996)	Baker (2004)

a phenomenon Bird refers to as "the tabloidization of news in the United States" (1998:33). For example, one article conjured images of ethnographers as stalkers with the title "Every Move You Make." "All over the world," the narrative begins, "there are teams of people videotaping other people doing their laundry, making breakfast, playing with their kids and taking a shower. They're not voyeurs, they're ethnographers" (Bowman 2010). For those aware of anthropology's conception of the "researcher as instrument," this lack of authorial reflexivity can come as both surprise and disappointment. Acknowledging that all five "Ws" are important, I focus on the "what" and "who" offered within the articles reviewed, as they are vital sites of rhetorical construction.

What's What

Signaling is critical to the media's representation of business anthropology. Writers frequently attempt to signal their cultural capital with a Geertzian wink,[7] alluding to key names, phrases, and concepts associated with the field of anthropology in apparent camaraderie with its practitioners. However, in doing so, they can skirt responsibility for understanding the concepts on which they report. Titles like "Coming of Age in Palo Alto" (Hafner 1999), "Anthropologists Go Native in the Corporate Village" (Kane 1996), "Consumer Rituals of the Suburban Tribe" (Osborne 2002), and "Consumers in the Mist" (Khermouch 2001; Wellner 2003) are good indicators that the narrative that follows may conflate or confuse.

For example, when the author of the one of two articles titled "Consumers in the Mist" (a misplaced reference to naturalist Dian Fossey's book chronicling her study of mountain gorillas) writes, "If the term *ethnographic* research conjures up sepia-tinged images from your Anthropology 101 textbook, you're on the right track. Look it up in an encyclopedia and you'll probably find a picture of its best-known practitioner, Margaret Mead" (Wellner 2003), it would come as no surprise if the reader became skeptical about the possible relevance of a profession described as antiquated (via the allusion to "sepia-tinged images"). The author of the earlier article of the same title (Khermouch 2001) reveals his own conflation of cultural anthropology with archaeology[8] with the article's subtitle ("Mad Ave.'s Anthropologists Are Unearthing Our Secrets") as well as a later subhead, "Digging Deep" (Khermouch 2001:94). Other warning signs that an article may misrepresent its subject: a cursory definition of business anthropology or ethnography; perfunctory, "thin" description of ethnographic field activities (particularly without reference to the importance of skillful cultural analysis after fieldwork); and a too-easy happy ending in which the act of merely beholding a shopper in situ solves complex business problems. An excellent example is found in an article published in *BusinessWeek* in 2006 by Spencer Ante. Weaving in and out of caricature, the article's large illustration (spread across two pages) features scientists in laboratory costume—white coats, nerdy black eyeglasses—to signal that ethnography is a scientific method, just in case the title of the article, "The Science of Desire," did not. The pile of glaring stereotypes thickens as the ersatz scientists are depicted looming over and peering into a dollhouse populated by the "average" American family: mother in the kitchen, father sitting on the couch reading the paper, brother at the computer, and sister on the phone.[9] While this misconstrued representation might have been corrected with meaningful comments from the many well-regarded business anthropologists and scholars interviewed for the article, their brief accounts are undermined in both text and illustration by misrepresentations reminiscent of the earliest ethnographies' misplaced exoticization of "primitive" people. "We know what you're thinking," suggests the author, "corporate ethnography can sound a little flaky. And a certain amount of skepticism is in order whenever consultants hype trendy new ways to reach the masses" (Ante 2006:102). Ante goes on to bemoan the amount of time ethnographic research can take, a point he illustrates by noting that Tony Salvador of Intel "spent two years traipsing around the developing world, including a memorable evening in the Ecuadorean Andes when the town healer conducted a ceremony that included spitting the local hooch on him" (Ante 2006:102). If Salvador did not describe his job to the interviewer as "traipsing and getting spit upon" (and one assumes he did not), it begs the question of what purpose is served by such caricature; yet, it continues. In a photograph illustrating a sidebar from the same article, Intel's Eric Dishman looks deviously (or is it fearfully?) over his shoulder at a lab simulating the "home environment," and still another illustrative photograph depicts anthropologist Timothy de Waal Malefyt, then at advertising giant BBDO, glowering into the camera dressed, Indiana Jones–style, in a leather jacket and rakish fedora.

Ante's article equally raises questions about some of the methods he describes firms deploying in the name of business anthropology (one hopes as inaccurately as the anthropologists are depicted). For instance, strategic product development consultancy IDEO is reported to have learned about the experiences of Marriott's customers by asking guests to "graph what they were doing hour by hour." Similarly, the account of Intel's purported innovation for seniors with Alzheimer's—a personal computer that flashes the photo and name of a person calling to remind the individual who the caller is—runs the risk of rendering "consumer insight" as oversimplification.

One way to counterbalance the potential confusion surrounding business anthropology's objectives and methods is description by exclusion; that is, articulating what business anthropology and ethnography are *not*. The vast majority of articles emphasize that ethnography, anthropology's signature method, is not "traditional" research, and invariably compare the information ethnography can provide to surveys and focus groups.

In an *Advertising Age* article titled "The Limits of Market Research Methods: Study Up," the author argues that ethnography is misused, in part, because it isn't understood and takes as her duty to disabuse readers of misconceptions. "First, let's be clear about what it is. Ethnography is the study of culture. Not individuals (psychology) or populations (demography) or nations (politics/history) or trends (cool-hunting)" (Demos 2007). Ultimately, Demos' critique of applied ethnography revolves around the failure of many studies to balance participation and observation, a point well taken. "Participation on its own is just as problematic as observation. Filming an interview or conducting an interview in someone's home—these techniques often fly under the flag of ethnography, but fall short of the actual method" (Demos 2007). However, while she specifies many details of video observation, she too fails to offer a specific corrective for the participation portion of the equation.

According to popular business media, corporate anthropology is not a lot of things. As noted earlier, many anthropologists in business are confused with archaeologists, and spend considerable effort explaining the differences. Susan Squires, profiled in a piece titled "Corporate Anthropology: Dirt-free Research," reports that her role was so often confused with archaeology that she began calling herself an "evaluator" (Walsh 2001). Like Demos (2007), Walsh cautions that business anthropology is not "coolhunting," and in an article in Brandchannel (Colyer 2003), marketing professor Richard Elliott stresses that is it also not "a magic bullet." With such fervent clarification, one might be seduced into believing a claim found in a piece in *The Economist* titled "Off with the Pith Helmets" (2004), which contends that the problem of misrepresentation is slowly ameliorating. Yet one glance at a 2013 article in *The Atlantic* titled "Anthropology Inc." (Wood 2013) is enough to dispirit the most optimistic anthropologist in business; the article's accompanying illustration is so steeped in exaggerated and recycled tropes[9] one can only hope that its intention is ironic. In this latest example of distortion, a digital camera, set up on a tripod to supplement the notes taken by earnest observers clutching clipboards, is the only clue that the article is describing current practice. Without it, the reader could mistake the image of scientists hovering over a family's dinnertime ritual—their subjects, literally constructed (the illustrator is a collage artist) to conform to the visual domestic dialect of midcentury middle America—for a Norman Rockwell painting.

Who's Who

Several issues related to the "who" of corporate anthropology and ethnography are significant, including who is authoring the account, who is reported to be an ethnographer and/or/versus an anthropologist, and who is commissioning the work. Considering each of these perspectives is vital, as each implies a frame (see Goffman 1974) that provides—or imposes upon—the reader with distinct interpretations of meaning, relevance, and relationship from which to understand business anthropology practices and to assess its study findings.

Authoring the Account

Authorship is of course, both etymologically and structurally, closely related to authority and thus legitimacy, a perennial concern for both business anthropologists (see DePaula et al. 2009) and scholar-ethnographers (see Crapanzano 1986). In the sample I examined, the articles were written by a variety of journalists, social scientists, and hybrid professionals who could both conduct and report upon anthropological practice. Whereas articles published in the 1950s and 1960s were generally written by academics, in the 1980s and 1990s newspaper and magazine staff writers were more likely to write accounts, and their necessarily limited engagement with their subject matter may be partly responsible for the frequently blurred distinctions among field of study and method. For example, Paco Underhill, author of the book *Why We Buy* (1999), is frequently called a "retail anthropologist" (e.g., Green 1999) because he observes shopping behavior, although the anthropology appellation is one that he distances himself from (see chapter 1 in Underhill [1999]: "A Science is Born"). Similarly, anthropologist Donna Flynn, profiled in a *USA Today* article for her work at former employer Microsoft, is described as an "ethnographer . . . [who] uses her training as a PhD in *archeology* to analyze for ordinary folks from London to Beijing make daily use of their cellphones" (Acohido 2007; emphasis added).

While I acknowledge that the staff reporters and freelance writers who are assigned stories for popular business news outlets must quickly engage the attention of a notoriously busy and distracted readership known for inspiring the "executive summary," such pressure cannot excuse the kinds of narratives (or illustrations) of the type characterized here as tabloidization. In egregious cases, the writers seem particularly eager to highlight the exoticism of the work they chronicle and often do so, ironically enough, by taking information out of context and thereby transgressing one of one of anthropology's core concerns. These authors selectively leverage extant stereotypes, portraying practitioners as "an executive PhD . . . [and] corporate indulgence" (Walsh 2001); flaky; or simply irrelevantly erudite. For example, "Sometimes I feel like my job is Captain Obvious" is the opening quote in an article about danah boyd, a "digital anthropologist" who "plays Margaret Mead with America's youth" according to an article in *Forbes* (Hill 2011). The profile goes on to describe boyd in a tone that reflects its writer's discomfort with his subject's self-presentation, begging the question if this is because boyd defied his expectations or because she met them. For example:

> The petite 33-year old expert on the Internet and youth is wearing a loose tan sweater, dangle silver jewelry and a trademark fuzzy hat that resembles the ears of a white Pomeranian puppy. That lower-case spelling of her name? Not a typo. She had it legally changed . . . because of "political irritation at the importance of capitalization." Roll your eyes and LOL, but boyd is a highly sought-after ethnographer (Hill 2011).

If glib characterization can be at least partially attributed to an outsider's lack of awareness, an enlightened author provides a welcome opportunity for elucidation. Such was the case when Steve Barnett, who holds a PhD in cultural anthropology, was asked to pen a column for *Advertising Age* called "Observing" from 1986 to 1988. In addition to his anthropological training, Barnett's byline identified him as chairman of research for the various communications and consulting agencies he worked for during the period he was a columnist. While Barnett's path-breaking articles could be construed as anthropological in topic (e.g., observation, ritual, hunting and gathering), the content was accessible and free from social science jargon. As is to be expected in a publication focused on advertising, in the *Advertising Age* column Barnett's identity as a marketing consultant tends to be foregrounded, rendering his academic training secondary. Even in one of the most explicitly anthropologically referential columns, titled "Hunters and Gatherers" (Barnett 1988), in which he discusses the division of labor by gender and why (Barnett asserts) men do not clean up as they cook, there is no reference to scholarly studies or little-known, small-scale cultures; his observations are presented as personal rather than theory-driven. Yet as both an academically trained anthropologist who has written traditional texts (e.g., Barnett and Magdoff 1986) and a market and consumer analyst (Levin 1992; Lewin 1986) who has described himself as "the anthropologist who created business ethnography" (Barnett 2002), Barnett's representation as both author and subject throughout the 1980s provides grist for consideration of the audiencing (Fiske 1992) of anthropology in the popular business press. What is the balance of responsibility of an author to his or her subject versus audience? Like other subjects of articles about business anthropology, Barnett is sometimes misrepresented as (or relegated to) being engaged in a fuzzy mix of social science and loitering. For example, in one article he is described as someone who "conducts polls and 'hangs out in small-town beauty salons, bars and bowling alleys' to observe and interview women" (Hinds 1988). Yet as author of his own narratives, Barnett also embodies a mixture of disciplinary personas. In a column titled "Two Views on Aging," Barnett (1987) references his observation of seniors in Europe and a textual analysis of an American sitcom before arriving at the thesis that when it comes to aging, Americans fight nature and allow marketers to determine their desired consumption objects:

> Defiance [against the aging process] . . . is turning the U.S. into an age-graded country. Age-grading describes societies (until now typically tribal) where people associate most closely with their peers, not their family. In a tribal society, age-grades are visibly separated by personal presentation. Traditionally in parts of the Midwest, blue hair signals older women. Now, there is an older male costume of loose jogging clothes plus walking shoes.

> Demographic-based marketing contributes to consumers identifying with an age-grade. Cadillacs are for older, affluent Americans. To break that stereotype, Cadillac is vigorously trying to appeal to a younger market with the new Allante convertible (Barnett 1987:60).

Blending anthropological subjects (tribal societies) with marketing practices (demographic segmentation), the "two views" Barnett offers could not only refer to the column's subject—Europeans versus Americans—but equally to anthropology and marketing. Yet his treatment of the former also confounds. For the advertising executives reading the column, what does the reference to a former tribal society afford? Moreover, since the reference to women's blue hair is misappropriated, taken together with its masculine parallel, the characterizations have a mocking quality, especially compared with the description of elegant windsurfing senior Europeans that opens the column. As such, Barnett seems to be walking a fine line between offering the observational insight of an anthropologist and marketing his expertise as leader of a market research firm. In retrospect, the role ambiguity Barnett cultivated may be considered both pioneering for introducing a new generation of "ad men" to the specialized perspective that cultural anthropology affords and indirectly implicated in exacerbating confusion over the same.

Like their professional forefather, practicing business anthropologists and ethnographers increasingly have been writing their own stories. For example, in 2010 and early 2011, members of PARC published articles on ethnography in *UX Magazine* (see Belloti 2010; Chockshi et al. 2011; and Glasnapp 2010). The motives behind these articles are unclear; it is possible that their authors hope to correct previous misrepresentations (a purpose which also may have motivated anderson [2009]), or they may be seeking exposure and the halo of expertise that publication brings, a prospect more likely when the authors work for consulting agencies (e.g. Bellotti 2010; Chokshi et al. 2011; Demos 2007; Durante and Feehan 2006; Glasnapp 2010). In either case, the authorial voice is increasingly an emic one.

Anthropologists, Ethnographers, & Voyeurs, Oh My!

Such self-referential authorship is imperative, because the record shows that relegating representation is fraught with peril. The profile of danah boyd referenced earlier is a prime example of the distortion that can result when business anthropology is glossed as methodological interpolation. While acknowledging her intellectual skill and professional accomplishment in the article (boyd is a senior researcher at Microsoft and holds a master's degree from MIT as well as a PhD from UC Berkeley), the author does not contain the urge to condescend, nor does he (or his editors) notice that he has conflated anthropology (by branding boyd a latter-day Margaret Mead) with ethnography. My concern is that such accounts are not rare outliers. An equally mocking article from *Fast Company* begins with this wince-inducing passage:

> Girl walks into a bar. Says to the bartender, "Give me a Diet Coke and a clear sight line to those guys drinking Miller Lite in the corner." No joke. The "girl" is Emma Gilding, corporate ethnographer at Ogilvy & Mather, one of the world's top advertising agencies. Her assignment is to hang out in bars across the country, watching guys throw back beers with their friends. And wipe those smirks off your faces. This is research (Tischler 2007).

The portrait of Gilding[10] that follows is not entirely derisive, but it is clearly skeptical. Gilding was undoubtedly unaware her work would be presented within the metaphor of a genre of jokes, yet because the research groups she developed were for advertising and marketing agency Ogilvy & Mather, it is likely that the media attention she received was still more welcome than it might have been if received by an organization's internal research group. Indeed, described in a company press releases as a "famed ethnographer" (Flatley 2005), Gilding's firm is likely at least partly responsible for the reporter's misrepresentation of her work. Characteristic of a cadre of consulting practices whose work can be difficult to evaluate because it evokes anthropology but may not necessarily cleave to the field's traditional methods or theories (see Baba, this volume), some practitioners use language or make hyperbolic claims to garner the media's—and prospective clients'—attention. For example, a press release about Gilding's IN:SITE group billed it as "*the first* communications-focused *cultural anthropology* think tank to discern the difference between what people say they do, and what they actually do" (Flatley 2005; emphasis added). The point is not to insinuate that the work Gilding's group did was less than stellar, but to wince at a description that, as written, seems to downplay the object of the sentence (think tank) while suggesting that the group is the first to discern that there is a difference between what people say they do and what they actually do. Moreover, the IN:SITE group membership highlights the problem of representation in the field: while anthropologists are not licensed as, for example, medical doctors are, it is disquieting that there is no evidence that anyone on the IN:SITE team has advanced education or training in cultural anthropology.

It is unsettling when practitioners are as implicated in distorting conceptions of who anthropologists and ethnographers are and how they behave as the journalists who sensationalize their practices. Adaptation in any field is inevitable, whether due to a shift in the context in which the work is done, or simply as a byproduct of changing ideologies over time. However, the potential misappropriation of concepts, methods, or the sheer co-optation of a profession is problematic, both for those who commission studies and those whose understanding of standard practice may result from reading an article.[11]

In addition to misidentification, articles which mix and match voices and perspectives of business anthropology can intensify the mystery or suspicion of its practitioners' work. An article that appeared in *Advertising Age* (Levin 1992:3) notes, "the discipline has its doubters, mainly because of misunderstandings about the role of cultural anthropology in society." As an example, he quotes marketing professor and anthropologist John Sherry as saying that the "general public still conceives of anthropology as archeologists or Indiana Jones kinds of things" (Levin 1992:3). Unfortunately, while the professor may have provided it, in the final text there is no clarification by Sherry of how he hopes the general public will understand the field. Instead, readers are given anecdotes: first, of letter carriers as symbols of connection; and then of the benefit of conducting a shop-along study, which the article describes as "observational research—a frequently used anthropological technique known more simply as hanging around supermarkets" (Levin 1992:3). Indeed, in the course of this article, anthropology is presented as myriad things: as a tool for finding hidden brand meaning; as being different and broader than a consumer psychology approach, but also capable of uncovering the "psychological rewards" that brands provide; as defining the connections between product categories and users; and as something which is not archaeology. The article closes with a cautionary tale of "cultural anthropology going too far"; a lawsuit filed against Nissan (later dropped) by a couple who accused the company of sending a spy to live with them. Amid this broad amalgam and conflation of concepts, what can the reader hope to understand?

Who Wants to Know?

Who commissions the research are also important means to confer—or destroy—legitimacy. Although many still provide the context of a project, early reports in particular took pains to cite examples of major companies engaging in ethnographic research. The not-so-subtle rhetoric device of naming General Foods, Johnson & Johnson, and Colgate-Palmolive (Alsop 1986); Xerox, Nissan, and General Motors (Deutsch 1991); and Hallmark Cards, McDonald's, Steelcase, and Texas Instruments (Posner 1996), among others, as engaging business anthropologists, is that if these successful and powerful companies find the research to be legitimate (or at least worthy of resource allocation), then it must surely be.

Yet another means of ratifying the anthropological endeavor is through the organizational function or role interested or engaged in anthropological practice. For example, in *InfoWorld*, a trade magazine for IT managers, an article cites an electrical engineer and computer scientist at Intel who became "a convert"[12] after working with social scientists and learning to appreciate their skills (Epstein 2000); *Inc.* magazine, targeted at entrepreneurs, ran an article that included stories of ethnographic insight that "opened up the eyes" of the general manager of a small group of boutique hotels. That same article also featured a quotation from the director of engineering of a medical device manufacturer, in which he enthuses, "Ethnographic research isn't glamorous and it takes a lot of standing around, but when you get that 'a-ha!' it's worth it" (Wellner 2003). The latter instance, however, exemplifies the double-edged sword that popular reports about ethnography represent, for while the hotelier had hired anthropologists to conduct his study, the article's author asserts that a DIY approach can be equally effective.

> Most professional ethnographers have years of training. But that doesn't mean you can't do it yourself. . . . [Medical company's] employees put on surgical scrubs and headed into operating rooms, where they obsessively chronicled every detail of an anesthesiologist's activities. It became clear that their original big, bulky design simply would not work in actual hospitals. For one thing, doctors preferred to look at their equipment as little as possible and focus instead on the patient. They also realized the product had to be strong enough to withstand a lot of abuse (Wellner 2003).

The description of the medical device company's research appears to describe a study of human factors and user interface design rather than the interpretation of behavior in cultural context and/or participant observation that are often hallmarks of anthropological ethnographic practice. Some of this trend is exacerbated by industrial and user interaction designers' use of different ethnographic methods that, while entirely valid and appropriate, are often derived from a different tradition than of cultural anthropology. As the authors of a book titled *Doing Design Ethnography* explain in their introduction, "This book is about one perspective on ethnography in design, derived from a very specific branch of sociology called ethnomethodology. Ethnomethodology was first on the scene, first to be used at Xerox PARC, [and] first to demonstrate the salience of ethnography to systems design" (Crabtree et al. 2012:1–2). The intent here is not to debate the merits of anthropological ethnographic methods compared with those of design, or ethnomethodology's ethnographic methods versus those emanating from other anthropological and sociological analytic frameworks, but to point out that given the many types of activities that inform the collection of methods that fit under the ethnographic umbrella, authors can easily mistake one tradition for another and make ill-informed statements that can result in unsuitable recommendations.

Indeed, contestation over what, fundamentally, constitutes "authentic" anthropological identity and practice must contribute to the disorientation of journalists and corporate managers alike when forging understanding and trust of business anthropology. Key concerns here include: the modification of traditional methods (How long in the field is long enough? Does conducting an interview in someone's living room constitute fieldwork? [see Wellner 2002]); privacy (Is videotaping individuals without their knowledge on the street or in a store a violation? [see Bowman 2010; Miller 1990] Is probing subjects for six hours about their activities and transgressions intrusive? [Wood 2013]); accountability (What happens if the results of the study are not what the client, whether internal or external, wants to hear? [see Ante 2006]); and representation (Does a PowerPoint slide deck of topline concept and photographs or a two-minute video condensed from purposively edited footage constitute an ethnography? [see Wakeford 2006]).

There is no fixed resolution to these issues, and it is the work of every field to engage in its own particular discourses and dialectics. Nevertheless, although the social sciences are marked by polyvocality, the rise of applied anthropology would seem to warrant *augmented* vocality on the part of professional groups such as the National Association for the Practice of Anthropology (NAPA) in specifying codes of practice.[13]

A friend of mine who is a physicist (and has a healthy sense of humor) sighs heavily when lay acquaintances ask him what he thinks of the situation-comedy television program *The Big Bang Theory*. He explains that while introducing physics to a mass audience is both desirable and laudable, there is little gained if the portrait it offers is mere caricature. This may be the pedagogue in him speaking, concerned with false impressions given to prospective scientists, but I think more likely there is something else in play. While I do not believe for a moment that he is afraid of being mocked, it is one thing to tease those within one's own in-group, and another to have outsiders recklessly determine what others will know and believe about you. This is, in part, what scholars such as Hall (1997) were concerned with: the power of discourse as a system of representation that constructs meaning. When journalists represent anthropologists in business as Keystone Cops, circling a woman as she showers in a bikini under the blinking recording light of a video camera and asking questions such as "Would you say that the shower has 'necessity status' for you?" and "So, you think the [soap] pump is a kind of control mechanism?" (Osborne 2002), they trivialize the meaning of human experience. Similarly, a report on an American design firm's process to "connect with" Chinese consumers ("Inside Lenovo's Design Quest"; *BusinessWeek* 2006) and characterized by the reporter as "among the best of its breed" due to an approach the firm branded (itself perhaps a signal of suspect practice) "Search for the Soul" describes among other activities: the firm studying Chinese billboards while listening to rock, pop, classical, and traditional Chinese music "blasting in the war [conference] room"; bringing in a Chinese history professor to lecture on cultural differences between the United States and China; and collecting "Chinese objects of desire—wallets, lighters and cell-phone holders." Such desultory activities risk deprecating the meaning, richness, and complexity of culture. Whether or not those profiled in these articles are what some might describe as "real" business anthropologists or ethnographies is not germane. It is the representations of the field's practices that are circulated and consumed, and by that criterion alone, they are rendered representative.

Given cultural anthropology's own crisis of representation (Marcus and Fischer 1986), it would seem disingenuous to harshly judge another field's portrayal of its subject. Yet it is perhaps precisely *because* of cultural anthropology's struggle for reflexivity that the implications of simplification or stereotype in the media should be conspicuous. While it is beyond the task of this essay to reiterate the scholarship on representation—a topic which has been amply theorized (e.g., Hall 1997)—it is worth underscoring the media's powerful social influence. As Coman, offering an anthropological perspective of mass media, notes, the "mass media [is] at the center of the process of social construction of reality as an institution that generates specific discourses and logics. The products incorporating such values are distributed to the public and are assumed by the public as edifying images about the world" (Coman 2005:46). In other words, although journalists themselves may not intend it, their narratives are powerful shaping mechanisms for their audiences' understanding.

Earlier in this chapter, I suggested that the incessant "discovery" of anthropology in commercial contexts signaled it as inexorably anomalous. Similarly, Suchman proposes that the media's ongoing fascination has to do with "the unlikely juxtaposition of anthropology as *investigator* of exotic Other with anthropologist *as* exotic Other in the mundane, familiar halls of the corporate workplace" (Suchman 2007). I concur with Suchman's eventual assessment, which is to read business anthropologists' examination of contemporary consumers as expressive of the tension that emanates from Othering the Self. Indeed, any call for anthropologists suggests that the familiar is strange. In an age marked by both self-absorption and hyperreflexivity (e.g., the creation and ascent of blogs and videos documenting the lived experience of everyday life as well as accompanying personal analysis and commentary) and the disenfranchisement of Big Data—a state in which individuals are both eerily parsed by their every mouse click or swipe of a smartphone and clustered together as faceless components of global segments[14]—the very act of commercial entities employing people to find or "expose" underlying meaning can be inherently destabilizing. This is evident in the metaphors sometimes used to characterize clients' perceptions of ethnography, such as "a crystal ball or magical resolution" (Sunderland and Denny 2007), which speak to the dual modes of fascination and fear provoked by the occult, or at least tacit, nature of consumer culture.

The corrective (but by no means singular) is perhaps that the time has come for anthropologists and ethnographers working in business to author their own thick descriptions of their work; the text you are holding (or reading online) is an excellent example. Another is found on the Context-based Research Group's website.[15] The firm offers an explanation of the firm's anthropological perspective and a definition of ethnography; it also provides downloadable copies of "self-funded [ethnographic] studies on topics of social and economic significance" that prospective clients can read and evaluate.

Perhaps most important, anthropologists in business should highlight and explicate the analysis that is central to the value their work provides. This is the one key component that the "template" described at the beginning of this chapter omits. Nowhere, whether in the illustrative account of the successful application of qualitative methods, the revelatory instance of deep insight, the enumeration of the deficiencies of extant research methods, or the urgency provoked by the turbulence of the times, is there any account or commentary provided on the act of data analysis. This is critical, because insightful analysis is both more likely with thorough training and the site of value creation for the client. It can distinguish "mere observation" of consumers—which indeed, many managers can and should engage in—from the analysis that those trained in both recognizing and mapping the socially constituted, symbolically rendered meanings and processes, and in doing so with multiple forms of data and while negotiating multiple perspectives and levels of analysis. Rather than disparage an existing research method for its deficiencies, we can instead condemn maladroit practitioners or insufficient praxis.

Providing responsible representations of well-executed applied anthropology is vital: to the health of the field, to attendant understanding of the field of anthropology as a whole, and to the understanding of well-intentioned marketers who seek to provide relevant products to the marketplace. These representations must be promulgated now, lest an enterprising writer decides to pitch a sitcom about a group of bearded and Birkenstocked roommates—anthropologists named Bronek, Claude, Franz, and Cliff—who compete for the attentions of two women named Margaret and Mary, who live with a shrewdness of apes[16] across the hall.

REFERENCES

Acohido, Byron. 2007. "Microsoft Cultures Creativity in Unique Lab." *USA Today* July 11. http://usatoday30.usatoday.com/tech/techinvestor/corporatenews/2007-07-10-windows-mobile_N.htm (accessed January 2, 2014).

Alsop, Ronald. 1986. "People Watchers' Seek Clues to Consumers' True Behavior." *Wall Street Journal* September 4, p. 29.

anderson, ken. 2009. "Ethnographic Research: A Key to Strategy." *Harvard Business Review* 87(3):24.

Ante, Spencer. 2006. "The Science of Desire." *BusinessWeek* June 5:98–106.

Baker, Stephen. 2004. "Online Extra: Reaching the Connected Generation." *BusinessWeek* July 11. http://www.businessweek.com/stories/2004-07-11/online-extra-reaching-the-connected-generation (accessed January 2, 2014).

Barnett, Steve. 2002. "Letter to the Editor: The Study of Shopping." *New York Times* May 4. http://www.nytimes.com/2002/05/04/opinion/l-the-study-of-shopping-874728.html (accessed January 2, 2014).

_____ 1988. "Observing: Hunters and Gatherers." *Advertising Age* March 7.

_____1987. "Two Views on Aging." *Advertising Age* October 12.

Barnett, Steve, and Magdoff, J. 1986. "Beyond Narcissism in American Culture of the 1980s." *Cultural Anthropology* 1:413–24.

Bellotti, Victoria. 2010. "Ethnography in Industry: Objectives?" *UX Magazine* June 1 (Article no. 532). http://uxmag.com/articles/ethnography-in-industry-objectives (accessed December 31, 2013).

Bird, S. Elizabeth. 1998. "News We Can Use: An Audience Perspective on the Tabloidisation of News in the United States." *Javnost/The Public* 5(3):33-49.

Bowman, Jo. 2010. "Every Move You Make." *CNBC Magazine* April.

Boyd, Harper W., Jr., and Sidney J. Levy. 1963. "New Dimension in Consumer Analysis." *Harvard Business Review* 41:129–40.

BusinessWeek. 2006. "Inside Lenovo's Design Quest." September 24. http://www.businessweek.com/stories/2006-09-24/inside-lenovos-design-quest (accessed December 2, 2013).

Chokshi, Sonal, Eric Vinkhuyzen, Victoria Bellotti, and Brigitte Jordan. 2011. "Busting the Myth of the Giant Green Button: A Brief History of Corporate Ethnography." *UX Magazine* January 27. http://uxmag.com/articles/busting-the-myth-of-the-giant-green-button (accessed December 31, 2013).

Clifford, James. 1986. "Introduction: Partial Truths." In *Writing Culture: The Poetics and Politics of Ethnography*, edited by J. Clifford and G. E. Marcus, 1–26. Berkeley, CA: University of California Press.

Colyer, Edwin. 2003. "Taking a Closer Look at Your Customers." *Brandchannel* July 21. http://www.brandchannel.com/features_effect.asp?pf_id=167 (accessed December 31, 2013).

Coman, Mihai. 2005. "Cultural Anthropology and Mass Media: A Processual Approach." In *Media Anthropology*, edited by Eric W. Rothenbuhler and Mihai Coman, 46–55. Thousand Oaks, CA: Sage.

Crabtree, Andrew, Mark Rouncefield, and Peter Tolmie. 2012. *Doing Design Ethnography*. London: Springer-Verlag.

Crapanzano, Vincent. 1986. "Hermes' Dilemma: The Masking of Subversion in Ethnographic Description." In *Writing Culture: The Poetics and Politics of Ethnography*, edited by J. Clifford and G. E. Marcus, 51–76. Berkeley, CA: University of California Press.

DePaula, Rogerio, Suzanne L. Thomas, and Xueming Lang. 2009. "Taking the Driver's Seat: Sustaining Critical Enquiry While Becoming a Legitimate Corporate Decision-Maker." *Ethnographic Praxis in Industry Conference Proceedings* 2009(1):2–16.

Demos, Alison. 2007. "The Limits of Market-Research Methods: Study Up—Ethnography Is Often Misused. *Advertising Age* October 8. http://adage.com/article/cmo-strategy/limits-market-research-methods/120917/ (accessed December 31, 2013).

Deutsch, Claudia. 1991. "Coping with Cultural Polyglots." *New York Times* February 24, p. 25.

Dichter, Ernest. 1962. "The World Customer." *Harvard Business Review* 40(4): 113–22.

Durante, Richard and Michael Feehan. 2006. "Watch and Learn: Ethnography Yields Useful, Strategic Insights." *Marketing News* February 1.

Epstein, Eve. 2000. *InfoWorld*.

Fiske, John. 1992. "Audiencing: A Cultural Studies Approach to Watching Television." *Poetics* 21:345–59.

Flatley, Marianne. 2005. "Omnicom Companies Launch IN:SITE." Press release, October 12. www.prweb.com/printer/295907.htm (accessed August 15, 2012).

Gardner, Burleigh B., and Sidney J. Levy. 1955. "The Product and the Brand." *Harvard Business Review* 33(March–April):33–9.

Geertz, Clifford. 1973. *The Interpretation of Cultures*. New York: Basic Books.

Glasnapp, James. 2010. "Ethnography in Industry: Methods Overview." *UX Magazine* November 10 (Article no. 578). http://uxmag.com/articles/ethnography-in-industry-methods-overview (accessed December 31, 2013).

Goffman, Erving. 1974. *Frame Analysis*. New York: Harper Colophone Books.

Green, Penelope. 1999. "Mirror, Mirror: The Anthropologist of Dressing Rooms." *New York Times* May 2. http://www.nytimes.com/1999/05/02/style/mirror-mirror-the-anthropologist-of-dressing-rooms.html?pagewanted=all&src=pm (accessed January 2, 2014).

Hafner, Katie. 1999. "Coming of Age in Palo Alto." *New York Times* June 10. http://www.nytimes.com/1999/06/10/technology/coming-of-age-in-palo-alto.html.

Hall, Stewart. 1997. "The Work of Representation." In *Representation: Cultural Representations and Signifying Practices*, edited by S. Hall, 13–69. London: Sage.

Hill, Kashmir. 2011. "Forbes Focus: Digital Anthropologist." *Forbes* February 28. http://www.forbes.com/sites/kashmirhill/2011/02/28/danah-boyd-digital-anthropologist/ (accessed December 31, 2013).

Hinds, Michael deCourcy. 1988. "Feminist Businesses See the Future, and Decide It's Unisex." *New York Times* (Consumer's World) November 12. http://www.nytimes.com/1988/11/12/style/consumer-s-world-feminist-businesses-see-the-future-and-decide-it-s-unisex.html (accessed December 31, 2013).

Holt, Douglas. 2002. "Why Do Brands Cause Trouble?" *Journal of Consumer Research* 29(1):70–90.

Jordan, Ann T. 2010. "The Importance of Business Anthropology: Its Unique Contributions." *International Journal of Business Anthropology* 1(1):7–17.

Kane, Kate A. 1996. "Anthropologists Go Native in the Corporate Village." *Fast Company* 5(October/November):60.

Kermouch, Gerry. 2001. "Consumers in the Mist." *BusinessWeek* February 25. http://www.businessweek.com/stories/2001-02-25/consumers-in-the-mist (accessed December 31, 2013).

Levin, Gary. 1992. "Anthropologists in Adland: Researchers Now Studying Cultural Meaning of Brands." *Advertising Age* 63(8):3.

Lewin, Tamar. 1986. "Cultural Consultant Steve Barnett: Casting an Anthropological Eye on American Consumers." *New York Times* May 11. http://www.nytimes.com/ 1986/05/11/business/cultural-consultant-steve-barnett-casting-anthropological-eye-american-consumers.html (accessed January 2, 2014).

Levy, Sidney J. 1959. "Symbols for Sale." *Harvard Business Review* 37 (July–August):117–24.

______. 2006. "History of Qualitative Research Methods in Marketing." In *Handbook of Qualitative Research Methods in Marketing*, edited by R. W. Belk, 3–16. Northampton, MA: Edward Elgar Publishing.

Levy, Sidney J., and Dennis Rook. 1999. *Brands, Consumers, Symbols and Research: Sidney J. Levy on Marketing*. Thousand Oaks, CA: Sage.

Marcus, George E., and Michael M. J. Fischer. 1986. *Anthropology as Cultural Critique*. Chicago, IL: University of Chicago Press.

McCracken, Grant. 2006. "Ethnography and the 'Extra Data' Opportunity." *Ethnographic Praxis in Industry Conference Proceedings* 1:1–3.

Miller, Annetta, with Bruce Shenitz and Lourdes Rosado. 1990. "You are What You Buy." *Newsweek* 115(23):59–61.

Osborne, Lawrence. 2002. "Consuming the Rituals of the Suburban Tribe." *New York Times* January 13, pp. 28–31.

Posner, Bruce G. 1996. "The Future of Marketing Is Looking at You." *Fast Company*. October 31, p. 105.

Society of Professional Journalists. 1996. "Code of Ethics." http://www.spj.org/pdf/ethicscode.pdf (accessed December 29, 2012).

Suchman, Lucy. 2007. "Anthropology as 'Brand': Reflections on Corporate Anthropology." Paper presented at the Colloquium on Interdisciplinarity and Society, February 24, Oxford University, United Kingdom.

Sunderland, Patricia L., and Rita M. Denny. 2007. *Doing Anthropology in Consumer Research*. Walnut Creek, CA: Left Coast Press.

The Economist. 2004. "Off with the Pith Helmets." March 11. http://www.economist.com/node/2476910 (accessed January 2, 2014).

Underhill, Paco. 1999. *Why We Buy: The Science of Shopping*. New York: Simon & Schuster.

Tischler, Linda. 2004. "Every Move You Make." *Fast Company*. April.

Turkle, Sherry. 2011. *Alone Together: Why We Expect More from Technology and Less from Each Other*. New York: Basic Books.

Wakeford, Nina. 2006. "PowerPoint and the Crafting of Social Data." *Ethnographic Praxis in Industry Conference Proceedings* 1:94–108.

Walsh, Sharon. 2001. "Corporate Anthropology: Dirt-free Research." *CNN.com*. May 23. http://edition.cnn.com/2001/CAREER/dayonthejob/05/23/corp.anthropologist.idg/index.html?_s=PM:CAREER (accessed December 31, 2013).

Wasson, Christina. 2000. "Ethnography in the Field of Design." *Human Organization* 59(4):377–88.

Wellner, Alison Stein. 2003. "Watch Me Now." *Advertising Age* October 1, pp. S1–S8. http: //adage.com/article/american-demographics/watch/44651/ (accessed December 31, 2013).

_____ 2003. "Consumers in the Mist." *Inc.* April. http://www.inc.com/magazine/ 20030401/25306.html (accessed December 31, 2013).

Wilson, Allan R. 1952. "Qualitative Market Research." *Harvard Business Review* January.

Winick, Charles. 1961. "Anthropology's Contributions to Marketing." *Journal of Marketing* 25(5):53–60.

Wood, Graeme. 2013. "Anthropology Inc." *The Atlantic* February 20. http://www.theatlantic.com/magazine/archive/2013/03/anthropology-inc/309218/ (accessed January 2, 2014).

NOTES

The author would like to acknowledge the excellent feedback and suggestions offered by the *Handbook*'s editors as well as reviewers Christina Wasson and Bob Yovovich.

1 I searched in business databases such as ProQuest Business and Factiva for news items by using terms such as "anthropology," "ethnography," and "business anthropology" as well as combination terms such as "anthropology" AND "market research" (and multiple adjectival variants). My search focused on the kind of mainstream print media that a manager might encounter in the course of their professional activities, and eschewed highly technical or narrowly specialized forums such as blogs or particular industry newsletters. These would also make rich data sources for future inquiry, but are beyond the scope of the current study. Because the popular business press is not always indexed in aggregating databases, in addition to those searches I conducted magazine- and newspaper-specific searches. The titles were selected for their popularity (circulation) and editorial content/target audience, and searched with similar key words and terms as noted. Although this

review suffers from inevitable limitations (including, among others, the focus on American print publications), it contains sufficient material for scrutiny, providing an ample supply from which to explore how business anthropology is portrayed in the narratives of trade and popular print outlets consumed by managers and consumers alike.

2 Students of ethnography will recognize the phrase "establishing rapport" as part of the standard training for fieldwork. Generally, it refers to the expectation that the ethnographer should establish a positive, trusting relationship with those who are being studied. I use the phrase here to highlight the notion of relationship between reporter and other.

3 Evidence that the Winick (1961) article was well received by at least some colleagues came from none other than Sidney Levy. In his own article, Levy (1978) enthuses, "[Winick's] summary of what anthropology is about and how it might be used is excellent in laying a groundwork and a plea for greater communication between the fields of anthropology and marketing" (1978:557).

4 Although in an interesting review of one of Dichter's books that appeared in *Journal of Marketing* around this time the author notes, with thinly veiled disdain towards Dichter's apparent omniscience, that although Dichter "trained as a psychologist and started in this role, he has now become an authority on social anthropology, sociology, semantics, symbolism and history, since these are now seen as part of motivation research" (Martineau 1961:109).

5 This is not intended to equate anthropology with "a novel form of market research" (Suchman 2007), but rather to make sense of the recurring discovery of anthropology by business and business reporting.

6 Sunderland and Denny (2007) emphasize this paradox when referring to "ethnography as the '*new*' means for companies to '*really understand consumers*'" (2007:14); Jordan (2010) refers to her work early as a business anthropologist as the "*re-development*" of a new field (2010:14), and Wasson notes that "although the field of design has only recently '*discovered*' ethnography, anthropologists have been looking at related issues for many years" (2000:379).

7 In *The Interpretation of Cultures,* Clifford Geertz (1973; borrowing from Ryle) illustrates how members of a culture are equipped to make sense of cultural categories through the example of eyelid twitches. That is, he describes how one knows to ignore the functional twitch of an eye that is a mere *blink* but to attend to the conspiratorial meaning conveyed (with the very same physical movement) with a *wink,* only by virtue of literacy with a given cultural code. I am asserting that many of the journalists co-opting anthropology's constructs assume that they are winking effectively, but are often misappropriating codes that they don't fully control.

8 Anthropology is the study of humans, but which aspect of "humanness" one studies can make a vast difference. In what has become known as the "four-field" approach, the discipline of anthropology in the United States is often defined as composed of four distinct sub-specializations: sociocultural anthropology, physical anthropology, linguistic anthropology, and archaeology (see http://www.aaanet.org/about/whatisanthropology.cfm). Most students of anthropology learn a bit of each of these areas. However, under this taxonomy, while archeologists can be categorized as anthropologists, only a portion of anthropologists consider themselves to be archaeologists.

9 Sunderland and Denny (2007) unpack a similar illustration for an article in *US News & World Report* (2007:43–4). While they forgive the image's creator for his or her ignorance, the similarity of the image accompanying the Ante (2006) piece, a virtually interchangeable illustration on anderson's (2009) article and a variation thereon in Wood's piece for *The Atlantic* (2013) is enough to wonder if art directors (or editors) have created their own visual trope for ethnography.

10 Gilding is no longer at IN:SITE.

11 For a cheeky and provocative articulation of this issue, see McCracken's keynote address, in which he proclaims: "My profession has a problem. It is awash in hacks and pretenders. I am guessing that 1 in 3 ethnographers is more or less incompetent. It is easy to identify some of the offenders. Some of them actually claim to be 'self-trained.' Others are focus-group moderators simply renamed. Some actually claim competence on the grounds that they 'roomed with an anthropology major in college'" (McCracken 2006:1).

12 The "conversion" metaphor is a common one, and interesting for its implication that the believer is acting on faith rather than evidence.

13 NAPA does post its ethical guidelines, but the Association's leadership might consider launching a campaign of dissemination; for example, asking members to post a link on their own websites or other information and promotional materials. Guidelines are available at http://practicinganthropology.org/about/ethical-guidelines/.

14 Some of these inherent contradictions are explored in Turkle's (2011) *Alone Together.*

15 Please see the Context Research Group's website at http://www.contextresearch.com.

16 A "shrewdness" is the term for a group of apes, just as fish congregate in schools, and birds flock together.

27

How "the User" Frames What Designers See: What Cultural Analysis Does To Change the Frame

MEGAN NEESE

Marketing teams talk about consumers. Research teams talk about respondents. Engineering teams talk about targets. Designers talk about users. These terms tend to be used simultaneously and somewhat interchangeably in corporations so that a single study can be applicable to a variety of departments. But are they really all the same?

I believe that the word choices highlight assumptions researchers accept as givens and that these assumptions influence what they subsequently learn from their studies. In particular for designers, expecting to meet "the user" informs how they see and what they hear. This chapter takes a look at who this "user" is, how the term came about, and how designers consider the user in the design process. I dig into the design process and the ideals that many designers are striving to achieve with their work. With that context, I consider how ethnography and cultural analysis can impact the design process. Then returning to the premise of "the user," I look critically at how this point of view shapes design work. In the end, cultural analysis can help to frame a design concept, bring designers closer to their ideals, and ultimately help develop designs that satisfy a broader range of users.

As the representative designer on a number of cross-functional and cross-departmental research projects, I've been asked more times than I can count: "What do you mean 'user'?" and "Can't we use 'customer'?" My favorite among these inquiries was the proclamation, "It's a weird word; it reminds me of a drug addict."

The "user" is an articulation of the person the designer imagines will be interacting with their design when it is complete. By watching users use things,

---

Handbook of Anthropology in Business, edited by Rita Denny and Patricia Sunderland, 521–539.

designers can identify problems. They look for points of frustration and confusion as a way to identify unmet needs. For example, comments such as "This is difficult to clean" or "This button is confusing" provide a clear direction for design development. Often such problems can be detected through observation even if the user does not verbalize them.

At the core, designers are seeking to understand what a concept or product means or might mean to its users so that they can build upon that meaning, enhance it, or change it. Cultural analysis can reframe the game for designers. But many, including designers, see ethnography as synonymous with observation: a method that can be equally well executed by a social psychologist, sociologist, design researcher, or professional moderator. This oversimplification prevents and, in fact, severely restricts designers from gaining the full benefit of ethnography for understanding a product's meaning. Integrating ethnography into the design process could help to generate more meaningful concepts and therefore more effective, universal, and timeless design.

THE HISTORY OF THE TERM

Human Factors in Industrial Design

During the early growth of industrial design as a profession in the United States, Henry Dreyfuss stood out as a pioneer for human considerations in the design process. His book *Designing for People* ([1955] 2003) and Alvin Tilley's capture of his work, *Measure of Man* (1960), introduced the design industry to human factors. In this work he eloquently described how considerations of human factors could influence the work of designers. Although Dreyfuss never explicitly used the term "user," his introduction of human factor considerations to design fundamentally shaped contemporary approaches; that is, user-centered design. I explore Dreyfuss' inspiration, the evolution of his philosophy over time, and introduction of the term "user" to understand the mindset of contemporary "user centered" designers.

Dreyfuss was inspired by the field of human factors, a derivative of human engineering: a term used in the military to build efficiencies through understanding human constraints.

> Before World War II, engineers and architects had some physical guidelines (space required to climb ladders and stairs, space for maintenance access, space for dining); these were usually based on the average man. . . . World War II required new and complex war machines, and the concept that these machines, not personnel, win wars gave way to efficient man-machine relationships (Tilley 2002:9).

Design standards for man-machine relationships became a mainstream focus with the growth of the industrial design profession, and Dreyfuss ran a successful practice on this premise for the next 60 years. He compiled measurement data over the history of his career from various public sources such as the US Department of Health and Human Services, The Society of Automotive Engineers, and NASA, and presented it in percentiles of the population. These percentiles were meant to enable designers to develop clear boundaries for their design considerations. As Dreyfuss explained, "The few at either end of the normal curve may be so extreme that an encompassing design could become too large or expensive to produce" (Mueller 2013). For example, considering the hand sizes of people in the 0 to 5 and 95 to 100 percentiles when designing a pair of scissors may not be feasible.

Over time, this percentile data grew to include all sorts of seemingly minute dimensional details. Dreyfuss laid out the typical physical development phases of children, typical range of motion, and typical design considerations for objects such as desk height, foot pedal angle, and button-pressing force. What is often less noted about his data is the extent to which he included guidelines about environment and context. For example, he provided measures of color reflectivity by material, color temperature by degrees Kelvin, illumination levels by light source, and typical decibel levels of dentist drills, snowmobiles, and vacuum cleaners (which he compares against "typical" decibel levels that cause fatigue or hearing loss). Factor by factor, designers were encouraged to define the bounds for whom they were designing and provide an optimal experience for that segment of the population. In large part, the term "user" has evolved out of this literal visualization of diagrammatic fiftieth-percentile people, but Dreyfuss never called them "users." Instead, they are always referred to in a specific context, such as travelers on a train, housewives ironing, or cooks in a kitchen.

Charles Eames never referred to "users" either, but he famously spoke about the role of the designer in a user-centered way. In one of his more well-known quotes, he says: "The role of the designer is that of a very good, thoughtful host, all of whose energy goes into trying to anticipate the needs of his guests" (Lane 2012:1). He spoke extensively about "needs" and "constraints" that directed and informed design work. Eames presumed that we should focus on the constraints and needs of a specific project. In this way, the idea of selecting a percentile range of people for whom to design limited the creative potential of considering constraints unique to the project itself. Even Dreyfuss, who produced the percentiles and intended for them to be standalone references, struggled to use these charts without personifying them in great detail. Indeed, "Joe and Josephine" helped guide 60 years of design work at the Dreyfuss firm.

> No matter what they are doing, we observe their every position and reaction. They are part of our staff, representing millions of consumers for whom we are designing, and they dictate every line we draw. Joe and Josephine did not spring lightly to our walls from the pages of a book on anatomy. They represent many years of research by our office, not merely into their physical aspects but into their psychology as well. . . . Joe and Josephine have numerous allergies, inhibitions and obsessions (Dreyfuss [1955] 2003:26–7).

Joe and Josephine helped to bring the Dreyfuss firm's diagrammatic percentiles to life. By making the "average" man and woman quantifiable, they became easier to imagine and easier to keep in mind during the design process. Eames took this notion further such that each project had its own sense of self, based on a set of needs and constraints specific to the context in which that product would live. In this way, a chair for the office environment would include different considerations than would seating for a public airport.

User-Centered Design in Computer Science

Although industrial designers began including considerations for people in the design process at the turn of the twentieth century, the term "user" was developed in the field of computer science and later co-opted as "user-centered design" by many design disciplines, including industrial design. Donald Norman is generally credited with popularizing the term "user." His first publication that popularized the term "user" was *User Centered System Design* (Norman and Draper 1986). The publication was a summary of a collection of projects that had been conducted at the University of California, San Diego, where he taught. The projects brought together two common interests within the university: psychology and artificial intelligence. Norman and his research partner Paul Smolensky put together a team of grad students, postdoctoral fellows, research faculty in the Institute for Cognitive Science, and experts across the industry and country with the goal of understanding issues, raising questions, and identifying methods for designing in a "user-centered" way. The premise of the book was a budding dialog within the computer science industry at the time: "People are so adaptable that they are capable of shouldering the entire burden of accommodation to an artifact, but skillful designers make large parts of this burden vanish by adapting the artifact to its users" (Norman and Draper 1986:1).

In *User Centered System Design,* the book title is explained in this way: "Paul Smolensky generated the name of the project alliteratively with the name of the University: so from UCSD, the University, has come UCSD, the project, and, eventually, the name of the book: User Centered System Design" (Norman and Draper 1986:1). It is difficult to determine the exact source of the term "user" from this book, and it seems a stretch to believe that it may have literally come from a desire to align with the acronym UCSD, but it is definitely within this book that the term "user" really took shape (Norman and Draper 1986). It was swiftly adopted by many design professions, including industrial design, as a means of shorthand for considering a person's needs in the design process, a concept that had long been understood and employed by Dreyfuss, Eames, and many others by the time of Norman's publication.

THE PROCESS OF DESIGN

Considering the user has become increasingly important in design education and professional practice. However, it is important to understand that it is not sufficient—or even always top priority—to consider the user. Considerations such as manufacturability or cost often weigh against user needs. The set of considerations a designer is faced with is often dependent upon the company, the project, the client, and the business plan. Although there is no standard set of considerations, there *are* some widely agreed-upon principles of composition that drive many of the more common ones.

Tension is one principle of composition. Tension is generally about implicit relationships between elements of a design and how to demonstrate those relationships in a meaningful way. Tension can be static, or it can be dynamic. Static tension may be created with symmetry or a central focus that connotes stability, orientation, strength, or power. Dynamic tension may be created with juxtaposition or contrast that connotes movement, dynamism, or change (Bradley 2012). Simply making something symmetrical does not make a composition balanced, nor does it provide tension. Working through how to achieve tension in a particular design is part of how an idea develops over time.

Through iterative sketching, designers focus on working through principles such as tension until they figure out an appropriate solution. Sketching often generates new ideas; after arriving at one solution, designers often start asking new questions to incorporate new considerations. "This works, but what if the handle were over there? Would it be easier to hold?" Here is a way to connote movement, but did it come at the cost of another principle of composition, such as order?

Order may be achieved with rhythm or balance that connotes familiarity, logic, or comprehension. If the design solution achieves dynamic tension at the cost of order, the composition may feel unbalanced or discordant—or just right—for the purpose and context of that design. Designers may consider a series of composition principles and find that many are in conflict with one another or with the desired outcome. At what point a designer finds resolution and begins to finalize a design depends on the project and on the individual.

Everyday objects around us embody their designer's chosen level of resolution. Chairs can be works of art, sculptures that demonstrate the possibilities of thoughtful and holistic composition. They display tension, balance, contrast, and material use; they engage the voids in space that the chair is sitting within as part of the composition itself. Yet these very chairs can be difficult and uncomfortable to sit in because of how that designer prioritized which considerations in coming to a resolution decision. This decision-making process is one of the most fundamental elements of personal voice in the design process: it demonstrates the individual's design intent. The user is only one of potentially many considerations that a designer must choose to reject or accept and prioritize.

The field of user-centered design presumes that the more designers understand and internalize the user, the better they will be able to consider the user during the design process. This is because the design process is iterative; ideas can be greatly transformed and enhanced by integrating new considerations and conflicts. Iterative thinking is a trainable skill that is honed in design schools through the method of critique. During a critique, design students pin up sketches and ideas for professors and the rest of the class to analyze. Their work is discussed and challenged by the group to encourage further thinking and idea development. Being challenged to include an increasingly long list of considerations helps to improve the depth of the student's thinking. Integrating user needs into the design process acts in the same way. As an idea continues to mature over time, new inputs from users may inspire new considerations and new thinking.

For example, the Post-it note was designed in a very slow and generative manner that still required a single moment of user inspiration. After five years of experimentation and development with sticky acrylic spheres that provided temporary adhesiveness but could be removed without leaving a residue, one of the inventors, Art Fry, got up to sing in his church choir when he realized that the paper bookmark he had used to save his spot in rehearsal had fallen out and he had no idea what page the rest of the choir was singing from. He wished for a bookmark that would stick to the paper but wouldn't pull the paper apart. Back at work he then added this consideration to the design process so that the spheres might work on something as light as paper and not tear apart the paper that it was attached to. Eventually this effort turned into the Post-it notes that we see littered all over offices today (Partnoy 2012). Art's participation in a church choir was an important element of the design process that integrated a new unforeseen consideration to the design of the Post-it note.

DESIGN IDEALS

All designs live within a context and a time. The considerations that are brought into the design process are a demonstration of a designer's understanding of that context and that time. But even the best, most thoughtful design solutions live within a context and time that can fade or change such that the solution may not maintain relevance. A few products are able to maintain an astounding sense of relevance over time. Rows and rows of Charles and Ray Eames' Tandem Sling Seat,[1] designed in 1962, are still manufactured new and specified by architects in contemporary airport interiors. A leading modern design furniture catalog, Design Within Reach,[2] is consistently full of new manufacturing runs of iconic design works developed in another time.

To design an object that is able to withstand shifts in time is often considered to be a pinnacle moment in one's design career. To some designers the notion of "timelessness" is a demonstration of compositional purity. However, industries such as computing, electronics, and robotics have a tight relationship with technological developments that are quickly surpassed by new capabilities of next-generation and all-new technologies. Even if the visual qualities and usability aspects of a design are "timeless," the rapid depreciation of the technology itself will undermine its ability to remain relevant. For example, the first iPhone may still be an elegant solution in today's market, but the drag of its now-obsolete components makes it contextually irrelevant. For industries such as electronics, timelessness is rarely even a design goal.

Instead, "Universal Design" has emerged as a philosophy within the design industry to address the idea of a product's ability to travel across contexts without traveling through time (see Erickson, this volume). The driver pushing toward universality is for a design to span multiple cultural contexts or extreme differences in age or ability.

> The relativity of aesthetic values does not mean that there cannot be "good" design. Good design is a visual statement that maximizes the life goals of the people in a given culture (or, more realistically, the goals of a certain subset of people in the culture) that draws on a shared symbolic expression for the ordering of such goals. If the system of symbols is relatively universal, then the design will also be judged good across time and cultures (Buchanan 1973:125).

Looking for needs and symbols that can work across cultures, contexts, and needs can help expand the reach of a design. For example, the OXO Good Grips potato peeler,[3] was originally designed for an arthritic woman who found it painful to peel potatoes with a traditional peeler. The need for a more comfortable grip resonated with many nonarthritic users who came to enjoy the improved ergonomic grip and soft rubberized material (Cagan and Vogel 2002).

One of the current trends in the interaction design field is a drive toward "human fluency" or "NUIs" (natural user interfaces). NUIs work to reduce the need for people to learn how to use or "adapt to" a device. Gesture-based interfaces (considered to be NUIs) in today's electronic products demonstrate how a single device can span user demographics and training levels. The design of gesture-based controls in the iPhone interface has allowed a much larger span of ages to intuitively navigate through a phone's basic interface premise, and has reduced the need for training less tech-savvy users. For example, Chinese characters can be quickly written on the iPhone interface, whereas previous computing technology required characters to be input phonetically; in some cases, an entirely new translation of one's native language had to be learned to interact with the basic functions of a smartphone.

Just like the concept of "timelessness," achieving some level of "universality" is often lauded as a pinnacle moment in a designer's career. To achieve either feat, a designer must have not only a keen sense of the time and context in which they live, but a broader perspective on the world, the future, and the desires of people in times and contexts other than his or her own. Designers who have been able to think in this way are often credited with developing the qualities of timelessness or universality. Although some product categories are naturally a better fit for a timeless or universal solution, designers cannot help but imagine they have some control over their ability to direct this fate. In an interview with Charles Eames at the Musée des Arts Décoratifs, Palais de Louvre, in 1972, Madame. L. Amic asked him, "Is design ephemeral?" to which he responded, "Some needs are ephemeral, most designs are ephemeral." She then asked him, "Ought design to tend towards ephemeral or towards permanence?" He replied, "Those needs and designs that have a more universal quality tend towards relative permanence" (Wunsch 2008).

Design schools emphasize the need for designers to think beyond their own context and their own time. Schools often assign projects to purposely require students to think about the needs of people who are very unlike them. Students may be asked to design diaper bags for young mothers, pillboxes for nursing-home residents, or solar cookers for grand-mothers in rural India. The student-teacher dialog surrounding these types of projects is often focused on how students are making assumptions about needs and contexts that differ sharply from their day-to-day life in college. How will a nursing-home patient be able to open the pillbox if they have severe arthritis? Did the student identify considerations that they themselves would not have or instinctively know?

Projects will often reflect a single element of this curiosity; a student will focus on the weight of an object, or the grip, or the legibility of a font size. In the end, the concept may be a pillbox that identifies the size and color of each pill for blind patients, or one that signals an alarm for forgetful dementia patients. These single dimensions help illustrate clarity of thought that is clearly different from one's own college context. Eventually this thinking can be further dimensionalized through broader debate and contextual inquiry. By slowly adding factors of cultural context, industry initiatives, governmental regulations, and social trends, young designers can increasingly empathize with complex contexts to inform their work. In this way, empathic thinking is methodically learned in design programs and later causally related to the research method of ethnography.

Designers think of research as a means to contextualize their ideation. The notion of designing something that designers would consider either timeless or universal relies on an understanding of context. If context were a plane in space, two lines on that plane could be universality and timelessness. Just trying to understand context in both of those dimensions could endlessly drive generative design thinking (Figure 27.1). Knowing where to draw boundaries in context is essential; you simply cannot design for everybody and every time. However, describing very strict boundaries can box a designer in. Project criteria that point to a very discrete set of contextual needs limit a designer to develop solutions only for that specific case. This discredits the potential for a designer to integrate dimensions and possibilities that could make an idea more universal or more timeless. In the end, leaving some contextual boundary considerations open to challenge and inspire a designer is not detrimental, yet context is always the landing point for ideas because it is the ground on which ideas must be realized. A designer will have to watch, listen, and ask themselves: "Does this work? Does this fit? Is this meaningful? Is this what I intended for the user to do?" As design ideas are developed, so is the need to bring them to life so that these questions can be explored.

Prototypes can be sketched in much the same way that simple forms are drawn on paper: rapidly, with inexpensive materials such as paper and tape. As these ideas come to life in three-dimensional form, designers are able to

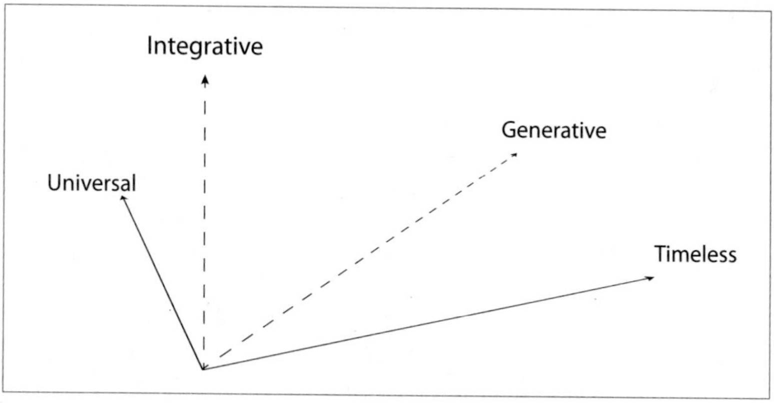

Figure 27.1. Context drives designers to think further.

see them differently and identify new considerations. Much like the drawing process, designers slowly increase the resolution of these prototypes with the resolution of the idea itself. The process is long and iterative. The idea of doing one swift "study" is difficult to harmonize with the design process. Ideally, a designer might live with a user for months and continuously plant new prototypes in their lives to see how they are used in context. This kind of philosophy has gotten Apple into trouble, with employees losing prototype iPhones months before their public release. However dangerous from a marketing standpoint, it is impressive to see that Apple is truly putting early prototypes to use.

Prototyping in its truest sense is part of the iterative design process, not simply a "test" as to whether consumers will buy something. Like the process Apple seems to be employing, designers believe in the need to play with their ideas and work them through in-context understanding as a means of improving them. This is easily mistaken for formal research. Historically, the reason for building a prototype hinged on understanding constraints and considerations of the design itself, the dimensional quality of it, the feeling of it, the manufacturability of it, rather than the current pressure to understand marketability.

> The pressures to ensure designs were meticulously worked out before production also led to a new scale of experimental modeling. When working on the Boeing 707 in the early 1950s, for example, Teague constructed a complete working interior mock-up with lighting and sound effects simulating flight, in which "passengers" were seated for the time space of prospective journeys, served by the full complement of airline staff. The experiment cost half a million dollars, but many details were improved, and prospective airline purchasers had the opportunity to satisfy themselves of the aircraft's practicability (Heskett 1980:135).

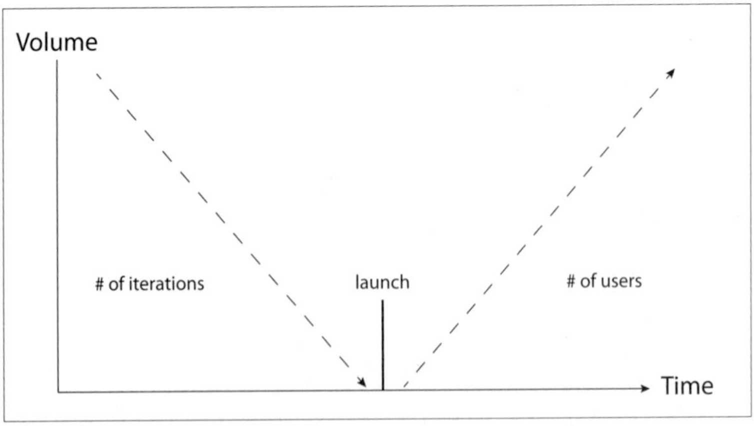

Figure 27.2. Classic prototyping model.

A classic prototyping model shown in Figure 27.2 demonstrates a gap between the design process and the launch of the product itself. The iteration process relies upon a series of critiques and experiments that demonstrate how the ideas will live in-context, but does not literally ask the end-user to rate the success of the design. Designers are often challenged to prove how their ideas will fair in the market. Automobile prototypes, for example, are clinic-tested with consumers (note the switch to the market research terminology) in a large ballroom. Consumers walk around the prototypes, interact with them, and then give each a rating (see "testing" in Figure 27.3). They're asked to judge whether or not they would purchase the item. Designers cringe. The approach relies on a belief that people have the ability to take themselves out of the clinic context, know themselves really well, and ultimately interpret design work. It ignores the impact of powerful industries such as marketing, advertising, and public relations. It also ignores the realities of everyday life and decision-making, including common biases such as our tendency to choose things that are familiar and our aversion to loss. Most important, it ignores the possibility of the influence on public taste: public taste is developed, persuaded, and slowly integrated into what we eventually desire.

> Without consensus-building efforts of the art theorist or critic, each person would evaluate objects in terms of his or her private experiences. In each culture however, public taste develops as visual qualities are eventually linked with values. The visual taste of an epoch is a subset of its worldview, related to the norms and values that regulate the rest of life. Like other values, visual values can be unanimous or contested, elite or popular, strong or vulnerable, depending on the integration of the culture (Csikszentmihalyi 1973:125).

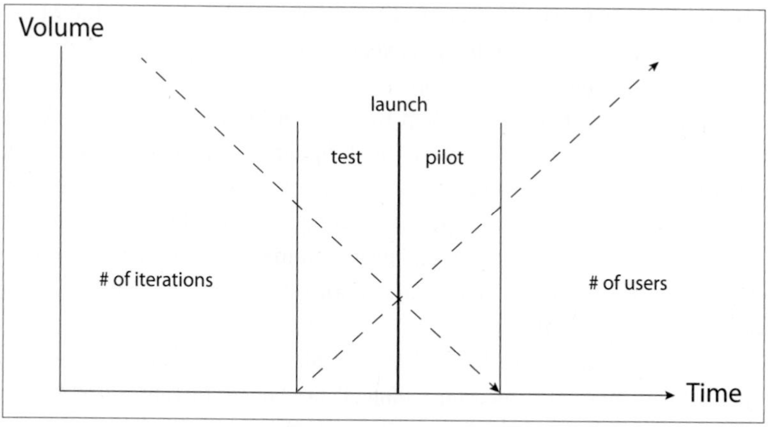

Figure 27.3. Prototype testing model.

In addition, too frequently designers are constrained by budgets, time, and confidentiality such that they are given only one or two chances to test out their ideas. This forces designers to decide on a specific resolution at which ideas may be shared. Because sketches are difficult to read and imagine, and the context of this research is often grossly unrelated to the reality of a product's life, designers typically lean towards sharing fully resolved concepts to wow people. Much of the learning process is then taken into the studio and out of the research realm.

A DESIGNER'S VIEW ON ETHNOGRAPHY

For a designer, ethnography can be a breath of fresh air. Unlike clinic testing, focus-grouping, and a pile of other quantitative methods it tends to be the only research in a corporate context that designers have an inherent desire to engage in. However, the intent designers have for participation may be quite different than anthropologists might imagine. Designers know what they're looking for. For designers, the entire purpose of this activity is to inform needs identification and personification. Until the user can be internalized, like a Method actor would "feel their part," it can be hard to know the right design even when it hits you in the face.

A Method actor seeks a really deep and informed description of the character to play the part. The goal for designers is for the user to be well-considered in the design process, so well-considered that the design itself demonstrates a firm understanding of the user such that the user actually feels considered. To begin adding user considerations to their already existing list of considerations, they want to meet someone who they imagine might be the user. This cannot be just anybody: it has to be somebody imaginable, inspiring, and interestingly complex. Typically, they're assuming they'll only find one such person over the course of a few weeks of research. The person can then become their prototypical "Josephine." If they're imaginable, they will stay top-of-mind; they'll be memorable, digestible, and therefore more informative and powerful in the design process. This person will help to add considerations the designer had not yet thought of, will help to guide the designer in one direction or another, and help ultimately decide when the design is enough—is done—because it is fitting to their needs. Wall-sized posters, human-sized cardboard cutouts, piles of purchased objects (clothing, bags, jewelry, home decor), entire rooms decorated to demonstrate taste, videos, and photo diaries are strewn throughout design offices to depict this person.

It took five years of leading "ethnographic" projects or hiring teams of people to lead them and reading *Doing Anthropology in Consumer Research* (Sunderland and Denny 2007) to realize cultural analysis could reframe the considerations for designers. Finding a single person to embody the essence of a design was far closer to a social psychology approach than it was to an ethnographic approach. As a designer looking for a persona, I had been attempting to profile the perfect person and understand how they think rather than learn about the concept of the object I was trying to design. I was surprised to learn that ethnography could define concepts themselves. Concepts had always felt very difficult to define.

"Concept" is a confusing term in design; it is often used to refer to an idea. This idea can be almost anything: it can be a paradigm shifting, it can be holistic, it can be one-dimensional, it can be a simple feature change. A "wall full of concepts" can sometimes mean a wall full of sketches because they're all ideas for something. I like to argue that concept is something greater than an idea. A concept articulates something larger that includes a premise for that thing existing at all; it includes strategy and context, and hints at uniqueness.

Ironically, I believe that a concept should not be discernible as a single idea. For example, the concept that supports the idea of the Bodum double-walled glass (Figure 27.4) might be something along the lines of "reverse insulation." It implies that it might be a handle-less mug, as that is the need that it is solving; but it is not limited to being a mug, and it is not reliant upon a form or a material. In this definition, a concept can set the premise for the entire design process. It poses a challenge, implies a set of considerations, and helps frame the intent of a design. This framing can direct and engage a designer in the same way a persona can without limiting the scope to a perfect user. Paradoxically, concepts are more dynamic, less presumptive, and at the same time more specific as to the purpose of the design.

A concept can be shaped by cultural analysis. By understanding the symbolic meaning of the object itself, a concept can then play to or challenge that meaning. It seems essential that the design process would relate in some way to the meaning of the object, but this is not frequently the case. It also seems natural that design research would start by focusing on the objects themselves and

Figure 27.4. Bodum double-walled glass.

work out slowly to interpret larger meanings, values, and norms, but this is not typical. As many designs are ultimately striving to be timeless and universal, it seems fitting that design would think on the scale of social, but normally it is honed on a single persona.

Some of the most artistic, provocative, and thoughtful design work today embodies (or articulates) the meaning that anthropologists are trained to identify. For example, at the start of the Apple iPhone 5 video, Jonathan Ive talks about the relationship that we have with our iPhones and says, "we take changing it really seriously" (Ive 2012). He is obviously not interested in the needs, whims, and ideals of a single high-tech user or the latest industry trends, but has internalized some larger social notion of what this object means to people and how difficult it will be to do a design iteration justice. The thoughtful changes in the product demonstrate this larger social understanding.

The design process at Apple came to life recently in their design patent lawsuit (Apple Inc. v. Samsung Electronics Co. Ltd.) over Samsung's infringement of iPhone patents. A long series of prototypes were shown that each studied new considerations. Over time, the product came to fruition in its own context, without reacting to momentary trends or industry norms. This kind of work is difficult to do. This is where anthropology can help. Designers are often given briefs that assume a certain set of norms about a product category. Stepping out of the existing categorical bounds requires an understanding of the product at a much deeper level. Taking a social and cultural focus removes the designer's typical one-persona lens and provides a forum for the team to talk more conceptually about the essence of the product space.

Some of the most influential ethnographic work that I have followed did exactly this. The results helped me understand things like the essence of "smallness" or the notion of "motherhood" in relation to specific categories of cars. These concepts were thoughtful and meaningful interpretations of what I had previously thought of as a platform, an engine, and 16 panels of sheet metal.

My questions about who was the most high-tech, sporty, exciting person in the recruiting list faded away. This process made way for direction and inspiration that was far afield of the typical automotive context. For example, we had been arguing for months about whether or not a new family vehicle should be built on a rear-wheel drive or front-wheel drive platform. The trade-off boiled down to a decision about how sporty the driving experience should feel to the user. The persona we developed did not help us to move forward, as "she" was not able to articulate an ideal driving experience and often wanted the best of both worlds.

The ethnography work took us out of this argument; the anthropologists began talking about the role of the vehicle as it related to the concept of "motherhood." By first understanding motherhood, we could then build a vehicle to support that notion. This created a forum for discussion about some of our fundamental assumptions that were unconsciously driving our stance on issues such as which platform and which engine. Unpacking motherhood helped us frame the concept of the car without instantly jumping to ideas for the product itself. Motherhood was about managing a series of ever-changing relationships (with families, friend, peers, work, and place). The vehicle was ideally a companion to help them navigate this complexity with grace. It was an oasis of self-sufficiency, a place for private conversations, a mediator that helped them to survive each day. Design work focused on addressing notions of management, self-sufficiency, and connectedness with mastery and grace. These solutions did not surface from an interrogation into what the customer wanted and result in a test as to whether or not our ideas would be a success in the market. Instead, this held true to a more fundamental purpose of design: how could we design for the concept of motherhood?

> Designers are exploring concrete integrations of knowledge that will combine theory with practice for new productive purposes. . . . The design of material objects includes traditional concern for the form and visual appearance of everyday products, clothing, domestic objects, tools, instruments, machinery, and vehicles—but has expanded into a more thorough and diverse interpretation of the physical, psychological, social, and cultural relationship between products and human beings. . . . [T]his area is rapidly evolving into an exploration of the problems of construction in which form and visual appearance must carry a deeper, more integrative argument that unites aspects of art, engineering, natural science, and the human sciences (Buchanan 1973:4).

In this sense, design is asked to assume a role of helping to be more thoughtful and to develop more meaningful and relevant work. It is a question of design ethics. Do we as designers owe to the people who will be using our products a thoughtful inquiry into existing symbolic meanings? Should we be aware of what it is that we are changing? With what level of awareness should we be designing? These questions are a natural fit for issues of environmentalism and sustainability, but should they not also be considered culturally? What do we do as designers to inhibit and exhibit an understanding of cultures in the work that we do? Sometimes we unknowingly affect, offend, or degrade cultural meaning. Can we instead sustain it, engage with it, or improve it?

Droog Design in the Netherlands, which roughly translates to "dry wit," is known for presenting work that purposely engages with symbolic meaning, often playfully or provocatively, to challenge our assumptions, and make us wonder, laugh, and cry. It also tends to be some of the most conceptual,

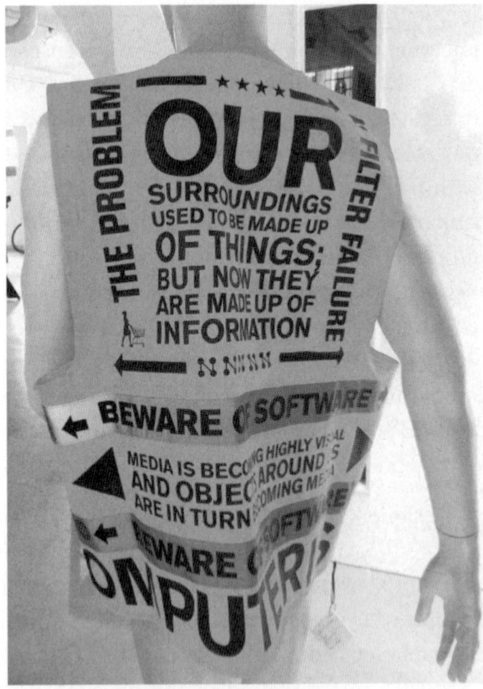

Figure 27.5. "Beware of Software" vest by Mieke Gerritzen with Droog Design.

Figure 27.6. "Sugar Cage" by Sofie Lachaert and Luc d'Hanis with Droog Design.

elemental, universal, and timeless work in the design industry. Here are a few of my recent favorites: a safety vest to warn us about spyware,[4] (Figure 27.5), a cage for storing your sugar cubes,[5] (Figure 27 .6), and cognac glasses that sway[6] (Figure 27.7). Some of their most famous pieces include Frank Tjepkema's "do break" vase,[7] which is lined with silicon so that the ceramic on the outside is broken and the silicon holds it together in a unique fractured pattern, and Tejo Remy's "chest of drawers,"[8] a pile of single drawers haphazardly piled and then firmly belted together.

These objects have recognizable symbolic meanings, but each challenges our assumptions and engages us in a larger cultural context. For example, in Figure 27.5, a safety vest is visually loud to garner attention and portray a need for heightened awareness from others. Safety vests are typically used to heighten the awareness of people about the presence of other people. However, software is neither human nor visible. Thus, playing with a familiar symbolic reference challenges us to consider software in a more human context. Similarly, placing sugar in a birdcage, as in Figure 27.6, presents an ironic twist on sugar storage by referencing a symbol of something that must be protected. A piece such as this may engage us in a common discourse about the ramifications of a sugar-laden diet. These concepts are difficult to embody in a single persona because they reference symbolic meanings that expand beyond a specific-use case. They work at a level that is more timeless and universal because they apply a cultural point of view rather than a specific response to a list of needs.

In the example of the cognac glass (Figure 27.7), a designer considered the need for a cognac drinker to swirl cognac. By lightly swirling a glass of cognac, the surface area of the cognac coating the glass expands and the molecules of cognac are jostled; together, these increase the evaporation of cognac and enhance the sensation of smell. Providing an opportunity for a drinker to increase the surface area of cognac and jostle molecules is all that the designer technically had to do. Referencing the shape of a spinning top broadened the

Figure 27.7. Cognac glasses by Rikke Hagen with Droog Design.

symbolic meaning of the design. Now people who did not drink cognac had a common cultural reference, the notion of spinning the object. Unpacking symbolic meanings can inspire more timeless and universal design thinking because a cultural point of view allows designers to think beyond the bounds of a specific brief and dig into the conceptual essence of what it is that they are designing without being tied to a specific user or a specific set of needs.

I think most design in corporations focuses on the tangible, functional, measurable needs of their known consumers. Just as Dreyfuss advocated, many have chosen a percentile of the population to consider in the design process. Anthropology offers us something additional; it pushes us to think on a social scale and in terms of cultural meanings and practices, to step out of specific segments and simplifications of a large, broad, messy population. This disruption and discussion can be very powerful. In a business world where we are actively trying to figure out how to make a few strong, resonant, and affordable global products that work across cultures, we will have to stop assuming that we can split up the world into nice little slices of a pie and then design things for each little slice. We need to wrestle with the complexities, values, meanings, and symbols that live within and across these different cultures and complicate our strategic picture. We can still think about a user and their needs, but it should not be done in lieu of a larger cultural study that looks at meaning, helps us to define concept, and frees designers to think of something that may resonate across cultures and times.

REFERENCES

Bradley, Steven. 2012. "How To Create Visual Tension in Your Designs." Vanseo Design (blog), January 10. http://www.vanseodesign.com/web-design/visual-tension/ (accessed September 9, 2013).

Buchanan, Richard. 1973. "Wicked Problems in Design Thinking." In *The Idea of Design*, edited by Victor Margolin and Richard Buchanan, 3–20. Boston, MA: MIT Press.

Cagan, Jonathan, and Craig Vogel. 2002. *Creating Breakthrough Products*. Upper Saddle River, NJ: Prentice Hall.

Csikszentmihalyi, Mihaly. 1973. "Design and the Order in Everyday Life." In *The Idea of Design*, edited by R. Buchanan and Victor Margolin, 118–126. Boston, MA: MIT Press.

Dreyfuss, Henry. (1955) 2003. *Designing for People*. New York, NY: Allworth Press.

Heskett, John. 1980. *Industrial Design*. London: Thames & Hudson.

Ive, Jonathan. 2012. Apple Inc, iPhone launch video. http://www.apple.com/iphone/#video (accessed September 15, 2012).

Lane, Sarah. 2012. Architecture and Design Museum of Los Angeles Show Announcement: "Eames Designs: The Guest Host Relationship." http://www.aplusd.org/files/AD_EamesRelease.pdf (accessed February 18, 2012).

Mueller, J. L. 2013. "Universal Design of Products." http://www.jlmueller.com/products.html (accessed December 23, 2013).

Nelson, George. (1977) 2003. *How to See: A Guide to Reading Our Man-Made Environment*. Stamford, CT: Design Within Reach.

Norman, Donald, and Stephen Draper. 1986. *User Centered System Design: New Perspectives on Human-Computer Interaction.* Hillsdale, NJ: Lawrence Erlbaum Associates.

Partnoy, Frank. 2012. Wait: *The Art and Science of Delay.* New York, NY: Public Affairs.

Sunderland, Patricia, and Rita Denny. 2007. *Doing Anthropology in Consumer Research.* Walnut Creek, CA: Left Coast Press.

Tilley, Alvin R. 2002. *The Measure of Man and Woman: Human Factors in Design.* New York: John Wiley & Sons.

Wunsch, Mark 2008. "Design Q&A Session with Charles Eames," interviewed by Mme. L. Amic. http://markwunsch.com/blog/2008/09/27/design-q-a-with-charles-eames.html (accessed September 9, 2013).

NOTES

1 http://www.hermanmiller.com/products/seating/public-seating/eames-tandem-sling-seating.html.

2 http://www.dwr.com/.

3 http://www.oxo.com/p-223-swivel-peeler.aspx.

4 http://www.droog.com/webshop/wearables/beware-of-software-vest/.

5 http://www.droog.com/webshop/studio-work/sugar-cage/.

6 http://www.droog.com/webshop/tableware/cognac—liqueur-glass/.

7 http://studio.droog.com/studio/all/do-create-on-location/do-break-by-frank-tjepkema—peter-van-der-jagt/.

8 http://www.droog.com/webshop/studio-work/chest-of-drawers/.

28

Recognizing Agile

NATALIE HANSON

Here is my "Top Ways To Know You're Working in an Agile Environment" list:

- You hear people talking about "sprints," but no one appears to be running around the office.
- You hear references to "scrum," but people seem more interested in American football than rugby.
- You hear people talking about a "backlog," but the bathrooms seem to be in working order. The only other references about plumbing or water are in reference to "Waterfall," and in this case most references are critical.
- Teammates are talking about "user stories" or "epics," but they are pointing to index cards. You're not at all clear how an entire story could fit on such a small piece of paper.
- You're asked to participate in a "release planning" meeting, but the team is not talking about lanterns or balloons (or birds for that matter).
- You're being asked to attend daily "stand-up" meetings, and you're concerned that your new company cannot afford chairs.
- You signed up to do research, but all of a sudden you're being called "that user experience (UX) person." You have no idea what they are talking about, or why they think the UX designer should share an office with you.

This was the teaser for a series of posts I wrote about Agile and user experience (UX) on my blog (www.nataliehanson.com). This chapter, focused on the application of Agile methods for software development, is built on those blog posts. It begins by providing a brief overview of what Agile is and the conditions under which it emerged. However, the primary focus of the chapter is to

Handbook of Anthropology in Business, edited by Rita Denny and Patricia Sunderland, 540–555.

ensure that researchers understand the cadence of Agile software development and the language used by practitioners (largely engineers) to describe how they work. The chapter provides suggestions for ways that UX professionals can effectively engage in contexts where Agile practices are present. Throughout, there are recommendations that range from where to focus research efforts to where research is ideally placed in the organizational structure.

A BRIEF OVERVIEW OF AGILE

In software development, Agile is an approach that is focused on delivering software more quickly and incrementally and with greater stakeholder involvement. It places a heavy emphasis on team engagement in planning, goal setting, and joint execution.

In the early days of software development, processes often mirrored those of automotive manufacturing: all the requirements were defined up front and then delivered in their entirety through to production. In the industry, this approach came to be known as a "waterfall." In other words, the requirements cascaded from business stakeholders down a long chain through product managers, business analysts, and technical analysts to the developers, who were then asked to build the solution based on written requirements. Unfortunately, the process was like a very expensive game of Telephone; the protracted series of hand-offs made it nearly impossible for the developers to understand the original, underlying goals of the work they were tasked with.

Over time, it became clear that this approach led to all kinds of challenges; most notably, long delays in getting a fully functioning product ready and a significant disconnect between what was requested and what was actually built. As the high-tech industry made a transition from technology for technology's sake to a more fast-paced, market-centric approach, this would become increasingly problematic.

The advent of object-oriented programming enabled engineers to think of their work in smaller components and required them to find ways of working together more effectively. In the late 1980s and early 1990s, cost pressure in the industry required companies to either develop software at a lower cost, or improve quality and throughput by finding better ways to deliver software. For more background on these pressures and the subsequent response by computer scientists, see "Lean, Agile" (Harvey 2004).

In 2001, a group of individuals (Beck et al.) disillusioned with prevalent software development practices got together and penned the Manifesto for Agile Software Development:

> We are uncovering better ways of developing software by doing it and helping others do it. Through this work we have come to value: *Individuals and interactions* over processes and tools; *Working software* over comprehensive documentation; *Customer collaboration* over contract negotiation; *Responding to change* over following a plan. That is, while there is value in the items on the right, we value the items on the left more.

The signers of the manifesto sought to evolve their work as engineers by ensuring they were adequately involved in understanding what they would build and then remained engaged with business stakeholders and users throughout the development lifecycle to make sure that the product was not just technically sound, but also met both specifications and user needs.

Agile practitioners use some specialized language to describe their ways of working, which may make it challenging to engage with at first. The value of an end-user's perspective today is generally understood and appreciated as being critical to the development process, but it is incumbent on the user-centered design and research professionals to understand Agile practices. Blogs and books are just starting to emerge about the ways that research and design professionals can contribute in this context. The goal of this chapter is to educate and guide researchers about how engage effectively in teams where Agile ways of working are present.

AGILE PRINCIPLES & PRACTICES

The Agile Manifesto resulted in a set of 12 principles[1] that provide practical guidance on *how* the vision of the manifesto will be achieved, including early and frequent delivery of software, regular face-to-face collaboration between business stakeholders and developers, and the fostering of a self-organizing and motivating work environment for developers. Perhaps most important, the final principle is one of change and continuous improvement as a competitive advantage. These tenets have much in common with Lean, both in the aspirational tone and the content.[2]

One of the key outcomes of an Agile approach to software development is to get a Minimum Viable Product (MVP) out the door as quickly as possible and—like the pull model in Lean—use those experiences to shape the product priorities and direction. The reasoning behind this approach is that the first product (or major new capabilities) to market enables the team to secure first-mover advantage, which usually translates into a significantly greater share of a new or emerging market. This approach also seeks to ensure that the team produces on a regular cadence against the defined requirements, and that the outcomes are validated with the business user or the market incrementally, leading to a better fit between what is being built and what the market demands. This is possible in part because business stakeholders do not disappear after a requirements document is completed; those individuals (or a well-informed proxy like a product manager) remain available on a biweekly basis (or even more frequently) to ensure that questions from the project team are answered in a timely way.

Over time, this new way of working resulted in a host of other changes in how software development projects are structured and managed. For example, development teams that take an Agile approach typically meet on a daily basis to talk about the status of what they are working on, where they might need help, and so on; that daily meeting is called a "scrum." The term comes from rugby; unlike American football, where the ball is passed or handed off for an individual to progress down the field, in rugby the ball moves down the field protected by a cluster of teammates.

All members of the project team—from business stakeholders to product managers to developers—participate in early definition of the product so the engineers can remain true to the vision of the solution as they seek the best technical approach. At the highest level, this approach has four major elements (Figure 28.1).

The largest box in Figure 28.1 represents the "roadmap," which might be planned at a high level one to two years in advance. Within the roadmap is a

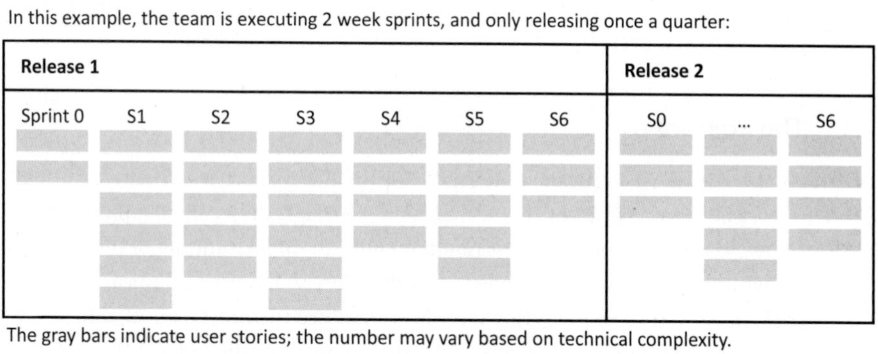
In this example, the team is executing 2 week sprints, and only releasing once a quarter:
Release 1
Release 2
Sprint 0
S1
S2
S3
S4
S5
S6
S0
...
S6
The gray bars indicate user stories; the number may vary based on technical complexity.

Figure 28.1. The product roadmap consists of releases, which in turn consist of sprints.

series of "releases." Releases comprise a series of "sprints," which in turn are composed of "user stories."

Each milestone in that roadmap is deliberately *not* defined at the beginning: objectives further out are left at a high level. This is sometimes described as an inverted pyramid. Activities in line of sight are at the top and defined in the most detail; the work further out is only generally understood and planned.

The rationale of this approach is to ensure that immediate priorities and next steps are clearly defined for everyone involved. This also allows time for further discovery—about markets, users, or technology—in areas that may not be sufficiently understood. Until those early building blocks have stabilized, building a house of cards on top of them is not recommended. That means that Big Up-Front Design (BUFD; more about that later in this chapter) is a risky proposition. Not having the complete picture may be disconcerting for those who have never worked in this way! In fact, there are some things (such as the overall information architecture or navigation of the application) that may difficult (if not impossible) to execute in a piecemeal way.

The benefit to this approach is that it enables the team to remain flexible and adapt to changing circumstances (e.g., unexpected technical hurdles) while still sharing the same desired outcome. The challenge for all UX professionals (including researchers) in these teams is that it does require continuous involvement and attention as priorities, approaches, and planned deliverables shift.

AGILE PRACTICES & RESEARCHER ENGAGEMENT

In the following sections I describe key stages of the Agile software development approach at a high level, as well as some of the typical activities at each step. I also elaborate how a researcher might expect to engage.

The Roadmap

At the outset, a common understanding of the project is achieved through a workshop or a series of them, if needed. Through these, the team achieves a shared vision, or roadmap. This might include an understanding of the markets for which the product is intended (and therefore what price points and project costs need to be considered), what capabilities are the most critical, and so on. This exercise might be conducted only once a year, maybe twice if there is a lot of ambiguity or change. This is not necessarily a research-led activity (although it could be; more on that later); oftentimes the product owner (who could be a business stakeholder or a product manager) leads this effort.

The Release

The shared roadmap is broken into releases based on business objectives, what is technically feasible, and so on. Again, the most current part of the roadmap (e.g., three to six months out) may be well defined, but beyond that the team typically sticks to more general descriptions of what will follow.

What if you arrive into a project team that has already established a roadmap, and perhaps plans for the next release or two? The key is to align with other resources that are planning more than one sprint ahead, such as a systems architect or a business analyst. Recognize that many teams have a "Sprint 0" (zero), which is a planning window that overlaps with the end of the previous release. So rather than Figure 28.1, the roadmap might look something like Figure 28.2.

There are numerous presentations and articles that argue in favor of this approach, including O'Brien's (2011) "The Secret of Agile UX" and Colfelt's (2010) "Bringing User Centered Design to the Agile Environment." After some elaboration on both user-centered design and Agile methods, Colfelt recommended proposing *some* up-front research and iteration (either in advance of development or at least a few sprints ahead), as I've shown in Figure 28.3.

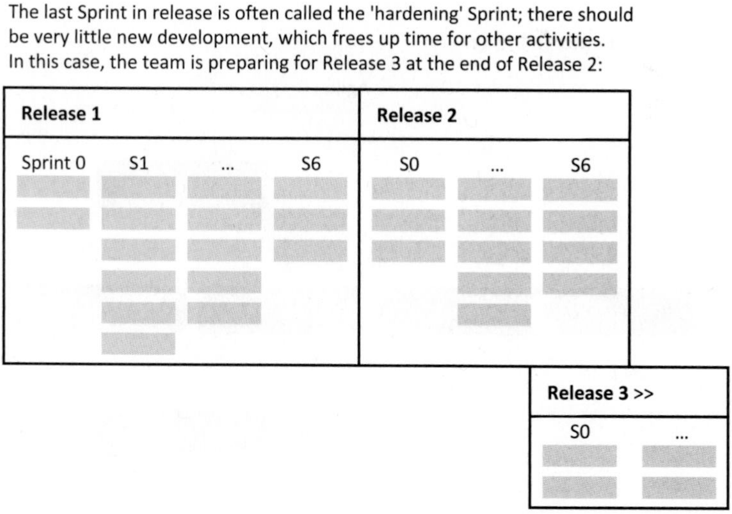
The last Sprint in release is often called the 'hardening' Sprint; there should be very little new development, which frees up time for other activities.
In this case, the team is preparing for Release 3 at the end of Release 2:
Release 1
Sprint 0
S1
...
S6
Release 2
S0
...
S6
Release 3 >>
S0
...

Figure 28.2. Sprint 0 planning may run in parallel with the final sprint(s) of a previous release.

My experience and recommendations are similar, though from a staffing perspective it is really tough (read: almost impossible) to have a single researcher who can look at foundational research questions early in the iteration or product lifecycle and expect that the same individual can test and validate with users during the active development cycle. Whether you're an individual contributor or a UX team lead, at some point you'll have to make tough decisions about how you can best contribute. Let's assume that the product vision is set and some good information exists about the target users. I will discuss alternate scenarios later in this chapter. For the moment, that means you can focus your UX capacity on getting the best possible product out the door.

A good team player (you want to be a good team player, don't you?!) will keep in mind what the rest of the team is trying to accomplish. The goal is to achieve an MVP (or a Minimum Usable Design [MUD]). Remember that, as Paul Scrivens (2012) put it, "Design is never finished." Unless a product is approaching end-of-life or the team is being disbanded for some reason, there are always opportunities to engage and provide user insights. Since the team is trying to get a minimum viable product out the door, user-centered design testing and validation should focus on supporting that goal. Aligning UX to the minimal viable (or valuable) product may be harder than you think (Ramsey

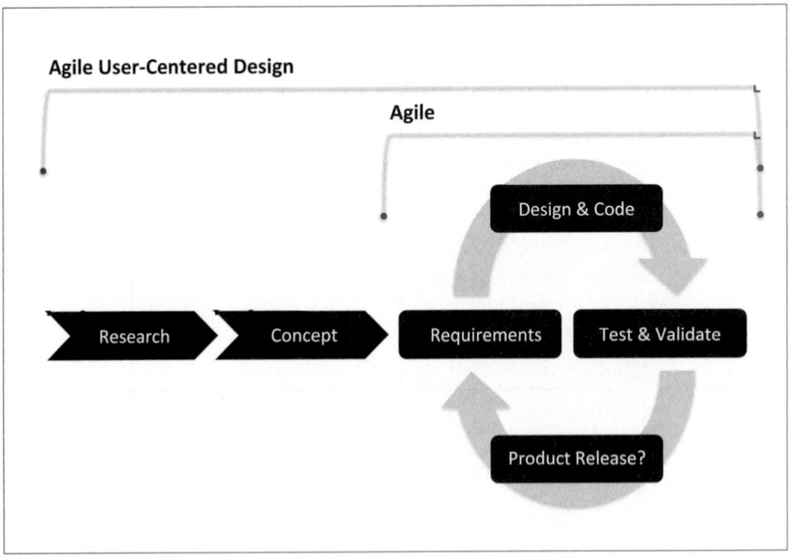

Figure 28.3. Some blend of up-front research and iterative testing during the product lifecycle is key to effectively supporting a software development team. Diagram adapted from Colfelt (2010).

2012). What has to be in? What can't be out? If a UX designer is contributing to that product vision, the improvements to the design need to be given the same consideration. Some authors have called this Test-Driven Design (TDD) (Innes 2012), Minimum Viable Design, or MUD (Scrivens 2012). But the short version is that testing needs to be considered at the outset. In addition to being practical, it will ensure that the UX team garners the respect of the larger team. In an article called "Have You Tried Talking To Your Customers?" blogger and chief operating officer Des Traynor (2011–2013) writes, "The quality of a product depends not just on the ability to generate ideas but also the ability to test and iterate through them based on good feedback."

So if you find yourself in the deep end, where do you begin collecting and providing that feedback to the project team? Options include testing the existing product, using paper prototypes to test divergent design ideas, or reviewing customer support data to identify opportunities for further improvement. As with other project phases, the key to making a contribution is to understand the roadmap, what releases are forthcoming, what is known (or not) about the epics or user stories that are on the horizon, and even what user problems or bugs have been reported.

How do you ensure your insights get incorporated into what the team has planned? As described earlier, both releases and sprints have a planning phase (sometimes formally established as Sprint 0), which may overlap with the tail end of the previous release. Agile project teams use an artifact called a "backlog" to collect all of the key themes that were established in the initial planning meetings, as well as new issues that emerge over time based on feedback from customers or members of the team.

Although release and sprint planning are regular occurrences, in general they do not attain the same level of breadth as the early planning sessions, where the vision and roadmap has been established. However, in these meetings the items in the backlog are refined and reprioritized as needed. Although these meetings may be extremely detailed and technical, engaging in them is critical for understanding and influencing what the development team does next. This approach also makes it possible to incorporate both small and larger issues into the backlog for inclusion into an upcoming release or sprint, as appropriate.

The outcome of a release is something that is usually complete enough that it can be released to the market. The release is executed through a series of shorter working bursts called "sprints."

The Sprint

Sprints are two- to four-week increments during which the developers are required to produce fully functioning features or capabilities that can be demoed, reviewed, and validated by the whole team during a sprint review. This truly means the whole team: business stakeholders, researchers, product management, quality assurance (testing), and the developers.

This style of working is what I think most characterizes Agile, and the piece that is also the most different from the traditional waterfall approach to software development. Teams meet in scrums (or "stand-up meetings") on most if not all working days. They check in about what they have completed, what remains to be done, and where they are stuck or might need to interact with another member of the team. Although these may appear to be very technical discussions, these are often the moments where clarifying questions may be asked about the rationale or the behavior of a certain feature. If a researcher or designer is not present, it's quite possible that the work will deviate from its original intent, and be hard to address later.

Each of the developers selects or is assigned user stories to work on during the sprint. During the sprint planning, they often use an exercise called "poker planning" to estimate the amount of time the work will require and to determine with which other team members they will need to collaborate. In all cases, they will work with a testing (quality assurance [QA]) resource to agree on how their work will be technically tested before release.

At the end of the sprint, the team should be able to demo a piece of functionality that is complete and shippable. This is another great time to participate and see if the emerging product is consistent with what researchers have learned from the user community.

User Stories

When I was first exposed to Agile, I remember being thrilled that the team was talking about users, and user stories. I thought, "Wow! They are already taking a user-centric approach to development!" That excitement was quickly followed by surprise and dismay when I realized that these stories were not "owned" by the UX team, but rather that they were defined and elaborated by the whole team.

Many authors have described the centrality of user stories in the Agile development process. These artifacts are a radical departure from the monolithic requirements documents of the past, as they are jointly created, refined, and iterated as the team's understanding evolves. In its simplest form, the user story describes the individual engaged in a task, what they are trying to accomplish, and why. In the early days of Agile, stories were written on index cards. As practices have matured, most stories are now documented electronically, often in specialized software where they are eventually broken down into work tasks for the various technical team members. This approach also enables the team to track completeness, which has been achieved if all the criteria of INVEST (Independent, Negotiable, Valuable, Estimable, and Testable), as defined by Mike Cohn in his 2004 book *User Stories Applied*, have been met.

The stories are likely the last moment in which user insights will be discussed in a form that is understandable to a non-developer, and so they are a critical locus of engagement for researchers. User stories provide a great means for researchers to engage with the project team, because well-written user stories focus not on tasks, but truly on the people who will use the software and their desired outcomes. As Tony Ulwick (2013) indicates, we should not conduct research in the service of a specific feature: rather, our starting point should be to achieve an understanding of our target users. Otherwise, the risk is that we come to the conclusion that people want a quarter-inch drill, when in fact what they truly want is a quarter-inch hole. Along the same lines, user researchers can contribute to the creation of user stories by ensuring that stories focus on *experience* and *outcomes*, and not just on tasks. In two very detailed articles about the role of UX professionals in creating user stories, Anders Ramsay (2011a, 2011b) maintains that we can help make the transition. For example, a user story might read: "I often order the wrong part, because the part numbering system is confusing. It wastes time and makes me look stupid in front of customers." Instead, a researcher who understands the users' goals could suggest: "Help me make users feel confident their donation is going towards the actual cause, so they'll want to encourage others to donate."

In the modified example, the language focuses on *outcomes*, so that the user can recommend (and/or the designer can look for) multiple ways to solve that problem. This reminds me of a quote attributed to Mathieu Lehanneur,[3] who said, "Do not ask a designer to design a bridge, but ask him to design a way to cross the river." In a similar vein, Sarah Doody (2011) writes about the importance of understanding the reason for and the value of a product in a person's life. User experience teams often report into product management, which in turn is often placed within the engineering organization. Doody quotes Marty Cagan: "Ultimately, an engineering organization is focused on execution and that culture is not optimized for the process of discovery, curiosity, and play, all of which are fundamental to those who engage in storytelling." The researcher has a critical role to play in ensuring that the user's perspective, and experience is not lost as the product is engineered.

AGILE: IMPLICATIONS FOR UX RESEARCHERS

One of the pleasures of working in both Lean and Agile working environments is that they are extremely flexible, adaptable, and emergent. There is lots of room for experimentation. However, that also means that the summaries I have provided here are not exhaustive.

It has been shown over and over again that the greatest return on investment (ROI) for user experience is in the early stages of product development. The goal is to ensure that the right thing is being built/aligned with the needs of markets and users. That means that research plays a critical role very early on in product direction and definition. Ideally—but rarely!—you'll be involved as a market is being identified and a product is just materializing.

But at the same time, as sites like Little Big Details,[4] reinforce, the devil is in the details when it comes to delivering a good experience through software. That means UX team members have to be engaged throughout, with strong transitions between research and design resources. Of course it depends on what the team is doing when you join. Are you there at inception, or do you join two years into the development of a maturing product?

In reality, you'll probably land smack in the middle of a project, and be thrown into the deep end. The team will be nearing the end of a sprint for one release, planning for the first sprint of the next release. You'll have to figure out what is known, what is not, and where you can best contribute. In the following section, I'd like to provide some specific examples of ways that researchers can engage at each of the major stages in the development lifecycle of a software product.

In a controversial article titled "Act First, Do the Research Later," Don Norman (2011) argues that a project may not plan the time or make a commitment to the research that is required. Researchers should be engaged in shaping those decisions, and being engaged in that decision-making process requires us to describe (and often quantify) the impact of our recommendations, much as market researchers do. But it is common for teams to be formed around a given market or product opportunity, which means that some significant decisions have already been made before that team is formed. Norman argues that researchers are often engaged relatively late in the planning and decision-making process, which limits the strategic impact of our findings. In other words, building a research plan when the market, users, or sales potential have already been defined is too late in the game. Norman argues that research skills need to change to earn a seat at the boardroom table, where those early and most critical decisions are made.

The only way to achieve this is to develop knowledge beyond your own discipline and methods and into the business issues that your research is intended to address. Only in this way will you truly establish trust with executives to earn a seat at that decision-making table. The reality is that you are most likely to make an impact with your findings when the research is sponsored by senior members of the organization. I have experienced over and over again that small, critical contributions in one project lead to repeat work and an increasingly strategic working relationship over time. In some cases, I was able to repurpose or repackage earlier findings as a relationship matured. For example, what started as user research for a series of websites expanded over a several-year period into ethnographic research, and my team was eventually asked by senior management to summarize two to three years of findings to help with that group's strategic direction.

The challenge is always to balance the effort between the forward-thinking research in advance of a release and doing some quick, iterative testing to inform adjustments to the product as it's going out the door. The way I would characterize the former is "build the right thing," and the latter as "build the thing right," as shown in Figure 28.4.

Again, both types of research have value, though different methods and skills surely will be needed at different stages. Ethnographic methods might be desirable early on due to the richness and complexity of the findings, but when your team is just trying to ship a non-buggy product on time, some quick prototype or usability testing will do.

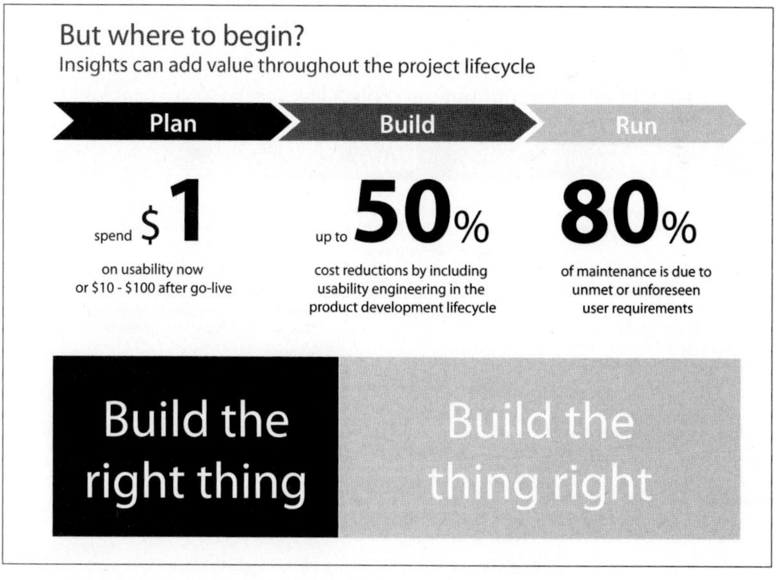

Figure 28.4. The need to balance effort between forward-thinking research and quick, iterative testing during active development.

In Figure 28.5 are listed specific examples about the role UX team members can play at these different stages. Note the waves at bottom, which represent the areas of highest engagement (and value) for UX research, UX design, and UX (or front-end) development, respectively.

Although you may have a preference about where you want to be engaged (as I do), you can't always be in both places. So, where to begin? Well, it depends on who hired you and how much they trust the value of user insights. Here are some considerations:

- It takes more knowledge of (and trust in) UX to spend the time doing research up front . . . because it takes longer for the impact of those findings to influence what ships. That type of research is also best suited for ethnographic methods, and perhaps also for innies (researchers that are members of the organization) rather than outies, as the delay in time-to-value may be tough for an external consulting team that's trying to sell ongoing research.
- In an organization that is really committed to Agile, they may be unwilling to support Big Up-Front Design (BUFD). In fact, BUFD is often a four-letter word with hard-core Agile teams. Those teams are very likely working with UX generalists (not dedicated research and design experts) if they

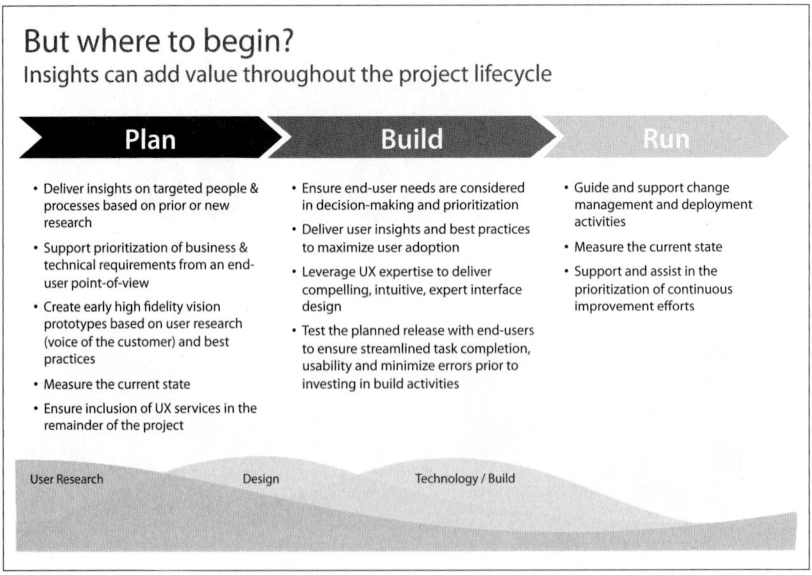

Figure 28.5. Insights can add value throughout the product lifecycle.

have a dedicated UX function at all. See, for example, the "UX for Devs Manifesto" blog post from Ambrose Little (2012), which seeks to explain to developers how to take responsibility for engaging users. Or this value proposition as maintained in 2013 for the Lean UX conference in New York: "The days of relying on a UX Designer for the whole experience are done. Collaboration has won out, and every team member needs to know how to contribute to product development" (Evans 2013). UX team members are strongly encouraged to find ways of working more efficiently than they have been historically by simplifying processes or eliminating steps such as paper prototypes. Furthermore, the team expects that all of the UX tasks will be planned and executed incrementally like the development tasks. Depending on the level of maturity in your UX organization and in your UX standards/libraries (as well as in your development organization), this is extremely challenging, but some practitioners swear by it (Little 2013).

- Some teams working in larger organizations recognize that it is not possible to orchestrate complex (e.g., enterprise-level) software development in this way. As I mentioned earlier, it make sense in those cases for UX practitioners to align with others thinking about the big picture; for example, product managers, systems architects, and business analysts.

The challenges you face and the way you most effectively engage with the project team has everything to do with how they are practicing Agile, how much they know (or have experience in) working with UX, and many other factors that are not (and will not be!) within your control. Your best chance for success is to understand the forces at play and adapt. To quote Charles Darwin: "It's not the strongest in the species that survives, nor the most intelligent that survives. It is the one that is most adaptable to change."[5]

IN CLOSING

Agile deeply shapes the organization in which it is implemented, and role of the hiring manager is critical here. Research is best aligned with senior management or with product management, where findings are delivered *before* development work gets under way so that research can inform *what* is built, not just *how* it should work and behave. Although both add value to the product in the long run, the former is more strategic (and also better suited to ethnographic methods). If the UX professional is hired by a development manager, there may be an expectation that research and design are deeply embedded in engineering activities. It is possible to deliver value, but the rapid cycles and very specific feedback require rethinking methods and historically lengthy research project timelines. On the design side, some efficiency will be critical, and can be achieved through reuse of templates, design standards, and so on.

Engaging in these settings means having some awareness of what external pressures and perceptions the company may be contending with. It's important to understand those factors, as they will have a profound influence on the organization. Take the initiative to read project artifacts and white papers, talk to product managers, learn to speak a language accessible to executive decision-makers. In other words, be a thoughtful participant observer.

Keep a critical eye and ear on the discourse of your work environment; whether you're there on a temporary basis or as an employee, that awareness will be critical. Agile without stakeholder or user involvement misses the mark and cannot deliver its true value or potential. More and more (especially in the software development arena), Lean and Agile may come together (as in Eric Ries' [2011] *The Lean Startup* and Dean Leffingwell's [2011] *Agile Software Requirements*). It can be beneficial to understand the historical roots of these trends and why they are drawn upon as industries evolve and change.

The biggest challenge for researchers, I think, is to recognize these shifts in the business setting, learn about the implications for their work, and actively explore new ways to engage and contribute. I hope this chapter, and the series of blog posts on which it was built, will help achieve those goals.

REFERENCES

Beck, Kent, Mike Beedle, Arie van Bennekum, Alistair Cockburn, Ward Cunningham, Martin Fowler, et al. 2001. "Manifesto for Agile Software Development." agilemanifesto.org/ (accessed October 14, 2013).

Cohn, Mike. 2004. *User Stories Applied: For Agile Software Development*. Boston: Addison-Wesley.

Colfelt, Anthony. 2010. "Bringing User Centered Design to the Agile Environment." Blog post: http://boxesandarrows.com/bringing-user-centered-design-to-the-agile-environment.

Doody, Sarah. 2011. "Why We Need Storytellers at the Heart of Product Development." *UX Magazine* Article No. 655, April 14. http://uxmag.com/articles/why-we-need-storytellers-at-the-heart-of-product-development.

Evans, Williams. 2013. "LeanUX NYC: A Conference for Designers, Innovators, and Entrepreneurs." vimeo.com/66002231 (accessed October 14, 2013).

Harvey, David. 2004. "Lean, Agile." Paper presented at the "The Software Value Stream" Workshop, Object Technology Conference, St. Neots, UK, March 28–31. OT2004 Revision: 43, January. http://www.davethehat.com.

Innes, Jon. 2012. "Test Driven Design: The Missing UX Ingredient in Agile." Guest post on User Zoom, March 5. http://www.userzoom.com/test-driven-design-missing-ux- ingredient-agile/.

Leffingwell, Dean. 2011. *Agile Software Requirements: Lean Requirements Practices for Teams, Programs, and the Enterprise*. Boston, MA: Addison-Wesley Professional.

Little, Ambrose. 2012. "UX for Devs Manifesto." Blog post, Infragistics. http://www.infragistics.com/community/blogs/ambrose_little/archive/2012/07/01/ux-for-devs-manifesto.aspx.

_____. 2013. "Whyyy Are You Still Designing With Static Wireframes?!? Blog post, Infragistics. http://www.infragistics.com/community/blogs/indigo-studio/archive/2013/ 01/23/whyyy-are-you-still-designing-with-static-wireframes.aspx.

Norman, Don. 2011. "Act First, Do the Research Later." Blog post, Core77, August 1. www.core77.com/blog/columns/act_first_do_the_research_later_20051.asp. (accessed December 2012).

O'Brien, James. 2011. "The Secret of Agile UX." Presented at UX Camp London, July 9. Presentation on Slideshare at http://www.slideshare.net/sparrk/agile-ux-how-to-avoid-big-design-up-front-by-pretending-not-to-do-big-design-up-front.

Ramsey, Anders. 2011a. "The UX of User Stories, Part 1." Blog post. http://www.anders ramsay.com/2011/07/16/the-ux-of-user-stories-part-1/.

_____. 2011b. "The UX of User Stories, Part 2." Blog post. http://www.andersramsay.com/2011/07/24/the-ux-of-user-stories-part-2/.

_____. 2012. "The UX of Minimum Viable Products (MVPs)." Blog post. http://www.andersramsay.com/2012/09/24/the-ux-of-mvps/.

Ries, Eric. 2011. The Lean Startup: How Today's Entrepreneurs Use Continuous Innovation to Create Radically Successful Businesses. New York: Crown Business.

Scrivens, Paul. 2012. "MUD: Minimal Usable Design." Smashing Magazine May 29. http: //www.smashingmagazine.com/2012/05/29/mud-minimum-usable-design/.

Traynor, Des. 2011–2013. "Have You Tried Talking to Your Customers?" Blog post, Inside Intercom. http://insideintercom.io/have-you-tried-talking-to-your-customers/.

Ulwick, Tony. 2013. "Silence the Voice of the Customer." Blog post, Innovation Management. http://www.innovationmanagement.se/2013/06/25/silence-the-voice-of-the-customer/.

NOTES

1 See Beck et al. (2001) at http://agilemanifesto.org/principles.html.

2 If you are unfamiliar with Lean, you can read some of my posts on the topic on my blog: http://www.nataliehanson.com/tag/lean/).

3 http://bpennington.tumblr.com/post/19001126693/do-not-ask-a-designer-to-design-a-bridge-but-ask.

4 http://littlebigdetails.com/.

5 http://www.brainyquote.com/quotes/authors/c/charles_darwin.html.

29

Business Anthropology in China

TIAN GUANG

INTRODUCTION

China is roaring into the twenty-first century with the force of a locomotive: its gross domestic product (GDP) has almost doubled every six years. Great changes being made by the Chinese people influence both the domestic business environment in China and the international economy (Wu 2009; Yu et al. 2006). Thirty-four years ago China had a centralized planning system that remained largely closed to international trade; the market mechanism played a limited role in production and consumption. In the late 1970s and early 1980s, China launched its economic reform (known as "socialism with Chinese characteristics") and reinvigorated the Open Door Policy, which brought China into a market-oriented economy, created a rapidly growing for-profit sector, and made China a major player in the global economy. The market mechanism has completely transformed the business environments in China (Tian 2008). Measured by purchasing power parity (PPP), China in 2009 stood as the second-largest economy in the world after the United States, although in per capita terms the country is still lower middle-income (Central Intelligence Agency 2010; Saxon 2006).

As the economy in China evolves and changes, business strategy must also adapt. There is no doubt that the economic transition in China is affecting business strategies across a wide range of industries—telecommunications, automotive, hospitality, airline, textiles, and cosmetics (Alon 2003; Gerth 2010)—and across a wide range of activities, such as how to upgrade products and services to meet international market needs, how to reach the target market and establish the positioning of products and services, and how to conduct advertising and promotions internationally and cross-culturally. Chinese business leaders

---

Handbook of Anthropology in Business, edited by Rita Denny and Patricia Sunderland, 556–571.

are attuned to the changes taking place every day in the world marketplace. They fully understand that to market their products and services effectively around the world they must have a better understanding of international market environments from a cross-cultural perspective (Paliwoda and Ryans 2008; Terpstra and Sarathy 2001; Yu et al. 2006). Particularly since China became a formal member of the World Trade Organization in 2001, Chinese business leaders increasingly have turned to business schools for help and have asked them to upgrade their curricula to reflect a rapidly changing business environment. It is critical for business schools to meet the needs of the complex and changing economic system and the needs of the business world for future talent.

Reforming curriculum construction and design became a key challenge for business schools, as these components largely determine the quality of education and have a direct impact on the employment of business school graduates, as well as the satisfaction of the business world with those graduates. Social networks play a very important role in the Chinese business world; thus, superior curricula, and the social networks that link these students, facilitate the movement of graduates into good corporate jobs.

An important trend in this era of global innovation in business schools is the application of basic principles and methods of traditional disciplines such as anthropology to the concrete practice of business management education (Villeneuve 2003). According to Chinese scholars who advocate the applications of anthropology in business administration, these initiatives will have profound impacts on business education in China (Qi et al. 2012). This chapter traces some of the milestones in the development of "business anthropology" in China. I examine the historical development of anthropology in China, particularly economic anthropology, then contextualize business anthropology within both anthropology and business school realms.

THE DEVELOPMENT OF ECONOMIC ANTHROPOLOGY IN CHINA

Anthropology as a field of social science emerged in China in the early 1900s. Peking University was the first institution to offer a course on anthropology in 1917; it was followed by Xiamen University, Nankai University, Fudan University, Hujiang University, and Jinling University in the early 1920s (Zhou and Liu 2006). Most early anthropology courses in China covered basic theories and methods in physical anthropology and archaeology, with limited ethnographic works on sociocultural anthropology. The Academia Sinica in Beijing established the first department of anthropology in 1928, but throughout the 1930s and 1940s, it was generally the departments of history, literature, or sociology in Chinese universities that started to offer ethnology and sociocultural anthropology courses in a piecemeal fashion. These courses were influenced by traditions emanating from Japan at first, and later by traditions from the West, including links between Yanjing University and the University of Chicago and scholarly visits in the 1930s and 1940s from Radcliffe-Brown, Robert Park, and Robert Redfield (see Guldin 1994; Smart 2011). Then, after the establishment of the People's Republic of China in 1949, the government restructured the higher education system and, as a result, anthropology was no longer recognized as a discipline.

In the late 1970s, the Ministry of Education revived and systematically restored anthropology, along with sociology, throughout China's universities. Starting from the early 1980s some leading universities, such as Xiamen University, Sun Yat-Sen University, Yunan University, and Peking University, as well as others, either reestablished or newly started anthropology departments. Therefore, it is safe to say that today anthropology in China is still in its recovery stage, and as such, business anthropology studies are indeed just starting (Guldin 1990). Also, as Josephine Smart has indicated, the development of anthropology in China has been by no means easy, and its rocky journey of uneven development is symptomatic of the ongoing tensions between nationalism, globalization, and reaction against Western hegemony. As a result, Smart suggests that it is not meaningful to speak of anthropology as a unified discipline of four subfields in China (Smart 2011).

According to Guldin (1994), prior to the establishment of the People's Republic of China, Western approaches dominated anthropology development in China. When the Soviet model replaced the Western approach in the mid-1960s, Mao Zedong Thought became the new standard against which the value of social science was evaluated. During this period, anthropological studies focused on minorities and educational programs, and were designed primarily to train leaders working in minority areas because the Chinese central government needed support from minorities to achieve economic goals and the security of the country. Change came in the late 1970s, when the economic reform and open door policy that brought such sweeping economic transformations also initiated a new direction in the development of anthropology in China, one which established a Chinese model that incorporated foreign elements (Guldin 1994). According to Zhou Daming, a noted contemporary anthropologist in China, the study of rural development and *Nongmingong* also became fashionable for anthropologists in the late 1970s and early 1980s (Zhou 2003). *Nongmingong* is a particular social class and phenomenon that emerged at the end of the 1970s with economic reform and refers to urban peasant workers who migrated to cities for employment. Prior to economic reform, peasants were not allowed to search for employment in cities (Zhou and Sun 2009).

China's recent economic growth has been powerful but uneven, and in 1999 the China Western Development Strategy was initiated to address the disparity between the booming eastern coast and the lagging west, which includes many ethnic minority regions. The strategy includes boosting investment and infrastructure, ecological protection, and education. Traditional economic development theories cannot provide complete solutions to these complex challenges. The fields of economic anthropology and ethnic economics (a subfield of economics in China with a focus on the study of economic development in the minority areas), with different and more holistic sociocultural perspectives, are a new source of valuable and meaningful solutions. Fan Xiaoqing (2009) has argued that ethnic economics research should be included in economic anthropology studies; she pointed out the similarities and convergence between these fields, which are closely linked in their focus on the economy of China's ethnic minority regions. These connections have attracted the attention of scholars from both fields. As early as 1987, Weng Qianlin wrote that ethnic economics scholars should learn from the theories from the emerging disciplines in the West, such as development economics and economic anthropology, to promote the joint development of theory and practices of ethnic economics (Weng 1987; also Tian and Luo 2013:351–3).

A number of important events and publications in the 1990s promoted the development of the two fields. The Institute of Sociology and Anthropology of Peking University undoubtedly played a leading role in promoting the localization of economic anthropology. In 1995, it organized a high-level seminar called "Social-Cultural Anthropology" during which the Taiwanese scholar Jiang Bin delivered a keynote speech to introduce his counterparts in mainland China to the key viewpoints and arguments of the two schools of economic anthropology: realism and formalism (Tian and Luo 2013:334). In 1996, Wang Yanxiang published articles on national economy and economic anthropology in the *Journal of the Central University for Nationalities* to introduce the development of Western economic anthropology and to explore the similarity and differences between China's ethnic economics and economic anthropology (Shi 2002). In 1997, Wang Mingming from Peking University wrote *Shehui Renleixue yu Zhongguo Yanjiu* (*Social Anthropology and Sinology*) to introduce to Chinese scholars the work on China's rural areas by US scholar G. William Skinner. In the same year, *Economic Anthropology*, written by the renowned Japanese anthropologist Shinichiro Kurimoto, was translated into Chinese and officially published in China. This book was the first comprehensive introduction to the disciplinary development, areas of research, and academic genres of economic anthropology for Chinese academics (Tian and Luo 2013:334).

FROM ECONOMIC ANTHROPOLOGY TO BUSINESS ANTHROPOLOGY

More than 30 years after China's market reforms initiated its explosive economic development, China's products and businesspeople travel to all corners of the world. However, China lags in-depth research on globalized markets, business organization, and cultural analyses of other countries. Chinese businesspersons have faced considerable problems in other countries, including having their products confiscated or burned, causing tremendous loss for Chinese companies. Many of these problems are attributable to, or exacerbated by, cultural misunderstanding. The growing awareness among Chinese business leaders of the need to understand international market environments from a cross-cultural perspective and to develop new business strategies across a wide range of industries (Paliwoda and Ryans 2008) has also fostered the recent emergence of business anthropology in China.

The business school at Shantou University started to offer a business anthropology course to its undergraduate students in 2011; the anthropology department at Yunnan University began to enroll graduate students in business anthropology in 2013. The application of anthropology in the field of business management is also new: Zhang Jijiao, an anthropologist from the Institute of Ethnology and Anthropology of China Social Science Academy, along with anthropologists Chen Yunpiao and Zhou Daming from the School of Sociology and Anthropology at Sun Yat-Sen University, are pioneers in this field (Qi et al. 2012).

Initiatives such as these have their roots in the convergence of economic anthropology and ethnic economics outlined in the previous section. At the same time, business anthropology in China is drawing from other, earlier anthropological studies by Chinese as well as international scholars that have relevance to the business world today. For example, from 1918 to 1919, American anthropologist Daniel Klup conducted a study on country life in south China. While studying the peasants' economic life, Klup made a detailed descriptive analysis of the business system and daily operations in a small town named Fenghuang Village (Klup 2011). The famous Chinese anthropologist Fei Xiaotong conducted a similar study in the 1930s. By observing local residents' consumption, production, distribution, and exchange behaviors, Fei concluded that the traditional Chinese economic structure is a mixture of agriculture and small industry, not a pure agricultural social module. Although Fei's study is not about business per se, it analyzes peasants' economic and business life, and can be considered a precursor of business anthropology in the Chinese context (Fei 1939).

Applications of anthropology to business issues in the West are having an impact on Chinese scholars in the field of anthropology (Yu 2012). The *Chinese*

Newspaper of Social Science reports that business anthropology enlarges the scope of the research area for anthropologists, and Chinese scholars are beginning to realize the potential of anthropological applications to business (Zhong and Liu 2012). Several recent endeavors are worth noting. Qi Xiaoguang, the first scholar in China to earn a doctoral degree focused on business anthropology (conducted at the Ethnology and Sociology School at Minzu University), applies anthropological fieldwork methods to study issues of corporate culture faced by international companies in China (Qi 2011). Chen Gang, a professor of anthropology at Yunnan Financial and Economic University, and his colleagues use anthropological approaches to study the tourism in Yunnan Province and suggest that the Yunnan tourism industry should mobilize local ethnic resources to develop the tourism business intensively (Bai and Chen 2012). Wang Chunxia, a law professor at Zhejiang Financial and Economic University, has shown how different religious thoughts and customs have influenced business practices in Macau Chinese business communities (Wang 2012). Li Dekuan, a professor in the anthropology doctoral program at Ningxia University, studies the significance of ethnicity in human resources management in business firms that either hire minority employees or conduct business operations in minority concentrated areas (Li 2012). Chen Yuqi studies the resistance movement of contemporary Nongmingong and indicates the importance of corporate social responsibility in China (Chen 2012). Family, kinship, and social networks are also crucial considerations. Yu Yonghong conducted his doctoral studies at the Sociology and Anthropology School at Sun Yat-Sen University on family businesses, and demonstrates the significance of social networks for family businesses' growth (Yu 2012). The International Congress of Anthropological and Ethnological Sciences (ICAES) in China has an Enterprise Anthropology group led by Zhang Jijiao, who has conducted a series of studies on Chinese enterprises. Zhang's ethnographic study on traditional brand enterprises has demonstrated that business models and management styles in most of those companies are typically centered with family operations (Zhang and Keong 2011).

As a major promoter of business anthropology, I returned to China in 2011 while on sabbatical leave from Medaille College in the United States, with the goal of educating business schools and anthropology departments in Chinese universities about the importance of business anthropology (Tian 2010). Zhou Daming was one of the first anthropology professors in China to agree that business anthropology is much needed in China and to realize the potential of the field as China transitions from a traditional agricultural to an industrialized and commercial society. Particularly worthy of note is the pioneering study conducted by Zhou and his students in the mid-1990s of *Nongmingong* as a unique social economic phenomenon in the modern Chinese business world.

One component of the research examined group differences among *Nongmingong* and suggested that business leaders must be aware of these in their everyday business management operations (Zhou and Sun 2009).

Zhou, who holds a leadership position at the Sociology and Anthropology School at Sun Yat-Sen University, took my suggestion and agreed to host the first international conference on business anthropology in China at Sun Yat-Sen University in May 2012. At the same time, the Central Minzu University and the People's University jointly hosted a conference on business anthropology in Beijing. The mainstream public media in China reported on both conferences. At both events, some Chinese scholars agreed that in the near future companies would ideally set up a new senior management position, perhaps with the title of Chief Anthropologist (see McCracken 2009), to guide the long-term development of the company together with other senior executives. More important, the Chief Anthropologists could promote internal harmony within the company to improve the working efficiency of employees, a goal of the current government (Wu 2012; Zhong and Liu 2012).

THE DEVELOPMENT OF BUSINESS ANTHROPOLOGY EDUCATION PROGRAMS IN CHINA

Business anthropology is in its infancy in China, and at present only Shantou University formally offers business anthropology training. But the emergence of courses and curricula in the field has been energetic at undergraduate and graduate levels, and the future is bright. A 2003 inventory showed that a total of 63 departments, institutes, or research centers in greater China (including Hong Kong and Taiwan) offered degree-granting programs or research facilities for anthropology and/or ethnology. Among these 63 institutions, 14 offered a PhD program in anthropology and/or ethnology, which is particularly impressive given that doctoral training in anthropology in China is a post-1980s phenomenon (Smart 2003, 2011). The view in the field of business administration today is that anthropological theories and methods are appropriate to be used in corporate culture and organizational behavior, human resource management, marketing, consumer behavior, product design and development, business competitive intelligence, and transnational business management (Lan and Tian 2011a, 2011b).

Yunnan University began recruiting graduate students in business anthropology in 2013. At same time, the anthropology department at Sun Yat-Sen University, the business school at North Minzu University, the anthropology department at South-central Minzu University, the anthropology program at Ningxia University, the anthropology program at Jishou University, and the anthropology program at Yunan Financial and Economic University, among others, planned to offer business anthropology courses at the undergraduate level in the near future. In the following sections, I examine the design of the business anthropology course and the teaching process at Shantou University, where I am on the faculty, to illustrate business anthropology training in the Chinese context.

For China, Ann Jordan's seminal textbook *Business Anthropology* (2003); Robert Guang Tian, Michael P. Lillis, and Alfons van Marrewijk's *General Business Anthropology* (2010); and Tian Guang and Zhou Daming's *Gonshang Renleixue Tonglun* (*General Business Anthropology*), published by Ningxia People's Press in 2013, provide a foundation for undergraduate teaching of business anthropology.

Shantou University Business School is one of the few registered members of The Association to Advance Collegiate Schools of Business (AACSB) International in China, one of the most respected international business educational program accreditation bodies; it is also one of the few Chinese business schools certified by the European Foundation for Management Development (EFMD). In 2011, Shantou University Business School, which is dedicated to international strategy development of business management education and focuses on the introduction of curricula and teaching materials of Western business schools, began offering business anthropology as a professional elective to senior undergraduate students.

In designing the business anthropology course, we set up five expected learning outcomes. The first is to understand the basic theory, methods, and recent developments of business anthropology and to know how to apply the theory and method into the specific practice of industry and commerce management. The second is to find and understand the specific problems in the practice of industry and commerce that can be solved through anthropology principles and methods and to put forward operational suggestions for management. The third is to carry out specific field research to identify and apply relevant anthropological theories and methods to solve practical problems. The fourth is to find and study the cultural factors affecting the company structure and concrete business operation and to put forward corresponding solutions for the development of the company culture. The fifth expected learning outcome is to understand how cultural differences are at play in international industry and commerce and to gain mastery of such differences to manage successfully in international contexts. The main objectives of the course were to cover the history and methods of business anthropology and examine cultural factors and business practices. In addition, we covered general anthropology, cultural change, and innovation; the application of ethnographic research in

Table 29.1. Outline and major content of business anthropology.

Outline	Detailed Teaching Contents
Introduction to Business Anthropology	(1) Basic knowledge of the contemporary business world; (2) basic anthropological knowledge; (3) characteristics of business anthropology; (4) special contribution of business anthropologists
The Application of Ethnography in Business Management	(1) Main features of ethnography; (2) steps in ethnographic study; (3) the fieldwork issues and professional ethics; (4) research and application of business ethnography
Marketing and Anthropology	(1) Anthropological perspective on markets; (2) anthropology promotion of the marketing; (3) cross-cultural issues in global marketing; (4) anthropology and social marketing
Anthropology and Consumer Behavior	(1) Consumer behavior as a category of social science research; (2) cultural consumer behavior; (3) anthropological understanding of characteristics of consumer behavior; (4) anthropological consumer behavior studies and applications
Anthropology and Product Design	(1) Product design and process issues; (2) contribution of anthropology to the design industry; (3) ethnography and experience design; (4) cooperation of anthropologists and product designers
Anthropology, Competitive Intelligence, and Knowledge Asset Management	(1) Introduction to business competitive intelligence; (2) anthropological research on competitive intelligence; (3) strategy of cross-cultural competitive intelligence; (4) intellectual property and anthropology
Globalization, International Trade, and Anthropology	(1) The study of the globalization process; (2) cross-cultural issues in international trade; (3) cross-cultural business communication; (4) anthropological interpretations of international cooperation
Anthropology and Entrepreneurs Research	(1) Theory of entrepreneurship; (2) management of family business; (3) ethnicity and entrepreneurship; (4) entrepreneurs and gender issues
Business Education and Prospects of Business Anthropology	(1) Application of anthropology in business management education; (2) professional business anthropologists; (3) forecasting of business anthropology
Case Study	(1) Specific case studies; all cases should reflect the practical value of the principles and methods of anthropology in the field of business administration.

business management; marketing and anthropology; anthropology and consumer behavior; anthropology and product design; anthropology, competitive intelligence, and knowledge management; globalization, international trade, and anthropology; anthropology and entrepreneurial research; business management education; and prospects of business anthropology.

Table 29.1 provides detailed course information, outlining the major theories and concepts covered in the business anthropology course. The course design received a first-rate award by the China National Educational Administrative Association in the summer of 2013. Teaching activities included classroom lectures, student participation and discussion, case analysis, and field research culminating in a term paper. Because business anthropology is an emerging interdisciplinary subject, mature teaching materials on this subject are still relatively limited and the selection of materials constrained. We prepared the syllabus and proposed this new course by building on relevant syllabi for courses at Wayne State University and the University of North Texas in the United States and VU University Amsterdam in the Netherlands, and combining that with the instructional norms of the Business School at Shantou University.

Teaching Process & the Interactions with Students

Wang Weilian points out that the use of interactive and group activities in the teaching process requires effective communication and dialog between teachers and students, as well as among students (Wang 2011). Chinese students are often reluctant to participate in class discussion due to Chinese teaching and learning traditions in which the students are supposed to listen to the teacher's lecture; asking questions is perceived as impolite (Zhang and Xu 2003). Likewise, even when a teacher asks direct questions, students tend not to answer to avoid possible loss of face if the answer is not correct. To help students become comfortable participating in the business anthropology class, the instructor explained and described the teaching content according to the syllabus and put forward some questions for students to answer; over the course of the whole semester, the instructor required that every student must answer no fewer than 10 questions out loud in class. In addition, the instructor encouraged communication and interaction with the use of the digital academy platform, so that students not only could upload their own work and release information, but also put forward their suggestions on the course design and progress.

Observation is a principal method in anthropological business research. However, students often may not automatically make the connections between the business strategies and the practice of anthropological business research (Tian 2001; Tian and Walle 2009). To help them understand the principles of business anthropology, a term project assignment was designed that strengthened the linkages between anthropology and business. Through case studies and the term project, the students learned to carry out specific observational field research to identify and apply relevant anthropological theory and method to solve practical problems.

The term field project, the key activity of the course, has both individual and collaborative components. Students start individually doing literature reviews and initial participant observation, then construct research questions as a group. Next, the group designs the approaches for conducting further observations, as well as the questions for in-depth interviews and questionnaires. The instructor guides discussion and the final choice of the research instruments. Students then individually carry out systematic observations, administer questionnaires, and conduct in-depth interviews; afterward, they work in small study groups to conduct preliminary analysis of their data and deliver the data and analysis to the class data pool for further processing. Students are encouraged to strive for a final term paper suitable for publication in academic journals. In the academic year 2012–2013, four of the student research reports were accepted by academic journals through a double-blinded peer reviewing process, and six were accepted for oral presentation at two international academic conferences.

This open teaching method with interaction greatly mobilizes the enthusiasm of students to learn. For example, after the course, one student independently designed a research project for the study of relations between the motivation of youth entrepreneurs and business results. Moreover, the student creatively blended participant observation methods and interview data in innovative ways.

Students learn that culture plays an important role in everyday business operations. Through case studies and the term project, they gain the skills and knowledge to find and study the cultural factors that affect company structures and concrete business operations. For example, in doing a term research project on food service effectiveness on the Shantou University campus, students discovered that the measurement of academic performance and accomplishments dominate the university culture, whereas food service quality is a secondary or even the tertiary concern of the university leadership. By contrast, food service is a top concern for students. Accordingly, the research report stressed the importance of food service to students' success at the university. This solution framed the issue in a way that made it culturally relevant to the university leadership (Hu et al. 2012). As the instructor, I emphasized this kind of cultural difference exists in international industry and commerce. One group of students indicated that one of the most important learning outcomes for them was that they began to collect cultural difference data in their daily readings to better prepare them for their future international business practice.

CONCLUSION & SUGGESTIONS

The business world is complex and quickly changing. The business school that regards cultivating future talents as its responsibility must adjust its curriculum and teaching content constantly. The requirements of the business world for future leaders are complex, so cross-fertilization among the humanities, social sciences, and natural sciences are a dominant trend in the discipline. Business education in many countries shows that the arts and sciences now have a significant influence on the curriculum in business administration (Lu and Han 2007). In China, the education system has long divided liberal arts from science, which results in inadequate integration of liberal arts and science in the curriculum of most business schools. To change the isolation of business in higher education in China, business schools should prioritize the incorporation of liberal arts and science as soon as possible to ensure the comprehensive development of students' knowledge and abilities.

The experience of developing business anthropology at Shantou University Business School is one successful example of how to advance this cross-fertilization. I expect Shantou University's course to become a model for other universities. The support of the leadership of business school at Shantou University, along with the accumulated teaching experiences and networking among business and anthropology professors in China, will lead more business schools and anthropology departments across the country to add business anthropology to their curricula. Business anthropology is poised to become one of the more popular courses at Chinese universities.

One of the most pressing issues that we must tackle immediately is the lack of teaching materials in Chinese. The texts adopted by instructors are mainly designed and written for US students. Because the field in China is just now emerging, there are not enough scholars conducting research and writing on Chinese cases, or publishers who prioritize such texts. We must organize experts to compile business anthropology teaching materials in Chinese as soon as possible, and in accordance with the reality of the business practice in China, to provide references for business anthropology teaching. In addition, business anthropology seminars and teaching demonstration sections should be conducted to promote the Shantou University course to other Chinese business schools.

In short, we must connect business education reform with the international standards while simultaneously meeting the specific needs of Chinese business management practices. Business schools in China must seize this opportunity—developing educational goals, school operation models, curriculum, faculty, international networks, and networks among Chinese business schools and arts and sciences departments—to constantly improve the quality of business management education. In my view, the addition of business anthropology courses is a simple but feasible first step that will undoubtedly accelerate the pace of reforming business education to meet international standards and enhance the international competitiveness of China's management education.

REFERENCES

Alon, Ilan. 2003. *Chinese Economic Transition and International Marketing Strategy.* Santa Barbara, CA: Praeger Publishers.

Bai, Ting, and Gang Chen. 2012. "Business Anthropology and Tourist Product Marketing." In *Business Anthropology*, edited by Guang Tian and Daming Zhou, 282–92. Yinchuan: Ningxia Renmin Press.

Central Intelligence Agency. 2010. *The World Fact Book.* https://www.cia.gov/library/publications/the-world-factbook/geos/ch.html (accessed September 15, 2012).

Chen, Yuqi. 2012. "China Corporate Social Responsibilities and *Nongmingong* Retaliation Movement." In *Business Anthropology,* edited by Guang Tian and Daming Zhou, 255–67. Yinchuan: Ningxia Renmin Press.

Fan, Xiaoqin. 2009. "Economic Anthropology Research in China." *Journal of Huaihua University* 28(12):21–4.

Fei, Xiaotong. 1939. *Peasant Life in China.* London: Kegan Paul, Trench, Trubner.

Gerth, Karl. 2010. *As China Goes, So Goes the World: How Chinese Consumers Are Transforming Everything.* New York, NY: Hill and Wang.

Guldin, Gregory Eliyu, ed. 1990 *Anthropology in China.* Armonk, NY: M. E. Sharpe.

_____. 1994. *The Saga of Anthropology in China: From Malinowski to Moscow to Mao.* NY: M. E. Sharpe.

Hu Mingzhi, Du Yanqiu, Liu Sha, Liu Yuan, Niu Haiyang, and Wang Yifan. 2012. "Food Services and Student Life: A Business Anthropological Case Study." *Journal of Higher Education Theory and Practice* 12(5)123–40.

Jordan, A. 2003. *Business Anthropology.* Prospect Heights, IL: Waveland Press.

Klup, Daniel H. 2011. *Civics: An Inductive Study Socially Developed of the Elements of Community Welfare in China.* Translated by Zhou Daming. Beijing: Zhisshi Chanquan Press.

Lan, X., and G. Tian. 2011a. "The Rising of Business Anthropology and The Application of Anthropology in Business Education." *Journal of China Management Information* (4):70–75.

_____. 2011b. "The Application of Ethnographic Methods in Business Practice." *Journal of Fujian Forum* (4):65–6.

Li, Dekuan. 2012. "The Cultural Orientation of China Minority Human Resources Management." In *Business Anthropology*, edited by Guang Tian and Daming Zhou, 209–23. Yinchuan: Ningxia Renmin Press.

Lu, Y., and X. Han. 2007. "A Comparative Study of Foreign and Domestic Business School Course Structure and Design." *Journal of China University Education* (1): 26–8.

McCracken, Grant. 2009. *Chief Culture Officer: How to Create a Living, Breathing Corporation.* New York: Basic Books.

Paliwoda, Stanley J., and John K. Ryans. 2008. *International Business vs. International Marketing.* Cheltenham, UK: Edward Elgar Publishing.

Qi, Xiaoguang. 2011. "Issues of Corporate Culture in the Context of Economic Globalization from the Perspective of Business Anthropology." *Journal of Shijiazhuang Economic University* 34(4):58–61.

Qi, Xiaoguang, Xiaona Wang, and Zhenyu Liu. 2012. "A Dialogue between Management Science and Anthropology: The Development of Business Anthropology." *Journal of Dalian Maritime University Social Sciences Edition* 11(3):48–51.

Saxon, Mike. 2006. *An American's Guide To Doing Business In China: Negotiating Contracts and Agreements*. Avon, MA: Adams Media.

Shi, Lin. 2002. *Economic Anthropology*. Beijing: Publication House of the Central University for Nationalities.

Smart, Josephine. 2011. "In Search of Anthropology in China: A Discipline Caught in the Web of Nation Building Agenda, Socialist Capitalism, and Globalization." Unpublished working paper, University of Calgary, Canada.

Smart, Josephine, and Allen Smart. 2003. "China Studies in Anthropology." Paper presented at the Conference on Historicizing Anthropology in Canada, Trent University, Peterborough, Ontario, Canada, February 20–23.

Terpstra, V., and R. Sarathy. 2001. *International Marketing*. 8th edition. Chicago IL: Dryden Press.

Tian, Guang. 2008. A *Critique of Pan-Market*. Fort Worth, TX: Fellows Press of America.

Tian, G., and K. Luo. 2013. *Introduction to Economic Anthropology*. Yinchuan: Ningxia People's Publishing House.

Tian, Guang, and Daming Zhou. 2013. *Gonshang Renleixue Tonglun* (*General Business Anthropology*). Beijing: China Finance and Economy Press.

Tian, Robert. 2001. "Anthropological Approach to the Consumer Science: A Practical Course Processes." *High Plains Applied Anthropologist* 21(2):157–65.

_____. 2010. "The Unique Contributions and Unique Methodologies: A Concise Overview of the Applications of Business Anthropology." *International Journal of Business Anthropology* 1(2):70–88.

Tian, R., M. Lillis, and A. H. van Marrewijk. 2010. *General Business Anthropology*. Miami, FL: North American Business Press.

Tian, Robert, and Alf Walle. 2009. "Anthropology and Business Education: Practitioner Applications for a Qualitative Method." *International Journal of Management Education* 7(2):59–67.

Villeneuve, M. 2003. "Business Education." *Business NH Magazine* 20(6):12–13.

Wang, Chunxia. 2012. "Religion and Business Operations." In *Business Anthropology*, edited by Guang Tian and Daming Zhou, 224–36. Yinchuan: Ningxia Renmin Press.

Wang, Mingming. 1997. *Shehui Renleixue yu Zhongguoyanjiu* (*Social Anthropology and Sinology*). Beijing: Sanlian Shudian.

Wang, Weilian. 2011. "Principles and Methods for Single Course Curriculum Design." In *Shantou University Instructor Training Documentations*, 1–14. Shantou University Academic Affairs Office, China.

Weng, Qianlin. 1987. "Theories and Practice: On Ethnic Economics Research Methods." *Journal of Qinhai Social Science* 1987(6):27–32.

Wu, Yan. 2012. "China Needs Business Anthropology." *China Minzu Newspaper*, June 28, p. 3.

Wu, Zhongming. 2009. *China in the World Economy*. New York: Routledge.

Yu, Hong. 2012. "The Growth and Development of Business Anthropology." In *Business Anthropology*, edited by Guang Tian and Daming Zhou, 91–104. Yinchuan: Ningxia Renmin Press.

Yu, Yonghong. 2012. "China Family Business Firms Social Networks." In *Business Anthropology*, edited by Guang Tian and Daming Zhou, 268–81. Yinchuan: Ningxia Renmin Press.

Yu, Li Anne, Cynthia Chan, and Christopher Ireland. 2006. *China's New Culture of Cool: Understanding the World's Fastest-Growing Market*. Berkeley, CA: New Riders Press.

Zhang, Jijiao, and V. Phin Keong. 2011. *Enterprise Anthropology: Applied Research and Case Study*. Beijing: Intellectual Copyright Press.

Zhang, Y., and L. Xu. 2003. "Comparative Study of China and Foreign Education." *Journal of Jilin Education Science, Higher Education Study* (2):32–4.

Zhong, Zhe, and Ning Liu. 2012. "Business Anthropology Expanding the Study Scope of Anthropology." *China Newspaper of Social Science*, July 20, p. 1.

Zhou, Daming. 2003. "A Review of a Century of Anthropology in China," In *Anthropology in the 21st Century*, edited by Daming Zhou, 3–13. Beijing: Minzu Publisher.

Zhou, Daming, and Changyun Sun. 2009. "Group Differences among *Nongmingong*: A Follow-up Ethnographic Case Study." *International Journal of Business Anthropology* 1(1):79–94.

Zhou, Daming, and Chaohui Liu. 2006. "A Centennial Review of Anthropology in China." *China Sociology and Anthropology*. http://bbs.netbig.com/thread-2110706-1-1.html (accessed September 2013).

30

In Pursuit of Strategy: Anthropologists in Advertising

ROBERT J. MORAIS

A number of years ago, when I was the chief strategic officer of an advertising agency, I accompanied our creative director to a presentation on consumer trends by the marketing consultancy Yankelovich Monitor. Immediately after the session ended, the creative director turned to me and commented on the elegance and persuasiveness of the talk. Then he added, "But they didn't tell us what to do with it." The "it" to which he referred was the information that Yankelovich had so artfully packaged, and the creative director was making both a critical and crucial point. The transposition of research findings into actionable advertising strategies was my job at the time; I understood that marketing research is valuable, but his remark was a cogent reminder that researchers who delineate how their findings can be applied to strategic marketing initiatives are indispensable.

The connection between research and advertising strategy has been central to advertising development for decades. The Ogilvy Awards, presented by the Advertising Research Foundation (ARF) in honor of advertising legend David Ogilvy, "celebrate the extraordinary and/or creative use of research in the advertising development processes of research firms, advertising agencies, and advertisers."[1] The Jay Chiat Awards, named for another advertising icon, "recognize brilliant strategic thinking."[2] These honors accentuate the advertising industry's belief that advertising research matters most when it affects strategies that generate outstanding advertising. I propose here that anthropologists who work in advertising should consider the preeminence of the research-strategy linkage and collaborate with their clients on strategy after a research project is completed rather than leave the developmental stream prematurely.

Handbook of Anthropology in Business, edited by Rita Denny and Patricia Sunderland, 571–587.

This chapter is driven by a personal observation: anthropologists who work in advertising and marketing research often make profound strategic contributions. However, many of them do not take an active part in strategy codification, specifically in the hands-on crafting of strategic documents, unless they are employed by advertising agencies as account planners or in strategy consulting firms (e.g., ReD Associates) that institutionalize the process (Wood 2013; for a recent example of strategic involvement in the nonprofit sector, see Sturges 2013). Although anthropologists in advertising and marketing research bring distinctive methodologies and analytical concepts to the table and provide research-based insights to strategic business needs (Malefyt and Morais 2012; Suchman 2007; Sunderland and Denny 2007), too often their strategic contribution ends before the blueprint for marketplace initiatives begins. A concern throughout this chapter is that when anthropologists are absent throughout the process of strategy formulation, the power and influence of their contributions is curtailed. Moreover, this missed opportunity occurs at a time when successful business strategies are elusive and ever more pressing. The marketing of brands is highly competitive and commercial pressures demand deep-thinking, highly engaged strategists. There is competition, too, among research suppliers for client projects, and an expanding and commoditized field of self-trained ethnographers is a threat to academy-trained, theoretically armed anthropologists who engage in commerce. I suggest that greater participation in strategic codification will distinguish anthropologists from competitors. It will help distance us from a research-only role that marginalizes some practitioners. It will advance anthropologists' professional careers and enlarge the influence of anthropological thinking, especially in the marketing and advertising domains, because as anthropologists increase our strategic involvement, we will inevitably develop a larger body of literature about how to practice strategic work and project an identity that identifies us as strategic experts. Equally important, anthropologists' clients will be equipped to market their brands more effectively, with the happy result that marketing executives will hire even more anthropologists.

To be clear, I should underscore that many anthropologists of and working in business (see Moeran, this volume) think and contribute strategically. The published evidence is plentiful (see, for example, Arnould and Price 2006; Arnould and Wallendorf 1994; Baba 2006; Malefyt and Moeran 2003; Malefyt and Morais 2012; Squires and Byrne 2002; and Sunderland and Denny 2007; in addition to other authors in this volume), and the Ethnographic Praxis in Industry Conference has played a major role in furthering strategic discussion among anthropologists in industry. At the same time, input by anthropologists to the process of strategic development after a research project is completed—the "what to do with it" phase in a formulation sense—tends not to be anthropologists' *modus operandi* or within their purview, at least not in the marketing and advertising arenas. Some have tackled the anthropology-strategy connection directly; for example, anderson (2009) addresses ethnography and strategy in the *Harvard Business Review;* Grant McCracken's *Chief Culture Officer* (2009) is essentially about anthropologists' strategic engagement, and his blog, www.cultureby.com, often intersects with advertising strategic planning; and Malefyt and Morais discuss strategy and business understanding in *Advertising and Anthropology* (2012). And yet, explicit references to strategy are rare in several substantial and influential works by anthropologists writing about advertising and marketing. The recent four-volume collection, *Advertising: Critical Readings,* edited by Brian Moeran (2010), does not contain a chapter or extended discussion on strategy. Two general books on business anthropology barely mention strategy at all (A. Jordan 2013; Tian et al. 2010). Sunderland and Denny's *Doing Anthropology in Consumer Research* (2007) contends, and richly demonstrates, that "good ideas" emanate from their work (2007:63–4), but the book does not include the word "strategy" in its index. Given that strategy is ubiquitous in business, anthropologists do themselves and their enterprises a disservice when they do not feature it as part of their professional offering. While this is understandable for anthropologists who focus on the distinctiveness of their methodological and theoretical approaches in commercial domains, it is not advisable.

This chapter is less about the idea of strategy than the actions that create it. Most anthropologists' research reports include insights and recommendations, many of which are strategic in orientation. But in my experience, advertising and marketing clients incorporate what they perceive as the strongest of a researcher's insights, cherry-picking those that suit management agendas and ignoring ideas if they are not deemed valuable. Anthropologists' research-derived strategic recommendations can also be given less attention because anthropologists are viewed as research, not strategic, experts, so they are not included in the strategic formulation stage. Taking an active role in the writing of strategy, rather than a "hand-off" of research findings with some strategic implications, would not only help ensure that anthropologists' best insights are heard during the time that strategic blueprints are crafted; it also would provide them with intimate client interaction—and respect—during the difficult, delicate, combative, and vital strategic development process.

PATHWAYS TO STRATEGY

In marketing and advertising research studies, placing research within a strategic business frame begins with a definition of the client's near-term learning needs, followed by immersion in their broader business issues. An anthropologist working in a commercial realm must have an answer for how the planned research will advance the client's objectives for product innovation, target communication enhancements, and/or sales growth. Anthropologists employed by advertising agencies and marketing firms are better equipped when they are briefed on the client's marketplace agenda, aware of the competitive landscape, and know which strategic and tactical initiatives have and have not been effective in the past.

Anthropologists who work in advertising agencies or on advertising assignments must be familiar with how ad agency account planners function and be versed in planners' primary deliverable: the creative brief. Anthropologists employed by marketing organizations should request or conduct a SWOT analysis, a commonly used quadrant framework that depicts a brand's strengths, weaknesses, opportunities, and threats (Kotler and Armstrong 2012:53–4). Anthropologists who engage in brand innovation need to be familiar with pertinent consumer trends, competitive innovations, their client's research and development (R&D) capabilities, and client management ideas concerning how and when they want to enter a new category (being first to market or a market follower). These knowledge areas will enable an anthropologist to comprehend the landscape of the research s/he has been hired to conduct. Certainly, many anthropologists understand the business context of their projects, but not all have the time or penchant for in-depth business analysis. My experience has taught me that without this level of awareness, and an appreciation of how clients balance hard-edged business analysis with leaps of insight, meaningful strategic engagement is not possible (compare with Cochoy, this volume). And, finally, anthropologists must be cognizant of their client's corporate culture as a way to facilitate their work and in light of anthropological studies on corporations (see, for example, Cefkin [2009] and B. Jordan [2013], in addition to many of the works cited earlier).[3]

The Meaning of Strategy

In the advertising industry, "strategy" typically refers to the plan that delivers an agreed-upon vision for a brand; "tactics" are the means by which the plan is delivered (media choices, for example); "execution" is the creative expression of the strategy in the form of television commercials, print advertisements, online communications, etc. Writing about strategic formulation in marketing, Kotler and Armstrong characterize marketing strategy as "the marketing logic by which the company hopes to create . . . customer value and achieve . . . profitable relationships" (Kotler and Armstrong 2012:48). For an example of how a leading

Figure 30.1. Advertising agency strategic planning model.

1	2	3	4	5	6
WHAT ARE THE SPECIFIC BUSINESS GOALS?	WHERE WILL THE BUSINESS COME FROM?	WHO ARE THE CUSTOMERS ASSOCIATED WITH THIS GROWTH?	WHAT DO THEY DO TODAY? WHY? (POINT A)	WHAT DO WE WANT THEM TO DO? (POINT B)	WHAT INFORMATION, DEMONSTRATION OR EXPERIENCE DO CUSTOMERS NEED TO MOVE FROM A TO B?
Describe volume/value/share goals that communications are expected to help the brand achieve.	What is the source of new business? If we plan to grow the category, how will consumption increase? If the plan is to steal share, from which competitors do you plan to take business?	Describe the customer in detail—as a living human, not just a target. Create a full-color portrait of what it is like to be this person that will put creatives on "first name terms" with the target.	Now, relative to the brand itself, how does the customer "buy"? What attitudes, knowledge, perceptions, etc. drive this behavior? What influences are driving perceptions? WHAT HAVE YOU CONCLUDED IS THE UNMET NEED?	Relative to business goals and source of business. How do we need to change what people do? What new information about the brand could change perceptions, attitudes, etc. so that people will change what they do?	CHECKPOINT **For communications for a particular product within a campaign portfolio:** Check that this an idea that will **advance** the overall campaign—not just restate it. **For all communications:** Check that the message is: • Differentiated • Relevant • Credible • Futureproof

Source: Major worldwide advertising agency; name withheld to protect confidentiality

advertising agency situates the strategic planning process within a business context, see Figure 30.1. This illustration is a particularly good one; not all advertising agencies are this systematic. In addition, processes for the development of specific types of strategies—marketing, advertising, promotional, pricing, and so on—vary across organizations. Anthropologists must understand their client's definition and use of strategy for a given research assignment. Not doing so is more than operationally problematic; incorrect assumptions about what strategy means for a client company can be hazardous to one's career.

STRATEGIC ENGAGEMENT IN A RESEARCH CONTEXT

Even smart marketers can lose sight of their strategic goals during the course of a marketing research project. An anthropologist who is informed by the broader business objective can make a decisive contribution when the original intent of a study is endangered. For example, one client of my marketing research firm, a manufacturer of products for breastfeeding mothers, wanted to develop a merchandising strategy for the retailer Target that would induce the chain to stock more of the client's brands. As focus groups with breastfeeding mothers progressed, several of the marketing managers pressed my company's moderator to spend an inordinate amount of time on consumers' reactions to product offerings rather than a more strategically productive exploration of respondents' in-store shopping needs.[4] After the first of four scheduled focus groups, and with the client's larger strategic objective in mind, I proposed that we redirect the questioning to center on consumers' in-store "pain points" and possible solutions. I spoke to the backroom observers, paying special attention to the vice president of marketing, and suggested that we discover the "seven things" (an arbitrary number provided to make the point) that would help improve breastfeeding mothers' in-store shopping experience. This exploration, I argued, would help the client develop a shopping solution story and a merchandizing plan to "sell" to Target. The redirection was broadly anthropological in that it was driven by consumer experience rather than product perception; it was strategic because it would deliver the client's goal of building a narrative about improving how mothers would feel about shopping at Target. I felt that this recommendation, offered when my clients were losing sight of the reason for fielding the research, was a professional risk, but one worth taking. The marketing vice president expressed appreciation for the redirection; the focus groups proceeded as I suggested, the findings yielded the insights and strategies needed, and my company was rewarded with additional research projects. The Target meeting informed by this study went extremely well according to the client, and our research approach was repeated for another marketing channel, drugstore chains, with a similar outcome.

SUSTAINED STRATEGIC INVOLVEMENT: CREATIVE BRIEFS

That anthropologists contribute to advertising strategy is well accepted, at least among those who practice in marketing and advertising. Here, I advocate for anthropologists taking a step beyond insight generation and strategic recommendations to become closely involved in the *drafting* of the creative brief. Although I am focusing on strategy, anthropologists can contribute on strate-

Table 30.1. How anthropologists can contribute to creative briefs.

Component	Contribution
Objective	Formulation as it ties to cultural issues that affect a client's business
Target	Expression beyond demographics and psychographics to reflect cultural issues
Insight	Core of what anthropologists deliver
Brand Positioning	Application of research to differentiate a brand from competition and compel consumers to consider purchase
Promise	Conversion of insights into a deeply meaningful consumer benefit
Support	Reason to believe the promise based upon consumer belief systems, values, practices
Executional Considerations	Codes, symbols, rituals, narratives, etc.
Mandatories	Essential language and symbols

gic, tactical, and executional levels, all of which are elements of a creative brief, as illustrated in Table 30.1. Insights and observations might inform, for example, the tactical selection of media choices, such as online social media sites, or advertising executional ideas, such as showing families interacting in specific ways. There is no standard creative brief format; some of the components included in Table 30.1 might or might not appear in any given agency's brief. This chart includes the most common creative brief elements. The areas that describe where and how an anthropologist can contribute to a brief are meant to illustrate, rather than rigidly define, the scope of an anthropologist's participation. Anthropologists who have worked with advertising clients can envision additional ways to inform a creative brief. This kind of close, sustained strategic involvement will help ensure that anthropologists' thinking will be included when creative development commences.

Following are two cases in which I contributed actively to the formal advertising strategic development process.

A Multidimensional Approach to Sore Throat Remedy Advertising

Consumers experience brands across psychological, social, and functional dimensions, and I often adopt a multidisciplinary approach that explores these domains (Morais and Malefyt 2010). I managed strategic research for a client's brand in the US over-the-counter sore throat medicine category that focused on the multiple ways consumers build and experience trust in a brand.[5] The team selected trust as the conceptual jumping-off point because it is a prime mover, as a sentiment and an attitude, for brand selection in the sore throat category. Consumers considering sore throat brands for purchase weigh many factors: brand reputation and image, efficacy, personal experience and loyalty, and recommendations from doctors, family, and friends. Price and promotions, such as coupons, are in the equation, too. However, judgments regarding brand value are governed primarily by individuals' emotions and perceptions as well as the broader cultural context of rules, beliefs, and ideas that affect consumer consumption.

The challenge in this project was to discover a consumer-driven, cognitively and experientially informed taxonomy of trust and then determine which trust components could drive purchase of the client's brand. With the right insight and advertising execution, the brand could potentially "own" a distinctive kind of trust and stand apart in the competitive sore throat remedy category. The research entailed in-depth one-on-one interviews, with lines of questioning drawn from a variety of perspectives. We began with indirect areas of inquiry that elicited personal stories in which respondents reflected upon sore throat experiences, especially moments of pain and relief. We also asked them to tell stories about a range of positive and negative trust episodes throughout their lives, an approach with foundations in clinical psychology and life history analysis in anthropology. In addition, respondents were directed to talk about the social (and implicitly cultural) implications of sickness, and to discuss the functional properties of the sore throat brands they preferred. This research enabled us to discover several dimensions of trust that we then had respondents connect to their brand: trust based on psychologically driven needs, such as "I trust that I will feel like myself again," and deep feelings about caregivers, especially their mothers; trust based on needs for social interaction and culturally driven affiliation such as "I trust that I will be able to get out and be in the world again"; and functionally driven trust based on experience with the brand and its ability to soothe a sore throat. Using these findings as a foundation, I worked closely with the advertising agency on the crafting of a creative brief that delineated several executional variations on trust. I remained involved in the project through the development of television advertising in video storyboard format and quantitative consumer assessment of the videos, which was conducted by my firm. Advertising based on the trust respondents placed in their mothers surpassed a research hurtle for consumer purchase intention, and was launched into the marketplace.

Leadership for an Orange Juice Advertising Strategy

A client in the orange juice category was experiencing slowed brand growth in the Canadian market and sought fresh consumer knowledge as a foundation for a more effective advertising strategy. A day of focus groups was planned: two groups with the client's brand users, two groups with competitive brand users. During discussions with the client insight manager, I learned that several members of the client and advertising agency teams held divergent views of the target consumers. To mediate the various constituencies' positions, prior to fielding the focus groups, I tasked the marketing group and the advertising agency with the generation of hypotheses about their brand user characteristics. These hypotheses were sent to me by email. At the midway point in the research day, between the second and third focus groups, I facilitated a discussion among the backroom observers that revisited the original hypotheses and produced new ideas for assessment during the second part of the day. Some of the initial hypotheses were rejected by the group—a discussion process that ensured future consensus—and new hypotheses were generated that everyone agreed merited exploration.

The focus groups incorporated several concepts and techniques from anthropology and psychology. These methods were chosen to help the research team crystallize consumers' identity by accessing and analyzing their physical and sociocultural worlds as well as their attitudes, beliefs, and perceptions.

- Respondents were asked to bring and share photos of their homes, such as the interiors of their refrigerator and food and cleaning supply cabinets, and snapshots of their daily lives. Given that focus groups were the preferred methodology, and this client was intrigued by ethnography but did not want to engage in it fully, I judged—and experienced—this method to be an effective way to bring the respondents' home lives vividly into the focus group sessions.
- Identification by the respondents of people in their lives who they admired. They then explained which personal traits they did and did not share with these role models.
- A binary opposition exercise during which consumers placed themselves on a continuum of opposite traits: extravagant/frugal, manufactured/authentic, rule follower/rule breaker. They first described where they currently saw themselves and then where they aspired to be. My firm has found that a creative binary opposition mode of inquiry, derived from structuralism and the semantic differential in psychology, is a valuable heuristic device.

- A triadic sorting exercise in which three brands of orange juice were exposed in a series of pairs and contrasted with an opposing brand. Respondents were asked to identify commonalities and differences and explain which of the brands best represented them as people. This elicitation-technique, based upon concepts in cognitive anthropology and psychology, provides access to respondents' classification systems and the logic and sentiments behind them.
- Projective storytelling, during which respondents described the traits of an imagined person who drinks a particular juice brand.

The methods and theory adapted for this project from psychological and cognitive anthropology and from personality and social psychology were made explicit to the client, and they enabled the research team to uncover a large array of thought-starters for an advertising creative strategy. Respondents' core values included authenticity and independence. They sought to be personally less conventional, more adventurous, more distinctive in their personal style, more rule-breakers than rule-followers. Their busy, stressful lives frustrated their ability to be their "true" or "better" selves. In a sense, they felt victimized by their culture. The research team used these and other findings to identify strategic advertising options. The strongest ideas for the brand (identified here as "OJ") linked with the research findings about consumers' identities, their worldviews, and their ways of managing their day-to-day lives:

- OJ as a way of accessing one's better self
- OJ as a signifier for simplifying one's life in a complex culture
- OJ as a representation for a less stressful life and for achieving peace and calm
- OJ as "one good thing" that enables consumers to take better care of themselves physically
- OJ as an expression of one's independence and "road less traveled" personal philosophy

During discussions about this study, follow-up focus groups, and quantitative research on category attitudes and usage conducted by my company, the client insight manager and I had numerous conversations about how to interpret and use the findings strategically. On one occasion, she commented that she could hear me "shifting between advertising strategy and anthropology" as we spoke, and she expressed her appreciation for the dual perspective. This process was a way to highlight my own and my firm's value. We not only conducted consumer research; we also led the advertising strategic development process. Ultimately, the insights from this research were stalled in a morass of corporate indecision and politics, and the initiative was not launched. In spite of this (all too common) frustration, the lesson is clear: an anthropologist who is versed in advertising strategy and willing to lead the strategic development process can bring substantial value to a client.

ETHNOGRAPHY & IDEATION

Anthropologists in marketing and advertising can also distinguish themselves and demonstrate strategic leadership as facilitators of group ideation even when they do not literally write strategic documents. These face-to-face meetings, known colloquially as brainstorming sessions, last a half-day to two days, and include marketing and advertising executives. The facilitator structures the meeting and leads the participants through a series of exercises that yield numerous ideas and culminate in selection of the most promising ones by the assembled group. A session might generate ideas for new products, formulate thinking about company innovation, or create alternate brand positionings and advertising strategies. Although group brainstorming as developed by Osborn (1957) has been criticized (see, for example, Feinberg and Nemeth 2008), many companies find ideation sessions to be highly productive. The very "messiness" of these meetings, at which the facilitator elicits ideas in rapid succession, can drive creativity and innovation. In my experience, the combination of research and strategically focused ideation is especially potent (Woodland et al. 2003; also see Morais 2001). Leading these sessions is a means of extending the function of an anthropologist beyond a research role. For example, Context-Based Research Group, led by anthropologist Robbie Blinkoff, offers

> . . . working sessions with clients who want to take the insights to the next step. After our presentation and informal discussion we lead a structured group brainstorm around the findings to identify the top insights that the group feels can lead to the most innovative and/or strategically viable solutions (www.contextresearch.com/context/about/about_process.cfm).

The case that follows illustrates how ethnography was used as a springboard for innovative thinking during an ideation session. The ethnographies were designed expressly to provide inspiration for the sessions. The case demonstrates how an anthropologist can assume a leadership position in a sphere that links closely to business strategy.

A consumer packaged-goods company sought to extend a well-known kitchen and bathroom cleaner to new functions and new forms. Following a client request, and with an understanding of the competitive category and my client's brand equities, I designed and led in-home ethnographies and a subsequent ideation session. The ethnographies were conducted over several days, during which teams composed of researchers and client executives visited homes for three-hour stretches. We observed and video-recorded women cleaning their kitchens and bathroom floors, sinks, walls, tubs, showers, toilets, and vanities. As the women cleaned, they narrated their process, discussing problems, needs, and wishes for better solution, and the team ethnographers probed further, incorporating observational and conversational interviewing techniques from anthropologically informed ethnography. The teams closely observed the respondents' cleaning methods, along with their challenges, frustrations, and successes, and noted where opportunities for brand innovation emerged.

The ethnographies helped the teams identify consumer trouble spots and potential openings for new products, brand functions, and innovative delivery systems. A report on the findings of the ethnographies, including video, was presented and followed immediately by several hours of idea generation. Client executives from marketing, R&D, and design participated in the sessions. Facilitation included a variety of techniques selected to stimulate thinking among the attendees. For example, thought experiments such as *How to, I wish, What if, Best Idea, and Worst Idea* (which was inverted by the group to become a "strong" idea) were assigned and executed. I captured all of the group's ideas on an easel in real time, and then led a prioritization exercise. The ethnographies inspired multiple new products; many more concepts were created during the ideation session. Leadership of both the research and ideation components of the innovation process reinforced my role as a strategic partner to this client.

A WAY FORWARD

Strategy & Its Risks for Professional Relationships

Based upon my experience, the advertising strategic development process occurs in a thicket of business challenges, client directives, management edicts, organizational gamesmanship, personal agendas, and interpersonal tensions, not to mention the emotional highs that follow triumphs and the lows that accompany defeats (see Malefyt and Morais 2012). Moreover, anthropologists engaged in marketing and advertising often have two "masters": brand marketing and insight managers employed by the manufacturer, and executives employed by the advertising agency. They must navigate relationships with both constituencies. Since leaving the advertising industry and joining a marketing research firm, I have been particularly wary of the "turf" of advertising agencies when I am engaged in strategically oriented research projects. I know from my advertising agency experience that agency executives feel compelled to control strategy. More than a few agency executives exhibit a NIH ("not invented here") rejection of a researcher's strategy recommendations, however valid they may be. Even when strategic insights from a researcher are accepted, advertising agencies often find ways to claim ownership of them. My business partner applied the psychological concept of learned helplessness in a research study and generated consumer insights that informed an advertising strategy. The advertising agency embraced my partner's recommendations, but relabeled the analytical framework "resigned complacency" and presented the insights as their own. The agency should have granted my firm—and the established psychological approach—recognition, but I understand their perspective. Clients look to their advertising agencies for strategic insight and leadership, and agency executives often view consultants, including research companies, as threats to both their brand stewardship and their client relationship.

A relationship management issue that speaks to both strategic engagement and broader anthropologist-client interaction is the question of how theory should be discussed when anthropologists engage in marketing and advertising projects. Anthropologists in marketing and advertising often view their projects through a particular methodological or theoretical lens, such as semiotics, ritual, cognition, etc. The case studies presented in this essay were driven less by a singular methodological or theoretical framework than an eclectic approach, incorporating cognitive anthropology and life history analysis, for example, as well as drawing on concepts and methods from psychology. In other studies, I have applied anthropological theory with greater precision (Malefyt and Morais 2012). When anthropological or other theory informs a marketing research analysis, I have found that client pragmatism, understanding, and patience usually requires that its role be implicit rather than explicit (for a similar point of view, see Sunderland 2013:131). For example, if I speak to clients about transformations during breakfast cereal consumption, I may be thinking about liminality, but I do not refer to the term. There are rare clients who appreciate theory, and I am happy to discuss it, but most of my clients prefer hearing about insights rather than the scholarship that inspired them. Although they are attracted to anthropology as a perspective, I risk glazed eyes if my presentations and reports become too academic.

Ultimately, to win acceptance from advertising agency executives, anthropologists must manage the relationship with sensitivity. Insights should be offered rather than declared. Leadership must be demonstrated, not seized. I have learned the hard way that research consultants occupy a place outside the intimate client–advertising agency bond. Assuming a strategic stance too aggressively has resulted in not being invited to work again with a client because the advertising agency resisted my position as a strategic contributor. There is also the possibility that the anthropologist's strategic overture may be summarily rejected. Clients and advertising agency executives may prefer that the anthropologist provide insight and not deviate from a researcher role. In these cases, one can only champion a strategic insight gently or suffer being told to "back off" and never be hired again.

Account Planning as a Behavioral Model

For anthropologists interested in best practices for integrating research with strategy, advertising agency account planning is a valuable model. Account planning (also known as brand planning, brand strategy, and other related terms) emerged during the 1960s in the United Kingdom and gained traction in the United States midway through the 1980s. Advertising agencies realized that an executive role focused on informing and guiding the creative development process by being the expert on consumers would enhance their work strategically and executionally, and cement their relationship with clients. The primary responsibility of the account planner is to initiate, design, and manage consumer research and translate research learning into inspired creative briefs. One of the best descriptions of the role of the account planner and the relationship between advertising research and advertising strategy is in Jon Steel's *Truth, Lies & Advertising* (1998). Other notable resources on advertising account planning include Cooper's *How to Plan Advertising* (1997), Kelley and Jugenheimer's *Advertising Account Planning: A Practical Guide* (2006), Lannon and Baskin's *A Master Class in Brand Planning* (2007), and Weichselbaum's *Readings in Account Planning* (2008). The account planning model is valuable because it makes clear the conceptual connection between research and strategy. It also illustrates a way of working. Account planners use consumer learning to inform strategic blueprints and creative executions. Academic anthropologists who conduct ethnography and embed their findings in anthropological theory are doing much the same thing. Anthropologists in marketing and advertising do this, too. However, in commerce, the next step after a research report, which often includes creative fodder (executional ideas) and strategic implications, is a formal strategic document or, perhaps, an ideation session. Anthropologists who think of these steps as an extension of their research project and remain involved in the strategic process, including the writing of creative briefs, will mirror the account planning model while they work as partners with planners.[6]

Repositioning Anthropologists

For many anthropologists engaged in marketing and advertising, this proposal may lie outside their comfort zone. Intense involvement in the creation of strategies will demand skills and sensibilities they may feel unsuited for professionally and temperamentally. Some anthropologists may not be inclined to venture so deeply into the production of marketing and advertising plans. Their professional identity as researchers may preclude traversing the space between learning and insight generation on the one hand and codification of strategies on the other hand. They may not want to join the contentious intellectual and emotional battles that the crafting of strategic documents often entails.

More intimate and sustained strategic engagement will compel some anthropologists to reposition themselves from researchers to researcher-strategists. It will require, in essence, a reengineering of their professional careers.[7] They will need to summon their interpersonal navigation skills to deal with clients and advertising agency collaborators with agendas that make the process of strategic formulation a highly charged time. Those who embrace a more overt and involved strategic role will find, for the most part, appreciative clients. As one of my clients said, "It's nice to do research, but the goal of the research is to guide us somewhere." To the extent that anthropologists add codification of strategy to their research skill set, they will, I believe, become more valued business partners. Their current clients will be more inclined to rehire them, and new clients will seek their contributions.

REFERENCES

anderson, ken. 2009. "Ethnographic Research: A Key to Strategy." *Harvard Business Review* 87(3)3:24.

Arnould, Eric J., and Linda L. Price. 2006. "Market-Oriented Ethnography Revisited." *Journal of Advertising Research* 46(3)3:251–62.

Arnould, Eric J., and Melanie Wallendorf. 1994. "Market-Oriented Ethnography: Interpretation Building and Marketing Strategy Formulation." *Journal of Marketing Research* 31(4):484–504.

Baba, Marietta. 2006. "Anthropology and Business." In *Encyclopedia of Anthropology,* edited by H. J. Birx, 83–117. Thousand Oaks, CA: Sage Publications.

Bryant, Adam. 2012. "Corner Office: Mike Sheehan." *The New York Times.* Sunday Business. June 3, p. 2.

Cefkin, Melissa, ed. 2009. *Ethnography and the Corporate Encounter: Reflections on Research in and of Corporations.* New York: Berghahn Books.

Cooper, Alan, ed. 1997. *How to Plan Advertising.* 2nd edition. London: Cassell.

Feinberg, Matthew, and Charlan Nemeth. 2008. "The 'Rules' of Brainstorming: An Impediment to Creativity?" *Institute for Research on Labor and Employment: Working Paper* Series. Berkeley: University of California. www.irle.berkeley.edu/workingpapers/167-08.pdf.

Jordan, Ann. 2013. *Business Anthropology.* 2nd edition. Prospect Heights, IL: Waveland Press.

Jordan, Brigitte, ed. 2013. *Advancing Ethnography in Corporate Environments: Challenges and Emerging Opportunities.* Walnut Creek, CA: Left Coast Press.

Kelley, Larry D., and David W. Jugenheimer. 2006. *Advertising Account Planning: A Practical Guide.* Armonk, NY: M. E. Sharpe.

Kotler, Philip, and Gary Armstrong. 2012. *Principles of Marketing,* 14th edition. Boston: Pearson Prentice Hall.

Lannon, Judie, and Merry Baskin, eds. 2007. *A Master Class in Brand Planning: The Timeless Works of Stephen King.* West Sussex, UK: Wiley.

Malefyt, Timothy de Waal, and Brian Moeran, eds. 2003. *Advertising Cultures.* Oxford, UK: Berg.

Malefyt, Timothy de Waal, and Robert J. Morais. 2012. *Advertising and Anthropology: Ethnographic Practice and Cultural Perspectives*. Oxford, UK: Berg.

McCracken, Grant. 2009. *Chief Culture Officer*. New York: Basic Books.

Moeran, Brian, ed. 2010. *Advertising: Critical Readings*. Oxford, UK: Berg.

Morais, Robert J. 2001. "Analytical Ideation: Power Brainstorming." *Brandweek* January 15, p. 22.

______. 2010. *Refocusing Focus Groups: A Practical Guide*. Ithaca, NY: Paramount Market Press.

Morais, Robert J., and Timothy de Waal Malefyt. 2010. "How Anthropologists Can Succeed in Business: Mediating Multiple Worlds of Inquiry." *International Journal of Business Anthropology* 1(1):45–56.

Osborn, Alex F. 1957. *Applied Imagination*. New York: Scribner.

Peters, Tom. 1999. *The Brand You 50: Fifty Ways To Transform Yourself from an "Employee" into a Brand that Shouts Distinction, Commitment, and Passion!* New York: Alfred A. Knopf.

Ries, Al, and Jack Trout. 1981. *Positioning: The Battle for Your Mind*. New York: McGraw-Hill.

Squires, Susan, and Bryan Byrne, eds. 2002. *Creating Breakthrough Ideas: The Collaboration of Anthropologists and Designers in the Product Development Industry*. Westport, CT: Bergin and Garvey.

Steel, Jon. 1998. *Truth, Lies & Advertising: The Art of Account Planning*. New York: John Wiley and Sons, Inc.

Sturges, Keith M. 2013. "Building Consensus in (not so) Hostile Territory: Applying Anthropology to Strategic Planning." *Practicing Anthropology*. 35(1):35–9.

Suchman, Lucy. 2007. "Anthropology as Brand: Reflections on Corporate Anthropology." Paper presented at the Colloquium on Interdisciplinary and Society, Oxford University, United Kingdom, February 24.

Sunderland, Patricia. L. 2013. "The Cry for More Theory." In *Advancing Ethnography in Corporate Environments: Challenges and Emerging Opportunities*, edited by Brigitte Jordan, 122–35. Walnut Creek, CA: Left Coast Press.

Sunderland, Patricia. L., and Rita M. Denny. 2007. *Doing Anthropology in Consumer Research*. Walnut Creek, CA: Left Coast Press.

Tian, Robert, Michael Lillis, and Alfons Van Marrewijk. 2010. *General Business Anthropology*. Toronto: North American Business Press.

Weichselbaum, Hart, ed. 2008. *Readings in Account Planning*. Chicago: Copy Workshop.

Wood, Graeme. 2013. "Anthropology, Inc." *The Atlantic* March:48–56.

Woodland, Cara, Arnold Spector, and Robert Morais. 2003. "Getting More Golden Eggs Without Killing the Goose." *Quirk's Marketing Research Review* December:46–49.

NOTES

The author wishes to acknowledge the valuable suggestions from reviewers of a previous draft of this chapter.

1 See rethink12.thearf.org/pages/ogilvy_awards.

2 See www.jaychiatawards.com.

3 The work on corporate culture by anthropologists notwithstanding, for many business executives, corporate culture is a "you know it when you experience it" phenomenon. For an example of how an advertising agency chief executive officer describes his firm's culture, see Bryant (2012).

4 My company, Weinman Schnee Morais, is a marketing research firm that conducts a wide range of qualitative and quantitative studies (www.wsm-inc.com). Many, but not all, of the projects that I have worked on have been explicitly or implicitly anthropological. Moreover, some studies have entailed ethnography; others have incorporated anthropological and other social and behavioral science approaches in nonethnographic settings, such as focus groups and one-on-one interviews

(Malefyt and Morais 2012; Morais 2010). As I discuss later in this chapter, my approach is eclectic and adapted to both the project and the client.

5 This project was initiated while I was a principal at Weinman Schnee Morais. However, I had worked previously with this client when I was chief strategic officer at advertising agency Carrafiello Diehl & Associates. My history as an advertising executive along with my close relationships with previous advertising agency colleagues perhaps enabled me to engage on the strategic front with greater ease than is typical for marketing researchers.

6 My proposal for more extensive strategic engagement would mean that many anthropologists might increase their fees. There is a risk that some clients will balk at paying anthropologists more. If this occurs, I recommend that the time devoted to strategy be merchandized to the client as "added value," and that fees be increased modestly.

7 The idea of repositioning stems from Ries and Trout (1981). As with all marketing positioning, anthropologists must consider the wants and needs of their target customers; in this case, clients and advertising executives. Also see Peters (1999) for a perspective on personal branding.

31

Nationalism, Identity, & Consumption

SAKARI TAMMINEN, OTTO UTTI, & JOHANNES SUIKKANEN

INTRODUCTION

In our experience, "quick ethnography" deployed for business development purposes often overlooks national symbolic systems and narrative structures as an explanatory factor in consumption[1] preferences. Further, the widely influential postmodern paradigm in social science regards national symbolics and identities based on them as outdated, and instead considers people's identities as "fluid," with individuals periodically choosing and building new identities mainly through globalized forms of consumption (e.g., Bauman 2000). This fluidity is often viewed as a constituent element in the postmodern lifestyle in the wake of the putative death of grand narratives (of which nationhood is one), the *locus classicus* being the works of Bourdieu (1984), Bauman (1992, 2000), and Lyotard (1984). We argue in this chapter that national symbolic systems, and identities based on them, are crucial for understanding consumption. Business anthropologists would therefore do well to operationalize anthropological theories on nationhood and national identity in both consumer research and branding.

Anthropologists theorizing nationalism and globalization now see identity not as a fixed entity attached to a stable nation-state, but as hybrid and increasingly deterritorialized, characterized global flows, for example, of capital, information, aesthetics, and imaginaries (Appadurai 1996; Featherstone 1987; Lyotard 1984). National identity is nonetheless powerful and surprisingly "sticky" for many people: for the past 200 years (Anderson 1983; Gellner 1983; Hobsbawm 1990; Smith 1986, 1999), nations have been naturalized as though they were the most basic political, social, cultural, and—by some accounts—biological categories of human existence. As nations and nationalisms rapidly

Handbook of Anthropology in Business, edited by Rita Denny and Patricia Sunderland, 588–602.

evolve around the world, there is likewise little consensus in the literature theorizing national identity and its relationship to consumer landscapes.

National identity, and especially its relation to brands, consumption, and "the market," has been previously explored from two different viewpoints. The first viewpoint emphasizes brands and their symbolical representation of specific national values. The perspective is most informed by "brand management" needs; thus, the analysis of the case studies often result either in showing how some brands do have a "authentic brand root" mediating or even co-creating the national culture in its historical sense, or pointing to the need to borrow brand authenticity through "localization" or "transnationalization" practices in the cases of multinational brands (Cayla and Eckhardt 2008; Dong and Tian 2009; Pearson 2000; Rubin et al. 2008). The second viewpoint attempts to bring the consumption of national symbols into the heart of consumer culture theory. Here, the analysis concentrates on untangling national myths and their reproduction as part of consumption, be that through fantasy-driven mythological narratives tied to particular locales and their overall offering, anticonsumption movements with nationalist underpinnings, or more mundane, everyday items immersed in national imagery (Belk and Costa 1998; Peñaloza 2001; Thompson and Tian 2008; Varman and Belk 2009).

At the level of language and symbols, nationalism constitutes a field of discourse (Calhoun 1998). It is a realm of innumerable enunciations, diverse institutions, and the semantics that accompany them, all readily at hand for many purposes. National identities have traditionally shared, among other things and with some exceptions, an idea of a distinct homogeneous population (with a particular language and forms of labor), their native territory, and a shared history. But at the level of everyday production and reproduction of "nation" and "nationhood" in all its banality (Billig 1995), nations and their virtues are today increasingly (re)produced in consumption practices and desires. Interestingly, when studying their relations, one soon stumbles on a similarity at the root both of national and of consumer ideologies. Both stress *distinction practices* as their key defining characteristics. For the German father of national ideology, Johan Gottfried von Herder ([1784] 1968), the existence and legitimacy of a particular nation depended on its capacity to actively produce something *unique* (a racial/biological production, linguistic and cultural patterns, history, or an economic or material resource) among the global family of nations. In consumer society, the key is not national but individual distinction practices (social, cultural, and economic) expressed through consumption. The two ideologies thus share the idea of making distinctions, but vary in their scale and differ in their modes of practice.

The two are intertwined so that national becomes both regional and individual as individual actions are conditioned by the pervasive national ideologies, rendering consumption multileveled in theory and practice. For example, global companies often tap into national "brands" and borrow from the discourses of the national identity in their efforts to boost the appeal of their products: "Designed in California," "Made in Germany," "Made in Switzerland." When these markers go beyond the legal requirements for stating the country of origin, they become branding efforts that commodify national virtues.[2] Nations produce distinct forms of labor (e.g., quality, creativity, or assembly), life (populations and their bodily forms), and language (filled with local symbols and narratives), and consumers choose from and consume these in readily available products. Some of the illustrative works on the role of national symbols and narratives in consumer products and their consumption can be found (in addition to the studies listed in this chapter) in the analysis of the North American whiskey Jack Daniel's (Holt 2006), French Camembert cheese (Boisard 2003), and the Peruvian soft drink Inca Cola (Alcalde 2009).

Successful positioning and branding of products can, and often does, draw on national narratives and imagery for creating recognizable—and indeed desirable—goods. The creative act of positioning brands brings to mind what Hobsbawm and Ranger (1983) describe as the techniques by which national traditions are innovated. According to them, novel pasts are created as "a set of practices, normally governed by overtly or tacitly accepted rules and of a ritual or symbolic nature, which seek to inculcate certain values and norms of behaviour by repetition, which automatically implies continuity with the past" (Hobsbawm and Ranger 1983:1). However, while national narratives are invented, they do not remain stable over time; instead, they tend to be reinvented as the surrounding symbols and practices of that nation change too. In this, national symbolic systems (including language, public advertising images, architecture, and music) can be either revitalized or rendered useless, depending on how well the creative team can tap into the historically changing trajectories of national symbolic systems.

This chapter looks into how the production of national identities today is engaged in interplay with the consumption-identity landscape in Finland. The reason for introducing Finland as an example for the powerful force of national ideology is that Finnish consumer culture has developed very recently and quickly compared with that of many other Western nations. This has resulted in a consumer-culture landscape that has as its backdrop a historical nationalism still alive and present in the consumer culture, one that has advanced apace to a postmodernism that produces and reproduces the individual and her desires in two paradoxical but not irreconcilable national narratives: the nationalist and postnationalist. Thus, the identification of national symbolic systems is among the keys for understanding brand and consumer spaces (e.g., generational, physical, and digital) and, hence, for performing successful business anthropology (including brand positioning) not only in Finland but also around the world. Regardless of the global, transnational flows that some social theorists see as a hallmark of the so-called postmodern age (Lash et al. 1997), it is virtually impossible for any individual to be "un-national" in the cultures of today.

CONFIGURING THE NATIONAL CONSUMER: FINNISH PARTICULARITIES

> No one is anyone, and some aren't even that.
>
> —Old Finnish proverb

"Consumer culture" is young by any standard in Finland. If consumer culture in the Western world emerged as a collection of practices that create and display individual identities through consumption after World War II (Edwards 2000), in Finland the birth of such cultural forms dates from only the early 1980s, the years after the heyday of the Soviet Union. That sequence of events made it possible for Finland to detach itself from the arms of the "Sleeping Bear" to the east and identify itself with the West and its political order. The crystallization of this de- and re-politicization occurred when Finland joined the European Union and European Monetary Union and further with adoption of the euro. This also meant the rapid reorganization of the national cultural form and made possible the full-blown consumerization of the culture at both the collective and individual levels.

Thus, the same developments that guided the Western consumer culture in general over the course of the postwar twentieth century—globalization, deregulation of financial and consumer markets, and mass migration toward post-industrial cities—took place within an interesting cultural context in Finland, its roots in traumatic wars both won and lost. Today, Finland is a country most worried about its competitiveness in the global market with its international brand visibility. The nation advertises itself globally as the true home of both Santa Claus and the most advanced technology companies, ranging from players in heavy industry to suppliers of mobile Internet technologies providing pure virtual consumption.

Despite this quick development, consumer culture in Finland is still steeped in ubiquitous and very powerful narratives of national identity devised to steer the cultural and political creation of a homogeneous, egalitarian, and politically progressive postwar Finnish identity. The old proverb quoted in this section illustrates this point nicely. For a long time, no individual distinctions within the national population were expected; neither were they culturally tolerated. A Finnish homogeneity of culture is thus anchored in the readily available folklore and ideograms, all directed to serve a national narrative of independent nationhood and its homogeneous population.

The most prevalent way of expressing the national ideal of internal homogeneity and the key characteristics of this national population is associated with two key dimensions of Finnish culture: the land and the people as expressed in war stories. First, the territory of Finland is large (the sixth largest in Europe) yet hosts only 5.4 million inhabitants, and is surrounded by a thousand lakes and forests (about 86 percent of the land is covered by forest). Second, the national story is still retold through Finland's successful war efforts against its eastern neighbor, Russia. War stories are central to Finnish national identity because they encapsulate two central aspects of Finnish nationhood: defense of the pure and pristine "natural" territory and the definition of its people as clever, tough, and resilient.

Here, two wars are relevant: the "Winter War" against Russia in 1939 and 1940, and the "Continuation War" from 1941 to 1944. These two wars led to the emergence of superior Finnish figures: men as cunning, resilient soldiers and women as both a hardworking national backbone and volunteer paramilitary figures directly supporting the army. Accordingly, battles in these wars were seen as won through superiority born of cunningness, joint effort between the two genders, and a particularly Finnish notion of resilience that evokes the old Finnish virtue of *sisu*, which, in the absence of an easy translation, can be said roughly to refer to a strength of will, determination, perseverance, and "guts."

It was these "natural characteristics" that made survival in the cold, snowy winters possible. These undergirded the military tactics resembling guerrilla warfare that crushed the Russian enemy. The Finnish population and its natural territory, the heavily forested land of a thousand lakes, maintained its independence against the Russian invaders. The legends growing out of these bloody wars, in which Finland was vastly outnumbered by the Russians yet won against all odds, still live on among the most powerful cultural undercurrents influencing consumption and branding two generations later.

In our work for Finnish clients during the past year, we have seen how the mythological murmurs echoing from the wars against Russia still dominate branding efforts, whether clearly obvious or not. When the national myths are used overtly, the rationale behind their use is market share and the general appeal of the brand in mass markets. Since Finland's population is small, tapping into the mythologies often seems the best choice for framing communication about consumer products. For others, this ubiquitous cultural undercurrent influences branding and positioning from so-called fast-moving consumer goods (FMCGs) to mobile games offered by Finnish companies locally and globally.

While the mythological narrative of war, national characteristics, and the people and the land surrounding them are not necessarily negative branding assets, the powerful cultural undertow it creates makes it hard for companies to seek out other desirable branding positions. Finnish companies readily fall back to the historical narratives in their branding when seeking the maximum resonance of their products with the home market. For consumers, this means that choosing from a limited repertoire of brands for cultural consumption leaves very few options for individual choices outside the historical narrative, thus creating a self-reinforcing cycle of mythological reproduction whether the consumers themselves desire it or not. This is especially true when national symbolic systems and narratives are not understood as dynamic and changing over time, with products as a particular form of media in themselves that operate along the historical trajectory of national identity.

Let us turn to our first example illustrating how this national narrative steers the cultural logic of branding and consumption in Finland today. It shows the branding efforts across business and industry boundaries in both business-to-business and business-to-consumer marketing.

Consider the Finnish spirits market and its overarching branding ideals. Finns have a reputation of being good drinkers, and to some extent this is true (see, for example, Pyörälä 1995). In terms of volume, Finns are the top alcohol consumers in the Nordic region, consuming the equivalent of slightly more than 10 liters of pure alcohol per adult per year. Relative to the rest of Europe, Finland's annual consumption is in the top of the mid-range band. Average consumption has more than doubled in 30 years for a number of structural and cultural reasons (among them are declining costs of alcohol as a consequence of taxation policies, the ready availability of alcohol due to the introduction of mild alcohol to food stores in the late 1980s, and general commodification of alcohol consumption as cultural practice). At the same time, spirit consumption accounts for about 25 percent of all alcoholic-beverage consumption in Finland, making spirits a large-volume business (Official Statistics of Finland 2012).

When we view branding from an anthropological perspective, the communication of the top-selling Finnish spirits clearly is taking a cue from nationalistic ideals (see Figure 31.1). The brands communicate and reproduce the mythologies of the Finnish wars of independence, the mental makeup of "Finnish people" by displaying the ideal *sisu* character, natural landscape (forests), and—if the consumer still is unsure of the brand's identity—the national flag. There is, of course, another anthropological insight behind the symbols used: your body becomes what it consumes; in this case, that national culture and its virtues. Finnish spirits are the brands that reproduce both the nation and the ideal national consumer, in both their symbolic and bodily senses.

Figure 31.1. Branding the nation. Among the top-selling Finnish-brand liquors are, from left to right, Finlandia, Vodka of Finland; Suomi Viina ("Finnish Spirit") alongside the national flag; and Sisu Viina ("Sisu Spirit"), resonating with the ideal of the natural willpower of the Finns and dubbed the "Dry Vodka of Finland," together with the official emblem of Finland (a lion with a sword). The branding involves all of the key national elements: the nationalistic naming, visual identity built around national flags and emblems, the warring lion, and the easily identifiable Finnish landscape imagery, with the forest a key element in the national economy and national pride.

Very little deviation from this branding strategy is seen in the vodka category, or in many other FMCG categories for that matter.[3] In attempts to reach the widest possible audience, this branding strategy assumes both that everyone shares the national ideals and that consumers desire these ideals. This, of course, is not true, rendering the nationalistic branding strategies effective only with part of the Finnish market.

THE EMERGENCE OF GLOBAL & POSTNATIONAL CONSUMER BRANDS

If the grand narrative of Finnish consumer culture is still closely tied to war stories and Finnish concepts of the ideal person, this narrative has been increasingly abandoned in favor of other narratives. The new national narratives are more in tune with the globally operating individual consumer and the surrounding consumption culture. However, in addition to "uprooted" global brands and the resulting figure of the global consumer, another brand and consumer configuration has emerged at the border between the old national brands and newer, multinational ones. This is what we call postnational consumerism. These brands and their consumers are not tied to an independent and isolated Finnish culture; instead, the goal is to tap into the "global" in a new way, one in which the symbols of "rooted" nationhood and the "uprooted" global are reconfigured. This is a reconfiguration of the national identity as a relational cultural achievement, in which the core set of national semantics is articulated against global symbolic systems of fashion, aesthetics, and new media.

Consider, for example, the Finland-based start-up company Unmonday,[4] which produces high-tech design wireless speakers and takes a global perspective in its marketing. The company has an interesting branding strategy: they invert the key symbol of the country, the Finnish forests. While in the historical national imagery forests were something to be protected (especially against the Russians), they are now repopulated with music and fashionably designed speakers (see Figure 31.2). The high-tech speaker brand reappropriates the forest and "unleashes" the sound to flow freely in the (imaginary) Finnish landscape. Forests become populated with one of the key symbols of the new, postnational consumption objects: music and high-tech speakers made in Finland. The appeal of unusual, and revitalized, Finnish national imagery of this sort ("the Finnish brand") was tested both nationally and globally when the company raised money in fall 2012. It succeeded in attracting project backers from Finland and all around the world, with more than US$1 million as a seed fund from both individual consumers and investors. The company is now beginning mass production of its speakers.

Accordingly, a completely new mode of production and consumption of the commodified nationhood has emerged in the past few years, one in which distinctions are produced concurrently through rearranged national symbols and individual identities. This can be seen in the marketplace by focusing on how new companies produce their brands and younger generations respond to these refashioned national symbolic systems. Some consumer products do not communicate the old Finnish myths about war and independence in their historical forms. Instead, they mix the historical narratives with the ideals of urbanization, digitalization, and internationalism at the heart of this northern country. The shift in symbolism visible through the analysis of brands resonates interestingly with a recent national survey about the various generations' experiences in Finland. The survey illustrates how Finnish consumers, depending

Figure 31.2. The inverted national ideal of forests in Unmonday's imagery (unmonday.com).

Table 31.1. National survey results on key generational experiences in Finland (Torsti 2012).

Year of Birth	Key Generational Experiences Related to Finland	Age and Population Size in 2012
1945–1958	• Kekkonen (the strong unifying president after war) • Finland in WWII • The Cold War • Collapse of the Soviet Union	54–67 years 1,160,672 people 28.3% of the population
1959–1974	• Accession to the EU • Death of Kekkonen • End of the Cold War	38–53 years 1,040,677 people 25.4% of the population
1975–1984	• Accession to the EU • Rapid development of IT and media technologies • Collapse of the Soviet Union	28–37 years 685,340 people 16.7% of the population
1985–1994	• Rapid development of IT and media technologies • Terrorism	18–27 years 659,864 people 16.1% of the population

on their age, share very different key national experiences, complete with a cutoff point pinpointed at the emergence of the consumer society around the 1980s (see Table 31.1). This generation-linked change is, of course, not a very new idea in anthropological literature focusing on the rapid spread of consumer culture around the globe, which attests to the same development worldwide (e.g., Davies 2005).

One interesting element in all of this is the way the younger generation is moving away from the all-encompassing war mythologies, while the older generations still may find the national war myths resonating with their experiences. This means that the Finnish population is polarized in the way people see their place as Finns in the world. If we return to the spirit-positioning strategies, it is easy to see now why the same old national narrative of the land, the national character, and the independence gained through war against the Russians is perhaps not the best way to position the product if both old and new generations are targeted: young Finnish people do not consider "Finland" to be an isolated, independent country. Instead, they locate it relationally as part of the globalized world, mediated through political development and the power of information technologies.

Thus, we see that the usual branding strategy now seems to resonate differently with different age groups; one might wish to target the groups with different messages and, perhaps, with two different products. Yet, while a superficial look at the younger generations might indicate that nothing in these older narratives resonates with them, this is not the case. A closer look reveals that, even if younger people are global consumers, the national narratives are still very powerful for them, but take on new, more nuanced forms, blending with a more global outlook (e.g., supranational languages of fashion and categories of taste). This is a case of global hybridization: while the structure of the new national experiences has been reorganized, the key elements of the national symbolic system are still at play here.

Therefore, we suggest, an alternative branding strategy is available. The illustrative case of Unmonday and its branded speakers is one example of this. But one could equally consider the worldwide hit game Angry Birds, produced by Rovio Entertainment Ltd. The game has been touted as one of the great global successes and the crown jewel of Finnish entrepreneurship in the aftermath of the rapid decline of mobile phone manufacturer Nokia. The game, in its various versions, has occupied the top spot in 67 countries across mobile platform boundaries and is still, three years after its initial launch, one of the most downloaded and top-grossing games globally.

The game involves birds whose eggs have been stolen by the bad piggies. Armed only with a slingshot and launching birds at pigs, the player tries to destroy the pigs and recapture the stolen eggs (Figure 31.3). The game is designed in an almost childish and comical style, yet something very familiar to the Finnish national narrative about the Winter War is found in its official description: "The survival of the Angry Birds is at stake! [. . .] Use logic, skill, and brute force to crush the enemy."

The war rhetoric, of course, is universal in its promotion of victory by destroying the enemy, but the key here is to take a closer look at how the destruction should take place. When this branding slogan is situated within the Finnish context, the message very clearly resonates with the historical narrative. Logic, skill, and sometimes brute force are exactly the tactics Finns used in wars against Russia, the big "other" for the Finnish culture and a narrative source for a great many popular book series and films in Finland, which also had international resonance.[5] At the same time, Angry Birds has become a sign of "new Finnishness," even to the extent that the wife of the company executive producing the game wore an Angry Birds ball gown at the most prestigious state event, the Independence Day Dinner at the presidential palace in 2011, thus breaking the formal dress code by advertising the brand at the event (see Watson 2011).

Figure 31.3. A screenshot of the Angry Birds description page on Rovio Ltd.'s website illustrates how pictorial and textual narratives play together in weaving together the figure of "cunning warrior": a character attribute that saves Angry Birds from Bad Piggies. It is also a narrative trope that mirrors the national survival story of Finland, one that depends heavily on the cunning character of Finnish soldiers.

We claim that the cross-cutting Finnish mythology of war is successfully reappropriated here and at play also in the current marketing of Angry Birds, although now as a virtual consumption object. The symbolic reconstruction of the Finnish warrior is achieved through the birds and their superior fighting skills.

The two illustrative cases of revitalization of the key symbols and narratives of Finnish nationhood show how branding in the postnational consumer era can still draw its power from the national imagery. This creative repositioning work, however, needs to play with the symbolic orders of the national and global consumer cultures if it is to be successful in its efforts (see Table 31.2). Studying national historical symbolic systems and narratives might just do the trick in many situations, for we still live in a world where nations are one of the most important sources for collective and *individual* identities.

Table 31.2. A tentative map of the relationships among national, global, and postnational consumption styles in Finland.

Consumption Styles	Both Collective, National Distinction…	…and Individual, Consumer-Based Distinction
Old Generations: National Consumption	Desire for historically driven symbolic distinction from the family of nations • Grand narratives • Historical continuity • Bounded spatial territory and its landscape symbols • Limited set of characteristics of the population	*Recognized but not desired in their uprooted form of global culture*
New Generations: Global Consumption	*Recognized but not desired in their historical forms*	Drive toward global consumption without national roots • Fragmented narratives fit for the selected style and aesthetics of subcultures • Immediate availability • Relational, digitally mediated landscapes • Unlimited, virtual characteristics of the individual
Hybridized Styles of Consuming Nationhood: Postnational Consumption	Commodified and updated national symbols reappropriated by the language of the global production/consumption • The semantics: creative reappropriation of the national core set of narrative mythical elements (e.g., the cunning player, the musical forests) • The syntax: relational identities that are not only tied to the national collective narratives, but play with the global syntax of fashion, aesthetics, and subcultures (fashion photography of the forests, virtual war spaces)	

BUSINESS ANTHROPOLOGY & THE CASE OF CONSUMABLE NATIONHOODS

In this chapter, we have argued that, despite the global marketing of consumer products and the transnational branding efforts that accompany them, and despite fluidity of consumer identities, national identities still play a big role both for companies and for consumers, be this by branding or through other means of (re)packaging and communicating national narratives. This is certainly true in Finland, our experience shows, but we claim also that it is generalizable to other parts of the world.

Though Finland's consumer culture is quite new and renders the country a somewhat special case in the Western world, the prevalence of national identities means that, particularly for business anthropologists worldwide, the value of understanding the specific national narratives/mythologies and their interplay with consumer culture should not be underestimated or overlooked.

National identities remain one of the "stickiest" political, social, and cultural categories of human invention. By exploring the interplay between national identities and consumer culture, we illustrated how the historical Finnish national narratives/mythologies continue to be powerful and desirable objects of symbolic consumption, especially for the older generations. For the younger, more globally oriented generations, the national narratives/mythologies are no less important; they just take a postnational form in both company brands and reconfigured styles of consumption: a hybrid form wherein national symbols are reappropriated, inverted, or mangled through an ironic attitude.

All of this points to the importance of the national factor in consumer anthropology. Everywhere in the world, researchers must carefully analyze how respondents enact the national culture: how does nationhood translate into consumption, and how does it materialize in the objects desired? Unless nationhood and its dynamic, hybrid components are understood through careful historical and ethnographic analysis, consumer research will fail to capture essential frames for consumption.

REFERENCES

Alcalde, M. Cristina. 2009. "Between Incas and Indians: Inca Kola and the Construction of a Peruvian-Global Modernity." *Journal of Consumer Culture* 9:31–54.

Anderson, Benedict. 1983. *Imagined Communities: Reflections on the Origin and Spread of Nationalism*. London and New York: Verso.

Appadurai, Arjun. 1996. *Modernity at Large: Cultural Dimensions of Modernity*. Minneapolis: University of Minnesota Press.

Bauman, Zygmunt. 1992. *Intimations of Postmodernity*. London, New York: Routledge.

______. 2000. *Liquid Modernity*. Cambridge, UK: Polity Press.

Belk, Russell, and Janeen Costa. 1998. "The Mountain Man Myth: A Contemporary Consuming Fantasy." *Journal of Consumer Research* 25(3):218–40.

Billig, Michael. 1995. *Banal Nationalism*. London: Sage.

Boisard, Pierre. 2003. *Camembert: A National Myth*. Berkeley: University of California Press.

Bourdieu, Pierre. 1984. *Distinction*. Boston: Harvard University Press.

Calhoun, Craig. 1998. *Nationalism*. Minneapolis: University of Minnesota Press.

Cayla, Julien, and Giana Eckhardt. 2008. "Asian Brands and the Shaping of a Transnational Imagined Community." *Journal of Consumer Research* 35:216–30.

Davies, Deborah. 2005. "Urban Consumer Culture." *The China Quarterly* 183(3):677–94.

Dong, Lily, and Kelly Tian. 2009. "Chinese National Identity." *Journal of Consumer Research* 36:504–23.

Edwards, Tim. 2000. *Contradictions of Consumption*. Buckingham, UK: Open University Press.

Featherstone, Mike. 1987. *Consumer Culture and Postmodernism*. London: Sage.

Gellner, Ernest. 1983. *Nations and Nationalism*. Ithaca, NY: Cornell University Press.

Graeber, David. 2011. *Debt: The First 5,000 Years*. Brooklyn, NY: Melville House.

Hobsbawm, Eric. 1990. *Nations and Nationalism since 1780: Programme, Myth, Reality*. Cambridge, UK: Cambridge University Press.

Hobsbawm, Eric, and Terence Ranger. 1983. *The Invention of Tradition*. Cambridge, UK: Cambridge University Press.

Holt, Douglas B. 2006. "Jack Daniel's America: Iconic Brands as Ideological Parasites and Proselytizers." *Journal of Consumer Culture* 6:355–77.

Lash, Scott, Roland Robertson, and Mike Featherstone, eds. 1997. *Global Modernities*. London: Sage.

Lyotard, Jean-Francois. 1984. *The Post-Modern Condition: A Report on Knowledge*. Minneapolis: University of Minnesota Press.

Pearson, David. 2000. "Editorial. The Local, National and Global Communities: Identifying with One or All." *Brand Management* 8:5–10.

Peñaloza, Lisa. 2001. "Consuming the American West: Animating Cultural Meaning and Memory at a Stock Show and Rodeo." *Journal of Consumer Research* 28:369–98.

Pyörälä, Eeva. 1995. "Comparing Drinking Cultures: Finnish and Spanish Drinking Stories in Interviews with Young Adults." *Acta Sociologica* 28(3):217–19.

Official Statistics of Finland (OSF). 2012. "Alcoholic Beverage Consumption" [e-publication]. Helsinki: National Institute for Health and Welfare (THL). http://www.stat.fi/til/ajkul/index_en.htm (accessed January 31, 2013).

Rubin, James, Majken Schultz, and Mary Jo Hatch. 2008. "Coming to America: Can Nordic Brand Values Engage American Stakeholders?" *Brand Management* 16:30–39.

Smith, Anthony D. 1986. *The Ethnic Origins of Nations*. Oxford, UK: Blackwell Publishers.

_____. 1999. *Myths and Memories of the Nation*. Oxford, UK: Oxford University Press.

Thompson, Craig, and Kelly Tian. 2008. "Reconstructing the South: How Commercial Myths Compete for Identity Value through the Ideological Shaping of Popular Memories and Countermemories." *Journal of Consumer Research* 34:595–613.

Torsti, Pilvi. 2012. *Suomalaiset ja historia* (*Finns and History*). Helsinki: Gaudeamus.

Varman, Rohit, and Russell Belk. 2009. "Nationalism and Ideology in an Anticonsumption Movement." *Journal of Consumer Research* 36:686–700.

von Herder, Johann Gottfried. (1789) 1968. *Reflections on the Philosophy of the History of Mankind*. Chicago, IL: University of Chicago Press.

Watson, Leon. 2011. "Wife of Rovio Boss Turns Up to the Palace Wearing an Angry Birds Dress." *Daily Mail* December 8. http://www.dailymail.co.uk/news/article-2071128/Wife-Rovio-boss-turns-palace-wearing-Angry-Birds-dress.html.

NOTES

1 By "consumption," we mean buying and selling things, including services and activities that are paid for. Some anthropologists, among them Graeber (2011), worry that the term is fraught and theoretically suspect, but in this chapter it is used in the everyday sense of things bought and sold.

2 While legislation plays a part in the origin statements of a given product, companies regularly use the nation's brand in their marketing efforts. For example, in the United States, non-US products are required by law to state their country of origin. In the European Union, similar law requires non-EU products to state their origins. However, products are not required to state their specific national origins within any EU country; the label "Produced in the EU" is sufficient. Still, many products within EU markets feature a label of their national origins for branding purposes (e.g., "Made in Germany," "Made in France," "Made in Sweden," or "Made in Finland").

3 Some examples from other categories: the best-known Finnish chocolate brand uses the national flag's blue as the symbol of the national nature and independence (see www.fazer.com/Brands/Karl-Fazer/Karl-Fazer/); Raisio, producer of the country's most popular breakfast flakes, uses a Finnish blonde farmer's daughter as its all-around mascot or brand character (see www.raisio.com/www/page/ElovenaFrontpage); and the country's biggest dairy company, Valio, advertises its products as "coming from Finland, the cleanest country in the world" (see http://ammattilaiset.valio.fi/portal/page/portal/ammattilaiset).

4 See http://www.unmonday.com.

5 Examples include the 1940 Pulitzer-winning Broadway play *There Shall be No Night*, the 2007 novel *The Burnt-out Town of Miracles*, and the 2012 HBO production *Hemingway and Gelhorn*, staring Nicole Kidman. See these and also other popular culture examples at http://en.wikipedia.org/wiki/Winter_War_in_popular_culture.

32

Rethinking Russian History & Identity Through Consumer Culture

LYUBAVA SHATOKHINA

Utro krasit yarkim svetom
Morning paints red
Steni drevnego Kremlya.
The walls of ancient Kremlin.
Prosipaetsya s rassvetom
With a sunrise awakes
Vsya sovetskaya zemlya.
The whole Soviet land.
Pust' v koshelkakh u nas ne gusto,
May our purses be not full,
No khlebom slavitcya moya zemlya.
But our land is known for bread.
Edim salat s morskoi kapustoi,
We eat a salad with laminaria,
Ved' v magazinakh netu ni(...)chego!
As there is (a bloody) nothing in our shops!

("Mama Russia" song by the popular Russian girls' band Kombinatcia, 1991)

After the collapse of the Soviet Union, Russia found itself thrown into a global market economy without anchor or life jacket. The country faced a dilemma: whether to import a foreign economic model or produce its own unique version. Despite the lack of roots and traditions of a market economy and all the

Handbook of Anthropology in Business, edited by Rita Denny and Patricia Sunderland, 603–618.

political, economic, and cultural challenges and contradictions of this transformation, Russia adapted relatively easily to the new logic of consumption (Jackson 2004) with its abundance of goods and services. Yet, ironically, although from the outside Russia's economic model and ways of consumption have come to resemble those of other capitalist countries, after two decades, Russia is still a country in transition. Important issues of national identity and the representation of the history of Russia and the Soviet Union remain unresolved. National identity crises within the country and among the countries of the former Soviet Union continue.

One of the new and troublesome issues that emerged after the collapse of the Soviet Union was connected to the nation-building projects of the Russian Federation and its newly sovereign neighboring states. When the USSR existed, ethnic belonging and cultural and linguistic differences were muted; after the collapse of the Soviet Union, the newly independent states increasingly played their nationalist cards. Instead of creating new sorts of identities that could cement together these rather segmented entities, these new states reestablished and reinvented national boundaries. For those citizens of the former Soviet Union who were used to a completely different notion of identity based on the rhetoric of class solidarity and the construction of communism, the reemergence and reinvention of national and ethnic differences was paradoxical and problematic.[1]

In Russia, citizens were pushed and encouraged by politicians, businessmen, and cultural elites to recompose new "us" and "them" identities.[2] The points of reference for new identities proclaimed in official discourse and the mass media sometimes contradicted people's everyday life experiences. The long-held uneasiness of the questions "Who do we belong to?" and "What does it mean to be Russian?" that were muted during the Soviet period by the grand narrative of the project of building communism was unleashed and used for different sorts of manipulation. The rhetoric and ideas of "national" and "foreign," "local" and "global," "ally" and "enemy" were used as well to make sense of the new world of market exuberance.

I have observed that tensions over national identity, history, and marketization have entered into consumer culture and found expression in product marketing and design. Although there is no single, clear-cut, and well-determined consumer culture in Russia, in this chapter I illuminate some prevailing themes that are grounded in the specifics of the country's economic, social, and cultural development. There are strategies, tactics, and practices of consumption that, whether inherited from the past or strategically constructed in response to the present, are culturally and historically specific and national in character (de Certeau 1984). Thus, in Russia, market research and the ethnography of consumption deal not only with questions of consumption, marketing, and design, but also with a wide variety of practices, symbols, and artifacts that reflect some of the main unresolved questions of post-Soviet Russian identity.

This chapter examines Russia's contemporary consumer culture through a set of snapshots—narratives and analytical semiotic sketches—that refract and serve as footings for understanding current practices, discourses, and artifacts of consumption. As with the concept of "culture" in general, Russia's very complex, entangled, and contested cultural system cannot be grasped in its entirety or represented as a seamless whole. Yet, despite the tensions between anthropology's critiques of bounded notions of "culture" and the concrete and practical needs of an applied research model, I still believe that there is room for anthropologists to maneuver. The examples I discuss speak not only of particular cases, but also of the larger picture. I suggest that consumption practices not only provide a lens for illuminating tensions in traditions and transition, but that consumption has become a stage for the engagement and contestation of identity.

These sketches are, of course, drawn from my own position as an insider and a bearer of the culture under investigation. As a graduate of a sociology department, I was recruited to provide cross-cultural translation for two consulting agencies doing research in Russia: one based in Finland and one in the United States. The whole idea behind having me on a team was to have a person who could be a cultural "native" by right of birth and a cultural "mediator" by right of professional training. Being "native" means one has the ability to understand things by being in people's shoes and to use culturally bound intuitions that make any member of a particular society an expert in the culture in which he or she was socialized. The Achilles' heel in the perspective of an "insider" lies in the inability to have enough distance to avoid seeing things simply as "a matter of course" or "going without saying." The lack of distance also can lead an observer to see small details well, but fail to grasp the larger picture. In my work, I was lucky enough to have colleagues, partners, and friends among scholars who were not native Russians and who not only shared with me their own perspective on things, but also taught me how to approach the subject from the standpoints of different cultures, disciplines, and schools of thought. Also, my current graduate training in anthropology has given me additional tools to view everyday life practices and narratives of my own society from both an insider and outsider perspective.

NARRATING THE PARADOXES OF RUSSIAN CONSUMER CULTURE

Even today, at the level of everyday life and routine, many Russians continue to feel that things are in constant flux. In reaction to this experience of instability, they make desperate efforts to create and connect to a grand narrative that will provide a sense of shared identity and point of reference. This tendency of creation, re-creation, and revitalization of grand narratives could be illustrated by ethnic belonging and religious revival trends in Russia that took shape after the collapse of the Soviet Union. This also could be seen in the variety of everyday interpretations of Russian history, from time immemorial to recent developments one can witness in different types of conversations in varied social settings (waiting for the bus, at the doctor, in a shop, at parties). When I was working as a shop assistant in a bookstore, there were people each day who would ask whether we had books about "this murderer" or "this villain," and these terms could refer to very different people: Peter the Great, Rasputin, Stalin, or El'tsin (Boris Yeltsin).

Moreover, it was not only new types of official discourses and grand narratives that confounded post-Soviet citizens and complicated the development of identities in the postsocialist landscape, but also new social and economic realities that ushered in novel practices, logics, and tactics of everyday life (Ries 2009). The abrupt shift from deficit to abundance, from stability to uncertainty, from equality to disparity were factors driving people to remodel their behavior in response to new social, economic, and cultural standards.

Nevertheless, the shift was not absolute and total. Despite the drastic rupture of the Soviet collapse, there is still a certain dependency on Soviet practices and narratives that hold legitimacy for many Russians (Shevchenko 2002). Even people whom I interviewed who, like me, lack real-life experience and vivid memories of the Soviet past, would, from time to time, claim that the way things are today is a result of the way they used to be during the Soviet period. Surprisingly, when explaining their contemporary conditions and behaviors, people tend to point to persistent legacies from Soviet times. The atmosphere of mistrust toward authorities and the perception of the "system" (including bureaucrats, officials, and institutions) as inefficient and unreliable—characteristic beliefs of Soviet citizens—have continued into the current era. As a result, people continue to rely on the old, familiar, trust-based networks; self-sufficient lifestyle practices; and alternative means of dealing with authorities and institutions (including bribery, nepotism, and avoidance) that they used in the Soviet era.[3]

The multifaceted shifts inside the country, global and local development, and generational change also provided a setting and the conditions for the assemblage of a mode of consumption that connects both new practices and rhetoric with inertia that goes back to the Soviet period. Moreover, Russia is a country that is far from homogeneous. There is much diversity among the different regions of the country and among the populations inside these regions. Moscow and, somewhat less prominently, St. Petersburg, are often seen as points of reference for market and consumer trends. It is in these cities that most consumer research takes place. However, Russians are quick to point out that "Moscow is not Russia," and that St. Petersburg has always been known for doing things "its own way." That is why the issues I discuss in this chapter are mainly applicable for the cases of St. Petersburg and Moscow, and could not be absolutely relevant for the rest of Russia's regions.

Good Old Times

> They need to talk about good times in Soviet history in order to have something to be proud of (*Nado govorit o horoshih vremenakh Sovetskoi istorii, kotorimi mozhno gorditcja*).
>
> —Male focus group participant from Moscow

Of all the different stories and interpretations of Russian history I heard while doing consumer research in Russia, there was one particular narrative that struck me with its ubiquity and popularity across very different groups and contexts. In trying to connect their present consumer experience to a particularly favorable and emotionally intense moment from the country's history, people often spoke about the first man in space, Uri Gagarin (Figure 32.1). This was in contrast to subjects such as the Russian revolution, World War II, or the collapse of the Soviet Union, which different people discussed and interpreted in different ways and which often carried a certain level of discomfort. When these historical subjects were raised in focus groups, people were often hesitant and resistant to discuss them in concrete or critical ways. Often they would say, "Oh, let's not touch upon this topic" ("*oi, nu davaite ne budem*"). Even speaking within the context of their homes, research participants were reluctant to take any definite position on the issue of Russian history. Only the figure of Uri Gagarin was an absolutely uncontroversial, and positive part of "our history." Even in pop culture one of the most popular retro-style ("good old days") songs is "Gagarin, I Loved You . . ." ("*Gagarin, ya vas lyubila . . .*") by the pop band Underwood, inspired by the famous eponymous documentary released in 1991 by Valentina Rudenko.

Gagarin was probably a safe and uncontested historical figure because he embodies a resolution of some of the major contradictions of modern Russian history. First, Gagarin represents Russia (the Soviet Union at that time) as a superpower without the connotation of aggressor. Second, he speaks to the idea that the Russian people are talented, hardworking, and determined. The implication here is that the country's current poor economic and social conditions are not the result of a lack of moral power, creativity, or knowledge, but rather a matter of historical circumstance. In fact, Gagarin and his flight into space symbolize the peak of Russia's development and triumph, which are direct counters to the notion that the communist revolution, with all its social

Figure 32.1. Uri Gagarin souvenirs. Nevsky Prospect, St. Petersburg, Russia. Photo by Lyubava Shatokhina.

experiments, diverted Russia from main path of civilized development. Thus, Gagarin personifies the greatness of the nation, while avoiding the bitter taste of revolutionary backwardness, Stalinist atrocities, and the ugliness of the present.

The Paradox of the Soviet

> Soviet is good and bad at the same time (*Sovetskoe odnovremenno I khorosho, i plokho*).
>
> —(Male focus group participant from Nizhny Novgorod

Although attitudes towards the Soviet past are ambivalent and contested, there are pervasive narratives connected with consumer behavior that imbue the socialist era with some positive aspects. As Nancy Ries (1997) observed, Russian people are particular experts in the genre of lamentation. Parallel to a distinct inclination to overdramatize and complain and to depict personal situations in dark colors, Russians have a set of narratives that exhibit tendencies of idealization and embellishment, especially in their reminiscences about the "lost paradise" and the "golden age" of the Soviet era, often idealized in bucolic ways. As articulated by Russian consumers, contemporary depictions of Soviet consumption practices have two paradoxical motifs. One is of an unbearable condition of deficit. At the same time, the tendency for many of these narrators is, over time, to speak less about the deficiencies of the socialist economy and more about its positive sides. As one young man from St. Petersburg said during a focus group discussion, "Sovdepia[4] is attractive but not that popular. In 10 years it is going to be very popular" ("*Sovdepia privlekatelna no ne populyarna. No cherez decyat let budet ochen populyarna*"). Even many young people who barely remember the Soviet past are likely to talk about the high level of state control over production in a positive way, noting the guaranteed quality of goods.

Russian producers have exploited this nostalgia for and revision of the socialist system to create positive brand images.[5] For example, some ice-cream manufacturers played on these feelings of trustworthiness, high standards, and attachment to a "golden age" (be it of the Soviet Empire or of personal childhood) by naming their products "USSR" (*SSSR*), "Back in the Old Days" (*Kak Ran'she*), and "48 Kopek,"[6] for example. Many companies use the "Soviet brand" less overtly, instead simply mimicking the simplistic design of Soviet goods or putting the GOST label (the Soviet sign for state quality control)[7] on their goods. While talking during a focus group about one particular brand whose history dates back to the Soviet era, one Muscovite in his 50s explained that "this is a famous brand, predictable quality, a habit that was driven into us, the USSR is good, everything was according to GOST" ("*Eto izvestni brand, predzkazyevoe kachestvo, privichka kotoruyu v nas ee zabili, SSSR—khotosho, vse bilo po GOSTu*"). The very sentence as a unit is paradoxical by mixing the highly negative phrase "was driven into us" (*zabili v nas*), which has a certain character of enforcement and pressure from above, with the general positive attitude toward the socialist past itself and the quality of goods associated with it. This type of contradiction is an almost inevitable and persistent feature of people's narratives about the Soviet Union in contemporary Russia.

NATION BUILDING VIEWED FROM THE MARKET SHELF

After the collapse of the Soviet Union, "the disappearance of the idea of Soviet cultural homogeneity was replaced by an emphasis on the Russian national heritage" (Baiburin et al. 2012:6) in Russia and in the Newly Independent States. The motto of people's unity under state socialism was transformed by the free market into values of diversity, authenticity, and the pursuit of individuality. At the level of branding, advertising campaigns, and consumption decision-making narratives and practices, such rhetoric, symbols, and ideas were also becoming more and more visible. These contemporary ideologies started to appear as sets of images, stereotypes, and narratives introduced and articulated through the design of products and in ad campaigns. Consumer goods were packaged and wrapped in the ideologies that were in the air, sometimes counterintuitively. Neringa Klumbyte discusses a striking example of such a counterintuitive market strategy in an article about a situation following Lithonia's declaration of independence from the Soviet Union (2010). In spite of the official rhetoric of the state's policy stigmatizing the Soviet era "as a time of colonization, oppression, suffering, annihilation, and economic and cultural backwardness" (Klumbyte 2010:23), a brand of "Soviet" sausages appeared to have great market success in Lithonia. Nevertheless, the major trend following the emergence of new nation states after the collapse of the Soviet Union was in emphasizing the ethnic, cultural, and historical specificity of goods and consumption styles. For example, beer branding and marketing campaigns in Georgia were openly built on announcing the idea of "our beer" that was "grounded in ethnographic images of Georgianess" (Manning and Uplisashvili 2007:632). Many more illustrations of the creation, reinvention, implementation, and popularization of goods labeled and marketed as "ours," as well as the invention of "local" practices and "indigenous" traditions, can be found in Russia and former USSR countries.

Marketing strategies based on identities, lifestyles, and values have a very specific interest in cultural codes of belonging. For producers, a very important part of business strategy is to understand or to construct, to make it clear or to persuade consumers that there is a readable distinction between "us" and "them," and that this distinction should be preserved and even heightened via their goods' branding and marketing. In the case of Russia, where the concept of lifestyle is not yet that strong compared with countries with long-established traditions of capitalism and individualism, and where the existence of grand narrative identities is still problematic, a producer who manages to create a brand that is able to empower or revitalize belonging finds a gold mine. Discourses are currently based partly on the concepts of ethnic belonging (cultural heritage ideas), imperial rhetoric, and old songs about the division between East and West.[8]

A/Olenka, Post-Soviet Identities on Candy Wrappers

As national identity started to play an increasingly important role in people's attempts to legitimize their identities and affiliate themselves with larger groups, it also became more prominent in the presentation of consumer goods. As Robert L. Craig explains, "By connecting the ideology of consumerism with ethnicity, advertising becomes a discourse about ethnicity" (Craig 1991:34). In Russia, advertisers and marketers began to deal not only with issues of class belonging and lifestyle preferences, but also with ethnic boundaries and so-called cultural differences. Marketers and producers of goods came to play a role in helping people find their own ways of belonging and making choices in the new consumer culture, and the market became increasingly a site for the production and reproduction of ethnic stereotypes, icons, and categories.

A well-known and iconic chocolate bar called "Alenka," which was a familiar brand in the Soviet era, exemplifies the creation of ethnic belonging and distinction via consumer goods. The wrapper of this chocolate brand catches the eye by depicting a cute little girl with a cherubic face, big blue eyes, blond hair, and Russian-style kerchief on her head (Figure 32.2). The familiar visual representation of "Russianness," along with the Soviet-era simplicity of the wrapper's design, make this chocolate bar a favorite souvenir for tourists travelling to Russia.[9] At the same time, Ukraine, thanks to its Soviet past, also has its own version of the Alenka chocolate bar, manufactured by a local producer. However, the Ukrainian "Alenka" is spelled with an "O"—"Olenka"—and the cute little girl on its wrapper has dark brown eyes, dark brown hair, a slightly different style of kerchief (the distinctive *vishivanka*, a traditional ornamented shirt) and a prominent "authentic" red-bead necklace. The play with national symbols on both wrappers is rather straight and obvious, but what are more interesting are the visual representations of national character embodied in the images of two girls. While the Russian Alenka is depicted in a visual code that could be interpreted as representing her as a highly spiritualized fragile creature longing for protection and love (the mother of my Norwegian friend told me, after consuming the chocolate, she wants to keep the wrapper because the girl on it is "so cute and fragile"), the Ukrainian Olenka is vivid and full of joy. With her smile and her eyes looking not directly out but in a flirtatious manner, she is open for play and companionship. She gives a sense of motion rather than a static iconography. The Ukrainian Olenka—a southern girl full of passion—and the Russian Alenka—northern and spiritual—are both bound together by a Soviet-style background. The brand's name and history are particularly straightforward examples of what the postsocialist nation-building project looks like.

After learning of the two ethnic faces of the A/Olenka chocolate bar, I happened to discover a Belorussian variant with a similar brand name and iconic image. Despite having a slightly different name—"Lyubimaya Alenka" ("beloved Alenka")—and variations in design, the Belorussian version of the chocolate wrapper still has a lot of striking similarities to the Russian and Ukrainian versions, and even more striking differences. Though there is the same idea of a stereotyped "Slavic-looking" girl (blue eyes, blond hair, pale skin) with her head in a kerchief that is set on a simplistic (read: Soviet) background, the creators of the Belorussian image seemingly were not as much into the "ethnic" image as their Russian and Ukrainian colleagues. In fact, Lyubamaya Alenka is a sexy young lady with extremely long lashes and plump, half-opened scarlet

Figure 32.2. Russian, Ukrainian, and Belorussian chocolate wrapper designs. Photo by Lyubava Shatokhina.

lips. Her kerchief (red, spotted with white), hair, and makeup resemble much more a retro-style pin-up than an ethnically grounded image. Her sexy look is somehow balanced by large eyes, covered hair, and a hint of naivete, so that the general iconic message could not be read as openly aggressive.

If one looks closer to the general message sent by chocolate bar producers, one can try to read between the lines or, in this case, between the images. First of all, the existence of the Soviet brand's successors suggests that Soviet legacies are still resonant semiotic tropes. By using simplistic "socialist" designs and familiar brand names, marketers seem to be keeping a common past and shared modes of consumption in play, including ideas about Soviet quality of goods. What deserves more focused attention in this case, however, are the differences. While Russian and Ukrainian producers emphasized the distinctly "ethnic" specificity of their product's image, their Belorussian colleagues seem to be inspired by a different mythology, namely Soviet nostalgia rather than ethnic revival. Thus the dividing lines between "us" and "them" could be different depending on what one wants to emphasize: ethnic belonging or political/historical affiliations.

"It Belongs to Us!" (*"On nash!"*)

National identity on the consumer market is not always as obvious and visible as in the Russian and Ukrainian chocolate bars, especially when it concerns relations with former Soviet republics. Here, the boundary between "us" and "them," between Russia and other countries, is situational and contextual, rather than settled and clear-cut. The fact of having a period of shared history alternately interpreted by some as peaceful coexistence and by some as invasion and oppression makes the process of defining "us" and "them" problematic. While politicians might use notions of "allies" and "enemies," and businessmen refer to "partners" and "competitors," people in their day-to-day lives operate with the rather confusing labels of "our" and "foreign," drawing imaginary borders that have real consequences in defining the boundaries between groups, between "us" and "them." In a context such as the one in contemporary Russia, where official discourse does not provide people with answers about how to make this division or gives answers that are confusing and contradictory, citizens start to come up with their own tactics of explaining the differences and boundaries between "us" and "them."

While conducting research on Armenian cognac in Russia in 2011, my colleague and I realized how entangled and contingent the borderline between "us" and "them" was. During focus group discussions and in-home interviews we found persistent ambivalence. Although everyone knew that Armenia was no longer a part of Russia, they continued to refer it as "ours." The strong affiliation with Armenia is illustrated in the straightforward response of a female focus group participant from St. Petersburg, who noted that "Armenia is a part of our country" ("*Armenia chast' nashei strani*"). This affiliation is seen, as well, in acknowledgments of a shared culture, past, and religion (Christianity). The degree of "otherness" was expressly dependent on the context of comparison. When dealing with the differences between Russian cognac and Armenian cognac, the latter was seen as familiar, but foreign. When discussing Armenian cognac versus French cognac, the former was seen as 100 percent "ours": that is, Russian.

Not only were these distinctions situational, but the very rhetoric of the two comparisons was absolutely different. When speaking about the difference between the Russian and Armenian products, respondents were mostly concerned with the past and with notions of "Soviet products as having high quality control" ("*Sovetskie producti visokogo kachestva*") (male focus group, Moscow); it made little difference whether the product was Russian or Armenian. When comparing French and Armenian cognacs, however, the tension in the room went off the scale, and people started throwing around such phrases as, "Russians do not give a shit about French quality!" ("*Russkim nasrat' na frantsuskoe kachestvo!*") or "Why French quality? We have our own! . . . We do not need the world's recognition!" ("*Pochemu frantsuskoe kachestvo? U nas ect' nashe cobstvennoe! . . . Nam ne nuzhno nikakoe mirovoe priznanie!*") (male focus group, St. Petersburg). In fact, "world recognition" was very much important for all the participants interviewed. As in all groups, the most common and cherished story was about Winston Churchill's preference for Armenian cognac over others. This very mercurial and contextual nature of understanding boundaries between "us" and "them" is without a doubt connected to both the Russian imperial past and "transitional" present. Of course, this kind of hierarchy or intensification of identities, actualized differently and for different reasons in different contexts, is not just a hallmark of the contemporary Russian consumer culture. This clearly illustrates Frederic Barth's (1969) claim that identities are defined at the borders: they are contextual, situational, and emerging in a concrete dialog.

"Khorosho tam gde nas net" ("The Grass Is Always Greener on the Other Side"), or Why Finnish Always Means "Better"

While distinctions between the countries of the former Soviet Union and Russia are problematic when talking about post-Soviet Eastern Europe, comparisons with the West and Asia give Russian people a sharper contrast to their own identity. The answer to the endless debates Russians have had for centuries[10] about whether "we" belong to the East or the West, to Europe or Asia, lies in actions rather than words.

This is illustrated particularly well in the curious tendency of residents of St. Petersburg to prefer Finnish goods to Russian goods, and, even more strikingly, to travel to Finland to buy Finnish or other "Western" goods, rather than buying them in Russia. St. Petersburg residents often joke about the behavior of Russian consumers abroad. These types of narratives, however, are, in fact, often not simply jokes. For example, many people often talk about the "legendary" quality of the Finnish dish soap, Fairy (Figure 32.3), which, in comparison to the same product produced in Russia, washes better, lasts longer, and costs less. While many people spoke ironically and sarcastically about Russians' practices of buying detergents in Finland, they had themselves often bought this "legendary" dish soap, at least once. In response to my straightforward question of "why," people tended to give me the same straightforward answer: "because it is Finnish."

To decode this answer, one should know that in the minds of these consumers, Finland is a symbol of the West, which itself is a symbol that rhymes with civilization, progress, high standards of living and quality, trust in relations towards authorities, stability, and tradition. To buy Finnish means to buy into a Western culture crystallized into an idealized picture of the "good life." Though territorially very close to Russia, Finland is nonetheless seen to be an "Other" world where everything (including consumer goods) is different and better.

But what does this "other" say about "us," then? First of all, it suggests that Russians are not satisfied with the goods they have here. Second, it says that

Russians are eager to adopt some aspects of Western culture, at least when it comes to consumption. Third, as some people have even started small private businesses buying products in Finland and reselling them in Russia, it tells us that Russians are streetwise enough to make a profit out of the perception of Russian consumer goods' "backwardness" and the disillusion and distrust for the country's current quality standards. Yet, while the high quality of Finnish goods is presumably undoubted by Russian consumers, the Finnish lifestyle is not that attractive to Russians. There is a consistent idea that weaves through talk about Finland: that it is too boring, too predictable, too monotonous. There is a clear lack of excitement about Finland as a possible tourist or immigration destination among Russians, something I heard while conducting research on travel to Finland. This point raises some more paradoxes of Russian-ness. While longing for stability and predictability, many Russians still feel excitement about the unpredictability and challenges of life. While believing that the Finnish Fairy soap is better, Russians still rely on their own bad Russian dish soap to give them something to fight for and a reason to tell stories about how they suffer for improvement while complaining that things will never get better. So for all their admiration and respect for the West, Russians still need "our own" way of being.

These attitudes toward Finland and its consumer goods reflect a general perspective on the meanings of and distinctions between culture and civilization in Russia (Patico 2005). In this respect, the notion of "culture" could be seen as opposing the notion of "civilization," which could be traced to the ideas of German Romanticism. While culture in this reading is presented as immaterial, spiritual, and idealist, civilization is material, objectified, and pragmatic. Sensing that their own country lacks "civilization"—defined in terms of high living standards, quality material goods, and advanced and sophisticated consumer traditions—Russians compensate for this by drawing on the concept of culture, which is understood as embodying spiritual values

Figure 32.3. "Legendary" Fairy Finnish detergent in a St. Petersburg kitchen. Photo by Lyubava Shatokhina.

Figure 32.4. The many faces of "traditional" Russian doll souvenirs featuring Obama, Medvedev, Putin, Lenin, and Stalin in a row (bottom right). Vyborg, Russia. Photo by Lyubava Shatokhina.

and morality, as well as interpersonal relations, which are perceived as stronger compared with the "formal and heartless" West. To bridge the gap between spiritual values and material well-being, a theme that is so often depicted in Russian classic literature,[11] there is the notion of "*kul'turnost*" (Kelly and Volkov 1998), a concept that embraces both being a decent person and a life of comfortable indulgence. The idea of *kul'turnost* is thus very promising for producers seeking a category that will solve one of the multiple paradoxes of Russian culture.

This chapter thus suggests that to understand Russian identities as they play out in consumer culture, one should look both at the present-day practices and meanings of consumption while keeping in mind history and the influence of deeply held traditions. Here I would agree with Norwegian anthropologist Finn Sivert Niel'sen (2004), who described the late Soviet culture as a culture of "limbo," a liminal position that lacks clear-cut structure and puts people in a constant struggle to set rules and roles, and at the same time denies and fights these determined rules and roles. In a way, Russian people still live in a world of highly entangled and unpredictable settings that are manifested in Russian culture through paradoxical behavior and contradictory narratives both in the private and public spheres. At the same time, Russians' struggles for identity and over the meanings of "Russian-ness" have become even more complex and ambivalent over the course of recent decades of drastic political and cultural change (Figure 32.4). Decoding the "mysterious Russian spirit" is not a matter of finding one core identity or explanation. Rather, it requires seeing how multiple identities play themselves out in the constant flux of consumer reasoning, argumentations, actions, and decision-making practices. Here, the project of demystification is not particularly appropriate, as "mystification" itself is a very important part of "being Russian." When we conducted interviews with Russians and presented ourselves as an international research team or scholars who work for a foreign client, people were always a bit skeptical about the outcomes of this encounter. Explicitly or implicitly, they let us know that "you will never understand," or that there are things that strangers ("others") will never grasp, be they political, historical, or cultural. We Russians got used to the idea of being very special—not like others—and we have ambivalent feelings of simultaneous guilt and pride about this. At the same time, it is not impossible to address questions of Russian identity, as the answer always shows itself through mundane actions and interactions, narratives, and discourses.

REFERENCES

Baiburin, Albert, together with Kelly Catriona and Vakhtin Nikolay. 2012. *Russian Cultural Anthropology After the Collapse of Communism.* London: Routledge.

Barth, Federic. 1969. *Ethnic Groups and Boundaries.* Boston: Little, Brown.

Boym, Svetlana. 2001. *The Future of Nostalgia.* New York: Basic Books.

Craig, L. Robert. 1991. "Designing Ethnicity: The Ideology of Images." *Design Issues* 7(2):34–42.

de Certeau, Michel. 1984. *The Practices of Everyday Life.* Berkeley: University of California Press.

Duncan, J. S. Robert. 2005. "Contemporary Russian Identity between East and West." *The Historical Journal* 48(1):277–94.

Jackson, Peter. 2004. "Local Cultures in a Globalizing World." *Transactions of the Institute of British Geographers (New Series)* 29(2):165–78.

Kelly, Catriona, and Vladimir Volkov. 1998. "Directed Desires: *Kul'turnost* and Consumption." In *Constructing Russian Culture in the Age of Revolution, 1881–1940*, edited by Catriona Kelly and David Shepherd, 291–313. New York: Oxford University Press.

Klumbyte, Neringa, 2010. "The Soviet Sausage Renaissance." *American Anthropologist* 112(1):22–37.

Ledeneva, Alena. 1998. *Russia's Economy of Favours:* Blat, *Networking and Informal Exchange.* London: Cambridge University Press.

Manning, Paul, and Ann Uplisashvili. 2007. "'Our Beer': Ethnographic Brands in Postsocialist Georgia." *American Anthropologist* 109(4):626–41.

Niel'sen, Finn Sivert. 2004. *Glaz Buri.* St. Petersburg, Russia: Aleteya.

Patico, Jenifer. 2005. "To Be Happy in a Mercedes: Tropes of Value and Ambivalent Vision of Marketization." *American Ethnologies* 32(3):479–96.

Ries, Nancy. 1997. *Russian Talk: Culture and Conversation during Perestroika.* Ithaca, NY: Cornell University Press.

_____. 2009. "POTATO ONTOLOGY: Surviving Postsocialism in Russia." *Cultural Anthropology* 24(2):181–212.

Rivkin-Fish, Michele. 2009. "Tracing Landscapes of the Past in Class Subjectivity: Practices of Memory and Distinction in Marketizing Russia." *American Ethnologist* 36(1):79–95.

Shevchenko, Olga. 2002. "'Between the Holes': Emerging Identities and Hybrid Patterns of Consumption in Post-Socialist Russia." *Europe-Asia Studies* 54(6):841–66.

NOTES

1 The ideas and policy considering the "national question" and ethnic belonging articulated as a part of state ideology differed greatly, especially at the early stage of Soviet rule. Nevertheless, the overarching idea that eventually took an upper hand in these debates was in favor of internationalist logic that downplayed the role of national and ethnic particularism.

2 Be it local versus foreign producer, "authentic" Russian culture ("tradition") versus West or East, Orthodox religion versus Muslim religion, these efforts were made to set borders to strengthen the imagined entity inside the proclaimed boundaries.

3 An illustrative example of this kind of alternative means of dealing with authorities and institutions in Russia is the phenomenon of blat (Ledeneva 1998).

4 *Sovdepia* is an unofficial pejorative term of the Soviet regime and lifestyle that carries connotation of low living standards and ignorance.

5 And of course, not only producers, but also political and cultural elites contributed to the promotion of "restorative nostalgia" (Boym 2001).

6 Forty-eight kopeks was the price for ice cream in the Soviet Union. Many people still see Soviet ice cream as inexpensive, tasty, and made without any chemical and "artificial" ingredients.

7 The GOST (an acronym for *gosudarstvenny standart* [state standard]) label was used in the Soviet Union as the sign of state quality control. Today, this certification continues to represent security and stability, although it has been undermined by mistrust towards the modern Russian government.

8 For more on these belonging strategies in modern Russian politics, see Duncan (2005).

9 At least some of my friends from abroad were extremely fascinated with this chocolate design, and were sure that it will make a unique and telling present from Russia.

10 The most articulated and representative discussion took place in the nineteenth century between so-called *"Zapadniki"* (Pro-Western) and *"Slavyanophils"* (Pro-Slavic) groups in the context of the nation-state building project, although it was discussed before that and continues to play a big role in current debates on politics and culture in Russia.

11 Russians do like to use classic literature examples to explain some modern realities and to legitimate their own moral and behavioral preferences. See Rivkin-Fish (2009).

33

Brand Fortitude in Moments of Consumption

NINA DIAMOND, MARY ANN MCGRATH, JOHN F. SHERRY, JR., ROBERT V. KOZINETS, ALBERT M. MUNIZ, JR., & STEFANIA BORGHINI

Home is a symbolic environment that helps create, maintain, and express personal and social identities. McCracken's (1989) work on "homeyness" illustrates how and by what cultural logic the symbolic properties of homes act on individuals. It also demonstrates how these properties give definition to the family unit and help the individual household member "mediate his or her relationship with the larger world, refusing some of its influences, and transforming still others" (McCracken 1989:179). The notion of home space shaping perceptions and organizing experiences, behaviors, and identities is also reflected in the work of Claiborne and Ozanne (1990), Cuba and Hummon (1993), Sherry (2000), and Thrift (1997). Of central concern in all of this work are the boundaries across which we are allowed to pass material and symbolic resources. Implicit in the selection of these resources and their disposition are the ways in which the family conceptualizes itself as a social unit and views the world outside the home. Material resources brought into the home are often laden with meaning produced by commercial agents and extended via public discourse, but they also accrete significance derived from the private discourses and rituals of the household. The objects themselves may or may not leave the home; however, the meanings attached to many of them will ultimately re-enter the public sphere. These meanings will wield influence—of greater or lesser magnitude—on the world outside, and substantiate status claims of the household and its members.

Most work on how objects are withdrawn from the public sphere and incorporated into the routines and rituals of daily life within a household describes how they are assigned personal and social meanings and are thereby stripped of

Handbook of Anthropology in Business, edited by Rita Denny and Patricia Sunderland, 619–637.

commodity status. Silverstone's (1994) "proto-model" of the consumption process represents a particularly detailed and theoretically significant articulation of this phenomenon in which we ground our own contribution. Silverstone describes six "moments" in a "cycle of consumption." The first three moments, "Commodification," "Imagination," and "Appropriation," relate to components of the consumption process that have been amply addressed in the academic literature. The latter three, however, pertain to aspects of consumption that are underrepresented in the literature and, we believe, are less well understood. These are "Objectification," "Incorporation," and "Conversion." Objectification relies on the classificatory schemata that serve to organize a household's understanding of itself and its place in the outside world. According to Silverstone, "objectification is expressed in usage, but also in the physical disposition of objects within the spatial environment of the home" (1994:127) and the construction of microenvironments intended to contain meaning-laden objects.

Incorporation has to do with the role an object comes to play within the "moral economy" of the household; how it serves to express values and distinctions that are meaningful within family culture. Incorporation also describes when, how, and in what relational contexts objects are used by household members, and the roles these objects play within the routines and rituals of daily life. Conversion resembles appropriation (acquisition/purchase) in that it too defines the relationship between the inner world of the family and the organizations and institutions of society at large. It is through conversion that material and symbolic resources that have been subjected to transformational work by the household gain currency in the world outside and come to represent a form of cultural capital for use by household members.

Silverstone's conception is rooted in Kopytoff's (1986) model of consumption as a process in which objects appropriated by household members from the public sphere move into and out of a commoditized state rather than suffering irreversible loss of commodity status by becoming singularized. Appadurai underscores this processual nature, depicting a commodity as "not one kind of thing rather than another, but one phase in the life of some things" (1986:17). Kopytoff (1986) reminds us that at the moment of commercial exchange all things are commodities; to be saleable is to be common, not singular. However, every commodity embodies the possibility of being drawn into the flow of social relations and thereby becoming singular, unique, and inalienable by acquiring personalized meanings. The cultural categories within which singularized objects will reside are determined by the communities toward whose unique ends they are being put to use. Kopytoff believes that the relevance and utility of these categories may ebb and flow, and their boundaries may expand and contract with changes in the social milieu; however, the entry of objects into these categories constitutes their removal, however temporary, from the commoditized realm. We contend, however, that there is another possibility.

We propose that branded objects idiosyncratically classified by the members of a particular household may concurrently occupy a place within the brand (commodity) category from which they originated. While theoretical work by Kopytoff (1986) and Silverstone (1994), and empirical work by Epp and Price (2010) demonstrates that the same object may have commodity status during one phase of its social history and exist as a singularity during another, none of these authors addresses the role of brands. More importantly, implicit in their work is the assumption that while a singularized object may be recommodified once it leaves the home (see, for example, Hermann [1997] and Lastovicka and Fernandez [2005]), it cannot at once be singularity and commodity. Our study of the American Girl brand led us to question that assumption and to explore the possibility that objects can at the same moment manifest the defining characteristics of commodities and of singularities by virtue of a property of the brands they represent.

Our analysis revealed patterns of consumer sentiment and practice that not only further energized the American Girl brand beyond its retail setting, but also imbricated it in an emplacement process of homebuilding. We describe the property that allowed the brand to resist dilution of its essence and gradually assume greater influence within the household as *brand fortitude*. Through objects bearing its name, the brand becomes both an affecting presence (Armstrong 1974) that consumers use to build life-worlds and a repository of the energy generated in that building. *Brand fortitude* is a more nuanced and sociological construct than brand attachment and, although the two share a similar hedonic, ideological, and functional charge (Park et al. 2008), the materiality of the object experience is far more central to fortitude.

THE AMERICAN GIRL BRAND AT HOME

The American Girl brand was conceived and executed by entrepreneur Pleasant Roland in 1984 (Morris 2003; Sloane 2002). By the time it was purchased by Mattel in 2005 for more than $700 million, the popular brand had morphed into a phenomenon with almost unprecedented appeal to preteen girls and female family members. The brand originated with a small set of doll characters and a series of books about their heroic exploits in various historical contexts. The American Girl books' storylines eschew the action-adventure formulae typical of boys' fiction (Cassell and Jenkins 1998), instead presenting universally relevant social and moral dilemmas typical of girls' literature. Each girl/doll is introduced in a historical keystone volume, and her adventures are chronicled in a dedicated but thematic series that emphasizes generosity, resourcefulness, resiliency, and resolve deployed against the exigencies of girlhood during one or another historical era. These stories represent common currency among girl-owners and their families, and constitute a wellspring of premises for shared play.

Over time, American Girl significantly expanded with the addition of more dolls and books as well as an extensive array of clothing, accoutrements, and accessories. Dolls, stories, accoutrements, and accessories had also become familiar to girls from a variety of backgrounds and social strata. We followed this "stuff" of American Girl retailing into homes, using traditional ethnographic techniques to explore American Girl consumers' contextualized understandings of the brand.[1]

American Girl products are integrated into the lives of households and their individual members in a manner similar to that described by Wallendorf and Arnould (1991) and Coupland (2005) for commercially prepared foods that were personalized by the surreptitious disposal of packaging and the addition of special ingredients or the substitution of unbranded and uniquely meaningful packaging for the manufacturer-created variety. Yet unlike the branded food products referenced by these authors, which become generic and stripped of brand meaning as they are integrated into the home, American Girl products seem not only to retain their branded character over time, but also to brand the homes and hearts of their owners. Rather than being stripped away, the marketer-authored meanings remain, coexisting with those created by members of the household.

In what follows, we parse our findings across Silverstone's (1994) last three moments of consumption: objectification, incorporation, and conversion. We present our themes in the form of illustrative ethnographic vignettes, each of which imparts the flavor of brand interactions and the ways in which the American Girl brand both changes (via powerful marketer-created meanings) and is changed by (via meaning-creation activities of the family and its members) the household culture. Rather than being diminished by its tenure in the home, the brand derives strength and dimensionality from its existence beyond the retail setting, its structure reinforced by the incorporation of personal and family meanings. Our description of consumers' interactions with American Girl products illustrates the ways in which brand fortitude manifests itself within the inner sancta of informants' lives.

Silverstone's Fourth Moment: Objectification

Our informants' attitudes toward American Girl dolls, books, accoutrements, and accessories are charged with a sense of responsibility similar to that evidenced by Lois Roget, McCracken's (1988) "curatorial consumer." Like Ms. Roget, the girls seem "bound by familial duty to store, display, and conserve these objects" (McCracken 1988:44). They do so in such a way as to maintain the marketer-created meanings of the brand, while at the same time imbuing the branded objects with individual and family significance. It is apparent that material components of the American Girl brand serve as containers for family memories, even as they continue to embody commercially derived meanings.

Brand & doll recapitulate family ethnohistory

Lisa is a six-year-old girl who lives with her family in a large complex of garden apartments on Chicago's South Side. Lisa shares the apartment with her mother, father, and younger brother. Her grandmother lives next door.

Lisa tells us that Addy, the Civil War–era African-American doll, was given to her by her grandmother, who purchased the doll before Lisa was born and presented it to her when she was "old enough to appreciate it." Her grandmother was attracted to the brand because its focus on history and heroic femininity would help Lisa understand her heritage. What Lisa knows of the period immediately preceding the Civil War has been gleaned from the Addy books her grandmother reads to her and from the stories her grandmother tells. In one of her grandmother's stories, according to Lisa, the children of slaves were made to pick flowers and, if there were worms on the flowers, the children were forced to eat them. She demonstrates how she had helped her doll, Addy, "cough up the worms" by holding her upside down and smacking her hard on the back.

Heroic femininity is a leitmotif of many of the tales in the American Girl brand universe. As a result, such themes loom large in many of the meanings girls ascribe to the dolls. The brand also provides a template for harnessing the child's personal creativity. Dolls often serve as objects of contemplation for children, as well as objects on which they are encouraged to act. We see the influence of this contemplative aspect of the American Girl dolls and their ethnohistory at work in the home of six-year-old Lisa. Such resonant connections were not uncommon among our informants. The African-American escaped slave girl, Addy, is Lisa's only doll. If she were to get another, she says it would probably be Kaya, the Native American American Girl doll, because Lisa herself is part "Indian." Her grandmother has mentioned the possibility of buying the Kaya doll to help Lisa understand that component of her heritage, just as she purchased Addy and told Lisa stories about slavery to reify the African-American aspect of her identity.

A collection in its entirety represents something distinct from its individual parts, to which the collector may also be attached (Belk 1995; Belk et al. 1991). In the same way, we see American Girl products being singularized by girls and their families, even as household members maintain a relationship with the brand and all it stands for. McCracken (1988) pointed out that an object may become irreplaceable via everyday possession rituals that both extract meaning from and give meaning to it. Similarly, a brand like American Girl may both draw from and contribute to meanings residing within a household as an extensive collection of objects bearing its name are used, maintained, stored, displayed, and discussed by household members. The brand retains its potency, even as the products bearing its name are reclassified into categories whose significance derives from the emotionally charged agendas of individuals and family members.

The Addy and Kaya dolls may be viewed as members of a class of objects subsumed under the American Girl brand name. The brand is conceived by Lisa's grandmother and mother as a vehicle for connecting Lisa to her family's racial and ethnic identity and history; it represents something distinct from the dolls, just as the curator's relationship with her collection in its entirety may be distinct from her relationship with the objects that comprise it. History is at the core of the American Girl brand, and the brand's historical character enhances its utility—and that of each of the dolls—to the adult members of Lisa's family. While the marketer-created stories about individual doll characters and their historical contexts are elaborate and detailed, the brand structure they represent is a loose one that is permeable to material authored by the household community. As we will see, this permeability is a key aspect of one of two important structural characteristics of the brand.

Brand & store pervade home

Three sisters aged 7, 10, and 12 share a spacious upscale residence with their parents. Within a communal play area, the double doors of a closet open to reveal a cornucopic, yet meticulously organized, collection of American Girl dolls, clothes, furnishings, and various miniatures. The interior of a large closet was arranged in such a way that it resembled an elaborate retail display. The middle daughter Maeve, age 10, had initiated the organization:

> In February, we had to take [lower] shelves out so they have room for their beds. There were shelves [in this closet] and the beds didn't fit. First we set it up in our rooms. We kept getting things for, like, our birthdays and things and we didn't have enough room. And so we, um, thought it would be an idea to put it here, so we took some shelves out of that area 'cause the posts are a little too tall. And we named that [pointing to an upper shelf] the party room."

Similar rationales were provided for the arrangement of accessories for other doll characters; individual drawers were assigned to hold clothes belonging to each doll, and the shelves mirrored elements of the historical dioramas and merchandise displays of the store. One shelf held desks, books, and accessories for school; another, the accretions of Native American culture and religion; and a third held skates, skis, a bowling ball, and other sports equipment. We posit that the apparent mimicry of merchandising strategy derives from the potent brand flagship store experience; this experience seems to have facilitated the emplacement of the brand and the translation of retail brand ideology (Borghini et al. 2009) from store to home. Commercially derived brand narratives are enacted at home through display as well as play. These tendencies are not uncommon, and they exist in contradistinction to those manifested by Wallendorf and Arnould's (1991) and Coupland's (2005) informants.

Brand transcends time & space

Rebecca ("Becca"), age 11, lives in a modest home in a Chicago suburb. Becca feels that the original American Girl dolls are special because of their stories. She sees each doll character as "somebody we can look up to," and has found inspiration in all of the American Girl stories. She tells us that the tales are of girls managing through hard times ("Kit and her family lived through the Depression"), standing up for their principles, or surviving the loss of a loved one ("Samantha's parents had died"). All of the characters were nonetheless "able to lead happy lives." To Becca the stories also represent "pieces of history" from which she has learned about the "times" in which the doll characters lived.

Although she continues to read and reflect on the stories about her American Girl dolls, Kit and Samantha, Becca admits that she has more interest now in the narratives she herself composes and enacts. In one of her invented stories, Kit and Samantha are in college and share the single set of American Girl "school things" she owns. Other dolls are recruited to join the class, which Becca teaches. When her friend Tammy visits with her American Girl doll, Molly, the girls often cast the three doll characters in the role of adopted daughters. Becca says, "We pretend that we found them on the street and we took them in. . . . It's very good to care for people." The narratives are new, but the values and priorities that undergird them are those pervading the marketer-created narratives in the books. Becca relates: "We usually make up our own stories, me and her, like they're usually our daughters, and we have various jobs. So like sometimes we're artists, and then they like judge our paintings and help us. . . . It's like on and on and on, we're cooks and they test our food."

The dolls are subjects: they are taken in and nurtured, and attend the school at which Becca teaches. But the dolls are also objects that subjectify Becca and Tammy: they are judges of the girls' heroic artistic and culinary efforts. The scenarios act as portals for the girls to try on different identities, to manifest imaginary selves through a physical context. In this sense, the brand is redefined through play; the storied meanings of the physical dolls become multistoried through personalizing practices enabled by aspects of what might be conceived as the brand architecture, namely the permeability of its surface and the availability of interstitial space among its components. As the American Girl brand is integrated into the home through play, its marketer-provided meanings temporarily recede in importance, disarticulated from their material substrate, only to reemerge as circumstances and setting change.

For example, girls often enact the roles of the doll characters in scripted "plays." Holding the dolls, they utter lines adapted from marketer-created narratives in the books. Annie, age 8, says, "My mom invited some of my friends to come to my house for an American Girl tea party. So we played and had lots of fun and we did a play about Samantha. We were acting the characters out, so I was Samantha and my friend Carolyn played Nelly." However, even unmoored from the brand meaning of a particular character living in a particular historical period, an American Girl doll does not become simply a doll, a girlishly shaped projective vehicle. Throughout this unmooring, the loose relation between the material thing and the brand attached to it is never truly severed. Girls continue to play with "Molly" and "Addy" and their branded accessories. The doll is an inescapably physical medium, which allows it to transform and alternate as the girl's double, family member, audience, teacher, judge, and friend, as well as a character in a brand-generated narrative. This was evident in the descriptions and observations of many girls' play styles. Consider Olivia's comments:

> I pretended it was Christmas, I pretended that [Molly] broke her leg. I thought it'd be fun so [instead of taking her to the doll hospital at American Girl Place] I pretended like there was a hospital at my house. I pretended that she was walking down the stairs and rolled down and then I picked her up and I ran around the whole house at least two times and put her in one room and put a cast on her and said, "Hello, she is in the recovery room." And we waited and waited and waited like we were in a real hospital. And then I went in to see her, she's in the recovery room. I pretended to pick her up and put her in the wheelchair, and then I got the crutches.

Like Becca, Olivia goes beyond the historical narratives, stretching her imagination—and the use of marketer-created accoutrements—with a story about injury followed by successful treatment. Her narrative represents an improvisation around the theme of care and healing in which the doll's needs become the focus of a multiplayer family drama. These alternative effects are culturally complex. From a purist or managerial standpoint, they might be said to diminish the American Girl brand because they do not tie directly to a marketer-created narrative. However, we observe that this home-based reinvention of characters and contexts also enhances the value of the dolls, the doll play, and the brand itself by deepening and broadening girls' understanding of, and ability to apply, the precepts that undergird the brand.

Although seemingly reminiscent of the debranding processes described by Wallendorf and Arnould (1991) and Coupland (2005), original or idiosyncratic play does not render the American Girl brand invisible; instead, such play seems to make it magnetic, capable of drawing congruent entities toward it and engulfing and incorporating them. In addition, there exists an abundance of interstitial space among the components of the American Girl architecture; the interstices represent lacunae to be filled with cultural material authored by those for whom the brand has meaning. Through mimicry and schooling, the brand is affected by contagion, cornucopic display, and a host of sacralizing tendencies (see Belk et al. 1989) intrinsic to American Girl. It is through this unmooring of brand and object, this personalizing suspension of managerial linkages, that the brand's wider attractive force is activated. Rather than making the brand generic, this loosening of programmed linkages causes an association of the singular and unlabeled. It is in large part the "openness" of the brand—its ability to incorporate and house consumer-generated material—that is the source of its power and its ability to sustain itself over time.

Material girls

Doll play is a material experience. The literal nature of this material relationship was apparent in our in-home interview with Maggie and Meghan, two seven-year-old best friends. In two corners of Maggie's room stand small trunks, each open to display a shelf containing an array of tiny accessories and a horizontal pole on which are arranged miniature hangers holding doll dresses and outfits. There are three doll beds of traditional style, each with a nightstand and lamp, and a large doll crib with a colorful mobile hanging above its American Girl Bitty Baby occupant. There are cases of American Girl doll clothes and accessories on the shelves of a wooden bookcase that also hold a library of American Girl books. Additional cases of clothing and accessories lie open on the floor.

Maggie and Meghan speak knowledgeably about a period of American history in which one of the dolls lived, and confide that they enact scenarios based on the historical narratives contained in the books, as well as others that take place in the present. Maggie says, "We play in her time, and then in our time, so back and forth." However, when clothing is mentioned, the conversation becomes notably more animated. Reference is made to an "apple-picking outfit" and we ask Maggie and Meghan to tell us more about it, which prompts both girls to leap to their feet. They kneel next to cases of clothing from the American Girl collection and pull garments from the satin-lined interiors, turn them right-side out, fasten their closures, smooth them, and display them against their own chests or midriffs so we can better appreciate them. This self-identifying pressing of doll outfits against live girl bodies reminds us that material objects like these are not merely cognitive categories linked to conformity or resistance, but deeply embodied aspects of the social world (Küchler and Miller 2005). It is this very physicality which, we postulate, energizes the ludic forces that enable products bearing powerful brand names like American Girl to resist decommodification, and instead become more broadly and deeply relevant agents in consumers' own cultural worlds.

Like other emotionally compelling entertainment brands, American Girl has multiple material manifestations that colonize domestic space. Books, dolls, accoutrements, and accessories are artfully arranged in bookcases, on dressers, and in designated areas on the floor, or arrayed on closet shelves. We observe that these objects are integrated into the lives of individual household members, and woven through the social fabric of the extended family group that includes girls, mothers, grandmothers, sisters, aunts, girlfriends, and the occasional father or grandfather. Here is revealed another structural characteristic of the brand: soundness. The components of the American Girl brand architecture are woven together in such a way that they enhance and extend one another, giving the form intelligibility and a degree and kind of logical and aesthetic order that facilitates engagement. By managerial design, the multitude of constituent parts articulate with and complement one another to form a cohesive and coherent whole.

Silverstone's Fifth Moment: Incorporation

Polyvocal brand

The American Girl brand has come to play a unique role in the relationship between a middle-aged man, Alan, and his daughter, Olivia. Alan took Olivia to American Girl Place for a birthday shopping expedition. Along with several requested additions to her extensive collection of dolls, clothes, and accessories, he purchased a blonde "Just Like You" doll and a 1960s outfit consisting of a pair of bell-bottom jeans and sandals, a tie-dyed T-shirt, a peace symbol necklace, a flowered headband, and round glasses with pink lenses. While still in the store, he requested that the American Girl Salon stylist braid the new doll's hair to look like that of the doll wearing the outfit in the display. Upon arriving home, he took the doll from her package and dressed her in the 1960s outfit. He then placed her on a shelf in his home office directly above his desk between a collection of commemorative photos, referred to by his family as "the wall of heroes" and what he calls "my army stuff." His daughter found this puzzling, though not off-putting. She told us, "My friends said it's for you, it's not like he's going to keep it, of course he's going to give it to you . . . five weeks later I said he's not giving it to me!" She and her friends sometimes visit the office and her father talks about the doll he privately calls "my icon," but to whom he has (under duress from his daughter) assigned the moniker "Flower Girl." He describes the historical period in which the doll character lived, and plays songs from that time. The children listen in wonder, and refer in conversation with one another and their families to "Olivia's dad's American Girl doll."

The doll's meaning to the father is complex and nuanced, and the immediacy of its physical presence is clearly important to him:

> The thing that's kind of funny is that I never experienced any of this (because) I was over there (in Vietnam). She (Flower Girl) is just such a perfect symbol: rose-colored glasses, flowers in her hair . . . she takes me back to the entire period in time that was very different. I mean, I could buy a picture of three hippies grooving in Haight Ashbury from some photo collection, but that wouldn't have the intimacy of the doll . . . .

Alan continues by noting why he believes a "hippie" doll is unlikely to bear some other brand name, apparently equating a variety of races and ethnicities with a plurality of sociopolitical perspectives.

> I can't imagine someone other than American Girl making a doll like this. . . . [Y]ears where there were only white, Christian, whatever: as WASP as could be, then the era of making a black doll in addition to the white doll. . . . they (American Girl) were different, willing to explore the range, where before there was no notion that people come from different ethnicities, different heritages. But they came out with dolls that say America is a country of immigrants, came out with the whole range because that's what America is. . . .

The doll sustains Alan's reveries and reflections, helping him conduct a life review. It also allows him to create for his daughter and her friends a multimedia guided tour of a historical era he had selectively experienced firsthand, but which he now uses the brand to recover. The brand animates history for the storyteller and his audience. Alan may be said to become a "ceremonial grandma" (Sherry et al. 2008), embodying the history he transmits to the girls, his status rising in their eyes on the brand's account. The line extension, American Girl of Today, is designed to allow consumers to choose an American Girl doll with skin color, hair color, and eye color similar to their own. Alan's retrofitting of a product from that line in such a way as to appropriate the ethos of the historical line and blur the boundaries between the two further illustrates the plasticity of the brand and the opportunities it provides for personalization.

Interiority of the brand.

Sasha is the 10-year-old only child of Russian immigrant parents living in a two-bedroom apartment in a working-class suburb. She invited us into her room, the most sparsely decorated of those we visited, to talk about American Girl. Unlike other informants, Sasha did not have an American Girl doll in her possession. She related the sad tale of losing Molly, telling us that she had taken the doll to the park, become distracted as she played with friends, and accidentally abandoned it. On realizing her error and racing back to retrieve the doll, she found it gone. Sasha's family's circumstances precluded immediate replacement of the doll and provided little assurance that another would be hers in the future. Though still mourning her loss and the opportunity to pass the doll along to her own daughter, she had enthusiastically agreed to be interviewed when a neighbor referred her to us. Despite Molly's absence, Sasha indicated that the doll and the brand were still very much part of her life; after describing how she continued to read the American Girl books, she pointed to her chest and echoed a phrase we had heard from other girls who were still in possession of their dolls: "She's in me." The doll and the brand seem to become intertwined with the experience of girlhood and sense of self.

Silverstone's Last Moment: Conversion

Disruptions & disjunctions

Branded objects may create static in household value systems capable of impairing value-laden communication among family members. Parents express anxiety about gifts representing alien brand values entering the home, and acknowledge that often such gifts "manage to get lost." Mindful of the propensity of toys to travel with children, parents are concerned not only about the entry into their homes of the wrong toys, but about these toys reemerging cloaked in brand and household ideology in full view of neighbors and friends. As Diana, an African American and mother of Keisha, tells us, "She's not getting that (a doll whose brand ethos is incompatible with that of the household) because where are we gonna take it?" Over time, Diana has "lost" several white dolls given to Keisha by others.

For Diana, the American Girl brand is interwoven with personal and cultural "baggage" that threatens the core values of the household. Although her knowledge of American Girl is limited to what she's seen in ads on city buses (only white faces), she professes dislike of the brand, claiming that it should be rechristened "European Girl." She feels that role models are critical in the socialization of girls, and her principal reservation about the brand is that it glamorizes "whiteness" to the exclusion of "role models of color." While pressure from her friends and her daughter has prompted Diana to consider a visit to American Girl Place, it is clear that Keisha's choices on that occasion will be constrained. Diana tells us that she will be permitted to select "any non-European doll of color." The issue of cultural heritage will loom large in this future shopping expedition and influence the microenvironment the two share with other American Girl Place visitors, and potentially (if attentive and conscientious staff overhear them) the brand itself.

Homecomings & reinfusions

American Girl dolls often accompany their owners back to the store, where girls and their families are reinfused with brand ideology by once again standing before the historical dioramas, perusing the displays of merchandise, visiting the doll hospital and styling salon, conversing over tea at the café, and seeing the play. Allison, who, with her younger sister Kathryn owns three American Girl dolls, tells us, "It was like a play about friendship, so I wanted to see how they acted it out. . . . They made a friendship quilt like in Kirsten's birthday story and they acted out each of the squares, one (story) for each of the American Girls." Verbal exchanges among women and girls evidence the fact that many, like Allison and Kathryn, return to the store not to shop, but to share the American Girl experience and reflect on the values embodied by the brand.

Just as important as reconnecting with the marketer-created meanings at American Girl Place is the display and exchange of idiosyncratic meanings acquired during the dolls' residence in households. Often these occasions represent opportunities for girls and family members to show off clothing and accessories purchased on previous visits, perhaps combined in unique and personal ways. Sometimes, however, dolls return to the fold wearing outfits handmade by a family member or purchased from an unauthorized source (e.g., the "18-inch-doll" section of a mass merchandise outlet). These customizations of the branded commodity are tolerated, although as we learned from Jane, the mother of five-year-old Christine, this tolerance has limits. Jane's daughter was refused service at the hair salon because, as the stylist confided, the doll in her arms wasn't "a real American Girl doll." It is not only dolls that return to the store transformed; young doll owners (and the occasional mother) can be observed to have remade themselves at home in the images of particular doll characters, sporting similar hairstyles, pairs of glasses, and items of clothing. These infinitely variable personalizations of the brand become components of the context within which brand meaning is conveyed and brand and family narratives co-created.

UNPACKING BRAND FORTITUDE

Articulating Brand Fortitude

American Girl products—branded, commercial entities—are reinterpreted by household communities, "classified and reclassified" (Kopytoff 1986) into idiosyncratic categories that have relevance and utility for the communities and their individual members. We observe with Silverstone (1994) that these branded objects accrete private meanings that reflect individual and household priorities, and when they reenter the public sphere they do so cloaked in significance acquired during their sojourns in the home. We also note, however, that marketer-created brand discourses are very much in evidence throughout this process.

We view Silverstone's six moments of consumption as a single stage in the overall process that Kopytoff (1986) calls the "cultural biography" of an object and endorse Kopytoff's notion, echoed in Silverstone's theoretical work, that an object is not exclusively either a mass-produced commodity or a home-based singularity: that it can represent a commodity in one phase of its life cycle and a singularity in another. We go further, however, and contend that objects bearing some brand names can at the same time manifest the defining characteristics of both commodities and singularities. We use the *brand fortitude* construct to represent what it is about these brands that make this possible; that is, what enables "dual citizenship in the Land of Commodities and the Land of Singularities." Our findings lead us to believe that two structural characteristics of brands constitute what we have termed *fortitude*: *soundness* and *openness*.

The Structural Characteristics of Brand Fortitude

The American Girl brand manifests itself in many and varied physical forms, including dolls, books, clothing, and accessories for dolls and humans, and historical and contemporary accoutrements (furniture, pets and pet accessories, outdoor recreation and sports equipment, musical instruments, school supplies, and personal technology, among others). In addition, a multitude of narratives represented in books, plays, magazines, catalogs, television "specials," and films animate the individual doll characters and give rise to compelling meta-narratives about morality and personal integrity, heroic femininity, homebuilding, and American-ness. *Soundness* relates both to the sheer number of physical and narrative elements that comprise the brand architecture and their variety of form and content. *Soundness* also reflects the degree to which these constituent parts articulate with and complement one another to form a coherent whole. Our findings demonstrate how consumers relate to the constituent parts of this complex brand in ways that are unique to them and their individual and collective projects and priorities, yet still reflect the brand's core premises. Doll forms are situated historically and otherwise using a variety of intertextual linkages, items of clothing and accoutrements are assigned central roles in morality plays, and the messages of how-to-live books are closely attended to by girls and by parents anxious to mitigate the influence of the negative role models they perceive as dominating the landscape of contemporary girlhood. The components of the American Girl brand architecture are woven together in such a way that they enhance and extend one another, giving the structure intelligibility and a degree and kind of logical and aesthetic order that facilitates engagement with the meanings built into the brand by its creator and sustained by its managers.

We observe the effects of structural *soundness* in the way Becca abstracts commonalities and derives life lessons from the large and diverse array of stories contained in the American Girl books. She applies what she's learned from these stories about facing adversity with courage and conviction and manifesting kindness and consideration toward others in her doll play, as well as in her relations with friends and family. We also see *soundness* at work as we talk with Maggie and Meghan, and with Maeve and her sisters, all of whom are surrounded by the American Girl dolls, accoutrements, and accessories that populate the intimate spaces they share. These products and the brand name under which they are united are imbued with a mélange of clearly articulated, yet interrelated marketer-created significances.

Brand fortitude additionally assumes *openness*, reflecting both degree of surface permeability and amount and distribution of interstitial space among the structure's components. We contend that brands whose structures manifest *openness* are permeable and hospitable to meanings authored by consumers. It is the permeability of such a brand's surface that enables cultural material authored by consumers to enter, and the presence of interstices or lacunae among the components that allows material that penetrates the structure to lodge in it, ultimately becoming integral to the brand architecture and contributing to its strength and permanence.

The effects of *openness* are evident in the use by Lisa's grandmother of American Girl–created stories of Addy, the African-American doll, and her Civil War–era clothing and accoutrements to animate and reify the family's ethnohistory. Alan uses the "Girl of Today" doll he has outfitted in marketer-created hippie garb to recover a lost part of himself and to forge novel connections with his daughter, Olivia, and her friends.

The ability of the American Girl brand to attract, admit, and accommodate material authored by its constituents—girls and their families—is evident in the vignettes presented in this chapter (see also Diamond et al. [2009] and Acosta-Alzuru and Kreshel [2002]). While American Girl, as a toy and entertainment brand, might seem particularly well suited to the insertion of consumer-generated material, *fortitude* and its defining properties of *soundness* and *openness* is demonstrated by other brands that do not fit the toy/entertainment description. For example, the Japanese household products brand MUJI,[2] which has a significant global presence and an unusually extensive product line, manifests what we have called "structural soundness" in that its multitude of conceptual and material component parts articulate in such a way as to support—if not actually comprise—a lifestyle guided by an explicit design philosophy. Like MUJI and American Girl, Coleman has an extensive product line that occupies large areas of consumers' homes. More important, its products play a role in emotion-laden patterns of domestic discourse and practice related to the sharing of outdoor recreation activities with family and friends. For these reasons, the products and the brand itself carry a multitude of individual and household meanings that comfortably coexist with—and enhance and extend—those proffered by the marketer. Like American Girl books, dolls, and accessories, Coleman products are rarely referenced without mention of the brand name under which they are united; consumers say "our Coleman stove" or "my Coleman tent" rather than "the stove" or "the tent."

Maintaining the vitality of a brand within the confines of a consumer's private space depends upon the continual investment and recovery of meaning in tangible objects; tangibility grounds all practices of branding in our framework. The American Girl brand moves within time, space, and culture. It is updated with each contextualized connection and marketing appeal. From the first taste of historical fiction to the continual deployment of dolls, accoutrements, and accessories within private spaces, through the teaching and judging themes of doll play to the dressing and grooming of the dolls, our observations return inexorably to the material basis of branding. The physical world of the brand, the sights, shape, textures, colors, smells, and embodied "feel" of the products are vital and immediate aspects of it. These aspects are continually reintegrated ideologically. The product exists without the brand, but the brand cannot exist without the product.

A FEW FINAL THOUGHTS

We would note that in addition to being different and distinct from brand attachment (Park et al. 2008) in ways identified earlier in this chapter, brand fortitude must be distinguished from another related construct, *brand meaning resonance* (Fournier et al. 2008). Fournier and her colleagues explored the process by which meaning affect brand equity, and the factors that mediate this process. Their investigation led them to conclude that "brands die when their meanings lose significance in consumers' lives" (Fournier et al. 2008:35). Meaning resonance helps sustain significance and operates on three levels: personal, cultural, and organizational. Personal resonance is "the goodness-of-fit between a brand's architecture of claimed meanings and the meanings the consumer seeks in his/her personal life." Cultural resonance "reflects the degree to which claimed brand meanings reflect, reinforce and shape meanings from the collective social space that links consumers to others in a shared language and interpretation of experience" (Fournier et al. 2008:40). Although our investigation reveals that the American Girl brand achieves meaning resonance on both personal and cultural levels, it additionally suggests that meaning resonance represents something different from brand fortitude, and is best characterized as a facilitator or enabler of fortitude. Meaning resonance increases the likelihood that branded objects will be recontextualized and reclassified in ways uniquely suited to the interests of individuals and groups, and thus incorporated into the symbolic environments that support the creation of individual and group identities. It does not, however, address the ability of branded objects singularized in this manner to resist the stripping away of marketer-created brand meaning; this is the role of brand fortitude.

As we seek to understand a world where the market power of brands and branding appears foundational, and where both the consumption and marketing of brands assumes a nearly infinite variety of forms, scholars and practitioners require flexible and culturally grounded theories as guides. How to preserve, evolve, adapt, and transform marketer-created meanings in such a way as to make the products and services that bear their names more valuable to consumers is an issue of considerable significance to marketing practitioners.

The rise of mass customization and "markets-of-one" (Gilmore and Pine 2000) reflects not just advances in digital technology that enable effective online marketing and inventory management, but also—and more important—customer preferences for niche markets that are capable of satisfying narrow interests. These circumstances make it incumbent on marketers of broadly targeted brands, especially those with global presence or aspirations, to create products and services that retain their marketer-created meanings even as they are singularized by becoming implicated in consumers' day-to-day lives. One way to accomplish this is by building *fortitude* into brands by using the structural properties of *soundness* and *openness* described in this chapter.

We contend that by building fortitude into brands, marketers not only help ensure that commodity meaning will not erode or be destroyed during branded objects' tenure in households; they also afford consumers the opportunity to enhance the value of their products and services via singularizing, de-alienating discourses and practices.

REFERENCES

Acosta-Alzuru, C., and P. J. Kreshel. 2002. "I'm an American Girl . . . Whatever That Means: Girls Consuming Pleasant Company's American Girl Identity. *Journal of Communication* 52:139–61.

Appadurai, Arjun, ed. 1986. *The Social Life of Things: Commodities in Cultural Perspective*. Cambridge, UK: Cambridge University Press.

Armstrong, Robert. 1974. *The Affecting Presence*. Urbana, IL: University of Illinois Press.

Belk, Russell. 1995. *Collecting in a Consumer Society*. NY: Routledge.

Belk, Russell, Melanie Wallendorf, and John Sherry Jr. 1989. "The Sacred and Profane in Consumer Behavior: Theodicy on the Odyssey." *Journal of Consumer Research* 16:1–38.

Belk, Russell, Melanie Wallendorf, John Sherry Jr., and M. Holbrook. 1991. "Collecting in a Consumer Culture." *Association for Consumer Research* (Special Volume) 178–215.

Borghini, Stefania, Nina Diamond, Robert Kozinets, Mary Ann McGrath, Albert Muñiz, Jr., and John Sherry, Jr. 2009. "Why Are Themed Brandstores So Powerful? Retail Brand Ideology at American Girl Place." *Journal of Retailing* 85:363–75.

Cassell, J., and H. Jenkins. 1998. *From Barbie to Mortal Kombat: Gender and Computer Games*. Cambridge, MA: MIT Press.

Claiborne, C. B., and J. L. Ozanne. 1990. "The Meaning of Custom-Made Homes: Home as a Metaphor for Living. *Advances in Consumer Research* 17:367–74.

Coupland, J. C. 2005. "Invisible Brands: An Ethnography of Households and the Brands in Their Kitchen Pantries." *Journal of Consumer Research*. 32(1):106–18.

Cuba, Lee, and David Hummon. 1993. "Constructing a Sense of Home: Place Affiliation and Migration Across the Life Cycle." *Sociological Forum* 8(4):547–72.

Diamond, Nina, John Sherry, Jr., Albert Muñiz, Jr., Mary Ann McGrath, Robert Kozinets, and Stefania Borghini. 2009. "American Girl and the Brand Gestalt: Closing the Loop on Socio-Cultural Branding Research." *Journal of Marketing* 73(3):118–34.

Epp, Amber, and Linda Price. 2010. "The Storied Life of Singularized Objects: Forces of Agency and Transformation." *Journal of Consumer Research* 36:820–37.

Fournier, Susan, Michael Solomon, and Basil Englis. 2008. "When Brands Resonate." In *Handbook on Brand and Experience Management*, edited by B. Schmitt and D. Rogers, 35–57. Northampton, MA: Edward Elgar.

Gilmore, James, and B. Joseph Pine. 2000. *Markets of One: Creating Customer-Unique Value through Mass Customization*. Boston: Harvard Business Press.

Hermann, Gretchen. 1997. "Gift or Commodity: What Changes Hands in the U.S. Garage Sale?" *American Ethnologist* 24(4):910–30.

Kopytoff, Igor. 1986. "The Cultural Biography of Things: Commoditization as Process." In *The Social Life of Things: Commodities in Cultural Perspective*, edited by A. Appadurai, 64–91. Cambridge, UK: Cambridge University Press.

Küchler, Susanne, and Daniel Miller, eds. 2005. *Clothing as Material Culture*. London: Berg.

Lastovicka, John, and Karen Fernandez. 2005. "Three Paths to Disposition: The Movement of Meaningful Possessions to Strangers." *Journal of Consumer Research* 31(4):813–23.

McCracken, Grant. 1988. *Culture and Consumption: New Approaches to the Symbolic Character of Consumer Goods and Activities*. Bloomington, IN: Indiana University Press.

__________ 1989. "Homeyness: A Cultural Account of One Constellation of Consumer Goods and Meaning." In *Interpretive Consumer Research*, edited by E. Hirschman, 168–83. Provo, UT: Association for Consumer Research.

Morris, Andrew P. 2003. "Selling History With Dolls." *Ideas on Liberty* 53(May):16–19.

Park, Cheol, Deborah Macinnis, and Joseph Priester. 2008. "Brand Attachment and a Strategic Brand Exemplar." *Handbook on Brand and Experience Management*, edited by B. Schmitt and D. Rogers, 3–17. Northampton, MA: Edward Elgar.

Sherry, John, Jr. 2000. "Place, Technology, and Representation." *Journal of Consumer Research* 27:273–8.

Sherry, John, Jr., Stefania Borghini, Albert Muñiz, Jr., Mary Ann McGrath, Nina Diamond, and Robert Kozinets. 2008. "Allomother as Image and Essence: Animating the American Girl Brand." In *Explorations in Consumer Culture Theory*, edited by J. F. Sherry Jr. and E. Fischer, 137–49. London: Routledge.

Silverstone, Roger. 1994. *Television in Everyday Life*. New York: Routledge.

Sloane, Julie. 2002. "New Twists on Timeless Toys." *Fortune* (October 1):70.

Thrift, Nigel. 1997. "Us and Them: Reimagining Places, Re-Imagining Identities." In *Consumption and Everyday Life*, edited by H. Mackay, 159–202. Thousand Oaks, CA: Sage.

Wallendorf, Melanie, and Eric Arnould. 1991. "'We Gather Together': Consumption Rituals of Thanksgiving Day." *Journal of Consumer Research* 18:13–31.

NOTES

The authors thank Julien Cayla, Timothy Malefyt, Sarah Wilner, Rita Denny, and Patti Sunderland for helpful comments on earlier versions of this chapter.

1 Toward this end, members of our multinational, multigenerational, multiethnic, and multi-institutional research team spent time in the living spaces of 16 brand devotees residing in the greater Chicago metropolitan area. Over the three-year duration of a larger research project, team members also conducted observations of and interviews (of varying depth) with several hundred consumers at other sites in which the brand was manifest, including sponsored events and American Girl Place stores in Chicago and New York.

2 See http://www.muji.com.

34

Live Fieldnoting: Creating More Open Ethnography

TRICIA WANG

OPENING UP FIELDNOTES

In an essay published in 1997, "The Cathedral and the Bazaar: Musings on Linux and Open Source by an Accidental Revolutionary," Eric Raymond contrasted top-down and bottom-up software design. Software code released in the "cathedral" model gives an exclusive group of programmers access to the code, whereas software released in the "bazaar" model gives access to anyone who wants the code. Raymond's central argument is that the visibility and accessibility embedded in a bazaar development process allows a greater number of people to participate in improving software, and thereby produces better code. I believe that a more open fieldnote process likewise produces better fieldwork and richer ethnography.

Like computer programmers who emphasized the value of a bazaar approach for coding, ethnographers can benefit from a more open ethnographic process. A bazaar model of ethnography embraces a more immediate response to fieldnotes, where responses are given not just as a critique, but in the spirit of improving the fieldwork. A bazaar model finds value in audience; it creates new possibilities for involving research participants and stakeholders who cannot come to the fieldsite in the fieldwork experience. In my view, lowering barriers to participation is a critical opportunity for building deeper understanding.

In this chapter, I describe my approach to live fieldnoting, in which I developed ways to share some of my ethnographic fieldnotes in real time using social media tools. I found that live fieldnoting helps establish and maintain relationships with participants; empowers participants because sharing my ethnographic process openly allows them to feel that they are truly participating in the research instead of just being studied; decreases the psychosocial alienation I (and many ethnographers) experience in the field; demands a new kind of

Handbook of Anthropology in Business, edited by Rita Denny and Patricia Sunderland, 638–657.

visual attention to the field (as opposed to textual); brings a wider audience with me into the fieldsite in real time; creates valuable opportunities for dialog with an audience of non-ethnographers and non-specialists; and produces new forms of data such as geotagged location-based data, time-stamped data, and embeddable image files.

After describing my fieldnoting practice and offering concrete examples of how I use live fieldnotes in my research, I then explore a number of challenges and key methodological questions (including privacy) raised by this process. I argue that just as the challenges raised by the critiques of anthropology as text led to new ways of thinking about how social scientists interacted with fieldsites, participants, and data (Handleman 1994; Tyler 2008) the questions raised by a more bazaar-style of ethnography and the use of social media during the ethnographic process raise questions and bring insights and innovations that are advancing the field. Finally, I propose some best practices for this type of fieldwork, and close by framing the process in the larger context of continued relevance for ethnography in a networked world.

LIVE FIELDNOTING: DEFINITION & PROCESS

I grew up with the internet and lived the transition from Web 1.0 to Web 2.0. I have long embraced the practices and principles of Lawrence Lessig's Free Culture Movement, including open sharing and decreasing barriers to content modification through the internet (Lessig 2005). Free Culture emerged out of a reaction against overly restrictive copyright laws that served private, not public interests. For more than 10 years I have put my work and digital artifacts under Creative Commons licenses whenever possible.[1] In 2011, I moved to China to conduct independent research. Since I was not working for a client,[2] it was an ideal time to experiment with a more open form of writing fieldnotes. I adopted many of the Free Culture Movement's principles around openness and transparency and applied them to my work.

One important tool was Instagram, a photo-sharing app for Androids and iPhones. Instagram made photo sharing effortless: the app was free; it was easy to use; it connected to other social media services; and a lot of other people were already using it.[3] In particular, the ability to share my photographs simultaneously across multiple social media platforms, such as Twitter, Foursquare, or Tumblr (a principle known as COPE: "Create Once, Publish Everywhere"[4]) made Instagram an ideal platform to experiment with sharing fieldnotes.

Instagram's ease of use, wide adoption, and social features made it an ideal research app to quickly post real-time fieldwork updates. From the second I landed in China to my last day of fieldwork, I posted at least one photograph to Instagram every day. Instagram then pushed my photos to Twitter, Flickr, Facebook, and Tumblr. Each Instagram contained a picture and a text description. My first Instagram from China documented the reaction I had when I stepped into the arrival hall at Shanghai Pudong International Airport (Figure 34.1). Over a period of 14 months, I posted more than a thousand Instagrams from my various fieldsites in China (Figures 34.2–34.5).[5]

Using Instagram led to many discussions with colleagues about my fieldwork and my use of social media to document it. For one thing, I realized that my use of Instagram was similar to other well-established Web 2.0 practices, such as live blogging and tweeting. When other ethnographers also started to use Instagram for live fieldnotes, I realized that we were creating a new lens for ethnographic observations.[6] I have named this process of continuously sharing text and visual coverage of an ethnographer's fieldwork "live fieldnoting."[7]

Live fieldnotes are real-time observations that an ethnographer shares from a fieldsite through a mobile social networking app over a cellular/wifi network to create a record of data from the field in the form of photos and text to tactically establish and maintain the ethnographer's relationship with her/his participants and audience. The term "sharing" also encompasses a broad set of social media practices, such as liking, posting, broadcasting, pushing, tagging, favoriting, indexing, and forwarding. In my case, the live fieldnote is created with an image-sharing app on a mobile phone. The app can push the post to other social networking services. Images are accompanied by a description of the image with relevant metadata (tags and location). The description includes context: the nature of the interaction itself, the objects in the picture, the place of the interaction, and the people in it. The description can also include the ethnographer's perspective, such as an explanation of the meaning of the interaction to participants, an interpretation of the interaction, and sometimes an analysis of the interaction (for example, Figures 34.6 and 34.7). All live fieldnotes are time-stamped with a unique URL, and may contain metadata (hashtags[8] and location geodata, making them searchable, archivable, and filterable). As such, live fieldnotes are more descriptive than brief shorthand "scratch notes" (Ottenberg

Figure 34.1. You know you've landed in Shanghai when you see people holding signs for "FOXCONN" at international arrivals. March 10, 2011 #bytesof china.

Figure 34.2. Tommy Hilfiger's stepbrother in China started Tommy Welai. #bytesofchina.

Figure 34.3. I finally found an awesome anti-porn, gambling, drugs poster at an internet cafe! The poster's Chinglish is: Caring for Life: Refusing "Pornography" "Gambling" "Drugs". I think it's ironic that they have all no-no's in quotation marks though I am sure they don't mean it that way. But seri-ously quotation marks perfectly describe China—what counts as "legal" is very vague and the distance between policy and prac-tice is wide. "Pornography" is illegal, but that's a large part of the activity in internet cafes and just outside there are brothels, KTVs [karoke], and sex workers with plenty of business. #China #bytesofchina.

Figure 34.4. Oh what memories this military hospital brings back. Just 3 years ago i did participant observation with women get-ting abortions, and on the day we came here in May, there was a big red banner: "Mother's Day Special—discounts on abortions." #bytes ofchina.

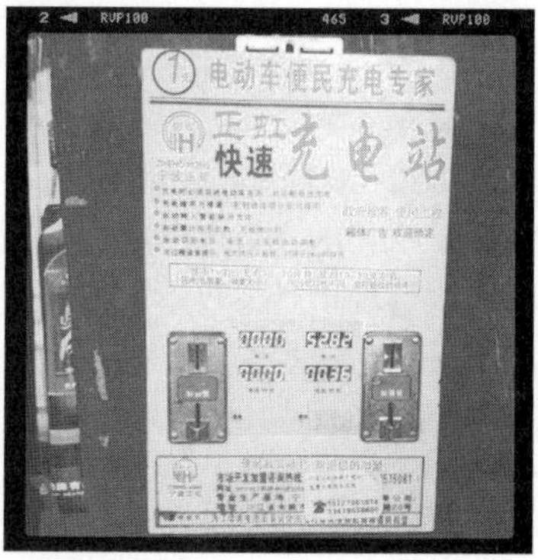

Figure 34.5. Electric scooter charging station, 1rmb = 10min = 3 miles. Wuhan, China #bytes ofchina.

Figure 34.6. When they showed me the basin of warm water they had prepared for me to wash my face, I automatically blurted out, "it's ok, i don't need to wash my face tonight," despite the fact that I had been walking around in a village all day & knew that my face had a layer of dirt on it. I've been in almost every kind of bathroom situation possible, but this was the first time that in such a newly modeled toilet in a village w/ a face washing basin next to the toilet. I have never washed my face squatting next to pee & poop. But then I said just suck it up tricia, it's clean water which is rare & just don't breathe. Plus I felt bad that they had prepared warm water, so it would've been rude of me to decline. For a moment i contemplated faking my face wash by dumping the water into the toilet. If I declined, I would make them feel bad for their bathroom not being clean enough for me. I have to remind myself in these moments it's important to let go. #bytesofchina.

Figure 34.7. The best part of fieldwork is the eating part. But usually this involves a lot of drinking and one of the local customs with the Dong minority group is that before the real drinking starts, everyone has to drink 3 shots—first shot is for the heavens, second cup is for the earth, third cup is for the ancestors. Before you drink the first cup you pour a few drops into the ground for the heavens and ancestors to drink. Then the REAL drinking starts after everyone is buzzed. Drinking and eating lasts usually about 6 hours. But this table set up is incredibly uncomfortable. The 3 inch high stools are made for midgets. I don't know how i will last all night. I am so screwed. I just want to sit on the table 火铺. Hunan, China #bytesofchina.

1990:148), but not as thorough as "fieldnotes proper" (Sanjek 1990b:187) that are typically written for an "audience of one" (Sanjek 1990a:99).

While live fieldnoting uses a digital platform, it still fulfills the core practices of ethnographic fieldnotes. In the opening chapter of *Writing Ethnographic Fieldnotes*, the process of ethnographic research is presented as a two-part process:

> First, the ethnographer enters into a social setting and gets to know the people involved in it; usually, the setting is not previously known in an intimate way. The ethnographer participates in the daily routines of this setting, develops ongoing relations with the people in it, and observes all the while

> what is going on. Indeed, the term "participant-observation" is often used to characterize this basic research approach. But, second, the ethnographer writes down in regular, systematic ways what she observes and learns while participating in the daily rounds of life of others. Thus the researcher creates an accumulating written record of these observations and experiences. These two interconnected activities comprise the core of ethnographic research: Firsthand participation in some initially unfamiliar social world and the production of written accounts of that world by drawing upon such participation (Emerson et al. 2011:1).

Live fieldnoting fulfills the two processes that the authors of *Writing Fieldnotes* consider to be central to ethnographic research: participation and documentation. With live fieldnotes, the documentation is both visual and textual and in the accumulated form serve to create a foundation for a "thick description" (Geertz 1993). While Geertz and many other ethnographers textually established their presence in the fieldsite and authority after the fact, live fieldnoting emphasizes the ways ethnographers visually establish their presence in the fieldsite in the moment to an audience that is not also present.

Although sharing photographs instantly through a cellular phone is a relatively recent practice made by possible by affordable smartphones and data plans, live fieldnotes themselves are not a new genre of ethnography per se. Their value is most aligned with public ethnography (Burawoy 2005; Farmer 2004), and the practice is similar to those emphasized in visual ethnography (Collier and Collier 1986; Hockings 2009; Pink 2006). Live fieldnoting embraces immediacy. Rapid and continuous sharing brings stakeholders—be they participants, other ethnographers, clients, or just interested people—closer to the site of action. The goal is to communicate the observation as quickly as possible, connecting audiences to the actual time the interaction was observed.

Previous researchers have also used the technologies available to them to share field observations. Jan Chipchase was one of the earlier ethnographers to post pictures of his fieldwork to his blog with text. Working at the time for Nokia, he provided design observations while on the move. His posts tended to be a mix of observations, compelling questions, and high-quality pictures (see Teitler, this volume).[9] In 2003, Ethnographic Research, Inc., experimented with setting up a secure site for clients to see text updates from the field (Julie Peggar, personal communication, 2013). In 2007, danah boyd shared results from her fieldsite on her blog while her fieldwork was still in progress. She was one of the first formally trained ethnographers in academia to use the internet to engage the public at large with anthropological/sociological fieldwork. Chipchase's and boyd's blogs were also a means for establishing their own presence and authority.

BENEFITS OF LIVE FIELDNOTING

In this section I offer examples of the practice and benefits of live fieldnoting. I used live fieldnotes to maintain relationships with participants and to add contextual information such as recent events (Figure 34.8). In this picture, @futuremeng, one of my key research participants, and I were traveling to Shanghai together to register his server. @futuremeng uses four of the same social media sites that I use: Instagram, Twitter, Facebook, and Weibo. Before I even captured this moment, he had already mentioned me through a post on Weibo (a Chinese version of Twitter) that we were traveling together. I then followed up with a post on Instagram explaining what we were doing.

Live fieldnoting this moment is an expected interaction in the ritual of building trust and relationships with youth (and most typical social media users). In fact, it would have been *unnatural* if I did not post on social media that we were together because he had already initiated the exchange. Being added or mentioned by name or handle on a participant's social media platforms is a key symbol of a participant trusting the researcher. I do not use "@" or add a participant on any social media platform until they initiate. I allow them to give me the indicator of trust, and then I take their cue by adding and using the "@" sign to mention them in return.

I use Instagram in my fieldwork with participants in the same way that I use social media in my everyday life: as a way to establish relationships with people. As an ethnographer I call it live fieldnoting, but I was doing what all youth would do in that situation: posting a picture online. Critically, however, engaging in social media participant observation by adding and mentioning @futuremeng in my posts made him feel like he was a part of my research. It also allows me to engage in the rituals of nurturing a long-term relationship with @futuremeng.

This fieldnote also contains important contextual information that generates a record trail of my location. I took this train two months

Figure 34.8. I am taking a train to shanghai w/ @futuremeng, we got stuck on front carriage #2. the train ministry is sneaky, they removed carriage #1 because no one wants to be in the first carriage after the train accident. If we get in accident we'll be the first to fall off the track! August 11, 2011.

after the largest high-speed train accident in China, which I refer to in my notes. At the time, citizens were still very concerned that the trains were not safe enough to ride. In addition, I was also interviewing people who the Chinese government considered to be sensitive. In the case that I could not be located or if there was another accident, my live fieldnotes provided important information. I logged the geodata on Instagram and Foursquare. I also showed the train ticket information that included the carriage number and departure and arrival city and time.

I also used live fieldnotes to take visual images of my data collection process, which created intentional redundancy in my documentation process, and improved my overall relationship to the research process. In this post, I took a picture of my data wall in the research center I set up in my home (Figure 34.9). In the post, I am expressing a deep fear that I have about leaving my fieldsite, a fear that many researchers can relate to. After I posted this image, my friend Clive Thompson under the username @pomerian99 left a message for me: "That is a truly superb Wall Of Crazy. I wish I had a wall big enough in my house to make one. . . ." I replied to his message, "This is the biggest place I've ever lived in—I could never afford an apt this size in NYC or even a first tier Chinese city like shanghai or beijing." Just being able to converse with @pomerian99 made me feel less lonely and took away some of my anxiety about reconstructing this wall in the United States. It also gave me a visual guide to refer to for the wall's reconstruction.

I used live fieldnotes to capture conversation dialog. In this fieldnote, I was on a train and overheard three men talking loudly to each other (Figure 34.10). I wrote this fieldnote as I was listening to their conversation and, akin to a tweet, benefitted from the immediacy of response. Within the hour, I received two comments. One person wrote, "This is hilarious." Another commenter, Kenyatta Cheese under the username @kenyatta, wrote, "China's real name registration is the Facebook Connect of the real world." After spending more than one year in China, I had lost sight and perspective of how people in the West were experiencing identity and privacy issues on social media. @kenyatta's comment helped me understand how to talk about my observations with people outside of China.

I live-fieldnoted observations about how people live and present themselves. In this fieldnote, I jotted down notes of what a man on an escalator in front of me was wearing (Figure 34.11). By the time I got off the escalator, I had already posted the fieldnote to Instagram. While a seemingly inconsequential observation, this post is a helpful visual that bring me back to my fieldsite. Live fieldnoting makes it easy to document these everyday interactions that ethnographers use to understand consumerism, fashion, and the self-presentation practices of our research participants.

Figure 34.9. It's hard to believe that in 1 week I'm taking this entire sticky note universe down & moving it to its new home in Brooklyn, NYC. Just thinking about it makes me cry. I'll be moving my brain & I'm afraid I'll never be able to put it together again. April 4, 2012.

Figure 34.10. A man walks by on the train offering 1 hour of DVD player rentals for 10rmb. The man sitting said, "what if I run off with the DVD player?" The vendor replies, "where will you run to? We're on a train. Plus now you train tickers require real name registration." the vendor leaves and all the men discuss how it's possible that people don't steal the DVD players. China May 21, 2012.

I also live-fieldnote memorable moments with participants. In this picture with a publicly known activist, Hooligan Yan, I mention several of the experiences we had together throughout the years. I also mention her mood and fears, all things that she had talked about publicly (Figure 34.12). Hooligan Yan posted this photo of us the day that I took it. She asked me to send the photo to her so that she could post it to her social media. I posted this photo one month after I took it. I did not geotag this photo because when we met up, she did not want the police to know where she was at the time we met. In fact, before meeting with her, I took out the SIM card of my cellphone so that my movement would not be traced and to prevent any remote monitoring through my cellphone.

These are a selection of several ways I use live fieldnotes. Most of the notes are no longer than one to two sentences. Some of them are even incomplete sentences with spelling and grammatical errors. I am often writing my fieldnotes while I'm walking, waiting for a bus, or riding a train. Often times I am rushing to write my notes before the mobile 3G data connection disappears. The images often come out shaky or dark because cameras on mobile phone do not produce images that are as stable as a point-and-shoot. I also avoid using flash, as I find it to be disruptive. There are many instances where I am unable to Instagram the fieldnotes at the very moment I take the picture. In these cases, I jot down the notes in my notebook app on my cellphone and then copy and paste the notes over to Instagram once I am able to post.

It is not possible (nor it is it preferable) to live-fieldnote all fieldwork observations or interactions. I estimate that I live-fieldnote about 1 percent of fieldwork. Yet the details of daily life and my interactions with participants I documented with such posts are a rich and multitextured complement to the private narrative fieldnotes, interviews, and pictures that I collected in the field.

Figure 34.11. Male wearing blue paisley pants with white Adidas sneakers, girlfriend has blue toenail polish. Fashion, consumer. Wuhan, China June 8, 2012.

Figure 34.12. [As I wrapped up my fieldwork, it was very painful to say good-bye to participants.] One day I will write the story of Hooligan Yan, the woman who drew me to Wuhan and who continues to force China to talk about a whole population that is usually silent—sex workers. We've been in police cars and witnessed beatings, and here we are, reflecting on what a new administration may bode for the future of China. Hooligan Yan says she wants a stable life, but she fears that she will always be a drifter. I can relate to her as we say goodbye and prepare for the last few weeks of data collection & story gathering. This will be the first of many temporary good bye in the next months. March 2, 2012.

And sharing my live fieldnotes moved my work closer to the bazaar-style model of ethnography the field so deeply needs.

PRIVACY ISSUES

Live fieldnoting on social media can bring value to both the researcher and participant. But any discussion of the benefits must take into account privacy and ethical concerns that come with increased visibility. Researchers have brought up important concerns about privacy for social media users (boyd 2008; boyd and Marwick 2009; Taddicken 2012; Weber 2012). Social media makes interactions more visible, which worries many ethnographers. Ethnographers have also expressed worry that social media will make their participants vulnerable, will introduce unnecessary attention to their fieldsite, or will expose their data to marketers or researchers who will use it without proper attribution or misuse it.

Ethnographers, regardless of whether they use social media tools, must always be deeply attuned to privacy implications. The same research protocols that an ethnographer applies to gathering and publicizing data also need to be applied to live fieldnotes. It is critical that the use of live fieldnotes does not violate human research protocols, put participants at risk, or breach trust between participants and researchers. If the interaction being observed is sensitive or very personal, do not live-fieldnote it. Whenever live fieldnotes involve a participant, permission is needed. In the same way that participants' consent is needed for research reported in books, journal articles, or blog posts, consent is needed for live fieldnotes.

One of the most important concerns when recording fieldnotes in any form during fieldwork is that participants understand what the ethnographer is doing, that they are comfortable with it, and that they understand the implications of visibility. After I receive consent, I always tell participants that I'm writing down fieldnotes in my phone when I live-fieldnote in front of them. I purposefully show them my cellphone screen while I'm typing. This is my policy for all forms of fieldnotes: writing in notebooks, recording audio, or live fieldnoting. When explaining live fieldnoting to participants, I inform them of the social media platforms I use. I then show them the live fieldnote on the specific social media platform. I do now show my participant's faces, unless they are already public figures, or if they have already posted photos of our faces onto their own social media outlets. Most important, as I had mentioned in the previous section, I only mention a participant's social media handle if they initiate interaction on social media.

For those working with sensitive populations or conditions, it is still possible to live fieldnote. You can take pictures of abstract images, such as the sky, participant's hands, what you ate, or the tip of an object. You can write general reflections about what you are doing or ideas without revealing pertinent data. The exact location does not have to be mentioned or logged.

Sam Ladner has pointed to the issue of temporality and queried what happens when participants want mentions of their name deleted from social media.[10] From my experience, social media makes it easier for participants and researchers to stay connected. Participants could easily reach out to an ethnographer via social media and ask them to delete all instances of the live fieldnote. Practically speaking, digital data is easier to remove than published data. It is critical for ethnographers to be accessible to their participants in the case that they would like a live fieldnote removed.

CHALLENGES AS OPPORTUNITY

In my conversations with ethnographers, they tell me social media creates artificial interactions because it is not face-to-face. Considering that ethnographers initially thought that the phonograph (Brady 1999) and telephone threatened the quality of fieldwork, it is not surprising that ethnographers are currently expressing ambivalence towards social media. As Sunderland (1999) pointed out in her article on the telephone as a medium of fieldwork, any assumptions of "real" interaction fetishizes a particular kind of social relation. All interactions, including ones that are digitally mediated, are just as real as proximate and physical interactions.[11]

Some ethnographers are concerned with sharing "raw" fieldnotes.[12] Ethnographers' focus on a "finished" analysis in the form of a monograph or a set of insights is problematic because it creates a false sense of completion. There is no construct of "finished" in a bazaar model of software programming because code always in constant beta, meaning the code is always in the process of being improved for users. Since Apple's first release of their operating software in 1999, OS X 1.0, seven major releases have followed with many bug fixes and patches in between each update. There is no "finished" OS X operating system because it is constantly being improved for new devices, software, and users. Ethnographers would benefit from adopting some principles of software programming. Opening up some of our own fieldwork processes would generate not only increased feedback, but also multiple interpretations to our data, and create opportunities to connect with likeminded researchers.

Incorporating new data collection or sharing tools can unsettle established practices in the field. Like the phonograph and telephone, social media also introduces new concerns. Instead of fearing the visibility that social media creates, ethnographers can use live fieldnoting as an opportunity to reexamine social media as a discursive tool.

Live fieldnoting, by virtue of its iterative and broadcast qualities, leads me to richer analysis of my work. Any stakeholder from participants to other ethnographers and even audience members (e.g., clients, friends, followers) can comment, offer interpretations, like, and so on. My participants were actively involved in my fieldnotes. They were notified through social media alerts when they were mentioned. They left comments, they favorited, and they reposted my fieldnotes. Their comments made me see my fieldsite with a different lens and other times the comments challenged me to reexamine my claims. Other researchers reached out to me to tell me that they had similar questions or that they observed a similar situation but arrived at a different conclusion. Several time readers sent tweets to me confirming what I saw or offering their own experiences. Participants have corrected a piece of data or clarified my data. Sometimes they offered another way of understanding the interaction. Some of the best feedback came from nonspecialists who asked me questions or made comments on something that I had overlooked.

While some ethnographers may see these dissenting voices as a threat to their discursive or analytic monopoly, in my view a much bigger threat is to keep ethnographic data obscure and undiscoverable. Ongoing participant involvement in my live fieldnotes prevented me from privileging my interpretations, challenged me to be rigorous in my data collection, and enhanced my ethnographic practice.

Transforming Fieldsite & Audience

Live fieldnoting subverts the traditional definition of participant observation, which refers only to the ethnographer participating in what is being observed. The very act of live fieldnoting changes the nature of the fieldwork because an audience is sharing the ethnographer's experience by proxy. My fieldsite no longer consisted of just my participants and me, but also my audience, who was sharing my experiences with me in real time. Live fieldnoting made it easier for my social media followers to participate in my participant observation. Instead of only showing the audience my fieldwork in the form of an end product, I showed them a behind-the-scenes process of making observations. My fieldsite became their fieldsite.

I would also note the impact my audience had on me while in the field. If there were reports in the news about an event in my fieldsite, I would make a greater effort to address it and show how my participants were reacting to it. I was not cut off from the news while conducting fieldwork.[13] I felt accountable for making my fieldnotes accessible and relevant to a wider public. But at the same time, I did not allow the audience's preferences shape all my choices. I posted images that I thought were interesting or necessary for my own documentation process.

Live fieldnotes present an alternative timescale for ethnographers to talk about their work. Social media can be one of many ways for ethnographers to communicate her/his fieldwork experience (Behar 1996) and "reduce the puzzlement" of a given social context (Geertz 1993:16). According to John van Maanen, ethnography is the "practice of representing the social reality of others through the analysis of one's own experience in the world of these others" (van Maanen 1988:ix). Social media tools make it possible for ethnographers to initiate the "reduce the puzzlement" process while they are collecting data because the social media culture values instantaneous sharing.[14]

Instead of viewing the visibility that social media bring with fear, I suggest that we see it an opportunity for interaction with field participants. Given that we are doing research in a time when an increasing number of our participants use social media as a significant part of their identity-making process and interaction with the world, it is absolutely necessary for ethnographers to interact with participants through social media.

Ethnography & Knowledge Production in a Networked World

Ethnographers too often use digital technology to record fieldnotes for ourselves, not for others; to store data, not to broadcast data. Computational technologies are treated as tools for ethnographic methods,[15] not as platforms for ethnographic storytelling. Yet over the last few years, the emergence of social media platforms has transformed the way people acquire and share information. Social media, such as Facebook, Twitter, and Tumblr, have rich ecosystems built on collaboration between communities, developers, users, and partners (Simon 2011). While many communities have taken to these platforms and integrated them into their workflow, ethnographers have largely declined to do so. Journalists, politicians, and even the medical field are using social media apps to share information and stay connected to their stakeholders while in the field. A rich archive of multimedia captures the excitement of fieldwork not just for the ethnographer, but also for a general audience.

Moreover, the core practices of ethnographic observation and analysis are too often invisible or devalued. Christine Hine argues that for ethnography to remain relevant, it needs to be adaptive so that it can thrive in a world of internet technologies (Hine 2000:154). Hine's point should not just be applied to the topics of ethnographic research, but also to the way we conduct ethnography. Ethnography needs to embrace a code of openness; otherwise, it risks undermining its own purpose. We need to approach ethnography as a bazaar, not as a cathedral.

Over the last few decades, there have been challenges to the production of traditional ethnographic knowledge production. Scholars concerned with the disquieting trend of ethnography becoming too insular, prosaic, and academic have raised concerns and offered alternative approaches. Vulnerable ethnography (Behar 1996),[16] experimental ethnography (Wolf 1992),[17] public ethnography (Bailey 2008; Burawoy 2005), adaptive ethnography (Hine 2000), and community-based ethnography (Stringer et al. 1997) are all part of a larger effort to explore an ethnography that speaks to nonspecialists, is not limited to the confines of academia or industry, and embraces a diversity of analytic texts. These approaches signal a turn to a more experimental and open ethnography. A more open ethnography can produce more relevant insights because it relies not on one person for the insights, but a network of people.

The internet consists of open and closed code. It is not a matter of which kind is better, but rather how to extract the best of both approaches for a vibrant online community. Similarly, ethnography should consist of a diversity of outputs from the lengthy monograph to a crisp report and to a short live fieldnote. It is not a matter of privileging one form over the other, but a matter of balancing different forms because each of these forms speak to a different audience. When there is little opportunity or discussion of writing for an audience beyond other ethnographers or clients, we risk marginalizing ethnographic practices.

We already see evidence of a more open ethnography in the form of projects such as The Asthma Files, which allows any ethnographers to contribute data, open sources the data, and collaborates with stakeholders such as epidemiologists, public health experts, and urban planners.[18] We see it in the conversations about an open ethnography on blogs such as *Ethnography Matters,* where these issues are discussed. We see it in listservs like *Anthrodesign,* that bring together designers and applied ethnographers.[19] We see it in the work of scholars who share their data online before publishing it in traditional spaces (boyd 2007; Ford 2012). We see it in the

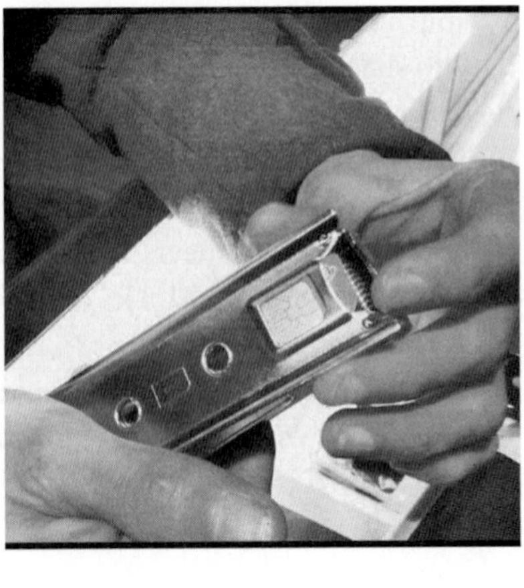

Figure 34.13. Cellphone vendors retrofit sim cards to fit iPhone 4 with a sim card cutter. What's fascinating is that someone invented this tool and now every cellphone vendor uses it in China. This is a bottom up innovation that wouldn't usually be seen as "innovative" but it is. China #bytesofchina.

#GoOpenAccess #pdftribute movement around to make published journal article accessible beyond institutional paywalls (Burrell 2013).[20] These examples reflect a larger effort among ethnographers to speak to other disciplines and to reach a wider audience.

While there are still many issues to explore with the confluence of social media and professional ethnographic practices, my hope is that by sharing my live-fieldnoting experiment we can begin a dialog about these challenges as a community. This chapter raises only a few dilemmas that come with making some of our fieldnotes more visible, though I believe that with near universal access to digital services, we are approaching a point where ignoring social media creates more risks then benefits. Live fieldnoting's use of social media reconfigures the relationship between the ethnographer, the audience, and the participants. Yet this reconfiguration, part of a needed shift towards a bazaar-style approach to learning in and sharing data about our sites, yields important new ethnographic insights. We can no longer avoid discussion of social media as a medium for communicating research, especially when social media is a primary medium of communication in the everyday lives of our participants.

We live in a globally interconnected world where very few places remain off the grid. In an era of networked knowledge, "the smartest person in the room is the room" (Weinberger 2012). The future of knowledge does not depend on individual experts, it depends on networks. It requires a complex level of collaboration that is made possible with the internet. We have to rethink the production of ethnographic knowledge in the age of the internet.

Instead of the trope of the lone ethnographer going to a far-off place to conduct fieldwork and then reporting back a few years later, the new reality is that the ethnographer goes to many places, online and offline, to conduct fieldwork and sends continuous updates that contribute to a network of knowledge. This new ethnographer embraces instant feedback not only from her/his audience

Figure 34.14. I spent a day doing ethnography with a cellphone vendor. His main clients are students. He tell me that he uses an iPad to seduce them into buying android phones. He showed me several website where consumers can download free android apps. Selling a mobile in China requires that you display the expertise of finding "free download." The culture of "free download" is incredibly pervasive that moving consumers to paid content will not only require mas-sive value change to paying for apps, but economic changes in consumer's household spending income. China #bytesofchina.

but from the participants themselves, and in some cases the feedback will challenge the ethnographer's interpretations. This new ethnographer produces multiple representational forms with their data, from live fieldnotes on social media to blogging and to more traditional forms of data and to mixed methods. This new ethnographer treats all forms of social interactions as an everyday occurrence (Figures 34.13 and 34.14). This new ethnographer collaborates with people from different industries and backgrounds and contributes to local problems and public issues of great significance. Ultimately, a more open ethnography is not about creating new tools to help us analyze our data; it is about rethinking our culture around the tool that has been with us the longest: our observations and interactions with the everyday world.

REFERENCES

Bailey, Carol A. 2008. "Public Ethnography." In *Handbook of Emergent Methods*, edited by S. N. Hesse-Biber and P. Leavy, 265–82. New York: The Guilford Press.

Behar, Ruth. 1996. *The Vulnerable Observer: Anthropology that Breaks Your Heart*. Boston: Beacon Press.

boyd, danah. 2007. "Viewing American class divisions through Facebook and MySpace." danah boyd (blog). http://www.danah.org/papers/essays/ClassDivisions.html (accessed June 2, 2013).

____. 2008. "Facebook's Privacy Trainwreck: Exposure, Invasion, and Social Convergence." *Convergence: The International Journal of Research into New Media Technologies* 14(1):13–20.

boyd, danah, and Alice Marwick. 2009. "The Conundrum of Visibility: Youth Safety and the Internet." *Journal of Children and Media* 3(4):410–14.

Brady, Erika. 1999. *A Spiral Way: How the Phonograph Changed Ethnography*. Jackson: University Press of Mississippi.

Burawoy, Michael. 2005. "For Public Sociology." *American Sociological Review* 70(1):4–28.

Burrell, Jenna. 2013. "#GoOpenAccess for the Ethnography Matters Community." Ethnography Matters (website). http://ethnographymatters.net/2013/01/17/goopenaccess-for-the-ethnography-matters-community/ (accessed February 10, 2013).

Collier, John, and Malcolm Collier. 1986. *Visual Anthropology: Photography As a Research Method*. Albuquerque: University of New Mexico Press.

Emerson, Ralph M., Rachel I. Fretz, and Linda L. Shaw. 2011. *Writing Ethnographic Fieldnotes*. Chicago, IL: University of Chicago Press.

Farmer, P. 2004. *Pathologies of Power: Health, Human Rights, and the New War on the Poor*. Berkeley: University of California Press.

Ford, Heather. 2012. "Beyond Reliability: An Ethnographic Study of Wikipedia Sources." Ethnography Matters (website). ethnographymatters.net/2012/07/31/beyond-reliability-an-ethnographic-study-of-wikipedia-sources/ (accessed September 1, 2012).

Geertz, Clifford. 1993. *The Interpretation of Cultures: Selected Essays (1973)*. London: Fontana.

Gitelman, Lisa, ed. 2013. *Raw Data Is an Oxymoron*. Cambridge, MA: MIT Press.

Handelman, Don. 1994. "Critiques of Anthropology: Literary Turns, Slippery Bends." *Poetics Today* 15(3):341–81.

Hine, Christine. 2000. *Virtual Ethnography*. Thousand Oaks, CA: Sage.

Hockings, P., ed. 2009. *Principles of Visual Anthropology*. Berlin: Walter de Gruyter.

Hsu, Wendy. 2012. "On Digital Ethnography: What Do Computers Have To Do with Ethnography? Ethnography Matters (website). http://ethnographymatters.net/2012/10/27/on-digital-ethnography-part-one-what-do-computers-have-to-do-with-ethnography/ (accessed July 10, 2013).

Jurgenson, Nathan. 2011. "Digital Dualism versus Augmented Reality." Cyborgology (website). http://thesocietypages.org/cyborgology/2011/02/24/digital-dualism-versus-augmentedreality/ (accessed March 10, 2012).

Lessig, Lawrence. 2005. *Free Culture: How Big Media Uses Technology and the Law To Lock Down Culture.* New York: Penguin Press.

Ottenberg, Simon. 1990. "Thirty Years of Fieldnotes: Changing Relationships to the Text." In *Fieldnotes: The Makings of Anthropology*, edited by R. Sanjek, 139–60. Ithaca, NY: Cornell University Press.

Pink, Sarah. 2006. *Doing Visual Ethnography*. Thousand Oaks, CA: Sage.

Raymond, E. S. (1999) 2001. *The Cathedral and the Bazaar: Musings on Linux and Open Source by an Accidental Revolutionary*. Sebastopol, CA: O'Reilly Series.

Sanjek, Roger. 1990a. "A Vocabulary for Fieldnotes." In *Fieldnotes: The Makings of Anthropology*, edited by R. Sanjek, 92–138. Ithaca, NY: Cornell University Press.

______. 1990b. "The Secret Life of Fieldnotes." In *Fieldnotes: The Makings of Anthropology*, edited by R. Sanjek, 187–272. Ithaca, NY: Cornell University Press.

Simon, Phil. 2011. *The Age of the Platform: How Amazon, Apple, Facebook, and Google Have Redefined Business*. Henderson, NV: Motion Publishing.

Stringer, Ernest T., Mary F. Agnello, Sheila C. Baldwin, Lois M. Christensen, and Deana L. P. Henry. 1997. *Community-Based Ethnography: Breaking Traditional Boundaries of Research, Teaching, and Learning.* Mahwah, NJ: Psychology Press.

Sunderland, Patricia. L. 1999. "Fieldwork and the Phone." *Anthropological Quarterly* 72(3):105–17.

Taddicken, Monika. 2012. "Privacy, Surveillance, and Self-Disclosure in the Social Web: Exploring the User's Perspective via Focus Groups." In *Internet and Surveillance: The Challenges of Web 2.0 and Social Media*, edited by C. Fuchs, K. Boersma, and A. Albrechtslund, 255–72. New York: Routledge.

Tyler, Stephen A. 2008. "Ethnography, Intertextuality and the End of Description." *The American Journal of Semiotics* 3(4):83–98.

Weber, Rolf H. 2012. "How Does Privacy Change in the Age of the Internet?" In *Internet and Surveillance: The Challenges of Web 2.0 and Social Media*, edited by C. Fuchs, K. Boersma, and A. Albrechtslund, 273–96. New York: Routledge.

Weinberger, David. 2012. *Too Big To Know: Rethinking Knowledge Now That the Facts Aren't the Facts, Experts Are Everywhere, and the Smartest Person in the Room Is the Room*. New York: Basic Books.

Wolf, Margery. 1992. *A Thrice-Told Tale: Feminism, Postmodernism, and Ethnographic Responsibility.* Stanford, CA: Stanford University Press.

van Maanen, John. 1988. *Tales of the Field: On Writing Ethnography*. Chicago, IL: University of Chicago Press.

NOTES

I'd like to thank Jelena Kranovic, Arvind Venkataramani, and Philip Howard for reading the first rough draft of this essay and giving amazing advice. Jelena encouraged me to think about copyright licenses and to provide a more clear terminology around sharing. Arvind helped me focus the essay and prodded me to think about how live fieldnotes could support ethnographic practices. Philip pointed out the practical benefits of having a rich archive of media once out of the field. A big thank you to my team of co-contributors at EthnographyMatters.net! Without you guys I wouldn't even have the space for sharing all these ideas! I received great comments on my original blog post (http://ethnographymatters.net/2012/08/02/writing-live-fieldnotes-towards-a-more-open-ethnography/). In particular, Sam Ladner pointed out very practical issues with ethics and time, Tom Boellstorff got me thinking about the nature of published ethnographies, and Annette Markham identified the instantaneous nature of immediate uploads. Leah Muse-Orlinoff, a humongous glitter unicorn thank you for restructuring the essay and selecting live fieldnotes. Claire Rice, you brought a copy-editor's clarity and sliced through my text like a bear on crack. Lastly, Patricia Sunderland and Rita Denny gave excellent advice as editors and without their initial invite, I would not have turned my initial blog musings on Ethnography Matters into this more well thought out essay.

1 Lawrence Lessig created Creative Commons, a nonprofit organization that distributes a range of licenses free of charge to the public that allows people to legally distribute, build, and share creative work. These licenses give creators an additional option to the "all rights reserved" copyright license with a "some rights reserved" license.

2 Upon returning from fieldwork, I've consulted several clients to transform how they share insights using the live-fieldnoting process. Even though live fieldnotes for clients are only shared internally, it still creates immense value to share fieldnotes in real time with coworkers who are unable to go to the fieldsite. While most fieldsite teams consist of three to ten people, a much larger group, often spread between several departments, is tracking and interacting with the live fieldnotes.

3 Instagram users create public or private accounts and can upload photos in square format with the choice of applying filters that change the colors and qualities of the photos. Users can follow other accounts and view, comment, and like other photos.

4 Karen McGrane talks about NPR's COPE model on her website: karenmcgrane.com/2012/09/04/adapting-ourselves-to-adaptive-content-video-slides-and-transcript-oh-my/ (accessed February 22, 2013). The philosophy of COPE can be traced back to the early days of video-blogging, when early pioneers of the form worked on universal embeds that prioritized views on any platform over views on the creator's site.

5 Experimenting with live fieldnotes was possible for me because I was not working for a client. I often hear that from industry ethnographers that they could never live fieldnote. My response is that there is nothing stopping an ethnographer from conducting fieldwork outside of one's work. If anything, nonclient ethnographic work is critical to keeping an ethnographer's soul alive. My experiment was to push fieldnotes to the most open extreme. But different levels of openness can also be explored within an institution. Fieldnotes can be live within a research team and then within a company. Industry ethnographers have a lot of opportunity to not only produce insights for a company, but to bring a company's consumers alive for a company's employees. Live fieldnotes can be a way for researchers to share their fieldwork with people in other departments and even researchers who work inside a lab or with quantitative data.

6 Look to An Xiao Mina (@anxiaostudio) and Zach Hyman (@SqInchAnthro) as ethnographers who are using Instagram to live fieldnote.

7 Social fieldnoting or participatory fieldnoting are other possible names for live fieldnoting.

8 I used the hashtag #bytesofchina on all live fieldnotes for my China research.

9 You see early examples of this work on his blog in 2002 (http://janchipchase.com; accessed January 10, 2013), but it wasn't until 2005 that he really started getting into it.

10 See http://ethnographymatters.net/2012/08/02/writing-live-fieldnotes-towards-a-more-open-ethnography/#comment-1025.

11 To think otherwise would be a form of digital dualism, where the real is associated with the physical and the unreal is associated with the virtual (Jurgenson 2011).

12 As Gitelman (2013) argues in Raw Data Is an Oxymoron, all forms of data are culturally mediated.

13 Often I had reporters reach out to me about current events in the news and in my live fieldnotes.

14 The de facto assumption is that pictures are of moments that have just happened, hence the "Insta" in Instagram; otherwise, users add the hashtag "#latergram" as a way to communicate that this event took place at an earlier time. While some ethnographers can see this as loss of control and lack of pacing the fieldwork, I see this as way to be more connected to participants and audience.

15 For example, ethnographer Wendy Hsu (2012) gives a detailed explanation for how she used computer programming in the analysis of her fieldwork.

16 Ruth Behar passionately makes a case against the depersonalizing trend within ethnography and defends "different kinds of witnessing" (1996:26). In particular, she outlines the practice of a vulnerable and highly subjective ethnographer.

17 Margery Wolff asserts that ethnography can produce different styles of texts that are valid. In *A Thrice-Told Tale* (1992), she presents three texts, from fiction to fieldnotes to a journal article, that draw on the same set of events to illustrate that ethnographic output can take multiple forms even when drawing on the same content.

18 See theasthmafiles.org/ (accessed January 28, 2013).

19 See anthrodesign.com (accessed January 28, 2013).

20 See pdftribute.net (accessed January 29, 2013).

35

Ethnography in Digital Spaces: Ethnography of Virtual Worlds, Netnography, & Digital Ethnography

ALESSANDRO CALIANDRO

INTRODUCTION

With the rise of Web 2.0, the internet has become not only a means of *mass communication*, but also a means of *mass consumption*. Millions of users surf social media daily looking for information about consumer goods and to shop (eMarketer 2013). Thanks to the interactive possibilities of social media, online consumers go further than looking, discussing brands and products among themselves, proposing evaluations and modifications in use, using them as vehicles to create communities or to express their own identity; in a word, they produce culture through consumer goods (Belk 1988). It is in the strategic interest of companies to take note of the production of culture from the bottom up for two reasons: to link *user-driven innovation* to their business and marketing processes (Carù and Cova 2007) and to bridge the gap between the meanings that companies assign to their brand and products and those actually produced by consumers (Walsh 2011).

The most appropriate method to understand the culture that consumers produce within their daily life practices on social media is undoubtedly web-based ethnography. In the last few years, various styles of web-based ethnography have been developed, each of them identified by different labels: "virtual ethnography" (Hine 2000), "Internet ethnography" (Miller and Slater 2001), "netnography" (Kozinets 2002), "cyber-ethnography" (Teli et al. 2007), "digital ethnography" (Murthy 2008), and "ethnography of virtual worlds" (Boellstorff et al. 2012). Often, these terms are used as synonyms; sometimes rightly so, some other times wrongly so. Nevertheless, my aim in this chapter is not so much to bring order to this terminological jungle once and for all; more modestly, I would like to focus on three particular styles of web-based ethnog-

Handbook of Anthropology in Business, edited by Rita Denny and Patricia Sunderland, 658–679.

raphy: the ethnography of virtual worlds, netnography, and digital ethnography, because each is an ethnographic style grounded on distinct theoretical and methodological paradigms, and each represents a trajectory for ethnographic engagement in business arenas.

ETHNOGRAPHY OF VIRTUAL WORLDS

Theoretical Frameworks

Ethnography of virtual worlds involves the study of MMORPGs (massively multiplayer online role-playing games) such as World of Warcraft or Second Life. Boellstorff et al., in their handbook *Ethnography and Virtual Worlds*, define virtual worlds as computer-generated physical environments that are characterized by four distinguishing features: (1) they instill in the users a sense of *worldness*; (2) they are, by their nature, *multiuser*; (3) they are *lasting* (they continue to exist even when the users log off); and (4) they allow the users to "*embody* themselves, usually as avatars" (Boellstorff et al. 2012:7). Thus, according to this definition, digital environments present on social networks, online communities based on forums, and first-person shooter games cannot be classified as virtual worlds.

Virtual worlds can be considered as cultural artifacts in the sense that they take shape both as technological objects manufactured by the combined work of various actors (programmers, designers, players) and as social spaces defined by the weave of interactions that take place within and by the meaning assigned to them from the people involved in such interactions. Inside those worlds, users can engage in communal activities (participate in a class) (Dalgarno and Lee 2010) as much as in individual experiences, such as strolling alone in a virtual forest (Pearce 2009). In the same way, users can maintain emotionally intense relations with each other or, conversely, detached ones (Nardi 2010). Such complexity and completeness of personal and social experiences make life in virtual worlds very similar to the "real" one.

The relationship between real and virtual represents a central theoretical tangle of almost all the ethnographic studies of virtual worlds that is therefore important to unravel. Among anthropologists there is a significant agreement about the fact that—although life in virtual environments is characterized by peculiar experiences (consider the possibility of constantly changing gender) that de facto separate it from the offline world—the interactions that take place within have a real impact on people's daily lives (Schiano et. al 2011). It is not unusual, for instance, that in virtual worlds users find spouses, friends, and emotional support for their physical or psychological discomfort; nor is it uncommon to feel they can express their real selves in a manner that is not allowed in "the world out there" (Boellstorff 2008). This is the reason, according to Boellstorff, it would be more correct to distinguish between "virtual world" and "actual world" and not between "real" and "virtual world," insofar as "it is in being virtual that we are human: since it is human "nature" to experience life through the prism of culture, human being has always been virtual being" (Boellstorff 2008:5).

Methodological Approaches

Ethnographers who study MMORPGs tend to call their research style "ethnography of virtual worlds" and not "virtual ethnography" (Hine 2000). This is due to the fact that the paradigm of ethnographic research is, by its nature, flexible and therefore it "does not undergo fundamental transformation or distortion in its journey to virtual arenas because ethnographic approaches are always modified for each field site, and in real time as the research progresses" (Boellstorff et al. 2012:4). Nevertheless, the ethnographic procedure in virtual worlds presents some methodological peculiarities that deserve to be highlighted.

The study of MMORPGs implies a total immersion in virtual environments; at a practical level, this means that while an ethnographer who studies nuclear technicians doesn't need to become a nuclear technician to understand their culture, a similar proposition does not apply to the ethnographers of virtual worlds, for whom becoming MMORPG players is key to study the cultural processes that structure them. The *medium* that makes the immersion in virtual worlds possible is the "avatar," "the central point at which users intersect with a technological object and embody themselves, making the virtual environment . . . real" (Taylor 2002:41). The ethnographer's choice of avatar is therefore very important and should never be left to chance, since it is through the avatar that the researcher communicates to others the way he wants to be perceived. For example, Taylor (2008) reports how, in her ethnography of the MMORPG Everquest, the choice of embodying a dwarf—a harmless and funny creature—helped her relate to strangers. What has been said up to now, therefore, recalls and strengthens the idea of Boellstorff et al. (2012), according to whom participant observation represents the *heart* and *soul* of the ethnographical method in virtual worlds. In fact, a face-to-face interview with a World of Warcraft player would make it impossible to understand the feeling of enthusiasm experienced when one kills a "raid boss" with their own guild (Nardi 2013). The choice to make participant observation the main technique ethnographers adopt to explore virtual worlds is therefore necessary to study these environments in *their own terms*, through methods and techniques that are natural to them and in some ways suggested by the environments themselves (Boellstorff 2008).

Implications for Ethnographers

Ethnographic studies pertaining to virtual worlds highlight the role of participants as *prosumers* (Castranova 2005): that is, the ability of consumers to transform their own consumer actions into productive processes. Second Life, for example, is a virtual world completely founded on the concept of user-created content (Ondrejka 2004). Linden Lab (the Second Life holding company), as a matter of fact, supplies users only with a basic platform consisting of a set of landscapes and some tools to control and modify the avatars; all the rest—buildings, stores, and so on—is the result of the users' work. These procedures of coproduction can be equated to real forms of "immaterial labor" (Virno 2002), since they generate two peculiar outputs: intangible goods as data, information, and knowledge; and what Lazzarato (1996) calls "ethical surplus": a social and emotional bond through which the production of value becomes possible. The value of virtual worlds—what makes them appealing to consumers—dwells in the spectacular settings they are immersed in and in the emotional intensity that characterizes the social interaction they are involved with: two *assets* entirely created by the same consumers (Arvidsson 2006). This represents a significant economic advantage for the companies that own them, since access to the virtual worlds is not free, but rather dependent on the payment of a fee. Furthermore, the ethical surplus generated by the consumers assures enormous advantages in terms of cost savings in customer care. The great social and emotional involvement that characterizes the interactions between players ensures that they mutually support each other in regard to game-related issues (Kow and Nardi 2009). Obviously, not only companies but consumers too are gaining economic advantages from virtual worlds. Consumers are often involved in commercial activities, the most common ones being those dealing with retail sales, both of virtual products (for example clothes for avatars) and analog products (for example, real clothes sold through avatars). In the same way, users also sell labor, as in the case of sex workers who offer both online and offline services (Lynch 2010).

Business implications also go beyond the boundaries of virtual worlds. For instance, Google Glass, a wearable computer with an optical head-mounted display that creates a layered world in front of the user, immerses users in an "augmented reality" world (Jurgenson 2012) made both by virtual and material objects. In this case, it is obvious that to capitalize on the potential of this product, the ethnographic methods and insights become crucial. "Gamification" is now a practice of management applied to a wide range of business contexts (such as call centers, e-commerce, mobile app design, recruitment, etc.). It was developed by game designers and is implemented mainly by managers who are skilled in the use of MMORPGs (Zichermann and Cunningham 2011). Of course, consumers can also take advantage of the skills they acquire in playing MMORPGs. Reeves et al. (2008) convincingly argue in their article "Leadership's Online Labs" that users who are able to manage teams of players within virtual worlds are more likely to become successful leaders in the future.

The impact of widespread productive consumption practices on the lifestyles and attitudes of virtual world users is the object of various theoretical observations. To this end, the concept of "digital virtual consumption" by Denegri-Knott and Molesworth (2010) is particularly interesting. According to the two sociologists, digital virtual consumption stands apart from imaginary or virtual consumption insofar as "the object of consumption does not only reside in the consumer's mind, but is experienced as owned and used within parameters of specific digital virtual spaces" (Denegri-Knott and Molesworth 2010:109–10). In this sense, virtual worlds would be privileged places for digital virtual consumption, as they are liminal spaces—somewhere between the imagination and the material—where consumers can actualize their fantasies of consumption, realizing purchasing desires unlikely to be fulfilled either because they are beyond their economic means (for example, luxury goods), or because they are purely fictional (for example, a magic wand). In this way, motivating and increasing the players' fantasies of consumption, virtual worlds take shape as platforms apt to "educate" the users to a consumerist lifestyle (Molesworth and Denegri-Knott 2007). Think, for example, about Sims Online, where all the characters are consumers whose happiness is directly caused by possessing material objects: the purpose of the game, actually, is to best manage one's own characters and to have them prosper (Arvidsson 2006). It is therefore clear that it is strategic for companies to control these worlds through product placement, space branding or, more simply, owning the world itself.

In spite of the undeniable advantages in terms of marketing and business, there are many ethical questions that have been raised about digital virtual consumption, especially concerning the risks of exploitation and manipulation of the consumers (Zwick et al. 2008). In their critique, Watkins and Molesworth (2013) see the co-creation of digital virtual goods within social media platforms and MMORPGs as an intensive form of exploitation of users, noting that "markets aren't only exploiting consumers' immaterial labour for financial gains—and may proceed to charge them a surplus for the fruits of their own labour—but, once purchased, consumers are denied full control over the digital virtual goods they worked so hard to cultivate" (Watkins and Molesworth 2013:4). Because consumers do not legally own the goods they possess, not only must they pay continuously for accessing the goods they created (via the login), but they cannot use them freely, for instance by selling their own avatars to other players. According to Watkins and Molesworth, this kind of exploitation proves to be particularly deceitful because it hinges on what they call "possession work," the "the investment of time and energy by consumers in order to bring digital virtual goods into existence, as well as the ongoing [affective] labour required in order to continually experience them as singular" (Watkins and Molesworth 2013:1).

NETNOGRAPHY

Theoretical Frameworks

Netnography is a neologism that combines the words "ethnography" and "internet." The term was coined by the marketing scholar Robert Kozinets (2002) and refers to a particular style of web-based ethnography that he developed within the theoretical domains of consumer culture theory (Arnould and Thompson 2005) and "tribal marketing" (Kozinets 1999). Netnography can therefore be defined as an ethnographic method that, through the use of naturalistic analysis techniques (immersive and unobtrusive), allows the researcher to immerse himself in online conversations between consumers in an empathetic way, re-creating their culture and their shared identities (Bilgram et al. 2011; also see Kozinets, this volume). Netnography's primary field sites are communities of online consumers (Kozinets 2002).

Netnographic research focuses on two main typologies of online communities: "brand communities" (Muñiz and O'Guinn 2001) and "communities of practice" (Wenger 1998). These communities are groups of online consumers that share a passion for either a brand (e.g., Nutella [Cova and Pace 2006]) or for certain consumption practices (e.g., sports bikes [Reto 2008]). Netnography proves to be an effective instrument in theorizing identities of online consumers. Based on the netnographic paradigm, consumers' identities are defined by the roles they assume within their own communities of reference (Pongsakornrungsil and Schroeder 2010). With this in mind, Kozinets suggests an interesting model in which consumers can be subdivided into four categories: Devotee, Insider, Newbie, and Mingler. These four "ideal types" differentiate based on the level of involvement and know-how they transfer to the community.

Methodological Approaches

At an epistemological level, netnography can be placed within the paradigm of "virtual methods" (Hine 2005). Virtual methods consist of adapting traditional research strategies developed offline (such as surveys), within the online environments. Netnography, actually, is a "promiscuous" (Kozinets 2010) and "hybrid" (Garcia et al. 2009) method; promiscuous in the sense that it relies on a wide range of virtual techniques (virtual surveys, interviews via chat, interviews by email, etc.), and hybrid in the sense that it skillfully combines virtual techniques with analogical techniques (for example, participant observation online and offline). The main virtual techniques used by netnographers are surveys, interviews, and participant observation.

Virtual surveys are very useful in understanding general patterns linked to online communities, both *global* (for example, how many people in the United States participate in an online community?) and *local* (for example, what is the gender composition of the Apple community?) (Li and Bernoff 2008).

Virtual interviews are text-based interviews subdivided into two macro-categories: synchronous and asynchronous (James and Busher 2009). Synchronous interviews—for example, the ones conducted through online chats in forums or social networks—require the temporal presence of both interviewer and interviewee. This type of interview is very effective when the netnographer wants to establish an empathetic contact with members of the community and obtain spontaneous answers from them (O'Connor and Madge 2003). Asynchronous interviews, on the other hand, do not envisage the temporal co-presence between interviewer and interviewee. A classic example of asynchronous interview is one conducted by email: a technique particularly appropriate when deep introspection by the interviewee is crucial (James 2007).

Virtual participant observation of online communities follow two main strategies: a completely nonintrusive one, where the researcher limits himself to observing the interactions of the community by "lurking" (Bruckman 2006); or a participatory one, where the researcher interacts with members of the community and shares their daily online interactions (Walstrom 2004). Usually, the first type of observation is preparatory to the second, in the sense that the netnographers, before immersing themselves in the interactions of the community, generally start their fieldwork with long periods of lurking to familiarize themselves with the rules and the communication codes of the community they intend to study (Muñiz and Schau 2005).

Implications for Ethnographers

Netnography is an effective resource for marketers because of its ability to immerse the practitioner in online communities and to reconstruct their cultures and their shared consumption identities (Schau et al. 2009). The wealth and depth of netnographic insights ensure that they can be translated in a strategic way to a range of marketing and business activities: advertising and communication design, product design and innovation, lead-user detection, and trend watching. To better understand the way such translations can occur, I describe a few netnographic case studies.

Advertising & communication design: Toyota Swagger Wagon

In 2009, Toyota decided to rely on a viral campaign to launch its new Sienna minivan. The campaign revolves around an ironic YouTube video[1] showing two young parents who, dancing to a rap beat with tough expressions, sing to the world about how much they owe the Toyota Swagger Wagon for the fact that they became cool people. The campaign had immediate success: 7 million views and 11 million subscriptions to the Sienna channel. A good part of the success was due to the fact that the company was able to listen directly to the consumers through the use of netnographic techniques: creating a fan page on Facebook and implementing face-to-face interviews with the most active users within that fan page. In this way, Toyota discovered that the addressed target (millennial parents) shared a complex subcultural universe, characterized by specific dreams, rituals, and languages: the postmodern dream of the suburban family, the values of comfort and certainty woven with those of flexibility and luxury, and the use of a particular hip-hop slang (Iamandi and Postolache 2011). Toyota's cleverness was therefore to align this system of cultural meanings with its brand and to present it to its own creators through viral advertising.

Product design & innovation: Nivea Black & White deodorant

In 2011, netnographers Bilgram, Bartl, and Biel, hired by Nivea, monitored the conversations of various online communities linked to cosmetics, fashion, and bodybuilding (Bilgram et al. 2011). By carefully exploring these conversational places and interacting with the users inhabiting those places, they discovered that consumers shared a desire to have not only a deodorant that wouldn't stain, but most of all a deodorant that would let white clothes stay white and black clothes stay black. As a result, Nivea immediately started the planning and production of a new, successful deodorant: Nivea Black & White.

Lead-user detection: Athletic shoe fans

According to Belz and Baumach (2011), netnography is, unlike traditional quantitative surveys in which the responders essentially self-select themselves, an effective instrument to identify lead-users because it is able to locate trendsetters in their habitual context of interaction: their communities. An emblematic case is found in Füller et al. (2007), who conducted research among communities of basketball shoe fans. The three netnographers focused on the website niketalk.com, where they bumped into the "Designer's Roll Call," informal contests where the most creative users challenge themselves in a design competition on themes such as "Invent the basketball shoe for the year 2050." In spite of the informal role, the users took these contests very seriously and posted very graphically and technologically complex design projects on the website. According to the netnographers, among these users, the one who stood out was Alphaproject, a young designer whose talent was very much appreciated and who was a very active member of the community. Not only Füller and his team noticed Alphaproject; so did Nike, who eventually hired him.

Trend-watching: intercultural marriage

Application of netnography to trend-watching is exemplified by Nelson and Otnes (2005), who studied communities devoted to intercultural marriages. According to the researchers' observations, brides who frequent these communities share two kinds of problems: a *material* one and a *symbolic* one. At a material level, brides complain of the lack of wedding service suppliers able to handle bilingual and multicultural ceremonies, from typographers unable to print invitations in two or more languages simultaneously to catering companies that can't supply more than one type of ethnic cuisine at a time. At a cultural level, the problem for brides was trying not to offend the various cultural sensitivities of their guests. To avoid small "diplomatic incidents," online brides co-created and developed ad hoc strategies, such as choosing bilingual DJs with a multiethnic musical culture, or picking artifacts and ethnic rituals that have significance primarily for the couple alone, since it is impossible to perfectly combine different religious and cultural traditions. In this case, through netnographic research, it is not only possible to observe emergent trends of consumption, but also the practical strategies used to meet them.

Conclusions

In the case studies presented, we can conclude that (to put it simply) the distinct value of netnography is in its capacity to bring into existence a sort of huge "Focus Group 2.0." Compared with traditional focus groups, a Focus Group 2.0 presents four crucial advantages: (1) it's free; (2) it allows researchers and companies to listen to the voices of hundreds of consumers at once; (3) it provides researchers and companies with naturalistic data, insofar as they are spontaneously generated by online consumers; and (4) it allows companies to coproduce strategies of marketing and business with consumers in a very immediate and effective way.

DIGITAL ETHNOGRAPHY

Theoretical Frameworks

Digital ethnography is an emerging style of online ethnography that studies the cultural conditions of a contemporary *networked society* through the internet. As an emerging methodology, digital ethnography is less formalized, in academic terms, compared with ethnography of virtual worlds and netnography. Nonetheless, its theoretical and methodological profile can be clearly defined from a wide scientific literature that focuses on how the architecture of digital environments (and their functions, such as links, retweets, or hashtags) shapes users' behaviors, their interactions, and their cultural processes (boyd et al. 2010; Horst and Miller 2012; Kien 2009; Marres 2004; Papacharissi 2011).

Digital ethnography is an ethnography grounded by *digital methods* rather than one based on the internet itself. In *The End of the Virtual: Digital Methods*, Richard Rogers (2009) distinguishes between digital methods and virtual methods. Virtual methods adapt methodological strategies developed offline to online environments. Proper digital methods, on the other hand, take the nature and affordances of the digital environment seriously. Such online groundedness entails following the medium: how digital devices like search engines and social media platforms, and functions like Instagram's tags or Twitter's retweets, structure flows of information and communication. It entails embracing the natural logic the internet applies to itself in gathering, ordering, and analyzing data. Digital methods as developed by Richard Rogers (2013) and Noortje Marres (2012) are inspired by Bruno Latour's (2005) call to "follow the natives," understanding social formations as the results of actors' activity, rather than as a priori starting points for the analysis. Because it is a socioanthropological method, digital ethnography doesn't obviously confine itself to following the medium, but also studies the uses users make of digital environments and their functions and observes the social formations, cultures, and shared identities that naturally emerge from such use practices (Wesch 2009).

A main field site of digital ethnography is the "digital public"—a social space concurrently constructed "through the networked technologies and the imagined collective that emerges as result of the intersection of people, technology and practice" (boyd 2011:39). A public can be defined as a mediated association among strangers who are united by a temporary emotional intensity directed towards a common object (Tarde 1902), such as a brand. In this sense, according to Arvidsson (2013), members of a public are not kept together by direct interaction, but by a social imaginary created and reelaborated by the members themselves that is spread and put into circulation within the same public. This makes the public a social space generated by the reflexive circulation of a discourse. Unlike the concept of community, the concept of a public allows the ethnographer to face the extreme variety of interactional processes happening on the internet that are not always as persistent and dense as the communal ones (Postill 2008). For instance, consider a social network such as Facebook or Twitter. Various studies, both quantitative and qualitative (Kwak et al. 2010; Parks 2011), have shown that people have loose relationships on social networks, using them not so much to interact and discuss with others in a strict sense, but rather as means to maintain and manage their own social network through *self-presentation* strategies (Marwick and boyd 2011). Here, self-presentation is another key concept for digital ethnography, which conceives online social identity not so much as a particular role played within a circumscribed community, but as a procedural occurrence that emerges, in a natural way, from different set manners through which the users construct and keep their *face* (Goffman 1959) in front of a digital public (Donath and boyd 2004).

Methodological Approaches

Digital ethnography uses various techniques inspired by natively digital methods: those methods the internet uses to organize itself (Rogers 2013). These include network analysis, co-word analysis, semantic analysis, and discourse analysis. Here I focus on network analysis and discourse analysis, illustrating each through two case studies connected to consumption culture. Specifically, I show how network analysis and discourse analysis are preferred techniques in exploring the social and semantic structures of publics and in understanding the construction of identity within publics.

Network Analysis

Online network analysis is very useful in modeling connections between social actors and identifying those who are most influential (if applied to sites/users) (Bakshy et al. 2011), and in analyzing co-occurrences between terms, thus reconstructing the semantic structure of a discourse (if applied to texts) (Marres and Weltrevede 2012). An interesting example is the digital ethnography by Barina (2013) about participants who talk about corporate social responsibility on Twitter. The research started by downloading 240,584 English tweets following the keywords/hashtags #CSR and #sustainability. From this set of tweets, Barina chose first of all the users who received more mentions (@) and retweets (RT), thus identifying the most influential subjects within the discourse about corporate social responsibility and Twitter. Subsequently, through the analysis

Figure 35.1. Network of the most influential actors in regard to CSR (@+RT received). Image courtesy of Stefania Barina.

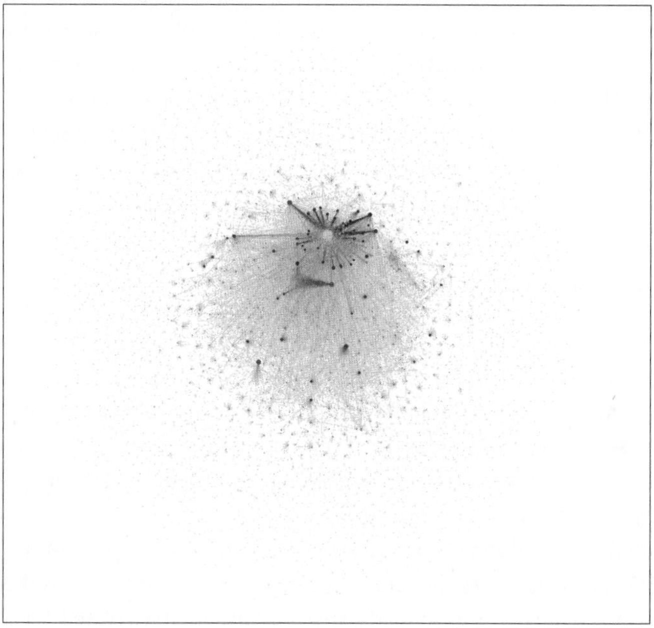

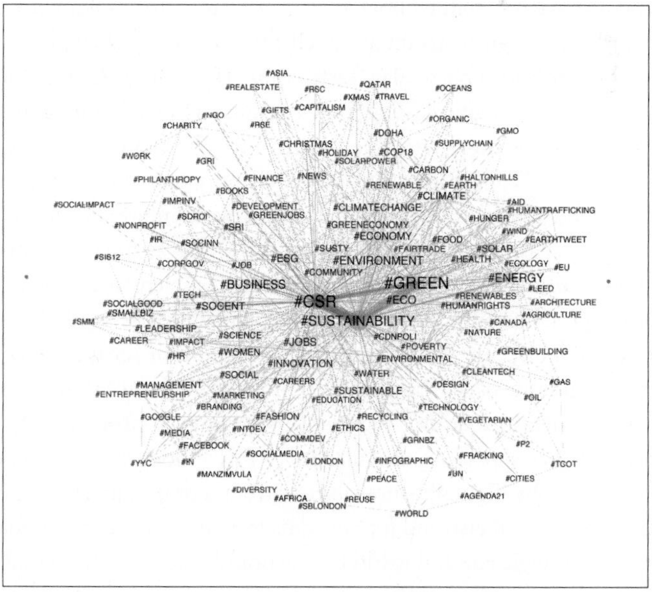

Figure 35.2. CSR hashtag network. Image courtesy of Stefania Barina.

of co-occurrences among hashtags, the hashtag network spontaneously associated by the users with the corporate social responsibility concept was reconstructed. This analysis produced some very interesting cultural insights, as it showed how the corporate social responsibility public on Twitter is composed of a wide but scattered network, dominated by a small group of influential accounts (Figure 35.1) mainly involved in marketing and communication activities (such as @Csrwire or @Taigacompany), that spread a discourse divided into two main topics (Figure 35.2): business issues (#business #jobs, #marketing), and environmental issues (#sustainability, #environment).

Discourse Analysis

Digital discourse analysis considers social media a cultural text in which the concept of "text" has to be understood broadly, like a language composed by written signs, images, and audio traces. Discourse analysis considers texts as sites of sociocultural practice that simultaneously constitute "social identities, social relations, systems of knowledge and belief" (Fairclough 1995:55). Although it specifically concerns the construction of identity, discourse analysis conducted on social media doesn't look so much at the content of the texts created by users as the uses they make of the texts (and of the tools the platform provides to create them) to spread a specific "presentation of Self" (Papacharissi 2009). With this purpose, various studies on the relation between brand and social media have highlighted how often users, more than talking *about* brands, use brands both as an instrument of self-presentation (Schau and Gilly 2003) and a way to indicate a particular "taste ethos" (Liu 2007). A case study on this subject matter is the digital ethnography conducted by Caliandro and Arvidsson (2013) for the infant-care brand Chicco. Through the analysis of 2,489 messages with the keyword "Chicco" posted by a public of Italian online moms on different forums and blogs, it emerged that moms were interested not so much in collectively discussing the value to assign the brand as they were in using the brand talk as a means of self-narration through which to describe their own maternal experiences. By analyzing the recurrent themes within the narrative plot of online moms, the researcher reconstructed four ideal types of maternal identity: "pragmatic mom," "passionate mom," "anxious mom," and "imprisoned mom." These identities do not represent psychological profiles, but rather discursive topoi that spread a particular maternity ethos. In this case, therefore, digital ethnography highlights how users have not only expressed an imaginary around the brand, but also and foremost, have constructed a social imaginary in relation to a strategic cultural world for the brand: one of motherhood.

The two digital ethnographic case studies presented here point to a new social phenomenon, which is the emergence of the consumer as a producer of metadata. This occurrence is quite different from what we saw in the ethnography of virtual worlds, where the consumer is a producer of new identities, and in netnography, where the consumer is a producer of new social connections in communities. Metadata are data whose function is to specify the meaning of other data. For instance, consider Twitter's hashtags, which are markers through which users naturally develop a specific conversation thread; users essentially categorize their own tweets. Practices of self-classification are also implicit, as we saw in the case of mothers: when mothers situate their opinions on childcare products within a certain ethos of maternity, they are fundamentally trying to convey to their publics the *authentic* meaning of their behaviors of consumption. In my opinion, this new role of the consumer has an interesting methodological implication: by producing metadata, the consumer becomes an actor whose actions align with the practices of researchers and managers in categorizing and analyzing data. Of course this makes the online consumer researches even more complex, but that shouldn't be an issue, as ethnographers are known for their ability to cope with complexity.

Implications for Ethnographers

The most demanding challenge facing companies and researchers today on the internet is Big Data, where the challenge is to extract sense from the chaotic amount of data daily produced and re-created on the web. The challenge to companies is twofold: (1) to interpret the massive disorganized flow of comments, likes, and retweets users associate with brands and products in a coherent way so they can be translated into real business strategies (Kozinets et al. 2010); and (2) to manage the data correctly so they can be translated into a company's good reputation (Hearn 2010). Given its theoretical and methodological background, digital ethnography is a valuable tool to meet these challenges. In a classic "seeding" strategy (Hinz et al. 2011), for example, digital ethnography can supply the brand with the right coordinates to spread its message through the simultaneous identification of: (1) the public to seed it to; (2) the imaginary to wrap it in; (3) the influential people able to magnify it; and (4) the strategies of users' self-presentation to leverage to viralize it.

Beyond the economic consequences, the outputs of digital ethnography also have ethical implications. As we saw, research on the brand allows publics developing around the brand to materialize; these publics tend to construct, more than an imaginary on the brand, a social imaginary starting from the brand. Such a conceptual shift entails, in my opinion, a shift from tribal marketing to "societing" (Badot et al. 2007),[2] in the sense that companies that today stay on Web 2.0 mustn't limit their impact to circumscribed communities of consumers (supporting and strengthening the existing social bonds and

Figure 35.3. Overlap between the actor-networks of sustainability and Coca-Cola. Image courtesy of Davide Beraldo.

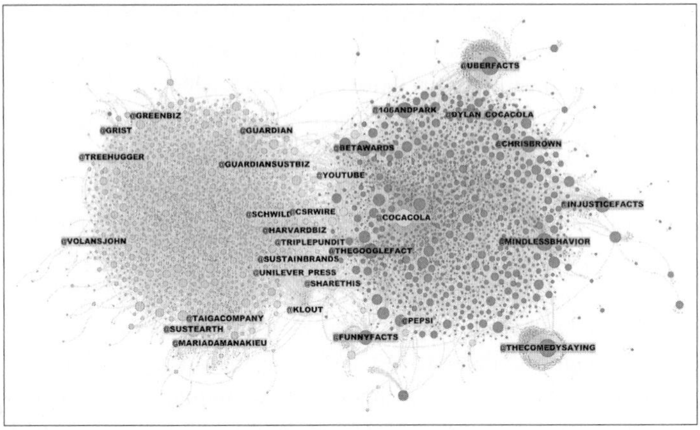

rewarding them with additional experiences of consumption), but must also have an impact on society, broadly speaking. The notion of societing is apt, since by societing we mean the set of practices through which consumers, publics, and companies cooperate to face the problems of contemporary globalized society (global warming, labor exploitation, sustainability, etc.), thus producing social innovation beyond marketing and the welfare state (Cova 2013). Is it possible to do all this now? Which road should be followed? Or, better yet, what type of help can ethnography provide? To try to answer these questions, I present the results of a digital ethnography study undertaken on the Coca-Cola brand (Beraldo 2012).

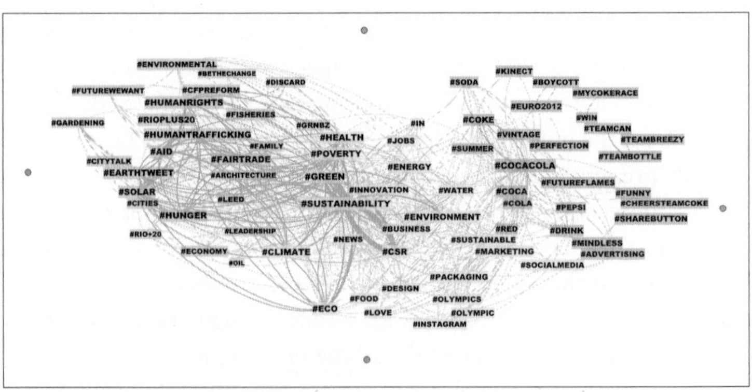

Figure 35.4. Overlap between the hashtag networks of sustainability and Coca-Cola. Image courtesy of Davide Beraldo.

Figure 35.3 shows two Twitter networks: the network on the right shows all the users who talk about Coca-Cola; the network on the left shows all users who talk about sustainability. As one can see, there is no significant overlap between the two publics (@sharethis is a tool that allows the integration of contents coming from social media on a personal website): those who talk about Coca-Cola don't talk about sustainability, and vice versa, considering them two separate cultural worlds. Nevertheless, observing the hashtag networks in Figure 35.4, one can see that some hashtags act as a bridge between the discourse users spontaneously formulate around Coca-Cola and the discourse articulated around the concept of sustainability, such as #green, #water, #poverty, #climate, #health, and #environment. Therefore, although distinct, publics of Coca-Cola and of sustainability present some potential points of contact. These simple visualizations thus highlight a gap in the imaginary between Coca-Cola and sustainability, but at the same time they indicate possible discursive *paths* to start from and to travel along to bridge the gap.

CONCLUSIONS

In this chapter, we deal with three ethnographic methods (ethnography of virtual worlds, netnography, and digital ethnography), and we focus mainly on their differences, which are summarized in Table 35.1.

Moving from the ethnography of virtual worlds to digital ethnography, methods increasingly rely on software and digital tools. In the ethnography of virtual worlds, researchers are required to immerse themselves in the world they intend to study; in netnography, researchers immerse themselves in the consumers' conversations and communities as well, but this immersion is often mediated by a variety of software for quantitative analysis (such as those for implementing virtual survey or for coding texts). Digital ethnography also relies completely on digital tools, which provide researchers with large amounts of data and the means for visualizing and analyzing them. In this instance, it might seem that the role of researchers becomes less and less relevant, since software takes care of the job. I would suggest the opposite. First, research design and the setting of objectives remain complex tasks that require socioanthropological skills and experience. Second, even if the digital tools are able to download and analyze data, it is perfectly useless, for example, to have a long list of retweets or to visualize a complex network of hashtags if one can't *interpret* them or shed a light on the practical *uses* users make of these metadata or on the *meanings* they assign to them, or again on the *cultural connections* that link them together. The more that digital tools for social analysis become widespread and complex, the more the work and expertise of social researchers is needed. So, given these

Table 35.1. Summary of frameworks.

Method	Ontological Framework (the Web is assumed to be …)	Epistemological Framework	Theoretical Framework	Iconic Examples	Conception of the Consumer
Ethnography of virtual worlds	A realm apart, parallel to the actual world	Grounded on the traditional ethnographic paradigm	Fieldsite: virtual world Identity: avatar	World of Warcraft, Second Life, The Sims Online, Everquest	Divided between virtuality and actuality
Netnography	A place where individuals gather and form communities, subcultures, and build social ties	Grounded on virtual methods	Fieldsite: community Identity: social role within the community	Nutella community, sport bikes community, communities of basketball shoes fans	Integration of online and offline
Digital ethnography	A nexus of interactions hosted by social media	Grounded on digital methods	Fieldsite: public Identity: self-presentation in front of a public	Facebook, Twitter	Made of data, fully digital

premises, we can anticipate the rise of an Ethnographer 2.0 that is a *hybrid* researcher able to integrate quantitative and qualitative approaches as well as the analysis and the interpretation of digital data.

REFERENCES

Arnould, Eric J., and Craig J. Thompson. 2005. "Consumer Culture Theory: Twenty Years of Research." *Journal of Consumer Research* 31(March):868–82.

Arvidsson, Adam. 2006. *Brands: Meaning and Value in Media Culture.* London: Routledge.

Arvidsson, Adam. 2013. "The Potential of Consumer Publics." *Ephemera* 13(2):367–91.

Badot, Olivier, Bernard Cova, and Ampelio Bucci. 2007. "Beyond Marketing Panaceas: In Praise of Societing." In *Critical Marketing: Defining the Field*, edited by M. Saren, P. Maclaran, C. Goulding, R. Elliott, A. Shankar, and M. Catterall, 85–98. Oxford, UK: Butterworth-Heinemann.

Bakshy, Eytan, Winter A. Mason, Jake M. Hofman, and Duncan J. Watts. 2011. "Everyone's an Influencer: Quantifying Influence on Twitter." Paper presented at the Fourth ACM International Web Search and Data Mining Conference (WSDM), February 9–12, Hong Kong, China. Available at misc.si.umich.edu/media/papers/wsdm333w-bakshy.pdf.

Barina, Stefania. 2013. "Mapping CSR on Twitter." MA thesis, Università degli Studi di Milano, Italy.

Belk, Russell. 1988. "Possessions and the Extended Self." *Journal of Consumer Research* 15(September):139–68.

Belz, Frank-Martin, and Wenke Baumbach. 2010. "Netnography as a Method of Lead User Identification." *Creativity and Innovation Management* 19(3):304–13.

Beraldo, Davide. 2012. "Nuovi Movimenti nell'Ambiente Social-Mediatico: Rete e Flussi Glocali del Meta Movimento #occupay" ["New Social Movements in the Social Media Environment: The #occupay Movement"]. MA thesis, Università degli Studi di Milano, Italy.

Bilgram, Volker, Michael Bartl, and Stefan Biel. 2011. "Getting Closer to the Consumer—How Nivea Co-Creates New Products." *Marketing Review St. Gallen* 1:34–40.

Boellstorff Tom. 2008. *Coming of Age in Second Life: An Anthropologist Explores the Virtually Human.* Princeton, NJ: Princeton University Press.

Boellstorff, Tom, Bonnie Nardi, Celia Pearce, and T. L. Taylor. 2012. *Ethnography and Virtual Worlds: A Handbook of Method.* Princeton, NJ, and Oxford, UK: Princeton University Press.

boyd, danah. 2011. "Social Networking Sites as Networked Publics: Affordances, Dynamics and Implication." In *A Networked Self: Identity Community and Culture on Social Network Sites*, edited by Z. Papacharissi, 39–58. London: Routledge.

boyd, danah, Scott Golder, and Gilad Lotan. 2010. "Tweet Tweet Retweet: Conversational Aspects of Retweeting on Twitter." Paper presented at the Proceedings of HICSS-42, Persistent Conversation Track, Kauai, HI: IEEE Computer Society, January 5–8.

Bruckman, Amy. 2006. "Teaching Students to Study Online Communities Ethically." *Journal of Information Ethics* 15(2):14–17.

Caliandro, Alessandro, and Adam Arvidsson. 2013. "Brand Publics: A Digital Ethnography of how Consumers Co-Create Brand Value Online." Paper presented at the Proceedings of the Anthropology of Markets and Consumption Conference, March 2013, Irvine, CA. Available at merage.uci.edu/events/merage/anthromarkets/Agenda (accessed June 1, 2013).

Carù, Antonella, and Bernard Cova. 2007. *Consuming Experience.* London: Routledge.

Castranova, Edward. 2005. *Synthetic Worlds: The Business and Culture of Online Games.* Chicago, IL: University Press of Chicago.

Cova, Bernard. 2013. "Societing Ovvero la Piccola Storia di un Grande Concetto tra Marketing e Sociologia" ["Societing, the Little Story of a Big Concept"]. In *Societing Reloaded: Pubblici produttivi e innovazione sociale*, edited by A. Arvidsson and A. Giordano, 1–5. Milano, Italy: Egea.

Cova, Bernard, and Stefano Pace. 2006. "Brand Community of Convenience Products: New Forms of Customer Empowerment—The Case "My Nutella The Community." *European Journal of Marketing* 40(9/10):1087–105.

Dalgarno, Barney, and Mark Lee. 2010. "What Are the Learning Affordances of 3-D Virtual Environments?" *British Journal of Educational Technology* 41:10–32.

Denegri-Knott, Janice, and Mike Molesworth. 2010. "Concepts and Practices of Digital Virtual Consumption." *Consumption, Markets & Culture* 13(2):109–32.

Donath, Judith, and danah boyd. 2004. "Public Displays of Connection." *BT Technology Journal* 22(4): 71–82.

eMarketer. 2013. "Seniors Still Lukewarm on Web Activity." eMarketer (website), March 26. www.emarketer.com/Article/Seniors-Still-Lukewarm-on-Web-Activity/1009757 (accessed June 1, 2013).

Fairclough, Norman. 1995. *Media Discourse*. London: Edward Arnold.

Füller, Johann, Gregor Jawecki, and Hans Mühlbacher. 2007. "Innovation Creation by Online Basketball Communities. *Journal of Business Research* 2:60–71.

Garcia, Angela C., Alcea I Standlee, Jennifer Bechkoff, and Yan Cui. 2009. "Ethnographic Approaches to the Internet and Computer-Mediated Communication." *Journal of Contemporary Ethnography* 38(1):52–84.

Goffman, Erving. 1959. *The Presentation of Self in Everyday Life*. New York: Doubleday.

Hearn Alison. 2010. "Structuring Feeling: Web 2.0, Online Ranking and Rating, and the Digital Reputation Economy." *Ephemera* 10(3/4):421–48.

Hine, Christine. 2000. *Virtual Ethnography*. London: Sage.

_____. 2005. *Virtual Methods: Issues in Social Research on the Internet*. Oxford, UK: Berg.

Hinz, Oliver, Bernd Skiera, Christian Barrot, and Jan U. Becker. 2011. "Seeding Strategies for Viral Marketing: An Empirical Comparison." *Journal of Marketing* 75(6):55–71.

Horst, Heather, and Daniel Miller. 2012. *Digital Anthropology*. London: Bloomsbury Academic.

Iamandi, Corina, and Petronela Postolache. 2011. "A Case of Strategic Online Communication in Postmodernism: Using Facebook to Create Virtual Brand Communities." MBA thesis, Aarhus School of Business, Denmark.

James, Nalita. 2007. "The Use of Email Interviewing as a Qualitative Method of Inquiry in Educational Research." *British Educational Research Journal* 33:963–76.

James, Nalita, and Hugh Busher. 2009. *Online Interviewing*. London: Sage.

Jurgenson, Nathan. 2012. "When Atoms Meet Bits: Social Media, the Mobile Web and Augmented Revolution." *Future Internet* 4(1):83–91.

Kien, Grant. 2009. *Global Technography: Ethnography in the Age of Mobility*. New York: Peter Lang.

Kow, Yong M., and Bonnie Nardi. 2009. "Culture and Creativity: World of Warcraft Modding in China and the US." In *Online Worlds: Convergence of the Real and the Virtual*, edited by B. Bainbridge, 21–41. Heidelberg, Germany: Springer.

Kozinets, Robert V. 1999. "E-Tribalized Marketing? The Strategic Implications of Virtual Communities of Consumption." *European Management Journal* 17(3):252–64.

_____. 2002. "The Field Behind the Screen: Using Netnography for Marketing Research in Online Communities." *Journal of Marketing Research* 39:61–72.

_____. 2010. *Netnography: Doing Ethnographic Research Online*. Los Angeles: Sage.

Kozinets, Robert V., Kristine de Valck, Andrea C. Wojnicki, and Sarah J. S. Wilner. 2010. "Networked Narratives: Understanding Word-of-Mouth Marketing in Online Communities." *Journal of Marketing* 74(2):71–89.

Kwak, Haewoon, Changhyun Lee, Hosung Park, and Sue Moon. 2010. "What Is Twitter: A Social Network or News Media?" In *Proceedings of the 19th International Conference on the World Wide Web*, 591–600. New York: ACM.

Latour, Bruno. 2005. *Reassembling the Social: An Introduction to Actor-Network-Theory*. Oxford, UK: Oxford University Press.

Lazzarato, Maurizio. 1996. "Immaterial Labour." In *Radical Thought in Italy: A Potential Politics*, edited by M. Hardt and P. Virno, 189–210. Minneapolis: University Press of Minnesota.

Li, Charlene, and Josh Bernoff. 2008. *Groundswell: Winning in a World Transformed by Social Technologies*. Boston: Harvard Business Press.

Liu, Hugo. 2007. "Social Network Profiles as Taste Performances." *Journal of Computer-Mediated Communication* 13(1): article 13. Available at http://jcmc.indiana.edu/vol13/issue1/liu.html (accessed June 4, 2013).

Lynch, Michael J. 2010. "Sex Work in Second Life: Scripts, Presence, and Bounded Authenticity in a Virtual Environment." *Social Thought and Research* 31:37–56.

Marres, Noortje. 2004. "Tracing the Trajectories of Issues, and Their Democratic Deficits, on the Web: The Case of the Development Gateway and Its Doubles." *Information Technology and People* 17(2):124–49.

______. 2012. *Material Participation: Technology, the Environment and Everyday Publics*. Basingstoke, UK: Palgrave Macmillan.

Marres, Noortje, and Esther Weltrevede. 2012. "Scraping the Social? Issues in Real-Time Research." In *Proceedings of the International Conference Evaluation in the Media*, March 2012, Assemblee Nationale, Paris. Available at https://wiki.digitalmethods.net/pub/Dmi/PapersPublications/Marres_Weltrevede_Scraping_the_Social_draft.pdf (accessed June 1, 2013).

Marwick, Alice E., and danah boyd. 2011. "I Tweet Honestly, I Tweet Passionately: Twitter Users, Context Collapse, and the Imagined Audience." *New Media and Society* 13:96–113.

Miller, Daniel, and Don Slater. 2001. *The Internet: An Ethnographic Approach*. London: Berg.

Molesworth, Mike, and Janice Denegri-Knott. 2007. "Digital Play and the Actualization of the Consumer Imagination." *Games and Culture* 2:114–33.

Muñiz, Albert M., and Thomas C. O'Guinn. 2001. "Brand Community." *Journal of Consumer Research* 27:412–32.

Muñiz, Albert M., and Hope J. Schau. 2005. "Religiosity in the Abandoned Apple Newton Brand Community." *Journal of Consumer Research* 31:737–47.

Murthy, Dhiraj. 2008. "Digital Ethnography: An Examination of the Use of New Technologies for Social Research." *Sociology* 42(5):837–55.

Nardi, Bonnie. 2010. *My Life as a Night Elf Priest: An Anthropological Account of World of Warcraft*. Ann Arbor: University of Michigan Press.

______. 2013. "Consuming Games: The Production of Subjective Experience in World of Warcraft." *Proceedings of the Anthropology of Markets and Consumption Conference*, March 2013, Irvine, CA. Available at merage.uci.edu/events/merage/anthromarkets/Agenda (accessed June 1, 2013).

Nelson, Michelle R., and Cele C. Otnes. 2005. "Exploring Cross-Cultural Ambivalence: A Netnography of Intercultural Wedding Message Boards." *Journal of Business Research* 58(1):89–95.

O'Connor, Henrietta, and Clare Madge. 2003. "Focus Groups in Cyberspace: Using the Internet for Qualitative Research." *Qualitative Market Research: An International Journal* 6(2):133–43.

Ondrejka, Cory R. 2004. "Escaping the Gilded Cage: User Created Content and Building the Metaverse." http://ssrn.com/abstract=538362 (accessed June 1, 2013).

Papacharissi, Zizi. 2009. "The Virtual Geographies of Social Networks: A Comparative Analysis of Facebook, LinkedIn and ASmallWorld." *New Media & Society* 11(1/2):199–220.

______. 2011. *A Networked Self: Identity Community and Culture on Social Network Sites*. London: Routledge.

Parks, Malcom R. 2011. "Social Network Sites as Virtual Communities." In *A Networked Self: Identity Community and Culture on Social Network Sites*, edited by Z. Papacharissi, 105–23. London: Routledge.

Pearce, Celia. 2009. *Communities of Play: Emergent Cultures in Online Games and Virtual World.* Cambridge, MA: MIT Press.

Pongsakornrungsil, Siwarit, and Jonathan E. Schroeder. 2010. "Understanding Value Co-Creation in a Co-Consuming Brand Community." *Marketing Theory* 11(3):303–24.

Postill, John. 2008. "Localizing the Internet Beyond Communities and Networks." *New Media & Society* 10(3):413–31.

Reto, Felix. 2008. "Product Relationships, Brand Meanings, and Symbolism For Mainstream Brands: the Case of the Sports Bike Community." *Latin American Advances in Consumer Research* 2:10–15.

Reeves, Byron, Thomas W. Malone, and Tony O'Driscoll. 2008. "Leadership's Online Labs." *Harvard Business Review* 86(5):58–66.

Rogers, Richard. 2009. *The End of the Virtual.* Amsterdam, the Netherlands: Amsterdam University Press.

_____. 2013. *Digital Methods*. Cambridge, MA: MIT Press.

Schau, Hope J., and Mary C. Gilly. 2003. "We Are What We Post? Self-Presentation in Personal Web Space." *Journal of Consumer Research* 30:385–404.

Schau, Hope J., Albert M. Muñiz, and Eric J. Arnould. 2009. "How Brand Community Practices Create Value." *Journal of Marketing* 73:30–51.

Schiano, Diane, Bonnie Nardi, Thomas Debeauvais, Nicolas Ducheneaut, and Nicholas Yee. 2011. "A New Look at World of Warcraft's Social Landscape." In *Proceedings of the 6th International Conference on Foundations of Digital Games, June 28–July 1*, 174–79. doi/10.1145/2159365.2159389.

Tarde, Gabriel. 1902. *Psychologie Economique*. Paris: Félix Alcan.

Taylor, T. L. 2002. "Living Digitally: Embodiment in Virtual Worlds." In *The Social Life of Avatars: Presence and Interaction in Shared Virtual Environments*, edited by R. Schroeder, 40–62. London: Springer-Verlag.

_____. 2008. "Becoming a Player: Networks, Structures, and Imagined Futures." In *Beyond Barbie and Mortal Kombat: New Perspectives on Gender, Games, and Computing*, edited by Y. Kafai, C. Heeter, J. Denner, and J. Sun, 50–65. Cambridge, MA: MIT Press.

Teli, Maurizio, Francesco Pisanu, and David Hakken. 2007. "The Internet as a Library-of-People: For a Cyberethnography of Online Groups." *Forum: Qualitative Social Research* 8(3): Article 33.

Virno, Paolo. 2002. *A Grammar Of The Multitude: For an Analysis of Contemporary Forms of Life.* Cambridge, MA: MIT Press.

Walsh, Mike. 2011. "Why Do Companies Need Anthropologists?" Blog post, Mike-Walsh.com, March 1. www.mike-walsh.com/blog/bid/50374/Why-Do-Companies-Need-Anthropologists (accessed June 1, 2013).

Walstrom, Mary K. 2004. "Ethics and Engagement in Communication Scholarship: Analyzing Public, Online Support Groups as Researcher/Participant-Experiencer." In *Virtual Research Ethics: Issues and Controversies*, edited by E. A. Buchanan, 174–202. Hershey, PA: Information Science Publishing.

Watkins, Rebecca, and Mike Molesworth. 2013. "The Ongoing Exploitation of Consumers' Possession Work via the Permanent Deferral of DVG Ownership." Paper presented at the Interpretive Consumer Research Workshop, Brussels, Belgium, April 2013.

Wenger, Etienne. 1998. *Communities of Practice: Learning, Meaning, and Identity*. Cambridge, UK: Cambridge University Press.

Wesch, Michael. 2009. "YouTube and You: Experiences of Self-Awareness in the Context Collapse of the Recording Webcam." *Explorations in Media Ecology* 8(2):19–34.

Zichermann, Gabe, and Christopher Cunningham. 2011. *Gamification by Design: Implementing Game Mechanics in Web and Mobile Apps*. Sebastopol, CA: O'Reilly Media.

Zwick, Detlev, Samuel K. Bonsu, and Aron Darmody. 2008. "Putting Consumers to Work: 'Co-Creation' and New Marketing Governmentality." *Journal of Consumer Culture* 8(2):63–96.

NOTES

I would like to greatly thank Stefano Pace for his valuable and inspiring advice. Also, I would like to thank Massimo Airoldi and Adam Arvidsson for their academic and emotional support.

1 See http://www.youtube.com/watch?v=ql-N3F1FhW4.

2 The term "societing" is a neologism coined by Olivier Badot, Ampelio Bucci, and Bernard Cova in 1993, which combines the words "society" and "marketing." It essentially means "making society" or "adding something to society." The strategies of societing, unlike those of marketing, tend to push companies to be active actors within the specific social context in which they are situated (Badot et al. 2007).

Section V

MUSES FOR ENGAGEMENT

INTRODUCTION

RITA DENNY & PATRICIA SUNDERLAND

> And yet, you still have to perform it, and it may prove difficult. In other words, the proper strategy is often found only if life can be rehearsed and replayed, which is possible with videogames but often problematic in real life!
>
> —Franck Cochoy (Chapter 36)

What we want to call out in this final collection of chapters are the sources of inspiration and motivation, the muses that keep people able and willing to work in the intersections of anthropology or sociology and business and to do it well. Muses include academic developments and theorizing, popular culture, online communities that digital platforms afford, and/or the personal engagement afforded by ethnographic fieldwork. As well, there is angst. We call out both inspiration and angst to contemplate the performative dimension of engagement in the intersection of anthropology and business. Doing so is a way to foreshadow a future.

If the muses are many and particularistic, a common theme running through these chapters is making anthropological objects of the work. The authors of these chapters lean in to their expertise—preserving a sense of difference, of being an outsider—while simultaneously seeking to contribute to a requested end. Both Cochoy and Malefyt, stymied by the prosaic, find muses in their disciplines. When asked to give a colloquium on "strategy" to academic business colleagues, a topic not in his typical purview but seriously theorized within the discipline of management, sociologist Cochoy tells us his muse was his procrastinating, videogame-playing self, and from there he launched into ancient (and "more prestigious" as he wryly notes) sources—Greek mythology and the Bible—all of which are suffused through the lens of actor-network theory. Cochoy introduces the notion of equipped serendipity as a way to conceive strategic action. Equipped with a plan, forecast, or "over" view ("angel's view"),

Handbook of Anthropology in Business, edited by Rita Denny and Patricia Sunderland, 683–688.

implementation is a "sharp angle view": the one available when in the thick of things (contextualized by situations, objects, people, spaces in actual practice), where the unforeseen, the serendipitous, occurs. Strategic action, Cochoy argues, rests on an interplay and tension between these two points of view (and two forms of knowledge production), in which we can never be entirely one or the other; just having a plan has performative consequences.

Faced with a task on men's shaving, Malefyt found inspiration in the academic literature of sensory anthropology. His chapter offers an astute analysis of the radically different conceptualizations of the senses by marketing and anthropology. Malefyt suggests that the idea of brand ritual is a way to mediate marketing's ontological divide between cognition (mind) and the senses (body). Attending to sensory experiences through a lens of ritual, Malefyt suggests, might reorient marketers' actions from "strategic deployment" of a brand's sensory qualities to a renewed consideration of products in individuals' lives. As did Cochoy in delivering his analysis to colleagues, Malefyt pushes his analysis through to the prosaic deliverable: in his case, positioning a shaving brand. In both cases, a goal was to provide a means for audiences to think differently about what they already knew well.

In Høyem's "true, semifactual" tale, he is marooned in a suburban sprawl of fast food where "language is devoid of content" and words are "rhetorical cotton candy." Without the ballast of words in the bookless world Høyem describes, his own speech falters, despair creeps into his voice and into his conversations. If Høyem's chapter speaks to love of the discipline, "stories of such eloquent enchantment," it also poetically captures the significant role of people in enabling the work: the humanity at the heart of the ethnographic enterprise. In these chapters the people involved are sometimes a resource of like-minded others, colleagues-as-clients, colleagues-as-team, or the participants drawn into fieldwork. Relationships with people fuel inspiration and are a salve for angst. Even Høyem's despair finds respite when conversing with his anthropological boss about books that can make you cry, or with T. S. Elliot about the need for a strong soul.

In Teitler's chapter on the blogosphere, bloggers post as a way to think with and through ideas; as a nexus for collaborative thinking; as a vehicle for sharing resources; and, when outraged by shoddy practices or a pundit's opinion, readers (and blogs) become tacit support groups not bounded by geography or places of employment. Bloggers engage with fellow travelers sometimes to offset the difficult. Beyond the intellectual isolation described by Høyem, authors in these chapters capture lots of moments of insecurity: How to behave as an "anthropologist" within organizations when, as Dornadic notes, "not sheltered by the canons of the discipline"? How to contribute when you don't know the literature or expert worlds of others? Without enough time? When working in interdisciplinary spaces takes you beyond what you love? When fieldwork is a source of despair? When criticism feels incipient? When one's creation—netnography in Kozinet's chapter—succumbs to the drift and "gravitational pull" of corporate practices, rendering a cultural analysis of online communities into a quantified bulletin board? Energy is garnered through interactions with others. "With energy and imagination, the little applied miracles that make us most human," Kozinets maintains, "gravity [of corporate discourses] can be overcome."

Moynié in his reflexive essay on "ethnographic mojo" contemplates what makes for the intense connection he establishes with respondents during fieldwork. A "desire [for] their desire," he maintains, is at the heart of his connection with people in the field, and it entails an intensity akin to seduction. The quality and level of that connection with people translates directly into the quality of his work. Without it, he is not only lost but bereft: a chance encounter with an idolized Flemish musician, Arno, in a Brussels bar late at night ends in humiliation when Arno rejects Moynié's presence and desire. Told with great poignancy, it speaks to Moynié's commitment to intense connection. Darrah and Dornadic also remind us that contracts might be with companies but the work is peopled: diffused authority, tacit assumptions, desires (and perhaps fears), and evolving agendas are normative. In conceiving anthropological work as a service, Darrah and Dornadic recognize that the deliverable is not an off-the-shelf product but rather evolves through engagement; that the objectives are sometimes tacit; and that things change. One needs to learn the registers of business and fathom opaque production processes of organizations. The point, as they note, is that consulting work is a co-created process that has power to transform; it affects lives.

The idea that the ethnographic process is one of co-construction is formalized in O'Dell and Willim's chapter. Drawing inspiration from Fortun (2012), Kelty (2009), Latour (2010), Marcus (1990), and Vannini (2012), they argue for a conceptualization of ethnography as *compositional practice* (think film or music) versus *writing* (think book). The idea of composition for O'Dell and Willim foregrounds the human relationships that are material components of the creative process, including one's audience. Applied cultural analysis "has to engage to convince." Kozinets, in his chapter on the development of netnography, observes that netnography captured managers' imaginations because it is "vivid, pictorial, emotional, visceral, current, and real." There is an affective dimension in what is produced in the ethnographic process, O'Dell and Willim argue: "The surprise effects, the affective and the sensuous aspects of ethnography, have to be kept alive throughout the research process. It's when you feel the composition doing something to your gut that you are putting the piece together in a convincing and innovative manner. To successfully compose ethnography you have to, in other words, connect with an audience and not just represent a culture."

These chapters also point to the importance of improvisation: loosening up, allowing for other things, adapting to exigency. Improvisation, serendipity in Cochoy's conceptualization, is sometimes something one learns to embrace, as in Dornadic's case in working with designers at Roche. While being effective consultants means being ethnographers of the companies that hire them, the unpredictable is inevitable. Given the exigencies of corporate life, Darrah and Dornadic argue one must be willing to cede control, become comfortable with ambiguity and "loosely holding and then abandoning tentative hypotheses." But more often, or perhaps increasingly, improvisation is a structural element of the process. Moynié, not knowing anyone in Lincoln, Nebraska, made himself and his quest (understanding food in life) visible by going to the barber shop on Friday, the bar on Saturday, and church on Sunday, and then being invited to a brunch organized by some of those he'd met along the way (perhaps on Monday). His "ethnographic mojo" is grounded in the idea of improvisation. O'Dell and Willim's idea of composition also tacitly accepts improvisation as a structural component.

These themes—making the work an anthropological object, recognizing the humanity enabling the enterprise, improvising in the process—comprise a strategy for doing fieldwork. Cochoy's notion of "equipped serendipity" is apt in this context. The authors in this volume and section inevitably lean in to their own expertise: Høyem's "strong soul," steeped in disciplinary knowledge, is the angel's view (synoptic reality) in Cochoy's words. Responding to the conditions on the ground is Cochoy's sharp-angle view (or bounded rationality), where the unpredictable changes things. The development of a netnographic consulting practice that Kozinets relates entailed a series of serendipitous moments. Saying yes to tasks that would take Darrah from anthropologist-as-researcher to video producer surely wasn't in the original plan. And, as Cochoy as well as O'Dell and Willim argue, we cannot help but be transformed in the doing.

The chapter by O'Dell and Willim, describing the development of a master's degree program in applied cultural analysis recently instituted at Lund University and the University of Copenhagen, provides a muse for the future. It is worth contemplating how the marketplace begat a new form of pedagogy and a reconceiving of ethnographic practice. The program's development was spurred by a Swedish government push to make scholarly knowledge useful to society at the same time that students by the early 2000s were opting out of ethnology and into programs with clear job prospects. Prototypically, the program reflects a leaning-in: cultural analysis is the distinctive voice and common core, while the diverse backgrounds of students are considered honored competencies. The challenge as they continue to see it is to get away from thinking about ethnography as a linear process and embrace the idea that ethnography consists of "messy, nonlinear performances in which diverse bits and pieces of information are put together and moved around." Rather than "writing" as the organizational metaphor, think composition. What is important to note is that composition is not a matter of boardroom deliverable, but rather a matter of the ethnographic process itself, "something that must take different forms and make use of different utterances in varied contexts." The theoretical grounding is never lost: the program trains students to be in the business of "cultural dubbing," but recognizes that understanding is relational and the actors multiple.

The performative aspect of cultural dubbing, the emotional connecting with an audience, espoused by O'Dell and Willim, challenges the prevailing and fundamental sense of the anthropological self as researcher, a view of anthropologists that business shares as well. Dornadic was shut out of a design meeting because it wasn't about research; design can subsume the ethnographic contribution as "research." A popular and trade press constrains contribution through caricature of the discipline and tropes of discovery (again, "research"). We should take note: what O'Dell and Willim are advocating is a more fluid and nuanced and variable role of ethnographers. The divide between academic and applied is moot, they would say; what matters are the *multiple* contexts for engagement (whether political, social, entrepreneurial, academic, corporate, governmental), that cultural analysts are facile in moving among terrains, and whether there is heart (and skill) for diverse forms of engagement. Acquiring skills that allow for flows among contexts, a vision that "leans in" to the sociocultural while engaging with diverse interlocutors, is both vision and foreseeable challenge. If anthropologists want to be more than the adjunct "research" voice and not be subsumed by prevailing discourses of design, engineering, marketing, C-suite, economics, or psychology, perhaps we should start composing, eloquently.

Anthropologists operating in the intersections with business perform the future. We are not benign in whatever choices made. Reconceiving what we do, whether as a service model (Darrah and Dornadic), composition (O'Dell and Willim), or a process of equipped serendipity, is necessary if anthropologists want to affect discourses, registers, and theorizing of brands, design, marketing, management consulting, or consumption. To persuasively contest forms of knowledge production requires being in and of it and retaining a commitment to an alternative disciplinary muse, as Malefyt's and Kozinets' chapters both illustrate. The task of reconfiguring is less in seeing "anthropologists" as a static entity and more in conceiving anthropologists as agents of transformation, as Darrah and Dornadic note. Getting beyond the silo of "researchers" conscripted to particular communities of practice might be more easily accomplished in Sweden or France, where boundaries between academy and publics are perhaps more permeable than elsewhere. We don't deny the hurdles in translating ethnographic work for wider publics; Fassin (2013) captures the merit and conundrum in doing so. It also takes a long time to *be* an anthropologist in corporate spaces in the form of making the work an anthropological object. Being in corporations or working for them or being in business *is* fieldwork, and it takes time to attend to the paraethnographic practices of colleagues (Holmes and Marcus 2006); it takes time to master discourses, practices, and power hierarchies. Tett (2009) is an illustration of the worthiness of this endeavor. It takes time to develop the ability; but in the meantime, all actions perform. For a future field, it is a moment for strategic realignment.

REFERENCES

Fassin, Didier. 2013. "Why Ethnography Matters: On Anthropology and Its Publics." *Cultural Anthropology* 28(4):621–46.

Fortun, Kim. 2012. "Ethnography in Late Industrialism." *Cultural Anthropology* 27(3): 446–64.

Holmes, Douglas R., and George E. Marcus. 2006. "Fast Capitalism: Para-Ethnography and the Rise of the Symbolic Analyst." In *Frontiers of Capital*, edited by Melissa S. Fisher and Greg Downey, 33–57. Durham, NC: Duke University Press.

Kelty, Cristopher, with contributions from Hannah Landecker, Ebru Kayaalp, Anthony Potoczniak, Tish Stringer, Nahal Naficy, Ala Alazzeh, Lina Dib, and Michael G. Powell. 2009. "Collaboration, Coordination, and Composition." In *Fieldwork Is Not What It Used To Be: Learning Anthropology's Method in a Time of Transition*, edited by J. D. Faubion and G. E. Marcus, 184–206. Ithaca, NY: Cornell University Press.

Latour, Bruno. 2010. "An Attempt at a 'Compositionist Manifesto.'" *New Literary History* 41:471–90.

Marcus, George. 1990. "The Modernist Sensibility in Recent Ethnographic Writing and the Cinematic Metaphor of Montage." *Society for Visual Anthropology (SVA) Review* 6(1):2–12.

Tett, Gillian. 2009. *Fool's Gold*. New York: Free Press.

Vannini, Phillip. 2012. *Ferry Tales: Mobility, Place, and Time on Canada's West Coast*. Oxon, UK: Routledge.

36

From Strategy to Equipped Serendipity: Lessons from Ezio, the Black Angel of Florence

FRANCK COCHOY

> Mad with rage and shame,
> Ezio then donned the garb of his father,
> vowing not to remove his hood
> until his family's death has been avenged.
> The Black Angel of Florence took off the heads
> of all the conspirators without respite, in silence
> (http://deadorchestra.forum-actif.net/t256-ezio-auditore-di-florenza)

Once upon a time, a colleague contacted me for a workshop where I was supposed to address the issue of strategy in business settings. Strategy is a serious management discipline with dedicated departments in business schools, professional associations (The Association of Strategic Planning, Strategic Planning Society, etc.), and academic journals (*Strategic Management Journal*, *Journal of Economics and Management Strategy*, *Strategic Organization*, etc.). This discipline analyzes how companies set their goals, what means and tactics they employ to fulfill them, and so on. It thus studies how business actors shape the relationship between organization and their environment (Selznick 1957), try to control the future (Chandler 1962), reduce the gaps between plans and current reality (Ansoff 1965), and play on the three dimensions of cost leadership, differentiation, and focus (Porter 1980). But since as a sociologist I knew little of this literature and had no prior experience in theorizing strategy, I met my colleague's request by adopting the strategy of relying on my own experience as a practical but as-yet unsuccessful strategist. Indeed, I took the risk of addressing the problem of strategy not from the management literature, but from the example of my personal adventures within a famous video game, Assassin's Creed II. In this

Handbook of Anthropology in Business, edited by Rita Denny and Patricia Sunderland, 689–703.

game, the player inhabits the character of Ezio, an assassin who some (see opening epigraph) have described as "the Black Angel of Florence."

This choice is the unexpected result of a long-lasting private joke. Indeed, when my colleague asked me to contribute to a collective discussion on strategy, I worried about tackling a subject I knew little about. To reassure me, he kindly sent me some explanations and encouragements. But when writing his email, my colleague's fingers made a mistake so that a word was misspelled:

> Thanks again for your positive reply. Of course I did not expect you to be a "disciplined strategist." This is exactly why I thought of you in the first place! As academic discipline, strategy is still fairly functional, and our event attempts to introduce some new perspectives and *theoretical angels* to the study of strategy as a socio-political practice that deals with uncertainty, representations of the future that alter the present, and intentionality (email to the author, June 19, 2011; italics added).

I wondered if there could be any connection between theoretical "angels" and theoretical "angles." And just for the fun of it, I promised to have a try. However, after several weeks, I realized I couldn't find any satisfactory solution. I had no theoretical angels, and hence no reliable strategy. As a consequence, I remained for months doing nothing, endlessly postponing the moment I would start to address the issue. At one point I even abandoned it. Allow me an embarrassing confession. Like Robinson Crusoe in Michel Tournier's novel *Friday*, I sometimes disconnect from my professional goals and plans, and succumb to a terrible and shameful vice. Robinson stopped managing his island and wallowed in the mire, behaving like a pig rather than like a civilized person (Tournier 1985). Similarly, every six months or so, I withdraw from my academic duties and fall back into an old, childish video game addiction. When this happens, I become completely trapped in it; I lose dozens of hours and just cannot escape. It's a really pleasurable, yet dangerous and frightening experience. But I hope that a fall may sometime turn into salvation. This is at least where my dark angel comes from.

Assassin's Creed II is a game where you, as a player, have to embody Ezio di Auditore, an assassin during the Italian Renaissance. As Ezio, you interact with prominent craftsmen and strategists, like Leonardo da Vinci and Machiavelli. You have to murder several important characters who belong to the Night Templars to avenge your father, whom they have killed, and more broadly to prevent them from taking over political power. The action takes place in beautiful medieval cities, like Venice and Florence. I played Assassin's Creed II for several days during the fall holidays, neglecting my professional duties and emergencies, until I was trapped in a deadlock, starting the same mission over and over again, trying different approaches, tactics, and strategies, but failing each time to succeed, until I got the solution on the internet. At the same time, I was ashamed for the time lost, and I recalled that I had to work on strategy and respect my commitment to remain faithful to my private joke with my dear colleague.

In a sense, my goal in this chapter is to show that a strategy is interesting only to the extent that it doesn't work. To do so I will first start from a general discussion. I will theorize from the video game, but soon move to more ancient and legendary figures taken from the Greek language and mythology. Indeed, a strategy to deal with strategy without being accused of knowing nothing about the related academic knowledge is to rely on older and more prestigious references than the ones quoted in the strategy literature.

AN ASSASSIN'S STRATEGY: FORECASTING & PROACTING

The mission of the game on which I want to focus occurs close to the end of the game, in the penultimate thirteenth sequence, where Ezio must wrestle control of Florence from Savonarola, who has captured the city in the absence of the Medici, and regain possession of the treasured Apples of Eden. This mission is called "Port Authority." You start the mission from a roof where you look down to the river and the boat of a merchant who works for Savonarola. Your task is to assassinate the merchant who is standing up in the middle of his boat, well protected by 10 guards. This mission and the problems it raises fit well the issue I want to address for at least two reasons. First, and as I said, the use of this example to deal with strategy is completely serendipitous, but this is very helpful, since I intend to show that strategy and serendipity are strongly connected, both generally and reflexively. Second, studying video games is the best way to access the inner workings of pure strategy. In the game, behavioral patterns are largely predictable, since they depend on given algorithms. Everything is goal oriented, and involves a set of very clear, very simple ingredients and logic.

Strategy combines forecasting and proacting. Forecasting conveys the idea of fate, of a passive submission to an order that I cannot control but that is rather imposed upon me. Proacting is just the contrary: it is about shaping the future as I wish it to be. Designing a strategy is thus about playing with deterministic models to accomplish one's project. Taking Ezio as an example, the character's success consists in finding a right combination of pure deterministic behaviors, encapsulated in algorithms, and interaction, enacted in the game.

When watching the video,[1] I realized that articulating forecasting and proacting, shaping future outcomes as I wanted them to be, is not a problem per se. Ezio needs to kill the merchant, but there are guards. Some of them are immobile at the rear, middle, and front of the boat and look to the bow; others are patrolling along the two sides of the boat. After killing the three guards posted

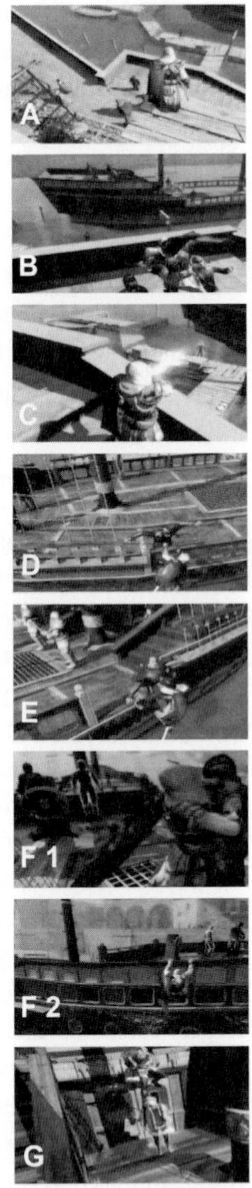

Figure 36.1. Walk through the Assassin's Creed II "Port Authority" mission.

outside of the boat (Figure 36.1B and 36.1C), I realize that I first have to discreetly murder a few of the patrolling guards. To do so, I have to plunge in the water, swim to the opposite side of the boat, and grasp them by surprise in climbing on the sides of the ship (Figure 36.1D and 36.1E). Second, I see that if I kill one of the two remaining moving guards on the rear ship (Figure 36.1F1), then quickly hide away again on the side (Figure 36.1F2), the closest ones, even previously immobile, will be diverted and quit their position to seek the attacker (Figure 36.1F2) and, a few seconds later, leave the boat. I may then reach the position from where I may reach my goal (Figure 36.1G). This is a very clear framework: "If I do this, I guess that my opponents will do that, so that I can do this, etc. until I fulfill my goal." Hence, the YouTube video provides a pure and basic definition and example of what a strategy is. Adopting a strategy is to define a sequence of actions (and tactics) not limited to the strategist's behavior but leading to the completion of his goal. This sequence rests on the hypothesis that other actors X, Y, and Z will behave in such and such ways, respectively (W_x, W_y, and W_z) (forecasting), but that they will shift these behaviors if I perform the series of actions A_1, A_2, or A_n (proacting). The A and W actions are arranged so that the goal is achieved.[2]

The sequence looks very simple, and several approaches can be tested, and so on. But what is remarkable and should be stressed is that, even in this purely computerized and simplified form, the strategy is very hard to find, then to perform. Indeed, if there is a YouTube video, it is because so many players, after dozens of repetitive attempts, have failed to succeed.[3] This is easy to see: the video I used has been watched by 3,883 players between August 2010 and December 2013.[4] There are several other videos and alternative solutions for the same mission; one of them has been viewed by no less than 115,569 players.[5] When you lack strategy, one of the best strategies is to take one from someone else! In other words, strategy is often a delegated option. Moreover, when someone posts a video, it is not

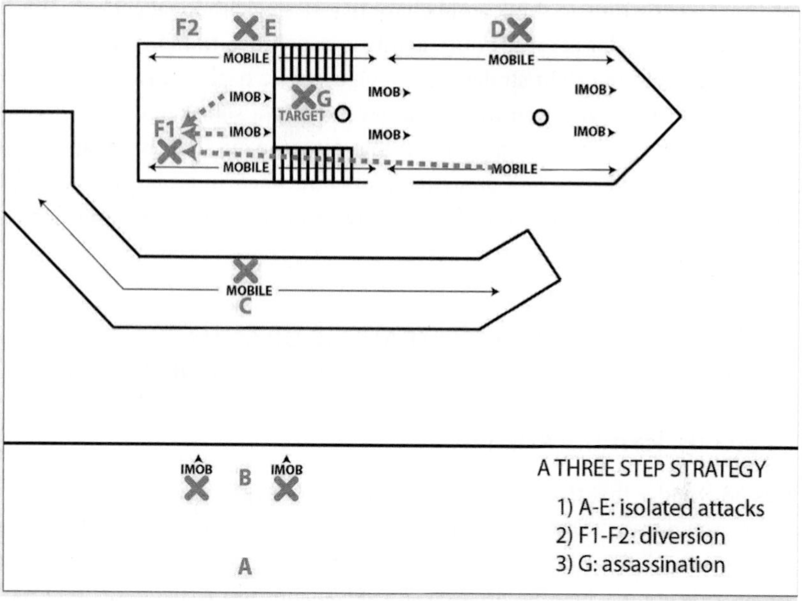

Figure 36.2. Ezio's angel's view.

because of pure strategic altruism, but because the one who succeeded knew how hard it was, even for him, and was proud to show he could succeed within a prime example of what Nicolas Dodier (1995) has referred to as "technical abilities arenas." Finally, it is very important to note that the solution is not provided as a plan, but as a video. The video displays the strategy and its enactment at the same time. In so doing, it implicitly acknowledges that there is a gap between the two. And yet, you still have to perform it, and it may prove difficult. In other words, the proper strategy is often found only if life can be rehearsed and replayed, which is possible with videogames but often problematic in real life!

Hence, a strange puzzle: on the one hand, just watching the video and extracting the plan looks highly simple; if I have dared to start with this example, it is because it looks like the zero degree of warship strategy: it stages a single soldier instead of an army; it involves rather deterministic behaviors derived from basic artificial intelligence algorithms, with a slight dose of randomness; and it rests on a single trick (a diversion) instead of many. And yet, the strategy still doesn't work, or at least there is little chance that it will work on the first attempt (Figure 36.2).

What is the problem? Why is it so difficult to identify a proper strategy and then to implement it successfully? Of course, a simple reason is that only a few players take the time to think and behave in a strategic rational pattern. When the risk of dying doesn't really hurt, acting is easier than thinking. It's an excellent way to find the right strategy, through a classic trial-and-error approach. But more surprisingly, even when you have the right solution, it often doesn't work, at least at the very beginning. In that case, the question is not about the relevance of forecasting and proacting, but about their interplay: the strategic plans are overrun by the course of practice and the many events occurring through interaction (Shove et al. 2012).

DAEDALUS & HIPPOMENES' STRATEGIC DILEMMAS: FROM BOUNDED RATIONALITY TO EQUIPPED SERENDIPITY

Daedalus, Icarus, & Ariadne

It is no wonder that the player who posted the strategy video chose "Icare533" as his pseudonym! Thanks to Icarus (*Icare* in French), we know that the relevant opposition is not between micro and macro perspectives, large-scale or small-scale approaches, but, to use Gérard Genette's terms, between "internal" and "external" focalization (Genette [1972] 1980): the task at stake is about how to draw maps and how to walk gaps, and our possible success depends on our ability to articulate the two.

Icarus is the son of Daedalus, a genius inventor and architect who conceived the Labyrinth, where he trapped the Minotaur, and who also invented the two alternative ways to escape it: he gave Ariadne the idea of equipping Theseus with a ball of thread so that he could enter the labyrinth, kill the Minotaur, and get out safely; and he designed the feathered wings by which he and his son Icarus could escape the very same labyrinth where King Minos placed them, and quit the island of Crete.

Three very important points deserve to be noted. First, Daedalus delegates stratagems. The delegation is both social and technical. In each case, the purpose is not restricted to the strategist's own goal and forces, but is extended through the enrollment of other persons, like Ariadne and Icarus, and other things, like a ball of thread and a pair of feathered wings. In so doing, Daedalus introduces a tension between strategy and distributed agency.[6] Second, Daedalus shows us that the best strategy to deal with a sophisticated piece of architecture is never a map. Daedalus is an architect, but paradoxically he doesn't trust or follow maps. Using the thread doesn't refer to the spatial labyrinth's structure, but rather to a horizontal and one-dimensional view: instead of following a map, the idea is to follow one's path; this trick prefigures the modern GPS, whose very logic is about converting plans into a continuous line you just have to follow. Symmetrically, with the feathered wings, Daedalus invents the angel's anatomy before its Christian reign, and more importantly the angel's view: with wings you are like an angel; you can see the maze from the sky. However, and paradoxically, seeing it from the top means forgetting it since you do not need to struggle with the maze any more to escape it: as soon as the map view is useful, it becomes useless. Third, even focused or not, the angel's view is little help: Daedalus and Icarus move from the maze to the sky; Ezio moves from the sky to the puzzle. But in either case, the overhanging position doesn't work, or rather, it did not work at the first attempt: it took millennia to safely succeed with Daedalus' trick and invent the airplane; thousands of players and game sessions are needed for many unsuccessful players to solve the Port Authority mission.

To understand better what is at stake here, I propose shifting angles and stories; I now move from the astute trio of Daedalus, Ariadne, and Icarus to the tragic couple of Atalanta and Hippomenes.

Atalanta & Hippomenes

Atalanta was a Greek woman with two qualities: she was incredibly beautiful, and she ran faster than anyone. But an oracle told her that if she ever married, she would be doomed. Atalanta thus decided to renounce love. To save herself from her fate, she proposed that suitors should attempt to win a race against her. If one wins, she will marry him; if he loses, he will be killed. One young man called Hippomenes watched the series of races and subsequent executions that invariably followed, and he thought the suitors were mad to risk death just for the chance of marrying Atalanta . . . until he went closer and saw how beautiful she was. He tried to seduce her, revealing his identity as the great-grandson of the god of the seas: Poseidon. Atalanta experienced a tragic tension: she fell in love with Hippomenes, but urged him to renounce a race she knew she had no choice but to win. But Hippomenes asked for the help of Aphrodite, the goddess of love, who gave him three golden apples (the same fruit is still the target of the video game Assassin's Creed, even if borrowed from the Bible rather than Greek mythology!). During the race, each time Atalanta took the lead, Hippomenes tossed an apple; the latter attracted Atalanta, who lost time to pick it up. At the very end of the race Atalanta hesitated to fetch the third apple, but Aphrodite forced her to do so; in addition, she had made the last apple heavier to slow Atalanta down. As a consequence, Hippomenes won the race, and Atalanta with it. But Hippomenes forgot to thank Aphrodite for her intervention and made love with Atalanta in a sacred temple. So in vengeance and as punishment, Aphrodite changed the couple into two statues in a lion shape.[7]

At first glance, this story seems to stage an oversimplified, chauvinist, and stereotyped opposition between male rationality and female futility. Hippomenes is a man with a purpose and a strategy. The purpose is to have the girl; the strategy rests on a thoughtful articulation of three steps: seducing Atalanta by (1) using Poseidon's reputation, (2) garnering Aphrodite's support, and (3) releasing the apples to win the race hence the wedding. We find the typical framework I described earlier: capitalizing on your opponent's behavioral patterns (here, curiosity) and playing on it: diverting Atalanta so that you win the race. In face of the strategic man, we have the futile woman. Atalanta is depicted as a weak girl incapable of sticking with her objective because she is unable to resist unexpected, frivolous temptations. This is just another variant of a long tradition of tales and myths where women are trapped in the shams of their curiosity. This story about the dangers of seductive apples and female curiosity obviously echoes the Bible, but also other mythological stories, such as Pandora and Psyche, and more recent narratives of Bluebeard, Lady Godiva, or the Lady of Shalott (Cochoy 2011).

However, a closer look shows that the situation is far more complex than it first seems. Atalanta is not fully curious: she remains focused on the race until the last, when Aphrodite forced her to pick up the third (heavier) apple. Moreover, Atalanta is also a terrific strategist, as evidenced with her vicious game aimed at protecting herself in cruelly benefiting from men's naive and pretentious self-confidence in their supposed superior physical force. Symmetrically, Hippomenes is not fully strategic, but rather fickle and distracted: before the race, he withdraws from his decision not to compete; he succumbs to Atalanta's charms, just as she is later attracted by the apples; then he forgets to reward Aphrodite for her help at the expense of his life. All in all, instead of being opposed, the two characters experience the very same tension between the rationality of strategic action and the seeming irrationality of serendipitous encounters.

Since we now understand the first element of this tension, we now move to the second. "Serendipity" is a term coined in reference to the three Princes of Serendip. Their father, the king, sent them to discover the world, and along their path they observed the traces of a camel. In looking carefully at these traces, such as grass eaten on only one side of the road; a wet place; a female smell; and the spots of two hands sustaining a heavy body, they inferred that the camel was blind, carrying a pregnant woman, and so on. According to Robert Merton and Elinor Barber (2004), who reviewed the history of serendipity, this word precisely refers to the ability to make sense of unexpected discoveries. Serendipity introduces a tension between two routes toward knowledge: one aims at fulfilling a predefined scientific objective; the other rests, on the contrary, on openness and curiosity.[8]

Then, how should we interpret Atalanta and Hippomenes' story? Of course, the original meaning points without ambiguity to the inescapable fate imposed by the gods, to the vacuum of proactive strategies as well as human frivolity. However, what makes the universality and eternity of myths is their ahistorical character, their ability to propose signifying structures that go beyond the culture of their origins. In this respect, we are entitled to dare another reading, focused not on the cultural intention of unknown authors of lost ages, but on the working of the text itself (Barthes 1977). In the very same way that, as Camus wrote, "one must imagine Sisyphus happy" (Camus 2004), one should imagine Atalanta and Hippomenes successful. Atalanta got not only the mysterious apples but a husband, and she eventually knew what love was, against the will of the gods; Hippomenes won the race, but more important, he succeeded in having Atalanta forever: they didn't die, but instead stayed together as immortal lions. The gods have strategies, but they also did not succeed: Aphrodite was not honored, and the oracle was not obeyed. Of course, what each character is getting is completely different than what he or she expected: Hippomenes thinks he got Atalanta, but the Atalanta he gets is not the one he expected: she has been transformed from a beautiful fast racer into a curious lion lover. At the same time, Atalanta fell in love with a dry, calculating agent who finally ended up as a distracted lion lover. That's another aporia of strategy: even when you succeed, what you obtain is often not exactly what you expected, since in most cases you cannot get it without having it transformed by your very quest.

In other words, the myth of Atalanta conveys two lessons: first, there is a tension between strategy and unexpected encounters; second, attaining a strategic objective is also having it change. This complements the lessons of the myths of Ariadne and Icarus where strategy appears strongly connected to the two opposite yet complementary views from the sky and from the guy, to coin a phrase.

LESSONS LEARNED: FROM BOUNDED RATIONALITY TO EQUIPPED SERENDIPITY

As our stories show, strategic action rests on a tension between two points of view. The first one is the right angle/overhanging view from the sky that I have proposed to call the "angel's view." This view leads to a two-dimensional representation of reality; it is that of the map or plan (a word which also means "map" in French), of what Herbert Simon (1947) called "synoptic rationality."

Along the angel's view of synoptic rationality, time is suspended and space is fully accessible. You know and you see everything, so that you may decide how to act optimally, but at some later point in time. It is the position Daedalus adopts when he conceives the feathered wings, of Atalanta when she organizes her fatal races, of the Assassin's Creed players who watch a video posted on the internet and try to organize and memorize the steps to get rid of deadlock. The other point of view is one-dimensional: it is the line of the path, of the several close and shifting angles we adopt when moving into the real and mundane world. Herbert Simon (1957) calls this perspective "bounded rationality." From this angle, a synoptic view is not accessible; bits of information are given selectively along a sequence, one has to deal with the limitations of our body and brain, etc. I propose to call this perspective the "sharp-angle view." In this case, time flows; thinking and acting cannot be separated; we get information about what to see and what to do, step by step, from the sharp angle of ground-level sight; and we have to make sense of this limited and sequential information in the course of our action. This is the position adopted by Icarus when he starts flying, Theseus when he enters the maze, Atalanta when she runs after Hippomenes and the apples, and the player engaging with mouse, keyboard, and screen to commit virtual assassination. We may have a strategy about the resources we need, about the pace we should take, but each step is then a discovery. In doing so, we are immersed in Simon's "bounded rationality."

But the experience of the video game as well as the other stories I related tend to show that these two visions, rather than being opposite and exclusive as decision theory would present them, are rather jointly involved in the pursuit of any goal-oriented action. We cannot discard the economists' conception too quickly. Michel Callon (1998) has argued that economic sociology has been ill served by its focus on the truthfulness or falseness of economic theory. According to Callon, economists have not only invented calculating agents, but they have also found the means to make them exist. Indeed, economics is not about describing the world of monetary exchanges and telling us what it is or what it is not; it is rather about shaping it. To put it in the terms of linguistic theory, economics is not a constative, but a performative science. In the very same way, strategic action is not so much about describing the state of affairs, but about equipping managerial action; hence, the dilemma of strategic action.

On the one hand, for the fulfillment of some goals, we need plans. Performing synoptic rationality is the aim of actors; this rationale is performative. Even if we—as anthropologists, sociologists, or management theorists—don't like the mapped plans of rational, synoptic action, even if we think them to be inaccurate, we have to admit that despite our tastes and arguments, the world is full of plans (Thévenot 2001), business plans (Giraudeau 2010), business models (Doganova and Eyquem-Renault 2009), algorithms (Muniesa 2011), search engines (Bourreau and Licoppe 2007), and so on. As a consequence, we have to acknowledge that these "angel view" tools heavily assist economic action, which is nonetheless rather oriented along the "sharp-angle view" of paths. At first, setting a plan may seem unrealistic, given the distance between the model and the underlying facts, but once it is produced, it is part of the game becomes real, although translated.

On the other hand, even when actors act in accordance with a plan, it is interesting to note that the latter is often accessible only through action. Even for Ezio, the Dark Angel, the angel's view is only a fleeting instant. As soon as the character is in the water or on the sides of the boat, the story changes. When actors start acting to fulfill their goals along a path, whether or not they had the benefit from an angel's view, they often encounter unexpected items or events that may not only contradict their quest, but sometimes can modify the very goals they are looking for. In this respect, Hippomenes' sudden interest in Atalanta or Atalanta's unexpected curiosity for golden apples wonderfully foreshadows more recent theorizations along which we often discover our goals along the course of our action (March 1991; Stark 2009).

As a result, the problem is neither to condemn strategic plans nor to deny their existence; the problem is not to choose between the angel's view of synoptic knowledge and the sharp-angle view of bounded rationality, but to study how and under what conditions they may converge. Most of the time, both views are involved. In other words, instead of opposing the synoptic rational dream of the economist to the bounded rationality of the active decision-maker, the examples I have reviewed suggest the existence of a third term that I propose: "equipped serendipity." This latter feature, which introduces a synthetic "stereoscopic" kind of strategic view, is probably more connected to contemporary high-tech action than old mythological or historical stories. Remember the video game: the player acts like the character, but his or her view does not exactly coincide with Ezio's one; the angle of sight is slightly different, and both views enrich each other. Moreover, just before playing, the player may have seen a video or read a solution on a forum (or paused the game to do so); the same player also benefits from a small map with a compass on the right of the screen, an estimate of his life, a tool measuring his reputation as a suspicious person, and even an "eagle vision," which supplements the character's view with a powerful infrared-like vision thanks to which the enemies become red, and the allies blue! This is what I call "equipped serendipity."

When playing, I am engaged in a serendipitous adventure that is closer to bounded than synoptic rationality. However, this experience is not fully reducible to bounded rationality for two reasons. First, I can withdraw from my goal, stop the game, or start another quest, like writing this chapter! This is why I think it is better to speak in terms of serendipity rather than rationality. Second and more important, I am not as deprived of external strategic synoptic tools as Simon's bounded rationality theory supposes: cognition is not isolated but rather assisted by a whole series of plans, tools, and other devices

(Hutchins 1995). This is why I suggest talking about equipped serendipity. Instead of being abandoned to a serendipitous journey, the equipment we benefit from helps us to combine the sharp-angle immersed view and the remote angel's view. Of course, one may object that this equipped serendipity refers to the virtual world of computer games rather than the real world of serious tasks. But looking at games is also a means to better grasp a pervasive feature of contemporary work or market settings, with all the screens, networks, information, and tools that now assist our actions (see, for instance, the association between two-dimensional barcodes and smartphones, which help contemporary customers to explore their environment further [Cochoy 2012]).

CONCLUSION

We now reach the end of this strange journey in a strategic realm where in fact no real angel flies, if one may speak of a "real" angel! I now understand why I couldn't find any solution to the Assassin's Creed Port Authority mission, or rather why the solutions I relied on proved inauthentic and tricky. The angels I enrolled preceded (in the case of Icarus) or followed (in the case of Ezio) the real ones. Icarus and Ezio are artificial angels. Just as Daedelus attached feather wings onto Icarus' body, Leonardo da Vinci designed Ezio's wings. But the very same Leonardo da Vinci also painted the well-known *Annunciation* with Gabriel, the angel who announced the conception of Jesus Christ to the Virgin Mary.[9]

"Real angels" are not strategists acting on their own, but rather messengers who speak for God. They are at the heart of communication, network, and action. As such, they received special attention from Michel Serres (1999), the French philosopher who was so influential in actor-network theory. If it were not blasphemous, I would say that the entities closest to angels in my account are neither Ezio nor Icarus, or their fellow mythological fictitious characters, but the body parts and technical equipment of my colleagues and myself. We ordinary fellows have no real wings but keyboards, mice, and fingers, and sometimes the unexpected interaction between these elements leads us to write things that have nothing to do with our conscious strategies (if any). Material artifacts and human flesh convey things, messages (as in those of brands); they evidence agency. As a result, their almost discrete and faithful mediation reshapes the strategies of all the other actors. It is also these angels who are invisibly flitting around us and sometimes subtly interacting with us, for instance when they mix up our fingers. Our fingers make mistakes and risk us losing pace and fail in fulfilling our Assassin's Creed plan (but in so doing they also helpfully "save" the researcher to get out of his vice), or give the pleasure of inverting the letters and thereby shift dry theoretical angles into some more poetic, and I hope heuristic, theoretical angels. All in all, the story I have told "of strategy as a socio-political practice that deals with uncertainty, representations of the future that alter the present, and intentionality," as a colleague's email urged me to do, is a serendipitous/reflexive tale from the beginning to the end. Without my colleague's misspelled words, there would have been no angels brought into strategy theorizing; without a video game, I couldn't have found the means to make different types of angels fly; without the somewhat miraculous apparition of a book proposal one day and the benevolence of several other angels, there would have been no chapter. In the end, the best strategy for finding a strategy, and for understanding what a strategy really is, may be forgetting strategy per se, and rather embracing and equipping serendipity, with a little help from other actors in one's network and actor-network theory.

REFERENCES

Ansoff, Igor. 1965. *Corporate Strategy*, New York: McGraw Hill.

Barthes, Roland, 1977. "From Work to Text." In *Image-Music-Text*, edited by R. Barthes, 155–64. New York: Hill and Wang.

Bourreau, Marc, and Christian Licoppe. 2007. "On-line Bidding and On-line Buying on the Same Website: Implications and Consequences of the Internet Homepage Proximity of Two Modes of Commercialization." In *Internet and Digital Economics*, edited by N. Curien and E. Brousseau, 510–36. Cambridge, UK: Cambridge University Press.

Callon, Michel. 1986. "Some Elements For A Sociology of Translation: Domestication of the Scallops and the Fishermen of St-Brieuc Bay." In *Power, Action and Belief: A New Sociology of Knowledge?* edited by J. Law, 196–223. Sociological Review Monographs Series. London: Routledge and Kegan Paul.

_____. 1998. "An Essay on Framing and Overflowing: Economic Externalities Revisited by Sociology." In *The Laws of the Markets*, edited by M. Callon, 244–69. Sociological Review Monographs Series. Oxford, UK: Blackwell.

Camus, Albert. 2004. *The Plague, The Fall, Exile and the Kingdom, and Selected Essays*. New York: Alfred A. Knopf.

Chandler, Alfred. 1962. *Strategy and Structure: Chapters in the History of Industrial Enterprise*. New York: Doubleday.

Cochoy, Franck. 2011. *De la curiosité, L'art de la séduction marchande* [*Of Curiosity, The Art of Market Seduction*]. Paris: Armand Colin.

_____. 2012. "The Pencil, the Trolley and the Smartphone: Understanding the Future of Self-Service Retailing through its Sociotechnical History." In *Nordic Retail Research, Emerging Diversity*, edited by J. Hagberg, U. Holmberg, M. Sundström, and L. Walter, 215–33. Göteborg, Sweden: BAS.

Dodier, Nicolas. 1995. *Les Hommes et les machines, La conscience collective dans les sociétés technicisées* [*Men and Machines, Collective Consciousness in Technicized Societies*]. Paris: Métailié.

Doganova, Liliana, and Marie Eyquem-Renault. 2009. "What Do Business Models Do? Innovation Devices in Technology Entrepreneurship." *Research Policy* 38(10):1559–70.

Elster, Jon. 1979. *Ulysses and the Sirens*. Cambridge, UK: Cambridge University Press.

Genette, Gérard. (1972) 1980. *Narrative Discourse: An Essay in Method*. Oxford, UK: Blackwell.

Giraudeau, Martin. 2010. "Organiser l'avenir: Une sociologie historique des business-plans" ["Organizing Future: A Socio-Historical Account of Business-Plans"]. PhD dissertation, University of Toulouse, France.

Harrison, Peter. 2001. "Curiosity, Forbidden Knowledge, and the Reformation of Nature Philosophy in Early Modern England." *Isis* 92(2):265–90.

Hutchins, Edwin. 1995. *Cognition in the Wild*. Cambridge, MA: MIT Press.

Latour, Bruno. 2005. *Reassembling the Social: An Introduction to Actor-Network Theory*. Oxford, UK: Oxford University Press.

March, James G. 1991. "How Decisions Happen in Organizations." *Human-Computer Interaction* 6:95–117.

Merton, Robert K., and Elinor Barber. 2004. *The Travels and Adventures of Serendipity*. Princeton, NJ: Princeton University Press.

Muniesa, Fabian. 2011. "Is a Stock Exchange a Computer Solution? Explicitness, Algorithms and the Arizona Stock Exchange." *International Journal of Actor-Network Theory and Technological Innovation* 3(1):1–15.

Porter, Michael E. 1980. *Competitive Strategy: Techniques for Analyzing Industries and Competitors*. New York: Free Press.

Selznick, Philip. 1957. *Leadership in Administration: A Sociological Interpretation*. Evanston, IL: Row, Peterson.

Serres, Michel. 1999. *La Légende des anges* [*The Legend of Angels*]. Paris: Flammarion.

Shove, Elizabeth, Mika Pantzar, and Matt Watson. 2012. *The Dynamics of Social Practice: Everyday Life and How It Changes*. London: Sage.

Simon, Herbert. 1947. *Administrative Behavior*. New York: Macmillan.

______. 1957. *Models of Man, Social and Rational: Mathematical Essays on Rational Human Behavior in a Social Setting*. New York: John Wiley and Sons.

Stark, David. 2009. *The Sense of Dissonance: Accounts of Worth in Economic Life*. Princeton, NJ: Princeton University Press.

Thévenot, Laurent. 2001. "Pragmatic Regimes Governing the Engagement with the World." In *The Practice Turn in Contemporary Theory*, edited by K. Knorr-Cetina, T. Schatzki, and V. Savigny Eike, 56–73. London: Routledge.

Tournier, Michel. 1985. *Friday*. New York: Pantheon Books.

NOTES

The author warmly thanks Jennifer Collier, Rita Denny, Martin Kornberberger, Patricia Sunderland, and two anonymous reviewers for their various contributions, input, and encouragements to the development of this chapter. While writing this chapter, the author benefited from the support of the Center for Retailing, Handels Business School, University of Gothenburg, Sweden.

1 See http://www.youtube.com/watch?v=a5eVq5mSbkE.

2 Of course, in the video the strategy is not explicitly formulated, but emerges as a pure deduction of the observation of its actual execution. Such deduction is not easy; that's why it's so hard to learn from what others have done: one is limited to the view "from the guy." She who posts the video is executing the plan with the strategy in mind, but in some cases the imitator may see only tactics, with no view "from the sky" (I am very grateful to one of the reviewers for this observation).

3 This is all the more remarkable because this mission did not belong to the original game, but was sold as an add-on that probably interested a population of fans much smaller than the general public. It was later included in the main quest, but since it occurs at the very end, not all players reach it.

4 http://www.youtube.com/watch?v=a5eVq5mSbkE (accessed December 13, 2013).

5 http://www.youtube.com/watch?v=eoYmsmvlVaQ (accessed December 13, 2013).

6 According to actor-network theory, the well-known theoretical framework my entire account rests upon, social action is not restricted to human beings. To put it in anthropological terms, there is no "great divide" between an active culture and a passive nature; action combines the input (or

agency) of human and nonhuman actors and actants (Latour 2005). In other words, these entities are all trying to follow their own goals and/or to express their own inner logics (a purpose for a human; a force for an object, etc.), and some of them try to better fulfill their "programs" by benefitting from the action of the others in "enrolling them" in vast "socio-technical networks" (Callon 1986). By such reasoning, the strategy of any given actor has to cope with the competing action logics and "distributed agency" of the surrounding entities.

7 Summary from Ovid's *Metamorphoses,* Atalanta and Hippomenes, 10, 519–739.

8 Since Eve's temptation for the Tree of Knowledge and the subsequent Fall, curiosity has remained a "forbidden knowledge," a dangerous, vain, and faulty attempt to challenge God's knowledge (Cochoy 2011; Harrison 2001). At best, it was envisioned as a useless, fascinating distraction and a proof of the "weaknesses of will." As Jon Elster (1979) showed, by relevantly relying on the experience of a legendary sailor, Ulysses, one can navigate such roads only through the delegation of one's will to external bounds: listening to the Sirens becomes acceptable, provided the hero puts wax in his seamen's ears and asks them to attach him to the mast.

9 See http://www.virtualuffizi.com/uffizi1/Uffizi_Pictures.asp?Contatore=126.

37

An Anthropology of the Senses: Tracing the Future of Sensory Marketing in Brand Rituals

TIMOTHY DE WAAL MALEFYT

In 2010, one of our clients, a men's grooming and hair care company, approached my in-agency insight group, Cultural Discoveries at BBDO advertising in New York City, to conduct in-home interviews among men who regularly shaved. They were puzzled over a new premium-priced shaving brand they had recently acquired. They wanted ethnographic research to explain why the small segment of men who regularly purchased this high-end shaving product were strong advocates of the brand, when most of their target group disliked shaving altogether. Who were these high-involvement brand advocates that expressed great satisfaction with the premium product in a consumer category that was notorious for low involvement and purportedly difficult to market?

We set out to bring these shaving enthusiasts "to life" and find out what this premium brand offered men. We interviewed and observed 24 men aged 18 to 49 in the tri-state (New York, New Jersey, and Connecticut) region, half of whom bought the premium product, and half of whom purchased a minimum of shaving equipment. We discovered that shaving for the brand enthusiasts was a highly engaging activity they enjoyed doing. Their daily grooming routine led them to feel like "better men" in what they described as a performance-oriented, competitive work world. Clothes, hair, and shaving played a key role in defining who they were in their presentation of self to others (Goffman 1959). Grooming not only transformed these men to be "ready for the day," but also identified them as men who cared about and paid attention to appearance. In this regard, their personal involvement with shaving translated into enhancing the social self.

But beyond solving a functional problem of providing an enhanced solution to daily grooming, as the company sought, their descriptions revealed deeper,

Handbook of Anthropology in Business, edited by Rita Denny and Patricia Sunderland, 704–721.

more engaged sensory involvement with the brand. What we observed as their shaving routine was actually a brand ritual. Indeed, the sequential four-step process as marked on the brand packaging, which stipulates that men follow a preshave, lathering, shaving, and aftershave process, helped identify the brand as potentially ritualistic. But it wasn't just the instructions on the package. Men who engaged in the shaving ritual showed greater focus, self-awareness, and concern for process: they used a different vocabulary of shaving terms, committed more time to the effort, and shared their thoughts and skills with other men. This did not occur with the other men we spoke to who used the "regular" shaving brand.

Our research confirmed what the company already had known: shaving for many men was drudgery, "a chore" to be minimized or skipped when possible. Many men only referenced the positive aspects of shaving in terms of the absence of negatives (no nicks or cuts). The "regular" shaving product mostly delivered on this with its vibrating five-blade system that *removed* the effort for the user. Yet, for other men, shaving was a ritual in which effort was *cherished*. Shaving involved multiple sensory interactions grounded in skill and acquired expertise. Men in the ritual spoke of focusing closely on what they were doing while shaving; they described sensory details such as the importance of sounds, movement, and scents during shaving. Some played special tunes, like classic Frank Sinatra songs, while other men enjoyed the sound and feel of stirring the brush in the cup, "wisking it fast" and "frothing up the lather." Still other men attended to the light scraping sound of the blade held at just the right angle as it glided over their skin (for example, see "How To Shave with a Single-Blade Razor" on YouTube).[1] For others, the choice among various brand scents was evocative. Smelling Citrus Lemon, Lavender, Sandalwood, or Ocean Kelp demarcated a transition from unclean to clean (Howes 1987), or, in their terms, "to feel ready" for the day. Men also tuned into brand packaging with more acuity. Some spoke of the high-end moisturizing preshave lotion's glass jar as being more "old-fashioned" and "genuine" than if it were made of plastic. The cursive writing, the list of natural ingredients, and the directions on the packaging were also noted as enhancing the brand's value to them. One respondent said, "Things that are important are given instructions. This says that they care about the details." In the process of enjoying the brand and shaving experience, these men drew out the best of its qualities.

Beyond following the four-step process on the brand package, some men embellished the ritual sequence by adding their own refinements to enhance the sensory experience. One added a few drops of olive oil to the shaving lather to "further soften whiskers." Another mentioned prewarming a frothing cup with hot water for better foam. Another discovered a double-edged German-manufactured blade called Merkur, which could be adjusted and gave a "higher quality shave" than other brands. This man shared his discovery with friends at work and others on a men's shaving website.

In the end, our learning about the sensory experience of brands showed a marked contrast between men, not only in what they purchased and how much they spent, but between those for whom shaving was a ritual and for those it was not. Our study helped develop a new marketing strategy for the high-end shaving product, suggesting that certain men might appreciate the effort in shaving as part of a grooming ritual. The campaign focused on the sensual aspects of shaving, affirming men who embraced shaving as savants, experts, and connoisseurs of grooming. The campaign reclaimed the shaving experience as a manifestation of one's performative skills leading to "the perfect shave," and as designed for a select community of fellow shavers, a "brotherhood" who relished the act. In the end, it was the sensory aspects of the brand that consumers embraced, which led us to discover brand rituals in shaving as a key aspect of remarketing the brand, experientially.

This chapter provides an overview of the rising interest in sensory approaches to human behavior. It compares sensory approaches as investigated by anthropologists who treat the senses as a form of social and cultural interaction, and marketing approaches in business that seek to maximize consumer experience with a brand through targeting specific sensory responses to consumption. The two approaches are shown to hinge their ideas and practices on very different concepts of agency of the mind and body. The anthropological approach seeks a more holistic and integrative understanding of the ways in which humans actively make sense of their world. The marketing approach seeks to categorize and distinguish human experience in terms of expanding consumption opportunities in novel ways. This chapter concludes by offering suggestions on ways that corporate anthropologists who engage in consumer research can integrate both approaches and use sensory-rich cultural frameworks to better map out consumer involvement with brands through the investigation of consumer brand rituals.

AN ANTHROPOLOGY OF THE SENSES

Anthropologists have recently turned their attention to human sensory experience as a means for understanding the complexities of contemporary social life. The sensorium, which straddles the divide between mind and body, cognition and sensation, is claimed to be a cultural construction that is "socially made and mediated" (Hsu 2008:433). A growing body of scholarly research reveals that the senses are lived, experienced, and understood differently by various people in different places and at different times (Bendix 2005; Brenneis 2005;

Classen 1993; Geurts 2002; Howes 1991, 2003, 2005a; Hsu 2008; Ingold 2000; Stoller 1989, 1997; Synnott 1991). In particular, anthropologists are interested in how culture-specific concepts and practices of a people's sensory experience generate day-to-day social interaction and mark what is meaningful in life, whether in ritual, performance, food, celebration, sports, work, play, or in notions of self and personhood.

At the same time, as commercial products have become more numerous, consumers more selective, and the marketplace more competitive, marketers have discovered the human senses as a means to elicit deeper, more personal experiences for consumers with their products, brands, and services. The senses represent a novel means for stoking human emotions and forging stronger consumer connections to brands that cannot be explained in words. Marketers are seeking sensory interactions with consumers in every mode of consumption. They claim that the greater the number of consumers' senses engaged or the deeper the targeting of a particular sense, the stronger an emotional impression is made with a branded product (Gobé 2009; Hultén et al. 2009; Krishna 2010; Lindstrom 2010; Postrel 2003; Roberts 2005). As such, the sensorium takes on heightened importance for marketers today as a means for making their brands and products stand out in a competitive field. Moreover, while anthropological and marketing approaches to the senses appear at odds with one another, anthropological analysis, such as in ritual, can offer a practical and insightful bridge. We can explore these approaches further to investigate what they each offer for consumer research.

SENSORY BEGINNINGS IN ANTHROPOLOGY

An "anthropology of the senses" was established in the 1980s and 1990s by the early work of Constance Classen (1993, 1998), David Howes (1991, 2003, 2005a), Paul Stoller (1989, 1997), Steven Feld (1982), and Steven Feld and Keith Basso (1996). Sensory studies currently cover a range of topics, including the senses and the anthropology of everyday life (Seremetakis 1994), the sensual revolution (Howes 2005a), sensuous scholarship (Stoller 1997), sensuous geography (Rodaway 1994), a sociology of the senses (Synnott 1993; Vannini et al. 2012), the senses and perception (Ingold 2000), senses of place (Feld and Basso 1996), the sensorium of contemporary arts and sensory architecture (Jones 2006; Malnar and Vodvarka 2004), sensory ethnography (Pink 2004, 2009) and a cultural history of the senses (Classen 1993, 1998, 2012). David Howes calls for a "sensory revolution" (2005a) challenging linguistic theory that underpins most cultural analysis, and advocates a new sensory subdiscipline within anthropology. Other scholars call for more integrative practice of the senses, augmenting studies of culture, ethnography, and social interaction with sensual perspectives (Bendix 2005; Brenneis 2005; Hertzfeld 2001; Hsu 2008). Both views advocate for a more multisensory orientation towards theory, cultural understanding, and fieldwork practices.

Sensory anthropologists distinguish themselves from other approaches to the senses by taking a decidedly social and cultural approach. They claim sensory experience is generated *between* and *among* people, places, and events, rather than *in* an individual's body (Hsu 2008). As opposed to dividing the body and mind, and treating the senses as vehicles that merely channel information to the brain as many marketers do, anthropologists and sociologists regard the active interplay among sensory experience, emotion, memory, and cognition as deeply contingent upon situated meaning, or context. A sociocultural approach notes that "as we sense we also make sense" (Vannini et al. 2012:15). Scholars variously explore how human sensing is an interactive and interpretive process that is primarily activated in social situations. They explore the interactive ways that the senses are socially patterned within each culture; how the senses are culturally ordered and variously ranked across cultures; and the ways in which the senses are linked to emotion, memory, and experience.

In how the senses are socially patterned within culture, scholars note that its members generally only perceive those sensations that are socially marked by a particular culture. From Bourdieu's universal concept of the *habitus*, Thomas Csordas (1990) advocates embodiment as a cultural concept for analysis. Elizabeth Hsu more recently (2008:437) likened socially patterned sensing to the ways linguists distinguish phonetic (outside) from phonemic (inside) sound patterns of a given language. In particular, people pay attention to, or sense, those aspects in life that are marked and given meaning by a culture: what scents are acceptable and which are not; what good food tastes like and what is repulsive; what is pleasing to the eye and what is not, and so forth. As such, particular cultural situations evoke specific sensory experiences and appropriate responses. Michael Hertzfeld (2001:244) informs us that, "To stare at someone may signify rudeness, curiosity, flattery or domination, depending on the circumstances and the culture," and that these cultural codes will vary even more by adding personal idiosyncrasies. The senses thus play a vital role in producing and maintaining different modalities and meaning of perception, place, and experience within cultures.

Other directions in sensory scholarship explore the ways in which one culture ranks and orders the senses in particular hierarchies with various meanings that are different from those in other cultures. These studies reveal how various sensory orders expand upon and challenge the classic Western five-sense structure. The Western sensory order typically ranks vision and audition as "higher" senses of rational reason, while the senses of smell, taste, and touch are ranked "lower" and associated with irrational emotions and feelings (Synnott 1991). However, other cultures inform different sensory orders. Kathryn Lynn Guerts (2002), for instance, reports how the Anlo-Ewe–speaking children in southeastern Ghana (Africa) learn to incorporate all their senses, including a sixth sense of balance to navigate their world, which is different from Western children, who are taught to rely on vision and audition as primary modes for learning. Steven Feld (1982) reveals how the Kaluli of Papau, New Guinea, develop fine acoustical skills to traverse dense rainforests, and their acoustic orientation to the world also structures their folklore, dance, and body décor. Helena Wulff (2011) notes that what generally might be considered a "common universal fact," such as the color green, can be injected with particular cultural meaning. Ireland is often identified as "The Green Isle" or "The Emerald Isle" for its green landscape. Yet, the different ways people "see green" in Ireland reveals that color is an identity marker that is highly charged politically and culturally, from the ban on "the wearing of the green" during British colonialism, to green signifying the color of the Republican Revolutionary Organization, to green as a marketed and branded indicator in outsiders' construction of Irishness, such as turning the Chicago River green for the St. Patrick's day celebration, or drinking green beer. Not only are the senses experienced differently by different cultures, but time and context also shift the meaning of apparently "universal" color schemes.

Sensory anthropologists also investigate the link between the senses, emotions, and memory, along with concepts of personhood. Elizabeth Hsu posits that as sensory experiences are produced, enacted, and perceived in combination with each other, they are also intertwined with emotion, meaning, and memory (2008:440). Sense and sentiment are deeply linked, "often difficult to articulate verbally, embedded in webs of association and memory, and not easily translatable," writes Donald Brenneis (2005:142). For one, he continues, the language commonly used for describing sensory experience is that of feeling and the emotions (Brenneis 2005). Furthermore, the same questions that vex anthropologists studying emotions are similar to questions about the senses, such as to what extent are emotions or the senses a "natural" response to stimuli, versus what is learned and shaped by culture? Anthropologists studying emotions note, as in studies of the senses, that emotions are thought in the West to reside *within* the individual, whereas emotions are thought in much of the Pacific regions to reside *between* people (Lutz 1988). Furthermore, like emotions, sensory experiences can evoke strong memories such as the "smell of greenness" signaling the annual celebration of the arrival of spring in Diane Young's (2005) account of the Pitjantjantnara people of Australia. Emotions and the senses here relate to notions of personhood, or what David Howes refers to as the power of "emplacement" (2005a), and are a resource for shaping, revealing, and transforming the self in appropriate social settings. Fred Myers (1979) claims that in

Australian Aboriginal Pintupi concepts of emotions, what one feels relative to a situation are moral systems that inform and orient one's disposition towards social life—how one should behave and interpret such feelings—affecting notions of self and personhood. In these ways, anthropologists studying culture put stock in the deeply contextualized aspects of sensory experience, which link the senses to particular events, feelings, place, and identity in shaping the everyday social life of people.

Just as an anthropology of the senses has been established to reveal the multiple ways in which people of various cultures map out life through an experience of the senses, so marketers are likewise interested in the ways brands, services, and consumer retail encounters can be mapped out differently, or expanded upon, through increased attention to several or all of consumers senses.

THE MARKETING OF THE SENSES

Corporations have recently paid increased attention to consumer experience through sensory modalities. "Sensory appeals are everywhere, they are increasingly personalized and they are intensifying," writes journalist Virginia Postrel (2003:5). Swedish business consultants Bertil Hultén and colleagues note that recent sensory awareness has launched "a new epoch in marketing," where "the five senses will be at the center of a firm's marketing strategy and tactics" (2009:2). Brands in competitive space, writes Martin Lindstrom (2010), need to stand out as distinctive; they must deliver a full sensory and emotive experience. Kevin Roberts, CEO of Saatchi and Saatchi, believes that the senses are a new frontier for marketers to advance their wares on consumers because the senses are ". . . direct, provocative and immediate. . . . The senses speak to the mind in the language of emotions, not words" (2005:105). The so-called "management of sensation" (Howes 2007) has now become an obsession in contemporary consumer capitalism. The thought is that by charging messages and commercial situations with sensations in every media modality, marketers can bypass "reason" by means of provoking a direct response to emotions. As such, they reinforce rather than revise traditional Western sensory orders.

The emphasis on sensory marketing today is spurred not only by increased brand competition, but also from changing views of the individual in contemporary society. For instance, Hultén and colleagues claim that marketing in a postmodern society has generated a new emphasis on human values. New information and rapid communication technology allow for greater circulation of globalization, diversity, and pluralism of ideas, knowledge, and brands (Hultén et al. 2009:25). Individuals, they claim, can craft new identities, forge new images of the self and their experiences, real and virtual, continuously in this reflexive world. Mass production has been replaced with customization, and calls for firms to more deeply satisfy individual needs and wants to succeed. Sensory marketing is based on a deeper level of an individual's sensory experience with a brand. It supersedes mass and relationship marketing because it involves expanded consumer engagement through dialog, interactivity, multidimensional communication, and digital technology (Hultén et al. 2009:5). An important feature of this new economy of the self, they claim, is an emphasis on design and style rather than content and substance.

Journalist Virginia Postrel, in *Substance of Style* (2003), expands on this idea, and links the recent marketing interest in the senses to the rise of a new aesthetic age. Highly styled and designed objects no longer serve a function alone, but are increasingly appreciated for their aesthetic value. She substantiates this claim through examples of newly designed products that range from colorful pagers and artfully designed computers to comfortable-grip toothbrushes for which consumers are willing to pay a premium. The sensual look and feel of things, she writes, will determine their success or failure, from architecture through fashion and products to people's appearance (2003:34–65). She maintains that design and style aesthetics are what evoke an emotional response from consumers and relate directly to personal preferences. Starbucks is a prime example of an aesthetically designed brand sensorium that, beyond serving coffee, creates an environment that attends to rich textures, colors, aromas, taste treats, and music, and so induces a respite from the hectic world. Starbucks "is to the age of sensory aesthetics what McDonalds was to the age of convenience or Ford was to the age of mass production" (Postrel 2003:20).

It appears from the perspectives of Postrel (2003) and Hultén and colleagues (2009) that sensory approaches to marketing do more than just respond to the personal aesthetic demands of the individual. They involve a high level of *reflexivity* that create for a firm both a new identification with their branded object, as well as a new subject in the consumer, to discern qualities of the brand previously unconsidered. The human sensorium importantly offers marketers a new lens by which to view their brand, and construct the consumers' body as a new private territory on which to expand their brand (Malefyt 2007). This highly customized and individualized marketing approach evidences what Howes calls "the progressive privatization of sensation" (2005b:287–88).

From a branding perspective, sensory marketing makes sense: it generates an entirely new mode of commodity production that requires marketers to reconsider what consumers *actually* experience with their product. Marketers must take into account more than what they are accustomed to, relative to a brand's distinctive features. It gives new life to a brand, a fresh way to envision consumers, and new marketing possibilities. Brands become meaningful to consumers through an experience with the brand that stimulates a sense or multiple senses in particular ways. It also reveals that consumers identify brands, not necessarily through logos and names (Klein 2000), but through experiences with them. It forces a firm to reconsider its product as an experience in itself instead of through functions, attributes, and features (Hultén et al. 2009:6).

A reflexive marketing perspective means that marketers are challenged to rethink their brands in new ways. They may question, for instance, when true enjoyment of a product really begins. What makes a particular brand of soda enjoyable? Beyond when a consumer might first taste a soda, enjoyment may begin when holding a cold, wet can; cracking open the tab with a burst; and smelling the soda as it is poured and fizzes up over the crackling sound of ice to the top of a glass. The evocative experience of enjoying a soda encompasses more than the soda taste that marketers have traditionally marketed to consumers. In other words, sensory awareness informs a marketer that by attending to consumer interaction with brands, enjoyment of a brand extends beyond its intrinsic or symbolic features. Moreover, the sensory value of the brand cannot be ascertained in advance or from a distance, but because it is subjective, can only be discovered through direct experience (Postrel 2003:xiv).

Marketers have since learned that attraction to a new car is not necessarily how it is designed, how fast it goes on a highway, or the number of safety features built into it, but rather how the doors sound in closing, the scent inside the car, or the variety of textures that contrast or harmonize within its interior (Lindstrom 2010:25–6). Arizona jeans are known for their unique smell, as is Play-Doh, Crayola crayons, and other brands that evoke strong memories in their sensual appeal. Sensory cues, Lindstrom claims, are even perceived as making a product appear more authentic (2010:12), such as Heinz ketchup sold in a heavy solid glass bottle rather than a light plastic container: "the slow heavy pour" gives the brand the appearance of containing higher-quality ingredients (Lindstrom 2010:13). In these examples, brands are reportedly given new life by marketers for sensual qualities that have traditionally been overlooked or underemphasized.

Nevertheless, however we might evaluate these branded claims, the focus on sensory marketing is not, in fact, on consumers. Rather, it is on how marketing strategies of companies use the senses to "perform" their products, brands, and services to consumers, in expectation of eliciting greater response from them. Marketers appear more concerned with mediating effects and the resulting responses generated by various sensory prompts than by fulfilling a more holistic brand experience for consumers that a sensory approach potentially affords. Marketing scholar Aradhna Krishna (2010), for instance, affirms that "*products* are sensual in nature" and that "the more a firm can create, accentuate, or highlight the sensuality of their products, the more appealing these products can be for consumers" (2010:1). Creating sensations or "bringing attention to existing sensations," she maintains, can increase products or services appeal to consumers. Marc Gobé affirms this approach when he says "successful sensory appeals only occur through intelligent strategy" (2009:71). The products, then, are the *active agents* strategized by brand managers to evoke a new or heightened response from consumers, rather than inquiring how consumers might gain greater fulfillment in their lives from interaction and use with the product. Marketing and anthropological approaches to the senses thus assume fundamentally different concepts of agency between objects in relation to the body, mind, and senses. For anthropologists, agency is located in *social interaction* and is highly contingent on context; for marketers, agency is situated in the *strategic deployment of brand qualities* that evoke a desired response from consumers. Nevertheless, I hope to show that anthropological analysis as revealed in consumer research on brand rituals can be a point of convergence for these two divergent approaches.

From a marketing standpoint, it may appear self-evident that five distinct senses correspond directly with particular body parts: eyes/sight, ears/hearing, nose/smell, mouth/taste, and skin/touch. But this clear division and compartmentalization is confounded when, for instance, we consider that 70 to 80 percent of taste cannot operate without smell, and that the texture of a food or beverage enhances its taste. Likewise, sight and sound typically work together when approaching an object. The senses coordinate in sequence: we see an apple, pick it up, feel its smooth texture, and taste and smell its qualities (Howes 2009). Furthermore, there is discussion of our "other senses" beyond the classic five senses that are not externally oriented, but rather provide information on our internal world. For instance, we can speak of our senses of balance, movement, and temperature; our sense of pain; or senses of thirst and hunger (Vannini et al. 2012:6). The opportunity for anthropologists conducting consumer research on brands is to discover and expand upon the *total sensory experience*, which is greater than the sum of any isolated sense. A sociologist, for instance, recalls his total experience of coffee enjoyment is greater than any one, two, or several isolated sensory cues that might be described separately:

> I genuinely enjoy the total sensual experience of fresh-brewed morning coffee. The taste of coffee incorporates its smell, but the smell of the coffee I drink is quite different from the tantalizing aroma of brewing coffee, a scent that, in fact, seems to awaken my senses. Even though the two aromas are different, I know that the smell of brewing coffee anticipates and lubricates how I both taste and smell coffee when I drink it. . . . [T]he flavor of coffee also includes the feel of hot liquid. In the morning, it has to be hot. I occasionally enjoy iced coffee, but iced coffee would never satisfy me in the morning, regardless of environmental temperature. Even the weight and

> feel of the mug are significant. I find it hard to get a satisfying swig from those dainty, undersized, bourgeois espresso cups. Conversely, if the mug is too large the coffee is cold before I'm finished. . . . I prefer a mid-sized, thick ceramic mug" (Vannini et al. 2012:5).

Taste, smell, feel, weight, and temperature of coffee, in addition to the situatedness of the morning-time experience, blend into a total sensual, contextual, and temporal experience of coffee, and are not limited solely to taste or aroma, as marketers would have it.

Unfortunately, many brand managers develop strategic plans either intended to bypass consumers' rational mind and appeal emotionally to their unconscious sensory bodies, or to distance the brand from direct involvement and social interaction through product messaging that reinforces mainly brand features and attributes, not user experience. For example, brand advertising for the corporation's "regular" shaver we studied stresses only the functional benefits of shaving (clean, close, efficient), while minimizing sensory involvement of its users. No wonder men may learn to dislike shaving! The advertising's focus on shave completion highlights a five-blade vibrating system meant to reduce time, minimize effort, and by association, uninvolve the user. If "the best a man can get" is a *rational* call for men seeking success out of life, missing is the sensory journey and *emotional* involvement a man might enjoy in getting there. In either case, marketing divides the sensory experience that consumers perceive as unified and whole.

Most marketing approaches, in fact, intentionally distinguish corporeal sensations of the body from cognitive processes of the mind. The "mind" of the consumer is believed to make choices, decide on products, or rationalize not to purchase them, whereas the body and corporeal senses are regarded as passive spectators that *react* to stimuli, unconscious vehicles for recording external stimuli and sending information to the brain. Marketing experts affirm this when they write, "all our knowledge comes to us *through the senses*" (Roberts 2005:105). Lindstrom notes that our moods, feelings, and products we use are "continuously imprinted on our 5-track sensory recorder" (2010:14). "As humans," he continues, "we are most *receptive* when we are operating on all five senses . . ." (Lindstrom 2010:15). Gobé advises, ". . . odor can be used to *manage* brand strategy" (2009:99). In this capacity, marketers reduce the senses to passive receiving channels that can be tapped to increase consumer persuasion and motivate choice, especially since they influence emotion and work unconsciously. The strategy for marketers is to either "manage" a particular sense or corral many senses together in one powerful, coordinated effort; the result, writes Lindstrom, of creating a "synergy across the senses," is like a "cascading domino effect" (2005:38), and the consumer is won.

Indeed, marketing consultant Dan Hill (2003) further distinguishes between body and mind, emotion and reason, when he alleges that more "truth" can be obtained from consumers when marketers focus on consumers' bodies, not their minds. In his words, "the human body won't lie" (Hill 2003:98). Reading the body is "quick, immediate and intuitive" (Hill 2003:102), and avoids (misleading) conscious rationalizations, since, for Hill, "it's critical to know the truth from the lies," and "people lie" (2003:5). By Hill's account, beneath "the surface" of rational thought the five senses interpret the world and dictate emotional responses to the environment and different stimuli (2003:2). By analogy, if the consumer's "head" is misleading for marketers, then they should target the "heart" and create "lovemarks" Roberts (2005). Marketing to the senses extends this "divide and conquer" analogy by regarding the senses as a new frontier of divisible units.

Marketing as a system works on the principle of division. Segmentation, in marketing terms, is a widespread practice that nearly all corporations conducting consumer research use today. This approach not only divides the human body from the mind and rational thinking from emotional response, but also from the greater population of its target consumers. Sunderland and Denny (2007) note that segmentation began with dividing consumers based on demographics (gender, age, income, marital status, and so forth), and later included lifestyle, psychographics, and value mindsets as variables to identify and target likely and potentially profitable consumer segments of the population. Categorizing the world into smaller units makes what is otherwise messy into something more manageable and also reflects the corporate practice to "separate fiefdoms" that might otherwise compete (Sunderland and Denny 2007:243).

In another sense, categorization is a response to the marketers' dilemma of too much information. The world we live in, including consumers as a subject of investigation, is not neatly divided into divisible units, but is overlapping, convoluted, and complex. Yet, even though it is essentially continuous, we seem to prefer to experience the world in discrete chunks. By sheer convention we perceive and make sense out of experience by creating distinct clusters. This process is what Zerubavel calls "lumping" and "splitting" (1996:421). The quality of in-betweenness, of not being able to categorize something distinctly, is culturally disruptive and dealt with through ritual (Douglas 1966) or other cultural systems that create order. In fact, Bowker and Star (2000) detail how a system's classificatory scheme works to mitigate ambiguity. Classification makes relevant and visible those ambiguous features that are desirable, while making irrelevant and obscure other features that are less desirable (Bowker and Star 2000:320).

Classifying consumer categories into units of behavior also helps reinvigorate and reinforce the self-serving system that marketing creates. Classification schemas help sustain a system, both through active feedback of selecting appropriate information and by organizing an infrastructure around that information (Bowker and Star 2000:320). Thus, consumer segmentation in business is a form of *knowledge production*. The ontological divide between consumer mind and body has sustained research departments and corporate practices within organizations for decades. Strategic ideas about crafting marketing campaigns rely on duality. Frequently, this is couched in terms of rational and emotional approaches to targeting (i.e, the "head" and the "heart"). Since marketers believe the consumers' head is overwhelmed with too many messages, features, and brands to choose from (their own and competing others), targeting the heart ostensibly bypasses reason and evokes emotion instead. Sensory marketing is a further deployment of this classificatory segmentation in ways that help produce (or reproduce) the marketing system itself. Rather than eliminating the trend to fragment human subjects into distinct compartmentalized targets, it extends preexisting categories and experiences into more divisions, divided among the five senses. Such division furthers a distrust of consumers ("they lie") and distances marketers from the social interactions and fully lived situations in which brands are meaningful to people.

BRAND RITUALS: MARKETING THE SENSES FOR CORPORATE ANTHROPOLOGISTS

Nevertheless, a way to reincorporate the cultural relevance of human interaction with product use back into the consumer's whole sensory experience is to frame consumption in terms of subject matter that marketers can attend to. Sarah Pink relates in her book *Home Truths* (2004) how she conducted an ethnography on home cleaning, commissioned by Unilever Corporation, to investigate a range of sensory reactions to home care products, including detergents. Another way anthropologists working in corporate research can inform their corporate clients of consumers' sensory engagement with brands is by drawing their attention to brand rituals.

Rituals, such as enjoying morning coffee or men's daily shaving, are useful cultural categories to better understand consumers' sensual connection to brand experiences, since rituals are "action[s] thick with sensory meaning" (Grimes 1995:965). Rituals blend a total sensual, contextual, and temporal experience of a brand to provide an integrative bridge between cultural analysis of anthropologists studying sensual experiences and marketers seeking to maximize their brand value through emotional connections with products.

By definition, ritual behaviors reformulate experience and create a sense of control and new order out of existing materials (Schechner 2002). As such, they respond to the marketers desire for understanding consumers' ordered and structured behavior, and also show emotional connections to products and brands as they transform participants through symbolic and sensory space (Douglas 1966; Turner 1969). Rituals may be highly stylized, or casual and informal. They often occur in special places, at regular times, and include sequences of words and actions laid down by someone other than the current performer (Vannini et al. 2012:44). Rituals also convey information about participants and their cultural traditions. Memories become inscribed into present actions. Performed year after year, generation after generation, they translate enduring messages, values, and sentiments into observable action (Rappaport 1979). The performative, emotive, and discursive aspects of ritual are thus readily observable in cultural analysis and useful for marketers to understand integrative and holistic consumer behavior towards a brand.

Rituals have many predominant features that marketers can attend to. For instance, as in shaving, marketers can appreciate how their brands "perform" when consumers become more aware of the brand's attributes and attend to the performance of its features to a greater degree. Sensory interactions with brands can thus be explored in terms of "skills" (Ingold 2000) that are learned and developed by consumers in rituals over time. These skills are actively deployed to interpret, evaluate, and "perform" the brand to self and others.

Concerning emotional attachment to brands, rituals are highly evocative of memories and nostalgic sentiments. A ritual connects a prescribed event or ceremony to social norms, roles, and scripts, such as certain kosher wine brands served in Jewish wedding rituals (Sutton 2001), which are passed down among people or across generations. Aesthetic preferences for specific sensations of a brand, such as taste, stipulate what is expected, what is meaningful, and what is emotionally evocative for its participants.

Men in our ritual shaving study, for instance, related their current shaving practices to past memories, images, and reminisces, real and imagined, which drew them further into a sentimental experience with shaving. One man commented, "Even though my grandfather is not here, I feel a certain bond with him. This is the way he would have shaved." Another man described the scent of the lotion and the feeling of lathering up as "bringing him back to an old-time barber shop, where the barber was like a skilled craftsman, respected in his profession."

Consumers also develop vocabularies for articulating brand experiences, and translate experience into descriptions for the way a brand functions or ought to function. The sensory aspects of a brand come to the fore in rituals, and become communicable to others. Brands prosper from community actions where members discuss shared sensory sensibilities and refined sensory acuities of a brand experience. For instance, wine clubs, archery clubs, or bowling leagues may regularly meet to discuss, critique, practice, and compete through shared discourses of their favorite brands (Vannini et al. 2012:7–8). The study of rituals can thus offer marketers a way to observe, understand, and communicate a brand to communities and individuals through shared sensory attributes and shared brand language involved in these activities.

For instance, our investigation on shaving rituals showed that some men joined online shaving groups, where they discussed their experiences of shaving and compared one brand's characteristics with another. Discussions with other men about shaving experiences allowed these men to develop linguistic descriptors and shaving vocabularies in which they described particular sensations, evaluated experiences, and shared product insights with others. This strengthened their own brand opinions and the experience of shaving for others. Comparing new or recently found products, and advising others on techniques, reveal the performative potential of the self in brand rituals that is waiting to be drawn out by certain brand qualities, not the reverse, as marketers have it, with the brand as sole focus. In fact, brands can become more potent through a deeper understanding of shared and performed sensory aspects of user communities that discover more out of a brand than a manufacturer might have intended, and thus inform others to do the same. Product innovation is often initiated, perfected, and then "democratized" among a community of avid users (Von Hippel 2005).

Rituals thus offer a way to inscribe sensory meaning, emergent memories, and expected outcomes of brands into recurrent actions. They also invite communities of users to become brand advocates, multiplying the marketing effect of a brand. Attending to the way shaving enthusiasts in our study recalled and demonstrated sensory cues with a branded product helped develop a marketing strategy for an advertising campaign that relaunched a premium shaving product for the men's grooming company.

CONCLUSION

This chapter has described two distinct approaches to the senses: one anthropological, the other consumer marketing. However, I have advocated that, in ritual, an anthropological approach can *conjoin* with a marketing approach to show that distinct brand features, sequential order, and consumer sensations reveal a *total sensory experience.* It also rejects the typical binary opposition between sensation (bodily experience) and perception (cognition), or in marketing terms of rational and emotional, because a dualist conceptualization treats the mind as a separate intelligent agent, while the body is a "passive spectator recording external stimuli" (Vannini et al. 2012:43). By investigating the sensual features of a brand, and integrating responses from consumers within the *full* social and interactive dimensions of a brand, a corporation can better discern the way people actually experience and appreciate its brand. This helps contextualize the brand beyond product features and attributes, within a broader social and material world that is meaningful to people, and with better results for the brand, consumer, and corporation.

This chapter has also shown that brands *perform* a heightened sensory role in rituals, so when consumers acquire skills and expertise, they can develop brand experience to a greater degree. A brand's particular characteristics come to the fore in ritual, and are open to sensory evaluation and adaptation by the user. An apparent mundane activity such as men's shaving can become a creative act, evoking new shaving vocabularies to describe sensations, evaluations, perceptions, and aesthetic preferences. When brand users are cognizant of the ritualistic rules that call for interaction, they engage in reflexive appreciation of the brand by talking with others. The power of the brand lies in its potential to transform an individual and evoke multiple forms of sociality. Discussions among men who value shaving thus reproduce and magnify the experience, memory, and sensory order to appreciate and extend the brand farther.

Increasingly, there are opportunities for anthropologists to work for corporations or in advertising agencies to conduct sensory-oriented research (Malefyt and Morais 2012a). A great deal of marketing attention is paid to *what* consumers sense, with scant attention to *how* they sense. Anthropologists employed in market research firms and ad agencies can show that the senses are a fundamental domain of cultural expression, and offer a medium, such as rituals, performances, sports, or other event-bound cultural expressions through which the values and practices of an individual or group are enacted (Howes 2003:xi). Moreover, attuning to one's own senses in fieldwork can bring about additional creative ideas, new awareness, and a deeper sense of place for a brand in use (Malefyt and Morais 2012b:74–89). Further studies on the anthropology of the senses will inform how the senses develop communities, activities, and socialized engagement in the world, often through rituals that center around brands.

An anthropology of the senses thus has a practical place for those interested in consumer research and studies of consumption. The cultural inclusion of the senses in various contexts of consumption illustrates the active, interpretive, and continuous engagement of the human sensorium, with the process of meaning-making that occurs between consumers and brands, people and environments, memory and practice, and individual and community. Consumer research, such informed, can help firms discern the ways in which "the senses mediate the relationship between self and society, mind and body, idea and object" (Bull et al. 2006:5). Business anthropologists enlighten their clients and benefit consumers by attending closely to the senses, those of others as well as their own.

REFERENCES

Bendix, Regina. 2005. "Introduction: Ear to Ear, Nose to Nose, Skin to Skin: The Senses in Comparative Ethnographic Perspective." Thematic issue "The Senses," edited by R. Bendix and D. Brenneis, *Etnofoor* 18(1):3–14.

Bull, Michael, Paul Gilroy, David Howes, and Douglas Kahn. 2006. "Introducing Sensory Studies." *Senses and Society.* 1:5–8.

Bowker, Geoffrey, and Susan Leigh Star. 2000. *Sorting Things Out.* Cambridge, MA: MIT Press.

Brenneis, Donald. 2005. "Afterward: Sense, Sentiment, and Sociality." *Etnofoor* 18(1):142–9.

Classen, Constance. 1993. *Worlds of Sense: Exploring the Senses in History and Across Cultures.* London: Routledge.

_____. 1998. *The Color of Angels: Cosmology, Gender and the Aesthetic Imagination.* London: Routledge.

_____. 2012. *The Deepest Sense: A Cultural History of Touch.* Champaign: University of Illinois Press.

Csordas, Thomas. 1990. "Embodiment as a Paradigm for Anthropology." *Ethos* 18:5–47.

Douglas, Mary. 1966. *Purity and Danger*. London: Routledge.

Feld, Steven. 1982. *Sound and Sentiment.* Philadelphia: University of Pennsylvania Press.

Feld, Steven, and Keith Basso. 1996. *Senses of Place.* Santa Fe, NM: School of American Research.

Geurts, Kathryn Linn. 2002. *Culture and the Senses.* Berkeley: University of California Press.

Gobé, Marc. 2009. *Emotional Branding.* New York: Allworth Press.

Goffman, Ervine. 1959. *The Presentation of Self in Everyday Life.* New York: Doubleday.

Grimes, Ronald. 1995. *Readings in Ritual Studies.* Englewood Cliffs, NJ: Prentice-Hall.

Hill, Dan. 2003. *Body of Truth.* New York: John Wiley.

Hertzfeld, Michael. 2001. *Anthropology: Theoretical Practice in Culture and Society.* Oxford, UK: Blackwell.

Howes, David, ed. 1987. "Olfaction and Transition: An Essay on the Ritual Use of Smell." *Canadian Review of Sociology and Anthropology* 24(3):398–416.

_____. 1991. *The Varieties of Sensory Experience.* Toronto, Canada: University of Toronto Press.

_____. 2003. *Sensual Relations.* Ann Arbor: University of Michigan Press.

_____, ed. 2005a. *Empire of the Senses.* Oxford, UK: Berg.

_____. 2005b. "Hyperesthesia, or, the Sensual Logic of Late Capitalism." In *Empire of the Senses*, edited by D. Howes, 281–303. Oxford, UK: Berg.

_____. 2007. "Multi-Sensory Marketing in Cross-Cultural Perspective (Part I): From Synergy to Synaesthesia." *Percepnet–Ciencia* January 22. http://www.percepnet.com/cien01_07_ang.htm.

_____. 2009. *The Sixth Sense Reader.* Oxford, UK: Berg.

Hsu, Elisabeth. 2008. "The Senses and the Social: An Introduction." *Ethnos* 73(4):433–43.

Hultén, Bertil, Niklas Broweus, and Marcus Van Dijk. 2009. *Sensory Marketing.* Hampshire, UK: Palgrave MacMillan.

Ingold, Tim. 2000. *The Perception of the Environment.* New York: Routledge.

Jones, Caroline. 2006. *Sensorium: Embodied Experience, Technology and Contemporary Art.* Cambridge, MA: MIT Press.

Klein, Naomi. 2000. *No Logo.* New York: Picador.

Krishna, Aradhna, ed. 2010. *Sensory Marketing: Research on the Sensuality of Products.* New York and London: Routledge.

Lindstrom, Martin. 2010. *Brand Sense.* New York: Free Press.

Lutz, Catherine. 1988. *Unnatural Emotions.* Chicago, IL: University of Chicago Press.

Malefyt, Timothy de Waal. 2007. "From Rational Calculation to Sensual Experience: The Marketing of Emotions in Advertising." In *The Emotions: A Cultural Reader*, edited by H. Wulff, 321–38. Oxford, UK: Berg.

Malefyt, Timothy de Waal, and Robert J. Morais, eds. 2012a. *Advertising and Anthropology: Ethnographic Practice and Cultural Perspectives.* Oxford, UK: Berg.

______. 2012b. "Creativity, Person and Place." In *Advertising and Anthropology*, edited by T. Malefyt and R. Morais, 74–89. Oxford, UK: Berg.

Malnar, Joy Monice, and Frank Vodvarka. 2004. *Sensory Design.* Minneapolis: University of Minnesota Press.

Myers, Fred. 1979. "Emotions and the Self: A Theory of Personhood and Political Order among Pintupi Aborigines." *Ethos* 7(4):343–70.

Pink, Sarah. 2004. *Home Truths.* Oxford, UK: Berg.

______. 2009. *Doing Sensory Ethnography.* London: Sage.

Postrel, Virginia. 2003. *The Substance of Style.* New York: HarperCollins.

Rappaport, Roy. 1979. *Ecology, Meaning and Religion.* Richmond, CA: North Atlantic Books.

Roberts, Kevin. 2005. *Lovemarks.* New York: Powerhouse Books.

Rodaway, Paul. 1994. *Sensuous Geographies.* London: Routledge.

Schechner, Richard. 2002. *Performance Studies: An Introduction.* New York: Routledge.

Serematakis, Nadia, ed. 1994. *The Senses Still.* Boulder, CO: Westview.

Stoller, Paul. 1989. *The Taste of Ethnographic Things: The Senses in Ethnography.* Philadelphia: University of Pennsylvania Press.

______. 1997. *Sensuous Scholarship.* Philadelphia: University of Pennsylvania Press.

Sunderland, Patricia, and Rita Denny. 2007. *Doing Anthropology in Consumer Research.* Walnut Creek, CA: Left Coast Press.

Sutton, David. 2001. *Remembrance of Repasts: An Anthropology of Food and Memory.* Oxford, UK: Berg.

Synnott, Anthony. 1991. "Puzzling over the Senses: From Plato to Marx." In *The Varieties of Sensory Experience*, edited by D. Howes, 239–56. Toronto, Canada: University of Toronto Press.

______. 1993. *The Body Social.* New York: Routledge.

Turner, Victor. 1969. *The Ritual Process.* New York: Aldine.

Vannini, Phillip, Dennis Waskul, and Simon Gottschalk. 2012. *The Senses in Self, Society, and Culture.* London: Routledge.

Von Hippel, Eric. 2005. *Democratizing Innovation.* Cambridge, MA: MIT Press.

Wulff, Helena. 2011. "Ways Of Seeing Ireland's Green: From Ban To The Branding Of a Nation." Paper presented at the Annual Meeting of the American Anthropological Association, Montreal, Canada, November 16–20.

Young, Diana. 2005. "The Smell of Greenness: Cultural Synaesthesia in the Western Desert." *Etnofoor* 18(1):61–77.

Zerubavel, Eviatar. 1996. "Lumping and Splitting: Notes on Social Classification." *Sociological Forum.* 11:421–33.

NOTE

1 "How to Shave with a Single-Blade Razor," YouTube, March 19, 2008. http://www.youtube.com/watch?v=ufG1dPmVo8Q.

38

Doing Anthropology, Doing Business

CHARLES N. DARRAH & ALICIA DORNADIC

GETTING STARTED

When we began working with businesses and other organizations, perhaps naively we thought the challenges were known and understood. Clients and employers would be interested in us because we were anthropologists, and so our job was to conduct ethnographic research, offer interpretations based on anthropological theory, and provide emic perspectives of different categories of people. Success would depend upon our mastery of anthropology and its application, as we dispelled clients' misunderstandings about its scope and potential contributions. Although this focus was understandable and even useful, we soon realized that success (or failure) was also due to factors beyond the discipline. In fact, we found ourselves increasingly focusing on an ancillary bundle of skills that enabled us to better incorporate anthropology into our practice. We came to see ourselves as providers of services that, while grounded in anthropology and the social sciences, have only loose connections to our academic training.

We begin with several vignettes drawn from our individual experiences of moving from academic to business settings. For Dornadic, an applied anthropologist launching a career, these experiences are of immediate and practical importance. For Darrah, an academic anthropologist who also works for clients, they inform how he teaches classes and develops curricula for students who in their own ways will take something of anthropology beyond the university. Second, we discuss several sets of skills that, for us, have become essential to our practices in organizations and our ability to draw upon our backgrounds in anthropology. These skills are not inconsistent with anthropology, but their salience to our practice came as a surprise and we continue to refine and

Handbook of Anthropology in Business, edited by Rita Denny and Patricia Sunderland, 722–736.

develop them. Third, we conclude by exploring the concept of service systems to frame how we link anthropology to the needs of clients and employers. This approach helps us expand anthropology's reach and relevance; it allows us to retain the qualities that distinguish us from other disciplines in regards to data, analysis, and interpreting worldviews, while earning us a place inside new and exciting arenas of study and production.

VIGNETTES

Vignette 1: Diabetes Research for Designers (Dornadic)

Roche Diagnostics gave me my first "real" paycheck out of graduate school. Freshly minted with a master's in applied anthropology, I was branded an anthropologist from the day I was hired into Roche's New Concept Incubator group, which also included designers, scientists, and engineers. The team's main purpose was to create products and services for people living with Type II diabetes that could be fed into Roche's larger "product pipeline." I had been an intern with the team the previous summer, but now I had a degree and expertise that was supposedly distinctive within the team. My manager would sometimes ask me in brainstorming sessions, "What would anthropology think about this?" Not only did I have a degree, but also the responsibility to speak for a discipline. In fact, my background was veiled with such mystery that I was asked to provide an "Anthropology in a Nutshell" informal lunch presentation for the team.

I often assigned myself overtly anthropological tasks. I collected and assessed secondary research and relevant existing literatures, wrote recruitment screeners, conducted open-ended and semi-structured interviews, analyzed design concepts, and coded previously conducted observations and interviews, all the while challenging definitions and categories related to diabetes care; usually, I worked alone. Other tasks I took on opportunistically as I gingerly stepped beyond the limits of academic anthropology. They were more collaborative in nature, and I figured out how to perform them as I went along. I participated in brainstorming sessions, reviewed and expanded on concepts with designers, designed and led co-creation workshops, and conducted usability testing. I analyzed business goals, yet never quite understood how projects were evaluated, to whom the group reported, or how projects were funded. I was only sure that we shouldn't wear our usual jeans and T-shirts when senior managers flew in from Switzerland. I constantly asked myself if I was spending my time wisely and how I could be better using my skills towards the team's goals.

Part of figuring out my role meant I had to decide how to participate with the designers and how to allocate time to research-based activities. Does an anthropologist draw? Should I be sketching, fleshing out design concepts with the rest of the team? Or, even when we were *performing* the same activities, should I be thinking about them in the same way as the designers? For example, what would an anthropologist think about this or that specific design idea based on research, or about the process of discussing the idea? Sometimes my sense of my responsibilities did not correspond to those of the team leader. One day, he came into my office: "Hey, I have a meeting with the development team in five minutes. You can join if you like." Quickly, I had to evaluate whether the meeting could possibly pertain to my role and skills, or whether I would spend the time wondering how to extricate myself. Always interested in learning more, I usually enthusiastically agreed to attend to seize an opportunity to contribute and demonstrate my willingness to support the team. Although my presence was usually welcomed, I could also be reminded about the normally unspoken limits to my involvement. At some point, the team was focused on delivering a specific product and we were getting deeper into "design sprints" of heavy, rapid brainstorming, prototyping, and refining. I was explicitly told not to participate because research was not the focus.

One day I found myself in a meeting with two industrial designers, Megan and Cara, who were working on blood glucose monitoring concepts. They wanted to know about research to understand "user behavior" in ways that would help them further develop their concepts. I simultaneously deplored and embraced the term "user" (see Neese, this volume). It isolates individual behavior, often stripping research participants of their social context, which was a rich aspect of anthropology that drew me into the discipline in the first place. I initially had the same problem when developing personas. I asked, "Why not use the real people that we spent so much time observing and interviewing?" "Real people are just too messy. Too complicated, too specific to design for," was the response from an industrial design intern. As much as I wanted to show them the anthropological light, I found I could only "educate" my peers for so long before alienating myself from the team.

I combed interview transcripts, my previous analyses, and relevant literature on the topic to prepare for my blood glucose monitoring meeting. What I couldn't anticipate was what Cara and Megan would show me. They brought some rough sketches to the meeting and described their rationale and decision-making. I listened, asked questions, explored their concepts with them, gave feedback, and suggested possible changes. I told them which concepts I thought were stronger, and addressed more pressing issues, which concepts made sense for Roche, etc. I left the meeting knowing that I had addressed their concerns, but I had contributed something even more important: I had helped them think more creatively about both problem and solution. I could not claim co-ownership of the ideas, and it was up to the designers whether to incorporate suggestions, but my imprint was on those designs. I felt that I had been useful because I maintained my anthropological stance while helping advance the designs. My identity as the anthropologist in the group was solidifying, reinforced by my separate activities and chats about anthropology. I remained valuable by remaining apart from the team, engaging in different kinds of activities, but also by being a participating member of the team simultaneously. It became a matter of balancing the anthropological and nonanthropological activities. The more I stepped away from anthropology, the more involved I felt I could be in team activities. The truer to anthropology I remained, the more unusual, unique, *and* useful was my perspective to the team.

Vignette 2: Research & Design for the Insurance Business (Dornadic)

My entry into Roche was validated by my anthropology degree, but the Allstate Research and Planning Center simply wanted someone familiar with both ethnography and design practices. The job posting asked for a graduate of a program in "product design, human factors, interaction design, sociocultural anthropology, psychology, or the like." This was a great opportunity for me to practice my anthropology and to expand into design roles without having to constantly consider whether something was anthropological or not. Now it didn't matter.

About half my responsibilities related to projects initiated within the Research Center, whereas the other half were projects requested by internal clients, mainly from the corporate headquarters 2,000 miles away. I was part of the qualitative research group, and there was already a standard research and design process in place and an established format for presenting reports; the work process and products here were more standardized than at Roche's New Concept Incubator group.

One of my roles was to design and facilitate workshops within the company. I remember being particularly concerned with presenting data accurately and relaying multiple points of view in context, but also in a way that would garner enthusiasm and help generate concepts for the future. I was energized by these workshops. I had learned to love brainstorming when I was at Roche, and it was invigorating to go beyond research to create new possible futures at Allstate. Once, going over the ideas generated from one such workshop, a colleague sighed: "We have tons of ideas. We don't need ideas. We need leadership to build a strategy and a means to implement the ideas." Although I had been concerned about my personal contribution and how to produce work in which I took pride, ultimately it was organizational processes that simultaneously enabled and inhibited what was produced.

As with my work at Roche, I first had to be in charge of presenting reliable and valid data. Then I was expected to interpret the implications of those data for designs and for the business, and to make jumps from the data to possible future products, services, and internal processes. I was deemed able to do this because of my anthropology background, but I realized quickly what was necessary to implement these changes extended far beyond what I had been prepared to undertake in school. Both of my experiences, at Roche and Allstate, had me questioning what it meant to participate in business as an anthropologist. And what about when I am completing tasks that aren't anthropological: is there a gray area in identity? These identity questions forced me to pay attention to organizational processes and goals in ways that would allow me to be effective and to draw upon anthropology, but these identity boundaries mattered more to me than to my team.

Vignette 3: Tech Savvy & "the Ethnographies" (Darrah)

In 2003, I was invited to present a keynote talk at the Office Ergonomics Research Committee, an organization that supported quantitative and experimental research with both design and legal implications. Inviting me was seen as an experiment in which they would listen to someone who ventured "into the wild" to study how people worked. After my presentation, Bill Dowell of Herman Miller Incorporated (HMI) asked if I could come to Michigan to discuss reanalyzing several research projects my colleagues and I had conducted previously to provide some robust speculations about the future of work. I agreed and headed for Grand Rapids, collecting a rental car one dark and snowy night and driving the 20 miles to a corporate lodge. Over the next few days I met with various members of the team, an external designer, and others whose roles I never quite figured out. I grabbed a copy of *The Office: A Facility Based on Change* (Propst 1968) as I was leaving, and six weeks later a colleague and I returned to make a presentation to 25 "Hermanoids," as Bill referred to his colleagues. The report was well received, especially its organization. I explained that I had used *The Office* for inspiration due to its iconic status within the company.

Over the next two years, Bill asked me to conduct several projects with clients where HMI had placed prototypes of public fixtures that could be placed amid the individual "pods" of open office environments. In effect, HMI and the clients created grand experiments in which workspaces were dramatically modified to understand how people adapted to new affordances and constraints. I conducted participant observation and semi-structured interviews, and prepared reports that complemented HMI's survey work by explicating the social interactions and structures within which those surveys were given, exploring the nuances of perspective and meaning that could not be captured in surveys and the interactions of variables that were otherwise treated as discrete. Referred to within HMI as "ethnographies," I was always reminding people that they were rapid assessments, a distinction that mattered more to me than them.

Vignette 4: Journey to Buffalo Grove (Darrah)

In 2007, I was asked to develop a small interview project that would contribute to thinking about Convia, an HMI technology that would provide programmable power and data infrastructures for buildings. Where traditional electrical infrastructure is hardwired and costly to modify, Convia would allow building users to alter the configuration of lighting and power using a point-and-click wand and modular "smart" connectors. It would be programmable at the level of the individual work area, the department, and the entire building. In effect, Convia would impart some "intelligence" to built environments, allowing users to control them and to sense and respond to user needs. It was the very range of control that raised questions that could be addressed through the "ethnographic interviews," which were now associated with giving voice to occupants or users of spaces. Control, for example, could be extended to the level of individual devices—chairs, desks, etc.—in the office and to the office, which could become the site for scenes or configurations customized to the requirements of different users or tasks. The frequency and magnitude of changes in conditions seemed limitless, but they had associated costs, raising the question of who was willing to pay how much to be able to exercise what forms of control within what period of time.

It was the coupling of technological programmability and its opportunities for control over workplace conditions and costs for sensors, actuators, and system architecture that presented both opportunities and constraints. The questions that arose were fascinating, at least to this anthropologist. How and under what conditions do people adapt to their work environments, and when do they expect more from it? What triggers efforts to adapt the environment, rather than adapting to it? What skills do people need to control environments in a social context and in ways that add value, and according to whom? How will people take to a programmable environment that could simultaneously provide opportunities for individuals to customize their work environments and for managers to exercise ubiquitous surveillance?

The result was a project that included interviews with ten workers in four companies; interviewees included software engineers, finance executives, a facilities director, and three project managers. The interviews focused on daily activities and interactions, and included visioning exercises in which interviewees were asked about their offices as "concierges" dedicated to supporting their work. The analysis suggested characteristics of work that had not been captured in surveys, but that provided opportunities for product development. For example, interviewees described morning routines to start devices that left workers vulnerable to interruptions and questions by coworkers, and which made it difficult to initiate daily agendas. Tracking the organizational locations of people, the status of projects, and even the reputations of rooms for supporting specific activities emerged as a form of tacit work, as did tasks of controlling current work environments. Protecting time and space for conducting personal business was also an essential task for those workers whose jobs were especially time consuming: taking care of personal tasks while at work was not seen as malingering, but as a hallmark of the conscientious employee who remained accessible to coworkers rather than requesting time off to run errands.

A report was prepared and presented, and I headed for a daylong meeting at the Convia headquarters in Buffalo Grove, Illinois, with its staff and my client, the team from Herman Miller. The meeting was cordial, but probably frustrating for everyone. At the time, Convia was a technology moving into production, and the company's approach was driven by engineering and marketing considerations. The pressure to sell to facilities managers pushed the product towards cost savings more than supporting work tasks. The "Hermanoids" were perplexed by an apparent inattention to HMI's tradition of humane, elegant design, and I felt that programmability was more aligned with cost-cutting surveillance than creating spaces that could support innovations in work. In retrospect, I was giving voice not only to the data, but also to the HMI team's concerns about product design and traditional corporate values.

Vignette 5: Lights! Camera! Action! (Darrah)

In 2010, Darrah and graduate student Nicole Conand were invited to a meeting convened by the John and James Knight Foundation for the purpose of telling stories about local people who were working to effect community change. We were cast as the experts at eliciting and analyzing the stories, and Suzanne St. John-Crane, the executive director of local public access station CreaTV San Jose, would be the expert at telling them. Thus began months of weekly meetings and discussions, as we learned about video-making and St. John-Crane learned about ethnography. Gradually, the three of us with CreaTV's producer formed a team dedicated to the project. In the end, Conand and I were drawn more deeply into video production as we took on more and more tasks, most of which were unfamiliar. We logged film, wrote outlines, edited scripts, and provided the voiceover. Yet we could not do the final editing, and we lacked other skills in sound and film. The video would not have been made without us, but we were participating in a production process requiring specific skills and using its own vocabulary: even how to label our contribution was difficult, and we relied on others who better understood it. Fortunately, we succeeded: the video was made and won an award, and we are now collaborating with CreaTV on another project. Specifically, we are working again with St. John-Crane, who values what we contribute. This is partially the capacity for deeper, somewhat unconventional interviewing and richer, more provocative story lines. But it is also our willingness to go beyond narrow definitions of our roles to take on more tasks to complete a project.

DOING ANTHROPOLOGY?

Many people we were encountering knew about anthropology and thought the discipline was fascinating and potentially useful, but the challenge was in how to proceed. They and we were attached to the salience of our identities as anthropologists: they because our presence stimulated requests for explanation or justification; and we because we wondered what to do next. Our methods, theories, and knowledge could be alien to clients and employers who thought they were similarly qualified to understand social settings. Yet we also knew that we could not deploy our full set of methods since they could be too time consuming and unnecessary, given the scope of the problem.

The issue of anthropological identity was further complicated because moving into a business or organization was to become entangled in networks that we did not understand. True, we did enter organizations, and their names were often on contracts and paychecks. But organizations themselves are complex; Darrah was neither simply in Herman Miller, nor Dornadic in Allstate. Even more striking, it was in our working relationships with particular individuals where our relationship with the organization was enacted. In fact, it was such individuals who typically acted as interpreters of our activities and findings, translating our skills and knowledge in ways that made sense to others. These relationships were critical to success and difficult to program: they were based on task performance, but also on the intangibles of friendship and mutual respect.

Clear lines between us as anthropologists and our clients or employers were also complicated by projects that were housed in organizations, but cut across their boundaries. We noticed that tasks and roles often had less to do with organizations per se than with projects that mobilized engagement and resources. Loyalty was often to projects, and although we always knew the difference between being in or out of the organization, we also knew that engagement with a project could be more compelling than organizational loyalty or disciplinary identity.

Finally, we also realized that we poorly understood the production processes that we were encountering within organizations. How those processes functioned and corresponded to divisions of labor, and how we—and those with whom we were working—fit into them were initially opaque. Accordingly, we could deliver as required, but what we delivered fit into something larger that we did not always comprehend. Fitting into those processes as they intersected with projects was what we pondered and discussed, not any gaps between anthropology and daily work. Ultimately, what determined our effectiveness within organizations was not whether we were anthropological or not, but had more to do with grappling with multiple and often inconsistent intentions and aspirations; participating in conversations that alternated between intensely focused and often seemingly one-way commands, and genuinely open discussions about the research-product relationship; recognizing the roles of multiple modes of representation; and allowing ourselves to "go native" by taking creative leaps and sometimes building new bridges (Cross 2007).

Intentions & Aspirations

We are often brought into business to clarify the intentions and aspirations of some population "out there," but clarifying the intentions and aspirations of the client turns out to be equally, if not more, important.

Often, our clients and partners wish to understand something external to their organization that confounds simple assumptions and quantitative indicators. The result can be conflicting pressures to simplify and complicate the lessons; demands for fundamental essences and the effects of diverse conditions uneasily coexist.

Clients have varying expectations. Some, drawing upon memories of their undergraduate days, see anthropology—ethnography, in particular—as a solution to a problem that has proven resistant to other disciplines or methodologies, only to find that they are unclear about what we can provide. Others, who know much less about anthropology or the social sciences, may actually have clearer expectations about what we can and cannot offer. They often hope we can conduct research that brings the organization closer to people and problems by providing new kinds of data. Here the expectation is intimacy through ethnography, with the hope that something previously unimagined will result. In other cases, we are invited in because a situation is presented as extraordinarily complex, often due to overwhelming, abundant data. Here our role is more as *anthropologists* who reputedly eschew simplistic explanations because the discipline is holistic and integrative. The hope is that such a perspective will provide a new, insightful synthesis. The expectation is less intimacy here than that anthropology's holism will allow people to make sense of data that seemingly conceal as much as they reveal. Regardless, we have found ourselves deemed useful when there is something "out there" that begs for intimacy or integration. For example, in working with designers, we have not only assisted by conducting research that reveals characteristics of people that we then design or plan for, but rather we find ourselves "peopling" designs. This includes helping the clients imagine how people would act within designs that have been created, particularly how designs may be constrained by notions of typical or normal users. Peopling the designs also requires us to appreciate how users, as figments of organizational imaginations, are effectively created by spaces, services, and products.

Because our findings enter a flow of other research in organizations, they do not simply provide answers, regardless of how well specified the problem space is. The challenge is that research is already viewed as a cost to be minimized, and so we are often asked to show that investing in us pays dividends. Critically, while we are focusing on what is out in the world, we are always thrust backwards and forwards into organizational processes. Regardless of where we start, we wind up as ethnographers of the organization that retained us. Our insights matter, but so too does our ability to understand the often tacit aspirations and intentions of the client. Furthermore, the people we speak with may act as if the company is a single "we," but it is not. Depending on whom we chat with, the company may be very different, which has consequences for our work.

Conversing

We can do good research for clients, but opportunities to do it are provided through conversations.

When we began, our work was framed by collections of formal documents, such as nondisclosure agreements and contracts. Other times they were informal, such as work performed on the basis of a telephoned "handshake." Regardless, our attention was directed to figuring out exactly what we needed to learn to satisfy the client. It was a world of deliverables and managing mutual expectations. Naturally enough, these activities were accompanied by conversations with clients, but they began as the means to accomplish the end of delivering the needed data and analysis. Of course, we got to know people better, and as we did, more information about interests, background, and family was exchanged. All this was ordinary, but it suggests a subtle transformation in our practice. It was not that the real work of data collection and analysis became subordinated to conversation, but the real work could not be contained and specified apart from the larger ongoing conversations about it.

These conversations have shaped our practice as they carry us from contribution to contribution. They begin with clear organizational distinctions between "us" (the researchers) and "them" (the clients). The conversations contribute to producing the palpable sense of a project that has its own life and needs, and that almost exhibits agency. These small conversations humanize what is otherwise a contractual or at least instrumental relationship, but they do much more. They can yield insights into tacit assumptions about the work being undertaken and about where it might "go" in the future. Other people with only peripheral involvement in the project may become conversationalists in ways that allow us to learn the backstory of the project and to audition to join future project teams. We have each, for example, been approached for advice by people we do not know but who have heard about our work in a project. Conversations reiterate that, contracts aside, we do not simply work for this or that organization, but with particular people whose careers can be harmed or helped through our involvement.

This emphasis on conversations is not to diminish the importance of the scope of work that brought us together with a client, but most clients do not initially fully understand our discipline and capabilities. We have come to see projects as simultaneously built around meeting deadlines by performing the specified work and as a conversation in which that work changes as new opportunities and capabilities are revealed on both sides. It is through the conversation that the practice of anthropology is better interpreted by those we are working with and that they find new ways to use us—and we, them.

Conversations thus allow us to explore new terrain and the interstices between familiar domains, but they also challenge our identities as professionals. We are not sheltered by the canons of our discipline and are much more in the realm of improvisation. While some may embrace this journey, it requires different skills than those at the center of academic anthropology.

Representing

We love detailed description and holistic analysis, but the challenge is to represent data and ideas so our clients can do something different.

We are hired to conduct research, perform analyses, and develop ideas. The last is important: ideas supported by research are prized because they help people justify decisions to their bosses and move forward, although if we could provide ideas without the cost of research, our clients would surely rejoice. Those ideas remain private matters, and they rarely emerge through sudden inspiration. A challenge is to externalize them so they can be shared. Here we encounter issues of representation, not simply of representing the people we study, but of the ideas we develop. For us, trained as we are in anthropology, writing is the preferred form (compare with O'Dell and Willim, this volume). After all, participation in cultural anthropology is based on the ability to write as much as on collecting field data. But writing is insufficient because the clients often lack time to read detailed accounts of behavior. They also lack the disciplinary frame of reference to appreciate why description is anything more than "interesting." Expressing half-formed ideas is a challenge, and our thinking about it is influenced by how other disciplines have already settled on ways of sharing. Architects, for example, generate what Lawson (2004) calls consultation, experiential, fabulous, and proposition drawings to communicate with others in the design process. These drawings are about thinking through the design challenge and many reflect the complex, holistic way that designers must meet conflicting constraints. They are visual hypotheses, and some of the best are drawn roughly and with broad strokes precisely because doing so leaves the design process open to further reflection. Fine lines, much like meticulously detailed written descriptions, may imply unwarranted precision and finality. Likewise, Gaver (2011) recommends use of rough drawings and collage in his design workbooks so that resulting drawings are not stylistically "owned" by or associated with individual designers.

This line of reasoning has had implications for our practice. First, it suggests that artistry may matter less than the sharing, communication, and discovery that are enabled by different modalities of representation. If we find an anthropological equivalent to the "thick and messy lines," we will be able to share more and be involved longer in the process. Second, it suggests that the project itself is created through a process of exchanging representations that may be incommensurate, but which are collectively used to "think through." Not only may the modes of representation differ, but also the uses to which they are put. Third, the drawings and sketches produced are artifacts that are as useful as evidence of thinking as they are of artistic skill, and the result is a production process with much going on behind the scenes.

Appreciating modalities of drawing is broadly applicable in our practice. Sketching skills can matter, just like our data collecting, analytical, and interpretive skills, but not in the same way through the entire process. Explicating production processes also allows us to identify how very specific skills can make the difference between being overlooked and being credited, with enormous consequences for subsequent work.

Creating

Clients can be fascinated that we are anthropologists, but ultimately they don't care: they just want us to contribute.

Data collection, analysis, interpretation, and critique, we have been told by some colleagues, are anthropological, and even evaluation may be grasped within the disciplinary embrace. But a line is seemingly crossed when we create something that is to exist in the world. Yes, anthropologists in business produce artifacts. "Both academic and non-academic anthropologists produce much more than publications. Videos, photos, notes from discussions, quotes from research participants, and diagrams . . . [which] are debated and reworked with various insiders and semi-insiders" (Nafus and anderson 2010:142). However, even this is more akin to data representation and further from producing the end design. From this perspective, we may be anthropologists, but whatever our practice is, it is most assuredly not entirely anthropological, which can be discomforting to at least some of our academic colleagues, although applied anthropologists have long participated in creating artifacts, spaces, and policies. The distinction between what is and is not anthropology, and even the fact that we raise the question, is befuddling to our clients or coworkers. They value anthropology not because they want to be anthropologists, but because it helps them in *their* professional practices.

As we take on unfamiliar roles and tasks, and even imagine ourselves in other disciplines, we return to anthropology. Ultimately, we have found that our own creative contributions are not about leaps or bridges toward new products, or the discovery that we can in fact sketch, but rather a renewed focus on social arrangements that are reinforced by existing built environments and institutions, and which, we remind those for whom we work, can be different than they are.

THE MARX BROTHERS

Few of the people we have worked with know about anthropology in depth. They are, however, hopeful and not hostile toward it, and they remain understandably grounded in their own practices. Much of what we do—and would like to do better—can fruitfully be conceptualized as offering services in which anthropology plays an important, but limited, role. The challenge we now appreciate is less about selling a discipline than focusing on how to make others value the services we can provide. Our perspective is, we argue half-jokingly, that of the Marx Brothers, Karl and Groucho. Karl draws our attention to the struggle to create and control a means of production, in this case a service system that is informed by anthropology. The concept of a service system helps us think through what we have to offer that reflects the distinctive characteristics of anthropology *and* the ability to transcend them to best help clients and partners. Ironically, just as it pushes us from dwelling on anthropology, it also underlies a robust and useful discipline.

Our discussion of services is necessarily brief and selective; we refer interested readers to several useful introductions to services (Bitner et al. 2000; Bryson et al. 2004; Lusch and Vargo 2006; Teboul 2006). We also provide an overview of some characteristics of services that we believe are salient to our practice.

First, services are not produced, stored, and delivered, but service providers and consumers co-create both the service and its value. Services are known by the transformations they produce in individuals or things, and they cannot be stockpiled: their production and consumption is simultaneous. An implication is that the process of service production and the quality of the resulting services requires the active participation of both producers and consumers. Service providers, including applied anthropologists, can *claim* to provide a service, but it is still up to the client or partner as a consumer to decide whether the desired transformation has occurred. Effecting transformations is far removed from admonitions to avoid affecting the people we study. Here, a service perspective encourages us to shift focus from our performances as anthropologists to our contribution to a transformation that may affect lives in different ways. Second, we cannot arrive bearing predefined services. We cannot assume we know the assumptions and values of the stakeholders, the flows of information and other resources that might be changed, or even what we can or should offer. So we must be comfortable with ambiguity, suspending our assumptions, exploring, and loosely holding and then abandoning tentative hypotheses. Likewise, we must be willing and able to cede control because we are working with others whose help we need to be able to act. They may have authority, but control may also be distributed across dozens of decisions and routines situated in time and space. Never do we find direct central control over the system, even though some may claim they do. The nature of such systems means that individuals may control only limited spheres of action, and that we discover systems as we interact with them.

Third, service systems reflect logics of instrumentality and payment. They cannot proceed through reciprocity alone because the enduring, stable relationships which reciprocity presumes are not present. Reciprocity among participants may occur and be locally important, but in general the scale and complexity of service systems means that reciprocity cannot bind together the whole system. Therefore, the value propositions (what different people seek by participating in the service system) must be made explicit. We must be able to articulate not only what we can produce, but what its value might be, and often do so in dollars.

Fourth, how people learn to recognize and acquire information about services, and then to decide that they are worth purchasing, is essential and successful providers seldom leave it to chance. Systems that elicit cooperation among producers and consumers of services may be understood by the concept of conventions (Becker 1982) that standardize expectations about routines, outcomes, values, etc. They help produce the very consumers who recognize and value some services while ignoring others. Likewise, circuits of knowledge "provide individuals with 'maps of meaning' [that] are a central component driving the relationship between the production and consumption of services" (Bryson et al. 2004:169).

If creating service systems allows us to be stable, valued contributors, then thinking about service encounters compels us to retain the qualities that our clients tell us differentiate us from others: the ability to collect unfamiliar data, to provide different kinds of analyses, and, above all, to reinterpret taken-for-granted categories of thought about the social world. This cannot be produced on demand, for it relies on humor, edginess, freshness, irreverence, insight, and flexibility. Groucho suggests that we are well served by not taking ourselves too serious and by thinking on the fly. How we build these encounters into service systems is the challenge, and it involves making service encounters more like the field, with all its sloppiness and potential for discovery.

REFERENCES

Becker, Howard. 1982. *Art Worlds*. Berkeley, CA: University of California Press.

Bitner, Mary Jo, Stephen W. Brown, and Matthew L. Meuter. 2000. "Technology Infusion in Service Encounters." *Journal of the Academy of Marketing Science* 28(1):138–49.

Bryson, John R., Peter W. Daniels, and Barney Warf. 2004. *Service Worlds: People, Organisations, and Technologies*. New York: Routledge.

Cross, Nigel. 2007. *Designerly Ways of Knowing*. Basel, Switzerland: Birkhauser Verlag AG.

Gaver, William. "Making Spaces: How Design Workbooks Work." Paper presented at the Annual Conference on Human Factors in Computing Systems, Vancouver, BC, Canada, May 7–12, 2011.

Lawson, Bryan. 2004. *What Designers Know*. New York: Routledge.

Lusch, Robert F., and Stephen L. Vargo. 2006. *The Service-Dominant Logic of Marketing: Dialog, Debate, and Directions*. Armonk, NY: M. E. Sharpe.

Nafus, Dawn, and ken anderson. 2010. "Writing on Walls: The Materiality of Social Memory in Corporate Research. In *Ethnography and the Corporate Encounter: Reflections on Research in and of Corporations*, edited by Melissa Cefkin, 137–57. New York: Berghahn Books.

Propst, Robert. 1968. *The Office: A Facility Based on Change*. Zeeland, MI: Quarto.

Teboul, James. 2006. *Service Is Front Stage: Positioning Services for Value Advantage*. New York: Palgrave MacMillan.

39

Glimpses from the Blogosphere

SARAH TEITLER

With the spread of web-publishing tools in the late 1990s, blogging no longer required specialized or technical knowledge and became available to anyone with access to a computer, blogging platform, and the desire and/or need to publish: to speak their mind, show their activities, sell their products or ideas. Usually blogs are informal, spontaneous, personal, and immediate. They are a quick and barrier-free way to reach an audience (or build one); an opportunity for authors to interact with readers (or the reverse); and a platform for instantaneous response.

My goal in these glimpses is to illustrate a range of topics deployed, of voices, and, implicitly, the uses of this informal, immediate, often thoughtful, persona-building venue. For anthropologists and ethnographers working in business, blogs are not only a primary venue for "publishing" and creating visibility, but also serve to build a community afforded by the digital activities of writers and readers.

TAKING STANDS, BUILDING PUBLICS

A prevailing preoccupation of blogs is on defining and defending the use of anthropology or ethnographic methods. Informality of the venue begets tonal clarity: one hears frustration, commiseration, helpful outreach, and authorial voice. If bloggers are taking stands, they are also building identities (and publics).

"Does Corporate Ethnography Suck?" This provocation was posted by Sam Ladner, senior user researcher at Microsoft, writing as a guest blogger on *Ethnography Matters* (Ladner 2012).[1] In the post (Figure 39.1), she addresses

Handbook of Anthropology in Business, edited by Rita Denny and Patricia Sunderland, 737–752.

Figure 39.1. A guest post by Sam Ladner on *Ethnography Matters*. Image courtesy of *Ethnography Matters*, licensed under Creative Commons.

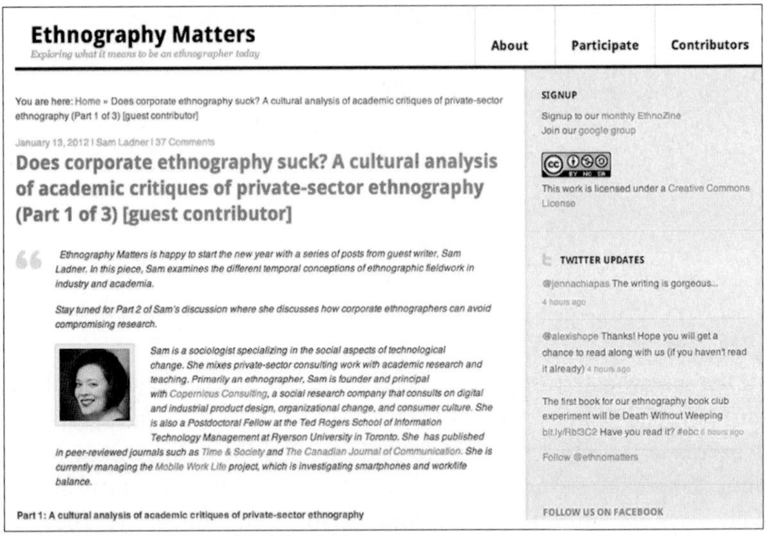

questions about the quality and rigor of the field. The initial post of this three-part series generated more than 30 comments the following week, with Ladner and her readers for the most part responding thoughtfully to one another. The comments addressed definitions of ethnography, additional shortcomings of corporate research that originate on the client side, the role of different audiences, different forms and approaches to storytelling, and questions raised by language choice.

Ladner argues that corporate ethnography is frequently poorly done. She finds valid the assertions of academically trained social scientists that private-sector practitioners often lack training, that ethnography and cultural analysis in the corporate context is often reduced to shallow onsite research, that results can be "meaningless," and the presentations "stupefying." She isn't saying corporate ethnography isn't worth doing: she's saying it's frequently poorly done. Starting her series with a broad critique of how corporate ethnography is practiced, Ladner enhances her authority by voicing a truth many would just as soon ignore.

Rachel Annechino, associate research scientist at the Prevention Research Center/PIRE, and an editor of *Ethnography Matters* (Figure 39.2), argues the legitimacy of qualitative research in response to *On the Media* host Bob Garfield's negative assessment, which can be reduced to: ". . . qualitative research, focus groups and the like, are not research at all" (Garfield 2011). You can hear the incredulity of her voice in the title of her post ("Qualitative research is not research at all?"), and her resignation as she writes: "Sigh. This is wrong on so many levels, and anyone who is interested in ethnography already knows why, but just to touch on some of the problems" (Annechino 2011). In addition to refuting his assertions point by point, Annechino advocates "mixed methods research," using quantitative and qualitative research together. She also provides examples of the extent to which quantitative research often requires culturally informed qualitative methods in its design and analysis.

None of the issues raised or addressed in Annechino's blog post are new; they are a constant in corporate work. What the blog form adds to the conversation is easy access to sources cited and references, resources that colleagues can access when confronting these same, tired issues in their own workplaces. In her post, Annechino provides links to the *On The Media* segment she is responding to, the original study that was the subject of the radio piece, and blog posts and articles supporting her argument. Links are provided to audio and/or text files of almost all the sources Annechino references. Providing this immediate access to references and sources is a service to the community.

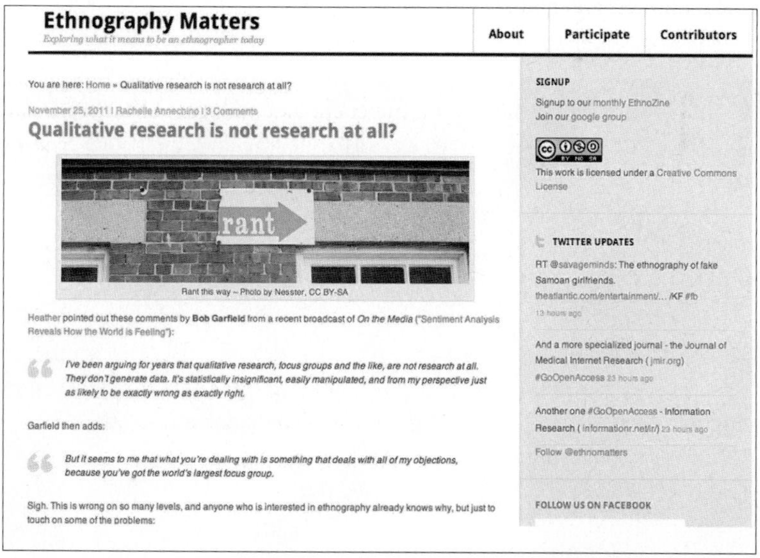

Figure 39.2. *Ethnography Matters* is a collective blog with a focus on using ethnography in technology research and design. Rachelle Annechino, Jenna Burrell, Heather Ford, and Tricia Wang started the blog in 2011 to counter what they see as a trend towards viewing "users as numbers, as digits, as data and as markets." Image courtesy of *Ethnography Matters,* licensed under Creative Commons.

Jan Chipchase, executive creative director of global insights at frog design, shares aspects of his peripatetic life on his blog-like website. The contents are eclectic: images of objects that inspire, musings on what the future might hold, research methods and challenges (Figure 39.3). Chipchase's photos are a real treat, visually striking and ethnographically rich. In an online essay titled "Imperialist Tendencies" (Chipchase 2012a), Chipchase defends corporate anthropology from a common critique, which he paraphrases provocatively in the following manner: What is it like working for BigCorps pillaging the intellect of people around the world for commercial gain? How do you sleep at night as the corporations you work for pump their worthless products into the world?

In the form of an extended essay, and written in response to questions from the audience at Pop!Tech 2011, Chipchase first sets out detailed guidelines he has established for running participatory design sessions and the approach he has developed for setting the "right" tone for research. Addressing accusations of "design imperialism" as illustrated in the questions above, Chipchase in turn critiques the assumptions about low-income consumers implicit in the questions, problematizes the notions of "rationality" and "rational consumer behavior," and through vivid example describes the complexity inherent in working in global markets and global contexts.

Figure 39.3. Jan Chipchase shares aspects of his peripatetic life on his blog-like website. Image courtesy of Jan Chipchase, licensed under Creative Commons.

Tricia Wang's *culturalbytes* is generationally and stylistically unique (Figure 39.4). The blog is one of many that Wang maintains, and provides a portrait of a scholar-in-training working though ideas, offering critiques, and engaging with current theoretical as well as political issues with whole-hearted gusto. Wang, a global tech ethnographer, posted as she prepared for her oral exams and for her fieldwork in sociology. She posted as she read new books, met new people, and tried out new ways of organizing her materials. The blog is chock-a-block full of links and extended excerpts, and is infused with a voracious appetite for engagement.

Wang's post about her 2011 SXSW presentation is a spirited discussion of the festival itself, and a critique of the "techno-utopianism" and lack of historical context that is so pervasive in discussions of the internet and digital technologies more broadly (Wang 2012). Working against that tide, Wang describes wanting to give a talk that "would not only illustrate my analysis and research on Internet users in China, but also provide historical context for what we're seeing in China." Wang's post reminds readers of the extent to which the bread and butter of an ethnographic approach (contextual, cultural, grounded) remains a rarity.

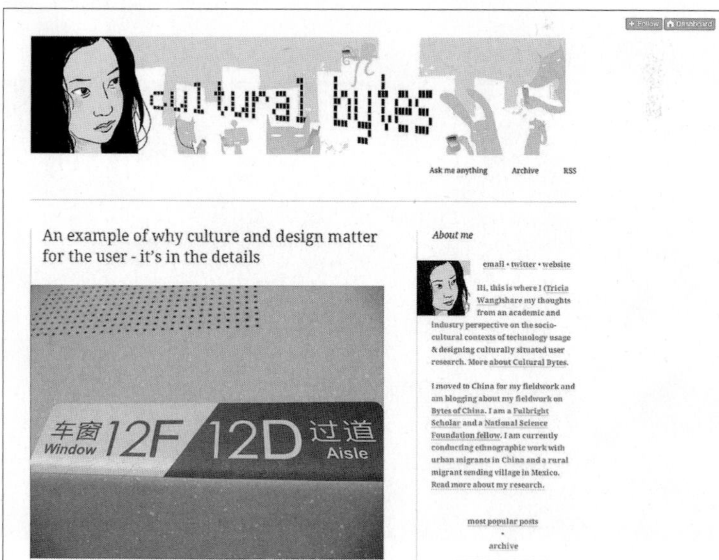

Figure 39.4. Tricia Wang writes on the sociocultural contexts of technology usage and designing culturally situated user research at *Culturebytes*. Image courtesy of Tricia Wang.

The focus of economic anthropologist Erin B. Taylor, a researcher at the Universidade de Lisboa who trained in Australia and did her dissertation research in the Caribbean, is material culture, mobile money, and socioeconomic development (Figure 39.5). She blogs about mobile money in its diverse manifestations and meanings, her ongoing research, and "debates of the day" in the field of anthropology (Big Data, small data, and the questions of ethics and exclusions often overlooked in the discussions, for example). Taylor is also a founding editor and member of *Popanth: Hot Buttered Humanity*, a site that "translates anthropological discoveries for popular consumption" (*Popanth* 2012–2013). With essays, film and book reviews, and forums, the language is clear and the tone enthusiastic, challenging readers' assumptions and using "cross-cultural stories to help you discover things about yourself and the world you live in." More broadly aimed than many of the blogs discussed here, Popanth's goal is to popularize the field of anthropology generally by providing "the public" with accessible examples of the field's offerings.

Figure 39.5. Big Data, big numbers: a DARPA photo from economic anthropologist Erin Taylor's blog. Image by Defense Advanced Research Projects Agency (DARPA) via Wikimedia Commons.

TRADING LESSONS

Writing specifically about what they do and recounting stories from the field, bloggers create a more nuanced portrait of business ethnography and their own approach to the work. Blogs provide a space for researchers to share their knowledge, insights, and lessons learned. Sometimes these blog posts are quite literally lessons: lectures or presentations delivered via YouTube or SlideCast.

Jenna Burrell, an associate professor in the School of Information at UC Berkeley and an *Ethnography Matters* blogger/editor, offers a "scavenger hunt style" list of questions to help "ramp up research quickly and get richer context for more specific research questions" in an urban fieldwork context (Burrell 2012). The foci of the questions run the gamut from the built environment to celebrity culture, bodily ideals and the sound landscape (Figure 39.6). Her list ends memorably with, "What insults do drivers shout at each other in traffic?" One can imagine the comfort the list might bring to an overwhelmed researcher at the start of a project in a large city, providing an entry point and first step into the tumult of urban culture.

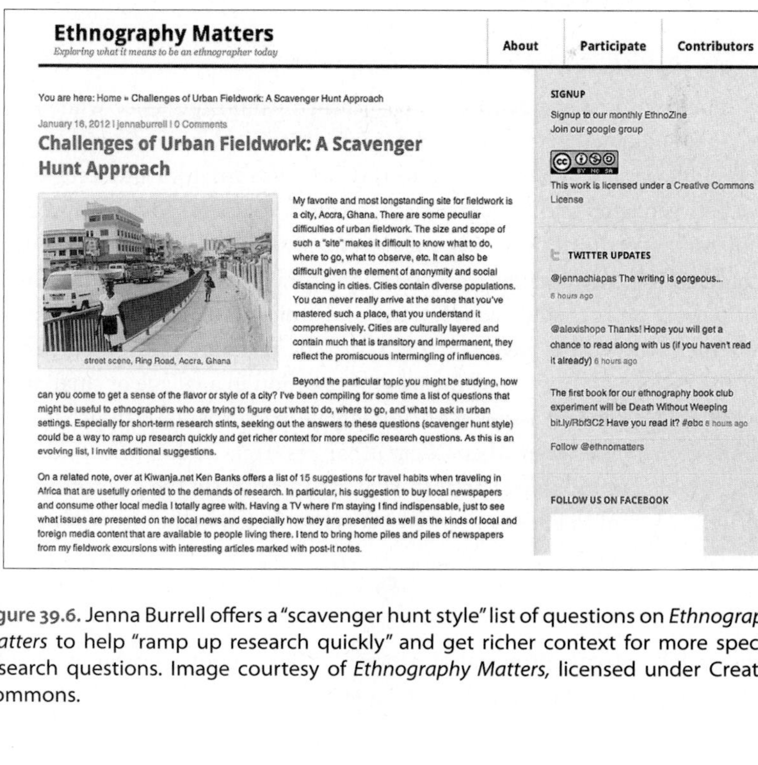

Figure 39.6. Jenna Burrell offers a "scavenger hunt style" list of questions on *Ethnography Matters* to help "ramp up research quickly" and get richer context for more specific research questions. Image courtesy of *Ethnography Matters,* licensed under Creative Commons.

Figure 39.7. In addition to photos and personal musings, Jan Chipchase offers lessons learned in the field; in his case, often "financially constrained communities." Image courtesy of Jan Chipchase, licensed under Creative Commons.

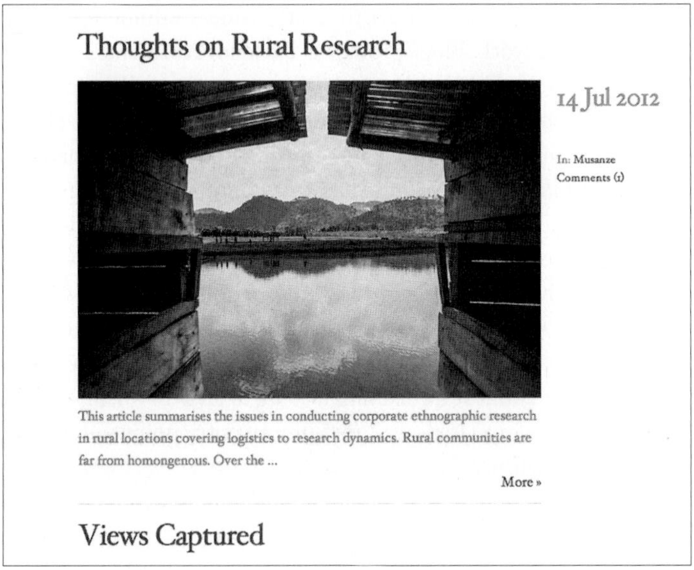

Jan Chipchase often shares what he has learned from experience while doing research in "financially constrained communities" in China, Brazil, Nigeria, and Rwanda, among others (Figure 39.7) (Chipchase 2012b). Describing differences between rural and urban research, he offers logistical advice for working in unfamiliar territories (tapping organizations already on the ground, using remote sensing, researching transportation infrastructure, being mindful of local "tempo" and schedule conventions, and anticipating advance permission requirements) as well as advice on the "research dynamics" one might encounter (expectations of "outsiders," the taint of rejection in a village or small town, how to handle consent issues with nonliterate participants). Chipchase also reminds readers that even when doing urban research, in countries with large agrarian populations, understanding what is happening in the countryside is a crucial component to understanding what is happening in the city.

Designer John Payne, principal at Moment, offers another lesson in how to do ethnography (or at least understand it enough to incorporate an "ethnogra-

Figure 39.8. A chart developed in a workshop led by John Payne illustrating the hand signals used in concert with the "human microphone" by members of the Occupy Wall Street movement. Image courtesy of Occupy Wall Street, licensed under Creative Commons.

phish" approach to one's design work). In a three-part post on *Ethnography Matters*, Payne describes a workshop he taught to interaction designers on ethnography as applied to user experience design (Payne 2012). The research site was "Liberty Square" in lower Manhattan, then home to the Occupy Wall Street movement. The research goal of Payne's workshop was to "understand how the occupiers communicated and coordinated within the group and with other occupy sites around the world" and to use that information "to inform the design of digital products that could help that communication and coordination process" (Figure 39.8).

The posts on the workshop not only describe the research methods used and conceptual frameworks that informed the short study, but also the analysis, concept work, and product proposals that came after, giving readers a good sense of the process from start to finish. Payne's posts are especially helpful to anyone thinking about how to set up a research class, or to create a research project of one's own, as he is thorough in describing why he designed the workshop the way he did and chose those particular methods.

Sharing stories from the field provides another picture of the process of research. "War Stories" is a series of posts on the Portigal company blog. The blog is an eclectic assemblage of news about the principal Steve Portigal, photos of his and colleagues' trips, observations from daily life, and opinions about and links to articles and videos on design, customer research, technology, consumption, and other related subjects. The "War Stories" series, written by researchers

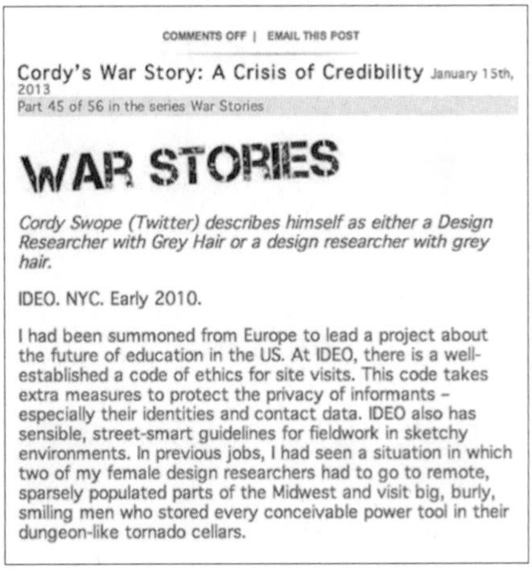

COMMENTS OFF | EMAIL THIS POST

Cordy's War Story: A Crisis of Credibility January 15th, 2013

Part 45 of 56 in the series War Stories

WAR STORIES

Cordy Swope (Twitter) describes himself as either a Design Researcher with Grey Hair or a design researcher with grey hair.

IDEO. NYC. Early 2010.

I had been summoned from Europe to lead a project about the future of education in the US. At IDEO, there is a well-established a code of ethics for site visits. This code takes extra measures to protect the privacy of informants – especially their identities and contact data. IDEO also has sensible, street-smart guidelines for fieldwork in sketchy environments. In previous jobs, I had seen a situation in which two of my female design researchers had to go to remote, sparsely populated parts of the Midwest and visit big, burly, smiling men who stored every conceivable power tool in their dungeon-like tornado cellars.

Figure 39.9. Researchers share stories from the field in the Portigal company blog series "War Stories." Image courtesy of Steve Portigal.

working on a wide range of projects all over the world, describes research derailed (and only sometimes put back on the tracks) and unexpected personal challenges (that are met or not) (Figure 39.9). They are sometimes humorous, providing a glimpse of the lighter side of research.

In "The Tools We Use" (Annechino 2012), *Ethnography Matters* provides links to sites with comprehensive software reviews, along with audio recorders, transcription devices, organizing and coding applications, reference managers, presentation tools, and the like. In her contribution to the series, Rachelle Annechino describes providing study participants with sketch pads and colored markers and asking them to draw maps, with great results. Annechino has also blogged on how to conduct a good interview, which is also the subject of several posts on the *Portigal* blog (Portigal 2012). Gavin Johnston, on *Anthrostrategy*, explores asking participants to write fiction and poetry as a way to elicit "deep meaning" (Johnston 2011).

Working with data that is not generated via participant observation is increasingly common, as more and more research projects include digital ethnography (studying social networks, for example, and other web-based communities). Writing on *Ethnography Matters*, Heather Ford describes her own uncertainty about how to approach the numbers, statistics, and patterns that emerged in her research on Wikipedia (Ford 2011). Her shift from numbers aversion to an understanding that numbers are problematic only to the extent that they are used with no regard for the context from which they are extracted was facilitated by "Numbers Have Qualities Too: Experiences with Ethno-Mining" (anderson et al. 2009), in which the Intel-based researchers introduce the concept of "ethno-mining" (joining database mining and ethnography). Her understanding was aided further by the notion of "trace ethnography" (Geiger and Ribes 2011), a methodology that avoids the quantitative/qualitative dichotomy and combines participant observation and log data "to reconstruct patterns and practices of users in distributed sociotechnical systems," focusing in this case on Wikipedia. Links to these papers are both made available within Ford's post, again a service to the community of readers.

WRITING IN THE SELF

Although all the blogs cited are professional blogs, some bloggers create (or reveal) more of a persona than others. The persona behind the blog usually gains shape in a post motivated by a daily event, frustration, a newspaper article, advertisement, TV, or shopping experience that then catalyzes a larger idea.

PacEth, a market and design research firm, recently posted a story on their

Thursday, February 9, 2012

Bring Home a Piece of Sweden from Ikea. Really?

Publicado por PacEth: Applied Anthropology Just About Everywhere

IKEA's Selfish Decision About Food, and What It Means to an Ex-Pat Swedish Anthropologist (Helena Ottoson, Pacific Ethnography, Port of Los Angeles)

In October of 2011 I went to IKEA to purchase my usual Swedish goodies. I ended up leaving in disbelief when none of the products I expected to find were there anymore. As an ex-pat Swede I was angry and disappointed that I could no longer purchase my Delicato pastries, my Marabou chocolate, or my Kalle's Kaviar.

However, I soon realized that I was not the only disgruntled customer. The Swedish ex patriots around the world were in uproar! Facebook pages such as "IKEA, please keep selling the brands we love" (as of February 7, 1,133 likes), "Only IKEA brand food? No, thank you!" (as of February 7, 1,661 likes) were started by angry IKEA shoppers. Articles in the blogosphere discussing the topic ended up with pages of angry comments.

Figure 39.10. A post on the PacEth blog by a Swedish researcher in the United States about IKEA's decision to stop carrying "local" (i.e., Swedish) products. Image courtesy of PacEth.

blog by Helena Ottoson, a Swedish member of the firm who was inspired to blog when she discovered that her local IKEA (in the United States) had stopped carrying "local" (i.e., Swedish) products (Ottoson 2012). Personal disappointment soon gave way to the anthropologist inside, and Ottoson researched (and writes about) how Swedes all over the world are responding, and how the change may in turn affect the IKEA brand (Figure 39.10). Other PacEth blog posts take as their starting points the personal search for non-genetically modified foods, and food labeling in the United States and Sweden.

Amy Santee, anthropologist and consumer experience researcher, and the voice of *Anthropologizing*, includes posts that focus on the consumer or participant experience of research, and her own experiences as both a customer and a researcher. *Anthropologizing* is a "mixed-bag of articles on anthropology, culture, consumption, and applied research methods." The style and language of the posts are informal and situated in Santee's daily life. A post on couponing culture, for example, starts with Santee's admission that one of her prime pleasures in going to the gym is watching reality TV, including TLC's *Extreme Couponing* (Santee 2012) (Figure 39.11).

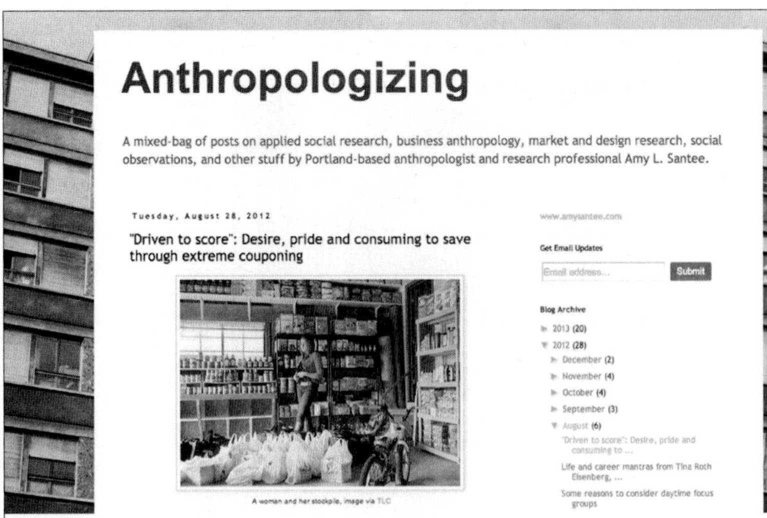

Figure 39.11. Amy Santee includes posts on the consumer or participant experience of research on her blog, including her dual roles as a consumer and a researcher. Image courtesy of Amy Santee.

Grant McCracken, long-time blogger, anthropologist, and early advocate of bringing cultural analysis to marketing and branding, writes at *Cultureby*, a blog that "sits at the intersection of anthropology and economics". A well-known figure in the field, his persona is further established online with posts that reference personal experience and local events. McCracken posts regularly on corporate and popular culture, with an emphasis on branding. He blogs on what he describes as a paradigm shift in marketing, illustrated by new approaches to branding: Oreo's "new looks" campaign (red cookies with track marks to celebrate the Mars Rover, for example) replaces the idea of a constant and simple brand for one that is "conversational and respiratory" (McCracken 2012c) (Figure 39.12). Spencer Falls and Sarah Carroll ("Sparah"), a fictional couple with all the trappings of a celebrity lifestyle, are a creation of Virgin Mobile and illustrate brand as embodied form, the "brand creature" (McCracken 2012b). McCracken also writes on changing cultural forms (Bjork's *Biophilia*,

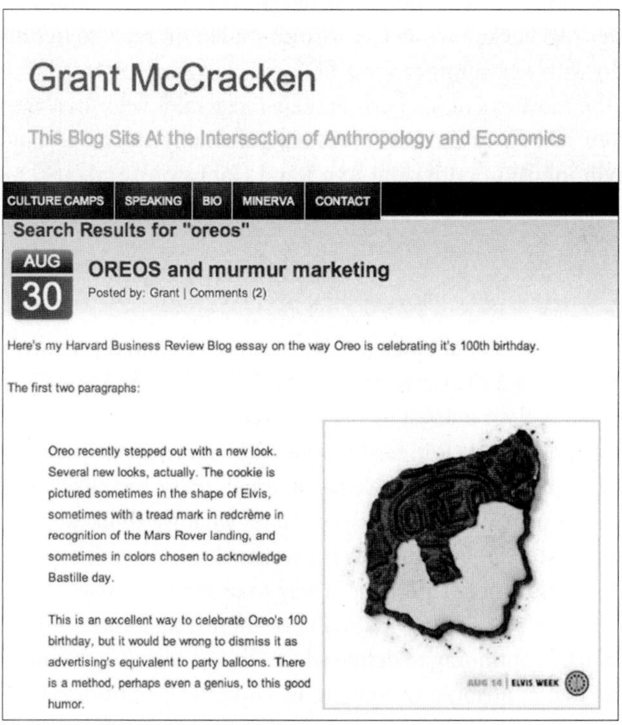

Figure 39.12. Grant McCracken's *Cultureby* focuses on corporate and popular culture, with an emphasis on branding. Image courtesy of Grant McCracken.

for example) and why he likes the TV shows he does, among many other surprising and thought-provoking tidbits.

Bloggers also write about the books they are reading and the conferences they attend. *Ethnography Matters* has several series related to recommended reading materials. In the new series "Syllabus as Essay" (Marwick 2013), Fordham assistant professor Alice Marwick provides a thoughtful and informative essay on her "Social Media" syllabus, what she chose to assign and why, and how students responded. An equally interesting series is "The Ethnographer's Summer Reading List," where different guest bloggers post what they are reading, sometimes as a simple list, sometimes with an accompanying essay to guide the reader through.

Bloggers also put on their sites what might be thought of as motivating or inspiring posts. Tricia Wang often posts brief (and not-so-brief) excerpts from the writing of Jean Baudrillard, news sources, Michel Foucault, colleagues, and friends. Some of the posts in Portigal's "War Stories" series fit the bill, as does a letter McCracken wrote to a former student in reply to her query about what to do with her summer (and life), encouraging her to stay mobile and follow in the footsteps of his hero Francis Fitzgerald, who "cast the net wide" (McCracken 2012a). In a related vein are personally assertive or questioning posts: Gavin Johnston criticizing Ayn Rand (Johnston 2012), and Amy Santee wondering about "bearing witness" and personal responsibility (Santee 2012a).

At their best, professional blogs provide a sense of shared practice and create community among a disparate group of individuals from varied backgrounds that are united in their interest in, and appreciation for, the use of anthropology and ethnographic methods in business and design contexts.[2] They provide links to material we might not otherwise see on topics that we are likely interested in, and sometimes provide a new perspective on what we think we already know. From a writer's standpoint, blogging is a way to think through one's ideas as well as a way to assess others' interests, "a way to probe the universe" (McCracken 2013:108). Blog posts can help maintain, or improve, or contest the "brand" of the approach by continuing to define what it is and what it isn't, and to generate discussions that contribute to making us all better practitioners. In so doing bloggers are also establishing their own visibility and publics that transcend geography, institutions, and disciplines.

REFERENCES

anderson, ken, Dawn Nafus, Tye Rattenbury, and Ryan Aipperspach. 2009. "Numbers Have Qualities Too: Experiences with Ethno-Mining." *EPIC* 2009:123–40.

Annechino, Rachelle. 2011. "Qualitative Research Is Not Research At All?" *Ethnography Matters* (blog), November 25. ethnographymatters.net/2011/11/25/qualitative-research -is-not-research-at-all.

_____. 2012. "The Tools We Use: Bring Some Colored Markers." *Ethnography Matters* (blog), August 28. ethnographymatters.net/2012/08/28/bring-some-colored-markers.

Burrell, Jenna. 2012. "Challenges of Urban Fieldwork: A Scavenger Hunt Approach." *Ethnography Matters* (blog), January 16. ethnographymatters.net/2012/01/16/challenges-of-urban-field work-a-scavenger-hunt-approach.

Chipchase, Jan. 2012a. "Imperialist Tendencies." Blog post, January 13. janchipchase.com /content/ essays/imperialist-tendencies.

_____. 2012b. "Thoughts on Rural Research." Blog post, July 14. janchipchase.com/2012/07/ thoughts-on-rural-research.

Ford, Heather. "Data Conversations: Can Ethnographers Do Numbers?" *Ethnography Matters* (blog), November 23. ethnographymatters.net/2011/11/23/data-conversations-can-ethnographers-do-numbers.

Garfield, Bob. 2011. "Sentiment Analysis Reveals How the World Is Feeling." *On the Media* (blog), November 11. onthemedia.org/2011/nov/11/sentiment-analysis-reveals-how-world-feeling.

Geiger, Stuart, and David Ribes. 2011. "Trace Ethnography: Following Coordination through Documentary Practices." Presented at the 44th Annual Hawaii International Conference on Systems Sciences, Koloa, Kauai, Hawaii, January 4–7, 2011. http://www. stuartgeiger.com/trace-ethnogra phy-hicss-geiger-ribes.pdf.

Johnston, Gavin. 2011. "Poetry as a Research Tool." *Anthrostrategist* (blog), October 13. anthrostrat egy.com/2011/10/13/poetry-as-a-research-tool.

_____. 2012. "No, I Am Not John Galt." *Anthrostrategist* (blog), January 17. anthrostrategy.com/ 2012/01/17/no-I-am-not-john-galt.

Ladner, Sam. 2012. "Does Corporate Ethnography Suck? A Cultural Analysis of Academic Critiques of Private-Sector Ethnography (Part 1 of 3)." *Ethnography Matters* (blog), January 13. ethnogra phymatters.net/2012/01/13/does-corporate-ethnography-suck-a-cultural-analysis-of-academic -critiques-of-private-sector-ethnography-part-1- of-2/.

Marwick, Alice. 2013. "On Teaching Social Media to Undergraduates [Syllabus as Essay]." *Ethnography Matters* (blog), January 9. ethnographymatters.net/2013/01/09/on-teach ing-social-media-to-undergraduates-syllbus-as-essay.

McCracken, Grant. 2012a. "Ethnographic Walk-About (or, What to Do with the Rest of Your Summer)." Blog post, July 5. cultureby.com/2012/07/ethnographic-walk-about-or-what-to-do-with-the-rest-of-your-summer.html.

_____. 2012b. "The Evolution of the Brand Creature." Blog post, August 9. cultureby.com /2012/08/ the-evolution-of-the-brand-creature.html.

_____. 2012c. "OREOS and Murmur Marketing." Blog post, August 30. cultureby.com/ 2012/08/ oreos-and-murmur-marketing.html.

_____. 2013. "How To Be a Self-Supporting Anthropologist." In *A Handbook of Practicing Anthropology*, edited by Riall Nolan, 104–13. West Sussex, UK: Wiley-Blackwell.

Ottoson, Helena. "Bring Home a Piece of Sweden from Ikea. Really?" *PacEth* (blog), February 9. http://www.ethnographers.net/2012/02/bring-home-piece-of-sweden-from-ikea.html.

Payne, John. 2012. "Teaching Ethnography for User Experience: A Workshop on Occupy Wall Street." *Ethnography Matters* (blog), August 31. ethnographymatters.net/2012/ 08/31/teaching-ethnog raphy-for-user-experience-a-workshop-on-occupy-wall-street.

Popanth. 2012–2013. "What on Earth Is Popanth?" *Popanth: Hot Buttered Humanity* (blog). http:// popanth.com/about/.

Portigal, Steve. 2012. "Seventeen Types of Interviewing Questions." *Portigal* (blog), February 14. portigal.com/blog/seventeen-types-of-interviewing-questions.

Santee, Amy L. 2012a. "'Bearing Witness': The Context of Choice, Behavior Change, and Changing the System." *Anthropologizing* (blog), July 16. amysantee.blogspot.com/ 2012/07/bearing-witness-context-of-choice.html.

_____. 2012b. "'Driven to Score': Desire, Pride and Consuming To Save through Extreme Couponing." *Anthropologizing* (blog), August 28. amysantee.blogspot.com/2012/08/driven-to-score-desire-consumption-and.html.

Wang, Tricia. 2012. "Slides/Notes For My SXSW Talk on My Research in China & Some Thoughts about SXSW." *culturalbytes* (blog), March 21. culturalbyt.es/post/4008760 175/sxsw.

BLOGS CITED

Anthrostrategy.com

Amysantee.blogspot.com

Culturalbyt.es

Cultureby.com

Copernicusconsulting.net

Erinbtaylor.com

Ethnographers.net

Ethnographymatters.net

Janchipchase.com

Popanth.com

Portigal.com/blog/

NOTES

1 Ladner has her own blog at copernicusconsulting.net.

2 While not itself a blog, the anthrodesign listserv (anthrodesign.com), founded by anthropologist Natalie Hanson in 2002, is another great resource for those interested in the intersection of design, business, and anthropology. The list functions as an online community and interactive bulletin board where subscribers post and discuss theoretical and practical questions, upcoming events, and current interests. Not all participants are anthropologists, but all share an interest in applying ethnographic techniques and social sciences theory to industrial, software, and other types of product and organizational design.

40

Between the Idea & the Reality Falls the Shadow: A True, Semifactual Tale of Professional Despair

MARTIN HØYEM

> Imagine yourself suddenly set down surrounded by all your gear, alone on a tropical beach close to a native village, while the launch or dinghy which has brought you sails away out of sight.
>
> —Bronislaw Malinowski, *Argonauts of the Western Pacific*

I tried not to think about Malinowski. Tried not to think about a tropical beach. I was sitting in a fast-food restaurant on the outskirts of Phoenix, Arizona, looking out through the windows with the massive graphics pasted onto the glass—four-foot-tall, hand-drawn, pastel-colored letters advertising "We're hiring!" to the parking lot outside. My boss, who had just dropped me off, was backing out of his parking spot with his beat-up Toyota Corolla. "Call me when you want me to pick you up," he had told me. "I'll go and do . . . do something."

So here I was. I had been sent over for a few days to help a fast-food restaurant chain better comprehend their customers. *Better comprehend their customers.* That's how they had put it. Help them figure out how to sell more burgers and fries was more like it.

I looked around the place while I contemplated my situation. I had five days to do what I had been taught would take at least one year to do. Five days to embed myself in the society I was to study. Understand the traditions and customs of the culture on its own terms. Bring back exceptional percipience.

"Hey, I like your tattoos, man. Are you like a rock star or something?" A young man, around 30 years old, was next to me in line as I was trying to figure

Handbook of Anthropology in Business, edited by Rita Denny and Patricia Sunderland, 753–762.

out what to order. As a matter of fact, it wasn't so much that I was trying to figure out *what* to order: I was trying to figure out *how* to order. In some people's eyes this probably makes me a snob: I take pride in my inexperience with establishments of this type, places where your lunch comes with a malfunctioning plastic toy made in Vietnam. The industry itself likes to call them "QSR": Quick Service Restaurants. I find the term "junk-food joint" to be just as accurate. I don't really get them. Like, I don't get their menus, those billboard-sized things, backlit and richly illustrated, on the wall above and behind the cashiers. Obviously they have been designed according to somebody's idea of user friendliness—let's use *big* letters, *big* pictures—but they still manage to confuse me. It's the rush that gets me. It's just decency, isn't it—in a restaurant—to read the whole menu before you make your choice? But the physical space of these places makes me feel like I don't have time. Like, *they're waiting.* "Hurry up!" The line I was standing in was moving too fast: there wouldn't be time to carefully weigh my options before I reached the front of the line. I needed to take a pick, quickly. And now this stranger was throwing me off with inquisitions about my appearance.

I looked over at him. His facial expression implied he meant the question sincerely. Was I like a rock star? Or something?

"No, I'm not a rock star," I said. I gave him a friendly smile, then looked back up at the menu. "I'm an anthropologist."

Hopefully that will shut him up, I thought. It was my turn at the counter.

"One number two," I said, with faked confidence. In desperation I had decided to just copy the order of the lady who had been in front of me in the line. "Medium. With Coke."

One day my boss and I talked to the manager of another franchise of this same fast-food restaurant chain, out somewhere in the thick of the suburban sprawl.

"I used to work at the race track in Santa Anita," the man told us, as we sat with him at one of the tables in his restaurant. He was probably in his 50s, and looked so nondescript to me that "nondescript" describes him pretty well.

"But the race track was just too depressing," he continued. "A bunch of losers, really, too many dead-end lives. I decided to quit and come here to do this instead."

I looked around his joint. The air was heavy with grease. The view out the window was a parking lot. The wall-to-wall carpet . . . it struck me as odd to have wall-to-wall carpet in a fast-food restaurant, like those English restrooms with a shaggy little rug on the floor, wrapped around the base of the toilet, it just seemed wrong . . . . The wall-to-wall carpet was pistachio and salmon, a color scheme and pattern out of vogue since 1987. This place was heartbreakingly depressing.

That race track must have been something, I thought, and took a sip of the milkshake-like substance I had asked for with my meal. This drink, by the way—or is it an ice cream?—was, I had been told, quite the centerpiece of this particular fast-food chain's offerings. I later found out that it contains almost three times as many calories as a similarly sized Coca-Cola. If you think I'm trying to suggest that you should choose a Coca-Cola, because a cup of Coca-Cola is a healthy choice . . . well, I'm not. I guess what I'm saying is that if you're trying to put on a few extra pounds, this drink I was sipping is the ticket. But here's the thing: I kept hearing—from our clients, and from the customers we talked to as well—that the food at this chain was healthier than the food you would get at other fast-food places. "This stuff is better for you," was the chorus. When I later asked the executives at the corporate headquarters if they had any nutritional data to back up this claim of being "better," they simply replied "no" and left it at that.

These kids . . . these kids were maybe 14. Maybe 15. One of them, a tiny boy who looked like a mouse, couldn't do much else than giggle the whole time. One of the others . . . I'll call him the alpha, although the word "alpha" probably conveys a much more dominant figure than this guy was ever cut out to be. He, too, looked like a mouse, like the rest of them. But I'll call him alpha because he seemed to be the one doing all the talking. Except they weren't really talking until I came up and started asking questions. They were stoned out of their minds, too busy being high to bother with speech. I could actually smell the pot on their breath.

So these kids—five or six of them—had come in from the parking lot entrance with their skateboards, and once inside they hauled the boards along with them and walked up to the counter. Then, with experienced efficiency and the sort of authority that comes with a long history of junk-food shopping, they placed their orders, paid, and brought the food over to a table tucked away in the narrow hallway next to the restrooms, over where it smells a little bit of pee and chlorine.

As soon as I saw them walk in I had decided to try to recruit them for our studies. Now, awkwardly crouching down next to their table, I moved fast and asked them if they could tell me about the stuff they were eating.

"Look," I told them. "We're doing this study on fast-food restaurant customers, so I wondered if I could ask you some questions about your food."

The alpha's answers were short: so short that calling them "answers" might be stretching it a bit. He was trying to impress his friends by cutting me off with curt replies.

"Fries are good. Ketchup is good. Meat is good. Bread is good. Coke is good."

The tiniest one giggled, astonished by the pure brilliance of the alpha's response. The others continued to silently fill their faces with French fries and burgers and Coca-Cola.

They didn't buy it. They thought I was a freak: a pervert hanging around in a place like this to hook up with young kids for dubious reasons. Perhaps they had previous experience with this.

"Yeah, right, fast-food study. . . ." They smirked knowingly at each other.

Without looking up, the tiny mouse giggled again and kept eating his fries, one by one.

Leave us alone, they said, without saying it.

I did. I walked back to my table.

What would Malinowski do? I thought to myself, as I sat down to pretend I was writing in my notebook.

I took a deep breath.

This was a sad place. A sad, sad place.

One morning, a couple of days earlier, I had decided I was in the mood to go to a bookstore. So I walked up to the clerk at the front desk of my motel and asked if she could direct me to one.

"No, I'm sorry," she said. "I don't know. I don't do that."

I looked at her, puzzled. She looked back at me.

What did she mean she doesn't do that? Doesn't do *what*? Go to bookstores? *Read?!* I was too confused to follow up.

"All right. . . . Thanks. I guess I'll see if I can just stumble upon one by chance, then."

I walked outside.

They probably have a strong oral tradition, I decided.

I sincerely hoped they did. The only bookstore I found that day was called Path of Light. It sold different types of Bibles, books about reading the Bible, and books about people who had read the Bible and found it rewarding.

Words are material to my character.

I think about those texts I read as a student, created by the pioneers of anthropology. That was the stuff, stories of such eloquent enchantment! Where the Social Scientist disappears into some faraway jungle, then reappears only after a year—a full year—returning from the field changed, wiser, replete with beautiful stories and deep insights.

Those were the books that made me decide I wanted to become an anthropologist. So I set out to learn how to do all that: how to gather empirical data, how to carefully weigh evidence, how to stitch data together so they form an argument, a logic expressed in spoken or written words, explaining how things connect. I aspired to analytical excellence and brilliant logical feats.

All that gave me great comfort.

Language devoid of content, on the other hand, makes me panic. That dreadful rhetorical cotton candy. Faux linguistic sophistication.

It's sinister.

Like these kids at the fast-food joint, they shook me. But the problem wasn't that their speech was full of circumlocution and pretentious jargon. Theirs was a language stripped to the bone: not brilliantly, like Hemingway, but by what seemed the lack of reflection. Like a strung-out Confucius. Within seconds of approaching them and feebly trying to chat them up, their attitude made everything I believe in vaporize. Those years of training were gone in a second. The world tumbled down. I tumbled along.

Back at my table I picked at my burger and looked around, took a slurp of my Coke through the straw. Margaret Mead had it easy, I told myself. Ruth Benedict. Boas. . . . They never had to deal with this.

"What happened?"

It was the guy from earlier, from the line. He was sitting at the table next to mine. I hadn't noticed.

"Is everything all right?" he asked, conspiratorially.

"Yeah," I said. "Everything is all right." I pulled myself together and looked at him. "I'm trying to talk to people about fast food. . . . We're doing this study. I'm an anthropologist."

"Yes," he said. "You already told me." He looked at me. "I thought anthropologists just dig in the dirt and study broken pieces of pottery?"

"Some of us do. But that's archaeology. Me, I'm a social anthropologist. I study the culture of people who are still around. Living cultures." I looked at him. He looked like he was waiting for more, so I continued. "Traditionally anthropologists like me would go into some jungle or to some Pacific island or somewhere exotic like that, and study the people they found there, but these days . . . these days we hang around in places like this, I guess."

He nodded.

"Why?" he asked, and took a bite of his burger.

"Well, the owners of this fast-food restaurant chain asked us if we could help them figure out their customers, so that's why I'm here."

He chewed.

"You interested in answering some questions?" I asked. "We'll pay you for your time."

He was sipping from his soda. "Sure," he said, with his lips still wrapped around the straw.

I moved over to his table, and opened my notebook. "So. . . . Let's see. Let me just get some initial data down." I was talking like an imbecile myself, now, trying to sound like I knew what I was doing. "Like, what do you do? You know . . . for a living?"

"I work at Fender," he answered. "Fender guitars. It's right up the street from here."

"Wow," I said.

"Yes, it's pretty cool. I'm just an accountant, though."

"Well, still. It's Fender," I insisted.

"Right. I like to say it's only paperwork, but the paperwork rocks."

I smiled. He was holding his burger with both hands, and leaned down to take another sip of his drink.

"But I also write poetry." He nodded down towards the table, pointing with his eyes. Next to his serving tray, there was a notebook and a pencil. "I'm working on a collection of poems. Each poem will be written in a junk-food restaurant."

I raised both eyebrows.

"Interesting," I said, approvingly.

"I just wrote a poem right now. I called it 'Drink dispenser chance encounter. . . .' I'm not sure how well it rolls off the tongue, though. I might have to change it."

He held out his hand, over the table.

"I'm Christian," he said.

A little bewildered, I shook it.

"That's all right. I'm an atheist, myself." I hesitated, then added sheepishly: "But I don't mind people having a religion."

"No," he said. "My name . . . my name is Christian."

"Oh, sorry," I said. I wrote "Christian" in my notebook. "Pleased to make your acquaintance, Christian."

Some nights before, after a day of slow and messy fieldwork, my boss and I had gone to a bar to grab some grub and a few beers. We started talking about books we loved and about reading and I had told him about how my wife recently handed me a copy of Hamsun's *Victoria* opened up to a passage somewhere in the middle of the book, and she had asked me to read it out loud for her, and I did, but then the text had made me cry and I was sobbing so hard I wasn't able to finish the page.

"The last book that made me cry," I told my boss, "was *Patterns of Culture.*"

"Ruth Benedict," he said. "Really?"

"Yeah. There's a passage in there, a short monologue by Ramon, the chief of the Paiute Indians. He gives Benedict this nice metaphor on culture, where he says *'In the beginning God gave to every people a cup, a cup of clay, and from this cup they drank their life. They all dipped in the water. But their cup was different. Our cup is broken now. It has passed away.'*"

I paused and poured beer into my glass.

"And then Benedict goes on to explain, she writes something like *'Our cup is broken. Those things that had given significance to the life of his people, the domestic rituals of eating, the obligations of the economic system, the succession of ceremonials in the villages, possession in the bear dance, their standards of right and wrong—these were gone, and with them the shape and meaning of their life.'*"

I took a sip of my beer. My boss smiled and nodded.

"I read that, and I cried," I said. "Granted I'm a sentimentalist, but I'll still argue that *Patterns of Culture* is a well-written book. It made me remember why I was drawn to anthropology to begin with."

The bar we were sitting in was nothing special, but it was a nice evening and we enjoyed ourselves.

"Are we going to say something about how sad these places are?" I asked my boss, as we settled in for breakfast a few days later. We had driven over to a diner nearby, because we needed to be—as my boss expressed it—"orange-juiced and caffeinated."

My boss lives in the desert in southern California and sometimes sleeps on his sailboat in the Los Angeles harbor. He speaks four languages, and is a smart man.

"Are we going to say something about how sad these places are?" My boss repeated my question, rolling it around in his mouth while he contemplated what I had said. He paused.

"We are going to say something about it if we hear people say they think the place is sad," he said. "Auto-ethnography can be fine, but we're really here to find out how *other* people feel, not how *we* feel."

"So you don't think these places are sad?" I asked, not willing to let go. " You don't see that? You don't agree?" To me this was so prominent that I couldn't believe anybody else could feel any differently.

"I don't know," he said, as the waitress brought over our coffee, juice, and pancakes. He waited until she had left before he continued. "They certainly aren't places where you sit and talk about books that make you cry. But I don't know if all places should be."

Christian had agreed to meet me a few days later, at another branch of the same fast-food chain, this one further from his job. When I arrived, he was already there. He waved from his table as I came in through the door.

I smiled at him as I walked over. Same wall-to-wall carpet on the floor, same pattern in pistachio and salmon. Same view out the windows, different parking lot.

I had a list of questions I was supposed to ask for our study. And I had an envelope with money I had promised him for his time. That envelope made me feel dirty, impure, so I was eager to get it off my hands, off my mind.

"Hi, there," I said, as I sat down at his table. "How's it hanging?"

"Not bad," he said. "Not bad at all. . . ."

I looked over at him. He twirled his cup of Coca-Cola with his plastic straw, listening to the ice cubes spin, then slowly lifted the cup and took a sip. His eyes focused on something far back in his skull. In the background I could hear a man pointing out how he didn't want any pickles with his burger, quite insistent on this distinction. Yesterday they had given him pickles, even though he had told them not to, and this was very upsetting. I looked over towards the counter, where the guy was standing. He was doughy-looking, clean-shaven, dressed in khaki-colored cargo shorts, cheap tassel loafers with no socks, and a washed out T-shirt advertising a local car show four years back.

"I'm very sorry about that, sir," said the short, middle-aged lady behind the counter. She had a thick accent. I made a guess she was an immigrant from somewhere in Latin America. "I make sure you don't get pickles."

"Also," the man continued, "I'd like the slice of tomato to be placed under the hamburger patty, not on top. Continental style."

"Continental style, sir?"

"Yeah, like they do in France. I saw that on TV."

I looked back at Christian. Fluid was seeping out of a little crack near the top of his cup, close to the plastic lid. He didn't notice.

"Your cup . . . " I said, and pointed. "Your cup is broken."

He lifted it up to look, turned it around.

"You're right. It *is* broken."

He stood up and started walking towards the condiment counter.

"No worries," he said. "I'll just get a new one."

I had a dream last night. Actually I had the same dream twice in a row, which bothers me. I'm not sure what my mind is trying to tell me; it's given up on my imagination, I guess. . . .

I was in an art gallery—or perhaps it was a church—it was hard to tell. There were many beautiful rooms, and a small crowd, and I was with T. S. Eliot. I had just bumped into him. He was friendly and open to conversation. I told him I liked "The Hollow Men."

"*Mistah Kurtz—he dead,*" I said, putting some extra effort into the accent and pronunciation, while simultaneously trying to sound like I made no effort.

"Conrad. Such a master," T. S. Eliot said.

"One of my favorite books," I offered. "Did you see the movie adaptation? Coppola . . ."

"Yes," he nodded. "It was okay. The book is better."

"Yeah, it is," I said. "Usually the book is better. But you know, sometimes . . . sometimes the movie is actually better. Or reality. Reality can be better."

"No," he said firmly, not even looking at me. "The book is always better."

We made our way out the main entrance of the gallery, and stopped on the stairs leading down to an entryway squeezed between the building we had just come out of and the neighboring one. They were both granite buildings, with an aura of nobility and history. The evening was warm. Nice.

"What do you do for a living?" T. S. Eliot asked me.

"I'm an anthropologist," I said.

"Oh, really? Interesting stuff! Very, very interesting!"

"Yeah. But sometimes. . . ." I let the unfinished sentence hang in the air.

"Anthropology is such a noble pursuit," he said. "Very important."

"Yeah, I know, but it doesn't always pay the bills, does it now?"

"The reality is, Martin, all those reasons you had when you started out studying anthropology, they might not always make sense to others. Just like painting doesn't always make sense. Like music doesn't. Poetry." He looked at me. "But you don't do anthropology to pay the bills. You do it because it's a thing of beauty. And also because you believe that humankind can do better, and that even in times when we feel we might not understand, it is still of great consequence that we try. You do anthropology because, frankly, it seems to be the only decent thing to do. You and me, Martin, we are the dreamers of dreams. We are world-losers and world-forsakers. But we are also the movers and shakers."

"Movers and shakers, huh?" I said. "I like that."

"So here's the score, Martin. If you want to survive doing anthropology, you're going to need a little extra. A little extra soul, perhaps. Otherwise you can't have any hope of keeping your integrity and dignity intact."

I looked at him, silently.

He continued: "I read somewhere . . . I think it was in a fortune cookie . . . that life is a tragedy for those who feel, and a comedy for those who think."

"What does that mean?"

"I don't know. Maybe nothing. What I'm trying to say is that perhaps one day you might find yourself, miserable, in a fast-food joint, let's say in Phoenix, Arizona, trying to engage strangers in conversation, because some business hired you to find out how to sell more greasy food. And it's simple as this, Martin: you might need a strong soul, then. Because, if you don't have a strong soul, you'll just get your heart shattered to smithereens."

That was the end of my dream. And then I had the exact same dream over again. Except this time the conversation had a better flow to it. And I was T. S. Eliot.

41

Seduction in the Field: Meditations on Building Rapport through the Ethnographic Camera Lens

BRUNO MOYNIÉ

MY EXPERIENCE, IN THE FIELD

My professional life is split nearly exactly into two clean parts. On the one end, I travel extensively to various places around the world—which we are calling here "the field"—to meet with people and record aspects of their life on camera. On the other, I stay isolated in my office—or within walking distance from it—for weeks, editing away the material I have collected during my travels. I am an ethnographic filmmaker.

I apply my craft to three distinct fields that all have people at the center. First, I specialize in applied ethnography for marketing and design research. I follow people, interview them in their day-to-day contexts, and observe their behaviors to unearth insights about their product or service experience or usage. For instance, I observed six American families and the way they eat because the Wendy's restaurant chain wanted to gain a deeper understanding of its clientele, their relationship to food in general, and to fast food in particular, as well as to get some understanding of how their customers chose between Wendy's restaurants and their main competitors. A clip from a 49-minute film about one family is available on my company website.[1]

Second, I do classic television documentaries. For example, I made a documentary that explores concepts of "traditional" meals and the dynamics involved in the changes that are occurring throughout the world toward a globalization of contemporary foods and ways of eating across five different countries.[2] Another project that took me around the globe was the *"J'aime les mots"* ("I love words") series.[3] I asked people from various part of the French-speaking world to react to one expression, proverb, or word commonly used or invented in other parts of the planet by other French-speaking cultures. The point of this playful show is for people to guess and try to understand—expand

Handbook of Anthropology in Business, edited by Rita Denny and Patricia Sunderland, 763–774.

on or find the etymology of—the word/expression/proverb at hand from their perspective and their own cultural context.

My third field is my own art, projects focused mainly around people's narratives on an array of topics. In one case, I was interested in hearing the stories attached to artifacts that people collect throughout their lives, as the most seemingly insignificant objects often prove to carry surprisingly deep emotions (explore the interactive project website: www.theobjectsproject.com). Another project features portraits of unusual French-speaking individuals who form an unexpected community in the almost mythical town of Fargo, North Dakota (www.fargoisnotfargo.com/).

To do work in all three of these fields, I find myself engaging in something I can only call a "seduction." By this, I mean to be a good ethnographer, you must genuinely need the affection of your participants. You must "desire their desire."

It is well established that the success of ethnographic fieldwork relies generally on the capacity to establish good rapport and build meaningful relationships with research participants. Similarly, and especially since the emergence of reflexive ethnography, we have acknowledged that a certain level of intimacy helps to erase the distinction between "self" and "other" and "the cultural boundaries that obscure the common humanity of researchers and their informants" (Sluka 2006; see also Rabinow 1977).

Indeed, irrespective of its context, my work is always about meeting with people I generally do not know beforehand, and then filming them. The purpose is not so much to work so that they do not notice my presence, but rather to achieve a level of comfort such that they forget about the camera that comes between us, even though the reality is that it is the device that I use to record their behaviors or what they have to say, both through actions and through words. I do this in various countries, and across diverse social classes, genders, and age groups.

Over two decades of work, techniques have changed, and enhancing my technical skills is certainly a challenge. However, although technical skills are required for good ethnographic filmmaking, one needs another, deeper set of skills: the ability to entice people to share their hopes and feelings with you. I learned this idea from Jean Rouch, one of the founders of the *cinéma verité* school of filmmaking, with whom I had the privilege to study in Paris in the mid-1980s. Projecting his own films to a class at the Cinémathèque, he constantly mentioned the friendships he had built, faithfully maintained, and relied on with the people he had filmed or collaborated with. It was intuitively evident from his persona that he was a charismatic "people person." His friends/collaborators were often invited to class sessions. I have no recollection of him giving us advice on "being a good friend" or even trying to discuss it theoretically, yet this idea has stayed with me through my practice: one must want to be with other people for them to be open with you.

The American anthropologist Charles Wagley speaks to the juncture that is the subjective gray space of science, art, and the interpersonal variables that are unavoidably a part of the human-centered and human-directed research that is fieldwork. He writes: "In the security of our studies and in the classroom, we claim that anthropology is a social science. . . . But, at its source, in the midst of the people with whom the anthropologist lives and works, field research involves the practice of an art in which emotions, subjective attitudes and reactions, and undoubtedly subconscious motivations participate" (Wagley 1960:414–5).

DESIRING THEIR DESIRE: MY "ETHNOGRAPHIC MOJO"?

This sounds like confessing that there is "artsy" skill to one's work, when everything is supposed to be part of a well-established process. It may also sound somewhat shameful. In fact, it could be said that my work is part of an extreme qualitative approach where the unpredictable, subtle, and sometimes contradictory human animal doesn't always bend to rigorous processes. Nevertheless, I never hide the fact that this "artsy" dimension is crucial in my work. What I am trying to convey here is the emotional drive underlying the rapport that is established between the observer and those being observed.

This is what I usually refer to as—and will call here with stern humor—my "ethnographic mojo." My ethnographic mojo piques my participants' interest, but to do so, *I have to be interested in them.* My ethnographic mojo requires me to "desire their desire." As ethnographers, we must thirst for that connection. We must make our participants want to talk to us, but we must also want to engage with them!

A lot has been said on the sexual dimension of this desire, but that is not per se what I am referring to (compare with Kulick and Wilson 1995). I do not deny the sexual dimension, but instead I believe that it is part of something bigger: something of the same nature but broader. I strongly believe that, as Dorinne Kondo writes: "All too often standards of scientific objectivity in ethnography have masked points of view that are merely distant and unsympathetic" (Kondo 1986:84).

I am not the first to consider this "magical" connection between ethnographer and participant. It is an emotional labor that we sometimes fail at completing. Bronislaw Malinowski considered "living with" participants to be one of the most important skills an ethnographer can have (1922). It was only after he died that we learned that Malinowski himself did not consistently feel a deep desire to have a rapport with his participants, and he found it almost impossible to "want" to be with them all the time (1967). Other anthropologists also have struggled to connect with their participants. Ethnographer Jean Briggs (1970) stopped "desiring" the approval of her adopted Inuit family . . . and found herself dumped outside the village for months!

Desiring their desire is one of the hardest things we can do as ethnographers. This is also true for commercial ethnographers. One of our most important tasks is to show our clients what their customers are doing, thinking, and feeling. If we do not have a desire for our participants, we cannot learn what really moves them emotionally. It is acutely important for ethnographic filmmaking, which requires participants to relax in front of a camera (Agafonoff 2006; see also Leibovitz 2008).

Desiring our participants' desire may not be necessary to do an excellent job; perhaps it is just a very personal way of doing things. But I highly doubt it. I know that it directly correlates to and affects the quality of my work. Without it, the results are simply not the same.

THE ROOTS OF MY MOJO

Allow me to share how I discovered my "desire to be desired." I was trained through respectable institutions: in France at the University of Provence, or Paris X, and in Canada at l'Université de Montréal and Concordia, in social anthropology, filmmaking, and finally ethnographic filmmaking. For my very first "ethnographic field" trip, a professor in Aix-en-Provence decided that we needed a field experience to conclude our academic year studying ethnography from a Marxist perspective. He took us all to a small village in the Alps and asked us to find a "field."

First, I tried the local bar where my ambition was broadly to "study the locals," particularly the masculine conviviality that is known to take place there. On that day, I ordered one single espresso, a common custom among students, and sat in a corner all day, while the only woman in the bar—the one behind the counter—gave me her darkest look. My experiment had turned into a pathetic failure. When I came back to our "camp," a local student (I was from a completely different region in France) enlightened me: he suggested I go back to the same bar the next day and offer a round of pastis, the local drink. And so I did. However, when I walked like a cowboy toward the bar and ordered the round, the woman tending bar—who had already spotted me the day before as an impoverished outsider—asked, with a dry voice: "What brand?" She went on to give me her nastiest gaze, full of disdain. She could read the hesitation on my face. She added "Yeah . . . whatever." I was terminally disqualified, and this was my last round of pastis ever.

The following day I decided to "study" a local farmer's family routine. As the man took me around his field, I realized that I knew nothing about farming, had no idea what was growing where or when. I looked pathetic, an urban boy trying too hard. I must have looked so depressed that he offered me a cup of coffee inside the farm to comfort me. His wife was making marmalade and welcomed me in. I was not trying to "study" anything any more; I was just there, relaxed and happy to be in such a quaint rural setting. I felt "at home," as if I were in my grandmother's kitchen. As soon as I started to feel this way, their behavior changed. I was not interviewing them anymore, and they were no longer in *representation* roles either. Rather, we were in a *conversation*, and this made a world of a difference.

We started an exchange about the marmalade: how she prepared it, what techniques, copper cauldron or not. On this subject, I had something to share because I had been raised in my grandmother's kitchen! The next thing I knew, I was leaving the farm with plenty of preserves of all sorts and studying culinary techniques and local food in this village.

If I tell this anecdote, it is because—for the first time—I touched something that never stopped growing in me ever since.

It was not about my good manners.

It was not about my academic knowledge.

It was not about my sense of observation.

It was definitely not yet about how to shoot or record it.

It was not even about my behavior per se.

It was much more about an emotional state of mind, about a way of "being there" and finding an angle to relate to these people that was genuine. This is what created the connection for the rest of the fieldwork to follow.

Since then and over the years, it has become obvious to me that I have *one real talent* that relies neither on my cinematographer's skills nor on my academic ethnographic background. Instead, it is in the quality and level of the connection I often succeed in establishing with people. When I "desire their desire," I am fully engaged, ready to hear them, and they respond in kind. In my work, I have found this much more useful and important than theoretical perfection.

Just because you have the "perfect" words for something doesn't mean you'll get the best interview. I have found that badly worded questions—especially in my adopted language of English—are not always a problem. What *is* a problem is if I am not listening to *their words* (compare with Briggs 1986). In fact, recent research has found that interactional rapport can actually be measured by how much people mirror one another's words and body language (Pentland 2008). When I "desire their desire," I use their words. I use their gestures. And they respond.

But furthermore, when I am in this state of "being there" and this seductive dimension is open, a sensuous state is created that also allows me to be more receptive to the whole array of the field itself. Those multiple flows of information, many of them absorbed subconsciously, can prove so elusive and difficult to describe with words alone. I have always found them easier to seize through the camera.

As Antonius Robben writes: "Ethnographic fieldwork is generally presented in a written text, even though people's sensory experience of the world reaches far beyond verbal or written expression. This literary bias has resulted in the ethnographic neglect of the senses and the privileging of writing over other means of representation such as photography, film and sound recordings" (Robben 1996:385).

THEORIZING "FIELD SEDUCTION"

Why do these connections occur on such a broad spectrum of varying degrees? Is it in what both the ethnographer and the respondent "read" as social clues, tastes, and statements? Is it purely a psychological phenomenon? As an ethnographic filmmaker, I am of course tempted to explain this mainly through the cultural filter, but I cannot deny the deeply psychological aspect of it.

Of course, in the end, it is both the cultural and the psychological that must be understood when examining these connections, or, more accurately, it is the psychological *within* the cultural that filters both how we "read" others and how others "read" us. Both individually and collectively we derive meaning from the quality of our connections to others, the strength of which need not be built on our similarities with them alone. Indeed, difference itself can be a strength of this connection. As George Simmel (1950) argues, "the stranger's" very strangeness is what makes it possible for people to share intimate details with him. Irrespective of our similarities or differences, we have various mechanisms for creating and maintaining connections, and these mechanisms are invariably brought to bear in deriving ethnographic insight.

For me, this phenomenon is similar to the seduction process, and by "seduction" I do not mean sexual seduction but rather the process of intense connection. Simmel, too, notes that "strangeness" breeds a certain eroticism:

> A trace of strangeness in this sense easily enters even the most intimate relationships. In the stage of first passion, erotic relations strongly reject any thought of generalization: the lovers think that there has never been a love like theirs; that nothing can be compared either to the person loved or to the feelings for that person (Simmel 1950:406).

This sudden, rapturous connection I create with my participants is similar to this "first passion," and indeed, it happens with total strangers.

In order for this connection to occur for me, for this "mojo" to do its magic, I must have this need to be attracted to the people with whom I am working. When the attraction is present, I seem instinctively to find infinite resources and energy to make them like me. I "desire their desire" in a psychological way.

I could get by with just their *attention*, but what I really need is people's *affection*! I often wonder if this is what other ethnographers experience: the need to be desired. Are there characteristics and personality traits that are common among our "breed" and set us apart?

I sharply remember, earlier in my life, being driven by the same need and trying pathetically to fit in at all cost. Some of this desire stems from being a cultural "misfit" and some from a psychological need. Of course the attempts I made to fit in required even more efforts in communities that were remote from my original *petit-bourgeois* provincial French one. I instinctively mirrored people and sometimes even adopted language accents or body language. This is precisely what retail workers have been shown to do to establish rapport with their customers (Gremler and Gwinner 2008). It is perhaps even an innate, unconscious behavior (Lakin and Chartrand 2003).

So there is an instinctual element to this process of getting closer, as well as a cultural *savoir-faire*. I am torn between two tendencies here: one to rationalize the mojo and the other to let go and keep doing it the way I have always done it, without trying too hard in case any deliberate efforts to harness it would make the magic vanish.

NOW, WHAT IS IT THAT "HAPPENS"?

As an ethnographer, it is normal to know and understand how to fit in, how to get accepted easily, and how to develop a natural empathy with people. It is difficult for me to imagine an ethnographer being solely an academic with little love for the field. However, in my case, sometimes the love is out of control! My teacher in urban studies, discovering my behavior during my research "field" in parts of the African community of Paris, told me: "*You are not integrated, you are assimilated!*" From her perspective, that was *not* a compliment; she was suggesting I lacked the necessary distance to conduct a more scientific and less impressionistic form of ethnography. She was, in fact, accusing me of "going native," but for me, this is a necessary danger of ethnography (compare with Bryman and Teevan 2005).

The emotional bond that people create with me is sometimes a bit disproportionate, particularly given the short period I often spend with them. Anyone with whom I work notices it, almost everywhere on the planet. People do not just invite me into their homes; they offer me their deepest emotional predisposition. They commonly tell me that it feels as if we have known each other for much longer than we actually have.

Yet, this bond can also get uncomfortable and even raises ethical questions. Anthropologists are and should be concerned that their goals do not compromise those of their participants (McCorkel and Myers 2003). Sometimes I feel as though I have taken advantage of what I have to call a "seduction technique": that in reaching this emotional level during an ethnographic encounter I may have involuntarily cheated the people I came across by leading them to believe this was an exceptional encounter.

Another danger is that, once initiated, my mojo does not end after I leave a family whose life I shared during research. It literally overflows. From my exchange with a taxi driver to the one with a customs officer, the magic carries on. People have few inhibitions in telling me about their personal lives, and make me share mine. I truly love this feeling, though it can be just plain exhausting!

The truth is that I have now reached a stage when I also feel the need to control this phenomenon. To understand how it works, where it comes from, and to pinpoint the elements behind it, whether they are psychological or cultural. I sometimes even wonder if it does not have to do with pheromones, but then people think that I may be a bit crazy. I do not blame them, but we should not deny these dimensions. "Seventy percent of the body's sense receptors cluster in the eyes," and smells also have a recognized influence (Ackerman 1991:230).

Since I have acknowledged that this "thing" might well be my best asset in the course of my work process, I have started to reflect on it, and what really intrigues me is to nail down how it works. I should state, of course, that it does not always work. The connection sometimes flops. Because it is a skill that has a strong impact on the quality of my work, you can understand why I wish I could just grasp it.

I wish I could turn it on and off. Modulate it. Control it. Guide it. And stop it.

But it does not work this way.

It is difficult to reproduce this magic on command. On the rare occasions when it does not work, I know, and can almost smell it instantly. When this happens, a certain level of professionalism—as well as human civility—kicks in and allows for the production of a reasonably good work. But it remains a mediocre moment. No spark, no confidence, no trust.

When it does work, it works well. The Wendy's research I mentioned earlier has been an exemplary study on all accounts, including—and starting with—the methodology.

We followed six families across the United States. There were four anthropologists simultaneously in the field: one in Phoenix, one in Queens, New York, one in Atlanta, and me in Lincoln, Nebraska. We did not use any recruiting companies. Rather, we chose to spend one week each in the field meeting with people in various places, randomly, as classic ethnographers would. Using a kind of snowballing sampling technique in which one individual led us to the next, we built our own "fresh" network of respondents. Predictably, the restaurants themselves were not the best places to recruit potential participants. Most people are in a hurry in these contexts. Plus, who wants to be disturbed on his lunch break? However, many other places where the "mood" led me were excellent "connectors." As I like to put it, in Lincoln, I literally went from the barbershop on Friday, to the topless bar on Saturday, to church on Sunday!

One of the teachers on Rouch's team would say, "*la dilettante paye!*" ("being a dabbler pays!"). Sure enough, wherever I went I interviewed people, I took notes, and I shared them daily on our research blog used by the client and the other research team members (who were following the same process in their respective regions). In Lincoln, this snowballing method was so successful that after a week of research, in a place where I arrived with zero connections, I reached a point where I was invited for brunch in one household with 15 people that gathered just to meet and exchange with me on the topic of food in their lives and what it meant there.

I also got the chance to select the family I later filmed as most representative of our findings. Or rather, I let the respondents "find me." Because this family fit our criteria *and* the right chemistry existed between us, the film about them was the most successful of the series of six films created for the project. Families in the other films were chosen by other ethnographers, and although the results were good, it took me longer to establish a similar rapport with those families, and our connections never reached the level of the one I developed with the family that "chose me." In the end, whereas the films featuring the participants selected in a traditional way are 10 to 20 minutes long, the one set in Lincoln is 40 minutes.

The remarkable thing is, just because you know about the very things that constitute whatever makes human relations intimate doesn't mean that you can readily and successfully apply this knowledge. Nor can you compensate if you do not *also* have the "gift" or, I would say, the "need" for it.

THE MOJO'S EXPONENTIAL & VOLATILE FACTORS

This phenomenon is "exponential." It also can crash suddenly.

I am never better at connecting with others than when I am starving for it. So staying isolated and locked in my editing room for weeks is the best way to recharge my "connective thirst"! Similarly, everything that contributes to set me into a good mood—where I am open to others and want to dive into life—will contribute to the quality of the rapport I will be able to establish. Moreover, it will "snowball." A person I meet on the train on my way to an interview, or a bit of happy chitchat: these things send me at a good speed that will only keep increasing and amplifying as I meet more people throughout the day. Conversely, a hostile encounter has a dulling effect; it will take a while to bring dynamics with others back to full speed again.

There is one example I recall vividly. In Europe to start a long shooting session that would take me to Africa, then Asia, my first stop was Brussels. As many of us do too often, whether we acknowledge it or not, I like to play the game of reducing places to a couple of clichés, at least initially, before letting myself be submerged in the complexity that always ensues. Music is an important part of my life, and so I reduced Brussels to the place from which some of my favorite singers come: Jacques Brel, Dick Annegarn, Arno, and many others.

Arno is a famous Flemish character that has a kind of a Tom Waits feel to his voice and, in addition to his immense talent, he is famous for his stutter and his heavy drinking! I arrived in Brussels jetlagged but deeply moved to be back in my old Europe after many years in North America. My local assistant set me up in my hotel and recommended a bar where I could go hang out after dinner. A couple of hours later, as I sat down in this small jazz bar that was obviously made for local regulars, who did I see right in front of me? Arno!

The little star-struck boy in me woke up immediately, all shaken and impressed by the surreal, dreamlike moment. It was like going to New York City for the first time as a Parisian and seeing Lou Reed in the first joint you walk into. I hesitated, then mustered the courage to sit next to him, shamelessly pretending that I did not recognize him. His reaction? It still haunts me to this day. Furiously annoyed and dismissive, he slurred: "WHY? AREN'T THERE ANY OTHER SEATS AVAILABLE??"

Mortified, I went to sit as far from him as I could; I probably chain-smoked a pack of Belga and gobbled down more than a couple Ti' Punch Rum shots. Me, the man who prides himself as being The Great Connector, desiring to be desired, was completely shot down. When I had the chance to meet one of my all-time favorite artists, a simple man that I very much relate to, I was incapable of unlocking that "click."

This event was unrelated to the purpose of my travels, yet it had drastic consequences on my work for at least a week. I had lost my trust in being able to do it. I thought I didn't have it anymore. It had been slapped cold and killed instantaneously, thus making me feel insecure, undesirable, fragile, and obviously not well intentioned or lovable. Arno had totally destabilized me, and my mojo—my precious mojo—had crashed!

I had to climb, painfully, up the ladder of connectivity again.

My intense "desire to be desired" may not be a widespread trait among ethnographers. But I believe that we all know this feeling, this phenomenon, on some level: that this magic is an elixir of our craft. Consider your own "desire to be desired" next time you are in the field. Turn it on, or off, and see what happens. Your own ethnographic mojo may very well appear.

REFERENCES

Ackerman, Diane. 1991. *A Natural History of the Senses.* New York: Knopf Doubleday Publishing Group.

Agafonoff, Nick. 2006. "Adapting Ethnographic Research Methods to ad hoc Commercial Market Research." *Qualitative Market Research: An International Journal* 9(2):115–25. doi:10.1108/13522750610658766.

Briggs, Jean L. 1970. *Never in Anger: Portrait of An Eskimo Family.* Boston, MA: Harvard University Press.

Bryman, Alan, and James Teevan. 2005. *Social Research Methods: Canadian Edition.* Don Mills, Canada: Oxford University Press.

Gremler, Dwayne D., and Kevin P. Gwinner. 2008. "Rapport-Building Behaviors Used by Retail Employees." *Journal of Retailing* 84(3):308–24. doi:10.1016/j.jretai.2008.07.001.

Kondo, Dorrine. K. 1986. *Dissolution and Reconstitution of Self: Implications for Anthropological Epistemology.* Cultural Anthropology 1(1):74–88.

Kulick, Don, and M. Wilson. 1995. *Taboo: Sex, Identity and Erotic Subjectivity in Anthropological Fieldwork.* London: Routledge.

Lakin, Jessica L., and Tanya L. Chartrand. 2003. "Using Nonconscious Behavioral Mimicry To Create Affiliation and Rapport." *Psychological Science* 14:334–39. http://www.ncbi.nlm.nih.gov/pubmed/12807406.

Leibovitz, A. 2008. *Annie Leibovitz at Work.* New York: Random House.

Malinowski, Bronislaw. 1922. "Introduction: The Subject, Method and Scope of This Inquiry." In *Argonauts of the Western Pacific: An Account of Native Enterprise and Adventure in the Archipelagoes of Melanesian New Guinea*, edited by B. Malinowski, 1–25. London: Routledge.

_____. 1967. *A Diary in the Strict Sense of the Term.* Stanford, CA: Stanford University Press.

McCorkel, Jill, and Kristen Myers. 2003. "What Difference Does Difference Make? Position and Privilege in the Field." *Qualitative Sociology* 26(2):199–231.

Pentland, Alex. 2008. *Honest Signals: How They Shape Our World.* Cambridge, MA: MIT Press.

Rabinow, Paul. 1977. *Reflections on Fieldwork in Morocco.* Berkeley, Los Angeles: University of California Press.

Robben, Antonius C. G. M. 1996. "Ethnographic Seduction, Transparence and Resistance in Dialogues about Terror and Violence in Argentina." *Ethos* 24(1):71–106.

Simmel, Georg. 1950. "The Stranger." In *The Sociology of Georg Simmel*, edited by Kurt H. Wolff, 402–8. New York: Free Press.

Sluka, Jeffery A. 2006. *Fieldwork Relations and Rapport in Ethnographic Fieldwork: An Anthropological Reader.* Oxford, UK: Blackwell Publishing.

Wagley, Charles. 1960. *Champukwi of the Village of the Tapirs.* New York: Harper and Row.

FURTHER READING

Altork, K. 1995. "Walking the Fire Line: The Erotic Dimension of the Fieldwork Experience." In *Taboo: Sex, Identity and Erotic Subjectivity in Anthropological Fieldwork*, edited by Don Kulick and Margaret Willson, 107–39. London: Routledge.

Barley, Nigel. 1983. *Adventures in a Mud Hut: An Innocent Anthropologist Abroad.* New York: Vanguard Press.

Berreman, G. D. 1972. *Prologue: Behind Many Masks: Ethnography and Impression Management.* Berkeley, Los Angeles: University of California Press.

Bowen, E. S. 1964. *Return to Laughter: An Anthropological Novel.* Norwell, MA: Anchor Press.

Collier, J., and M. C. Collier 1986. *Visual Anthropology: Photography As a Research Method.* Albuquerque: University of New Mexico Press.

Dwyer, Kevin. 1982. *Moroccan Dialogues: Anthropology in Question.* Baltimore, MD: Johns Hopkins University Press.

Lorde, A. 1978. *Uses of the Erotic: The Erotic as Power.* Freedom, CA: The Crossing Press.

McCracken, Grant. 1988. *The Long Interview.* London: Sage Publications.

Newton, Esther. 2000. *Margaret Mead Made Me Gay: Personal Essays, Public Ideas.* Durham, NC: Duke University Press.

Powdermaker, Hortense. 1967. *Stranger and Friend: The Way of an Anthropologist.* London: Secker and Warburg.

Spradley, J. 1979. *The Ethnographic Interview.* New York: Holt, Rinehart and Winston.

Stoller, P and C. Olkes. 1989. *The Tastes of Ethnographic Things: The Senses in Anthropology.* Philadelphia: University of Pennsylvania Press.

van Maanen, J. 1988. *Tales of the Field: On Writing Ethnography.* Chicago, IL: University of Chicago Press.

Wengle, J. L. 2011. *Ethnographers In The Field. The Psychology of Research.* Tuscaloosa: The University of Alabama Press.

Whitney, A. 2012. "The Secret Subject: Michel Foucault, Death and The Labyrinth, and The Interview as Genre." *Criticism* 54(4):567–81.

Whitehead T. L., and L. E. Conaway. 1986. *Self, Sex, and Gender in Cross-Cultural Fieldwork.* Champaign: University of Illinois Press.

NOTES

I would like to acknowledge Sam Ladner and Charley Scull for their help on an earlier version of this chapter.

1 www.mondemoderne.com/films/wendys.htm.

2 An excerpt from this production is on Vimeo (vimeo.com/49798966).

3 An excerpt in French is also on Vimeo (vimeo.com/55985965).

42

Applied Netnography: An Appropriate Appropriation?

ROBERT V. KOZINETS

THE SITUATION'S GRAVITY

Everything, it seems, has a drift. Ideas, it would seem—if you get my drift—also have their own gravity. For more than 10 years now, I have not only been pondering the interrelation of the commercial and the communal in the sphere of academic research, I have actually been observing it up close. Close as in microscope close. Close as in part of the phenomenon itself close.

In 1995, I was a PhD student at Queen's University in Kingston, Ontario. I had begun working on a dissertation about the marketing implications of media fan communities, particularly those in the *Star Trek* fan community. After some very interesting exposure to the method of ethnography by the evangelical organizational behavior professor John Dowling, I felt it would offer me the best means to study these communities and their combined commitment to the show, its brands, and one another.

Ethnography, as most of the readers of this volume readily recognize, is a technique that has been deployed for cultural understanding. In one particular incarnation or another, ethnography has been used by social scientists, or perhaps more accurately social scholars, for 2,300 years or more, since the time of Herodotus of Halicarnassus at least. Ethnography grounds research in the complexly combined act of participating-while-observing, spurring the researcher to personally assume positions of cultural encounter and communal experience before attempting the tricky work of analyzing, understanding, and cogently explaining cultural practices, embedded objects, symbol systems, and practices.

As I gained membership in the fan groups I was studying, I gathered data on where the community was communicating. Lo and behold, I heard several times that the "real action"—as in the really juicy, detailed, content-rich, and

Handbook of Anthropology in Business, edited by Rita Denny and Patricia Sunderland, 775–786.

emotionally involving discussions and debates—were increasingly occurring online. At that time, in 1995 and 1996, very few of the people I knew were online. The World Wide Web and the browser (Netscape's Mosaic) were brand-new, highly risky, and charged with geekier-than-geeky cultural connotations. Intransigently unwilling since childhood to be left out of important social gatherings, I was already one of these pioneers, using a private service called CompuServe to access the wonders of bulletin boards, chatrooms, and even the playspaces of multiuser "dungeons." The Trek fans pointed me in the direction of their favorite server, Prodigy. Finding these services, and exploring the early internet with miraculous but maddeningly slow service, I felt a little bit like Howard Carter opening the tomb in the Valley of the Kings. What I found was a vast treasure of consumer data with what seemed to me to be profound implications for business and marketing: and for society itself.

Immediately, I realized that I was ill equipped for the task at hand. Embarrassingly so. I was, to come clean, barely an ethnographer at that point. I was an MBA student taking a PhD in marketing, studying science fiction media fans by going to fan club meetings and conventions, taking photographs, and talking to himself into a tape recorder. What I knew about anthropology I had learned almost entirely from an undergraduate class, journal articles, heaps of books, and a few meetings with anthropologists. My audodidactic addiction.

And Houston, there was another problem when I tried to adopt the tried-and-true ethnographic approaches used by Herodotus for this new and technologically mediated world. It seems notionally clear that online communications are just another form of communication. But because they are textual, visual, dynamic, hyperlinked, and complex, online communications are granted a spacelike quality, captured and magnified by science fiction seer William Gibson's coining of the influential term "cyberspace."

UNDERSTANDING CYBERSPACE

Online communications are not simply an extension of the cultural communications of people's everyday lifeworlds, but also an augmentation that transforms and is transformed by the transmission in particular ways. The online environment mediates messages, allows archiving, accommodates accessibility, and optionally permits pseudonymity or even anonymity (Kozinets 2010). These characteristics mean that the social world of *Star Trek* fans that I access and analyze from my computer screen is quite different from the one that I reach by, for instance, sitting in a Burger King with a group of fans after a club meeting, even if the exact same people are participating in the conversation.

Those are challenges that need to be carefully accounted for by specific research procedures. I developed netnography to do so, systematically and with a degree of rigor. Methodologically, my work has focused and adjusted the research approach for this impending alteration in the way people socialize (at least it seemed impending to me).

Thus was netnography originated, necessity being ever the motivator of invention. Netnography is a qualitative, interpretive research methodology that adapts the traditional ethnographic techniques of anthropology and applies them to the study of social media. Netnography is about depth, not necessarily about breadth. Netnography is not interested in counts or representativeness: quantities are best left to other techniques. Netnography adds specific practices to those traditional techniques that include locating communities and topics, narrowing data, handling large digital datasets, analyzing digitally contextualized data, and navigating difficult online ethical matters and research procedures. Because the online context alters so many aspects of the research experience, the nature of researcher immersion and ethnographic (or "netnographic") participation are also treated rigorously within netnography

It thus constitutes a specific set of related ethnographic, data analysis, ethical, and representational practices. Those practices are performed in relation to the freely shared social and cultural matter that people communicate over the internet. Netnography offers a less-intrusive approach even than ethnography. It is certainly more naturalistic than surveys, experiments, focus groups, and personal interviews. It is also much less costly and timelier than many other methods. Its focus is penetrating cultural analysis.

Like so many things, it was invented during a precarious balancing on the shoulders of titans. I scoured anthropology and sociology for information and elaboration of other researchers who were undertaking work in the area. There were a number of very interesting psychological studies that I drew on, such as the work by Joseph Walther. In anthropology I found that surprisingly little had been written, although I was inspired by some of the conceptual work of Arturo Escobar. The real action was happening inside of cultural studies, with the work of pioneers like Nancy Baym, Annette Markham, and Henry Jenkins. These developments, as well as the gaps I found in this literature, would continue to play a part in the present and future of netnography.

That new designation, a portmanteau smashing together "internet" and "ethnography," helped to clarify the distinct approach, because although some scholars had been engaging ethnographically with the internet at that time, the particular techniques they used and the rationale for using them remained obscure. So it was that, with considerable encouragement from a supportive community of scholarly peers, I continued to develop the technique. Throughout this scholarly development, however, there had been another, shadow development slowly percolating, equally important but underexposed. This was the growing interest of business in netnography.

THE INTERESTS OF BUSINESS

I am unsure of the exact origins of the interest of business in netnography. While working on my dissertation in 1996, I fielded a call from California to discuss the marketing of the new *Star Trek* movie with a Paramount executive. I remember some interest in the findings of my netnography and in the technique itself. I also remember briefly overviewing and presenting netnography to a gathering of broadcast industry executives in San Francisco in 2000 at the National Association of Broadcasters annual meeting. One of my students, a trademark lawyer by trade, suggested that I trademark the term "netnography" so as not to lose control of its use. In fact, I began teaching netnography to business school students almost as soon as I began teaching, in 1997. It was certainly in the business school classroom that the practical advantages of netnography started to become apparent. But, in terms of actual companies wanting to use netnography, not much really happened for a long time. Relatively speaking, not much is happening even today. The dot-com boom came, and then the dot-com bubble burst. For the most part, managers and researchers quickly lost interest in most aspects of the internet, certainly in the weird science of "online communities." Why should they care? Online communities would languish in the back alleys of newsgroups and chat rooms for at least seven more years, until the rise of Facebook and Twitter.

In 2003, Harvard Professor John Deighton was leading a Marketing Science Institute conference in Toronto. He invited me to come and talk about netnography to a group of practitioners and academics. I gave a talk called "Netnography: Online Anthropology for a Digital Age," which was fairly similar to talks that I still give about netnography in a variety of places. The big difference, in fact, between the presentations that I used to give about netnography and the ones I do now is that I do not have to explain: (1) what online communities/social media are, and (2) why online communities and social media have important implications for business and marketing. In those pre-Facebook and -Twitter days, when blogs were the "new new" thing, the ability of the internet to do anything for business beyond e-commerce was seriously in doubt. Even e-commerce was viewed as being a bit sketchy. So my presentation used my research on coffee connoisseurs online to show how consumers influence each other's purchase decisions and even create their own online cultures.

At that conference, there were two businesspeople who became my first two clients. One was in the pharmaceutical industry, and later hired me to do some fascinating netnography about the implications of social media to their business. The other was Bob Woodard, VP of Global Consumer and Customer Insights at Campbell Soup. A little later, Bob invited me to speak at Campbell Soup's Global Insights Summit the next year. A little while after the conference,

Bob invited me to write a more applied article about netnography for the *Journal of Advertising Research* (Kozinets 2006). A while after that, I began working with some of the Marketing Insights team at Campbell Soup to investigate how and why people swap recipes and soup stories, analyzing how these experiences fit into their daily lives, and trying to help orchestrate online experiences that were coordinated with these processes and motivations.

For the Campbell Soup project, netnography seemed uniquely suitable. The people at Campbell had a website where consumers could go to share recipes, but the site was simply not performing as desired. I suggested netnography be deployed to fully understand the consumer experience of the site and the needs underlying it. As a participant-observer in that space, I became a denizen of the online social world of recipe and meal-planning sites. The related definition of this new social space was critical, as it led me to first define and then sniff out the best sites. It turned out that a range of factors contributed towards the feeling of online *communitas*, and that a number of these factors could fall under management control. Following are a few details about the Campbell Soup study, drawn directly from an article on netnography in the *MIT Technology Review* (Kozinets 2011a):

> The studies my colleagues and I designed and carried out at Campbell looked at the "natural environment" of the online world. But our work didn't stop at the company's social-media efforts; it involved a detailed look at a vast range of interactions going on around meal planning and recipe sharing. We sought out and studied competitive companies and their efforts. We located and listened to bloggers. We checked out forums and newsgroups. We examined video blogs on YouTube and beyond. We came up with statements about brand impact, best practices, missed opportunities, failed efforts, and key trends. The results gave Campbell a set of powerful recommendations that helped the company create a responsive new version of the site. Unique monthly visitors shot up from 120,000 before the main relaunch in October 2008 to more than one million by January 2009, according to QuantCast. The number, emotional depth, and topical breadth of interactions increased. The company was able to build its brands into meal-planning routines, creating online features such as "tips for busy cooks," "portion control," and "search by mood" (for example, users can search for recipes described as "hearty" or "comforting"). There was a new, family-like feel to the redesigned Campbell's Kitchen, a strong sense that this was a helpful, responsive place to visit.

The netnography had revealed to managers the delicate balancing act and interests of community management in a way that was vivid, pictorial, emotional, visceral, current, and real. It exposed the Campbell brand in all of its strength and weakness. It gave designers and managers a range of practical suggestions for implementation to increase community participation and loyalty. Although it was qualitative in focus, its implementation had measurable results. It was, in short, some very early applied research conceptualizing and applying notions of social media engagement, and as such it was powerful, successful management research. As recounted here, Campbell acted on it, redesigned the website, and the results were dramatic and desirable (see Kozinets 2011a). Shortly afterward, I began an international innovation project for American Express that also yielded some fascinating new ideas that fed international finance product innovation and expansion. Other clients followed.

Working together with my firm, Netnografica, my clients and I found a range of different applications for netnography. Netnography could be used to let the voices and stories of the consumer drive innovation processes in companies, such as allowing a bank to offer new products along the lines suggested by its most devoted customers. Netnography could be applied to a detailed unpacking of brand meaning that proved useful to positioning and repositioning. For example, it was used to develop a consumer-inspired advertising campaign to market a classic, but somewhat "worn out" consumer brand, the mouthwash Listerine (see Kozinets 2011b). Consistently, netnography helped reveal the complex cultural terrain whose understanding permits a more realistic mapping of online marketspaces.

Consider how a pharmaceutical company might need to understand the dynamics and complex space of health care treatment in the age of the internet (another consulting project I was fortunate to work on and successfully complete). With deep attention to language, symbol, and image, netnography helped translate cultural codes. For example, an automobile manufacturer might want to understand how the cultural understanding of the nature of driving and cars have changed in the era of "hybridness" and "electric carness." And on practical, tactical levels, netnography helped reveal the powerful and influential players in a given community or culture, the sites they frequent and follow, and also inform about their strategies and motivation. Could netnography be used to reveal something as mundane and taken for granted as deodorant? I had been asked this question for almost a decade. Bilgram et al. (2011) show how a netnographic approach was used to help Beiersdorf discover and then deliver a successful new Nivea product in a new market position in the mature and competitive deodorant marketplace. A coauthored academic study I did with Matchstick and Nokia revealed the complex way that word-of-mouth marketing campaigns were transformed by the "dual role" of the consumer-messenger and offered numerous suggestions for more effective implementation of word-of-mouth marketing and social media marketing campaigns (Kozinets et al. 2010).

These practical studies and applications fascinated me. At the same time, several other things were occurring. Around 2007, Michael Osofsky, a brilliant Silicon Valley entrepreneur, somehow found me, and we began corresponding. At the time, Michael had created a firm called Accelovation, which was geared at using social media information to help companies accelerate their innovation processes. I was impressed with the idea, and Michael wanted to see the connections between netnography and the social search tool he was building and marketing.

GROWTH & DEVELOPMENT

With the exception of Christine Hine's (2000) "virtual ethnography," there was rather limited development of any methodological alternative to netnography (Bengry-Howell et al. 2011; Kozinets 2012). Hine (2000) conceptualized "virtual" ethnography, described her procedures as a necessarily partial type of ethnography, and illustrated them without methodological proscription.

The alternative to netnography, it seems, was a "default mode" of online ethnography, the conduct of ethnography online without lucid specification of procedures or standards. Although various other names were used and proposed, such as digital ethnography and webnography, these labels appeared without coherent statements of their difference from either a generic laissez-faire "do what you like" approach to online ethnography or the more specific procedures of netnography (see Caliandro, this volume). In terms of development of the method, there have been some interesting and growing efforts. For example, Langer and Beckman (2005) asserted that looser ethical standards would be desirable for netnographic inquiry. Rokka (2010) explored the relationship between netnography and the notion of a translocal site of the social. Belz and Bumbauch (2010) developed netnography as a form of lead user analysis. Bilgram et al. (2011) contributed to this ongoing discussion by showing how netnography was useful in sourcing ideas for corporate innovation. And Kozinets (2010) intended to broaden the appeal and use of netnography to others outside of the marketing field by carefully delineating pragmatic research approaches to the real challenges of online ethnographic research: locating communities and topics, narrowing data, handling large digital datasets, researcher immersion and participation, and navigating difficult online ethical matters and research procedures. The role for netnography as a discipline has been to offer specific practices to ensure comparability and rigor across varieties of research.

As blogs, then microblogs, and then the social networking sites of Facebook, Twitter, Foursquare, Pinterest, Instagram, and others attained greater popularity, advertising and marketing attention and dollars began to flow into social media. Marketing and consumer research scholars in Holland, the United

Kingdom, France, Norway, Germany, Turkey, and Brazil began at various points to take notice (some, like Kristine de Valck, Cele Otnes, Michelle Nelson, Janice Denegri-Knott, Pauline Maclaran, Margaret Hogg, Miriam Caterrall, Stephen Brown, and Markus Giesler, were early entrants) and to build the base of netnography beyond the United States and Canada. Netnographies began to appear in every marketing and consumer research journal. Dissertations used netnography. Netnography is also spreading to other fields, broadening from management studies to education, sociology, gaming studies, urban geography, nursing and health care, cultural studies, and anthropology (Bengry-Howell et al. 2011; Kozinets 2012).

Meanwhile, in Germany, an ambitious young professor by the name of Johann Füller began introducing netnographies to the professional market. His company, Hyve, was promoting and selling professional netnographies. Like Michael Osofsky, his primary positioning for the approach was as a means to gather community insights to help companies innovate. According to his brochure, "innovation leaders like Adidas, Beiersdorf, Gore, Hubert Burda Media, Miele, and Swisscom used the NetnographyInsights© method to promote innovation in the areas of sport, water treatment, personal care/cosmetics, media, cooking/food, and telecommunication. HYVE successfully utilizes this method within the consumer goods area as well as in the industrial goods sector." This was all news—exciting news—to me. Johann later invited me to visit Hyve in Germany, and his firm also organized a conference devoted to netnography called Netnography08. The conference had as one of its mandates to spread information through industry on the usefulness of the technique.

THE CALL OF THE QUANT

Historical drift is the notion that organizations and institutions, and perhaps even ideas and approaches, have a tendency to drift away from their original intention and focus.

That sense of drift has been following netnography for a while. Practically for as long as it has been adopted beyond my own work, a drift in both academia and in the world of marketing research and practice has been apparent to me.

In fact, it is not really a drift. It is a gravitational pull. Perhaps a tug at first, but now it feels a bit like a tractor beam.

When I developed netnography for publication in the *Journal of Marketing Research*, I included a section where I counted how long I had spent on the netnography, how many posts I had viewed and used in the analysis, and how many unique user names were included in these postings. This seemed to me to be sensible, but it began a slow march towards the quantification of netnography's qualitative data that is the essence of this gravitational pull. I now regard it as an error in judgment, an early and ultimately confusing compromise that should not have been made.

I felt and still feel this pull when I negotiated sample sizes and sampling strategies with clients. I see this pull when I look at corporate netnographic analyses, which are often full of counts and quantities. I experience it in my use of social search engines, many of which conveniently quantify a range of social media data. Social search companies such as Radian6, Sysomos, Lithium, and AC Nielsen BuzzMetrics are based upon data-mining of the linguistic/textual elements of online conversations, natural language processing of their content, automatic coding, and provision of reports to corporations and managers. Much of this information has been used to provide a real-time, real-world "monitoring" of brand and product-related topics and sentiments on the internet. Even more impressively, it has been used to build a variety of different "marketing dashboards" that allegedly allows managers to see a highly abstracted and quantified version of what is being said in social media.

The institution of business, it seems to me, is based upon quantification. Numbers objectify and solidify. They reveal big picture patterns. They are scientific. And above all, perhaps, they allow mathematical manipulation that can result in prediction and control. Numbers help managers to manage. Money is the ultimate number. And all numbers can be marshaled to help better manage those all-important financial numbers.

But as necessary and useful as they no doubt often are, numbers are not what netnography is about. As I describe it in this chapter, netnography is focused on cultural insights, which cannot be described quantitatively. As delightful and tempting as quantification can be, it is not netnography's forte, and in fact, netnography performed properly deliberately draws the attention away from the realm of quantification. Would a word cloud, a pie chart, or a bar graph of word counts and adjectives from Abraham Lincoln's biography be sufficient to understand this great man? Then why we would find it sufficient to understand the lives and voices of hundred or thousands of our consumers? Word clouds, like all clouds, obscure the light, which in this case is composed of the brilliant stories that consumers shared with one another to illuminate their experiences and their lives.

NETNOGRAPHY & CULTURAL UNDERSTANDING

Netnography was designed from the beginning as a way to gain, enhance, and continuously deepen cultural understanding. From the standpoint of our everyday sense of understanding one another, of our general sense of meaning as we move through our lives (other than our quantified work-life), culture is, quite simply, everything. If we do not understand a language, words are simply gobbledygook. If we do not grasp the rules of a culture, we are helpless, useless, weird, an idiot. Small children laugh at us for mistakes we do not even comprehend. Misunderstanding culture is pathetic.

In the world of consumption, it works the same, as Sidney Levy, Grant McCracken, Russell Belk, Dennis Rook, and many of the contributors to this book have all spent careers emphasizing. To investigate consumers and consumption in this way is to understand consumption's role as a source of power, meaning, education, ritual, and practice; as natural, special, and profound in context. Cultural insights sit on these foundations of understanding.

A trained cultural analyst will treat every utterance and object of consumption as an artifact that speaks a language. Every rite revolving around a consumption activity is a message to be decrypted, a gibberish to be translated into sense. Online, this means that colors, fonts, textures, photographs, images, sounds, audio, video, and every other aspect of shared files become important revelators of data.

Moreover, cultural understanding inheres in a strange way in human understanding. Moments of genuine and inspirational understanding are rarely based on matters of fact. They emerge instead most naturally through stories and images that craft narratives. Understanding is an act of imagination at least as much as of information. Consumer ethnography is insight-generation that locates itself in the interstitial space between thought, observation, action, participation, and representation.

With consumption increasingly happening and being influenced by mobile communications and distributed internet access, consumer insights must increasingly turn to them to understand the changing reality of contemporary consumers. Social media as a cultural space is growing and changing. Alongside it, consumer culture itself is dynamic, expansive, multifarious, and global. Contexts are critical. Networks are critical. Meanings are critical.

ESCAPING GRAVITY

In our current time, netnography is still a largely unknown approach. In a world where few ethnographies are conducted by those in business or by business academics, it should be no surprise that even fewer netnographies are performed. However, from this small base, some growth is occurring. A number of private firm have begun to offer netnographies. For the most part, these seem to involve various types of social search and marketing dashboard types of output. Quantification persists. But I am hopeful.

Institutional theorists call this sort of gravitation pull towards the regulative systems, cognitive forms, and normative arrangements of an industry or institution "mimetic isomorphism." Essentially, this theory suggests that an idea like netnography would be altered by various practitioners to be more like existing offerings, to quantify its findings, to abstract and totalize, to reduce rich and varied cultural context to universalized content, to speak the current language of quantification, and to offer managers prediction and control rather than human understanding. The reasons for quantification are rather simple. Quantification simplifies the complex. If I throw a party and simply want to know how many people are at the party, perhaps so that I can serve them food, this is an achievable and fairly simple goal. However, if I want to construct a party with the right dynamics, the right "feel," to make it a memorable occasion where people will make new friends, perhaps even meet the love of their life: that is a much taller order. At that point, I need to start understanding the qualities of people, their differences, and how their differences fit together. It becomes a much more tender and probabilistic venture, this creating of complex social experiences. It requires that we understand and balance and predict with a large number of qualities. It is far riskier, far less certain, but the rewards can be much more profound.

There will always be a niche for genuine insight. It is likely the highest bar, the highest level to which marketing research and business acumen can strive. But it is more than just good business to appreciate a need for human understanding. It is actually life-affirming.

Netnography can be a channel, then, to deeper understanding and to business creativity. At the very core of understanding and innovation is the common need to be able to look into the world and truly see, truly hear, and deeply sniff the complex, rich mélange of culture, content, context, and consumption that is the social lifeworld of marketing.

With energy and imagination, the little applied miracles that make us most human, gravity can be overcome.

REFERENCES

Belz, Frank-Martin, and Wenke Baumbach. 2010. "Netnography As a Method of Lead User Identification." *Creativity and Innovation Management* 19(3):304–13.

Bengry-Howell, A., R. Wiles, M. Nind, and G. Crow. 2011. "A Review of the Academic Impact of Three Methodological Innovations: Netnography, Child-Led Research and Creative Research Methods" [research paper]. National Centre for Research Methods Hub, University of Southampton.

Bilgram, Volker, Michael Bartl, and Stefan Biel. 2011. "Getting Closer to the Consumer: How Nivea Co-Creates New Products." *Marketing Review St. Gallen* 28(1):34–40.

Hine, Christine. 2000. *Virtual Ethnography*. London: Sage.

Kozinets, Robert V. 2006. "Click To Connect: Netnography and Tribal Advertising." *Journal of Advertising Research* 46:279–88.

______. 2010. *Netnography: Doing Ethnographic Research Online*. London: Sage.

Kozinets, Robert V. 2011a. "Netnography: The Marketer's Secret Ingredient." *MIT Technology Review* October 14. http://www.technologyreview.com/business/26434/.

_____. 2011b. "Netnography: The Marketer's Secret Weapon." White paper distributed by Netbase corporation. http://info.netbase.com/rs/netbase/images/Netnography_WP.pdf.

_____. 2012. "Marketing Netnography: Prom/ot(ulgat)ing a New Research Method." *Methodological Innovations Online (MIO)* 7:37–45. http://www.pbs.plym. ac.uk/mi/index.html.

Kozinets, Robert V., Kristine de Valck, Andrea Wojnicki, and Sarah Wilner. 2010. "Networked Narratives: Understanding Word-of-Mouth Marketing in Online Communities." *Journal of Marketing* 74:71–89.

Langer, Roy, and Suzanne C. Beckman. 2005. "Sensitive Research Topics: Netnography Revisited." *Qualitative Market Research: An International Journal* 8(2):189–203.

Rokka, Joonas. 2010. "Netnographic Inquiry and New Translocal Sites of the Social." *International Journal of Consumer Studies* 34(4):381–7.

43

Applied Cultural Analysis: Ethnography as Compositional Practice

TOM O'DELL & ROBERT WILLIM

Folke sits on a two-meter-high chair in the corner of a Norwegian man's kitchen, observing, taking notes, and drawing up diagrams. Both he and the man he studies have been given clear instructions: the observer must be allowed to come and go as he pleases, must not be spoken to, and must never be included in the daily chores or routines of the people he is supposed to be studying. But things don't go as planned.

Isak, the elderly man Folke is supposed to observe, has a change of heart. Regretting his choice to volunteer for the project, he refuses to allow Folke into his home, and only after several days of patiently waiting outside does Folke gain entry. Then, after a few days of being observed, Isak secretively turns the tables on his observer, and drills a hole in the ceiling just above Folke's chair. From his bedroom closet on the second floor Isak can now peer through the hole and watch what Folke is reading, writing, and drawing in his notebooks. Isak even goes so far as to begin sketching diagrams (in Folke's own diary and without his knowledge) of Folke's movements in the kitchen. And while Folke is not aware of all the activities going on around him, he is sure of one thing: things aren't going very well. Very slowly the relationship between the two men begins to thaw, and despite clear instructions, they do begin to speak to one another.

Elsewhere in the village another researcher, Folke's colleague Green, has gone so far as to begin drinking with his "study object." Late one night, having run out of alcohol, Green comes to Folke to "borrow" a bottle or two. Folke reprimands him, and Green replies:

> **Green:** Not allowed to drink. Not allowed to talk. Shit, Folke, what the hell are we doing? We sit up there on our pedestals and think that we understand everything. How can we think that we can understand anything about

Handbook of Anthropology in Business, edited by Rita Denny and Patricia Sunderland, 787–799.

> people simply by observing them? . . . We have to talk to each other. People have to communicate . . .
>
> **Folke:** Our research is based upon a positivistic approach.
>
> **Green:** Positivistic? I've decided to quit. That's the most positivistic thing I can do.

Green turns and stumbles away into the dark. Feeling slightly bad, and sorry for Green, Folke shouts out into the night, "I've talked too! I've talked to my host too!"

This is a scene from the film *Kitchen Stories*, inspired by the work of the Swedish Home Research Institute, which focused from 1944 to 1957 on the study of women's routines in the kitchen with the goal of rationalizing those kitchens and the activities of the women in them. Folke and 10 colleagues have been assigned to Norway to study the way in which single men use their kitchens, and *Kitchen Stories* is a warm, humorous film about the relationship between two very different men from two different Scandinavian countries. For ethnographers interested in applied cultural research, however, the film addresses a number of issues that are continuously being discussed. These include the manner in which scholars influence the fields they study, stand in relation to the people and phenomena that they observe, and indeed are observed and under the scrutiny of those they study. But beyond this, it is also a reminder of one of the few early arenas in which applied social or cultural research was conducted in the Swedish context.

As it turns out, applied forms of cultural analysis have a rather shallow history in Scandinavia in general, and in Sweden more specifically. Sure, scholars such as the Myrdals gained international recognition for their work, but they were more the exception than the rule. And when applied research was conducted, it tended to be quantitatively oriented, fixated with the activity of experts measuring, graphing, and counting their object of study. This is perhaps not so surprising in light of the fact that over the course of the twentieth century engineers were the people who were generally considered the "experts" capable of solving the nation's problems, and so when researchers from the social sciences were enlisted to alleviate social and urban problems, their work tended to follow that of their peers from the schools of engineering and natural sciences, taking a highly positivistic and quantitative approach.

In recent years, however, the situation has begun to change, and new forms of applied cultural research are taking the stage. In this chapter, we describe the development of a new field of study, applied cultural analysis, which is expanding in Sweden and other parts of Scandinavia. As part of this process, we (the authors) are working to reframe ethnography as a compositional process; the second section of this chapter explains what this entails. We conclude with some examples of teaching and rendering ethnography as a compositional practice.

MOVING TOWARD THE REALM OF THE APPLIED

The postwar period in Sweden was marked by the rapid expansion of the middle classes, which was facilitated by a slew of social policies implemented by the Social Democrats aimed at more evenly distributing the wealth of the nation in a manner that would allow for such an expansion. But beyond this, it was also characterized by the strong belief that knowledge could lead to change (Frykman 1981). And while organizations such as the Swedish Home Research Institute were established, the bulk of research undertaken in Sweden was funded by the government but conducted under the auspices of the university system. Although applied forms of anthropology developed early in the twentieth century in the United States, nothing of the sort ever took hold in Sweden.[1] Research emanating from departments of ethnology in Sweden was firmly anchored in the academy, focusing upon the mapping of peasant traditions and the spread of folklore. In this sense, they had a rather positivistic ambition of charting cultural processes (see Ehn and Löfgren 1996). A shift occurred in the early 1970s as influences from American anthropology and French cultural theory (from scholars like Michel Foucault and Pierre Bourdieu) captured the imagination of a younger generation of ethnologists, who began using their work to provide a voice to weaker groups in society (compare with Arnstberg 1997; Daun 1970). Ethnologists who did not remain in the academy usually found they could apply their knowledge in Swedish museums and cultural institutions, but work in the private sector was viewed with deep skepticism.

This situation was at least partially changed in the years around the new millennium in conjunction with two interconnected phenomena. First, the Swedish government began pressing scholars to explain how their knowledge could be made useful for society. The government was interested primarily in marketable assets. Second, students increasingly were enrolling in programs that led to clear career paths (O'Dell 2009), and their interest in ethnology was rapidly dissipating. Whereas an introductory course in ethnology could attract close to a hundred students at Lund University in the mid-1990s, just 10 years later, faculty there found themselves meeting as few as six students in ethnology classrooms.

Whereas the old motto was "publish or perish," ethnologists were increasingly facing a new one: "Adapt your educational program and change your attitude or perish!" At Umeå University, in the far north of Sweden, a program in "cultural entrepreneurship" was established that focused on educating and preparing young Swedes for work in the creative industries and cultural economy.

At the other end of the country, in the far south, the departments of ethnology at the University of Copenhagen and Lund University collaborated to develop an international program, the Master of Applied Cultural Analysis (MACA). In the MACA program, each department accepts 20 students, and although many of them have backgrounds in anthropology or ethnology, others have had exposure to cultural theory but majored in subjects as diverse as art history, business administration, and journalism.

A number of challenges emerged in the initial development of the MACA program. One was how to harness the wide array of skills, competencies, and experiences of a diverse student cohort from different scholarly and national backgrounds and guide the group down a path that, over the course of two years, would lead to the development of a new type of ethnographer: not an anthropologist or an ethnologist, but a cultural analyst specialized in working in applied contexts. Pedagogically, students were expected to master a common core in cultural theory to ground their discussions with one another, and they were also expected to master a set of practices and inquisitive dispositions that would fit under the banner of "applied ethnography." From a disciplinary standpoint, we deeply believed that this necessitated a different education than they would receive in any other department of anthropology or ethnology in Scandinavia.

CULTURAL ANALYSIS & PROCESSES OF COMPOSITION

To implement our vision for the new MACA program, we in Lund had to make use of our ethnological backgrounds and past experiences. Indeed, these would have to be an important platform from which to begin our work. Doreen Massey, arguing that cultural theorists should more thoroughly investigate the borderland between culture and economy, cautioned that this work should not turn cultural theorists into bad economists, but instead engender good cultural analyses of economic issues. Massey's lesson was not to abandon your background, but embrace it and move it in new directions (Massey 1999).

As it turned out, the diversity of the student body complemented the manner of working with cultural analysis that ethnologists based in Lund developed. Since the 1980s, cultural analysis in Lund implied maintaining an eclectic theoretical disposition combined with a slightly different approach to ethnography than that found in more traditional forms of European anthropology. A broad body of cultural theory from geography and gender studies to philosophy and beyond were readily absorbed and reworked to grasp and understand often overlooked and inconspicuous processes of everyday life (Ehn and Löfgren 2010). Methodologically, our focus has seldom been on the immersive, long period of fieldwork so often evoked within anthropology departments. Instead, our methods have been characterized by a kind of *bricolage* approach.

Where academic anthropologists generally regard ethnography as a means of studying other people over an extended period of time (Moeran 2005:3), Swedish ethnology has increasingly aligned itself over the years with those who believe ethnography is best defined as a plurality of methods "based on fieldwork using a variety of mainly (but not exclusively) qualitative research techniques" (Davies 2008:5).

Ethnologists in Sweden have embraced ethnography through historically anchored fieldwork or serial forms of it rather than long periods of continuous fieldwork (see Bergquist and Svensson 1999; Ehn and Löfgren 2010). The shift towards serially organized fieldwork among ethnologists was in part facilitated by the fact that the demands placed on scholars studying their own cultural surroundings were different than those faced by scholars entering less familiar contexts (Labaree 2002; Pripp and Öhlander 2011:125f). Where anthropologists worked to understand "Others" and make sense out of the different ways of life they observed, ethnologists usually engaged the ethnographic process by first attempting to exoticize the segments of Swedish daily life that they observed to distance themselves from it so they could understand the practices they were observing as well as the emotional impact it had upon them (Arnstberg 1997:24; Ehn and Löfgren 2001).

From the perspective of anthropology, there are questions about the degree to which ethnography must be closely associated with participant observation (Sillitoe 2007:156), and how long one actually has to work "in the field" for one's work to qualify as ethnography (Pink 2004:9). As Sunderland and Denny have argued, "We once bristled over short lengths because they conflicted with the assumption in anthropological research that understanding requires considerable time . . . yet we bristle less now . . . [due to] a realization and appreciation that sometimes length does not matter" (Sunderland and Denny 2007:267). Many of us working within ethnology in Sweden were well accustomed to the idea of doing short stints of fieldwork. A weekend at a car meet, a day at a boardroom meeting, or an afternoon at a horse race: these were all accepted ways of working. The short duration of the ethnographic encounter was not a problem in and of itself since it could be combined with a wider *bricolage* of materials and theoretical perspectives. In developing MACA, the *bricolage* method of doing cultural analysis that had developed in our department of ethnology seemed to be not only a natural way of moving, but even a productive and good way of de-dramatizing notions of the exoticism of field encounters, and the appropriate length of fieldwork.

Thus, the problem in developing a field of applied cultural analysis was not bound to issues concerning the duration of fieldwork; it was one of moving students with rather different scholarly backgrounds from a point of naive empiricism to analytical insight. In line with this, an important challenge was to move ethnography from the world of text to a more multimodal set of practices. Here we have developed an approach where we conceptualize ethnography and cultural analysis as compositional practices.

What does this mean? At a very trivial level, it implies an emphasis on teaching students that methods cannot be separated from theory. They are entwined and must be taught, treated, and used as such. In the academy, ethnography is all too often treated and taught as a textual practice, despite the *Writing Culture* exchanges about moving beyond the text (Clifford and Marcus 1986). What happens if we shift the metaphoric register of our discussions away from writing and into the realm of that which we can compose? Here it is possible to draw inspiration from Bruno Latour's *Compositionist Manifesto* (2010) as well as Christopher Kelty's writings about collaboration, coordination, and composition (2009). As Latour points out:

> Even though the word "composition" is a bit too long and windy, what is nice is that it underlines that things have to be put together (Latin *componere*) while retaining their heterogeneity. Also it is connected with composure. . . . [I]t is not too far from "compromise" and "compromising" retaining with it a certain diplomatic and prudential flavor (Latour 2010:3).

As we see it, a problem with the traditional anthropological view of ethnographic practice is that it still creates an all-too-linear impression of how ethnographies are assembled: moving from the planning stages at the desk, to the extended period of fieldwork, and back to the desk or the write-up. Thinking of ethnography as a compositional practice allows us to accept ethnographic work as messy, nonlinear performances in which diverse bits and pieces of information are put together and moved around.

Kelty, for his part, has advocated that the word "composition" might capture the complexity of activities that are the results of ethnographers today using a plethora of digital tools based on the infrastructure of the internet:

> We say "composition" here because it is more inclusive than "writing" (paintings, musical works, and software all need to be composed, as poetry and novels do). Writing implies the textual and narrative organization of languages . . . but it leaves out the composition of images and sounds, or especially how other kinds of objects are composed as part of an ethnographic project . . . (Kelty 2009:186).

As we see it, applied cultural analysis has to engage to convince. It needs to connect to the senses in a very different way than the latest book from a "top university publisher." You cannot ignore the importance of text, or the form it should take in different contexts, but ethnography has to be considered more seriously as a multimodal process (see also Malefyt, this volume). Here, we are partly drawing on George Marcus' thoughts on intellectual montage. Two decades ago he argued for ways of coupling cinematic imaginations to ethnographic writing and modernist sensibilities in ethnographic writing (Marcus 1990). By discussing intellectual montage, a concept derived from filmmaker Sergei Eisenstein, he discussed experimental ethnography at the end of the twentieth century and the uses of polyphony, fragmentation, and reflexivity in writing. At the core of these experiments lay combinatory montage practices and creative juxtapositions. But we would argue for a need to extend his vision of intellectual montage further. We need to switch the register of our metaphors even more dramatically to reimagine how we conceptualize ethnographic work. We think, all too often, of the formation of texts in terms of continuous "rewriting," while the making of films involves cutting, editing, and compositing, and music production is characterized by the layering, looping, and remixing of sound. When working with time-based media, the issue of duration is at the core of the compositional practices. You have to consciously deal with tempo and synchronization through techniques like time-stretching and quantization when working with sound and video.

How might we use the concepts from different modes of creation and expression to think of ethnographies in terms of such phenomena as mixing and layering (among other things) as well as rewriting? Rather than viewing the realities that force many of us to conduct short stints of fieldwork to gather ethnographic materials as a weakness, it might be more productive to teach students that they can actually layer different types of materials and theoretical perspective as well as using previous encounters in the field as a point of departure for ongoing projects.

HOW DO YOU COMPOSE ETHNOGRAPHY?

Composing ethnography means working in a manner akin to what Kim Fortun advocated as "ethnography in late industrialism":

> . . . ethnography that "loops," using ethnographic techniques to discern the discursive risks and gaps of a particular problem domain so that further ethnographic engagement in that domain is responsive and creative, provoking new articulations, attending to emergent realities. Ethnographic findings are thus fed back into ethnographic engagement. This mode of ethnography stages collaboration with interlocutors to activate new idioms and ways of engaging the world. It is activist, in a manner open to futures that cannot yet be imagined (Fortun 2012:460).

The looping that Fortun mentions can be related to the activist strands she evokes. But it is occurring in a number of contexts. In the world of applied cultural analysis, people are often conducting relatively short periods of ethnographic work for clients. They often let previous studies inform current and coming studies. Knowledge, experiences, and findings are looped or reiterated between the projects conducted by ethnographic consultants.

Fortun is concerned with the manner in which ethnographic findings are fed back into ethnographic engagement. In research we undertook on applied cultural analysis outside of academia, we have found numerous examples of similar practices. Anthropologists and ethnologists sometimes specialize in a limited number of empirical arenas that they repeatedly return to and that speak back to one another. One practitioner, for example, was very adept at conducting cultural analysis of media and the manner in which they are used and perceived by people in the course of their daily lives. Another emphasized his skills in both the study of food and cell phones, while a third person was very focused upon issues of sustainability. Within these empirical areas, their knowledge and findings were constantly being reiterated and looped.

To imagine this work as a compositional practice, however, we want to stretch the idea of looping within ethnography to compare it with the practices of other creative work, like making music. When creating music with digital media, the sound clip is a piece of sound that can be manipulated, stretched, layered, and looped; the looped sound results in a pattern that can be altered through various subtle or more dramatic modulations. The addition of sound effects (like echoes, reverb, filters, etc.) can create surprises or different atmospheres. This, we argue, is essentially what we do as we sift our data through a variety of theoretical perspectives and continually work to help clients understand their products and services in new ways that they can in part recognize, but in part have never seen before.

Composing ethnography also conceptually accommodates the reality of teamwork. Where traditional anthropological fieldwork implied the movement of a single anthropologist into the field for a longer period of study to "get it all," composing ethnography can imply several people working together, and here it can be an advantage to work with people with different cultural backgrounds and academic educations. To once more refer to the world of music: a marching band, for example, needs coordination, teamwork, and discipline. But if everyone wants to be the tuba player, it's not much of a band. So composing ethnography also implies a need to appreciate and use multiple and different competencies, and to coordinate them. To this end, MACA students spend the first year of the program working in groups. This often creates friction and causes problems in the beginning, but over the course of the year students learn that the art of composing ethnography requires a large degree of group management and the skill of appropriately delegating work and responsibilities to group members. Learning the managerial skills of the composer and conductor are, in other words, part and parcel of the competencies we strive to imbue in students.

Along the way, as students move ever closer to obtaining a degree, they are urged to consider their work as applied cultural analysts in terms of "cultural dubbing," which we envision as a move that forces the ethnographer to change both the voice and register of a cultural representation to make an impression. As such, cultural dubbing is not a single analytical act, but a polymorphic transformative movement that involves processes of both transcription and translation, but also moves beyond them. It is a process in which academic knowledge, when presented in the context of the boardroom, is translated into new forms accentuated with terms derived from business administration textbooks and presented not as a 200-page text, but as a PowerPoint presentation with perhaps eight slides and a video. It is also a process in which the "business pitch" or "final presentation" is viewed as much more than a representation. To be successful, we argue, it should be an emotionally laden *evocative performance* that aims to engage and convince. And even here, the art of the evocative performance is a talent students are forced to confront, learn, and experiment with in conjunction with their coursework on theory, methodology, and project management.

A way to further stress the shift we are advocating is by refocusing the thrust of our activity from one of *writing culture* to one of *rendering culture*. Rendering fits well with conceptualizing ethnography as composition as well as a multimodal practice. Composition focuses more on ethnography as a creative process than as a representational practice, even as the realist ambition is always to some extent incorporated in ethnography. Here our thoughts resonate with the approach Phillip Vannini took in his book *Ferry Tales*:

> I am less interested in ethnographic *representation* than I am in ethnographic *creation*. . . . [B]ecause research is more than representation, my writing and analysis aims less at explaining "findings" and more at *rendition*—aiming to create new stories, rather than replicate old ones (Vannini 2012:28).

The focus on rendition and composition highlight the potential of experimental ethnography to align itself with applied contexts, but it also highlights practices of *worldmaking*. This resonates with some of the arguments brought up by John Law and John Urry (2004) in the article "Enacting the Social." They argue that social science is performative, that it contributes to the process of making worlds. Social enquiry and its methods "do not simply describe the world as it is, but also enact it" (Law and Urry 2004:391). Methods always interfere with what is studied. The examples they present are, among others, Michel

Callon's writings about how "*theories* of markets have been crucial in helping to produce the realities that they purportedly describe" (Law and Urry 2004:394). Social enquiry methods as well as economic theory are performative and create the market realities that they describe (Callon et al. 2002).

According to Law and Urry, ethnography can "help to make worlds." This could mean ethnography as a force of production, or—if we use the language of the business world or applied research—ethnography as leading to "actionable results." The point is that the composition of ethnography can lead to very different forms of "deliverables" depending upon the context (O'Dell and Willim 2013). It's not just that a traditional conference paper does not work in a boardroom context, but that even the small tools used by applied ethnographers, ranging from PowerPoint presentations to cleanly arranged videos, have to be chosen and invoked in manners that are thoroughly and reflexively thought through. Composing ethnography is not an activity done by academics *or* practitioners; it requires a relational appreciation of ethnography as being something that must take different forms and make use of different utterances in varied contexts.

UNWITTINGLY ON THE COATTAILS OF PUBLIC ANTHROPOLOGY

In many ways, the ability to move in the direction of public anthropology was presaged by that shift Swedish ethnology took in the early 1970s in which ethnologists realized the role they could play in giving a voice to others. Where American anthropologists began writing about and discussing public anthropology in the 1990s, Swedish ethnologists moved in this direction two decades earlier. Important to this shift was a new insistence on the availability of the ethnographic text and the language of the ethnologist. Highbrow, abstract academic language full of jargon and theoretical concepts were frowned upon. A good ethnography should be readily accessible to any high school student: that was (and is) the motto. Simultaneously, ethnologists moved into public awareness by making appearances on television and radio programs, as well as being quoted in the daily newspapers. Swedish ethnologists are for the most part unfamiliar with the concept of "public anthropology." Instead, the current generation of ethnologists received their undergraduate and graduate educations in a context in which public engagement and activism was part of the ethnological habitus.

Strangely enough, most of the skills required to work in this way were never explicitly taught to students. The movement towards a compositional ethnography is an intentional and explicit attempt to emphasize the manner in which ethnographic representations can be put together in very different ways to produce different understandings depending upon the requirements of the context at hand. Our own work spans the continuum from highly experimental artistic forms of digital representations (such as Willim's piece *Surreal Scania*,[2] made together with video artist Anders Weberg, that depicts Scania—the southern province of Sweden—in a highly experimental manner intended to provoke the question of the limits of place marketing as well as its potential) to more conventional documentary-style ethnographic video, which is becoming an increasingly common mode of representation used by both students and scholars. But it also includes our participation in the production of different forms of educational programs for national television and radio, and engagement in various events such as "knowledge slams" that throw academics, local politicians, and entrepreneurs into cocktail party–like performances to stimulate dialog and the sharing/development of ideas and innovations around specific themes.[3] These can be encounters in which ethnographic video, sound recordings, slide shows, and staged performances provide a backdrop for the conversation that develops.

The key point is that composing ethnography requires us to dare to move in different directions than anthropologists and ethnologists have done before. Applied cultural analysts have to be highly competent writers. But they also have to train to present their work orally in a manner that speaks to the specific client/audience in question. Thinking in terms of composing ethnography forces us to acknowledge that the "representation of culture" is an important aspect of what we do, but what we do is much more than this.

Applied cultural analysis is evocative and multimodal; it engages audiences in ways that go beyond the realm of the cerebral. To be convincing it has to make the self-apparent seem enticingly or disturbingly new. Compositions have to engage the specific audience they are addressing. We are arguing that ethnography has to do the same, and high-flying language presented in thick textbooks isn't always enough. But this is not just a question about the form or media of what is being composed. It is when ethnography manages to walk the thin line between that which is trivially obvious and that which offers credible insight into a certain field of study (and suggests the thought provokingly uncanny) that it becomes truly successful. The surprise effects, the affective and the sensuous aspects of ethnography, have to be kept alive throughout the research process. It's when you feel the composition doing something to your gut that you are putting the piece together in a convincing and innovative manner. To successfully compose ethnography you have to, in other words, connect with an audience and not just represent a culture.

REFERENCES

Arnstberg, Karl-Olov. 1997. *Fältetnologi* [*Field Ethnology*]. Stockholm: Carlsson.

Bergquist, Magnus & Birgitta Svensson. 1999. *Metod och mine: Etnologiska tolkningar och rekonstruktioner* [*Methods and Memory: Ethnological Interpretations and Reconstructions*]. Lund, Sweden: Studentlitteratur.

Callon Michel, Méadel Cécile, and Rabeharisoa Vololona. 2002. "The Economy of Qualitities." *Economy and Society* 31(2):194–217.

Clifford, James, and George Marcus. 1986. *Writing Culture: The Poetics and Politics of Ethnography.* Berkeley: University of California Press.

Daun, Åke. 1970. *Upp till kamp i Bårskärsnäs: Ett etnologiskt studie av ett samhälle inför industrinedläggningen* [*Engaging the Struggle in Bårskärsnäs: An Ethnological Study of a Society Facing Industrial Shutdowns*]. Stockholm: Prisma.

Davies, Charlotte. 2008. *Reflexive Ethnography.* New York: Routledge.

Ehn, Billy, and Orvar Löfgren. 1996. *Vardagslivets etnologi: Reflektioner kring en kulturvetenskap* [*The Ethnology of Everyday Life: Reflections Around A Cultural Science*]. Stockholm: Natur och kultur.

_____. 2010. *The Secret World of Doing Nothing.* Berkeley: University of California Press.

Fortun, Kim. 2012. "Ethnography in Late Industrialism." *Cultural Anthropology* 27(3): 446– 64.

Frykman, Jonas. 1981. "Pure and Rational. The Hygenic Vision. A Study of Cultural Transformation in the 1930s. The New Man." *Ethnologia Scandinavica* 21:36-63.

Kelty, Cristopher, with contributions from Hannah Landecker, Ebru Kayaalp, Anthony Potoczniak, Tish Stringer, Nahal Naficy, Ala Alazzeh, Lina Dib, and Michael G. Powell. 2009. "Collaboration, Coordination, and Composition." In *Fieldwork Is Not What It Used To Be: Learning Anthropology's Method in a Time of Transition*, edited by J. D. Faubion and G. E. Marcus, 184–206. Ithaca, NY: Cornell University Press.

Labaree, Robert. 2002. "The Risk of 'Going Observationalist': Negotiating the Hidden Dilemmas of Being an Insider Participant Observer." *Qualitative Research* 2(1):97–122.

Latour, Bruno. 2010. "An Attempt at a 'Compositionist Manifesto.'" *New Literary History* 41:471–90.

Law, John, and John Urry. 2004. "Enacting the Social." *Economy and Society* 33(3):390–410.

Marcus, George. 1990. "The Modernist Sensibility in Recent Ethnographic Writing and the Cinematic Metaphor of Montage." *Society for Visual Anthropology (SVA) Review* 6(1):2–12.

Massey, Doreen. 1999. "Negotiating Disciplinary Boundaries." *Current Sociology* 47(4):5–12.

Moeran, Brian. 2005. *The Business of Ethnography: Strategic Exchanges, People and Organizations.* Oxford, UK: Berg.

O'Dell, Tom. 2009. "What's the Use of Culture?" *Culture Unbound* 1(1):15–29.

O'Dell, Tom, and Robert Willim. 2013. "Transcription and the Senses: Cultural Analysis when It Entails More than Words." *Senses and Society* 8(3):314–33.

Pink, Sarah. 2004. "Applied Visual Anthropology Social Intervention, Visual Methodologies and Anthropology Theory." *Visual Anthropology Review* 20(1):3–15.

Pripp, Oscar, and Magnus Öhlander. 2011. "Observation" ["Participant Observation"]. In *Etnologiskt Fältarbete* [*Ethnological Fieldwork*], edited by L. Kaijser and M. Öhlander, 113–46. Lund, Sweden: Studentlitteratur.

Sillitoe, Paul. 2007. "Anthropologists Only Need Apply: Challenges of Applied Anthropology." *Journal of the Royal Anthropological Institute* 13:147–65.

Sunderland, Patricia, and Rita Denny. 2007. *Doing Anthropology in Consumer Research.* Walnut Creek, CA: Left Coast Press.

Vannini, Phillip. 2012. *Ferry Tales: Mobility, Place, and Time on Canada's West Coast.* Oxon, UK: Routledge.

NOTES

We would like to thank Riksbankens Jubileumsfond (RJ) for the financial support we have received for the research project "Runaway Methods: Ethnography and its New Incarnations." It is with the aid of this funding that we have been able to produce this chapter. We would also like to thank The Crafoord Foundation for additional financial support.

1 The situation was slightly different in the field of sociology, where people such as the Myrdals did conduct work with an applied orientation. The Myrdals, however, were more of an exception than the rule, and even they were tightly bound to the university system.

2 *Surreal Scania*, as well as a number of other works by Willim and Weberg, such as *Elsewhereness* and *Sweden for Beginners*, has been featured at exhibitions, festivals, and conferences around the world. These works, as well as other works by Willim such as *Fieldnotes*, work to problematize the notion of place, and examine notions of fieldwork and the ends of ethnography. For some examples, see http://www.robertwillim.com/portfolio/.

3 Our engagement in the national media includes the fact that we are interviewed and cited regularly in national newspapers and magazines about diverse cultural issues. But beyond print media, both O'Dell and Willim appear regularly on national radio and television shows. O'Dell, for example, has appeared in everything from talk show debates about the Americanization of Swedish holidays to the production of 20-minute-long popularly oriented lectures on the manner in which magic and economic forces are entangled in modern society. And Willim and his research have been featured on numerous evening television shows. He has also produced a TV series based on ethnological perspectives. On a more local level, both O'Dell and Willim frequently participate in public talks, local debates, and knowledge slams. Knowledge slams are meetings that are regularly organized in Lund, at times by the university, at times by the municipality, and are intended to help bridge the gap between the academy and actors in the local setting. Knowledge slams can address widely diverse issues, from the manner in which Lund can become a more hospitable place to live in, to the question of how school children can be inspired to be culturally innovative. In addition to these types of meetings, both O'Dell and Willim are regularly engaged in advisory roles by national agencies as well as municipal and regional authorities to help those actors meet the challenges they happen to be struggling with as well as helping them to develop new cultural activities and services. These are examples of the types of projects that we have been involved in, but they are not unique to us. Most of our ethnological colleagues in Lund are involved in very similar activities. In this sense, we mean to draw attention to the fact that ethnologists in Lund have a rather different form of access to both a national public audience as well as local and regional ones than most of our colleagues at universities in the United States do.

Index

Note: Italicized page numbers indicate illustrations and their captions.

About the Editors & Contributors

EDITORS

Rita Denny and **Patricia Sunderland** are anthropologists and founding partners of Practica Group, LLC, a consumer research and strategic consultancy based in New York City and Chicago. Internationally recognized as among the pioneers in bringing ethnographic research and anthropological, cultural analysis to the contemporary commercial sphere, their insights have helped shape products and brands for many Fortune 500 clients. Traversing boundaries between the disciplines of anthropology and marketing, and the many practices of both in business realms, they are sought after as seminar leaders for training programs and guest speakers at both business and academic venues and conferences. Their path-breaking book *Doing Anthropology in Consumer Research* is widely assigned to undergraduate and graduate students in anthropology, communications, and marketing in the United States, Europe, and Asia, and is a CHOICE Outstanding Academic Book.

CONTRIBUTORS

Nick Agafonoff is a specialist market ethnographer and documentary filmmaker with more than 15 years of experience as a commercial practitioner. He has directed hundreds of ethnographic and video insight programs for a diverse range of private and public sector clients. Agafonoff is a full member of the Australian Market and Social Research Association, and holds a Masters of Media Arts and Production (University of Technology Sydney) and an honors degree in sociology (Australian National University).

Kateřina Ailová is the Chief Innovation Officer at IdeaSense, Czech Republic. Her work includes developing innovation ecosystems and innovative product, service, and customer experience concepts. Her other specialties are in design thinking, ethnography, usability research, semiotics, customer and employee co-creation, brand positioning, and strategy. She is a PhD candidate in cultural anthropology at Brandeis University (USA) and has an MA from Charles University (Czech Republic).

Sophie Alami has conducted qualitative studies covering a wide range of market sectors with a developing expertise in health for the past 20 years. After nearly a decade analyzing consumer behavior in Morocco, she returned to Paris in 2002 and cofounded Interlis, a private research firm. She received an MA in intercultural studies and a PhD in sociology from Paris Descartes University. She comes from a multicultural background of Moroccan and French origins.

Eric J. Arnould is Professor of Marketing at Southern Denmark University. As a practicing anthropologist since 1973, he has consulted for a variety of public and private organizations in Africa and the United States. His many papers on consumer culture theory as applied to consumption and marketing processes, development in Africa, and services marketing appear in social science and managerial periodicals and books. His 2005 paper coauthored with Craig Thompson on consumer culture theory helped catalyze the formation of the Consumer Culture Theory Consortium.

Marietta L. Baba is Dean of the College of Social Science, and Professor of Anthropology and of Human Resources and Labor Relations at Michigan State University. Previously, Baba was Professor and Chair of the Department of Anthropology, and founding director of the Business and Industrial Anthropology program at Wayne State University in Detroit, MI. Her research interests include the anthropology of work, organizations, and institutions, the anthropology of policy, and the history and theory of applied and practicing anthropology.

Sam Barton worked at Added Value London for five years and has since returned to the bosom of academia, pursuing a PhD in urban geography at University College London (UCL). During his time with the Cultural Insight team at Added Value, he worked on disparate issues including marketing to women, men's facial hair, and the cultural meaning of fish. Commercial semiotics was such a fascination that he made it his dissertation topic for a master's degree in material and visual culture at UCL.

Stefania Borghini is Associate Professor of Marketing at Università Bocconi, Milan. Her research interests are related to consumers' behavior in the marketplace and their connections with brands and retail spaces in particular. Her current projects focus on children's and women's consumer behavior. In her studies, she adopts a consumer culture perspective and privileges ethnographic methods.

Alessandro Caliandro is a postdoctoral researcher in sociology and Director of Research at the Centro Studi Etnografia Digitale at the State University of Milan,

Italy. He is also Chief of the Digital Ethnography Department of Viralbeat, a social media marketing company.

Julien Cayla is a Research Fellow at the Institute on Asian Consumer Insight, an Assistant Professor of Marketing at Nanyang Technological University in Singapore, and a Visiting Professor at Kedge Business School in France. In his research, he integrates anthropological theories and methodologies to the study of marketing in the global marketplace. His work has been published in outlets such as *MIT Sloan Management Review,* the *Journal of Consumer Research,* and the *Journal of Marketing.*

Melissa Cefkin is a research manager at IBM with a focus on work and consumption practices in complex technical and organizational contexts and experience in design and consulting. She was previously at Sapient Corporation and the Institute for Research on Learning and served on the Board of Directors for the Ethnographic Praxis in Industry Conference (EPIC). Editor of *Ethnography and the Corporate Encounter* (Berghahn 2009) and author of numerous publications, Cefkin is a frequent presenter internationally and holds a PhD in anthropology from Rice University.

Jaroslav Cír studied psychology and sociology at University of Toronto. In 1999 he joined Unilever in Prague, working as the head of market research for central and eastern Europe. At the beginning of 2005, he moved to London as the global Consumer and Market Insight Director for Rexona. In 2009, Cír established A Perfect Crowd, a marketing consultancy and market research agency specializing in co-creation and crowdsourcing.

Franck Cochoy is Professor of sociology at the University of Toulouse and a member of CERTOP-CNRS, France. He works in the field of economic sociology, with a focus on the human and technical mediations that frame the relationship between supply and demand.

Martha Cotton is a partner at gravitytank, where she leads the Research Discipline. She began her career at E-Lab in 1990s, and since then has worked across a wide variety of industries as an applied ethnographer and business consultant. Cotton holds a BA in English from Indiana University and an MA in performance studies from Northwestern University. She is currently adjunct faculty at Northwestern University's Kellogg School of Management and the McCormick School of Engineering.

Bernard Cova is a Professor of Marketing at Kedge Business School Marseilles, France, and a Visiting Professor at Università Bocconi, Milan, Italy. A pioneer in the Consumer Tribes field since the early 1990s, he has published in major consumer research and marketing academic journals. He has collaborated with companies such as Alfa Romeo, Citroën, Ducati, and Orange through action research programs.

Charles N. Darrah is an applied anthropologist and chair of the Department of Anthropology at San Jose State University. His research focuses on work and workplaces, families, and technology. He cofounded the Silicon Valley Cultures Project and the Human Aspiration and Design Laboratory (HADLab) at San Jose State University, and Design Practices Collaborative.

Dominique Desjeux is Professor of Anthropology at the Sorbonne, Paris Descartes University, where he directs the Professional Doctoral Program in social sciences. He is an international consultant, working in China, Africa, Brazil, the United States, and Europe. He has written many books and articles from his research on innovations in business, distribution, consumption, and waste.

Nina Diamond is Associate Professor of Marketing at DePaul University and the Kellstadt Graduate School of Business, where she teaches courses in new product management, strategy, consumer behavior, and consumer culture. She has published in the *Journal of Marketing, Journal of Retailing, Qualitative Market Research,* and *Journal of Marketing Education.* Diamond is also a consultant partner in the BRS Group, where she works with Fortune 500 companies on consumer needs identification, marketing strategy, new product development, and marketing communication projects.

Lisa DiCarlo is a cultural anthropologist who studies innovation and social change. She spent 10 years at Babson College teaching in the liberal arts and entrepreneurship programs. As Entrepreneur-in-Residence at Clark University's Center for Innovation and Entrepreneurship, she developed courses on anthropology and innovation. She is currently Visiting Assistant Professor in Sociology, and teaches in the Business, Entrepreneurship and Organizations program at Brown University.

Alicia Dornadic is a design researcher and writer who partners with organizations and individuals to make products, services, and UX. She has held positions at Allstate Insurance and Roche Diagnostics. She holds a BA in fine arts from New York University and an MA in applied anthropology from San Jose State University.

Patricia Ensworth is President of Harborlight Management Services LLC, a consultancy specializing in project/program management, business analysis, requirements engineering, and quality assurance. She is the author of *The Accidental Project Manager: Surviving the Transition from Techie to Manager* (Wiley 2001), and numerous essays and articles in both technical and general interest publications. Ensworth is a faculty member at the American Management Association, leading project management seminars and workshops for public courses and private client engagements.

Kenneth C. Erickson is an applied anthropologist. He helms a research boutique, Pacific Ethnography, which conducts field research in China, Brazil, India, and the United States. He is presently an apprentice stoneware potter and full-time clinical faculty member in the Sonoco Department of International Business at University of South Carolina's Darla Moore School of Business. Erickson received his PhD in anthropology from the University of Kansas.

Kateřina Svatoň Gillárová is a PhD student of sociology at the Institute of Sociological Studies, Charles University, in Prague. She is also a researcher and a managing partner at Idealisti, a branding agency based in Prague. Her main areas of interest are technology and society, new methodological approaches (netnography, visual methods), youth studies, and consumer ethnogrphy. Svatoň Gillárová is a frequent contributor to professional magazines and books and regularly speaks at international conferences.

Natalie Hanson has been working and researching at the intersection of business strategy, technology, social science, and design for nearly 15 years. Her research explores the ways in which institutions respond to macroeconomic, industry, and regional trends, and how those changes affect employees. In 2002, Hanson founded an online community called Anthrodesign (http://www.anthrodesign.com), where participants engage in dialog about cross-disciplinary collaboration, with a focus on the use of field research (ethnographic) methods in the business context.

Jay Hasbrouck is a social anthropologist whose insights drive the design of products, services, concepts, and systems. His interests include sustainability, health care, visual culture, and cultural landscape. He has conducted research in Mexico, Egypt, Germany, South Korea, Brazil, Japan, Malaysia, China, and the United States for clients in health care, government, technology, tourism, and home care. Hasbrouck received an MA in visual anthropology and a PhD in social anthropology, both from the University of Southern California.

Belinda Heath is a sociocultural researcher, analyst, and writer. Her academic interests span across poststructuralist sociology, feminist theory, material cultural studies, and ethnography. Heath's MA studies (University of Technology Sydney) investigated tensions between regional and national aesthetic values in Kagoshima, Japan. Currently, she is exploring constructs of esteem, class-belonging, personal value, and social agency for minimum wage–earning women in Sydney.

Vidar Hepsø has worked as an ethnographer and project manager in the Norwegian oil and gas industry for more than 20 years. He has studied crane operators, process and production engineers, subsurface-reservoir specialists, and, recently, marine biologists. His main interests are within science and technology studies. Most of his publications are within emerging collaborative practices enabled by new information and communication technologies. He received his PhD in anthropology from the Norwegian University of Science and Technology, and is also an adjunct professor at the same institution.

Martin Høyem is a cultural anthropologist and the founder, creator, publisher, and editor of *American Ethnography Quasimonthly.* He has done fieldwork and anthropological research on lowriders in Los Angeles. He has also done ethnography among fast food restaurant guests in Arizona and Florida, and studied underwear shoppers in big box retail stores.

Cato Hunt is Director of Cultural Insight, Added Value London. With a degree in art history and psychology and an MBA, a career in commercial semiotics seemed a natural fit, once she learned this was actually a job she could get paid for. Hunt has spent her career helping clients build meaningful, culturally vibrant brands. An expert at blending approaches across ethnography, semiotics, and cultural analysis, she loves nothing more than thinking about the future of fashion or the meaning of breakfast.

Ann T. Jordan is Professor of Anthropology at the University of North Texas, specializing in business anthropology, especially organizational anthropology. Her work includes studies of organizational change, mergers, self-managed work teams, global organizational networks, and health care systems. She has also conducted research in Native American studies and in globalization in the Kingdom of Saudi Arabia. Her most recent books are *A Companion to Organizational Anthropology,* coedited with Douglas Caulkins (2013), and *Business Anthropology,* second edition (2013).

Lucy Kimbell is Associate Fellow at Said Business School, University of Oxford, where she has been teaching in the MBA program since 2005. She publishes research on design thinking and designing for service. Recent work includes a study at the University of Brighton mapping social design research and practice. In another guise, she makes performative art that looks a bit like social research methods.

Kathi R. Kitner is an anthropologist and has been a Senior Research Scientist with Intel Labs since 2006, researching how various cultural constructs act as conduits for technology usage and adoption. She has explored vibrant data, urban experiences, and mobility and development in South Africa, India, and Latin America. Before Intel, she studied the uneven process of globalization, tourism, and resilience in Venezuela and Mexico; pathways to heroin addiction in Miami; and social change in United States and Caribbean fishing communities.

Robert V. Kozinets is Professor of Marketing at York University's Schulich School of Business, where he is also Chair of the Marketing department, and has authored more than 80 research publications, including many in the world's top marketing journals, a textbook, and three books. He is also a blogger and a change agent supporting global organizations such as L'Oréal, Amex, TD Bank, Merck, Nissan, and Sony in their innovation, research, and social media initiatives.

Timothy de Waal Malefyt is visiting Associate Professor at Fordham University Business School in New York. Previously, he was Director of Cultural Discoveries for BBDO Advertising in NYC, and Senior Planner at D'Arcy, Masius, Benton & Bowles in Detroit. He is coeditor of *Advertising Cultures* (2003), coauthor of *Advertising and Anthropology* (2012), and series editor of the new Business Anthropology series from Left Coast Press. He is cited in ABC News, *BusinessWeek*, and *The New York Times.*

Maryann McCabe is founder and principal of Cultural Connections LLC, a market research consultancy. She has worked with companies and advertising agencies in the United States, Japan, and Europe on branding, positioning, and new product development. Based on ethnographic research for clients, she has published articles in academic journals on US cultural practices. She is Senior Lecturer, University of Rochester, Department of Anthropology, and received a PhD in anthropology from New York University.

John L. McCreery is a partner at The Word Works, Ltd. and an anthropologist who studied Daoist magic in Taiwan. His postacademic career has included 13 years as a copywriter and creative director for Japan's second largest advertising agency and the writing of *Japanese Consumer Behavior: From Worker Bees to Wary Shoppers*. His current project combines social network analysis with ethnographic and historical research to explore the world of top Tokyo advertising creatives.

Heather McGowan is an innovation strategy consultant with specific expertise in leading transformational change in higher education. From 2008 to 2012, McGowan was Assistant Provost for the creation of the Kanbar College of Design + Engineering + Commerce (DEC) at Philadelphia University. Previously, McGowan was Associate Director of the Center for Design and Business at the Rhode Island School of Design (RISD). McGowan holds a BFA in industrial design from the Rhode Island School of Design and an MBA from Babson.

Mary Ann McGrath is a Professor of Marketing in the Quinlan School of Business at Loyola University Chicago, and currently serving in the capacity of Director of the Intercontinental MBA Program. Between April 2009 and July 2010 she served as Professor of Marketing at the China Europe International Business School (CEIBS) in Shanghai, China. A former mathematics teacher and marketing consultant, she studies consumer and marketplace behaviors.

Brian Moeran is Professor of Business Anthropology at the Copenhagen Business School and Visiting Professor at the University of Hong Kong. His research has focused on advertising, ceramics, fashion magazines, publishing, and smell cultures, primarily in Japan. He is also Editor-in-Chief of the Open Access *Journal of Business Anthropology.*

Robert J. Morais is a Principal at Weinman Schnee Morais Inc., a New York–based marketing research firm. He holds a PhD in anthropology and has worked for more than 30 years in the advertising and marketing research industries. Morais is the author of *Refocusing Focus Groups: A Practical Guide* (2010) and coauthor of *Advertising and Anthropology: Ethnographic Practice and Cultural Perspectives* (2012).

Bruno Moynié is one of the foremost anthropologist filmmakers working in the marketing and design research industry, has training in social anthropology and ethnographic film, and has produced documentary films for nearly 20 years. His experience and charisma give him unique capacities to immerse himself in different places, create strong rapport, and capture genuine human activities up close. Whether shooting in Toronto (where he resides), Europe, Asia, the United States, or Africa, Moynié thinks of himself first as a world citizen.

Albert M. Muñiz, Jr. is Professor of Marketing at DePaul University. His interests are in sociological aspects of consumer behavior and branding, including consumer-generated content and value creation in consumption communities. He has researched consumer brand communities for nearly two decades, and his work has been published in *Business Horizons, European Journal of Marketing, Journal of Advertising, Journal of Consumer Research, Journal of Interactive Marketing, Journal of Marketing, Journal of Retailing,* and *Journal of Strategic Marketing.*

Dawn Nafus is an anthropologist at Intel Corporation, where she conducts research to build new markets and strategies. She researches cultural notions of time, measurement, and technology. Nafus received her PhD from the University of Cambridge.

Megan Neese is a Senior Manager of Future Lab at Nissan Motor Limited, a global cross-functional team tasked with identifying new business opportunities for the Nissan, Infiniti, and Datsun brands. Prior to this, Neese held similar design strategy positions at BMW Group DesignworksUSA, Samsung Design America, and Nissan North America. Neese sits on the Board of Directors for IDSA and holds a BA in industrial design and MA in product development from Carnegie Mellon University.

Tom O'Dell is Professor of Ethnology in the Department of Arts and Cultural Sciences at Lund University, Sweden. Among his previous publications is *Culture Unbound: Americanization and Everyday Life in Sweden* (Nordic Academic Press, 1997), *Experiencescapes: Tourism, Culture, and Economy* (Copenhagen Business School Press, 2004, together with Peter Billing), and *Spas and the Cultural Economy of Hospitality, Magic and the Senses* (Nordic Academic Press, 2012).

Dipak R. Pant is an experienced field anthropologist and (accidental) economist, and the founder of the Interdisciplinary Unit for Sustainable Economy, LIUC, Castellanza (VA), Italy. Pant provides environmentally sustainable and socially sound economic policy and development guidelines for governmental, industrial, commercial, and nongovernmental organizations in many parts of the world. He has served as visiting professor and guest contributor in university departments, business schools, and natural history museums. Pant serves on the editorial boards of *EnerGeo* (Italy) and *Place Branding* (UK).

Neal H. Patel is Executive Director of the Human and Social Dynamics Laboratory with Google's Advanced Technology and Projects (ATAP) team. Patel joined Google in 2008, authoring influential research projects including Project Oxygen—a study quantifying the impact of effective people management—featured in *The New York Times* and recently in the *Harvard Business Review*. As a part of ATAP, Patel develops programs for high-tech innovation that transform research practice while advancing strategic business application.

Simon Roberts works at Stripe Partners, an innovation and strategy consultancy. Since completing his PhD on the satellite television revolution in north India, his career has focused on applying anthropology to business and policymaking. In 2002 he founded Ideas Bazaar, the United Kingdom's first ethnographic research company. Between 2006 and 2011 Simon helped establish an R&D lab for Intel Corporation's Digital Health division. Roberts is on the Board of EPIC (Ethnographic Praxis in Industry Conference) and co-chaired the 2012 and 2013 events.

Sarah Rottenberg is the Associate Director of the Integrated Product Design master's program and a lecturer in the School of Design at the University of Pennsylvania. She is also an innovation strategy consultant, training clients in design research methods, helping them understand their customers' needs, and facilitating product and business design. Rottenberg has a BS in Foreign Service from Georgetown University and an MS in Social Sciences from the University of Chicago.

Charley Scull is a cultural and visual anthropologist, documentary filmmaker, and, since 2012, a partner with Practica Group. His work, which frequently includes the prominent use of video, spans both the corporate and nonprofit sectors and features a range of topics, including health care, immigration and work, consumer market research, environmental communications, and recent work on public green spaces. Scull earned his PhD in anthropology from the University of Southern California and lives in Brooklyn, New York.

Lyubava Shatokhina is currently a resident researcher and graduate student in anthropology at the European University at St. Petersburg. Having earned a first master's degree in philosophy of culture and a second in sociology, she then pursued anthropology, a discipline that bridges the gap between theory and practice. For the past three years she has been working as an assistant researcher for applied anthropologists in the field of Russian consumer culture.

John F. Sherry, Jr. is Herrick Professor of Marketing and Department Chair, and Professor of Anthropology (concurrent) at the University of Notre Dame. He is a Fellow of the American Anthropological Association and the Society for Applied Anthropology, studying brand strategy, experiential consumption, and retail atmospherics. Sherry is President of the Consumer Culture Theory Consortium, and past President of the Association for Consumer Research. His work appears in numerous journal articles and books.

Susan Squires is Assistant Professor of Anthropology, at the University of North Texas, leading course-based research projects in the medical and technology sector. Her past work at Trinity College (Dublin) investigated how to support older Irish adults in their homes, mapping workflow of computational scientists, and ethnographic research for health and technology companies. Her edited book, *Creating Breakthrough Ideas* (2002), chronicles the application of her research theory and methodology as used by anthropologists in business and design.

Johannes Suikkanen is the cofounder and managing partner of Gemic, a Helsinki- and Berlin-based strategy and innovation consultancy. Working at the intersection of business strategy and cultural analysis, he advises global corporations on innovation, marketing, and customer centricity. Suikkanen holds a master's degree in business and culture studies from Copenhagen Business School.

Sakari Tamminen is the cofounder of Gemic, a Helsinki- and Berlin-based strategy and innovation consultancy. Besides leading client engagements, Tamminen teaches customer-centric product and service development at Aalto University in Helsinki, and anthropology of science at the University of Helsinki. His academic interests include the impact of new biotechnologies to societies. Tamminen received his PhD in social psychology and anthropology from Helsinki University, and a predoctoral (Licenciate) degree in user-centric design from the Aalto University School of Engineering.

Sarah Teitler is an ethnographer and user researcher. She has conducted research to understand the relationships between users and systems, consumers and products, and people and places. Teitler has taught at New York University and Purchase College, and her videos have shown at festivals in the United States and abroad. She received master's degrees in anthropology (with a certificate in ethnographic film) and interactive telecommunications from New York University.

Craig J. Thompson is the Churchill Professor of Marketing at the University of Wisconsin School of Business, where he served as department chair from 2005 to 2008. Thompson's research focuses on consumers' identity-constituting relationships to marketplace resources; how class and gender socialization influence consumer preferences, behavioral predispositions, and identity projects; and the ideological shaping of market systems and corresponding networks of consumption practices. He is an associate editor for the *Journal of Consumer Research* and on the editorial advisory board for *Consumption, Markets, & Culture.*

Tian Guang is a specially appointed professor at Shantou University and Dean of the Advanced Institute of Applied Anthropology at Jishou University. He is one of the major scholars in business anthropology in China and serves as the editor for the *International Journal of Business Anthropology.* Author or coauthor of 24 books and more than 100 journal articles, he has received awards for published papers and for service from organizations in Canada, China, and the United States.

Otto Utti is a Partner at Gemic, a Helsinki- and Berlin-based strategy and innovation consultancy. His work focuses on helping companies innovate in strategy, marketing, and product development through a deep and meaningful understanding of human needs, aspirations, and practices. Utti received a master's degree in political economy from the London School of Economics and a bachelor's degree in political science from the University of York (UK).

Tricia Wang is a global tech ethnographer transforming the way organizations conduct research. She advises corporations and start-ups on cutting-edge ethnographic research methods to improve strategy, policy, services, and products. She has worked with Fortune 500 companies such as Nokia and GE and numerous institutions including the UN and NASA. Wang received her PhD in sociology from the University of California San Diego, and is a Fulbright and National Science Foundation Scholar. She is the cofounder of ethnographymatters.net. Wang is also the proud owner of an internet-famous creature, ellethedog.com.

Christina Wasson is a Professor of Anthropology at the University of North Texas. Her work is motivated by a passion to investigate three "C"s: communication, collaboration, and community-building. Much of her research compares these processes across face-to-face and virtual settings. Current contexts of investigation include business teams, environmental scientists and stakeholders, and students' learning experiences in the university setting. Wasson formerly worked for E-Lab and was a founding member of the Ethnographic Praxis in Industry Conference (EPIC) steering committee.

Robert Willim is Associate Professor of Ethnology in the Department of Arts and Cultural Sciences at Lund University, Sweden. Among his previous publications are *Magic, Culture and The New Economy* (Berg Publishers, 2005, with Orvar Löfgren) and *Industrial Cool—Om postindustriella fabriker* (Lund University, 2008, in Swedish). Parallel with his work as an ethnographer and cultural analyst, he is working as an artist.

Sarah J. S. Wilner is Assistant Professor of Marketing at Wilfrid Laurier University. Her research focuses on "consumer insight": what it is, how it's obtained, what's done with it, and who decides. In particular, she studies product design and development processes, including the contributions of corporate ethnographers. She continues to regret that business anthropology was not presented as a career option when she got her anthropology degree in the 1980s. Wilner received her PhD in marketing from York University (Canada).

Keiko Yamaki is Associate Professor at Hiroshima University. Her interest in cultural differences in service grew out of experience as a cabin crewmember for Cathay Pacific and Lufthansa. For her PhD, she chose the School of Cultural and Social Studies at SOKENDAI, Japan's national Graduate University for Advanced Studies, for which MINPAKU, Japan's National Museum of Ethnology, is the center. She chose this path because she wanted to join the Anthropology of Administration Group.